Managing Human Resources

Productivity, Quality of Work Life, Profits

Twelfth Edition

Wayne F. Cascio
The Business School
University of Colorado Denver

McGraw Hill

MANAGING HUMAN RESOURCES:
PRODUCTIVITY, QUALITY OF WORK LIFE, PROFITS, TWELFTH EDITION

 This book is printed on acid-free paper.

1 2 3 4 5 6 7 8 9 LWI 24 23 22 21

ISBN 978-1-260-68135-2 (bound edition)
MHID 1-260-68135-1 (bound edition)
ISBN 978-1-264-06936-1 (loose-leaf edition)
MHID 1-264-06936-7 (loose-leaf edition)

Director: *Michael Ablassmeir*
Associate Portfolio Manager: *Laura Hurst Spell*
Marketing Manager: *Lisa Granger*
Content Project Managers: *Melissa M. Leick, Emily Windelborn*
Buyer: *Sandy Ludovissy*
Content Licensing Specialist: *Gina Oberbroeckling*
Cover Image: *Shutterstock/fizkes*
Compositor: *Aptara®, Inc.*

Library of Congress Cataloging-in-Publication Data

Names: Cascio, Wayne F., author.
Title: Managing human resources : productivity, quality of work life,
    profits / Wayne F. Cascio, The Business School, University of Colorado,
    Denver.
Description: Twelfth edition. | New York, NY : McGraw-Hill Education,
    [2022] | Includes index.
Identifiers: LCCN 2020031868 | ISBN 9781260681352 (hardcover) | ISBN
    9781264069361 (spiral bound) | ISBN 9781264069354 (ebook) | ISBN
    9781264069392 (ebook other)
Subjects: LCSH: Personnel management.
Classification: LCC HF5549 .C2975 2022 | DDC 658.3–dc23
LC record available at https://lccn.loc.gov/2020031868

To Tanni Lee
Endless Joy

ABOUT THE AUTHOR

Wayne F. Cascio

WAYNE F. CASCIO is a Distinguished University Professor Emeritus in The Business School at the University of Colorado Denver. He earned his B.A. degree from Holy Cross College, his M.A. degree from Emory University, and his Ph.D. in industrial/organizational psychology from the University of Rochester.

Professor Cascio is past chair of the Society for Human Resource Management Foundation and the Human Resources Division of the Academy of Management, past president of the Society for Industrial and Organizational Psychology, and a past member of the Academy of Management's Board of Governors. He is a Fellow of the National Academy of Human Resources, the Academy of Management, the American Psychological Association, and the Australian Human Resources Institute. He received the Distinguished Career award from the HR Division of the Academy of Management in 1999; an honorary doctorate from the University of Geneva, Switzerland, in 2004; and the Michael R. Losey Human Resources Research Award from the Society for Human Resource Management in 2010. In 2013 he received the Distinguished Scientific Contributions Award from the Society for Industrial and Organizational Psychology, and in 2016 he received the George Petitpas [Lifetime Achievement] Award from the World Federation of People Management Associations. In 2020 he received the Ulrich Impact award from the HR Division of the Academy of Management for excellence in the application of theory and research in practice.

Professor Cascio currently serves as a consulting editor of the *Journal of International Business Studies* (JIBS), and from 2007 to 2014 he served as a senior editor of the *Journal of World Business*. He also serves as chair of the SHRM Certification Commission and as a member of the Australian HR Institute's National Certification Council. He has consulted with a wide variety of organizations on six continents, and periodically he testifies as an expert witness in employment discrimination cases. Professor Cascio is an active researcher and writer. He has published more than 200 articles and book chapters, as well as 33 books.

CONTENTS IN BRIEF

CONTENTS

BOXES AND SPECIAL FEATURES

PREFACE

I did not write this book for students who aspire to be specialists in human resource management (HRM). Rather, I wrote it for students of general management whose jobs inevitably will involve responsibility for managing people, along with capital, material, and information. A fundamental assumption, then, is that all managers are accountable to their organizations in terms of the impact of their HRM activities, and they are expected to add value by managing their people effectively. They also are accountable to their peers and to their subordinates in terms of the quality of work life that they are providing.

As a unifying theme for the text, I have tried to link the content of each chapter to three key outcome variables–productivity, quality of work life, and profits. This relationship should strengthen the student's perception of HRM as an important function affecting individuals, organizations, and society.

Each chapter incorporates the following distinguishing features:

- In keeping with the orientation of the book toward general managers, each chapter opens with "Questions This Chapter Will Help Managers Answer." This section provides a broad outline of the topics that each chapter addresses.
- Following the chapter opener is a two-part vignette, often from the popular press, that illustrates "Human Resource Management in Action." Events in the first part of the vignette are designed to sensitize the reader to the subject matter of the chapter. The events lead to a climax, but then the vignette stops–like a two-part television drama. The reader is asked to predict what will happen next and to anticipate alternative courses of action.
- Then the text for the chapter appears–replete with concepts, research findings, court decisions, "HR Buzz" boxes, and international comparisons.
- Each chapter includes an "Ethical Dilemma." Its purpose is to identify issues relevant to the topic under discussion where different courses of action may be desirable and possible. The student must choose a course of action and defend the rationale for doing so.
- As in the 11th edition, "Implications for Management Practice" provide insights into the ways in which issues presented in the chapter affect the decisions that managers must make. "Impact" boxes in each chapter reinforce the link between the chapter content and the strategic objectives–productivity, quality of work life, and the bottom line–that influence all HR functions.
- Near the end of the chapter, the vignette introduced at the outset continues, allowing the reader to compare his or her predictions with what actually happened.

Ultimately, the aim of each chapter is to teach prospective managers to *make decisions* based on accurate diagnoses of situations that involve people–in domestic as well as global contexts. Familiarity with theory, research, and practice enhances the ability of students to do this. Numerous real-world applications of concepts allow the student to learn from the experiences of others, and the dynamic design of each chapter allows the student to move back and forth from concept to evidence to practice–then back to evaluating concepts–in a continuous learning loop.

WHAT'S NEW IN THE TWELFTH EDITION?

HR texts have sometimes been criticized for overemphasizing the HR practices of large organizations. There is often scant advice for the manager of a small business who "wears many hats" and whose capital resources are limited. To address this issue explicitly, I have made a conscious effort to provide examples of effective HRM practices in small businesses in almost every chapter.

This was no cosmetic revision. I examined every topic and every example in each chapter for its continued relevance and appropriateness. I added dozens of new company examples and "HR Buzz" boxes to illustrate current practices, updated legal findings from each area, and cited the very latest research findings in every chapter. I added hundreds of new references since the previous edition of the book, and I removed older ones that are less relevant today. As in previous editions, I tried to make the text readable, neither too simplistic nor too complex.

The book still includes 16 chapters, but in light of the coronavirus pandemic of 2020, I added lots of new material related to its effects on work, workplaces, and workers. As in previous editions, and to provide more topics for class discussion, the average number of discussion questions in each chapter is 10. In each chapter, I reviewed, and in many cases revised, "Applying Your Knowledge" cases and exercises, and although many of the chapter-opening vignettes ("Human Resource Management in Action") retain the same titles, I have updated each one to reflect current information and content. Key terms are boldfaced as they are discussed in the text and they are linked to the Glossary so that students can locate definitions quickly. Each chapter also includes a consolidated list of key terms.

A final consideration is the treatment of international issues. Although there are merits to including a separate chapter on this topic, as well as to interspersing international content in each chapter, I do not see this as an either-or matter. I have done both, recognizing the need to frame domestic HR issues in a global context (e.g., recruitment, staffing, compensation, labor-management relations). At the same time, the book covers international issues (e.g., cultural differences, recruiting, staffing, training, performance management, and compensation of expatriates) in more depth in a separate chapter.

NEW TOPICS IN THE TWELFTH EDITION

Chapter 1–I've updated the chapter-opening case: "Globalization at Work: Wealth, Jobs, and Worker Displacement," to emphasize that free trade and globalization are not good for everyone. In the section on responses of firms to the competitive business environment, I added a new HR Buzz box, "Working Post Pandemic." This is necessary as a new factor–a biological hazard–has the potential to enter the environments of organizations everywhere. Finally, I thoroughly updated Case 1-1, "PepsiCo: Winning with Purpose."

Chapter 2–"HR Technology" reflects the rapid changes in technology, along with a discussion of factors that affect the adoption and implementation of workplace technologies. A new HR Buzz box, "Biometrics and Employee Privacy," should stimulate lively interaction in the classroom, as should the emerging capabilities of HRIS. Along with a description of HR technology, trends, the chapter also includes a new discussion of how leading companies are addressing the need to upgrade the strategically relevant skill sets of their employees as technology evolves.

Chapter 3–This chapter, on people analytics, begins with a new chapter-opening case, "New Developments in People Analytics," with special emphasis on using next-generation people analytics software to assess unconscious bias, gender equity, and diversity and inclusion. The chapter retains its discussions of the promise and perils of Big Data, along with the LAMP model to guide workforce measurement. In the discussion of turnover costs, a revised section describes the kinds of information companies are using to predict the likelihood that an employee will leave. Overall, the chapter reflects the most current thinking and research about people analytics.

Chapter 4–The chapter-opening vignette, on retaliation, has been thoroughly updated, as has every section of employment case law, including the Supreme Court's 2020 decision that outlaws discrimination against gay and transgender individuals. There is also a new Case 4-1, "Second-Chance Employment," featuring organic-bread company, Dave's Killer Bread. The area of employment law is dynamic, and this chapter reflects the latest findings and guidance for employers.

Chapter 5–"Diversity and Inclusion (D&I)" features a revised chapter-opening case, "The Business and Ethical Cases for Diversity Are Not Enough to Bring about Real Change." It sets the stage for a discussion of the many dimensions of diversity and how increased D&I in the workforce complements evolving changes in organizations and markets. There is also advice for managers about how to handle questions and concerns about D&I and new examples that illustrate how progressive companies are maximizing the benefits of D&I.

Chapter 6–The opening case on leadership succession reflects a timeless topic. I have updated it, along with every other section in the chapter, and tried to show tighter linkages between strategic workforce planning and business strategy. I've also completely rewritten the HR Buzz boxes, "Technology Innovation Leads to Changes in Job Design" and "Small Businesses Confront Succession Planning." Finally, Case 6-1, "Workforce Forecasts for a Small Business," is completely new.

Chapter 7–In addition to a thoroughly updated chapter-opening vignette on the promise and perils of social media, the chapter retains its focus on a supply-chain approach to the recruiting-staffing process. Job-posting via social media receives special attention, as does the HR Buzz box on online job search. A new HR Buzz box, "Record Low Unemployment Spurs Creative Recruitment Tactics" and an updated discussion of applicant tracking systems help students grasp important management issues in the recruiting process.

Chapter 8–The chapter begins with an updated treatment of organizational culture and the powerful effect it has on current and prospective employees. Treatments of each of the various screening methods and staffing techniques, from employment applications to drug screening, integrity tests, personality measures, and interviews (including video interviews), reflect the most current research and sound professional practice. A new section highlights Walmart's use of virtual reality in the selection of middle managers for its stores.

Chapter 9–Following an updated treatment of technology-delivered instruction, the chapter discusses training trends, such as the effects of digital technology on work, the growing demand for personal and professional development, and training as an important aspect of an employer's brand. There is a new international application, "The Rise of Robotics, AI, and Upskilling–Globally," and also an updated HR Buzz box, "Action Learning at UPS." As in the 11th edition, Case 9-1 focuses on the on-boarding and training of young leaders at Chinese e-commerce giant Alibaba.

Chapter 10–Firms are not abandoning formal judgments about employee performance, but they are making them much more frequently. Like German fashion retailer Zalando, they're also using apps to create dashboards that allow employees to see, in one place, all of the feedback they have received for both development and evaluation. I've also updated the Ethical Dilemma box, "Employment Decisions Based on Performance," and incorporated the most recent research findings on each aspect of performance management.

Chapter 11–Beginning with the thoroughly updated chapter-opening vignette on "The Trust Gap," the chapter presents a nontechnical introduction to compensation from a strategic perspective–that is, as a pivotal control and incentive mechanism that managers use to attain business objectives. I've updated the HR Buzz box, "What Are You Worth? Salary-Comparison Sources," as well as the one on the Wells Fargo scandal, and a third to show the flip side of stock-based compensation. That is, I added material to show how the drop in the 2020 market fueled by the coronavirus caused hundreds of millions in losses.

Chapter 12–The chapter-opening vignette emphasizes how benefits are changing as a result of trends such as a multigenerational workforce, the global pandemic that pushed work and home lives under the same roof, the need to integrate financial wellness with physical and emotional health, and the digitization of benefits. The chapter emphasizes key strategic considerations in the design of benefit programs, and it presents the very latest research and trends in each key area of employee benefits. I've also added a new section on maternity and paternity leaves and updated changes to the Affordable Care Act.

Chapter 13–A continuing emphasis in this chapter is that organizations will be more successful if they adopt collaborative approaches to labor-management relations than if they doggedly pursue "us-versus-them" approaches. Despite ongoing drops in membership and more right-to-work states, unions remain as powerful social, political, and organizational forces. I've updated the HR Buzz box, "Why There Are Fewer Strikes in the United States," and Figure 13-5 on union membership in other countries has been updated as well.

Chapter 14–Workplace due process and justice on the job are timeless and ever evolving. The chapter illustrates these themes via examples of social-media policies, lifestyle discrimination, and at-will employment. It also includes the latest research and legal rulings about employment contracts, noncompete clauses, and termination for cause. New sections illustrate the complexity of personal privacy in an age of biometric data, smartphones that can track the spread of the the coronavirus pandemic, and the European Union's General Data Protection Regulation.

Chapter 15–I've updated the chapter-opening vignette on substance abuse and the tough policy choices it presents for managers, but a major change is the new issues that businesses face in light of the coronavirus pandemic. Two new ethical dilemmas ask, "What to Do When Scared Workers Don't Want to Report for Work Due to a Pandemic?" and "Should Employees Be Punished for Unhealthy Lifestyles?" A new section focuses on managing a workforce in a time of crisis, and a new HR Buzz box asks, "What If a Worker Is Injured While Working from Home?"

Chapter 16–The chapter emphasizes that although globalization is a dominant force, managers need to pay careful attention to the backlash against it. I've updated the international application on HR practices in the European Union, added new sections on "Classifying Cultures" and "Consultation with European Works Councils," and a new HR Buzz box on local-language proficiency. I've simplified the explanation of the balance-sheet approach to expatriate compensation and also added a new section on the U.S.–Mexico–Canada Agreement that replaced NAFTA.

HELP FOR INSTRUCTORS AND STUDENTS

Several important supplements are available to help you use this book more effectively.

INSTRUCTOR LIBRARY

The Connect Instructor Library is your repository for additional resources to improve student engagement in and out of class. You can select and use any asset that enhances your lecture. The Instructor Library includes

- Instructor's Manual.
- PowerPoint files.
- Test Bank.

ORGANIZATION AND PLAN OF THE BOOK

The text is based on the premise that three critical strategic objectives guide all HR functions: productivity, quality of work life, and profits. The functions–employment; development; compensation; labor-management accommodation; and safety, health, and international implications–in turn, are carried out in multiple environments: competitive, legal, social, and organizational.

Part 1, "Environment," includes Chapters 1 through 4. It provides the backdrop against which students will explore the nature and content of each HRM function. These first four chapters paint a broad picture of the competitive, technological, legal, and organizational environments in which people-management activities take place. They also describe key economic and noneconomic factors that affect productivity, quality of work life, and profits. This is the conceptual framework within which the remaining five parts (12 chapters) of the book unfold.

Logically, "Employment" (Part 2) is the first step in the HRM process. Diversity and inclusion, planning for people, recruiting, and staffing are key components of the employment process. Once employees are on board, the process of "Development" (Part 3) begins, with workplace training, on-boarding, and performance-management activities.

Parts 4, 5, and 6 represent concurrent processes. That is, "Compensation" (Part 4), "Labor-Management Accommodation" (Part 5) and "Support and International Implications" (Part 6) are all closely intertwined, conceptually and in practice. They represent a network of interacting activities such that a change in one of them (e.g., a new pay system or a collective-bargaining agreement) inevitably will have an impact on all other components of the HRM system. It is only for ease of exposition that the book presents them separately in Parts 4, 5, and 6.

ACKNOWLEDGMENTS

Many people played important roles in the development of this edition of the book, and I am deeply grateful to them. Ultimately, any errors of omission or commission are mine, and I bear responsibility for them.

Several people at McGraw-Hill were especially helpful. Associate Portfolio Manager Laura Hurst Spell, Marketing Manager Lisa Granger, and Senior Content Developer Gabriela Velasco provided advice, support, and encouragement. Senior Content Project Manager Melissa Leick and Full Service Project Manager Sarita Yadav were ever vigilant to ensure that all phases of the book's production stayed on schedule. It has been a pleasure to work with each of these individuals. Finally, the many reviewers of the current and previous editions of the text provided important insights and helped improve the final product. Their guidance and feedback have helped make the book what it is today, and they each deserve special thanks:

- Caitlin Demsky, Oakland University
- Christopher McChesney, Indian River State College
- Sandra J. Miles, Murray State University
- Regina Yanson, Francis Marion University

Wayne F. Cascio

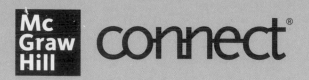

Instructors: Student Success Starts with You

Tools to enhance your unique voice

Want to build your own course? No problem. Prefer to use our turnkey, prebuilt course? Easy. Want to make changes throughout the semester? Sure. And you'll save time with Connect's auto-grading too.

65%
Less Time
Grading

Laptop: McGraw Hill; Woman/dog: George Doyle/Getty Images

Study made personal

Incorporate adaptive study resources like SmartBook® 2.0 into your course and help your students be better prepared in less time. Learn more about the powerful personalized learning experience available in SmartBook 2.0 at **www.mheducation.com/highered/connect/smartbook**

Affordable solutions, added value

Make technology work for you with LMS integration for single sign-on access, mobile access to the digital textbook, and reports to quickly show you how each of your students is doing. And with our Inclusive Access program you can provide all these tools at a discount to your students. Ask your McGraw Hill representative for more information.

Padlock: Jobalou/Getty Images

Solutions for your challenges

A product isn't a solution. Real solutions are affordable, reliable, and come with training and ongoing support when you need it and how you want it. Visit **www.supportateverystep.com** for videos and resources both you and your students can use throughout the semester.

Checkmark: Jobalou/Getty Images

Students: Get Learning that Fits You

Effective tools for efficient studying

Connect is designed to make you more productive with simple, flexible, intuitive tools that maximize your study time and meet your individual learning needs. Get learning that works for you with Connect.

Study anytime, anywhere

Download the free ReadAnywhere app and access your online eBook or SmartBook 2.0 assignments when it's convenient, even if you're offline. And since the app automatically syncs with your eBook and SmartBook 2.0 assignments in Connect, all of your work is available every time you open it. Find out more at
www.mheducation.com/readanywhere

> *"I really liked this app—it made it easy to study when you don't have your textbook in front of you."*
>
> - Jordan Cunningham,
>   Eastern Washington University

Calendar: owattaphotos/Getty Images

Everything you need in one place

Your Connect course has everything you need—whether reading on your digital eBook or completing assignments for class, Connect makes it easy to get your work done.

Learning for everyone

McGraw Hill works directly with Accessibility Services Departments and faculty to meet the learning needs of all students. Please contact your Accessibility Services Office and ask them to email accessibility@mheducation.com, or visit
www.mheducation.com/about/accessibility
for more information.

Top: Jenner Images/Getty Images, Left: Hero Images/Getty Images, Right: Hero Images/Getty Images

ENVIRONMENT

To manage people effectively in today's world of work, one must understand and appreciate the significant competitive, technological, and legal issues. The purpose of Chapters 1 through 4 is to provide insight into these issues. They provide both direction for and perspective on the management of human resources in the 21st century.

1

HUMAN RESOURCES IN A GLOBALLY COMPETITIVE BUSINESS ENVIRONMENT

Questions This Chapter Will Help Managers Answer

LO 1-1 How have global flows of information and knowledge changed the ways we live and work?

LO 1-2 What people-related business issues must managers be concerned about?

LO 1-3 Which features will characterize the competitive business environment in the foreseeable future, and how might we respond to them?

LO 1-4 What people-related problems are likely to arise as a result of changes in the forms of organizations? How can we avoid these problems?

LO 1-5 What are the HR implications of our firm's business strategy?

GLOBALIZATION AT WORK: WEALTH, JOBS, AND WORKER DISPLACEMENT*

Globalization–the ability of any individual or company to compete, connect, exchange, or collaborate globally–is exploding. The ability to digitize so many things, to send them anywhere and to pull them in from everywhere via our mobile phones and the Internet, has unleashed a torrent of global flows of information and knowledge. Global flows of commerce, finance, credit, social networks, and more are interlacing markets, media, central banks, companies, schools, communities, and individuals more tightly together than ever before. That same connectivity is also making individuals and institutions more interdependent. As author Tom Friedman notes, "Everyone everywhere is now more vulnerable to the actions of anyone anywhere"[1] (2016, p. 27).

Think about just a few of these global flows: friends (Facebook); renters (Airbnb); opinions (Twitter); e-commerce (Amazon, Tencent, Alibaba); crowdfunding (Kickstarter, GoFundMe, Indiegogo); ideas and instant messages (WhatsApp, WeChat); peer-to-peer payments (PayPal, Venmo); pictures (Instagram); college courses (MOOCs); design tools (Autodesk); music (Apple, Pandora, Spotify); video (Netflix); searches for knowledge (Google); and cloud-based tools (Salesforce.com).

Trade was once largely confined to advanced economies and their large, multinational companies. Today, a more digital form of globalization has opened the door to developing countries, to small companies and start-ups, and to billions of individuals. Millions of small and midsize enterprises worldwide have turned themselves into exporters by joining e-commerce marketplaces such as Alibaba, Amazon, eBay, and Flipkart. Approximately 18 percent of the global goods trade is now conducted via international e-commerce, up from 10 percent just since 2017. This is globalization 3.0, or digital globalization. Today, even the smallest firms can compete with the largest multinationals. Individuals are using global digital platforms to learn, find work, showcase their talent, and build personal networks. According to the McKinsey Global Institute, some 900 million people have international connections on social media, and 360 million take part in cross-border e-commerce. Digital platforms for both traditional employment and freelance assignments are beginning to create more global labor markets. That allows companies to find the best person for a job anywhere in the world. In this increasingly digital era of globalization, large companies can manage their international operations in leaner, more efficient ways. Using digital platforms and tools, they can sell into fast-growing markets while keeping virtual teams connected in real time.

These developments signal that globalization is deepening and expanding, as most of the world continues to pursue free trade. Emerging economies are knitting closer ties among themselves as China, India, and others gain in wealth, clout, and confidence. The World Trade Organization estimates that more than half of exports from developing countries now go to emerging economies, up from 38 percent

Sources: Friedman, T. L. (2016). *Thank You for Being Late: An Optimist's Guide to Thriving in the Age of Accelerations.* New York: Farrar, Straus & Giroux. Free exchange. (2016, Feb. 6). Trade in the balance. *The Economist*, p. 69. Autor, D. H., Dorn, D., and Hanson, G. H. (2016). The China shock: Learning from labor-market adjustment to large changes in trade. *Annual Review of Economics*, 8, pp. 205–40. Schuman, M. (2016, July 31). The world is still flat. *Bloomberg Businessweek*, pp. 8, 9. Goodman, P. S. (2016, Sept. 28). More wealth, more jobs, but not for everyone: What fuels the backlash on trade. *The New York Times.* Retrieved from *www.nytimes.com/2016/09/29/business/economy/more-wealth-more-jobs-but-not-for-everyone-what-fuels-the-backlash-on-trade.html?r=0* on September 30, 2016. McKinsey Global Institute. (2016, Feb.) Digital globalization: The new era of global flows. Retrieved from *http://www.mckinsey.com/business-functions/digital-mckinsey/our-insights/digital-globalization-the-new-era-of-global-flows* on April 7, 2016. Lipsman, A. (2019, June 27). Global e-commerce. Retrieved from *https://www.emarketer.com/content/global-ecommerce-2019* on February 19, 2020.

in just two decades. Economists since Adam Smith have argued that trade makes countries richer. It creates larger markets, which allows for greater specialization, lower costs, and higher incomes. Yet the news is not all good because trade comes with no assurances that the benefits will be shared equitably.

Although global trade has reduced inequality at a worldwide level, it has played some part in increasing it at a national level. It certainly has increased the profitability of big firms, relative to labor, because *Fortune* 500 corporations can relocate capital and labor to the most economically advantageous places, even as workers struggle to adapt to change. Whereas highly skilled workers in the industrialized world have enjoyed rising opportunities and incomes, workers with low-level skills have borne the costs, suffering joblessness, bleak opportunities, and intense competition.

In the United States, conventional economics has long held that workers would move into new, more enriching areas of the labor market when jobs in their communities went elsewhere. Yet as a recent study has shown, that is not always the case. Looking at the effect of the rise of China on American labor from the 1990s onward (which they termed a "trade shock"), labor economists David Autor, David Dorn, and Gordon Hanson found that workers' adjustment to trade shocks was stunningly slow, with local unemployment rates remaining elevated for a full decade or more after the onset of a trade shock. Bottom line: Free trade and globalization are not good for everyone. There are groups of workers that suffer because of free trade—and they often suffer for a long time. In the conclusion to this case, we will examine some possible solutions to these problems.

Challenges

1. What are some of the benefits of increased flows of digital information and knowledge?
2. In the United States, about 6 million manufacturing jobs disappeared in the first decade of the 21st century. What factors other than free trade and foreign competition might explain that?
3. What might governments do to cushion the blow from job losses?

THE ENTERPRISE IS THE PEOPLE

Organizations are managed and staffed by people. Without people, organizations cannot exist. Indeed, the challenge, the opportunity, and the frustration of creating and managing organizations frequently stem from the people-related problems that arise within them. People-related problems, in turn, frequently stem from the mistaken belief that people are all alike, that they can be treated identically. Nothing could be further from the truth. Like snowflakes, no two people are exactly alike, and everyone differs physically and psychologically from everyone else. Sitting in a sports arena, for example, will be tall people, small people, fat people, thin people, people of color, white people, elderly people, young people, and so on. Even within any single physical category there will be enormous variability in psychological characteristics. Some will be outgoing, others reserved; some will be intelligent, others not so intelligent; some will prefer indoor activities, others outdoor activities. The point is that these differences demand attention, so that each person can maximize his or her potential, organizations can maximize their effectiveness, and society as a whole can make the wisest use of its human resources.

This book is about managing people, the most vital of all resources, in work settings. Rather than focus exclusively on issues of concern to the human resource specialist, however, we will examine human resource management (HRM) issues in terms of their impact on management in general. A changing world order has forced us to take a hard look at the ways we manage people. Research has shown time and again that HRM practices can make an important, practical difference in terms of three key organizational outcomes: productivity, quality of work life, and profit. **Productivity** is a measure of the output of goods and services relative to the input of labor, capital, and equipment. The more productive an industry the better its competitive position because its unit costs are lower. **Quality of work life (QWL)** refers to employees' perceptions of their physical and mental well-being at work. **Profit** refers to financial gain, the income remaining after total costs are deducted from total revenue. Each chapter in this book considers the impact of a different aspect of human resource management on these three broad themes. To study these impacts, we will look at the latest theory and research in each topical area, plus examples of actual company practices.

This chapter begins by considering what human resource management is all about, how it relates to the work of the line manager, and how it relates to profits. Then we will consider some current competitive challenges in the business environment, emphasizing the importance of business and human resources (HR) strategy—both of which have direct implications for productivity and quality of work life. Let's begin by considering the nature of HRM.

MANAGING PEOPLE: A CRITICAL ROLE FOR EVERY MANAGER

Managers are responsible for optimizing all of the resources available to them—material, capital, and human.[2] When it comes to managing people, however, all managers must be concerned to some degree with the following five activities: staffing, retention, development, adjustment, and managing change.

Staffing comprises the activities of (1) identifying work requirements within an organization; (2) determining the numbers of people and the skills mix necessary to do the work; and (3) recruiting, selecting, and promoting qualified candidates.

Retention comprises the activities of (1) rewarding employees for performing their jobs effectively; (2) ensuring harmonious working relations between employees and managers; and (3) maintaining a safe, healthy work environment.

Development is a function whose objective is to preserve and enhance employees' competence in their jobs through improving their knowledge, skills, abilities, and other characteristics; HR specialists use the term *competencies* to refer to these items.

Adjustment comprises activities intended to maintain compliance with the organization's HR policies (e.g., through discipline) and business strategies (e.g., cost leadership).

Managing change is an ongoing process whose objective is to enhance the ability of an organization to anticipate and respond to developments in its external and internal environments, and to enable employees at all levels to cope with the changes.

Needless to say, these activities can be carried out at the individual, work-team, or larger organizational unit (e.g., department) level. Sometimes they are initiated by the organization (e.g., recruitment efforts or management development programs), and sometimes they are initiated by the individual or work team (e.g., voluntary re-tirement, safety improvements). Whatever the case, the responsibilities for executing them are highly interrelated. Together, these activities constitute human resource management, **HRM.** To understand how each of the major activities within HRM relates to every other one, consider the following scenario.

As a result of a large number of unexpected early retirements, the Hand Corpora-tion finds that it must recruit extensively to fill the vacated jobs. The firm is well aware of the rapid changes that will be occurring in its business over the next 3 to 5 years, so it must change its recruiting strategy in accordance with the expected changes in job requirements. It also must develop selection procedures that will identify the kinds of competencies required of future employees. Compensation poli-cies and procedures may have to change because job requirements will change, and new incentive systems will probably have to be developed. Because the firm cannot identify all the competencies that will be required 3 to 5 years from now, it will have to offer new training and development programs along the way to satisfy those needs. Assessment procedures will necessarily change as well, because different com-petencies will be required in order to function effectively at work. As a result of carrying out all this activity, the firm may need to lay off, promote, or transfer some employees to accomplish its mission, and it will have to provide mechanisms to en-able all remaining employees to cope effectively with the changed environment.

It is surprising how that single event, an unexpectedly large number of early retirees, can change the whole ballgame. So it is with any system or network of in-terrelated components. Changes in any single part of the system have a reverberating effect on all other parts of the system. Simply knowing that this will occur is healthy because then we will not make the mistake of confining our problems to only one part. We will recognize and expect that whether we are dealing with problems of staffing, training, compensation, or labor relations, all parts are interrelated. In short, the systems approach provides a conceptual framework for integrating the various components within the system and for linking the HRM system with larger organi-zational needs.

To some, the activities of staffing, retention, development, and adjustment are the special responsibilities of the HR department. But these responsibilities also lie within the core of every manager's job throughout any organization, and because line managers have **authority** (the organizationally granted right to influence the actions and behavior of the workers they manage), they have considerable impact on the ways workers actually behave.

Thus, a broad objective of HRM is to optimize the usefulness (i.e., the productivity) of all workers in an organization. A special objective of the HR department is to help line managers manage those workers more effectively. As Jack Welch, legendary former CEO of General Electric, noted: "Look, HR should be every company's 'killer app.' What could possibly be more important than who gets hired, developed, promoted, or moved out the door? Business is a game, and as with all games, the team that puts the best people on the field and gets them playing together wins. It's that simple."[3]

This is consistent with the findings of Deloitte's 2019 Human Capital Trends. When CEOs were asked to name the top four measures of success for their enter-prises, they identified (1) the impact on society, including income inequality, diver-sity, and the environment; (2) customer satisfaction; (3) employee satisfaction/retention; and (4) financial performance (revenue, profit).[4] Meeting the people-management challenge is a responsibility that is shared by the HR department and line managers, as shown in Table 1-1.

Table 1–1		
HRM ACTIVITIES AND THE RESPONSIBILITIES OF LINE MANAGERS AND THE HR DEPARTMENT		
Activity	**Line management responsibility**	**HR department responsibility**
Staffing	Providing data for job or competency analyses and minimum qualifications; integrating strategic plans with HR plans; interviewing candidates, integrating information collected by the HR department, making final decisions on entry-level hires and promotions	Job/competency analysis, workforce planning, recruitment; compliance with civil rights laws and regulations; application forms, written tests, performance tests, interviews, background investigations, reference checks, physical examinations
Retention	Fair treatment of employees, open communication, face-to-face resolution of conflict, promotion of teamwork, respect for the dignity of each individual, pay increases based on merit	Compensation and benefits, employee relations, health and safety, employee services
Development	On-the-job training, job enrichment, coaching, applied motivational strategies, performance feedback to subordinates	Development of legally sound performance management systems, morale surveys, technical training; management and organizational development; career planning and counseling; talent analytics
Adjustment	Discipline, discharge, layoffs, transfers	Investigation of employee complaints, outplacement services, retirement counseling
Managing change	Provide a vision of where the company or unit is going and the resources to make the vision a reality	Provide expertise to facilitate the overall process of managing change

In the context of Table 1-1, note how line and HR managers share people-related business activities. Generally speaking, HR provides the technical expertise in each area, while line managers (or, in some cases, self-directed work teams) use this expertise in order to manage people effectively. In a small business, however, line managers are responsible for both the technical and managerial aspects of HRM. In a recent survey of chief HR officers, one described his or her greatest challenge as follows: "Creating a true sense of ownership among the senior leaders regarding their roles as 'Chief Talent Officers.' Recognizing that having the right people in critical leadership roles is not an HR thing, or responsibility, but rather it is a business imperative and must be truly owned by the leaders of the respective businesses/functions."[5]

WHY DOES EFFECTIVE HRM MATTER?

At a broad level, HRM is concerned with choices—choices that organizations make from a wide variety of possible policies, practices, and structures for managing employees.[6] More specifically, there exists a substantial and growing body of research evidence showing a strong connection between how firms manage their people and the economic results they achieve. For example, a recent meta-analysis (a quantitative summary of empirical results) conceptualized HR practices as falling into one of three primary dimensions: skill-enhancing, motivation-enhancing, or opportunity-enhancing. Skill-enhancing HR practices include comprehensive recruitment, rigorous selection, and extensive training. Motivation-enhancing HR practices include developmental performance management, competitive compensation, incentives and rewards, extensive benefits, promotion, and career development. Opportunity-enhancing HR practices empower employees to use their skills and motivation to achieve organizational objectives. They include practices such as flexible job design, work teams, employee involvement, and information sharing.[7] The authors hypothesized that these three dimensions of HR systems are indirectly related to financial outcomes through human capital, employee motivation, voluntary turnover, and operational outcomes. Operationally, financial outcomes included return on assets, return on equity, market return, sales growth, and overall financial performance. Human capital was measured using established scales and the education level of a workforce. Employee motivation was reflected by collective job satisfaction, organizational commitment, organizational climate, perceived organizational support, and organizational citizenship behavior. Finally, operational outcomes included productivity, quality, service, innovation, and overall operational performance.

Meta-analysis revealed that the three dimensions of HR systems had different effects. This result was counter to an earlier belief that all HR practices in an HR system function in the same pattern. Skill-enhancing HR practices were more strongly related to human capital, whereas motivation- and opportunity-enhancing HR practices were more strongly related to employee motivation. Human capital and employee motivation, in turn, were strongly related to voluntary turnover and to operational outcomes, and operational outcomes were strongly related to financial outcomes. Not only are HR practices distinct, but they operate through different pathways as well.

Another study, done by accounting professors at Wharton and Stanford, used data from 153 publicly traded companies to assess the impact of several HR management practices on stock returns 12 months later.[8] They found that a 10 percent increase in a measure of goal-setting activity at firms was associated with a 6 percent increase in industry-adjusted stock returns. A 6 percent stock boost also was associated with a 10 percent increase in a measure of the extent to which managers used the full spectrum of the rating scale when evaluating employees. In short, managers in companies that are clear with employees about work expectations and that provide honest feedback on a regular basis drive successful performance. Needless to say, the extent to which these practices actually will pay off depends on the skill and care with which the many HR practices available are implemented to solve real business problems and to support a firm's operating and strategic initiatives.

Such high-performance work practices provide a number of important sources of enhanced organizational performance.[9] People work harder because of the increased involvement and commitment that comes from having more control and say in their work. They work smarter because they are encouraged to build skills and competence. They work more responsibly because their employers place more responsibility in the hands of employees further down in the organization. What's the bottom line in all of this? HR systems have important, practical impacts on the survival and financial performance of firms, and on the productivity and quality of the work life of the people in them.

Now that we know what HRM is, and why it matters, the next step is to understand some significant features of the competitive business environment in which HRM activities take place. Four such features are globalization, technology, sustainability, and demographic changes.

FEATURES OF THE COMPETITIVE BUSINESS ENVIRONMENT

Globalization

We noted earlier that **globalization** is the ability of any individual or company to compete, connect, exchange, or collaborate globally. Markets in every country have become fierce battlegrounds where both domestic and foreign competitors fight for market share. For example, Coca-Cola earns more than 75 percent of its revenues from outside the United States! The world's 500 largest companies in 2019 generated $32.7 trillion in revenues and $2.15 trillion in profits. Together, they employ 69.3 million people worldwide and are represented by 34 countries.[10]

The Backlash against Globalization

In no small part, the booming economies of recent years in developed countries have been fueled by globalization. Open borders have allowed new ideas and technology to flow freely around the globe, accelerating productivity growth and allowing companies to be more competitive than they have been in decades. Yet there is a growing fear on the part of many people that globalization benefits big companies instead of average citizens, as stagnating wages and growing job insecurity in developed countries create rising disenchantment. In theory, less-developed countries win from globalization because they get jobs making low-cost products for rich countries. Rich countries win because, in addition to being able to buy inexpensive imports, they also can sell more sophisticated products, like financial services, to emerging economies. The problem, according to many experts, is that workers in the West are not equipped for today's pace of change, in which jobs come and go and skills can quickly become redundant.[11] In the public eye, multinational corporations are synonymous with globalization. In all of their far-flung operations, therefore, they bear a responsibility to be good corporate citizens, to preserve the environment, to uphold labor standards, to provide decent working conditions and competitive wages, to treat their employees fairly, and to contribute to the communities in which they operate. Doing so will make a strong case for continued globalization.

Implications of Globalization for HRM

Globalization is a fact of organizational life, as countries, companies, and workers are interconnected as never before. Global trade connects the fate of every industry and laborer, no matter how small or seemingly self-sufficient, to the decisions of bureaucrats in China, shipbuilders in Korea, and bankers everywhere.[12] To illustrate, consider how the ripple effects of the coronavirus outbreak in China in 2020 affected global business and markets. When the virus shut down parts suppliers in China, it affected industries as diverse as airlines, automobiles, and consumer electronics. It affected supply chains in industries around the world as assembly lines from Asia to Europe depend upon parts moving swiftly from China into their plants.[13]

Another feature of globalization is that cheap labor and plentiful resources, combined with ease of travel and communication, have created global labor markets. This is fueling mobility as more companies expand abroad and people consider foreign postings as a natural part of their professional development. Beyond the positive effects that such circulation of talent brings to both developed and developing countries, it enables employment opportunities well beyond the borders of one's home country. This means that competition for talent will come not only from the company down the street, but also from the employer on the other side of the world. It will be a seller's market, with talented individuals having many choices. Countries as well as companies will need to brand themselves as employers of choice in order to attract this talent.[14]

Along with these trends, expect to see three more. The first is increasing workforce flux as more roles are automated or outsourced and more workers are contract-based, are mobile, or work flexible hours. This may allow companies to leverage global resources more efficiently, but it also will increase the complexity of management's role. Second, expect more diversity as workers come from a greater range of backgrounds. Those with local knowledge of an emerging market, a global outlook, and an intuitive sense of the corporate culture will be particularly valued. Not surprisingly, talented young people will more frequently choose their employers based, at least in part, on opportunities to gain international experience. Finally, technical skills, although mandatory, will be less defining of the successful manager than the ability to work across cultures and to build relationships with many different constituents.[15]

Technology

We live in a global world where technology, especially information and communication technology, is changing the manner in which businesses create and capture value, how and where we work, and how we interact and communicate. Consider five technologies that are transforming the very foundations of global business and the organizations that drive it: cloud and mobile computing, big data and machine learning, sensors and intelligent manufacturing, advanced robotics and drones, and clean-energy technologies. These technologies are not just helping people to do things better and faster, but also enabling profound changes in the ways that work is done in organizations.[16]

Information and ideas are keys to the new creative economy because every country, every company, and every individual depends increasingly on knowledge. Artificial intelligence and robotics have increasingly taken over such tasks as bookkeeping, clerical work, and repetitive production jobs in manufacturing. At the same time, countless white-collar jobs, such as many in customer service, have disappeared. Fortunately, history shows that technology-driven job destruction does not decrease overall employment—even while making some jobs obsolete. Ultimately, as workers adjust their skills and entrepreneurs create opportunities based on the new technologies, the number of jobs rebounds.[17] Business leaders cannot wait until evolving technologies disrupt the status quo. Rather, they need to understand how the competitive advantages on which they have based their strategies might erode or be enhanced a decade from now by emerging technologies. They need to understand how technologies might bring them new customers or force them to defend their existing bases, or inspire them to invent new strategies.[18]

In the creative economy, the most important intellectual property is not software or music. Rather, it is the intellectual capital that resides in people. When assets were physical things like coal mines, shareholders truly owned them. But when the most vital assets are people, there can be no true ownership. The best that corporations can do is to create an environment that makes the best people want to stay.[19] Therein lies the challenge of managing human resources.

Impact of New Technology on HRM

Technology is changing the nature of competition, work, and employment in ways that are profound and that need to be managed actively. As just one example, Levi Strauss & Co. is introducing robotic software to its finance function. According to the

New technology has changed the ways we work.
mapodile/Getty Images

company's chief financial officer: "The idea is not to eliminate jobs. We are going to upskill employees and have them spend more time on analysis."[20] More generally, firms will need to consider the cost of developing and deploying automation solutions for specific tasks in the workplace, the availability and cost of labor, and regulatory and social acceptance of automation.

According to the McKinsey Global Institute, by 2030 as many as 30–40 percent of workers in developed countries may need to move into new occupations or upgrade their skill sets significantly. Skilled workers in short supply will become even scarcer. Companies that fail to address their underlying talent needs may fail to achieve their digital aspirations. At the same time, senior managers have a great opportunity to collaborate with employees to create a prosperous, fulfilling future, as they work through employee transitions.[21] Amazon, for example, has pledged $700 million to train 100,000 employees for higher-skilled jobs in technology.[22] PricewaterhouseCoopers is upskilling all of its 50,000 employees. Walmart runs 201 academies inside Walmart Supercenters and modular classrooms in store parking lots where employees receive training. That upskilling effort resulted in the promotion of 215,000 employees in 2018.[23] At a broader level, worker upskilling, reskilling, and in some cases, supportive employee transitions out of the workforce, will be major HR challenges facing firms for the foreseeable future.

Sustainability

Sustainability is often defined as the "ability to meet the needs of the present without compromising the ability of future generations to meet their needs."[24] For many organizations, this suggests a different way of doing business. In addition to economic considerations of growth and profit, sustainability considerations suggest that decision makers should assess social and environmental risks and opportunities when making all business decisions. It is an evolving business practice that incorporates sustainable development into a company's business model. This approach is often referred to as the "triple bottom line," the simultaneous delivery of positive results for people, planet, and profit.[25]

Sustainability is more than simply meeting responsibilities to society, for it also can create sustained competitive advantage. Indeed, research suggests that responsible approaches to social and environmental issues are likely to pay off in a number of tangible ways.[26] Consider just two examples. Since 2005, Pepsico has presented its sustainability goals in annual reports that focus on three broad themes: human sustainability (promote healthy food and drinks), talent sustainability (work to attract top talent and to create a diverse company culture), and environmental sustainability. Thus, by 2025 it plans to reduce added sugar and fat in its products, to make 100 percent of its packaging recyclable, and to reduce the waste it generates by 50 percent. Computer technology company Dell integrates alternative materials in its products and packaging, actively recycles used electronics, and partners exclusively with responsible suppliers. A key goal for 2020 is to reduce the energy intensity of its products by 80 percent.[27]

Other payoffs include improvements in reputation, productivity, talent acquisition, employee retention and engagement, cost-effectiveness, risk avoidance or mitigation, innovation and market expansion, and access to capital.[28] While 90 percent of executives see sustainability as important, however, only 60 percent of their companies have a sustainability strategy.[29] The relationship between sustainability investments and organizational performance is complex, and other factors, such as industry positioning and market structure, also affect the strength of the relationship.[30]

In practice, sustainability affects an organization's business model, structure, and processes in at least three ways. One, organizations consider a wider set of stakeholders when setting strategy. In addition to financial shareholders, other stakeholders include employees, customers, suppliers, regulators, and local communities. Sustainable organizations seek them out to understand their expectations, concerns, and risks relating to operations before developing a sustainability strategy. Two, stakeholders help with the implementation of such a strategy, as employers partner with external organizations. These may include community organizations, governmental and nongovernmental organizations (NGOs), and industry alliances. Such partnerships may help advance sustainable development because the demands of global corporate sustainability often exceed the capability of a single organization to respond.[31] Three, sustainability affects corporate practices and requires greater involvement and accountability of boards of directors, and it requires business transparency, as illustrated in the growing number of organizations that issue annual sustainability reports.

Implications of Sustainability for HRM   From a people-management perspective, the challenge is to hire and develop managers who can deal with present as well as future sustainability issues facing their organizations. *One way to encourage that is to tie executive compensation to sustainability goals and results.*[32] Alcoa, for example, ties 5 percent of its executives' annual bonuses to the company's goals to reduce carbon-dioxide emissions. Xcel Energy ties a full one-third of its CEO's annual bonus to goals that include renewable energy, emissions reductions, energy efficiency, and clean technology. That is a powerful marker of a company's environmental leadership, and a strong signal about company culture.

Some companies have achieved notable results, Kickstarter, the world's largest funding platform for creative projects—nearly 340,000 projects—developed an online environmental resource center for early-stage entrepreneurs. The resource center provides production-specific environmental tools to help reduce the environmental impact associated with the manufacturing and shipping of projects. More importantly, it integrates sustainability into the design from the very start. To address carbon emissions by its suppliers, Novartis created an interactive dashboard to visualize and track total greenhouse-gas emissions from its upstream activities (material inputs needed for production) and downstream activities (production and distribution). The dashboard can identify potential emission hotspots and take action by increasing supplier-engagement initiatives to reduce its environmental impact.[33] For companies that are serious about achieving sustainability gains, here are four key steps: (1) Make a public commitment, (2) the CEO should lead by example, (3) help employees understand the link between sustainable products and processes and strategic business goals, and (4) embed sustainable behaviors and processes throughout the business and offer incentives for line managers to deliver results.

The HRM function also has the potential to contribute important skills in areas such as change management and cultural stewardship.[34] Embedding a sustainability strategy deeply into an organization's culture and management practices is an ongoing challenge. Practices such as values-based recruitment using employer branding informed by sustainability initiatives, helping employees and managers link performance targets to sustainability initiatives, and linking variable pay to those initiatives, accomplish two objectives. They support the broader business approach to sustainability and they create and deliver core HRM processes sustainably.

Demographic Changes and Increasing Cultural Diversity

The number and the mix of people available to work are changing rapidly, as Figure 1-1 illustrates. By 2040 the non-Hispanic white population is projected to drop below 50 percent, with Hispanics making up more than a quarter of the population, and Asians, African Americans, and other ethnic groups constituting the rest. The share of foreign-born people living in the United States (more than 44 million or 13.6 percent of the population) is approaching a record high, but 25 nations and territories have higher shares of immigrants.[35] Globally, the United Nations estimates that by 2060, for every 100 people of working age, there will be 30 people who are 65 and older. That is more than double the ratio of old-to-young people today. Because of low birthrates, the age wave is more acute in developed countries, increasing the cost of social programs and limiting economic growth. Younger migrants may ease the pain.[36]

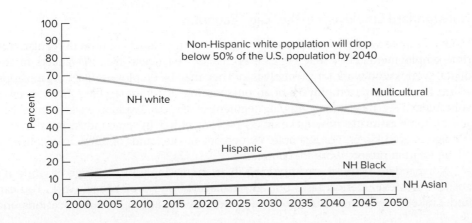

Figure 1–1

U.S. population by race, 2000 to 2050.

Source: National Association of Corporate Directors. (2014, Jan. 16). *The US Demographic Tsunami: What Directors Need to Know,* p. 6.

Implications for HRM

These trends have two key implications for managers: (1) The reduced supply of workers (at least in some fields) will make finding and keeping employees a top priority. (2) The task of managing a culturally diverse workforce, of harnessing the motivation and efforts of a wide variety of workers, will present a continuing challenge to management.

The organizations that thrive will be the ones that embrace the new demographic trends instead of fighting them. That will mean even more women and minorities in the workforce–and in the boardrooms. Workforce diversity is not just a competitive advantage. Today it's a competitive necessity.

RESPONSES OF FIRMS TO THE NEW COMPETITIVE REALITIES

In today's world of fast-moving global markets and fierce competition, trends such as the following are accelerating the shift toward new forms of organization in the 21st century[37]:

- Old thinking: Minimize the costs of transactions by hiring in-house expertise. New thinking: Create and maintain an optimal portfolio of resources inside as well as outside the organization.
- The decline of routine work (sewing-machine operators, telephone operators, word processors) coupled with the expansion of complex jobs that require flexibility, creativity, and the ability to work well with people (managers, software-applications engineers, artists, and designers).
- Pay tied less to a person's position or tenure in an organization and more to the market value of his or her skills.
- A change in the paradigm of doing business from making a product to providing a service, often by part-time or temporary employees.
- Outsourcing of activities that are not core competencies of a firm (e.g., payroll, benefits administration, relocation services).
- The redefinition of work itself: constant learning, more higher-order thinking, less nine-to-five mentality.

In response to these changes, many firms are doing one or more of the following: using nonstandard employees, restructuring (including downsizing), and building flexibility into work schedules and rules. Let's briefly consider each of these.

Nonstandard Employees in the "Gig" Economy

More and more workers are operating outside the traditional confines of regular, full-time employment. They may be "free agents" or "e-lancers" (i.e., freelancers in the digital world) who work for themselves, or they may be employees of an organization a firm is allied with, employees of an outsourcing or temporary-help firm, or even volunteers. Freelancers are a growing segment of the U.S. workforce (see Figure 1–2) and by some estimates now make up 35 percent of it.[38] In some industries, that percentage is even larger. For example, 90 percent of the hands-on crew in an offshore oil-exploration project work for contractors.[39]

Nonstandard workers are appearing in an increasingly broad range of work. It's not just low-level clerical tasks but also managerial and professional work. You can find LinkedIn freelance profiles for directors of marketing communications and

Figure 1–2

Where do you work?

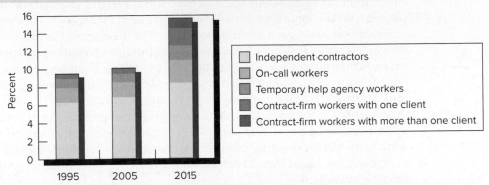

Source: Weber, L. (2017, Feb. 3). The end of employees. *The Wall Street Journal*, p. A10.

freelance chief executive officer (CEO), chief financial officer (CFO), and chief operating officer (COO) jobs on Indeed.com. Nonstandard workers may be less costly than their regular full-time counterparts, especially because they typically are not eligible for benefits. Nonstandard work allows the workforce to expand or contract faster when demand is volatile.[40] Nonstandard work allows organizations to tailor the skill sets they need without hiring and firing full-time employees.

Two factors combine to make nonstandard work more feasible for organizations and workers. The first is technology. Internet-based communication tools, including collaborative workspaces and the opportunity for remote monitoring by companies, make nonstandard work attractive to individuals as well as organizations.[41] Second, creativity and problem-solving skills play critically important roles in production and value creation in today's knowledge-based economy, and those can originate either inside or outside organizational boundaries. For example, consider the hundreds of thousands of applications that exist for the iPhone, iPad, and Android operating systems. The developers of those "apps" do not work for Apple, Google, or a phone manufacturer. Freelancers develop them in exchange for royalties from sales. For certain specialized skills, the best way to obtain and keep them current is a freelance or nonstandard work ecosystem.[42] To illustrate, Siemens invented a pediatric hearing aid. Because its expertise was not marketing, it forged a partnership with a company that excels at marketing–Walt Disney Corp. Disney developed the storybooks, character-themed packaging, and displays for physicians' offices to help market the product.[43]

These factors have combined to create a virtuous circle. That is, the more nonstandard work exists as a model of how to do work and to conduct a career over a lifetime, the more legitimate it becomes as a work form and life pattern. The more legitimate it becomes, the more firms and employees will choose to engage in it.[44]

At the same time, there are risks associated with nonstandard workers. Will they be as committed as full-timers? Will their rapid turnover require extensive orientation and training of new ones? Will they stick around long enough to develop the kind of depth of understanding of people and operations that will enable them to contribute meaningfully? Can work arrangements appropriately protect workers and balance worker and organizational rights and needs?

One example of a new organizational form that is evolving from these changes is the **virtual organization**, where teams of specialists come together to work on a project—as in the movie industry—and then disband when the project is finished. Virtual organizations are already quite popular in consulting, in legal defense, and in sponsored research. They are multisite, multiorganizational, and dynamic.[45] More common in the information age, however, is the **virtual workplace**, in which employees operate remotely from each other and from managers.[46] They work anytime, anywhere—in real space or in cyberspace. The widespread availability of e-mail, teleconferencing, collaborative software, and intranets (within-company information networks) facilitates such arrangements. Compelling business reasons, such as reduced real estate expenses, increased productivity, higher profits, improved customer service, access to global markets, and environmental benefits drive their implementation.[47] Jobs in sales, marketing, project engineering, and consulting seem to be best suited for virtual workplaces because individuals in these jobs already work with their clients by phone or at the clients' premises. Indeed, research at Manpower Inc. found that 30 percent of the tasks in a multinational enterprise could be done virtually.[48]

Restructuring, Including Downsizing

Restructuring can assume a variety of forms, of which employment downsizing is probably the most common. Companies can restructure by selling or buying plants or lines of business by altering reporting relationships, or by laying off employees. **Downsizing,** the planned elimination of positions or jobs, has had, and will continue to have, profound effects on organizations, managers at all levels, employees, labor markets, customers, and shareholders.[49]

There was a time when layoffs were seen as an emergency strategy, the last resort in a downturn or crisis. Today, however, layoffs are a standard tool for doing business. Downsizing continues, in good times and in bad, regardless of whether the economy is expanding or contracting, for it has become etched into corporate cultures. During the Great Recession (2007–2009), downsizing was global in scope, with 8.5 million layoffs in the United States and more than 50 million worldwide. During turbulent economic times, even countries that traditionally have avoided layoffs (e.g., South Korea, Japan, Taiwan, and Hong Kong) have embraced the practice. Export-oriented and labor-intensive firms in China, and firms in both manufacturing and service industries in Britain, Canada, Australia, New Zealand, South Africa, South America, and Eastern Europe, participated as well. Not surprisingly, therefore, employment downsizing has attained the (dubious) status as one of the most high-profile, significant, and pervasive management issues of our time. Over the past three decades, downsizing has occurred in virtually all industries and sectors of the economy, and it has affected businesses, governments, and individuals around the world.[50]

Sometimes layoffs are necessary, as when an organization is overstaffed or if a particular business no longer fits into a firm's long-term strategy. Thus, IBM spun off its printer business, Lexmark, and its PC business to Lenovo because neither printers nor PCs fit into its long-term business strategy. Both continue to be successful businesses elsewhere. In many cases, though, the direct and indirect costs are extremely high. Direct costs include items such as severance costs, as well as pension and benefits payouts. Indirect costs, which may be far higher, include low morale, risk-averse survivors, decreased productivity, lack of staff when the economy rebounds, loss of institutional memory, unanticipated voluntary turnover among survivors, and damage to a company's brand as an employer of choice.[51] According to former Honeywell CEO David Cote, "Most managers underestimate how much disruption layoffs create;

they consume everyone in the organization for at least a year. Managers also typically overestimate the savings they will achieve and fail to understand that even bad recessions usually end more quickly than people expect."[52]

When people are fearful about their jobs, they tend to become risk averse, narrow-minded, and self-absorbed. Those are exactly the wrong characteristics needed in tough times. The longer-term questions are "How are we as a company going to emerge when the tough times end? Will we be able to penetrate new markets, generate new customers, and introduce new products or services?" Disengaged, fearful employees don't generally help their firms to do those things. The message to employers is clear: Don't try to shrink your way to prosperity. Instead, the best way to prosper is to create and innovate to grow your business.

Flexibility

More than half of employed U.S. adults don't take all of the vacation days they earn for the year, even though 96 percent of workers claim to see the virtue in taking time off.[53] Time is employees' most precious commodity, and they want the flexibility to control their own time–where, when, and how they work. They want balance in their lives between work and leisure. Flexibility in schedules is the key, as organizations strive to retain talented workers. Indeed, 40 percent of retired Americans say they would rejoin the workforce, if hours were more flexible.[54]

In practice, the concept of "flexibility" reflects a broad spectrum of possible work arrangements, as Table 1–2 makes clear. Unfortunately, flexibility is frequently viewed by managers and employees as an exception or employee accommodation, rather than as a new and effective way of working to achieve business results. A face-time culture, an excessive workload, manager skepticism, customer demands, and a fear of negative career consequences are among the barriers that prevent employees from taking advantage of policies they might otherwise use and that prevent companies from realizing the full benefits that flexibility might bestow.[55]

Table 1–2

IMPLEMENTING FLEXIBILITY: A SPECTRUM OF PRACTICE

Individual Accommodations

Special arrangements, or "deals," are granted on a case-by-case basis and are often kept secret.

Policies and Programs in Place

Policies and programs exist, but flexibility is used only in "pockets" across the organization.

Flexibility's Many Faces

Widespread use of formal and informal flexibility meets business and individual needs.

New Ways of Working

A results-driven culture, where flexible work practices are utilized as a management strategy to achieve business results, ensues.

Source: Corporate Voices for Working Families. (2011, Feb.). Business impacts of flexibility: An imperative for expansion (updated, 2011), p. 16. Retrieved from *www.cvwf.org/publication-toolkits/business-impacts-flexibility-imperative-expansion-updated-2011* on September 29, 2011.

ETHICAL DILEMMA
Conflict between American and Foreign Cultural Values

Each chapter of this book contains a brief scenario that illustrates a decision-making situation that could result in a breach of acceptable behavior. Such situations pose ethical dilemmas. To be ethical is to conform to moral standards or to conform to the standards of conduct of a given profession or group (e.g., medicine, auditing). **Ethical decisions about behavior** take account not only of one's own interests but also, equally, the interests of those affected by a decision. What would you recommend in response to the following situation?[a]

You are the director of HR for a large, southwestern teaching hospital. This hospital has a cooperative program with a major teaching hospital in Saudi Arabia. Each year several doctors from your hospital spend the year in Saudi Arabia, teaching and doing research. The stay in Saudi Arabia is generally considered both lucrative and professionally rewarding.

This morning you had a visit from two of the doctors in the hospital who had been rejected for assignment to Saudi Arabia. They were very upset, as they are both very qualified and ambitious. You had carefully explained to them that although the selection committee was impressed with their abilities, the members had decided that because they were Jewish, it would be best if they were disqualified from consideration. In spite of vigorous protest from the two doctors, you had held your ground and supported the committee's decision. However, as you sit at home, reading, that evening, the situation replays itself in your mind, and you think about the decision and feel a little uncertain.

Is the director of HR correct in supporting the committee's decision? What criteria should the committee, and the director of HR, use to make a decision such as this? What would you recommend?

[a]Taylor, S., and Eder, R. W. (2000). U.S. expatriates and the Civil Rights Act of 1991: Dissolving boundaries. In M. Mendenhall and G. Oddou (Eds.), *Readings and Cases in International Human Resource Management* (3rd ed.). Cincinnati, OH: South-Western College Publishing, pp. 251-79.

HR BUZZ
WORKING POST PANDEMIC

The coronavirus pandemic of 2020 rocked our world like nothing else. It affected how, where, and when people work, as well as how we live. To be sure, the concerns of people working remotely or at home are different from those at an office, a retail store, a hotel, or a factory. Here we focus on physical spaces where people come to work, and where workplace safety and health are paramount concerns. Here are some possible changes.

Checking employees' temperatures as they arrive each day may be required, while social distancing may become a company mandate. Meeting rooms may have capacity limits. To maintain social distancing in an office, many companies will keep large numbers of employees working at home and schedule shifts at widely separated desks in the office, with the help of software applications for booking space at desks and in meeting rooms. Density sensors (people counters) that attach to building entrances, floors, or rooms can count the numbers of people in the cafeteria, the coffee-break room, office floors, or the elevator lobby.

They can send alerts to smartphones or computers to let office managers and employees know if space is available. That information also can be noted on digital screens posted at entrances. As Alex Gorsky, CEO of Johnson & Johnson, noted so clearly, "Every business leader in some way is going to be a health care leader going forward."

Deep-cleaning practices at many workplaces will follow guidelines from the Centers for Disease Control and Prevention (www.cdc.gov/coronavirus/2019-ncov/community/guidance-business-response.html). There will likely be no more hand-shakes, and cross-training will increase so that employees can handle more than one aspect of the business. This is a positive effect of the pandemic because during an emergency, employees will be able to redeploy rapidly to perform essential tasks with little or no learning time, which should allow organizations to maintain their productivity and effectiveness, even with a skeleton crew.

Pay for essential workers will likely change. During the pandemic, many front-line, customer-facing workers made heroic efforts to keep their organizations (and countries) from collapse. These included health-care workers, ambulance drivers, EMTs, and paramedics, as well as long-haul truck drivers, grocery workers, retail-store employees, and fulfillment-center workers and drivers who delivered customer orders from online sites. Most pay systems compensate employees for the additional risks associated with hazardous working conditions that include, among others, biological hazards such as viruses or bacteria that can cause adverse health effects. In the future, expect to see risk premiums and additional benefits added to the pay of essential workers.

Many executives who were skeptical about employees working from home found that remote work can actually be productive, in some cases, more so than work done in an office location. As a result, companies as varied as JPMorgan Chase, Toyota, and Facebook plan to make remote work permanent for many employees.

Many workplaces avoided permanent layoffs by "sharing the pain" of pay cuts or temporary furloughs. That may well become part of the playbook of executives the next time disaster strikes or an economic recession hits. Most importantly, organizations everywhere learned that having a plan to maintain business continuity through a disaster, including written protocols and avoiding sole-source supply chains, is essential. These features will characterize a bright, if different, future for workplaces everywhere.

Sources: Oliver, S. (2020, June 9). Ways to make the office more healthful. *The Wall Street Journal*, p. R2. Wilkie, D. (2020, May 1). Into the future: How a pandemic might reshape the word of work. *SHRM Online*. Retrieved from *www.shrm.org/resourcesandtools/hr-topics/people-managers/pages/coronavirus-future-of-work-.aspx* on May 1, 2020. The post-crisis world: what changes are coming? (2020, May 5). *Knowledge@Wharton*. Retrieved from *https://knowledge.wharton.upenn.edu/article/post-crisis-world-changes-coming/* on May 5, 2020. McCullah, S. (2020, May). 9 predictions on how COVID-19 will permanently affect the workplace. *HR Professionals Magazine* 10(5), p. 26. Smith, A. D. (2020, Apr. 22). Revise policies to facilitate return to work. *SHRM Online*. Retrieved from *www.shrm.org/resourcesandtools/legal-and-compliance/employment-law/pages/coronavirus-facilitate-return-to-work.aspx* on Apr. 22, 2020.

Three features are keys to making the business case for increased flexibility: talent management (specifically, attraction and retention); human capital outcomes (increased satisfaction and commitment, decreased stress); and financial, operational, and business outcomes. Consider the first of these, attraction and retention.

At IBM, responses to a recent global work-life survey from almost 42,000 IBM employees in 79 countries revealed that lack of work-life fit—of which flexibility is a significant component—is the second leading reason for potentially leaving IBM, behind compensation and benefits. In the Corporate Finance organization, for example, 94 percent of all managers reported positive impacts of flexible work options on the company's ability to retain talented professionals. In light of these findings showing the strong link between flexibility and retention, IBM actively promotes flexibility as a strategy for retaining key talent.

People make organizations go. How the people are selected, trained, and managed determines to a large extent how successful an organization will be. As you can certainly appreciate by now, the task of managing people in today's world of work is particularly challenging in light of the competitive realities we have discussed. In 2020 a new factor entered the environments of organizations everywhere: the coronavirus pandemic. It affected their ability to compete, and in the case of many small businesses, their ability to survive. The HR Buzz box highlights a number of workplace changes that have emerged from this painful experience.

Each chapter of this book focuses on a different aspect of HRM and considers its impact on three important outcomes: productivity, quality of work life, and profits. An "Impact of" (topic under discussion) box at the end of each chapter offers specific implications for each of these outcomes.

BUSINESS TRENDS AND HR COMPETENCIES

Over the past decade, organizations have become more complex, dynamic, and fast-paced. As a result, senior managers recognize that attracting, retaining, and managing people effectively is more important than ever. In fact, the results of a recent study by the Society for Human Resource Management that included input from more than 1,200 HR professionals from 33 nations, and survey responses from 32,000 participants, identified nine competencies or elements for HR success. The nine competencies are grouped into four broader clusters: **technical** (HR expertise in people, organizations, the workplace, and strategy); **business** (business acumen, critical evaluation, and consultation); **leadership** (leadership and navigation, ethical practice); and **interpersonal** (communication, relationship management, global and cultural effectiveness). Each competency also includes sub-competencies and behaviors, along with proficiency standards by career level: early, mid, senior, and executive levels. The competencies and their definitions are as follows[56]:

1. **Human resource expertise.** The knowledge of principles, practices, and functions of effective human resource management. It includes expertise in people, organizations, the workplace, and strategy.
2. **Business acumen.** The ability to understand and apply information to contribute to the organization's strategic plan.
3. **Critical evaluation.** The ability to interpret information to make business decisions and recommendations.
4. **Consultation.** The ability to provide guidance to organizational stakeholders.
5. **Leadership and navigation.** The ability to direct and contribute to initiatives and processes within the organization.
6. **Ethical practice.** The ability to integrate core values, integrity, and accountability throughout all organizational and business practices.

7. **Communication.** The ability to effectively exchange with stakeholders.
8. **Relationship management.** The ability to manage interactions to provide service and to support the organization.
9. **Global and cultural effectiveness.** The ability to value and consider the perspectives and backgrounds of all parties.

The Society for Human Resource Management (SHRM) offers HR certification of these competencies at two levels: SHRM-CP (certified professional) and SHRM-SCP (senior certified professional). SHRM's assessment of these competencies through knowledge as well as situational judgment items reflects the ability to know as well as the ability to do. For more information, see *www.shrm.org/certification/about/ certification-commission/pages/default.aspx.*

IMPACT OF EFFECTIVE HRM ON PRODUCTIVITY, QUALITY OF WORK LIFE, AND THE BOTTOM LINE

For most of the last two decades, downsizing set the tone for the modern employment contract. As companies frantically restructured to cope with slipping market share or heightened competition, they tore up old notions of paternalism. They told employees, "Don't expect to spend your life at one company anymore. You are responsible for your own career, so get all the skills you can and prepare to change jobs, employers, even industries. As for the implicit bond of loyalty that might have existed before, well, forget it. In these days of fierce global competition, loyalty is an unaffordable luxury."[a]

Today, faced with the retirements of large numbers of baby boomers, and impending labor shortages, employers have changed their tune. Now it's "Don't leave. We need you. Work for us—you can build a career here." Employers are going to great lengths to persuade employees that they want them to stay for years. According to a recent survey, employees are less loyal to their companies, and they tend to put their own needs and interests above those of their employers. More often, they are willing to trade off higher wages and benefits for flexibility and autonomy, job characteristics that allow them to balance their lives on and off the job. Almost 9 out of every 10 workers live with family members, and nearly half care for dependents, including children, elderly parents, or ailing spouses.[b] Among employees who switched jobs in the last 5 years, pay and benefits rated in the bottom half of 20 possible reasons why they did so. Factors rated highest were "nature of work," "open communication," and "effect on personal/family life." What are the implications of these results? When companies fail to factor in quality-of-work-life issues and quality-of-life issues when introducing any of the popular schemes for improving productivity, the only thing they may gain is a view of the backs of their best people leaving for friendlier employers.[c]

---

[a]DeMeuse, K. P., and Dai, G. (2012). Reducing costs and enhancing efficiency or damaging the company: Downsizing in today's global economy. In C. Cooper, A. Pandey, and J. C. Quick (Eds.), *Downsizing: Is Less Still More?* Cambridge, UK: Cambridge University Press, pp. 258–90. *See also* Wethe, D. (2017, Feb. 5). Drilling is back. What about the workers? *Bloomberg Businessweek*, pp. 14, 15.

[b]Ma, S. (2017, Jan. 16). Digital economy invents new jobs. *China Daily*, pp. 1, 13. *See also* Galinsky, E., Aumann, K., and Bond, J. T. (2009). *Times Are Changing: Gender and Generation at Work and at Home.* New York: Families and Work Institute.

[c]Naughton, K., Dawson, C., Welch, D., & Coppola, G. (2019, April 29). What Gen Z wants. *Bloomberg Businessweek*, pp. 12–17. *See also* Maurer, R. (2016, Mar. 16). From paycheck to purpose: How millennials are changing work. Retrieved from *www. shrm.org/resourcesandtools/hr-topics/talent-acquisition/pages/ from-paycheck-to-purpose-how-millennials-are-changing-work.aspx* on March 20, 2016.

IMPLICATIONS FOR MANAGEMENT PRACTICE

The trends we have reviewed in this chapter suggest that the old approaches to managing people may no longer be appropriate responses to economic or social reality. A willingness to experiment is healthy. To the extent that the newer approaches do enhance productivity, QWL, and profits, everybody wins. Competitive issues cannot simply be willed away, and because of this we may see even more radical experiments in organizations. The traditional role of the manager may be blurred further as workers take a greater and greater part in planning and controlling work, not simply doing what managers tell them to do. Consider professional service and Big Four accounting firm Ernst & Young (E&Y).[a] It is a global organization of member firms in more than 140 countries, headquartered in London, England, and it employs more than 152,000 people. According to former Global Chairman and CEO Jim Turley, "I think the business case was first around retaining talent. Whatever firm has the best talent wins in our space. So attracting and retaining the best talent is a critical business imperative. . . . You ask yourself, is it better to have a flexible culture and keep all the great talent in the firm and use it as a vehicle to attract and retain more talent, or do we want to keep the more rigid ways that we used to operate in and have people walking out the door?" That kind of progressive thinking is consistent with survey results that show 89 percent of Gen Y, and 79 percent of Gen X, feel that flexible work arrangements and the opportunity to give back to society trump the sheer size of the pay package. To get started, Ernst & Young focused on managers' responses to

requests for flexibility from their direct reports. Instead of asking "why," the firm encouraged its managers to ask "why not?" Flexibility became more of a right for all, rather than a privilege for a few. Since much of the work at Ernst & Young is team-based, as in audit teams, flexible work arrangements have to fit within that team-based environment. Team calendars help facilitate that. At Ernst & Young, flexibility pervades the company's culture, even at the rank of partner. More than 200 of them are on some form of flexible work arrangement. Among the firm's 26,000 U.S. employees, 2,500 are on flexible schedules. Of those, 15 percent are men and 85 percent are women. In any given year, about 1,000 employees take parental leave, and 50 percent of those are men. Also in any given year, about 200 employees who work formal flexible schedules are promoted to positions of partner, principal, executive director, or director. That sends a strong signal that flexibility will not stifle one's career-advancement opportunities at E&Y. What about implementing flexible work arrangements in other cultures, where laws and social norms may vary significantly from those in the headquarters country? At Ernst & Young, the message is clear: Be the best you can be at implementing flexibility in your culture because doing so will be critical to attracting and retaining the best talent available.

[a]Society for Human Resource Management Foundation. (2017, Feb. 7). *Ernst & Young: Creating a Culture of Flexibility.* Alexandria, VA: Author. Available at *https://www.youtube.com/watch?v=z9ixbBJ0YMA*

Human Resource Management in Action: Conclusion

GLOBALIZATION AT WORK: WEALTH, JOBS, AND WORKER DISPLACEMENT

According to the Federal Reserve Bank of Dallas, Americans saw their choice of products expand by one-third in recent decades. Trade is how bananas, raspberries, and pineapples appear on store shelves in the dead of winter. Clothes, appliances, and many other goods are cheaper in Walmart stores in America because many of those products are sourced overseas. If iPhones were made in America, they would be more expensive than those assembled in China from parts made in Germany, Japan, and Korea.

Yet economic stagnation in many parts of the world has fueled an antitrade backlash, from British laborers who blame trade for declining pay to former factory workers in America's Midwest who have seen their incomes and standards of living drop over the past decade. Many major nations are grappling with weak growth, tight credit, and anxiety over the future. At the same time, automation has grown in sophistication and reach. In the United States, about 6 million manufacturing jobs disappeared in the first decade of the 21st century, but only 13 percent of those losses can be explained by trade. The rest were casualties of automation, including artificial intelligence, robots, and sensors that have enabled about 25 percent greater production from factory operations with roughly the same number of workers as a decade earlier. In short, rapid technological change, coupled with economic stagnation, has caused more job losses in middle America than free trade.

Here is a major concern. In the past, human beings and societies adapted steadily to change, but the rate of technological change is now accelerating so fast that it has risen above the average rate at which most people can absorb all these changes. Many just cannot keep pace anymore. In the past, it took 10–15 years to understand a new technology, and to build out laws and regulations to safeguard society. Now, technology is turning over every 5–7 years. Think about what this means for education. It's certainly not finished after 12, 16, or even 20 years because as the pace of change increases, the only way to retain a lifelong working capacity is to engage in lifelong learning.

Workers displaced from their jobs as a result of automation, trade, or outsourcing obviously need help in adjusting their lives and careers. What is the role of governments? In wealthy countries such as Germany, the Netherlands, Sweden, and Denmark, unemployment benefits, housing subsidies, and government-provided health care are far more generous than those in the United States. They cushion the costs of job losses in the short term, and they provide training to give dislocated workers the skills they need to compete.

In the United States, Trade Adjustment Assistance is a program designed to support workers whose jobs are casualties of overseas competition by paying for job training. Yet a study of the effects of the program 4 years after workers completed training found that only 37 percent of those employed were working in the industries they retrained for. Many of those enrolled in the training had lower incomes than those who simply signed up for unemployment benefits and looked for other work. What can be done?

Displaced workers need more intensive training to prepare them for new jobs. This is where public-private-sector partnerships can pay off if workers are trained for jobs in fields that government forecasts indicate are likely to grow in the future. Workers themselves may have to be willing to move to take advantage of those employment opportunities. There need to be less expensive options for university education, and vocational schools need to be more available. If companies can devise ways for labor and management to cooperate and to share more equitably in the profits that globalization creates, then everyone will be better off.

SUMMARY

People are a major component of any business, and the management of people (or human resource management, HRM) is a major part of every manager's job. It is also the specialized responsibility of the HR department. In fact, we use the term *strategic HRM* to refer to the wisest possible use of people with respect to the strategic focus of the organization. HRM involves five major areas: staffing, retention, development, adjustment, and managing change. Together they compose the HRM system, for they describe a network of interrelated components. The HRM function is responsible for maximizing productivity, quality of work life, and profits through better management of people.

The competitive business environment of the 21st century reflects factors such as an aging and changing workforce in a high-tech workplace that demands and rewards ever-increasing skill, and increasing global competition in almost every sector of the economy. In response, organizations are using nonstandard employees, often in virtual work arrangements, restructuring (including downsizing), and building flexibility into work schedules and rules. This implies a redistribution of power, greater participation by workers and nonemployees, and more teamwork. The challenge of attracting, retaining, and motivating people has never been greater.

One of the most pressing demands we face today is for productivity improvement—getting more out of what is put in; doing better with what we have; and working smarter, not harder. Nevertheless, increased productivity does not preclude a high quality of work life (QWL). *QWL* refers to employees' perceptions of their physical and psychological well-being at work. It involves giving workers the opportunity to make decisions about their jobs, the design of their workplaces, and ensuring work-life fit. Its focus is on employees and managers operating a business together. HR professionals can help by demonstrating competencies in HR expertise, relationship management, consultation, leadership and navigation, communication, diversity and inclusion, ethical practice, critical evaluation, and business acumen.

KEY TERMS

productivity	HRM
quality of work life (QWL)	authority
profit	globalization
staffing	virtual organization
retention	virtual workplace
development	restructuring
adjustment	downsizing
managing change	ethical decisions about behavior

DISCUSSION QUESTIONS

1-1. What are the HRM implications of employing nonstandard workers in the "gig" economy?

1-2. How will demographic changes and increasing diversity in the workplace affect the ways that organizations manage their people?

1-3. Considering everything we have discussed in this chapter, describe management styles and practices that will be effective for your country's businesses in the next decade.

1-4. What difficulties do you see in shifting from a hierarchical, departmentalized organization to a leaner, flatter one in which power is shared between workers and managers?

1-5. How can effective HRM contribute to improvements in productivity and quality of work life?

1-6. How can effective HRM contribute to sustainability?

1-7. If you could only work on three of the nine key HR competencies, what would they be, and why did you choose those three?

1-8. The pace of developments in new technologies is becoming faster than the abilities of workers to adjust to them. What recommendations would you make to high-level policymakers in organizations and government to address this issue?

1-9. It has often been said that people don't leave bad companies; they leave bad bosses. What can managers do to enhance employee retention?

1-10. How does the effective management of people provide a competitive advantage to organizations?

APPLYING YOUR KNOWLEDGE

PepsiCo: "Winning with Purpose"   *Case 1–1*

A broad objective at PepsiCo is to win sustainably in the marketplace and to accelerate its top-line growth, while keeping its commitment to do good for the planet and for the communities it serves. That objective builds on decades of progress it has made since PepsiCo was founded in 1965.[57] The company's purpose is defined by three pillars of sustainable growth:

1. *Products*, helping to improve health and well-being through the products it sells. To do that, here are three of its goals for 2025: At least two-thirds of its global beverage portfolio volume will have 100 calories or fewer from added sugars per 12-oz. serving; at least three-quarters of its global food portfolio volume will not exceed 1.1 grams of saturated fat per 100 calories; and it will provide access to at least 3 billion servings of nutritious foods and beverages to underserved communities and consumers.

2. *Planet*, to ensure that PepsiCo's operations don't harm the natural environment. For example, by 2025 it plans to design 100 percent of its packaging to be recoverable or recyclable; to improve the water-use efficiency of its direct manufacturing operations by 25 percent (in addition to the 25 percent improvement it achieved from 2006 to 2016); and to replenish 100 percent of the water it consumes in its manufacturing operations within high-water-risk areas. The goal is to transform PepsiCo

into a company with a net-zero impact on the environment, for it believes that young people today will not patronize a company that does not have a sustainable strategy.

3. *People,* which attempts to create a corporate culture in which employees "not just make a living, but also have a life." This includes a continued focus on achieving gender parity in PepsiCo's management roles and pay equity for women. Seven behaviors define the PepsiCo way of working: be consumer-centric, act as owners, focus and get things done fast, voice opinions fearlessly, raise the bar on talent and diversity, celebrate success, and act with integrity. PepsiCo's ambition is to empower people and social development across its operations, its global supply chain, and communities.[58]

PepsiCo's vision of winning with purpose acknowledges the importance of corporate social responsibility and stakeholder strategy. The company is convinced that it has a tremendous opportunity–as well as a responsibility–not only to make a profit but to do so in a way that makes a difference in the world.[59]

Has the approach of "winning with purpose" impacted PepsiCo's financial performance? PepsiCo has increased its dividends for 46 straight years. Over the past five years, while the total return (stock appreciation plus dividends) of the S&P 500 increased 65.64 percent and that of arch-rival Coca-Cola increased 45.49 percent, PepsiCo's increased 76.03 percent.[60]

Questions

1. One measure used to assess competitive advantage is shareholder value creation. How would you assess PepsiCo's performance?
2. If you were to apply a triple-bottom-line approach to assessing competitive advantage, would you reach the same conclusion? Why or why not?
3. PepsiCo's vision is to deliver top-tier financial performance over the long term by integrating sustainability into its business strategy. How might this approach apply to firms in other industries?

REFERENCES

1. From Friedman, T. L. (2016). *Thank You for Being Late: An Optimist's Guide to Thriving in the Age of Accelerations.* New York: Farrar, Straus & Giroux.
2. Campbell, J. P., Dunnette, M. D., Lawler, E. E. III, and Weick, K. E., Jr. (1970). *Managerial Behavior, Performance, and Effectiveness.* New York: McGraw-Hill. *See also* Welch, J., and Welch, S. (2006, July 17). So many CEOs get this wrong. *Bloomberg Businessweek,* p. 92.
3. From Welch, J. (2005) (with Welch, S.). *Winning.* New York: Harper Business.
4. 2019 Deloitte human capital trends. Retrieved from https://www2.deloitte.com/content/dam/insights/us/articles/5136_HC-Trends-2019/DI_HC-Trends-2019.pdf on Feb. 1, 2020.
5. Wright, P. M., and Stewart, M. (2011). *From Bunker to Building: Results from the 2010 Chief Human Resource Officer Survey.* Ithaca, NY: Cornell Center for Advanced Human Resource Studies, p. 13.

6. Cascio, W. F. (2007a). The costs–and benefits–of human resources. *International Review of Industrial and Organizational Psychology* 22, pp. 71-109.

7. Jiang, K., Lepak, D. P., Hu, J., and Baer, J. C. (2012). How does human resource management influence organizational outcomes? A meta-analytic investigation of mediating mechanisms. *Academy of Management Journal* 55, pp. 1264-94. *See also* Crook, T. R., Todd, S. Y., Combs, J. G., Woehr, D. J., and Ketchen, D. J., Jr. (2011). Does human capital matter? A meta-analysis of the relationship between human capital and firm performance. *Journal of Applied Psychology* 96, pp. 443-56. *See also* Huselid, M. A. (1995). The impact of human resource management practices on turnover, productivity, and corporate financial performance. *Academy of Management Journal* 38, pp. 635-72.

8. Berrgren, E., and Strezo, M. (2011, May). How companies leverage business-execution software to drive excess shareholder return. SuccessFactors White Paper, San Mateo, CA. *See also* Frauenheim, E. (2011, May 31). SuccessFactors research ties performance management to stock market success. *Work Force Management*. Retrieved from *www.workforce.com* on June 2, 2011.

9. Boselie, P., Dietz, G., and Boon, C. (2005). Commonalities and contradictions in HRM and performance research. *Human Resource Management Journal* 15, pp. 67-94. *See also* Pfeffer, J., and Veiga, J. F. (1999). Putting people first for organizational success. *Academy of Management. Executive* 13(2), pp. 37-49.

10. The *Fortune* global 500. (2019). Retrieved from *https://fortune.com/global500/* on Feb. 20, 2020.

11. Northeastern University/Gallup. (2019). *Facing the future*. Retrieved from *https://www.northeastern.edu/gallup/* on Dec. 2, 2019. *See also* Fridman, 2016, op. cit. *Thank You for Being Late: An Optimist's Guide to Thriving in the Age of Accelerations*. New York: Farrar, Straus & Giroux.

12. World Economic Forum. These are the biggest risks facing the world in 2020. Retrieved from *https://www.weforum.org/agenda/2020/01/top-global-risks-report-climate-change-cyberattacks-economic-political/* on Feb. 20, 2020. *See also* Bloomberg Businessweek: Year in review. (2011, Jan. 2). *Bloomberg Businessweek: Year in Review*, p. 9.

13. Yap, C-W., & Emont, J. (2020, Feb. 24). Global economy shows strain as virus starts to take a toll. *The Wall Street Journal*, pp. A1, A6.

14. Economist Intelligence Unit. (2014, Feb.). *What's Next: Future Global Trends Affecting Your Organization*. Alexandria, VA: SHRM Foundation. *See also* International Labour Organization. (2014). *Global Employment Trends 2014: Risk of a Jobless Recovery?* Geneva, Switzerland: Author.

15. McGovern, M. (2017). *Thriving in the Gig Economy: How to Capitalize and Compete in the New World of Work*. Wayne, NJ: Career Press/New Page Books. *See also* Economist Intelligence Unit (2014), op. cit. *See also* Lublin, J. S. (2011, Apr. 11). Hunt is on for fresh executive talent: Cultural flexibility in demand. *The Wall Street Journal*, pp. B1, B9.

16. Montealegre, R., & Cascio, W. F. (In press.). Managing in the age of external intelligence. *Organizational Dynamics. See also* Cascio, W. F., & Montealegre, R. (2016). How technology is changing work and organizations. *Annual Review of Organizational Psychology and Organizational Behavior 3*, pp. 349-75. Annual Reviews.

17. Hancock, B., Lazaroff-Puck, K., & Rutherford, S. (2020, Jan.). Getting practical about the future of work. Retrieved from *https://www.mckinsey.com/business-functions/organization/our-insights/getting-practical-about-the-future-of-work* on Jan. 24, 2020. *See also* Aeppel T. (2015, Feb. 24). What clever robots mean for jobs: Experts rethink belief that tech always lifts employment as machines take on skills once thought uniquely human. *The Wall Street Journal*. Retrieved from *http://www.wsj.com/articles/what-clever-robots-mean-for-jobs-1424835002*.

18. Hancock et al., 2020, op. cit. *See also* Murray A. (2015, May 1). The new industrial revolution. *Fortune*, p. 6. *See also* McKinsey Global Institute. (2013, May). Disruptive technologies: Advances that will transform life, business, and the global economy. Retrieved from *http://www.mckinsey.com/insights/business_technology/disruptive_technologies* on Aug. 20, 2013.

19. Daugherty, P. R., & Wilson, H. J. (2018). *Human + Machine: Reimagining Work in the Age of AI.* Boston: Harvard Business Review Press. *See also* Friedman (2016), op. cit.

20. Minaya, E. (2018, Apr. 11). Levi's CFO turns to robots to help keep the books. *The Wall Street Journal,* *https://blogs.wsj.com/cfo/2018/04/11/levis-cfo-turns-to-robots-to-help-keep-the-books/.*

21. Hancock et al., 2020, op. cit.

22. Matsakis, L. (2019, July 11). Amazon pledges $700 million to teach its workers to code. *Wired.* Retrieved from *https://www.wired.com/story/amazon-pledges-700-million-training-workers/* on July 13, 2019.

23. Tyler, K. (2020, Feb. 22). Upskill or fade away. *SHRM Online.* Retrieved from *https://www.shrm.org/hr-today/news/all-things-work/pages/upskill-or-fade-away.aspx.* on Feb. 22, 2020.

24. Vos, L. (2019, Aug. 30). What is sustainability in business? Retrieved from *https://learn.g2.com/sustainability-in-business* on Feb. 21, 2020. See also WCED. (1987). *Our Common Future.* Oxford, UK: Oxford University Press.

25. Benoit, D. (2019, Aug. 20). Top CEOs see a duty beyond shareholders. *The Wall Street Journal,* pp. A1, A7. Schooley, S. (2019, April 22). What is corporate social responsibility? *Business News Daily.* Retrieved from *https://www.businessnewsdaily.com/4679-corporate-social-responsibility.html* on Feb. 21, 2020. *See also* Cohen, E., Taylor, S., and Muller-Camen, M. (2013). *HRM's Role in Corporate Social and Environmental Sustainability.* Alexandria, VA: SHRM Foundation.

26. Vos, 2019, op. cit. See also Orlitsky, M., Schmidt, F. L., and Rynes, S. L. (2003). Corporate social and financial performance: A meta-analysis. *Organization Studies* **24**(3), pp. 403–41.

27. Vos, 2019, op. cit.

28. See Cohen et al. (2013), op. cit., for a comprehensive review.

29. Kiron, D., Unruh, G., Kurschwitz, N., Reeves, M., Rubel, H., & Zum Felde, A. M. (2017, May 23). Corporate sustainability at a crossroads. *MIT Sloan Management Review.* Retrieved from *https://sloanreview.mit.edu/projects/corporate-sustainability-at-a-crossroads/* on Feb. 21, 2020.

30. Bain (2015), op. cit. *See also* Siegel, D. S. (2009). Green management matters only if it yields more green: An economic/strategic perspective. *Academy of Management Perspectives* **23**(3), pp. 5–16.

31. Kiron et al., 2017, op. cit. *See also Doing Well by Doing Good: Global Sustainability at Aditya Birla Group, https://www.youtube.com/watch?v=yYEwnUqTqJw.*

32. To learn how to do this, see Birchman, S., & Jones, B. (2019, July 19). 5 steps for tying executive compensation to sustainability. *Harvard Business Review.* Retrieved from *https://hbr.org/2019/07/5-steps-for-tying-executive-compensation-to-sustainability* on Feb. 21, 2020. *See also* Shumsky, T. (2019, June 24). More companies link executive pay to sustainability targets. *The Wall Street Journal.* Retrieved from *www.wsj.com/articles/more-companies-link-executive-pay-to-sustainability-targets-11561379745.*

33. Hill, D. (2018, Oct. 31). How the biggest corporate sustainability trends of 2018 have really paid off. *Forbes.* Retrieved from *https://www.forbes.com/sites/edfenergyexchange/2018/10/31/how-the-biggest-corporate-sustainability-trends-of-2018-have-really-paid-off/#6a28296a6592* on Feb. 21, 2020.

34. Babcock, P. (2015, Oct. 29). Accelerating HR's role in CSR and sustainability. *SHRM Online.* Retrieved from *https://www.shrm.org/resourcesandtools/hr-topics/behavioral-competencies/ethical-practice/pages/hr-role-csr-sustainability.aspx* on Feb. 21, 2020. *See also* Huffman, A. H.,

and Klein, S. (Eds.). (2013). *Green Organizations: Driving Change with I-O Psychology*. New York: Taylor & Francis. *See also* Pfeffer, J. (2010). Building sustainable organizations: The human factor. *Academy of Management Perspectives* **24**(1), pp. 34–45.

35. Cilluffo, A., & Cohn, D. (2019, April 11). 6 demographic trends shaping the U.S. and the world in 2019. *Pew Research Center*. Retrieved from *https://www.pewresearch.org/fact-tank/2019/04/11/6-demographic-trends-shaping-the-u-s-and-the-world-in-2019/* on Feb. 21, 2020.

36. The first world is aging. (2015, Oct. 1). *Fortune*, p. 16. *See also* Jordan, M. (2015, Sept. 28). Asians to surpass Hispanics as largest foreign-born group in U.S. by 2055. *The Wall Street Journal*. Retrieved from *www.wsj.com/articles/asians-to-surpass-hispanics-as-largest-foreign-born-group-in-u-s-by-2055-1443412861* on Sept. 29, 2015. *See also* Qi, L. (2017, Jan. 26). China lays out population forecast. *The Wall Street Journal*, p. A7.

37. Hancock et al., 2020, op. cit. *See also* 2019 Deloitte human capital trends, op. cit. *See also* Lee, L. (2011, May 16). Streamlining HR: Let somebody else do it. *The Wall Street Journal*, p. R6.

38. Maurer, R. (2018, Dec. 5). Just how many gig workers are there, anyway? *SHRM Online*. Retrieved from *https://www.shrm.org/resourcesandtools/hr-topics/talent-acquisition/pages/how-many-gig-workers-are-there.aspx* on Dec. 6, 2018. See also Pofeldt, E. (2016, Oct. 6). Freelancers now make up 35% of U.S. workforce. *Forbes*. Retrieved from *www.forbes.com/sites/elainepofeldt/2016/10/06/new-survey-freelance-economy-shows-rapid-growth/#30cc8ec8737c* on Feb. 14, 2017.

39. Barrett, P. M., and Elgin, B. (2015, Aug. 10). The Arctic or bust. *Bloomberg Businessweek*, pp. 58–63.

40. Wilkie, D. (2018, Sept. 25). Managing expectations: How to balance gig workers and regular employees. *SHRM Online*. Retrieved from *https://www.shrm.org/resourcesandtools/hr-topics/employee-relations/pages/managing-gig-workers-.aspx* on Sept. 26, 2018. See also Davis-Blake, A., and Uzzi, B. (1993). Determinants of employment externalization: A study of temporary workers and independent contractors. *Administrative Science Quarterly* **38**(2), pp. 195–223.

41. Chapman, L. (2017, April 23). Hacking the need for a full-time job. *Bloomberg Businessweek*, pp. 33, 34. See also Cascio, W. F., and Montealegre, R. (2016). How technology is changing work and organizations. *Annual Review of Organizational Psychology and Organizational Behavior* 3, pp. 349–75.

42. McGovern (2017), op. cit. *See also* Boudreau, J. W., Jesuthasan, R., and Creelman, D. (2015). *Lead the Work*. Hoboken, NJ: Wiley. *See also* Meyer, K. J., Somaya, D., and Williamson, I. O. (2012). Firm-specific, industry-specific, and occupational human capital and the sourcing of knowledge work. *Organization Science* **23**(5), pp. 1311–29.

43. Boudreau et al. (2015), op. cit.

44. Boudreau et al. (2015), op. cit. *See also* Ashford, S. J., George, E., and Blatt, R. (2007). Old assumptions, new work: The opportunities and challenges of research on nonstandard employment. *Academy of Management Annals* **1**(1), pp. 65–117.

45. Maynard, M. T., Gilson, L., Jones-Young, N. C., and Vartiainen, M. (2017). Virtual teams. In G. Hertel, D. Stone, R. Johnson, and J. Passmore (Eds.), *The Wiley-Blackwell Handbook of the Psychology of the Internet at Work*. Chichester, UK: Wiley-Blackwell. *See also* Ferrazzi, K. (2014, Dec.). Getting virtual teams right. *Harvard Business Review*. Retrieved from *https://hbr.org/2014/12/getting-virtual-teams-right* on Feb. 4, 2015.

46. Chapman, 2017, op. cit. See also Ferrazzi, K. (2012, Oct. 8). How to build trust in a virtual workplace. *Harvard Business Review*. Retrieved from *https://hbr.org/2012/10/how-to-build-trust-in-virtual* on Dec. 5, 2012. *See also* Raghuram, S., Tuertscher, P., and Garud, R. (2010, Dec.). Mapping the field of virtual work. *Information Systems Research*, pp. 983–99.

47. Loten, A. (2019, May 30). "Talent war" at home prompts U.S. employers to take another look abroad. *The Wall Street Journal*. Retrieved from *www.wsj.com/articles/talent-war-at-home-prompts-u-s-employers-to-take- another-look-abroad-11559257791* on May 30, 2019.

48. Lau, Y. (2020, Jan. 30). Six liquid workforce trends employers will see in 2020. *Forbes.* Retrieved from *https://www.forbes.com/sites/forbeshumanresourcescouncil/2020/01/30/six-liquid-workforce-trends-employers-will-see-in-2020/#665f26bb4ea5* on Feb. 22, 2020. See also Cascio, W. F. (2011, Oct. 15). *The Virtual Global Workforce: Leveraging Its Impact.* Louisville, KY: SIOP Leading-Edge Consortium.

49. Cascio, W. F., Chatrath, A., & Christie-David, R. (In press.). Antecedents and consequences of employment and asset restructuring. *Academy of Management Journal. See also* Cascio, W. F. (2010). *Employment Downsizing and Its Alternatives: Strategies for Long-Term Success.* Alexandria, VA: Society for Human Resource Management Foundation. *See also* DeMeuse, K. P., Marks, M. L., and Dai, G. (2011). Organizational downsizing, mergers and acquisitions, and strategic alliances: Using theory and research to enhance practice. In S. Zedeck (Ed.), *Handbook of Industrial and Organizational Psychology.* Washington, DC: APA Books, pp. 729-68.

50. Sucher, S., & Gupta, S. (2018, May-June). Layoffs that don't break your company. *Harvard Business Review*, Reprint R1803K. *See also* Cascio, W. F. (2012). How does downsizing come about? In C. L. Cooper, J. C. Quick, and A. Pandey (Eds.), *Downsizing: Is Less Still More?* Cambridge, UK: Cambridge University Press, pp. 51-75. *See also* Datta, D. K., Guthrie, J. P., Basuil, D., and Pandey, A. (2010). Causes and effects of employee downsizing: A review and synthesis. *Journal of Management* **36**, pp. 281-348.

51. Koenig, R. (2019, April 25). Layoffs leave scars on survivors, too. *US. News & World Report.* Retrieved from *https://money.usnews.com/careers/applying-for-a-job/articles/how-to-cope-as-a-layoff-survivor* on Apr. 26, 2019. *See also* How layoffs hurt companies. (2016, Apr. 12). *Knowledge@Wharton.* Retrieved from *http://knowledge.wharton.upenn.edu/article/how-layoffs-cost-companies/* on Apr. 14, 2016. *See also* Cascio (2010), op. cit.

52. Cote, D. (2013, June). Honeywell's CEO on how he avoided layoffs. *Harvard Business Review.* Retrieved from *http://hbr.org/2013/06/honeywells-ceo-on-how-he-avoided-layoffs/ar/1* on June 17, 2013.

53. Carino, M. M. (2019, July 12). American workers can suffer vacation guilt—if they take vacations at all. Retrieved from *www.marketplace.org/2019/07/12/american-workers-vacation-guilt/* on Feb. 22, 2020.

54. Travers, M. (2019, Oct. 30). 40% of retired Americans say they would rejoin the workforce, if hours were more flexible. *Forbes.* Retrieved from *https://www.forbes.com/sites/traversmark/2019/10/30/how-to-keep-more-americans-in-the-workforce/#489134e76bc8* on Nov. 11, 2019. *See also* Behson, S. (2014, Mar. 24). Increase workplace flexibility and boost performance. *Harvard Business Review.* Retrieved from *https://hbr.org/2014/03/increase-workplace-flexibility-and-boost-performance* on July 1, 2015. *See also* Families and Work Institute and SHRM. (2012). *Workflex: The Essential Guide to Effective and Flexible Workplaces.* Alexandria, VA: Author.

55. Shellenbarger, S. (2019, Oct. 15). When family-friendly firms really aren't. *The Wall Street Journal*, p. R7. See also Corporate Voices for Working Families. (2011). Business impacts of flexibility: An imperative for expansion. Retrieved from *http://www.cvwf.org/publication-toolkits/business-impacts-flexibility-imperative-expansion-updated-2011* on Aug. 3, 2011.

56. Society for Human Resource Management. (2015). *The SHRM Body of Competency and Knowledge.* Alexandria, VA: Author. *See also* Society for Human Resource Management. (2016). *The SHRM Competency Model: A Roadmap for Success.* Alexandria, VA: Author.

57. Source: *https://www.pepsico.com/about/mission-and-vision*, retrieved on Feb. 23, 2020.

58. Sources: *https://thepepsicoway.com/*, retrieved on Feb. 23, 2020. *See also* PepsiCo launches 2025 sustainability agenda designed to meet changing consumer and societal needs. (2016, Oct. 17). Retrieved from *http://www.pepsico.com/live/pressrelease/pepsico-launches-2025-sustainability-agenda-designed-to-meet-changing-consumer-a10172016* on Feb. 21, 2017.

59. Nunes, K. (2016). PepsiCo sets 2025 sustainability agenda. SOSLAND Publishing Company.

60. This minicase is based on: Bowman, J. (2019, June 26). Is PepsiCo stock a buy today? *The Motley Fool. Retrieved from www.fool.com/investing/2019/06/26/is-pepsico-stock-a-buy-to-day.aspx* on Feb. 23, 2020. *See also* PepsiCo sets 2025 sustainability agenda. (2016, Oct. 17). *Food Business News. See also* Pepsi banks on young guns to disrupt snacks and soda market (2015, Sept. 9). *The Economic Times. See also* Werbach. A. (2011, July 11). Pepsi vs. Wall St.: Why should a soda company try to be "good for you"? *The Atlantic. See also* Pepsi gets a makeover. (2010, Mar. 25). *The Economist.*

2 HR TECHNOLOGY

Questions This Chapter Will Help Managers Answer

LO 2-1 How is technology changing work and organizations?

LO 2-2 How does HR technology affect the management of people?

LO 2-3 How can managers leverage HR technology to maximize efficiency and effectiveness?

LO 2-4 What key considerations should guide the selection of a vendor for an organization's human resource information system?

LO 2-5 What challenges will managers confront when implementing HR technology?

HOW TECHNOLOGY IS CHANGING WORK AND ORGANIZATIONS*

As we noted in Chapter 1, We live in a global world where **technology**, especially information and communication technology, is changing the manner in which businesses create and capture value, how and where we work, and how we interact and communicate. Research by Cisco Systems Inc. indicates that by the end of 2030, almost 500 billion devices will be connected to the Internet. Given the amount of time the average American spends online—23.6 hours a week—smart and connected devices will become ubiquitous.[1] These devices and the technologies that power them are not just helping people to do things better and faster, but they are enabling profound changes in the ways that work is done in organizations. As one observer noted, "Together these innovations are hurtling us toward a new industrial revolution. Savvy corporate leaders know they have to either figure out how these technologies will transform their businesses or face disruption by others who figure it out first".[2]

The last great wave of technological innovation was all about social interaction. The next one may well feature the emerging general technology paradigm known as **ubiquitous computing**. This concept is not about one technology. Rather, it reflects information and communication environments in which computer sensors (such as radio frequency identification tags, wearable technology, smart watches) and other equipment (tablets, mobile devices) are unified with various objects, people, information, and computers as well as the physical environment. The combination of these developments is giving us a new kind of world, "one that is hyperconnected and data saturated, a world where an Internet of everyone is linked to an Internet of everything."[3] These new technologies, disruptive as they are, did not just appear overnight. Rather, many other developments in technology preceded them, and their effects on work and organizations over the past several decades have been profound. Consider just a few, brief examples to illustrate how applications of ubiquitous computing may disrupt work and work systems in organizations:

- As employees wear clothing and other wearables embedded with computer chips and sensors, they no longer need to carry a computer separately to meetings. They are armed with up-to-date information, their decisions are guided by analysis of the information provided by cloud computing, and they can resolve operational issues in creative ways that were not possible before.
- Computer networks allow employees to work from the office, their home, or anywhere. Employees are routinely collaborating with people they have never met, in places they have never visited, and are staying connected with the office anywhere and anytime. This has enabled the emergence of ubiquitous working environments supporting different types of working styles and conditions.

°*Sources:* Cascio, W. F., and Montealegre, R. (2016). How technology is changing work and organizations. *Annual Review of Organizational Psychology and Organizational Behavior* 3, pp. 349-75. Mantas, J.B. (2019, Nov./Dec.). Intelligent approaches to AI. *NACD Directorship*, pp. 40-45. Accenture Security-NACD. (2019, Oct. 22). A board primer on artificial intelligence. Retrieved from *https://www.accenture.com/ acnmedia/ PDF-110/Accenture-A-Board-Primer-AI-Final.pdf#zoom=50* on Oct. 25, 2019. Salama, V. and Fuhrman, V. (2018, July 20). Firms vow to train millions of workers. *The Wall Street Journal*, p. A3. Murray, A. (2015). The new industrial revolution. *Fortune*, May 1, p. 6. Wooldridge, A. (2015). The Icarus syndrome meets the wearable revolution. *Korn/Ferry Briefings on Talent and Leadership* 6, pp. 27-33. Coovert, M. D., and Thompson, L. F. (Eds.). (2014). *The Psychology of Workplace Technology*. New York: Routledge. Ryan, R. M., and Deci, E. L. (2017). *Self-Determination Theory: Basic Psychological Needs in Motivation, Development, and Wellness*. New York: Guilford.

- Computer programs, intelligent robots, and other devices are used to perform an increasing variety of tasks with a high level of technical skills and with benefits that include lower costs, higher quality, improved safety, and environmental protection. People, however, participate in defining, creating, and maintaining these automated programs, machines, and other devices.
- Employees can integrate their use of Facebook, Twitter, Google, and other social media into their daily routines, and companies can integrate social media into their intranets so that they can share internal information and knowledge with employees, and even with suppliers and customers if desired.
- Through the use of smartphones, GPS, earphones, and microphones, employees can access online education and training materials anytime not only from their own companies, but also from universities in or outside their home countries.

To some, ubiquitous computing is a threat because of its impact on jobs. It is by no means the first technology to have such effects. From steam engines to robotic welders and ATMs, technology has long displaced humans–often creating new and higher-skill jobs in its wake. The invention of the automobile threw blacksmiths out of work but created far more jobs building and selling cars. Over the past 30 years, the digital revolution has displaced many of the middle-skill jobs that underpinned 20th-century middle-class life. Today, nearly one in five Americans are employed in jobs that did not exist in 1980. Artificial intelligence builder, robot manager, mobile app designer, 3-D printing engineer, drone pilot, social-media manager, genetic counselor–these are just a few of the careers that have appeared in recent years. What can we expect in the future? What factors affect the adoption and implementation of workplace technologies? What are the best ways for managers to address these issues? In the conclusion to this case, we will consider what research tells us about how to proceed.

Challenges

1. How can managers maximize the positive effects of technology at work?
2. What advice would you offer a young person about the effects of technology on his or her career?
3. How has ubiquitous computing changed the way you live and work?

TECHNOLOGY AND ITS IMPACT ON HR MANAGEMENT

By any standard, technology is changing the ways we live and work. According to the Oxford English Dictionary, the term *technology* refers to the application of scientific knowledge for practical purposes, especially in industry–for example, "advances in computer technology."[4] The focus of this chapter is on HR technology–specifically, the use of technology of all types and in all HR areas, both to support the HR function itself as well as business goals. As we think about the impact of that technology, let's examine its effects in nine key areas of HR management: business leadership, compensation and benefits, diversity, employee relations, labor relations, organization and employee development, safety and security, recruitment and staffing, and HR risk management.

Business Leadership[5]

Technology is an ever-present focus for leaders because it is constantly evolving and because it affects the ability of their organizations to be competitive, to stay ahead of the curve. Indeed, some organizations use technology to disrupt the status quo of their industries–think Amazon, Skype, and Apple's App Store. Some technology requirements involve basic business functions, such as word processing, planning, accounting, budgeting, legal compliance, research, and communications. Yet a vast and ever-increasing array of software, web-based, and mobile applications has also affected higher-level functions and helps organizations achieve their strategic objectives. Predictive talent analytics help organizations move from simply describing what is to predicting important outcomes, such as the number of employees expected to quit at various levels in the coming year or over the longer term.

Compensation and Benefits[6]

Many employers use technology in benefits administration. **Decision-support systems (DSS)** help employees make the best choices from among an array of benefits, given their individual situations (e.g., married, single, with dependents, no dependents). Self-service websites enable employees to go online to make changes to their benefits or to record change-in-life events, such as marital status or the birth of a child. When employees opt in, automated systems facilitate retirement contributions by making regular deductions from a worker's pay and directing each person's contributions according to his or her wishes.

HR technology is widely used in administering pay systems. State-of-the-art systems link time and attendance records to payroll systems, and those systems operate with little to no human intervention. To eliminate paper checks entirely, many payroll systems pay workers electronically. In addition, HR technology allows organizations to operate multiple incentive systems across business units, and it facilitates seamless pay-for-performance programs by integrating compensation plans with performance management tools.

Diversity

Technology is helping organizations of all sizes to increase diversity. For example, the Mom Source Network uses virtual networks to connect moms looking to return to the workforce with women who are currently working. Other vendors specialize in delivering "blind" résumés or profiles by removing names, photos, nationality, and other details that can be used to identify people, as well as creating blind assessments or reducing bias in background-checking processes.[7] People with physical disabilities also play important roles in increasing diversity in organizations, and advances in **assistive technology** have dramatically increased job opportunities for them. Organizations benefit because they are able to recruit from a broader pool of applicants. Here are just a few examples of such tools for visually or hearing-impaired individuals[8]:

- For those with visual impairments, screen readers like JAWS or Window-Eyes read the content of computer screens to users and provide speech and Braille output for many popular computer applications. Screen-magnification programs like ZoomText or Magic enlarge text or images for easier viewing. Another new tool is OrCam, a small camera mounted on glasses that converts visual information–such as that from newspapers, computer screens, restaurant menus, or street signs–into the spoken word, relaying information to users through built-in mini speakers.

- For those who are deaf or who have hearing impairments, programs like Ava can be used on smartphones or tablets. Ava transcribes what is being spoken in one-to-one or group conversations. Microphones on mobile devices pick up voices, and the Ava software converts words into text, presented on the user's phone or tablet display. To respond, a deaf or hearing-impaired person uses a keyboard supplied with Ava to type what he or she wants to say, and it is then projected through speakers on the phone.

Employee Relations

The move to a technology-driven, mobile workforce where employees are accessible at all times via mobile phone and e-mail is a double-edged sword. On the one hand, it allows employees to work flexible hours or remotely. On the other hand, it can promote overwork and burnout. The challenge for managers is to promote a culture that balances that fine line. Social media present a special challenge for HR. Although business-related social-networking sites are great sources for talent sourcing, networking, and advertising, there is also a need for organizations to devise social-media policies that will protect their brands from slander or libel from employees or competitors.

HR technology is extremely helpful in conducting employee surveys via a company's intranet or the Internet, and integrated talent management systems can tie performance management to compensation as well as to learning and development. The result is a holistic system with the capability to train, track, and reward performance. In the area of learning and development, technology-delivered instruction– the presentation of text, graphics, video, audio, or animation in digitized form–is catching on fast. One example of this is **gamification**.[9] Gaming technology is being used to engage employees and direct behavior through interactive games and competitions. A final application of technology in employee relations is **biometrics**– unique physical and behavioral features (such as fingerprints or eye pupils) that can be sensed by devices and interpreted by computers to bond digital data to personal identities. Biometrics can increase efficiency, prevent fraud, and ensure the safety of workers. At the same time, however, organizations using them must balance employee privacy and security.

Labor Relations

In the context of collective bargaining, software has long been used to address "what if?" questions and to cost out various proposals, such as those involving wage increases, along with contributions to benefit options such as paid leave, health and other types of insurance, pensions, and various retirement-savings vehicles. At the same time, technology in the form of e-mail, social media, and various websites has changed union strategies for organizing, communicating with members and nonmembers, and creating virtual picket lines.[11] It is important to note, however, that employees may not use their employer's e-mail system for those purposes. The National Labor Relations Board has held that employees have no legally protected right to use an employer's e-mail system for organizing or other legally protected, concerted activity.[12]

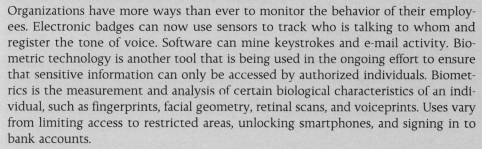

BIOMETRICS AND EMPLOYEE PRIVACY   HR BUZZ

Organizations have more ways than ever to monitor the behavior of their employees. Electronic badges can now use sensors to track who is talking to whom and register the tone of voice. Software can mine keystrokes and e-mail activity. Biometric technology is another tool that is being used in the ongoing effort to ensure that sensitive information can only be accessed by authorized individuals. Biometrics is the measurement and analysis of certain biological characteristics of an individual, such as fingerprints, facial geometry, retinal scans, and voiceprints. Uses vary from limiting access to restricted areas, unlocking smartphones, and signing in to bank accounts.

Laws don't prevent companies from capturing such data, but to maximize transparency and employee trust, consider taking the following steps:

- Create a written policy that describes in detail how the company uses biometric data.
- Establish retention schedules and guidelines for permanently destroying biometric data within a certain period of time.
- Obtain written releases from employees before collecting and storing their biometric data.
- Develop reasonable procedures to store, transmit, and protect biometric data from disclosure.
- Invite employees to provide input on what and how to communicate about the information their employers capture. Trust and transparency are key ingredients that all employees should demand and that all employers should provide to safeguard employee privacy.[10]

Organization and Employee Development

Three areas in particular have benefited from HR technology: workforce planning, e-learning, and tools to promote collaboration. People analytics is playing an ever more significant role in workforce planning, for example, by identifying talent gaps in workforce forecasts, high-potential employee segments that are at risk of leaving, and the potential redeployment of surplus employees in existing talent segments. The following is a brief example.

Using basic data on promotions, attrition, headcount by level, and anticipated organizational growth rate makes it possible to project the "shape" of an organization (the percentage of employees at each level) at the end of a year, at the end of two years, or after three-plus years. With the proper formulas in place, users can input anticipated future attrition/promotion and organizational growth rates to model different scenarios. By assigning salaries to employees at each level, one can see the financial impact of having an organizational shape that looks like a typical pyramid (with fewer employees at each level as one moves up the organization) or a more uniform distribution across levels, which would occur if the organization was not hiring but employees continued to receive promotions.[13]

Technology-based **electronic (e-) learning** can often generate savings in time and cost over traditional, classroom-based learning. The percentage of training resources devoted to e-learning is clearly increasing, with 64 percent of organizations now using virtual classrooms.[14] One type of e-learning is short digital learning sessions that are available at employees' convenience and delivered through

micro-learning apps.[15] E-learning companies such as Grovo, Udemy Inc., and LinkedIn Learning offer micro-learning formats for corporate-skills training (e.g., how to use a piece of accounting software, how to manage conflict). Duolingo offers them for language skills. Typically, they comprise a mix of video and interactive lessons that take fewer than five minutes to complete, and they include a quiz. Users can access micro-learning apps either online or via their smartphones. Evidence indicates that e-learning does work,[16] but its effectiveness depends on the delivery method as well as the skill or task being trained.

With respect to collaborative tools, there are two broad groups: web-based and collaborative media platforms. Web-based tools include blogs, wikis, and social networking sites where people mine and exchange information. These tools have been adapted for secure use by businesses, and vendors have infused many of these features into their software. **Collaborative media platforms** are specialized tools for various disciplines, from sales to supply-chain management. They also support various HR processes—for example, recruitment and performance management (360-degree feedback that incorporates ratings from superiors, peers, and subordinates). Other tools in this category include file-sharing sites and other spaces where teams can collaborate on projects to share information in a private, secure setting.

Safety and Security

The most common use of HR technology is a **human resource information system (HRIS)**. We will have much more to say about HRIS in later sections, but the key point here is that HRIS allow organizations to sort information so that it can be used for record keeping, reporting, and business decision making. Consider just a few examples. The acquisition and analysis of injury and illness data can help to improve workplace safety and security by identifying trends or common causes. Incident-management technology can facilitate the computation and analysis of the costs of various types of injuries. HRIS also facilitate the documentation and management of training activities, many of which are required in safety-sensitive or other positions. Beyond that, they facilitate electronic communications, digital access to key login information, data management from security cameras, and, by incorporating proper safeguards, employee protection from identity theft.

Recruitment and Staffing

A vast and ever-increasing array of technology is available to assist organizations with recruitment and staffing management: applicant-tracking software, web-based applications, cloud computing, mobile apps, and video products. Organizations compete in talent markets, domestic and global, and technology often helps them attract and hire the best talent from those markets. Indeed, organizations that do not have some type of online-application process are at a competitive disadvantage because most job seekers now apply online.

At a general level, HR technology is used widely to source talent, to track applicants through the various steps of the recruitment-selection process, and to facilitate background investigations, job analyses, and applicant screening. Social media like LinkedIn and web-based search engines enable firms to identify candidates.[17] Savvy recruiters are constantly looking for ways to poach high performers, and HR technology makes it easier than ever to find them.

In recruiting, the most robust **applicant-tracking systems** record and analyze data to meet equal employment opportunity (EEO) and government-contractor requirements. They track where each applicant is in the recruitment process, and they generate reports that analyze the relative performance of alternative recruitment sources and strategies. To market their job openings more strategically, some employers are using real simple syndication (RSS) to reach job seekers via e-mail or text message as soon as a new job is posted. Finally, **self-service portals** allow applicants to manage multiple applications at once as their multimedia résumés display text, photos, videos, and sound. Sites like Glassdoor.com and TheJobCrowd.com allow job seekers to research an employer's brand and decide if they even want to apply for a job there. Those sites provide information about the cultures and values of an organization and its senior managers, interview questions, and salaries. The sites are like "Trip Advisor" for jobs.

When it comes to applicant screening, thousands of employers use **e-Verify**, a free web-based tool from the Social Security Administration and the Department of Homeland Security to verify a match between employees' names, Social Security numbers, and immigration information. Desktop job-search engines like Google allow employers to conduct background checks, supplemented by third-party background screeners using Internet-based tools and databases. Private blogs and postings on social-networking sites like Facebook, LinkedIn, and Twitter provide additional information to consider. Aptitude tests administered online, such as for computer programming, basic math, and verbal comprehension, make applicant screening more efficient. Finally, electronic on-boarding systems handle tasks like assigning parking passes, desktops, laptops, or tablet computers, uniforms, e-mail addresses, and security badges. Some employers with globally distributed workforces, like IBM, use technology-delivered learning to teach new employees about corporate culture and business processes. Avatars of new employees attend meetings, view presentations, and interact with other avatars in a virtual IBM community.

HR Risk Management

HR risk refers to the uncertainty arising from changes in a wide range of workforce and people-management issues that affect a company's ability to meet its strategic and operating objectives.[18] Such risks typically fall into four main categories: strategic, compliance, operational, and financial risks. With respect to HR technology, the primary concern is operational risks that might impede a firm's ability to meet its operating and strategic objectives. Two key subareas include policies and procedures that define internal controls and vendor management and sourcing.[19] In the digital age, a major area of internal controls is the responsibility to ensure that employees' personal information is protected. Risks run the gamut from the release of sensitive data to the wrong manager to major security breaches or hacks that expose employees' personal information to external, unknown sources.

Sensible policies and security protocols can minimize the risk of security breaches. Here are three examples: (1) **multifactor authentication** (requiring not only a password and user name but also something that only a user has, such as a code sent to his or her smartphone in order to log in to a website); (2) encrypting sensitive data, and (3) restricting the type of data that can be shared in the cloud or on social media. Finally, organizations should be vigilant with vendors that require personal data. Some organizations require all vendors to meet or exceed specified levels of IT security protocols as a condition of doing business with them. It's also important to understand what steps a vendor will take in the event of a breach.[20]

Ethical Dilemma
Is It Unethical to Fail to Provide Cybersecurity?

Data breaches, regulatory demands, and compliance requirements are driving the global market for cybersecurity services and products. With the average cost of a data breach being $4 million, there is no room for complacency.[21] In 2019 there were a whopping 5,183 data breaches for a total of 7.9 billion exposed records.[22] Not surprisingly, therefore, organizations worldwide spent more than $124 billion on information security services and products. Budgeting for cloud security increased 148 percent between 2017 and 2019, while general data-security budgeting increased 38 percent.[23] Digitized data are a tempting target, as almost 90 percent of the total value of the *Fortune* 500 now consists of intellectual property (IP) and other intangible assets. Organizations are at risk from the loss of IP, destroyed or altered data, outright theft of employees' personal data, and loss of public confidence. Have senior leaders in your organization established an enterprise-wide, cyber-risk management framework with adequate staffing and budget? Is it unethical to fail to do that? After all, the median number of days that an organization is compromised before identifying a cyber-breach is 146. Of even greater concern is that 53 percent of cyberattacks are first identified by law enforcement or third parties, compared with 47 percent that are discovered internally.[24]

LEVERAGING HR TECHNOLOGY—HUMAN RESOURCE INFORMATION SYSTEMS (HRIS)

A key feature of all modern HRIS systems is the use of **relational databases** that store data in separate files that can be linked by common elements, such as name, Social Security number, hiring status (full- or part-time), training courses completed, job location, mailing address, or birthdate, among others. A relational database lets a user sort the data by any of the fields.

HRIS have come a long way. Early applications were built for computer-system specialists. Managers, employees, and even HR professionals were far removed from the process. High costs convinced small companies to stick with their filing cabinets, Rolodexes, or Excel spreadsheets. Today's more affordable systems allow managers to make informed decisions, often based on predictive analytics, about a wide range of issues in talent management. HRIS can be as simple as a small, internally developed employee database or as complex as a fully integrated enterprise resource planning (ERP) system offering economies of scale to larger companies.

Both large and small companies are eager to take advantage of the new technology. Large employers want to upgrade their aging **on-premise systems** (platforms housed in privately controlled data centers) to cloud-based **software-as-a-service (SaaS) systems**: subscription-based software paid on a month-to-month basis. Small employers want to upgrade after years of using spreadsheets. Buyers in both groups need to be savvy consumers in order to choose wisely from the wide array of HRIS platforms that are available. Figure 2-1 shows seven key issues to consider.

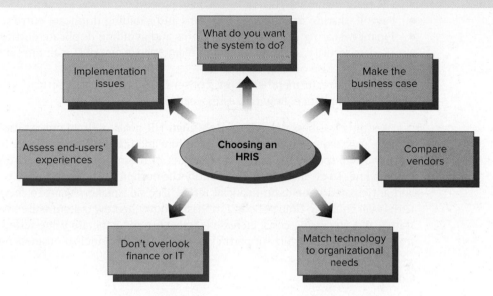

Figure 2–1

Items to consider when choosing an HRIS.

What Do You Want the System to Do?

An HRIS should last 5–7 years. To do that, it's important to identify today's needs as well as tomorrow's. The first step is to develop a deep understanding of top management's long-term goals and objectives in order to create buying criteria for a long-term solution.[25] An organization poised for aggressive growth will have different needs than one that is shedding assets and reducing its operations. Perhaps the biggest regret among dissatisfied buyers is that they focus only on automating transactional activities, such as payroll processing or legal/regulatory and compliance activities, focusing on the short term. Yet suppose a firm plans to expand its operations to international markets in the next 3–5 years? Will its HRIS offer linkages to payroll providers around the world? Begin by identifying immediate problems to solve as well as longer-term challenges.

Immediate problems might include reducing human error in data management, reducing cycle time in recruitment, or remaining compliant with regulatory or legal requirements. Longer-term challenges might be to create a positive employer brand by enhancing each applicant's experience, gaining a first-mover advantage in recruiting, or improving new-hire on-boarding experiences. Know what features your HRIS needs to have, as well as those that might be nice to have, over short- and longer-term horizons. Beyond that, what kind of a budget do you have to work with? Who will have access to the HRIS? What security controls do you need? Will the HRIS need to be compatible with other systems (e.g., accounting)?

Make the Business Case

In addition to the needs of HR, the business case for an HRIS will be stronger if you can address the concerns of senior managers and show how the software will affect other departments. In short, try to anticipate issues that will affect key players. Here are some examples[26]:

- HR team members–current versus new processes; interfacing with legacy software.
- Payroll–sharing data between systems and avoiding duplicate entries.
- Finance–sharing data between systems and avoiding duplicate entries.
- IT–data security, software setup and maintenance, use of IT staff time and resources.
- Managers–ease of use, workflows.
- Executive team members–cost, consensus, data security, return on investment (ROI), compliance, new processes, team buy-in.

A strong business case will closely align HR goals with an organization's business strategy (e.g., reducing the time it takes to hire and make a new employee fully productive) and will specify the anticipated impact of the new system on the organization's bottom line. To do that, HR must quantify the current level of services as well as future and anticipated benefits in financial terms. Decision makers want to see financial returns over multiple time periods. Emphasize how the new system will reduce administrative and processing costs, increase efficiencies, and generate value-added knowledge from data analytics, while supporting an organization's principal business needs.

Compare Vendors

Consider three broad strategies for adopting HR technology: (1) an integrated system from a single vendor, (2) **best of breed** (select the best applications in each area from multiple vendors), and (3) outsource HR technology infrastructure to a third-party vendor.[27] There is no single best system, as organizations vary in their needs, resources, and priorities. When comparing vendor systems, start by identifying a small number of main uses of the HRIS–say, three or four–and ask each vendor to demonstrate how it addresses each one. How much support for each of these uses can you expect from each vendor? Smaller organizations with limited internal staff and resources to draw on need strong implementation and customer support from the vendor of choice. This is what led SwervePoint, a small, promotional merchandising company in Danvers, Massachusetts, to choose Namely's HRIS. At the opposite end of the spectrum, Hitachi gave a small number of very complex scenarios to each vendor and asked how its system would handle it. It wanted to see, for example, how each HRIS would handle different organizational structures, as well as situations where employees are loaned to other divisions in Hitachi, in some cases, in other countries. This rigorous evaluation process led Hitachi to select Workday as its HRIS vendor.[28]

Here are two other recommendations. One, people demonstrating the software know how to hide usability issues. Test each system yourself before you spend money and roll out the software companywide. Two, beware of a vendor that is unwilling to say, "Our system doesn't do that." If the answer to every question is yes, then something is probably wrong.[29]

Match Technology to Organizational Needs

There is enormous variation across vendors in terms of the capabilities their HRIS offer. This is why it is absolutely essential to specify in advance what you want an HRIS to do. Knowing "need-to-have" HRIS features in advance helps protect an organization from paying for nonessential, but perhaps "nice-to-have," features. Do you want an **HR dashboard**, for example, that displays a series of measures that indicate HR

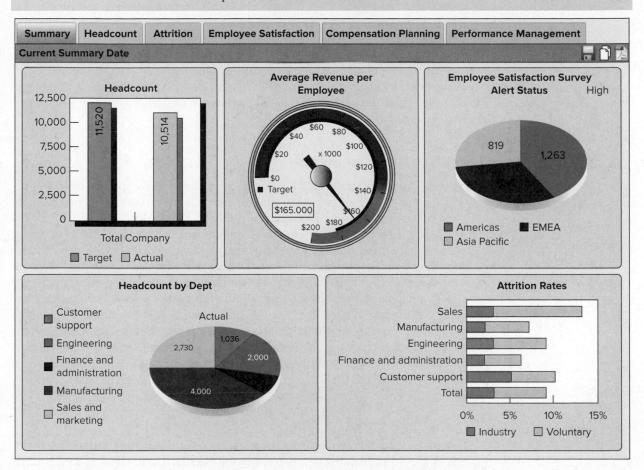

Figure 2–2

Examples of HR metrics in a dashboard format.

goals and objectives (e.g., for diversity or employee development) and the progress toward meeting them? Figure 2-2 is just one example of such dashboard metrics.

At the high end, Heineken and Lufthansa, for example, chose SAP's Success Factors, an SaaS system, that offers capabilities such as 2,000 built-in metrics, analytics capabilities to correlate workforce data with financial and other non-HR data to generate actionable insights, and built-in "wizards" to reduce errors in employee self-service functions. Other vendors for large organizations include Kronos Workforce Ready, UltiPro Enterprise, Oracle HCM Cloud, or Workday HCM. Mid-sized organizations often turn to vendors such as Namely, Zenefits, Viventium, or Espresso HR. Naturally, they do not incorporate as many features as those targeted to large firms. Small organizations, in contrast, might choose an HRIS from Eddy, Breathe, Paycor Perform, or Boomr that allows them to transition from spreadsheets to an affordable HRIS. Employee information can be consolidated from multiple locations into a single view. They typically support activities such as recruitment, on-boarding, time and attendance, compliance, compensation, employee and manager self-service, and performance management.[30] These are examples of just a few of hundreds of vendors. Can you appreciate why it is so important in advance to have a well-defined "shopping list" of features you are willing to pay for?

Don't Overlook Finance or Information Technology (IT)

When choosing an HRIS, a big mistake for any organization, large or small, is to fail to include representatives from finance and IT in the vendor-selection process. It is too late to bring them in *after* a system is purchased. Instead, IT should provide critical information about the types of features and platforms it is able to support, including software setup and maintenance, as well as requirements for data security. Finance needs to endorse the business case for an HRIS, particularly the expected payoffs for the organization. Beyond that, a basic concern for finance is for an integrated payroll module or for an HRIS that will work smoothly with the payroll system that is already in place.

Assess End Users' Experiences

When comparing alternative HRIS, it is critical to assess the experiences of end users. This is one reason a demonstration-only from different vendors is not enough. Various types of users need to experience the HRIS features for themselves. For example, there is a big difference between HR professionals using an HRIS to automate a process and increase efficiency versus employees and managers who need to rely on it for their own purposes. If employees or managers will use the system, there are high expectations for a user-friendly, consumer-grade technology experience. For example, employee self-service modules allow employees to view and update their personal information in the HRIS and perhaps access a decision-support system to make informed choices regarding employee benefits that best match their current situations. Managers may use the system to modify or approve time sheets or performance reviews. Inputs from all three groups can provide valuable information when choosing an HRIS that best fits an organization's needs.[31]

Implementation Issues

You've chosen a vendor and signed a contract. Now comes the final step, implementing the new system. Successful implementation is critical, and the first step is to be crystal clear about the underlying objectives for the new HRIS. To accomplish work in the digital age, the majority of new HRIS are in the cloud, and the top four reasons for replacing an HRIS are:[32]

- To have a single system of record for HR data.
- To ensure reliable, consistent reporting for compliance and legal obligations.
- To standardize HR data across multiple geographies or business units.
- To move away from legacy systems that were not meeting organizational needs.

These become important criteria for assessing the effectiveness of the new HRIS. A detailed treatment of system integration is beyond the scope of this chapter, but a key issue for the integration team is to verify the accuracy and integrity of the data in the new system. Are the data stored in the correct location? Can users query the data? Are data available to individuals with appropriate security clearances? Members of the software team and the functional HR team should test each module to ensure that it works as intended and that it produces accurate data.[33]

Upgrading or purchasing a new HRIS is a multifaceted undertaking, and there are many potential roadblocks that can hinder success. Following the seven steps outlined above and in Figure 2-1 can help ensure that this HR technology will perform successfully for years to come.

CHALLENGES FACING HR TECHNOLOGY

This section discusses five emerging challenges in HR technology: (1) new skills and roles for HR staff, (2) increasing expectations and demand for data, (3) more distant HR staff, (4) need to improve the quality of decisions, and (5) increasing the comfort level of *all* employees with HR technology.[34]

New Skills and Roles for HR Staff

In small organizations, HR generalists will be responsible for managing the HRIS as well as the growth in services that it supports. They will need to have technical skills as well as interpersonal skills because they will have to develop relationships with vendors as well as users. In larger organizations, HR staff will focus on policy decisions, complex or sensitive employee issues, and analysis of people-related business issues that have financial implications for the firm. In today's team-driven, collaborative work environments, HR professionals are interacting more frequently with other parts of the organization in tasks such as configuring cloud software and integrating disparate technology systems. To do that well, they need technical skills as well as soft skills in communication, empathy, and active listening.[35] Expectations for both types of skills will rise as the roles of HR professionals change in the digital age.

Increasing Expectations and Demand for Data

As consumers who use smartphones, smart televisions, or consumer electronics, we have come to expect intuitive, easy-to-use software. As employees, we want the same high-quality experiences when we use employee self-service features of an HRIS. When we can manage more personal data and use the HRIS to answer questions and make decisions, we will begin to ask new questions and seek broader information. For example, in choosing employee benefits, instead of simply reading about the features that each provider offers, and then choosing benefits that seem to provide the best match to one's current family or life situation, new applications allow users to ask "what if?" questions: "What if I have a wife and two young children?" "What if I have an elderly parent to care for?" "What if I am single and approaching retirement?" Using artificial intelligence, the software can configure one or more packages of benefits that best fit each employee's current situation. The result is that employees make better informed, more intelligent choices as they optimize the set of benefits they choose.

More Distant HR Staff

As more HR content becomes available online, and as employee self-service becomes the norm rather than the exception, there is naturally less contact between employees and HR professionals. Particularly in organizations with newly adopted HRIS, employees may miss the personal contact they previously enjoyed with HR staff. Working with a computer to complete tasks they used to accomplish collaboratively in person may seem a little awkward at first. Communications and relationships with HR staff may become more distant. To deal with this, HR staff should be highly visible and accessible in the workplace, so that they can interact with employees as needed.

IMPACT OF HR TECHNOLOGY ON PRODUCTIVITY, QUALITY OF WORK LIFE, AND THE BOTTOM LINE

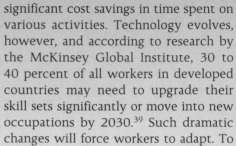

Internet-enabled smartphones, tablets, and personal computers, together with company intranets, including employee self-service capabilities facilitated by HR technology, allow employees to work from their offices, their homes, or anywhere else. Tools to promote collaboration—web-based or collaborative media platforms—also facilitate the ability to work remotely. This has enabled stunning gains in personal productivity and has reduced the need to acquire information through personal interactions with middle managers or HR representatives. Frontline workers now have essentially unlimited access to data that used to be difficult to obtain or required more senior managers to interpret.[38] At the same time, advances in assistive technology have dramatically increased job opportunities for people with disabilities. Organizations benefit through their ability to recruit from a broader pool of applicants. Whether it's recruiting, staffing, performance management, or employee relations, HR technology has enabled workers at all levels to be more productive, and it has demonstrated bottom-line benefits through significant cost savings in time spent on various activities. Technology evolves, however, and according to research by the McKinsey Global Institute, 30 to 40 percent of all workers in developed countries may need to upgrade their skill sets significantly or move into new occupations by 2030.[39] Such dramatic changes will force workers to adapt. To ease the stress, employers should lead the way in training and upskilling the current workforce—rather than engaging in layoffs and new rounds of recruiting. Evidence indicates that employers as varied as Amazon, Facebook, Guardian Life Insurance Co, Nationwide, Siemens, the Home Depot, and Chevron are doing just that. They are also forming partnerships with high schools, community colleges, universities, and state and local governments.[40] The message to companies is clear: Address the skills gap now or fall short of your digital aspirations.

Need to Improve the Quality of Decisions

HR technology can dramatically improve the time and cost per transaction as HR staff, employees, and line managers gain access to increased data to support decisions. An unanticipated consequence, however, is that the logic behind the decision may become less transparent.[36] For example, consider the use of managerial self-service in the award of annual bonuses to employees. Unless managers are aware of processes and policies, such as timelines for completing performance reviews and limits on the size of bonuses based on each employee's position in his or her pay range, they may become frustrated with the HRIS because it will not allow them to do what they want to do. As a result, the overall quality of a decision may not improve. To avoid this situation, ensure that all employees and managers understand the processes and policies that are embedded in the self-service features of the HRIS.

Increasing the Comfort Level of *All* Employees with HR Technology

HR technology exists to make workflows more efficient, increase accuracy, simplify mundane tasks, and ideally, to improve the employee experience and company performance. While many of today's employees are "digital natives" who have grown up with technology as a central feature of their lives, this is not true for everyone in today's multigenerational workforce. Employee reactions to new software tools may range from excitement to wariness. To deal with that, do three things well. Be crystal clear in communications about why the technology is being introduced, explain how it will benefit both the company and the employee, and make it easy for employees to seek help, if they have trouble using the new tools.[37] Employees will appreciate the attention, and the payoff in improved productivity will be immediate.

HR TECHNOLOGY TRENDS

In this final section of the chapter, we will consider briefly five emerging trends in HR technology: (1) expansion of social networking; (2) growth of compliance and reporting requirements; (3) more renting, less buying of services; (4) growth in the use of data analytics and dashboards; and (5) more transparent HR policies, increasing concerns about data privacy.[41]

Expansion of Social Networking

As the popularity of social-networking sites grows, more and more organizations are integrating information from them. This is a trend that is too big for many organizations to ignore. To illustrate, Facebook's Workplace is a platform that helps employees collaborate and connect internally using chat, group conversations, and video calls. Its Jobs and Mentorships platforms allow users to search for jobs and to find mentors within specific groups on the Facebook network.[42] As another example, consider LinkedIn. LinkedIn operates the world's largest professional network on the Internet, with more than 660 million members in more than 200 countries and territories.[43] For a fee, organizations can sign up for a LinkedIn "Recruiter" account that allows access to the entire LinkedIn network. Designed specifically to match an organization's staffing workflow, Recruiter's user interface includes more than 20 advanced search filters. On the supply side, potential applicants can receive e-mail alerts for new jobs posted on LinkedIn that match advanced search criteria that they specify, or postings that are recommended to them from a feature called "Jobs You May Be Interested In."[44]

Growth of Compliance and Reporting Requirements

In country after country, organizations continue to be affected by national and local compliance requirements, legal and regulatory, that require HR to collect and report additional information. Firms increasingly will need to adapt their HRIS in order to remain compliant. Pending changes in tax codes, financial regulations, equal employment opportunity compliance, and health care–just to note a few areas–all suggest that compliance and reporting demands will increase. Multinational investment banking and financial services corporation Citigroup Inc. has nearly 30,000 employees working on regulatory and compliance issues,[45] many of which are related to HR. Can you imagine trying to navigate this environment without a well-functioning HRIS?

More Renting, Less Buying of Services

One of the biggest HR trends in the last few years has been the adoption of subscription-based cloud systems, which were intended to reduce the need for IT to maintain HR software, provide a more integrated suite of tools, improve data management, improve the user experience, and deliver faster innovation. Organizations have experienced varying degrees of success in each of these areas.[46] One of the disadvantages to using an SaaS approach, however, is that the software is not customizable to the specific needs of an organization. Firms either find a solution that best matches their needs or change their processes to fit a particular system. Full integration of old and new systems can be challenging. Only 5 percent of Deloitte's 2019 Human Capital Survey respondents reported that they have a fully integrated HR cloud platform. Most of the others have some combination of cloud and on-premise software, and 29 percent have no systems at all. In short, the quality of the user experience and the level of integration vary considerably. At the same time, there has been an explosion of intelligent tools and experience platforms. More than 1,400 HR technology vendors are in the market, many focused on using AI, cognitive interfaces, advanced analytics, sentiment analysis, and other new technologies designed to make work easier. While many of the challenges with HR technology remain, the pace of development has quickened, giving organizations a tremendous range of options in their plans for the future.[47]

Growth in the Use of Data Analytics and Dashboards

"People analytics–using insights from data to support decision-making–offers tremendous potential to organizations to drive business strategy, improve productivity and performance, and personalize and enhance the employee experience."[48] Despite that rosy forecast, three key challenges remain: (1) turning analytical insights into business actions, (2) aggregating multiple data sources, and (3) lack of appropriate analytical skills.[49] HRIS are particularly well suited to address challenge 2, whereas the other two depend on acquiring and retaining the right talent. Organizations will move from using **descriptive analytics** to understand what happened in the past and why, to **predictive analytics** to model what will happen, and ultimately to **prescriptive analytics** to develop multiple scenarios about the future.[50] This will enable managers to use HR data to make better decisions about the workforce. At the same time, HR dashboards (see Figure 2-2), which provide high-level, real-time, graphically formatted data to managers, will become integral features of talent management.

More Transparent HR Policies, Increasing Concerns about Data Privacy

As more data-privacy laws are enacted, joining the likes of the General Data Protection Regulation (a regulation in European Union law) and the California Consumer Privacy Act, HR leaders and technology solutions will play a growing role in helping to strike the right balance between employee trust and data privacy. Few organizations manage as much personal information as do employers. At the same time, employees want more transparency and control over their personal data. "Providing the right level of transparency, and the right level of protection for employee data, will be on ongoing challenge. As employers make data easier to access, the risk of jeopardizing employees' privacy increases. Managing this risk has become more complex as HR applications often link to systems outside the organization, such as benefits vendors, online job-search sites, and distance-learning providers."[51]

HR technology–most prominently in the form of HRIS–has changed the ways that HR services are delivered and managed. Self-service portals promise faster execution of employee and manager transactions, with more informed users. HR functions that can protect the integrity and privacy of employees' data, while ensuring that all users are comfortable with the system, will add genuine value to their organizations.

IMPLICATIONS FOR MANAGEMENT PRACTICE

Technology in general, and HR technology in particular, has come a long way in the past several decades. Here are five key implications for managers: (1) Employees want assurances that their personal data will be protected. Be able to explain HR policies and specific steps your organization is taking to ensure that. (2) At a broader level, cybersecurity is an enterprise-wide risk-management issue, not just an IT issue. To address it, make it your business to know about the leading practices for cybersecurity, including insider threats, and where your organization differs from those. Offer ongoing, companywide awareness and training programs around cybersecurity.[52] (3) In the on-boarding process for new hires, ensure that all individuals, not just "digital natives," are comfortable and competent when using the company's intranet and HRIS. (4) Demand break-even or return-on-investment analyses for investments in HR technology. Begin by quantifying the cost savings associated with reduced time for HR transactions. (5) Identify three or four key HR metrics and have HR staff develop dashboards that illustrate results or current status graphically. There are certainly additional steps managers can take to harness the power of HR technology, but these five are fundamental to improved productivity, quality of work life, and profits.

HOW TECHNOLOGY IS CHANGING WORK AND ORGANIZATIONS

Human Resource Management in Action: Conclusion

Artificial intelligence (AI) is rapidly becoming part of our lives. Mobile phones, PCs, Google, Alexa, and even smart televisions use AI, attempting to make decisions for us. Hiring-based decisions may be based on facial expressions, word choice, or tone of voice. To trust those decisions, there needs to be confidence in the data input to the AI application, the method used to train it, the rationale for how the system reaches every conclusion, the ability to verify or validate that those conclusions are aligned with the original intent of the algorithm, and that every step along the way is aligned with an organization's purpose and ethical standards. Humans therefore need to be looped in to critical AI-supported tasks to enforce a company's values and ethics.

As AI seeps deeper and deeper into organizational operations, what is the role of managers and executives? Unlike effective managers, machines have not yet learned to tolerate high levels of ambiguity or to inspire people at every level. Consider ambiguity. The bigger and broader the question to be addressed, the more likely it is that human synthesis will be central to problem solving because, although machines can provide many pieces, they cannot assemble the big picture. The big picture represents the glue that holds a company together.

With respect to the adoption and implementation of technology, it can be used to enable or to oppress people at work. Self-determination theory is a particularly useful guide. That theory holds that self-motivation and well-being will be enhanced when innate needs for autonomy, competence, and relatedness are satisfied, and they will be diminished when these needs are thwarted. Autonomy is the need to control one's actions, to be a causal agent in one's life. Competence is the need to experience mastery and to affect one's outcomes and surroundings. Relatedness is the need to feel interpersonally connected with others.

In practice, at least four considerations influence the adoption and implementation of workplace technologies. First, are they natural and easy to use? **Usability** concerns the interface between humans and technology, and it can be measured in terms of efficiency (time to complete a task), effectiveness (error rate), and user satisfaction. A second consideration is self-efficacy. People who feel competent to use, or to learn to use, new technology are likely to experience less anxiety when that new technology is introduced. A third consideration is economic. Does the new technology promise competitive advantage to an organization or to an individual in his or her personal life? If so, the organization or individual is more likely to implement it. Finally, it also is important to consider the role of social factors in the acceptance of technology. If friends, coworkers, or family members are using a particular technology—for example, a smartphone-payment system—peer pressure increases the likelihood of one's own adoption of it.

If technology is to enable people at work, it should foster self-motivation and well-being, key elements of self-determination theory; enhance productivity; and promote job satisfaction, organizational commitment, and citizenship behaviors among workers.

SUMMARY

Technology is changing the manner in which businesses create and capture value, how and where we work, and how we interact and communicate. In this chapter, we examined the effects of technology in nine key areas of HR management: business leadership, compensation and benefits, diversity, employee relations, labor relations, organization and employee development, safety and security, recruitment and staffing, and HR risk management. The most central use of technology in HRM is an organization's human resource information system (HRIS). An HRIS provides a single, centralized view of the data needed to execute HR processes, such as recruiting, applicant tracking, payroll, time and attendance, training, performance management, benefits administration, and employee self-service. Many different HRIS platforms are available, but to choose the one that is best for any given organization, it is necessary to address seven key issues: (1) decide what you want the system to do, (2) make the business case for an HRIS, (3) compare vendors, (4) match technology to organizational needs, (5) don't overlook finance or information technology (IT), (6) assess end users' experiences, and (7) address implementation issues. HRIS also bring challenges, such as new skills and roles for HR staff members, increasing expectations and demand for data, more distant HR staff, the need to demonstrate improvements in the quality of decisions, and the need to increase the comfort levels of all employees with HR technology. The chapter closed by considering five emerging trends in HR technology: the expansion of social networking; the growth of compliance and reporting requirements; more renting, less buying of services; growth in the use of data analytics and dashboards; and more transparent HR policies, leading to increasing concerns about protecting the integrity and privacy of employees' data.

KEY TERMS

ubiquitous computing

decision-support systems (DSS)

technology

assistive technology

gamification

biometrics

electronic (e-)learning

micro-learning apps

collaborative media platforms

applicant-tracking systems

self-service portals

e-Verify

HR risk

multifactor authentication

relational databases

on-premise systems

software-as-a-service (SaaS) systems

best of breed

HR dashboard

descriptive analytics

predictive analytics

prescriptive analytics

usability

human resources information system

DISCUSSION QUESTIONS

2-1. Describe how technology has changed the ways that you live and work.

2-2. Always-on technology, such as e-mail and smartphones, has promises as well as perils. Discuss alternative strategies for avoiding overwork and burnout.

2-3. If an organization decides to use biometrics for security reasons, what can it do to protect personal privacy?

2-4. Technology alone is not sufficient to ensure a successful implementation of an HRIS. What else is necessary?

2-5. Identify three types of security procedures that can help to minimize the risk of security breaches.

2-6. What are some examples of HR risks?

2-7. What are the advantages and disadvantages of on-premise versus SaaS HRIS?

2-8. How might HRIS affect employees, managers, and HR team members?

2-9. You have been charged with choosing an HRIS. What key factors will you consider?

2-10. Recommend three strategies for protecting employees' personal information.

APPLYING YOUR KNOWLEDGE

Automation and AI Reshape the Workplace   *Case 2–1*

The robots are coming! The robots are coming! Well, not so fast. While only about 5 percent of all occupations are at risk of being entirely automated by 2025, many jobs will be transformed as people rework their old roles to include collaborating with AI and other forms of digital technology.[53] Just because automation or AI are available, however, does not mean that organizations will adopt them. The pace of adoption, and thus the impact on workers, will vary across different activities, occupations, and wage and skill levels. Factors that will determine the extent of worker displacement include the ongoing development of technological capabilities; the cost of technology; competition with labor, including skills and supply-and-demand dynamics; performance benefits, including and beyond labor-cost savings; and social and regulatory acceptance.

Workers themselves are not down on new technology in the workplace. In an Accenture survey of more than 10,000 workers, 87 percent felt optimistic about how technology will change their jobs in the next 5 years. Nearly the same number said they feel ready for those changes. About half of the respondents were described as high skill, with the rest split evenly between low- and medium-skill levels. The challenge for employers will be to provide the kind of high-quality training employees at every level need to keep their skills fresh.[54] As we have seen, many employers are answering the call.[55] The bottom line is that jobs will change dramatically, and that will force organizations–and workers–to adapt to the changes.

Questions

1. As a manager, what can you do to help employees adapt to changes wrought by automation and AI?
2. What responsibility, if any, do organizations bear for helping workers adapt to technological changes?
3. How would you advise workers themselves to adapt to changes in their jobs due to automation and AI?
4. Might organizations use their strategies for adaptation to technological change as a retention strategy? How?

REFERENCES

1. Sardon, M. (2020, Jan. 6). Fund themes investors are likely to bet on. *The Wall Street Journal*, pp. R5, R6.
2. Murray A. (2015, Apr. 22). The new industrial revolution. *Fortune*, p. 6.
3. Wooldridge A. (2015). *The Icarus syndrome meets the wearable revolution.* Korn/Ferry Breifings Talent Leaders, p. 29.
4. Oxford living dictionaries. Retrieved from *https://en.oxforddictionaries.com/definition/technology* on Dec. 29, 2016.
5. Lupushor, S. (2019). People analytics is finally here and we have a lot to celebrate. *People + Strategy, 42*(1), p. 14. See also *Introduction to the Discipline of Human Resources Technology.* (2015, Aug. 25). Retrieved from *www.shrm.org/resourcesandtools/tools-and-samples/toolkits/pages/introtechnology.aspx* on Oct. 27, 2016.
6. Goth, G. (2019, Sept. 23). Data-driven benefit-selection tools are just getting started. *SHRM Online.* Retrieved from *https://www.shrm.org/resourcesandtools/hr-topics/benefits/pages/data-driven-benefit-selection-tools-just-getting-started.aspx* on Sept. 24, 2019. *See also* Grensing-Pophal, L. (2019, Oct. 1). Analytical tools to help HR manage benefits, reduce costs. *SHRM Online.* Retrieved from *https://www.shrm.org/resourcesandtools/hr-topics/benefits/pages/analytical-hr-tools-manage-benefits-reduce-costs.aspx* on Oct. 2, 2019.
7. Zielinski, D. (2019, Aug. 27). How HR technology supports diversity and inclusion. *SHRM Online.* Retrieved from *https://www.shrm.org/resourcesandtools/hr-topics/technology/pages/how-hr-technology-supports-diversity-inclusion.aspx* on Aug. 28, 2019.
8. Zielinski, D. (2016, Dec. 20). New assistive technologies aid employees with disabilities. Retrieved from *www.shrm.org/resourcesandtools/hr-topics/technology/pages/new-assistive-technologies-aid-employees-with-disabilities.aspx* on Dec. 21, 2016.
9. Thielsch, M. T., and Niesenhaus, J. (2017). User experience, gamification, and performance. In G. Hertel, D. Stone, and J. Passmore (Eds.), *The Psychology of the Internet at Work*, Vol. 8, *Wiley-Blackwell Handbook Series on Industrial and Organizational Psychology.* New York: Wiley-Blackwell. *See also* Roberts, B. (2014, May). Gamification: Win, lose, or draw? *HRMagazine*, pp. 28–35.
10. Sheikh, K. (2019, July 8). Biometric technology in the workplace: No harm, no foul? *Spark Newsletter.* Retrieved from *https://www.adp.com/spark/articles/2019/07/biometric-technology-in-the-workplace-no-harm-no-foul.aspx#* on Feb. 24, 2020. *See also* Zielinski, D. (2018, Aug. 23). Use of biometric data grows, though not without legal risks. *SHRM*

Online. Retrieved from *https://www.shrm.org/resourcesandtools/hr-topics/technology/pages/biometric-technologies-grow-.aspx* on Aug. 24, 2018. *See also* Alsever, J. (2016, Mar. 15). Is software better at managing people than you are? *Fortune*, pp. 41, 42.

11. Green, K. (2019, Feb. 19). How unions use technology to organize strikes today. *Union-Track*. Retrieved from *https://www.uniontrack.com/blog/unions-use-technology* on Feb. 24, 2020.

12. *Introduction to the Discipline of Human Resources Technology* (2015), op. cit.

13. Cascio, W. F., Boudreau, J. W., & Fink, A. (2019). *Investing in People* (3rd ed.). Upper Saddle River, NJ: Pearson.

14. *Association for Talent Development (ATD) State of the Industry Report.* (2016). Alexandria, VA: Author. *See also* Bersin by Deloitte. (2015). *Corporate Learning Factbook 2015*. San Francisco, CA: Deloitte Development, LLC.

15. Cascio, W. F. (2019). Training trends: Macro, micro, and policy issues. *Human Resource Management Review* 29, pp. 284–97.

16. Cheng, T., and Chen, C. C. (2015). The impact of e-learning on workplace on-the-job training. *International Journal of e-Education, e-Business, e-Management, and e-Learning* 5(4), pp. 212–25.

17. How to use social media for applicant screening. (2016, Aug. 10). Retrieved from *www.shrm.org/resourcesandtools/tools-and-samples/how-to-guides/pages/howtousesocialmediaforapplicantscreening.aspx* on Oct. 12, 2016.

18. Young, M. B., and Hexter, E. S. (2011). *Managing Human Capital Risk*. Research Report No. 1477-11-RR. New York: The Conference Board.

19. Cascio, W. F., and Boudreau, J. W. (2014). HR strategy: Optimizing risks, optimizing rewards. *Journal of Organizational Effectiveness: People and Performance* 1(1), pp. 77-97.

20. Cragle, F. R. III. (2015, July 10). How HR leaders can prevent and mitigate cyber loss. Retrieved from *www.shrm.org/resourcesandtools/hr-topics/technology/pages/how-hr-can-prevent-cyber-loss.aspx* on Jan. 2, 2017.

21. IBM Security. (2019). 2019 Cost of a data breach study. Retrieved from *www.ibm.com/security/data-breach?p1=Search&p4=p50370570729&p5=b&cm_mmc=Search_Google--1S_1S--WW_NA--%2Bbreach%20of%20%2Bdata_b&cm_mmca7=71700000061027912&cm_mmca8=aud-384354108630:kwd-295901324379&cm_mmca9=EAIaIQobChMI4IOE8JLr5wIVA9vACh1OKAKREAAYASAAEgLM9vD_BwE&cm_mmca10=405839889594&cm_mmca11=b&gclid=EAIaIQobChMI4IOE8JLr5wIVA9vACh1OKAKREAAYASAAEgLM9vD_BwE&gclsrc=aw.ds* on Feb. 24, 2020.

22. Hodge, R. (2019, Dec. 27). 2019 data breach hall of shame: These were the biggest data breaches of the year. *CNET*. Retrieved from *https://www.cnet.com/news/2019-data-breach-hall-of-shame-these-were-the-biggest-data-breaches-of-the-year/* on Feb. 24, 2020.

23. RSA conference. (2019). The future of companies and cybersecurity spending. Retrieved from *https://www.saconference.com/industry-topics/blog/the-future-of-companies-and-cyber-security-spending* on Feb. 24, 2020.

24. Clinton, L. (2017). *Cyber-Risk Oversight*. Washington, DC: National Association of Corporate Directors.

25. Bamboo HR. (2020). The complete HRIS buyer's guide for 2020. Retrieved from *file:///Users/waynefcascio/Downloads/The%20Complete%20HRIS%20Buyers%20Guide.pdf* on Feb. 24, 2020. *See also* Zielinski, D. (2016, Oct.). An HRMS for everyone. *HRMagazine*, pp. 47–50.

26. The complete HRIS buying guide for 2020, op. cit.

27. The complete HRIS buying guide for 2020, op. cit. *See also* Johnson, R. D., and Geutal, H. G. (2014a). *Transforming HR through Technology*. Alexandria, VA: SHRM Foundation Effective Practice Guidelines Series.

28. Zielinski (2016), op. cit.

29. The complete HRIS buyer's guide for 2020, op. cit.

30. HRMS World. (2020). Find and compare HRMS software. Retrieved from *https://www.hrmsworld.com/hrms-product-comparison.html* on Feb. 24, 2020.

31. The complete HRIS buyer's guide for 2020, op. cit. Zielinski (2016), op. cit. *See also* How to select an HRIS. (2015, Aug. 11). Retrieved from *www.shrm.org/resourcesandtools/tools-and-samples/how-to-guides/pages/howtoselectanhrissystem.aspx* on Oct. 12, 2016.

32. Wright, A. D. (2016, July 29). 5 steps to managing an HRIS implementation. Retrieved from *www.shrm.org/resourcesandtools/hr-topics/technology/pages/5-steps-to-managing-an-hris-implementation.aspx* on Oct. 12, 2016.

33. Designing and managing a human resource information system. (2015, Aug. 25). Retrieved from *www.shrm.org/resourcesandtools/tools-and-samples/toolkits/pages/managingahumanresourceinformationsystem.aspx* on Oct. 14, 2016.

34. Johnson, R. D., and Geutal, H. G. (2014b). *Leveraging HR Technology for Competitive Advantage.* Alexandria, VA: Society for Human Resource Management.

35. Zielinski, D. (2019, May 28). HR tech pros need soft skills, too. *SHRM Online.* Retrieved from *https://www.shrm.org/resourcesandtools/hr-topics/technology/pages/soft-skills.aspx* on May 29, 2019.

36. Goth (2019), op. cit.

37. Feffer, M. (2019, Sept. 9). How to boost employee adoption of new HR tech. *SHRM Online.* Retrieved from *https://www.shrm.org/resourcesandtools/hr-topics/technology/pages/how-to-boost-employee-adoption-of-new-hr-tech.aspx* on Sept. 10, 2019.

38. Mims, C. (2015, Apr. 20). Data is now the new middle manager. *The Wall Street Journal,* pp. B1, B2.

39. Hancock, B., Lazaroff-Puck, K., and Rutherford, S. (2020, Jan.). Getting practical about the future of work. *McKinsey & Co.* Retrieved from *https://www.mckinsey.com/business-functions/organization/our-insights/getting-practical-about-the-future-of-work* on Feb. 1, 2020. *See also* Weber, L. (2017, Jan. 18). Increasingly, automation reshapes workplace tasks. *The Wall Street Journal,* p. B5.

40. Soergel, A. (2020, Feb. 20). Companies invest in partnerships, workforce training to bridge skills gap. *U.S. News & World Report.* Retrieved from *https://www.usnews.com/news/economy/articles/2020-02-20/amazon-facebook-home-depot-among-companies-paying-to-train-workforce* on Feb. 24, 2020.

41. Zielinski, D. (2020, Jan. 2). What to expect: 2020 HR tech trends. *SHRM Online.* Retrieved from *https://www.shrm.org/resourcesandtools/hr-topics/technology/pages/2020-hr-tech-trends.aspx* on Jan. 4, 2020. *See also* Johnson and Geutal (2014a), op. cit.

42. Zielinski, D. (2019, Jan. 29). The technology giants are moving into HR. *SHRM Online.* Retrieved from *https://www.shrm.org/resourcesandtools/hr-topics/technology/pages/facebook-google-microsoft-moving-into-hr-technology.aspx* on Jan. 30, 2019.

43. About LinkedIn. Retrieved from *https://about.linkedin.com/* on Feb. 25, 2020.

44. LinkedIn talent solutions. Retrieved from *https://business.linkedin.com/talent-solutions/recruiter* on Jan. 10, 2017.

45. Citi will have almost 30,000 employees in compliance by year-end. (2014, July 14). Retrieved from *http://blogs.marketwatch.com/thetell/2014/07/14/citi-will-have-almost-30000-employees-in-compliance-by-year-end/* on Jan. 10, 2017.

46. Volini, E., Schwarz, J., & Roy, I. (2019, April 11). HR cloud: A launch pad, not a destination. *Deloitte Insights.* Retrieved from *https://www2.deloitte.com/us/en/insights/focus/human-capital-trends/2019/hr-cloud.html* on Feb. 25, 2020.

47. Volini et al. (2019), op. cit.

48. Green, D. (2019). The rise of people analytics. *People + Strategy, 42*(1), p. 9.

49. Ibid. *See also* Ransbotham, S., Kiron, D., and Prentice, P. K. (2015, Apr.). The talent dividend. *MIT Sloan Management Review,* pp. 2-11, Reprint No. 56480. *See also* What's driving the demand for data scientists? (2019, Mar. 8). *Knowledge@Wharton.* Retrieved from *https://knowledge.wharton.upenn.edu/article/whats-driving-demand-data-scientist/* on Mar. 9, 2019.

50. Ransbotham et al., 2015, op. cit.

51. Zielinski, D., (2020, Jan. 2), op. cit. *See also* Johnson, R. D., and Geutal, H. G. (2014a). *Transforming HR through Technology.* Alexandria, VA: SHRM Foundation Effective Practice Guidelines Series.

52. Carey, G., & Turner, B. (2020, Feb. 7). Best online cyber security courses of 2020: Free and paid certification programs, degrees and masters. *Techradar*. Retrieved from *https://www.techradar.com/best/best-online-cyber-security-courses* on Feb. 25, 2020. *See also* Clinton (2017), op. cit.

53. Sources: Morath, E. (2020, Feb. 24). AI threat targets higher-paying jobs. *The Wall Street Journal*, p. A2. *See also* Waldrop. M. M. (2018, July 28). The future of work: Will robots take my job? *Knowable Magazine*. Retrieved from *https://www.knowablemagazine.org/article/technology/2018/future-work-will-robots-take-my-job* on Aug. 1, 2018. *See also* Daugherty, P.R., and Wilson, H. J. (2018). *Human + Machine: Reimagining Work in the age of AI*. Boston, MA: Harvard Business Review Press.

54. Weber (2017), op. cit.

55. Soergel (2020), op. cit.

3

PEOPLE ANALYTICS: THE FINANCIAL IMPACT OF HRM ACTIVITIES

Questions This Chapter Will Help Managers Answer

LO 3-1 How can HR measures improve talent-related decisions in organizations?

LO 3-2 If I want to know how much money employee turnover is costing us each year, what factors should I consider?

LO 3-3 How do employees' attitudes relate to their engagement at work, customer satisfaction, and employee retention?

LO 3-4 What's the business case for work–life programs?

NEW DEVELOPMENTS IN PEOPLE ANALYTICS*

People analytics–using insights from data to support decisions about people-related business issues–offers great potential to organizations to drive business strategy, improve productivity and performance, and personalize and enhance the employee experience. Because conventional sources of competitive advantage no longer differentiate firms in the global marketplace, flexibility, speed, innovation, and talent are now critical. Many firms are substantially increasing the level of accountability in the line manager's role in talent management, and one of the outcomes of such accountability is increased demand for the insights and information that people analytics can generate. Widespread interest in innovations such as Google's *Project Oxygen* (what makes a good boss?) and data analysis in sports (inspired by the book and later the film, *Moneyball*) have boosted applications of analytics in many organizations.

In sports, for example, the market for data analytics is expected to reach $4 billion by 2022 as new applications help teams win in virtually every sport. Teams are also using electronic tickets–and even fingerprint or retinal scans–to understand the movements and purchasing behavior of fans to optimize ticket pricing and staffing on game days. In business settings, HR professionals now have access to advanced analytics software that either comes packaged as part of a vendor's technology suite or is available from providers that specialize in analytics products. Workday, for example, uses artificial intelligence and machine learning to automate analysis and deliver data insights to HR leaders on what's happening in their organizations, narrating those issues in natural language called a "story." The story is delivered with accompanying metrics and charts to make it easy for a decision maker to understand.

Many firms administer employee-engagement surveys that provide feedback to managers but no guidance on what to do next with the findings. To address that, Qualtrics recently launched a guided-action planning tool that helps HR leaders work with line managers to drill down to the manager's focus areas with specific tasks, resources, and action plans to help drive improvements on their teams.

Beware of a trap, however, if an HR team presents people data only as a "prettier form" of reporting, with visually enhanced dashboards, charts, and graphs. That's not what success looks like. The real challenge is to use those data to answer business questions that are strategically relevant and important. Data need to be accurate and current, the team analyzing the data needs a variety of experience and skills, and decision makers need to have real-time access to the insights the data offer.

Other key issues are data security and access. To address those concerns, analytics products from SAP Success Factors include features such as an authorization process that makes it possible to control the display of information and to change the authorization to access people data from highest to lowest levels. Another function is "data purge," which allows organizations to define the kinds of people data that should be deleted–and when. This is a key requirement of the General Data

Sources: Green, D. (2019). The rise of people analytics. *People + Strategy* 42, pp. 9, 10. Zielinski, D. (2019, Winter). Get smarter about people analytics. *HRMagazine*, pp. 24-29. Abhas, R. (2019, Jan. 31). How data analysis in sports is changing the game. *Forbes.* Retrieved from *https://www.forbes.com/sites/forbestechcouncil/2019/01/31/how-data-analysis-in-sports-is-changing-the-game/#28e368193f7b* on Mar. 1, 2020. Huselid, M. (2018). The science and practice of workforce analytics: Introduction to the HRM special issue. *Human Resource Management* 57, pp. 679-84.

Protection Regulation, a legal regulation on data protection and privacy in the European Union and the European Economic Area. It also addresses the transfer of personal data outside of those areas.

One area where HR leaders have sought more sophisticated analytics is in measuring the impact of their diversity and inclusion initiatives. In the conclusion to this case, we will see the kinds of tools that firms are using to address those concerns.

Challenges

1. What might account for the growing interest in people analytics?
2. How can HR leaders improve their ability to ask strategically relevant questions?
3. How might analytics promote competitive advantage through people?

In business settings, it is hard to be convincing without data. If the data are developed systematically and comprehensively and are analyzed in terms of their strategic implications for the business or business unit, they are more convincing. The chapter-opening vignette described some new developments in people analytics, but the most important feature of any analytical project is whether answers to the question being asked will enhance the competitiveness of a business. All of the material in this chapter is based on a simple principle that HR measurement is valuable to the extent that it improves vital decisions about talent. **Talent** refers to the potential and realized capacities of individuals and groups, including those within the organization and those who might join the organization.[1] We will begin the chapter with a discussion of the promise and perils of big data. Then we will present a broad framework for HR measurement, followed by an examination of the costs and benefits of HR activities in five key areas: employee attitudes, absenteeism, turnover, work–life programs, and collaboration and sharing knowledge.

BIG DATA: PROMISE AND PERILS

We live in a digital age and a smartphone world. Data are more widely available than ever before. To use the data wisely, however, decision makers must never lose sight of two paradoxes: (1) Many organizations are drowning in data but starved for information. (2) Data-driven decisions are evidence-based, yet there is still a great need for informed judgment and intuition.

Users of big data seek to glean insights from analyzing the data and to use those insights to gain competitive advantage in the marketplace. **Big data** is the collection and analysis of the digital history created when people shop or surf the Internet, but it also includes the tests and measures of aptitudes, behaviors, and competencies that employers compile about applicants and employees.[2] Three key features distinguish big data from more traditional approaches to analytics: volume, velocity, and variety.[3] In terms of volume, the sheer amount of data that businesses can access has accelerated because most information is now in digital format and comes from many different sources. The nearly universal use of the Internet and mobile technology has changed the ways we interact (think social media), shop (think e-commerce), run errands (think mobile banking, Uber Eats, or downloadable print or audio books), and entertain ourselves (think video streaming). EMC Corp., a data-storage vendor, estimates that the amount of worldwide digital information doubles every 2 years. By volume alone we are in the midst of a "big data" digital transformation.[4]

The variety of data includes sources of data both internal and external to HR and an enterprise. Examples include salary studies, industry benchmarks, and data published in print and digital media. Some of it is structured, like the information contained in relational databases in HR (see Chapter 2), accounting, and enterprise resource planning systems. Other information is unstructured, like that found in answers to open-ended questions on employee-engagement surveys, social-media posts, blogs, wikis, e-mails, and videos. *Velocity* refers to the speed of data creation. Real-time, or nearly real-time, information makes it possible for an organization to be more agile than its competitors and to make the data actionable for business value.

Although the promise of big data is real, perils in the form of managerial challenges also abound. Here are four such perils: Senior managers have to embrace big data, there is a pressing need to hire data scientists who can find meaningful patterns in the data, it is easy to mistake correlation for causation, and data alone never substitute for good judgment. Perhaps the biggest challenge is to be able to link the findings from big data to the competitive strategy of a business.[5]

Competitive strategy refers to the decisions, processes, and choices that organizations make to position themselves for sustainable success.[6] Those decisions, processes, and choices define a firm's competitive position in the marketplace. Strategy answers questions such as the following: Why should customers buy from your company, as opposed to one of your competitors? What do you do better than anyone else? What do you offer that is valuable, rare, and difficult to imitate? Competitive strategy is about choices and trade-offs that firms make. It is about being different. It means deliberately choosing a different set of activities in order to deliver a unique mix of value to the customer. Ultimately, the purpose of strategy is to win in the marketplace.

A firm's competitive strategy and its HR strategy are interdependent. **HR strategy** refers to the decisions, processes, and choices organizations make regarding how they manage their people. HR strategies align with competitive strategy by creating the capacity in the workforce and how it is organized that is necessary to achieve the organization's strategic objectives.[7] At a broader level, HR strategy requires a focus on planned major changes in the organization and on critical issues such as the following:

- What are the HR implications of the firm's competitive strategy?
- What external constraints and requirements do we face in order to achieve our strategy?
- What are the implications for management practices, management development, and management succession?
- What can be done in the short term to prepare for longer-term needs?

To the extent that managers can see and take action on the connections between the insights generated by big data and the strategy of a business, there is great opportunity to gain competitive advantage. Here are three HR applications of big data:

- To improve the retention of night clerks in its convenience stores, Wawa experimented with increasing pay or increasing hours worked. Increasing pay had little effect but increasing hours so that the clerks could qualify for benefits cut employee turnover by 24 percent.

- After finding that 30 percent of employees who got second opinions from top-rated medical centers ended up foregoing spinal surgery–which can cost $20,000 or more–Walmart hired Castlight Healthcare to identify and communicate with workers suffering from back pain.
- Casino operator Caesar's wanted to know how much to pay prized employees to keep them from leaving. After analyzing pay and engagement scores for 5,000 workers who left, it found that attrition was 16 percent higher for those who earned below the midpoint of their salary range. Raising salary to the midpoint reduced attrition to 9 percent, but raising it higher than that had no effect and was just as effective as paying 10 percent above the midpoint.[8]

Our next section presents a broad framework designed to enhance talent-related decisions by making HR measures more strategic.

THE LAMP MODEL: FOUNDATION FOR WORKFORCE MEASUREMENT[9]

The letters in **LAMP** stand for *logic, analytics, measures,* and *process,* four critical components of a measurement system that drives strategic change and organizational effectiveness. Measures represent only one component of this system. Although they are essential, without the other three components, the measures and data are destined to remain isolated from the true purpose of HR measurement systems. The model is shown graphically in Figure 3–1, which shows that HR measurement systems are only as valuable as the decisions they improve and the organizational

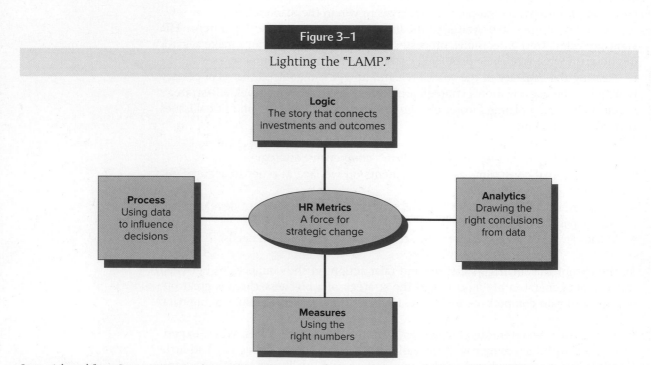

Figure 3–1

Lighting the "LAMP."

Source: Adapted from Cascio, W. F., Boudreau, J. W., and Fink, A., (2019). *Investing in people: Financial impact of human resource initiatives* (3rd ed.), p. 13. Alexandria, VA: SHRM Publishing.

effectiveness to which they contribute. That is, such systems are valuable to the extent that they are a force for strategic change. Let's examine how the four components of the LAMP framework define a more complete measurement system. A brief description of each of these elements follows.

Logic: The "Story" That Connects Investments and Outcomes

Suppose you want to convince senior leaders to invest in a work-life program at your firm. You might begin by sketching a diagram or flowchart that shows how those investments lead to behavioral outcomes like reduced stress and burnout, coupled with improved employee engagement. Those outcomes, in turn, might lead to ones that senior leaders really care about, such as improvements in customer satisfaction and loyalty, internal customer service, and operating and financial performance. Without a compelling *logic*, it's just not clear where to look for insights into what the numbers (HR measurement data) mean. Conversely, with well-grounded logic, it is easier to help leaders outside of HR to understand and use the measurement systems to enhance the talent-related decisions they make.

Can you appreciate the value of this approach, as opposed to a simple linkage between better management practices and profits? Making the linkages explicit allows managers to understand more fully the intermediate connections and how investments in them might enhance profits.

Analytics: Drawing Appropriate Conclusions from Data

Analytics transforms HR logic and measures into rigorous, relevant insights. Statistics and research design are analytical strategies for drawing correct conclusions from data, while *measures* comprise the numbers that populate the statistical formulas. Yet it is easy to be misled. To illustrate, assume that a researcher observes a positive correlation between employee engagement and employee performance. The correlation by itself does not prove that higher employee engagement causes better performance, nor does it prove that improving one will improve the other. It could be that effective or ineffective employee performance actually *causes* effective or ineffective employee engagement. The correlation could also result from a third, unmeasured factor, such as an employee incentive plan. That plan might be related to *both* employee performance and employee engagement. A high correlation between employee engagement and employee performance can be due to any or all of these effects. Sound analytics can reveal which way the causal arrow actually is pointing.

Measures: Getting the Numbers Right

The *measures* part of the LAMP model has received enormous attention in HR. In fact, if you type "HR measurement" into a search engine, you will get more than 300 million results! Scorecards, summits, dashboards, data mines, data warehouses, and audits abound. Indeed, the array of HR measurement technologies is daunting. Consider the measurement of employee turnover. There is much debate about the appropriate formulas to use in estimating turnover and its costs, or the precision and frequency with which employee turnover should be calculated. Today's turnover-reporting systems can calculate turnover rates for virtually any employee group and business unit.

Armed with such systems, managers "slice and dice" the data in a wide variety of ways (ethnicity, skills, performance, and so on), with each manager pursuing his or her own pet theory about employee turnover and why it matters. Are their theories any good? If not, better or more precise measures won't help. That is why the logic component of the LAMP model is so vital to sound measurement; it tells a story about potential causes and consequences, and it identifies measures that are most appropriate.

In fact, the logic guiding the measurement of turnover is straightforward. It begins with the assumption that employee turnover is not equally important everywhere. Where turnover costs are very high, or where turnover represents a significant risk to the revenues or critical resources of the organization (such as when departing employees take clients with them or when they possess unique knowledge that cannot be re-created easily), it makes sense to track turnover very closely and with greater precision. However, this does not mean simply reporting turnover rates more frequently. It means focusing attention on mission-critical jobs or those that are pivotal in importance. **Pivotal jobs** exist where a change in the number or quality of employees in them has a major effect on business outcomes. Lacking a common logic about how turnover affects business or strategic success, well-meaning managers might draw conclusions that are misguided or dangerous. Conversely, they can make strategically sound decisions when guided by a logical framework in which the measures are embedded. When they do that, they get the numbers "right."

Process: Creating Actionable Insights

Process is the final element of the LAMP framework. It is the process of using data to influence key decision makers. It is "storytelling with data." That influence process begins by convincing managers that the analysis of people-related business processes is possible as well as informative. For example, calculating the costs of employee turnover can reveal millions of dollars that can be saved by reducing turnover. For many leaders outside of HR, a turnover-cost analysis may be their first realization that talent has tangible effects on the economic and accounting processes with which they are familiar. Certainly, it is valuable for leaders to see that the same analytical logic used for financial, technological, and marketing investments can apply to human resources. Then, the door is open to more sophisticated analyses beyond the costs.

Education is also a core element of any change process. Application of the LAMP process reveals that it is a powerful tool for educating leaders outside of HR, and for embedding HR measures in their mental frameworks. When that happens, meaningful data provide the basis for people-related business decisions.[10]

In summary, we began this section by asking how we might make HR measures more strategic. As Figure 3-1 shows, the answer is by embedding the measures into a broader framework of logic, analytics, measures, and process that will enable HR metrics to serve as a force for strategic change. In other words, the LAMP framework makes the metrics matter. We will use it to illustrate the costs and benefits of several important areas within HR in the remainder of this chapter. Before we do that, however, we need to say a bit more about people analytics.

People Analytics

People analytics, sometimes known as HR, talent, or workforce analytics, is a set of quantitative approaches that answer two simple questions: (1) What do we need to know about our organization and workforce to run the company more effectively?

(2) How do we turn that knowledge into action?[11] The quantitative approaches use descriptive, visual, and statistical analyses of data related to HR processes and organizational performance, together with external economic benchmarks, to establish business impact and enable data-driven decision making.[12] Unfortunately, many firms do not use analytics. Why not?

Some executives fail to see the competitive advantage they can achieve through their workforce. They see employees as a cost of doing business, a common denominator that all their competitors must deal with. What they fail to realize is that organizations do not manage people identically. Progressive management practices can make a huge difference in the ability to attract and retain talent, and talent is the key to growth in many organizations.

To be most useful, executives must be able to see the implications of workforce analytics for their own actions or decisions.[13] Yet many view access to the needed information as too difficult and time consuming. Perhaps the major reason for this is that talent analytics almost always requires integration of data from financial, operational, sales, and HR information systems. A third reason is that organizations often lack logical models to show how analytics can help them compete. To illustrate, consider the model of employee engagement in Figure 3-2.

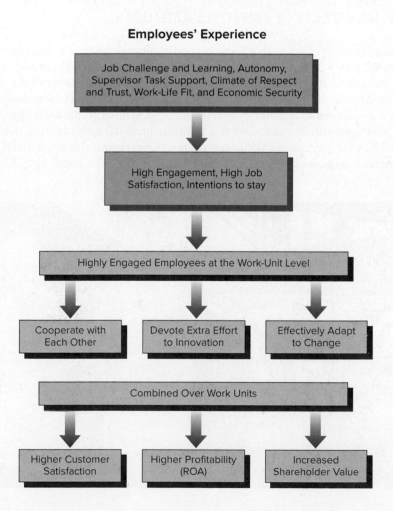

Employees' Experience

Job Challenge and Learning, Autonomy, Supervisor Task Support, Climate of Respect and Trust, Work-Life Fit, and Economic Security

High Engagement, High Job Satisfaction, Intentions to stay

Highly Engaged Employees at the Work-Unit Level

Cooperate with Each Other

Devote Extra Effort to Innovation

Effectively Adapt to Change

Combined Over Work Units

Higher Customer Satisfaction

Higher Profitability (ROA)

Increased Shareholder Value

Figure 3–2

Linking investments in employee engagement to firm-level outcomes.

Source: Cascio, W. F., Boudreau, J. W., & Fink, A. A. (2019). *Investing in People: Financial Impact of Human Resource Initiatives,* 3rd ed. Alexandria, VA: SHRM Publishing.

The objective is to connect investments in programs that contribute to employee engagement with outcomes that senior executives value, such as higher customer satisfaction, higher profitability, and increased shareholder value. The **logic diagram** in Figure 3–2 helps to illustrate those connections. Employers invest in training programs that promote job challenge and learning, autonomy, supervisor task support, a climate of respect and trust, work–life fit, and economic security. *If* employees experience those features of their work environment, *then* they should be highly engaged and satisfied with their jobs and should intend to stay. At the level of the individual work unit, highly engaged employees cooperate with each other, they devote extra effort to innovation, and they adapt effectively to change. If those kinds of behaviors extend over all work units, they result in higher customer satisfaction, higher profitability, and increased shareholder value. Can you see how the logic diagram helps to sew the top and bottom of the figure together? It links investments in programs designed to enhance employee engagement to financial and nonfinancial outcomes that decision makers care about. In the remainder of this chapter, we will use these ideas to present both hypothetical and actual company examples in five important areas: employee attitudes, absenteeism, turnover, work–life programs, and the value of collaboration and sharing of knowledge.

FINANCIAL EFFECTS OF EMPLOYEE ATTITUDES

Attitudes are internal states that focus on particular aspects of or objects in the environment. Examples include attitudes about working conditions, jobs, or pay. Attitudes include three elements: *cognition*, the knowledge an individual has about the focal object of the attitude; the *emotion* an individual feels toward the focal object; and an *action* tendency, a readiness to respond in a predetermined manner to the focal object.[14]

For example, **job satisfaction** is a multidimensional attitude; it is made up of attitudes toward pay, promotions, coworkers, supervision, the work itself, and so on.[15] Another attitude is **organizational commitment**, a bond or linking of an

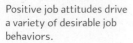

Positive job attitudes drive a variety of desirable job behaviors.
Iakov Filimonov/Shutterstock

individual to the organization that makes it difficult to leave.[16] It is the emotional engagement that people feel toward an organization. Commitment can be to the job or to the firm and can be a commitment to contribute, to stay, or both.

The concept of employee engagement is closely related to commitment. It can be defined as a positive, fulfilling, work-related state of mind that is characterized by vigor, dedication, and absorption.[17] Engagement behaviors operate at the individual, team, and organizational levels.[18] Engagement fuels discretionary efforts and concern for quality. It is what prompts employees to identify with the success of their companies, to recommend them to others as good places to work, and to follow through to make sure problems get identified and solved.

Managers are interested in employees' attitudes principally because of the relationship between attitudes and behavior. They assume that employees who are dissatisfied with their jobs, disengaged at work, and not committed strongly to their organizations will tend to be absent or late for work, to quit more often, and to place less emphasis on customer satisfaction than those whose attitudes are positive. Poor job attitudes therefore lead to lowered productivity and organizational performance. Evidence indicates that this is the case and that management's concern is well placed.[19]

Employee Attitudes, Customer Behavior, and Profits at Sysco Corporation

Sysco Corporation, the largest food marketer and distributor in North America, used behavior-costing methodology to study the relationship among employee attitudes, customer behavior, and profits. Behavior costing assumes that measures of attitudes are indicators of subsequent employee behaviors.[20] Those behaviors can be assessed using cost-accounting procedures, and they have economic implications for organizations. Sysco's approach shows how all of the elements of the LAMP model come together. Sysco began with a logical framework that describes how it creates value from its human capital (see Figure 3-3). The framework is based on an earlier service-profit-chain model.[21]

Logic: Linking Management Practices to Financial Outcomes

As Figure 3-3 shows, effective management practices drive employee satisfaction (and engagement). A satisfied and engaged workforce, in turn, enables a company to pursue excellence in innovation and execution. The logical proposition is that higher

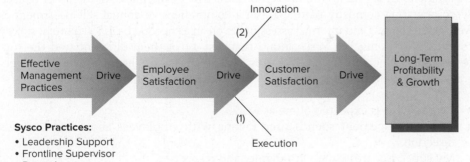

Figure 3–3

Sysco's value-profit chain.

HR in Alignment: The Link to Business Results. (2017, Jan. 30). *YouTube.* Retrieved from *https://www.youtube.com/watch?v=15kS-330k A* on Feb. 1, 2018.

employee satisfaction-engagement drives innovation and execution, which in turn enhances customer satisfaction, customer purchasing behavior, and eventually long-term profitability and growth. Certainly, management needs to put in place the systems, people, technology, and processes that will initiate and sustain innovation and execution–the principal components of an effective value-profit chain. Technology and processes are easily copied by competitors, but a highly skilled, committed, and fully engaged workforce is difficult to imitate.

Analytics: Connecting the Model to Management Behaviors

Sysco's basic management model–the set of practices that describe how the company seeks to engage the hearts and minds of employees with its employer brand–has been termed the 5-STAR management model.[22] Its focus is on taking care of people: extending the same respect to employees as managers do to their external customers.

The framework is general enough to apply to any type of company structure or business model, and it gives businesseswide discretion in actual implementation. As Figure 3-3 shows, the five principles of the STAR model ("Management Practices" in Figure 3-3) are as follows:

- Ensuring that leaders offer direction and support.
- Strengthening frontline supervisors.
- Rewarding performance.
- Addressing employees' quality of life.
- Including employees by engaging them and leveraging diversity.

Employee attitudes are integral components of the STAR model because, as a set, those attitudes reflect employee satisfaction-engagement, a key component of the value-profit chain. At a broader level, Figure 3-3 shows how Sysco creates value from its human capital. It shows clearly the intermediate linkages between employee attitudes and financial performance. Indeed, the logic of the model is so compelling that it is taught to every manager and employee from the first day on the job.

Measures

To measure the attitudes of its employees, Sysco developed a work climate/employee-engagement survey built around each of the 5-STAR principles. All members of each Sysco operating company participate in a comprehensive annual self-assessment as well as impromptu and informal assessments on an as-needed basis.[23] The total survey comprises 61 items, but Sysco found that just 14 of them differentiated the top-performing 25 percent of its operating companies (more than 150, based on geographical location) from the bottom 25 percent. Here are some examples:

- I know what is expected of me at work.
- Upper management spends time talking with employees about our business direction.
- My supervisor treats me with dignity and respect.
- I have received constructive feedback on my performance within the last 6 months.
- I am proud to work for Sysco.

Consider an additional item in the survey: "My supervisor removes obstacles so I can do my job better." A multiyear study of hundreds of knowledge workers in a variety of industries that tracked their day-to-day activities, emotions, and motivations through 120,000 journal entries strongly supported this driver of engagement. The study found that "workers reported feeling most engaged on days when they made headway or received support to overcome obstacles in their jobs."[24] They reported feeling least engaged when they hit brick walls. In short, small wins at work were as meaningful as large achievements.

Analytics Combined with Process: The Sysco Web Portal

Sysco uses organizationwide rewards to encourage the managers of the autonomous operating companies to share information with each other and to transfer best practices within the organization. Sysco built a "best business practices" web portal on its intranet to provide a platform for organizationwide improvement. The web architecture offered a framework for managers to do two things: (1) share information on their own operating company's successful practices and (2) learn from the best practices of other Sysco operating companies. This is important because the company's in-house research showed that operating companies with the most satisfied employees consistently receive the highest scores from their customers and have higher retention of marketing associates and drivers. Table 3-1 shows these results.

The data in Table 3-1 are tantalizing, but it is important to emphasize that causes and effects are not clear. Are customers more loyal because employees are more satisfied and engaged? Or are employees more satisfied and engaged in their work in operating companies with loyal customers who make their work more rewarding? The data in Table 3-1 cannot tell us that. What they do suggest is that continued improvements in logic, analytics, measures, and process are vital, even in advanced systems like Sysco's.

Monetary Payoffs

Table 3-1 does not include cost savings associated with improvements in the retention of marketing associates and drivers, but those cost savings are significant. They reflect the economic impact of positive attitudes about staying at the company. In 2000, retention rates for marketing associates and drivers were 75 percent

Table 3–1

SATISFIED EMPLOYEES DELIVER BETTER RESULT

	High				Low
Associate satisfaction	4.00–5.00	3.90–3.99	3.75–3.89	3.55–3.74	<3.55
Customer loyalty score	4.55	4.40	4.25	4.15	4.05
Retention, marketing associates	88%	85%	81%	75%	76%
Retention, drivers	87%	81%	81%	75%	76%

Source: Carrig, F. K., and Wright, P. M. (2006). *Building Profit through Building People.* Alexandria, VA: Society for Human Resource Management.

and 65 percent, respectively. By 2005, those retention rates had improved to 88 percent and 87 percent, respectively. Sysco then estimated the replacement and training costs of these three groups of employees as $50,000 per marketing associate and $35,000 per driver.

Assuming 100 employees per business unit, from 2000 to 2005, each business unit saved (in terms of costs that were not incurred) $650,000 among marketing associates and $770,000 among drivers, for a total savings of $1.42 million ($1.92 million in 2020 dollars). Corporate wide savings in retention over all categories of employees from 2000 to 2005, assuming 10,000 employees, totaled $156.5 million ($212 million in 2020 dollars).[25] Such savings contributed to the firm's long-term profitability and growth.

Integrating the Value–Profit Chain into Organizational Systems

Today, top executives at Sysco meet on a quarterly basis to review the metrics. What led Sysco executives to pay attention to the human capital indices? HR researchers found a high multiple correlation ($R^2 = 0.46$) among work climate/ employee engagement scores, productivity, retention, and pretax earnings 6 months later. This means that 46 percent of the variation in pretax earnings was associated with variation in the combination of the three employee-related variables.

Sysco leaders began to pay attention when they realized that the human capital indices served as indicators of subsequent financial results that the executives could see in their own operating companies. Although exact cause–effect relationships have not been determined, the business model that the company uses assumes that employee satisfaction-engagement drives customer satisfaction, which drives long-term profitability and growth. In short, Sysco has been able to determine not only what practices and processes are helping to drive the human capital indices but also how those, in fact, influence the financial metrics over time. Such powerful insights have focused and improved the overall management process.

COSTING EMPLOYEE ABSENTEEISM

In any human resource costing application, it is important first to define exactly what is being measured. From a business standpoint, **absenteeism** is any failure of an employee to report for or to remain at work as scheduled, regardless of reason. The phrase "as scheduled" is very significant, for it automatically excludes vacations, holidays, jury duty, and the like. It also eliminates the problem of determining whether an absence is "excusable" or not. Medically verified illness is a good example. From a business perspective, the employee is absent and is simply not available to perform his or her job; that absence will cost money. How much money? According to a Mercer survey of 276 companies, if one excludes planned absences (vacations, holidays), the total direct and indirect costs consume 9 percent of payroll.[26] Direct costs include actual benefits paid to employees (such as sick leave and short- and long-term disability), whereas indirect costs reflect reduced productivity (delays, reduced morale of coworkers, and lower productivity of replacement employees).

Thus, a 1,000-employee company that averages $65,000 in salary and benefits per employee would have an annual payroll of $65 million. Of that, 9 percent is $5.85 million, or about $5,850 per employee when direct and indirect costs are both considered. Figures like that get management's attention.

Why are employees absent? In the United States, the five leading causes are personal illness (34 percent), family-related issues (22 percent), personal needs (18 percent), entitlement mentality (13 percent), and stress (13 percent).[27]

In costing absenteeism, an important qualification is necessary. Specifically, if workers can vary their work time to fit their personal schedules, if they need not "report" to a central location, and if they are accountable only in terms of results, then the concept of "absenteeism" may not have meaning. Teleworkers often fit this description. Building on this idea, we begin by presenting the logic of employee absenteeism, that is, how absenteeism creates costs (Figure 3-4).

In this figure, "pivotal" jobs are those in which a change in the availability or quality of talent has the greatest impact on the success of an organization, such as mechanics at an airline or new-product designers at a company that thrives on innovation. Opportunity costs are "opportunities foregone" that might have been realized if the absent employees were at work. These might include increased productivity or sales. Figure 3-4 may serve as a "mental map" for decision makers, to help them understand the logic of employee absenteeism.

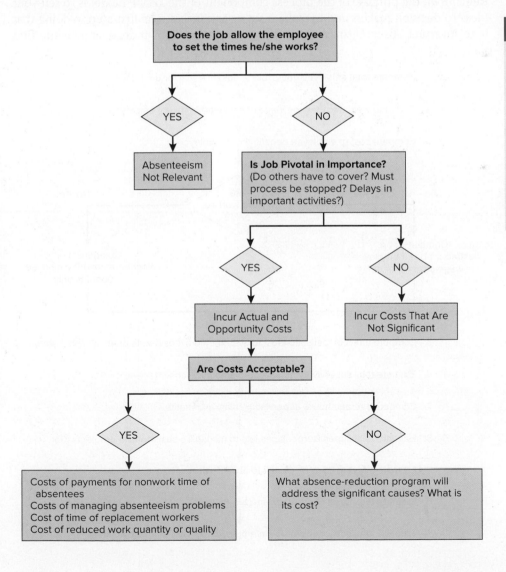

Figure 3–4

The logic of employee absenteeism: How absenteeism creates costs.
Source: Cascio, W., Boudreau, J., and Fink, A. (2019). *Investing in People: Financial Impact of Human Resource Initiatives* (3rd ed.). Alexandria, VA: SHRM Publishing.

Analytics and Measures for Employee Absenteeism

In the context of absenteeism, *analytics* refers to formulas (e.g., those for absence rate, total pay, supervisory time) and to comparisons to industry averages and adjustments for seasonality. Analytics also includes various methodologies (e.g., surveys and interviews with employees and supervisors) used to identify the causes of absenteeism and to estimate variation in absenteeism across different segments of employees. Measures, on the other hand, focus on specific numbers (e.g., finding employee pay-and-benefit numbers or time sampling to determine the lost time associated with managing absenteeism problems). Figure 3-5 is a flowchart that shows how to estimate the total cost of employee absenteeism over any period. Free online software that performs all of the calculations necessary to estimate absenteeism costs is available at *http://iip.shrm.org*.

Process: Interpreting the Costs of Absenteeism

Remember, the purpose of the process component of the LAMP model is to sell your ideas to decision makers and to make insights actionable. The first step in doing that is to interpret absenteeism costs in a meaningful manner. Indeed, among the first

Figure 3–5

Total estimated cost of employee absenteeism.
Source: Cascio, W., Boudreau, J., and Fink, A. (2019). *Investing in People: Financial Impact of Human Resource Initiatives* (3rd ed.). Alexandria, VA: SHRM Publishing.

1. Compute total employee hours lost to absenteeism for the period.

2. Compute weighted average wage or salary/hour/absent employee.

3. Compute cost of employee benefits/hour/employee.

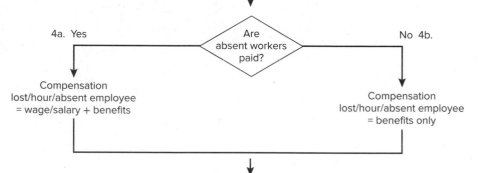

4a. Yes — Are absent workers paid? — No 4b.

Compensation lost/hour/absent employee = wage/salary + benefits

Compensation lost/hour/absent employee = benefits only

5. Compute total compensation lost to absent employees (1 × 4a or 4b, as applicable).

6. Estimate total supervisory hours lost to employee absenteeism.

7. Compare average hourly supervisory salary + benefits.

8. Estimate total supervisory salaries lost to managing absenteeism problems (6 × 7).

9. Estimate all other costs incidental to absenteeism.

10. Estimate total costs of absenteeism (Σ5, 8, 9).

11. Estimate total cost of absenteeism/employee (10 ÷ total no. employees).

questions management will ask upon seeing absenteeism-cost figures are, What do they mean? Are we average, above average, below average? Unfortunately, there are no industry-specific figures on the costs of employee absenteeism. Certainly, these costs will vary depending on the type of firm, the industry, and the level of employee that is absent (unskilled versus skilled or professional workers). As a benchmark, however, consider that the average employee in the United States misses 2.8 percent of scheduled work time, or an average of 5.4 unscheduled absences per year.[28] The percentage of scheduled work time missed is higher in the public sector (3.4 percent) than in the private sector (2.7 percent).[29]

It is also important to note that the dollar figure determined using Figure 3–5 (we will call it the "Time 1" figure) becomes meaningful as a baseline from which to measure the financial gains realized as a result of a strategy to reduce absenteeism. At some later time (we will call this "Time 2"), the total cost of absenteeism should be measured again. The difference between the Time 2 figure and the Time 1 figure, minus the cost of implementing the strategy to reduce absenteeism, represents net gain.

Another question that often arises at this point is, Are these dollars real? Because supervisors are drawing their salaries, anyway, what difference does it make if they have to manage absenteeism problems? To be sure, many calculations in HR measurement other than absenteeism involve an assessment of the value of employees' time (e.g., those involving exit interviews, attendance at training classes, or the time taken to screen job applications). One way to account for that time, in financial terms, is in terms of total pay to the employee. The idea is to use the value of what employees earn (salaries, benefits, and overhead costs) as a proxy for the value of their time.

Total pay, however, is generally not synonymous with the fixed costs, variable costs (e.g., those that vary with employee productivity, such as sales commissions), or opportunity costs of employee time. It is a convenient proxy but must be used with great caution. In most situations, the costs of employee time simply don't change as a result of their allocation of time. They are paid no matter what they do, as long as it is a legitimate part of their jobs.

The more correct concept is the opportunity cost of the lost value that employees would have been creating if they had not been using their time to manage absenteeism problems. That cost is obviously not necessarily equal to the cost of their wages, benefits, and overhead. It is so difficult to estimate the opportunity cost of employees' time, however, that it is very common for accounting processes just to recommend multiplying the time by the value of total pay (including benefits and overhead). The important thing to realize is the limits of such calculations, even if they provide a useful proxy.[30]

COSTING EMPLOYEE TURNOVER

Organizations need a practical procedure for measuring and analyzing the costs of employee turnover, especially because top managers view the costs of hiring, training, and developing employees as investments that must be evaluated just like other corporate resources. The objective in costing human resources is not just to measure the relevant costs but also to develop methods and programs to reduce the costs of human resources by managing the more controllable aspects of those costs.

Earlier we discussed the logic of turnover–namely, that it is not equally important everywhere in an organization and that in talent pools where turnover costs are very high, or where turnover represents a significant risk to the revenues or critical resources of the organization (such as when departing employees take clients with them or when they possess unique knowledge that cannot be re-created easily), it makes sense to track turnover very closely and with greater precision. Even a very rigorous logic with good measures can flounder, however, if the analysis is incorrect.

Turnover occurs when an employee leaves an organization permanently. Not included as turnover within this definition, therefore, are transfers within an organization and temporary layoffs. The rate of turnover in percent over any period can be calculated by the following formula:

$$\frac{\text{Number of turnover incidents per period}}{\text{Average workforce size}} \times 100\%$$

In the United States, for example, annual turnover rates vary considerably across industries (e.g., from 60.5 percent in retail and wholesale to 20.9 percent in high-tech, to 16 percent in banking and financial services, to 11.8% percent in energy) and economic conditions. These percentages include voluntary, involuntary, and retirement separations.[31] Voluntary turnover (an estimated at 47 million workers in 2020)[32] is controllable by the organization, while uncontrollable turnover is "involuntary" (e.g., due to retirement, death, or spouse transfer). Furthermore, turnover may be *functional*, where the employee's departure produces a benefit for the organization, or *regrettable*, where the departing employee is someone the organization would like to retain.

High performers who are difficult to replace represent regrettable turnovers; low performers who are easy to replace represent functional turnovers. The crucial issues in analyzing turnover, therefore, are not how many employees leave, but rather the performance and replaceability of those who leave versus those who stay–and the criticality of their skills.[33]

In costing employee turnover, first determine the total cost of all turnover and then estimate the percentage of that amount that represents controllable, regrettable turnover–resignations that represent a net loss to the firm and that the firm could have prevented. Thus, if total turnover costs $1 million and 50 percent is controllable and regrettable, $500,000 is the Time 1 baseline measure. To determine the net financial gain associated with the strategy adopted prior to Time 2, compare the total gain at Time 2 (say, $700,000) minus the cost of implementing the strategy to reduce turnover (say, $50,000) with the cost of turnover at Time 1 ($500,000). In this example, the net gain to the firm is $150,000. Now let's see how that total cost is derived.

Analytics: The Components of Turnover Costs

There are three broad categories of costs in the basic turnover costing model: separation costs, replacement costs, and training costs. This section presents only the cost elements that make up each of these three broad categories. Those who wish to investigate the subject more deeply may seek information on the more detailed formulas that are available.[34]

Separation Costs
Following are four cost elements in separation costs:

1. *Exit interview,* including the cost of the interviewer's time and the cost of the terminating employee's time.

2. *Administrative functions related to termination*–for example, removal of the employee from the payroll, termination of benefits, and turn-in of company equipment.

3. *Separation pay,* if applicable.

4. *Increased unemployment tax*–a relevant concern for firms doing business in the United States. Such an increase may come from either or both of two sources. First, in states that base unemployment tax rates on each company's turnover rate, high turnover will lead to a higher unemployment tax rate. Suppose a company with a 10 percent annual turnover rate was paying unemployment tax at a rate of 6.2 percent on the first $7,000 of each employee's wages in 2019. But in 2020, because the company's turnover rate jumped to 15 percent, its unemployment tax rate may increase to 6.6 percent. Second, replacements for those who leave will result in extra unemployment tax being paid. Thus, a 500-employee firm with no turnover during the year will pay the tax on the first $7,000 (or whatever the state maximum is) of each employee's wages. The same firm with a 20 percent annual turnover rate will pay the tax on the first $7,000 of the wages of 600 employees.

The sum of these four cost elements represents the total separation costs for the firm.

Replacement Costs

The eight cost elements associated with replacing employees who leave are the following:

1. *Communicating job availability.*

2. *Pre-employment administrative functions*–for example, accepting applications and checking references.

3. *Entrance interview,* or perhaps multiple interviews.

4. *Testing* and/or other types of assessment procedures.

5. *Staff meetings,* if applicable, to determine if replacements are needed, recheck job analyses and job specifications, pool information on candidates, and reach final hiring decisions.

6. *Travel and moving expenses*–for example, travel for all applicants and travel plus moving expenses for all new hires.

7. *Post-employment acquisition and dissemination of information,* for example, all the activities associated with in-processing new employees.

8. *Medical examinations,* if applicable, either performed in-house or contracted out.

The sum of these eight cost elements represents the total cost of replacing those who leave.

Training Costs

This third component of turnover costs includes four elements:

1. *Informational literature*–for example, an employee handbook.

2. *New-employee orientation* (sometimes called on-boarding).

3. *Instruction in a formal training program.*

4. *Instruction by employee assignment*–for example, on-the-job training.

Table 3–2

PRODUCTIVITY LOSS OVER EACH THIRD OF THE LEARNING PERIOD FOR FOUR JOB CLASSIFICATIONS

Classification	Weeks in learning period	Productivity loss during each third of the learning period		
		1	2	3
Management and partners	24	75%	40%	15%
Professionals and technicians	16	70	40	15
Office and clerical workers	10	60	40	15
Broker trainees	104	85	75	50

Note: The learning period for the average broker trainee is 2 years, although the cost to the firm is generally incurred only in the first year. It is not until the end of the second year that the average broker trainee is fully productive.

The sum of these four cost elements represents the total cost of training replacements for those who leave.

Note that a major cost associated with employee turnover, *reduced productivity during the learning period*, is generally not included along with the cost elements *instruction in a formal training program* and *instruction by employee assignment*. The reason for this is that formal work-measurement programs are not often found in employment situations. Thus, it is not possible to calculate accurately the dollar value of the loss in productivity during the learning period. If such a program does exist, then by all means include this cost. For example, a major brokerage firm did a formal work-measurement study of this problem and reported the results shown in Table 3-2. The bottom line is that we want to be conservative in our turnover-cost figures, so that we can defend every number we generate.

The Costs of Lost Productivity and Lost Business

By all means, include the costs of lost productivity and lost business in the fully loaded cost of employee turnover, if your organization can tally those costs accurately. Such costs are not easily estimated in many jobs, and that is why they are not routinely included in the cost of turnover. Seven additional cost elements might be included[35]:

- The cost of additional overtime to cover the vacancy.
- The cost of additional temporary help.
- Wages and benefits saved due to the vacancy (these are subtracted from the overall tally of turnover costs).
- The cost of reduced productivity while the new employee is learning the job.
- The cost of lost productive time due to low morale of remaining employees.
- The cost of lost customers, sales, and profits due to the departure.
- Cost of additional (related) employee departures.

The Total Cost of Turnover

The sum of the three component costs—separation, replacement, and training—represents the total cost of employee turnover for the period in question. Other factors can also be included in the tally, such as the difference in compensation between leavers and their replacements, but that is beyond the scope of this book.[36]

Remember, *the purpose of measuring turnover costs is to improve management decision making.* Once turnover figures are known, particularly among segments of the workforce deemed "pivotal," managers have a sound basis for choosing between accepting current turnover costs and instituting some type of turnover-reduction strategy, including the following: anticipate who might leave, taking into account the criticality of his or her skill set, and take action to prevent the departure[37]; provide realistic job previews and flexible schedules, and hold managers and supervisors accountable for retention[38]; conduct and follow up on employee surveys; and institute merit-based rewards to retain high performers.[39]

A number of companies are actively trying to predict how likely an employee is to leave. Using artificial intelligence and predictive analytics, IBM can predict with 95 percent accuracy which employees will leave, then sends their managers advice on how best to engage, and therefore, to retain them.[40] The following are some of the types of information that Workday software considers, based on its analysis of data from selected customers representing 100,000 individuals over 25 years: time since last promotion; bonus as compared to last year; time since last raise; each employee's performance and potential; performance and potential of that employee's manager; attrition under the employee's manager; time off taken; stock grants over time; team size; and location of the employee, his or her team, and his or her manager.[41]

Think about the fully loaded cost of turnover. It includes not just separation and replacement costs, but also an exiting employee's lost leads and contacts, the new employee's depressed productivity while he or she is learning, and the time coworkers spend guiding him or her. The combined effect of those factors can easily cost 150 percent or more of the departing person's salary.[42] At Ernst & Young (now EY), this is the cost to fill a position vacated by a young auditor.[43] In fact, pharmaceutical giant Merck & Company found that depending on the job, turnover costs were 1.5 to 2.5 times the annual salary paid.[44]

In terms of process, there are opportunities in this area for enterprising managers to make significant bottom-line contributions to their organizations: Work with leaders to help them build a logical framework, to understand the "story" that connects the numbers in the calculation of costs with important effects or outcomes for the organization. Then tie the fully loaded turnover costs among pivotal employees to the ability of the organization to achieve its long-term strategic objectives.[45]

Is Employee Turnover Good or Bad for an Organization?

Many people assume that a low rate of employee turnover is good, and the lower the better. Actually, the answer is a little more complicated than that. It depends on where in an organization the turnover happens (in a pivotal talent pool or not), on whether the employee who leaves is a good or poor performer, and on how easy it is to replace him or her. Even in a firm with a low turnover rate—say, 4 percent per year—it can be extremely costly if those who leave are members of pivotal talent pools in mission-critical jobs, are high performers, and are difficult to replace.

More generally, *reducing* employee turnover tends to have the largest effects on organizational success under three conditions:

- Turnover costs are high and reducing turnover can save those costs.
- Those leaving are much more valuable than their replacements.
- There is great uncertainty about the availability or quality of replacements.

Conversely, *increasing* employee turnover tends to have the largest effects on organizational success under the opposite conditions:

- Turnover costs are low and reducing turnover saves little.
- Those leaving are much less valuable than their replacements.
- There is certainty about the availability or quality of the replacements.

FINANCIAL EFFECTS OF WORK–LIFE PROGRAMS

A **work–life program** is any employer-sponsored benefit or working condition that helps an employee to manage work and nonwork demands.[46] Although originally termed *work-family* programs, this book uses the term *work–life* programs to reflect a broader perspective of this issue. *Work–life* recognizes the fact that employees at every level in an organization, whether parents or nonparents, face personal or family issues that can affect their performance on the job. At a general level, such programs span five broad areas[47]:

1. *Child- and dependent-care benefits* (e.g., onsite or near-site child- or elder-care programs, summer and weekend programs for dependents).
2. *Flexible working conditions* (e.g., flextime, job sharing, teleworking, part-time work, compressed workweeks).
3. *Leave options* (e.g., maternity, paternity, and adoption leaves; sabbaticals; phased reentry; or retirement schemes).
4. *Information services and HR policies* (e.g., cafeteria benefits; life-skill educational programs such as parenting skills, health issues, financial management, retirement, exercise facilities, professional and personal counseling).
5. *Organizational cultural issues* (e.g., an organizational culture that is supportive with respect to the non-work issues of employees, coworkers, and supervisors who are sensitive to family issues).

The Logic of Work–Life Programs

There are consequences, both behavioral and financial, to decisions to offer, or not to offer, one or more work–life programs. If an organization chooses not to offer such programs, there may be negative consequences with respect to job performance. Some of these potential impacts include heightened stress, more burnout, a higher likelihood of mistakes, and more refusals of promotions by employees already feeling the strain of pressures for balance between their work and nonwork lives.

Assuming an organization does offer one or more work–life programs, Figure 3-6 shows that the financial and nonfinancial effects of those programs depend on several factors. These include the range, scope, cost, and quality of the programs; support for the programs from managers and supervisors; and the extent and quality of

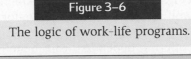

Figure 3–6

The logic of work–life programs.

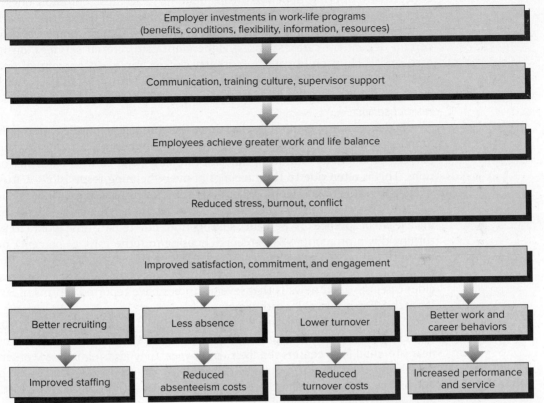

Source: Cascio, W. F., Boudreau, J. W., and Fink, A. (2019). *Investing in People: Financial Impact of Human Resource Initiatives* (3rd ed.). Alexandria, VA: SHRM Publishing.

communications about them to employees. If those conditions are met, it is reasonable to expect reduced stress, burnout, and work–life conflict among employees; increased satisfaction, commitment, and motivation to perform well; and improved financial, operational, and business outcomes.

Analytics and Measures: Connecting Work–Life Programs and Outcomes

Meta-analytic results (a quantitative summary of 59 studies) show that merely offering work–life programs is related to greater perceptions of organizational support, and these perceptions improve job attitudes and performance. The more programs offered, the more positive the effects.[48]

For purposes of illustration, we will consider the financial effects of only two of the many possible work–life interventions: dependent care and flexible work arrangements.

Dependent Care

In the United States, about one in five full-time employees is a caregiver for an older relative, and nearly 75 percent of these employees have children under the age of 18. Being a member of the working "sandwich" generation–those raising children as well as serving as caregivers for older relatives–comes with a steep emotional and financial price tag.[49] Some employers are trying to alleviate these concerns by offering dependent-care benefits. The most common ones include paid or unpaid leave, a **dependent-care assistance plan** (DCAP, a form of flexible spending account that provides a tax-free vehicle for employees to pay for certain dependent-care expenses), dependent-care referral services, onsite child care, and backup child care.[50] Currently, for example, 59 percent of employers offer DCAPs, and 25 percent allow a parent to bring a child to work in an emergency, but just 11 and 10 percent, respectively, offer a child-care or elder-care referral service.[51]

Evidence indicates, though, that there is a compelling business case to be made for offering dependent-care benefits. Caregiving for children or elders can affect employees' productivity, attendance, health-care costs, and turnover at many organizations. This is often due to their feelings of overwhelming responsibility, frustration, stress, and distraction at work. According to studies by MetLife, employed caregivers take a toll on productivity by coming to work late or leaving early (57 percent), taking a leave of absence (17 percent), shifting from full- to part-time work (10 percent), turning down promotions (4 percent), choosing to retire early (3 percent), or giving up work entirely (3 percent). Those who live farther away are likely to rearrange their work schedules (44 percent) and miss workdays (36 percent). With respect to elder care, the good news is that several studies have reported returns of $3 to $14 for each $1 spent on elder-care benefits.[52]

With respect to child-care programs, companies are getting creative. American Express and insurance company USAA not only offer lactation rooms and onsite or near-site child care centers for their employees, they also reimburse workers when they bring their children on business travel.[53] Citigroup owns or participates in 12 child-care centers in the United States. Employees pay about half the cost. In two follow-up studies, Citigroup found the following[54]:

- A 51 percent reduction in turnover among center users compared to noncenter users.
- An 18 percent reduction in absenteeism.
- A 98 percent retention rate of top performers.

Finally, a study of the **return on investment (ROI)** of backup child care at JPMorgan Chase revealed the following. Child-care breakdowns were the cause of 6,900 days of potentially missed work by parents. Because backup child care was available, these lost days were not incurred. When multiplied by the average daily salary of the employee in question (expressed in 2020 dollars), gross savings exceeded $2.84 million. The annual cost of the backup child-care center was $1,263,340, for a net savings exceeding $1.58 million and an ROI (economic gains divided by program costs) of better than 125 percent.[55]

It is important to emphasize that simply offering child care is no guarantee of results like those described. Employers considering offering such a benefit should understand child-care service delivery, the cost of care and its availability, what is available in the local market, and any challenges it presents. In addition, employers need to consider the business case for offering child care.[56] Depending on the nature of the business, the goal may be to improve recruitment and retention, support the advancement of women, reduce absenteeism, retain high performers, or be an

Company-sponsored day care is a valuable benefit for working parents.
Terry Vine/Blend Images LLC

employer of choice. Then they should measure what matters, considering key drivers of the business and the goals established for the program.

Flexible Work Arrangements

Although 69 percent of U.S. employers offer telework on an ad hoc basis and 57 percent offer flextime during core business hours, firms such as Ernst & Young (EY) and Price Waterhouse Coopers (PwC) and have built flexibility into the very culture of their organizations. Fully 90 percent of PwC employees have incorporated some type of flexibility into their work schedules.[57]

To help inform the debate about flexible work arrangements, consider the financial and non-financial effects that have been reported for these key outcomes: *talent management* (specifically, better recruiting and lower turnover) and *human-capital outcomes* (increased satisfaction and commitment, decreased stress), which affect cost and performance, leading to *financial, operational,* and *business outcomes.* Here are some very brief findings in each of these areas from a study of 29 American firms.[58]

Talent Management   IBM's global work–life survey demonstrated that flexibility is an important aspect of employees' decisions to stay with the company. Responses from almost 42,000 IBM employees in 79 countries revealed that work–life fit—of which flexibility is a significant component—is the second leading reason for potentially leaving IBM, behind compensation and benefits. Conversely, employees with higher work–life fit scores (and therefore also higher flexibility scores) reported significantly greater job satisfaction and were much more likely to agree with the statement "I would not leave IBM."

In the Corporate Finance organization, 94 percent of all managers reported positive impacts of flexible work options on the company's "ability to retain talented professionals." In light of these findings showing the strong link between flexibility and retention, IBM actively promotes flexibility as a strategy for retaining key talent.

Human-Capital Outcomes—Employee Commitment   At Deloitte, one employee-survey item asked whether employees agreed with the statement "My manager grants me enough flexibility to meet my personal/family responsibilities." Those who agreed that they have access to flexibility scored 32 percent higher in commitment than those who believed they did not have access to flexibility. Likewise, AstraZeneca found that commitment scores were 28 percent higher for employees who said they had the flexibility they needed, compared to employees who did not have the flexibility they needed.

Financial Performance, Operational and Business Outcomes—Client Service   Concern for quality and continuity of client or customer service is often one of the concerns raised about whether flexibility can work in a customer-focused organization. To be sure that compressed workweeks did not erode traditionally high levels of customer service, the Consumer Healthcare Division of GlaxoSmithKline surveyed customers as part of the evaluation of its flexibility pilot program. Fully 89 percent of customers said they had not seen any disruption in service, 98 percent said their inquiries had been answered in a timely manner, and 87 percent said they would not have any issues with the program becoming a permanent work schedule.

Such studies make it possible to reframe the discussion and to position flexibility not as a "perk," an employee-friendly benefit, or an advocacy cause but as a powerful business tool that can enhance talent management, improve important human capital outcomes, and boost financial and operational performance.[59]

Cautions in Making the Business Case for Work–Life Programs

Although the results of the studies just presented may seem compelling, remember that senior leaders have to buy in to the logic and analyses that underlie the adoption of work–life programs. At a general level, here is a three-pronged strategy to consider in securing that kind of buy-in[60]:

1. Make the business case for work–life initiatives through data, research, and anecdotal evidence.
2. Offer to train managers on how to use flexible management approaches—to understand that for a variety of reasons some people want to work long hours, way beyond the norm, but that's not for everybody. The objective is to train managers to understand that individual solutions will work better in the future than a one-size-fits-all approach.
3. Use surveys and focus groups to demonstrate the importance of work–life fit in retaining talent.

Beyond that, recognize that no one set of facts and figures will make the case for all firms. It depends on the strategic priorities of the organization in question. Figure 3-6 provides a diagnostic logic for conversations about this. One might start by discussing whether the organization's likely payoff will be primarily through talent management, human-capital outcomes (improved employee satisfaction, commitment, and engagement), business operations, or the costs of alternative programs. Start by finding out what your organization and its employees care about right now, what the workforce is going to look like in 3 to 5 years, and therefore what they are going to need to care about in the future.[61]

Second, don't rely on isolated facts to make the business case. Considered by itself, any single study or fact is only one piece of the total picture. Think in terms of a multi-pronged approach:

- External data that describe trends in your organization's own industry.
- Internal data that outline what employees want and how they describe their needs.[62]
- Internal data, perhaps based on pilot studies, that examine the financial and nonfinancial effects of work-life programs. As one executive noted, "Nothing beats a within-firm story."[63]

Finally, recognize that some decision makers may be skeptical even after all the facts and costs have been presented to them. That suggests that more deeply rooted attitudes and beliefs may underlie the skepticism—such as a belief that addressing personal concerns may erode service to clients or customers, that people will take unfair advantage of the benefits, or that work-life issues are just women's issues.[64] To inform that debate, HR leaders need to address attitudes and values, as well as data, on costs and benefits of work-life programs. As one set of authors noted, "Every workplace, small or large, can undertake efforts to treat employees with respect, to give them some autonomy over how they do their jobs, to help supervisors support employees to succeed on their jobs, and to help supervisors and coworkers promote work-life fit."[65]

Ultimately, a system of work-life programs, coupled with an organizational culture that supports that system, will help an organization create and sustain competitive advantage through its people.

FINANCIAL EFFECTS OF COLLABORATION AND SHARING KNOWLEDGE[66]

Global competition and the rapidly changing financial environment are driving the need to innovate constantly and effectively. The ability to develop and share insights around the globe has become an increasingly important element of competitive advantage. At the same time, measuring the return on investment (ROI) from innovation and knowledge sharing is one of the most difficult activities to conduct and, therefore, to justify. Here is how one company did it.

At a major Asian airline, one of the CEO's top-five strategic initiatives was to create a companywide approach to capture and efficiently distribute critical learning, knowledge, and best practices that had been developed over many years. The key driver of that initiative was the changing demographics of the airline's workforce. It expected nearly 60 percent of its employees to retire within the next 5 years. The CEO's concern was that the top-rated customer service of the airline, and therefore its basic competitiveness, would suffer as the rapidly growing, younger workforce would not be able to tap into all of the learning and best practices that the company's older employees had developed over decades. Before funding this initiative, the board of directors demanded that a credible case showing rapid ROI be put in place and confirmed.

Upon direction from the CEO, the HR and finance departments developed a quantifiable business case to support the substantial investment required to implement new technology, methods, and processes to capture and share organizational knowledge. Measurement teams included representatives from HR, finance, and senior operations leaders, including IT technicians.

Logic and Analytics

As part of their on-the-job observations, the measurement teams found that the vast majority of senior flight attendants and pilots (both pivotal pools of talent) had purchased their own mobile devices and were using them to organize themselves for upcoming flights. This led to a field study in which the company gave several teams of flight attendants (the test group) Wi-Fi access to airline-passenger systems on their mobile devices. Instead of doing their flight preparations in offices, they used their mobile devices onboard the plane at the gate (Wi-Fi was already available onboard). Meanwhile, several other teams of flight attendants (the control group) performed traditional office- and paper-based flight preparations.

Those pre-flight preparations included tasks such as determining the number of special-assistance passengers and special meals, the number of infants, premium-customer services, and seat-assignment issues. Pre-flight preparations were the key to smoothly running flights. Traditionally, they required not only office space but also a significant amount of time to review paper-based reports. Two potential payoffs from the technology were (1) to reduce the need for office space and (2) to decrease the time spent on pre-flight paper-based preparations while improving the accuracy of data by sharing best practices.

The total sample included 200 flight attendants and 100 pilots. Both the test and control groups had mobile devices and access to publicly available information, but 100 flight attendants and 50 pilots in the test group also received a new set of collaboration tools. Those tools were designed to help them leverage lessons learned and other organizational information to speed up their preparation for flights. Both the test and control groups also had access to the airline's airport and onboard Wi-Fi, intranet, and external systems for full connectivity.

The measurement teams developed seven baseline measures of productivity for both the test and control groups: (1) time spent in airport-office preparation, (2) number and type of activities performed in airport preparation, (3) time spent in onboard preparation, (4) the number and type of activities performed in onboard preparation, (5) customer-satisfaction ratings of flight attendants, (6) the number of hits on the mobile devices for flight-related information, and (7) the number of on-time departures.

Measures

Over a 3-month period, the teams measured the seven baseline indicators for both the test and control groups. This was time intensive and required significant travel by the members of the measurement teams. They kept the data in spreadsheets, and then consolidated all data into a single repository for analysis by finance specialists. The measurement teams used networked laptops onboard aircraft and in the airport, leveraging the significant investment that the airline had made in Wi-Fi technology.

Test-group crews doubled their productivity, relative to the baseline measures and to the control group. They literally spent half the time in flight preparations that the control group did and rarely used airport offices for flight preparations. Instead, they preferred to use the networked mobile-device technology at hotels and onboard the aircraft. Flight attendants in the test group made extensive use of instant messaging and message boards to reach other attendants for advice and information. They also reported having more time available to focus on passengers and a greater ability to answer questions more accurately with the data at hand. Customer-satisfaction scores in the test group were 27 percent higher than those in the control group. The finance department's analyses identified two main areas of cost savings: the need for fewer flight attendants on some flights and the elimination of very expensive office space around the world.

Process

The measurement teams presented their findings and the projected ROI to the somewhat surprised board of directors. The board authorized investment in the full program of collaboration and social-networking tools, as well as in the learning tools that would be required. The CEO was delighted that this critical but difficult-to-measure HR issue was being resolved.

Over the following 12 months, the airline expanded the program and the measurement approach to all 12,000 customer-facing service professionals. As for the ROI, the program paid for itself in less than 6 months.

Most organizations assume that they cannot quantify the value of collaboration and sharing of knowledge. In this case, HR worked with the finance department to develop the analytics needed to quantify a business case for investment. Overall, the program had a powerful impact on the airline's ability to address a major business challenge: the impending retirements of large numbers of customer-facing employees. Use of a logical, data-based approach, coupled with dramatic results from a pilot test, enabled a skeptical board to endorse a program in which the

IMPACT OF HUMAN RESOURCE MANAGEMENT ACTIVITIES ON PRODUCTIVITY, QUALITY OF WORK LIFE, AND THE BOTTOM LINE

There is a growing consensus among CEOs in many industries that the future success of their firms may depend as much on the skill with which human problems are handled as on the degree to which their firms maintain leadership in technical areas.[a] For example, every year, *Fortune* magazine conducts an annual survey of the "100 Best Companies to Work For." If satisfied, engaged employees really do fuel corporate profits, one would expect "100 Best" employers to outperform broad indexes of firms that are publicly traded—and they do.[b]

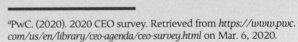

In one well-controlled study, for example, researchers compared the organizational performance of *Fortune*'s "100 Best Companies to Work For" with two sets of other companies, a matched group and the broad market of publicly traded firms, over a 6-year period.[c] They found that organization-level employee attitudes of the 100 Best firms were both highly positive and stable over time. They also found that the return on assets and market-to-book value of the equity of publicly traded companies included on the 100 Best list were generally better than those of a matched comparison group. That finding established an important link between employee attitudes and organization-level financial performance.

As for stock returns, the same study found that the 100 Best companies outperformed the broad market when considering cumulative (longer-term) returns (82 percent versus 37 percent over a 3-year period), although not consistently for annual returns. The authors concluded, "At the very least, our study finds no evidence that positive employee relations come at the expense of financial performance. Firms can have both."[d]

[a]PwC. (2020). 2020 CEO survey. Retrieved from *https://www.pwc.com/us/en/library/ceo-agenda/ceo-survey.html* on Mar. 6, 2020.

[b]See, for example, Edmans, A. (2009, Aug. 12). Does the stock market fully value intangibles? Employee satisfaction and equity prices. Retrieved from *http://ssrn.com/abstract=985735* on May 28, 2010. Cappelli, P. (2008, June 26). The value of being a best employer. Retrieved from *http://www.hreonline.com* on June 26, 2008. Filbeck, G., and Preece, D. (2003). *Fortune*'s Best 100 companies to work for in America: Do they work for shareholders? *Journal of Business Finance & Accounting* 30(5), pp. 771–97.

[c]*Source:* Fulmer, I. S., Gerhart, B., and Scott, K. S. (2003). Are the 100 Best better? An empirical investigation of the relationship between being a "great place to work" and firm performance. *Personnel Psychology*, 56, p. 965–93.

[d]Ibid.

benefits were not immediately obvious. Best of all, the airline was able to preserve the methods and institutional knowledge developed over many years for a new generation of workers.

<table>
<tr><td>

Human Resource Management in Action: Conclusion

</td><td>

NEW DEVELOPMENTS IN PEOPLE ANALYTICS

In the past, the demand for data focused primarily on compliance with the requirements of government agencies, such as the Equal Employment Opportunity Commission. Today the desire of firms for high-quality data is tied every bit as much to the relationship between diversity and inclusion (D&I) and positive business outcomes. HR leaders are increasingly focused on issues like analyzing compensation data to ensure gender equity, eliminating unconscious bias in hiring or promotion decisions, and ensuring that members of underrepresented populations feel included in the organization. When comparing the pay of men and women in similar roles, for example, some pay-equity software tools make it easy to analyze the relative weight of variables like job and organization tenure, geographic location, work experience, training, and skill sets in predicting the pay of similarly situated men and women.

</td></tr>
</table>

More advanced applications include organizational network analysis (ONA) to assess difficult-to-measure inclusion rates of members of underrepresented groups in their companies. Traditionally, such analyses were conducted through paper-and-pencil surveys, perhaps asking participants about their key mentors or advisors or which top experts they might consult. More recently, technologies have emerged to capture and map these relationships from communications platforms within an organization, such as email, instant messaging, and collaborative platforms. ONA analyzes factors like participation in internal collaboration networks, e-mail communication patterns, or data from software-based e-calendars to assess how diverse populations are being included in conversations and decision making or being identified as high-potential employees.

Clearly, next-generation people-analytics software can be extremely valuable in helping HR to gather and analyze key data. Always remember, though, that success in using analytics still rests more with people than with technology. Asking the kinds of strategically relevant questions that senior leaders really care about, with results that can translate directly to actionable recommendations to improve the business, will always be the top priority.

ETHICAL DILEMMA
Survey Feedback: Nice or Necessary?

Is it unethical to ask employees for their opinions, attitudes, values, or beliefs on an attitude survey and then subsequently not give them any feedback about the results? We know that survey results that are not fed back to employees are unlikely to be translated into action strategies and that it is poor management practice to fail to provide feedback.[a] Is it unethical as well? (*Hint:* See the definition of ethical decision making in Chapter 1.)

[a]Macey, W. H., & Fink, A. A. (2020). *Employee Surveys and Sensing: Challenges and Opportunities.* New York, NY: Oxford University Press. Levinson, A. (2014). *Employee Surveys That Work.* Oakland, CA: Berrett-Kohler.

IMPLICATIONS FOR MANAGEMENT PRACTICE

How can such substantial gains in productivity, quality, and profits as we have described in this chapter occur? They happen because high-performance management practices provide a number of sources for enhanced organizational performance:[a]

1. People work harder because of the increased involvement and commitment that come from having more control and say in their work. Managers who adopt democratic leadership styles influence employees' perceptions of personal control over their work.
2. People work smarter because they are encouraged to build skills and competence. Managers have considerable influence over the opportunities for professional growth and development of their employees.
3. Finally, people work more responsibly because more responsibility is placed in the hands of employees further down in the organization. Again, managers who delegate responsibility appropriately can foster such feelings of responsibility on the part of their subordinates. These practices work not because of some mystical process but because they are grounded in sound social science principles that are supported by a great deal of evidence. Managers should use them to create win-win scenarios for themselves and for their people.

[a]Ogbonnaya, C., & Valizade, D. (2018). High performance work practices, employee outcomes and organizational performance. *The International Journal of Human Resource Management.* Retrieved from *https://www.tandfonline.com/doi/full/10.1080/09585192.2016.1146320?src=recsys* on Mar. 7, 2020. Rousseau, D. M. (Ed.). (2012). *The Oxford Handbook of Evidence-Based Management.* Oxford, UK: Oxford University Press. Pfeffer, J., and Veiga, J. F. (1999). Putting people first for organizational success. *Academy of Management Executive,* 13(2), pp. 37-48.

SUMMARY

The overall theme of this chapter is that HR measurement is valuable to the extent that it improves vital decisions about talent and how it is organized. To have strategic impact, HR measures must be embedded within logical frameworks that drive sound decisions about talent. *Talent* refers to the potential and realized capacities of individuals and groups, including those within the organization and those who might join it. *People analytics* uses insights from data to support decisions about people-related business issues.

The chapter began with a discussion of the promise and perils of big data. Three key features distinguish big data from more traditional approaches to analytics: volume, velocity, and variety. As an organizing framework, we presented the LAMP model: logic, analytics, measures, and process. *Logic* is the "story" that connects investments to outcomes. *Analytics* transforms HR logic and measures into rigorous, relevant insights that enable researchers and managers to draw correct conclusions from data. Whereas statistics and research design are analytical strategies for drawing correct conclusions from data, *measures* comprise the numbers that populate the statistical formulas. *Process* is the final element of the LAMP framework. It is story-telling with data in an effort to influence key decision makers. The purpose of the process phase is to create actionable insights that lead to genuine strategic change.

Payoffs from determining the cost of employee behaviors lie in being able to demonstrate a financial gain from the wise application of human resource management methods. The remainder of the chapter used the LAMP framework to present both hypothetical and actual company examples of such measurement in five areas: employee attitudes, absenteeism, turnover, work–life programs, and collaboration and sharing of knowledge.

KEY TERMS

talent	attitudes
big data	job satisfaction
competitive strategy	organizational commitment
HR strategy	absenteeism
LAMP	turnover
pivotal jobs	work–life program
people analytics	dependent-care assistance plan
logic diagram	return on investment (ROI)

DISCUSSION QUESTIONS

3-1. What are the key elements of the LAMP model? What does each contribute?

3-2. Given the positive financial returns from high-performance work practices, why don't more firms implement them?

3-3. Why is management interested in the financial effects of employee attitudes?

3-4. Discuss three controllable and three uncontrollable costs associated with absenteeism.

3-5. Why should efforts to reduce turnover focus only on controllable costs?

3-6. In making the business case for work–life programs, what points would you emphasize?

3-7. What might be some examples of jobs or business models where increasing (or decreasing) turnover makes sound business sense?

3-8. How would you answer the question "Is employee turnover good or bad for an organization?"

3-9. If you wanted to quantify the financial effects of collaboration and sharing knowledge in a hospital, how might you proceed?

3-10. As a recruiter, your boss says to you, "Don't worry about not filling that open position. We're saving money." Under what circumstances might it be *more costly* not to fill an open position?

3-11. Why don't more fathers take paternity leave, even when their employers offer it?

APPLYING YOUR KNOWLEDGE

Case 3–1   **Absenteeism at ONO Inc.**

ONO Inc. is a small auto-supply company with 11 employees. In addition, there are two supervisors and Fred Donofrio, the owner and general manager. Last year, ONO did $7.5 million in business and earned $375,000 in profits ($552,000 before taxes). The auto-supply business is extremely competitive, and owners must constantly be on the lookout for ways to reduce costs to remain profitable.

Employee salaries at ONO average $27.90 an hour, and benefits add another 33 percent to these labor costs. The two supervisors earn an average of $37.40 an hour, with a similar level (percentage) of benefits. Employees receive 2 weeks of vacation each year and 12 days of paid sick leave.

Over the last 2 years, Fred Donofrio has noted an increasing rate of absenteeism among his 11 employees. (There seems to be no similar problem with the two supervisors.) Last week, he asked Cal Jenson, his most senior supervisor, to go through the records from last year and determine how much absenteeism had cost ONO. Further, he asked Cal to make any recommendations to him that seemed appropriate depending on the magnitude of the problem.

Cal determined that ONO had lost a total of 539 employee labor-hours (67.375 days) to absenteeism last year. (This figure did not, of course, include vacation time.) Further, he estimated that he and the other supervisor together had averaged 1.5 hours in lost time whenever an employee was absent for a day. This time had been spent dealing with the extra problems (rescheduling work, filling in for missing workers, etc.) that an absence created. On several occasions last year, ONO had been so short of help that temporary workers had to be hired or present employees had to work overtime. Cal determined that the additional costs of overtime and outside help last year totaled $15,260. Cal is now in the process of preparing his report to Fred Donofrio.

Questions

1. What figure will Cal Jenson report to Fred Donofrio for the amount that absenteeism cost ONO last year?
2. Is absenteeism a serious problem at ONO? Why or why not?
3. What recommendations for action could Cal Jenson make to Fred Donofrio?

REFERENCES

1. Cascio, W. F., Boudreau, J. W., & Fink, A. (2019). *Investing in People: Financial Impact of Human Resource Initiatives* (3rd ed.). Alexandria, VA: SHRM Publishing.
2. King, A. G., and Mrkonich, M. (2016, Oct. 7). The legal risks of "big data": What HR should know. Retrieved from *https://www.shrm.org/resourcesandtools/legal-and-compliance/employment-law/pages/legal-risks-of-big-data.aspx* on Oct. 8, 2016.
3. McAfee, A., and Brynjolfsson, E. (2012, Oct.). Big data: The management revolution. *Harvard Business Review*, pp. 60–67.
4. Maurer, R. (2020, Jan. 15). Organizations will need data analytics to survive. *SHRM Online*. Retrieved from *https://www.shrm.org/resourcesandtools/hr-topics/technology/pages/organizations-will-need-data-analytics-to-survive.aspx* on Jan. 16, 2020. *See also* Roberts, B. (2013, Oct.). The benefits of big data. *HRMagazine*, pp. 21–30.
5. Cascio et al. (2019), op. cit. *See also* Fleming, O., Fountaine, T., Henke, N., & Saleh, T. (2018, May). Ten red flags signaling your analytics program will fail. *McKinsey Analytics*. Retrieved from *https://www.mckinsey.com/business-functions/mckinsey-analytics/our-insights/ten-red-flags-signaling-your-analytics-program-will-fail* on June 1, 2018.
6. Lawler, E. E. III, and Worley, C. G., with Creelman, D. (2011). *Management Reset: Organizing for Sustainable Effectiveness*. San Francisco: Jossey-Bass.
7. Cascio, W. F., and Boudreau, J. W. (2012). *Short Introduction to Strategic Human Resource Management*. Cambridge, UK: Cambridge University Press.

8. Silverman, R. E. (2016, Feb. 16). Bosses tap outside firms to predict which workers might get sick. *The Wall Street Journal.* Retrieved from *www.wsj.com/articles/bosses-harness-big-data-to-predict-which-workers-might-get-sick-1455664940* on Feb. 17, 2016. *See also* Walker, J. (2012, Sept. 20). Meet the new boss: Big data. Companies trade in hunch-based hiring for computer modeling. *The Wall Street Journal,* pp. B1, B2.

9. Material in this section is drawn from Cascio, W. F., Boudreau, J. W., & Fink, A. (2019). *Investing in people: Financial impact of human resource initiatives* (3rd ed.). Alexandria, VA: SHRM Publishing.

10. Wattendorf, K. (2018, Aug. 1). How to use analytics to make smarter decisions. *SHRM Online.* Retrieved from *https://www.shrm.org/hr-today/news/hr-magazine/book-blog/pages/how-to-use-analytics-to-make-smarter-decisions.aspx* on Aug. 2, 2018. *See also* Boudreau, J. W., and Cascio, W. F. (2017). Human capital analytics: Why are we not there? *Journal of Organizational Effectiveness: People and Performance* 4(2), pp. 119–26.

11. Hoffmann, C., Lesser, E., and Ringo, T. (2012). *Calculating Success: How the New Workplace Analytics Will Revitalize Your Organization.* Boston: Harvard Business Review Press.

12. Marler, J. H., and Boudreau, J. W. (2017) An evidence-based review of HR analytics. *The International Journal of Human Resource Management* 28(1), pp. 3–26.

13. Boudreau and Cascio (2017), op. cit.

14. Schleicher, D. J., Hansen, D., and Fox, K. J. (2011). Job attitudes and work values. In S. Zedeck (Ed.), *APA Handbook of Industrial and Organizational Psychology* (Vol. 3). Washington, DC: American Psychological Association, pp. 137–89. *See also* Breckler, S. J. (1984). Empirical validation of affect, behavior, and cognition as distinct components of attitude. *Journal of Personality and Social Psychology* 47, pp. 1191–205.

15. Judge, T. A., Weiss, H. M., Kammeyer-Mueller, J. D., and Hulin, C. L. (2017). Job attitudes, job satisfaction, and job affect: A century of continuity and change. *Journal of Applied Psychology* **102**(3), pp. 356–74. *See also* Schleicher et al. (2011), op. cit.

16. Klein, H. J., Molloy, J. C., and Cooper, J. T. (2009). Conceptual foundations: Construct definitions and theoretical representations of workplace commitments. In H. J. Klein, T. E. Becker, and J. P. Meyer (Eds.), *Commitment in Organizations.* New York: Taylor & Francis. *See also* Mathieu, J. E., and Zajac, D. M. (1990). A review and meta-analysis of the antecedents, correlates, and consequences of organizational commitment. *Psychological Bulletin* 108(2), pp. 171–94.

17. Schaufeli, W. B., Bakker, A. B., and Salanova, M. (2006). The measurement of work engagement with a short questionnaire: A cross-national study. *Educational and Psychological Measurement* 66, pp. 701–16.

18. Kelleher, R. (2014). *Employee Engagement for Dummies.* Hoboken, NJ: Wiley. *See also* Macey, W. H., and Schneider, B. (2008). The meaning of employee engagement. *Industrial and Organizational Psychology: Perspectives on Science and Practice* 1, pp. 3–30.

19. Judge et al. (2017), op. cit. *See also* Macey and Schneider (2008), op. cit. *See also* Ryan, A. M., Schmit, M. J., and Johnson, R. (1996). Attitudes and effectiveness: Examining relations at an organizational level. *Personnel Psychology* 49, pp. 853–83. *See also* Cohen, A. (1993). Organizational commitment and turnover: A meta-analysis. *Academy of Management Journal* 36, pp. 1140–57. *See also* Ostroff, C. (1992). The relationship between satisfaction, attitudes, and performance: An organizational-level analysis. *Journal of Applied Psychology* 77, pp. 963–74.

20. Mirvis, P. H., and Lawler, E. E. III. (1977). Measuring the financial impact of employee attitudes. *Journal of Applied Psychology* 62, pp. 1–8.

21. Heskett, J. L., Jones, T. O., Loveman, G. W., Sasser, W. E., Jr., and Schlesinger, L. A. (1994, Mar./Apr.). Putting the service-profit chain to work. *Harvard Business Review* 72, pp. 164–74.

22. Carrig, K., and Wright, P. M. (2006). *Building Profit through Building People: Making Your Workforce the Strongest Link in the Value-Profit Chain.* Alexandria, VA: Society for Human Resource Management.

23. Ibid.

24. Fox, A. (2010, May). Raising engagement. *HRMagazine,* pp. 35–40.

25. Carrig and Wright (2006), op. cit.

26. Society for Human Resource Management. (2014, Mar. 3). Managing employee attendance. Retrieved from *http://www.shrm.org/templatestools/toolkits/pages/managingemployeeattendance.aspx* on Mar. 19, 2014.

27. Society for Human Resource Management (2014), op. cit.

28. U.S. Department of Labor, Bureau of Labor Statistics. (2018). Absences from work of employed full-time wage and salary workers by occupation and industry. Retrieved from *www.bls.gov/cps/cpsaat47.htm* on Oct. 22, 2018.

29. Ibid.

30. Cascio et al. (2019), op. cit.

31. Agovino, T. (2019, Feb. 23). To have and to hold. *SHRM Online.* Retrieved from *https://www.shrm.org/hr-today/news/all-things-work/pages/to-have-and-to-hold.aspx* on Feb. 24, 2019.

32. Ibid.

33. Cascio et al. (2019), op. cit.

34. Cascio et al. (2019), op. cit.

35. Dooney, J. (2005, Nov.). Cost of turnover. Retrieved from *www.shrm.org* on Feb. 6, 2006.

36. For more on this subject, see Cascio et al. (2019), op. cit.

37. Cossack, S., Guthridge, M., and Lawson, E. (2010, Aug.). Retaining key employees in times of change. *McKinsey Quarterly.* Retrieved from *http://www.mckinseyquarterly.com/Retaining_key_employees_in_times_of_change_2654* on Dec. 30, 2010.

38. Agovino (2019), op. cit. *See also* Allen, D. G. (2008). *Retaining Talent.* Alexandria, VA: SHRM Foundation.

39. For more on this, see Klotz, A. C., & Bolino, M. C. (2019, July 31). Do you really know why employees leave your company? *Harvard Business Review.* Retrieved from *https://hbr.org/2019/07/do-you-really-know-why-employees-leave-your-company* on Aug. 7, 2019. *See also* Hom, P., Lee, T. W., Shaw, J. D., & Hausknecht, J. P. (2017). One hundred years of employee turnover theory and research. *Journal of Applied Psychology* 102, pp. 530–45. *See also* Griffeth, R. W., Hom, P. W., and Gaertner, S. (2000). A meta-analysis of antecedents and correlates of employee turnover: Update, moderator tests, and research implications for the next millennium. *Journal of Management* 26, pp. 463–88.

40. AI predicts which staff will quit. (2019, July). *HRM Magazine* (Australia) 56, p. 9.

41. Greenwald, T. (2017, Mar. 18). How AI is transforming the workplace. *The Wall Street Journal,* pp. R1, R2.

42. Frye, L. (2017, May 9). The cost of a bad hire can be astronomical. *SHRM Online.* Retrieved from *https://www.shrm.org/resourcesandtools/hr-topics/employee-relations/pages/cost-of-bad-hires.aspx* on May 10, 2017. *See also* Abbott, J., De Cieri, H., and Iverson, R. D. (1998). Costing turnover: Implications of work/family conflict at management level. *Asia Pacific Journal of Human Resources* 36(1), pp. 25–43.

43. Hewlett, S. A., and Luce, C. B. (2005, Mar.). Off-ramps and on-ramps: Keeping talented women on the road to success. *Harvard Business Review,* pp. 43–54.

44. Solomon, J. (1998, Dec. 29). Companies try measuring cost savings from new types of corporate benefits. *The Wall Street Journal,* p. B1.

45. Boudreau, J. W. (2017, Dec. 5). HR analysts: Unleash your inner storyteller. *Clarity.* Retrieved from *https://www.visier.com/clarity/hr-analysts-storyteller/*on Dec. 7, 2017.

46. Arthur, M. (2003). Share price reactions to work–family initiatives: An institutional perspective. *Academy of Management Journal* 46, pp. 497-505. *See also* Edwards, J. R., and Rothbard, N. P. (2000). Mechanisms linking work and family: Clarifying the relationship between work and family constructs. *Academy of Management Review* 25, pp. 178-99.

47. Bardoel, E. A., Tharenou, P., and Moss, S. A. (1998). Organizational predictors of work–family practices. *Asia Pacific Journal of Human Resources*, pp. 1-49.

48. Casper, W. J., and Butts, M. M. (2010, Sept.). Work-family support programs as a strategic human resource initiative: A meta-analysis of effects on organizational outcomes. Final research report submitted to the SHRM Foundation, Alexandria, VA.

49. AARP. (2019, Oct. 1). Surprising out-of-pocket costs for caregivers. Retrieved from https://www.aarp.org/caregiving/financial-legal/info-2019/out-of-pocket-costs.html on March 6, 2021. See also Bliss, W. (2013, May 5). Managing work/life fit: Elder care. Retrieved from *http://www.shrm.org/templatestools/toolkits/pages/managingworklifefitelder-care.aspx* on March 20, 2014.

50. Daniel, T. A. (2013, May 5). Managing work/life fit: Dependent care. *http://www.shrm.org/templatestools/toolkits/pages/managingworklifefitdependentcare.aspx* on Mar. 20, 2014.

51. Society for Human Resource Management. (2019). SHRM employee benefits 2019. Retrieved from *https://www.shrm.org/hr-today/trends-and-forecasting/research-and-surveys/pages/benefits19.aspx* on Mar. 6, 2020.

52. Bliss (2013), op. cit.

53. Wilkie, D. (2018, May 9). Paying to fly nannies on work trips? Companies get creative with child-care benefits. *SHRM Online*. Retrieved from https://www.shrm.org/resource-sandtools/hr-topics/employee-relations/pages/child-care-benefits-.aspx on March 6, 2020.

54. Gurchiek, K. (2007, Mar. 5). Child-care "investment" creates competitive advantage. *HR News*. Retrieved from *www.shrm.org* on May 25, 2010.

55. O'Connell, B. No baby sitter? Emergency child-care to the rescue, compensation & benefits forum. Retrieved from *www.shrm.org* on May 25, 2010.

56. Rose, M. K. (2018, Nov. 9). How offering child care benefits can boost a company's bottom line. *The Dallas Morning News*. Retrieved from *https://fwddfw.com/why-offering-child-care-benefits-is-good-for-business/* on March 6, 2020. *See also* Gurchiek (2007), op. cit.

57. PwC. Flexibility². Retrieved from About Us, PwC United States, *https://www.pwc.com/us/en/about-us/diversity/pwc-work-life-balance.html* on Mar. 6, 2019. *See also* SHRM Foundation. (2017, Feb. 7). *Ernst & Young: Creating a culture of flexibility.* Available at *https://www.youtube.com/watch?v=z9ixbBJ0YMA.*

58. Corporate Voices for Working Families. (2011, Feb.). Business impacts of flexibility: An imperative for expansion. Retrieved from *http://www.cvwf.org/publication-toolkits/business-impacts-flexibility-imperative-expansion-november-2005* on Sept. 28, 2011.

59. Ibid.

60. Families & Work Institute. (2012). *Workflex: The Essential Guide to Effective and Flexible Workplaces.* Alexandria, VA: Society for Human Resource Management.

61. Pires, P. S. (2005). Sitting at the corporate table: How work–family policies are really made. In D. F. Halpern and S. E. Murphy (Eds.), *From Work-Family Balance to Work-Family Interaction: Changing the Metaphor.* Mahwah, NJ: Erlbaum, pp. 71-81.

62. Families & Work Institute. (2013). *2013 Guide to bold new ideas for making work work.* Alexandria, VA: Society for Human Resource Management.

63. Ibid. *See also* Roberts, B. (2009 Oct.). Analyze this! *HRMagazine*, pp. 35-41.

64. Fisman, R., and Luca, M. (2017, Mar. 3). Why we don't value flextime enough. *The Wall Street Journal.* Retrieved from *www.wsj.com/articles/why-we-dont-value-flextime-enough-1488547616* on Mar. 7, 2017. *See also* Weber, L. (2013, June 13). Why dads don't take paternity leave. *The Wall Street Journal*, pp. B1, B7.

65. Aumann, K., and Galinsky, E. (2009). *The 2008 National Study of the Changing Workforce: The State of Health of the American Workforce: Does Having an Effective Workplace Matter?* New York: Families and Work Institute.

66. The example in this section is based on material presented in chapter 5 of Hoffmann, C., Lesser, E., and Ringo, T. (2012). *Calculating Success: How the New Workplace Analytics Will Revitalize Your Organization.* Boston: Harvard Business Review Press.

4 THE LEGAL CONTEXT OF EMPLOYMENT DECISIONS

Questions This Chapter Will Help Managers Answer

LO 4-1 How are employment practices affected by the civil rights laws and Supreme Court interpretations of those laws?

LO 4-2 What should be the components of an effective policy to prevent sexual harassment?

LO 4-3 What obligations does the Family and Medical Leave Act impose on employers? What rights does it grant to employees?

LO 4-4 When a company is in the process of downsizing, what strategies can it use to avoid complaints of age discrimination?

LO 4-5 What should senior management do to ensure that job applicants or employees with disabilities receive "reasonable accommodation"?

RETALIATION: GUIDANCE FOR EMPLOYERS AND SOME PREVENTIVE MEASURES*

The Equal Employment Opportunity Commission (EEOC) is the agency charged with enforcing federal laws against employment discrimination. It also issues enforcement guidance on a variety of topics, including retaliation. Retaliation claims now comprise more than half of all charges filed with the EEOC. Here, in brief question-and-answer format, are answers to some of the key topics in that guidance.

1. *What is retaliation?* Federal equal employment opportunity (EEO) laws prohibit employers, employment agencies, or unions from punishing applicants or employees for asserting their rights to be free from employment discrimination, including harassment. Asserting EEO rights is called "protected activity."

2. *What actions by applicants and employees are protected from retaliation?* Protected actions can take many forms, ranging from participating in an EEO complaint process to reasonably opposing discrimination. For example, it is unlawful to retaliate against applicants or employees for taking part in an internal or external investigation of employment discrimination, including harassment; filing or being a witness in a complaint or lawsuit alleging discrimination; communicating with a supervisor or manager about employment discrimination, including harassment; refusing to follow orders that would result in discrimination; resisting sexual advances, or intervening to protect others; requesting accommodation of a disability or for a religious practice; or asking managers or coworkers about salary information to uncover potentially discriminatory wages. The protections against retaliation apply not only to current employees (full-time, part-time, probationary, seasonal, and temporary) but also to applicants and to former employees.

3. *Does this mean that an employer can't ever punish someone who has engaged in EEO activity?* No, engaging in EEO activity does not shield an employee from discipline or discharge. Employers are free to discipline or to terminate workers if motivated by nonretaliatory and nondiscriminatory reasons that would otherwise result in such consequences–for example, due to poor job performance or low productivity.

4. *What if an employer never takes an official employment action against an employee? Could there still be retaliation?* Yes, an employer is not allowed to do anything in response to EEO activity that would discourage someone from resisting or complaining about future discrimination. For example, depending on the facts of a particular case, it could be retaliation if an employer reprimanded an employee or assigned a performance evaluation that was lower than it should have been; transferred the employee to a less desirable position; engaged in verbal or physical abuse; threatened to make, or actually made, reports to authorities (such as reporting immigration status or contacting the police); spread

Sources: U.S. Equal Employment Opportunity Commission. Charge statistics, FY1997 through FY 2019. Retrieved from *https://www.eeoc.gov/eeoc/statistics/enforcement/charges.cfm* on Mar. 10, 2020. Nagele-Piazza, L. (2018, March 26). How to prevent workplace retaliation claims. *SHRM Online.* Retrieved from *https://www.shrm.org/resourcesandtools/legal-and-compliance/employment-law/pages/how-to-prevent-a-workplace-retaliation-claim.aspx* on Mar. 27, 2018. U.S. Equal Employment Opportunity Commission. (n.d.). Small business fact sheet: Retaliation and related issues. Retrieved from *http://www.eeoc.gov/laws/guidance/retaliation-factsheet.cfm* on Mar. 22, 2017. U.S. Equal Employment Opportunity Commission. (2016, Aug. 29). EEOC enforcement guidance on retaliation and related issues. Retrieved from *http://www.eeoc.gov/laws/guidance/retaliation-guidance.cfm* on Mar. 22, 2017.

false rumors; or took action that made the person's work more difficult (e.g., punishing an employee for filing an EEO complaint by purposefully changing his work schedule to conflict with family responsibilities).

5. *Does the law address interference with the rights of people with disabilities?* The Americans with Disabilities Act (ADA) prohibits disability discrimination, limits an employer's ability to ask for medical information, requires confidentiality of medical information, and gives employees who have disabilities the right to reasonable accommodations at work. An employer cannot retaliate against an employee for raising ADA rights and cannot interfere with ADA rights by doing anything that makes it more difficult for an applicant or employee to assert any of these rights. For example, it is unlawful for an employer to use threats to discourage someone from asking for, or keeping, a reasonable accommodation, intimidating an employee into undergoing an unlawful medical examination, or pressuring an employee not to file a disability-discrimination complaint.

Challenges

1. If you were developing a training program about retaliation, what key elements would you include?
2. What can an employer do to avoid liability for retaliation?
3. Based on EEOC's guidance, what changes in company policies might be necessary?

SOCIETAL OBJECTIVES

As a society, we espouse equality of opportunity, rather than equality of outcomes. That is, the broad goal is to provide for all Americans–regardless of race, age, gender, religion, national origin, or disability–an equal opportunity to compete for jobs for which they are qualified. The objective, therefore, is EEO (equal employment opportunity), not EE (equal employment, or equal numbers of employees from various subgroups).[1] For Americans with disabilities, the nation's goals are to ensure equality of opportunity, full participation, independent living, and economic self-sufficiency.

Whenever the members of heterogeneous groups work together, the possibility of unfair discrimination exists. Civil rights laws have been passed at the federal and state levels to provide remedies for job applicants or employees who feel they have been victims of unfair discrimination. Understanding these laws, as well as the rights as well as the obligations of employers, job candidates, and employees, is critical for all managers, not just for HR professionals. As we will see, ignorance in this area can be very expensive. Let's begin by considering the meaning of EEO and the forms of unfair discrimination.

EEO AND UNFAIR DISCRIMINATION: WHAT ARE THEY?

Civil rights laws, judicial interpretations of the laws, and the many sets of guidelines issued by state and federal regulatory agencies have outlawed discrimination based on race, religion, national origin, age, sex, and physical disability. In short, they have attempted to frame national policy on **equal employment opportunity (EEO)**.

Although no law has ever attempted to define precisely the term **discrimination**, in the employment context it can be viewed broadly as the giving of an unfair advantage (or disadvantage) to the members of a particular group in comparison with the members of other groups.[2] The disadvantage usually results in a denial or restriction of employment opportunities or in an inequality in the terms or benefits of employment. In short, EEO implies at least two things:

1. *Evaluation of candidates for jobs in terms of characteristics that really do make a difference between success and failure* (e.g., in selection, promotion, performance appraisal, or layoffs).
2. *Fair and equal treatment of employees on the job* (e.g., equal pay for equal work, equal benefits, freedom from sexual harassment).

Despite federal and state laws on these issues, they represent the basis of an enormous volume of court cases, indicating that stereotypes and prejudices do not die quickly or easily. Discrimination is a subtle and complex phenomenon that may assume two broad forms:

1. **Unequal (disparate) treatment** is based on an intention to discriminate, including the intention to retaliate against a person who opposes discrimination, has brought charges, or has participated in an investigation or a hearing. There are three major sub-theories of discrimination within the disparate-treatment theory:
   a. Cases that rely on **direct evidence** of the intention to discriminate. Such cases are proved with direct evidence of other bias based on an open expression of hatred, disrespect, or inequality, knowingly directed against members of a particular group; or blanket exclusionary policies, such as exclusion of an individual whose disability (e.g., an inability to walk) has nothing to do with the requirements of the job she is applying for (financial analyst). Using different standards for different groups is evidence of intentional discrimination.
   b. Cases that are proved through **circumstantial evidence** of the intention to discriminate (see the *McDonnell Douglas v. Green* test), including those that rely on statistical evidence as a method of circumstantially proving the intention to discriminate against classes of individuals.
   c. **Mixed-motive cases** (a hybrid theory) that often rely on both direct evidence of the intention to discriminate on some impermissible basis (e.g., gender, race, disability) and proof that the employer's stated legitimate basis for its employment decision is actually just a pretext for illegal discrimination.
2. **Adverse-impact (unintentional) discrimination** occurs when identical standards or procedures are applied to everyone, despite the fact that they lead to different employment outcomes (e.g., selection, promotion, layoffs) for the members of a particular group, and they are unrelated to success on a job. For example, suppose that a minimum height requirement of 5 feet 8 inches for police cadets has an adverse impact on Asians, Hispanics, and women. The policy is neutral on its face but has an adverse impact. To use it, an employer must show that the height requirement is necessary to perform the job.

These two forms of illegal discrimination are illustrated graphically in Figure 4–1.

Figure 4–1

Major forms of illegal discrimination.

THE LEGAL CONTEXT OF HUMAN RESOURCE DECISIONS

Now that we understand the forms that illegal discrimination can take, let's consider the major federal laws governing employment. Then we will consider the agencies that enforce the laws, as well as some important court cases that have interpreted them. Space constraints do not permit a full treatment of all employment laws, particularly those that require nondiscrimination as a condition for receiving federal funds. In the following sections, therefore, we will discuss laws of broad scope that prohibit unfair discrimination.

The particular laws that we will discuss are the following:

Thirteenth and Fourteenth Amendments to the U.S. Constitution

Civil Rights Acts of 1866 and 1871

Equal Pay Act of 1963

Title VII of the Civil Rights Act of 1964

Civil Rights Act of 1991

Age Discrimination in Employment Act of 1967, as amended in 1986

Immigration Reform and Control Act of 1986

Americans with Disabilities Act of 1990, as amended in 2008

Family and Medical Leave Act of 1993

Uniformed Services Employment and Reemployment Rights Act of 1994

The Thirteenth and Fourteenth Amendments

The Thirteenth Amendment prohibits slavery and involuntary servitude. Any form of discrimination may be considered an incident of slavery or involuntary servitude and thus liable to legal action under this amendment.[3] The Fourteenth Amendment guarantees equal protection of the law for all citizens. Both the Thirteenth and Fourteenth Amendments granted to Congress the constitutional power to enact legislation to enforce their provisions. It is from this source of constitutional power that all subsequent civil rights legislation originates.

The Civil Rights Acts of 1866 and 1871

These laws were enacted on the basis of the provisions of the Thirteenth and Fourteenth Amendments. The Civil Rights Act of 1866 grants all citizens the right to make and enforce contracts for employment, and the Civil Rights Act of 1871 grants all citizens the right to sue in federal court if they feel they have been deprived of any rights or privileges guaranteed by the Constitution and other laws. It applies only to "persons within the jurisdiction of the United States" and does not extend to discriminatory conduct occurring overseas.[4]

Until recent times, both of these civil rights acts were viewed narrowly as tools for solving Reconstruction-era racial problems. This is no longer so. In *Johnson v. Railway Express Agency Inc.*, the Supreme Court held that although the Civil Rights Act of 1866 on its face relates primarily to racial discrimination in the making and enforcement of contracts, it also provides a federal remedy against racial discrimination in private employment.[5] It is a powerful remedy. The Civil Rights Act of 1991 amended the Civil Rights Act of 1866, so that workers are protected from intentional discrimination in all aspects of employment, not just hiring and promotion. The Civil Rights Act of 1866 allows for jury trials and for compensatory and punitive damages[6] for victims of intentional racial and ethnic discrimination. It covers both large and small employers, even those with fewer than 15 employees, and the Supreme Court has ruled that employees also may sue for retaliation under this law.[7]

The 1866 law also has been used recently to broaden the definition of racial discrimination originally applied to African Americans. In a unanimous decision, the Supreme Court ruled that race was equated with ethnicity during the legislative debate after the Civil War, and therefore Arabs, Jews, and other ethnic groups thought of as "white" are not barred from suing under the 1866 act. The Court held that Congress intended to protect identifiable classes of persons who are subjected to intentional discrimination solely because of their ancestry or ethnic characteristics. Under the law, therefore, race involves more than just skin pigment.[8]

The Equal Pay Act of 1963

This act was passed as an amendment to an earlier compensation-related law, the Fair Labor Standards Act of 1938. For those employees covered by the Fair Labor Standards Act, the Equal Pay Act requires that men and women working for the same establishment be paid the same rate of pay for work that is substantially equal in skill, effort, responsibility, and working conditions. Pay differentials are legal and appropriate if they are based on seniority, merit, systems that measure the quality or quantity of work, or any factor other than sex (e.g., shift differentials, completion of a job-related training program). Moreover, in correcting any inequity under the Equal Pay Act, employers must raise the rate of lower-paid employees, not lower the rate of higher-paid employees.[9]

Thousands of equal-pay suits have been filed (predominantly by women) since the law was passed. The EEOC receives about 1,000 equal-pay complaints per year.[10] For individual companies, the price can be quite high. For example, in 2011 Novartis Pharmaceutical Corporation settled a sex-discrimination lawsuit for $152.5 million.[11]

Title VII of the Civil Rights Act of 1964

The Civil Rights Act of 1964 is divided into several sections, or titles, each dealing with a particular facet of discrimination (e.g., voting rights, public accommodations, public education). Title VII is most relevant to the employment context because it prohibits discrimination on the basis of race, color, religion, sex, or national origin in all aspects of employment (including apprenticeship programs). Title VII is the most important federal EEO law because it contains the broadest coverage, prohibitions, and remedies. Through it, the Equal Employment Opportunity Commission (EEOC) was created to ensure that employers, employment agencies, and labor organizations comply with Title VII.

Some may ask why we need such a law. As an expression of social policy, the law was passed to guarantee that people would be considered for jobs not on the basis of the color of their skin, their religion, their gender, or their national origin, but rather on the basis of the abilities and talents that are necessary to perform a job.

In 1972, the coverage of Title VII was expanded. It now includes almost all public and private employers with 15 or more employees, except (1) private clubs, (2) religious organizations (which are allowed to discriminate on the basis of religion in certain circumstances), and (3) places of employment connected with an Indian reservation.

Finally, back-pay awards in Title VII cases are limited to 2 years prior to the filing of a charge. For example, if a woman filed a Title VII claim in 2014, and the matter continued through investigation, conciliation, trial, and appeal until 2019, she might be entitled to as much as 7 years' back pay, from 2012 (2 years prior to the filing of the charge) until the matter was resolved in her favor. The 2-year statute of limitations begins with the *filing* of a charge of discrimination.

The following are specifically exempted from Title VII coverage:

1. *Bona fide occupational qualifications (BFOQs).* Discrimination is permissible when a prohibited factor (e.g., gender) is a **bona fide occupational qualification** for employment–that is, when it is considered "reasonably necessary to the operation of that particular business or enterprise." The burden of proof rests with the employer to demonstrate this. Both the EEOC and the courts interpret BFOQs quite narrowly.[12] Preferences of the employer, coworkers, or clients are irrelevant and do not constitute BFOQs.
2. *Seniority systems.* Title VII explicitly permits bona fide seniority, merit, or incentive systems "provided that such differences are not the result of an intention to discriminate."
3. *Pre-employment inquiries.* Inquiries regarding such matters as ethnicity or gender are permissible as long as they can be shown to be job-related. Even if not job-related, some inquiries (e.g., regarding race or gender) are necessary to meet the reporting requirements of federal regulatory agencies. Applicants provide this information on a voluntary basis.

4. *Testing.* An employer may give or act upon any professionally developed ability test. If the results demonstrate adverse impact against a protected group, then the test itself must be shown to be job-related (i.e., valid) for the position in question. The Supreme Court established this standard in *Griggs v. Duke Power Co.*, a case we will discuss later in the chapter.

5. *Preferential treatment.* The Supreme Court has ruled that Title VII does not require the granting of preferential treatment to individuals or groups because of their race, sex, religion, or national origin on account of existing imbalances:

> The burden which shifts to the employer is merely that of proving that he based his employment decision on a legitimate consideration, and not an illegitimate one such as race. . . . Title VII . . . does not impose a duty to adopt a hiring procedure that maximizes the hiring of minority employees.[13]

6. *National security.* Discrimination is permitted under Title VII when it is deemed necessary to protect national security (e.g., against members of groups whose avowed aim is to overthrow the U.S. government).

Initially it appeared that these exemptions (summarized in Figure 4–2) would blunt the overall impact of the law significantly. However, it soon became clear that they would be interpreted very narrowly, by both the EEOC and the courts.

Litigating Claims of Unfair Discrimination

If someone decides to bring suit under Title VII, the first step is to establish a **prima facie case** of discrimination (i.e., a body of facts presumed to be true until proved

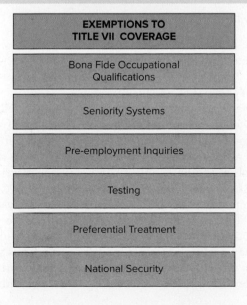

Figure 4–2

The six exemptions to Title VII coverage.

EXEMPTIONS TO TITLE VII COVERAGE

- Bona Fide Occupational Qualifications
- Seniority Systems
- Pre-employment Inquiries
- Testing
- Preferential Treatment
- National Security

otherwise). However, the nature of prima facie evidence differs depending on the type of case brought before the court. If an individual alleges that a particular employment practice had an *adverse impact* on all members of a class that he or she represents, prima facie evidence is presented when adverse impact is shown to exist. Usually this is demonstrated by showing that the selection rate for the group in question is less than 80 percent of the rate of the dominant group (e.g., white males) and that the difference is statistically significant. If the individual alleges that he or she was treated differently from others in the context of some employment practice (i.e., *unequal-treatment discrimination*), a prima facie case is usually presented either through direct evidence of the intention to discriminate or by circumstantial evidence. The legal standard for circumstantial evidence is a four-part test first specified in the *McDonnell Douglas v. Green* case,[14] wherein a plaintiff must be able to demonstrate the following:

1. She or he belongs to a protected class, such as a racial minority or a qualified individual with a disability.
2. She or he was somehow harmed or disadvantaged (e.g., by not receiving a job offer or a promotion).
3. She or he was qualified to do the job or to perform the job in a satisfactory manner.
4. She or he was treated less favorably than others outside the protected class.

Once the court accepts prima facie evidence, the burden of producing evidence shifts back and forth from plaintiff (the complaining party) to defendant (the employer). First, the employer is given the opportunity to articulate a legitimate, nondiscriminatory reason for the practice in question. Following that, in an unequal-treatment case, the burden shifts back to the plaintiff to show that the employer's reason is a pretext for illegal discrimination. In an adverse-impact case, the plaintiff's burden is to show that a less discriminatory alternative practice exists and that the employer failed to use it. Age-discrimination cases follow a similar process.

The Civil Rights Act of 1991[15]

Here are nine key provisions that are likely to have the greatest impact in the context of employment.

Monetary Damages and Jury Trials

A major effect of this act is to expand the remedies in discrimination cases. Individuals who feel they are the victims of intentional discrimination based on race, gender (including sexual harassment), religion, or disability can ask for compensatory damages for pain and suffering, as well as for punitive damages, and they may demand a jury trial. In the past, only plaintiffs in age-discrimination cases had the right to demand a jury.

Compensatory and punitive damages are available only from nonpublic employers (public employers are still subject to compensatory damages up to $300,000) and not for adverse-impact (unintentional discrimination) cases. Moreover, they may not be awarded in an Americans with Disabilities Act (ADA) case when an employer has engaged in good faith efforts to provide a reasonable accommodation. Thus, the 1991 Civil Rights Act provides the sanctions for violations of the ADA. The total amount of damages that can be awarded depends on the size of the employer's workforce:

Number of employees	Maximum combined damages per complaint
15 to 100	$ 50,000
101 to 200	100,000
201 to 500	200,000
More than 500	300,000

In *Kolstad v. American Dental Association*, the U.S. Supreme Court held that the availability of punitive damages depends on the motive of the discriminator rather than on the nature of the conduct (the extent to which it is "egregious" or "outrageous"). Further, employers should not be assessed punitive damages if they implement, in good faith, sound anti-discrimination policies and practices. It is not enough simply to distribute a well-crafted policy. Supervisors must be trained to use it, and there should be consequences for failing to do so.[16]

Adverse-Impact (Unintentional Discrimination) Cases
The act clarifies each party's obligation in such cases. As we noted earlier, if a plaintiff alleges adverse impact, he or she must identify a specific employment practice as the cause of it. If the plaintiff is successful in demonstrating adverse impact, the burden of producing evidence shifts to the employer, who must prove that the challenged practice is "job-related for the position in question and consistent with business necessity."

Protection in Foreign Countries
Civil rights laws also protect U.S. citizens from discrimination in a foreign facility owned or controlled by a U.S. company. However, the employer does not have to comply with U.S. discrimination law if to do so would violate the law of the foreign country.[17]

Racial Harassment
As we noted earlier, the act amended the Civil Rights Act of 1866, so that workers are protected from intentional discrimination in all aspects of employment, not just hiring and promotion.

Challenges to Consent Decrees
Once a court order or consent decree is entered to resolve a lawsuit, nonparties to the original suit cannot challenge such enforcement actions.

Mixed-Motive Cases
In a mixed-motive case, an employment decision was based on a combination of job-related factors and unlawful factors, such as race, gender, religion, or disability. Under the Civil Rights Act of 1991, an employer is guilty of discrimination if a plaintiff can show that a prohibited consideration was a motivating factor in a decision, even though other factors, which are lawful, also were used. More recently, however, the

Supreme Court ruled that it is not enough for a plaintiff to prove that age was one of the motivating factors in a decision to terminate him. Instead, the plaintiff must prove that, but for his age, the termination would not have occurred.[18]

Seniority Systems

The act provides that a seniority system that intentionally discriminates against the members of a protected group can be challenged (within 180 days) at any of three points: (1) when the system is adopted, (2) when an individual becomes subject to the system, or (3) when a person is injured by the system.

"Race-Norming"

The act makes it unlawful "to adjust the scores of, use different cutoff scores for, or otherwise alter the results of employment-related tests on the basis of race, color, religion, sex, or national origin." Prior to the passage of this act, within-group percentile scoring (so-called **race-norming**) had been used extensively to adjust the test scores of minority candidates to make them more comparable to those of non-minority candidates. Under race-norming, each individual's percentile score on a selection test was computed relative only to others in his or her race/ethnic group and not relative to the scores of all persons who took the test. The percentile scores (high to low) were then merged into a single list, and the single list of percentiles was presented to those responsible for hiring decisions.

Extension to U.S. Senate and Appointed Officials

The act extends protection from discrimination on the basis of race, color, religion, gender, national origin, age, and disability to employees of the U.S. Senate, political appointees of the president, and staff members employed by elected officials at the state level. Employees of the U.S. House of Representatives are covered by a House resolution adopted in 1988.

The Age Discrimination in Employment Act of 1967 (ADEA)

As amended in 1986, this act prohibits discrimination in pay, benefits, or continued employment for employees age 40 and over, unless an employer can demonstrate that age is a BFOQ for the job in question. It does not apply to job applicants.[19] A key objective of the law is to prevent financially troubled companies from singling out older employees when there are cutbacks. To win an age-discrimination case in federal court, however, an employee must prove that age was the determining factor for a layoff.[20] When there are cutbacks, older workers can waive their rights to sue under this law (e.g., in return for sweetened benefits for early retirement). Under the Older Workers Benefit Protection Act (OWBPA), an individual employee who does not have a pending claim has 21 days to consider such a waiver (45 days if terminated during a group reduction in force or if leaving voluntarily through a group incentive program), and 7 days after signing to revoke it.[21] Even after signing a waiver, employees age 40 and over can still sue for age discrimination if the employer did not comply with OWBPA requirements for obtaining a knowing and voluntary release.[22] Courts have made clear, however, that severance agreements will be upheld when agreements follow the rules and are written clearly and in a manner that will enable employees to understand what it is that they are agreeing to.[23]

The Immigration Reform and Control Act of 1986 (IRCA)

This law applies to every employer in the United States, even to those with only one employee. It also applies to every employee—whether full-time, part-time, temporary, or seasonal—and it makes the enforcement of national immigration policy the job of every employer. Three basic features of the law are particularly relevant to employers[24]:

1. Employers may not hire or continue to employ persons who are not legally authorized to work in the United States.
2. Employers must verify the identity and work authorization of every new employee. They may not require any particular form of documentation but must examine documents provided by job applicants (e.g., U.S. passports for U.S. citizens, "green cards" for resident noncitizens) showing identity and work authorization. Both employer and employee then sign a form (I-9), attesting under penalty of perjury that the employee is lawfully eligible to work in the United States. Experts advise firms to make copies of whatever documentation they accept for an individual's employment, such as a work visa or Social Security card. In addition, to show a good-faith effort to abide by the law, employers should do a self-audit of all I-9 forms, not just those of a particular ethnic group.[25]
3. Employers with 4 to 14 employees may not discriminate on the basis of citizenship or national origin. Those with 15 or more employees are already prohibited from national origin discrimination by Title VII. However, this prohibition is tempered by an exception that allows employers to select an applicant who is a U.S. citizen over a noncitizen when the two applicants are equally qualified.

Qualified employees with disabilities can make important contributions to organizations.
Inti St Clair/Blend Images LLC

Penalties for noncompliance are severe. For example, for failure to comply with the verification rules, fines range from $110 to $1,100 for *each* employee whose identity and work authorization have not been verified. The act also provides for criminal sanctions for employers who engage in a pattern or practice of violations, and a later executive order prohibits companies that knowingly hire illegal workers from receiving federal contracts.[26] In the first seven months of fiscal-year 2018, Immigration and Customs Enforcement made 1,204 worksite arrests, up from 311 in all of fiscal 2017.[27]

The Americans with Disabilities Act of 1990 (ADA)

Almost one in five people in the United States have at least one disability, using a broad definition of disability, according to the Centers for Disease Control and Prevention.[28] At the same time, the employment rate for working-age people with disabilities remains less than half that of those without disabilities (19.3 percent versus 66.3 percent).[29] The ADA protects people with disabilities from discrimination in employment, transportation, and public accommodation. It applies to all employers with 15 or more employees.[30]

As a general rule, the ADA prohibits an employer from discriminating against a "qualified individual with a disability." A qualified individual is one who is able to perform the **essential (i.e., primary) functions** of a job with or without accommodation. An employer's written job description is instrumental in determining essential functions.[31] **Disability** is a physical or mental impairment that substantially limits one or more major life activities, such as walking, talking, seeing, hearing, or learning. People are protected if they currently have an impairment and have a record of such impairment, or if the employer thinks they have an impairment (e.g., a person with diabetes under control).[32] Rehabilitated drug and alcohol abusers are protected, but current drug abusers may be fired. Alcoholics, in contrast, are covered and must be reasonably accommodated by being given a firm choice to rehabilitate themselves or face career-threatening consequences.[33] The law also protects people who have tested positive for HIV/AIDS.[34]

The ADA Amendments Act of 2008 overturned two Supreme Court decisions that interpreted ADA's definition of disability narrowly, and it broadened the definition of a disability by expanding the phrase "major life activities." Alongside long-recognized impairments such as blindness, the list now includes conditions such as cancer, diabetes, major depression, and epilepsy.[35] Although the amendments make it easier to claim a disability, a plaintiff still has to prove that he or she has one.[36] Companies do not have to lower work standards, tolerate misconduct, or give someone a make-work job.[37] Here are six major implications for employers[38]:

1. Any factory, office, retail store, bank, hotel, or other building open to the public will have to be made accessible to those with physical disabilities (e.g., by installing ramps, elevators, telephones with amplifiers). "Expensive" will be no excuse, unless such modifications will lead an employer to suffer an "undue hardship," considering the cost of the accommodation, the employer's size, financial resources, and the nature and structure of its operation.[39]
2. Employers must make "reasonable accommodations" for job applicants or employees with disabilities (e.g., by restructuring job and training programs, modifying work schedules, or purchasing new equipment that is "user friendly" to sight- or hearing-impaired people).[40] For example, Walgreens replaced

keyboards with touch screens based on large pictures and icons, not words, making it easier for sight-impaired people or those with cognitive disabilities to learn and complete tasks. **Qualified job applicants** (i.e., individuals with disabilities who can perform the essential functions of a job with or without reasonable accommodation) must be considered for employment. However, the ADA neither requires an employer to shift the essential functions of a job nor to create a new job as an accommodation.[41]

3. Pre-employment physicals are now permissible only if all employees are subject to them, and they cannot be given until after a conditional offer of employment is made. That is, the employment offer is made conditional upon passing of the physical examination. Further, employers are not permitted to ask about past workers' compensation claims or disabilities in general. However, after describing essential job functions, an employer can ask whether the applicant can perform the job in question.[42] Here is an example of the difference between these two types of inquiries: "Do you have any back problems?" clearly violates the ADA because it is not job specific. However, the employer could state the following: "This job involves lifting equipment weighing up to 50 pounds at least once every hour of an 8-hour shift. Can you do that?"

4. Medical information on employees must be kept separate from other personal or work-related information about them.

5. Drug-testing rules remain intact. An employer can still prohibit the use of alcohol and illegal drugs at the workplace and continue to give alcohol and drug tests. In 33 states, for example, medical marijuana use is legal, yet businesses still have the right to fire people who test positive for the drug because federal law provides no exception for the use of medicinal marijuana.[43]

6. Train supervisors, HR professionals, and anyone else who supervises employees, interviews candidates, and makes hiring decisions. Training should address who is covered under the ADA and its amendments, the process of interacting with someone who requests an accommodation, what accommodations are reasonable, and what is prohibited (harassment, retaliation). With respect to accommodations, keep the focus on performance or behavior without speculating or inquiring about the cause of a deficiency. Finally, identify HR or legal professionals whom supervisors or higher-level managers can contact for advice.[44]

Enforcement

The Equal Employment Opportunity Commission enforces the ADA.[45] In cases of intentional discrimination, the Supreme Court has ruled that individuals with disabilities may be awarded both compensatory and punitive damages up to $300,000 (depending on the size of the employer's workforce) if it can be shown that an employer engaged in discriminatory practices "with malice or with reckless indifference."[46]

The Family and Medical Leave Act of 1993 (FMLA)

The FMLA covers all private-sector employers with 50 or more employees, including part-timers who work 1,250 hours over a 12-month period (an average of 25 hours per week). The law gives workers up to 12 weeks' unpaid leave each year for birth, adoption, or foster care of a child within a year of the child's arrival; care for a spouse, parent, or child with a serious health condition; or the employee's own serious health condition if it prevents him or her from working. The employer is responsible for designating an absence or leave as FMLA leave, on the basis of information provided by the employee.[47] Employers can require workers to provide medical certification of such serious illnesses and can require a second medical opinion. Employers also can exempt from the FMLA key salaried employees who are among their highest-paid 10 percent. For leave takers, however, employers must maintain health insurance benefits and give the workers their previous jobs (or comparable positions) when their leaves are over.[48] Enforcement provisions of the FMLA are administered by the U.S. Department of Labor.

The FMLA also includes military families. Businesses are required to offer up to 26 weeks of unpaid leave to employees who provide care to wounded U.S. military personnel. Employers also must provide 12 weeks of FMLA leave to immediate family members (spouses, children, or parents) of soldiers, reservists, and members of the National Guard engaged in activities such as overseas assignments, recalls to active duty, or troop mobilizations.[49]

Uniformed Services Employment and Reemployment Rights Act of 1994

Employers, regardless of size, may not deny a person initial employment, reemployment, promotion, or benefits on the basis of that person's membership in the armed services. The Uniformed Services Employment and Reemployment Rights Act requires both public and private employers promptly to reemploy individuals returning from uniformed service (e.g., National Guard or activated reservists) in the position they would have occupied and with the seniority rights they would have enjoyed, had they never left. Employers are also required to maintain health benefits for employees while they are away, but they are not required to make up the often significant difference between military and civilian pay.[50]

To be protected, the employee must provide advance notice, oral or written. Employers need not always rehire a returning service member (e.g., if the employee received a dishonorable discharge or if changed circumstances at the workplace make reemployment impossible or unreasonable), but the burden of proof will almost always be on the employer. The Veterans Employment and Training Service of the U.S. Department of Labor administers this law.[51]

FEDERAL ENFORCEMENT AGENCIES: EEOC AND OFCCP

The Equal Employment Opportunity Commission is an independent regulatory agency whose five commissioners (one of whom is chairperson) are appointed by the president and confirmed by the Senate for terms of 5 years. No more than three of the commissioners may be from the same political party. Like the Office of Federal Contract Compliance Programs (OFCCP), the EEOC sets policy and in individual cases determines whether there is "reasonable cause" to believe that unlawful discrimination has occurred. If the EEOC finds reasonable cause, it can sue either on its own behalf or on behalf of a claimant. As far as the employer is concerned, the simplest and least costly procedure is to establish a system to resolve complaints internally. However, if this system fails or if the employer does not make available an avenue for such complaints, an aggrieved individual (or group) can file a formal complaint with the EEOC. The process is shown graphically in Figure 4-3.

Once it receives a complaint of discrimination (72,675 in 2019), the EEOC follows a three-step process: investigation, conciliation, and litigation.[52] As Figure 4-3

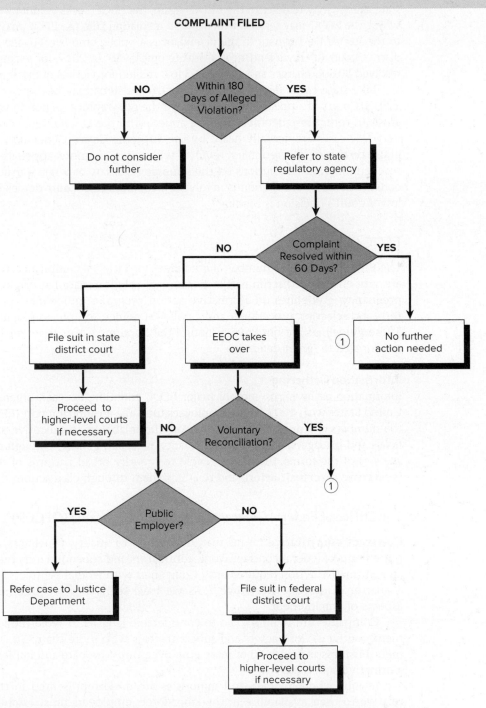

Figure 4–3

Discrimination complaints: The formal process.

indicates, complaints must be filed within 180 days of an alleged violation (300 days if the same basis of discrimination is prohibited by either state or local laws). If that requirement is satisfied, the EEOC immediately refers the complaint to a state agency charged with enforcement of fair employment laws (if one exists) for resolution within 60 days. If the complaint cannot be resolved within that time, the state agency can file suit in a state district court and appeal any decision to a state appellate court, the state supreme court, or the U.S. Supreme Court. As an alternative to filing suit, the state agency may re-defer to the EEOC. Again, the EEOC seeks voluntary reconciliation, where the EEOC may serve as a mediator. If mediation fails, the EEOC may refer the case to the Justice Department (if the defendant is a public employer) or file suit in federal district court (if the defendant is a private employer). In 2019, for example, the EEOC resolved 80,806 charges and secured $346.6 million for victims of discrimination.[53]

Like state-court decisions, federal-court decisions may be appealed to 1 of the 12 U.S. Courts of Appeal, corresponding to the geographical region in which the case arose. In turn, these decisions may be appealed to the U.S. Supreme Court, although very few cases are actually heard by the Supreme Court. Generally the Court will grant *certiorari* (discretionary review) when two or more appellate courts have reached different conclusions on the same point of law or when a major question of constitutional interpretation is involved. If the Supreme Court denies certiorari, the lower court's decision is binding.

EEOC Guidelines

The EEOC has issued a number of guidelines for Title VII compliance.[54] Among these are guidelines on discrimination because of religion, national origin, gender, and pregnancy; guidelines on affirmative action programs; guidelines on employment tests and selection procedures; and a policy statement on pre-employment inquiries. These guidelines are not laws, although the Supreme Court has indicated that they are entitled to "great deference."[55]

Information Gathering

Information gathering is another major EEOC function, for each organization in the United States with 100 or more employees must file an annual report (EEO-1) detailing the numbers of employees by job category (from laborers to executive/senior-level officials and managers), and then by ethnicity, race, and gender. Through computerized analysis of the forms, the EEOC is able to identify broad patterns of discrimination **(systemic discrimination)** and to attack them through class actions.[56]

The Office of Federal Contract Compliance Programs (OFCCP)

Contract compliance means that, in addition to quality, timeliness, and other requirements of federal contract work, contractors and subcontractors must meet EEO and affirmative action requirements. Companies with federal contracts employ nearly a quarter of the U.S. workforce.[57] As we have seen, these requirements cover all aspects of employment.

Companies are willing to go to considerable lengths to avoid the loss of government contracts. Contractors and subcontractors with more than $50,000 in government business and with 50 or more employees must prepare and implement written affirmative action plans.[58]

In jobs where women and minorities are underrepresented in the workforce relative to their availability in the labor force, employers must establish goals and timetables for hiring and promotion. Theoretically, goals and timetables are distinguishable from rigid quotas in that they are flexible objectives that can be met in a realistic amount of time (Figure 4–4).[59]

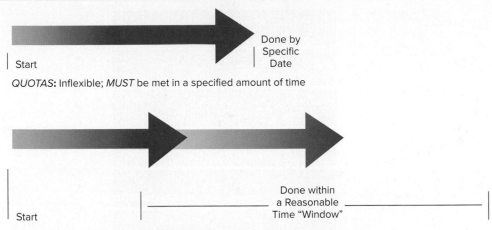

Figure 4–4

The distinction between rigid quotas and goals and timetables.

QUOTAS: Inflexible; *MUST* be met in a specified amount of time

GOALS AND TIMETABLES: Flexible; *MAY* be met in a realistic amount of time

When a compliance review by the OFCCP does indicate problems that cannot be resolved easily, it tries to reach a conciliation agreement with the employer. Such an agreement might include back pay, seniority credit, special recruitment efforts, promotion, or other forms of relief for the victims of unlawful discrimination.

The conciliation agreement is the OFCCP's preferred route, but if such efforts are unsuccessful, formal enforcement action is necessary. Contractors may lose their government contracts, the government may withhold their payments, or they may be debarred from any government contract work. How has the agency done? In FY 2019, for example, the OFCCP conducted 1,331 compliance reviews and recovered more than $40.5 million in back pay and other costs for employees.[60]

Affirmative Action Remedies

In three different cases, the Supreme Court found that Congress specifically endorsed the concept of non–victim-specific racial hiring goals to achieve compliance.[61] Further, the Court noted the benefits of flexible affirmative action rather than rigid application of a color-blind policy that would deprive employers of flexibility in administering human resources. We will have more to say about this in a following section.

EMPLOYMENT CASE LAW: SOME GENERAL PRINCIPLES

Although Congress enacts laws, the courts interpret the laws and determine how they will be enforced. Such interpretations define what is called **case law**, which serves as a precedent to guide future legal decisions. And, of course, precedents are regularly subject to reinterpretation.

In the area of employment, a considerable body of case law has accumulated since 1964. Figure 4-5 illustrates areas in which case law is developed most extensively. Lawsuits affecting virtually every aspect of employment have been filed, and in the following sections we will consider some of the most significant decisions to date.

Figure 4–5

Areas making up the main body of employment case law.

EMPLOYMENT CASE LAW
Unfair Discrimination by Sex, Race, Age, Religion, or National Origin
Seniority
Testing and Interviewing
Personal-History Information
Preferential Selection

Sex Discrimination

In a landmark Supreme Court decision in 2020, the Court ruled that an employer who fires a worker merely for being gay or transgender violates Title VII of the 1964 Civil Rights Act. "An individual's homosexuality or transgender status is not relevant to employment decisions. That's because it is impossible to discriminate against a person for being homosexual or transgender without discriminating against that individual based on sex. . . . An individual employee's sex is not relevant to the selection, evaluation, or compensation of employees."[62] This decision allows people who say they were discriminated against in the workplace based on their sexual orientation or gender identity to file lawsuits, just as people claiming race and sex discrimination may. The plaintiffs have to offer evidence, of course, and employers may respond that they had reasons unrelated to discrimination for their decisions.[63]

Another Supreme Court decision (*Johnson v. Santa Clara Transportation Agency*)[64] addressed the issue of the promotion of a woman over a marginally better-qualified man in traditionally sex-segregated jobs. The Supreme Court ruled unambiguously that in such jobs, a qualified woman can be promoted over a marginally better-qualified man to promote more balanced representation. The Court stressed the need for **affirmative action** plans (actions appropriate to overcome the effects of past or present policies, practices, or other barriers to equal employment opportunity) to be flexible, gradual, and limited in their effect on whites and men. The Court also expressed disapproval of strict numerical quotas except where necessary (on a temporary basis) to remedy severe past discrimination. This decision clearly put pressure on employers to institute voluntary affirmative action programs, but at the same time it also provided some welcome guidance on what they were permitted to do.

Sex-discrimination cases have been argued under both theories of unlawful discrimination: disparate treatment (e.g., sexual harassment) and adverse impact (e.g., physical ability tests).[65] Many cases involve allegations of gender stereotyping (unwitting preferences by managers).[66] Gender stereotypes are not a thing of the past, and they will play important roles in future employment-law litigation.

Pregnancy

The EEOC's interpretive guidelines for the Pregnancy Discrimination Act (passed in 1978) state:

> A written or unwritten employment policy or practice which excludes from employment applicants or employees because of pregnancy, childbirth, or related medical conditions is in prima facie violation of Title VII.[67]

Each year, the EEOC receives about 2,800 complaints related to pregnancy. In 2019, it resolved 2,996 of them and recovered $22.4 million in monetary benefits for the complaining parties, excluding benefits recovered through litigation.[68]

Under the law, an employer is never *required* to give pregnant employees special treatment. If an organization provides no disability benefits or sick leave to other employees, it is not required to provide them for pregnant employees.[69] The actual length of maternity leave, however, is an issue to be determined by the woman's and/or the company's physician.

As of 2014, The Pregnant Workers Fairness Act requires employers to make reasonable accommodations to known limitations for pregnant applicants or employees, so long as those do not cause an undue hardship for the employer.[70] For many women, unfortunately, getting pregnant is often the moment they are knocked off the professional ladder.[71] At the same time, however, many employers are doing their best to accommodate pregnant women through flexible work scheduling and generous maternity leave policies.[72] Given that about 75 percent of the 68 million working women in the United States will become pregnant (three-quarters of whom will return to work),[73] combined with the tight labor markets that employers face for many types of skills, there really is no other choice.

Sexual Harassment

What is **sexual harassment**? According to the EEOC, it is "unwelcome sexual advances, requests for sexual favors, and other verbal or physical conduct of a sexual nature when submission to or rejection of this conduct explicitly or implicitly affects an individual's employment, unreasonably interferes with an individual's work performance, or creates an intimidating, hostile, or offensive work environment."[74]

Actually, the "no frills" definition can be put into one word: *unwelcome*. According to the courts, for behavior to be treated as sexual harassment, the offender has to know that the behavior is unwelcome. If a person wants to file a grievance, therefore, it is important to be able to prove either that he or she told the perpetrator to back off or that the action was so offensive the harasser should have known it was unwelcome.

Sexual harassment is not really about sex. It's about power—more to the point, the abuse of power.[75] In the vast majority of cases on this issue, females rather than males have suffered from sexual abuse at work.[76] Such abuse may constitute illegal sex discrimination, a form of unequal treatment on the job. How prevalent is it? Roughly 7,500 harassment complaints were filed with the EEOC in 2019, and $68.2 million (up from $40.7 million in 2016) was recovered for charging parties and other aggrieved individuals.[77] Fully 90 percent of *Fortune* 500 companies have dealt with sexual harassment complaints, and more than a third have been sued at least once. It is perilous self-deception for a manager to believe that sexual harassment does not exist in his or her own organization.

ETHICAL DILEMMA
Secret Recording of Supervisors: It May Be Legal, but Is It Ethical?

As smartphones have become common, so also has recording by employees of work conversations without their employers' knowledge or permission. Such recording, often done to support whistle-blower lawsuits or claims of discrimination or sexual harassment, outrages and exasperates employers. Defenders counter that secret recording sometimes is the only way to bring out the truth.

Federal law allows secret recording, as long as one of the people being recorded knows about it. However, in 12 states, the law requires that everyone being recorded must know that he or she is being recorded (so-called dual-consent states).[a]

Most companies confronted with a recording quickly settle out of court. In one case, for example, a pregnant saleswoman's coworkers told her outright that they would force her off the job by making life hard on her at work. The workers were afraid the pregnancy would stop the woman from racking up sales, and they all would lose a bonus as a result. Once the woman sued for pregnancy discrimination, the coworkers lied about threatening her. They said, "We were all happy for

her—we gave her a big hug when we found out she was pregnant." But the woman produced a secret recording she had made of the threats and won a $180,000 settlement.

What is a business to do? Issue a policy against covert recording. That way, employees who do so can be fired for breaking company rules. In one-party-consent states, companies can turn the tables on employees by using the recordings against them. If a recording is leaked online, however, it can cause a public relations nightmare for an employer. The cheapest and best protection of all is to advise coworkers and managers to avoid saying things they would be embarrassed to go into on a witness stand ... or to see on the evening news.[b]

---

[a]Summary of consent requirements for taping telephone conversations. Retrieved from *aapsonline.org/judicial/telephone.htm* on Mar. 25, 2017. Smith, A. (2018, Aug. 8). Employees secretly record managers for litigation. *SHRM Online.* Retrieved from *https://www.shrm.org/resourcesandtools/legal-and-compliance/state-and-local-updates/pages/secret-recordings.aspx* on Aug. 9, 2018.

[b]Ibid. Smith, A. (2016, Mar.1). Employers can't prohibit all recording at work. Retrieved from *www.shrm.org/resourcesandtools/hr-topics/labor-relations/pages/recordings.aspx* on Mar. 7, 2016.

Although many behaviors can constitute sexual harassment, there are two main types:

1. Quid pro quo (you give me this; I'll give you that).
2. Hostile work environment (an intimidating, hostile, or offensive atmosphere).

Quid pro quo harassment exists when the harassment is a condition of employment. For example, consider the case of *Barnes v. Costle*: The plaintiff rebuffed her director's repeated sexual overtures. She ignored his advice that sexual intimacy was the path she should take to improve her career opportunities. Subsequently, the director abolished her job. The court of appeals found that sexual cooperation was a condition of her employment, a condition the director did not impose upon males. Therefore, sex discrimination had occurred and the employer was liable.[78]

The U.S. Supreme Court has gone even further. In two key rulings, *Burlington Industries Inc. v. Ellerth*[79] and *Faragher v. City of Boca Raton*,[80] the Court held that employers always are potentially liable for a supervisor's sexual misconduct toward an employee, even if they knew nothing about that supervisor's conduct. More recently, the Supreme Court ruled in *Vance v. Ball State University* that an employee is a "supervisor" only if he or she is empowered by the employer to take tangible employment actions against the victim. The Court rejected the view that "supervisors" include those whom the employer vests with authority to direct and oversee the victim's daily work. The distinction is important, because under Title VII, an employer's liability for workplace harassment often depends on the harasser's status.[81]

Hostile-environment harassment was defined by the Supreme Court in the case of *Meritor Savings Bank v. Vinson*.[82] Vinson's boss had abused her verbally as well as sexually. However, because Vinson was making good career progress, the district court ruled that the relationship was a voluntary one having nothing to do with her continued employment or advancement. The Supreme Court disagreed, ruling that whether the relationship was "voluntary" was irrelevant. The key question was whether the sexual advances from the supervisor were "unwelcome." If unwelcome, and if they are "sufficiently severe or pervasive to be abusive,"[83] then they are illegal.

This case was groundbreaking because it expanded the definition of harassment to include verbal or physical conduct that creates an intimidating, hostile, or offensive work environment or interferes with an employee's job performance. Employers may also be liable for the harassing actions of coworkers or customers, if they fail to take reasonable steps to stop the harassing behavior.[84]

In *Pennsylvania State Police v. Suders*,[85] the Supreme Court emphasized that an employer has no defense when a supervisor harasses an employee and an adverse-employment action results. In hostile-environment cases, however, the employer may avoid liability if it can prove that (1) it exercised reasonable care to prevent and promptly correct any sexually harassing behavior and (2) the plaintiff failed to use any preventive or corrective methods provided by the employer. The key is to establish and follow a thorough anti-harassment program in the workplace.[86]

Preventive Actions by Employers

What can an employer do to escape, or to at least limit, its liability for the sexually harassing acts of its managers or workers? An effective policy should include the following features[87]:

- The chief executive officer must state firmly that sexual harassment will not be tolerated. Then actions must follow words to demonstrate that the CEO is working to create a culture of respect for all.
- Create a workable definition of sexual harassment. Publicize it using multiple channels. Include concrete examples of inappropriate behaviors (e.g., derogatory comments, demeaning jokes, visual messages, nicknames that refer to a person's membership in any protected group).
- Create an effective complaint procedure that includes multiple ways to file complaints (supervisor, high-level manager, HR or legal representative, hot line). The more choices employees have, the less reasonable will be their failure to complain. Every employee must sign a written acknowledgment of receipt of the policy.
- Be clear about sanctions for violators and protection for those who make charges.
- Promptly and confidentially, investigate every claim of harassment, no matter how trivial.
- Preserve all investigative information.
- Train all managers and supervisors regularly, including top managers, to model appropriate behavior and to recognize and respond to complaints. Outline their responsibilities and obligations. Each person needs to sign a written acknowledgment of his or her participation in the training.
- Follow-up to determine if harassment has stopped.[88]

Age Discrimination

The EEOC's guidelines on age discrimination emphasize that in order to defend an adverse-employment action against employees age 40 and over, an employer must be able to demonstrate a "business necessity" for doing so. That is, it must be able to show that age is a factor directly related to the safe, efficient operation of a business. To establish a prima facie case of age discrimination with respect to termination, for example, an individual must show that[89]

1. She or he is within the protected age group (40 years of age and over).
2. She or he is doing satisfactory work.
3. She or he was discharged despite satisfactory work performance.
4. The position was filled by a person younger than the person replaced.

For example, in *Schwager v. Sun Oil Company of PA*, the company reorganized and had to reduce the size of its workforce. The average age of those retained was 35 years, while the average age of those terminated was 45.7 years. Schwager was close to retirement but the company was able to demonstrate that it considered factors other than age in his termination. The local manager had to let one person go, and he chose Schwager because he ranked lowest in overall job performance among salespeople in his district. Job performance, not age, was the reason for Schwager's termination. Employers can still fire unproductive workers, but the key is to base employment decisions on ability, not on age.[90] In addition to reductions in force, age-discrimination complaints may arise following employment decisions that involve discipline, selection, or promotion. They can be brought under disparate-treatment or adverse-impact theories of discrimination.[91] Several Appeals Courts have ruled, however, that age-based adverse- impact claims are available only to employees. Job applicants have to prove intentional discrimination.[92]

If a case gets to a jury, aggrieved employees have a 78 percent success rate at both state and local jury trials. At the federal level, 15,573 charges of age discrimination were filed with the EEOC in 2019, and the agency recovered $75.7 million for aggrieved individuals.[93]

"Overqualified" Job Applicants

Employers sometimes hesitate to hire an individual who has a great deal of experience for a job that requires few qualifications and may be only an entry-level job. They assume that an overqualified individual will be bored in such a job or is using the job only to get a foot in the door, so that he or she can apply for another job at a later time. Beware of violating the Age Discrimination in Employment Act! An appeals court has ruled that rejection of an older worker because he or she is overqualified may be a pretext to mask the real reason for rejection–the employee's age.[94]

The key to success seems to be careful assessment prior to hire. Begin by defining *overqualified*. Is it too much experience, salary expectations? How much is too much? Is there anything you can do to position the job to take better advantage of this applicant's experience? Can you change or modify it? Can the person be fast-tracked into a new position? Most importantly, give applicants a realistic preview of what the job will be–the good, the bad, and the ugly. You want to note all the advantages but also the things that might make the job less satisfying for an overqualified person. Doing so allows the candidate to make his or her own judgment. Finally, ask, "Is there anything in this job that you feel wouldn't engage you?"[95]

"ENGLISH-ONLY" RULES—NATIONAL ORIGIN DISCRIMINATION?

LEGALITIES

Rules that require employees to speak only English in the workplace have come under fire in recent years. Employees who speak a language other than English claim that such rules are not related to the ability to do a job and have a harsh impact on them because of their national origin. The EEOC and many courts agree that blanket English-only rules that lack business justification amount to unlawful national origin discrimination.[a]

Employers should be careful when instituting such a rule. Although it is not necessarily illegal to make fluency in English a job requirement or to discipline an employee for violating an English-only rule, employers must be able to show there is a legitimate business need for it. For example, it's a safety issue when medical workers or firefighters do not understand or cannot make themselves understood.[b] Avoid requiring the use of English at all times and in all areas of the workplace. Inform employees in advance of the circumstances where speaking only in English is required and of the consequences of violating the rule. (Conversely, many employers would be delighted to have a worker who can speak the language of a non-English-speaking customer.) Otherwise, the employer may be subject to discrimination complaints on the basis of national origin.

---

[a]Cornell Law School (n.d.). Speak-English-only rules. Retrieved from *https://www.law.cornell.edu/cfr/text/29/1606.7* on Mar. 13, 2020. Tuschman, R. (2013, Nov. 15). English-only policies in the workplace: Are they legal? Are they smart? *Forbes.* Retrieved from *http://www.forbes.com/sites/richardtuschman/2012/11/15/english-only-policies-in-the-workplace-are-they-legal-are-they-smart/* on Mar. 28, 2014. Wilkie, D. (2013, Nov. 14). English-only rules at work: Discrimination or business necessity? Retrieved from *http://www.shrm.org/hrdisciplines/diversity/articles/pages/english-only-eeoc.aspx* on Mar. 21, 2014.

[b]Bell, J. (2017, April 21). English-only rules in the workplace can be a legal minefield. *SHRM Online.* Retrieved from *https://www.shrm.org/resourcesandtools/legal-and-compliance/state-and-local-updates/pages/english-only-rules-in-the-workplace-can-be-a-minefield.aspx* on May 1, 2019.

Seniority

Seniority is a term that connotes length of employment. A **seniority system** is a scheme that, alone or in tandem with "non-seniority" criteria, allots to employees ever-improving employment rights and benefits as their relative lengths of pertinent employment increase.[96]

Various features of seniority systems have been challenged in the courts for many years.[97] However, one of the most nettlesome issues is the impact of established seniority systems on programs designed to ensure equal employment opportunity. Employers often work hard to hire and promote members of protected groups. If layoffs become necessary, however, those individuals may be lost because of their low seniority. As a result, the employer takes a step backward in terms of workforce diversity. What is the employer to do when seniority conflicts with EEO?

The U.S. Supreme Court has been quite clear in its rulings in two landmark decisions: *Firefighters Local Union No. 1784 v. Stotts*[98] (decided under Title VII) and *Wygant v. Jackson Board of Education*[99] (decided under the equal protection clause of the Fourteenth Amendment). The Court ruled that an employer may not protect the jobs of recently hired African American employees at the expense of whites who have more seniority.[100]

Voluntary modifications of seniority policies for affirmative action purposes re-main proper, but where a collective bargaining agreement exists, courts have made it clear that the union must be a party to any decree that modifies a bona fide senior-ity system.[101] What about seniority and the ADA? In *US Airways v. Barnett*,[102] the Supreme Court ruled that that an employer is not required to grant an employee with a disability a job in place of an employee with more seniority–if a seniority system normally is used as a fundamental factor in such decisions. The Court empha-sized that seniority does not always trump the ADA, and that such a question must be resolved on a case-by-case basis.[103]

Testing and Interviewing

Title VII clearly sanctions the use of "professionally developed" ability tests. Never-theless, it took several landmark Supreme Court cases to clarify the proper role and use of tests. The first was *Griggs v. Duke Power Co.*, which was decided in favor of Griggs.[104] Duke Power was prohibited from requiring a high-school education or the passing of an intelligence test as a condition of employment or job transfer because it could not show that either standard was significantly related to job performance. The ruling also included four other general principles:

1. The law prohibits not only open and deliberate discrimination but also prac-tices that are fair in form but discriminatory in operation. That is, Title VII prohibits practices having an adverse impact on protected groups, unless they are job-related. This is a landmark pronouncement because it officially estab-lished adverse impact as a category of illegal discrimination.

   For example, suppose an organization wants to use prior arrests as a basis for selection. In theory, arrests are a "neutral" practice because all persons are equally subject to arrest if they violate the law. However, if arrests cannot be shown to be job-related, and if a significantly higher proportion of African Americans than whites are arrested, the use of arrests as a basis for selection is discriminatory in operation.

2. The employer bears the burden of proof that any requirement for employment is related to job performance.[105] As affirmed by the Civil Rights Act of 1991, when a charge of adverse impact is made, the plaintiff must identify a specific employment practice as the cause of the discrimination. If successful, the bur-den shifts to the employer.

3. It is not necessary for the plaintiff to prove that the discrimination was inten-tional; intent is irrelevant. If the standards result in discrimination, they are unlawful.

4. Job-related tests and other employment selection procedures are legal and useful.

The confidentiality of individual test scores has also been addressed both by the profession[106] and by the courts. Thus, the Supreme Court affirmed the right of the Detroit Edison Company to refuse to hand over to a labor union copies of aptitude tests taken by job applicants and to refuse to disclose individual test scores without the written consent of employees.[107]

As is well known, interviews are commonly used as bases for employment deci-sions to hire or to promote certain candidates in preference to others. Must such "subjective" assessment procedures satisfy the same standards of job relatedness as more "objective" procedures, such as written tests? If they produce an adverse impact against a protected group, the answer is yes, according to the Supreme Court in *Watson v. Fort Worth Bank & Trust*.[108]

This need not involve a formal validation study, although the Court agreed unanimously that it is possible to conduct such studies when subjective assessment devices are used.[109] The lesson for employers? Be sure that there is a legitimate, job-related reason for every question raised in an employment or promotional interview. Limit questioning to "need to know," rather than "nice to know," information, and monitor interview outcomes for adverse impact. Validate this selection method. It is unwise to wait until the selection system is challenged.

Personal History

Frequently, job-qualification requirements involve personal background information. If the requirements have the effect of denying or restricting equal employment opportunity, they may violate Title VII. Here are a few examples of allegedly neutral practices that have been struck down by the courts on the basis of non-job relevance:

- Recruitment practices based on present employee referrals, where the workforce is nearly all white to begin with.[110]
- Height and weight requirements.[111]
- Arrest records, because they show only that a person has been accused of a crime, not that she or he was guilty of it; thus, arrests may not be used as a basis for selection decisions,[112] except in certain sensitive and responsible positions (e.g., police officer, school principal).[113]
- Conviction records, unless the conviction is directly related to the work to be performed (e.g., a person convicted of embezzlement applying for a job as a bank teller).[114] In addition, employers should consider carefully the nature and gravity of the offense, the time that has passed since the conviction and/or completion of the sentence, and the nature of the job held or sought. As of 2019, 35 states and more than 150 cities and counties have passed "ban the box" laws that require organizations to remove the check box that asks if a candidate has ever been convicted of a crime. Instead, they require employers first to conduct a job interview to see if someone is qualified, and then do a background investigation and analysis of whether a conviction is job-related.[115]
- Salary-history questions. To encourage employers to focus more on a job seeker's skill set, 15 states and many cities now prohibit employers from asking them to reveal their salary history. To avoid potential problems, many employers routinely post salary ranges for all jobs.[116]

Despite such decisions, personal-history items are not unlawfully discriminatory per se, but to use them you must show that they are relevant to the job in question. Just as with employment interviews, collect this information on a "need to know," not on a "nice to know," basis.

Preferential Selection

In an ideal world, selection and promotion decisions would be color blind. Thus, social policy as embodied in Title VII emphasizes that so-called **reverse discrimination** (discrimination against whites and in favor of members of protected groups) is just as unacceptable as is discrimination by whites against members of protected groups.[117] Indeed, this riddle has perplexed courts and the public since the dawn of affirmative action more than 50 years ago: How do you make things fair for oppressed groups while continuing to treat people as equal individuals?[118] Court cases, as well as the Civil Rights Act of 1991, have clarified a number of issues in this area:

1. Courts may order, and employers voluntarily may establish, affirmative action plans, including goals and timetables, to address problems of underutilization of women and minorities. Individuals who were not parties to the original suit may not reopen court-approved affirmative action settlements.
2. The plans need not be directed solely to identified victims of discrimination but may include general, classwide relief.
3. Although the courts will almost never approve a plan that would result in white people losing their jobs through layoffs, they may sanction plans that impose limited burdens on whites in hiring and promotions (i.e., plans that postpone hiring and promotion).

What about numerically based preferential programs? The U.S. Supreme Court has issued two landmark rulings that clarified this issue. Both cases represented challenges to admissions policies at the University of Michigan, one involving undergraduate admissions (*Gratz v. Bollinger*) and one involving law-school admissions (*Grutter v. Bollinger*).[119] The undergraduate admissions policy was struck down because it was too mechanistic. It awarded 20 points of the 150 needed for admission (8 points more than is earned for a perfect SAT score) to any member of an officially recognized minority group. Such a disguised quota system denied other applicants the equal protection of the law guaranteed by the Fourteenth Amendment to the Constitution, and thus it was ruled illegal.

Cast a wide net to search for qualified talent, but make hiring/promotion decisions based on merit.
Tom Merton/age fotostock

However, the Court also was mindful of arguments from leading businesses, educational institutions, and former military officials that a culturally diverse, well-educated workforce is vital to the competitiveness of the U.S. economy and that an integrated officer corps produced by diverse military academies and ROTC programs is vital to national security. The Court upheld the law school's approach to enrolling a "critical mass" of African Americans, Latinos, and Native Americans, under which the school considers each applicant individually and sets no explicit quota.

The Court emphasized that diversity is a "compelling state interest" but that universities may not use quotas for members of racial or ethnic groups or put them on separate admissions tracks. The law school's admissions policy satisfied these principles by ensuring that applicants are evaluated individually.

The net effect of the two rulings is to permit public and private universities to continue to use race as a "plus factor" in evaluating potential students–provided they take sufficient care to evaluate individually each applicant's ability to contribute to a diverse student body.[120] The Court made clear that its rationale for considering race was not to compensate for past discrimination but to obtain educational benefits from a diverse student body. Corporate hiring policies also will have to reflect the Court's double message: Diversity efforts are acceptable, but quotas aren't.[121]

IMPACT OF LEGAL FACTORS ON PRODUCTIVITY, QUALITY OF WORK LIFE, AND THE BOTTOM LINE

There are both direct and indirect costs associated with unlawful discrimination. For example, sexual harassment can create high levels of stress and anxiety for both the victim and the perpetrator. Job performance may suffer, and absenteeism, sick leave, and turnover may increase–boosting labor costs for employers. Discrimination against present employees or job applicants can lead to costly lawsuits. Litigation is a time-consuming, expensive exercise that no organization wants.[a] Organizations have been hit with lawsuits affecting virtually every aspect of the employment relationship, and many well-publicized awards to victims have reached millions of dollars.

Let's not view the legal and social aspects of the HR management process exclusively in negative terms. In most instances, the flip side of unlawful discrimination is good HR practice. For example, it is good practice to use properly developed and validated employment-selection procedures and performance management systems. It is good HR practice to treat people as individuals and not to rely on stereotypes (e.g., about women, ethnic groups, older workers, workers with disabilities). Finally, it just makes good sense to pay people equally, regardless of gender, if they are equally qualified and are doing the same work.[b] These kinds of HR practices can enhance productivity, provide a richer quality of work life, and contribute directly to the overall profitability of any enterprise.

[a]Gates, A. (2017, Dec.). 10 simple steps to avoid discrimination lawsuits. *HR Professionals Magazine* 7(12), p. 39. Malone, M. Consequences of discrimination in the workplace. Retrieved from *http://everydaylife.globalpost.com/consequences-discrimination-workplace 3934.html* on Mar. 28, 2014.

[b]Nagele-Piazza, L. (2018, May 8). Conducting gender pay audits in a changing landscape. Retrieved from *https://www.shrm.org/resourcesandtools/legal-and-compliance/state-and-local-updates/pages/conducting-gender-pay-audits-in-a-changing-landscape.aspx* on May 9, 2018.

Human Resource Management in Action: Conclusion

RETALIATION: GUIDANCE FOR EMPLOYERS AND SOME PREVENTIVE MEASURES

Retaliation claims more than doubled between 1997 and 2019, from 22.6 percent of all charges to 53.8 percent. In fiscal year 2019, the EEOC received 39,110 charges of retaliation discrimination, the vast majority of which involve actions such as discharge and suspension.

Perhaps the best way to avoid liability for retaliation is to prevent it from ever happening. Two management actions can help: (1) create an anti-retaliation policy (or update an existing one) and (2) provide specific training to supervisors on retaliation, using the EEOC's guidance to explain what actions might constitute it.

Experts recommend that an anti-retaliation policy include the following six elements:

1. Implement and follow a zero-tolerance anti-discrimination and anti-retaliation policy. Emphasize to employees at all levels that retaliatory acts will lead to discipline and/or discharge.
2. Illustrate the types of conduct the policy prohibits.
3. Provide a mechanism, such as a toll-free telephone number, for reporting possible acts of retaliation.
4. State that complaints will be maintained as confidential to the extent practicable, and that they will be investigated promptly and resolved.
5. After the initial investigation, follow up to ensure complainants feel comfortable in the workplace and do not perceive retaliation.

With respect to training, an effective program will include the following:

1. Describe the company's anti-harassment policy clearly.
2. Use examples and stories to explain what acts could be viewed as retaliatory, as *retaliation* might be even more difficult to define than *harassment*.
3. Explain the consequences of engaging in retaliation.
4. Encourage supervisors to check with HR or legal counsel before taking an action that might have negative consequences for an employee.

Updated policies, effective training, and thoughtful attention to possible retaliatory actions by supervisors and higher-level managers can help safeguard an organization from potential legal liability.

IMPLICATIONS FOR MANAGEMENT PRACTICE

A manager can easily feel swamped by the maze of laws, court rulings, and regulatory-agency pronouncements that he or she must navigate. Although it is true that in the foreseeable future there will continue to be legal pressure to avoid unlawful discrimination, as we saw in Chapter 1, there will be great economic pressure to find and retain top talent. Managing that talent effectively is a competitive necessity, and employers know it. Now is the time to begin developing the kinds of corporate policies and interpersonal skills that will match the needs and challenges of today's demanding work environments.

SUMMARY

Congress enacted the following laws to promote fair employment. They provide the basis for discrimination suits and subsequent judicial rulings:

- Thirteenth and Fourteenth Amendments to the U.S. Constitution.
- Civil Rights Acts of 1866 and 1871.
- Equal Pay Act of 1963.
- Title VII of the Civil Rights Act of 1964.
- Age Discrimination in Employment Act of 1967 (as amended in 1986).
- Immigration Reform and Control Act of 1986.
- Americans with Disabilities Act of 1990 (as amended in 2008).
- Civil Rights Act of 1991.
- Family and Medical Leave Act of 1993.
- Uniformed Services Employment and Reemployment Rights Act of 1994.

The Equal Employment Opportunity Commission (EEOC) and the Office of Federal Contract Compliance Programs (OFCCP) are the two major federal regulatory agencies charged with enforcing these nondiscrimination laws. The EEOC is responsible for both private and public nonfederal employers, unions, and employment agencies. The OFCCP is responsible for ensuring compliance from government contractors and subcontractors.

A considerable body of case law has developed, affecting almost all aspects of the employment relationship. We discussed case law in the following areas:

- Sex discrimination, sexual harassment, and pregnancy.
- Age discrimination.
- "Overqualified" job applicants.
- Seniority.
- Testing and interviewing.
- Personal history (specifically, pre-employment inquiries).
- Preferential selection.

The bottom line is that as managers we need to be very clear about job requirements and performance standards, we need to treat people as individuals, and we must evaluate each individual fairly, relative to those job requirements and performance standards.

KEY TERMS

equal employment opportunity (EEO)	essential functions
discrimination	disability
unequal treatment	qualified job applicants
direct evidence	systemic discrimination
circumstantial evidence	contract compliance
mixed-motive cases	case law
adverse-impact discrimination	sexual harassment
affirmative action	quid pro quo harassment
bona fide occupational qualification	hostile-environment harassment
prima facie case	seniority system
race-norming	reverse discrimination

DISCUSSION QUESTIONS

4-1. If you were asked to advise a private employer (with no government contracts) of its equal employment opportunity responsibilities, what would you say?

4-2. As a manager, what steps can you take to deal with the organizational impact of the Family and Medical Leave Act?

4-3. Prepare a brief outline of an organizational policy on sexual harassment. Be sure to include complaint, investigation, and enforcement procedures.

4-4. What steps would you take as a manager to ensure fair treatment for older employees?

4-5. Collect two policies on EEO, sexual harassment, or family and medical leave from two different employers in your area. How are they similar (or different)? Which aspects of the policies support the appropriate law?

4-6. To comply with the provisions of the Pregnant Workers Fairness Act, what types of reasonable accommodations might an employer make for a pregnant employee?

4-7. What are some of the key differences between adverse-impact discrimination and disparate-treatment discrimination?

4-8. Your boss, the chief HR officer, asks for advice on how to avoid charges of age discrimination when conducting a layoff. What would you recommend?

4-9. How might an employer ensure that the term *overqualified applicant* is not just a code for *too old*?

4-10. You are the CEO of a midsize manufacturing company. You want to be sure that all your supervisors understand the concept of retaliation and that your company is not accused of it. What actions might you take?

APPLYING YOUR KNOWLEDGE

Case 4–1   *Second-Chance Employment*

Attitudes about hiring job applicants with criminal convictions are shifting. One company that believes in second-chance hiring is Dave's Killer Bread, because when people with a criminal background return from prison, their path to a better future greatly depends on a job—a second chance. After 15 years in prison, that's just what Dave's Killer Bread co-founder Dave Dahl got when his older brother Glenn welcomed him back to the family bakery. Dave went on to create what has become the No. 1-selling organic bread and inspire a legacy of second chances at the company. Today, between 30 and 40 percent of the more than 250 employee-partners at the company's Oregon bakery have a criminal background. They hold positions ranging from entry-level jobs to managers who are responsible for critical bakery operations. See *http://www.daveskillerbread.com/about-us#about-us-1*.

Second-chance hiring sounds great in theory, but employers that conduct background checks during the hiring process must walk a fine line between restrictions on background checks and not conducting such checks at all.

Your task:

Develop a policy on second-chance hiring. Be sure to tailor your policy to the EEOC's guidance, "Consideration of arrest and conviction records in employment decisions under Title VII of the Civil Rights Act of 1964," accessible at *https://www.eeoc.gov/eeoc/newsroom/wysk/arrest_conviction records.cfm*.

REFERENCES

1. Von Drehle, D. (2003, June 24). Court mirrors public opinion. *The Washington Post*, p. A1.
2. Player, M. A. (2004). *Federal Law of Employment Discrimination in a Nutshell* (5th ed.). St. Paul, MN: West.
3. Friedman, A. (1972). Attacking discrimination through the Thirteenth Amendment. *Cleveland State Law Review* 21, pp. 165–78.
4. Peikes, L., and Mitchell, C. M. (2006, Aug.). 2nd Circuit: Employee working abroad has no remedy for extraterritorial discriminatory conduct. *HRMagazine News*, p. 1.
5. *Johnson v. Railway Express Agency Inc.* (1975). 95 S. Ct. 1716.
6. Punitive damages are awarded in civil cases to punish or deter a defendant's conduct and are separate from compensatory damages, which are intended to reimburse a plaintiff for injuries or harm.
7. *CBOCS West Inc. v. Humphries.* (2008). 128 S. Ct. 1951.
8. Civil rights statutes extended to Arabs, Jews. (1987, May 19). *Daily Labor Report*, pp. 1, 2, 6.
9. Stites, J. (2005, May). Equal pay for the sexes. *HRMagazine*, pp. 64–69.
10. Equal Employment Opportunity Commission. Charge statistics: FY 1997 through FY 2019. Retrieved from *https://www.eeoc.gov/eeoc/statistics/enforcement/charges.cfm* on Mar. 9, 2020.
11. Society for Human Resources Management. (2011, Jan. 19). Novartis pays $152.5 million for bias. Retrieved from *www.shrm.org/LegalIssues/StateandLocalResources/Pages/NovartisPays-1525MillionforBias.aspx* on June 14, 2011. *See also* Wilson, D. (2010, May 17). Women win a bias suit against Novartis. *The New York Times*. Retrieved from *http://www.nytimes.com/2010/05/18/business/18novartis.html?scp=1&sq=Women%20win%20a%20bias%20-suit%20against%20Novartis&st=cse* on May 18, 2010.
12. Smith, A. (2017, Oct.26). Title VII prohibits discrimination against men. *SHRM Online*. Retrieved from *https://www.shrm.org/resourcesandtools/legal-and-compliance/employment-law/pages/title-vii-discrimination-men.aspx* on Oct. 27, 2017. See also Thompson, C. (2008, Mar.). Standard should not have been applied to hearing test. *HRMagazine*, p. 88.
13. *Furnco Construction Corp. v. Waters* (1978). 438 U.S. 567.
14. *McDonnell Douglas v. Green* (1973). 411 U.S. 972.
15. Civil Rights Act of 1991, Public Law No. 102-166, 105 Stat. 1071 (1991). Codified as amended at 42 U.S.C., Section 1981, 2000e *et seq.*
16. Valenza, G. (1999, Nov.-Dec.). The Supreme Court creates a safe harbor from liability for punitive damages. *Legal Report*. Washington, DC: Society for Human Resource Management, pp. 5–8.
17. Lau, S. (2008, Feb.). U.S. laws abroad. *HRMagazine*, p. 33.
18. *Gross v. FBL Financial Services Inc.* (2009). 129 S. Ct. 2343.
19. Smith. A. (2019, Oct. 9). Supreme Court declines to decide if ADEA covers job applicants. *SHRM Online*. Retrieved from *https://www.shrm.org/resourcesandtools/legal-and-compliance/employment-law/pages/supreme-court-adea-job-applicants.aspx* on Oct. 10, 2019.
20. Winerip, M. (2013, Dec. 7). Pushed out of a job early. *The New York Times*. Retrieved from *http://www.nytimes.com/2013/12/07/booming/pushed-out-of-a-job-early.html?r=0* on Dec. 14, 2013.
21. Segal, J. A. (2008, July). Severance strategies. *HRMagazine*, pp. 95–98.
22. Ibid.
23. *Parsons v. Pioneer Hi-Bred Int'l Inc.* (2006, May 19). 8th Cir., No. 05-3496.
24. Chichoni, H. (2011, Feb.). I-9 compliance crackdowns. *HRMagazine*, pp. 63–68.
25. Henderson, J. (2017, Feb.). Six tips to help employers maintain I-9 compliance. *HR Professionals Magazine*, p. 24.
26. Heathfield, S. M. (2017, Feb. 15). What every employer should know about the I-9 Form. Retrieved from *www.thebalance.com/i-9-form-employment-eligibility-verification-form-1918902* on July 11, 2017.
27. Meckler, L. (2018, May 15). Workplace inspections rise in pursuit of illegal hirings. *The Wall Street Journal*, p. A3.

28. Calfas, J. (2015, July 30). CDC: 1 in 5 American adults live with a disability. *USA Today.* Retrieved from *http://www.usatoday.com/story/news/nation/2015/07/30/american-adults-disability/30881975/* on Mar. 25, 2017.

29. U.S. Bureau of Labor Statistics. (2020, Feb. 26). Persons with a disability: Labor force characteristics summary. Retrieved from *https://www.bls.gov/news.release/disabl.nr0.htm* on Mar. 10, 2020.

30. ADA National Network. (n.d.). An overview of the Americans with Disabilities Act. Retrieved from *https://adata.org/factsheet/ADA-overview* on Mar. 10, 2020.

31. Rhodes, J. (2018, Sept. 4). Job description didn't establish essential function. *SHRM Online.* Retrieved from *https://www.shrm.org/ResourcesAndTools/legal-and-compliance/employment-law/Pages/Court-Report-job-description-did-not-establish-essential-function.aspx* on Sept. 5, 2018. *See also* Danaher, M. G. (2013, Apr. 26). Employer's job description instrumental in determining essential duties. Retrieved from *http://www.shrm.org/LegalIssues/FederalResources/Pages/Employers-Job-Description-Instrumental-Determining-Essential-Duties.aspx* on May 15, 2013.

32. Courtner, M. (2020). ADA's "regarded as" test. *HR Professionals Magazine, 10*(1), pp. 20, 21. *See also* Equal Employment Opportunity Commission. Americans with Disabilities Act, questions and answers. Retrieved from *www.eeoc.gov/eeoc/publications/adaqa1.cfm* on Mar. 25, 2017.

33. Ibid. *See also* Batiste, L. C. (2011). Accommodation and compliance series: Employees with drug addiction. Retrieved from *http://askjan.org/media/drugadd.html* on June 14, 2011.

34. Americans with Disabilities Act of 1990, Public Law No. 101–336, 104 Stat. 328 (1990). Codified at 42 U.S.C., Section 12101 *et seq.*

35. Weber (2014), op. cit.

36. Achille, R. S. (2013, Dec. 5). ADAAA requires proof of disability. Retrieved from *www.shrm.org* on Mar. 23, 2014.

37. Gibson, T. (2016, Nov.). Treading the muddy waters of the ADAAA. *HR Professionals Magazine,* pp. 34, 35. *See also* EEOC, Americans with Disabilities Act, questions and answers, op. cit.

38. Segal, J. A. (2010, June). ADA game changer. *HRMagazine,* pp. 121–26. *See also* Willman, S. K. (2003, Jan.–Feb.). Tips for minimizing abuses of the Americans with Disabilities Act. *Legal Report.* Alexandria, VA: Society for Human Resource Management, pp. 3–8. *See also* Janove, J. W. (2003, Mar.). Skating through the minefield. *HRMagazine,* pp. 107–13.

39. EEOC. The ADA: Your responsibilities as an employer. Retrieved from *www.eeoc.gov/facts/ada17.html* on Mar. 24, 2017. *See also* Smith, A. (2016, June 22). Don't flunk the reasonable accommodation duty. Retrieved from *www.shrm.org/hr-today/news/hr-news/pages/dont-flunk-the-reasonable-accommodation-duty.aspx* on June 27, 2016.

40. Mook, J. (2007, Jan.). Accommodation paradigm shifts. *HRMagazine,* pp. 115–20. *See also* Campbell, W. J., and Reilly, M. E. (2000). Accommodations for persons with disabilities. In J. F. Kehoe (Ed.), *Managing Selection in Changing Organizations.* San Francisco: Jossey-Bass, pp. 319–67.

41. Binkley, R. (2019). Are shortened work weeks a required ADA accommodation? *HR Professionals Magazine 9*(7), pp. 30, 31.

42. EEOC, The ADA: Your responsibilities as an employer, op. cit.

43. Nagele-Piazza, L. (2020, Jan. 21). Workplace drug testing: Can employers still screen for marijuana? *SHRM Online.* Retrieved from https://www.shrm.org/resourcesandtools/legal-and-compliance/state-and-local-updates/pages/can-employers-still-test-for-marijuana.aspx on Jan. 22, 2020.

44. Binkley (2019), op. cit. *See also* Zellers, V. (2009, Jan.). Make a resolution: ADA training. *HRMagazine,* pp. 81–83.

45. U.S. Department of Labor. (n.d.). Americans with Disabilities Act. Retrieved from *https://www.dol.gov/general/topic/disability/ada* on Mar. 10, 2020.

46. *Kolstad v. American Dental Association.* (1999). 119 S. Ct. 2118.

47. Rhodes, J. (2017, Mar. 15). Employee denied FMLA leave for sick grandparent can go to jury. Retrieved from *www.shrm.org/resourcesandtools/legal-and-compliance/employment-law/pages/fmla-leave-sick-grandfather-in-place-of-parent.aspx* on Mar. 22, 2017.

48. McCutchen, T. D. (2013, July 12). Managing family and medical leave. Retrieved from *www.shrm.org* on Mar. 23, 2014. *See also* Cadrain, D. (2010, July). A leave law that just won't go away. *HRMagazine*, pp. 49–52.

49. U. S. Deptartment of Labor, Wage and Hour Division. (n.d.). Fact Sheet #28M: The military family leave provisions under the Family and Medical Leave Act . Retrieved from *https://www.dol.gov/sites/dolgov/files/WHD/legacy/files/whdfs28m.pdf* on Mar. 10, 2020.

50. Smith, A. (2017, Mar. 9). Have workers in the military? The 4 USERRA requirements you should know. Retrieved from *www.shrm.org/resourcesandtools/legal-and-compliance/employment-law/pages/4-userra-requirements.aspx* on Mar. 23, 2017. *See also* Thelen, J. (2006, Mar.–Apr.). Workplace rights for service members: The USERRA regulations deconstructed. *Legal Report*, pp. 1–8.

51. Jackson Lewis. (2014, Mar. 5). Employers must treat employees on military leave like those on comparable leaves. Retrieved from *http://www.shrm.org/legalissues/federalresources/pages/employees-military-leave.aspx* on Mar. 27, 2014. *See also* The Uniformed Services Employment and Reemployment Rights Act of 1994, Public Law 102–353; H. R. 995.

52. EEOC. EEOC releases fiscal year 2019 enforcement and litigation data. Retrieved from *https://www.eeoc.gov/eeoc/newsroom/release/1-24-20.cfm* on Mar. 10, 2020. *See also* EEOC. What you can expect after filing a charge. Retrieved from *https://www.eeoc.gov/employees/process.cfm* on Mar. 10, 2020.

53. EEOC enforcement and litigation statistics, FY 1997 through FY 2019. Retrieved from *https://www.eeoc.gov/eeoc/statistics/enforcement/all.cfm* on Mar. 11, 2020.

54. EEOC's regulations are published annually in Title 29 of the Code of Federal Regulations, Parts 1600 through 1699. They are available online through the U.S. Government Printing Office.

55. *Albemarle Paper Company v. Moody.* (1975). 442 U.S. 407.

56. Smith, A. (2019, Sept. 17). How do the EEOC and OFCCP use EEO-1 reports? *SHRM Online.* Retrieved from *https://www.shrm.org/resourcesandtools/legal-and-compliance/employment-law/pages/eeoc-ofccp-use-eeo-1-reports.aspx* on Sept. 18, 2019.

57. Weber (2014), op. cit.

58. U. S. Department of Labor. (2019, Aug. 1). OFCCP at a glance. Retrieved from *https://www.dol.gov/ofccp/CAGuides/files/At-A-Glance-WEB_080119_CONTR508c.pdf* on Mar. 10, 2020.

59. See, for example, Smith, A. (2013, Aug. 28). OFCCP backs away from rigid affirmative action requirements for people with disabilities. Retrieved from *http://www.shrm.org/legalissues/federalresources/pages/ofccp-rules.aspx* on Oct. 8, 2013.

60. U.S. Department of Labor. (2019). OFCCP by the numbers. Retrieved from *https://www.dol.gov/ofccp/BTN/* on Mar. 10, 2020.

61. *Wygant v. Jackson Board of Education.* (1986). 106 S. Ct. 1842. *See also Local 28 Sheet MetalWorkers v. EEOC.* (1986). 106 S. Ct. 3019. *See also Local 93 Firefighters v. Cleveland.* (1986). 106 S. Ct. 3063.

62. Bravin, J., and Kendall, B (2020, June 16). Justices rule LGBT workers are protected. *The Wall Street Journal*, pp. A1, A2.

63. Liptak, A. (2020, June 16). Civil rights law protects gay and transgender workers, Supreme Court rules. *The New York Times.* Retrieved from *www.nytimes.com/2020/06/15/us/gay-transgender-workers-supreme-court.html* on June 16, 2020.

64. *Johnson v. Santa Clara Transportation Agency.* (1987, Mar. 26). 107 S. Ct. 1442, 43 FEP Cases 411.

65. Randazzo, S. (2016, July 26). Qualcomm to pay $19.5 million to settle claims of bias against women. *The Wall Street Journal.* Retrieved from *www.wsj.com/articles/qualcomm-to-pay-19-5-million-to-settle-claims-of-bias-against-women-1469571756* on July 27, 2016. *See also Carter v. Wells Fargo Advisors LLC*, C.A. No. 09-01752, D. D. C. 2011. *See also* Smith, A. (2011, June 10). Wells Fargo settles sex discrimination claim for $32 million. Retrieved from *http://www.shrm.org/legalissues/federalresources/pages/wellsfargo.aspx* on July 25, 2012.

66. Fiske, S. T. (2010). Interpersonal stratification: Status, power, and subordination. In S. T. Fiske, D. T. Gilbert, and G. Lindzey (Eds.), *Handbook of Social Psychology* (5th ed.). New York: Wiley, pp. 941–82. *See also* Crosby, F. J., Stockdale, M. S., and Ropp, S. A. (Eds.). (2007). *Sex Discrimination in the Workplace.* Malden, MA: Blackwell. *See also* Gutek, B. A.,

and Stockdale, M. S. (2005). Sex discrimination in employment. In F. J. Landy (Ed.), *Employment Discrimination Litigation*. San Francisco: Jossey-Bass, pp. 229-55.

67. Guidelines on discrimination because of sex, 29CFR1604.10. Employment policies relating to pregnancy and childbirth (revised July 1, 2003).

68. EEOC. Pregnancy discrimination charges FY2010–FY2019. Retrieved from *https://www.eeoc.gov/eeoc/statistics/enforcement/pregnancy_new.cfm* on Mar. 12, 2020.

69. EEOC. Enforcement guidance: Pregnancy discrimination and related issues. (2015, June 25). Retrieved from *www.eeoc.gov/laws/guidance/pregnancy_guidance.cfm* on Mar. 12, 2020.

70. S.942-113th Congress (2013-2014). Pregnant Workers Fairness Act. Retrieved from *http://beta.congress.gov/bill/113th-congress/senate-bill/942* on Mar. 28, 2014. *See also* Danaher, M. G. (2017, June 28). Employer pays $100,000 after firing just-hired pregnant applicant. *SHRM Online*. Retrieved from www.shrm.org/resourcesandtools/legal-and-compliance/employment-law/pages/court-report-just-hired-fired-pregnant-employee.aspx on June 29, 2017.

71. Kitroeff, N., and Silver-Greenberg, J. (2018, June 15). Pregnancy discrimination is rampant inside America's biggest companies. *The New York Times*. Retrieved from *https://www.nytimes.com/interactive/2018/06/15/business/pregnancy-discrimination.html* on Mar. 12, 2020.

72. Fox, A. (2014, Feb. 1). How to accommodate pregnant employees. *SHRM Online*. Retrieved from www.shrm.org/hr-today/news/hr-magazine/pages/0214-pregnancy-accommodation.aspx on Feb. 14, 2014. *See also* Families & Work Institute and Society for Human Resource Management. (2014). *2014 Guide to Bold New Ideas for Making Work Work*. Alexandria, VA: SHRM.

73. What to expect when you're expecting. (2008, May 26). *BusinessWeek*, p. 17.

74. EEOC. (2018, July 1). Guidelines on discrimination because of sex. Code of Federal Regulations. Retrieved from *https://www.govinfo.gov/content/pkg/CFR-2018-title29-vol4/xml/CFR-2018-title29-vol4-part1604.xml* on Mar. 12, 2020.

75. North, A. (2019, Oct. 4). 7 positive changes that have come from the #MeToo movement. Retrieved from *https://www.vox.com/identities/2019/10/4/20852639/me-too-movement-sexual-harassment-law-2019* on Mar. 12, 2020.

76. Calderone, F. (2019, July). Men too. *HRM Magazine, 56*(7), pp. 37, 38. *See also* What does "sexual harassment" mean today? (2017, Jan. 31). *Knowledge@Wharton*. Retrieved from *http://knowledge.wharton.upenn.edu/article/sexual-harassment-mean-today/* on Feb. 1, 2017.

77. EEOC settlements reflect #MeToo era. (2020, Spring). *HRMagazine* **65**(1), p. 9. *See also* EEOC. Charges alleging sex-based harassment, FY2010–FY2019. Retrieved from *https://www.eeoc.gov/eeoc/statistics/enforcement/sexual_harassment_new.cfm* on Mar. 12, 2020.

78. *Barnes v. Costle*. (1977). 561 F. 2d 983 (D. C. Cir.). *See also* Nagele-Piazza, L. (2016, Oct. 5). Texas Roadhouse ends sexual harassment suit for $1.4M. *SHRM Online*. Retrieved from *https://www.shrm.org/resourcesandtools/legal-and-compliance/employment-law/pages/texas-roadhouse-sexual-harassment-settlement.aspx* on Oct. 6, 2016.

79. *Burlington Industries, Inc. v. Ellerth*. (1998, June 26). 118 S. Ct. 2257.

80. *Faragher v. City of Boca Raton*. (1998, June 26). 118 S. Ct. 2275.

81. Deschenaux, J. (2013, June 24). High court narrowly defines "supervisor." Retrieved from *http://www.shrm.org/legalissues/federalresources/pages/high-court-narrowly-defines-supervisor.aspx* on Mar. 18, 2014.

82. *Meritor Savings Bank v. Vinson*. (1986). 477 U.S. 57.

83. Ibid.

84. Cadrain, D. (2014, Mar. 12). Employee wins judgment against coworker for sexual harassment. Retrieved from *http://www.shrm.org/legalissues/stateandlocalresources/pages/kan-employee-wins-judgment-against-co-worker-sexual-harassment.aspx* on Mar. 28, 2014. *See also* France, A. H. (2011, Feb. 16). 10th Circuit: dismissal of claim of sexual harassment by non-employee reversed. Retrieved from *http://www.shrm.org/LegalIssues/FederalResources/Pages/10thCircuitDismissal.aspx* on June 14, 2011.

85. *Pennsylvania State Police v. Suders*. 93 Fair Employment Practices Cases (BNA) 1473 (2004).

86. Bolden-Barrett, V. (2017, Aug. 21). Ford pays $10M to settle sexual harassment charges at Chicago plant. *HRDive*. Retrieved from *https://www.hrdive.com/news/ford-pays-10m-to-settle-sexual-harassment-charges-at-chicago-plants/503026/* on Aug. 23, 2017. See also What does "sexual harassment" mean today? (2017), op. cit.

87. Smith, A. (2017, Mar. 15). Use four harassment checklists, EEOC Commissioner says. Retrieved from *www.shrm.org/resourcesandtools/legal-and-compliance/employment-law/pages/eeo-commissioner-use-four-harassment-checklists.aspx* on Mar. 16, 2017. *See also* Segal, J. (2016, Nov.). 17 tips for anti-harassment training. *HRMagazine*, pp. 74, 75.

88. For an example of an actual policy, see Sexual harassment policy and complaint/investigation procedure. (n.d.). Retrieved from *https://www.shrm.org/resourcesandtools/tools-and-samples/policies/pages/cms_000554.aspx* on Mar. 13, 2020.

89. *Schwager v. Sun Oil Company of PA.* (1979). 591 F. 2d 58 (10th Cir.).

90. Ibid. See also Danaher, M. G. (2009). Termination for obsolete skill set does not constitute age discrimination. *HRMagazine*, p. 73.

91. Sterns, H. L., Doverspike, D., and Lax, G. A. (2005). The Age Discrimination in Employment Act. In F. J. Landy (Ed.), *Employment Discrimination Litigation*. San Francisco: Jossey-Bass, pp. 256-93. *See also* Bravin, J. (2005, Mar. 31). Court expands age-bias claims for work force. *The Wall Street Journal*, pp. B1-B3.

92. Smith, A. (2019, Feb. 4). 7th Circuit curtails applicants' age-discrimination lawsuits. *SHRM Online*. Retrieved from *https://www.shrm.org/resourcesandtools/legal-and-compliance/employment-law/pages/applicant-age-discrimination-lawsuits-curtailed.aspx* on Feb. 5, 2019. *See also* Cohen, P. (2019, June 7). New evidence of age bias in hiring, and a push to fight it. *The New York Times*. Retrieved from *https://www.nytimes.com/2019/06/07/business/economy/age-discrimination-jobs-hiring.html* on June 10, 2019.

93. EEOC. Age Discrimination in Employment Act charges filed with the EEOC, FY 1997-FY 2019. Retrieved from *https://www.eeoc.gov/eeoc/statistics/enforcement/adea.cfm* on Mar. 13, 2020.

94. Wilkie, D. (2013, Nov. 19). "Overqualified": Is it code for "too old"? Retrieved from *http://www.shrm.org/hrdisciplines/diversity/articles/pages/older-workers-discrimination.aspx* on Mar. 21, 2014.

95. Hastings, R. R. (2008, Dec. 1). Overcoming the 'Overqualified' label. Retrieved from *http://www.shrm.org/HRCareers/Pages/shrm_123107.aspx* on June 15, 2011. *See also* Wells, S. J. (2004, Oct.). Too good to hire? *HRMagazine*. Retrieved from *http://www.shrm.org/hrmagazine/articles/1004/1004covstory.asp* on June 15, 2011.

96. What is seniority and how is it determined? (2009, May 7). Retrieved from *http://www.shrm.org/TemplatesTools/hrqa/Pages/Whatisseniority.aspx* on June 15, 2011. *See also* *California Brewers Association v. Bryant.* (1982). 444 U.S. 598, p. 605.

97. See, for example, *Franks v. Bowman Transportation Co.* (1976). 424 U.S. 747. *See also International Brotherhood of Teamsters v. United States.* (1977). 432 U.S. 324. *See also American Tobacco Company v. Patterson.* (1982). 535 F. 2d 257 (CA-4). *See also* Gordon, M. E., and Johnson, W. A. (1982). Seniority: A review of its legal and scientific standing. *Personnel Psychology* 35, pp. 255-80.

98. *Firefighters Local Union No. 1784 v. Stotts.* (1984). 104 S. Ct. 2576.

99. *Wygant v. Jackson Board of Education.* (1986). 106 S. Ct. 1842.

100. Greenhouse, L. (1984, June 13). Seniority is held to outweigh race as a layoff guide. *The New York Times*, pp. A1, B12.

101. Britt, L. P., III. (1984). Affirmative action: Is there life after Stotts? *Personnel Administrator* 29(9), pp. 96-100.

102. *US Airways, Inc. v. Barnett.* (00-1250) 535 U.S. 391 (2002) 228 F. 3d 1105.

103. Americans with Disabilities Act, as amended. (2016, July 16). Retrieved from *www.shrm.org/hr-today/public-policy/hr-public-policy-issues/pages/americanswithdisabilityactof1990,asamended.aspx* on Mar. 26, 2017.

104. *Griggs v. Duke Power Company.* (1971). 402 U.S. 424.

105. Smith, A. (2016, June 14). DOL cracks down on company's use of hiring tests. Retrieved from *www.shrm.org/resourcesandtools/legal-and-compliance/employment-law/pages/dol-cracks-down-on-companys-use-of-hiring-tests.aspx* on June 18, 2016.

106. Society for Industrial and Organization Psychology, Inc. (2018). *Principles for the Validation and Use of Personnel Selection Procedures* (5th ed.). Bowling Green, OH: Author. *See also* Committee on Psychological Tests and Assessment, American Psychological Association. (1996, June). Statement on the disclosure of test data. *American Psychologist* 51, pp. 644–48.

107. Justices uphold utility's stand on job testing. (1979, Mar. 6). *The Wall Street Journal*, p. 4.

108. *Watson v. Fort Worth Bank & Trust.* (1988). 108 S. Ct. 299.

109. Schmitt, N. W., Arnold, J. D., and Nieminen, L. (2017). Validation strategies for primary studies. In J. L. Farr and N. T. Tippins, *Handbook of Employee Selection* (2nd ed.). New York: Routledge, pp. 34–55. *See also* McPhail, S. M. (Ed.). (2007). *Alternative Validation Strategies.* San Francisco: Jossey-Bass.

110. *EEOC v. Radiator Specialty Company.* (1979). 610 F. 2d 178 (4th Cir.).

111. *Dothard v. Rawlinson.* (1977). 433 U.S. 321.

112. *Gregory v. Litton Systems Inc.* (1973). 472 F. 2d 631 (9th Cir.). *See also* Pearson, J. (2014, Jan. 21). Arrested: By the time they turn 23 years old, many men have become involved with the criminal justice system for non-traffic offenses. *The Denver Post*, p. 2A.

113. *Webster v. Redmond.* (1979). 599 F. 2d 793 (7th Cir.).

114. *Hyland v. Fukada.* (1978). 580 F. 2d 977 (9th Cir.). *See also* Smith, A. (2012, Jan. 11). Pepsi settles dispute over criminal background checks for $3.13 million. Retrieved from *http://www.shrm.org/legalissues/federalresources/pages/pepsisettles.aspx* on Mar. 28, 2013.

115. Avery, B. (2019, July 1). Ban the box: U.S. cities, counties, and states adopt fair hiring practices. *National Employment Law Project.* Retrieved from *https://www.nelp.org/publication/ban-the-box-fair-chance-hiring-state-and-local-guide/* on Mar. 13, 2020. *See also* Epperson, M. P., & O'Neill, M. O. (2019, May). Second-chance employment. *HR Professionals Magazine* **9**(5), pp. 14, 15.

116. Sammer, J. (2019, June 5). Employers adjust to salary-history bans. *SHRM Online.* Retrieved from *https://www.shrm.org/resourcesandtools/hr-topics/compensation/pages/employers-adjust-to-salary-history-bans.aspx* on June 6, 2019.

117. Smith, A. (2017, Oct. 26). Title VII prohibits discrimination against men. *SHRM Online.* Retrieved from *https://www.shrm.org/resourcesandtools/legal-and-compliance/employment-law/pages/title-vii-discrimination-men.aspx* on Oct. 27, 2017. See also *McDonald v. Santa Fe Transportation Co.* (1976). 427 U.S. 273.

118. Von Drehle, D. (2003, June 24). Court mirrors public opinion. *The Washington Post*, p. A1.

119. *Gratz v. Bollinger.* (2003, June 23). 539 U.S. 244. *See also Grutter v. Bollinger.* (2003). 539 U.S. 306.

120. Liptak, A. (2016, June 23). Supreme Court upholds affirmative action program at University of Texas. Retrieved from *www.nytimes.com/2016/06/24/us/politics/supreme-court-affirmative-action-university-of-texas.html* on Mar. 26, 2017. See also Liptak, A. (2014, Apr. 22). Court backs Michigan on affirmative action. *The New York Times.* Retrieved from *www.nytimes.com/2014/04/23/us/supreme-court-michigan-affirmative-action-ban.html?r=0* on May 5, 2014.

121. Kronholz, J., Tomsho, R., and Forelle, C. (2003). High court's ruling on race could affect business hiring. *The Wall Street Journal*, pp. A1, A6.

2

EMPLOYMENT

Now that you understand the competitive, technical, and legal environments within which HR management activities take place, it is time to address several major aspects of the employment process: encouraging workforce diversity and inclusion, identifying the numbers and mix of skills of people required to do the work, recruiting candidates, and hiring employees. Chapter 5 addresses diversity and inclusion. Chapter 6 focuses on strategic workforce planning and its link to business strategy, including leadership succession. Chapter 7 considers the planning, implementation, and evaluation of recruitment operations. Finally, Chapter 8 examines initial screening and employee selection—why they are important, how they are done, and how they can be evaluated.

5 | DIVERSITY AND INCLUSION

Questions This Chapter Will Help Managers Answer

LO 5-1 Are there business and ethical reasons I should pay attention to diversity and inclusion (D&I)?

LO 5-2 What are leading companies doing in this area?

LO 5-3 What works when it comes to changing employee attitudes and behaviors toward D&I?

LO 5-4 How can I maximize the potential of a gender and racially/ethnically diverse workforce?

LO 5-5 What can I do to accommodate women and older workers?

THE BUSINESS AND ETHICAL CASES FOR D&I ARE NOT ENOUGH TO BRING ABOUT REAL CHANGE*

Diversity, the ability to live and work with people who are different from us, matters because we increasingly live in a global world that has become deeply interconnected. It should come as no surprise, then, that an increasing body of evidence shows that companies with more diverse workforces perform better financially. For example, using data from 1,000 major companies across 12 countries, McKinsey & Co. examined metrics such as financial results and the composition of top management and boards. The findings were compelling.

- Companies in the top quartile for racial and ethnic diversity are 33 percent more likely to outperform competitors on profits than those in the bottom quartile.
- Companies in the top quartile for gender diversity are 21 percent more likely to outperform competitors on profits than those in the bottom quartile. Having gender diversity on executive teams is consistently positively correlated with higher profitability across geographies
- Companies in the bottom quartile on both gender and ethnic diversity underperform their industry peers by 29 percent on profitability
- The unequal performance of companies in the same industry and the same country implies that diversity is a competitive differentiator that shifts market share toward more diverse companies.

Although correlation does not equal causation (greater gender and ethnic diversity in senior-executive teams does not translate automatically into more profit), the correlation does indicate that when companies commit themselves to diverse leadership, they are more successful. The fact is, diversity is not just about mirroring a country's demographics. It's also about innovation and performance. It stands to reason—and has been demonstrated in other studies—that more diverse companies are better able to win top talent and improve their customer orientation, employee satisfaction, and decision making, leading to a virtuous cycle of increasing returns.

Diversity beyond gender and ethnicity/race (such as diversity in age and sexual orientation) as well as diversity of experience (such as military veterans or those with a global mind-set and cultural fluency) are also likely to bring some level of competitive advantage for firms that are able to attract and retain such talent. Sounds logical, doesn't it? Yet diversity alone is not the answer. The best companies also practice inclusion.

The Society for Human Resource Management defines **inclusion** as a work environment in which all individuals are treated fairly and respectfully, have equal access to opportunities and resources, and can contribute fully to the organization's success. More succinctly: Diversity is being invited to the party; inclusion is being asked to dance. It's no exaggeration to say that the full potential of diversity can only be realized when all members of an organization feel included, that they belong, and that they are respected for who they are and what they offer.

Sources: Hunt, V., Yee, L., Prince, S., & Dixon-Fyle, S. (2018, Jan.). Delivering through diversity. *McKinsey & Co.* Retrieved from *https://www.mckinsey.com/business-functions/organization/our-insights/delivering-through-diversity* on Mar. 10, 2020. Garrett, G. (2018, Aug. 30). Why diversity is about much more than numbers. *Knowledge@Wharton.* Retrieved from *https://knowledge.wharton.upenn.edu/article/why-diversity-is-about-much-more-than-numbers/* on Aug. 31, 2018. Dobbin, F., and Kalev, A. (2016, July-Aug.). Why diversity programs fail, and what works better. *Harvard Business Review*, pp. 52-60. Parsi, N. (2017, Feb.). Diversity and innovation. *HRMagazine* 62(1), pp. 39-45.

Certainly the business case for D&I is important, but achieving it is harder than completing a typical organizational transformation due to barriers such as unconscious bias. Dealing with those who are like us–who understand what we mean without needing much explanation, who share experiences and an outlook–feels comfortable and reassuring. Most people are not consciously hostile to those who are not at the table, but the biases that keep us from including new kinds of people often exist outside our field of awareness. A focus on inclusion explicitly addresses such barriers and includes visible commitment from the leadership team. In the conclusion to this case, we will examine what some progressive companies are doing to overcome the hurdles.

Challenges

1. What is the ethical rationale for fostering diversity and inclusion?
2. Is there additional information beyond the information presented here that you feel is necessary to make the business case for diversity and inclusion?
3. What steps can you take as a manager to become more effective in a work environment that is more diverse than ever?

As we noted in Chapter 1, the U.S. workforce is diverse–and it will become more so.[1]

- The demographics of the United States are changing so dramatically that over the coming decades it will be impossible for employers to fill their ranks with members of the traditional workforce–white males. By 2040, an estimated 70 percent of American workers will be either women or members of what are now racial minorities.
- More than half the U.S. workforce now consists of racial minorities (i.e., non-white), **ethnic minorities** (i.e., people classified according to common traits and customs), immigrants, and women.
- Women's share of the labor force slightly exceeded that of men in 2019 (50.04 percent of jobs). Yet a gap in the labor-force participation rate of men and women 16 and up persists. It was 57.7 percent for women versus 69.2 percent for men.[2]
- White non-Hispanics accounted for 64.6 percent of the labor force in 2014. That percentage will drop to 59.6 by 2024.
- From 2014 to 2024, Asians' share of the labor force will increase from 5.6 to 6.4 percent, the Hispanic share will increase from 15.5 to 18.3 percent, and the African American share will increase slowly from 12.4 to 12.9 percent.
- The labor force will continue to age, with the 55-and-older group moving from 34.2 to 38.2 percent from 2014 to 2024. Over the same time period, the percentage in the 25- to 54-year age group will shrink from 50.2 to 47.9 percent, and for the 16- to 24-year age group, it will shrink from 15.6 to 13.8 percent.

These demographic facts do not indicate that a diverse workforce is something a company ought to have. Rather, they tell us that all companies already do have–or soon will have–diverse workforces. As we have seen in our chapter-opening vignette, D&I presents an opportunity for firms to compete and win in the global marketplace.

THE MANY DIMENSIONS OF WORKFORCE DIVERSITY

To celebrate diversity is to appreciate and value individual differences. **Managing diversity** means establishing a heterogeneous workforce (including white men) to perform to its potential in an equitable work environment where no member or group of members has an advantage or a disadvantage.[3] This is a pragmatic business strategy that focuses on maximizing the productivity, creativity, and commitment of the workforce while meeting the needs of diverse consumer groups.

Think back to our discussion of Title VII of the 1964 Civil Rights Act in Chapter 4. Title VII makes it illegal to discriminate against employees on the basis of sex, race, religion, color, or national origin. Subsequently, many employers focused narrowly on ridding their workplaces of discrimination based on a set of visual cues–race, gender, or the wearing of religious garments at work. Yet diversity has many more dimensions than those few, as Figure 5-1 illustrates.[4]

As Figure 5-1 shows, visible characteristics are the most obvious dimensions of diversity, but there are many more, including those that are visible or invisible (e.g., veteran status, sexual orientation, religion, or language). Finally, there are invisible dimensions that complete the full mosaic of diversity. These include characteristics like education, life experiences, functional area at work (accounting, information technology, finance, marketing, sales, HR), family status, and perspectives.

In fact, each of us has many different group affiliations or identities. For example, an employee may be the "older person" in the morning meeting, "the mom" at lunch, "the bean counter" on the afternoon teleconference, and the "Asian American" in a train car filled with non-Asians, all in the course of a single day. The challenge for organizations, and for the managers who run them, is to leverage this diversity in ways that will capitalize on the strengths that each person brings, and to encourage

Figure 5–1

The Many Dimensions of Diversity

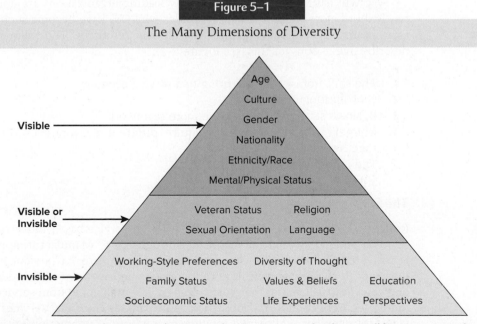

Source: Bersin by Deloitte, 2014. Cited in Bersin, J. (2015, Dec. 6). Why diversity and inclusion will be a top priority for 2016. *Forbes.* Retrieved from *www.forbes.com/sites/joshbersin/2015/12/06/why-diversity-and-inclusion-will-be-a-top-priority-for-2016/#2a8e53d12ed5* on Jan. 14, 2016.

Figure 5–2

Increased diversity in the workforce meshes well with evolving changes in organizations and markets.

behaviors that will make the organization an employer of choice as well as one that can generate products or services that make it successful in the marketplace.

We will have more to say about how leading organizations are doing this currently, but before we do that, let's consider why D&I have become such key considerations in managing an organization's human resources. The following sections describe five reasons for this (see Figure 5–2):

1. The shift from a manufacturing to a service economy.
2. Globalization of markets.
2. Business strategies that require more teamwork.
4. Mergers and alliances that require different corporate cultures to work together.
5. The changing labor market.

The Service Economy

Roughly 71 percent of U.S. employees work in service-based industries, and that figure is projected to stay at that level through 2024.[5] Manufacturing employment is projected to drop slightly from 8.1 percent in 2014 to 7.1 percent in 2024. Productivity in this sector continues to increase, whereas the need for additional labor decreases. Virtually all of the growth in new jobs will come from service-producing industries. Service-industry jobs, such as in banking, financial services, health services, tourism, hospitality, and retailing, imply lots of interaction with customers. Service employees need to be able to "read" their customers–to understand them, to anticipate and monitor their needs and expectations, and to respond sensitively and appropriately to those needs and expectations. In the service game, "customer literacy" is an essential skill.

A growing number of companies now realize that their workforces should mirror their customers. Similarities in culture, dress, and language between service workers and customers create more efficient interactions between them and better business for the firm. Bank of America in Baltimore discovered this when it studied the customer-retention records for its branches. The branches showing highest customer loyalty recruited locally to hire tellers, who could swap neighborhood gossip.[6]

When companies discover they can communicate better with their customers through employees who are similar to their customers, those companies then realize they have increased their internal diversity. And that means they have to make every employee feel that he or she belongs. According to the global head of D&I at BlackRock, the world's largest asset manager, diversity is a universal concept that translates in many cultures as "belonging-ness." People want to work at companies where D&I is baked into their DNA.[7]

The Globalization of Markets

As organizations around the world compete for customers, they offer customers choices unavailable to them domestically. Customers everywhere worship two words, *cheap* and *available*. With more options to choose from, customers have more power to insist that their needs and preferences be satisfied. To satisfy them, firms have to understand those needs and preferences. Some firms have established a strong local presence (e.g., advertisements for Japanese-made cars that showcase local dealerships and satisfied American owners); others have forged strategic international alliances (e.g., Google and Italian eyewear maker Luxottica).[8] In domestic as well as international markets, diversity is a fact of modern organizational life. Successful leaders know that and they are working hard to manage it effectively

Business Strategies That Require More Teamwork

To survive, to serve, and to succeed, organizations need to accomplish goals that are defined more broadly than ever before (e.g., world-class quality, reliability, and customer service), which means carrying out strategies that no one part of the organization can execute alone. For example, if a firm's business strategy emphasizes speed in every function (in developing new products, producing them, distributing them, and responding to feedback from customers), the firm needs to rely on teams of workers. Teams mean diverse workforces, and the best teams share three characteristics: (1) Members are tolerant of their teammates' perspectives; (2) members represent diverse personalities (e.g., introverts and extroverts, improvisers and organizers); and (3) members feel they can share thoughts, ideas, and concerns without fear of ridicule or punishment. They feel "psychologically safe."[9]

Firms have found that only through work teams can they execute newly adopted strategies stressing better quality, innovation, cost control, or speed. Indeed, virtual teams—domestic or global—promise new kinds of management challenges. In a virtual team, members are dispersed geographically or organizationally. Their primary interaction is through some combination of electronic communication systems. They may never "meet" in the traditional sense. Further, team membership is often fluid, evolving according to changing task requirements. This has created a rich opportunity for members from diverse backgrounds to learn to work productively together.[10]

Coordinating team talents to develop new products, better customer service, or ways of working more efficiently is a difficult, yet essential, aspect of business strategy.

Mergers and Strategic International Alliances

The managers who have worked out the results of all the mergers, acquisitions, and strategic international alliances occurring over the past 20 years know how important it is to knit together the new partners' financial, technological, production, and marketing resources.[11] However, the resources of the new enterprise also include people, and this means creating a partnership that spans different corporate cultures.

A key source of problems in mergers, acquisitions, and strategic international alliances is differences in corporate cultures.[12] According to two studies, integrating culture is the top challenge in mergers and acquisitions.[13] Corporate cultures may differ in many ways, such as the customs of conducting business, how people are expected to behave, and the kinds of behaviors that get rewarded.

When two foreign businesses attempt a long-distance marriage, the obstacles are national cultures as well as corporate cultures. Fifty percent of U.S. managers either resign or are fired within 18 months of a foreign takeover.[14] Many of the managers report a kind of "culture shock." As one manager put it, "You don't quite know their values, where they're coming from, or what they really have in mind for you."[15] Managing D&I effectively is crucial as companies combine their efforts to offer products and services to customers in far-flung markets.

The Changing Labor Market

You can be sure of this: Over the next 25 years, the U.S. workforce will comprise more women, more immigrants, more people of color, and more older workers (see Figure 5-3). In fact, more than 500 million people, double the number today,

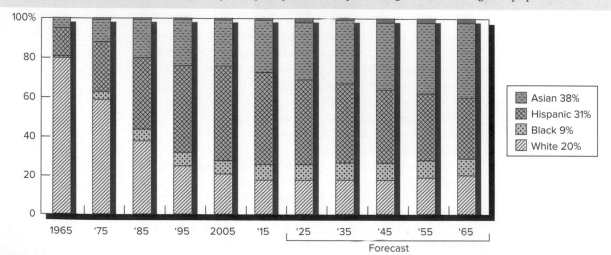

Figure 5-3

The U.S. will become even more diverse over the next several decades. Asians are projected to become the largest immigrant group, surpassing Hispanics as a percentage of the immigrant population.

Legend:
- Asian 38%
- Hispanic 31%
- Black 9%
- White 20%

Source: Jordan, M. (2015, Sept. 28). Asians to surpass Hispanics as largest foreign-born group in U.S. by 2055. *The Wall Street Journal.* Retrieved from *www.wsj.com/articles/asians-to-surpass-hispanics-as-largest-foreign-born-group-in-u-s-by-2055-1443412861* on Oct. 8, 2015.

Chapter 5 Diversity and Inclusion

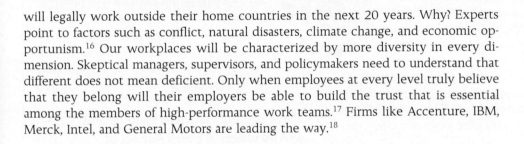

A WORD ABOUT TERMINOLOGY

In recent years, few topics have sparked as much debate as "politically correct" language. Choosing the right words may take a bit more thought and effort, but it is imperative to do so in business communication. After all, it makes no sense to alienate employees and customers by using words that show a lack of respect or sensitivity.

Consider three examples. Instead of referring to dark-skinned people (whose ethnic origins may be Hispanic or African) as "Black," it is more appropriate to refer to them as "Hispanic Americans" or "African Americans." Instead of referring to people with physical or mental impairments as "the disabled" or "the handicapped" (terms that emphasize what a person cannot do rather than what he or she can do), it is more appropriate to refer to them as "people with disabilities." As for gender, the term "transgender" is actually more complicated as a new generation redefines the two-gender reality most people are accustomed to. Facebook, with more than 2.4 billion users, has about 60 options for users' gender.[19] Showing respect and sensitivity to differences by means of the language we use in business is the first step toward building up the capabilities of a diverse workforce.

will legally work outside their home countries in the next 20 years. Why? Experts point to factors such as conflict, natural disasters, climate change, and economic opportunism.[16] Our workplaces will be characterized by more diversity in every dimension. Skeptical managers, supervisors, and policymakers need to understand that different does not mean deficient. Only when employees at every level truly believe that they belong will their employers be able to build the trust that is essential among the members of high-performance work teams.[17] Firms like Accenture, IBM, Merck, Intel, and General Motors are leading the way.[18]

D&I AT WORK

Reports of discrimination correlate with a tendency to feel "burned out," a reduced willingness to take initiative on the job, and a greater likelihood of planning to change jobs. Not surprisingly, therefore, a large-scale study of more than 475,000 professionals and managers from 20 large corporations found that minorities and women quit companies much more often than white males do, especially during the early period of employment, although over time, racial differences in quit rates disappear.[20] Such turnover represents millions of dollars in lost training and productivity.

So how should you handle questions and concerns about D&I? Here are some suggestions: *inquire* ("What makes you say that?"), *show empathy* ("It is frustrating when you can't understand someone"), *educate* (debunk myths, provide facts, explain), *state your needs or expectations* ("Let's develop an approach we can both live with"), and *don't polarize people or groups* ("What might be other reasons for this behavior?"). Sometimes people respond differently to the same situation because of their culture. Culture is the foundation of group differences. In the following sections, we will examine the concept of culture and then focus briefly on some key issues that characterize three racial/ethnic groups (African Americans, Hispanic Americans, and Asian Americans), women, and the five generations that make up the U.S. workforce. As in other chapters, we will present examples of companies that have provided progressive leadership in this area.

WHY IS A D&I STRATEGY SO DIFFICULT TO IMPLEMENT?*

Despite their importance, D&I strategies are difficult to implement, and they often do not deliver the benefits they promise. Why is this the case? Many companies underestimate the time and effort required to implement a D&I strategy. Rather than working toward integrating it into the organization's broader business strategy and all HR activities, companies sometimes see D&I as just another "stand-alone project," or they fail to address more issues, such as management style, hierarchy, and culture. What is the best way to overcome this? Experts advise organizations to include five crucial steps.

1. Identify Key Stakeholders

The CEO and other senior leaders must be D&I "culture carriers," involved and credible through their actions. They should be visible at workshops, training programs, and question-and-answer sessions on D&I. The process starts with the CEO, but there must be buy-in both up and down the organization chart. Executives, managers, and rank-and-file employees must understand the purpose of D&I and how it will help them do their jobs more effectively

2. Build In Accountability

The role of managers is critical. Ask them to provide quarterly or semiannual reports on what they are doing to promote diversity and inclusion. Some large organizations have created a diversity office or appointed a chief diversity officer. Doing so creates a kind of social accountability. When people know that they might have to explain their decisions, they are less likely to act on bias.

3. Communicate D&I on a Continuous Basis

Communicating about why diversity is crucial for the success of the business is important. It must be frequent and include a variety of channels, such as social media, newsletters, intranet, seminars, meetings, and posters.

4. Create a Formal Project Plan

Include measurable objectives that are integrated with the rest of a company's strategic objectives and operations. Here's just one example. In 2014, San Francisco start-up Slack Technologies was building an office-collaboration chat tool. One of its executives wrote a manifesto committing the company to hiring "people with as many diverse experiences and backgrounds as we can." It infused that approach into every HR activity as it grew from 80 employees and $10 million in revenue in 2014, to 1,664 people and $401 million in revenue in 2019. Its performance management program for all managers and employees functions as an accountability mechanism.

5. Move beyond Hiring to Include Diversity and Inclusion in Every Aspect of Employment

Bias can thwart diversity at every step of the hiring process—recruiting, screening, interviewing, and on-boarding. Inclusion is bigger than hiring alone, however. As we noted earlier, it's about feeling that one belongs in an organization. To make that happen, it's important that employees and managers work together, really engaging with each other, and that the organization rewards individuals and teams for smart risk taking. Encourage employees to discuss mistakes openly and to think about mistakes as learning opportunities rather than signs of incompetence.

*Sources: Slack Technologies. *Wikipedia.* Retrieved from *https://en.wikipedia.org/wiki/Slack_Technologies* on Mar. 17, 2020. Zenger, J., and Folkman, J. (2017, Oct. 26). Leaders aren't great at judging how inclusive they are. *Harvard Business Review.* Retrieved from *https://hbr.org/2017/10/leaders-arent-great-at-judging-how-inclusive-they-are* on Dec. 1, 2017. Babcock, P. (2017, Feb. 24). 5 key steps to starting a D&I program. Retrieved from *www.shrm.org/resourcesandtools/hr-topics/behavioral-competencies/global-and-cultural-effectiveness/pages/5-key-steps-to-starting-a-di-program.aspx* on Feb. 25, 2017. Parsi (2017), op. cit.

Culture—the Foundation of Group Differences

Culture refers to the characteristic behavior of people in a country or region. Culture helps people make sense of their part of the world. It provides them with an identity–one they retain even when they emigrate.[21]

When we talk about culture, we include, for example, family patterns, customs, social classes, religions, political systems, clothing, music, food, literature, and laws.[22] Understanding the things that make up a person's culture helps diverse peoples to deal more constructively with one another. Conversely, misunderstandings among people of goodwill often cause unnecessary interpersonal problems and have undone countless business deals. We will examine the concept of culture more fully in our final chapter.

"Valuing diversity and inclusion" means more than feeling comfortable with employees whose race, ethnicity, or gender differs from your own.[23] It means more than accepting their accents or language, their dress or food. It means learning to value and respect styles and ways of behaving that differ from yours. To manage D&I effectively, there is no room for inflexibility and intolerance–displace them with adaptability and acceptance.

African Americans in the Workforce

African Americans will make up about 12.7 percent of the U.S. civilian workforce by the year 2024.[24] Consider these facts:

- According to the U.S. Census Bureau, African Americans own 2.5 million businesses in the United States, employ more than a million people, and generate $187.5 billion in revenue. Overall, African American small business owners are younger and include more women than the general small business population.[25]
- **Buying power** of African American consumers–that is, their disposable income after taxes–reached $1.2 trillion in 2018.[26]
- Among the *Fortune* 500 largest firms, there were four African American chief executive officers in 2019. African Americans held just 10 percent of profit-and-loss jobs in large companies.[27]
- Top companies for African Americans include Methodist Le Bonheur Healthcare, Texas Health Resources, FedEx, Foot Locker, Delta Airlines, Kimpton Hotels and Restaurants, Quicken Loans, Aflac, and AT&T.[28]

Despite these encouraging trends, sometimes progress only comes through the legal system. For example, in November 2000, Coca-Cola Company agreed to a record $192.5 million settlement to a race-discrimination lawsuit that alleged wide disparities in pay, promotions, and performance evaluations.[29] Such settlements do lead to improvement, as Coca-Cola's own data show. Today, 20 percent of the company's U.S. workforce comprises African Americans, and 41 percent of the company is female, with three African Americans and three women on the Coca-Cola board of directors. Even more impressive, the company made DiversityInc's Top 50 Companies for Diversity® list for the 12th straight year.[30] Coca-Cola uses quarterly monitoring to ensure that individuals are being hired, retained, promoted, and rewarded on a fair and consistent basis. Why? Because with diversity and inclusion there is no endgame.

Employee networks can help ensure that products and services are relevant and culturally appropriate to various customer segments.

Sam Edwards/Age Fotostock

Hispanics in the Workforce

Hispanics, who will constitute 19.8 percent of the civilian labor force by the year 2024,[31] experience many of the same disadvantages as African Americans. However, the term *Hispanic* encompasses a large, diverse group of people who come from distinctively different ethnic and racial backgrounds and who have achieved various economic and educational levels. For example, a third-generation, educated, white Cuban American has little in common with an uneducated Central American immigrant of mainly Native American ancestry who has fled civil upheaval and political persecution. Despite the fact that their differences far outweigh their similarities, both are classified as Hispanic. Why? Largely because of the language they speak (Spanish), their surnames, or their geographic origins.

Mexicans, Puerto Ricans, and Cubans constitute the three largest groups classified as Hispanic. They are concentrated in four geographic areas: Most Mexican Americans reside in California and Texas, most Puerto Ricans in New York, and most Cuban Americans in Florida. These four states account for 73 percent of the firms owned by Hispanics. Hispanic entrepreneurs in the United States own more than 4.4 million businesses, contributing more than $700 billion each year to the U.S. economy.[32] Labor-force participation rates for Hispanics (as a group) are growing rapidly, as Figure 5-4 shows.

Hispanics are also getting wealthier, as mean household income reached $50,486 in 2018.[33] Buying power among Hispanics—that is, the total personal income available after taxes for goods and services—reached $1.7 trillion in 2019, accounting for nearly 11 percent of the nation's total buying power.[34]

To encourage greater diversity throughout its entire corporate structure, health-care benefits company Aetna is exemplary.

AETNA: EMBEDDING D&I INTO THE FABRIC OF THE BUSINESS*

Aetna is one of the nation's leading diversified health-care benefits companies, serving approximately 46.7 million people. More than 50,000 employees work for the company. Of those, 31 percent are people of color, and 76 percent are women. People of color hold 16 percent of management/supervisory positions, and 15 percent of senior leaders are people of color. Women hold 62 percent of management/supervisory positions, and 26 percent of senior leaders are women. That's 81 percent higher than U.S. companies overall.

Aetna employees live by a set of core values, known as the Aetna Way, which puts the people who use the company's services at the core of everything it does. Although business results are important, Aetna's senior managers believe that *how* the company achieves those results–how it makes a difference for the people it serves–is every bit as important. The four core values are integrity, employee engagement, excellence and accountability, and quality service and value. Notice how they all revolve around Aetna's customers. Each value also describes how employees are expected to behave.

- *Integrity:* Do the right thing for the right reason, honor commitments, and behave ethically.
- *Employee engagement:* Lead people to success, value diversity, and build confidence and pride in our company.
- *Excellence and accountability:* Make a fair profit, innovate, and anticipate the future–look, listen, and learn.
- *Quality service and value:* Make it easy. Eliminate hassles; make Aetna the standard by which others are judged; build trusting, valued relationships with all constituents.

The "ICE" Strategy

Aetna's D&I strategy is a unique marriage of values and business strategy with roots from more than 40 years ago. Its core components are integration, communication, and education (ICE). *Integration* means that all diversity components are working together across the enterprise (marketing, HR, Aetna's philanthropic foundation, investments, procurement, sales, etc.) and that they are fully integrated into the short- and long-term business-planning process. *Communication* is the creation and dissemination of information to all employees and customers. Finally, *education* means deepening the understanding of what the D&I strategy is, including its components, the role it plays in Aetna's business strategy, and tools to help its people be successful at every level.

Payoffs from Aetna's D&I Efforts

Aetna's business results are impressive. Its market value zoomed from $3.3 billion in 2001 to $57.1 billion in 2019, with sales of $60.6 billion. Undoubtedly, much of the turnaround in business results can be traced to a more focused business strategy, but at the same time, the CEO made D&I a key business imperative.

°Sources: Aetna story 2016. Retrieved from *http://www.aetnastory.com/about.html* on Apr. 2, 2017. Aetna. (2019). Forbes.com. Retrieved from https://www.forbes.com/companies/aetna/#7eec2c815b07 on Mar. 18, 2020. Cascio, W. F. (2009). *Aetna: Investing in Diversity.* Alexandria, VA: Society for Human Resource Management.

HR BUZZ

BOTTOM-LINE BENEFITS OF DIVERSITY AT PEPSICO*

In 2006, Indra Nooyi took the helm as CEO of PepsiCo, the largest U.S. company by market capitalization to put a woman in charge. Given PepsiCo's culture, that is no surprise. It is well known that diversity programs cannot succeed without commitment from the organization's top executives. Nooyi's predecessor, CEO Steve Reinemund, was certainly committed. He enforced aggressive hiring and promotion rules. Half of all new hires at PepsiCo have to be either women or ethnic minorities. And managers now earn their bonuses, in part, by how well they recruit and retain them. Today, 27 percent of PepsiCo's U.S.-based executives are women, and 36 percent are people of color. PepsiCo sells its products in more than 200 countries and territories. International markets now make up fully half of PepsiCo's $67.1 billion in revenue.

The diversity push is part of PepsiCo's game plan to understand better the disparate tastes of new consumers as it continues to expand globally. To do that, it needs to tap the creative, cultural, and creative skills of a variety of employees and to use those skills to improve company policies, products, and customer experiences. The Latino Employee Network at Frito-Lay, the snack-food division of PepsiCo, did just that. During the development of Doritos Guacamole-Flavored Tortilla Chips, members of the network provided feedback on the taste and packaging to help ensure that the product would be regarded as authentic in the Latino community. Their insight helped make the guacamole-flavored Doritos one of the most successful new-product launches in the company's history, generating more than $100 million in sales in its first year alone.

Sources: Clifford, C. (2016, Oct. 17). PepsiCo CEO: Hiring more women and people of color is a business imperative. Retrieved from *http://www.cnbc.com/2016/10/17/pepsico-ceo-hiring-more-women-and-people-of-color-is-a-business-imperative.html* on Apr. 2, 2017. PepsiCo revenue 2006-2019. Retrieved from *https://www.macrotrends.net/stocks/charts/PEP/pepsico/revenue* on Mar. 18, 2020.

Figure 5–4

Growth of the civilian Hispanic labor force (in millions), 1994–2024 (est.).

Source: U.S. Bureau of Labor Statistics. (2015, Dec.). Labor force projections to 2024: The labor force is growing, but slowly. *Monthly Labor Review.* Retrieved from *www.bls.gov/opub/mlr/2015/article/pdf/labor-force-projections-to-2024.pdf* on Mar. 21, 2017

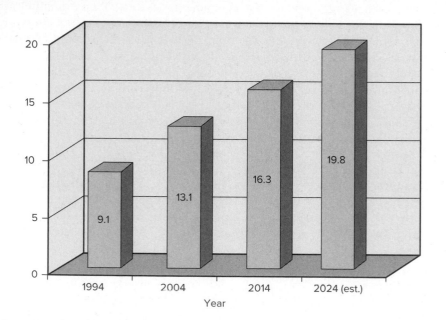

Asian Americans in the Workforce

The share of the workforce comprised by Asian Americans was 5.3 percent in 2012 and is expected to reach an estimated 6.3 percent by 2022, largely due to immigration.[35] Buying power among Asian Americans exceeded $1 trillion in 2018 and it is expected to reach $1.3 trillion by 2023. It is propelled by the fact that Asian Americans are better educated than the average American. Fully 50 percent of them ages 25 and over have a bachelor's degree or higher, compared with 28 percent of the total population. Thus, many hold top jobs, and the increasing number of successful Asian entrepreneurs also helps to increase the group's buying power.[36]

Which are the best companies for Asian Americans to work for? Several notable ones are Workday, St. Jude Children's Hospital, Salesforce, Hyatt Hotels, Genentech, Intuit, and American Savings Bank. All offer progressive HR policies. For example, At Workday, 96 percent of the finance and HR software company's employees feel they have meaningful responsibilities. It has a "find a need and fill it" policy, where employees are encouraged to try out new roles that might further their skills. At biotech and drug company Genentech, to ensure its scientists don't get burned out, the company offers six-week paid sabbaticals after six years. Employees can use them for their own research or vacations. Its Senior VP of development sciences spent her sabbatical teaching dance to children with disabilities.

At Salesforce, another best place to work for Asian Americans, members of the executive management team regularly meet with their organizations via town halls. The primary objective of these meetings is to hear directly from employees, listen to their ideas, and address their questions in intimate and engaging environments. Fully 75 percent of the time is allocated for live questions. Employees get immediate, face-to-face, unscripted responses, which is a powerful way to build trust and a sense of belonging.[37]

Women in the Workforce

A number of factors have encouraged women to raise their expectations and levels of aspiration sharply higher. Here are just a few: civil rights legislation, well-publicized judgments against large companies for gender discrimination in employment, the #MeToo and Time's Up movements, and Cheryl Sandberg's 2013 book, *Lean In.*[38] Today, women constitute 47 percent of the U.S. workforce, and they hold 52 percent of all managerial and professional positions. So much for the myth that women don't hold high-level business jobs because they supposedly don't aim high enough.[39] Five key forces account for these changes:

1. *Changes in the family.* Legalized abortion, contraception, divorce, and a declining birthrate have all contributed to a decrease in the number of years of their lives most women devote to rearing children. About 76 percent of mothers with children under 18 years of age work for pay outside the home, including 65 percent of mothers with children under 6 years old.[40] To lure them back to work, it's important that line managers create an open dialog that begins before maternity leave and focuses on how to approach the leave, communication preferences while on leave, and developing a plan for handovers at the start and end of leave. The most successful programs position parental leave as a brief interlude, not a major disruption, offer gradual returns to work, and set up mentoring programs that match new parents with high performers who are experienced caregivers.[41]

2. *Changes in education.* Since World War II, increasing numbers of women have been attending college. Women now earn 57 percent of all undergraduate degrees, 59 percent of all master's degrees, and 53 percent of all doctorates. Women also earn about 50 percent of all undergraduate business degrees and 55 percent of all MBAs.[42]

3. *Changes in self-perception.* Many women juggle work and family roles. This often causes personal conflict, and the higher they rise in an organization, the more that work demands of them in terms of time and commitment.[43] Many women executives pay a high personal price for their organizational status in the form of broken marriages or never marrying at all.[44] Thus, a major goal of **EEO for women** is to raise the awareness of these issues among both women and men, so that women can be given a fair chance to think about their interests and potential, to investigate other possibilities, to make an intelligent choice, and then to be considered for openings or promotions on an equal basis with men.[45]

4. *Changes in technology.* Advances in technology, both in the home (e.g., Siri, Alexa, or Google Assistant smartphone apps to control the home) and in the workplace (e.g., robotics), have reduced the physical effort and time required to accomplish tasks. Through technology, more women can now qualify for formerly all-male jobs, and, for some women and for some types of jobs, technology makes virtual work arrangements possible, thus helping the women to balance their work and personal lives.[46]

5. *Changes in the economy.* Although there has been an increasing shift away from goods production and toward service-related industries, there are increasing numbers of female employees in all types of industries. Here are some statistics characterizing these changes:
   - Today, women make up 40 percent of U.S. business owners (12.3 million businesses), generating $1.8 trillion in revenues.[47]
   - Women-owned businesses include the same types of industries as are in the *Fortune* 500.
   - About 60 percent of couples are dual earners.
   - The percentage of female C-Suite executives varies from about 20 percent (software, engineering, and industrial manufacturing) to 25 percent in banking and consumer finance, to 35 percent in health-care systems and services.[48]

The statistics presented thus far imply that women have made considerable economic gains over the past three decades. However, there are also some disturbing facts that moderate any broad conclusions about women's social and economic progress:

- Today, U.S. women who work full-time make about 80 cents for every dollar earned by men. The gap exists at all ages, but it is generally narrower when workers are young and widens more significantly as women age and as they advance into higher-paying careers. It has not changed for almost 20 years. Even after accounting for age, experience, and education, the pay gap among men and women in comparable jobs is still about 5 percent.[49]
- As a group, women who interrupt their careers for family reasons never again make as much money as women who stay on the job. How much? Women overall lose an average of 18 percent of their earning power when they take an

off-ramp. In business, it's 28 percent. The longer the time out, the more severe the penalty. Three or more years out and women lose 37 percent of their earning power.[50]

- Women in paid jobs still bear most of the responsibility for family care and housework.[51]

Conclusions Regarding Women in the Workforce

The clearest picture we need to see from the data reflecting all these changes is this: If all the working women in the United States were to quit their jobs tomorrow and stay at home to cook and clean, businesses would disintegrate. There is no going back to the way things were before women entered the workforce. What many people tend to think of as women's issues really are business and competitiveness issues. Companies that routinely don't offer child care and flexibility in work scheduling will suffer along with their deprived workers.[52] Women are not less committed employees; working mothers especially are not less committed to their work. Three-quarters of professional women who have quit large companies did so because of lack of career progress; only 7 percent left to stay at home with their children.[53]

It is important that executives see that creative responses to work-family dilemmas are in the best interests of both employers and employees. Adjustments to work schedules (flextime), extended maternity and paternity leaves, and quality day care based near the job come a little closer to workable solutions. The HR Buzz box below describes some practical steps that IBM is taking.

IBM—CHAMPION OF FAMILY-FRIENDLY POLICIES*   HR BUZZ

IBM has made *Working Mother* magazine's list of 100 Best Companies for Working Mothers for 33 consecutive years and is a member of the magazine's Hall of Fame. It continues to set lofty standards by researching new programs and policies, expanding and improving old ones, and extending such efforts worldwide. In keeping with its mission of becoming "the premier global employer for working mothers," IBM offers dependent care in 42 countries and is a huge proponent of schedule and career flexibility. Of its 350,000 employees, 100 percent use flextime.

It's similarly expansive in its approach to work-life matters, allowing its people to earn health insurance after working just 20 hours per week, revising its parental leave to give women up to 14 fully paid weeks off for a birth or 6 weeks for an adoption, and allowing new mothers to ship their breast milk home from business trips at the company's expense. Child-care partnerships and a life-coaching service help caregivers.

IBM's Special Care for Children Assistance Plan reimburses up to $50,000 per child toward services addressing a range of disabilities–mental, physical or developmental. IBM also ranks high on child care, supporting three on-site and 68 near-site centers–where employees' children have priority access–and more than 1,600 family child-care homes.

Source: "2019 Working Mother 100 Best Companies." Retrieved from *http://www.workingmother.com/best-companies-ibm* on Mar. 19, 2020.

Age-Based Diversity

At present, the U.S. workforce is populated by five generations of workers, each with different, often conflicting values and attitudes.[54] Following is a brief sketch of each.

- The **silent generation** (born 1928-1945) was born in the middle of the Great Depression. Too young to have fought in World War II, they were heavily in demand. Many went to the best colleges, were courted by corporations, rose rapidly, and were paid more than any other group in history. They embraced their elders' values and became good "organization men" (i.e., they gave their hearts and souls to their employers and made whatever sacrifices were necessary to get ahead). In return, employers gave them increasing job responsibility, pay, and benefits). Many members of the silent generation have retired, but others hold positions of power (e.g., corporate leaders, members of Congress).
- The **baby-boom generation** (born 1946-1964) currently accounts for 29 percent of the workforce, but it is not a homogeneous group. Experts typically divide it into early boomers (1946-1954) and late boomers (1955-1964). Each group was socialized differently and had different experiences while growing up. Generally speaking, boomers believe in rights to privacy, due process, and freedom of speech in the workplace; believe that employees should not be fired without just cause; and believe that the best should be rewarded without regard to age, gender, race, position, or seniority. Boomers represent a huge base of knowledge and talent in organizations. They bring years of management and leadership expertise that cannot be replaced easily.[55] Fortunately, they do not change jobs frequently. Median years of tenure on the job is only 2.8 for workers ages 25 to 34, but 10.1 for those aged 55 to 64.[56]
- **Generation X** (born 1965-1980), represents approximately 53 million Americans, or about one-third of the workforce.[57] Hurt more by parental divorce and having witnessed corporate downsizing first-hand, they tend to be independent and cynical and do not expect the security of long-term employment. On the other hand, they also tend to be practical, focused, and future oriented. They demand interesting work assignments and thrive on open-ended projects that require sophisticated problem solving. This is a computer-literate generation. Five characteristics define the kinds of work environments that Gen Xers find most rewarding: (1) control over their own schedules, (2) opportunities to improve their marketable skills, (3) exposure to decision makers, (4) the chance to put their names on tangible results, and (5) clear areas of responsibility.[58]
- **Generation Y**, also known as "Millennials" (born 1981-1996), comprise 35 percent of the U.S. workforce and will comprise three-quarters of the global workforce by 2025.[59] Each country's Millennials are different, but because of globalization, social media, the exporting of Western culture, and the speed of change, Millennials worldwide are more similar to one another than to older generations within their nations.[60] This is a group that grew up texting and instant messaging. They are more accepting of differences, not just among gays, women, and minorities, but among everyone. Their mantra is simple: Challenge convention; find new and better ways of doing things.[61] Millennials value what they do for work above all else. On average, they would be willing to give up $7,600 in salary every year to work at a job that provided a better environment for them.[62]
- **Generation Z** (born 1997-2012) is on track to be the most diverse and highly educated generation yet. Its members came of age in a post-September 11 world, saturated with news of terrorism, war, and economic distress. This has influenced

them to be goal oriented, planning careers and seeking job security earlier than previous cohorts. They are highly skeptical, inclined to fact-check everything. These are "true digital natives" who believe that smartphones are essential to living and working. Thus, they reach for their phones first to find the answer to a question, learn a new skill, apply for a job, or connect with friends. They will be attracted to careers that have both purpose and pragmatism. Like Millennials, they believe that jobs should have a greater meaning than just earning a paycheck.[63]

Intergenerational Conflict

Overall, the majority of employees in different generations work well together. At the same time, many myths exist about generational differences.[64] When conflict does occur, it seems to stem from three primary causes: work ethic (different generations have different perceptions of what makes an employee dedicated), organizational hierarchy (some members of younger generations bypassing the chain of command and some members of older generations believing that seniority trumps qualifications), and management of change (some members of older generations are perceived as reluctant to change, whereas members of younger generations seem eager to try new ideas constantly).

In terms of solutions, it appears that separating workers from different generations does not work. What does work is communicating information in multiple ways (oral and written, formal and informal), thereby addressing different generations' learning styles. Two other solutions are collaborative decision making ("co-creation") and training managers to handle generational differences. At the same time, it is important to recognize that all generations want to be treated with respect. They want leaders whom they can trust. Most people are uncomfortable with change, everyone wants to learn, and everyone likes feedback.[65]

D&I: MAXIMIZING BENEFITS

As we have seen, racial and ethnic minorities, women, and immigrants will account for increasingly larger segments of the U.S. labor force. And there are other large and growing groups—older workers, workers with disabilities, gay/lesbian workers, members of multiple generations—that also affect the overall makeup of the workforce. Businesses that want to grow will have to rely on this diversity. Let us consider some practical steps that managers can take to maximize the benefits of diversity and inclusion.

Racial and Ethnic Minorities

To derive maximum value from a diverse workforce, corporations now realize that it's not enough just to start a mentoring program or to put a woman on the board of directors. Rather, they have to undertake a host of programs—and not just inside the company. ChevronTexaco and Dow Chemical are building ties with minorities as early as high school. Rockwell Collins is building closer relationships with schools that have strong engineering programs as well as sizable minority populations.[66] More specifically, to attract and retain racial and ethnic minorities, consider taking the following steps:[67]

- Hire only search firms with solid track records for providing diverse slates of candidates for positions at all levels.
- Forge links with colleges and universities with significant numbers of minority students, and bring real jobs to the recruiting table.

- Consider labeling résumés by number and deleting names from them.
- Start formal mentoring and succession programs to ensure that minorities are in the leadership pipeline.
- Include progress on D&I issues in management performance reviews and compensation.
- Develop career plans for employees as part of performance reviews.
- Promote racial and ethnic minorities to decision-making positions, not just to staff jobs.
- Provide all employees with confidential outlets to air and settle grievances—for example, telephone and e-mail hot lines.

D&I should be linked to every business strategy—for example, recruiting, selection, placement (after identifying high-visibility jobs that lead to other opportunities within the firm), succession planning, performance management, and reward systems. Companies such as Four Seasons Hotels, Marriott, Qualcomm, and USAA do that extremely well.[68] Here are several other examples.

Female Workers

Here are five ways that firms today provide women with opportunities not previously available to them:[69]

1. **Extended leave**. Only half of working Americans are covered by the FMLA, and only 12 percent have access to paid leave. Some firms go much further.

HR BUZZ

Diverse by Design[a]

BALL, USAA, AND ABBOTT LABORATORIES*

Metal-packaging company Ball primarily hires engineers. Rather than mimic the engineering workforce in the United States—79.3 percent white, 83.8 percent male—it strives to create a workforce that looks like the world. It has developed relationships with organizations including the National Society of Black Engineers, the Society of Asian Scientists and Engineers, the Society of Hispanic Professional Engineers, and the Society of Women Engineers, assigning dedicated liaisons to each. *Forbes* ranked it the number 1 best employer for D&I in 2019.

USAA provides insurance, banking, investments, retirement products, and advice to 11.4 million current and former members of the U.S. military and their families. Of its executives, 32 percent are women, and 20 percent are minorities. Fully 94 percent of employees say they are proud to tell others they work at USAA.

At Abbott Laboratories, the drug maker has gone all out in its D&I efforts. Minorities now comprise 33 percent of new hires, 23 percent of the board of directors, and 20 percent of employees in career-tracking efforts, as well as 11 of the 50 top-paid executives. New-employee affinity groups include separate ones for Chinese, Ibero Americans, and African Americans, among others.

What do these firms have in common? All are sending strong signals that they value workforce diversity, inclusion, and equal opportunities for people to succeed and to prosper.

---

*Valet, V. (2019, Jan. 15). America's best employers for diversity. *Forbes*. Retrieved from *https://www.forbes.com/sites/vickyvalet/2019/01/15/americas-best-employers-for-diversity-2019/#11f755372bda* on Mar. 20, 2020. 50 best workplaces for diversity. (2016, Dec. 5). *Fortune*. Retrieved from *http://fortune.com/best-workplaces-for-diversity/* on Apr. 4, 2017.

Goldman Sachs offers 4 months of paid leave, GE offers 2 months to moms and 2 weeks to dads or other parents, and Facebook offers just over 4 months of paid leave to everyone. Google offers 5 months for mothers and 3 months for fathers or new adoptive parents. The number of new mothers who left the company subsequently dropped by half.

2. *Modify performance reviews for those on extended leave.* To reduce fears about taking family time, the U.S. arm of the global professional-services firm PWC LLP exempts new mothers and anyone else off work for 16 weeks or more from being measured against their peers for their performance review for that year. PWC now retains 98 percent of new mothers.

3. *Offer targeted programs to subsets of high-potential women.* Partnering with The Mom Project, oil and gas producer BP created a "returnship" program for experienced professionals who take career breaks. BP provides mentors and pays them to work on value-added projects that may lead to full-time employment. Boeing, Walgreens, GM, Goldman Sachs, JPMorgan Chase, and Morgan Stanley have instituted similar programs that are open to anyone looking to reenter the workforce after voluntarily taking a career break of more than 2 years.[70]

4. *Flexible work arrangements, including* **flexible scheduling** *and* **teleworking**. Through its Women's Interests Network, an 825-member task force with chapters in five states, American Express now has a universal framework for employees and their managers to implement flexible work arrangements at all of the company's 1,675 locations. Today, progressive employers like Ernst & Young (now EY) make access to flexibility a "conversational process" with all employees, not just to a favored few.[71]

5. *Offer women high-level sponsorship and profit-and-loss responsibility.* Chip maker Intel moves people around regularly and does not allow them to get stuck in staff roles. It operates a sponsorship to catapult more women into senior leadership, which usually requires P&L responsibility. Sponsors are senior players who open the doors to promotions and push their protégés through. Of its 394 vice presidents, 77 are women, compared to 27 of 141 in 2011.

Generations X, Y, and Z

Here are 10 suggestions for integrating Generations X, Y, and Z into the workforce:[72]

- Explain to them how their work contributes to the bottom line.
- Always provide full disclosure.
- Create customized career paths.
- Allow them to have input into decisions.
- Provide public praise and regular feedback, not just once a year.
- Forget the 9-to-5 schedule. At PwC, the firm asks managers how, exactly, they will help their team members work the hours that suit them.
- Encourage the use of mentors.
- Provide access to innovative technology and prepare your IT platform to accept BYOD (bring your own device). Get everyone involved. For example, IBM uses online brainstorming sessions called "jams" to create a virtual network of peers, mentors, and senior staff.

Different generations have much to learn from each other.
Radius Images/Alamy Stock Photo

- Consider new benefits and compensation strategies, such as help paying off student loans. Benefits are sent directly to a third-party vendor and applied to the principal, reducing the overall size of the loan.
- Offer opportunities for community involvement and lots of opportunities for training and leadership development.

In terms of compensation, it seems to be more important to Gen Xers. In contrast, Gen Yers rate six types of rewards at least as important as compensation: high-quality colleagues, flexible work arrangements, prospects for advancement, recognition from one's company or boss, a steady rate of advancement and promotion, and access to new experiences and challenges.[73] As for Gen Z, the two career goals most important to them are work–life fit and job security. Others are autonomy, leadership opportunities, dedication to a cause, and the chance to be creative.[74] As for community involvement, all three generations have high rates of volunteerism. They will look for opportunities to continue this in the context of the workplace.

Older Workers

Workers 50 and older contribute 40 percent of the U.S. gross domestic product (GDP).[75] Only 2 percent of them expect to retire before age 55.[76] To be sure, their experience, wisdom, and institutional memories (particularly about mission-critical procedures and processes) represent important assets to firms. Progressive organizations will continue to develop and use these assets effectively because they see them as important elements of the diversity mix. Here are six priorities to consider to maximize the use of older workers:[77]

1. *Age/experience profile.* Identify types of jobs where older workers can use their experience and talents most effectively.
2. *Job-performance requirements.* Define more precisely the types of abilities and skills needed for various posts. Whereas physical abilities decline with age, especially for heavy lifting, running, or sustained physical exertion, mental abilities generally remain stable well into a person's 80s. Clear job requirements

serve as the basis for improved staffing, job design, and performance-management systems.

3. *Performance management.* Beware of age biases that may be reflected in managers' attitudes. This is known as **age grading**: subconscious expectations about what people can and cannot do at particular times of their lives. In fact, most mature workers are still interested in self-improvement. Like other workers, they want feedback on how they could do their jobs better or extend their careers.[78]

4. *Incentives to stay or leave.* Management must decide if it wants to encourage some older workers to continue with the organization; it must also consider selectively encouraging turnover among those it doesn't want to continue. What effects will different incentives have on the workers management wants to continue and on the ones it doesn't?[79]

5. *Training and counseling.* Develop training programs to avoid **midcareer plateaus** (i.e., performance at an acceptable but not outstanding level, coupled with little or no effort to improve one's current performance), as well as to reduce **obsolescence** (the tendency for knowledge or skills to become out of date). Programs should reflect the special needs of older workers, who can learn but need to be taught differently (e.g., by using self-paced programs instead of lectures).

6. *Adjust jobs.* As an experiment, German auto maker BMW staffed an assembly line at a Bavarian factory exclusively with workers over 50. By making small changes—ergonomic chairs, less-rigid wooden floors, lenses to magnify smaller parts—it transformed the line into one of the factory's most efficient.[80]

Workers with Disabilities

Prospective employers want to know what job applicants can do for them, not what their limitations are. If you can show a prospective employer that you will bring in customers, design a new product, or do something else that makes a contribution, employers will hire you. Your disability won't matter if you can prove that you will contribute to the employer's bottom line. Organizations may not have jobs, but they always have problems. If you can show that you are a problem solver, then it won't matter if you are blue, green, or confined to a wheelchair.

Poll after poll of employers demonstrate that they regard most people with disabilities—roughly 57 million in the United States—as good workers, punctual, conscientious, and competent—if given reasonable accommodation. Despite this evidence, persons with disabilities are less likely to be working than any other demographic group under age 65. Whereas 68.5 percent of those without a disability are in the labor force, only 19.3 percent of those with a disability are.[81]

Perhaps the biggest barrier is employers' lack of knowledge. For example, many are concerned about financial hardship because they assume it will be costly to make architectural changes to accommodate wheelchairs and add equipment to aid workers who are blind or deaf. In fact, according to the Job Accommodation Network, about a third of the accommodations needed by employees and job applicants with disabilities cost absolutely nothing. The remaining two-thirds cost under $500, and tax incentives are available to help businesses offset those costs.[82] Consider several possible modifications:[83]

- Placing a desk on blocks, lowering shelves, and using a carousel for files are all inexpensive accommodations that enable people in wheelchairs to be employed.

- Install telephone amplifiers for hearing-impaired individuals or computer-screen readers that provide speech and Braille output for visually impaired individuals. Hearing aids with Bluetooth connectivity can be connected to smartphones to make it easier to hear phone conversations.
- Use flextime, job sharing, and other modifications to the work schedule to help persons with disabilities to continue to work.[84]

Actions like these enable persons with disabilities to work, gain self-esteem, and reach their full potential. That is a key objective of D&I.

Lesbian/Gay/Bisexual/Transgendered Employees

Throughout this chapter we have emphasized that D&I is a business issue: Either you attract, retain, and motivate the best talent or you lose business. Lesbian/gay/bisexual/transgendered (LGBT) employees, as a group, are highly educated; they

ETHICAL DILEMMA
If Diversity Training Activates Bias or Sparks a Backlash, Is It Still Worthwhile?

Although people are easily taught to respond correctly to a questionnaire about bias, they soon forget the right answers. In some cases, diversity training can activate bias or spark a backlash. Nonetheless, nearly half of midsize companies use it, as do nearly all of the *Fortune* 500.[a] Unfortunately, very few organizations conduct in-depth evaluations of their D&I training efforts. Yet a key concern for practitioners is to understand when and under what conditions D&I training is most beneficial. Fortunately, a substantial body of empirical evidence now exists to answer that question.[b]

D&I training generally falls into one of two broad categories: training designed to disseminate information and training designed to create behavioral change. Training to disseminate information informs employees of their organization's diversity strategy and expectations. This is cognitive-based change. Training to create behavioral change can be divided further into awareness and skill training. Awareness training attempts to increase trainees' awareness of their biases, including stereotypes. Skill training teaches specific skills and behaviors (e.g., do's and don'ts of interpersonal behavior at work).

Empirical evidence indicates that diversity training has modestly positive effects on both cognitive and behavioral change. Effects are much stronger, however, when such training incorporates active (e.g., group-based exercises) rather than passive (lecture, video) forms of instruction. Emphasize tolerance, with a goal of effective dialog through open and honest conversations. The behavior of employees and managers at every level, every day, must show that they live the values of tolerance and respect, and that D&I is more than just a slogan.

Diversity training that activates bias or sparks a backlash is clearly not worthwhile. Offering diversity training merely for the sake of "checking a box" that it has been completed is a waste of time. Conversely, we know what works; isn't it time to put evidence-based research findings about diversity training into practice?

[a]Dobbin, F., and Kalev, A. (2016, July-Aug.). Why diversity programs fail, and what works better. *Harvard Business Review*, pp. 52-60.

[b]Chang, E. H., et al. (2019). Does diversity training work the way it's supposed to? *Harvard Business Review*. Retrieved from *https://hbr.org/2019/07/does-diversity-training-work-the-way-its-supposed-to* on July 20, 2019. Gebert, D., Buengeler, C., & Heinitz, K. (2017). Tolerance: A neglected dimension in diversity training? *Academy of Management Learning & Education* 16, pp. 415–38. Kalinoski, Z. T., Steele-Johnson, D., Peyton, E. J., Leas, K. A., Steinke, J., and Bowling, N. A. (2013). A meta-analytic evaluation of diversity training outcomes. *Journal of Organizational Behavior* 34, pp. 1076-104.

constitute 4.5 percent of the population (about 11 million people). Their buying power in 2018 was almost $1 trillion and is growing by about 10 percent each year. LGBT consumers are very loyal to specific brands, wishing to support companies that support the gay community and that provide equal rights for LGBT workers.[85] Here's an example. Despite outside pressure not to do it, Walgreens made a $100,000 donation to support the Gay Games, a weeklong festival in Chicago that attracted 11,000 athletes. The company wanted to support its LGBT employees and to let gay and lesbian customers know that they are welcome at Walgreens.

Raytheon, a $22 billion-a-year defense contractor, is a high-profile supporter of gay rights. Why? Not because gay people buy missiles or radar; rather, it's because the competition to hire and retain engineers and other skilled workers is so brutal that Raytheon doesn't want to overlook anyone in the talent pool. This is one reason that 91 percent of *Fortune* 500 firms prohibit discrimination based on sexual orientation and that 418 of them now offer transgender-inclusive health-care coverage, compared to 49 in 2009.[86] Well-known companies such as Apple, REI, Nike, Google, IBM, Intel, Raytheon, and JPMorgan Chase are just a few companies that offer such benefits.[87]

In 2020, IBM achieved a perfect score of 100 on the Corporate Equality Index.[88] It is the number 1 financial supporter of gay-rights groups in the United States, and it supports employee LGBT groups in 23 other countries. It even convened a group of gay college students at the Human Rights Campaign to form a national organization of gay students in science and technology.[89] American Airlines's "Rainbow Team" of gay employees brought in $192 million in revenue in one year by targeting the gay community.

Examples like these reveal that some of the largest and most successful companies recognize that treating all workers equally makes good business sense. Research consistently shows that unfair and discriminatory work environments cripple an organization's ability to recruit and retain the best and the brightest. They also stifle job performance and productivity. D&I means that dignity, respect, and belongingness replace bias and exclusion.[90]

As we have seen, the workforce is now and will continue to be more and more diverse. Figure 5-5 presents a list of actions that managers can take to deal with these changes.

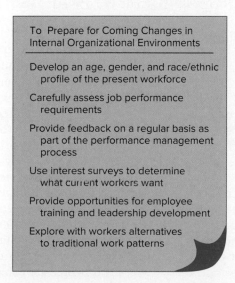

To Prepare for Coming Changes in Internal Organizational Environments

Develop an age, gender, and race/ethnic profile of the present workforce

Carefully assess job performance requirements

Provide feedback on a regular basis as part of the performance management process

Use interest surveys to determine what current workers want

Provide opportunities for employee training and leadership development

Explore with workers alternatives to traditional work patterns

Figure 5–5

Priority listing of suggested actions to manage effectively changes in the workforce.

IMPACT OF D&I ON PRODUCTIVITY, QUALITY OF WORK LIFE, AND THE BOTTOM LINE

All employees–no matter who, no matter at what level–want to be treated with respect. They want to know that their employer values the work they do. Managers at every level need to show people what respectful behavior at work looks like so that all employees can feel supported and have the opportunity to be successful.[a] And when D&I is managed well–as at Accenture, Boston Scientific, IBM, and Ernst & Young–productivity and the quality of work life improve. So do stock prices. Researchers examined the effect on stock prices of announcements of U.S. Department of Labor awards for exemplary diversity programs and announcements of damage awards from the settlement of discrimination lawsuits. Announcements of awards were associated with significant, positive excess returns that represent the capitalization of positive information concerning improved business prospects. Conversely, damage awards were associated with significant negative stock-price changes, which represent the capitalization of negative economic implications associated with discriminatory corporate practices.[b] As we noted earlier, D&I has evolved from being the correct thing to do to being the essential thing to do. It's a mistake, however, to think there is a cookie-cutter approach. Rather, the path to D&I success must take into account each organization's unique goals, resources, number of employees, business locations, product lines, and customer bases.[c]

[a]How companies can develop anti-bias strategies that work. (2018, May 11). Knowledge@Wharton. Retrieved from *https://knowledge.wharton.upenn.edu/article/how-companies-can-develop-anti-bias-strategies-that-work/* on May 12, 2018. Meister, J. C., and Willyerd, K. (2010). *The 2020 Workplace*. New York: HarperCollins.

[b]Wright, P., Ferris, S. P., Hiller, J. S., and Kroll, M. (1995). Competitiveness through management of diversity: Effects on stock price valuation. *Academy of Management Journal* 38, pp. 273-87.

[c]Forbes Coaches Council. (2018, Aug. 13). Practice what you preach: How any organization can truly embrace diversity. Forbes. Retrieved from *https://www.forbes.com/sites/forbescoachescouncil/2018/08/13/practice-what-you-preach-how-any-organization-can-truly-embrace-diversity/#2052c6b652c3* on Aug. 14, 2018. Hastings, R. R. (2010, Oct.). Business needs inform diversity strategies. Retrieved from *www.shrm.org/hrdisciplines/Diversity/Articles/Pages/BusinessNeedsInformDiversity-Strategies.aspx* on June 20, 2011.

IMPLICATIONS FOR MANAGEMENT PRACTICE

1. Workforce diversity is here to stay. There is no going back to the demographic makeup of organizations 20 years ago. To be successful in this new environment, learn to value and respect cultural styles and ways of behaving that differ from your own.

2. Recognize that there are tangible business reasons that D&I should be a high priority: (*a*) It is an opportunity to deepen an understanding of the marketplace as well as the needs of various customers, and to penetrate new markets. (*b*) Demographic changes are coming so rapidly that employers will have to meet their hiring needs with a diverse labor force.

3. To maximize the potential of all members of the workforce, link concerns for D&I to every business strategy: recruitment, staffing, placement, succession planning, performance management, and rewards.

4. To retain talented women and minorities, follow the lead of firms like Intel and Pepsi Bottling Group in developing long-term career plans that include stretch assignments–and don't be afraid to share the plan with the employees in question. As Pepsi Bottling Group's CEO noted, "Give them a lot of profit-and-loss responsibility, and show them that you care. If you do that, then most of your great people are going to stay."[91]

THE BUSINESS AND ETHICAL CASES FOR DIVERSITY ARE NOT ENOUGH TO BRING ABOUT REAL CHANGE

To boost their numbers of women and members of underrepresented groups, many firms are setting goals for hiring and promotion and tying executive compensation to meeting diversity goals Twitter has set specific hiring goals. Collaboration hub Slack practices "intentional hiring." Facebook is giving recruiters double the credit for "diversity hires." Uber is setting D&I goals for 2022 that are tied to the compensation of some of its senior leaders.[92]

Others are focusing on boosting innovation by finding the right mix of individuals to work on teams and creating the conditions in which they can excel. At Bank of America, participants in volunteer service projects reported that volunteering with their coworkers increased their ability to get along with people from diverse backgrounds. At Bloomberg LP in New York City, employee resource groups called Communities align themselves with key business initiatives. In HR, for example, they have been instrumental in developing recruitment strategies targeting graduates from historically Black colleges and universities, veterans, women, and LGBTQ individuals.[93]

Mentoring is another way to engage managers and chip away at their biases. Great mentors help teach their protégés through active listening, support, and challenging them to be better. Does it work? Salesforce found that 95 percent of employees with mentors were promoted within 18 months. Mentoring programs tend to make the managerial ranks much more diverse, too. On average, they boost the representation of Asian, African American, and Hispanic men and women by 9 to 24 percent. Reverse mentoring (younger workers mentoring older colleagues) also promotes D&I. Thus, millennials at a major airline worked with HR to develop a reverse mentoring program to foster inter-generational collaborations.[94]

Task forces, including cross-functional ones, generate three benefits important to D&I programs: (1) They promote accountability; (2) they engage employees and managers who previously might have been cool to such projects; and (3) they increase personal contact among the women, minorities, and white men who participate.

Is there a payoff? On average, companies that use diverse task forces see 9 to 30 percent increases in the representation of white women and of each minority group in management over the following 5 years. Unfortunately, only 20 percent of medium and large employers have task forces. The good news is that we know what works. We just need to do more of it.

SUMMARY

More than half the U.S. workforce now consists of racial and ethnic minorities, immigrants, and women. White, native-born males, as a group, are still dominant in numbers over any other group, but today women constitute nearly half the entire workforce. The labor force will continue to age through 2024, as more Baby Boomers continue to work. By contrast, the growth rate of the 25- to 54-year age group will be essentially flat, and that of the young age group consisting of 16- to 24-year-olds will actually be slightly negative (−1.4 percent).

Managing D&I means encouraging a heterogeneous workforce–which includes white men–to perform to its potential in an equitable work environment in which no one group enjoys an advantage or suffers a disadvantage. At least five factors account for the increasing attention companies are paying to diversity: (1) the shift from a manufacturing to a service economy, (2) the globalization of markets, (3) new business strategies that require more teamwork, (4) mergers and alliances that require different corporate cultures to work together, and (5) the changing labor market. Each of these factors can represent opportunities for firms whose managers and employees work to create inclusive company cultures and who appreciate cultural differences among other employees and managers.

To attract and retain women, as well as persons with disabilities, companies are making extended leaves available to them, modifying performance reviews for those on extended leaves, offering targeted programs to subsets of high-potential women, providing flexible work arrangements, and offering high-level sponsorship of high-potential women along with profit and loss (P&L) responsibility. In addition, many companies now offer the same benefits to same-sex couples that are offered to heterosexual couples.

A different aspect of diversity is generational diversity–important differences in values, aspirations, and beliefs that characterize the silent generation, the baby-boom generation, and Generations X, Y, and Z. To manage older workers effectively, develop an age profile of the workforce, monitor the actual requirements of jobs, provide feedback on a regular basis, provide opportunities for employee training, modify jobs, and explore alternatives to traditional work patterns.

Finally, to support D&I, do the following things well: Focus on bringing in a wide range of talent; treat every employee with dignity and respect to promote belongingness; establish mentoring programs among employees of same and different races; hold managers accountable for meeting D&I goals; develop career plans for employees as part of performance reviews; promote women and minorities to decision-making positions, not just to staff jobs; and provide confidential outlets to air and settle grievances.

KEY TERMS

diversity	Generation Y
inclusion	Generation Z
ethnic minorities	extended leave
managing diversity	flexible scheduling
culture	teleworking
buying power	age grading
EEO for women	midcareer plateaus
silent generation	obsolescence
baby-boom generation	
Generation X	

DISCUSSION QUESTIONS

5-1. In your opinion, what are some key business reasons for emphasizing diversity and inclusion?

5-2. Why is there no simple relationship between D&I and business performance?

5-3. How would you respond to someone who has questions or concerns about D&I?

5-4. What would be the broad elements of a company policy to promote D&I?

5-5. What are some possible sources of intergenerational friction? How might you deal with those?

5-6. Suppose you were asked to identify key components of a successful D&I-training program. What would you say?

5-7. Why is cultivating D&I an ethical imperative?

5-8. Develop a research question or hypothesis where talent analytics might reveal the financial and nonfinancial effects of D&I.

5-9. Describe a management policy designed to promote a culture of inclusion.

5-10. It has been said that D&I only endures when it is baked into the way a company does business every day. As a newly appointed CEO of a cosmetics company, how would you ensure that D&I is "baked in"?

APPLYING YOUR KNOWLEDGE

The Challenge of D&I*   *Case 5–1*

Talk, talk, talk. As Ken Hartman, an African American midlevel manager at Blahna Inc. recalls, that's all he got from the white men above him in top management–despite the fact that Blahna had long enjoyed a reputation as a socially responsible company. But that reputation didn't mean much to Hartman as he watched other African American managers he thought were highly qualified get passed over for plum jobs and as his own career seemed stalled on a lonely plateau. Top management always mouthed D&I, Hartman said, "but in the end, they chose people they were comfortable with for key positions."

Meeting the Challenge

Is this situation uncommon? Not at all. In the last decade, however, it has become increasingly apparent that managing D&I effectively is critical for organizations that seek to improve and maintain their competitive advantage. Building and sustaining a truly inclusive organization–one that makes full use of the contributions of all employees–is not just a nice idea; it is good business sense that yields greater innovation and productivity. Although Denny's Corporation had to experience and settle several costly discrimination cases to begin to see the value in D&I, today Denny's serves as an example of what other organizations should strive for. Half of its board of directors, as well as half of its senior-management team members, are women or members of minorities, along with 15.8 percent of African Americans and 41.2 percent of Hispanics among its 9,315 company employees. In 2019, minorities made up 68 percent of the company's overall workforce, and 52 percent of management. Fully 49 percent of its restaurants are minority-owned, 22 percent are women-owned, and 5 percent are LGBT-owned.[95] The company has won many awards and justifiable praise from numerous media outlets for its genuine efforts to make diversity and inclusion a part of the very fabric of its business.

The Strategy at Blahna Inc.

Ken Hartman's firm, Blahna Inc., has finally gotten the message. The company is now using D&I to head off conflict and reduce turnover among employees it can ill afford to lose.

Several years ago, Blahna formed a 20-member D&I Committee, chaired by a vice president. It was chartered to consider why women and minorities weren't better represented at all levels

*Sources: Klein, D. (2019, Aug.). At Denny's, the brand revolution continues. Retrieved from *https://www. fsrmagazine.com/chain-restaurants/dennys-brand-revolution-continues* on Mar. 21, 2020. Adamson, J. (2000). *The Denny's Story: How a Company in Crisis Resurrected Its Good Name and Reputation*. New York: Wiley. White, E. (2006, Mar. 20). Fostering diversity to aid business. *The Wall Street Journal*, p. B3.

of the organization. Although the company had a good record of hiring women and minorities, turnover was two to three times higher for these groups than it was for white males.

Sample exit interviews revealed that women and minorities left because they didn't feel valued in their day-to-day work, didn't have effective working relationships, or didn't sense that the work they were being given to do would lead to the fulfillment of their career goals. White males, on the other hand, left for business-related reasons, such as limited opportunities for future advancement.

As a result of this initial investigation, Blahna formed a 25-person advisory committee. The committee developed a multi-pronged approach for dealing with D&I issues—including building bridges with the broader community outside the company. Within the company itself, a key strategy involved training conducted by diversity consultants Hope & Associates.

To date, 60 percent of Blahna's 11,000 employees have gone through a 2-day D&I seminar and 40 percent have gone through a more extensive 6-day training. "The premise of the training is that the more different you are, the more barriers there can be to working well together," explains Blahna's chief diversity officer. Training sessions focus on group discussions that emphasize tolerance, creating a culture of belongingness, and inclusion.

A key part of the training offered by Hope & Associates is the implementation of a "consulting pairs" process that is designed to help trainees take what they've learned in training and apply it on the job. When a conflict first arises between two peers or between a manager and an employee, a consulting pair is called in to facilitate discussion and problem solving. The unique feature of this approach is that the consulting pair is selected to match as closely as possible the backgrounds of the individuals who are involved in the conflict. Of course, all proceedings are strictly confidential.

The result? Ken Hartman is a happier guy these days. As president of one of Blahna's divisions, the 48-year-old executive is a step away from joining the ranks of senior management. Life has changed for him since the company "stopped talking about values like D&I and began behaving that way."

Questions

1. Why do many companies find D&I to be difficult?
2. What were the key elements in Blahna's successful D&I strategy?
3. Under what circumstances might the consulting-pairs approach be most useful?
4. What steps should management take to ensure that the consulting-pairs approach is working?

REFERENCES

1. Toosi, M. (2015, Dec.). Labor force projections to 2024: The labor force is growing, but slowly. *Monthly Labor Review*. Retrieved from *www.bls.gov/opub/mlr/2015/article/labor-force-projections-to-2024-1.htm* on Mar. 31, 2017.
2. Omeokwe, A. (2020, Jan. 10). Women overtake men as majority of U.S. workforce. *The Wall Street Journal*. Retrieved from *https://www.wsj.com/articles/women-overtake-men-as-majority-of-u-s-workforce-11578670615* on Jan. 10, 2020.
3. Society for Human Resource Management. Introduction to the human resources discipline of diversity. Retrieved from *http://www.shrm.org/hrdisciplines/Diversity/Pages/DiversityIntro.aspx* on June 20, 2011.
4. Roberson, Q., Ryan, A. M., & Ragins, B. R. (2017). The evolution and future of diversity at work. *Journal of Applied Psychology* 102(3), pp. 483–99.
5. Desilver, D. (2019, Aug. 29). 10 facts about the American workforce. *Pew Research Center*. Retrieved from *https://www.pewresearch.org/fact-tank/2019/08/29/facts-about-american-workers/* on Mar. 17, 2020. *See also* U.S. Department of Labor, Bureau of Labor Statistics.

(2015, Dec.). Employment projections 2014-2024 and employment by sector. Retrieved from *www.bls.gov/emp/ep_table_201.htm* on Mar. 31, 2017.

6. Sellers, P. (2003, Oct.) The diversity factor. *Fortune.*

7. BlackRock's diversity chief: Do your employees feel they belong? (2018, May 16). *Knowledge@Wharton.* Retrieved from *https://knowledge.wharton.upenn.edu/article/blackrocks-diversity-expert-employees-feel-belong/* on May 17, 2018.

8. Kokalicheva, K. (2015, Apr. 24). Google taps Luxottica for the next version of Glass. *Fortune.* Retrieved from *http://fortune.com/2015/04/24/google-luxottica-glass/* on Apr. 1, 2017.

9. Woo, S. (2019, Mar. 13). In search of a perfect team. *The Wall Street Journal,* p. R6.

10. Roepe, L. R. (2020). Scattered. *HRMagazine* 65(1), pp. 37-42. *See also* Dulebohn, J. H., and Hoch, J. E. (2017). Virtual teams in organizations. *Human Resource Management Review* 27, pp. 569-74. *See also* Watkins, M. D. (2013, June 27). Making virtual teams work: Ten basic principles. *Harvard Business Review.* Retrieved from *https://hbr.org/2013/06/making-virtual-teams-work-ten* on Mar. 2, 2017.

11. Gaughan, P. A. (2018). *Mergers, Acquisitions, and Corporate Restructurings* (7th ed.). Hoboken, NJ: Wiley. *See also* Schmidt, J. A. (2002). *Making Mergers Work: The Strategic Importance of People.* Alexandria, VA: Towers Perrin/Society for Human Resource Management Foundation.

12. Ladika, S. (2020). Melding two cultures. *HRMagazine* 65(1), pp. 59-64. *See also* Bird, M. (2015, Aug. 4). Merging two global company cultures. *Harvard Business Review.* Retrieved from *https://hbr.org/2015/08/merging-two-global-company-cultures* on Apr. 1, 2017. *See also* Once the deal is done: Making mergers work. (2017, Feb. 12). Available at *https://www.youtube.com/watch?v=k3Zf9nB9lJc.*

13. Gelfand, M., Gordon, S., Li C., Choi, V., and Prokopowicz, P. (2018, Oct.). One reason mergers fail: The two cultures aren't compatible. *Harvard Business Review.* Retrieved from *https://hbr.org/2018/10/one-reason-mergers-fail-the-two-cultures-arent-compatible* on Mar. 17, 2020.

14. Marks, M., and Mirvis, P. (2010). *Joining Forces: Making One Plus One Equals Three in Mergers, Acquisitions, and Alliances* (2nd ed.). San Francisco, CA: Jossey-Bass. *See also* McWhirter, W. (1989, Oct. 9). I came, I saw, I blundered. *Time,* pp. 72, 77.

15. Ibid.

16. Migration: A world on the move. *United Nations Population Fund.* Retrieved from *www.unfpa.org/migration* on Apr. 1, 2017. *See also* Fox, A. (2010, Jan.). At work in 2020. *HRMagazine.* Retrieved from *www.shrm.org/Publications/hrmagazine/EditorialContent/2010/0110/Pages/0110fox.aspx* on June 17, 2011.

17. Meinert, 2019, op. cit. Parsi (2017), op. cit. *See also* Berreby, D. (2015). Why old habits die hard. *Korn/Ferry Briefings on Talent and Leadership* 6(23), pp. 33-39.

18. Bolden-Barrett, V. (2019, Aug. 6). Accenture, IBM among top rated companies for D&I in Working Mother media index. *HRDive.* Retrieved from *https://www.hrdive.com/news/accenture-ibm-among-top-rated-companies-for-di-in-working-mother-media-in/560179/* on Feb. 1, 2020.

19. Steinmetz, K. (2017, Mar. 27). Infinite identities. *Time,* pp. 48-54.

20. Hom, P. W., Roberson, L., and Ellis, A. D. (2008). Challenging conventional wisdom about who quits: Revelations from corporate America. *Journal of Applied Psychology* 93, pp. 1-34.

21. Tarique, I., Briscoe, D., and Schuler, R. (2016). *International Human Resource Management* (5th ed.). New York: Routledge. *See also* Gelfand, M. J., Erez, M., and Aycan, Z. (2007). Cross-cultural organizational behavior. *Annual Review of Psychology* 58, pp. 479-514.

22. Abramson, N. R., & Moran, R. T. (2018). *Managing Cultural Differences* (10th ed.). New York: Routledge.

23. Barkman, S. J., and Speaker, H. L. Valuing diversity. Retrieved from *https://cals.arizona.edu/sfcs/cyfernet/nowy/sc_valdiv.html* on Apr. 1, 2017. *See also* Page, S. F. (2007). *The Difference: How the Power of Diversity Creates Better Groups, Firms, Schools, and Societies.* Princeton, NJ: Princeton University Press.

24. Toossi (2015), op. cit.

25. Lesonsky, R. (2020, Feb. 25). State of African-American-owned businesses. Retrieved from *https://www.score.org/blog/state-african-american-owned-businesses?gclid=EAIaIQobCh*

MI6Na4sdCk6AIVNPjBx3NAQoVEAAYASAAEgK7tfD_BwE on Mar. 18, 2020. *See also* Becker-Medina, E. H. (2016, Feb. 26). Women are leading the rise of Black-owned businesses. Retrieved from *https://www.census.gov/newsroom/blogs/random-samplings/2016/02/ women-are-leading-the-rise-of-black-owned-businesses.html* on Mar. 18, 2020.

26. Black impact: Consumer categories where African-Americans move markets. (2018, Feb. 15). Retrieved from *https://www.nielsen.com/us/en/insights/article/2018/black-impact-consumer-categories-where-african-americans-move-markets/* on Mar. 18, 2020.

27. Green, J. (2019, Oct. 10). Black executives hold few positions that lead to CEO jobs. *Bloomberg.com.* Retrieved from *https://www.bloomberg.com/news/articles/2019-10-10/ black-executives-hold-few-positions-that-lead-to-ceo-job* on Mar. 18, 2020.

28. The 10 best workplaces for African Americans. (2016, Dec. 5). *Fortune.* Retrieved from *http://fortune.com/2016/12/05/best-workplaces-diversity-african-americans/* on Apr. 1, 2017.

29. McKay, B. (2000, Nov. 17). Coca-Cola agrees to settle bias suit for $192.5 million. *The Wall Street Journal,* pp. A3, A8.

30. The Coca-Cola Company. Our progress. Retrieved from *http://www.coca-colacompany. com/our-company/diversity/our-progress* on Apr. 1, 2017.

31. Toossi (2015), op. cit.

32. CNBC. (2018, Sept. 25). Latinos: A powerful force turbocharging small-business growth and driving $700 billion into the U.S. economy. Retrieved from *https://www.cnbc. com/2018/09/25/latinos-are-a-powerful-force-fueling-small-business-growth-in-the-us.html* on Mar. 18, 2020.

33. Davidson, K. (2018, Sept. 12). Hispanic household income climbs. *The Wall Street Journal.* Retrieved from *https://www.wsj.com/articles/hispanic-household-income-climbs-1536792308* on Mar. 18, 2020.

34. The Hispanic potential buying power of $1.7 trillion dollars. (2019, Feb. 28). Retrieved from *https://www.nawrb.com/hispanic-buying-power/* on Mar. 18, 2020.

35. Toossi (2015), op. cit.

36. Lam, C. (2019, May 9). Asian American buying power topped $1 trillion in 2018, Nielsen report finds. *NBC News.* Retrieved from *https://www.nbcnews.com/news/asian-america/ asian-american-buying-power-topped-1-trillion-2018-nielsen-report-n1003061* on Mar. 18, 2020. *See also* Campbell, A. F. (2016, Aug. 24). Asian American buying power outpaces other ethnic consumer groups. *The Atlantic.* Retrieved from *www.theatlantic.com/business/archive/2016/08/the-overlooked-consumer-group-with-billions-to-spend/497105/* on Apr. 2, 2017.

37. 10 best workplaces for Asian Americans. (2019). *Fortune.* Retrieved from *https://fortune. com/best-workplaces-for-asian-americans/* on Mar. 18, 2020.

38. Suddath, C., and Greenfield, R. (2018, Mar. 12). 5 years of leaning in. *Fortune,* pp. 50–57.

39. Catalyst. (2019, June 5). Quick take: Women in the workforce–United States. Retrieved from *https://www.catalyst.org/research/women-in-the-workforce-united-states/* on Mar. 19, 2020.

40. U.S. Bureau of Labor Statistics. (2018, Apr. 18). Employment characteristics of families. 2018. Retrieved from *https://www.bls.gov/news.release/pdf/famee.pdf* on Mar. 19, 2020.

41. Collings, D., Freeney, Y., and van der Werff, L. (2018, Sept. 11). How companies can ensure maternity leave doesn't hurt women's careers. *Harvard Business Review.* Retrieved from *https://hbr.org/2018/09/how-companies-can-ensure-maternity-leave-doesnt-hurt-womens-careers* on Nov. 1, 2018. *See also* Weber, L. (2015, Sept. 30). How to get more women back into the workforce. *The Wall Street Journal,* p. R4.

42. Catalyst (2019), op. cit.

43. Chen, T-P. (2018, Oct. 23). A corporate ladder of attrition for women. *The Wall Street Journal,* p. R5. *See also* Waller, N., and Lublin, J. S. (2015, Sept. 30). What's holding women back in the workplace? *The Wall Street Journal,* pp. R1, R2.

44. Rampell (2010), op. cit. *See also* Sellers, P. (1996, Aug. 5). Women, sex, & power. *Fortune,* pp. 43–57.

45. Rifkin, G. (2015). Second-generation gender bias. *Korn/Ferry Briefings on Talent and Leadership* 6(23), pp. 44–53.

46. Cascio, W. F., and Montealegre, R. (2016). How technology is changing work and organizations. *Annual Review of Organizational Psychology and Organizational Behavior* 3, pp. 349-75.

47. Fundera. (2020). Women-owned businesses: Statistics and overview (2020). Retrieved from *https://www.fundera.com/resources/women-owned-business-statistics* on Mar. 19, 2020.

48. Chen, T-P. (2018), op. cit.

49. Suddath, C. (2017, June 26). Paid in semi-full. *Fortune*, pp. 42-49. *See also* Gerhart, B., and Newman, J. M. (2020). *Compensation* (13th ed.). New York: McGraw-Hill. *See also* Nagele-Piazza, L. (2020). The importance of pay equity. *HRMagazine* 65(1), pp. 16-18.

50. Hewlett, S. A., and Luce, C. B. (2005, Mar.). Off-ramps and on-ramps: Keeping talented women on the road to success. *Harvard Business Review*, pp. 43-54.

51. Suddath & Greenfield (2018), op. cit. *See also* Suddath (2017), op. cit.

52. Feintzeig, R. (2018, Oct. 23). Child care's impact on women's opportunities. *The Wall Street Journal*, p. R8. *See also* Sandberg, S. (2015, Sept. 30). When women get stuck, corporate America gets stuck. *The Wall Street Journal*, p. R3.

53. Deutsch, C. H. (2005, May 1). Behind the exodus of executive women: Boredom. *The New York Times*. Retrieved from *www.nytimes.com/2005/05/01/business/yourmoney/01women.html?scp=1&sq=Behind%20the%20exodus%20of%20executive%20women:%20Boredom&st=cse* on June 22, 2011.

54. The framework for this section was drawn from the following sources: Dimock, M. (2019, Jan. 17). Defining generations: Where Millennials end and post-Millennials begin. *Pew Research Center*. Retrieved from *https://www.pewresearch.org/fact-tank/2019/01/17/where-millennials-end-and-generation-z-begins/* on Mar. 19, 2020. *See also* Steinmetz, K. (2015, Oct. 26). Help, my parents are millennials. *Time*, pp. 36-43. *See also* Meister, J. C., and Willyerd, K. (2010). *The 2020 Workplace*. New York: HarperCollins.

55. Bersin, J., & Chamorro-Premuzic, T. (2019, Sept. 26). The case for hiring older workers. *Harvard Business Review*. Retrieved from *https://hbr.org/2019/09/the-case-for-hiring-older-workers* on Nov. 4, 2019. *See also* Green, J. (2016, Jan. 31). Chowing down on boomers' brains. *Bloomberg Businessweek*, pp. 19, 20.

56. Bureau of Labor Statistics, U.S. Dept. of Labor. (2018, Sept. 20). Employee tenure summary. Retrieved from *https://www.bls.gov/news.release/tenure.nr0.htm* on Mar. 19, 2020.

57. Fry, R. (2018, April 11). Millennials are the largest generation in the U.S. labor force. Pew Research Center. Retrieved from *https://www.pewresearch.org/fact-tank/2018/04/11/millennials-largest-generation-us-labor-force/* on Mar. 19, 2020.

58. Kane, S. (2019, Dec. 12). Common characteristics of Gen X professionals. *The Balance Careers*. Retrieved from *https://www.thebalancecareers.com/common-characteristics-of-generation-x-professionals-2164682* on Mar. 19, 2020. *See also* Stephey, M. (2008, Apr. 16). Gen-X: The ignored generation? Retrieved from *www.time.com/time/arts/article/0,8599,1731528,00.html* on June 4, 2011.

59. Catalyst. (2019, Nov. 7). Generations–Demographic trends in population and workforce. Retrieved from *https://www.catalyst.org/research/generations-demographic-trends-in-population-and-workforce/* on Mar. 19, 2020.

60. Stein, J. (2013, May 20). Millennials: The me, me, me generation. *Time*. Retrieved from *www.time.com/time/magazine/article/0,9171,2143001,00.html* on July 6, 2013.

61. Stein (2013), op. cit.

62. Alton, L. (2017, June 20). How Millennials are reshaping what's important in corporate culture. *Forbes*. Retrieved from *https://www.forbes.com/sites/larryalton/2017/06/20/how-millennials-are-reshaping-whats-important-in-corporate-culture/#633fd66b2dfb* on Aug. 3, 2017.

63. Knowledge@Wharton. (2019, Jan. 22). Make way for Generation Z in the workplace. Retrieved from *https://knowledge.wharton.upenn.edu/article/make-room-generation-z-workplace/* on Jan. 23, 2019. *See also* Francis, T., and Hoefel, F. (2018, Nov.). "True Gen": Generation Z and its implications for companies. Retrieved from *https://www.mckinsey.com/industries/consumer-packaged-goods/our-insights/true-gen-generation-z-and-its-implications-for-companies* on Dec. 16, 2018.

64. Bayern, M. (2019, Oct. 28). Crossing the generation divide: 5 different generations work side-by-side - and they like it. Retrieved from *https://www.techrepublic.com/article/crossing-the-generational-divide-5-different-generations-work-side-by-side-and-they-like-it/* on Oct. 30, 2019. *See also* Erickson, T. J. (2009, Feb.). Gen Y in the workforce. *Harvard Business Review,* Reprint R0902B.

65. Lindzon, J. (2016, Mar. 16). The problem with generational stereotypes at work. *FastCompany.* Retrieved from *www.fastcompany.com/3057905/the-problem-with-generational-stereotypes-at-work* on Apr. 3, 2017. *See also* SHRM. When work works toolkit. (2014). Retrieved from *https://www.shrm.org/communities/volunteerresources/pages/whenworkworkstoolkit.aspx* on Apr. 2, 2014. *See also* Deal, J. J. (2007). *Retiring the Generation Gap.* New York: Wiley.

66. White, E. (2006, Mar. 20). Fostering diversity to aid business. *The Wall Street Journal,* p. B3.

67. Babcock, P. (2017, Feb. 24). 5 steps to improve diversity recruiting. Retrieved from *https://www.shrm.org/resourcesandtools/hr-topics/talent-acquisition/pages/five-steps-improve-diversity-recruiting.aspx* on Feb. 28, 2017. *See also* Dunham, A. B., & Stout-Jough, S. (2020). Are ethics hotlines effective? *HRMagazine* 65(1), pp. 26, 27. *See also* Hastings (2010), op. cit.

68. Peters, K., and Bush, M. (2016, Dec. 5). How the best companies do diversity right. *Fortune.* Retrieved from *http://fortune.com/2016/12/05/diversity-inclusion-workplaces/* on Apr. 4, 2017.

69. Waller and Lublin (2015), op. cit. *See also* Glazer, E. (2015, Sept. 30). Big banks to female employees: We want you. *The Wall Street Journal,* p. R4. *See also* Suddath (2018), op. cit.

70. Gurchiek, K. (2018, Mar. 9). Returnships offer employers ways to find skilled, diverse employees. *SHRM Online.* Retrieved from *https://www.shrm.org/resourcesandtools/hr-topics/organizational-and-employee-development/pages/returnships-offer-employers-ways-to-find-skilled-diverse-employees.aspx* on Mar. 10, 2018.

71. SHRM Foundation. (2017, Feb. 7). *Ernst & Young: Creating a Culture of Flexibility.* Available at *https://www.youtube.com/watch?v=z9ixbBJ0YMA.*

72. Ellis, J. (2019, April 29). what Gen Z wants. *Bloomberg Businessweek,* pp. 12, 13. *See also* Francis & Hoefel (2018). op. cit. *See also* Groden, C. (2016, Mar. 15). Five things you can do to attract millennial talent. *Fortune,* pp. 181-83.

73. Grodin (2016), op. cit. *See also* Hewlett, S. A., Sherbin, L., and Sumberg, K. (2009, Jul.-Aug.). How Gen Y and Boomers will reshape your agenda. *Harvard Business Review* 68, pp. 71-76.

74. Francis & Hoefel (2018), op. cit. *See also* Maurer (2016), op. cit.

75. Malito, A. (2020, Jan. 31). The U.S. economy would be better off if more senior citizens had jobs. *Market Watch.* Retrieved from *https://news.yahoo.com/m/d356e80e-ef44-3946-be52-3fe487098996/the-u.s.-economy-would-be.html* on Feb. 1, 2020.

76. Brandon, E. (2016, June 10). The most popular ages to retire. *US News & World Report.* Retrieved from *http://money.usnews.com/money/blogs/planning-to-retire/articles/2016-06-10/the-most-popular-ages-to-retire* on Apr. 4, 2017.

77. Bersin and Chamorro-Premuzic (2018), op. cit. *See also* Chand, M., and Tung, R. L. (2014). The aging of the world's population and its effect on global business. *Academy of Management Perspectives* 28(4), pp. 409-29. *See also* SHRM Foundation. (2017, Jan. 31). *Investing in Older Workers: The National Institutes of Health.* Available at *https://www.youtube.com/watch?v=d0W4au6pSzo.*

78. Hirsch, A. S. (2019, Oct. 1). How attracting and retaining older employees can help your business. *SHRM Online.* Retrieved from *https://www.shrm.org/resourcesandtools/hr-topics/talent-acquisition/pages/attracting-and-retaining-older-employees.aspx* on Oct. 2, 2019. *See also* Hymowitz, C. (2016, Mar. 20). Where retirement isn't job one. *Bloomberg Businessweek,* pp. 25, 26.

79. Smith, A. (2016, Feb. 17). Old vs. not-quite-as-old: The gloves come off. Retrieved from *www.shrm.org/resourcesandtools/legal-and-compliance/employment-law/pages/old-vs-not-quite-as-old-the-gloves-come-off.aspx* on Feb. 24, 2016.

80. Fairless, T. (2019, July 16). Older employees breathe new life into Europe's labor market. *The Wall Street Journal.* Retrieved from *https://www.wsj.com/articles/older-employees-breathe-new-life-into-europes-labor-market-11563269401* on July 16, 2019.

81. U.S. Bureau of Labor Statistics. (2020, Feb. 26). Persons with a disability: Labor force characteristics summary. Retrieved from *https://www.bls.gov/news.release/disabl.nr0.htm* on Mar. 20, 2020. *See also* Weber, L. (2014, Mar. 18). Are you disabled? Your boss needs to know. *The Wall Street Journal*, pp. B1, B7.

82. Flewelling, J. (2014, Nov. 10). 4 myths about hiring employees with disabilities. *Denver Business Journal*. Retrieved from *http://www.bizjournals.com/bizjournals/how-to/human-resources/2014/11/4-myths-about-hiring-employees-with-disabilities.html* on Dec. 7, 2015.

83. For much more information on this, consult the Job Accommodation Network at *www.jan.wvu.edu*.

84. Zielinski, D. (2016, Dec. 20). New assistive technologies aid employees with disabilities. Retrieved from *www.shrm.org/resourcesandtools/hr-topics/technology/pages/new-assistive-technologies-aid-employees-with-disabilities.aspx* on Jan. 23, 2017. *See also* Schuman (2017), op. cit.

85. Schneider, J., and Auten, D. (2018, Aug. 4). The $1 trillion marketing executives are ignoring. *Forbes*. Retrieved from *https://www.forbes.com/sites/debtfreeguys/2018/08/14/the-1-trillion-marketing-executives-are-ignoring/#1ec5c6c0a97f* on Mar. 20, 2020. *See also* Newport, F. (2018, May 22). In U.S., estimate of LGBT population rises to 4.5%. *Gallup*. Retrieved from *https://news.gallup.com/poll/234863/estimate-lgbt-population-rises.aspx* on Mar. 20, 2020. *See also* Miller, A. (2014, Feb. 24). Equality makes business sense. *Fortune*, pp. S1–S2.

86. Human Rights Campaign. (2020). LGBTQ equality at the Fortune 500. Retrieved from *https://www.hrc.org/resources/lgbt-equality-at-the-fortune-500* on Mar. 20, 2020. *See also* Steinmetz (2017), op. cit. *See also* Milligan, S. (2015, Sept.). A remarkable transformation. *HRMagazine*, pp. 28–33.

87. Wells, G. (2016, Aug. 3). Apple says latest group of hires is more diverse. *The Wall Street Journal*. Retrieved from *www.wsj.com/articles/apple-says-latest-group-of-hires-is-more-diverse-1470245486* on Aug. 7, 2016. *See also* Gay partner benefits growing (2013), op. cit. *See also* Tkaczyk, C. (2010, June 14). 100 best companies to work for: REI. *Fortune*, p. 52.

88. The best big American companies for LGBT employees. (2020). *Forbes*. Retrieved from *https://www.forbes.com/pictures/mkl45fehh/the-best-big-american-companies-for-lgbt-employees-2/#2175910673b7* on Mar. 20, 2020. *See also* Hudson, D. (2016, Nov. 8). IBM named most LGBT-friendly employer in the world. Retrieved from *www.gaystarnews.com/article/ibm-named-lgbt-friendly-employer world/* on Apr. 4, 2017.

89. Ibid. *See also* IBM, Google among most gay-friendly firms: Survey. (2010, June 10). Retrieved from *www.torontosun.com/money/2010/06/10/14339156.html* on June 21, 2011.

90. Rogers (2018), op. cit. *See also* Appenteng, K. A., and Robertson, L. D. (2016, Feb. 22). Diversity is no longer as black and white as it once was. Retrieved from *www.shrm.org/resourcesandtools/hr-topics/behavioral-competencies/global-and-cultural-effectiveness/pages/diversity-not-black-and-white.aspx* on Mar. 15, 2017.

91. "Retain talent, but develop it, Pepsi Bottling chief says," (2008, Apr. 21). *USAToday*, p. 5B. *See also* Waller, N. & Lublin, J. S. (2015, Sep. 30). What's holding women back in the workplace? *The Wall Street Journal*. Retrieved from *www.wsj.com/articles/whats-holding-women-back-in-the-workplace-1443600242* on Oct. 1, 2015.

92. O'Brien, S. A. (2019, July 15). Uber will tie executive compensation to meeting diversity goals. *CNN Business*. Retrieved from *https://www.cnn.com/2019/07/15/tech/uber-diversity-report-2019/index.html* on July 15, 2019.

93. Dubey, R. and Hirsch, A. S. (2018, Mar. 19). Viewpoint: Building a business case for diversity and inclusion. *SHRM Online*. Retrieved from *https://www.shrm.org/resourcesandtools/hr-topics/behavioral-competencies/global-and-cultural-effectiveness/pages/viewpoint-building-a-business-case-for-diversity-and-inclusion.aspx* on Mar. 20, 2018.

94. Ibid.

95. Stanley, T. L. (2019, Apr. 29). Q&A: How Denny's advertising Is embracing inclusivity as more than a buzzword. *Adweek*. Retrieved from *https://www.adweek.com/brand-marketing/qa-how-dennys-advertising-is-embracing-inclusivity-as-more-than-a-buzzword/*. *See also* Denny's–diversity factsheet. (2019). Retrieved from *https://www.dennys.com/assets/files/diversity/Diversity-Fact-Sheet.pdf?v=2.1.4.408* on Mar. 20, 2020.

6

PLANNING FOR PEOPLE

Questions This Chapter Will Help Managers Answer

LO 6-1 How can business strategy be integrated with strategic workforce planning?

LO 6-2 How might job-design principles and job analysis be useful to the practicing manager?

LO 6-3 What is strategic workforce planning, and how should I begin that process?

LO 6-4 How can organizations balance "make," "buy," or "rent" decisions with respect to talent?

LO 6-5 How should organizations manage leadership succession?

LEADERSHIP SUCCESSION—A KEY CHALLENGE FOR ALL ORGANIZATIONS*

The death or illness of a chief executive is a crisis that most companies rarely face. McDonald's Corporation did so twice in just 7 months in what was widely viewed as a model of **succession planning**. When James Cantalupo died of a heart attack in April, within hours the board of directors appointed his second-in-command, Charles Bell, who had been groomed for the job. And when Bell resigned in late November after being diagnosed with colon cancer, the board named Vice Chairman James Skinner to the job. Leaving nothing to chance, it promoted U.S. operations chief Michael Roberts to president and chief operating officer, in line to succeed Skinner, 60. When Skinner retired 7 years later, the president and chief operating officer succeeded him in a predictable, smooth transition.

Unfortunately, McDonald's is the exception. Recent data indicate that 20 percent of public and 32 percent of private companies have no CEO succession plans in place. A higher percentage haven't even identified an interim CEO, in case the incumbent leaves abruptly. In contrast, firms such as 3M, Verizon, ExxonMobil, Goldman Sachs, Johnson & Johnson, United Parcel Service, and PepsiCo benefited enormously from building strong teams of internal leaders, which, in turn, resulted in seamless transitions in executive leadership.

Why don't more boards groom internal candidates for top leadership jobs? In part, because at the heart of succession lie personality, ego, power, and–most importantly–mortality. Moreover, some boards tend to look the other way on the succession question when the CEO makes the numbers and is singularly focused on pleasing Wall Street the next quarter, or when he or she purges talented subordinates rather than prepare them to take over. Here are several other, more concrete obstacles to leadership succession planning: poor dynamics between the board and the CEO; the lack of a well-defined process; poorly defined ownership of succession-planning responsibilities; a scarcity of internal, CEO-ready talent; and an inability to assess objectively any potential internal candidates.

Are boards serving shareholders when they let these barriers get in the way of leadership development and succession-planning efforts? Hardly. Companies that fire their CEOs forgo an average of $1.8 billion in shareholder value compared with companies that have planned successions.

Ideally, careful succession planning grooms people internally. Doing so maintains the intellectual capital of an organization, and it motivates senior-level executives to stay and to excel because they might get to lead the company someday. On the other hand, there are also sound reasons that a company might look to an outside successor. Boards that hire outsiders to be CEOs feel that change is more important than continuity, particularly so in situations where things have not been going well.

Sources: Faughnder, R. (2020, Feb. 25). Bob Iger steps down at Disney, Bob Chapek named new CEO. *Los Angeles Times.* Retrieved from *https://www.latimes.com/entertainment-arts/business/story/2020-02-25/bob-chapek-named-walt-disney-co-ceo-replacing-bob-iger* on Mar. 21, 2020. Consulting.us. (2020, Mar. 10). More than half of companies didn't have female candidate for CEO. Retrieved from *https://www.consulting.us/news/3908/more-than-half-of-companies-didnt-have-female-candidate-for-ceo* on Mar. 7, 2020. Sahadi, J. (2019, Sept. 6). A surprising number of companies don't have a CEO succession plan. Here's why. *CNN Business.* Retrieved from *https://www.cnn.com/2019/09/06/success/ceo-succession/index.html* on Mar. 21, 2020. Berns, K. V. D., & Klarner, P. 2017. A review of the CEO succession literature and a future research program. *Academy of Management Perspectives* 31, pp. 83-108. Fitzpatrick, D., Enrich, D., and Lublin, J. S. (2009, Oct. 2). BofA directors scramble to lay a succession plan. *The Wall Street Journal,* p. C1, C3.

Such was the case when Ford Motor Co. reached out to Alan Mulally, then CEO of Boeing Commercial Airplanes. It turned out to be a stroke of genius for Ford. Another situation in which an outsider makes sense is when a company has been engulfed in scandal. Hiring an outsider signals a change in direction, an effort to "re-float the boat."

In the conclusion to this case, we will see how several leading-edge firms avoid a crisis in succession planning by institutionalizing their leadership-succession processes. We'll also offer some concrete steps that any board can take.

Challenges

1. If planning for leadership succession is so important, why don't more organizations do it?
2. What sort of leadership-development process would you recommend?
3. As board chairperson, how might you overcome the resistance of a CEO to plan for succession?

To make intelligent decisions about HR strategy, the best ways to deploy and manage people, you need two types of information: (1) a description of the strategy that a firm will use to compete for business in the marketplace and (2) work design, including a description of the work to be done, the skills needed, and the training required for various types of work. Only then does it makes sense to plan for the numbers and skills mix of people required at some future time period. We consider the first of these needs, business strategy, HR strategy, and work design, in the sections that follow. We consider strategic workforce planning in the latter part of the chapter.

BUSINESS STRATEGY—FOUNDATION FOR ALL ORGANIZATIONAL DECISIONS

Business strategy consists of the decisions, processes, and choices that firms make to position themselves for sustainable success. Likewise, **HR strategy** consists of the decisions, processes, and choices that firms make about how to manage their people.[1] The goal is to ensure that all resources, including people, are deployed and managed in relation to their importance to strategic success and in a manner that allows an organization to sustain its competitive advantages. The final step is strategy execution, in which firms take the necessary actions to implement their strategies. After all, decisions are of little use unless they are acted upon. Strategy execution makes the intended strategy real.

How firms compete with each other and how they attain and sustain competitive advantage are the essence of what is known as strategic management.[2] Successful firms strive to develop sustainable competitive advantages by doing something that is valuable, rare, and difficult to imitate. For example, they may achieve competitive advantage through cost leadership or differentiation, or by focusing narrowly on a market segment. Consider differentiation as an example. Firms strive to create differences in their products or services by offering something that is perceived industrywide as unique and valued by customers–for example,

- Prestige (Ritz-Carlton hotels or BMW automobiles).
- Technology (Bose sound systems, Apple).
- Innovation (Amazon, Square, Tencent).
- Customer service (Lexus, Nordstrom department stores).

FedEx CEO and founder Fred Smith claims that the key to his firm's success is innovation. He contends that his management team did not understand its real goal when the firm started operating in 1971: "We thought that we were selling the transportation of goods; in fact, we were selling peace of mind."[3] Today, customers can track the progress of their packages right from their personal computers or from their mobile devices.

Ensuring Coherence in Strategic Direction

Organizations are more likely to be successful if everyone from the mailroom to the boardroom is striving for common goals and objectives. From general to specific, those goals form a hierarchy that includes vision, mission, and strategic objectives.

An organization's vision should be "massively inspiring, overarching, and long term."[4] Emotionally driven, it is a fundamental statement of an organization's values, aspirations, and goals. Here are some examples:[5]

- "To be the happiest place on earth" (Disneyland).
- "Restoring patients to full life" (Medtronic).
- "To be the world's best quick-service restaurant" (McDonald's).

A vision may or may not succeed. It depends on whether everything else happens according to a firm's strategy. In the case of Apple, the careful alignment of strategy formulation and execution led to its winning top honors in 2019 among the World's Most Admired Companies in the following categories: people management, social responsibility, the quality of management, the quality of its products/services, and global competitiveness.[6]

A mission statement differs from a vision statement in that it includes both the purpose of the company and the basis of competition and competitive advantage. Here is Costco's:

To continually provide our members with quality goods and services at the lowest possible prices. In order to achieve our mission we will conduct our business with the following Code of Ethics in mind:

- Obey the law.
- Take care of our members.
- Take care of our employees.
- Respect our suppliers
- Reward our shareholders.[7]

Costco has generated one of the most fanatically loyal customer bases the retail industry has ever seen.

The most important audience for a mission statement is employees because it helps build a common understanding of an organization's purpose and its intended competitive advantage in the marketplace. Strategic objectives operationalize the mission statement. They may be financial or nonfinancial, but in both cases they need to provide guidance on how an organization can fulfill or move toward its higher-level goals: vision and mission. For example, CVS Health plans to open 1,500 HealthHubs by 2021. Each will offer an expanded range of health services and wellness products for everyday care and chronic conditions.[8] This objective is **SMART**– it is *S*pecific, *M*easurable, *A*ppropriate (consistent with the vision and mission), *R*ealistic (challenging but doable), and *T*imely.

SMART objectives have several advantages. They help to channel the efforts of all employees toward common goals. They can motivate and inspire employees to higher levels of commitment and effort. Finally, they can provide a yardstick to measure performance, and thus the distribution of rewards and incentives.

Other objectives are even more specific. These are short-term objectives–essential components of action plans that are critical to executing a firm's chosen strategy. We will have more to say about action plans later in the chapter as we discuss strategic workforce planning.

Although planning business strategy clearly offers a number of benefits, there is also a potential downside in that it may lock companies into a particular vision of the future–one that may not come to pass. This poses a dilemma: how to plan for the future when the future changes so quickly. The answer is to make the planning process more democratic. Include a wide range of people, from line managers to customers to suppliers. Top managers must listen and be prepared to shift plans in midstream, if conditions demand it. Cisco Systems takes exactly this approach. It is not wedded to any particular technology because it recognizes that customers ultimately choose the technology that best fits their needs. It listens carefully to its customers and then offers solutions that customers want.

Business strategy provides an overall direction and focus for the organization as a whole, including for each functional area of the business. In this book, our primary focus is on managing people, and overall business strategy provides choices to guide the type of talent that will be necessary to win in the marketplace. HR strategy is much more specific with respect to the selection, deployment, and management of talent. The next section addresses the relationship between HR and business strategy in more detail.

RELATIONSHIP OF HR STRATEGY TO BUSINESS STRATEGY

Human resource (HR) strategy parallels and facilitates implementation of the strategic business plan. It requires a focus on planned major changes in the business and on critical issues such as the following: What are the HR implications of the proposed business strategies? What are the possible external constraints and requirements? What are the implications for management practices, management development, and management succession? What can be done in the short term to prepare for longer-term needs? In this approach to the strategic management of human resources, a firm's business strategy and its HR strategy are interdependent.[9]

Figure 6-1 is a model that shows the relationship of HR strategy to the broader business strategy.[10] Briefly, the model shows that planning proceeds top-down, while execution proceeds bottom-up. There are four links in the model, beginning

---

Figure 6–1

The relationship of HR strategy to the broader strategy of a business.

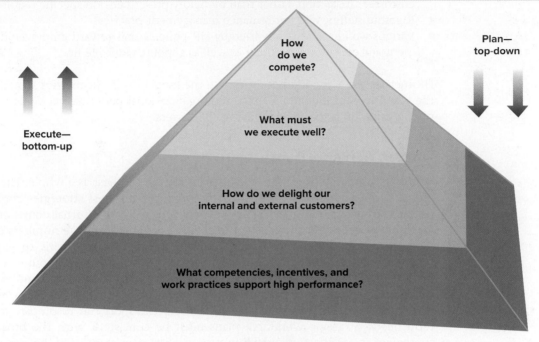

Source: HR in Alignment: The Link to Business Results, DVD.

with the fundamental question "How do we compete?" As we noted earlier, firms may compete on a number of nonindependent dimensions, such as innovation, quality, cost leadership, or speed. From that, it becomes possible to identify business processes that the firm must execute well in order to compete (e.g., speedy order fulfillment). When processes are executed well, the organization delights its internal and external customers through high performance. This may occur, for example, when an employee presents a timely, cost-effective solution to a customer's problem.

To manage and motivate employees to strive for high performance, the right competencies, incentives, and work practices must be in place. Execution proceeds bottom-up, as those competencies, incentives, and work practices inspire high performance, which makes everyone happy. This, in turn, means that business processes are being executed efficiently, enabling the organization to compete successfully for business in the marketplace.

At a general level, high-performance work practices include such workplace features as the following:[11]

- Worker empowerment, participation, and autonomy.
- The use of self-managed and cross-functional teams.

- Flat organizational structures.
- The use of contingent or "gig" workers.
- Flexible design of work defined by roles, processes, output requirements, and customer satisfaction, rather than by rigidly prescribed, job-specific requirements.
- Rigorous staffing and performance management practices.
- Various worker- and family-friendly HR policies that reward employee development and continuous learning as well as support work-life fit.

HR metrics serve as a kind of overlay to the model itself. HR metrics should reflect the key drivers of individual, team, and organizational performance. When they do, the organization is measuring what really matters.

Strategic Workforce Plans

Strategic workforce plans parallel the plans for the business as a whole. They focus on questions such as these: What do the proposed business strategies imply with respect to human resources? What kinds of internal and external constraints will (or do) we face? For example, the projected retirements of large numbers of older workers are an internal constraint on the ability of some firms to expand,[12] whereas a projected shortfall in the supply of college graduate computer scientists (relative to the demand for them by employers) is an external constraint. What are the implications for staffing, compensation practices, training and development, and management succession? What can be done in the short run to prepare for long-term needs? Strategic workforce plans must be consistent with the broader HR strategy of an organization, which in turn must be consistent with the overall strategy of the business. Figure 6-2 shows the relationship between business planning—long-range, mid-range, and annual—and parallel processes that occur in strategic workforce planning.

As Figure 6-2 shows, workforce plans are firm-level responses to people-related business issues over multiple time horizons. Such issues might include "What types of skills will managers need to run the business 3-5 years from now, and how do we make sure we'll have them?" At a broader level, issues include the impact of rapid technological change, more complex organizations (in terms of products, locations, customers, and markets), responses to external forces such as legislation and litigation, demographic changes, and increasing multinational competition. In this scenario, people-related business issues drive actions, and actions include programs and processes to address them.[13]

Realistically, HR concerns become business concerns only when they affect the line manager's ability to function effectively.[14] Such concerns may result from an immediate issue, such as downsizing or a labor shortage, or from a longer-term issue, such as management development and succession planning. On the other hand, people-related business issues such as the need for upskilling in response to new technology, growth or no-growth assumptions, or mergers, are issues that affect the competitiveness of an organization and its ability to survive. Progressive firms recognize that people-related business issues have powerful impacts on their strategic business and workforce plans.

We will have more to say about strategic workforce plans in a later section, but first we need to address the analysis of jobs and work as well as the kinds of personal characteristics they require. We begin by considering the concept of a job in in today's world of work.

Figure 6–2

Impact of three levels of business planning on workforce planning.

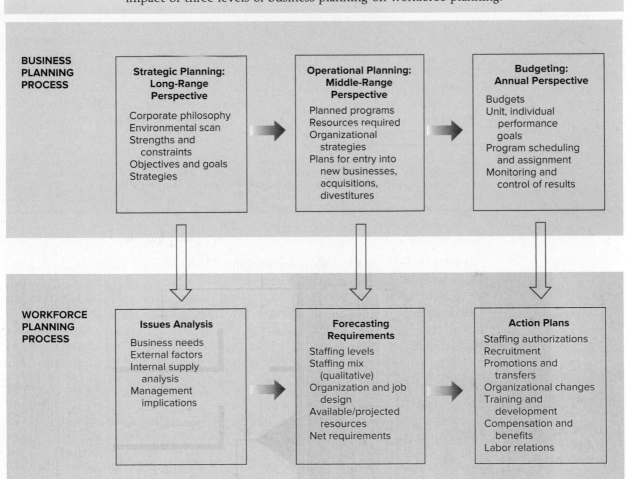

BUSINESS PLANNING PROCESS

Strategic Planning: Long-Range Perspective

Corporate philosophy
Environmental scan
Strengths and constraints
Objectives and goals
Strategies

Operational Planning: Middle-Range Perspective

Planned programs
Resources required
Organizational strategies
Plans for entry into new businesses, acquisitions, divestitures

Budgeting: Annual Perspective

Budgets
Unit, individual performance goals
Program scheduling and assignment
Monitoring and control of results

WORKFORCE PLANNING PROCESS

Issues Analysis

Business needs
External factors
Internal supply analysis
Management implications

Forecasting Requirements

Staffing levels
Staffing mix (qualitative)
Organization and job design
Available/projected resources
Net requirements

Action Plans

Staffing authorizations
Recruitment
Promotions and transfers
Organizational changes
Training and development
Compensation and benefits
Labor relations

JOBS AND WORK: CONSTANT CHANGE

Jobs and work are changing constantly. Sometimes the changes occur at a dizzying pace because fluid organizations fighting to stay competitive require their people to adapt constantly and quickly. Fully 70 percent of key people say their jobs change substantially every 2 to 3 years.[15] Despite all the changes, using a job as a way to organize and group tasks and responsibilities has not yet disappeared, especially in large organizations.[16]

JOBS, INDIVIDUALS, AND ORGANIZATIONS

Jobs are important to individuals: They help determine standards of living, places of residence, status (value ascribed to individuals because of their positions), and even a personal sense of self-worth. Jobs are important to organizations because they are the

HR BUZZ

YOU DO WHAT? HACKER HUNTER

Increasing cyber threats make cyber analysis a growth area for everyone from banks to start-ups, as recent hacks of Equifax, Yahoo!, and Facebook have added to the rush for more qualified staff. Hacker hunters face off against increasingly sophisticated hackers to protect critical financial and security information. They also develop strategies to resist attack, or to track down culprits after the fact. To do the job well, hacker hunters need a computer science–related degree as a baseline; they must be motivated to hack legally; and additional experience in risk management, forensics, or psychology is a plus. With the average data breach costing $3.9 million to fix, demand for hacker hunters will only grow.

Sources: Osborne, C. (2019, Dec. 12). These are the worst hacks, cyberattacks, and data breaches of 2019. *ZDNet.* Retrieved from *https://www.zdnet.com/article/these-are-the-worst-hacks-cyberattacks-and-data-breaches-of-2019/* on Mar. 24, 2020. Mahan, R. (2016, June 9). On the job: Hacker hunter. *Psychology Today.* Retrieved from *www.psychologytoday.com/articles/200811/the-job-hacker-hunter* on Apr. 7, 2017.

vehicles through which work is accomplished. Some jobs are highly unusual, as the example of the "hacker hunter" illustrates.

Earlier we noted the need to look at the design and content of jobs from the perspective of the entire organization. **Job design** examines how work is structured, organized, experienced, and enacted.[17] It should link closely to business strategy because the strategy might require new and different tasks, for example, by incorporating new technology or different ways of performing the same tasks. Here is an example.

Identifying the Work to Be Done and the Personal Characteristics Needed to Do the Work

A fundamental requirement in any organization is to describe the work to be done and the kinds of personal characteristics (knowledge, skills, abilities, personality dimensions) that are required to do the work. That is the purpose of job or work analysis. The results of that process are used in virtually every aspect of employment, from staffing to compensation.

One result of the process of job analysis is a **job description** (an overall written summary of task requirements). A second is a **job specification** (an overall written summary of worker requirements). In the past, such job definitions often tended to be quite narrow in scope. Today, however, some organizations are beginning to develop behavioral job descriptions or specifications of work-role requirements. They tend to be more stable, even as technologies and customer needs change.[18]

For example, instead of focusing on communication skills, such as writing, speaking, and making presentations, behavioral job descriptions incorporate broader behavioral statements, such as "actively listens, builds trust, and adapts his or her style and tactics to fit the audience." These behaviors will not change, even as the means of executing them evolve with technology. Instead of being responsible for simple procedures and predictable tasks, workers are now expected to draw inferences and render diagnoses, judgments, and decisions, often under severe time constraints.[19]

TECHNOLOGY INNOVATION LEADS TO CHANGES IN JOB DESIGN

HR BUZZ

Within the next three years, American manufacturers are on track to employ more college graduates than workers with a high school education or less. It's part of a shift toward automation that has increased factory output, provided opportunities for more women, and reduced prospects for lower-skilled workers. Pioneer Service Inc. is a 40-person machine shop outside of Chicago that has invested in new technology to create a bright future for its employees.

Pioneer makes complex components for the aerospace industry as well as for Tesla vehicles and other luxury cars. In 2012, when business dropped 90 percent after Pioneer's biggest clients, heating and cooling systems, switched to cheaper foreign suppliers, company president Aneesa Muthana hired Pioneer's first salespeople. They found vehicle makers that needed complex metal components that Pioneer could make more profitably than the parts for heaters and air conditioners. Pioneer had little experience with the advanced equipment needed, but Muthana persuaded suppliers to help her install the machines and train employees to use them. The cost of the new technology was more than $6 million, but the machines can make one complex part every 6 minutes, compared with 45 minutes on multiple machines previously. Learning how wasn't easy, and many longtime employees left. The switch to new technology paid off, though. Pioneer had its highest revenue last year. Production workers start at $14 an hour and rise to $27 an hour with experience. Half of Pioneer's 40 employees are women.

ColorBlind Images/Blend Images LLC

Source: Hufford, A. (2019, Dec. 9). American factories demand white-collar education for blue-collar work. *The Wall Street Journal.* Retrieved from *https://www.wsj.com/articles/american-factories-demand-white-collar-education-for-blue-collar-work-11575907185* on Dec. 9, 2019.

LEGALITIES

JOB ANALYSIS AND THE AMERICANS WITH DISABILITIES ACT (ADA) OF 1990

Job analyses are not legally required under the ADA, but sound professional practice suggests that they be done for three reasons:

1. The law makes it clear that job applicants must be able to understand what the essential functions of a job are before they can respond to the question "Can you perform the essential functions of this job?" A function may be essential because the reason the position exists at all is to perform that function (e.g., a baggage handler at an airport must be able to lift bags weighing up to 70 pounds repeatedly throughout an 8-hour shift). Alternatively, the function may be so highly specialized that it cannot be shifted to others (e.g., a licensed pharmacist must dispense doctors' prescriptions). Job analysis is a systematic procedure that can help to identify essential job functions.

2. Existing job analyses may need to be updated to reflect additional dimensions of jobs—namely, the physical demands, environmental demands, and mental abilities required to perform essential functions. Figure 6-3 shows a portion of a checklist of physical demands.

3. Once job analyses are updated as described, a summary of the results is normally prepared in writing in the form of a job description.[a] What may work even better under the ADA, however, is a video job description that illustrates the physical, environmental (e.g., temperatures, noise level, working space), or mental (e.g., irate customers calling with complaints) demands of jobs. Candidates who are unable to perform a job because of a physical or mental disability may self-select out, thereby minimizing the likelihood of a legal challenge.

If a candidate with a disability can perform the essential functions of a job and is hired, the employer must be willing to make "reasonable accommodations" to enable the person to work.[b] Here are some examples that the ADA defines as "reasonable" accommodation efforts:

- Restructuring a job so that someone else does the nonessential tasks a person with a disability cannot do.
- Modifying work hours or work schedules, so that a person with a disability can commute during off-peak periods.
- Reassigning a worker who becomes disabled to a vacant position.
- Acquiring or modifying equipment or devices (e.g., a telecommunications device for the deaf).
- Modifying examinations, training materials, or HR policies.
- Providing qualified readers or interpreters.

---

[a]Brannen, D. A. (2016, Feb. 17). Why you should have job descriptions. Retrieved from www.shrm.org/resourcesandtools/hr-topics/talent-acquisition/pages/why-you-should-have-job-descriptions.aspx on Mar. 14, 2016.

[b]U.S. EEOC. The ADA: Your responsibilities as an employer (addendum). Retrieved from *https://www.eeoc.gov/facts/ada17.html* on Mar. 24, 2020. Colella, A. J., and Bruyere, S. M. (2011). Disability and employment: New directions for industrial and organizational psychology. In S. Zedeck (Ed.), *APA Handbook of Industrial and Organizational Psychology* (Vol. 1). Washington, DC: American Psychological Association, pp. 473–503.

Use the symbols below to rate the following activities:

NP	Not present	Activity does not exist.
O	Occasionally	Activity exists up to 1/3 of the time.
F	Frequently	Activity exists about half of the time
C	Constantly	Activity exists 2/3 or more of the time.

1a. Strength (also enter the percentage of time spent in each activity)

_____ Standing   _____ percent

_____ Walking   _____ percent

_____ Sitting   _____ percent

1b. Also indicate the number of pounds that must be lifted, carried, pushed, or pulled.

_____ Lifting   _____ (weight)

_____ Carrying   _____ (weight)

_____ Pushing   _____ (weight)

_____ Pulling   _____ (weight)

 2. Climbing   _____

 3. Balancing   _____

 4. Stooping   _____

 5. Kneeling   _____

 6. Crouching   _____

 7. Crawling   _____

 8. Reaching   _____

 9. Talking (Ordinary)_____(Other)_____

10. Hearing (Ordinary conversation)_____(Other)_____

Figure 6–3

Portion of a physical-abilities checklist.

Job specifications should reflect *minimally* acceptable qualifications for job incumbents. Frequently, they do not, reflecting instead a profile of the *ideal* job incumbent. How are job specifications set? Typically, they are set by consensus among experts–immediate supervisors, job incumbents, and job analysts.[20] Such a procedure is professionally acceptable, but be careful to distinguish between required and desirable qualifications. The term *required* assumes that without this qualification, an individual absolutely would be unable to do the job (e.g., certification or licensure). *Desirable* is "nice to have," but it is not a "need to have" (e.g., for some jobs, education or experience requirements). Required qualifications will exist in almost all jobs, but know that they must meet a higher standard.

Competency Models

Competency models attempt to identify variables related to overall organizational fit and to identify personality characteristics consistent with the organization's vision and mission (e.g., drive for results, persistence, innovation, flexibility).[21] The goal is to link organizational strategy to desired individual characteristics. As such, they are written in terms that operating managers can relate to.

Competency models are a form of job or work analysis that focus on broader characteristics of individuals and on using these characteristics to inform HR practices. They focus on the full range of knowledge, skills, abilities, and other characteristics (e.g., motives, traits, attitudes, personality characteristics), so-called KSAOs, that are needed for effective performance on the job and that characterize exceptional performers. Ideally, such a model consists of a set of **competencies** that have been identified as necessary for successful performance, with behavioral indicators associated with high performance on each one.[22]

Is competency modeling different from job analysis? A rigorous comparison concluded that competency approaches typically begin with an organization's business context and competitive strategy and then establish a line-of-sight between individual competency requirements and the broader goals of an organization. Job analyses generally do not make this connection, but their level of rigor and documentation are more likely to enable them to withstand the close scrutiny of a legal challenge. As currently practiced, therefore, competency modeling is not a substitute for job analysis.

Neither job analysis nor competency modeling is a single approach to studying work, and there is much variability in the ways they are implemented in actual practice.[23] Moreover, no single type of description of work content (competencies, KSAOs, work activities, performance standards) is appropriate for all purposes, and purpose is a key consideration in choosing any particular approach to the study of work.

How Do We Study Job Requirements?

A number of methods are available to study jobs.[24] At the outset, it is important to note that none alone is sufficient. Rather, use a combination of them to obtain a total picture of the task and the physical, mental, social, and environmental demands of a job. Here are five common methods:

1. *Job performance.* With this approach, an analyst actually performs the job under study to get firsthand exposure to what it demands.
2. *Observation.* The analyst simply observes a worker or group of workers doing a job. Without interfering, the analyst uses a standard format to record the what, why, and how of the various parts of the job.
3. *Interview.* In many jobs in which it is not possible for the analyst actually to perform the job (e.g., airline pilot) or where observation is impractical (e.g., architect), it is necessary to rely on workers' own descriptions of what they do, why, and how. As with recordings of observations, use a standard format to collect input. In this way, all questions and responses can be restricted to job-related topics. More importantly, standardization makes it possible to compare what different people are saying about the job in question.
4. *Critical incidents.* These are vignettes comprising brief actual reports that illustrate particularly effective or ineffective worker behaviors—for example,

   On January 14, a customer asked Mr. Vin, the restaurant's wine steward, about an obscure bottle of wine. Without hesitation, he described the place of vintage and bottling, the meaning of the words on the label, and the characteristics of the grapes in the year of vintage.

   After collecting many of these little incidents from knowledgeable individuals, it is possible to categorize them according to the general job area they describe. The end result is a fairly clear picture of actual job requirements.

5. *Structured questionnaires.* These questionnaires list tasks, behaviors (e.g., negotiating, coordinating, using both hands), or both. Tasks focus on *what* gets done. This is a job-oriented approach. Behaviors, on the other hand, focus on *how* a job is done. This is a worker-oriented, or ability-requirements, approach. Workers rate each task or behavior in terms of whether or not it is performed, and if it is, they rate characteristics such as frequency, importance, level of difficulty, and relationship to overall performance. The ratings provide a basis for scoring the questionnaires and for developing a profile of actual job requirements.[25] The ability to represent job content in terms of numbers allows relatively precise comparisons across different jobs.[26]

The preceding five methods of job analysis represent the popular ones in use today. Table 6–1 considers the pros and cons of each method. Regardless of the method used,

Table 6–1

ADVANTAGES AND DISADVANTAGES OF FIVE POPULAR JOB-ANALYSIS METHODS

Method	Advantages	Disadvantages
Job performance	With this method there is exposure to actual job tasks as well as to the physical, environmental, and social demands of the job. Use it for jobs that can be learned in a relatively short period of time.	This method is inappropriate for jobs that require extensive training or are hazardous to perform.
Observation	Direct exposure to jobs can provide a richer, deeper understanding of job requirements than workers' descriptions of what they do.	If the work is primarily mental, observations alone may reveal little useful information. Critical, yet rare, job requirements (e.g., "copes with emergencies") may not be observed.
Interviews	This method can provide information about standard as well as nonstandard and mental work. Workers can report on activities that would not be observed often and that might not be available from any other source.	Workers may be suspicious of interviewers and their motives; interviewers may ask ambiguous questions. Thus, distortion of information is a possibility. Hence, the interview should never be used as the sole job-analysis method.
Critical incidents	This method focuses directly on what people do in their jobs, and thus it provides insight into job dynamics. Because the behaviors in question are observable and measurable, information derived from this method can be used for most applications of job analysis.	It takes considerable time to gather, abstract, and categorize the incidents. Also, because the incidents describe particularly effective or ineffective behavior, it may be difficult to develop a profile of average job behavior—the main objective in job analysis.
Structured questionnaires	This method is generally cheaper and quicker than other methods. Questionnaires can be completed off the job, thus avoiding lost productive time. Web-based questionnaires allow analysts to survey geographically dispersed job incumbents, in English as well as in other languages. Questionnaires offer a breadth of coverage and speed of analysis and feedback that are impossible to obtain otherwise.	Questionnaires are often time-consuming and expensive to develop. Rapport between analyst and respondent is not possible unless the analyst is present to explain items and clarify misunderstandings. Such an impersonal approach may have adverse effects on respondent cooperation and motivation.

Table 6–2

JOB-ANALYSIS METHODS AND THE PURPOSES BEST SUITED TO EACH

Method	Job descriptions	Development of tests	Development of interviews	Job evaluation	Training design	Performance review	Career-path planning
Job performance		X	X		X	X	
Observation	X	X	X				
Interviews	X	X	X	X	X	X	
Critical incidents	X	X	X		X	X	
Questionnaires:							
Task checklists	X	X	X	X	X	X	
Behavior checklists			X	X	X	X	X

the workers providing job information to the analyst must be experienced and knowledgeable about the jobs in question.[27] Trained job analysts tend to provide the highest levels of agreement about the components of jobs,[28] although there seem to be no differences in the quality of information provided by members of different gender or race/ethnic subgroups[29] or by high as opposed to low performers.[30] Incumbents, however, tend to provide higher ratings of abilities required in a job than do supervisors or trained job analysts.[31] In terms of the types of data actually collected, the most popular methods today are observation, interviews, and structured questionnaires.

Job Analysis: Relating Method to Purpose

Given such a wide choice among available job-analysis methods, the combination of methods to use is the one that best fits the *purpose* of the research (e.g., staffing, training design, performance reviews). Table 6-2 suggests some possible match-ups between job analysis methods and various purposes. For example, the job-performance method of job analysis is most appropriate for the development of tests and interviews, training design, and performance-review systems.

FROM JOB ANALYSIS TO STRATEGIC WORKFORCE PLANNING

Having identified the behavioral requirements of jobs, the organization is in a position to identify the numbers of employees and the skills required to do those jobs, at least in the short term. **Strategic workforce planning (SWP)** is the formal process that connects business strategy to human resource strategy and practices, and ensures that a company has the right people in the right place, at the right time, and at the right cost.[32] SWP focuses on firm-level responses to people-related business issues over multiple planning horizons (see Figure 6-2). With respect to each one, there are two key questions to address:[33]

(1) Which factors are likely to have the greatest impact on the ability of our organization to achieve its short- and long-range objectives?

(2) How might these effects change over the short, mid-range, and long terms?

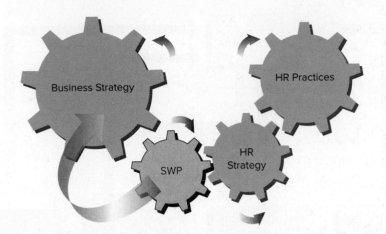

Figure 6–4

Model of strategic workforce planning in action.
Source: Young, M. B. (2010). *Strategic Workforce Planning in Global Organizations.* New York: The Conference Board.

In this framework, changes in the business environment drive issues, issues drive actions, and actions include programs and processes to address the business issues identified (see Figure 6-4).

The arrows in Figure 6-4 show what happens as SWP matures and business leaders understand its value. No longer is SWP simply driven by business strategy. It also becomes an input to business strategy, providing data, analytics, and insights to inform, and sometimes challenge, executive decision making.[34] In global organizations, SWP delivers value in four ways.[35]

1. *It uncovers significant differences among business units or locations,* such as which countries' workforces will grow or shrink, and by how much. It also reveals how the regional supply of talent compares to the demand, and where the company derives the highest return from its investments in human capital.
2. *It provides metrics and other tools to support business decisions.* For example, 3M uses productivity metrics to help determine which countries receive additional resources and which ones receive fewer. UBS uses scenario planning–the anticipated future, a bear market, and a bull market–and financial indicators to signal when the bank needs to switch its workforce plans.
3. *It enables leaders to compare the long-term implications of alternative business scenarios and HR options.* At UBS, for example, planners developed a cost model to illustrate the short-term trade-offs between various staffing options, as well as the long-term costs of failing to develop a coherent, regional talent strategy.
4. *It supports different kinds of planning at different levels of the organization.* SWP raises the discussion from a tactical to a strategic level and incorporates long-term considerations such as labor supply, regulatory changes, infrastructure, and costs.

Now let's consider in more detail how SWPs actually work.

Strategic Workforce-Planning Systems

Several specific, interrelated activities constitute an SWP system (see Figure 6-5):

- A *talent inventory* to identify the skills, abilities, and potential of the current workforce.

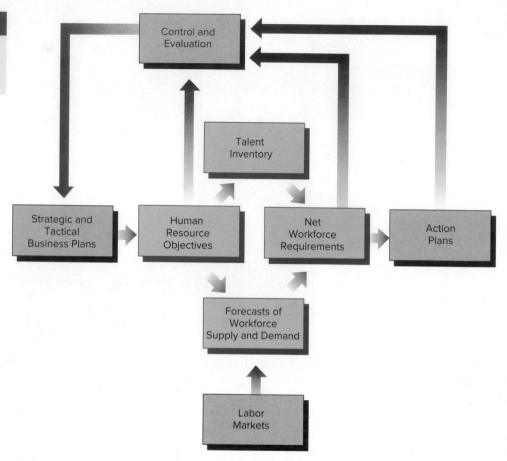

Figure 6–5

An integrated, strategic workforce-planning system.

- A *workforce forecast* to predict future people requirements based on an analysis of the future availability (supply) of labor and future demand for labor, informed by an analysis of external conditions (e.g., technologies, markets, competition).
- *Action plans* to enlarge the pool of people qualified to fill the projected vacancies through such actions as recruitment, selection, training, placement, transfer, promotion, development, and compensation.
- *Control and evaluation* to provide feedback on the overall effectiveness of the SWP system.

TALENT INVENTORY

A talent inventory is a fundamental requirement of an effective SWP system. It is an organized database of the existing skills, abilities, career interests, and experience of the current workforce. Prior to actual data collection, however, it's important to address some key questions:

1. Who should be included in the inventory?
2. What specific information must be included for each individual?

3. How can this information best be obtained?
4. What is the most effective way to record such information?
5. How can inventory results be reported to decision makers?
6. How often must this information be updated?
7. How can the security of this information be protected?

Answers to these kinds of questions will provide both direction and scope for subsequent efforts. For example, IBM uses a technology-powered staff-deployment tool called "Workforce Management Initiative."[36] It's a sort of in-house version of Monster.com, the online job site. Built on a database of 400,000 résumés, it lets managers search for employees with the precise skills they'll need for particular projects. The initiative has already saved IBM $500 million, and it has improved productivity. For example, when a health-care client needed a consultant with a clinical background, the system almost instantly targeted Lynn Yarbrough, a former registered nurse. That search would have taken more than a week in the old days.

The Workforce Management Initiative's greatest impact, however, may be its ability to help managers analyze what skills staffers possess and how those talents match up to the business outlook. It's part of a broader SWP effort. When a talent inventory is linked to other databases (i.e., in a relational database; see Chapter 2), the set of such information enables an optimal workforce strategy and an integrated talent supply chain.[37]

Information such as the following is typically included in a profile developed for each employee:

- Current position information.
- Previous positions in the company.
- Other significant work experience (e.g., other companies, military).
- Education (including degrees, licenses, certifications).
- Language skills and relevant international experience.
- Training and development programs attended.
- Community or industry leadership responsibilities.
- Current and past performance-review data.
- Disciplinary actions.
- Awards received.

Some common uses of a talent inventory include identification of candidates for promotion, leadership succession, assignments to special projects, transfer, and training as well as planning for recruitment, compensation, and careers. Information provided by individuals may also be included. At Schlumberger, for example, employees add their career goals, information about their families, past assignments, professional affiliations, publications, patents granted, and hobbies. IBM includes the individual's expressed preference for future assignments and locations, as well as interest in staff or line positions in other IBM locations and divisions.[38]

Talent inventories and workforce forecasts must complement each other; an inventory of present talent is not particularly useful for planning purposes unless it can be analyzed in terms of future workforce requirements. On the other hand, a forecast of workforce requirements is useless unless it can be evaluated relative to the current and projected future supply of workers available internally.

WORKFORCE FORECASTS

The purpose of **workforce forecasting** is to estimate an organization's requirements for talent at some future time period. Such forecasts are of two types: (1) the external and internal supply of talent and (2) the aggregate external and internal demand for that talent. We consider each type separately because each rests on a different set of assumptions and depends on a different set of variables.[39]

Internal supply forecasts relate to conditions *inside* the organization, such as the age distribution of the workforce, terminations, retirements, and new hires within job classes. In contrast, demand forecasts–internal and external–depend primarily on the behavior of some business factor (e.g., projected number of retail outlets, projected sales, product volume) to which human resource needs can be related. Unlike internal and external supply forecasts, demand forecasts are subject to many uncertainties–in domestic or worldwide economic conditions, in technology, and in consumer behavior, to name just a few. The *Occupational Outlook Handbook*, published by the U.S. Department of Labor, focuses on forecasting the aggregate demand for various occupations. In terms of the percentage increase in demand between 2018 and 2028, here are the top 20 fastest-growing occupations:[40]

Occupation	Growth Rate 2018–2028	2018 Median Pay (per year)
Solar photovoltaic installers	63%	$ 42,680
Wind turbine service technicians	57	54,370
Home health aides	37	24,200
Personal-care aides	36	24,020
Occupational therapy assistants	33	60,220
Information security analysts	32	98,350
Physician assistants	31	108,610
Statisticians	31	87,780
Nurse practitioners	28	107,030
Speech-language pathologists	27	77,510
Physical therapist assistants	27	58,040
Genetic counselors	27	80,370
Mathematicians	26	101,900
Operations research analysts	26	83,390
Software developers, applications	26	103,620
Forest fire inspectors and prevention specialists	24	39,600
Health specialties teachers, postsecondary	23	97,370
Phlebotomists	23	34,480
Physical therapist aides	23	26,240
Medical assistants	23	33,610

In the following sections, we will consider several firm-level workforce-forecasting techniques that have proven to be practical and useful.

Forecasting External Workforce Supply

The recruiting and hiring of new employees are essential activities for virtually all firms, at least over the long run. Whether due to projected expansion of operations or normal workforce attrition, forays into the labor market are necessary.

Several agencies regularly make projections of external labor market conditions and estimates of the supply of labor to be available in general categories. These include the Bureau of Labor Statistics of the U.S. Department of Labor, the National Science Foundation, the Department of Education, and the Public Health Service of the Department of Health and Human Services. For new college and university graduates, the National Association of Colleges and Employers conducts a quarterly salary survey of starting salary offers to new college graduates at the bachelor's degree level (*www.naceweb.org*), and salary offers reflect supply/demand conditions in the external labor market. Organizations in industries as varied as oil and gas, aviation, digital-media advertising, construction, and health care are finding such projections of the external labor market to be helpful in preventing surpluses or deficits of employees.[41]

Here's an example. Several years ago, some 47,000 jobs opened up worldwide in the field of computer animation. At the same time, only 14,000 animators graduated from art school. Such an imbalance between the supply and demand for new workers bids up starting salaries to the point where new hires may earn more than senior people at their companies! That's especially true of data scientists and artificial-intelligence experts. It's not just high-tech workers, either. Long-haul truckers and machinists who specialize in precision manufacturing are also in short supply. These new hires are known as "gold-collar" workers. They are educated, smart, creative, computer literate, equipped with portable skills–and in demand.[42]

Forecasting Internal Workforce Supply

A reasonable starting point for projecting a firm's future supply of labor is its current supply. Thus, when CNA Financial Corporation analyzed the demographics of various mission-critical jobs, it learned that 85 percent of its risk-control safety engineers, who inspect boilers and other machinery in buildings, were eligible for retirement. The company wanted to hold on to their specialized skills because they were so important to retaining current business. The forecast prompted the company to take action to ensure that projected deficits did not materialize.[43]

Perhaps the simplest type of internal-supply forecast is the **succession plan**, a concept that has been discussed in the planning literature for decades. Succession plans may be developed for management employees, nonmanagement employees, or both. In fact, an active succession-planning process is similar to an insurance policy; it should be there when you need it. When there is a crisis of leadership–for example, after a death or a departure–a robust succession-planning process provides needed assurance.[44]

As the chapter-opening vignette showed, there are some deep-seated reasons some firms don't deal with succession issues: personality, ego, power, and–most importantly–mortality.[45] Assuming that such barriers can be overcome, the actual mechanics for developing such a plan include steps such as the following: gaining alignment on business strategy, assessing current performance and readiness for promotion, identifying replacement candidates for each key position based on their fit with the firm's business strategy, identifying career-development needs, and

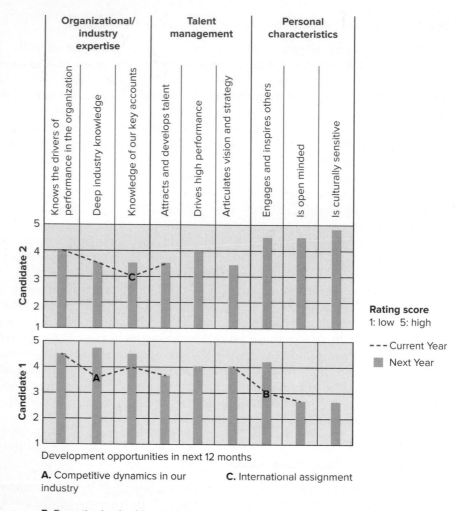

Figure 6–6

Sample senior-exec-utive criteria and ratings for use in leadership succession planning.

Source: Bjornberg, A., and Feser, C. (2015, May). *CEO succession starts with developing your leaders,* p. 4. Retrieved from *http://www.mckinsey. com/global-themes/ leadership/ceo-succession-starts-with-developing-your-leaders* on Apr. 2, 2017.

Development opportunities in next 12 months

A. Competitive dynamics in our industry

B. Executive leadership program

C. International assignment

integrating the career goals of individuals with company goals. The overall objective, of course, is to ensure the availability of competent executive talent in the future or, in some cases, immediately.[46] In view of its importance, let's examine leadership succession further in the next sections.

Leadership-Succession Planning

This is the one activity that is pervasive, well accepted, and integrated with strategic business planning among firms that do SWP.[47] In fact, leadership-succession planning is considered by many firms to be the sum and substance of SWP. A key requirement is to implement it in relation to a firm's future business strategy. Some candidates might fit today's strategy but not tomorrow's, and the focus on the future helps executives to rivet their attention where it needs to be. Figure 6-6 is an abbreviated example of a succession-planning chart for an individual manager.

Today's world is volatile, uncertain, complex, and ambiguous. Key questions to ask include, "Are we optimizing all possible types and sources of talent, to be properly hedged against the multiple futures and risks that our talent (and business) will face?"

The challenge is to understand the ways in which future scenarios are shifting, the risks inherent in the current talent base, and the options available to alleviate those risks as the scenarios unfold. Top leaders need to review their talent portfolios regularly as internal or external conditions change, for agility is the future of SWP.[48]

Leadership-succession processes are particularly well developed at 3M. With 2019 worldwide sales of $32.1 billion, two-thirds of which came from outside the United States, 3M sells 55,000 products, and it employs 93,000 people worldwide.[49]

At 3M, a common set of leadership behaviors links all management practices with respect to assessment, development, and succession:[50]

- Play to win.
- Prioritize and execute.
- Foster collaboration and teamwork.
- Develop others and self.
- Innovate.
- Act with integrity and transparency.

3M's leadership attributes describe what leaders need to know, what they need to do, and the personal qualities that they need to display. With respect to *assessment*, managers assess potential as part of the performance-review process. All managers also receive 360-degree feedback as part of leadership classes. Executive hires all go through an extensive psychometric assessment.

With respect to *development*, 3M's Global Academy of Innovative Development focuses on developing global leaders that add value to 3M, its customers, and the world we all live in. It is delivered as a key development strategy in the formation of a global leadership pipeline. 3M also uses "action learning"–experiential and real-time projects that are focused on developing creative solutions to business-critical problems or critical social challenges that achieve impact in the real-world. This is learning by doing. Participants present their final recommendations to senior-level

ETHICAL DILEMMA
Should Leadership-Succession Plans Be Secret?

This is a thorny issue. If firms keep strategic workforce planning information about specific candidates secret, planning may have limited value. Thus, at a software company, a senior executive on her way out the door for a president's job at a competitor was told that the firm had expected her to be its next president. Her response? "If I'd known, I would have stayed."

A somewhat different course of events transpired at another firm whose policy was to talk

openly about prospective candidates. There, employees learned what the company had in mind for them over the next 3 to 5 years. Subsequently, when they did not get the jobs they thought they were entitled to, employees felt betrayed. Some sued; others left. In your view, is it unethical to share planning information with employees and then not follow the plan? Conversely, do employees have a right to see such information?[51]

executives. After follow-up coaching and individual-development plans, leaders are assessed in terms of the impact of their growth on the organization strategically.

Succession planning focuses on a few key objectives: to identify top talent–that is, high-potential individuals–both within functions and corporatewide; to develop pools of talent for critical positions; and to identify development plans for key leaders. 3M's Executive Resources Committee assures consistency in both policy and practice in global succession planning for key positions, including the process for identifying, developing, and tracking the progress of high-potential individuals.

Lessons to Apply

Here are five key lessons from our brief review of leadership-succession processes:

1. The CEO must drive the talent agenda. It all begins with commitment from the top.
2. Identify and communicate a common set of leadership attributes to serve as a "road map" for people in leadership positions, and for all other employees. That way, everyone in the organization knows what is expected of leaders.
3. Use candid, comprehensive performance reviews as the building block for assessment, development, and management consensus about performance and potential.
4. Keep to a regular schedule for performance reviews, broader talent reviews, and the identification of talent pools for critical positions.
5. Link all decisions about talent to the strategy of the organization.

Forecasting Workforce Demand

In contrast to supply forecasting, demand forecasting is beset with multiple uncertainties–changes in technology; consumer attitudes and patterns of buying behavior; local, national, and international economies; number, size, and types of contracts won or lost; and government regulations that might open new markets or close off old ones, just to name a few. Consequently, forecasts of workforce demand are often more subjective than quantitative, although in practice a combination of the two is often used. Where should one begin?

Identify Pivotal Talent

Begin the process of demand forecasting by identifying pivotal jobs, those that drive strategy and revenue and differentiate your organization in the marketplace.[52] For example, materials-science firm Corning Inc., which employs 52,000 people worldwide, segmented jobs into four categories: strategic, core, requisite, and noncore. The objective? Deconstruct the business strategy to understand its implications for talent.[53]

Assessing Future Workforce Demand

To develop a reasonable estimate of the numbers and skills mix of people needed over some future time period–for example, 2–3 years–it is important to tap into the collective wisdom of managers who are close to the scene of operations. Consider asking them questions such as the following:[54]

- What are our key business goals and objectives for the next 2 years?
- What are the top three priorities we must execute well in order to reach our goals over that time period?

- What are the most critical workforce issues we currently face?
- What are the 3–5 core capabilities we need to win in our markets?
- What kinds of knowledge, skills, and abilities do we need to execute our strategy?
- What types of new positions will we need? What types will we no longer need?
- Which types of skills should we have internally, versus buy or rent?
- What actions are necessary to align our resources with priorities?
- How will we know if we are effectively executing our workforce plan?

How Accurate Is Accurate?

Accuracy in forecasting the demand for labor varies considerably by firm and by industry type (e.g., utilities versus women's fashions), roughly from a 5 to 35 percent

---

SMALL BUSINESSES CONFRONT SUCCESSION PLANNING*   HR BUZZ

Thus far, we have been discussing succession planning in large firms. But what about small firms, such as family-owned businesses? Only about 30 percent of family businesses survive into the second generation, 12 percent make it to the third, and only 3 percent into the fourth. Others were never designed for a long life. They start fast, grow quickly, and then are sold or merged with another. Yet family-owned businesses come in all varieties. Some are simple and never expand beyond a single location. Others span the globe and have interests in a broad variety of fields. With respect to leadership succession, experts advise families to do three things:

- Devote as much thought to getting the former boss to move on as to training his or her successor. For example, give the retiring boss something to fill his or her days, such as running a family charity.
- To ensure that heirs are ready for the jobs they inherit, make them prove themselves outside the family firm.
- Require both family and non-family executives to go through a "future leaders program," which uses tests, inventories, and assessment exercises to assess their abilities.

At the same time, this is no time for wishful thinking, hoping that an uninterested or incapable son or daughter will suddenly become full of passion and business skills. Provide clear, consistent communication to all family members, and allow all who are involved in the business in any way to have a voice. Sometimes family-owned firms look to outsiders, especially for new ideas and technology. Firms in that situation should start early, for it may take 3–5 years for the successor to become fully capable of assuming leadership for the company. Finally, remember that the best successions are those that end with a clean and certain break. In other words, once the firm has a new leader in the driver's seat, the old leader should get off the bus.

---

*Sources: Sekulich, T. (2018, Oct. 24). When succession goes awry–four famous examples of failure. *Tharawat Magazine*. Retrieved from *https://www.tharawat-magazine.com/facts/succession-goes-awry-four-famous-examples/* on Mar. 26, 2020. Schumpeter. (2016, Feb. 6). Succession failure. *The Economist*, p. 61. Berman, D. (2016, June 2). The difficult succession decision that family businesses face. *The Wall Street Journal*, p. B5. Gale, A. (2015, Oct. 7). Succession dramas roil Asian family dynasties. *The Wall Street Journal*, pp. A1, A6.

error factor. Factors such as the duration of the planning period, the quality of the data on which forecasts are based (e.g., expected changes in the business factor and labor productivity), and the degree of integration of SWP with strategic business planning all affect accuracy. At the same time, SWP is not a static process. Evidence indicates that as it matures, four things happen: (1) Organizational boundaries disappear or become less important; talent and skills are seen as a shared resource. (2) SWP gains broader support and ownership. (3) It incorporates tools from other functions and frameworks (e.g., finance, marketing, supply-chain management). (4) It becomes increasingly data driven–for example, modeling the feasibility and cost of executing alternative business scenarios.[55]

Integrating Supply and Demand Forecasts

If forecasts are to prove genuinely useful to managers, they must result in an end product that is understandable and meaningful. The goal is to develop a concise statement of projected staffing requirements that integrates supply and demand forecasts. In Figure 6–7, net workforce demand at the end of each year of a 3-year forecast is compared with net workforce supply for the same year. This yields a "bottom-line" figure that shows an increasing deficit each year during the 3-year period. This is the kind of evidence senior managers need in order to make informed decisions regarding the future direction of HR initiatives.

LinkedIn has created a labor-market-intelligence product, Talent Insights, to provide real-time insight on external supply, demand, and competition. More than 1,500 companies now use workforce planning data extracted from the site's 645 million members, 20 million jobs, and tens of thousands of standardized skills and job titles. According to LinkedIn, "We can show you what skills you lack on your team, where to find the people with those skills, and who you are competing with to get them."[56]

Figure 6–7		2018	2019	2020
Integrated workforce supply-and-demand forecast.	**Demand**			
	Beginning in position	313	332	351
	Increases (decreases)	19	19	19
	Total demand (year end)	332	351	370
	Supply (during year)			
	Beginning in position	313	332	351
	Minus promotions	(38)	(41)	(41)
	Minus terminations	(22)	(22)	(23)
	Minus retirements	(16)	(16)	(16)
	Minus transfers	(14)	(14)	(14)
	Subtotal	223	239	257
	Plus promotions in	28	28	28
	Total supply (year end)	251	267	285
	Surplus/deficit (year end)	(81)	(84)	(85)

Make or Buy?

Assuming a firm has a choice, however, is it better to *select* workers who already have the skills necessary to perform competently or to select workers who do not have the skills immediately but who can be *trained* to perform competently? This is the same type of "make-or-buy" decision that managers often face in so many other areas of business. As a general principle, to avoid mismatched costs, balance make and buy. Here are some guidelines for determining when buying is more effective than making.[57]

- How accurate is your forecast of demand?
  If not accurate, do more buying.
- Do you have the "scale" to develop?
  If not, do more buying.
- Is there a job ladder to pull talent through?
  If not long, do more buying.
- How long will the talent be needed?
  If not long, do more buying.
- Do you want to change culture/direction?
  If yes, do more buying.

IMPACT OF STRATEGIC WORKFORCE PLANNING ON PRODUCTIVITY, QUALITY OF WORK LIFE, AND THE BOTTOM LINE

The design of jobs, and the kinds of personal characteristics needed to do them, seems to be changing a lot these days. This is especially true of jobs at the bottom and at the top of today's organizations. Entry-level jobs now demand workers with new and different kinds of skills. Even simple clerical work now requires computer knowledge, bank tellers need more knowledge of financial transactions and sales techniques, and assembly-line workers need more sophisticated understanding of mathematics and better reading and reasoning skills. Executives need to be aware constantly of shifting competitive dynamics in their industries and of global trends that might alter those dynamics, and they need to be able to shift course rapidly, if necessary.[a] Such changes have direct implications for SWP and projected HR needs.

Here's just one example. The American Hotel and Lodging Association Education Foundation sponsors a lodging-management apprenticeship program. The program's 1,000 participants have the option of completing the program online or at a local community college. Fully 80 percent of them are frontline or midlevel associates selected for the upskilling program to help them advance into management careers. The program has a 94 percent retention rate, and apprentices see an 18 percent wage increase, on average, as they upskill. In PwC's 2019 Global CEO survey, 79 percent of CEOs reported that they are extremely or somewhat concerned about the availability of people with key skills as a threat to their businesses. Internal training, apprenticeships, and company-college partnerships are three ways to address those concerns.

---

[a]Hufford (2019), op. cit. Kahn (2018), op. cit. Maurer (2017), op. cit.
[b]Tyler, K. (2020, Feb. 22). Upskill or fade away. *SHRM Online.* Retrieved from *https://www.shrm.org/hr-today/news/all-things-work/pages/upskill-or-fade-away.aspx* on Feb. 23, 2020.

Recognize that in today's fast-paced business environment, "deep benches" of candidates waiting for opportunity represent inventory. Inventory in talent often "walks" for jobs elsewhere, and that represents the biggest loss possible. In forecasting the demand for labor, therefore, it is often better to underestimate the numbers of people needed because overestimation is now too expensive. Use outside hiring to fill in gaps, but recognize that the other extreme (hiring *only* from the outside) can also be harmful. Why? Because doing so yields no unique skills and no unique culture.

CONTROL AND EVALUATION OF SWP SYSTEMS

The purpose of control and evaluation is to guide SWP activities, identifying deviations from the plan and their causes. Qualitative and quantitative objectives can both play useful roles in SWP. Quantitative objectives offer objective data and the opportunity to measure deviations more precisely. Nevertheless, the nature of evaluation and control should always match the degree of development of the rest of the SWP process. In newly instituted SWP systems, for example, evaluation is likely to be more qualitative than quantitative, with little emphasis placed on control. SWP is more about:

- The extent to which HR staff and line managers are tuned in to workforce issues and opportunities, and the extent to which their priorities are sound.
- The quality of working relationships between HR staff and line managers who supply data and use SWP results. How closely do they work together on a day-to-day basis?
- The extent to which decision makers at every level are making use of SWP forecasts, action plans, and recommendations.
- The perceived value of SWP. Do decision makers view the information from SWP as useful to them in their own jobs?

IMPLICATIONS FOR MANAGEMENT PRACTICE

More and more, workforce issues are seen as people-related business issues. This suggests that as a manager you should do the following:

- Recognize that your company needs to compete just as fiercely in talent markets as it does in capital or customer markets.
- Talent management assumes that maximizing the talents of employees is a source of sustained competitive advantage. Be sure that your approach is linked tightly to sound HR practices.
- A study of 200 firms, both U.S.-based and global in scope, drawn from 40 industries over a 10-year time period revealed that many companies, unfortunately, are overlooking the importance of talent management. Executives are key assets, and their work to build and sustain talent is critical. It manifests in four broad categories: in strategy, structure, culture, and execution.
  - Bottom line: plan for people in the context of managing the business strategically.
  - Recognize that business and HR strategies are interdependent.[a]

[a]Cascio, W. F., and Boudreau, J. W. (2016). The search for global competence: From International HR to talent management. *Journal of World Business* 51(1), pp. 103-14. Joyce, W. F., and Slocum, J. W. (2012). Top management talent, strategic capabilities, and firm performance. *Organizational Dynamics* 41(3), pp. 183-93.

In more established SWP systems, key comparisons might include the following:

- Actual staffing levels compared to forecasted levels.
- Actual levels of labor productivity compared to anticipated levels.
- Action programs planned compared to those implemented. (Were there more or fewer? Why?)
- Action programs implemented–actual versus expected results (e.g., improved applicant flows, lower quit rates in pivotal jobs).
- Action-program costs compared to budgets.
- Ratios of action-program benefits to costs.

The advantage of quantitative information is that it highlights potential problem areas and can provide the basis for constructive discussion of the issues.

LEADERSHIP SUCCESSION—A KEY CHALLENGE FOR ALL ORGANIZATIONS

Human Resource Management in Action: Conclusion

Research shows that planning for CEO succession should be part and parcel of the way a company is managed. Grooming potential leaders is a process that takes years. It's not an ad hoc event. In fact, developing leaders with strategic vision and developing those who can implement strategy successfully are two critical challenges for every chief executive. The best ones tie learning-and-development activities directly to the business strategy. In fact, people development is becoming an important part of executive performance. PepsiCo is a good example. Historically, it allocated one-third of incentive compensation to the development of people, with the remainder allocated to results. Now the company allocates equal amounts of incentive compensation for people development and results. To avoid a future crisis in leadership succession, here are some key steps to take.[58]

1. *Ensure that the sitting CEO understands the importance of this task and makes it a priority.* At both Johnson & Johnson and Procter & Gamble, managers at every rank are graded in performance reviews on whether they've retained and advanced their most talented employees. Link some of the CEO's bonus to the development of internal candidates.
2. *Focus on an organization's future needs.* In today's changing business landscape, companies need leaders with strengths and talents that differ from those of the previous CEO–no matter how successful he or she was.
3. *Build an inclusive leadership pipeline.* Sadly, a large 2020 study found that more than half of organizations didn't assess a single female candidate when searching for their next CEO. A more inclusive leadership cadre delivers a wider variety of perspectives and wisdom.
4. *Provide broad exposure.* Allow rising stars to rotate through jobs, changing responsibilities every 3-5 years. Let them shadow more-senior managers (e.g., for several weeks at a time) to see how decisions actually get made.
5. *Provide access to the board.* Let up-and-comers make presentations to the board of directors. Managers get a sense of what matters to directors, and directors get to see the talent in the pipeline.

SUMMARY

We are witnessing vast changes in the nature of work and competition, and in the types and numbers of jobs available. To address those, pay careful attention to the linkages among strategic business planning, HR strategy, and strategic workforce planning. Business strategy provides an overall direction and focus for the organization as a whole, including for each functional area of the business. HR strategy parallels and facilitates implementation of the strategic business plan. It is the set of decisions, processes, and choices that firms make about how to manage their people. Strategic workforce planning is the formal process that connects business strategy to HR strategy and practices.

Business strategy and job design provide a basic blueprint for the organization in terms of organizing work to accomplish strategic objectives. Jobs can be designed to achieve several different objectives—for example, to maximize efficiency, to facilitate the performance of teams, to increase productivity, or to decreases in stress and turnover. In all cases, there is a need to identify the work to be done and the personal characteristics necessary to do the work. This is the purpose of job analysis.

A job description is a written summary of the task requirements of a particular job. A job specification is a written summary of people requirements - knowledge, skills, abilities, and other characteristics. Together they constitute a job analysis. A variety of methods are available to collect information about jobs and their requirements, such as job performance, observation, interviews, critical incidents, and structured questionnaires. All have advantages as well as disadvantages. Key considerations in the choice of methods are method-purpose fit, cost, practicality, and an overall judgment of the appropriateness of the methods for the situation in question.

Competency models are a form of job analysis—not a substitute for it—that link to business strategy, focus on broader characteristics of individuals, and use these characteristics to inform HR practices. They focus on the full range of knowledge, skills, abilities, and other characteristics (motives, traits, attitudes, personality characteristics), so-called KSAOs, that are needed for effective performance on the job and that characterize exceptional performers.

Information about jobs and business strategy are the key inputs to the SWP process. Several interrelated activities make up an integrated SWP system: (1) an inventory of talent currently on hand; (2) forecasts of talent supply and demand over short- and long-term periods; (3) action plans, such as hiring, training, or job transfer to meet forecasted HR needs; and (4) control and evaluation procedures.

KEY TERMS

succession planning	job specification
business strategy	competency models
HR strategy	competencies
SMART objectives	strategic workforce planning (SWP)
job design	workforce forecasting
job description	succession plan

DISCUSSION QUESTIONS

6-1. How are workforce plans related to business and HR strategies?

6-2. Discuss the similarities and differences between job analysis and competency models.

6-3. For purposes of succession planning, what information would you want in order to evaluate "potential"?

6-4. Why are forecasts of workforce demand more uncertain than forecasts of workforce supply?

6-5. When is it more cost-effective to "buy" rather than to "make" competent employees?

6-6. Why should the results of forecasting models be tempered with the judgment of experienced line managers?

6-7. The chairperson of the board of directors at your firm asks for advice about SWP. What would you say?

6-8. Discuss the kinds of employee information that managers might find to be particularly useful in a talent inventory.

6-9. Why is it important that job design include task, physical, knowledge, social, and contextual characteristics?

6-10. Why is it important to keep job descriptions up-to-date?

6-11. What are some advantages of having a common set of leadership attributes for all managers to strive for? Are there any downsides to this approach?

APPLYING YOUR KNOWLEDGE

Workforce Forecasts for a Small Business   *Case 6–1*

You are the owner of a 120-person cybersecurity business, Cyber-Lock Security, that works with small- and midsize organizations. A pivotal position in the firm is that of security software developer. The following table is a 3-year, integrated forecast of labor supply and demand for that position.

Integrated workforce supply-and-demand forecast for security software developers at Cyber-Lock Security.

	2019	2020	2021
Demand			
Beginning in position	53	68	86
Increases (decreases)	15	18	24
Total demand (year end)	68	86	110
Supply (during year)			
Beginning in position	53	68	86
Minus promotions	(4)	(6)	(9)
Minus terminations	(6)	(8)	(10)
Minus retirements	(3)	(5)	(7)
Minus transfers	(10)	(8)	(11)
Subtotal	30	41	49
Plus new hires during the year	31	48	53
Total supply (year end)	61	89	102
Surplus/deficit (year end)	(7)	3	(8)

Questions

1. In December 2019, the demand is for 68 security software developers, but you expect to have only 61. How will you address the deficit of 7 developers?
2. In December 2020 the demand is for 86 security software developers, and you expect to have 89. What will you do with the surplus of 3 extra software developers?
3. In December 2021 the demand is for 110 security software developers, but you expect to have only 102. Once again you are facing a deficit. How will you address the need for 8 more security software developers?

REFERENCES

1. Cascio, W. F., and Boudreau, J. W. (2012). *Short Introduction to Strategic Human Resource Management.* Cambridge, UK: Cambridge University Press.
2. Dess, G. D., McNamara, G., Eisner, A. B., & Lee, S-H. (2019). *Strategic Management: Creating Competitive Advantages* (9th ed.). New York: McGraw-Hill.
3. Rosenfeld, J. (2000, Apr.). Unit of one. *Fast Company & Inc.,* p. 98.
4. Lipton, M. (1996). Demystifying the development of an organizational vision. *Sloan Management Review* 37(4), pp. 83–92.
5. Dess et al. (2019), op. cit.
6. World's most admired companies. (2019). *Fortune.* Retrieved from *https://fortune.com/worlds-most-admired-companies/2019/apple/*on Mar. 23, 2020.
7. Farfan, B. (2019, Nov. 20). Top department store mission statements. Retrieved from *https://www.thebalancesmb.com/department-store-mission-statements-4068552* on Mar. 23, 2020.
8. CVS Health outlines strategy to accelerate growth. (2019, June 4). Retrieved from *https://cvshealth.com/newsroom/press-releases/cvs-health-outlines-strategy-accelerate-growth* on Mar. 23, 2020.
9. Cascio and Boudreau (2012), op. cit. *See also* Becker, B. E., Huselid, M. A., and Beatty, R. W. (2009). *The differentiated workforce: Transforming talent into strategic impact.* Boston: Harvard Business School Press. See also Becker, B. E., Huselid, M. A., and Ulrich, D. (2001). *The HR Scorecard: Linking People, Strategy, and Performance.* Boston: Harvard Business School Press.
10. The model is based on the work of Boudreau, J. W., and Ramstad, P. M. (2003). Strategic industrial and organizational psychology and the role of utility analysis models. In W. C. Borman, D. R. Ilgen, and R. J. Klimoski (Eds.), *Handbook of Psychology: Industrial and Organizational Psychology* (Vol. 12). Hoboken, NJ: Wiley, pp. 193–221. *See also* Boudreau, J. W. (1998). Strategic human resource management measures: Key linkages and the PeopleVantage model. *Journal of Human Resource Costing and Accounting* 3(2), pp. 23–35.
11. Brannick, M. T., Pearlman, K., and Sanchez, J. I. (2017). Work analysis. In J. L. Farr and N. T. Tippins (Eds.), *Handbook of Employee Selection* (2nd ed.). New York: Routledge Taylor & Francis Group, pp. 134–61.
12. Kujawa, P. (2019, Mar. 25). Employers' blind eye for boomers slowly opening to retirement realities. Workforce.com. Retrieved from *https://www.workforce.com/news/employers-blind-eye-for-boomers-slowly-opening-to-retirement-realities* on Mar. 23, 2020.
13. Dess et al. (2016), op. cit. *See also* Schuler, R. S., and Walker, J. W. (1990, Summer). Human resources strategy: Focusing on issues and actions. *Organizational Dynamics,* pp. 5–19.
14. Society for Human Resource Management Foundation. (2017, Feb. 6). From local to regional to global player–The evolution of Aramex International. Available at *youtube.com/watch?v=Yq1TCdICUuM.*
15. Maurer, R. (2017, Mar.). The big picture: Workforce planning requires leaders to look beyond their business needs. *HRMagazine,* p. 16.

16. Gerhart, B., and Newman, J. M. (2020). *Compensation* (13th ed.). New York: McGraw-Hill.
17. Parker, S. K., Morgeson, F. P., and Johns, G. (2017). One hundred years of work design research: Looking back and looking forward. *Journal of Applied Psychology* **102**(3), pp. 403–20. *See also* Grant, A. M., Fried, Y., and Juillerat, T. (2011). Work matters: Job design in classic and contemporary perspectives. In S. Zedeck (Ed.), *APA Handbook of Industrial and Organizational Psychology* (Vol. 1). Washington, DC: American Psychological Association, pp. 417–53.
18. Brannick et al. (2017), op. cit. *See also* Morgeson, F. P., and Dierdorff, E. C. (2011). Work analysis: From technique to theory. In S. Zedeck (Ed.), *APA Handbook of Industrial and Organizational Psychology* (Vol. 2). Washington, DC: American Psychological Association, pp. 3–41.
19. Brannick et al. (2017), op. cit. *See also* Morgeson and Dierdorff (2011), op. cit.
20. A systematic procedure for developing minimum qualifications was presented by Levine, E. L., May, D. M., Ulm, R. A., and Gordon, T. R. (1997). A methodology for developing and validating minimum qualifications (MQs). *Personnel Psychology* 50, pp. 1009–23.
21. Brannick et al. (2017), op. cit. *See also* Schippmann, J. S., Ash, R. A., Battista, M., Carr, L., Eyde, L. D., Hesketh, B., Kehoe, J., Pearlman, K., Prien, E. P., and Sanchez, J. I. (2000). The practice of competency modeling. *Personnel Psychology* 53, pp. 703–40.
22. Goffin, R. D., and Woychesin, D. E. (2006). An empirical method of determining employee competencies/KSAOs from task-based job analysis. *Military Psychology* 18(2), pp. 121–30. *See also* Mihalevsky, M., Olson, K. S., and Maher, P. T. (2007). *Behavioral Competency Dictionary*. La Puente, CA: Bassett Unified School District. *See also* Sackett, P. R., and Laczo, R. M. (2003). Job and work analysis. In W. C. Borman, D. R. Ilgen, and R. J. Klimoski (Eds.), *Handbook of Psychology: Industrial and Organizational Psychology* (Vol. 12). Hoboken, NJ: Wiley, pp. 21–37.
23. Brannick et al. (2017), op. cit. *See also* Morgeson and Dierdorff (2011), op. cit. *See also* Frame, M. C., and Schmieder, R. A. (2017). Competency modeling. In S. G. Rogelberg (Ed.), *The Sage Encyclopedia of Industrial and Organizational Psychology* (2nd ed., Vol. 1). Thousand Oaks, CA: Sage, pp. 198–201.
24. Brannick et al. (2017), op. cit. *See also* Brannick, M. T., Levine, E. L., and Morgeson, F. P. (2007). *Job and Work Analysis: Methods, Research, and Applications for Human Resource Management*. Thousand Oaks, CA: Sage.
25. Ibid. *See also* Fleishman, E. A., and Mumford, M. D. (1991). Evaluating classifications of job behavior: A construct validation of the ability requirements scales. *Personnel Psychology* 44, pp. 523–75.
26. Harvey, R. J. (1991). Job analysis. In M. D. Dunnette and L. M. Hough (Eds.), *Handbook of Industrial and Organizational Psychology* (Vol. 2). Palo Alto, CA: Consulting Psychologists Press, pp. 71–163.
27. Landy, F. J., and Vasey, J. (1991). Job analysis: The composition of SME samples. *Personnel Psychology* 44, pp. 27–50. *See also* DeNisi, A. S., Cornelius, E. T., III, and Blencoe, A. G. (1987). Further investigation of common knowledge effects on job analysis ratings. *Journal of Applied Psychology* 72, pp. 262–68. *See also* Friedman, L., and Harvey, R. J. (1986). Can raters with reduced job descriptive information provide accurate Position Analysis Questionnaire (PAQ) ratings? *Personnel Psychology* 39, pp. 779–89.
28. Dierdorff and Wilson (2003), op. cit.
29. Schmitt, N., and Cohen, S. A. (1989). Internal analyses of task ratings by job incumbents. *Journal of Applied Psychology* 73, pp. 96–104.
30. Conley, P. R., and Sackett, P. R. (1987). Effects of using high- versus low-performing job incumbents as sources of job-analysis information. *Journal of Applied Psychology* 72, pp. 434–37.
31. Morgeson, F. P., Delaney-Klinger, K., Ferrara, P., Mayfield, M. S., and Campion, M. A. (2004). Self-presentation processes in job analysis: A field experiment investigating inflation in abilities, tasks, and competencies. *Journal of Applied Psychology* 89, pp. 674–86.
32. Lublin and Francis (2016), op. cit. *See also* Bjornberg, A., and Feser, C. (2015, May). CEO succession starts with developing your leaders. *McKinsey Quarterly*. Retrieved from

http://www.mckinsey.com/global-themes/leadership/ceo-succession-starts-with-developing-your-leaders on Feb. 1, 2016.

33. Cascio, W. F., Boudreau, J. W., & Church, A. (2017). Using a risk-optimization lens: Maximizing talent readiness for an uncertain future. In C. Cooper & P. Sparrow (Eds.), *A Research agenda for human resource management: HR strategy, structure, and architecture* (pp. 55-77). London: Edward Elgar Publishers.

34. Young, M. B. (2010). *Strategic Workforce Planning in Global Organizations.* New York: The Conference Board.

35. Ibid. *See also* Sutherland, D., and Wilkerson, B. (2010, Feb.). *Leading-Edge Workforce Planning Using Simulation and Optimization.* New York: The Conference Board Council of Talent Management Executives.

36. Boudreau, J. W. (2010). *IBM's Global Talent Management Strategy.* Alexandria, VA: Society for Human Resource Management. *See also* Byrnes, N. (2005, Oct. 10). Starsearch: How to recruit, train, and hold on to great people. What works, what doesn't. *BusinessWeek,* pp. 68-78.

37. Zielinski, D. (2016, Oct.). An HRMS for everyone. *HRMagazine,* pp. 47-50.

38. Boudreau (2010), op. cit. *See also* Byrnes (2005), op. cit.

39. Maurer (2017), op. cit. *See also* Cappelli, P. (2008). *Talent on Demand: Managing Talent in an Age of Uncertainty.* Boston: Harvard Business School Press.

40. U.S. Bureau of Labor Statistics. (2019, Sept. 4). Fastest-growing occupations, 2018-2028. Retrieved from *https://www.bls.gov/ooh/fastest-growing.htm* on Mar. 24, 2020.

41. Everhart, C. D., II. (2017, Feb. 28). Impending pilot shortage, a developing national crisis. Retrieved from *www.military.com/daily-news/2017/02/28/impending-pilot-shortage-a-developing-national-crisis.html* on Apr. 8, 2017. *See also* Coy, P., and Ewing, J. (2007, Apr. 9). Where are all the workers? *BusinessWeek,* pp. 28-31. *See also* Aston, A. (2007, Jan. 22). Who will run the plants? *BusinessWeek,* p. 78.

42. Kahn, J. (2018, Feb. 19). The war for AI talent, and what counts. *Bloomberg Businessweek,* pp. 22, 23. *See also* Smith, J. (2018, Apr. 4). Trucking's big-rig life stays a tough sell. *The Wall Street Journal,* pp. B1, B2. *See also* Leopold, G. (2017, Jan. 24). Demand, salaries grow for data scientists. Retrieved from *www.datanami.com/2017/01/24/demand-salaries-grow-data-scientists/* on Apr. 8, 2017.

43. Kujawa, 2019, op. cit. See also Hirschman, C. (2007, Mar.). Putting forecasting in focus. *HRMagazine,* pp. 44, 49.

44. Schoenberger, C. (2015, June 3). How corporate boards deal with a lost successor. *Bloomberg Businessweek.* Retrieved from *www.bloomberg.com/news/articles/2015-06-03/how-corporate-boards-deal-with-a-lost-successor* on May 2, 2016.

45. Yung, C., & Ma, W. (2018, Mar. 17). Hong Kong icon passes the baton. *The Wall Street Journal,* p. B1. *See also* Ma, W., & Watts, J. M. (2017). Asian tycoons look to heirs. *The Wall Street Journal,* pp. B1, B6.

46. Lublin and Francis (2016), op. cit. *See also* Plank, W. (2014, Apr. 27). The do's and don'ts of CEO succession planning. *The Wall Street Journal.* Retrieved from *www.wsj.com/articles/SB10001424052702303987004579479680859042214 on* May 14, 2015. See also Beiertz, Y., Ogden, D., Simmons, T., and Speed, E. (2010). Seven succession-planning missteps boards should avoid. *Spencer Stuart Point of View,* pp. 1-4.

47. Nyberg, A. J., Schepker, D. J., Cragun, O. R., and Wright, P. M. (2017). Succession planning: Talent management's forgotten, but critical tool. In D. G. Collings, K. Mellahi, and W. F. Cascio (Eds.), *The Oxford Handbook of Talent Management* (pp. 318-342). Oxford, UK: Oxford University Press. *See also* Cascio et al. (2017), op. cit.

48. Stadtler, D. (2019, Oct. 10). 3 ways to modernize workforce planning. *SHRM Online.* Retrieved from *https://www.shrm.org/resourcesandtools/hr-topics/organizational-and-employee-development/pages/three-ways-to-modernize-workforce-planning.aspx. See also* Cascio et al. (2017), op. cit.

49. About 3M. Retrieved from *https://www.3m.com/3M/en_US/company-us/about-3m/* on Mar. 24, 2020.

50. Paul, K. B. (2017, October 22). 3M, U.S. talent development leader. Personal communication.

51. Church, A. H., & Rotolo, C. T. (2016). Lifting the veil: What happens when you are transparent with people about their future potential? *People + Strategy* 39(4), pp. 36-40.

52. Cascio, W. F., Boudreau, J. W. , & Fink, A. (2019). *Investing in People: Financial Impact of Human Resource Initiatives* (3rd ed.). Alexandria, VA: SHRM Publishing. *See also* Cascio, W. F., and Boudreau, J. W. (2016). The search for global competence: From international HR to talent management. *Journal of World Business* 51, pp. 103-14. *See also* Boudreau, J. W., and Ramstad, P. (2007). *Beyond HR: The New Science of Human Capital*. Boston: Harvard Business School Press.

53. Corning, who we are, what we do. (2020). Retrieved from *https://www.corning.com/worldwide/en/about-us/company-profile.html* on Mar. 26, 2020.

54. Hirschman (2007), op. cit., p. 46.

55. OptTek Systems Inc. (2017). OptForce: True workforce planning and optimization. Retrieved from *http://www.optforce.com/* on Apr. 8, 2017. *See also* Young (2010), op. cit.

56. Maurer, R. (2019, Oct. 1). LinkedIn announces move toward "holistic" talent platform. *SHRM Online*. Retrieved from *https://www.shrm.org/resourcesandtools/hr-topics/talent-acquisition/pages/linkedin-announces-move-toward-holistic-talent-platform.aspx* on Oct. 1, 2019.

57. Cappelli (2008a), op. cit.

58. Holliday, T. (2019, Nov.). Overcoming blunders organizations make in succession planning. *HR Professionals Magazine* 9(11), pp. 20, 21. *See also* National Association of Corporate Directors. (2017, Nov.-Dec.). Director's perspectives: Guidelines for making CEO succession count. *NACD Directorship*, pp. 76-81. See also Sahadi (2019), op. cit.

7 RECRUITING

Questions This Chapter Will Help Managers Answer

LO 7-1 What factors are most important to consider in developing a recruitment policy?

LO 7-2 Under what circumstances does it make sense to retain an executive search firm?

LO 7-3 Do alternative recruitment sources yield differences in the quality of employees and in their "survival" rates on the job?

LO 7-4 How can we communicate as realistic a picture as possible of a job and an organization to prospective new employees? What kinds of issues are most crucial to them?

LO 7-5 If I lose my current job, what's the most efficient strategy for finding a new one?

THE PERILS AND PROMISE OF SOCIAL MEDIA*

Social media are here to stay. They facilitate the social relationships that we have with other people, and the use of Internet technologies makes those relationships easier to develop and maintain. Social media include at least four major types: (1) social-networking sites, such as Facebook, LinkedIn, Instagram, and chat rooms; (2) blogs and microblogs, such as Twitter; (3) virtual worlds, such as Second Life; and (4) video-sharing websites, such as YouTube. Today 72 percent of companies use social media to advertise their jobs, 59 percent find they get more referrals, and 50 percent get more applications by using social media. The top channels? LinkedIn, Facebook, and Twitter, pulling in 96 percent of searching, 94 percent of contacting, and 92 percent of vetting candidates, respectively. Other networks, like YouTube, Reddit, and Quora, are proving to be rich sources of talent as well.

For prospective candidates, the new imperative is to present your professional skills as attractively as possible, packing your profile with keywords (e.g., *marketing manager, global sourcing specialist*) that will send your name to the top of recruiters' searches. At the same time, you can connect your online professional interactions in one place, joining groups on the site (e.g., based on companies, schools, and affinities). Statistics show that 74 percent of adult Internet users have profiles on at least one social-networking site, 80 percent of recruiters use the Internet as part of the screening process, and 43 percent of those have eliminated candidates based on information found. On the flip side, 19 percent found information that sold them on a candidate, such as communication skills or professional image.

A big appeal of social media is that they appear to be able to solve business challenges without any associated costs. Why hire a search firm when you can tap your personal/contact list to find candidates without charge? Why hire consultants when one of your "friends" can give you free advice? Why hire a coach when you can get a volunteer mentor from your current executives? Personal relationships with outsiders can become just as important as those with fellow employees. Will the promise of social media really play out as described? Maybe, but only if organizations can find ways to manage the risks that they entail.

The top five social-media risks to business identified in a recent study are malware, brand hijacking, lack of content control, noncompliance with rules over record keeping, and unrealistic expectations of Internet performance. Here are seven more: sexual harassment, defamation, libel, disclosure of confidential information or trade secrets, disclosure of customer lists, tort law violations (negative comments about employers), and theft of employer time. After all, the use of social media is not free. It only appears to be so because companies do not account for the time employees spend using social media. Studies show that at least some employees spend up to 3 hours per day on social-networking websites!

What should organizations do? The number of people fired over social media posts is rising, and employees need to understand that their actions on social media

Sources: Roddy, S. (2020, Mar. 5). Top four social media recruiting strategies to find top talent. *The Manifest.* Retrieved from *https://themanifest.com/staffing/agencies/top-4-social-media-recruiting-strategies* on Mar. 7, 2020. Bell, J. D. (2018, Sept.-Oct.). Anti-social behavior. *HRMagazine,* pp. 30-36. Forbes Human Resources Council. (2017, May 25). Why your business needs a social media policy and 8 things it should cover. *Forbes.* Retrieved from *https://www.forbes.com/sites/forbeshumanresourcescouncil/2017/05/25/why-your-business-needs-a-social-media-policy-and-eight-things-it-should-cover/#4942faf25264* on Mar. 30, 2020. Kumar, S. (2015, May 22). Why monitoring employees' social media is a bad idea. *Time.* Retrieved from *http://time.com/3894276/social-media-monitoring-work/* on Apr. 11, 2017.

may damage their reputations and cause them to lose their jobs. Companies need to develop policies about the use of social media at work, yet roughly 70 percent do not have them. In the conclusion to this case, we will consider what sound social-media policies should contain.

Challenges

1. From your perspective, what is the main appeal of social media in recruitment?
2. How can organizations manage the risks associated with social media?
3. How might a company measure the costs and benefits of social media in the workplace?

RECRUITMENT AS A STRATEGIC IMPERATIVE

Recruitment is a form of business contest, and it is fiercely competitive. Just as corporations strategize to develop, manufacture, and market the best product or service, so they must also vie to identify, attract, and hire the most qualified people. Recruitment is a business, and it is big business.[1] It demands serious attention from management because any business strategy will falter without the talent to execute it.

Certainly, the range of recruitment needs is broad. A small manufacturer in a well-populated rural area faces recruitment challenges that are far different from those of a high-technology firm operating in global markets. Both need talent—although different types of talent—to be successful in their respective markets. Regardless of the size of a firm, or what industry it is in, recruitment and selection of people with strategically relevant abilities is more important than ever. Let's begin by examining the big picture of the employee recruitment and selection process, along with some important legal issues. Then we'll focus specifically on the processes of planning, managing, and evaluating recruitment efforts. We will address the special issues associated with recruiting people for international assignments in Chapter 16.

A SUPPLY-CHAIN APPROACH TO THE RECRUITMENT–STAFFING PROCESS

Recruitment is an important component of the staffing supply chain.[2] A common misconception is that recruiting and staffing are separate activities, done in isolation. In fact, both are part of a system, a network of human resource activities. A useful way to view these activities is through the lens of a supply chain–a *supply chain for talent acquisition*. Figure 7-1 shows this approach graphically.

In Figure 7-1, groups of individuals (talent pools) flow through the various stages of the staffing process, with each stage serving as a filter that eliminates a subset of the original talent pool. The top row shows the results of the filtering process. It begins with a **potential labor pool** of individuals who might eventually become applicants, such as high school students who attend summer science camps sponsored by high-technology companies (box 1). A potential labor pool develops into an **available labor pool** once individuals acquire minimum qualifications for

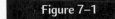

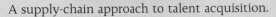

A supply-chain approach to talent acquisition.

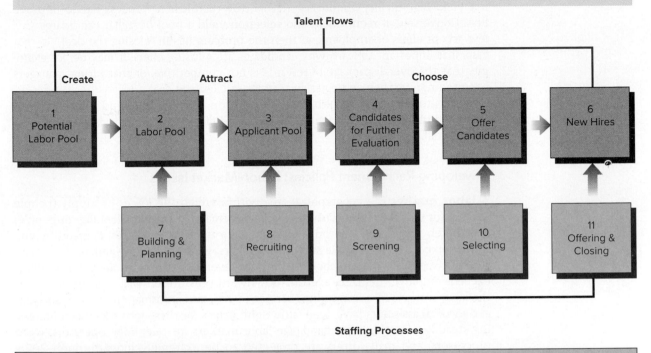

Source: Cascio, W. F., and Boudreau, J. W. (2011). Utility of selection systems: Supply-chain analysis applied to staffing decisions. In Zedeck, S. (Ed.) *APA Handbook of Industrial and Organizational Psychology* (Vol. 2). Washington, DC: American Psychological Association, p. 424.

jobs (box 2). Some of those individuals will actually apply for jobs and become **applicants** (box 3). Recruiters (box 8) then filter the applicant pool to identify candidates for further evaluation (box 4). **Screening** and **selection** (boxes 9 and 10) identify smaller pools of candidates who receive offers (box 5). Some will accept offers (box 11) and remain with the organization as new hires (box 6).

The "staffing processes" in the lower row show the activities that accomplish the filtering sequence, beginning in box 7 with building and planning (forecasting trends in external and internal labor markets, inducing potential applicants to develop qualifications to satisfy future talent demands), leading in box 8 to recruiting (attracting applicants who wish to be considered), then in box 9 to screening (identifying the clearly qualified and/or rejecting the clearly unqualified), moving in box 10 to selection (rating those not screened in or out earlier) and ending in box 11 with offering and closing (creating and presenting offers, and getting candidates to accept).

Note box 12 at the bottom of Figure 7–1 that identifies the metrics of cost, time, price, expected quality/quantity, and variation in quality/quantity. At every stage the quality or variability of the talent flows can be enhanced at some cost, but the objective is not to maximize quality and reduce variation and cost *at every stage*. Rather, it is to optimize *overall* costs, returns, and risks.

Viewing talent flows and staffing processes as a system facilitates this and shows where improvements can have the biggest impact. For example, if the quality of recruitment efforts is poor, then even a highly valid screening and selection process will not yield high-quality employees. Rather, the recruitment process has to improve first. Conversely, if recruitment and selection yield a pool of stellar candidates, but few accept offers of employment, then the problem lies in "closing the deal." In that case, it is important to learn why candidates are refusing offers. It may be, for example, that the overall package of rewards is not competitive, or that hiring managers need to improve their strategies and tactics to close the deal.

Recruitment policies ultimately depend on the structure and functioning of internal and external labor markets. Let us therefore discuss labor-market issues in more detail.

Developing Recruitment Policies: Labor-Market Issues

A **labor market** is a geographical area within which the forces of supply (people looking for work) interact with the forces of demand (employers looking for people) and thereby determine the price of labor.[3] In a tight labor market, demand by employers exceeds the available supply of workers, which tends to exert upward pressure on wages. In a loose labor market, the reverse is true: The supply of workers exceeds employer demand, exerting downward pressure on wages. In recent years, the labor markets for wind-turbine service technicians, information-security analysts, and medical assistants have been fairly tight; wages for these jobs have been increasing steadily.[4] On the other hand, the labor markets for telephone operators, word processors, and mail sorters are projected to be extremely loose through 2028, thereby reducing pressure for wage increases for these workers.

Unfortunately, it is not possible to define the geographical boundaries of a labor market in any clear-cut manner.[5] Employers needing key employees will recruit far and wide if necessary. Indeed, for certain types of jobs and certain firms, the Internet has made recruitment from global labor markets a reality. In short, employers do not face a single, homogeneous market for labor; rather, they operate in many labor markets, each with unique demand and supply.[6] Economists focus on this fact as the major explanation for wage differences among occupations and among geographical areas.

Of practical concern to managers, however, is a reasonably accurate definition of labor markets for planning purposes. Here are some factors that are important for defining the limits of a labor market:[7]

- Geography.
- Education and/or technical background required to perform a job.
- Industry.
- Licensing or certification requirements.
- Union membership.

Companies may use one or more of these factors to help define their labor markets. Thus, a zoo that needs to hire four veterinarians cannot restrict its search to a local area because the market is national or international in scope. Union membership is not a concern in this market, but licensing and/or certification is. Applicants are likely to be less concerned with where the job is located and more concerned with job design and career opportunities. On the other hand, suppose a brewery is

RECRUITMENT POLICIES

As a framework for setting recruitment policies, let us consider four different possible company postures:[a]

1. **Passive nondiscrimination** is a commitment to treat all races and both sexes equally in all decisions about hiring, promotion, and pay. No attempt is made to recruit actively among members of protected groups.
2. **Pure diversity-based recruitment** is a concerted effort by an organization to actively expand the pool of applicants so that no one is excluded. However, the decision to hire or to promote is based on the best-qualified individual, regardless of race or sex.
3. **Diversity-based recruitment with preferential hiring** systematically favors members of protected groups in hiring and promotion decisions. This is a "soft-quota" system.
4. **Hard quotas** represent a mandate to hire or promote specific numbers or proportions of members of protected groups.

Both private and government employers find hard quotas an unsavory strategy for rectifying the effects of past or present discrimination. Nevertheless, the courts have ordered temporary quotas in instances in which unfair discrimination has obviously taken place and where no other remedy is feasible.[b] Temporary quotas have bounds placed on them. For example, a judge might order an employer to hire two African American employees for every white employee until the number of African American employees reaches a certain percentage of the employer's workforce.

Passive nondiscrimination misses the mark. Many years ago the secretary of labor publicly cited a government contractor, the Allen-Bradley Company of Milwaukee, for failure to actively recruit African Americans. The company was so well known in Milwaukee as a good place to work that it usually had a long waiting list of friends and relatives of current employees. The company preferred to hire referrals from current employees, and it did almost no public recruiting for entry-level job openings. Because almost all of its employees were white, so were almost all the referrals.[c]

As noted in Chapter 3, preferential selection is a sticky issue. However, in several landmark cases the Supreme Court established the following principle:[d] Staffing decisions must be made on a case-by-case basis; race or sex may be taken into account, but the overall decision to select or reject must be made on the basis of a combination of factors, such as entrance-test scores and previous performance. That leaves us with pure diversity-based recruitment as a recruitment and selection strategy. Indeed, in a free and open competitive labor market, that's the way it ought to be.

---

[a]Seligman, D. (1973, Mar.). How "equal opportunity" turned into employment quotas. *Fortune*, pp. 160–68.

[b]Replying in the affirmative (1987, Mar. 9). *Time*, p. 66.

[c]*Furnco Construction Corp. v. Waters*, 438 U.S. 567 (1978).

[d]*Fisher v. University of Texas at Austin.* (2016, June 23). 579 U. S. _ (2016). *Gratz v. Bollinger.* (2003, June 23). 539 U.S. 244. *Grutter v. Bollinger.* (2003). 539 U.S. 306.

trying to hire a master plumber. The brewery will be looking at a labor market defined primarily by geographical proximity[8] and secondarily by people whose experience, technical background, and (possibly) willingness to join a union after employment qualify them for the job.

Internal versus External Labor Markets

Thus far, we have been focusing on external labor markets. Internal labor markets also affect recruitment policies (in many cases, more directly) because firms often give preference to current employees in promotions, transfers, and other career-enhancing opportunities. Each employing unit is a separate market. At United Parcel Service (UPS), for example, virtually all jobs above the entry level are filled by internal promotion rather than by outside recruitment. UPS looks to its current employees as its source of labor supply, and workers look to this internal labor market to advance their careers. In the internal labor markets of most organizations, employees peddle their talents to available "buyers."[9] Three elements constitute the internal labor market:

- Formal and informal practices that determine how jobs are organized and described.
- Procedures for identifying potential candidates.
- Methods for choosing among candidates.
- In an open internal labor market, every available job is advertised throughout the organization via "job posting," and anyone can apply. Preference is given to internal candidates by withholding outside advertising until the job has been on the internal market for several days. Finally, each candidate for a job receives an interview.

Recruitment Policies and Labor-Market Characteristics

A great deal of research suggests that employers change their recruitment policies as market conditions change.[10] For example, as labor becomes increasingly scarce, employers may change their policies in the following ways:

- Improve the characteristics of vacant positions—for example, by raising salaries, improving benefits, or increasing opportunities for training.
- Reduce hiring standards.
- Use more (and more expensive) recruiting methods.
- Extend searches over a wider geographical area.[11]

The remainder of the chapter focuses broadly on three themes: planning, managing, and evaluating recruitment efforts. Let's begin by considering recruitment planning.

RECRUITMENT PLANNING

Recruitment begins with a clear specification of (1) the number of people needed (e.g., through workforce forecasts) and (2) when they are needed. Implicit in the latter is a time frame—the duration between the receipt of a résumé and the time a new hire starts work. This time frame is sometimes referred to as the recruitment pipeline.

Table 7–1		
AVERAGE TIME SPAN FOR EVENTS IN A RECRUITMENT PIPELINE		
Sequence of events		
From	**To**	**Average number of days**
Résumé	Invitation	5
Invitation	Interview	6
Interview	Offer	4
Offer	Acceptance	7
Acceptance	Report to work	21
Total length of the pipeline		43

The flow of events through the pipeline is represented as in Table 7-1. The table shows that if an operating manager sends a requisition for a new hire to the HR department today, it will take almost a month and a half, 43 days on average, before an employee fulfilling that requisition actually starts work. Time to fill an open requisition is important in pivotal jobs, those where changes in the quantity or quality of people have a direct impact on firm success, but it can be misleading, especially if measures of the quality of new hires are ignored.[12] For example, it is useful to know that a firm's sales openings average 75 days to fill. It's even more valuable, however, to know that the difference between filling them in 75 vs. 50 days costs the firm $30 million revenue or that a 20 percent improvement in quality-of-hire will result in an $18 million productivity improvement.[13]

One study of *Fortune* 500 firms found that the average firm cut about 6 days off its hiring cycle by posting jobs online instead of in newspapers, another 4 days by taking online applications instead of paper ones, and more than a week by screening and processing applications electronically.[14] It's important to move quickly because delays in the timing of recruitment events are perceived very negatively by candidates, especially high-quality ones, and often cost job acceptances.[15]

INTERNAL RECRUITMENT

The first thing to note about internal recruitment is that organizational culture becomes more important, whereas employer brand and reputation become less important.[16] At the same time, there are four key advantages to recruiting internally.[17] (1) There is less transition time moving into new jobs. Current employees are already familiar with an employer's products, people, and operating procedures. (2) There is a greater likelihood of filling a position successfully. In contrast to external candidates, an employer has considerably more information about internal candidates (e.g., past performance, temperament, work ethic). (3) Filling a higher-level position internally is generally cheaper than filling it from outside. (4) Assuming that those promoted from within are seen as deserving, there is a positive impact on the motivation levels of other employees.

Operationally, here are five important questions about internal recruitment that all organizations need to address. To illustrate each one, consider the role of technical professionals and their potential moves to managerial positions.[18]

- How does the organization create a talent pool? For example, how does it prepare technical professionals for future management positions?
- How does the organization attract candidates for promotion? Do the most suitable technical professionals want to advance to management, or do they prefer to pursue technical work?
- How does the organization choose candidates to promote? Is it a reward for good technical performance or for their leadership abilities?
- How does the organization make offers to land candidates? How successful is the organization in convincing technical professionals to move into leadership positions?
- How does the organization bring new employees on board? How much support and training are technical professionals given after they assume their new positions to help them become effective leaders?

One of the thorniest issues confronting internal recruitment is the reluctance of managers to grant permission for their subordinates to be interviewed for potential transfer or promotion. In a 2016 survey, fully half of 665 firms reported talent hoarding as a serious problem.[19] To overcome this aversion, promotion-from-within policies must receive strong top-management support, coupled with a company philosophy that permits employees to consider available opportunities within the organization and incentives for managers to release them. At Ernst & Young (EY) and Johnson & Johnson, pay is now determined, in part, by how well a manager does at nurturing people. Technology consulting firm Avenade shifts leaders to new roles every few years to ensure that high-potential employees get noticed.[20]

Among the channels available for internal recruitment, the most popular ones are succession plans (discussed in Chapter 5), job posting, employee referrals, and temporary worker pools.

Job Posting

Advertising available jobs internally began as a way to provide equal opportunity for women and minorities to compete. It served as a method of getting around the "old-boy" network, where jobs sometimes were filled more by "who you knew" than by "what you knew." Today **job posting** is an established practice in many organizations, especially for filling jobs up to lower-executive levels.

Openings are published on company intranets, on internal social media, or in company newsletters. Interested employees must reply within a specified number of days, and they may or may not have to obtain the consent of their immediate supervisors.[21] Some job-posting systems apply only to a local office or plant, whereas other companies will relocate employees.

Using Jobs on Facebook, employers in the United States and Canada can post jobs, track applications, and communicate with job applicants. Initially, its job-posting features were geared toward small and midsize businesses but in 2019 Facebook partnered with SAP's recruiting platform to appeal to large corporate employers.[22] Here is how it works (see Figure 7-2).

Figure 7–2

Facebook's job board.

Sources: Maurer, R. (2017, March 2). Facebook's job board entry a "solid first step." Published by Society for Human Resource Management. *www.facebook.com.*

Postings appear on a company's Facebook page under a "new jobs" bookmark and on the newsfeeds of relevant Facebook users. Job seekers can apply for open positions by clicking the "Apply Now" button on the ad, which takes them to an editable form pre-populated with information from their Facebook profile. The form prompts applicants to write a short cover letter explaining why they are the best candidate for the position. Once submitted, employer page administrators receive the applications via Facebook Messenger.[23]

Job posting via social media is essentially a "help wanted" sign on the Internet, but a problem might arise from poor communication. The best posts highlight an organization, selling its strengths. They include salary ranges and gender-neutral language. Expedia found that such postings attract higher-quality candidates and fill five days faster. Most importantly, respond to every applicant who applies. Respectful communication and follow-up feedback are essential if job posting is to work properly.[24]

Employee Referrals

Referral of job candidates by current employees has been and continues to be a major source of new hires at many levels, including professionals. It is an internal recruitment method; that is, internal rather than external sources are used to attract candidates. Typically, such programs offer a cash or merchandise bonus when a current employee refers a successful candidate to fill a job opening. The logic behind employee referral is that "it takes one to know one." Interestingly, the rate of employee participation seems to remain unaffected by such efforts as higher cash bonuses, cars, or expense-paid trips.[25] This suggests that good employees will not refer

Employee referrals can be an excellent source of new hires at all levels.
Isadora Getty Buyou/Image Source

potentially undesirable candidates, even if the rewards are outstanding. Finally, considerable research evidence indicates that referrals result in consistently lower quit rates than other sources.[26]

What's New in Employee Referrals?[27]

Employee referrals deliver more than 30 percent of all hires. They are particularly effective with highly specialized positions that might be difficult to fill through conventional channels. That's because people tend to associate with others in their professions. The game-development division of Redmond, Washington–based Nintendo is typical. Says Nintendo recruiting specialist Helen Fu, "Most of our hires are referred by other employees. It's a specialized skill set, a tight-knit community." Referrals work for many other jobs as well. Prudential considers its employees "talent ambassadors." They can earn between $500 and $2,500 for each successful referral, depending on the job level. Hiring managers are not required to hire a referral over a more qualified candidate–decisions are based on skills, experience, and qualifications–but they give serious consideration to those candidates who are referred by Prudential employees.

At Vistaprint, a print company focused on business cards and brochures, the company's "Everyone Here Is a Recruiter" program offers a $1,500 referral award for each successful hire, and a home-theater system for the employee with the most referrals hired. More than 50 percent of new hires at the company come from employee referrals.

Another benefit of such a program is that it can provide the employer with a source of passive candidates–those workers who are not actively seeking new jobs.[28] This not only expands the employer's pool of potential candidates but also tends to produce higher-quality candidates. Zynga, the popular social-gaming company, relies heavily on employee referrals to find new talent. It uses software to match prospective hires with current employees who have worked with candidates previously, attended the same college, or share a similar interest, such as skiing. It then asks its employees to place an initial call to the target and talk about Zynga.

Be careful, though. Some competing businesses may retaliate against your company for stealing their happily employed workers via employee-referral programs. Assess the business impact as well as the legal risks before making an offer. If a person has an employment contract with his or her current employer, can that person be employed in a capacity that does not violate contract restrictions until they lapse? What is the likelihood that the former employer will take legal action and that it will be successful?

Some firms have created online alumni networks to find and rehire former employees. Consulting firms McKinsey and Bain actively recruit female alumni, many of whom presumably left to start families, by promoting flexible work options. From Dow Chemical to JPMorgan Chase, companies are urging former employees to maintain ties as members of the broader corporate team, almost like grads of the same alma mater, even if they end up moving to competing companies. Alumni networks follow an important principle of the knowledge economy: Personal connections transcend corporate boundaries. Not surprisingly, 15 percent of ex-employees "boomerang" back to their old firms.[29]

Research shows that employee referrals work for three major reasons. (1) Assuming that current employees value their reputations, they pre-screen referrals; (2) referrals are more likely to have accurate expectations about jobs, assuming they have discussed them with current employees; and (3) newly hired employee referrals have someone they can go to for coaching.[30] Although employee referrals clearly have advantages, it is important to note that from an EEO perspective, employee referrals are fine as long as the workforce is diverse in gender, race, and ethnicity to begin with. A potential disadvantage, at least for some firms, is that employee referrals tend to perpetuate the perspective, the belief systems, and, in some cases, the lack of diversity of the current workforce. This may not be the best way to go for organizations that are trying to change those things.

Temporary Worker Pools

Unlike workers supplied from temporary agencies, in-house "temporaries" work directly for the hiring organization and may receive benefits, depending on the number of scheduled hours worked per week. Think about the number of firms that hire temporaries around the holidays. In 2019, firms such as Macy's, JCPenney, Amazon, FedEx, UPS, Target, and Kohl's hired roughly 550,000 workers. At Amazon, about 15,000 became full-time employees after the holidays.[31]

The top reasons for hiring temporary workers are to work on specific projects (27 percent of respondents) and to provide extra staff during business or seasonal cycles (25 percent).[32] Temporary workers are part of the on-demand, or "gig," economy. They pursue alternative work through specialty consulting firms, staffing firms, and talent-matching platforms. Although exact data are hard to find, there is general agreement that more than 50 million people in the United States are working in the gig economy. The vast majority are Millennials.[33]

EXTERNAL RECRUITMENT

To meet demands for talent brought about by business growth, a desire for fresh ideas, or to replace employees who leave, organizations periodically turn to the outside labor market. Keep in mind, however, that the recruitment practices of large and small firms differ considerably. Larger firms tend to be more formal and bureaucratic than smaller firms. (See the company examples in the HR Buzz box below.) In addition, many job seekers have distinct preferences regarding firm size, and they actively seek those types of employers to the exclusion of those that do not meet their preferences. It might be argued, therefore, that large and small firms comprise separate labor markets.[34] In this section, we describe five of the most popular recruitment sources: university relations, virtual career fairs, executive search firms, employment agencies, and recruitment advertising, as well as special inducements.

HR BUZZ

RECORD-LOW UNEMPLOYMENT SPURS CREATIVE RECRUITMENT TACTICS*

As tight labor markets become the norm, companies, both large and small, high-tech and low-tech, are scrambling to find talent. In fields like machine learning, artificial intelligence, and cybersecurity, it is especially difficult.

Here are three big limitations: (1) Cutting-edge skills are evolving faster than universities can train people, (2) the supply of talented young people entering these fields is well below the demand for them, and (3) luring coveted talent away from their current job or city is difficult.

Stanley Black & Decker needed high-tech talent to help it run factories and to manage its supply chain. After studying where the right talent was already living and working, the 175-year-old maker of wrenches, hedge trimmers, and medical equipment opened an Atlanta office and hired about 100 digital experts. To attract more of them, it is boosting investments in corporate social responsibility and branding itself as an engine of innovation.

Manufacturers, especially small ones, often have a difficult time recruiting talent. Firms like Woodward Inc. and Keg Enterprises invite parents of high school students to a "Parents Night Out" to persuade today's highly involved moms and dads that manufacturing work can lead to satisfying and lucrative careers for their children—with the added benefit of keeping them nearby.

The Belden electric wire factory in Richmond, Indiana, with a third of its workers within 5 years of retirement, adopted a novel approach. It offers drug treatment, paid for by the company, to job applicants who fail a drug screen. Those who complete the treatment are promised a job. Located in a company town, its fate is intertwined with the community.

Other companies are using student-debt repayment and college-tuition benefits to lure recruits. Bright Horizons, a child-care provider, offers full tuition to employees pursuing associate or bachelor degrees in early childhood education. The company estimates it will get $1.67 in return on every dollar invested due to higher retention rates. Other firms—like Fidelity, Hulu, PwC, LiveNation, and Staples—offer student-loan-repayment programs. As you can see, creative recruiting tactics have become the norm in the ongoing struggle to attract and retain talent.

*Sources: GlassDoor.com. (2020, Feb. 5). 12 companies that will pay off student loans. Retrieved from *https://www.glassdoor.com/blog/12-companies-that-will-pay-off-student-loans/* on Apr. 1, 2020. Simon, R. (2020, Feb. 9). Smallest U. S. firms struggle to find workers. *The Wall Street Journal.* Retrieved from *https://www.wsj.com/articles/smallest-u-s-firms-struggle-to-find-workers-11581264011* on Feb. 9, 2020. Noguchi, Y. (2018, July 27). Now hiring: A company offers drug treatment and a job to addicted applicants. *NPR.* Retrieved from *https://www.npr.org/2018/07/27/631557443/now-hiring-a-company-offers-drug-treatment-and-a-job-to-addicted-applicants* on July 20, 2018. Weber, L. (2018, June 1). Industrial giants join battle for tech talent. *The Wall Street Journal,* pp. B1, B4. Levitz, J. (2017, Dec. 18). Factories tap parents to recruit workers. *The Wall Street Journal,* p. A3.

University Relations

What used to be known as "college recruiting" is now considerably broader in many companies. Companies have targeted certain schools that best meet their needs and have broadened the scope of their interactions with them.[35] Such activities may now include–in addition to recruitment–gifts and grants to the institutions, summer employment and consulting projects for faculty, and invitations to placement officers to visit company plants and offices. In 2018, for example, the ExxonMobil Foundation provided more than $50 million to U.S. universities and colleges.[36]

PricewaterhouseCoopers (PwC) is an example of a company that works on college campuses aggressively. It focuses on four main areas: early identification, team involvement, ongoing activities, and internships. During each visit, it uses virtual reality headsets so students can feel like they are sitting in on a meeting, or seeing D&I initiatives in action.[37] At the same time, a senior member of the company meets regularly with faculty and deans. That person treats the university as a client and is supported by a recruiter. To assess its efforts, PwC gathers data on the universities that yield the most new hires, new employees who receive the highest performance ratings, and new hires who remain with the firm for the longest period. PwC uses this information to decide whether it will continue to recruit at a university.

To enhance the yield from campus recruitment efforts, employers should consider the following research-based guidelines:[38]

1. Establish a "presence" on college campuses beyond just the on-campus interviewing period (as PwC has done).
2. Provide more detailed information about the characteristics of entry-level jobs, especially those that have affected the decisions of prior applicants to join the organization. Use actual employees in photos and videos to illustrate the employment brand. Thus, Booz Allen Hamilton launched a website featuring consultants as they work on projects. Visitors to the site can follow consultants' progress and see how they deal with clients, team members, and their friends and families outside of work. The weekly episodes are edited video clips rather than live-streaming video, and each one features interactive questions and answers plus detailed information about each of the project's consultants.[39]
3. Devote more time and resources to training on-campus interviewers to answer specific, job-related questions from applicants.[40]
4. Focus on job attributes that influence the decisions of applicants–for example, opportunities for creativity or to exercise initiative, promotional opportunities, location of work, and company culture. Fully 46 percent of Generation Y is prepared to forego pay or promotion to work for an organization with a good reputation. That number rises to 48 percent for Gen X and to 53 percent for baby boomers.[41] As for Generation Z, in North America, 51 percent identified flexible work as the career goal most important to them. Beyond that, their focus is not on the current job, but where it will lead.

Virtual Career Fairs

Driven in part by technology for popular video games that makes it possible to create ever more realistic scenarios, **virtual career fairs** now have the ability to use video, voice, and text to connect job seekers with recruiters and to span time zones and continents in the process. At a virtual job fair, online visitors see a setup that is very similar to a physical one. They can listen to presentations, visit booths, leave résumés and business cards, participate in live chats, and get contact information from recruiters, HR managers, and even hiring managers. A third party—a college, a publication, or an association—that brings together companies runs most such job fairs.

Goodwill Industries hosts an annual virtual career fair. Here's how it works. Job seekers first register at the Goodwill website, post their résumés, and then visit the online employer booths of their choice. Attendees can log in to the virtual career fair anytime. The event is free for job seekers; employers pay a fee for a virtual booth. Visitors to the online job fair see a large coliseum, where, with a click, they can go to an information booth, where an avatar welcomes them, and then they can visit employer booths featuring companies such as Sprint, Dell, and Cintas. Employers post available positions in their booths and link to their job-listing pages on their websites. If there are a lot of jobs available in a lot of markets, an HR representative can answer questions about them via chat or e-mail exchange. The virtual career fair site links to a Facebook page, has videos about participating employers, and offers real-time online chats with recruiters. Employers schedule the chat times, and up to five people can chat at any time in individual conversations. Here is another bonus: Candidates enjoy visiting several companies without leaving their desks, along with the knowledge that they will not run into the HR manager from their company at the next booth.[42]

Executive Search Firms

Organizations typically retain executive search firms to recruit for senior-level positions. The reasons for doing so may include a need to maintain confidentiality from an incumbent or a competitor, a lack of local resources to recruit executive-level individuals, or insufficient time. To use an executive search consultant most effectively requires time and commitment from the hiring organization. It must allow the consultant to become a company "insider" and to develop knowledge and familiarity with the business, its strategic plans, and its key players.[43]

Although using an executive search firm has advantages, employers evaluating a search firm should carefully consider the following indications that the firms can do competent work:[44]

- The firm has defined its market position by industries rather than by disciplines or as a jack-of-all-trades.
- The firm understands how your organization functions within the industries served.
- The firm is performance oriented and compensates the search salesperson substantially on the basis of assignment completion.
- Who will be doing the work? Some of the highest-profile firms may have some of the most junior staff involved in your search.
- How does your firm communicate with non-finalists? Most firms treat finalists well, but it says a lot about a firm when it also treats well those who have been removed from consideration.
- When are fees due? The retainer is traditionally paid at 30, 60, and 90 days. Indirect expenses, which cover such things as research tools, communication systems, postage, and printing, can be up to 10 to 12 percent of the search fee, although they are frequently capped at $9,000–$12,000. Know what you are signing up for.
- The firm is a member of the Association of Executive Search Consultants (AESC) and subscribes to AESC's professional practice guidelines and code of ethics.

Compared with other recruitment sources, executive search firms are quite expensive. Total fees may reach 30 to 35 percent of the compensation package of the new hire, although more clients are now negotiating fixed-fee arrangements. Fees are often paid as follows: a retainer amounting to one-third the total fee as soon as the search is commissioned; one-third 60 days into the assignment; and a final third upon completion, plus expenses. If an organization hires a candidate on its own prior to the completion of the search, it still must pay all or some portion of the search firm's fee, unless it makes other arrangements.[45]

Employment Agencies

Employment agencies find people to fill all kinds of jobs, from temporary to full time, in a number of different career fields. According to the American Staffing Association, employment agencies (or staffing companies) employ more than 3 million temporary and contract workers in an average week. Each year they hire 16 million employees at an average wage of more than $17 per hour. Some make more than $100 per hour.[46] To achieve the best results, cultivate a small number of firms and thoroughly describe the education, training, and experience of the candidates needed, the fee structure, and the method of resolving disputes.

Most major temporary agencies act also as employment agencies, usually with the employer paying the fees. Manpower, Kelly, Office Mates, and Olsten (among many others) have direct-hire (fee paid by employer) or temporary-to-hire fee arrangements. With the latter, either a temporary employee must stay on the payroll for temporaries a certain number of weeks or the employer must pay a fee, depending on the salary range of the new hire.[47]

Recruitment Advertising

When the Container Store needed to fill seasonal jobs, it did not post the openings in local newspapers, nor did it post them on job boards online. Instead, it sent 1.6 million e-mails seeking potential employees among customers who lived within 20 miles of any of its stores. That was in addition to other efforts on LinkedIn, Facebook, and Twitter and in stores.[48] Welcome to the new world of recruitment advertising.

Corporate home pages on the Internet are often designed with potential recruits in mind because they are frequently the first place job seekers look when they begin to evaluate companies. On their home pages, many companies highlight links to information about diversity and inclusion, employee benefits, and flexible work schedules. JPMorgan Chase, Electronic Arts, Accenture, and Enterprise Rent-a-Car are just some of the many companies that provide compelling materials on their websites about why people should work there.[49]

Special Inducements—Relocation Aid, Help for the Trailing Spouse, and Sign-On Bonuses

Especially with higher-level jobs, newly recruited managers expect some form of relocation assistance. A basic package includes household-goods assistance; an allowance (usually equivalent to 2–4 weeks' salary) to cover incidental expenses; help with the sale of the relocating employee's home; covering the employee's loss, if any, on the sale of the home; and transportation costs for the final move to the new location, including hotels and meals during transit.[50] At a cost of roughly $97,000

HR BUZZ

Online Job Search

HELP WANTED

It is no exaggeration to say that the Internet has revolutionized recruitment practice. For the nearly 20 percent of the world's workforce who change jobs each year, there are more than 50,000 sites globally, as well as the ability to research employers and to network.[a] Fully 92 percent of companies use social media for recruitment, and 45 percent of *Fortune* 500 firms include links to social media on their career-page sections.[b] This rapid evolution is expected to continue, with dynamic, customized job postings that use cookie-based targeting to communicate job advertisements to relevant individuals based on their online behaviors and the incorporation of mobile technology to access Internet-based job information.[c]

In short, the Internet is where the action is in recruiting. Despite the allure of commercial job search sites, evidence indicates that it took an average of about 15 applications to different employers to get a job through an online job site vs. 10 for those who applied directly to the company and 6 for those who were referred.[d] The best ones make it simple for candidates to apply for jobs. They provide a wealth of information about the company and leave candidates with a favorable impression.[e] Excluding niche job boards, the top 10 job sites in 2020 were Indeed, LinkedIn, Glassdoor, Job. com, Monster, CareerBuilder, Joblist, ZipRecruiter, Craigslist, and Linkup.[f]

Despite the reach and apparent ease that online searches offer, surprisingly few jobs get filled that way. Only about 1 percent of those who apply for jobs through job boards or internal career sites are offered positions, compared with almost 70 percent for networking with friends, family, or colleagues.[g] For that reason, online networking sites—such as LinkedIn, Facebook, Instagram, Pinterest, and Twitter—have become increasingly important to job seekers. Geared toward professional relationships, networking websites allow their members to build a web of social and business associates and to interact person-to-person with new contacts.[h] GlassDoor's job postings feature eye-catching multimedia company profiles balanced with anonymous feedback from current and former employees on the culture, salary, and CEO. Indeed. com goes even further. It examines thousands of job boards and employer sites free of charge and tells you what LinkedIn contacts you have at a company posting a job. That lets you follow up your job application with an e-mail to a colleague to request a referral or to set up an introduction.[i]

[a]Maurer, R. (2016, Jan. 14). Internet is primary resource for job seekers worldwide. Retrieved from *www.shrm. org/resourcesandtools/hr-topics/talent-acquisition/pages/internet-job-seekers-worldwide.aspx* on Jan. 26, 2016.

[b]Nelson, B. (2020). Attention, college grads: Everything they told you about social media is completely wrong. *Reader's Digest.* Retrieved from www.rd.com/advice/work-career/social-media-etiquette-for-job-seekers/ on Apr. 1, 2020.

[c]Maurer, R. (2016, Feb. 2). The most sought-after talent prefer mobile recruitment. Retrieved from *www. shrm.org/resourcesandtools/hr-topics/talent-acquisition/pages/talent-prefer-mobile-recruitment.aspx* on Feb. 14, 2016. Dineen, B. R., and Allen, D. G. (2014). Internet recruiting 2.0: Shifting paradigms. In K. Y. T. Yu and D. M. Cable (Eds.), *The Oxford Handbook of Recruitment,* Oxford, UK: Oxford University Press, pp. 382–401.

[d]Maurer (2016, Jan. 14), op. cit.

[e]Doyle, A. (2017, Jan. 31). Top 10 best job websites. Retrieved from *www.thebalance.com/top-best-job-websites-2064080* on Apr. 13, 2017.

[f]Careerblog. (2020, Mar. 3). Best job-search sites in 2020 [For every industry]. Retrieved from *https:// novoresume.com/career-blog/job-search-sites* on Apr. 1, 2020.

[g]Tomaszewski, M. (2020, Jan. 27). Job-search statistics for 2020. *Zety.* Retrieved from *https://zety.com/ blog/job-search-statistics* on Apr. 1, 2020.

[h]Thebalancecareers. (2020). Best social media sites for job searching. Retrieved from *https://www. thebalancecareers.com/best-social-media-sites-for-job-searching-2062617* on Apr. 1, 2020.

[i]Reviews.com. (2017, Jan. 25). The best job sites for 2017. Retrieved from *http://www.reviews.com/job-sites/* on Apr. 13, 2017.

to move an employee homeowner, and $72,600 to move a new-hire homeowner, employers are weighing carefully the talent-management benefits against the monetary costs of moving staff. Relocating employees and new hires who rent costs much less: about $24,000 and $19,000, respectively.[51] Homeowner or renter status is a basis for placing employees in different mobility tiers that contain different housing subsidies.[52]

Prodded by the emergence of the dual-career family—more than 60 percent of all families[53]—firms are finding that many managers and professionals, men and women alike, are reluctant to relocate unless the spouse will be able to find suitable employment in a new location. Spouse employment assistance typically includes job counseling, fees to placement agencies, contacts outside the company, and job-search assistance.[54]

An increasingly common recruiting inducement, independent of any relocation assistance, is the sign-on bonus. Originally used in the sports world, signing bonuses are now common among executives, professionals (particularly in high-technology firms), and middle-level executives, as companies seek to strengthen the eroding bonds between them and their employees. Executive-level hires receive the largest sign-on bonuses, with 41 percent paying $50,000 or more. Supervisors, professionals, and IT employees typically receive 5–10 percent of starting salary.[55]

What's a company to do if things don't work out and the new person simply walks away with the cash? Employers usually make bonus offers based on the employee agreeing to remain with the employer for a set period of time (e.g., 2 years). If the employee signs a repayment agreement, he or she will likely have to return the money if he or she leaves before that date.[56]

Summary of Findings Regarding Recruitment Sources

Now that we have examined some of the most popular sources for internal and external recruiting, it seems reasonable to ask, Which sources are most popular with employers and job applicants? Among employers, evidence indicates that:

- Informal contacts are used widely and effectively at all occupational levels. In fact, word-of-mouse (informal, web-based conversations about companies) are viewed as more credible and associated with higher organizational attractiveness than web-based testimonials.[57]
- Use of public employment services declines as required skills levels increase.
- The internal market is a major recruitment source except for entry-level, unskilled, and semiskilled workers.
- Larger firms are the most frequent users of walk-ins, write-ins, and the internal market. They clearly have a hiring advantage.[58]
- There is no consistent relationship between recruitment sources and person-job fit.
- Use of multiple recruitment sources together with informal sources provides more realistic and accurate information.[59]

In practice, most applicants use more than one recruitment source to learn about jobs. However, the accumulated evidence on the relationship among recruitment sources, turnover, and job performance suggests that such relationships are quite weak.[60] In light of these results, what may be more important than the source per se is how much support and information a source provides, or the extent to which a source embeds prescreening on desired applicant characteristics.[61] After all, today's job candidates require a consumer-grade recruiting experience similar to what they receive when shopping online.

DIVERSITY-ORIENTED RECRUITING

Special measures are called for in diversity-oriented recruiting. Although it might appear obvious that employers should use women and members of underrepresented groups (1) in their HR offices as interviewers; (2) on recruiting trips to high schools, colleges, and job fairs; and (3) in employment advertisements, these are necessary, but not sufficient, steps. One study found that although as many as 44 percent of African American candidates said they eliminated a company from consideration because of a lack of gender or ethnic diversity, three key attributes affected their decisions to apply or remain: the ready availability of training and career-development programs, a diverse upper management, and a diverse workforce. It's not just hiring. People want to feel like they belong.[62]

It's important to signal to prospective minority applicants that an organization values D&I. To do that, incorporate D&I into the corporate vision statement, have the CEO meet regularly with employee-resource groups and routinely review D&I metrics and progress.

Employers need to establish reliable contacts in the groups targeted for recruitment. This is known as *relationship recruiting*. Allow plenty of lead time for contacts to notify prospective applicants and for the applicants to apply for available positions.

Reach out to community or professional organizations, such as the Society of Mexican-American Engineers and Scientists, the National Society of Black Engineers, and the National Black MBA Association. Encourage leaders of those organizations to visit the employer and talk with employees. Offer internships to members of targeted groups. Finally, recognize two things: (1) It takes time to establish a credible, workable diversity-oriented recruitment program and (2) there is no payoff from passive nondiscrimination. Strive to create a consistent corporate image that will support recruiting efforts across the board.[63]

MANAGING RECRUITMENT OPERATIONS

Administratively, recruitment is one of the easiest activities to foul up—with potentially long-term negative publicity for the firm. Traditionally, recruitment was intensively paper based. Today, however, the entire process has been reengineered through cloud- or computer-based applicant tracking systems (ATS). An ATS is a databank for all hiring processes. Figure 7–3 shows the flow of work in such a system.

The process begins with a requisition from a hiring manager to authorize the filling of one or more positions within a job category. Once a job posting is created, it is published in a variety of potential hiring channels (e.g., company website, job boards, social media). As candidates apply, they receive acknowledgments, and the documents they submit proceed through rough screening on a pass/fail basis. Hiring managers then interview the most promising candidates and select the one or more who receive the highest ratings.

Over the years, ATS have evolved from résumé databases to well-rounded recruitment-optimization tools—cloud-based models that incorporate intuitive interfaces and tools that allow recruiters to cast a wider net for candidates.[64] For example,

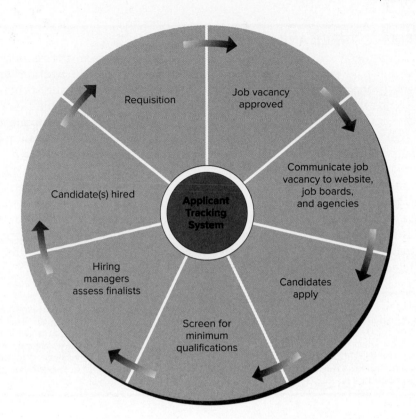

Figure 7–3

How work flows from requisition to hire in an applicant tracking system.
Source: (Adapted from) Gray, N. (2013, June 26). How to choose applicant tracking software to fast-track your recruiting. Retrieved from *www.job-science.com/blog/how-to-choose-applicant-tracking-software-to-fast-track-your-recruiting/* on Mar. 2, 2017.

HiringSolved is using artificial intelligence and machine learning to develop a conversational interface to a robust talent analytics platform–basically "Siri" for recruiting–to leverage massive data analysis and learning capabilities known as RAI. If a recruiter says, "I'm looking for data scientists with experience with Python within 25 miles of Chicago," RAI will respond with "I found 42 candidates that look good for the role. Here's a preview. Would you like to refine the search or e-mail these candidates?"[65] Other products, such as IBM Kenexa's Brass Ring, Oracle Taleo, or Greenhouse, can easily be integrated with "add-on" recruiting technologies from outside vendors, such as video interviewing, pre-hire assessments, and the sourcing of passive candidates. To attract those candidates, LinkedIn has a feature called "Open Candidates" that lets users announce to recruiters their openness to changing jobs while keeping that decision hidden from their current employers.[66]

As many as 80 percent of active candidates now use smartphones to search and apply for jobs, yet as many as 60 percent of them quit in the middle of filling out online job applications because of their length or complexity. The cost to organizations is the loss of top talent, poor word-of-mouth from candidates frustrated with the process, and higher costs to firms that use cost-per-click recruiting models. What can organizations do? A large-scale study by recruitment company Appcast revealed that completion rates drop by almost 50 percent when an application asks 50 or more questions vs. 25 or fewer questions.

Job-board company CareerBuilder cut drop-off rates in half by making three changes to its ATS. It no longer required candidates to register before applying, it streamlined its mobile-application process, and it allowed job seekers to apply to a company vs. for a specific job.[67] The HR Buzz box describes several additional features that some firms are offering as part of their ATS.

HR BUZZ

SYSTEMS TO TRACK AND CONTACT APPLICANTS

Most companies want to improve the candidate experience in the recruitment process. Fully 82 percent of candidates report that the ideal interaction with a company is one where innovative technologies are used behind the scenes and come second to personal, human interaction. At the same time, the ability to communicate automatically with candidates as their applications move from one stage to another is a valuable feature. Other ATS applications incorporate robust analytics. Companies want to know how long it takes candidates to move through interview stages, how that influences drop-out rates, and where recruiters spend the most time. IBM Watson helps recruiters measure the degree of effort required to fill certain job openings, helps prioritize job requisitions, accurately predicts the likelihood of candidates being successful, and performs social-media "listening" to create insights that help recruiters improve their messages to candidates.[a] As you can see from these few examples, ATS are evolving into more user-friendly, versatile tools that are capable of supporting advanced components of talent acquisition.

[a]O'Connell, B. (2019, Nov. 16). Five recruiting trends for the new decade. Retrieved from *https://www.shrm.org/hr-today/news/all-things-work/pages/five-recruiting-trends.aspx* on Nov. 16, 2019. *See also* Zielinski, D. (2017, March 24). Recruiting gets smart thanks to artificial intelligence. Retrieved from *www.shrm.org/hr-today/news/hr-magazine/0417/pages/recruiting-gets-smart-thanks-to-artificial-intelligence.aspx* on Apr. 8, 2017. *See also* Wright, A. D. (2017, Aug. 25). Job seekers are frustrated with automated recruiting. Retrieved from *https://www.shrm.org/resourcesandtools/hr-topics/technology/pages/candidates-soured-too-much-technology.aspx* on Aug. 25, 2017.

Evaluation and Control of Recruitment Operations

The reason for evaluating past and current recruitment operations is simple: to improve the efficiency of future recruitment efforts. After all, recruitment costs account for 15 percent of all HR spending. Here are just a few pre-hire metrics:[68]

- Cost of operations—that is, the costs of company recruiters, operational costs (e.g., staff travel and living expenses, agency fees, advertising expenses, brochures), and overhead expenses (e.g., rental of temporary facilities and equipment).
- Cost per hire, which averages $4,129 overall and $14,936 for executives.[69]
- Number and quality of résumés by source.
- Acceptance/offer ratio.
- Analysis of post-visit and rejection questionnaires.
- Salary offered—acceptances versus rejections.

The American National Standard for Cost per Hire allows organizations to determine accurate and comparable costs to staff a position using standard data and formulas. Here is the formula for Cost per Hire (CPH):

$$CPH = \left(\frac{\Sigma \text{ (External costs)} + \Sigma \text{ (Internal costs)}}{\text{Total number of hires in a time period}} \right)$$

Examples of external costs include advertising, marketing, recruitment-process outsourcing fees, and job-fair expenses. Examples of internal costs include the fully loaded costs of the recruiting staff, the time of the hiring manager, and the costs of recruitment software. The standard notes explicitly that some cost elements and the definition of a "hire" will vary across organizations.[70]

While any number of cost and quality analyses are possible, choose those that are strategically most relevant to your organization. In addition, strive to link staffing performance to business outcomes. For example, it is one thing to know that a firm's sales openings average 65 days to fill. It's another thing to know that the difference between filling them in 65 vs. 40 days costs the firm $30 million in revenue or that a 20 percent improvement in quality-of-hire will result in an $18 million productivity improvement.[71]

Several studies have examined the recruitment process from the perspective of applicants. They reveal, unfortunately, that many job applicants (1) have an incomplete and/or inaccurate understanding of what a job opening involves; (2) are not sure what they want from a position; (3) do not have a self-insight into their knowledge, skills, and abilities; and (4) cannot accurately predict how they will react to the demands of a new position. While applicants consider their work experience to be the most important factor in securing a job interview, hiring managers focus on accomplishments.[72]

What about a company's reputation? Evidence indicates that reputation provides firms with a competitive advantage by attracting more, and possibly higher-caliber, applicants.[73] Research findings also show that a company's reputation also affects applicants' willingness to pursue jobs because (1) they use reputation as a signal about the attributes of jobs (e.g., fun, challenging, lots of variety); (2) reputation affects the pride that individuals expect from joining the organization; and (3) applicants are willing to pay a premium in terms of lost wages to join firms with positive reputations.[74]

Recruitment is a market-exchange process in which employers attempt to differentiate their "products" (job opportunities) among "consumers" (job applicants) who vary in their levels of job-relevant knowledge, abilities, and skills.[75] Not surprisingly, therefore, the best predictors of applicant attraction are person–organization and person–job fit. Organizations as varied as ESPN, Accenture, Home Depot, IKEA, and the U.S. Army offer interactive assessments of fit.[76] The most important effects on interview outcomes, however, are candidates' perceived qualifications (e.g., ability to express ideas and demonstrated initiative).[77]

Timing issues in recruitment, particularly delays, are important factors in the job-choice decisions of applicants.[78] Research indicates that (1) long delays between recruitment phases are not uncommon; (2) applicants react to such delays very negatively, and (3) the most marketable candidates accept other offers if delays become extended. In short, top talent disappears quickly in a competitive marketplace. If you want to compete for it, streamline the decision-making process, so that you can move fast.

Realistic Job Previews

A conceptual framework that might help explain some of these research findings is that of the **realistic job preview (RJP)**.[79] An RJP requires that in addition to telling applicants about the nice things a job has to offer (e.g., pay, benefits, opportunities for advancement), recruiters must also tell applicants about the unpleasant aspects of the job—for example, required on-call hours or a high volume of e-mails. Research in actual company settings has indicated consistent results.[80] That is, when the unrealistically positive expectations of job applicants are lowered to match the reality of the actual work setting prior to hire, job acceptance rates may be lower but job performance, job satisfaction, and survival are higher for those who receive an RJP.[81] In the hospitality industry, Compass Group uses virtual, or 360-degree videos to demonstrate "day-in-the-life" perspectives about specific jobs. They can be viewed either online or at job fairs. Acceptances to its manager-in-training program have jumped from 30 to 45 percent since the virtual videos were introduced.[82] Over many studies, meta-analysis shows that RJPs improve retention rates, on average, by 9 percent.[83]

RJPs administered after hire as part of newcomer socialization also have positive effects. They help to reduce turnover, help new hires cope with work demands, and signal that the employer is concerned about the well-being of its new hires.[84]

A final recommendation is to develop RJPs even when there is no turnover problem (proactively rather than reactively). Use interactive, 360-degree video if possible, and show actual job incumbents.[85] Here are four research-based criteria for deciding what information to include in an RJP: (1) It is important to most recruits, (2) it is not widely known outside the organization, (3) it is a reason that leads newcomers to quit, and (4) it is related to successful job performance after being hired.[86]

Nevertheless, RJPs are not appropriate for all types of jobs. They seem to work best (1) when few applicants are actually hired (i.e., the selection ratio is low), (2) when used with entry-level positions (because those coming from outside to inside the organization tend to have more inflated expectations than those who make changes internally), and (3) when unemployment is low (because job candidates are more likely to have alternative jobs to choose from).[87]

ETHICAL DILEMMA
Online Résumés and Personal Privacy

Millions of people will transmit their résumés over the Internet this year. Is this a recruiting bonanza for employers? In one sense, yes, because they can scan online job boards using keywords to identify candidates with the skills and experience that they need. On the other hand, there are some very serious privacy concerns for job seekers and employee-relations concerns for employers.[a]

Résumés posted at one site can be traded or sold to other sites, they can be stolen by unscrupulous headhunters or duplicated and reposted by roving "spiders," and current employers can locate them. The Internet is so vast that many people think their résumés are safe there. Think again: A number of factors can wrest control from a job seeker. Here is one.

In the name of protecting company secrets, some organizations assign staff to patrol cyberspace in search of wayward workers. Their objective is to reassign employees who are posting their résumés online, and who therefore have one foot out the electronic door, off sensitive projects. Fair enough. But such a practice can also be viewed as an invasion of an employee's privacy and right to search for another job. What do you think? Is it ethical for current employers to search the Internet in an effort to identify employees who have posted their résumés online?

[a]Bryce, S. C., and Sanborn, A. (2019, Sept. 5). Should you upload your resume to LinkedIn or other social media? *Work It Daily.* Retrieved from *https://www.workitdaily.com/should-i-post-resume-online* on Apr. 2, 2020. Boatman, K. (n.d.). The dos and don'ts of posting your résumé online. Retrieved from *https://us.norton.com/yoursecurityresource/detail.jsp?aid=jobs* on Apr. 14, 2017. Ashford, K. (2006, Dec.). Is your résumé online? Watch out. *Money,* p. 36.

THE OTHER SIDE OF RECRUITMENT—JOB SEARCH

At some time, whether voluntarily or otherwise, almost everyone faces the difficult task of finding a job. Although many people land jobs through personal contacts or networking, 73 percent of 18- to 34-year-olds found their last job through social professional networks.[88] This is also true for executives, many of whom now make use of executive-networking sites such as LinkedIn, Indeed, and GlassDoor.[89] Keep this in mind as you read the following scenario.

Scenario 1: Unemployed

This scenario has happened all too frequently over the last decade (as a result of mergers, restructurings, and downsizings), and it is expected to occur often this decade as economic conditions change.[90] You are a midlevel executive, well regarded, well paid, and seemingly well established in your chosen field. Then—whammo!—a change in business strategy or a change in economic conditions results in your layoff from the firm from which you hoped to retire. What do you do? How do you go about finding another job? According to management consultants and executive recruiters, the following are some of the key things *not* to do, followed by some suggestions for posting an Internet résumé.[91]

- *Don't panic.* A search takes time, even for well-qualified middle- and upper-level managers. Seven months to a year is not unusual. Be prepared to wait it out.
- *Don't be bitter.* Bitterness makes it harder to begin to search; it also turns off potential employers.
- *Don't kid yourself.* Do a thorough self-appraisal of your strengths and weaknesses, as well as your likes and dislikes about jobs and organizations. Face up to what has happened, decide if you want to switch fields, figure out where you and your family want to live, and don't delay the search itself for long.
- *Don't drift.* Develop a plan, target companies, and go after them relentlessly. Realize that your job is to find a new job. Cast a wide net; consider industries (and countries) other than your own.
- *Don't be lazy.* The heart of a good job hunt is research. Use the Internet, public filings, and annual reports when drawing up a list of target companies. If negotiations get serious, talk to a range of insiders and knowledgeable outsiders to learn about politics and practices. You don't want to wind up in a worse fix than the one you left.
- *Don't be shy or overeager.* Because personal contacts are the most effective means to land a job, get the word out that you are available. At the same time, resist the temptation to accept the first job that comes along—unless it's absolutely right for you.
- *Don't ignore your family.* Some executives are embarrassed and don't tell their families what's going on. A better approach, experts say, is to bring the family into the process and deal with issues honestly.
- *Don't lie.* Experts are unanimous on this point. Don't lie, and don't stretch a point—either on résumés or in interviews.[92] Be willing to address failures as well as strengths. Discuss openly and fully what went wrong at the old job, and what you learned from that experience. One study found that work experience and dates of employment were the two most fibbed-about topics.[93]

- *Don't jump the gun on salary.* Let the potential employer bring this subject up first. But once it surfaces, thoroughly explore all aspects of your future compensation and benefits package. At the same time, a candid conversation with an outside recruiter about your present and desired salary is a good idea.[94]
- *Be careful when posting a résumé on the Internet.* Post a digital version on your own home page and place the word *résumé* in the website address to increase the chance of being noticed by Internet recruiters. These days, knowing how to assemble a résumé for online consumption is a skill you will need for almost any job search. Although it is important to use job-specific keywords, be careful! The latest ATS can distinguish between a keyword inserted in a résumé at random and one used to describe a person's work history. Use a keyword out of context and your résumé will be bumped to the bottom of the search results.[95]

Those who have been through the trauma of job loss and the challenge of finding a job often describe the entire process as a wrenching, stressful one. Avoiding the mistakes listed here can ensure that finding a new job need not take any longer than necessary.

Scenario 2: Employed but Searching for a New Job

People who are currently employed may decide to engage in a job search for any one or more of the following reasons: to establish a network, to demonstrate their marketability to their current employers, or to develop other job choices to compare with their current positions. A study using currently employed managers found that they engaged in more job-search behavior the more agreeable (trusting, compliant, caring), conscientious, and open to experience they were. Characteristics of one's current employment situation play a key role—for example, perceived fairness of pay and benefits, feelings about one's supervisor, satisfaction with career progress, and perceived alternative opportunities.[96] What are the implications of these results for organizations?

IMPACT OF RECRUITMENT ON PRODUCTIVITY, QUALITY OF WORK LIFE, AND THE BOTTOM LINE

A close fit between individual strengths and interests and organizational and job characteristics almost guarantees a happy "marriage." Because the bottom line of recruitment success lies in the number of successful placements made, however, a regular system for measuring and evaluating recruitment efforts is essential. Consider that the first-year turnover rate for new employees can be 50 percent or higher in some industries.[a] To hire and retain 100 employees, therefore, the organization will need 200. However, if an RJP can boost retention from 50 to 59 percent, then the company will only need to hire 159

new people. For large retailers and fast-food chains that typically hire more than 100,000 newcomers at a (conservative) cost of $400–$500 per hire, the savings in recruitment and hiring costs avoided may be in the tens of millions of dollars.

---

[a]U.S. Bureau of Labor Statistics. (2020, Jan.). Job openings and labor turnover, January 2020. Retrieved from *https://www.bls.gov/news.release/pdf/jolts.pdf* on Apr. 2, 2020. Zivkovic, M. (2020). The true cost of hiring an employee in 2020. *Togglhire.* Retrieved from *https://toggl.com/blog/cost-of-hiring-an-employee* on Apr. 2, 2020. Wanous, J. P. (2017). Realistic job preview. In S. G. Rogelberg (Ed.), *The Sage Encyclopedia of Industrial and Organizational Psychology* (2nd ed., Vol. 3). Thousand Oaks, CA: Sage, pp. 1311-4.

IMPLICATIONS FOR MANAGEMENT PRACTICE

Talent is what makes firms go. Recruitment is therefore a strategic imperative and an important form of business competition. The following elements should be part of any successful recruitment program:

- Always view recruitment as a long-term strategy.
- Offer a consumer-grade recruiting experience to job seekers.
- Develop a total-rewards package that genuinely appeals to the employees being hired.
- Audit the recruitment programs in place.

Brands and reputations have always been important in product markets. Today they are just as important in talent markets. Companies with well-known brands and excellent reputations want to leverage them in their recruitment efforts. For example, consider firms that are named to various "Best Employer" lists. They strive to make those lists because they receive twice as many applications as firms that don't. In addition, they enjoy employee turnover levels that are less than half those of their competitors.[a] In short, people want to work at places where they are treated well, places that are doing well, and places where they are proud to work. Organizations with features like that will always be perceived as employers of choice.

[a]Cascio, W. F., and Graham, B. Z. (2016). New strategic role for HR: Leading the employer-branding process. *Organization Management Journal* 13(4), pp. 182-92.

Assuming that the manager is someone you want to retain, communicate clearly that he or she is valued and that there are rich opportunities within the organization.

At the same time, employers know that top workers are often treated well and may not be searching actively for a new job. These are so-called passive prospects, and they are hot commodities. Locating them is easier now, given the availability of social professional networks such as LinkedIn.[97]

THE PERILS AND PROMISE OF SOCIAL MEDIA

Human Resource Management in Action: Conclusion

An effective social-media policy sets expectations for appropriate behavior online with respect to the employer. It should include the following elements:

1. State whether company recruiters or hiring managers can use social media to screen candidates or employees and the risks involved in doing that (e.g., the risk of discovering information about an individual's protected status under federal, state, or local laws).
2. Emphasize that company recruiters and hiring managers will only review publicly available information. Do not ask for passwords, and be consistent across candidates and employees.
3. State clearly that employees are not to divulge trade secrets or proprietary information. Provide specific examples of policy violations.

4. State that employees may be held accountable for content they post on the Internet, particularly if that content violates other company policies–for example, derogatory, defamatory, or inflammatory speech that offends reasonable people.
5. Be clear about the legal consequences for the employer and disciplinary actions for employees if rules are not followed.
6. State that the policy is not a static document and may be revised as laws and usage change or as new platforms are introduced. Ensure that employees have the most up-to-date social-media policy.
7. Educate employees about the benefits as well as the pitfalls of social networking. Help them to protect their privacy–for example, by using secure passwords, logging out of accounts while on public computers, and using common sense when creating new profiles and customizing settings.
8. Inform employees about the need for company approval prior to posting certain kinds of information, and from whom to seek it.
9. Emphasize to employees that they are brand ambassadors for the organization and that what they write may be disseminated to the world–even if they only share it with their "friends."
10. Encourage employees to think twice about posting comments they would not say out loud or that they would not want their bosses or family members to see.
11. Finally, do more than just post a policy and expect employees to read it. Develop interactive training that promotes a deeper understanding of the words in the policy.

SUMMARY

Recruitment is a form of business competition and it is fierce. It is an important component of the staffing supply chain. Recruitment begins with a clear statement of objectives, based on the number and types of knowledge, skills, abilities, and other characteristics that an organization needs to achieve its strategic business objectives. A recruitment policy must spell out clearly an organization's intention to evaluate and screen candidates without regard to factors such as race, gender, age, or disability. The actual process of recruitment begins with a specification of workforce requirements–numbers, skills mix, levels, and the time frame within which such needs must be met.

Recruitment may involve internal or external labor markets or both. Internal recruitment often relies on succession plans, job posting, employee referrals, or temporary worker pools. Many external recruitment sources are also available. In this chapter, we discussed five such sources: university relations, virtual job fairs, executive search firms, employment agencies, and recruitment advertising, with special emphasis on online job searches. In managing and controlling recruitment operations, consider using an applicant tracking system that calculates the cost of operations, analyzes the performance of each source, and estimates payoffs of successful recruitment efforts. Why? Because the number of hires who actually perform their jobs successfully determines recruitment success.

KEY TERMS

recruitment

potential labor pool

available labor pool

applicants

screening

selection

labor market

passive nondiscrimination

pure diversity-based recruitment

diversity-based recruitment with
  preferential hiring

hard quotas

job posting

virtual career fair

realistic job preview (RJP)

DISCUSSION QUESTIONS

7-1. How would you implement a strategy of pure diversity-based recruitment?

7-2. Discuss the conditions under which realistic job previews are and are not appropriate.

7-3. How would you advise a firm that wants to improve its recruitment efforts at universities?

7-4. Knowing that you have been studying the subject of recruitment, a friend asks you for advice on doing an online job search. What would you say?

7-5. Draft a recruitment ad to advertise a job opening at your company. Have a friend critique it, as well as–if possible–an HR professional from a local company. Incorporate their suggestions for improvement into a final draft.

7-6. You have just lost your middle-management job. Outline a procedure to follow in trying to land a new one.

7-7. How might social media help in recruiting passive job applicants, those not actively looking for a job?

7-8. Why is organizational culture particularly important in internal recruitment?

7-9. Your boss asks you to develop an employee-referral program for new hires. What might such a program look like?

7-10. You have been assigned to manage the recruitment visit of a prospective new hire for your 12-person organization. Develop a checklist of do's and don'ts to help ensure a successful visit.

APPLYING YOUR KNOWLEDGE

Transforming Data into Recruiting Intelligence[98]   *Case 7–1*

Arguably, the bottom line of recruiting success is the number of successful new hires. Organizations know that it is important to measure the outcomes of recruitment, but, unfortunately, most focus on measures that show how efficient they are: time to fill an open job or cost per hire. These are helpful but by no means indicate the impact that hiring decisions have on a company's ability to realize its business goals. For example, it's easy to say, "Our time-to-fill is 42 days." Wouldn't it be better to say, "We reduced our time-to-fill by 20 percent, which got our technology and engineering teams to finish their project a quarter earlier, resulting in $500,000 of savings, which contributed to $250,000 of revenue"?

Experts agree that to measure quality of hire effectively, it's important to calculate metrics both pre- and post-hire. Pre-hire, recruitment-focused quality measures include such things as candidate quality (education, experience, training), new-hire attrition, and candidate assessment scores. Consider questions such as the following: Do we have enough qualified candidates in the pipeline? Is our interview process effective? Are we closing deals with the candidates we want to hire? Measures of post-hire quality include outcomes such as time to become fully productive, rank among peers, and supervisory assessments of culture fit.

ATS enable firms to collect a wide range of data. The challenge is to distill them in ways that will convey business-critical information to decision makers.

Questions

1. You have just been named manager of recruiting at your firm. The senior executive team asks you to develop a "scorecard" that will enable it to assess the costs and benefits of recruitment efforts. What might such a scorecard look like?

2. The team wants you to distinguish measures of efficiency from measures of business impact. What kinds of metrics will you put in each column?

3. A recent survey found that nearly two-thirds of job seekers who felt they were treated poorly during the recruitment process were less likely to purchase goods and services from those employers. If 10 percent of job seekers at your firm are dissatisfied, how might you tally those costs?

REFERENCES

1. Lytle, T. (2020). Searching far and wide. *HRMagazine* **65**(1), pp. 44-49. *See also* Bloomberg. (2020, Jan. 9). Taco Bell offers $100,000 salaries and paid sick time. *Los Angeles Times.* Retrieved from *https://www.latimes.com/business/story/2020-01-09/taco-bell-higher-salaries-paid-sick-time* on Jan. 9, 2020.

2. International Organization for Standardization (ISO 30405: 2016). (2016, Sept.). Human resource management: Guidelines on recruitment. Retrieved from *www.iso.org/standard/64149.html* on Mar. 2, 2017. *See also* Cascio, W. F., and Boudreau, J. W. (2011). Utility of selection systems: Supply-chain analysis applied to staffing decisions. In S. Zedeck (Ed.), *APA Handbook of Industrial and Organizational Psychology* (Vol. 2). Washington, DC: American Psychological Association, pp. 421-44.

3. Ehrenberg, R. G., and Smith, R. S. (2018). *Modern Labor Economics* (13th ed.). New York: Routledge. *See also* Cahuc, P., Carcillo, S., and Zylberberg, A. (2014). *Labor Economics* (2nd ed.). Cambridge, MA: MIT Press.

4. U.S. Bureau of Labor Statistics. (2019). Fastest growing occupations, 2018 and projected 2028. Retrieved from *https://www.bls.gov/emp/tables/fastest-growing-occupations.htm* on Mar. 31, 2020.

5. Gerhart, B., & Newman, J. M. (2020). *Compensation* (13th ed.). New York: McGraw-Hill.

6. Ehrenberg and Smith (2018), op. cit.

7. Gerhart & Newman (2020), op. cit. *See also* Dineen, B. R., and Soltis, S. M. (2011). Recruitment: A review of research and emerging directions. In S. Zedeck (Ed.), *APA Handbook of Industrial and Organizational Psychology* (Vol. 2). Washington, DC: American Psychological Association, pp. 43-66.

8. Feintzeig, R. (2016, Feb. 23). Companies pay workers to live close to the office. *The Wall Street Journal.* Retrieved from *www.wsj.com/articles/companies-pay-workers-to-live-close-to-the-office-1456223402* on Feb. 24, 2016.

9. Ehrenberg and Smith (2018), op. cit. *See also* Bidwell, M. (2017). Managing talent flows through internal and external labor markets. In D. G. Collings, K. Mellahi, & W. F. Cascio (Eds.), *The Oxford Handbook of Talent Management.* Oxford, UK: Oxford University Press, pp. 281-98. *See also* Stewman, S. (1986). Demographic models of internal labor markets. *Administrative Science Quarterly* 31, pp. 212-47.

10. Ryan, A. M., and Delany, T. (2017). Attracting job candidates to organizations. In J. L. Farr and N. T. Tippins (Eds.), *Handbook of Employee Selection* (2nd ed.). New York: Routledge, pp. 165–81. *See also* Rynes, S. L., Reeves, C. J., and Darnold, T. C. (2014). The history of recruitment research. In K. Y. T. Yu and D. M. Cable (Eds.), *The Oxford Handbook of Recruitment*. Oxford, UK: Oxford University Press, pp. 335–60. *See also* Rynes, S. L., and Cable, D. M. (2003). Recruitment research in the twenty-first century. In W. C. Borman, D. R. Ilgen, and R. J. Klimoski (Eds.), *Handbook of Psychology: Industrial and Organizational Psychology* (Vol. 12). Hoboken, NJ: Wiley, pp. 55–76.

11. Lytle (2020), op. cit. *See also* Derezin, M. (2019, June 14). Companies can stay ahead in the talent war by recruiting from within, says this LinkedIn VP. *FastCompany*. Retrieved from *https://www.fastcompany.com/90363915/companies-can-stay-ahead-in-the-talent-war-by-recruiting-from-within-says-this-linkedin-vp* on June 15, 2019. *See also* Weber, L. (2016, Apr. 13). Firms flock to cities with top talent. *The Wall Street Journal*, p. B6.

12. Maurer, R. (2016, June 17). Targeted recruiting metrics will improve hiring. Retrieved from *www.shrm.org/resourcesandtools/hr-topics/talent-acquisition/pages/targeted-recruiting-metrics-will-improve-hiring.aspx* on June 20, 2016. *See also* Maurer, R. (2015, Nov. 18). The holy grail of recruiting: How to measure quality of hire. Retrieved from *m.org/resourcesandtools/hr-topics/talent-acquisition/pages/how-to-measure-quality-of-hire.aspx* on Nov. 20, 2015.

13. Maurer (2016), op. cit. *See also* Maurer (2015), op. cit.

14. For more on how the Internet has changed recruiting, see Dineen, B. R., and Allen, D. G. (2014). Internet recruiting 2.0: Shifting paradigms. In K. Y. T. Yu and D. M. Cable (Eds.), *The Oxford Handbook of Recruitment*. Oxford, UK: Oxford University Press, pp. 382–401.

15. Job applicants' pain can hurt companies. (2017, April 12). *The Wall Street Journal*, p. B5. *See also* Ryan and Delany (2017), op. cit. *See also* Rynes et al. (2014), op. cit. *See also* Bretz, R. D., and Judge, T. A. (1998). Realistic job previews: A test of the adverse self-selection hypothesis. *Journal of Applied Psychology* 83, pp. 330–37.

16. Ployhart, R. E., and Kim, Y. (2014). Strategic recruiting. In K. Y. T. Yu and D. M. Cable (Eds.), *The Oxford Handbook of Recruitment*. Oxford, UK: Oxford University Press, pp. 5–20.

17. Bidwell (2017), op. cit. See also Maurer, R. (2016, Feb. 1). 5 recruiting trends for 2016. Retrieved from *www.shrm.org/resourcesandtools/hr-topics/talent-acquisition/pages/5-recruiting-trends-2016.aspx* on Feb. 14, 2016.

18. Cascio and Boudreau (2011), op. cit.

19. Lublin, J. S. (2017, Apr. 12). When ability holds back advancement. *The Wall Street Journal*, p. B5.

20. Ibid.

21. Maurer, R. (2017, Mar. 2). Facebook's job board entry a "solid first step." Retrieved from *www.shrm.org/resourcesandtools/hr-topics/talent-acquisition/pages/facebook-jobs-linkedin.aspx* on Apr. 12, 2017.

22. Zielinski, D. (2019, May 9). Facebook goes big with enterprise ATS integrations. *SHRM Online*. Retrieved from *https://www.shrm.org/resourcesandtools/hr-topics/talent-acquisition/pages/facebook-enterprise-ats-integrations.aspx* on May 9, 2019.

23. Ibid. *See also* Zielinski, D. (2013, Mar.). Social media platforms are expanding employers' recruiting reach. *HRMagazine*, pp. 63–65.

24. Cutter, C. (2019, Aug. 22). Talking up a job requires new language. *The Wall Street Journal*, p. B6. *See also* Job applicants' pain can hurt companies (2017), op. cit.

25. Breaugh, J. A. (2012). Employee recruitment: Current knowledge and suggestions for future research. In N. Schmitt (Ed.), *The Oxford Handbook of Personnel Assessment and Selection*. New York: Oxford University Press, pp 68–87. *See also* Orgel, M. (2010, Feb. 10). It's who you know: Job seekers who don't network miss out on company referral programs. Retrieved from *http://www.marketwatch.com/story/job-seekers-aided-by-employee-referral-programs-2010-02-10* on July 7, 2011.

26. Griffeth, R. W., Tenbrink, A., and Robinson, S. (2014). Recruitment sources: A review of outcomes. In K. Y. T. Yu and D. M. Cable (Eds.), *The Oxford Handbook of Recruitment*. Oxford, UK: Oxford University Press, pp. 215–50.

27.   Maurer, R. (2017, June 23). Employee referrals remain top source for hires. *SHRM Online*. Retrieved from *https://www.shrm.org/resourcesandtools/hr-topics/talent-acquisition/pages/ employee-referrals-remains-top-source-hires.aspx* on June 23, 2017. *See also* Society for Human Resource Management. (2016, Dec. 20). Designing and managing successful employee referral programs. Retrieved from *www.shrm.org/resourcesandtools/tools-and-samples/toolkits/pages/tk-designingandmanagingsuccessfulemployeereferralprograms.aspx* on Dec. 21, 2016. *See also* Maurer, R. (2016, Feb. 10). How Dell revamped its employee referral program. Retrieved from *www.shrm.org/resourcesandtools/hr-topics/talent-acquisition/pages/dell-employee-referral-program.aspx* on Mar. 6, 2016.

28.   Ryan, L. (2017, Mar. 25). The real reason employers love "passive candidates." Retrieved from *www.forbes.com/sites/lizryan/2017/03/25/the-real-reason-employers-love-passive-candidates/#364400665006* on Apr. 1, 2017. *See also* Passive candidates–Engage now for informed hire later. (2015, Jan. 14). *HRZone*. Retrieved from *http://www.hrzone.com/ community-voice/blogs/spire-technologies/passive-candidates-engage-now-for-informed-hire-later* on May 1, 2015.

29.   Brin, D. W. (2018, May 2). Catching a boomerang? Pros and cons of rehiring former employees. SHRM Online. Retrieved from *https://www.shrm.org/resourcesandtools/hr-topics/ talent-acquisition/pages/pros-cons-rehiring-former-employees-boomerangs.aspx* on May 2, 2018. *See also* 15%: Ex-employees who return to the fold. (2015, Dec.). *Money*, p. 17. *See also* Kwoh, L. (2013, Feb. 20). McKinsey tries to recruit mothers who left the fold. *The Wall Street Journal*, pp. B1, B8.

30.   Breaugh (2014), op. cit. *See also* Griffeth, R. W., Hom, P. W., Fink, L. S., and Cohen, D. J. (1997). Comparative tests of multivariate models of recruiting sources effects. *Journal of Management* 23, pp. 19–36. *See also* Kirnan, J. P., Farley, J. A., and Geisinger, K. F. (1989). The relationship between recruiting source, applicant quality, and hire performance: An analysis by sex, ethnicity, and age. *Personnel Psychology* 42, pp. 293–308.

31.   Mullen, C. (2019, Dec. 6). As holiday shopping evolves, so does seasonal hiring. Retrieved from *https://www.shrm.org/resourcesandtools/hr-topics/talent-acquisition/pages/pros-cons-rehiring-former-employees-boomerangs.aspx* on Mar. 31, 2020. *See also* Kauflin, J. (2016, Nov. 1). Who's hiring the most, holiday season 2016. *Forbes*. Retrieved from *www.forbes.com/sites/ jeffkauflin/2016/11/01/whos-hiring-the-most-holiday-season-2016/#7518cfb33c7f* on Apr. 12, 2017.

32.   Schaefer, P. (2019, Nov. 26). The pros and cons of hiring temporary employees. *Business Know-how*. Retrieved from *https://www.businessknowhow.com/manage/hire-temp.htm* on Mar. 31, 2020. *See also* Olson, E. G. (2011, May 5). The rise of the permanently temporary worker. *Fortune*. Retrieved from *http://management.fortune.cnn.com/2011/05/05/the-rise-of-the-permanently-temporary-worker/* on Apr. 16, 2014.

33.   Mitic, I. (2019, Aug. 21.). Gig economy statistics: The new normal in the workplace. Fortunly.com. Retrieved from *https://fortunly.com/statistics/gig-economy-statistics#gref* on Mar. 31, 2020. *See also* McGovern, M. (2017). *Thriving in the Gig Economy*. Wayne, NJ: Career Press.

34.   Barber, A. E., Wesson, M. J., Roberson, Q. M., and Taylor, M. S. (1999). A tale of two job markets: Organizational size and its effect on hiring practices and job search behavior. *Personnel Psychology* 52, pp. 841–67.

35.   Gellman, L. (2016, June 24). Goldman rebuffs the Ivy League. *The Wall Street Journal*, pp. C1, C2. *See also* Estrada-Worthington, R. (2016). Graduate Management Admission Council: 2016 corporate recruiters survey report. Retrieved from *www.gmac.com/market-intelligence-and-research/research-library/employment-outlook/2016-corporate-recruiters-survey-report.aspx* on Apr. 4, 2017. *See also* Porter, J., and Lavelle, L. (2007, July 9). The professor is a head-hunter. *BusinessWeek*, pp. 80–84.

36.   ExxonMobil. (2019, May 4). ExxonMobil, employees, and retirees donate more than $50 million to U.S. colleges and universities. Retrieved from *https://corporate.exxonmobil. com/News/Newsroom/News-releases/2019/0514_ExxonMobil-employees-and-retirees-donate-more-than-50-million--to-US-colleges-and-universities* on Apr. 1, 2020.

37. Zielinski, D. (2019, Jan. 25). Recruiters, trainers find new uses for virtual reality. *SHRM Online*. Retrieved from *https://www.shrm.org/resourcesandtools/hr-topics/technology/ pages/recruiters-trainers-new-uses-virtual-reality-hr.aspx* on Jan. 25, 2019.

38. Breaugh (2014), op. cit. *See also* Dineen and Soltis (2011), op. cit.

39. Maurer (2016, Feb. 1), op. cit. *See also* Silverman, R. E. (2000, Oct. 31). The jungle: What's news in recruitment and pay. *The Wall Street Journal*, p. B18.

40. Maurer, R. (2018, March 21). Recruiters need to be ready to answer these candidate questions. *SHRM Online*. Retrieved from *https://www.shrm.org/resourcesandtools/ hr-topics/talent-acquisition/pages/recruiters-prepare-answer-candidate-questions.aspx* on Mar. 21, 2018.

41. Maurer, R. (2016, Mar. 1). 4 tips for recruiting Generation Z. Retrieved from *www.shrm. org/resourcesandtools/hr-topics/talent-acquisition/pages/4-tips-for-recruiting-generation-z. aspx* on Mar. 2, 2016. *See also* Generation Y goes directly to source in job hunt. (2011, Apr. 25). Retrieved from *http://www.shrm.org/Publications/HRNews/Pages/GenYGoesTo-Source.aspx* on July 7, 2011. *See also* Dineen and Soltis (2011), op. cit.

42. Gurschiek, C. (2013, May 3). Three-day virtual career fair kicks off May 6. Retrieved from *www.shrm.org/publications/hrnews/pages/goodwill-veterans-youth-women-lobfair.aspx* on Apr, 16, 2014.

43. Ryan Search & Consulting. (2013, June). Five questions you should ask before retaining an executive search firm. Retrieved from *http://www.ryansearch.net/blog/june_2013/five_ questions_you_should_ask_before_retaining_an_* on Nov. 9, 2016. *See also* Columbia Consulting Group. (2000). *Executive Search Guidelines*. New York: Author.

44. Ibid. *See also* Agility Executive Search. (n.d.). 10 key questions to ask your executive recruiter. Retrieved from *http://agilityexecutivesearch.com/10-key-questions-ask-executive-recruiter/* on Apr. 12, 2017. *See also* Association of Executive Search Consultants. (2014). Selecting a retained executive search firm. Retrieved from *http://members.aesc.org/ eweb/upload/Guidelines%20for%20Selecting%20an%20Executive%20Search%20Firm.pdf* on Apr. 16, 2014.

45. Bradford, K. (2019, Nov. 1). Executive search prices: What does executive search cost? *Intellerati*. Retrieved from *https://intellerati.com/executive-search-prices-executive-search-cost/* on Apr. 1, 2020. *See also* Wells, S. J. (2003, Apr.). Slow times for executive recruiting. *HRMagazine* 48(4), pp. 60–68.

46. American Staffing Association. (2019). Staffing industry statistics. Retrieved from *https:// americanstaffing.net/staffing-research-data/fact-sheets-analysis-staffing-industry-trends/staffing-industry-statistics/* on Apr. 1, 2020.

47. Jaracz, J. (n.d.). How employment agencies work. Retrieved from *https://money.howstuff-works.com/business/getting-a-job/employment-agencies.htm* on Apr. 1, 2020.

48. Morath, E. (2014, Oct. 27). Stores try filling jobs for holiday via tweets. *The Wall Street Journal*, pp. B1, B2. *See also* Talent wars: Corporate recruitment in the age of social media. (2014, Jan. 28). *Fortune*, pp. S1–S6.

49. Smith, J. (2017, Apr. 10). Online retailers heat up local labor markets. *The Wall Street Journal*, p. B5.

50. Woodward, N. H. (2007, Feb.). Surprise, surprise. *HRMagazine*, pp. 81–88.

51. Armstrong, M. (2018, March 1). Relocation statistics every business should know. *Urbanbound*. Retrieved from *https://www.urbanbound.com/relocation-statistics-to-know* on Apr. 1, 2020.

52. Franquiz (2013), op. cit. *See also* Krell, E. (2011, Mar.). Mobility officers on the move. *HRMagazine*, pp. 59–62.

53. U.S. Bureau of Labor Statistics. (2017, Apr. 27). Employment in families with children in 2016. Retrieved from https://www.bls.gov/opub/ted/2017/employment-in-families-with-children-in-2016.htm on April 1, 2020.

54. Global mobility: Dual-career assistance for international assignments. (2020). *ShieldGeo*. Retrieved from *https://shieldgeo.com/global-mobility-dual-career-assistance-international-assignments/* on Apr. 1, 2020.

55. Henricks, M. (2020, Jan. 24). What is a sign-on bonus? *SmartAsset*. Retrieved from *https://finance.yahoo.com/news/sign-bonus-005225869.html* on Apr. 1, 2020.

56. Kuhn, B. E. (2014, Apr. 9). Signing bonuses. Retrieved from *http://www.bryankuhnlaw.com/blog/2014/04/signing-bonuses.shtml* on Apr. 13, 2017.

57. Tomaszewski, M. (2020, Jan. 27). Job-search statistics for 2020. *Zety*. Retrieved from *https://zety.com/blog/job-search-statistics* on Apr. 1, 2020. *See also* Van Hoye, G., and Lievens, F. (2007). Investigating web-based recruitment sources: Employee testimonials versus word-of-mouse. *International Journal of Selection and Assessment* 15, pp. 372–82.

58. Bidwell (2017), op. cit. *See also* Knowledge@Wharton. (2014, Apr. 10). The hiring advantage of high-status firms. Retrieved from *knowledge.wharton.upenn.edu/article/hiring-advantage-high-status-firms/* on Apr. 12, 2014. *See also* Griffeth et al. (2014), op. cit.

59. Griffeth et al. (2014), op. cit.

60. Ibid. *See also* Carlson, K. D., Connerly, M. L., and Mecham, R. L. (2002). Recruitment evaluation: The case for assessing the quality of applicants attracted. *Personnel Psychology* 55, pp. 461–90. *See also* Williams, C. R., Labig, C. E., Jr., and Stone, T. H. (1993). Recruitment sources and post-hire outcomes for job applicants and new hires: A test of two hypotheses. *Journal of Applied Psychology* 78, pp. 163–72.

61. Maurer (2017, Feb. 23), op. cit. *See also* Rynes et al. (2014), op. cit.

62. Babcock, P. (2017, Feb. 24). 5 steps to improve diversity recruiting. Retrieved from *www.shrm.org/resourcesandtools/hr-topics/talent-acquisition/pages/five-steps-improve-diversity-recruiting.aspx* on Feb. 26, 2017. *See also* Volpone, S. D., Thomas, K. M., Sinisterra, P., and Johnson, L. (2014). Targeted recruiting: Identifying future employees. In K. Y. T. Yu and D. M. Cable (Eds.), *The Oxford Handbook of Recruitment*. Oxford, UK: Oxford University Press, pp. 110–25.

63. McConnell, B. (2019, March 25). 12 ways to improve your diversity recruiting strategy. *Recruitee*. Retrieved from *https://blog.recruitee.com/diversity-recruiting-strategy/* on Apr. 1, 2020. *See also* Wells, G. (2017, Mar. 29). Uber offers data on workforce diversity. *The Wall Street Journal*, p. B3. *See also* Parsi, N. (2017, Jan. 16). Workplace diversity and inclusion gets innovative. Retrieved from *www.shrm.org/hr-today/news/hr-magazine/0217/pages/disrupting-diversity-in-the-workplace.aspx* on Jan. 19, 2017.

64. O'Connell, B. (2019, Nov. 16). Five recruiting trends for the new decade. Retrieved from *https://www.shrm.org/hr-today/news/all-things-work/pages/five-recruiting-trends.aspx* on Nov. 16, 2019. *See also* Maurer (2017, Feb. 23), op. cit. *See also* Zielinski, D. (2017, Feb. 13). Recruiting gets smart thanks to artificial intelligence. Retrieved from *www.shrm.org/resourcesandtools/hr-topics/technology/pages/recruiting-gets-smart-thanks-to-artificial-intelligence.aspx* on Feb. 15, 2017.

65. Maurer, R. (2017, Feb. 2). "Siri" for recruiting set to debut this year. Retrieved from *www.shrm.org/resourcesandtools/hr-topics/talent-acquisition/pages/siri-for-recruiting-debut-2017-hiringsolved.aspx* on Feb. 3, 2017.

66. Maurer, R. (2016, Oct. 6). New LinkedIn feature helps users find a new job without alerting their employer. Retrieved from *www.shrm.org/resourcesandtools/hr-topics/talent-acquisition/pages/linkedin-unveils-new-features.aspx* on Oct. 8, 2016.

67. Zielinski, D. (2015, Oct.). 7 reasons to love your ATS. *HRMagazine*, pp. 31–36.

68. Cascio, W. F., and Aguinis, H. (2019). *Applied Psychology in Talent Management* (8th ed.). Thousand Oaks, CA: Sage.

69. Google Hire Team. (2019, July 25). How to accurately calculate your cost per hire. Retrieved from *https://hire.google.com/articles/cost-per-hire/* on Apr. 2, 2020.

70. ANSI/SHRM. (2012, Feb. 8). *Cost-per-Hire: American National Standard*. Alexandria, VA: Society for Human Resource Management.

71. Cascio, W. F., Boudreau, J. W., & Fink, A. (2019). *Investing in People: Financial Impact of Human Resource Initiatives* (3rd ed.). Alexandria, VA: SHRM Publishing.

72. Alonso, A. (2019, June 5). Job seekers unaware of what employers value in applicants. *SHRM Online.* Retrieved from *https://www.shrm.org/hr-today/news/hr-magazine/summer2019/pages/job-seekers-unaware-of-what-employers-value-in-applicants.aspx* on June 5, 2019. *See also* Breaugh (2014), op. cit.

73. The hiring advantage of high-status firms. (2014, Apr. 10). *Knowledge@Wharto*n. Retrieved from *http://knowledge.wharton.upenn.edu/article/hiring-advantage-high-status-firms/* on Apr. 10, 2014. *See also* Turban, D., and Cable, D. (2003). Firm reputation and applicant-pool characteristics. *Journal of Organizational Behavior* 24, pp. 733–51.

74. Glassdoor. (2019, July 10). New survey: company mission & culture matter more than salary. Retrieved from *https://www.glassdoor.com/blog/mission-culture-survey/* on Apr. 2, 2020. *See also* The hiring advantage of high-status firms (2014), op. cit.

75. Ployhart and Kim (2014), op. cit. *See also* Maurer, S. D., Howe, V., and Lee, T. W. (1992). Organizational recruiting as marketing management: An interdisciplinary study of engineering graduates. *Personnel Psychology* 45, pp. 807–33.

76. Ryan and Delany (2017), op. cit. *See also* Uggerslev, K. L., Fassina, N. E., and Kraichy, D. (2012). Recruiting through the stages: A meta-analytic test of predictors of applicant attraction at different stages of the recruiting process. *Personnel Psychology* 65, pp. 597–660.

77. Graves, L. M., and Powell, G. N. (1995). The effect of sex similarity on recruiters' evaluations of actual applicants: A test of the similarity-attraction paradigm. *Personnel Psychology* 48, pp. 85–98.

78. Harold, C. M., Uggerslev, K. L., and Kraichy, D. (2014). Recruitment and job choice. In K. Y. T. Yu and D. M. Cable (Eds.), *The Oxford Handbook of Recruitment.* Oxford, UK: Oxford University Press, pp. 47–72. *See also* Dineen and Soltis (2011), op. cit.

79. Cutter, C. (2019, Aug. 22). Talking up a job requires new language. *The Wall Street Journal,* p. B6. *See also* Landis, R. S., Earnest, D. R., and Allen, D. G. (2014). Realistic job previews: Past, present, and future. In K. Y. T. Yu and D. M. Cable (Eds.), *The Oxford Handbook of Recruitment.* Oxford, UK: Oxford University Press, pp. 423–36. *See also* Wanous, J. P. (2017). Realistic job preview. In S. G. Rogelberg (Ed.), *The Sage Encyclopedia of Industrial and Organizational Psychology* (2nd ed., Vol. 3). Thousand Oaks, CA: Sage, pp. 1311–14. *See also* Popovich, P., and Wanous, J. P. (1982). The realistic job preview as a persuasive communication. *Academy of Management Review* 7, pp. 570 78.

80. Hom, P. W. (2011). Organizational exit. In S. Zedeck (Ed.), *APA Handbook of Industrial and Organizational Psychology* (Vol. 2). Washington, DC: American Psychological Association, pp. 325–75. *See also* Breaugh (2008), op. cit. *See also* Premack, S. L., and Wanous, J. P. (1985). A meta-analysis of realistic job preview experiments. *Journal of Applied Psychology* 70, pp. 706–19.

81. Weller, I., Michalik, A., and Muhlbauer, D. (2014). Recruitment source implications for organizational tenure. In K. Y. T. Yu and D. M. Cable (Eds.), *The Oxford Handbook of Recruitment.* Oxford, UK: Oxford University Press, pp. 139–60. *See also* Phillips, J. M. (1998). Effects of realistic job previews on multiple organizational outcomes: A meta-analysis. *Academy of Management Journal* 41, pp. 673–90.

82. Grensing-Pophal, L. (2018, Mar. 30). Providing realistic job previews through 360-degree video. *SHRM Online.* Retrieved from *https://www.shrm.org/resourcesandtools/hr-topics/talent-acquisition/pages/realistic-job-previews-360-degree-video.aspx* on Mar. 31, 2018.

83. Earnest, D. R., Allen, A. G., and Landis, R. S. (2011). Mechanisms linking realistic job previews with turnover: A meta-analytic path analysis. *Personnel Psychology* 64(4), pp. 865–97. *See also* Hom, P. W., Griffeth, R. W., Palich, L. E., and Bracker, J. S. (1998). An exploratory investigation into theoretical mechanisms underlying realistic job previews. *Personnel Psychology* 51, pp. 421–51. *See also* McEvoy, G. M., and Cascio, W. F. (1985). Strategies for reducing employee turnover. A meta-analysis. *Journal of Applied Psychology* 70, pp. 342–53.

84. Maurer, R. (2017, March 31). New hires skip out when the role doesn't meet expectations. *SHRM Online*. Retrieved from *https://www.shrm.org/resourcesandtools/hr-topics/talent-acquisition/pages/new-hires-retention-turnover.aspx* on Apr. 1, 2017. *See also* Wanous (2017), op. cit. *See also* Landis et al. (2014), op. cit. *See also* Hom, P. W., Griffeth, R. W., Palich, L. E., and Bracker, J. S. (1999). Revisiting met expectations as a reason why realistic job previews work. *Personnel Psychology* 52, pp. 97–112.

85. HUMRRO. (2019, May 29). Virtual job previews. Retrieved from *https://www.humrro.org/corpsite/article/virtual-job-previews/* on May 29, 2019. *See also* Grensing-Pophal (2018), op. cit. *See also* Wanous, J. P. (1989). Installing a realistic job preview: Ten tough choices. *Personnel Psychology* 42, pp. 117-34.

86. Wanous (2017), op. cit. *See also* Landis et al. (2014), op. cit. *See also* Wanous (2007), op. cit.

87. Wanous, J. P. (1980). *Organizational Entry: Recruitment, Selection and Socialization of Newcomers*. Reading, MA: Addison-Wesley.

88. Ryan and Delany (2017), op. cit. *See also* Farrell (2012), op. cit. *See also* Van Hoye, G. (2012). Recruitment sources and organizational attraction: A field study of Belgian nurses. *European Journal of Work and Organizational Psychology* 21, pp. 376–91.

89. Y Scouts. (2019, Apr. 4). Top 4 best executive job search websites. Retrieved from *http://yscouts.com/top-4-best-executive-job-search-websites/* on Apr. 2, 2020.

90. Casselman, B., & Cohen, P. (2020, April 2). A widening toll on jobs. *The New York Times*. Retrieved from *https://www.nytimes.com/2020/04/02/business/economy/coronavirus-unemployment-claims.html* on Apr. 2, 2020. *See also* Cascio, W. F. (2017). Downsizing. In S. G. Rogelberg (Ed.), *The Sage Encyclopedia of Industrial and Organizational Psychology* (2nd ed., Vol. 1). Thousand Oaks, CA: Sage, pp. 323–26.

91. Yate, M. (2017, Aug. 22). Your career Q&A: The evolution of the traditional resume. Retrieved from *https://www.shrm.org/resourcesandtools/hr-topics/organizational-and-employee-development/career-advice/pages/your-career-qa-the-evolution-of-the-traditional-resume.aspx* on Aug. 22, 2017. *See also* Boswell, W. (2017). Job search. In S. G. Rogelberg (Ed.), *The Sage Encyclopedia of Industrial and Organizational Psychology* (2nd ed., Vol. 2). Thousand Oaks, CA: Sage, pp. 812-16.

92. West, T. (2020, March 30). The lies we tell at work—and the damage they do. *The Wall Street Journal*, pp. R12, R13. *See also* Gurchiek, K. (2019, Dec. 9). Lying on resume can sink career, lead to jail. *SHRM Online*. Retrieved from *https://www.shrm.org/resourcesandtools/hr-topics/talent-acquisition/pages/lying-on-resume-can-sink-career-lead-to-jail.aspx* on Dec. 9, 2019. *See also* Liu, J. (2019, Aug. 12). Millennials are twice as likely as other generations to lie on their resumes. *CNBC*. Retrieved from *https://www.cnbc.com/2019/08/12/millennials-are-most-likely-to-lie-on-their-resumesheres-why.html* on Apr. 2, 2020.

93. West (2020), op. cit. *See also* Liu (2019), op. cit. *See also* Efrati, A., and Lublin, J. S. (2012, May 6). Résumé trips up Yahoo's chief. *The Wall Street Journal*, pp. A1, A12. *See also* Fisher, A. (2004, July 12). Should you admit why you were fired? *Fortune*, p. 52.

94. Ryan, L. (2016, June 23). How do I bring up salary at a job interview? *Forbes*. Retrieved from *www.forbes.com/sites/lizryan/2016/06/23/how-do-i-bring-up-salary-at-a-job-interview/#3d7b79cf4431* on Apr. 14, 2017. See also Malhotra, D. (2014, Apr.). 15 rules for negotiating a job offer. *Harvard Business Review* 92(4), pp. 117-20.

95. Yate (2017), op. cit. *See also* Battle the bot: How to get your resume read by a real human being. (2017, Feb. 21). Retrieved from *https://blog.appleone.com/2017/02/21/battle-the-bot-how-to-get-your-resume-read-by-a-real-human-being/* on Apr. 14, 2017.

96. Boswell (2017), op. cit. *See also* Boudreau, J. W., Boswell, W. R., Judge, T. A., and Bretz, R. D., Jr. (2001). Personality and cognitive ability as predictors of job search among employed managers. *Personnel Psychology* 54, pp. 25-50.

97. Maurer (2016, Oct. 6), op. cit.
98. Maurer (2017, Feb. 23), op. cit. *See also* Maurer (2016, Feb. 1), op. cit. *See also* Maurer, R. (2016, June 17). Targeted recruiting metrics will improve hiring. Retrieved from *www.shrm.org/resourcesandtools/hr-topics/talent-acquisition/pages/targeted-recruiting-metrics-will-improve-hiring.aspx* on June 20, 2016. *See also* Maurer, R. (2015, Nov. 18). The Holy Grail of recruiting: How to measure quality of hire. Retrieved from *www.shrm.org/resourcesandtools/hr-topics/talent-acquisition/pages/how-to-measure-quality-of-hire.aspx* on Nov. 20, 2015.

8

STAFFING

Questions This Chapter Will Help Managers Answer

LO 8-1 How do business strategy and organizational culture affect staffing decisions?

LO 8-2 What screening and selection methods are available, and which ones are most accurate?

LO 8-3 How can we improve pre-employment interviews?

LO 8-4 Can work-sample tests improve staffing decisions?

LO 8-5 What are some advantages and potential problems to consider in using assessment centers to select managers?

ORGANIZATIONAL CULTURE—KEY TO STAFFING "FIT"*

Organizational culture–shared values, expectations, and behavior–sets the context of everything a company does. Often, boards of directors, senior executives, and the public pay attention to organizational culture only after a scandal exposes the toxic atmosphere that results in wrongdoing. In recent years, scandals at such well-known companies as Volkswagen, Uber, Wells Fargo, Wynn Resorts, and KPMG have led to serious legal and personal consequences for companies as well as individual executives.

Workplace culture has a profound effect on employees. Bad workplace culture can derail an organization, leaving employees frustrated and creating material bottom-line impact. Recent large-scale research by the Society for Human Resource Management quantified some of these consequences. While 76 percent of employees say their manager sets the culture of their workplace, fully one in five workers left a job due to workplace culture, and 58 percent of those individuals say that their managers were the main reason they ultimately left. The cost? A staggering $223 billion over the past 5 years.

Conversely, in strong workplace cultures leaders are trusted and admired. They build organizations that excel at results and at taking excellent care of their people and their customers. Their vision, mission, and strategy are clear. Core values drive the culture and are used in decision making. Roles, responsibilities, and criteria of success are unambiguous and communication is candid and straightforward. Not surprisingly, the world's most admired companies, such as Apple, Amazon, Berkshire Hathaway, Walt Disney, Starbucks, Microsoft, Alphabet, Netflix, JPMorgan Chase, and FedEx score high on these indicators.

Actually, understanding a company's culture boils down to two dimensions: people interactions and response to change. People interactions span the gamut from highly independent (autonomy, individual action, and competition) to interdependent (managing relationships, collaborative, coordinating group effort). Likewise, response to change varies from stability (maintaining the status quo, consistency, predictability) to flexibility (innovation, openness, diversity of ideas and actions).

In the conclusion to this case, we will see how some companies signal their cultures to job applicants and employees, and how you can size up an organizational culture before accepting a new job.

*Sources: Eisen, B. (2020, Feb. 23). Wells Fargo settles U.S. probes. *The Wall Street Journal*, pp. A1, A10. Lublin, J. S. (2020, Jan. 16). Check out the culture before a new job. *The Wall Street Journal*, p. B5. World's most admired companies. (2019). *Fortune*. Retrieved from *https://fortune.com/worlds-most-admired-companies/2019/* on Apr. 6, 2020. Mirza, B. (2019, Sept. 25). Toxic workplace cultures hurt workers and company profits. *SHRM Online*. Retrieved from *www.shrm.org/resourcesandtools/hr-topics/employee-relations/pages/toxic-workplace-culture-report.aspx* on Sept. 25, 2019. Eaglesham, J. (2019, Sept. 12). Auditor sentenced in KPMG case. *The Wall Street Journal*, p. B10. Berzon, A., Kirkham, C., Bernstein, E., & O'Keefe, K. (2018, Mar. 28). Wynn accusers fault firm culture. *The Wall Street Journal*, pp. A1, A10. Groysberg, B., Lee, J., Price, J., & Cheng, J. (2018, Jan-Feb). The culture factor. *Harvard Business Review*. Retrieved from *https://hbr.org/2018/01/the-culture-factor* on May 4, 2018. McCord, P. (2017). *Powerful: Building a Culture of Freedom and Responsibility*. Arlington, VA: Missionday. Warrick, D. D. (2017). What leaders need to know about organizational culture. *Business Horizons* 60(3), pp. 395-404. Bensinger, G. (2017, Mar. 22). Uber vows to change corporate culture. *The Wall Street Journal*, pp. B1, B2. Collins, J. (2008, May 5). The secret of enduring greatness. *Fortune*, pp. 73-76. Nocera, J. (2008, May 24). Parting words of an airline pioneer. *International Herald Tribune*. Retrieved from *www.redorbit.com*, on May 27, 2008.

Challenges

1. What can a company do to communicate its culture to prospective new hires?
2. Can an organization have more than one culture–for example, by department?
3. How might organizational culture affect the ways that employees deal with coworkers and customers?

The chapter-opening vignette describes the crucial role of organizational culture in attracting, retaining, and motivating employees to perform their best every day. As we shall see, the most progressive companies strive to convey their cultures to new hires as well as to current employees, and the fit of a prospective new hire with the organizational culture plays a major role in staffing decisions. There is also a constant need to align staffing decisions with business strategy. As we shall see in this chapter, there is a wide variety of tools for initial screening and selection decisions, and much is known about each one. We will examine the relative effectiveness of the tools, so that decision makers can choose those that best fit their long- and short-range objectives. Let us begin by considering the role of business strategy in staffing decisions.

ORGANIZATIONAL CONSIDERATIONS IN STAFFING DECISIONS

Business Strategy

Clearly, there should be a fit between the intended strategy of an enterprise and the characteristics of the people who are expected to implement it.[1] Apple Inc. cofounder Steve Jobs saw this connection quite clearly, as the following quote suggests:

> My passion has been to build an enduring company where people were motivated to make great products. Everything else was secondary. Sure, it was great to make a profit, because that was what allowed you to make great products. But the products, not the profits, were the motivation. . . . It ends up meaning everything–the people you hire, who gets promoted, what you discuss in meetings.[2]

Apple's competitive strategy is to make great products. Its HR strategy flows directly and naturally from that strategy ("it [strategy] ends up meaning everything–the people you hire, who gets promoted, what you discuss in meetings").

For strategic reasons, it is important to consider the stage of development of a business because many characteristics of a business–such as its growth rate, product lines, market share, entry opportunity, and technology–change as the organization changes. One possible set of relationships between the development stage and the management selection strategies is shown in Figure 8-1. Although a model such as this is useful conceptually, in practice the stages might not be so clearly defined, and there are many exceptions.

Organizations that are just starting out are in the *start-up* stage. They are characterized by high growth rates, basic product lines, heavy emphasis on product engineering, and little or no customer loyalty.

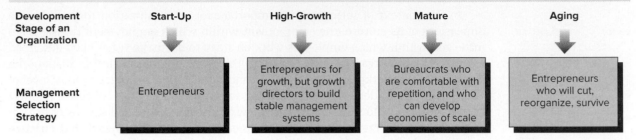

Figure 8–1

The relationship between the development stage of an organization and the management selection strategy that best "fits" each stage.

Organizations in the *high-growth* stage are concerned with two things: fighting for market share and building excellence in their management teams. They focus on refining and extending product lines, as well as building customer loyalty.

Mature organizations emphasize the maintenance of market share, cost reductions through economies of scale, more rigid management controls over workers' actions, and the generation of cash to develop new product lines. In contrast to the "freewheeling" style of an embryonic organization, there is much less flexibility and variability in a mature organization.

Finally, an *aging* organization struggles to hold market share in a declining market, and it demands extreme cost control obtained through consistency and centralized procedures. Economic survival becomes the primary motivation.

A different management style seems to fit each of these development stages best. In the start-up stage, there is a need for enterprising managers who can thrive in high-risk environments. These are known as entrepreneurs (Figure 8-1). They are decisive individuals who can respond rapidly to changing conditions.

During the high-growth stage, there is still a need for entrepreneurs, but it is also important to select the kinds of managers who can develop stable management systems to preserve the gains achieved during the embryonic stage. We might call these managers "growth directors."

As an organization matures, there is a need to select the kind of manager who does not need lots of variety in her or his work, who can oversee repetitive daily operations, and who can search continually for economies of scale. Individuals who fit best into mature organizations have a bureaucratic style of management.

Finally, an aging organization needs movers and shakers to invigorate it. Strategically, it becomes important to select (again) entrepreneurs capable of doing whatever is necessary to ensure the economic survival of the firm. This may involve divesting unprofitable operations, firing unproductive workers, or eliminating practices that are considered extravagant.

Admittedly, these characterizations are coarse, but they provide a starting point in the construction of an important link between the development stage of an organization and its staffing strategy. Such strategic concerns may be used to supplement job analyses as bases for staffing. This also suggests that job descriptions should be broadened into role descriptions that reflect the broader and more changeable strategic requirements of an organization.

Organizational Culture

Just as organizations choose people, people choose jobs and organizations that fit their personalities and career objectives and in which they can satisfy needs that are important to them.[3]

In the context of selection, it is important for an organization to describe the dimensions of its culture–the environment within which employment decisions are made and within which employees work on a day-to-day basis. It has been described as the DNA of an organization–invisible to the naked eye but critical in shaping the character of the workplace.[4] It exists at a fundamental, perhaps preconscious, level of awareness; is grounded in history and tradition; and is a source of collective identity and commitment.[5] In short, culture is the way that the values and actions of managers and employees create a unique business environment.[6] **Organizational culture** is embedded and transmitted through mechanisms such as the following:[7]

1. Formal statements of organizational philosophy and materials used for recruitment, selection, and socialization of new employees.
2. Promotion criteria.
3. Stories, legends, and myths about key people and events.
4. What leaders pay attention to, measure, and control.
5. Implicit and possibly unconscious criteria that leaders use to determine who fits key slots in the organization.

Organizational culture has two implications for staffing decisions. First, cultures vary across organizations; individuals will consider this information if it is available to them in their job-search process.[8] Companies such as IBM and Procter & Gamble have a strong marketing orientation, and their staffing decisions tend to reflect this value. Other companies, such as BMW and HP, are oriented toward research and development and engineering, whereas still others, such as McDonald's, concentrate on consistency and efficiency. Recruiters assess person/job fit by focusing on specific knowledge, skills, and abilities. They assess person/organization fit by focusing more on values and personality characteristics.[9] By linking staffing decisions to cultural factors, companies try to ensure that their employees have internalized the strategic intent and core values of the enterprise. In this way, they will be more likely to act in the interest of the company and as dedicated team members, regardless of their formal job duties.[10]

Second, other things being equal, individuals who choose jobs with organizations that are consistent with their own values, beliefs, and attitudes are more likely to be productive, satisfied employees. This was demonstrated in a study of 904 college graduates hired by six public accounting firms over a 7-year period. Those hired by firms that emphasized interpersonal-relationship values (team orientation, respect for people) stayed an average of 45 months. Those hired by firms that emphasized work-task values (detail, stability, innovation) stayed with their firms an average of 31 months. This 14-month difference in survival rates translated into an opportunity loss of at least $12.5 million (in 2019 dollars) for each firm that emphasized work-task values.[11]

The Logic of Personnel Selection

If variability in physical and psychological characteristics were not so prevalent, there would be little need for the selection of people to fill various jobs. Without variability among individuals in abilities, aptitudes, interests, and personality traits, we would expect all job candidates to perform comparably. Research shows clearly that as jobs become more complex, individual differences in output also increase.[12] Likewise, if there were 10 job openings available and only 10 qualified candidates, selection again would not be a significant issue because all 10 candidates would have to be hired. Selection becomes a relevant concern only when there are more qualified candidates than there are positions to be filled: Selection implies choice, and choice means exclusion.

Because practical considerations (safety, time, cost) make job tryouts for all candidates infeasible in most selection situations, it is necessary to predict the relative level of job performance of each candidate on the basis of available information. As we shall see, some methods for doing this are more accurate than others. However, before considering them, we need to focus on the fundamental technical requirements of all such methods–**reliability** and **validity.**

Reliability of Measurement

The goal of any selection program is to identify applicants who score high on measures that purport to assess knowledge, skills, abilities, or other characteristics that are critical for job performance. Yet we always run the risk of making errors in employee-selection decisions. Selection errors are of two types: selecting someone who should be rejected (erroneous acceptance) and rejecting someone who should be accepted (erroneous rejection). These kinds of errors can be avoided by using measurement procedures that are reliable and valid.

A measurement is considered to be reliable if it is consistent or stable–for example,

- *Over time*–such as on a hearing test administered first on Monday morning and then again on Friday night.
- *Across different samples of items*–say, on form A and form B of a test of mathematical aptitude or on a measure of vocational interests administered at the beginning of a student's sophomore year in college and then again at the end of her or his senior year.
- *Across different raters or judges working independently*–as in a gymnastics competition.

As you might suspect, inconsistency is present to some degree in all measurement situations. In employment settings, people generally are assessed only once. That is, organizations give them, for example, one test of their knowledge of a job, or one application form, or one interview. The procedures through which these assessments are made must be standardized in terms of content, administration, and scoring. Only then can the results of the assessments be compared meaningfully with one another. Reliability is typically expressed in terms of a correlation coefficient, e.g., between scores on Form A of a test and scores on Form B. Correlation is a measure of relationship between the two sets of scores. The magnitude of that relationship (typically expressed as **r**, for "relationship") varies from -1.0 to $+1.0$. When r is 1.00, the two sets of scores are related perfectly to each other. In "high-stakes" testing (e.g., licensure, certification), most tests demonstrate reliabilities that exceed 0.90. For more information about how reliability is actually estimated in quantitative terms several sources are available.[13]

Validity of Measurement

Reliability is certainly an important characteristic of any measurement procedure, but it is simply a means to an end, a step along the way to a goal. Unless a measure is reliable, it cannot be valid. This is so because unless a measure produces consistent, dependable, stable scores, we cannot begin to understand what implications high versus low scores have for later job performance and economic returns to the organization. Such understanding is the goal of the validation process. *Validity* is defined as the degree to which the inferences decision makers make about job performance from predictor measures (e.g., tests, interviews) are accurate.[14]

Although evidence of validity may be accumulated in many ways, *validity* always refers to the degree to which the evidence supports inferences that are drawn from scores or ratings on a selection procedure. It is the *inferences* regarding the specific use of a selection procedure that are validated, not the procedure itself.[15] Hence, a user must first specify exactly why he or she intends to use a particular selection procedure (i.e., what inferences he or she intends to draw from it). Then the user can make an informed judgment about the adequacy of the available evidence of validity in support of that particular selection procedure when used for a particular purpose.

Scientific standards for validation are described in greater detail in *Principles for the Validation and Use of Personnel Selection Procedures*[16] and *Standards for Educational and Psychological Testing.*[17] Legal standards for validation are contained in the *Uniform Guidelines on Employee Selection Procedures.*[18]

Quantitative evidence of validity is often expressed in terms of a correlation coefficient between scores on a predictor of job performance (e.g., a test or an interview) and a criterion that reflects actual job performance (e.g., supervisory ratings, dollar volume of sales). The greater the absolute value of $\mathbf{r}$, the better the prediction of criterion performance. In fact, the square of $\mathbf{r}$ indicates the percentage of variability in the criterion that is explained or accounted for, given a knowledge of the predictor. Assuming a predictor–criterion correlation of 0.40, $\mathbf{r}^2 = 0.16$ indicates that 16 percent of the variance in the criterion (job performance) can be explained, given a knowledge of the predictor. In employment contexts, predictor validities typically vary between about 0.20 and 0.50. In the following sections, we will consider some of the most commonly used methods for screening and selection decisions, together with validity evidence for each one.

SCREENING AND SELECTION METHODS

Employment Application Forms

Particularly when unemployment is high, organizations find themselves deluged with applications for employment for only a small number of available jobs. Many large companies, especially companies with solid reputations and strong company cultures, receive more than 1 million applications per year. Some receive many more. In 2019, Google received 3.3 million job applications and hired about 14,000 employees.[19] Of course, when applications are submitted electronically, it is possible to screen them for obvious mismatches by considering answers to questions such as "Are you willing to move?" and "When are you prepared to start work?" As we noted in Chapter 7, applicant tracking systems using advanced software can help screen candidates on items such as background and experience, thereby streamlining the selection process considerably.

An important requirement of all employment application forms is that they ask only for information that is valid and fair with respect to the nature of the job. Organizations should regularly review employment application forms to be sure that the information they require complies with equal employment opportunity guidelines and case law. For example, under the Americans with Disabilities Act, an employer may not ask a general question about disabilities on an application form or whether an applicant has ever filed a workers' compensation claim. However, at a pre-employment interview, after describing the essential functions of a job, an employer may ask if there is any physical or mental reason the candidate cannot perform the essential functions. Here are some guidelines that will suggest which questions to delete:

- Any question that might lead to an adverse impact on the employment of members of groups protected under civil rights law.
- Any question that cannot be demonstrated to be job-related or that does not concern a bona fide occupational qualification.
- Any question that could constitute an invasion of privacy.

There is little consistency among state laws, not to mention cities and counties, for the use of criminal records in hiring. Currently, 35 U.S. states and more than 150 cities and counties have passed "ban the box" laws that generally remove questions about criminal history from job applications and delay asking about it until after making a conditional offer of hire. The Society for Human Resource Management, as well as major retailers like Target and Walmart, are supporting efforts to increase the hiring of ex-offenders and to ensure that employers do not discriminate on the basis of criminal records.[20] Employers should consider the nature of the offense; the time that has passed since the applicant committed the offense or completed sentencing; and the nature of the job sought, including its essential functions.[21]

Recommendations, References, and Background Checks

Recommendations, along with reference and background checks, are used by 95 percent of employers to screen outside job applicants.[22] They can provide four kinds of information about a job applicant: (1) education and employment history, (2) character and interpersonal competence, (3) ability to perform the job, and (4) willingness of the past or current employer to rehire the applicant. Many organizations are not aware of how deep a check must go to identify serious problems. A casual check may reveal only that a candidate has wonderful references, no criminal record, and no liens against him or her. A more extensive probe, however, could uncover the fact that a candidate sued every company he ever worked for, or that he mismanaged assets but his former employer decided not to prosecute.[23]

ETHICAL DILEMMA
Are Work History Omissions Unethical?

Consider the following situation. A job applicant knowingly omits some previous work history on a company's application form, even though the form asks applicants to provide a complete list of previous jobs. However, the applicant is truthful  about the dates of previous jobs he does report. He leaves it to the interviewer to discover and ask about the gaps in his work history. The interviewer fails to ask about the gaps. Is the job applicant's behavior unethical?

Pre-employment background checks are an essential element of screening because they identify risks and validate claims made by prospective new hires. Here is what you need to know about the process.[24] The average background check costs $90 and typically takes 24–72 hours, but in-depth screening and multiple geographical locations could take longer. For example, if a former employer has gone out of business, or a candidate currently lives in New York but went to school in India and then worked in the U.K., it will take longer to complete the process. For reasons of privacy and possible discrimination, HR and hiring managers should not perform online or social media candidate screens. It's better to leave it to screening professionals, such as a firm accredited by the National Association of Professional Background Screeners.

With respect to a recommendation or reference check, it will be meaningful only if the person providing it (1) has had an adequate opportunity to observe the applicant in job-relevant situations, (2) is competent to evaluate the applicant's job performance, (3) can express such an evaluation in a way that is meaningful to the prospective employer, and (4) is completely candid.[25]

Unfortunately, evidence is beginning to show that there is little candor, and thus little value, in written recommendations and referrals, especially those that must, by law, be revealed to applicants if they petition to see them. Specifically, the Family Educational Rights and Privacy Act of 1974 gives students the legal right to see all letters of recommendation written about them. It also permits release of information about a student only to people approved by the student at the time of the request.

A meta-analysis of five studies found that the average inter-rater reliability for references is only 0.22. In fact, research indicates that there is more agreement between recommendations written by the same person for two different applicants than between two people writing recommendations for the same person![26] Other research suggests that if letters of recommendation are to be meaningful, they should contain the following information:[27]

1. *Degree of writer familiarity with the candidate*—that is, time known and time observed per week.
2. *Degree of writer familiarity with the job in question.* To help the writer make this judgment, the reader should supply the writer with a description of the job in question.
3. *Specific examples of performance*—that is, goals, task difficulty, work environment, and extent of cooperation from coworkers.
4. *Individuals or groups to whom the candidate is compared.*

When seeking information about a candidate from references or in a background check, or when contacting individuals identified through professional networking sites like LinkedIn or Jobster, consider the following guidelines:[28]

- Request job-related information only; put it in written form to prove that your hire or no-hire decision was based on relevant information.
- The Fair Credit Reporting Act requires third-party investigators to secure the applicant's written consent prior to doing a background check. If a decision not to hire results from negative information found through a background check, an employer is obligated to provide the applicant with the results and an opportunity to dispute them.

- Do not reach out to anyone that the candidate has asked not to be contacted. Likewise, unless the candidate expressly gives permission, do not contact any references from a candidate's current employer.[29]
- Evaluate the credibility of the source of the reference material. Not everything available online is factual. Under most circumstances, an evaluation by a past immediate supervisor will be more credible than an evaluation by an HR representative.
- Wherever possible, use public records to evaluate on-the-job behavior or personal conduct (e.g., records regarding criminal and civil litigation, driving, or bankruptcy).[30]

What kind of information will employers release and not release? Fully 98 percent will verify dates of employment for current or former employees. However, 68 percent will not discuss work performance, 87 percent will not discuss a disciplinary action, and 82 percent will not discuss character or personality.[31] What should you do if you are asked to provide reference information? Here are some useful guidelines:[32]

- Develop a written policy outlining procedures for checking references, and then follow it.
- Only one person, usually a trained HR professional, should be permitted to provide references. That person should be familiar with state laws where the employee resides and where the employer is located.
- Ask each applicant to provide at least three professional references.
- Obtain the applicant's written consent to contact former employers.
- Try to contact at least two of the references via telephone or e-mail.
- Document attempts to contact references, and note their responses.
- Provide only factual information and avoid giving opinions about the employee's suitability for a new job.

Sweetening of résumés and previous work history is common. How common? One study of 2.6 million résumés found that 44 percent contained exaggerations or outright fabrications about work experience; 23 percent listed bogus credentials; and 41 percent boasted fictional degrees.[33] The lesson: Always verify key aspects of previous history.

On the other hand, employers can be held liable for **negligent hiring** if they fail to check closely enough on a prospective employee who then commits a crime in the course of performing his or her job duties. The employer becomes liable if it knew, or should have known, about the applicant's unfitness to perform the job in question.[34] When courts receive negligent-hiring claims, they consider the following: (1) Would the risk have been discovered through a thorough background check? (2) Did the nature of the job cause greater risk? (3) Did the employer have a greater responsibility to conduct a thorough background investigation because of the nature of the job? (4) Was the action intentional?[35]

Currently, an employer has no legal duty or obligation to provide information to prospective employers. However, if an employer's policy is to disclose reference information, providing false or speculative information could be grounds for a lawsuit.[36] Reference checking is not an infringement on privacy. Rather, it is a sound evaluative tool that can provide objectivity for employers and fairness for job applicants. Figure 8-2 shows some facts about reference and background checks.

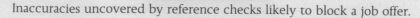

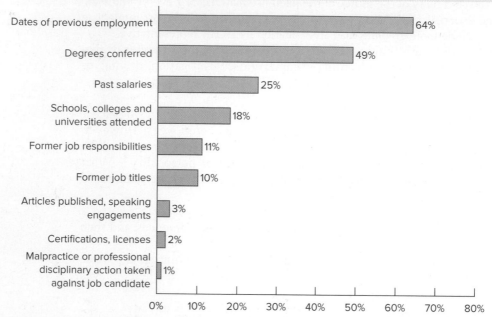

Inaccuracies uncovered by reference checks likely to block a job offer.

Meinert, D. "Seeing Behind the Mask." *HR Magazine*, 2011. Alexandria, VA: Society for Human Resource Management.

ASSESSMENT METHODS IN SELECTION

Evidence indicates that as the complexity of work increases, organizations use more selection methods and use selection methods that capture the applicant's capability to do the work.[37] For example, organizations frequently evaluate and select job candidates on the basis of the results of physical (e.g., drug testing) or psychological assessments (e.g., aptitude, work-sample, or personality tests). Tests are standardized measures of behavior.

A great deal of published research is available on almost all of the assessments we describe. What follows is a brief description of available methods and techniques, together with a description of their track records to date.

At the same time, four trends are unmistakable. (1) Assessment must be accessible—roughly half of job applicants now apply on mobile devices. (2) Assessment must be engaging and job-related—60 percent of mobile users won't complete it if it is too lengthy or complex. (3) Assessment must support brand identity and promises. Candidates demand to know your brand and what it means to them and to others with whom they share connections. (4) Feedback about the hiring process and related assessments is becoming a critical part of the hiring process itself.[38]

Drug Screening

Drug-screening tests, which began in the military and spread to the sports world, are now used by two-thirds of employers—with good reason. More than 70 percent of those abusing illicit drugs are employed. Drug users are almost four times as likely to be involved in a workplace accident as a sober worker and five times as likely to file a workers' compensation claim. Drug users miss more days of work, show up late, and change jobs more often. Absenteeism and involuntary turnover are the outcomes that drug testing forecasts most accurately.[39] The cost of a drug test, meanwhile, is usually less than $50.[40] The number of job applicants and workers who test positive has been about 4 percent since the mid-2000s, even as cocaine, methamphetamine, and marijuana have surged.[41]

Is such drug screening legal? Yes, according to the Supreme Court, in the case of railroad crews involved in accidents and (2) for U.S. Customs Service employees seeking drug-enforcement posts. Indeed, federal or state laws require that more than 10 million civilian workers, mostly in law enforcement or in industries regulated by the U.S. Department of Transportation, be tested.[42] What about marijuana use? While it remains illegal under federal law, as of 2020, 33 states have legalized medical use and 11 states and Washington, DC, allow recreational use as well.[43]

Although state laws vary, what is true in every state is that an employer has a legal right to ensure that employees perform their jobs competently and that no employee endangers the safety of other workers. So if illegal drug use may reduce job performance and endanger coworkers, the employer has adequate legal grounds for conducting drug tests. To avoid legal challenge, consider instituting the following commonsense procedures:[44]

1. Inform all employees and job applicants, in writing, of the company's policy regarding drug use.
2. Include the policy in all employment contracts.
3. Emphasize that drug screening will help ensure a safer workplace.
4. Forbid employees from reporting to work or working while under the influence of alcohol or drugs.
5. If drug testing will be used with employees as well as job applicants, tell employees in advance that it will be a routine part of their employment.
6. Employees who are more sensitive to job-safety issues are more likely to perceive drug screening as fair.[45]
7. If drug testing is done, it should be uniform—that is, it should apply to managers as well as non-managers.
8. Continue to comply with federal regulations.

Integrity Tests

Shrinkage—an industry term for losses due to employee theft, shoplifting, vendor fraud, and administrative errors—is estimated to make up about two percent of annual sales in the retail industry.[46] Employee theft alone is estimated to cause up to 30 percent of all business failures. It costs the nation's retailers $50 billion per year and the average family of four an extra $450 a year in higher prices.[47] With statistics like these, it should come as no surprise that employers representing retail stores, nuclear plants, law enforcement agencies, and child-care facilities regularly use **integrity tests**. There are two types.[48] Overt integrity tests (clear-purpose tests) are designed to assess directly a person's attitudes toward dishonest behaviors—for example, "Do you think most people would cheat if they thought they could get away with it?" The second type, personality-based measures (disguised-purpose tests), aim to predict a broad range of counterproductive behaviors at work (disciplinary problems, violence on the job, excessive absenteeism, and drug abuse, in addition to theft)—for example, "Do you like to take chances?"

IMPAIRMENT TESTING—DOES IT WORK?*

Impairment testing is used to determine which workers in safety-sensitive jobs put themselves and others at risk by directly measuring the workers' current fitness for duty. Impairment may be due to a variety of sources, such as fatigue or illness, not just from illegal drug use. Drug screening, by contrast, attempts to determine which workers have used specific substances known to cause impairment in the relatively recent past. Impairment testing may involve a software-based test of mental alertness, monitoring the ability of a worker's eyes to smoothly track an object moving horizontally, or monitoring his or her eyes' involuntary responses to light stimuli.

The tests can be administered via software downloaded onto mobile devices like smartphones or tablet computers. A study of almost every employer that has used impairment testing over the past 10 years revealed that 82 percent of the employers reported improvements in safety (reduced accidents) and no impact on productivity. Eighty-two percent of the employees in the study preferred impairment testing to urine testing, and 88 percent of employers expressed similar preferences.

Sources: Lauriski, D. (2018, Apr. 8). Advantages of impairment testing over drug testing to improve safety. *Predictive Safety.* Retrieved from *https://www.predictivesafety.com/blog/the-advantages-of-impairment-testing-over-drug-testing-to-improve-workplace-safety* on Apr. 7, 2020. Katz, J. (2010, Feb. 11). Impairment tests as a drug-screen alternative. *Industry Week.* Retrieved from *http://www.industryweek.com/public-policy/impairment-tests-drug-screen-alternative* on Apr. 22, 2014.

Do they work? Yes, as two meta-analyses (statistical cumulations of research results across studies) have demonstrated. The average validity of the tests, when used to predict supervisory ratings of performance and counterproductive work behaviors was 0.21 and 0.33, respectively. The results for overt integrity and personality-based tests were similar (0.23 and 0.30, respectively). However, the average validity of overt tests for predicting theft per se was much lower, 0.13. For personality-based tests, there were no validity estimates available for the prediction of theft alone. Thus, theft appears to be less predictable than broadly counterproductive behaviors, at least by overt integrity tests.[49] The validity of integrity tests for predicting drug and alcohol abuse per se is about 0.30,[50] and it is 0.25 for predicting absenteeism.[51] Finally, because there is no correlation between gender or race and integrity-test scores, such tests might well be used in combination with general mental-ability test scores to improve validity even further.[52]

Cognitive-Ability Tests

The major types of cognitive-ability tests used in business today include measures of general intelligence; verbal, nonverbal, and numerical skills; spatial relations ability (the ability to visualize the effects of manipulating or changing the position of objects); motor functions (speed, coordination); mechanical information, reasoning, and comprehension; clerical aptitudes (perceptual speed tests); and inductive reasoning (the ability to draw general conclusions on the basis of specific facts). When job analysis shows that the abilities or aptitudes measured by such tests are important for successful job performance, the tests are among the most valid predictors currently available (see Table 8–1).[53]

Table 8–1

AVERAGE VALIDITIES OF ALTERNATIVE PREDICTORS OF JOB PERFORMANCE

Measure	Validity*
General mental-ability tests	0.51
Work-sample tests	0.54
Integrity tests	0.41
Conscientiousness tests	0.31
Employment interviews (structured)	0.51
Employment interviews (unstructured)	0.38
Job-knowledge tests	0.48
Job-tryout procedure	0.44
Peer ratings	0.49
Ratings of training and experience	0.45
Reference checks	0.26
Job experience (years)	0.18
Biographical data	0.35
Assessment centers	0.37
Points assigned to training and experience	0.11
Years of education	0.10
Interests	0.10
Graphology	0.02
Age	−0.01

*Validity is based on cumulative findings that have been summarized using meta-analysis. Validity is expressed as a correlation coefficient that varies from −1 to +1.

Source: Adapted from Schmidt, F. L., and J. E. Hunter. "The Validity and Utility of Selection Methods in Personnel Psychology: Practical and Theoretical Implications of 85 Years of Research Findings." *Psychological Bulletin,* 1998, 24.

When some Walmart store workers want to apply for a higher-paying management role, the company fits them with a $250 virtual reality (VR) headset to see if they are the right candidate for the job. It is using a VR skills assessment as part of the selection process to find new middle managers, watching how workers respond in virtual reality to an angry shopper, a messy aisle, or an underperforming worker.

VR training is becoming more common in a variety of industries to educate a large number of workers quickly or assess the technical ability of high-skilled workers like electricians or pilots. But Walmart's use of the technology to gauge a worker's strengths, weaknesses, and potential is significant because it pushes VR evaluation out to a massive hourly workforce.[54] For administrative convenience and for reasons of efficiency, many tests today are administered via computer, either at a dedicated physical location (such as a company office) or using web-based assessments, available anytime.[55] In high-stakes testing situations—for example, licensure, certification, and university admissions—there is general agreement that unproctored Internet testing is not acceptable and that some cheating will occur. Steps can be taken to minimize test exposure and the motivation to cheat, however, such as not allowing retesting, issuing warnings about the consequences of cheating, or following unproctored testing with a proctored test.[56]

With respect to the selection of managers, there are many ways executives get the job done.[57] There is no agreed-upon list of executive competencies or attributes, and many that are listed are too broad or vague to guide assessment efforts (e.g., global strategic perspective, thinking outside the box, performance orientation). Successful executives have a pattern of attributes that an organization needs at the time of selection. These attributes form a unique profile, including some forms of intelligence (e.g., crystallized intelligence–knowledge of facts at lower levels; fluid intelligence–creativity–at executive levels); personality characteristics (extroversion, conscientiousness); values; and experience, knowledge, and effective interpersonal skills. The most common method of selecting executives remains the performance/potential review process by higher-level executives and the board of directors.[58]

Validity Generalization

A traditional belief of testing experts is that validity is situation specific. That is, a test with a demonstrated validity in one setting (e.g., selecting bus drivers in St. Louis) might not be valid in another, similar setting (e.g., selecting bus drivers in Atlanta), possibly as a result of differences in specific job tasks, duties, and behaviors. Thus, it would seem that the same test used to predict bus driver success in St. Louis and in Atlanta would have to be validated separately in each city.

Decades of research have cast serious doubt on this assumption.[59] In fact, it has been shown that the major reason for the variation in validity coefficients across settings is the size of the samples–they are too small. When the effect of sampling error is removed, the validities observed for similar test/job combinations across settings do not differ significantly. Hence, the results of a validity study conducted in one situation can be generalized, as long as it can be shown that jobs in the two situations are similar. Despite that general conclusion, methodological and statistical concerns remain.[60] On balance, however, the thousands of studies that have been done on the prediction of job performance and **validity generalization** allow us to establish reliable values for the average validity of most predictors (see Table 8-1).

Personality Measures

Personality is the set of characteristics of a person that account for the consistent way he or she responds to situations. Five personality characteristics particularly relevant to performance at work are known as the "Big Five": neuroticism, extroversion, openness to experience, agreeableness, and conscientiousness.[61] **Neuroticism**, the degree to which an individual is insecure, anxious, depressed, and emotional, is the opposite of emotional stability–calm, self-confident, and cool. **Extroversion** concerns the degree to which an individual is gregarious, assertive, and sociable versus reserved, timid, and quiet. **Openness to experience** concerns the degree to which an individual is creative, curious, and cultured versus practical with narrow interests. **Agreeableness** concerns the degree to which an individual is cooperative, warm, and agreeable versus cold, disagreeable, and antagonistic. **Conscientiousness** concerns the degree to which an individual is hard-working, organized, dependable, and persevering versus lazy, disorganized, and unreliable. Research conducted over the past several decades shows that these are valid predictors of performance, but their validities differ depending on the nature of the job and the type of criteria. Conscientiousness has been shown to be the most generalizable predictor across jobs, with an average validity of 0.28. Personality measures predict many important criteria in addition to job performance, such as counterproductive behaviors, managerial effectiveness, entrepreneurial performance, customer service, and life satisfaction. Validities tend to be highest when theory and job analysis information are used explicitly to select personality measures.[62]

Among employers, the most prevalent reasons for using personality tests are their contribution to improving employee fit with the job and organization and to reducing turnover while increasing productivity.[63] Personality measures add significant explanatory and predictive power beyond other predictors, such as cognitive ability, educational credentials, and work experience.[64] They are used primarily in the hiring or promotion of executives and middle managers (32 percent and 28 percent of organizations, respectively), and, to a lesser extent (17 percent) for entry-level, hourly-paid jobs.[65]

At this point, you are probably asking yourself about the relationship of the Big Five to integrity tests. Integrity tests have been found to measure mostly conscientiousness but also some components of agreeableness and emotional stability.[66] That is why their validities tend to be higher than those of individual Big Five characteristics alone.

The Issue of Faking

Can't applicants distort their responses in ways they believe will make a positive impression on the employer? The answer is yes.[67] Although *moderate* distortion may reduce predictive-related validities slightly, compared with validities obtained with job incumbents,[68] response distortion can have a dramatic effect on who is hired, even though it has no detectable effect on predictive validity.[69] On top of that, coaching can improve scores.[70] To control the effects of faking, warn job applicants in advance that distortion can and will be detected, that verification procedures exist, and that there will be a consequence for such distortion. Possible consequences might vary from elimination from the selection process to verification in a background check or oral interview. A review of eight studies that investigated the effects of such warnings found that, in all eight, warnings reduced the amount of intentional distortion in self-report instruments, relative to situations where no such warnings were given.[71]

Measures of Emotional Intelligence

Emotional intelligence (EI) is the ability to perceive, appraise, and express emotion.[72] It is a well-established component of successful leadership. To appreciate the nature of EI, consider one instrument designed to measure it, the Emotional Competence Inventory–ECI 360. It is a 72-item, multirater assessment that includes input from self, manager, direct reports, peers, customers/clients, and others.[73] Based on Goleman's Emotional Competence Framework, the ECI 360 is composed of four domains, each with associated competencies: (1) self-awareness (emotional self-awareness, accurate self-assessment, and self-confidence—i.e., *personal competence*), (2) self-management (emotional self-control, transparency, adaptability, achievement, initiative, and optimism—i.e., *social competence*), (3) social awareness (empathy, organizational awareness, and service), and (4) relationship management (inspirational leadership, influence, developing others, change catalyst, conflict management, teamwork, and collaboration).

In recent years, EI has received considerable attention in practitioner as well as academic literature. Although some claims of its validity and ability to predict job performance over and above other, more traditional measures (cognitive ability, personality characteristics) have been viewed skeptically in the academic community,[74] a review of three meta-analyses found average validities of 0.16, 0.21, and 0.17 with measures of performance.[75] Although EI does seem to predict organizational citizenship behaviors,[76] researchers have defined and measured it in several different ways. As a result, the jury is still out regarding the incremental value of using EI as a basis for hiring or promotional decisions.

Personal-History Data

Based on the assumption that one of the best predictors of what a person will do in the future is what he or she has done in the past, biographical information has been used widely and successfully as one basis for staffing decisions. Table 8-1 shows its average validity to be a very respectable 0.35. As with any other method, careful, competent research is necessary if biodata are to prove genuinely useful as predictors of job success.[77] For example, items that are more objective and verifiable are less likely to be faked,[78] although faking can be reduced by asking applicants to describe incidents to illustrate and support their answers.[79] The payoff is that biodata can add significant explanatory power over and above Big Five personality dimensions and general mental ability.[80]

At executive levels, general biographical data may be replaced by critical experiences (some preset list of experiences seen as necessary for success). Many organizations are focusing on key work experiences that have developed management talent during the previous 10 years and can guide planning for the next 10–15 years.[81]

Employment Interviews

By any measure, interviews are the most popular hiring tool across countries, jobs, and organizational levels. Yet employment interviewing is a difficult mental and social task. Managing a smooth social exchange while instantaneously processing information about a job candidate makes interviewing uniquely difficult among all managerial tasks.[82] Well-designed interviews can be helpful because they allow examiners to gather information on characteristics not typically assessed via other means, such as empathy and personal initiative.[83] For example, a review of 388 characteristics that were rated in 47 actual interview studies revealed that personality traits (e.g., *responsibility, dependability,* and *persistence,* which are all related to conscientiousness) and applied social skills (e.g., *interpersonal relations, social skills, team focus,* and *ability to work with people*) are rated more often in employment interviews than any other type of construct.[84] In addition, interviews can contribute to the prediction of job performance over and above cognitive abilities and conscientiousness[85] as well as experience.[86] Reviews of the state of the art of interviewing research and practice lead to the following recommendations:[87]

1. Base interview questions on a job analysis.
2. Ask the same general questions of each candidate. That is, use a structured interview.
3. Use detailed rating scales, with behavioral descriptions to illustrate scale points.
4. Take detailed notes that focus on behavioral information about candidates.[88]
5. Use multiple interviewers.
6. Provide extensive training on interviewing.
7. Do not discuss candidates or answers between interviews.
8. Use statistical weights for each dimension, as well as an overall judgment of suitability, to combine information.[89]

Personal interviews are a common feature of the hiring process in almost all organizations.
michaeljung/Shutterstock

VIDEO INTERVIEWS

Unable to interview a job candidate in person? Video interviewing is the next best thing, according to a recent poll of 700 executives. Nearly 75 percent of their companies are using real-time video platforms, like Skype or Zoom, to interview leading candidates, and 50 percent use video interviews to reduce the pool of candidates. Firms such as Goldman Sachs and Novartis Pharmaceuticals use video interviews to open up national and international talent pools that were inaccessible even several years ago. Conversely, job seekers increasingly incorporate video into their online portfolios and LinkedIn profiles as a way to stand out from their peers.

Video interviews could cause legal problems for employers who reject candidates from protected groups, but they also expedite the hiring process, ease the time impact on hiring managers,

reduce costs, and improve the candidate experience. At Novartis, there was some initial hesitation from hiring managers, but it tended to disappear after they had the opportunity to try it. Managers conducted 2,700 video interviews in 1 year, saving $475,000 and cutting travel by 220 trips. As for candidates, they felt the use of video interviews demonstrated that Novartis was a progressive company in the use of technology.

Sources: Shellenbarger, 2019, op. cit. Gellman, L. (2016, June 24). Goldman rebuffs the Ivy League. *The Wall Street Journal*, pp. C1, C2. Maurer, R. (2015, Aug. 21). Use of video for recruiting continues to grow. Retrieved from *www.shrm.org/resourcesandtools/hr-topics/talent-acquisition/pages/use-video-recruiting-grow.aspx* on Aug. 24, 2015. See also Ho, D.(2013, Oct. 23). Should companies require job applicants to submit videos to apply? Retrieved from *http://www.askamanager.org/2013/10/should-companies-require-job-applicants-to-submit-videos-to-apply.html* on Apr. 21, 2014.

The validity of the pre-employment interview will be reduced to the extent that interviewers' decisions are overly influenced by such factors as first impressions, personal feelings about the kinds of characteristics that lead to success on the job, and contrast effects, among other nonobjective factors. **Contrast effects** are a tendency among interviewers to evaluate a current candidate's interview performance relative to those that immediately preceded it. If a first candidate received a very positive evaluation and a second candidate is just average, interviewers tend to evaluate the second candidate more negatively than is deserved. The second candidate's performance is contrasted with that of the first.

Employers are likely to achieve nonbiased hiring decisions if they concentrate on shaping interviewer behavior.[90] One way to do that is to establish a specific system for conducting the employment interview. Building on the suggestions made earlier, here are some things to consider in setting up such a system:[91]

- To know what to look for in applicants, focus only on the competencies necessary for the job. Be sure to distinguish between entry-level and full-performance competencies.[92]
- Screen résumés and application forms by focusing on (1) keywords that match job requirements, (2) quantifiers and qualifiers that show whether applicants have these requirements, and (3) skills that might transfer from previous jobs to the new job.
- Use open-ended questions (those that cannot be answered with a simple yes or no response). For example, consider asking "What would you do if . . . ?" questions. These comprise a situational interview, which is based on the assumption that a person's expressed behavioral intentions are related to subsequent behavior.
- In a situational interview, candidates are asked to describe how they think they would respond in certain job-related situations. Alternatively, if they have prior experience, they are asked to provide detailed accounts of actual situations. For example, "You're a project manager? Tell me about a time you had a delayed project." Answers provide insight into the candidate's level of critical thinking, adaptability, awareness of his or her impact, and creativity.[93] Answers also tend to be remarkably consistent with actual (subsequent) job behavior.[94] Validities for both types of interviews vary from about 0.22 to 0.28.[95]
- Conduct the interview in a relaxed physical setting. Begin by putting the applicant at ease with simple questions and general information about the organization and the position being filled. Note all nonverbal cues, such as lack of eye contact and facial expressions, as possible indicators of the candidate's interest in and ability to do the job.[96]
- Don't ask about previous salary history. As of 2020, 17 states and 20 cities ban the question. The assumption is that if women have been paid less in prior jobs, asking about their pay history as a means of determining future pay is not fair. Instead, price the job, not the person, by establishing a range of pay and sharing that with the candidate. Then the interviewer can focus on where the candidate might fit into that range based on his or her experience, skills, and accomplishments.[97]

A systematic interview developed along these lines will minimize the uncertainty so inherent in decision making that is based predominantly on "gut feeling." It also will contribute additional explanatory power over and above cognitive ability and measures of conscientiousness,[98] and it will reduce differences in evaluation scores

Table 8–2

SOME EXAMPLES OF PROPER AND IMPROPER QUESTIONS IN EMPLOYMENT INTERVIEWS

Issue	Proper	Improper (and Why)
Criminal history	Have you ever been convicted of a violation of a law?	Have you ever been arrested? (An arrest is an accusation, not proof of guilt.)
Marital status	None	Are you married? Do you prefer Ms., Miss, or Mrs.? What does your spouse do for a living? (None of these questions is job-related.)
National origin	None	Where were you born? Where were your parents born? (Place of birth is not relevant; a person's legal right to work in the United States is.)
Disability	None	Do you have any disabilities or handicaps? Do you have any health problems? (Neither question is related to the requirements of a specific job.)
Sexual orientation	None	With whom do you live? Do you ever intend to marry? (Neither question is job-related.)
Citizenship status	Do you have a legal right to work in the United States?	Are you a U.S. citizen? Are you a foreign citizen?
Situational questions (assumption: job analysis has shown such questions to be job-related)	How do you plan to keep up with current developments in your field? How do you measure your customers' satisfaction with your product or services? If you were a product, how would you position yourself?	

among members of protected groups. Table 8–2 shows some examples of proper and improper interview questions, along with several examples of situational-type questions.

Work-Sample Tests

Work-sample tests, or situational tests, are standardized measures of behavior whose primary objective is to assess the ability *to do* rather than the ability *to know*. They may be motor-skills tests, involving physical manipulation of things (e.g., trade tests for carpenters, plumbers, electricians), or verbal-skills tests, involving problem situations that are primarily language or people oriented (e.g., situational tests for supervisory jobs).[99] Because work samples are miniature replicas of actual job requirements, they are difficult to fake, and they are unlikely to lead to charges of discrimination or invasion of privacy. They produce small minority/nonminority group differences in performance, a lack of bias by race or gender, and only modest losses in predictive validity, compared with traditional tests.[100] However, because the content of the test reflects the essential content of the job, the tests do have content-oriented evidence of validity.[101] Their use in one study of 263 applicants for city-government jobs led to a reduction of turnover from 40 percent to less than 3 percent in the 9 to 26 months following their introduction.[102] Nevertheless, because of time and equipment constraints, work-sample tests are probably not cost effective when large numbers of people must be evaluated. Because they measure "can-do" (ability, skill) but not "will-do" (motivation, person–organization fit), they should not be used as the sole method to hire people.[103]

Two types of situational tests are used to evaluate and select managers: group exercises, in which participants are placed in a situation where the successful completion of a task requires interaction among the participants, and individual exercises, in which participants complete a task independently. The context in which work-sample tests are administered is important, though. When used as stand-alone tests, work samples are designed to simulate actual job tasks. When used in the context of managerial selection, however, there is a de-emphasis on current knowledge and skill in a specific domain and a strong focus on the assessment of future potential.[104] The following sections consider three of the most popular situational tests: the leaderless group discussion, the in-basket test, and the situational-judgment test.

Leaderless Group Discussion

The **leaderless group discussion (LGD)** is simple and has been used for decades. A group of participants is given a job-related topic (e.g., which budget proposal to fund or which candidate to promote) and is asked simply to carry on a discussion about it for a period of time. No one is appointed leader, nor is anyone told where to sit. Instead of using a rectangular table (with a "head" at each end), a circular table is often used, so that each position carries equal weight. Observers rate the performance of each participant.

In the course of the discussion, participants gravitate to roles in which they are comfortable. Usually, someone structures the meeting, someone keeps notes, some brainstorm well, some show skill at developing others' ideas, and some participate little. Assessors can see a whole range of competencies related to communication, influence, collaboration, resolution of disagreements, problem solving, and relationship management.[105] Evidence indicates that it's not how much you communicate that matters. It's how well you communicate. The best leaders find common ground and ways to connect with followers.[106] Given the current emphasis on teamwork, as well as the ability to collaborate and compromise, the LGD is an excellent tool for assessing interpersonal skills.[107]

LGD ratings have forecast managerial performance accurately in virtually all the functional areas of business.[108] Previous LGD experience appears to have little effect on present LGD performance, although prior training clearly does.[109] Individuals in one study who received a 15-minute briefing on the history, development, rating instruments, and research relative to the LGD were rated significantly higher than untrained individuals. To control for this, all those with prior training in LGD should be put into the same groups.

In-Basket Test

The **in-basket test** is a situational test designed to simulate important aspects of a position. The test assesses an individual's ability to work independently. In general, it takes the following form: The test consists of memos, reports, notes, and other communications that the incumbent of a role being assessed (e.g., a bank manager) might receive in his or her in-basket on a given day. The subject who takes the test is given appropriate background information concerning the business, military unit, school, or whatever institution is involved. She is told that she is the new incumbent of the role and that she is to deal with the material in the in-basket. The background information is sufficiently detailed that the subject can reasonably be expected to take action on many of the problems presented by the in-basket documents. The subject is instructed that she is not to play-act; she is not to pretend to be someone else. She is to bring to the new job her own background of knowledge and experience, and her own personality, and she is to deal with the problems as though she were really the incumbent. She is not to say what she would do; she is actually to write letters and memoranda, prepare agenda for meetings, and make notes and reminders for herself, as though she were actually on the job. Often, she is given a time limit—say, 1 hour—to work through the items in her in-basket.[110]

Although the situation is relatively unstructured, each candidate faces the same complex set of materials. In-basket activities can therefore be considered a multidimensional work-sample test. Today, managers spend much less time handling memos in paper form and much more time in e-mail, digital media, and cellphone communication. Thus, participants' workspace for the in-basket test may include a computer and smartphone, through which they can communicate with others. The availability of such technology enhances the fidelity of the simulation, but it also greatly increases the workload on the assessors, who must keep track of such rapid communication via multimedia for several participants.[111]

The in-basket test generates documented output—for example, written recommendations, market analysis, meeting agendas, or reply memos. Assessors then score the test by describing (if the purpose is development) or evaluating (if the purpose is selection for promotion) what the candidate did in terms of such dimensions as self-confidence; abilities to organize, plan, and set priorities; written communications; and decision making, risk taking, and coordination with key resources. The dimensions to be evaluated are identified through job analysis prior to designing or selecting the exercise. The major advantages of the in-basket test, therefore, are its flexibility (it can be designed to fit many different types of situations) and the fact that it permits direct observation of individual behavior within the context of a job-relevant, standardized problem situation.

Decades of research on the in-basket test indicate that it validly forecasts subsequent job behavior and promotion.[112] It correlates 0.30 with cognitive ability, sharing only 9 percent of the variance in common.[113] Moreover, because performance on the LGD is not strongly related to performance on the in-basket test, in combination they are potentially powerful predictors of managerial success.

The Situational-Judgment Test

Situational-judgment tests (SJTs) consist of a series of job-related situations presented in written, verbal, or visual form. In many SJTs, job applicants are asked to choose best and worst options among several choices available. Consider the following item from an SJT used for selecting retail associates:[114]

> A customer asks for a specific brand of merchandise the store doesn't carry. How would you respond to the customer?
>
> 1. Tell the customer which stores carry that brand, but point out that your brand is similar.
> 2. Ask the customer more questions, so that you can suggest something else.
> 3. Tell the customer that the store carries the highest-quality merchandise available.
> 4. Ask another associate to help.
> 5. Tell the customer which stores carry that brand.
>
> *Questions for job applicants:*
>
> - Which of the options above do you believe is the *best* under the circumstances?
> - Which of the options above do you believe is the *worst* under the circumstances?

Can you see the similarity to situational interviews? In fact, situational interviews can be considered a special case of SJTs in which interviewers present the scenarios verbally and job applicants respond verbally.

SJTs are inexpensive to develop, administer, and score compared with other types of work samples.[115] With respect to SJT validity, a meta-analysis, based on 134 validity coefficients and 28,494 individuals, found the following average levels of validity for various types of skills: teamwork (0.38), leadership (0.28), interpersonal skills (0.25), and job knowledge and skills (0.19). In each of these skill domains, video-based SJTs had stronger relationships with job performance than paper-and-pencil SJTs.[116]

A major distinction in SJT response instructions is behavioral tendency ("what would you do?") versus knowledge ("what should you do?" or "rate the best/worst option"). "What would you do?" elicits responses that more closely resemble future behavior on a job, rather than mere knowledge of the best response. More importantly, SJTs make the prediction of job performance more accurate above and beyond cognitive ability, job experience, and conscientiousness while showing less adverse impact based on ethnicity, as compared with general cognitive-ability tests.[117]

Assessment Centers

The assessment-center approach was first used by German military psychologists during World War II to select officers. They felt that paper-and-pencil tests took too narrow a view of human nature; therefore, they chose to observe each candidate's behavior in a complex situation in order to develop a broader appraisal of his reactions. Borrowing from this work and that of the War Office Selection Board of the British army during the early 1940s, the U.S. Office of Strategic Services used this method to select spies during World War II. Each candidate had to develop a cover story that would hide her or his identity during the assessment. Testing for the ability to maintain cover was crucial, and ingenious situational tests were designed to seduce candidates into breaking cover.[118]

After World War II, many military psychologists and officers joined private companies, where they started small-scale assessment centers. In 1956, AT&T was the first to use the method as the basis for a 25-year study of managerial progress and career development.[119]

Today, about 22 percent of organizations assess senior- and midlevel managers on three broad dimensions: the ability (1) to innovate, (2) to manage change and complexity, and (3) to demonstrate global competency.[120] Assessment centers do more than just test people. The **assessment-center method** is a process that evaluates a candidate's potential for management based on three sources: (1) multiple assessment techniques, such as situational tests, tests of cognitive abilities, and interest inventories; (2) standardized methods of making inferences from such techniques because assessors are trained to distinguish between effective and ineffective behaviors by the candidates; and (3) pooled judgments from multiple assessors to rate each candidate's behavior.

Assessment centers have received much attention in the research literature. Developing and running a high-fidelity assessment center are complex and expensive, even if run many times. This has limited their use to large organizations and to positions where the risk is high of selecting the wrong person for a mission-critical job. Smaller organizations may use a less costly, hybrid approach that combines an online, vendor-provided simulation, followed by an in-person presentation on that simulation to an assessor or a hiring manager. That's the approach Advance Auto Parts took to find leaders for its 3,900 stores and 55,000 employees.[121] By relating each candidate's overall performance on the assessment-center exercises to such indicators as the management level subsequently achieved 2 (or more) years later or current salary, researchers have shown that the predictions for each candidate are very accurate.[122]

The assessment-center method offers great flexibility. It is is also being used to train and upgrade management skills, to encourage creativity among research and engineering professionals, to resolve interpersonal and interdepartmental conflicts, to assist individuals in career planning, to train managers in performance management, and to provide information for workforce planning and organization design.

Assessor training is another feature of the assessment-center method. Assessors are either line managers two or more levels above the candidates or professional psychologists. They are trained (usually for several days) in interviewing techniques, behavior observation, and development of a common frame of reference with which to assess candidates.[123] Assessors usually go through the exercises as participants before rating others.

This experience, plus the development of a consensus by assessors on effective versus ineffective responses by candidates to the situations presented, enables the assessors to standardize their interpretations of each candidate's behavior. Standardization ensures that each candidate will be assessed fairly—that is, in terms of the same "yardstick."[124]

Each candidate is usually evaluated by a different assessor on each exercise. Although assessors make their judgments independently, the judgments are combined into an overall rating on each dimension of interest. A summary report is then prepared and shared with each candidate.

These features of the assessment-center method—flexibility of form and content, the use of multiple assessment techniques, standardized methods of interpreting behavior, and pooled assessor judgments—account for the successful track record of this approach over the past six decades. It has consistently demonstrated high validity, with correlations between assessment-center performance and later job performance as a manager sometimes reaching the 0.50s and 0.60s.[125]

Assessment-center ratings also predict long-term career success (i.e., corrected correlation of 0.39 between such ratings and average salary growth 7 years later).[126] Both minorities and nonminorities and men and women acknowledge that the method provides them a fair opportunity to demonstrate what they are capable of doing in a management job.[127]

In terms of its bottom-line impact, two studies have shown that the use of assessment centers is cost-effective. Both demonstrated that the assessment-center method should not be measured against the cost of implementing it, but rather against the cost (in lost sales and declining productivity) of promoting the wrong person into a management job.[128] In a first-level management job, the gain in improved job performance as a result of promoting people via the assessment-center method is about $7,400 per year (in 2019 dollars). However, if the average tenure of first-level managers is, say, 5 years, the gain per person is about $37,000 (in 2019 dollars).

Despite its advantages, the method is not without potential problems, including the following:[129]

- Adoption of the assessment-center method without carefully analyzing the need for it and without adequate preparations to use it wisely.
- Blind acceptance of assessment data without considering other information on candidates, such as past and current performance.
- The tendency to rate only general exercise effectiveness, rather than performance relative to each behavioral dimension (e.g., by using a behavioral checklist).
- Lack of control over assessment information—for example, "leaking" assessment ratings to operating managers.
- Failure to evaluate the dollar benefits of the program, relative to costs.
- Inadequate feedback to participants.
- Not every competency can be simulated, especially those requiring long-term, cumulative actions, such as networking.[130]

Each of these problems can be overcome. Doing so will allow even more accurate prediction of each candidate's likely performance as a manager.

HR BUZZ

HOW GOOGLE SEARCHES . . . FOR TALENT*

Google's mission is to organize the world's information. A complementary objective is to be just as innovative on the people side of the business as on the product side. In fact, it has to be innovative. After all, Google, with more than $160 billion in 2019 revenues and about 114,000 employees, receives more than 8,200 job applications per day and is the ideal employer of almost one in five undergraduate students! The company sets very exacting hiring standards, which may include an elaborate online

*Sources: Alphabet revenue, 2006–2019. Retrieved from https://www.macrotrends.net/stocks/charts/GOOG/alphabet/revenue on Apr. 8, 2020. Scorza, J. (2015, Nov.). Inside Google. HR, pp. 26, 27. Friedman, T. L. (2014, Feb. 23). How to get a job at Google. The New York Times. Retrieved from http://www.nytimes.com/2014/02/23/opinion/sunday/friedman-how-to-get-a-job-at-google.html?r=0 on Mar. 9, 2014. Friedman, T. L. (2014, Apr. 19). How to get a job at Google, Part 2. The New York Times. Retrieved from http://www.nytimes.com/2014/04/20/opinion/sunday/friedman-how-to-get-a-job-at-google-part-2.html on Apr. 21, 2014.

survey that explores a job seeker's attitudes, behavior, personality, and biographical details going back to high school, multiple interviews, even homework assignments (a personal statement plus a marketing plan for a future Google product). Executives take the hiring process very seriously–and devote an average of 5–8 hours a week on it. The overall process has been described as "data-driven hiring."

Google uses "crowdsourcing"–based on the premise that any given group of people is always smarter than any given expert–in its hiring decisions. Here is how the process works. Google uses its applicant tracking system (ATS) to ask its current employees to weigh in on applicants who have submitted their résumés online. Information from the applications is parsed and stored in the ATS. The system then matches that information to data about existing Google employees–for example, based on the fact that they went to the same school.

Following the match, an e-mail automatically asks employees for internal references, which allows recruiters to tap employees who best understand the demands of the jobs and the nature of the culture in assessing the fit of potential hires. It allows current employees to build the community–even if they are not part of the formal interview process. This approach fits the Google culture perfectly because employees are being asked for their opinions.

As a general matter, beyond cognitive ability–the ability to learn things and solve problems–Google looks for five broad hiring attributes. The first is leadership–in particular, emergent leadership. That is, when faced with a problem and you are a member of a team, do you step in and lead at the appropriate time? Just as critically, do you step back and stop leading at the appropriate time? A second characteristic is intellectual humility, a willingness to learn from others and from one's experiences.

A third characteristic is collaboration. Google believes that talent comes in many forms and is built in many nontraditional ways. Today, 14 percent of the members of some teams never went to college. The fourth and fifth characteristics are adaptability and loving to learn and re-learn. Given the pace of change and the rapid obsolescence of knowledge, those characteristics will serve you well no matter where you go to work. Why are Google's hiring standards so demanding? Because the company believes that hiring the best talent will make it geometrically better than its competitors.

CHOOSING THE RIGHT PREDICTOR

In this chapter, we have examined a number of possible predictors of future performance that might be used in the staffing process. Determining the right ones to use depends on considerations such as the following:

- *The nature of the job.*
- An estimate of the *validity of the predictor* in terms of the strength of the relationship between applicants' scores on the predictor and their corresponding scores on some measure of performance.
- *The selection ratio,* or percentage of applicants selected.
- *The cost of the predictor.*

To the extent that job performance is multidimensional (as indicated in job-analysis results), use multiple predictors, each focused on critical competencies. Other things being equal, use predictors with the highest estimated validities; they will tend to minimize the number of erroneous acceptances and rejections, and they will tend to maximize workforce productivity. Look back at Table 8–1 for a summary of the accumulated validity evidence for a number of potential predictors.

It is important to take into account the **selection ratio** (the percentage of applicants hired) in evaluating the overall usefulness of any predictor. Low selection ratios mean that more applicants must be evaluated but only the "cream" of the applicant crop will be selected. Predictors with lower validity may be used when the selection ratio is low because it is necessary only to distinguish the very best qualified from everyone else.

Finally, the cost of selection is a consideration, but not a major one. Of course, if two predictors are roughly equal in estimated validity, then use the less costly procedure. However, the trade-off between cost and validity should almost always be resolved in favor of validity. Choose the more valid procedure because the major concern is not the cost of the procedure, but rather the cost of a mistake if the wrong candidate is selected or promoted. In management jobs, such mistakes are likely to be particularly costly.[131]

Human Resource Management in Action: Conclusion

ORGANIZATIONAL CULTURE—KEY TO STAFFING "FIT"

The best companies often create distinctive cultures. Thus, from its first day in 1997, Netflix founder Reed Hastings focused on the start-up's culture, making it a place he enjoyed coming to every day, with people who pushed him intellectually, and a company of which he could be proud.

At Netflix, five key principles guide talent management: (1) hire, reward, and tolerate only fully formed adults; (2) tell the truth about performance; (3) managers own the job of creating great teams; (4) leaders own the job of creating the company culture; and (5) good talent managers think like businesspeople and innovators.

At Southwest Airlines the fundamental business proposition is that its people come first. As cofounder Herb Kelleher commented,

> It used to be a business conundrum: Who comes first? The employees, customers, or shareholders? That's never been an issue to me. The employees come first. If they're happy, satisfied, dedicated, and energetic, they'll take real good care of the customers. When the customers are happy, they come back. And that makes the shareholders happy.[132]

Southwest lets its best customers get involved in the pre-employment interviews for flight attendants. The entire process focuses on a positive attitude and teamwork. Peers play active roles in the hiring of peers; for example, pilots hire other pilots, and baggage handlers other baggage handlers. In one case, Southwest pilots turned down a top pilot who worked for another major airline and did stunt work for movie studios. Even though he was a great pilot, he made the mistake of being rude to a Southwest receptionist. Teamwork also is critical. If applicants say "I" too much in the interview, they don't get hired. Clearly, culture is a major reason outsiders want to join the company and seasoned veterans want to remain.

Netflix and Southwest Airlines send powerful signals to job applicants and employees that culture counts in a big way. Sleuthing out the culture at many other companies is more difficult, yet no less important. Here are five strategies for doing that. (1) Identify who and what count. Employees look for signals in who gets rewarded, promoted, and let go. Applicants should ask if rules are consistent across departments or if stars operate under looser standards. (2) Grill recruiters and interviewers about suitability. Ask recruiters why the five previous people they placed were successful. Ask interviewers why other individuals left the role you are applying for. (3) Make sure that actions match promises. We discussed realistic job previews in Chapter 7. If a recruiter or an interviewer is not forthcoming about the good, the bad, and the ugly of a job, press until you get answers. (4) Seek a temporary consulting assignment. Just as internships are great ways for interns and employers to get to know each other, so also are temporary "gigs." (5) Walk the halls. Look for unspoken cues. Do employees smile at you or avoid eye contact? Trust your instincts. How would you feel about working with these people?

There is a simple lesson to learn from all of this. The ability to articulate a company's culture, to live it every day, and to make it real for applicants and for current employees is a key feature of the decisions of successful applicants to join, and for seasoned veterans to stay and to compete for promotions.

SUMMARY

In staffing an organization or an organizational unit, it is important to consider its developmental stage—start-up, high growth, mature, or aging—in order to align staffing decisions with business strategy. It also is important to communicate an organization's culture, because research shows that applicants will consider this information to choose among jobs if it is available to them. To use selection techniques meaningfully, however, it is necessary to specify the kinds of competencies that are necessary for success.

Organizations commonly screen applicants through recommendations and reference checks, information on application forms, and employment interviews. In addition, some firms use written ability or integrity tests, work-sample tests, drug tests, or measures of emotional intelligence. In each case, it is important to pay careful attention to the reliability and validity of the information obtained. Reliability is the consistency or stability of scores over time, across different samples of items, or across different raters or judges. Validity is the degree to which the inferences decision makers make about job performance from predictor measures (e.g., tests, interviews) are accurate.

IMPACT OF STAFFING DECISIONS ON PRODUCTIVITY, QUALITY OF WORK LIFE, AND THE BOTTOM LINE

Some companies avoid validating their screening and selection procedures because they think validation is too costly—and its benefits too elusive. However, a large body of research has shown that the economic gains in productivity associated with the use of valid selection and promotion procedures far outweigh the cost of those procedures.[a] Think about that. If people who score high on selection procedures also do well on their jobs, high scores suggest a close fit between individual capabilities and organizational needs. Low scores, on the other hand, suggest a poor fit. In both cases, productivity, quality of work life, and the bottom line stand to gain from the use of valid selection procedures.

Valid selection and promotion procedures also benefit applicants. Indeed, a more accurate matching of their knowledge, skills, ability, and other characteristics to job requirements helps enhance the likelihood of successful performance. This, in turn, helps workers feel better about their jobs and adjust to changes in them, as they are doing the kinds of things they do best. Moreover, because we know that there is a positive spillover effect between job satisfaction and life satisfaction, the accurate matching of people and jobs will also foster an improved quality of life, not just an improved quality of work life, for all concerned.

---

[a]Cascio, W. F., and Scott, J. C. (2017). The business value of employee selection. In J. Farr and N. T. Tippins (Eds.), *Handbook of Employee Selection* (2nd ed.). New York: Routledge, pp. 226-48. Cascio, W F., Boudreau, J. W., and Fink, A. (2019). *Investing in People* (3rd ed.). Alexandria, VA: SHRM Publishing.

IMPLICATIONS FOR MANAGEMENT PRACTICE

The research evidence is clear: Valid selection procedures can produce substantial economic gains for organizations. The implication for policymakers also is clear:

- Select the highest-caliber managers and lower-level employees, for they are most likely to profit from development programs.
- Do not assume that a large investment in training can transform marginally competent performers into innovative, motivated top performers.
- Lots of screening and selection procedures are available. Ask "tough" questions of vendors and HR specialists about the reliability, job relatedness, and validity of each one proposed for use.

- Recognize that no one predictor is perfectly valid, and therefore that some mistakes in selection (erroneous acceptances or erroneous rejections) are inevitable. By consciously selecting employees at all levels based on their fit with job requirements, the strategic direction of a business, and organizational culture, you will minimize mistakes and make optimum choices.

In the context of managerial selection, numerous techniques are available, but the research literature indicates that the most effective ones are cognitive-ability tests, personality and interest inventories, peer assessments, personal-history data, and situational tests. The use of situational tests, such as the leaderless group discussion, the in-basket, and business simulations, lies at the heart of the assessment-center method. Key advantages of the method are its high validity, fair evaluation of each candidate's ability, and flexibility of form and content. Other features include the use of multiple assessment techniques, assessor training, and pooled assessor judgments in rating each candidate's behavior.

Recent research indicates, at least for ability tests, that a test that accurately forecasts performance on a particular job in one situation will also forecast performance on the same job in other situations. Hence, it may not be necessary to conduct a new validity study each time a predictor is used. Research has also demonstrated that the economic benefits to an organization that uses valid selection procedures may be substantial. In choosing the right predictors for a given situation, pay careful attention to four factors: the nature of the job, the estimated validity of the predictor(s), the selection ratio, and the cost of the predictor(s). Doing so can pay handsome dividends to organizations and employees alike.

KEY TERMS

organizational culture	openness to experience
reliability	agreeableness
validity	conscientiousness
negligent hiring	emotional intelligence
shrinkage	contrast effects
integrity tests	work-sample tests
validity generalization	leaderless group discussion (LGD)
personality	in-basket test
neuroticism	assessment center method
extroversion	selection ratio

DISCUSSION QUESTIONS

8-1. Your boss asks how she can improve the accuracy of pre-employment interviews. What would you tell her?

8-2. Why are reliability and validity key considerations for all assessment methods?

8-3. How does business strategy affect management selection?

8-4. Discuss the do's and don'ts of effective reference checking.

8-5. As jobs become more team oriented, assessment centers will be used more often for nonmanagement jobs. Do you agree or disagree?

8-6. There are many possible staffing tools to help forecast later job performance. How do you decide which ones to use?

8-7. Your boss asks you to review the current application form at your organization. How will you decide which questions to keep, change, or delete?

8-8. Of the Big Five personality characteristics, why do you think conscientiousness is the most valid predictor across many types of jobs?

8-9. Why is emotional intelligence particularly important in service jobs?

8-10. Choose a job you know well. Develop three job-relevant situational interview questions ("What would you do if . . ." or "Tell me about a time when . . .") to use with applicants for that job.

APPLYING YOUR KNOWLEDGE

Exercise 8–1   *An In-Basket and an LGD for Selecting Managers*

There are several ways to make the right choices in the managerial- selection process. One popular approach is to attempt to assess what a managerial candidate can do, rather than what he or she knows.

Various kinds of work samples or situational tests can be used to assess what a candidate can do. In this exercise, you will have an opportunity to see how two of the most valid managerial work samples operate–in-basket tests and leaderless group discussions (LGDs). An attractive feature of this combination of predictors is that although both are valid, the scores on each do not correlate highly with each other. This suggests that in-baskets and LGDs tap different, but important, subsets of the managerial performance domain.

Part A: In-Basket Exercise

An in-basket exercise is designed to assess a candidate's problem-solving, decision-making, and administrative skills. Further, because all responses are written ones, the exercise can also assess written communication ability.

An in-basket exercise consists of a set of notes, memos, reports, and other communications to which a candidate must respond. These items would typically be presented in digital form. To give you a sense of how an in-basket operates, here is a sample set of such items, presented in the form of memoranda.

Procedure

You are to assume that you have just been appointed director of human resources at Ace Manufacturing Company and that your name is George (or Georgina) Ryan. The president of the firm is Arnold ("Arnie") Ace. You were to replace the current HR director, John Armstrong, in 2 weeks, when he was scheduled to be transferred to Hong Kong. However, a family emergency in South Africa has required that John leave the country immediately, and you must fill in for him as best as you can. You have taken an alternate flight on an important business trip to Washington, DC, and have stopped over in Los Angeles, where Ace's headquarters are located. It is Saturday morning, and no one else is available in the office. You must resume your flight to Washington, DC, within an hour.

Read through the items in your in-basket, decide what to do with each item, and record your decision on a separate sheet of paper. If any decisions require writing a letter or memo, draft the response in the space provided. Don't role-play how you think someone else might behave in this situation. Rather, behave exactly as you yourself would in each situation.

Item 1

MEMO TO: John Armstrong, HR Director
FROM: Jackie Williams, Downtown Business Club
SUBJECT: Speaking engagement next week

Thanks again for your willingness to speak to our Business Club next week. As you know, this group represents a good cross section of the L.A. business community as well as a number of Ace's best customers. We are all looking forward to what you have to say regarding the relationship between business and human resource strategies.

Item 2

MEMO TO: Mr. Ryan
FROM: Judy [human resources staff member]
SUBJECT: Tom Tipster's employment status

Just after Mr. Armstrong left yesterday, we received a call from the owner of Stockman's Bar and Grill saying that Tom Tipster had gotten drunk in the middle of the day again and damaged the bar. He said he'd hold off pressing charges until he talked to you (I explained that you were Mr. Armstrong's replacement). This is the third time that Mr. Tipster has gotten in trouble over his drinking problem. I think Mr. Armstrong was planning to fire him if he had another problem like this. You'd think that someone with 17 years of service at Ace would have more sense than to get into trouble like this, especially with four kids at home to feed!

Item 3

MEMO TO: John
FROM: Arnie
SUBJECT: EEO Report

Where is that EEO report you promised me? There's no way I want to face the investigators from Denver Wednesday without it!

Item 4

MEMO TO: John Armstrong
FROM: Lisa Buller, Administrator of Training Programs
SUBJECT: Time off

I need to take next Thursday off to fly to San Francisco on important personal business. Will this be OK?

Item 5

MEMO TO: Mr. John Armstrong
FROM: Arch Turnkey
SUBJECT: Thefts

As you know, my store is located between your downtown office extension and that of Deuce's. During the past several months we have had several cases of shoplifting from our store, and the police haven't been able to do anything about it. Further, several custodians from your facility have been observed acting funny (with dazed looks on their faces) and wandering around outside my store, looking in. I think that your people may be responsible for the recent shoplifting losses I have suffered. I would appreciate hearing from you within the next week. Otherwise, I will be forced to take appropriate measures to ensure protection of my store.

Item 6

MEMO TO: John
FROM: Alice Calmers, Director of Manufacturing
SUBJECT: Thursday's training program

I finally got everything rearranged for that training program on Thursday. You can't imagine how difficult it is to try to rearrange the schedules of 15 very busy supervisors to attend anything at the same time. I certainly hope that Lisa's presentation is going to be worth all this juggling of schedules!

Item 7

MEMO TO: John Armstrong
FROM: Ralph Herzberg, Manager of Customer Relations
SUBJECT: New training program

We have a serious problem in the customer relations department. It is common for a large number of calls to come in all at once. When this happens, the customer-relations-contact employee is supposed to take the customer's phone number and get back to him or her within an hour. We've found in the past that this is a reasonable target because, after a big rush of calls, things usually settle down for a while. But when we check up on the customer-contact employees, we find that they get back to the customer within an hour only about one-third of the time. Sometimes they don't get back to the customer until the next day! I sent a memo to all customer-contact employees about a month ago reminding them of the importance of prompt responses on their parts, but it did very little good. We need a training program from your department to improve this critical performance area. Can we get together early next week?

Responses

On a separate sheet of paper, provide your responses to each in-basket item. Then, as a group, discuss how the set of responses reflects problem-solving, decision-making, and administrative skills.

Item 1: Speaking engagement next week.
Item 2: Tom Tipster's employment status.
Item 3: EEO report.
Item 4: Time off.
Item 5: Thefts.
Item 6: Thursday's training program.
Item 7: New training program.

Part B: Leaderless Group Discussion (LGD)

Unlike the in-basket exercise, a leaderless group discussion exercise involves groups of managerial candidates working together on a job-related problem. The problem is usually designed to be as realistic as possible, and it is often discussed in groups of five or six candidates. No one in the group is appointed leader, nor is anyone told where to sit or how to act. Candidates are instructed simply to solve the problem to the best of their ability in the time allotted.

The LGD is used to assess such managerial traits and skills as aggressiveness, interpersonal skills, persuasive ability, oral communication skills, self-confidence, energy level, and resistance to stress.

Procedure

The problem that follows is typical of those in an LGD. However, to conserve time, we have simplified it somewhat. Divide about two-thirds of the class into groups of five or six participants; the remaining one-third should serve as observers. Participants should read the statement of the problem and attempt to arrive at a consensus solution within about 15 minutes. Assign two or three observers to each group and give each one or two participants to observe. At the end of the exercise, be prepared to discuss the kinds of management skills exhibited by participants in your group. Use the rating scale shown at the end of the exercise.

Bonus-Allocation Problem

Your organization has recently instituted an incentive bonus in an attempt to stimulate and reward key employee behaviors. The company has budgeted $120,000 for this purpose, to be spent every 6 months. You have been appointed to a committee responsible for determining the allocation of bonus funds to deserving employees over the previous 6-month period. A total of 25 employees were recommended by their supervisors. Decisions have already been made on 20 of them, and $95,000 of the original sum has been expended. Your task today is to decide on the size of the bonuses (if any) to be received by the remaining five employees. Summaries of the qualifications for the five employees are presented below.

Virginia Dewey

Head custodian, 15 years with the firm. High school diploma plus 22 years of relevant job experience. Manages a flawless custodial staff with low turnover and few union grievances. Present salary below average in most recent salary survey. Supports a family of six. Overlooked for salary increase last year.

Alfred Newman

Accounting clerk, 3 years with the firm. Has a 2-year college degree and 3 years of relevant work experience. Performs well under pressure of deadlines. Present salary is average in recent salary survey. Is known to be looking for other jobs.

Augusta Nie

Manager of business analytics, 7 years with the firm. Master's degree in computer science and 14 years of relevant work experience. Has developed the business analytics department into one of the most efficient in the company. Present salary is above average in recent salary survey. Has leadership potential and may be offered jobs from other firms. Will be difficult to replace.

Barry Barngrover

Machinist, 11 years with the firm. High school diploma and 11 years relevant job experience. Is the top performer in the milling-machine department and exhibits a positive company attitude. Present salary is average in a recent salary survey. Is single and seems to have all the money he needs to support his chosen lifestyle.

Harvey Slack

Human resources staff, 1 year with the firm. College degree from prestigious Ivy League school and 3 years of relevant work experience. Very knowledgeable in subject matter but has trouble getting along with older coworkers. Present salary is above average in a recent salary survey. His mentor is the firm's vice president for human resources, who is said to be grooming Harvey for the VP position. Has received several offers from other firms recently.

Rating Scale

Observation of Participant: A B C D E F

Step 1: Use a check mark to indicate each time the participant you are evaluating demonstrates the following behaviors:

Introduces a new idea.

Builds on the ideas of others.

Interrupts others.

Takes conversation in new direction.

Focuses the group onto the task.

Attends to relationship needs of the group.

Seeks ideas from others.

Contributes expert knowledge.

REFERENCES

1. Ployhart, R. E., and Weekley, J. A. (2017). Strategy, selection, and sustained competitive advantage. In J. L. Farr and N. T. Tippins (Eds.), *Handbook of Employee Selection* (2nd ed). New York: Routledge, pp. 115-33. *See also* Heneman, H. G., III, Judge, T., and Kammeyer-Mueller, J. D. (2015). *Staffing Organizations* (8th ed.). New York: McGraw-Hill.
2. Isaacson, W. "The Real Leadership Lessons of Steve Jobs." *Harvard Business Review* 90, no. 4 (2012): 97.
3. Ployhart, R. E., Schmitt, N., and Tippins, N. T. (2017). Solving the supreme problem: 100 years of selection and recruitment at the *Journal of Applied Psychology. Journal of Applied Psychology* 102, pp. 291-304. *See also* Kristof-Brown, A., and Guay, R. P. (2011). Person-environment fit. In S. Zedeck (Ed.), *APA Handbook of Industrial and Organizational Psychology* (Vol. 3). Washington, DC: American Psychological Association, pp. 3-50. *See also* Schneider, B., Smith, D. B., Taylor, S., and Fleenor, J. (1998). Personality and organizations: A test of the homogeneity of personality hypothesis. *Journal of Applied Psychology* 83, pp. 462-70. *See also* Schneider, B. (1987). The people make the place. *Personnel Psychology* 40, pp. 437-53.
4. Tetenbaum, T. (1999, Autumn). Beating the odds of merger and acquisition failure. *Organizational Dynamics*, pp. 22-36.
5. Schneider, B., Gonzalez-Roma, V., Ostroff, C., and West, M. A. (2017). Organizational climate and culture: Reflections on the history of the constructs in the *Journal of Applied Psychology. Journal of Applied Psychology* 102, pp. 468-82. *See also* Schneider B., Ehrhart, M. G., and Macey, W. H. (2013). Organizational climate and culture. *Annual Review of Psychology* 64, pp. 361-88.
6. Warrick, D. D. (2017). What leaders need to know about organizational culture. *Business Horizons* 60(3), pp. 395-404.

7. Schneider et al. (2013), op. cit. See also Schneider, B., Ehrhart, M. G., and Macey, W. H. (2011). Perspectives on organizational climate and culture. In S. Zedeck (Ed.), *APA Handbook of Industrial and Organizational Psychology* (Vol. 1). Washington, DC: American Psychological Association, pp. 373-414. *See also* Schein, E. H. (2010). *Organizational Culture and Leadership* (4th ed.). San Francisco: Jossey-Bass.

8. Feintzeig, R. (2016, Oct. 12). "Culture fit" may be key to your next job. *The Wall Street Journal*, pp. B1, B6. *See also* Kristof-Brown and Guay (2011), op. cit.

9. Kristof-Brown and Guay (2011), op. cit. See also Kristof-Brown, A. L. (2000). Perceived applicant fit: Distinguishing between recruiters' perceptions of person-job and person-organization fit. *Personnel Psychology* 53, pp. 643-71.

10. Potworowski, G. A., and Green, L. A. (2012). Culture and evidence-based management. In D. M. Rousseau (Ed.), *The Oxford Handbook of Evidence-Based Management*. Oxford, UK: Oxford University Press, pp. 272-92. See also Dickson, M. W., Mullins, M. W., and Deuling, J. K. (2017). Organizational culture. In S. G. Rogelberg (Ed.), *The Sage Encyclopedia of Industrial and Organizational Psychology* (2nd ed., Vol. 3). Thousand Oaks, CA: Sage, pp. 1099-103.

11. Sheridan, J. E. (1992). Organizational culture and employee retention. *Academy of Management Journal* 35, pp. 1036-56. See also O'Reilly, C. A. III, and Pfeffer, J. (2000). *Hidden Value: How Great Companies Achieve Extraordinary Results with Ordinary People*. Boston: Harvard Business School Press.

12. Sackett, P. R., Lievens, F., Van Iddekinge, C. H., and Kuncel, N. R. (2017). Individual differences and their measurement: A review of 100 years of research. *Journal of Applied Psychology* 102, pp. 254-73. *See also* Hunter, J. E., Schmidt, F. L., and Judiesch, M. K. (1990). Individual differences in output variability as a function of job complexity. *Journal of Applied Psychology* 75, pp. 28-42.

13. Cascio, W. F., and Aguinis, H. (2019). *Applied Psychology in Talent Management*. Thousand Oaks, CA: Sage, Ch 6. See also Putka, D. Reliability. In J. L. Farr & N. T. Tippins (Eds.), *Handbook of Employee Selection* (2nd ed.). New York: Routledge. pp. 3-33.

14. Schmitt, N. W., Arnold, J. D., and Nieminen, L. (2017). Validation strategies for primary studies. In J. L. Farr and N. T. Tippins (Eds.), *Handbook of Employee Selection* (2nd ed.). New York: Routledge, pp. 34-55. *See also* Schmitt, N., and Sinha, R. (2011). Validation support for selection procedures. In S. Zedeck (Ed.), *APA Handbook of Industrial and Organizational Psychology* (Vol. 2). Washington, DC: American Psychological Association, pp. 399-420.

15. Ibid. See also Cascio, W. F., and Aguinis, H. (2019). *Applied Psychology in Human Resource Management* (8th ed.). Thousand Oaks, CA: Sage.

16. Society for Industrial-Organizational Psychology. (2018). *Principles for the Validation and Use of Personnel Selection Procedures* (5th Ed.). Bowling Green, OH: Author.

17. American Educational Research Association, American Psychological Association, National Council on Measurement in Education. (2014). *Standards for Educational and Psychological Testing*. Washington, DC: American Educational Research Association.

18. Uniform guidelines on employee selection procedures. (1978). *Federal Register* 43, pp. 38290-315.

19. Fried, I. (2020, Jan. 9). Google received 3.3 million job applications in 2019. *Axios*. Retrieved from *https://www.axios.com/google-2019-applications-backlash-972203e4-8e86-4cec-aa26-195572c69e13*.html on Apr. 7, 2020.

20. Janove, J. (2019, Aug. 2). Employing the formerly incarcerated: A global perspective. *SHRM Online*. Retrieved from *https://www.shrm.org/resourcesandtools/legal-and-compliance/employment-law/pages/global-second-chance-employment.aspx* on Aug. 4, 2019. *See also* Vedantam, V. (2016, July 19). "Ban the box" laws: Do they help job applicants with criminal histories? *National Public Radio*. Retrieved from *www.npr.org/2016/07/19/486571633/are-ban-the-box-laws-helping-job-applicants-with-criminal-histories* on Apr. 18, 2017.

21. Gurschiek, K. (2019, May 10). Formerly incarcerated are an overlooked source of talent. *SHRM Online*. Retrieved from *https://www.shrm.org/resourcesandtools/hr-topics/*

behavioral-competencies/global-and-cultural-effectiveness/pages/formerly-incarcerated-are-an-overlooked-source-of-talent-.aspx on May 12, 2019.

22. Ahearn, T. (2018, July 2). NAPBS survey reveals 95 percent of employers conducting employment background screening in 2018. Retrieved from *https://www.esrcheck.com/wordpress/2018/07/02/napbs-survey-reveals-95-percent-employers-conducting-employment-background-screening-2018/* on Apr. 7, 2020.

23. Kroll, J., and Turecek, P. (2003, Jan.). Why background checks on executives are critical. *Director's Monthly*, pp. 11, 12. *See also* Krell, E. (2013, Apr.). Forecast for global background checks. *HRMagazine*, pp. 67-69.

24. Maurer, R. (2018, June 26). 7 HR questions (and answers) about employment screening. SHRM Online. Retrieved from *https://www.shrm.org/resourcesandtools/hr-topics/talent-acquisition/pages/hr-questions-answers-employment-screening.aspx* on June 26, 2018. *See also* cFirst Think Tank. (2018, Feb. 22). Pre-employment background screening in the U.S.: An overview. Retrieved from *https://www.cfirstcorp.com/pre-employment-background-screening-in-usa-an-overview/* on Apr. 7, 2020.

25. Cascio and Aguinis (2011), op cit.

26. Aamodt, M. G. (2017). Letters of recommendation. In S. G. Rogelberg (Ed.), *The Sage Encyclopedia of Industrial and Organizational Psychology* (2nd ed., Vol. 2). Thousand Oaks, CA: Sage, pp. 889-91.

27. Ibid. *See also* Knouse, S. B. (1987). An attribution theory approach to the letter of recommendation. *International Journal of Management* 4(1), pp. 5-13.

28. Brooks, C. (2016, Aug. 2). The pros and cons of social media background checks. Retrieved from *www.businessnewsdaily.com/9289-social-media-background-checks.html* on April 18, 2017. *See also* Meinert (2012), op. cit. *See also* Wells, S. J. (2008, Feb.). Ground rules on background checks. *HRMagazine*, pp. 47-54. *See also* Aamodt (2017), op. cit.

29. Grensing-Pophal, L. (2019, May 8). Creative and compliant ways to check references. *SHRM Online*. Retrieved from *https://www.shrm.org/resourcesandtools/hr-topics/talent-acquisition/pages/creative-compliant-ways-check-references.aspx* on Apr. 7, 2020.

30. Thurm, S. (2013, Aug. 13). Judge sinks lawsuit on screening hires. *The Wall Street Journal*, p. B7. *See also* Meinert (2012), op. cit. *See also* Athavaley, A. (2007, Sept. 27). Job references you can't control. *The Wall Street Journal*, pp. D1, D2.

31. Society for Human Resource Management. (2016, Oct. 4). Conducting background investigations and reference checks. Retrieved from *www.shrm.org/resourcesandtools/tools-and-samples/toolkits/pages/conductingbackgroundinvestigations.aspx* on Apr. 18, 2017.

32. Nagele-Piazza, L. (2018, Feb. 28). Can employers give a bad reference for a former employee? *SHRM Online*. retrieved from *https://www.shrm.org/resourcesandtools/legal-and-compliance/state-and-local-updates/pages/can-employers-give-a-bad-reference-for-a-former-employee.aspx*. See also Meinert, D. (2012, Dec.). Search and verify. *HRMagazine*, pp. 37-41.

33. Maurer, R. (2016, Oct.). Making every check count. *HRMagazine*, pp. 69, 70. *See also* Elliott, M. (2018, Nov. 19). Lying on your resume? Here's how you'll get caught. *Glassdoor*. Retrieved from *https://www.glassdoor.com/blog/lying-on-your-resume/* on Apr. 7, 2020.

34. Roberts, B. (2010, Dec.). Backgrounds to the foreground. *HRMagazine*, pp. 46-51. *See also* Ryan, A. M., and Lasek, M. (1991). Negligent hiring and defamation: Areas of liability related to pre-employment inquiries. *Personnel Psychology* 44, pp. 293-319.

35. Nagele-Piazza (2018), op. cit. *See also* Jackson, S., and Loftin, A. (2000, Jan.). Proactive practices avoid negligent hiring claims. *HR News*, p. 12.

36. Arnold, D. W. (1996, Feb.). Providing references. *HR News*, p. 16.

37. Tippins, N. T., Solberg, E. C., and Singla, N. (2017). Decisions in the operational use of employee selection procedures: Choosing, evaluating, and administering assessment tools. In J. Farr and N. T. Tippins (Eds.), *Handbook of Employee Selection* (2nd ed.). New York: Routledge, pp. 367-87. *See also* Fox, A. (2013, Aug.). Upon further assessment.... *HRMagazine*, pp. 39-45. *See also* Sackett, P. R., and Lievens, F. (2008). Personnel selection. *Annual Review of Psychology* 59, pp. 419-50.

38. Dugan, D. (2019, Aug. 9). The dos and don'ts of mobile recruiting. *Recruiter.com*. Retrieved from *https://www.recruiter.com/i/the-dos-and-donts-of-mobile-recruiting/*on Ap.l 7, 2020. *See also* Cascio, W. F., and Graham, B. Z. (2016). New strategic role for HR: Leading the employer-branding process. *Organization Management Journal* 13(4), pp. 182–92.

39. Juergens, J. (2019, Dec. 5). Alcohol and drugs in the workplace. *Addiction Center.com*. Retrieved from *https://www.addictioncenter.com/addiction/workplace/* on Apr. 7, 2020. *See also* Harris, M. M., and Heft, L. L. (1993). Pre-employment urinalysis drug testing: A critical review of psychometric and legal issues and effects on applicants. *Human Resource Management Review* 3, pp. 271–91.

40. Handrick, L. (2018, May 16). Employee drug screening: Compliance, providers, and cost. *Fit Small Business*. Retrieved from *https://fitsmallbusiness.com/employee-drug-screening/* on Apr. 7, 2020. *See also* HireRight. (2012, Feb. 6). Think the cost of drug testing is too high? Think again. Retrieved from *www.hireright.com/blog/2012/02/think-the-cost-of-pre-employment-drug-testing-is-too-high-think-again/* on Apr. 18, 2017.

41. Weber, L. (2018, May 9). Illicit drug use rises for workers. *The Wall Street Journal*, pp. B1, B5.

42. Zeidner, R. (2010, Nov.). Putting drug screening to the test. *HRMagazine*, pp. 25–30.

43. Nagele-Piazza, L. (2020, Jan. 17). Marijuana and the workplace: What's new for 2020? *SHRM Online*. Retrieved from *https://www.shrm.org/resourcesandtools/legal-and-compliance/state-and-local-updates/pages/marijuana-and-the-workplace-new-for-2020.aspx* on Jan. 17, 2020.

44. Ibid. *See also* Nagele-Piazza, L. (2020, Jan. 21). Workplace drug testing: Can employers still screen for marijuana? *SHRM Online*. Retrieved from *https://www.shrm.org/resourcesandtools/legal-and-compliance/state-and-local-updates/pages/can-employers-still-test-for-marijuana.aspx* on Jan. 21, 2020.

45. Paronto, M. E., Truxillo, D. M., Bauer, T. N., and Leo, M. C. (2002). Drug testing, drug treatment, and marijuana use: A fairness perspective. *Journal of Applied Psychology* 87, pp. 1159–66.

46. HS Brands Global. (2019, Apr. 1). Top causes of shrinkage in retail. Retrieved from *https://hsbrands.com/resource-center/articles/top-causes-of-shrinkage-in-retail/* on Apr. 7, 2020.

47. Employee theft statistics. (2017, Apr. 1). Retrieved from *www.statisticbrain.com/employee-theft-statistics/* on Apr. 18, 2017.

48. Murphy, K. R. (2017). Integrity testing. In S. G. Rogelberg (Ed.), *The Sage Encyclopedia of Industrial and Organizational Psychology* (2nd ed., Vol. 2). Thousand Oaks, CA: Sage, pp. 730–33. *See also* Rotundo, M., and Spector, P. E. (2017). New perspectives on counterproductive work behavior, including withdrawal. In J. L. Farr and N. T. Tippins (Eds.), *Handbook of Employee Selection* (2nd ed.). New York: Routledge, pp. 476–508.

49. Van Iddekinge, C. H., Roth, P. I., Rymark, P. H., and Odle-Dusseau, H. N. (2012). The criterion-related validity of integrity tests: An updated meta-analysis. *Journal of Applied Psychology* 97, pp. 499–530. *See also* Schmidt, F. L., and Hunter, J. E. (1998). The validity and utility of selection methods in personnel psychology: Practical and theoretical implications of 85 years of research findings. *Psychological Bulletin* 124, pp. 262–74. *See also* Wanek, J. E. (1999). Integrity and honesty testing: What do we know? How do we use it? *International Journal of Selection and Assessment* 7, pp. 183–95. *See also* Ones, D. S., Viswesvaran, C., and Schmidt, F. L. (1993). Comprehensive meta-analysis of integrity test validities: Findings and implications for personnel selection and theories of job performance. *Journal of Applied Psychology* (monograph) 78, pp. 679–703.

50. Schmidt, F. L, Viswesvaran, V., and Ones, D. S. (1997). Validity of integrity tests for predicting drug and alcohol abuse: A meta-analysis. In Bukoski, W. J. (Ed.), *Meta-analysis of drug abuse prevention programs*. NIDA Research Monograph 170. Washington, DC: U.S. Department of Health and Human Services, pp. 69–95.

51. Rotundo and Spector (2017), op. cit. *See also* Ones, D. S., Viswesvaran, C., and Schmidt, F. L. (2003). Personality and absenteeism: A meta-analysis of integrity tests. *European Journal of Personality* 17, pp. S19–S38.

52. U.S. Office of Personnel Management. (n.d.). Integrity/honesty tests. Retrieved from *https://www.opm.gov/policy-data-oversight/assessment-and-selection/other-assessment-methods/integrityhonesty-tests/* on Apr. 7, 2020. *See also* Roberts (2011), op. cit. *See also* Schmidt and Hunter (1998), op. cit.

53. Ones, D. S., Dilchert, S., Viswesvaran, C., and Salgado, J. (2017). Cognitive ability. In J. Farr and N. T. Tippins (Eds.), *Handbook of Employee Selection* (2nd ed.). New York: Routledge, pp. 251–76. *See also* Sackett and Lievens (2008), op. cit. For an excellent discussion and summary of results across jobs, settings, jobs, and countries, see Ones, D. S., Viswesvaran, C., and Dilchert, S. (2004). Cognitive ability in selection decisions. In O. Wilhelm and R. W. Engle (Eds.), *Handbook of Understanding and Measuring Intelligence*. London: Sage, pp. 448–77.

54. Nassauer, S., & Cutter, C. (2019, July 1). Walmart uses virtual reality before promoting workers. *The Wall Street Journal*, pp. B1, B2.

55. Reynolds, D. H., and Dickter, D. N. (2017). Technology and employee selection. In J. Farr and N. T. Tippins (Eds.), *Handbook of Employee Selection* (2nd ed.). New York: Routledge, pp. 855–73. *See also* Coovert, M., and Thompson, L. F. (Eds.). (2014). *The Psychology of Workplace Technology*. San Francisco: Jossey-Bass.

56. Walker, J. M., & Moretti, D. (2018). *Recent trends in preemployment assessment*. SIOP White Paper Series. Bowling Green, OH: Society for Industrial and Organizational Psychology. *See also* Johnson, J., and Oswald, F. L. (2017). Test administration and the use of test scores. In J. Farr and N. T. Tippins (Eds.), *Handbook of Employee Selection* (2nd ed.). New York: Routledge, pp. 182–204. *See also* Tippins, N. T., Beaty, J., Drasgow, F., Gibson, W. M., Pearlman, K., Segall, D. O., and Shepherd, W. (2006). Unproctored Internet testing in employment settings. *Personnel Psychology* 59, pp. 189–225.

57. Silzer, R. F., and Borman, W. C. (2017). The potential for leadership. In D. G. Collings, K. Mellahi, and W. F. Cascio (Eds.), *The Oxford Handbook of Talent Management*. Oxford, UK: Oxford University Press. *See also* Nye, C. D., Su, R., Rounds, J., and Drasgow, F. (2012). Vocational interests and performance: A quantitative summary of over 60 years of research. *Perspectives on Psychological Science* 7(4), pp. 384–403. *See also* Goldstein, H. W., Yusko, K. P., Braverman, E. P., Smith, D. B., and Chung, B. (1998). The role of cognitive ability in the subgroup differences and incremental validity of assessment center exercises. *Personnel Psychology* 51, pp. 357–74. *See also* Lord, R. G., DeVader, C. L., and Alliger, G. M. (1986). A meta-analysis of the relationship between personality traits and leadership perceptions: An application of validity generalization procedures. *Journal of Applied Psychology* 71, pp. 402–10.

58. Thornton, G. C. III, Johnson, S. K., and Church, A. H. (2017). Selecting leaders: Executives and high-potentials. In J. L. Farr and N. T. Tippins (Eds.), *Handbook of Employee Selection* (2nd ed.). New York: Routledge, pp. 833–52. *See also* Korman, A. K. (1968). The prediction of managerial performance: A review. *Personnel Psychology* 21, pp. 295–322. *See also* Kraut, A. I. (1969). Intellectual ability and promotional success among high-level managers. *Personnel Psychology* 22, pp. 281–90.

59. Lebreton, J. M., Schoen, J. L., and James, L. R. (2017). Situational specificity, validity generalization, and the future of psychometric meta-analysis. In J. L. Farr and N. T. Tippins (Eds.), *Handbook of Employee Selection* (2nd ed.). New York: Routledge, pp. 93–114. *See also* Schmidt, F. L., and Hunter, J. (2003a). History, development, evolution, and impact of validity generalization and meta-analysis methods, 1975–2001. In K. R. Murphy (Ed.), *Validity Generalization: A Critical Review*. Mahwah, NJ: Lawrence Erlbaum, pp. 31–65.

60. Lebreton et al. (2017), op. cit.

61. Hough, L. M., and Dilchert, S. (2017). Personality: Its measurement and validity for employee selection. In J. Farr and N. T. Tippins (Eds.), *Handbook of Employee Selection* (2nd ed.). New York: Routledge, pp. 298–325. *See also* Smith, D. B., Hanges, P. J., and Dickson, M. W. (2001). Personnel selection and the five-factor model: Reexamining the effects of applicant's frame of reference. *Journal of Applied Psychology* 86, pp. 304–15. *See also*

Salgado, J. F. (1997). The five-factor model of personality and job performance in the European community. *Journal of Applied Psychology* 82, pp. 30–43.

62. Hough and Dilchert (2017), op. cit. See also Oswald, F. L., and Hough, L. M. (2011). Personality and its assessment in organizations: Theoretical and empirical developments. In S. Zedeck (Ed.), *APA Handbook of Industrial and Organizational Psychology* (Vol. 2). Washington, DC: American Psychological Association, pp. 153–84. *See also* Ones, D. S., Dilchert, S., Viswesvaran, C., and Judge, T. A. (2007). In support of personality assessment in organizational settings. *Personnel Psychology* 60, pp. 995–1027. *See also* Rothstein, M., and Goffin, R. D. (2006). The use of personality measures in personnel selection: What does current research support? *Human Resource Management Review* 16, pp. 155–80. *See also* Barrick, M. R., and Mount, M. K. (2003). Impact of meta-analysis methods on understanding personality-performance relations. In K. R. Murphy (Ed.), *Validity Generalization: A Critical Review*. Mahwah, NJ: Lawrence Erlbaum, pp. 197–221.

63. Rockwood, K. (2020, Feb. 29). Assessing personalities. *SHRM Online*. Retrieved from *https://www.shrm.org/hr-today/news/all-things-work/pages/personality-assessments.aspx* on Mar. 1, 2020. *See also* Oswald and Hough (2011), op. cit.

64. Hough and Dilchert (2017), op. cit. *See also* Healy, M. C., and Handler, C. A. (2010). *2009 Survey of Online Pre-Employment Assessment: Complete Findings*. New Orleans: Rocket-Hire, LLC.

65. Rockwood (2020), op. cit.

66. Hogan, J., and Brinkmeyer, K. (1997). Bridging the gap between overt and personality based integrity tests. *Personnel Psychology* 50, pp. 587–99.

67. Hough and Dilchert (2017), op. cit. *See also* Peterson, M. H., Griffith, R. L., Isaacson, J. A., O'Connell, M. S., and Mangos, P. M. (2011). Applicant faking, social desirability, and the prediction of counterproductive work behaviors. *Human Performance* 24, pp. 270–90. *See also* Oswald and Hough (2011), op. cit. *See also* McFarland, L. A., and Ryan, A. M. (2000). Variance in faking across noncognitive measures. *Journal of Applied Psychology* 85, pp. 812–21. *See also* Rosse, J. G., Stecher, M. D., Miller, J. L., and Levin, R. A. (1998). The impact of response distortion on pre-employment personality testing and hiring decisions. *Journal of Applied Psychology* 83, pp. 634–44. *See also* Christiansen, N. D., Goffin, R. D., Johnston, N. G., and Rothstein, M. G. (1994). Correcting the 16PF for faking: Effects on criterion-related validity and individual hiring decisions. *Personnel Psychology* 47, pp. 847–60.

68. Hough, L. M. (1998). Effects of intentional distortion in personality measurement and evaluation of suggested palliatives. *Human Performance* 11, pp. 209–44. *See also* Hough, L. M. (1997). The millennium for personality psychology: New horizons or good old daze. *Applied Psychology: An International Review* 47, pp. 233–61. *See also* Hough, L. M., Eaton, N. K., Dunnette, M. D., Kamp, J. D., and McCloy, R. A. (1990). Criterion related validities of personality constructs and the effect of response distortion on those validities. *Journal of Applied Psychology Monograph* 71, pp. 581–95.

69. Peterson et al. (2011), op. cit. *See also* Mueller-Hanson, R., Heggestad, E. D., and Thornton, G. C. (2003). Faking and selection: Considering the use of personality from select-in and select-out perspectives. *Journal of Applied Psychology* 88, pp. 348–55. *See also* Rosse et al. (1998), op. cit.

70. Zickar, M. J., and Robie, C. (1999). Modeling faking good on personality items: An item-level analysis. *Journal of Applied Psychology* 84, pp. 551–63. *See also* Alliger, G. M., Lilienfeld, S. O., and Mitchell, K. E. (1996). The susceptibility of overt and covert integrity tests to coaching and faking. *Psychological Science* 11, pp. 32–39.

71. Hough (1998), op. cit.

72. Hughes, M., Patterson, L. B., and Terrell, J. B. (2005). *Emotional Intelligence in Action*. San Francisco: Pfeiffer. *See also* Goleman, D. (1998). *Working with Emotional Intelligence*. New York: Bantam. See also Goleman, D. (1995). *Emotional Intelligence: Why It Can Matter More Than IQ*. New York: Bantam.

73. Goleman, D., Boyatzis, R., and McKee, A. (2002). *Primal Leadership: Realizing the Power of Emotional Intelligence*. Boston: Harvard Business School Press.

74. Lievens, F., and Chan, D. (2017). Practical intelligence, emotional intelligence, and social intelligence. In J. Farr and N. T. Tippins (Eds.), *Handbook of Employee Selection* (2nd ed.). New York: Routledge, pp. 342-64. *See also* Joseph, D. L., Jin, J., Newman, D. A., and O'Boyle, E. (2015). Why does self-reported emotional intelligence predict job performance? A meta-analytic investigation of mixed EI. *Journal of Applied Psychology* 100, pp. 298-342. *See also* Mayer, J. D., Roberts, R. D., and Barsade, S. G. (2008). Emerging research in emotional intelligence. *Annual Review of Psychology* 59, pp. 501-36. *See also* Murphy, K. R. (2006). *A Critique of Emotional Intelligence: What Are the Problems and How Can They Be Fixed?* Mahwah, NJ: Erlbaum.

75. Cote, S. (2014). Emotional intelligence in organizations. *Annual Review of Organizational Psychology and Organizational Behavior* 1, pp. 459-88.

76. Organ, D. W., Podsakoff, P. M., and Podsakoff, N. P. (2011). Expanding the criterion domain to include organizational citizenship behavior: Implications for employee selection. In S. Zedeck (Ed.), *APA Handbook of Industrial and Organizational Psychology* (Vol. 2). Washington, DC: American Psychological Association, pp. 281-323.

77. Breaugh, J. A. (2009). The use of biodata for employee selection: Past research and future directions. *Human Resource Management Review* 19, pp. 219-31. *See also* Carlson, K. D., Scullen, S. E., Schmidt, F. L., Rothstein, H., and Erwin, F. (1999). Generalizable biographical data validity can be achieved without multi-organizational development and keying. *Personnel Psychology* 52, pp. 731-75. *See also* Kluger, A. N., Reilly, R. R., and Russell, C. J. (1991). Faking biodata tests: Are option-keyed instruments more resistant? *Journal of Applied Psychology* 76, pp. 889-96.

78. Becker, T. E., and Colquitt, A. L. (1992). Potential versus actual faking of a biodata form: An analysis along several dimensions of item type. *Personnel Psychology* 45, pp. 389-406.

79. Sackett and Lievens (2008), op. cit. *See also* Rothstein and Goffin (2006), op. cit. *See also* Schmitt, N., and Kunce, C. (2002). The effects of required elaboration of answers to biodata questions. *Personnel Psychology* 55, pp. 569-87.

80. Hausknecht, J. P., and Heavey, A. L. (2017). Selection for service and sales jobs. In J. L. Farr and N. T. Tippins (Eds.), *Handbook of Employee Selection* (2nd ed.). New York: Routledge, pp. 781-96. *See also* Mount, M. K., Witt, L. A., and Barrick, M. R. (2000). Incremental validity of empirically keyed biodata scales over GMA and the five-factor personality constructs. *Personnel Psychology* 53, pp. 299-323.

81. McCauley, C. D., and McCall, M. W., Jr. (Eds.). (2014). *Using Experience to Develop Talent: How Organizations Leverage on-the-Job Development*. San Francisco: Jossey-Bass.

82. Burnett, J. R., and Motowidlo, S. J. (1998). Relations between different sources of information in the structured selection interview. *Personnel Psychology* 51, pp. 963-83. *See also* Hakel, M. D. (1989). Merit-based selection: Measuring the person for the job. In W. F. Cascio (Ed.), *Human Resource Planning, Employment, and Placement*. Washington, DC: Bureau of National Affairs, pp. 2-135 to 2-158.

83. Cliffordson, C. (2002). Interviewer agreement in the judgment of empathy in selection interviews. *International Journal of Selection & Assessment* 10, pp. 198-205. *See also* Fay, D., and Frese, M. (2001). The concept of personal initiative: An overview of validity studies. *Human Performance* 14, pp. 97-124.

84. Huffcutt, A. I., Conway, J. M., Roth, P. L., and Stone, N. J. (2001). Identification and meta-analytic assessment of psychological constructs measured in employment interviews. *Journal of Applied Psychology* 86, pp. 897-913.

85. Hough and Dilchert (2017), op. cit. *See also* Cortina, J. M., Goldstein, N. B., Payne, S. C., Davison, H. K., and Gilliland, S. W. (2000). The incremental validity of interview scores over and above cognitive ability and conscientiousness scores. *Personnel Psychology* 53, pp. 325-51.

86. Day, A. L., and Carroll, S. A. (2002). Situational and patterned behavior description interviews: A comparison of their validity, correlates, and perceived fairness. *Human Performance* 16, pp. 25-47.

87. Huffcutt, A. I., and Culbertson, S. S. (2011). Interviews. In S. Zedeck (Ed.), *APA Handbook of Industrial and Organizational Psychology* (Vol. 2). Washington, DC: American Psychological Association, pp. 185-203. *See also* Schmidt, F. L., and Zimmerman, R. D. (2004). A counter-intuitive hypothesis about employment-interview validity and some supporting evidence. *Journal of Applied Psychology* 89, pp. 553-61. *See also* Moscoso, S. (2000). Selection interviews: A review of validity evidence, adverse impact, and applicant reactions. *International Journal of Selection and Assessment* 8(4), pp. 237-47. *See also* Campion, M. A., Palmer, D. K., and Campion, J. E. (1997). A review of structure in the selection interview. *Personnel Psychology* 50, pp. 655-702. *See also* Conway, J. M., Jako, R. A., and Goodman, D. F. (1995). A meta-analysis of inter-rater and internal consistency reliability of selection interviews. *Journal of Applied Psychology* 80, pp. 565-79. *See also* McDaniel, M. A., Whetzel, D. L., Schmidt, F. L., and Maurer, S. (1994). The validity of employment interviews: A comprehensive review and meta-analysis. *Journal of Applied Psychology* 79, pp. 599-616.

88. Middendorf, C. H., and Macan, T. H. (2002). Note-taking in the employment interview: Effects on recall and judgments. *Journal of Applied Psychology* 87, pp. 293-303. *See also* Burnett, J. R., Fan, C., Motowidlo, S. J., and DeGroot, T. (1998). Interview notes and validity. *Personnel Psychology* 51, pp. 375-96.

89. Ganzach, Y., Kluger, A. N., and Klayman, N. (2000). Making decisions from an interview: Expert measurement and mechanical combination. *Personnel Psychology* 53, pp. 1-20. *See also* Westen, D., and Weinberger, J. (2004). When clinical description becomes statistical prediction. *American Psychologist* 59, pp. 595-613.

90. Posthuma, R. A., Morgeson, F. P., and Campion, M. A. (2002). Beyond employment interview validity: A comprehensive narrative review of recent research and trends over time. *Personnel Psychology* 55, pp. 1-81.

91. Cascio and Aguinis (2019), op. cit. *See also* Campion et al. (1997), op. cit.

92. Tippins, N. T., Solberg, E. C., and Singla, N. (2017). Decisions in the operational use of employee selection procedures. In J. L. Farr and N. T. Tippins (Eds.), *Handbook of Employee Selection* (2nd ed.). New York: Routledge, pp. 367-87. *See also* Shippmann, J. S., Ash, R. A., Battista, M., Carr, L., Eyde, L. D., Hesketh, B., Kehoe, J., Pearlman, K., Prien, E. P., and Sanchez, J. I. (2000). The practice of competency modeling. *Personnel Psychology* 53, pp. 703-40.

93. Cohen, A. (2014, Jan. 9). What's your favorite hiring question? *Bloomberg Businessweek*, p. 69.

94. Dipboye, R. L., and Gaugler, B. B. (1993). Cognitive and behavioral processes in the selection interview. In N. Schmitt and W. C. Borman (Eds.), *Personnel Selection in Organizations*. San Francisco: Jossey-Bass, pp. 135-70. *See also* Weekley, J. A., and Gier, J. A. (1987). Reliability and validity of the situational interview for a sales position. *Journal of Applied Psychology* 72, pp. 484-87.

95. Motowidlo, S. J., Carter, G. W., Dunnette, M. D., Tippins, N., Werner, S., Burnett, J. R., and Vaughan, M. J. (1992). Studies of the structured behavioral interview. *Journal of Applied Psychology* 77, pp. 571-87.

96. Falcone, P. (2017, Apr. 13). Interview ice breakers: 7 questions to segue into meaningful candidate conversations. *SHRM Online*. Retrieved from *https://www.shrm.org/resourcesandtools/hr-topics/talent-acquisition/pages/interview-ice-breakers-7-questions-to-segue-into-meaningful-candidate-conversations.aspx* on Apr. 13, 2017.

97. Hawkins, J. (2020). Actions HR should take regarding the salary-history question. *HR Professionals Magazine, 10*(3), p. 38. *See also* Frank, L. (2017, Sept. 5). Why banning questions about salary history may not improve pay equity. *Harvard Business Review*. Retrieved from *https://hbr.org/2017/09/why-banning-questions-about-salary-history-may-not-improve-pay-equity* on Sept. 24, 2017.

98. Huffcutt and Culbertson (2011), op. cit. *See also* Cortina et al. (2000), op. cit.

99. Borman, W. C., Grossman, M. R., Bryant, R. H., and Dorio, J. (2017). The measurement of task performance as criteria in selection research. In J. L. Farr and N. T. Tippins (Eds.),

Handbook of Employee Selection (2nd ed.). New York: Routledge, pp. 429–47. *See also* Gebhardt, D. L., and Baker, T. A. (2017). Physical performance tests. In J. L. Farr and N. T. Tippins (Eds.), *Handbook of Employee Selection* (2nd ed.). New York; Routledge, pp. 277–97. *See also* Asher, J. J., and Sciarrino, J. A. (1974). Realistic work sample tests: A review. *Personnel Psychology* 27, pp. 519–33.

100. Roth, P. L., Bobko, P., and McFarland, L. A. (2005). A meta-analysis of work-sample test validity: Updating and integrating some classic literature. *Personnel Psychology* 58, pp. 1009–37. *See also* Schmitt, N., and Mills, A. E. (2001). Traditional tests and job simulations: Minority and majority performance and test validities. *Journal of Applied Psychology* 86, pp. 451–58.

101. Callinan, M., and Robertson, I. T. (2000). Work sample testing. *International Journal of Selection and Assessment* 8(4), pp. 248–60.

102. Cascio, W. F., and Phillips, N. (1979). Performance testing: A rose among thorns? *Personnel Psychology* 32, pp. 751–66.

103. Borman et al. (2017), op. cit.

104. Arthur, W., Jr., and Day, E. A. (2011). Assessment centers. In S. Zedeck (Ed.), *APA Handbook of Industrial and Organizational Psychology* (Vol. 2). Washington, DC: American Psychological Association, pp. 205–35.

105. Kello, J. (2017). Assessment center methods. In S. G. Rogelberg (Ed.), *The Sage Encyclopedia of Industrial and Organizational Psychology* (Vol. 1). Thousand Oaks, CA: Sage, pp. 74–77.

106. Pillay. S. (2016, Feb. 19). How leaderless groups end up with leaders. *Harvard Business Review*. Retrieved from *https://hbr.org/2016/02/how-leaderless-groups-end-up-with-leaders* on Apr. 20, 2017.

107. Ibid. *See also* Mohammed, S., and McKay, A. S. (2017). Selection for team membership. In J. L. Farr and N. T. Tippins (Eds.), *Handbook of Employee Selection* (2nd ed.). New York: Routledge, pp. 812–32.

108. Ibid. *See also* Bass, B. M. (1954). The leaderless group discussion. *Psychological Bulletin* 51, pp. 465–92. *See also* Tziner, A., and Dolan, S. (1982.) Validity of an assessment center for identifying future female officers in the military. *Journal of Applied Psychology* 67, pp. 728–36.

109. Kurecka, P. M., Austin, J. M., Jr., Johnson, W., and Mendoza, J. L. (1982). Full and errant coaching effects on assigned role leaderless group discussion performance. *Personnel Psychology* 35, pp. 805–12. *See also* Petty, M. M. (1974). A multivariate analysis of the effects of experience and training upon performance in a leaderless group discussion. *Personnel Psychology* 27, pp. 271–82.

110. Kello (2017), op. cit. *See also* Arthur and Day (2011), op. cit. *See also* Fredericksen, N. (1962). Factors in in-basket performance. *Psychological Monographs* 76(22, whole no. 541), p. 1.

111. Kello (2017), op. cit.

112. See, for example, Howard, A. (2010). The Management Progress Study and its legacy for selection. In J. Farr and N. T. Tippins (Eds.), *Handbook of Employee Selection*. New York: Routledge, pp. 843–64. *See also* Brass, G. J., and Oldham, G. R. (1976). Validating an in-basket test using an alternative set of leadership scoring dimensions. *Journal of Applied Psychology* 61, pp. 652–57. *See also* Tziner, A., and Dolan, S. (1982). Validity of an assessment center for identifying future female officers in the military. *Journal of Applied Psychology* 67, pp. 728–36.

113. Hoffman, B. J., Monahan, E., Lance, C. E., and Sutton, A. (2015). A meta-analysis of the content, construct, and criterion-related validity of assessment center exercises. *Journal of Applied Psychology* 100, pp. 1143–68.

114. Weekley, J. A., and Jones, C. (1999). Further studies of situational tests. *Personnel Psychology* 52, pp. 679–700.

115. Clevenger, J., Pereira, G. M., Wiechmann, D., Schmitt, N., and Harvey, V. S. (2001). Incremental validity of situational judgment tests. *Journal of Applied Psychology* 86, pp. 410–17.

116. Christian, M. S., Edwards, B. D., and Bradley, J. C. (2010). Situational judgment tests: Constructs assessed and meta-analysis of their criterion-related validities. *Personnel Psychology* 63, pp. 83–117.

117. Whetzel, D., Sullivan, T. S., and McCloy, R. A. (2020). Situational judgment tests: An overview of development practices and psychometric characteristics. *Personnel Assessment and Decisions* 6(1), pp. 1–16. *See also* Hough and Dilchert (2017), op. cit. *See also* Clevenger et al. (2001), op. cit. *See also* McDaniel, M. A., and Nguyen, N. T. (2001). Situational judgment tests: A review of practice and constructs assessed. *International Journal of Selection and Assessment* 9, pp. 103–13.

118. Arthur and Day (2011), op. cit. *See also* Howard (2010), op. cit. *See also* McKinnon, D. W. (1975). Assessment centers then and now. *Assessment and Development* 2, pp. 8–9. *See also* Office of Strategic Services (OSS) Assessment Staff .(1948). *Assessment of Men.* New York: Rinehart.

119. Howard (2010), op. cit. *See also* Bray, D. W. (1976). The assessment center method. In R. L. Craig (Ed.), *Training and Development Handbook* (2nd ed.). New York: McGraw-Hill, pp. 17-1 to 17-15.

120. *SHRM Talent acquisition benchmark report.* (2017). Alexandria, VA: Society for Human Resource Management. *See also* Thornton, G. C. III, Rupp, D. E., and Hoffman, B. J. (2015). *Assessment Center Perspectives for Talent Management Strategies* (2nd ed.). New York: Routledge.

121. Fox (2013), op. cit. *See also* Hough and Dilchert (2017), op. cit.

122. Hoffman, B. J., Kennedy, C. L., LoPilato, A. C., Monahan, E. L., & Lance, C. E. (2015). A review of the content, criterion-related, and construct-related validity of assessment center exercises. *Journal of Applied Psychology,* 100, 1143–1168.

123. Arthur and Day, 2011, op. cit. *See also* Lievens, F. (2001). Assessor training strategies and their effects on accuracy, interrater reliability, and discriminant validity. *Journal of Applied Psychology* 86, pp. 255–264.

124. Schleicher, D. J., Day, D. V., Mayes, B. T., and Riggio, R. E. (2002). A new frame for frame-of-reference training: Enhancing the construct validity of assessment centers. *Journal of Applied Psychology* 87, pp. 735–46. *See also* Kolk, N. J., Born, M. P., vander Flier, H., and Olman, J. M. (2002). Assessment center procedures: Cognitive load during the observation phase. *International Journal of Selection & Assessment* 10, pp. 271–78.

125. Erker, S. C., Cosentino, C. J., and Tamanini, K. B. (2017). Selection methods and desired outcomes. In J. L. Farr and N. T. Tippins. (Eds.), *Handbook of Employee Selection* (2nd ed.). New York: Routledge, pp. 738–59. *See also* Thornton, G. C., III, and Rupp, D. E. (2006). *Assessment Centers in Human Resource Management: Strategies for Prediction, Diagnosis, and Development.* Mahwah, NJ: Lawrence Erlbaum. *See also* Arthur, W., Day, E. A., McNelly, T. L., and Edens, P. S. (2003). A meta-analysis of the criterion-related validity of assessment center dimensions. *Personnel Psychology* 56, pp. 125–54. *See also* Dayan, K., Kasten, R., and Fox, S. (2002). Entry-level police candidate assessment center: An efficient tool or a hammer to kill a fly? *Personnel Psychology* 55, pp. 827–49. *See also* Gaugler, B. B., Rosenthal, D. B., Thornton, G. C., III, and Bentson, C. (1987). Meta-analysis of assessment center validity. *Journal of Applied Psychology* 72, pp. 493–511. *See also* Howard, A. (1974). An assessment of assessment centers. *Academy of Management Journal* 17, pp. 115–34.

126. Jansen, P. G. W., and Stoop, B. A. M. (2001). The dynamics of assessment center validity: Results of a 7-year study. *Journal of Applied Psychology* 86, pp. 741–53.

127. Howard (2010), op. cit. *See also* Hoffman, C. C., and Thornton, G. C. (1997). Examining selection utility where competing predictors differ in adverse impact. *Personnel Psychology* 50, pp. 455–70. *See also* Thornton, G. C., III, and Byham, W. C. (1982). *Assessment Centers and Managerial Performance.* New York: Academic Press. *See also* Huck, J. R., and Bray, D. W. (1976). Management assessment center evaluations and subsequent job performance of white and Black females. *Personnel Psychology* 29, pp. 13–30.

128. Cascio, W. F., and Ramos, R. A. (1986). Development and application of a new method for assessing job performance in behavioral/economic terms. *Journal of Applied Psychology* 71,

pp. 20-28. *See also* Cascio, W. F., and Silbey, V. (1979). Utility of the assessment center as a selection device. *Journal of Applied Psychology* 64, pp. 107-18.

129. Lefkowitz, J., and Lowman, R. L. (2017). Ethics of employee selection. In J. L. Farr and N. T. Tippins (Eds.), *Handbook of Employee Selection* (2nd ed.). New York: Routledge, pp. 575-98. *See also* Lievens, F. (2002). Trying to understand the different pieces of the construct validity puzzle of assessment centers: An examination of assessor and assessee effects. *Journal of Applied Psychology* 87, pp. 675-86. *See also* Klimoski et al. (1987), op. cit. *See also* Gaugler, B. B., and Thornton, G. C., III. (1989). Number of assessment center dimensions as a determinant of assessor accuracy. *Journal of Applied Psychology* 74, pp. 611-18. *See also* Reilly, R. R., Henry, S., and Smither, J. W. (1990). An examination of the effects of using behavior checklists on the construct validity of assessment center dimensions. *Journal of Applied Psychology* 43, pp. 71-84.

130. Thornton et al. (2017), op. cit. *See also* Howard (2010), op. cit.

131. Cascio, W. F., and Scott, J. C. (2017). The business value of employee selection. In J. Farr and N. T. Tippins (Eds.), *Handbook of Employee Selection* (2nd ed.). New York: Routledge, pp. 226-48. *See also* Fox (2013), op. cit.

132. Herb Kelleher, former CEO, Southwest Airlines.

DEVELOPMENT

Once employees are hired, their personal growth and development over time become a major concern. Change is a fact of organizational life, and to cope with it effectively, planned programs of employee training and performance management are essential. We address these issues in Chapters 9 and 10. Chapter 9 examines what is known about training developing, and onboarding management and non-management employees. Chapter 10 is concerned with performance management—particularly with the design, implementation, and evaluation of such systems. The overall objective of Part 3 is to establish a framework for managing the development process of employees as their careers in organizations unfold.

9

TRAINING AND ON-BOARDING

TECHNOLOGY-DELIVERED INSTRUCTION CATCHES ON*

We live in a digital age and a smartphone world. Consider the development of cloud computing as just one example. Cloud computing–the practice of using a network of remote servers hosted on the Internet to store, manage, and process data, rather than a local server, is exploding in popularity. It gives consumers, as well as enterprises, cheap, unlimited access to cutting-edge computing power and applications. On the consumer side (roughly 29 percent of cloud applications in use), sites such as Facebook, Twitter, YouTube, LinkedIn, and Pinterest are most popular. On the enterprise side (roughly 71 percent of such services), the top five sites are Amazon Web Services, Microsoft Azure, Google Cloud, IBM Cloud, and Oracle Cloud.

Mobile computing is moving faster than anyone might have expected. Today, more than 88 percent of all mobile devices are smartphones, and more than 6 billion of them are in use around the world. People check their phones as often as 150 times a day, and more business is now conducted via smartphone. What this means is that there is a pressing need to ensure that all HR functions, from recruitment to training and development, work well on mobile and tablet devices and that your organization's IT function has adopted a "BYO" ("bring your own") technology strategy.

Although technology is surely not the answer to all people-related business issues, it is critical to recognize how prevalent it is and the high expectations that employees, job candidates, suppliers, customers, and other stakeholders have that it will operate well. Technology also enables innovations in training design and delivery. One such innovation is technology-delivered instruction (TDI).

Whether training is web-based, delivered on a single work station, a tablet, or on a mobile device, TDI is catching on. Before we go any further, let's take a moment to define our terms. TDI is the presentation of text, graphics, video, audio, or animation in digitized form for the purpose of building job-relevant knowledge and skill. TDI includes asynchronous (meaning it is not delivered to every user at the same time) text-based courses, job aids, educational games, and video and audio segments, as well as synchronous media, such as video-conferencing and chat rooms.

TDI is booming. What's driving the trend? Both demand and supply forces are operating. On the demand side, rapid obsolescence of knowledge and training makes learning and relearning essential if workers are to keep up with the latest developments in their fields. In addition, there is a growing demand for just-in-time training delivery, coupled with demand for cost-effective ways to meet the learning needs of a globally distributed workforce. Finally, there is demand for flexible access to lifelong learning.

On the supply side, Internet access is becoming standard at work and at home, and advances in digital technologies now enable training designers to create interactive, media-rich content. In addition, increasing bandwidth and better delivery

*Sources: LinkedIn Learning. (2020). 2020 workplace learning report. Retrieved from https://learning.linkedin. com/content/dam/me/learning/resources/pdfs/LinkedIn-Learning-2020-Workplace-Learning-Report.pdf on Apr. 13, 2020. 2019 Deloitte global human capital trends. Retrieved from https://documents.deloitte.com/ insights/HCTrends2019 on Apr. 13, 2020. Association for Talent Development (ATD) State of the Industry Report. (2019). Alexandria, VA: Author. HostingTribunal.com. (2020). The latest cloud computing trends. Retrieved from https://hostingtribunal.com/blog/cloud-computing-trends/#gref on Apr. 13, 2020. Gurschiek, K. (2020, Jan. 2). Look for these training trends in 2020. SHRM Online. Retrieved from https://www.shrm. org/resourcesandtools/hr-topics/organizational-and-employee-development/pages/look-for-these-training-trends-in-2020.aspx on Jan. 3, 2020. Sitzmann, T. (2011). A meta-analytic examination of the instructional effectiveness of computer-based simulation games. Personnel Psychology 64, pp. 489-528.

platforms make TDI particularly attractive. Finally, there is a growing selection of high-quality products and services.

Features like these allow smaller companies, such as Arrow Electronics, to work with a vendor (BrandGames) to make a game that teaches customer-account managers customer-service skills and supply-chain management. They also led the Greater Seattle Chamber of Commerce to create an online learning center for its 2,200 members–most of whom employ fewer than 100 employees. Online learning also permits large firms, such as General Motors, to reach more than 175,000 employees at 7,500 dealerships in less than a week, using interactive distance learning (IDL) technology. IDL lets employees view a live course beamed in by satellite and ask questions of the instructor without leaving their dealerships, which slashes travel time and costs and improves quality, because GM can select its best instructors to teach each course.

Classroom courses are not going away (54 percent of training hours were delivered in face-to-face classrooms in 2019) and TDI does have its drawbacks, as we shall see in the conclusion to this case, but one thing is certain: TDI is changing corporate training forever.

Challenges

1. What are some of the key advantages of TDI?
2. Are some types of material or course work better suited than others to TDI?
3. What disadvantages or opportunity costs can you identify with this approach?

Traditionally, lower-level employees were "trained," whereas higher-level employees were "developed." This distinction, focusing on the learning of hands-on skills versus interpersonal and decision-making skills, has become too blurry in practice to be useful. Throughout the remainder of this chapter, therefore, we will use the terms *training* and *development* interchangeably. Training is big business, and the first half of this chapter examines some current issues in the design, conduct, and evaluation of training programs.

Change, growth, and sometimes displacement (e.g., through layoffs and restructuring) are facts of modern organizational life. Young people entering the workforce today typically change jobs at least seven times by their late 20s as they strive to figure out what they like, what they are good at, and where they can fit in and stand out.[1] Each new employer represents a transition. On-boarding, the subject of the second part of this chapter, can ease that transition considerably, with positive results both for the new employee and for the company. Trends such as leased employees and free-agent workers will make on-boarding even more important in the future. Let's begin by defining training and consider some emerging trends.

EMPLOYEE TRAINING

What Is Training?

Training consists of planned programs designed to improve performance at the individual, group, and/or organizational levels. Improved performance, in turn, implies that there have been measurable changes in knowledge, skills, attitudes, and/or social behavior.

When we examine the training enterprise as a whole, it is clear that training issues can be addressed from at least two perspectives. At the macro level, we can examine issues such as the following, among others: aggregate expenditures by the various providers of training (e.g., federal, state, and local governments, educational institutions, private-sector businesses), the degree of cooperation among the providers, incentives (or lack of incentives) for providing training, who gets training, and the economic impact of training.[2]

At the micro level, we may choose to examine issues such as what types of training seem to yield positive outcomes for organizations and trainees (i.e., *what works*); how to identify if training is needed and, if so, what type of training best fits the needs that have been identified; how to structure the delivery of training programs; and how to evaluate the outcomes of training efforts.

Unfortunately, organizations sometimes place too much emphasis on the techniques and methods of training and not enough on first defining what the employee should learn in relation to desired job behaviors. In addition, fewer than half of all organizations even try to measure the value of training, and fewer still (just 8 percent) calculate the return in monetary terms.[3] This may be changing, however, as "evaluating the effectiveness of learning programs" emerged as the top strategic focus in 2020 of learning and development professionals in 18 countries.[4]

In this section, we will do two things: (1) discuss several macro-level issues and (2) illustrate research-based findings that might lead to improvements in the design, delivery, and evaluation of training systems. Let's begin by considering some important training trends.

Training Trends

These are exciting times for training and development, as a number of trends, many well under way, are accelerating. Here are six of them[5]:

- *A growing demand for personal and professional development.* Among young adults, the most important feature they look for in a new job is opportunity for continuous learning.[6] Fully 94 percent say they would stay at a company longer if it invested in their learning and development. As for employers, tight labor markets in recent years have put pressure on them to invest in training. Fully 66 percent of them now do.[7] In addition to technical skills, employers are looking for people who can interact satisfactorily with customers and who demonstrate responsibility, flexibility, initiative, critical thinking, and a collaborative spirit. To be most effective though, training needs to be aligned with management's operating goals, which may include improved productivity, quality, or customer satisfaction.[8]
- *The effects of digital technology on work.* Technology, especially information and communication technology, is changing the manner in which businesses create and capture value, how and where we work, and how we interact and communicate. Technologies such as cloud and mobile computing, big data and machine learning, sensors and intelligent manufacturing, advanced robotics and drones, and clean-energy technologies are transforming the very foundations of global business and the organizations that drive it. They have enabled workers to decide where they work, when they work, and in some cases even how they accomplish work.[9] Employees can take a course on nearly any subject online without leaving their desks, or couch, or coffee shop. Indeed, the trend toward consumer-centric learning puts employees, not training departments, in charge.[10]

- *Structural changes in labor markets.* Today, many organizations employ workers from a variety of labor market sources. Some operate outside the traditional confines of regular, full-time employment. They may be "free agents" or "e-lancers" (i.e., freelancers in the digital world) who work for themselves, or they may be employees of an organization a firm is allied with, employees of an outsourcing or temporary-help firm, or even volunteers.[11] On any given day, experts estimate, as much as 36 percent of the American workforce may be nonstandard workers.[12]

- *Increased training opportunities for nonstandard workers.* One approach to demonstrating competence—and therefore job readiness and greater marketability of one's skills—is to accumulate "**stackable credentials**." CPA (certified public accountant) and CMA (certified management accountant) are well-known acronyms in the fields of accounting and finance, but other certifications, like digital badges and online course certificates, are appearing in many other fields. Expect to see more focus on credentialing for virtual and classroom delivery. Industry groups as well as schools currently grant such credentials, and each skill level of the stack builds on what came before.[13]

- *Training as an important aspect of an employer's brand. Brand* is shorthand for the goods and services that a company provides (e.g., "Coca-Cola," "CNN," "Ford"). *Brand* is also shorthand for the quality and distinctiveness of those goods and services. In general, the public is attracted to good-name brands and repelled by bad-name brands.[14] Websites like Glassdoor, Twitter, and Facebook make it very easy for employees to communicate the pros and cons of working at a company. Why worry about that? Because from the consumer's perspective, brands simplify choice, increase trust, reduce risk, and promise a particular level of value. Employers compete in talent markets, and employer brands play a critical role in recruiting and retaining talent.[15]

- *Teams.* As more firms move to employee involvement and teams in the workplace, team members need to learn behaviors such as asking for ideas, offering help without being asked, listening and providing feedback, and recognizing and considering the ideas of others.[16]

Indeed, as the demands of the information age spread, companies are coming to regard training expenses as a no-less-critical part of their capital costs than plants and equipment. Organizations that provide superior opportunities for learning and growth have a distinct advantage when competing for talented employees. Indeed, 94 percent say they would stay at a company longer if it invested in their learning and development.[17]

These trends suggest a dual responsibility: Managers at every level must encourage employee learning, and employees must take advantage of the learning opportunities provided (see the HR Buzz box). The payoffs? Better attraction and retention for employers, improved skills, heightened self-worth, and opportunities for advancement for employees. It's a win–win.

Impact of Training on Individuals, Teams, Organizations, and Society

Consider the following benefits of training, most of which have been demonstrated at the individual and team levels of analysis.[18]

1. *Meta-analyses (quantitative summaries of accumulated results across many studies) have demonstrated repeatedly that training has an overall positive effect on job-related behaviors or performance.*[19] The average effect size equals 0.62—that is, it

FUTURE WORK: AUTOMATION TECHNOLOGY*

The robots are coming! According to Boston Consulting Group, the pace of advanced robotics installation is expected to rise from 2 to 3 percent annual growth today to 10 percent annual growth within a decade. That presents major opportunities in automation technology, a field that requires skills in programming and maintaining or fixing industrial robots, or automated software. Marion, Ohio-based RAMTEC (Robotic Advanced Manufacturing Technical Education Collaborative), offers an au-tomation-certification program. It is a partnership among robotics companies, local manufacturers, and educators at Tri-Rivers Career Center. Here's how it works.

High school students enrolled for free at RAMTEC continue earning their traditional diplomas while also developing skills that local businesses, such as automaker Honda and robotics-refurbishing firm Robot Works, are demanding. Companies are pitching in. For example, robot manufacturer FANUC donated software training programs and sold cutting-edge robotics systems to RAMTEC at a steep discount. FANUC already trains about 9,000 people annually through its own network of paid courses but is running at 99 percent capacity. According to a company spokesperson, "We can't keep up. The only way to put a dent in the demand is to partner with education."

Here's more good news: Careers in advanced manufacturing automation pay well. Annual salaries for high school grads with certification from a center like RAMTEC range from $40,000 to $60,000 (compared to a median salary of $35,256 for those with only a high school diploma). For graduates with associate degrees from junior colleges with similar training, it's $50,000 to $70,000 (compared to $41,496 for those with only an associate's degree). The lesson? One way to keep the automation revolution from swallowing your job is to devise a role that turns the tables on tech.

Source: Bomey, N. (2017, Feb. 6). At Ohio training center, students embrace lucrative future of automation, robotics. *USA Today*, pp. 1B, 2B.

is 0.62 standard deviations better than performance without training[20]–but the effectiveness of training varies, depending on the delivery method and the skill or task being trained.

2. *Training can improve technical skills.* Generally, this occurs through improvements in declarative knowledge (facts, meaning of terms) as well as procedural knowledge (how to perform skilled behavior).

3. *Training can improve strategic knowledge*–that is, knowing when to apply a specific knowledge or skill.

4. *Training, and especially practice, helps to maintain consistency in performance.* Think of a chef who must cook various items on a menu over and over in a consistent manner, or a professional athlete who must perform at a consistently high level to be successful.

5. *Management development programs show positive effects.* They seem to affect two types of outcomes: knowledge–principles, facts, and skills (average effect sizes range from 0.96 to 1.37)–and changes in on-the-job behavior (average effect sizes range from 0.35 to 1.01).[21]

6. *Cross-cultural training improves expatriate adjustment and performance.* The actual effectiveness of such training in any given situation, however, depends on several

INTERNATIONAL APPLICATION
The Rise of Robotics, AI, and Upskilling—Globally*

People from all generations increasingly recognize that rapid technological change, while holding out the promise of valuable opportunities, also creates unforeseen impacts that can dramatically disrupt their careers and lead to major changes in the composition of the workforce. People become alarmed when they learn that by 2030, 3 to 14 percent of the global workforce worldwide could be forced out of their current occupations by robotics and artificial intelligence (AI). AI is an evolving constellation of technologies that enable computers to simulate elements of human thinking, including learning and reasoning. Today, nearly one in five Americans are employed in jobs that did not exist in 1980. Artificial intelligence builder, robot manager, mobile-app designer, 3-D printing engineer, drone pilot, social-media manager, genetic counselor–these are just a few of the jobs that have appeared in recent years.

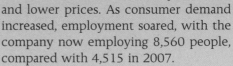

Most existing jobs will be transformed as people rework their old roles to include collaborating with digital technology in some form. While relatively few jobs now performed by humans will disappear completely as a result of full automation, almost everyone's job will change in meaningful ways as a result of advances in technology. Thus, the larger challenge is not mass unemployment, but rather upskilling to transition people, structures, and processes to a workplace enabled by the cooperation between humans and technology. Here are a few examples of companies that have managed the transition well.

Finnish firm Fiskars AB, manufacturer of iconic and once pricey orange-handled scissors, used automation to reach more customers. Workers at its Helsinki plant used to forge steel blades by hand in 2,700-degree furnaces–repetitive and dangerous work. When robots took over the tasks in 2011, technicians moved to quality control, testing the scissors to make sure the blades made the right "snip" sound as they sliced together and that they smoothly cut strips of fabric. After the partial automation, the firm was able to increase production and lower prices. As consumer demand increased, employment soared, with the company now employing 8,560 people, compared with 4,515 in 2007.

German multinational engineering and technology company Robert Bosch GmbH uses 140 robotic arms in its factories worldwide, up from zero in 2011. While it hires many designers, engineers, and scientists among its total staff of 400,000 employees, it has developed training courses for workers, teaching once single-skilled welders, joiners, and mechanics basic software-coding skills to enable them to use robots as tools, much like hammers or screwdrivers.

Because it takes time to work out how best to use robots, the slow pace of roll-outs can shield workers, providing time for retraining. That's what happened at clothing company Levi Strauss during

*Sources:: *MIT Technology Review*. (n.d.). What is artificial intelligence? Retrieved from *https://www.technologyreview.com/topic/artificial-intelligence/* on Apr. 14, 2020. Soergel, A. (2020, Feb. 20). Companies invest in partnerships, workforce training to bridge skills gap. *US News & World Report*. Retrieved from *https://www.usnews.com/news/economy/articles/2020-02-20/amazon-facebook-home-depot-among-companies-paying-to-train-workforce* on Feb. 21, 2020. Montealegre, R., and Cascio, W. F. (In press). Managing in the age of external intelligence. *Organizational Dynamics*. *https://doi.org/10.1016/j.orgdyn.2019.100733*. Wilkes, W. (2018, May 15). Big companies fine-tune the robot revolution. *The Wall Street Journal*, pp. A1, A8. Minaya, E. (2018, Apr. 11). Levi's CFO turns to robots to help keep the books. *The Wall Street Journal*. Retrieved from *https://blogs.wsj.com/cfo/2018/04/11/levis-cfo-turns-to-robots-to-help-keep-the-books/* on Apr. 11, 2018. Smith, A. (2018, July 10). Automation revolution will spur retraining to fill new jobs. *SHRM Online*. Retrieved from *https://www.shrm.org/resourcesandtools/legal-and-compliance/employment-law/pages/automation-revolution-retraining.aspx* on July 10, 2018. McKinsey Global Institute. (2017, Dec.). Jobs lost, jobs gained: Workforce transitions in a time of automation. Retrieved from *https://www.mckinsey.com/~/media/mckinsey/featured%20insights/Future%20of%20Organizations/What%20the%20future%20of%20work%20will%20mean%20for%20jobs%20skills%20and%20wages/MGI-Jobs-Lost-Jobs-Gained-Report-December-6-2017.ashx* on Mar. 4, 2019.

its introduction of robotic software to its finance function. Rather than eliminate jobs, the company chose to upskill employees and have them spend more time on financial analysis. Upskilling is a huge challenge and companies as varied as Amazon, JPMorgan Chase, Nationwide, Chevron, and Home Depot are spending millions to make their workforces "future-ready."

important variables: the timing of the training (predeparture, postarrival, postassignment), the spouse's adjustment, the attributes of the job (e.g., discretion), and the cultural "distance" between home and host countries.[22]

7. *Leadership training seems to enhance the attitudes and performance of followers.* Specifically, it seems to have a positive effect on the motivation, values, and self-efficacy (belief that one can accomplish a task) of followers.[23]

8. *Training in team communication and team effectiveness has positive effects on team performance and, in the case of airplane cockpit crews, safety.* It also seems to affect nontechnical skills (team building) as well as situation awareness and decision making. We will have more to say about this topic later in the chapter.

9. *Training is a key enabler of e-commerce.* This is one reason why Amazon plans to spend $700 million by 2025 to retrain a third of its U.S. workforce as automation, machine learning and other technology upends the way many of its employees do their jobs.[24] See the accompanying International Application box.

10. *Training improves the quality of a nation's labor force.* That, in turn, enhances a country's economic growth, as it attracts foreign direct investment. This has led many countries around the world (e.g., members of the European Union, Singapore) to adopt national policies to encourage wide delivery of training programs.

CHARACTERISTICS OF EFFECTIVE TRAINING PRACTICE

Despite the rosy picture painted in the previous section, keep in mind that if training is ill conceived, poorly planned, or inadequately executed, then it is likely to be ineffective and waste precious resources (time and money). Conversely, four characteristics seem to distinguish companies with the most effective training practices[25]:

- Top management is committed to training and development; training is part of the corporate culture. This is especially true of leading companies, such as Google, Disney, Marriott, and Cisco.
- Training is tied to business strategy and objectives and is linked to bottom-line results.
- Managers at all levels are actively involved. They stress continuous improvement, promote risk taking, offer one-on-one coaching, and afford opportunities to learn from successes and failures.
- There is commitment to invest the necessary resources, to provide sufficient time and money for training.

The Training Paradox

Some businesses, small and large, don't offer training because they think that by upgrading the skills of the workforce, their employees will be more marketable to competitors. That is true. However, if an employer provides lots of opportunities for learning and professional growth, employees who take advantage of them build more security with that employer. This is the **training paradox**: Increasing an individual's employability outside the company simultaneously increases his or her job security and desire to stay with the current employer (assuming that the employer creates challenging jobs and provides an exciting work environment).

How Training Relates to Competitive Strategies

Competitive strategies refer to the decisions, processes, and choices that organizations make to position themselves for sustainable success.[26] *HR strategy*, in turn, refers to the decisions, processes, and choices organizations make about managing people. Training is an important aspect of HR strategy, and a key objective of any training program is to tie workplace training to the strategy of a business. 3M is especially adept at this. For instance, it will set a goal to reduce product-development cycle time (i.e., to increase speed), then create a course on how to do it. This is not learning for its own sake; rather, all leadership-development courses are linked to business objectives.[27] Thus, if a company's strategy is to provide high-quality customer service, it is likely to emphasize, for example, training in problem solving, conflict resolution, negotiation, and team building. If its objective is innovation, then topics such as technical training, effective communications, and–for managers–training in feedback and communication are more typical. Although the potential returns from well-conducted training programs are hefty, sound design and execution are necessary to realize these returns. The remainder of this chapter examines some key issues that managers need to consider. Let us begin by examining the broad phases that constitute training systems.

WHAT DETERMINES EFFECTIVE TRAINING?

Research shows that a number of factors affect training effectiveness.[28] For example, training success is determined not only by the quality of training but also by an individual's readiness for it and the degree of organizational support. Characteristics of the individual as well as the work environment are important influences before training (e.g., the motivation to participate), during training (by affecting learning), and after training (by influencing the transfer of learning and skills from the training situation to the job).

Admittedly some individual characteristics, such as trainability (i.e., the ability to learn the content of the training) and personality are difficult, if not impossible, for organizations to influence through policies and practices. The organization clearly can influence others, however, such as job or career attitudes, a person's belief that he or she can learn the content of the training successfully, the attractiveness of outcomes, and the work environment.[29]

ASSESSING TRAINING NEEDS AND DESIGNING TRAINING PROGRAMS

One way to keep in mind the phases of training is to portray them graphically, in the form of a model that illustrates the interaction among the phases. One such model is shown in Figure 9–1.

Figure 9–1

A general systems model of the training and development process. Note how information developed during the evaluation phase provides feedback, and therefore new input, to the assessment phase. This initiates a new cycle of assessment, training and development, and evaluation.

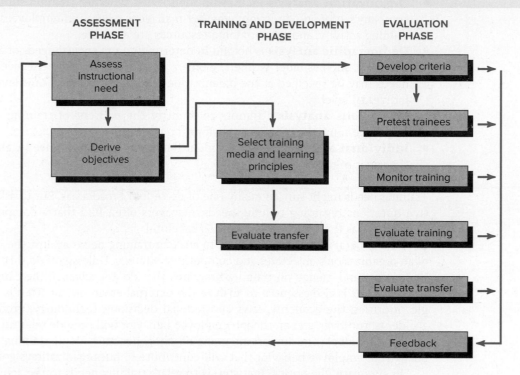

The **assessment (or planning) phase** serves as a foundation for the entire training effort. As Figure 9-1 shows, the **training and development phase** and the **evaluation phase** depend on inputs from assessment. The purpose of the assessment phase is to define what it is the employee should learn in relation to desired job behaviors. If this phase is not carefully done, the training program as a whole will have little chance of achieving what it is intended to do.

Assuming that managers specify the objectives of the training program carefully, the next task is to design the environment in which to achieve those objectives. This is the purpose of the training phase. Choose methods and techniques carefully and deliver them in a supportive, encouraging environment, based on sound principles of learning. More on this later.

Finally, if both the assessment phase and the training and development phase have been done competently, evaluation should present few problems. Evaluation is a twofold process that involves (1) establishing indicators of success in training as well as on the job and (2) determining exactly what job-related changes have occurred as a result of the training. If done well, evaluation provides a continuous stream of feedback that can be used to reassess training needs, thereby creating input for the next stage of employee development. Now that we have a broad overview of the training process, let us consider the elements of Figure 9-1 in greater detail.

Assessing Training Needs

The purpose of needs assessment is to determine if training is necessary. There are four levels of analysis for determining the needs that training can fulfill[30]:

- **Organization analysis** focuses on identifying whether training supports the company's strategic direction; whether managers, peers, and employees support training activity; and what training resources are available.
- **Demographic analysis** is helpful in determining the special needs of a particular group, such as older workers, women, or managers at different levels. Those needs may be specified at the organizational level, the business-unit level, or the individual level.
- **Operations analysis** attempts to identify the content of training—what an employee must do in order to perform competently.
- **Individual analysis** focuses on identifying employees who need training and the types of training they need.

Training needs might surface in any one of these four broad areas. But to ask productive questions regarding training needs, managers often find that a comprehensive model, such as that shown in Figure 9-2, is helpful.

At a general level, it is important to analyze training needs against the backdrop of an organization's objectives and competitive strategy. Unless you do this, you may waste time and money on training programs that do not advance the cause of the company.[31] It is also essential to analyze the external environment. Trends in strategic priorities, the economy, laws and judicial decisions, technology, productivity, accidents, turnover, and on-the-job employee behavior will provide relevant information at this level. The important question then becomes "Will training produce changes in employee behavior that will contribute to our organization's goals?"

In summary, the critical first step is to relate training needs to the achievement of key strategic business objectives. If you cannot make that connection, the training is probably unnecessary. However, if a training need does surface at the organizational level, a demographic analysis is the next step.

Demographic analysis provides information that may transcend particular jobs, even divisions, of an organization. With respect to managers, for example, level, function, and attitudes toward the usefulness of training all affect their self-reported training needs.[32] Taking this information into account lends additional perspective to the operations and person analyses to follow.

Operations analysis requires a careful examination of the work to be performed after training. It involves (1) a systematic collection of information that describes how work is done, (2) a determination of standards of performance for that work, (3) a description of how tasks are to be performed to meet the standards, and (4) a description of the competencies necessary for effective task performance. In fact, validated competency models can be very helpful in driving training curricula.[33] Job analyses, performance reviews, interviews with subject-matter experts (jobholders, supervisors, higher-level managers, even knowledgeable customers and suppliers), and analyses of operating problems (quality control, downtime reports, and customer complaints) all provide important inputs to the analysis of training needs.

Finally, there is individual analysis. Training needs often surface after comparing desired performance to an individual's actual performance. Performance standards, identified in the operations analysis phase, reflect desired performance. To compare

Figure 9–2

Training needs-assessment model.

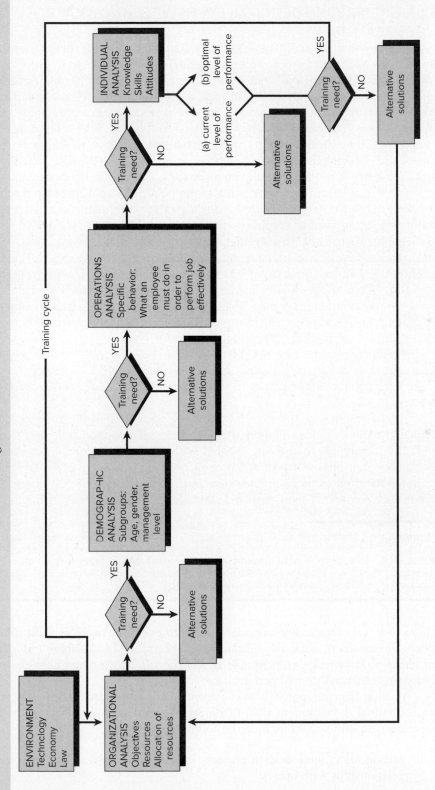

HR BUZZ

CLASSIC TRAINING DESIGN MEETS NEW TECHNOLOGY: BOEING'S 787 DREAMLINER*

Mechanics going through Boeing's 25-day training course for the 787 Dreamliner learn to fix all kinds of problems, from broken lights in the cabin to major malfunctions with flight controls. One thing they won't soon do is touch one of the planes while they are in training. Instead, using laptop and desktop computers inside a classroom with huge diagrams, the mechanics train on a system that displays an interactive 787 cockpit, as well as a 3-D exterior of the plane. Using a mouse, the mechanics "walk" around the jet, open virtual maintenance access panels, and go inside the plane to repair and replace parts. At the end of the course, the mechanics get all training materials on a tiny memory stick. Once they are in the field staring up at an actual Dreamliner, they will also use laptop PCs to diagnose and solve real problems with the planes. Boeing has already established eight Dreamliner training suites, including some in London, Seattle, Shanghai, Singapore, and Tokyo.

Boeing customer Japan Airlines (JAL) is developing training tools that use Microsoft's HoloLens technology. Images allow mechanics to experience a strikingly realistic environment using a pair of goggles hooked up to a nearby computer. A 3-D hologram image of a jet engine appears to hang suspended from the ceiling in the room. A student wearing HoloLenses may stand beside it and examine the engine up close and even take it apart, allowing the student to study its structure and connections to other nearby aircraft systems.

JAL mechanics can now see the inside of a Dreamliner 787 engine and take it apart without having to park and open up an aircraft. This technology could be a game-changer when it comes to training mechanics to fix the newest planes and engines.

Yes, Dreamliner training does use the latest whiz-bang technology, but don't be fooled into thinking that's all there is. Undergirding all of it is an extremely thorough, detailed training-needs analysis, coupled with careful consideration of alternative design and delivery options to optimize each trainee's learning. Given the time and expense incurred in training mechanics and pilots, Boeing and customers like JAL are using every one of these tools to maximize returns on their investments.

Sources: From P. Sanders, "Boeing 787 Training Takes Virtual Path," *The Wall Street Journal*, September 2, 2010, p. B8. Reproduced with permission of Dow Jones & Company via Copyright Clearance Center. McIntosh, A. (2016, Dec. 13). Japan Airlines explores Microsoft hologram technology to train Dreamliner mechanics. *Puget Sound Business Journal.* Retrieved from *www.bizjournals.com/seattle/news/2016/12/13/japan-airlines-explores-microsoft-hologram.html* on May 3, 2017.

those to actual performance, consider using ratings of employees by their supervisors, peers, or customers; objective indicators of performance (if available); and interviews, or tests (job knowledge, work sample, or situational). Training may help close the gap between actual and desired performance.

Another fruitful approach to the identification of individual training needs is an individual development plan (IDP). Such a plan provides a blueprint for self-development and should include the following:

1. *Statements of aims*—desired changes in knowledge, skills, attitudes, values, or relationships with others.

2. *Definitions*–areas of study, search, reflection, or testing, including lists of activities, experiences, or questions that can help achieve these aims.
3. *Ideas about priorities*–what should be learned first.

Individuals often construct their own IDPs, with assistance, in career-planning workshops, as they develop objectives for their work, or in assessment centers.

As a result of needs assessment, it should be possible to determine what workers do, what knowledge, skills, and abilities (KSAs) are essential to do what they do effectively, and what type of learning and instructional content are necessary to acquire those KSAs.[34] This information should guide all future choices about training methods and evaluation strategies.

Once training needs have been identified, the next step is to structure the training environment for maximum learning. Careful attention to the fundamental principles of learning will enhance this process.

PRINCIPLES THAT ENHANCE LEARNING

To promote efficient learning, long-term retention, and application of the skills or factual information learned in training to the job situation, training programs should incorporate the principles of learning developed over the past century. Which principles should they consider? It depends on whether the trainees are learning skills (e.g., drafting) or factual material (e.g., principles of life insurance).[35]

To be most effective, *skill learning* should include four essential ingredients: (1) goal setting, (2) behavior modeling, (3) practice, and (4) feedback. However, when the focus is on *learning facts*, the sequence should change slightly: (1) goal setting, (2) meaningfulness of material, (3) practice, and (4) feedback. Let's consider each of these in greater detail.

Motivating the Trainee: Goal Setting

A person who wants to develop herself or himself will do so; a person who wants to be developed rarely is. This statement illustrates the role that motivation plays in training–to learn, you must want to learn. Although cognitive ability predicts training success, so also does motivation. Conscientiousness (striving for excellence, having high standards of performance, setting challenging personal goals) and internal locus of control (belief that one controls one's own fate) are important determinants of motivation to learn. So also are the climate in which the trainee functions, and the support he or she receives from supervisor and peers.[36]

Perhaps the most effective way to raise a trainee's motivation is by setting goals. More than 500 studies have demonstrated goal setting's proven track record of success in improving employee performance in a variety of settings and cultures.[37] On average, goal setting leads to a 10 percent improvement in productivity, and it works best with tasks of low complexity.[38]

Goal theory is founded on the premise that an individual's conscious goals or intentions regulate her or his behavior.[39] Research indicates that once an individual accepts a goal and is committed to achieving it, difficult but attainable goals result in higher levels of performance than do easy goals or even a generalized goal such as "do your best."[40] These findings have three important implications for motivating trainees:

1. Make the objectives of the training program clear at the outset.
2. Set goals that are challenging and difficult enough that the trainees can derive personal satisfaction from achieving them, but not so difficult that they are perceived as impossible to reach.
3. Supplement the ultimate goal of finishing the program with subgoals during training, such as trainer evaluations, work-sample tests, and periodic quizzes. As trainees clear each hurdle successfully, their confidence about attaining the ultimate goal increases.

Although goal setting clearly affects trainees' motivation, so also do the expectations of the trainer. In fact, expectations have a way of becoming self-fulfilling prophecies, so that the higher the expectations, the better the trainees perform. Conversely, the lower the expectations, the worse the trainees perform. This phenomenon of the self-fulfilling prophecy is known as the **Pygmalion effect**. Legend has it that Pygmalion, a king of Cyprus, sculpted an ivory statue of a maiden named Galatea. Pygmalion fell in love with the statue, and, at his prayer, Aphrodite, the goddess of love and beauty, gave it life. Pygmalion's fondest wish–his expectation–came true.

Behavior Modeling

Much of what we learn is acquired by observing others. We will imitate other people's actions when they lead to desirable outcomes (e.g., promotions, increased sales, or more accurate tennis serves). The models' actions serve as a cue as to what constitutes appropriate behavior.[41] A model is someone who is seen as competent, powerful, and friendly and has high status within an organization. We try to identify with this model because her or his behavior is seen as desirable and appropriate. **Behavior modeling** tends to increase when the model is rewarded for behavior and when the rewards (e.g., influence, pay) are things the imitator would like to have. In the context of training (or coaching or teaching), we attempt to maximize trainees' identification with a model. To do this well, research suggests the following:

1. Portray the behaviors to be modeled clearly and in detail. Provide the trainees a list of key behaviors to attend to when observing the model and allow them to express the behaviors in language that is most comfortable for them. For example, supervisors learning how to coach employees received the following list of key behaviors[42]: (1) Focus on the problem, not on the person, (2) ask for employees' ideas on how to solve it, (3) listen openly, (4) agree on the steps that each of you will take to solve the problem, and (5) plan a follow-up date.
2. Rank the behaviors to be modeled in a sequence from least to most difficult, and be sure the trainees observe lots of repetitions of the behaviors being modeled.
3. Finally, have several models portray the behaviors, not just one.[43]

A large body of research demonstrates the effectiveness of behavior modeling in learning facts and procedures, as well as in changing behavior on the job.[44] It is particularly appropriate for teaching interpersonal and computer skills.[45] To a large extent, this is because behavior modeling overcomes one of the shortcomings of earlier approaches to training: telling instead of showing.

PYGMALION IN ACTION: MANAGERS GET THE KIND OF PERFORMANCE THEY EXPECT

To test the Pygmalion effect and to examine the impact of instructors' prior expectations about trainees on their subsequent style of leadership toward the trainees, a field experiment was conducted at a military training base.[a] In a 15-week combat-command course, 105 trainees were matched on aptitude and assigned randomly to one of three experimental groups. Each group corresponded to a particular level of expectation that was communicated to the instructors: high, average, or none (due to insufficient information). Four days before the trainees arrived at the base, the instructors were given a score (known as command potential, or CP) for each trainee that represented the trainee's potential to command others. The instructors were told that the CP score had been developed on the basis of psychological test scores, data from a previous course on leadership, and ratings by previous commanders. The instructors were also told that course grades predict CP in 95 percent of the cases. The instructors were then given a list of the trainees assigned to them, along with their CPs, and asked to copy each trainee's CP into his or her personal record. The instructors were also requested to learn their trainees' names and their CPs before the beginning of the course.

The Pygmalion hypothesis that the instructor's prior expectation influences the trainee's performance was confirmed. Trainees of whom instructors expected better performance scored significantly higher on objective achievement tests, exhibited more positive attitudes, and were perceived as better leaders. In fact, the prior expectations of the instructors explained 73 percent of the variability in the trainees' performance, 66 percent in their attitudes, and 28 percent in leadership. The lesson is unmistakable: Trainers (and managers) get the kind of performance they expect. This is not an isolated instance. The Pygmalion effect has been confirmed in many studies, using both male and female trainees.[b]

[a]Eden, D., and Shani, A. B. (1982). Pygmalion goes to boot camp: Expectancy, leadership, and trainee performance. *Journal of Applied Psychology* 67, pp. 194-99.

[b]Heslin, P. A., and Caprar, D. V. (2013). Goals and self-efficacy as mediators. In E. A. Locke and G. P. Latham (Eds.), *New Developments in Goal Setting and Task Performance*. New York: Routledge, pp. 213-30. Begley, S. (2003, Nov. 7). Expectations may alter outcomes far more than we realize. *The Wall Street Journal*, p. B1.

Meaningfulness of the Material

It's easier to learn and remember factual material when it is meaningful. **Meaningfulness** refers to material that is rich in associations for the trainees and is therefore easily understood by them. To structure material to maximize its meaningfulness,

1. Provide an overview of the material to be presented. Seeing the overall picture helps trainees understand how program units fit together and how each unit contributes to the overall training objectives.[46]
2. To clarify and reinforce key learning points, present the material by using examples, terms, and concepts that are familiar to the trainees. Show them how to use the content of the training to do their jobs better.
3. As complex intellectual skills are invariably made up of simpler ones, teach the simpler skills before the complex ones.[47] This is true whether teaching accounting, computer programming, or X-ray technology.

Practice (Makes Perfect)

Anyone learning a new skill or acquiring factual knowledge must have an opportunity to practice what he or she is learning.[48] **Practice**, the active use of training content, has three aspects: active practice, overlearning, and the length of the practice session. Let's consider each of these.

- *Active practice.* During the early stages of learning, the trainer should be available to oversee the trainee's practice directly. Traditional approaches focus on teaching correct methods (and avoiding errors), but a newer approach, known as error-management training, encourages trainees to make errors, then to engage in reflection to understand why they made them, and to develop strategies to avoid repeating them.[49]
- *Overlearning.* When trainees are given the opportunity to practice far beyond the point where they have performed a task correctly several times, the task becomes second nature and is "overlearned." **Overlearning** is critical[50] for tasks that must be performed infrequently and under great stress–for example, performing CPR on a patient who is not breathing. It is less important in types of work where an individual practices his or her skills on a daily basis (e.g., auto mechanics, electronics technicians).
- *Length of the practice session.* Suppose you have only 1 week to memorize the lines of a play, and during that week, you have only 12 hours available to practice. What schedule is best? Should you practice 2 hours a day for 6 days, 6 hours each of the final 2 days before the deadline, or some other schedule? The two extremes represent **distributed practice** (which implies rest intervals between sessions) and **massed practice** (in which the practice sessions are crowded together). Although there are exceptions, most of the research evidence indicates that for the same amount of practice, learning is better when practice is distributed rather than massed.[51]

Constructive feedback facilitates learning and supports a trainee's desire to perform well.
Echo/Getty Images

Feedback

Feedback is a form of information about one's attempts to improve. It is essential both for learning and for trainee motivation.[52] If trainees are to understand what leads to good as well as poor performance, however, the specificity of the feedback should vary.[53] Specific feedback benefits the learning of responses for good performance, but it may not help the learning of responses for poor performance. For example, in learning to operate a piece of equipment, less specific feedback may cause trainees to make errors that lead to problems, providing them with opportunities to learn which behaviors lead to problems, and how to fix them. Feedback affects team, as well as individual, performance.[54] Thus, application of performance-based feedback in a small fast-food store over a 1-year period led to a 15 percent decrease in food costs and a 193 percent increase in profits.[55]

To have the greatest impact, provide feedback as soon as possible after the trainee demonstrates good performance, especially to novices.[56] It need not be instantaneous, but there should be no confusion regarding exactly what the trainee did and the trainer's reaction to it. Feedback need not always be positive, but it will have the highest impact if provided by the trainee's immediate supervisor. In fact, if the supervisor does not reinforce what is learned in training, the training will be transferred ineffectively to the job—if at all.

Transfer of Training

Transfer of training refers to the extent to which competencies learned in training can be applied on the job. Transfer may be positive (i.e., it enhances job performance), negative (i.e., it hampers job performance), or neutral. Long-term training or retraining probably includes segments that contain all three of these conditions. Training that results in negative transfer is costly in two ways—the cost of the training (which proved to be useless) and the cost of hampered performance. To maximize positive transfer, do the following things before, during, and after training[57]:

1. Maximize the similarity between the training situation and the job situation. To encourage participation, use interactive activities.
2. Provide trainees as much experience as possible with the tasks, concepts, or skills being taught, so that they can deal with situations that do not fit textbook examples exactly.[58]
3. Provide a strong link between training content and job content ("What you learn in training today, you'll use on the job tomorrow").
4. In the context of team-based training, ensure that teams have open, unrestricted access to information; that the membership includes a variety of job functions and administrative backgrounds; and that the team can draw upon more members to accomplish its activities.[59]
5. Ensure that what is learned in training is used and rewarded on the job. Supervisors and peers are key gatekeepers in this process. If immediate supervisors or peers, by their words or by their example, do not support what was learned in training, don't expect the training to have much of an impact on job performance.[60]

Action learning, in which participants focus on real business problems in order to learn through experience and application, is an excellent vehicle for facilitating positive transfer from learning to doing.[61] It's not just for executives, either, as the HR Buzz box ("Action Learning at UPS") illustrates.

HR BUZZ

ACTION LEARNING AT UPS*

When UPS, affectionately known as "Big Brown," found that some 30 percent of its twenty-something driver candidates were flunking its traditional driver training, it had a serious problem on its hands: how to train Generation Y for a hard blue-collar job. Gen Yers make up more than 60 percent of the part-time loader workforce, from which it draws the majority of new-driver hires. To address the issue head on, UPS created a whole new approach.

UPS opened its first full-service training center, in Landover, Maryland. The 11,500-square-foot facility, known as Integrad, is much like a movie set, and it's aimed directly at young would-be drivers. It is fashioned around an approach known as "technology-enhanced, hands-on learning," or "teach me, show me, let me." Drivers learn UPS driving and service methods, they are shown how the methods work, and then they practice them in a realistic, hands-on fashion. UPS Integrad training uses a mixture of 3-D computer simulations, Webcast learning modules, and traditional classroom instruction to complement activity in a controlled environment in order to reinforce safety, delivery, and customer-service training. UPS's integrated delivery network requires a single driver to handle all types of packages—air, ground, domestic, international, commercial, and residential.

Odd-size packages and cramped space can make the UPS driver's job difficult.

Andrew Resek/McGraw-Hill Education

John Flournoy/McGraw-Hill Education

Sources: UPS Integrad driver training facility opens in Cologne, Germany. (2016, June 7). Retrieved from *www.pressroom.ups.com/pressroom/ContentDetailsViewer.page?ConceptType=PressReleases &id=1465302219941-350* on May 4, 2017. Levitz, J. (2010, Apr. 6). UPS thinks outside the box on driver training. *The Wall Street Journal*, pp. B1, B2.

There are many aspects to the rigorous training that UPS provides, but consider just one of those, the transparent UPS "package car." The car is stocked with rows of (weighted) packages. It may look like a big toy, but its purpose is serious. Package selection is the most fundamental part of a UPS driver's job, and yet it can seem impossible when you are staring into the gaping back door of a package car, scrambling to locate your five packages and trying to decide how you are going to get them out in the 65.5 seconds that the company's "human engineering" experts have allotted to you.

When learning package-selection techniques, demonstration in an actual package car is a lot more effective than a lecture: Watching an instructor deal with the same shelving system, odd-size packages, and cramped space that drivers have on the road—and then getting to try it yourself before your first trip out—proves invaluable.

Actual driving at Integrad is done at a mini-town that has real street and stop signs, a toy house and toy stores, a UPS dropbox, and even a loading dock. Tasks increase in difficulty, and facilitators and fellow trainees stand in as customers to test the drivers on their customer service.

Driver candidates also play a videogame that places them in the driver's seat and has them identify obstacles. They progress from computer simulations to "Clarksville," an artificial village of miniature houses and businesses on the property where they drive a real truck and must successfully execute five deliveries in 19 minutes.

Driver training is critical for UPS. More than 7,500 drivers and 1,500 driver supervisors have completed UPS Integrad training at the seven existing U.S. training locations. Has its high-tech approach to training worked? Before Integrad, 30 percent of driver trainees failed to complete the training, which takes a total of 6 weeks overall and includes 30 days driving a truck in the real world. Today the failure rate is only 10 percent. Action learning virtually ensures high positive transfer to the job, and the reduction in the failure rate is a huge win for the company, its drivers, and the customers it serves.

Team Training

Up to this point, we have been discussing training and development as an individual enterprise. Yet today, as we have noted, there is an increasing emphasis on *team* performance, with almost 90 percent of corporations worldwide using teams of one sort or another.[62] For example, cross-functional teams, intact or virtual, are common features of many organizations. A **team** is a group of individuals who are working together, with shared responsibility, toward a common goal. It is this common goal that really defines a team, and if team members have opposite or conflicting goals, the efficiency of the total unit is likely to suffer.[63] For example, consider the effects on a basketball team when one of the players *always* tries to score, regardless of the team's situation.

Although many different models of teamwork exist, effective teams share seven characteristics: *cooperation* (collective beliefs that they can succeed, strong team orientation), *coordination* (members ask, "What can I do to help you?"), *communication* (information protocol and clarity), *cognition* (clear roles and team norms), *coaching* (team leaders promote and share ground rules), *conflict* (to resolve it, teams have psychological safety granted by leaders), and *conditions* (team members have ready access to resources and information).[64]

A systematic approach to team training should include four steps[65]:

1. *Conduct a team-training needs analysis.* Such an analysis has two objectives: (a) to identify interdependencies among team members and the skills required to coordinate team tasks and (b) to develop knowledge of team-member roles and responsibilities).

2. *Develop training objectives that address both task-work and teamwork skills.* In general, effective teams demonstrate adaptability, shared awareness of situations, performance monitoring and feedback, leadership/team management, interpersonal skills, coordination, communication, and decision-making skills. Effective teams also share beliefs about the importance of teamwork skills, placing the team's goals above those of individual members, mutual trust, and shared vision.[66] Sequence the training so that trainees can master task-work skills before learning teamwork skills.

3. *Design exercises and training events based on the objectives from step 2.* Opportunities for guided practice and constructive feedback are particularly important for team training. They may include, for example, **team-coordination training** (focusing on teamwork skills that facilitate information exchange, cooperation, and coordination of job-related behaviors); **cross-training** (providing exposure to and practice with other teammates' tasks, roles, and responsibilities in an effort to increase shared understanding and knowledge among team members); and **guided team self-correction** (providing guidance to team members in reviewing team events, identifying errors, exchanging feedback, and developing plans for the future).

4. *Design measures of team effectiveness based on the objectives from step 2, evaluate the effectiveness of the team training, and use this information to guide future team training.*

Other research has revealed two broad principles regarding the composition and management of teams. First, individual skills are a necessary, but not sufficient, condition for effective team performance.[67] Individual training and development are still important, but only a partial solution because interactions among team members must also be addressed. This interaction is what makes team training unique—it always uses some form of simulation or real-life practice, and it always focuses on the interaction of team members, equipment, and work procedures.[68]

Second, managers of effective work groups tend to monitor the performance of their team members regularly, and they provide frequent feedback to them. This is as true of traditional teams as it is of virtual teams.[69] In fact, as much as 35 percent of the variability in team performance can be explained by the frequency of the use of monitors and consequences. Incorporating these findings into the training of team members and their managers should lead to better overall team performance.

Selecting Training Methods

New training methods appear every year. Whereas some are well founded in learning theory or models of behavior change (e.g., behavior modeling), others result more from technological than theoretical developments (e.g., presentation software, use of animation and sound, computer-based business simulations).

ETHICAL DILEMMA
Anger Management: Whose Responsibility Is It?*

Workplace stress is high these days, given the fact that many employers have reduced the size of their workforces, instituted pay cuts, or imposed furloughs. Often, remaining employees are saddled with increased workloads. As one expert put it, "Anger comes in two flavors: hot and cold contempt. Hot contempt is what we traditionally think of as anger: red face and bulging veins. But 90 percent of workplace anger is cold contempt: gossip, back-stabbing, withdrawal, simmering resentment, and the desire to see others fail." Either type of anger can cost a company in terms of lost productivity and higher health premiums. Should supervisors and higher-level managers be responsible for dealing with the anger issues of those who report to them? Some might argue that it is unreasonable to expect anyone other than a highly credentialed and experienced provider, schooled in clinical psychology, counseling, or medicine, to be able to deal effectively with issues like that. What do you think?

Source: Tyler, K. (2010, May). Helping employees cool it. *HRMagazine* 55(4), pp. 53–55.

To choose the training method (or combination of methods) that best fits a given situation, *first define carefully what you wish to teach.* That is the purpose of the needs-assessment phase. Only then can you choose a method that best fits these requirements. To be useful, the method should meet the minimal

As part of training in team building, a team of would-be chefs prepares a course for dinner, but without a recipe.
Don Hammond/Design Pics

conditions needed for effective learning to take place; that is, the training method should

- Motivate the trainee to improve his or her performance.
- Clearly illustrate desired skills.
- Allow the trainee to participate actively.
- Provide an opportunity to practice.
- Provide timely feedback on the trainee's performance.
- Provide reinforcement while the trainee learns, e.g., through automated, personalized conversations or chatbots that provide reminders, track goals, assess transfer, and support continued performance.[70]
- Be structured from simple to complex tasks.
- Be adaptable to specific problems.
- Encourage positive transfer from the training to the job.

As a manager, these are the kinds of questions you should be asking about any training program—that is, "Does it motivate the trainees?" "Does it clearly illustrate desired skills," and so forth.

EVALUATING TRAINING PROGRAMS

To evaluate training, you must systematically document the outcomes of the training in terms of how trainees actually behave back on their jobs and the relevance of that behavior to the objectives of the organization.[71] To assess the utility or value of training, we seek answers to questions such as the following:

1. Have trainees achieved a specific level of skill, knowledge, or performance?
2. Did change occur?
3. Is the change due to training?
4. Is the change positively related to the achievement of organizational goals?
5. Will similar changes occur with new participants in the same training program?[72]

In evaluating training programs, one could measure outcomes such as the reaction of trainees, what they have learned, how their behavior on the job has changed, or organizational results, such as reductions in costs, increases in sales, or improvements in quality.[73] A more complete framework, however, matches targets of evaluation (training content and design, changes in learners, and organizational payoffs) with data-collection methods (e.g., to assess changes in learners, use written tests, work samples, interviews, surveys). Figure 9-3 presents a model that illustrates these concepts. Targets and methods depend on the focus of the evaluation. For example, with respect to changes in learners, the focus might be on cognitive, affective, or behavioral changes. Finally, targets, focus, and methods are linked to the purpose of the evaluation—feedback (to trainers or learners), decision making, and marketing.

Consider organizational payoffs, for example. The focus might be on transfer of training (e.g., management support, opportunity to perform, on-the-job behavior change), on results (performance effectiveness or innovation),[74] or on the financial impact of the training (e.g., through measures of return on investment or utility analysis).

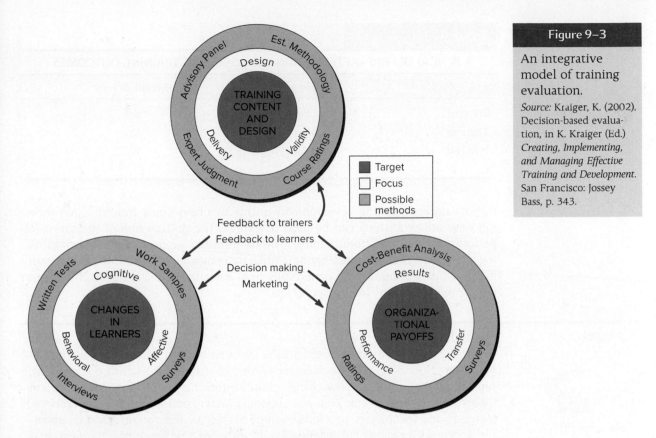

Figure 9–3

An integrative model of training evaluation.
Source: Kraiger, K. (2002). Decision-based evaluation, in K. Kraiger (Ed.) *Creating, Implementing, and Managing Effective Training and Development.* San Francisco: Jossey Bass, p. 343.

ADDITIONAL CONSIDERATIONS IN MEASURING THE OUTCOMES OF TRAINING

Regardless of the measures used, our goal is to be able to make meaningful inferences and to rule out alternative explanations for results (e.g., job experience, outside economic events, changes in supervision or performance incentives). To do so, it is important to administer the measures according to some logical plan or procedure (experimental design) (e.g., before and after training as well as to a comparable control group).

To rule out these rival explanations for the changes that occurred, it is essential to design a plan for evaluation that includes *before* and *after* measurement of the trained group's performance relative to that of one or more untrained control groups. (However, when it is relatively costly to bring participants to an evaluation and administration costs are particularly high, after-only measurement of trained and untrained groups is best.)[75] Match members of the untrained control group as closely as possible to those in the trained group. Table 9-1 shows a standard design for such a study. If the outcomes of the training are positive, the untrained control group at time 1 may become the trained group at a later time. It is important to note that the post-training appraisal of performance should not be done sooner than 3 months (or more) following the training, so that the trainees have an opportunity to put into practice what they have learned.

Finally, the impact of training on organizational results is the most significant, but most difficult, effect to demonstrate. *Measures of results are the bottom line of*

Table 9–1		
A TYPICAL BEFORE–AFTER DESIGN FOR ASSESSING TRAINING OUTCOMES		
	Trained group	**Untrained group**
Pretest	Yes	Yes
Training	Yes	No
Post-test	Yes	Yes

training success. Exciting developments in this area have come from research showing how utility analysis can be used to express the dollar value of improved job performance resulting from training.[76] Utility formulas are now available for evaluating the dollar value of a single training program compared to a control group, a training program re-administered periodically (e.g., annually), and a comparison between two or more different training programs.

HR BUZZ

Does It Pay Off?

EXECUTIVE COACHING

External coaches are often used to help talented executives who are in trouble because of behavioral or style deficiencies, or to help them lead critical transitions, such as having to lead a major change effort. Unfortunately, practice is far ahead of theory and research in this area, and there is a lack of consensus about definitions, methods, and techniques. In addition, there are no barriers to entry and no generally accepted standards for certification. In terms of coaching's effectiveness, it is difficult to identify causal connections between specific actions and outcomes like strategy execution and change management because the coaching process unfolds over a relatively long period of time.[a]

That said, executive coaching has the following characteristics. It is

- One-on-one.
- Relationship based.
- Methodology based (draws on specific tools and techniques as part of a relatively structured overall process).
- Provided by a professional coach.
- Scheduled in multiple sessions over time.
- Goal oriented for both organizational and individual benefits.
- Customized to the person.
- Intended to enhance the person's ability to learn and develop independently.[b]

The best coaching is aligned with an organization's overall talent-management strategy. It includes a clear understanding of talent and development needs, tools

---

[a]Vandaveer, V. V. (2017). Executive coaching. In S. G. Rogelberg (Ed.), *The Sage Encyclopedia of Industrial and Organizational Psychology* (2nd ed., Vol. 1). Thousand Oaks, CA: Sage, pp. 451-55. Peterson, D. B. (2011). Executive coaching: A critical review and recommendations for advancing the practice. In S. Zedeck (Ed.), *Handbook of Industrial and Organizational Psychology* (Vol. 2). Washington, DC: American Psychological Association, pp. 527 66.

[b]Ibid.

that might be used (including coaching), and a method for matching talent needs with appropriate solutions.

Does coaching work? A review of four studies revealed an average return on investment (ROI) of five to seven times its cost. There is reason to be skeptical, however, because it is extremely difficult to estimate accurately the future financial value of any capabilities acquired through coaching. Another study found five main areas of improvement: people management, relationships with managers, goal setting and prioritization, personal productivity and engagement at work, and communications with colleagues.[c]

Executive coaching incorporates multiple techniques already shown to be effective in learning. These include goal setting; feedback; accountability; behavioral practice; communicating performance expectations; enhancing self-efficacy; reflection; and establishing a trusting, supportive relationship.[d]

Coaching also improves managers' use of 360-degree feedback by helping them set specific goals for improvement and solicit ideas for improvement. Those actions lead to improved performance.[e]

Remember, not all coaches are equally proficient in what they do, and not every executive is equally likely to change from coaching.[f] The best coaches are empathetic, supportive, practical, and self-confident but do not appear to know all the answers or tell others what to do. To be receptive to coaching, employees need to be open-minded and interested, not defensive and closed-minded. Both parties must be willing to take risks in the relationship. To evaluate a prospective coach, consider asking questions such as the following.

- With whom have you worked, in what types of organizations and jobs, and at what levels?
- What processes do you build in to ensure that you get results?
- What kind of assessment will we go through to focus on the right things for me?
- What is your approach to help me learn new things?
- How can we know we have achieved what we set out to achieve?
- Whom would you turn down, and why?[g]

---

[c]Kombarakaran, F. A., Yang, J. A., Baker, M. N., and Fernandes, P. B. (2008). Executive coaching: It works! *Consulting Psychology Journal: Practice and Research* 60, pp. 78–90.

[d]Peterson (2011), op. cit.

[e]Smither, J. M., London, M., Flautt, R., Vargas, Y., and Kucine, L. (2003). Can working with an executive coach improve multisource ratings over time? A quasiexperimental field study. *Personnel Psychology* 56, pp. 23–44.

[f]Ibid.

[g]Tyler, K. (2000, June). Scoring big in the workplace. *HR*, pp. 96–106.

NEW-EMPLOYEE ORIENTATION: THE ON-BOARDING PROCESS

Orientation of new employees is a one-time event, welcoming them to the company and its culture. **On-boarding** is a series of events (including orientation) that helps them understand how to be successful in their day-to-day job and how their work contributes to the overall business. Because most turnover occurs during the first few months on the job (at Marriott, 40 percent of the new employees who leave do so during the first 3 months),[77] failure to provide thorough orientation and on-boarding can be a very expensive mistake.[78]

One definition of **orientation** is "familiarization with and adaptation to a situation or an environment." Among large employers in North America, 77 percent of their orientation and on-boarding programs last 3 months or less and 38 percent last only a week.[79] This is woefully inadequate, often little more than just a superficial indoctrination into company philosophy, policies, and rules; sometimes it includes the presentation of an employee handbook and a quick tour of the office or plant. This can be costly.

Going to work at a new company is not unlike visiting a foreign country. Either you are told about the local customs or you learn them on your own by a process of trial and error. An effective orientation and on-boarding program can help lessen the impact of this shock. The payoff? Higher levels of job satisfaction and commitment, along with reduced levels of employee turnover and a deeper understanding of a firm's goals, values, history, and people.[80]

The cost of recruiting, hiring, and training a new person is far higher than most of us realize. For example, Merck & Co., the pharmaceutical giant, found that—depending on the job—turnover costs are 1.5 to 2.5 times the annual salary paid for the job.[81] Moreover, because the turnover rate among new college hires can be as great as 50 percent during the first 12 months, such costs can be considerable.

A new employee's experiences during the initial period with an organization can have a major impact on his or her career. A new hire stands on the boundary of the organization—certainly no longer an outsider but not yet embraced by those within. There is great stress. The new hire wants to reduce this stress by becoming incorporated into the "interior" as quickly as possible. Consequently, during this period an employee is more receptive to cues to proper behavior than she or he is ever likely to be again. Such cues may come from a variety of sources, for example,

- Official literature of the organization.
- Examples set by senior people.
- Formal instructions given by senior people.
- Examples given by peers.
- Rewards and punishments that flow from the employee's efforts.
- Responses to the employee's ideas.
- Degree of challenge in the assignments the employee receives.

New employees are information rich but experience poor, eager to apply their knowledge to new processes and problems. Here are three typical problems that face every new employee:

1. *Problems in entering a group.* The new employee asks herself whether she will (a) be acceptable to the other group members, (b) be liked, and (c) be safe—that is, free from physical and psychological harm. These issues must be resolved before she can feel comfortable and productive in the new situation.
2. *Naïve expectations.* Organizations find it much easier to communicate factual information about pay and benefits, vacations, and company policies than information about **employee norms** (rules or guides to acceptable behavior),

company attitudes, or "what it really takes to get ahead around here." Yet employees ought to be told about these intangibles. The bonus is that being up front and honest with them produces positive results. As we saw in Chapter 7, the research on realistic job previews (RJPs) indicates that job acceptance rates will likely be lower for those who receive an RJP, but job survival rates will be higher.[82]

3. *First-job environment.* Does it help or hinder the new employee trying to climb aboard? Can peers be counted on to support the new employee? How and why was the first job assignment chosen? Is it clear to the new employee what she or he can expect to get out of it?

To appreciate the kinds of problems a new employee faces, consider how Dave Savchetz, plant manager of Ford Motor Company's Kansas City, Missouri, factory, described his first day on the job 20 years earlier[83]:

It was a shock. To be honest, it was pretty traumatic. You got hired in this group of 30 people you've never met, and you sign a form, and the foreman comes in, and you walk out into this factory. And it's just the first time, you know? Things are moving, and you just look around, and you go, "What's going on here?" Quite frankly, the first day I got lost.

In fact, the first year with an organization is the critical period during which an employee will or will not learn to become a high performer. The careful matching of company and employee expectations during this period can result in positive job attitudes and high standards, which then can be reinforced in new and more demanding jobs.

PLANNING, PACKAGING, AND EVALUATING AN ON-BOARDING PROGRAM

Typically, some time will elapse between the acceptance of a job and the actual start date. That is a good time to begin the orientation and on-boarding process. Send the new hire a pre-boarding packet that includes e-signature software and a customized portal to complete essential digital forms, to learn about teammates, and to begin developing short-term goals before the first day on the job. AI-driven virtual agents can answer commonly asked questions. Such a portal can customize workflows to match the organization's orientation needs and send automated reminders to ensure that on-boarding tasks are completed on time.[84] After an experience like that, the new employee probably feels extremely welcome and will be quite comfortable during the first day on the job.

At a broad level, new employees need specific information in the following areas[85]:

- Policies and culture—benefits (including self-service portals), standards, expectations, goals, history, politics (information about formal and informal power structures), and language (knowledge of the organization's acronyms, slang, and jargon).

- Social behavior, such as dress codes, approved conduct, the atmosphere at work, and getting to know fellow workers and supervisors.
- Technical aspects of the job so that the employees can become proficient and perform well.

Some employers now offer a rich online orientation experience. For example, technology vendor NCR Corp. established a year-long on-boarding program based on a web portal derived from Taleo's Transitions solution and integrated with Taleo's applicant-tracking system. NCR developed a virtual orientation to allow new hires to interact with one another with built-in social-networking capabilities tied to a virtual learning platform, CorpU. Managers can assign an on-boarding plan for each new hire, track his or her progress, and solicit feedback about the individual's performance. HR and marketing staff worked together to make the portal appealing and fun, as well as to ensure a consistent branded experience for all employees.[86]

Before their first day at Oracle, new employees receive a "Welcome to Oracle" e-magazine with a message from leaders, information about Oracle, values and opportunities that await them when they join, and stories from employees around the world. After their first day, they can link to the new-hire team for any questions, an internal social media channel to begin networking, and a website with a new-hire checklist for the first day, week, and month at the job. The checklist includes links to important videos and policy documents to review, and each item can be checked off as it is completed.[87]

We know from other companies' mistakes what works and what does not. For example, consider the infographic below, "The First 90 Days."

Orientation/On-Boarding Follow-Up

The worst mistake a company can make is to ignore the new employee after the first week or so on the job. Rather, have one-on-one follow-up questions at 30-, 60-, and 90-day intervals. Here are just three questions at each interval.[88] 30 days: What do you like about the job and organization so far? Have you faced any surprises since joining us? Is there anything you don't understand about your job or the organization now that you've had a month with us? At 60 days: Can you see how your job relates to the organization and its mission? Do you have all of the resources you need to do your job well? Does your supervisor offer constructive criticism? Finally, at 90 days ask, Have you had any uncomfortable situations with supervisors, coworkers, or customers? Are your ideas and suggestions valued? What can we do to make our on-boarding process stronger? Does on-boarding pay off? Yes, because 69 percent of employees are more likely to stay with their companies for at least 3 years if they experienced great on-boarding.[89]

Evaluating On-Boarding

At least once a year, review the orientation/on-boarding process to determine if it is meeting its objectives and to identify future improvements. To improve it, you need candid, comprehensive feedback from everyone involved. There are several ways to provide this kind of feedback: through roundtable discussions with new employees after their first year on the job, through in-depth interviews with randomly selected employees and supervisors, and through questionnaires for mass coverage of all recent hires. Now let's consider some important lessons that any company can use.

THE FIRST 90 DAYS

HR BUZZ

How to Make the First 3 Months Successful for a New Employee

Prior to Start:
- Create a welcome packet! Tell new employees when their first day will start and where they should go. Let them know about their upcoming orientation and inform them of any paperwork they need to bring (i.e., W-4, driver's license, passport, etc.)
- Create a workspace for the new employee. Whether it's a new office or a cubicle, a new employee will need basics, like a computer, network access, email, a phone, and even pens.

Week 1
- Make sure someone is available to greet and show the new employee around. No one wants to be kept waiting at the front door.
- Provide an introductory information packet that includes a directory, handbook, and company calendar.
- Arrange to have the employee's photo taken for their ID.
- Assign a mentor for the new employee.
- Arrange lunch; whether a group or just the boss takes the employee out to eat, don't let the new employee feel too lonely the first day.
- Ask the new employee to write a brief "About Me" to share with the rest of the team.

Week 2
- Discuss goals.
- Schedule time for the employee to meet with people in other departments that they'll be working closely with.
- Host a gathering for the employee to socialize with the rest of the team.

Week 3
- Make sure a manager stops by regularly to check in with the employee to answer any questions.
- Assess how the employee is doing in terms of adapting and picking up on the job.

Week 4
- Have the employee complete a survey about their first month.
- Revisit the goal and get the employee working on both short- and long-term projects.

Five to Six Weeks
- Keep having conversations with the employee. Are they happy? Overwhelmed? Still transitioning?

Three Months
- Organize a three-month review to discuss the employee's performance and discuss the next steps.
- Discuss the employee's successes and initial failures.
- Ask the employee if there are any areas that they see the department or company needing to improve.

° *Source:* SHRM. (2015, Dec.–2016, Jan.). The first 90 days: Help new employees start out on the right foot. *HRMagazine* 60(10), p. 27.

LESSONS LEARNED

Based on established research findings, as well as the recent experiences of a number of companies, we offer the following considerations to guide the process of orienting and on-boarding new employees. They apply to any type of organization, large or small, and to any function or level of job.[90]

1. The impressions formed by new employees within their first 60 to 90 days on a job are lasting.
2. Day one is crucial—new employees remember it for years. It must be managed well.
3. New employees are interested in learning about the total organization—and how they and their unit fit into the big picture. This is just as important as is specific information about their own jobs and departments. For example, new employees at Corning go through an intranet scavenger hunt that requires them to use information learned during orientation and to demonstrate that they are comfortable with using the company's intranet system.
4. Give new employees major responsibility for their own guided self-learning, with direction and support.
5. Avoid information overload—provide it in reasonable amounts.
6. Recognize that community, social, and family adjustment is a critical aspect of on-boarding for new employees.
7. Make the immediate supervisor ultimately responsible for the success of the entire process.
8. Thorough on-boarding is a "must" for productivity improvement. It is a vital part of the total management system—and therefore the foundation of any effort to improve employee productivity.

IMPACT OF TRAINING AND DEVELOPMENT ON PRODUCTIVITY, QUALITY OF WORK LIFE, AND THE BOTTOM LINE

Does training work? One investigation of 2,500 firms revealed that when the firms were ranked on per-employee training expenditures, those in the upper fourth of the distribution had 24 percent higher profit margins than those ranked in the lower fourth. As for various types of training, consider the following reported returns on investment (ROI): 5:1 (behavior modification), 4.8:1 (customer service), 13.7:1 (team training), 15:1 (role of the manager), and 21:1 (sales training).[a] At a more general level, although the potential returns from well-conducted training programs can be substantial, there is often considerable variability in the effectiveness with which any given training method or content area is implemented.[b] As we have seen, in-depth planning (through needs analysis) and follow-up program-evaluation efforts are necessary in order to realize these returns. As an example, consider results reported by NTT Data, based in Plano, Texas, and Tokyo.[c] The company developed a leadership-development game based on a careful needs analysis and established principles of learning. Employees work through modules on leadership skills, such as negotiation, time management, and delegation. Modules include readings, videos, puzzles, and scenario-based quizzes that help learners understand the contexts in which leadership decisions take place. As people complete modules, they advance to different levels and earn points that appear on a leaderboard.

About 700 of 7,000 employees completed a pilot program in 2012. By 2014, 50 had assumed team-lead roles, which is 50 percent more than had assumed those roles after traditional leadership training and coaching. Those 50 people generated 30 ideas that created $1 million in new revenue or cost savings for clients. Organizationwide, employee referrals increased by 30 percent, reducing recruiting costs by $500,000 per year. As this example shows, continual investments in training and learning are essential, as they have direct impacts on the productivity of organizations and on the quality of work life of those who work in them.

[a]Kraiger, K., and Nelson, T. (2017). Training. In S. G. Rogelberg (Ed.), *The Sage Encyclopedia of Industrial and Organizational Psychology* (2nd ed., Vol. 4). Thousand Oaks, CA: Sage, pp. 1637–39. Philips, J. J. (1996, Feb.). ROI: The search for best practices. *Training and Development*, p. 45. Arthur, W. J., Bennett, W. J., Edens, P., and Bell, S. T. (2003). Effectiveness of training in organizations: A meta-analysis of design and evaluation features. *Journal of Applied Psychology, 88*, pp. 234–245.

[b]Kraiger and Nelson (2017), op. cit. Aguinis, H., and Kraiger, K. (2009). Benefits of training and development for individuals and teams, organizations, and society. *Annual Review of Psychology* 60, pp. 451–474.

[c]Roberts, B. (2014, May). Gamification: Win, lose, or draw? *HR*, pp. 29–35.

These lessons are exciting and provocative. They suggest that we should be at least as concerned with preparing the new employee for the social context of his or her job and for coping with the insecurities and frustrations of a new learning situation as with the development of the technical skills necessary to perform well.

TECHNOLOGY-DELIVERED INSTRUCTION CATCHES ON

Human Resource Management in Action: Conclusion

Simulation games are one popular type of TDI. Instruction is typically delivered via a PC or tablet computer that immerses trainees in a decision-making exercise in an artificial environment in order to learn the consequences of their decisions. The games are intrinsically motivating, and people report a loss of time when playing their favorite ones. When used for training, they seem to pay off nicely. Meta-analysis results indicate that relative to a comparison group, post-training self-efficacy (belief that one can succeed) was 20 percent higher, knowledge of facts was 11 percent higher, skill-based knowledge was 14 percent higher, and retention was 9 percent higher for trainees taught with simulation games.

Trainees learned more when simulation games conveyed course material actively rather than passively, trainees could access the simulation game as many times as they desired, and the simulation game was a supplement to other instructional methods rather than stand-alone instruction. Trainees learned less, however, when the instruction the comparison group received as a substitute for the simulation game actively engaged them in the learning experience.

Here's an example. Cold Stone Creamery developed a simulation game to teach customer service and portion control in a virtual Cold Stone store. Players race against the clock to service customers in a timely fashion while maximizing the company's profit by avoiding wasting too much ice cream. The first week the simulation game was available, more than 8,000 employees—30 percent of the workforce—voluntarily downloaded the simulation game. Corporate trainers believe that the entertainment value will motivate employees to play the game continuously while teaching them retail sales, technical, and managerial skills.

There are drawbacks, however. Computer-based simulation games are expensive to develop, with complex games costing between $5 million and $20 million to create. Needless to say, in order to maximize payoffs, designers need to focus on content reuse, using software that streamlines the game-development process, and offsetting development costs with savings in travel costs for training that used to be delivered via classroom instruction. Here's another concern.

Although some people may relish the opportunity to squeeze in a little training via a computer at home, on a plane, or in a hotel room, others may regard after-hours training as an unwarranted intrusion on their personal time. Perhaps this is why 83 percent of employers provide time for training during the workweek. Some provide specific tools. Cisco Systems gives employees police tape to stretch across their cubicle doors. Others hand out signs saying "Learning in Progress." Such workday carve-outs will become more acceptable as learning becomes a part of every job—and of day-to-day life.

Suppose you are considering offering TDI to your employees. Experts say that it is critical to test drive each potential course from the vendor. Experience the course. See how easy it is to navigate the site, how fast it loads, and if it provides quality

---

IMPLICATIONS FOR MANAGEMENT PRACTICE

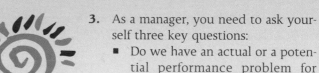

One of the greatest fears of managers and lower-level employees is obsolescence. Perhaps the **Paul principle** expresses this phenomenon most aptly: Over time, people become uneducated, and therefore incompetent, to perform at a level at which they once performed adequately.[a] Training is an important antidote to obsolescence, but it is important to be realistic about what training can and cannot accomplish.

1. Training cannot solve all kinds of performance problems. In some cases, transfer, job redesign, changes in selection or reward systems, or discipline may be more appropriate.

2. Because productivity reflects a system of inputs, such capital, material, energy, and labor, changes in individual or team performance are only one possible cause of changes in productivity.[b]

3. As a manager, you need to ask yourself three key questions:
   - Do we have an actual or a potential performance problem for which training is the answer?
     - Have we defined what is to be learned and what the content of training should be before we choose a particular training method or technique?
     - What kind of evaluation procedure will we use to determine if the benefits of the training outweigh its costs?

---

[a]Armer, P. (1970). The individual: His privacy, self-image, and obsolescence. *Proceedings of the Meeting of the Panel on Science and Technology, 11th "Science and Astronautics."* Washington, DC: U.S. Government Printing Office.

[b]Business Dictionary. (n.d.). Retrieved from *http://www.business-dictionary.com/definition/productivity.html* on Apr. 16, 2020.

take-home information. Are all elements of the course integrated? Is technical support available 24/7? An online course won't be of much use if employees can't access it or can't get help with it anytime they want. Finally, simulation games or any other type of TDI should not be used in training simply because the technology exists. Rather, determine training needs carefully, and identify the kinds of features that should be included in order to maximize learning.

A final issue is this. Who profits most from e-learning? A recent study found that employees who learned most from this type of learning environment were those who completed more of the practice opportunities made available and took more time to complete the experience.

SUMMARY

The pace of change in our society is forcing employees at all levels continually to acquire new knowledge and skills. In most organizations, therefore, lifelong training is essential. To be maximally effective, training programs should follow a three-phase sequence: needs assessment, implementation, and evaluation. First define clearly what is to be learned before choosing a particular method or technique. To do that, use organization analysis, demographic analysis, operations analysis, and analysis of the training needs of individual employees.

Then, relate training needs to the achievement of broader organizational goals. To design any training program, principles of learning—goal setting, behavior modeling, meaningfulness of material, practice, feedback, and transfer of training—are essential considerations. Choose a technique based on how well it fits identified needs and incorporates the learning principles.

In evaluating training programs, it is important to relate targets of evaluation (training content and design, changes in learners, and organizational payoffs) to data-collection methods (e.g., cost-benefit analyses, tests, ratings, surveys). However, the impact of training on organizational results is the bottom line of training success. Advances in utility analysis now make evaluations possible in terms of economic costs and benefits.

One of the most neglected areas of training is new-employee orientation and on-boarding. Clearly, a new employee's initial experience with a firm can have a major effect on his or her later success. To maximize the impact of these processes, provide specific information in three major areas: (1) company policies and company culture, (2) social behavior, and (3) technical aspects of the job. While some aspects of orientation can be handled via technology (e.g., forms completion, history of the organization), the more socially rich areas should not. Instead, use a formal, social-based program to do that, and be sure to involve HR as well as non-HR executives and employees in the process. Follow-up by HR and the immediate supervisor is essential (e.g., after 30, 60, and 90 days, and after 6 months and 1 year) to ensure proper quality control plus continual improvement.

KEY TERMS

training	practice
stackable credentials	overlearning
training paradox	distributed practice
assessment phase	massed practice
training and development phase	feedback
evaluation phase	transfer of training
organization analysis	action learning
demographic analysis	team
operations analysis	team-coordination training
individual analysis	cross-training
goal theory	guided team self-correction
Pygmalion effect	on-boarding orientation
behavior modeling	norms of behavior
meaningfulness	Paul principle

DISCUSSION QUESTIONS

9-1. Would you be able to recognize a well-designed training program if you saw one? What features would you look for?

9-2. How does goal setting affect trainee learning and motivation?

9-3. Outline an evaluation procedure for a training program designed to teach sales principles and strategies.

9-4. Why do organizations so frequently overlook the on-boarding of new employees?

9-5. Think back to your first day of the most recent job you have held. What could the organization have done to hasten your on-boarding and your adjustment to the job?

9-6. Given the growth of the "on-demand," or "gig," economy, we can no longer assume that "workers" in an organization are all employees. What are the implications of that for training and on-boarding?

9-7. Companies with the best training practices seem to share several characteristics in common. What are they?

9-8. Some companies don't want to offer training to employees because they fear that the employees will then leave. How might a firm use training as a strategy to retain employees?

9-9. Why is it critical first to identify what employees need to learn before deciding on a method to use in training them?

9-10. What can organizations do to enhance positive transfer from training to on-the-job application?

APPLYING YOUR KNOWLEDGE

Case 9–1   ***On-Boarding and Training Young Leaders at E-Commerce Giant Alibaba***

In the 3 months since he began working for Alibaba Group Holdings Ltd., Matt Shofnos, age 30, has improved his Mandarin, helped an American retailer target Chinese consumers, and donned a Captain America costume to meet the company's chief executive.

Alibaba has brought Mr. Shofnos and 31 other young workers from around the world to China for a year-long immersion in Chinese business and language and the company's culture. The company's executives are betting that the leadership program will produce China-trained, globally minded leaders able to make and manage partnerships with Western retailers, moving the e-commerce giant closer to its goal of earning 40 percent of revenue outside China in the next decade.

Alibaba has committed to running the program for at least 10 years and expects enrollment to grow to 100 annually. Participants, all new hires, typically join after business school or a few years working in fields such as marketing and technology. More than 3,000 applied to the inaugural class. Finalists underwent several rounds of interviews, including a visit to the company's Hangzhou headquarters. Recruits are paid competitively as they complete two 6-month rotations at Alibaba businesses such as shopping platform Tmall Global. They take classes on Chinese culture, politics, and economics and travel, visiting rural villages to observe how e-commerce has transformed local economies.

Participants must learn how to navigate life in China, including finding apartments, commuting to work, and learning Alibaba products, many of which are in Chinese. Veteran Alibaba workers, called "life buddies," greet arrivals at the airport and help them load useful smartphone apps.

After their second 6-month rotation, graduates are expected to return to Alibaba offices in their home regions in places such as New York and Paris. Having been integrated into "the mothership," the workers will help ensure an expanded Alibaba stays true to its Chinese roots and company culture.

Program participant Anna Kim, 28, was scheduled to attend the annual meeting of Alibaba affiliate Ant Financial Services Group. She expected the typical recitation of graphs and PowerPoint slides. What awaited her was a massive party in a stadium. "When I go to work, I don't know what kind of surprise is going to come my way," she said.

As for Matt Shofnos, he is still adjusting to life in Hangzhou, where something as simple as hailing a ride with the country's version of Uber can befuddle an outsider. Earlier in his career, he realized that being "an American company's China guy" wasn't going to happen, thanks to lackluster Mandarin skills. With Alibaba, he said, "I can absolutely be a Chinese company's American guy."

Questions

1. Based on material presented in the chapter, critique Alibaba's on-boarding and training program for young leaders.
2. What principles of learning has Alibaba built into its program?
3. Senior management wants you to develop a plan to evaluate the effectiveness of this program. How might you do that?

Source: Feintzeig, R. (2017, Jan. 11). Alibaba new hires get crash courses. *The Wall Street Journal*, p. B5.

REFERENCES

1. Cascio, W. F. (2019) Training trends: Macro, micro, and policy issues. *Human Resource Management Review* 29, pp. 284–97.
2. Association for Talent Development (ATD). (2019). *State of the Industry Report*. Alexandria, VA: Author.
3. Cermak, J., and McGurk, M. (2010, July). Putting a value on training. *McKinsey Quarterly*. Retrieved from *www.mckinsey.com/business-functions/organization/our-insights/putting-a-value-on-training* on Apr. 30, 2017.

4. LinkedIn Learning. *2020 workplace learning report*. Retrieved from *https://learning.linke-din.com/content/dam/me/learning/resources/pdfs/LinkedIn-Learning-2020-Workplace-Learning-Report.pdf* on Apr. 13, 2020.

5. Noe, R. A. (2020). *Employee Training and Development* (8th ed.). New York: McGraw-Hill. *See also* Cascio (2019), op. cit. *See also* Cascio, W. F. (2014). Investing in HRD in uncertain times now and in the future. *Advances in Developing Human Resources* 16(1), pp. 108–22.

6. LinkedIn Learning (2020), op. cit. *See also* Hirsch, A. S. (2016, Jan. 26). What emerging adults want in a job: 9 key requirements. Retrieved from *www.shrm.org/resourcesand-tools/hr-topics/employee-relations/pages/emerging-adults.aspx* on Apr. 28, 2016.

7. Soergel, A. (2020, Feb. 20). Companies invest in partnerships, workforce training to bridge skills gap. *US News & World Report*. Retrieved from *https://www.usnews.com/news/economy/articles/2020-02-20/amazon-facebook-home-depot-among-companies-paying-to-train-workforce* on Feb. 21, 2020. *See also* Minaya, E. (2019, Mar. 8). Companies seek to fill skills gap by retraining their own workers. *The Wall Street Journal*. Retrieved from *https://www.wsj.com/articles/companies-seek-to-fill-skills-gap-by-retraining-their-own-workers-11552041000* on Mar. 8, 2019. *See also* Coy, P. (2018, Oct. 29). Companies give worker training another try. *Bloomberg Businessweek*, pp. 36, 37.

8. Nathan, A. (2016, Mar. 10). 7 key steps for better training and development programs. Retrieved from *www.shrm.org/resourcesandtools/hr-topics/organizational-and-employee-development/pages/key-steps-for-better-training-development-programs.aspx* on May 6, 2016.

9. Gurschiek, K. (2020, Jan. 2). Look for these training trends in 2020. *SHRM Online*. Retrieved from *https://www.shrm.org/resourcesandtools/hr-topics/organizational-and-employee-development/pages/look-for-these-training-trends-in-2020.aspx* on Jan. 3, 2020. *See also* Montealegre, R., and Cascio, W. F. (In press). Managing in the age of external intelligence. *Organizational Dynamics*. *https://doi.org/10.1016/j.orgdyn.2019.100733*. *See also* Cascio, W. F., and Montealegre, R. (2016). How technology is changing work and organizations. *Annual Review of Organizational Psychology and Organizational Behavior*, pp. 349–75.

10. Weber, L. (2020, Jan. 7). Employers want to train workers but are swimming in options. *The Wall Street Journal*. Retrieved from *https://www.wsj.com/articles/employers-want-to-train-workers-but-are-swimming-in-options-11578393001* on Jan. 7, 2020.

11. Cascio, W. F., and Boudreau, J. W. (2017). Talent management of nonstandard employees. In D. Collings, K. Mellahi, and W. Cascio (Eds.), *Handbook of Talent Management*. Oxford, UK: Oxford University Press, pp. 494–520. *See also* Boudreau, J. W., Jesuthasan, R., and Creelman D. (2015). *Lead the Work*. Hoboken, NJ: Wiley.

12. McCue, T. J. (2018, Aug. 31). 57 million U.S. workers are part of the gig economy. *Forbes*. Retrieved from *https://www.forbes.com/sites/tjmccue/2018/08/31/57-million-u-s-workers-are-part-of-the-gig-economy/#5ee2ad137118* on Dec. 14, 2019.

13. Gurschiek (2020), op. cit. *See also* Weber (2020), op. cit. *See also* Harward, D. (2016). Key trends for 2016: Focusing on the science of learning to better engage the adult learner. *Training Industry Magazine*. Retrieved from *http://www.trainingindustry.com/ezine/current-issue/key-trends-for-2016-focusing-on-the-science-of-learning-to-better-engage-the-adult-learner.aspx* on May 20, 2016.

14. Lloyd, T. (2019, June 18). Defining what a brand is. Why is it so hard? *EmotiveBrand*. Retrieved from *https://www.emotivebrand.com/defining-brand/* on Apr. 13, 2020. *See also* Keller, K. L. (1993). Conceptualizing, measuring, and managing customer-based brand equity. *Journal of Marketing* **57**, pp. 1–22.

15. Cascio, W. F., and Graham, B. Z. (2016). New strategic role for HR: Leading the employer-branding process. *Organization Management Journal* 13(4), pp. 182–92.

16. Bersin, J. (2016, March 3). New research shows why focus on teams, not just leaders, is key to business performance. *Forbes*. Retrieved from *https://www.forbes.com/sites/joshbersin/2016/03/03/why-a-focus-on-teams-not-just-leaders-is-the-secret-to-business-performance/#4973598d24d5*. *See also* Cannon-Bowers, J. A., and Bowers, C. (2011). Team development and functioning. In S. Zedeck (Ed.), *Handbook of Industrial and Organizational Psychology* (Vol. 1). Washington, DC: American Psychological Association, pp. 597–650.

17. LinkedIn Learning (2020), op. cit. *See also* Soergel (2020), op. cit. *See also* Moore, E. (2019, May 16). 10 companies that offer incredible professional development programs. *Glassdoor.com*. Retrieved from *https://www.glassdoor.com/blog/companies-with-professional-development-programs/* on Apr. 13, 2020.

18. Aguinis, H., and Kraiger, K. (2009). Benefits of training and development for individuals and teams, organizations, and society. *Annual Review of Psychology* 60, pp. 451–74.

19. Arthur, W. J., Bennett, W. J., Edens, P., and Bell, S. T. (2003). Effectiveness of training in organizations: A meta-analysis of design and evaluation features. *Journal of Applied Psychology* 88, pp. 234–45. *See also* Cheng, T., and Chen, C. C. (2015). The impact of e-learning on workplace on-the-job training. *International Journal of e-Education, e-Business, e-Management, and e-Learning* **5**(4), pp. 212–25. *See also* Brown, K., and Sitzmann, T. (2011). Training and employee development for improved performance. In S. Zedeck (Ed.), *Handbook of Industrial and Organizational Psychology* (Vol. 2). Washington, DC: American Psychological Association, pp. 469–503.

20. In general, 0.2 is considered a "small" effect size, 0.5 a "medium" effect size, and 0.8 a "large" effect size; *see* Cohen J. (1988). *Statistical power analysis* (2nd ed.). Hillsdale, NJ: Lawrence Erlbaum.

21. Cullen, J., and Turnbull, S. (2005). A meta-review of the management development literature. *Human Resource Development Review* 4, pp. 335–55.

22. Littrell, L. N., Salas, E., Hess, K. P., Paley, M., and Riedel, S. (2006). Expatriate preparation: A critical analysis of 25 years of cross-cultural training research. *Human Resource Development Review* 5, pp. 355–88.

23. Dvir, T., Eden, D., Avolio, B. J., and Shamir, B. (2002). Impact of transformational leadership on follower development and performance: A field experiment. *Academy of Management Journal* 45, pp. 735–44.

24. Cutter, C. (2019, July 11). Amazon to retrain a third of its U. S. workforce. *The Wall Street Journal*. Retrieved from *https://www.wsj.com/articles/amazon-to-retrain-a-third-of-its-u-s-workforce-11562841120* on July 11, 2019.

25. LinkedIn Learning. (2020). 2020 workplace learning report. Retrieved from *https://learning.linkedin.com/content/dam/me/learning/resources/pdfs/LinkedIn-Learning-2020-Workplace-Learning-Report.pdf* on Apr. 13, 2020. *See also* Gurschiek, K. (2019, Sept. 4). Workers look to managers for training encouragement. *SHRM Online*. Retrieved from *https://www.shrm.org/resourcesandtools/hr-topics/organizational-and-employee-development/pages/workers-look-to-managers-for-training-encouragement.aspx* on Sept. 4, 2019.

26. Lawler, E. E. III, and Worley, C. G., with Creelman, D. (2011). *Management Reset: Organizing for Sustainable Effectiveness*. San Francisco: Jossey-Bass.

27. Society for Human Resource Management Foundation. (2017, Jan. 30). *Seeing Forward: Succession Planning and Leadership Development at 3M*. Available at *https://www.youtube.com/watch?v=XLNpp49bCvs*.

28. Sitzmann, T., and Weinhardt, J. (2015). Training engagement theory: A multilevel perspective on the effectiveness of work-related training. *Journal of Management* 20, pp. 1–25. *See also* Colquitt, J. A., LePine, J. A., and Noe, R. A. (2000). Toward an integrative theory of training motivation: A meta-analytic path analysis of 20 years of research. *Journal of Applied Psychology* 85, pp. 678–707.

29. Brown and Sitzmann (2011), op. cit. *See also* Quinones, M. A. (1997). Contextual influences on training effectiveness. In M. A. Quinones and A. Ehrenstein (Eds.), *Training for a Rapidly Changing Workplace*. Washington, DC: American Psychological Association, pp. 177–200.

30. Noe (2020), op. cit. *See also* Goldstein, I. L., and Ford, J. K. (2002). *Training in Organizations: Needs Assessment, Development, and Evaluation* (4th ed.). Belmont, CA: Wadsworth.

31. Nathan, A. (2016, Mar. 10). 7 key steps for better training development programs. Retrieved from *www.shrm.org/resourcesandtools/hr-topics/organizational-and-employee-development/pages/key-steps-for-better-training-development-programs.aspx* on Mar. 11, 2016. *See also* Brown and Sitzmann (2011), op. cit. *See also* Moore, M. L., and Dutton, P. (1978). Training needs analysis: Review and critique. *Academy of Management Review* 3, pp. 532–54.

32. Ford, J. K., and Noe, R. A. (1987). Self-assessed training needs: The effects of attitudes toward training, managerial level, and function. *Personnel Psychology* 40, pp. 39-53.

33. Noe (2020), op. cit. *See also* Noe, R. A. (2000). Toward an integrative theory of training motivation: A meta-analytic path analysis of 20 years of research. *Journal of Applied Psychology* 85, p. 678-707.

34. Blanchard, P. N., and Thacker, J. W. (2019). *Effective training: Systems, strategies, and practices* (6th ed.). Chicago: Chicago Business Press. *See also* Goldstein, I. L., and Ford, J. K. (2002). *Training in Organizations: Needs Assessment, Development, and Evaluation* (4th ed.). Belmont, CA: Wadsworth.

35. Wexley, K. N., and Latham, G. P. (2002). *Developing and Training Human Resources in Organizations* (3rd ed.). Upper Saddle River, NJ: Prentice Hall.

36. Noe (2020), op. cit. *See also* Gurchiek (2019), op. cit. *See also* Colquitt, LePine, and Noe (2000), op. cit.

37. Latham, G. P., and Locke, E. A. (2017). Goal-setting theory. In S. G. Rogelberg (Ed.), *The Sage Encyclopedia of Industrial and Organizational Psychology* (2nd ed., Vol. 2). Thousand Oaks, CA: Sage, pp. 556-59. *See also* Locke, E. A., and Latham, G. P. (Eds.). (2013). *New Developments in Goal Setting and Task Performance*. New York: Routledge. *See also* Latham, G. P. (2009). *Becoming the Evidence-Based Manager: Making the Science of Management Work for You*. Boston: Davies-Black. *See also* Locke, E. A., and Latham, G. P. (2002). Building a practically useful theory of goal setting and task motivation. *American Psychologist* 57, pp. 705-17.

38. Schmidt, F. L. (2013). The economic value of goal setting. In E. A. Locke and G. P. Latham (Eds.), *New Developments in Goal Setting and Task Performance*. New York: Routledge, pp. 16-20. *See also* Wood, R. E., Mento, A. J., and Locke, E. A. (1987). Task complexity as a moderator of goal effects: A meta-analysis. *Journal of Applied Psychology* 72, pp. 416-25.

39. Locke and Latham (2017), op. cit. *See also* Locke, E. A., and Latham, G. P. (2013). Goal setting theory, 1990. In E. A. Locke and G. P. Latham (Eds.), *New Developments in Goal Setting and Task Performance*. New York: Routledge, pp. 3-15. *See also* Locke, E. A. (1968). Toward a theory of task motivation and incentives. *Organizational Behavior and Human Performance* 3, pp. 157-89.

40. Klein, H. J., Cooper, J. T., and Monahan, C. A. (2013). Goal commitment. In E. A. Locke and G. P. Latham (Eds.), *New Developments in Goal Setting and Task Performance*. New York: Routledge, pp. 65-89. *See also* Klein, H. J., Wesson, M. J., Hollenbeck, J. R., and Alge, B. J. (1999). Goal commitment and the goal-setting process: Conceptual clarification and empirical synthesis. *Journal of Applied Psychology* 84, pp. 885-96. *See also* Locke, E. A., Latham, G. P., and Erez, M. (1988). The determinants of goal commitment. *Academy of Management Review* 13, pp. 23-39.

41. Bandura, A. (2013). The role of self-efficacy in goal-based motivation. In E. A. Locke and G. P. Latham (Eds.), *New Developments in Goal Setting and Task Performance*. New York: Routledge, pp. 147-57. *See also* Bandura, A. (1986). *Social Foundations of Thought and Action: A Social Cognitive Theory*. Englewood Cliffs, NJ: Prentice Hall.

42. Hogan, P. M., Hakel, M. D., and Decker, P. J. (1986). Effects of trainee-generated versus trainer-provided rule codes on generalization in behavior-modeling training. *Journal of Applied Psychology* 71, p. 469-73.

43. Goldstein, A. P., and Sorcher, M. (1974). *Changing Supervisor Behavior*. New York: Pergamon Press. *See also* Latham, G. P., and Saari, L. M. (1979). The application of social learning theory to training supervisors through behavior modeling. *Journal of Applied Psychology* 64, pp. 239-46.

44. Taylor, P. J., Russ-Eft, D. F., and Chan, D. W. L. (2005). A meta-analytic review of behavior-modeling training. *Journal of Applied Psychology* 90, pp. 692-709.

45. Davis, F. D., and Yi, M. Y. (2004). Improving computer-skill training: Behavior modeling, symbolic mental rehearsal, and the role of knowledge structures. *Journal of Applied Psychology* 89, pp. 509-23.

46. Wexley, K. N., and Latham, G. P. (2002). *Developing and Training Human Resources in Organizations* (3rd ed.). Upper Saddle River, NJ: Prentice Hall.

47. Gist, M. E. (1997). Training design and pedagogy: Implications for skill acquisition, maintenance, and generalization. In M. A. Quinones and A. Ehrenstein (Eds.), *Training for a Rapidly Changing Workplace*. Washington, DC: American Psychological Association, pp. 201–22. *See also* Gagné, R. M. (1977). *The Conditions of Learning*. New York: Holt, Rinehart & Winston.

48. William, K. J. (2013). Goal setting in sports. In E. A. Locke and G. P. Latham (Eds.), *New Developments in Goal Setting and Task Performance*. New York: Routledge, pp. 375–96. *See also* Ehrenstein, A., Walker, B. N., Czerwinski, M., and Feldman, E. M. (1997). Some fundamentals of training and transfer: Practice benefits are not automatic. In M. A. Quinones and A. Ehrenstein (Eds.), *Training for a Rapidly Changing Workplace*. Washington, DC: American Psychological Association, pp. 119–47.

49. Keith, N., and Frese, M. (2008). Effectiveness of error-management training: A meta-analysis. *Journal of Applied Psychology 93*, pp. 59–69.

50. Driskell, J. E., Willis, R. P., and Copper, C. (1992). Effect of overlearning on retention. *Journal of Applied Psychology 77*, pp. 615–22.

51. Donovan, J. J., and Radosevich, D. J. (1999). A meta-analytic review of the distribution of practice effect: Now you see it, now you don't. *Journal of Applied Psychology 84*, pp. 795–805. *See also* Goldstein and Ford (2002), op. cit. *See also* Tyler, K. (2000, May). Hold on to what you've learned. *HRMagazine*, pp. 94–102.

52. Ashford, S. J., and De Stobbeleir, K. E. M. (2013). Feedback, goal setting, and task performance revisited. In E. A. Locke and G. P. Latham (Eds.), *New Developments in Goal Setting and Task Performance*. New York: Routledge, pp. 51–64. *See also* Stajkovic, A. D., and Luthans, F. (2003). Behavioral management and task performance in organizations: Conceptual background, meta-analysis, and test of alternative models. *Personnel Psychology 56*, pp. 155–94. *See also* Martocchio, J. J., and Webster, J. (1992). Effects of feedback and cognitive playfulness on performance in microcomputer software training. *Personnel Psychology 45*, pp. 553–78.

53. Goodman, J. S., and Wood, R. E. (2004). Feedback specificity, learning opportunities, and learning. *Journal of Applied Psychology 89*, pp. 809–21.

54. Cannon-Bowers and Bowers (2011), op. cit. *See also* Pritchard, R. D., Jones, S. D., Roth, P. L., Steubing, K. K., and Ekeberg, S. E. (1988). Effects of group feedback, goal setting, and incentives on organizational productivity. *Journal of Applied Psychology 73*, pp. 337–58.

55. Florin Thuma, B. C., and Boudreau, J. W. (1987). Performance feedback utility in a small organization: Effects on organizational outcomes and managerial decision processes. *Personnel Psychology 40*, pp. 693–713.

56. Cascio, W. F., and Aguinis, H. (2019). *Applied Psychology in Talent Management* (8th ed.). Thousand Oaks, CA: Sage. *See also* Brown, K. G., and Ford, J. K. (2002). Using computer technology in training: Building an infrastructure for active learning. In K. Kraiger (Ed.), *Creating, Implementing, and Managing Effective Training and Development*. San Francisco: Jossey-Bass, pp. 192–233.

57. Ford, J. K. (2017). Transfer of training. In S. G. Rogelberg (Ed.), *The Sage Encyclopedia of Industrial and Organizational Psychology* (2nd. ed., Vol. 4). Thousand Oaks, CA: Sage, pp. 1652–55. *See also* Brown and Sitzmann (2011), op. cit. *See also* Burke, L. A., and Hutchins, H. M. (2008). A study of best practices in training transfer and a proposed model of transfer. *Human Resource Development Quarterly 19*, pp. 107–28. *See also* Machin, M. A. (2002). Planning, managing, and optimizing transfer of training. In K. Kraiger (Ed.), *Creating, Implementing, and Managing Effective Training and Development*. San Francisco: Jossey-Bass, pp. 263–301.

58. Baldwin, T. T., Ford, J. K., and Blume, B. D. (2009). Transfer of training 1988–2008: An updated review and agenda for future research. *International Review of Industrial and Organizational Psychology 24*, pp. 41–70.

59. Magjuka, R. J., and Baldwin, T. T. (1991). Team-based employee involvement programs: Effects of design and administration. *Personnel Psychology 44*, pp. 793–812.

60. Chiaburu, D. S., and Marinova, S. V. (2005). What predicts skill transfer? An exploratory study of goal orientation, training self-efficacy, and organizational supports. *International Journal of Training and Development 9*, pp. 110–23. *See also* Pidd, K. (2004). The impact of

320 Part 3 Development

workplace support and identity on training transfer: A case study of drug and alcohol safety training in Australia. *International Journal of Training and Development* 8, pp. 274–88.

61. Johnson, C. (2017, Jan. 30). *Succession Planning at 3M,* op. cit.

62. Ernst & Young. (n.d.) How companies use teams to drive performance. Retrieved from *www.ey.com/gl/en/issues/talent-management/how-companies-use-teams-to-drive-performance* on May 4, 2017. *See also* Vella, M. (2008, Apr. 28). White-collar workers shoulder to-gether–Like it or not. *BusinessWeek,* p. 58.

63. Mathieu, J. E., Hollenbeck, J. R., van Knippenberg, D., & Ilgen, D. R. (2017). A century of work teams in the *Journal of Applied Psychology. Journal of Applied Psychology* 102, pp. 452–67. *See also* Kramer, W. S., Thayer, A. L., and Salas, E. (2013). Goal setting in teams. In E. A. Locke & G. P. Latham (Eds.), *New Developments in Goal Setting and Task Performance.* New York: Routledge, pp. 287–310.

64. Woo, S. (2019, March 13). In search of a perfect team. *The Wall Street Journal,* p. R6. *See also* Weir, K. (2018, Sept.). What makes teams work? *Monitor on Psychology,* pp. 46–54.

65. Salas, E., Tannenbaum, S., Cohen, D., and Latham, G. P. (Eds.). (2013). *Developing and En-hancing High-Performance Teams.* New York: Wiley-Pfeiffer. *See also* Cannon-Bowers and Bowers (2011), op. cit. *See also* Salas, E., Burke, C. S., and Cannon-Bowers, J. A. (2002). What we know about designing and delivering team training: Tips and guidelines. In K. Kraiger (Ed.), *Creating, Implementing, and Managing Effective Training and Development.* San Francisco: Jossey-Bass, pp. 234–59.

66. Collins, J. (2009, May 25). How the mighty fall. *BusinessWeek,* pp. 26–38. *See also* Cannon-Bowers, J. A., Tannenbaum, S. I., Salas, E., and Volpe, C. E. (1995). Defining competencies and establishing team training requirements. In R. A. Guzzo and E. Salas (Eds.), *Team Ef-fectiveness and Decision Making in Organizations.* San Francisco: Jossey-Bass, pp. 333–80.

67. Salas et al. (2013), op. cit. *See also* DeChurch, L. A., and Mesmer-Magnus, J. R. (2010). The cognitive underpinnings of effective teamwork: A meta-analysis. *Journal of Applied Psy-chology* 95, pp. 32–53. *See also* Ganster, D. C., Williams, S., and Poppler, P. (1991). Does training in problem-solving improve the quality of group decisions? *Journal of Applied Psychology* 76, pp. 479–83.

68. Salas and Cannon-Bowers (2000), op. cit. *See also* Bass, B. M. (1980). Team productivity and individual member competence. *Small Group Behavior* 11, pp. 431–504. *See also* Colvin, G. (2006, June 12). Why dream teams fail. *Fortune,* pp. 87–92.

69. Maynard, M. T., Gilson, L., Jones-Young, N. C., and Vartiainen, M. (2017). Virtual teams. In G. Hertel, D. Stone, R. Johnson, and J. Passmore. *The Psychology of the Internet at Work.* Chichester, UK: Wiley-Blackwell, pp. 315–345. *See also* Walvoord, A., Redden, E., Elliott, L., and Coovert, M. (2008). Empowering followers in virtual teams: Guiding principles from theory and practice. *Computers in Human Behavior* 24, pp. 1884–906. *See also* Komaki, J. L., Desselles, J. L., and Bowman, E. D. (1989). Definitely not a breeze: Extend-ing an operant model of supervision to teams. *Journal of Applied Psychology* 74, pp. 522–29.

70. Han, V. (2017, October 12). Are chatbots the future of training? *SHRM Online.* Retrieved from *www.shrm.org/resourcesandtools/ hr-topics/technology/pages/are-chatbotst-the-future-of-training.aspx* on Oct. 13, 2017.

71. Noe (2020), op. cit. *See also* Kraiger, K. (2002). Decision-based evaluation. In K. Kraiger (Ed.), *Creating, Implementing, and Managing Effective Training and Development.* San Francisco: Jossey-Bass, pp. 331–75.

72. Brown, K., and Sitzmann, T. (2011). Training and employee development for improved performance. In S. Zedeck (Ed.), *Handbook of Industrial and Organizational Psychology,* Vol. 2. Washington, DC: American Psychological Association, p. 469–503.

73. Brown, K. G. (2017). Training evaluation. In S. G. Rogelberg (Ed.), *The Sage Encyclopedia of Industrial and Organizational Psychology* (2nd ed., Vol. 4). Thousand Oaks, CA: Sage, pp. 1639–42. *See also* Kirkpatrick, D. L. (1996). Great ideas revisited. *Training and Development* 50, pp. 54–59.

74. Sung, S. Y., and Choi, J. N. (2014). Do organizations spend wisely on employees? Effects of training and development investments on learning and innovation in organizations. *Jour-nal of Organizational Behavior* 35, pp. 393–412.

75. Kraiger, K., McLinden, D., and Casper, W. J. (2004). Collaborative planning for training impact. *Human Resource Management* 43, pp. 337–51. *See also* Arvey, R. D., Maxwell, S. E., and Salas, E. (1992). The relative power of training evaluation designs under different cost configurations. *Journal of Applied Psychology* 77, pp. 155–60.

76. Cascio, W. F., Boudreau, J. W., and Fink, A. (2019). *Investing in People: Financial Impact of Human Resource Initiatives* (3rd ed.). Alexandria, VA: SHRM Publishing. *See also* Cascio, W. F., and Aguinis, H. (2019). *Applied Psychology in Talent Management* (8th ed.). Thousand Oaks, CA: Sage. *See also* Cascio, W. F. (1989). Using utility analysis to assess training outcomes. In I. L. Goldstein (Ed.), *Training and Development in Organizations*. San Francisco: Jossey-Bass, pp. 63–88.

77. Klein, H. J., and Weaver, N. A. (2000). The effectiveness of an organizational-level orientation training program in the socialization of new hires. *Personnel Psychology* 53, pp. 47–66.

78. Hirsch, A. (2017, Aug. 10). Don't underestimate the importance of good onboarding. *SHRM Online*. Retrieved from *https://www.shrm.org/resourcesandtools/hr-topics/talent-acquisition/pages/dont-underestimate-the-importance-of-effective-onboarding.aspx* on Apr. 25, 2017. *See also* Bauer, T., and Erdogan, B. (2011). Organizational socialization: The effective onboarding of new employees. In S. Zedeck (Ed.), *Handbook of Industrial and Organizational Psychology* (Vol. 3). Washington, DC: American Psychological Association, pp. 51–64.

79. Maurer, R. (2018, Nov. 30). Survey: Onboarding programs are too short. *SHRM Online*. Retrieved from *https://www.shrm.org/resourcesandtools/hr-topics/talent-acquisition/pages/silkroad-survey-onboarding-programs-too-short.aspx* on Nov. 30, 2018.

80. Hirsch (2017), op. cit. *See also* Maurer, R. New employee onboarding guide. (n.d.). *Society for Human Resource Management*. Retrieved from *https://www.shrm.org/mlp/pages/new-employee-onboarding-guide.aspx* on Apr. 16, 2020. *See also* Bauer and Erdogan (2011), op. cit.

81. Cascio et al. (2019), op. cit. *See also* Solomon, J. (1988, Dec. 29). Companies try measuring cost savings from new types of corporate benefits. *The Wall Street Journal*, p. B1.

82. Hom, P. W. (2011). Organizational exit. In S. Zedeck (Ed.), *Handbook of Industrial and Organizational Psychology* (Vol. 2). Washington, DC: American Psychological Association, pp. 325–75. *See also* Phillips, J. M. (1998). Effects of realistic job previews on multiple organizational outcomes: A meta-analysis. *Academy of Management Journal* 41, pp. 673–90.

83. Savchetz, D., quoted in David, G. (2004, Apr. 5). One truck a minute. *Fortune*, p. 258.

84. Zielinski, D. (2019, Feb. 19). New onboarding technology cuts down manual tasks. *SHRM Online*. Retrieved from *https://www.shrm.org/resourcesandtools/hr-topics/technology/pages/new-onboarding-technology-cuts-down-manual-tasks.aspx* on Feb. 19, 2019.

85. Bamboo HR. (2020). *The new definitive guide to onboarding*. Retrieved from *https://www.bamboohr.com/resources/ebooks/the-new-definitive-guide-to-onboarding/* on Mar. 17, 2020. *See also* Maurer (2018), op. cit. *See also* Wesson, M. J., and Gogus, C. I. (2005). Shaking hands with a computer: An examination of two methods of organizational newcomer orientation. *Journal of Applied Psychology* 90, pp. 1018–26.

86. Robb, D. (2016, Dec.-Jan.). New-hire onboarding portals provide a warmer welcome. *HRMagazine*, pp. 58–60.

87. Janove, J. (2018, Dec. 10). Putting humanity into HR compliance: Onboarding shouldn't be like boarding a plane. *SHRM Online*. Retrieved from *https://www.shrm.org/resourcesandtools/hr-topics/employee-relations/humanity-into-hr/pages/putting-humanity-into-hr-compliance-onboarding-shouldnt-be-like-boarding-a-plane.aspx* on Dec. 10, 2018.

88. Falcone, P. (2018, April 24). Effective onboarding should last for months. *SHRM Online*. Retrieved from *https://www.shrm.org/resourcesandtools/hr-topics/talent-acquisition/pages/effective-onboarding-should-last-for-months.aspx* on Apr. 24, 2018.

89. Hirsch (2017), op. cit.

90. Bamboo HR (2020), op. cit. *See also* Maurer (2018), op. cit. *See also* Bauer and Erdogan (2011), op. cit. *See also* Watkins, M. (2003). *The First 90 Days: Critical Success Strategies for Leaders at All Levels*. Boston: Harvard Business School Publishing.

10 PERFORMANCE MANAGEMENT

Questions This Chapter Will Help Managers Answer

LO 10-1   What steps can I take, as a manager, to make the performance-management process more relevant and acceptable to those who will be affected by it?

LO 10-2   How can we best fit our approach to performance management with the strategic direction of our department and business?

LO 10-3   Should managers and nonmanagers be appraised from multiple perspectives—for example, by those above, by those below, by peers, and by customers?

LO 10-4   How can we train raters at all levels in the mechanics of performance management and in the art of giving feedback?

LO 10-5   What would an effective performance-management process look like?

PERFORMANCE REVIEWS ARE DEAD; LONG LIVE PERFORMANCE REVIEWS!*

The list of major U.S. companies that are abandoning the traditional, year-end performance review reads like a Who's Who: GE, Goldman Sachs, Deloitte, SAP, Accenture, Adobe, Gap, Medtronic, PwC, IBM, Microsoft; the list goes on and on. It seems like this is a performance management revolution–a fundamental change in the ways that companies manage their employees and the relationships that managers have with them. But wait–is this a stampede? Hardly. Recent surveys of employers in more than 50 countries indicate that 90 percent or more still undertake formal reviews of employee performance each year; 89 percent calculate an overall score for each worker and link pay to these ratings. Yet change is unmistakable.

Those at GE are typical. Here's the old approach:

- Employees had a formal performance review at the end of the year.
- Managers placed staff in categories ranging from "role model" to "unsatisfactory," with raises tied to ratings and reviews.
- From goal setting to manager approvals, reviews could take as long as 5 months to complete.

Under its new system,

- Managers and employees check in frequently throughout the year, holding a brief annual summary, rather than a review.
- Employees use a mobile app, PD@GE, to give one another feedback at any time.
- GE pilot-tested rating-free reviews with 30,000 employees.

   Without ratings, pay and bonus decisions may become more nuanced, according to company leaders. Though high performers can still be rewarded with annual raises and bonuses, managers can make finer distinctions among employees who fall in the middle of the spectrum. The hope is that more detailed feedback may spur middle-of-the-road employees to aim higher. Some employees may be happier without ratings, but research suggests managers have a trickier task. A survey of 9,000 managers and employees by advisory firm CEB found that employees felt the quality of review conversations suffered because managers struggled to explain to workers how they performed in the past and to provide specific steps for improvement.

°*Sources:* Hancock, B., Hioe, E., and Schaninger, B. (2018, Apr.). The fairness factor in performance management. *McKinsey Quarterly.* Retrieved from *https://www.mckinsey.com/business-functions/organization/our-insights/the-fairness-factor-in-performance-management* on May 1, 2018. Miller, S. (2017, Aug. 14). Employers try better ways to measure and reward performance. *SHRM Online.* Retrieved from *https://www.shrm.org/resourcesandtools/hr-topics/compensation/pages/better-ways-measure-reward-performance.aspx* on Aug. 14, 2017. Hoffman, L. (2017, Apr. 22). Goldman makes feedback shift. *The Wall Street Journal,* p. B1. Silverman, R. E. (2016, July 26). GE does away with employee ratings. *The Wall Street Journal.* Retrieved from *www.wsj.com/articles/ge-does-away-with-employee-ratings-1469541602* on July 27, 2016. Schumpeter. (2016, Feb. 20). Reports of the death of performance reviews are exaggerated. *The Economist,* p. 59. Goler, L., Gale, J., and Grant, A. (2016, Nov.). Let's not kill performance evaluations yet. *Harvard Business Review.* Retrieved from *https://hbr.org/2016/11/lets-not-kill-performance-evaluations-yet* on Dec. 2, 2016. CEB. (2016, May 12). The real impact of removing performance ratings on employee performance. Retrieved from *www.cebglobal.com/blogs/corporate-hr-removing-performance-ratings-is-unlikely-to-improve-performance/* on May 9, 2017.

In reality, firms are not getting rid of performance reviews; they are modifying them, hopefully for the better. Here are five changes that are proving particularly popular:

1. Companies are getting rid of "ranking and yanking," in which those with the lowest scores each year are fired. Research indicates that forced ranking does not boost productivity, cooperation with others, creativity, or personal improvement. It actually creates antagonism between managers and workers.
2. Annual reviews are being replaced with more frequent ones–quarterly or even weekly.
3. There is separation between performance reviews and pay reviews.
4. Some performance reviews are turning into "performance previews," focusing more on discovering and developing employees' potential than on rating their past work.
5. Technology in the form of apps and tools that workers and managers can use to track worker performance on a real-time basis, often with graphs and charts, is becoming widely accepted. Apps from firms such as Zugata, Reflektive, BetterWorks, and Small Improvements are just a few. They create a record of feedback that is more reliable than memory months after the fact.

In the conclusion to this case, we will examine the advantages and disadvantages of the changes we've described and will provide answers to the following challenges.

Challenges

1. It's one thing to get rid of numerical ratings, but managers still have to decide whom to promote, perhaps whom to let go, the relative sizes of pay raises, and bonuses. Will the new systems help them do those things more effectively?
2. Are there features of current performance-management systems that are worth keeping?
3. What types of safeguards might you suggest to ensure fairness, transparency, and accountability in performance-management systems?

The chapter-opening vignette reveals just how complex performance management can be because it includes both developmental (feedback) and evaluation (pay, promotions) issues, as well as both technical aspects (design of a performance-management system) and interpersonal aspects (check-in or feedback interviews). This chapter's objective is to present a balanced view of the performance-management process, considering both its technical and its interpersonal aspects. Let's begin by examining the nature of this process.

MANAGING FOR MAXIMUM PERFORMANCE[1]

Consider the following situations:

- An athlete searching for a coach who really understands her.
- A student scheduled to see his guidance counselor at school.

- A worker who has just begun working for a new boss.
- A work team and a supervisor about to meet to discuss objectives for the next quarter.

What do these situations all have in common? The need to manage performance effectively–at the level of either the individual or the work team. Think of **performance management** as a kind of compass, one that indicates a person's actual direction as well as a person's desired direction. Like a compass, the job of the manager (or athletic coach or school guidance counselor) is to indicate where that person is now, and to help focus attention and effort on the desired direction.

Unfortunately, the concept of performance management means something very specific, and much too narrow, to many managers. They tend to equate it with **performance appraisal** or rating exercise they typically do once a year to identify and discuss job-relevant strengths and weaknesses of individuals or work teams. This is a mistake! Would it surprise you to learn that a poll of 750 HR executives revealed that 58 percent of them graded their own performance-management systems a C or below? Many were frustrated that managers do not have the courage to give constructive feedback to employees. Indeed, only 30 percent of respondents agreed that employees have a sense of trust in their performance-management systems. Although HR professionals often devise the systems and follow up at the end, they cannot control how effectively managers execute reviews. Clearly, there is lots of room for improvement.[2]

On the other hand, there are solid organizational payoffs for implementing strong performance-management systems, empirical research has found. Organizations with such systems are 51 percent more likely to outperform their competitors on financial measures and 41 percent more likely to outperform their competitors on nonfinancial measures (e.g., customer satisfaction, employee retention, quality of products or services).[3]

Obviously, if performance management were easy to do, more firms would do it. One of the reasons it is difficult to execute well throughout an entire organization is that performance management demands daily, not annual, attention from every manager. It is part of a continuous process of improvement over time.

So what is the role of performance appraisal in the overall performance-management process? Performance appraisal is a necessary, but far from sufficient, part of performance management. Typically, appraisal is done annually, or in some firms, quarterly. *Performance management requires willingness and a commitment to focus on improving performance at the level of the individual or team every day.* A compass provides instantaneous, real-time information that describes the difference between one's current and desired course. To practice sound performance management, managers must do the same thing–provide timely feedback about performance while constantly focusing everyone's attention on the ultimate objective (e.g., world-class customer service).

At a general level, the broad process of performance management requires that you do three things well:

1. Define performance.
2. Facilitate performance.
3. Encourage performance.

Let's explore each of these ideas briefly.

Define Performance

A manager who defines performance ensures that individual employees or teams know what is expected of them and that they stay focused on effective performance.[4] How does the manager do this? By paying careful attention to three key elements: *goals, measures,* and *assessment.*

Goal setting has a proven track record of success in improving performance in a variety of settings and cultures.[5] How does it improve performance? Studies show that goals direct attention to the specific performance in question (e.g., percentage of satisfied customers), they mobilize efforts to accomplish higher levels of performance, and they foster persistence for higher levels of performance.[6] The practical implications of this work are clear: Set specific, challenging goals, for this clarifies precisely what is expected and leads to high levels of performance.[7] Several important qualifications are in order, though: (1) More goals are not better than fewer. Experts suggest setting no more than three to four goals.[8] (2) Some jobs are fluid and unpredictable, so goals must be agile. Setting goals provides context, direction, meaning, and energy. (3) Individual objectives do not work well when work is team based or when results depend on factors outside an employee's control.[9] When individual goal setting is appropriate, however, on average, studies show that you can expect to improve productivity 10 percent by using goal setting.[10]

The mere presence of goals is not sufficient. Managers must also be able to *measure* the extent to which goals have been accomplished. Goals such as "make the company successful" are too vague to be useful. Measures such as the number of defective parts produced per million or the average time to respond to a customer's inquiry are much more tangible.

In defining performance, the third requirement is *assessment.* Regular assessment of progress toward goals focuses the attention and efforts of an employee or a team. Adobe does this through quarterly "check-ins." Managers at The Gap hold monthly "touch-base" sessions. To define performance properly, therefore, you must do three things well: set goals, measure accomplishment, and provide regular assessments of progress. Doing so will leave no doubt in the minds of your people what is expected of them, how it will be measured, and where they stand at any given point in time. There should be no surprises in the performance-management process—and regular assessments help ensure that there won't be.

Facilitate Performance

Managers who are committed to managing for maximum performance recognize that one of their major responsibilities is to eliminate roadblocks to successful performance.[11] Another is to provide adequate resources to get a job done right and on time, and a third is to pay careful attention to selecting employees, all of which are part of **performance facilitation**.

What are some examples of *obstacles* that can inhibit maximum performance? Consider just a few: outdated technology, poorly maintained equipment, lack of timely information, inefficient design of workspaces, and ineffective work methods. Employees are well aware of these, and they are only too willing to identify them—if managers will only ask for their input. Then it's the manager's job to eliminate these obstacles.

Having eliminated roadblocks to successful performance, the next step is to *provide adequate resources*—capital resources, material resources, or human resources.

After all, if employees lack the tools to reach the challenging goals they have set, they will become frustrated and disenchanted. Indeed, one observer has gone so far as to say, "It's immoral not to give people tools to meet tough goals."[12] Conversely, employees really appreciate it when their employer provides everything they need to perform well. Not surprisingly, they usually do perform well under those circumstances.

A final aspect of performance facilitation is the *careful selection of employees*. After all, the last thing any manager wants is to have people who are ill-suited to their jobs (e.g., by temperament or training) because this often leads to overstaffing, excessive labor costs, and reduced productivity. In leading companies, like Apple and Google, even top managers are expected to get actively involved in selecting new employees. Both companies typically require even experienced software developers to go through several hours of intense interviews.[13] If you're truly committed to managing for maximum performance, you pay attention to all of the details—all of the factors that might affect performance—and leave nothing to chance. That doesn't mean that you are constantly looking over everyone's shoulder. On the contrary, it implies greater self-management, more autonomy, and lots of opportunities to experiment, take risks, and be entrepreneurial.

Encourage Performance

The last area of management responsibility in a coordinated approach to performance management is **performance encouragement.** To encourage performance, especially repeated good performance, it's important to do three more things well: (1) *provide a sufficient number of rewards that employees really value, (2) in a timely fashion, and (3) in a fair manner.*

Don't bother offering rewards that nobody cares about, like a gift certificate to see a fortune teller. On the contrary, *begin by asking your people what's most important to them*—for example, pay, benefits, free time, merchandise, or special privileges. Then consider tailoring your awards program so that employees or teams can choose from a menu of similarly valued options.

Next, *provide rewards in a timely manner*, soon after major accomplishments. If there is an excessive delay between effective performance and receipt of the reward, then the reward loses its potential to motivate subsequent high performance.

Finally, provide rewards in a manner that employees consider *fair*. Fairness is a subjective concept, but it can be enhanced by adhering to four important practices[14]:

1. Voice—collect employee input through surveys or interviews.
2. Consistency—ensure that all employees are treated consistently when seeking input and communicating about the process for administering rewards.
3. Relevance—as noted earlier, include rewards that employees really care about.
4. Communication—explain clearly the rules and logic of the rewards process.

In practice, there is much room for improvement. Thus, in a recent survey of 10,000 managers and employees, only 46 percent of the managers and 29 percent of the employees agreed with the statement "My last raise was based on performance."

In summary, managing for maximum performance requires that you do three things well: define performance, facilitate performance, and encourage performance. Like a compass, the role of the manager is to provide orientation, direction, and feedback. These ideas are shown graphically in Figure 10-1.

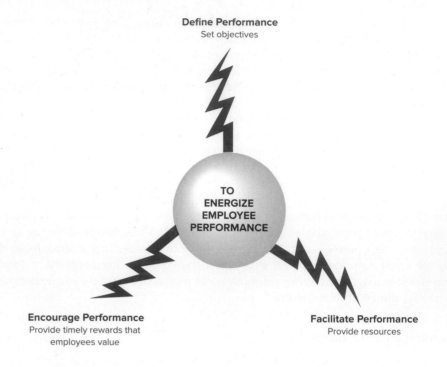

Figure 10–1

Elements of a performance-management system.

Performance Management in Practice

A study by RainmakerThinking of more than 500 managers in 40 different organizations found, unfortunately, that few managers consistently provide their direct reports with what Rainmaker calls the five management basics: clear statements of what's expected of each employee, explicit and measurable goals and deadlines, detailed evaluation of each person's work, clear feedback, and rewards distributed fairly. Can you see the similarity with the "Define, Facilitate, Encourage Performance" approach shown in Figure 10-1? Only 10 percent of managers provide all five of the basics at least once a week. Only 25 percent do so once a month. About a third fail to provide them even once a year![15] Clearly there is much room for improvement.

PURPOSES OF PERFORMANCE-MANAGEMENT SYSTEMS

Performance management has many facets. It is an exercise in observation and judgment, it is a feedback process, and it is an organizational intervention. It is an assessment process as well as an intensely emotional process. Above all, it is an inexact, human process. Not surprisingly, therefore, there is considerable dissatisfaction with many such systems.[16] If implemented well, however, they can serve several important purposes.

In general, there are two broad objectives of performance management systems: (1) to improve employees' work performance as they address their firms' strategic priorities and (2) to provide information to employees and managers for use in making work-related decisions. Here are five more specific purposes:

1. *They provide legal and formal organizational justification for employment decisions* to promote outstanding performers; to coach or counsel low performers; to train, transfer, or discipline others; to justify pay increases (or no increases); and as one

basis for reducing the size of the workforce. Performance management therefore serves as a key input for administering a formal reward and punishment system.

2. *They provide feedback to employees* and thereby serve as vehicles for personal and career development.

3. *They can help to identify developmental needs of employees* and to *establish objectives for training programs.*

4. *They can help diagnose organizational problems* by identifying training needs and the personal characteristics to consider in hiring, and they provide a basis for distinguishing between effective and ineffective performers.

5. *Data regarding employee performance can serve as criteria in HR research.* For example, test results can be correlated with performance ratings to evaluate the hypothesis that test scores predict job performance.[17] These ideas are shown graphically in Figure 10–2.

Should Organizations Abandon Performance Reviews?

Despite their shortcomings, performance reviews continue to be used widely, especially as a basis for tying pay to performance.[18] To attempt to avoid these shortcomings by doing away with reviews is no solution, for whenever people interact in organized settings, judgments about performance will be made–formally or informally. To illustrate, think of the last time you went to a concert, you watched a sporting event, a motorist cut in front of you, or you had to choose members of a project team. In each case, two processes were at work: observation and judgment. The real challenge, then, is to identify methods and techniques that are most likely to achieve the purposes we listed earlier. Let us begin by considering some of the fundamental requirements that determine whether a performance-management system will succeed or fail.

Requirements of Effective Performance-Rating Systems

Legally and scientifically, the key requirements of any performance-rating system are relevance, sensitivity, and reliability. In the context of ongoing operations, the key requirements are acceptability and practicality.[19] Let's consider each of these.

Figure 10–2

Purposes of Performance-Management Systems.

Relevance

Relevance implies that there are clear lines of sight between the performance standards for a particular job and organizational objectives and between the critical job requirements identified through a job analysis and the dimensions to be rated. In short, relevance is determined by answering the question "What really makes the difference between success and failure on a particular job, and according to whom?" The answer to the latter question is simple: the customer. Customers may be internal (e.g., your immediate boss, workers in another department) or external (those who buy your company's products or services). In all cases, it is important to pay attention to the things that the customer believes are important (e.g., on-time delivery, zero defects, information to solve business problems).

Performance standards translate job requirements into levels of acceptable or unacceptable employee behavior. They play a critical role in the job or work analysis–performance rating linkage, as Figure 10-3 indicates. Job analysis identifies *what* is to be done. Performance standards specify *how well* work is to be done. Such standards may be quantitative (e.g., time, errors) or qualitative (e.g., quality of work, ability to analyze market research data or a machine malfunction).

Relevance also implies the periodic maintenance and updating of job analyses, performance standards, and rating systems. Should the system be challenged in court, relevance will be a fundamental consideration in the arguments presented by both sides.

Sensitivity

Sensitivity implies that a performance-rating system is capable of distinguishing effective from ineffective performers. If it is not, and the best employees are rated no differently from the worst employees, then the system cannot be used for any administrative purpose. It certainly will not help employees to develop, and it will undermine the motivation of both supervisors ("pointless paperwork") and subordinates.

A major concern here is the purpose of the rating. One study found that raters process identical sets of performance-appraisal information differently, depending on whether a merit pay raise, a recommendation for further development, or the retention of a probationary employee is involved.[20] These results highlight the conflict between

---

ETHICAL DILEMMA
Employment Decisions Based on Performance

Performance rating actually encompasses two distinct processes: observation and judgment. Managers must observe performance, at least a representative sample of an employee's performance, if they are to be competent to judge its effectiveness.[a] Yet some managers assign performance ratings on the basis of small (and perhaps unrepresentative) samples of their subordinates' work. Others assign ratings based only on the subordinate's most

recent work. Is this ethical? And further, is it ethical to assign performance ratings (either good or bad) that differ from what a manager knows a subordinate deserves?

---

[a] Aguinis, H. (2019b). *Performance Management* (4th ed.). Chicago: Chicago Business Press. Moser, K., Schuler, H., and Funke, U. (1999). The moderating effect of raters' opportunities to observe ratees' job performance on the validity of an assessment center. *International Journal of Selection and Assessment* 7(3), pp. 355-67.

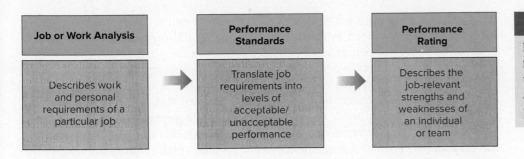

Job or Work Analysis		Performance Standards		Performance Rating
Describes work and personal requirements of a particular job	→	Translate job requirements into levels of acceptable/ unacceptable performance	→	Describes the job-relevant strengths and weaknesses of an individual or team

Figure 10–3

Relationship of performance standards to job or work analysis and performance rating.

ratings made for employment decisions and those made for employee development. Rating systems designed to support employment decisions demand performance information about differences *between* individuals, whereas systems designed to promote employee growth demand information about differences *within* individuals. The two different types of information are not interchangeable, and that is why performance-management systems designed to meet both purposes are more complex and costly.

Reliability

A third requirement of sound rating systems is **reliability**. In this context, it refers to consistency of judgment. For any given employee, ratings made by raters working independently of one another should agree closely. In practice, ratings made by supervisors tend to be more reliable than those made by peers.[21] Certainly, raters with different perspectives (e.g., supervisors, peers, subordinates) may see the same individual's job performance very differently, and this can actually make the feedback less useful and more problematic.[22] To provide reliable data, each rater must have an adequate opportunity to observe what the employee has done and the conditions under which he or she has done it; otherwise, unreliability may be confused with unfamiliarity.

Note that throughout this discussion there has been no mention of the validity or accuracy of raters' judgments. This is because we really do not know what "truth" is in performance appraisal. However, by making rating systems relevant, sensitive, and reliable—by satisfying the scientific and legal requirements for workable performance-rating systems—we can assume that the resulting judgments are valid as well.

Acceptability

In practice, **acceptability** is the most important requirement of all. We know, for example, that when senior managers emphasize the importance of the performance-management process—that is, when they "own" it—it is far more effective. When HR "owns" it, however, it is seen more as an administrative exercise.[23] Evidence also indicates that appraisal systems that are acceptable to those who will be affected by them lead to more favorable reactions to the process, increased motivation to improve performance, and increased trust for top management.[24]

Smart managers enlist the active support and cooperation of subordinates or teams by making explicit exactly what aspects of job performance they will be rated on. As we have seen, defining performance is the first step in performance management. Only then can we hope for acceptability and commitment.

Practicality

Practicality implies that appraisal instruments are easy for managers and employees to understand and use. Those that are not, or that impose inordinate time demands on all parties, simply are not practical, and managers will resist using them. As we have seen, managers need as much encouragement and organizational support as possible if thoughtful performance management is to take place.

In a broader context, we are concerned with developing employment-decision systems. From this perspective, relevance, sensitivity, and reliability are simply technical components of a system designed to make decisions about employees. However, just as much attention needs to be paid to ensuring acceptability and practicality. These five basic requirements of performance-rating systems should be embedded in the broader performance-management system because a lack of understanding of the context surrounding performance rating is likely to result in a failed system.

LEGALITIES

PERFORMANCE REVIEWS

There is a rich body of case law on this issue, and multiple reviews of it reached similar conclusions.[a] To avoid legal difficulties, consider taking the following steps:

1. Conduct a job analysis to determine the characteristics necessary for successful job performance.
2. Incorporate these characteristics into a rating instrument. This may be done by tying rating instruments to specific job behaviors (e.g., *behaviorally anchored rating scales*, as described later in this chapter), but the courts routinely accept less sophisticated approaches, such as simple graphic rating scales. Regardless of the method used, provide written standards to all raters.
3. Provide written instructions and train supervisors to use the rating instrument properly, including how to apply performance standards when making judgments. The uniform application of standards is very important. The vast majority of cases lost by organizations have involved evidence that subjective standards were applied unevenly to members of protected groups versus all other employees.
4. Establish a system to detect potentially discriminatory effects or abuses of the rating process.
5. Include formal appeal mechanisms, coupled with higher-level review of ratings.
6. Document the ratings and the reason for any termination decisions. This information may prove decisive in court, as long as it was not generated after the supervisor made the decision to terminate. Credibility is enhanced by documented ratings that describe specific examples of poor performance based on personal knowledge.[b]
7. Provide some form of performance counseling or corrective guidance to assist poor performers.

Here is a good example of step 6. In *Stone v. Xerox*, the organization had a fairly elaborate procedure for assisting poor performers.[c] Stone was employed as a sales representative and in fewer than 6 months had been given several written reprimands concerning customer complaints about his selling methods and failure to develop adequate written selling proposals. As a result, he was placed on a 1-month performance-improvement program designed to correct these deficiencies. This program was extended 30 days at Stone's request. When his performance still did not improve, he was placed on probation and told that failure to improve substantially would result in termination. Stone's performance continued to be substandard, and he was discharged at the end of the probationary period. When he sued Xerox, he lost.

Certainly, the type of evidence required to defend performance ratings is linked to the *purposes* for which the ratings are made. For example, if a rating of past performance is to be used as a predictor of future performance (i.e., promotions), evidence must show (1) that the ratings of past performance are, in fact, valid and (2) that the ratings of past performance are statistically related to *future* performance in another job.[d] At the very least, this latter step should include job-analysis results indicating the extent to which the requirements of the lower- and higher-level jobs overlap. Finally, to assess adverse impact, organizations should keep accurate records of who is eligible for and interested in promotion. These two factors, *eligibility* and *interest*, define the **applicant group.**

In summary, it is not difficult to offer prescriptions for scientifically sound, court-proof rating systems, but as we have seen, implementing them requires diligent attention by organizations plus a commitment to make them work. In developing a performance-rating system, the most basic requirement is to determine what you want the system to accomplish. This requires a strategy for the management of performance.

---

[a]Vranjes, T. (2016, Feb. 19). Reduce the legal risks of performance reviews. Retrieved from *www.shrm.org/resourcesandtools/legal-and-compliance/state-and-local updates/pages/reduce-the-legal-risks-of-performance-reviews.aspx* on Feb. 20, 2016. Meyrowitz et al. (2012), op. cit. Segal, J. A. (2010, Nov.). Performance management blunders. *HR*, pp. 75-78. Malos, S. B. (1998). Current legal issues in performance appraisal. In J. W. Smither (Ed.), *Performance Appraisal: State of the Art in Practice.* San Francisco: Jossey-Bass, pp. 49-94.

[b]*Paquin v. Federal National Mortgage Association* (1996, July 31). Civil Action No. 94-1261 SSH.

[c]*Stone v. Xerox* (1982). 685 F. 2d 1387 (11th Cir.).

[d]*United States v. City of Chicago* (1978). 573 F. 2d 416 (7th Cir.).

The Strategic Dimension of Performance Ratings

In the study of work motivation, a fairly well-established principle is that the things that get rewarded get done. At least one author has termed this "the greatest management principle in the world."[25] A fundamental issue for managers, then, is "What kind of behavior do I want to encourage in my subordinates?" GE, which is in the midst of a multiyear effort to remake itself into a leaner, innovation-driven company, emphasizes behaviors such as "stay lean to go fast" and "learn and adapt to win."[26]

To be most useful, therefore, the strategic management of performance must be linked to the strategies an organization (or a strategic business unit) uses to gain competitive advantage–for example, innovation, speed, quality enhancement, or cost control.[27] As one manager observed, "If you can't find hard measures of why something's strategically important, you let it go."[28]

Rating systems that focus on results are popular but a recent trend is to give equal weight to *how* the results were accomplished. The objective is to ensure that behaviors used to achieve the results are consistent with the values of an organization. This is termed "full-spectrum" leadership.[29]

In Japan, greater emphasis is placed on the psychological and behavioral sides of performance rating than on objective outcomes. Thus, an employee will be rated in terms of the effort he or she puts into a job; on integrity, loyalty, and cooperative spirit; and on how well he or she serves the customer. Short-term results tend to be much less important than long-term personal development, the establishment and maintenance of long-term relationships with customers (i.e., behaviors), and increasing market share.[30]

Once managers decide what they want the rating system to accomplish, their next questions are "What's the best method? Which technique should I use?" As in so many other areas of HR management, there is no simple answer. The following section considers some alternative methods, along with their strengths and weaknesses. Because readers of this book are more likely to be users than developers of rating systems, our focus is primarily on describing and illustrating them. For more detailed information, consult the references cited.

ALTERNATIVE METHODS OF APPRAISING EMPLOYEE PERFORMANCE

Many regard rating methods or formats as the central issue in performance appraisal; this, however, is not the case.[31] Broader issues must also be considered–such as *trust* in the appraisal system; the *attitudes* of managers and employees; the *purpose, frequency,* and *source* of appraisal data; and rater *training*. Viewed in this light, rating formats play only a supporting role in the overall appraisal process.

Behavior-oriented rating methods focus on employee behaviors, either by comparing the performance of employees to that of other employees (so-called **relative rating systems**) or by evaluating each employee in terms of performance standards without reference to others (so-called **absolute rating systems**). **Results-oriented rating methods** place primary emphasis on what an employee produces; dollar volume of sales, the number of units produced, and the number of wins during a baseball season are examples. Management by objectives (MBO) and work planning and review use this results-oriented approach.

Evidence indicates that ratings (i.e., judgments about performance) are not strongly related to results.[32] Why? Ratings depend heavily on the mental processes of the rater. Because these processes are complex, there may be errors of judgment in the ratings. Conversely, results depend heavily on conditions that may be outside the control of the individual worker, such as the availability of supplies or the contributions of others. Thus, most measures of results provide only partial coverage of the overall domain of job performance. With these considerations in mind, let's examine the behavior- and results-oriented systems more fully.

Behavior-Oriented Rating Methods

Narrative Essay
The simplest type of absolute rating system is the **narrative essay,** in which a rater describes, in writing, an employee's strengths, weaknesses, and potential, together with suggestions for improvement. This approach assumes that a candid statement from a rater who is knowledgeable about an employee's performance is just as valid as more formal and more complicated rating methods.

If essays are done well, they can provide detailed feedback to subordinates regarding their performance. On the other hand, comparisons across individuals, groups, or departments are almost impossible because different essays touch on different aspects of each subordinate's performance. This makes it difficult to use essay information for employment decisions because subordinates are not compared objectively and ranked relative to one another. Methods that compare employees to one another are more useful for this purpose.

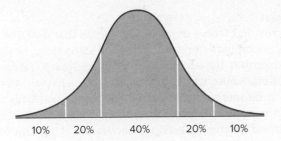

Figure 10–4

Example of a forced distribution: 40 percent of the ratees must be rated "average," 20 percent "above average," 20 percent "below average," 10 percent "outstanding," and 10 percent "unsatisfactory."

Ranking

Simple ranking requires only that a rater order all employees from highest to lowest, from "best" employee to "worst" employee. **Alternation ranking** requires that a rater initially list all employees on a sheet of paper. From this list, he or she first chooses the best employee (No. 1), then the worst employee (No. *n*), then the second best (No. 2), then the second worst (No. *n* - 1), and so forth, alternating from the top to the bottom of the list until all employees have been ranked.

Paired Comparisons

Use of **paired comparisons** is a more systematic method for comparing employees to one another. Here each employee is compared with every other employee, usually in terms of an overall category such as "technical/functional expertise." The number of pairs of ratees to be compared may be calculated from the formula $[n(n - 1)]/2$. Hence, if 10 individuals were being compared, $[10(9)]/2$, or 45, comparisons would be required. The rater's task is simply to choose the "better" of each pair, and each employee's rank is determined by counting the number of times she or he was rated superior. As you can see, the number of comparisons becomes quite large as the number of employees increases. On the other hand, ranking methods that compare employees to one another are useful for generating initial rankings for purposes of employment decisions.

Forced Distribution

Forced distribution is another method of comparing employees to one another. With this method, the overall distribution of ratings is forced into a normal, or bell-shaped, curve, under the assumption that a relatively small portion of employees is truly outstanding, a relatively small portion is unsatisfactory, and everybody else falls in between. That assumption may not reflect reality.[33] Figure 10-4 illustrates this method, assuming that five rating categories are used.

Forced distribution does eliminate clustering almost all employees at the top of the distribution (rater **leniency**), at the bottom of the distribution (rater **severity**), or in the middle (**central tendency**). Who tends to be most lenient? One study found that individuals who score high in agreeableness (trustful, sympathetic, cooperative, and polite) tend to be most lenient, whereas those who score high in conscientiousness (strive for excellence, high performance standards, set difficult goals) tend to be least lenient.[34]

Forced distribution can foster a great deal of employee resentment, however, if an entire group of employees *as a group* is either superior or substandard. If teamwork and social support are necessary to accomplish work, such systems can foster dysfunctional competition.[35] In general, they are seen as less fair than absolute rating systems.[36] They are most useful when a large number of employees must be rated and there is more than one rater.

Behavioral Checklist

Here the rater is provided with a series of statements that describe job-related behavior. His or her task is simply to check which of the statements, or the extent to which each statement, describes the employee. In this approach, raters are not so much evaluators as reporters whose task is to describe job behavior. Moreover, descriptive ratings are likely to be more reliable than evaluative (good–bad) ratings,[37] and they reduce the cognitive demands placed on raters.[38] One such method, the **Likert method of summed ratings**, presents a declarative statement (e.g., "She or he follows up on customer complaints") followed by several response categories, such as "always," "very often," "fairly often," "occasionally," and "never." The rater checks the response category that he or she thinks describes the employee best. Each category is weighted, for example, from 5 ("always") to 1 ("never") if the statement describes desirable behavior. To derive an overall numerical rating (or score) for each employee, the weights of the responses that were checked for each item are summed. Figure 10–5 shows a portion of a summed rating scale for rating teacher performance.

Critical Incidents

Critical incidents are brief anecdotal reports by supervisors of things employees do that are particularly effective or ineffective in accomplishing parts of their jobs. They focus on behaviors, not traits. For example, a store manager in a retail computer store observed Mr. Wang, a salesperson, doing the following:

> Mr. Wang encouraged the customer to try typing a message on a tablet computer using a virtual keyboard. Grammatical and spelling errors were highlighted but easy to fix using an "auto-correct" feature of office-suite software. As a result, Mr. Wang sold the customer the tablet computer and the office-suite software.

Such anecdotes force attention onto the ways in which situations determine job behavior and on ways of doing the job successfully that may be unique to the person described. Hence, they can provide the basis for training programs. Critical incidents also lend themselves nicely to "check-in" sessions and performance-review feedback because

Figure 10–5

A portion of a summed rating scale. The rater simply checks the response category that best describes the teacher's behavior. Response categories vary in scale value from 5 points (strongly agree) to 1 point (strongly disagree). A total score is computed by summing the points associated with each item.

	Strongly agree	Agree	Neutral	Disagree	Strongly disagree
The teacher was well prepared.					
The teacher used understandable language.					
The teacher made me think.					
The teacher's feedback on students' work aided learning.					
The teacher knew his or her field well.					

supervisors can focus on actual job behaviors rather than on vaguely defined traits. They are judging performance, not personality. Recording incidents on a daily, or even a weekly, basis is burdensome, but employee feedback apps that incorporate real-time inputs from peers, subordinates, supervisors, and even customers make this much less of a problem today than it once was.[39] Incidents alone, however, do not permit comparisons across individuals or departments. Graphic rating scales may overcome this problem.

Graphic Rating Scales

Many organizations use **graphic rating scales**.[40] Figure 10-6 shows a portion of one such scale. Many different forms of graphic rating scales exist. In terms of the amount of structure provided, the scales differ in three ways:

1. The degree to which the meaning of the response categories is defined (in Figure 10-6, what does *conditional* mean?).
2. The degree to which the individual who is interpreting the ratings (e.g., a higher-level reviewing official) can tell clearly what response was intended.
3. The degree to which the performance dimensions are defined for the rater (in Figure 10-6, what does *dependability* mean?).

Graphic rating scales may not yield the depth of essays or critical incidents, but they are less time consuming to develop and administer. They also allow results to be expressed in quantitative terms; they consider more than one performance dimension; and, because the scales are standardized, they facilitate comparisons across employees. Graphic rating scales have come under frequent attack, but when compared with more sophisticated forced-choice scales, the graphic scales have proven just as reliable and valid and are more acceptable to raters.[41]

Behaviorally Anchored Rating Scales

Graphic rating scales that use critical incidents to anchor various points along the scale are known as **behaviorally anchored rating scales (BARS)**. Their major advantage is

Figure 10–6

A portion of a graphic rating scale.

Rating factors	Level of performance				
	Unsatisfactory	Conditional	Satisfactory	Above satisfactory	Outstanding
Attendance					
Appearance					
Dependability					
Quality of work					
Quantity of work					
Relationship with people					
Job knowledge					

that they define the dimensions to be rated in behavioral terms and use critical incidents to describe various levels of performance. BARS therefore provide a common frame of reference for raters. An example of the job-knowledge portion of a BARS for police patrol officers is shown in Figure 10-7. BARS require considerable effort to develop,[42] yet there is little research evidence to support the superiority of BARS over other types of rating systems.[43] Nevertheless, the participative process required to develop them provides information that is useful for other organizational purposes, such as communicating clearly to employees exactly what good performance means in the context of their jobs.

Results-Oriented Rating Methods

Management by Objectives

Management by objectives (MBO) is a well-known process of managing that relies on goal setting to establish objectives for the organization as a whole, for each department, for each manager within each department, and for each employee. At Kraft Heinz, for example, employees display their personal objectives on their desks, while those of top executives, including the CEO, are posted widely. The objectives are data-driven, measurable, and linked to the goals of other employees to encourage teamwork as well as the company's values of ownership and transparency.[44]

To establish objectives, the key people involved should do three things: (1) meet to *agree on the major objectives* for a given period of time (because businesses no longer have clear annual cycles and it is important to engage in agile goal setting), (2) *develop plans* for how and when the objectives will be accomplished, and (3) *agree on the*

Figure 10-7
A behaviorally anchored rating scale to assess the job knowledge of police patrol officers.

JOB KNOWLEDGE (Awareness of procedures, laws, and court rulings and changes in them)

High (7, 8, or 9)
- Always follows correct procedures for evidence preservation at the scene of a crime
- Is fully aware of recent court rulings and conducts himself or herself accordingly
- Searches a citizen's vehicle with probable cause, thereby discovering smuggled narcotics

Average (4, 5, or 6)
- Arrests a suspect at 11:00 p.m. on a warrant only after ensuring that the warrant had been cleared for night service
- Distinguishes between civil matters and police matters
- Seldom has to ask others about points of law

Low (1, 2, or 3)
- Is consistently unaware of general orders and/or departmental policy
- Arrests a suspect for a misdemeanor not committed in his or her presence
- Misinforms the public on legal matters through lack of knowledge

Examples of the behavior of patrol officers who are usually rated high, average, and low on job knowledge by supervisors

measurement tools for determining whether the objectives have been met. Progress reviews are held regularly until the end of the period for which the objectives were established. At that time, those who established objectives at each level in the organization meet to evaluate the results and to agree on the objectives for the next period.[45]

To some, MBO is a complete system of planning and control and a complete philosophy of management.[46] In theory, MBO promotes success in each employee because, as each employee succeeds, so do that employee's manager, the department, and the organization. But this is true only to the extent that the individual, departmental, and organizational goals are compatible.[47] That is typically not the case.[48]

Work Planning and Review

Work planning and review is similar to MBO; however, it places greater emphasis on the periodic review of work plans by both supervisor and subordinate in order to identify goals attained, problems encountered, and the need for training.[49] Adobe's monthly "check-ins" and Gap Inc.'s monthly "touch-base" sessions are consistent with this approach.[50] Table 10-1 presents a summary of the rating methods we have just discussed.

Table 10-1

A SNAPSHOT OF THE ADVANTAGES AND DISADVANTAGES OF ALTERNATIVE APPRAISAL METHODS

Behavior-oriented methods

Narrative essay. Good for individual feedback and development but difficult to make comparisons across employees.

Ranking and paired comparisons. Good for making comparisons across employees but provides little basis for individual feedback and development.

Forced distribution. Forces raters to make distinctions among employees but may be unfair and inaccurate if a group of employees, as a group, is either very effective or ineffective.

Behavioral checklist. Easy to use, provides a direct link between job analysis and performance appraisal, can be numerically scored, and facilitates comparisons across employees. However, the meaning of response categories may be interpreted differently by different raters.

Critical incidents. Focuses directly on job behaviors, emphasizes what employees did that was effective or ineffective, but can be very time consuming to develop.

Graphic rating scales (including BARS). Easy to use, very helpful for providing feedback for individual development and facilitating comparisons across employees. BARS are time consuming to develop, but dimensions and scale points are defined clearly. Graphic rating scales often do not define dimensions or scale points clearly.

Results-oriented systems

Management by objectives. Focuses on results and on identifying each employee's contribution to the success of the unit or organization. However, MBO is generally short-term oriented, provides few insights into employee behavior, and does not facilitate comparison across employees.

Work planning and review. In contrast to MBO, emphasizes process over outcomes. Requires frequent supervisor/subordinate review of work plans. Does not facilitate comparisons across employees.

When Should Each Technique Be Used?

You have just read about a number of alternative appraisal formats, each with its own advantages and disadvantages. At this point, you are probably asking yourself, What's the bottom line–I know that no method is perfect, but what should I do? First, remember that the rating format is not as important as the relevance and acceptability of the rating system. Second, the following is some advice based on systematic comparisons among the various methods.

There is no clear "winner, and researchers generally agree that the type of rating scale per se does not lead to better ratings."[51] However, the researchers were able to provide several "if . . . then" propositions and general conclusions, including the following:

- If the objective is to compare employees across raters for important employment decisions (e.g., promotion, merit pay), then don't use MBO or work planning and review. They are not based on a standardized rating scheme for all employees.
- If you use a BARS, then also use a feedback app to incorporate real-time performance assessments. Multiple data points will improve the accuracy of the ratings and will help supervisors distinguish between effective and ineffective employees.[52]
- If objective performance data are available, then MBO is the best strategy to use. Remember, though, that *how* an employee or a manager achieves results is also important.
- In general, appraisal methods that are best in a broad, organizational sense–BARS and MBO–are the most difficult to use and maintain. No rating method is foolproof.
- Methods that focus on describing, rather than evaluating, behavior (e.g., BARS, summed rating scales) produce results that are the most interpretable across raters. They help remove the effects of individual differences in raters.[53]
- No rating method has been an unqualified success when used as a basis for merit pay or promotional decisions.
- When certain statistical corrections are made, the correlations between scores on alternative rating formats are very high. Hence, all the formats measure essentially the same thing.

WHO SHOULD EVALUATE PERFORMANCE?

The most fundamental requirement for any rater is that he or she has an adequate opportunity to observe the ratee's job performance over a reasonable period of time (e.g., 6 months). This suggests several possible raters.

The Immediate Supervisor   Among the nearly 80 percent of firms that conduct performance ratings, this person is the most common rater.[54] She or he is probably most familiar with the individual's performance and, in most jobs, has had the best opportunity to observe actual job performance. Furthermore, the immediate supervisor is probably best able to relate the individual's performance to what the department and organization are trying to accomplish, and to distinguish among various dimensions of performance.[55] Because she or he also is responsible for reward (and punishment) decisions, and for managing the overall performance-management process,[56] it is not surprising that feedback from supervisors is more highly related to performance than that from any other source.[57]

Peers   In some jobs, such as outside sales, the immediate supervisor may observe a subordinate's actual job performance only rarely (and indirectly, through written reports). In other environments, such as self-managed work teams, there is no supervisor. Sometimes objective indicators, such as the number of units sold, can provide useful performance-related information, but in other circumstances, the judgment of peers is even better. Peers can provide a perspective on performance that is different from that of immediate supervisors. Thus, a member of a cross-functional team may be in a better position to rate another team member than that team member's immediate supervisor. However, to reduce potential friendship bias while simultaneously increasing the feedback value of the information provided, it is important to specify exactly what the peers are to evaluate[58]–for example, "the quality of her help on technical problems." Even then, however, it is important to be aware of *context effects*. That is, ratings might differ, depending on the context in which the technical problems occurred–in a crisis versus a less stressful context.[59] Peer ratings can provide useful information, but in light of the potential problems associated with them, friendship bias and context effects, it is wise not to rely on them as the sole source of information about performance.

Subordinates   Appraisal by subordinates can be a useful input to the immediate supervisor's development,[60] and the ratings are of significantly higher quality when used for that purpose.[61] Subordinates know firsthand the extent to which the supervisor *actually* delegates, how well he or she communicates, the type of leadership style he or she is most comfortable with, and the extent to which he or she plans and organizes. Longitudinal research shows that managers who met with their direct reports to discuss their upward feedback improved more than other managers. Further, managers improved more in years when they discussed the previous year's feedback with their direct reports than in years when they did not. This is important because it demonstrates that what managers do with upward feedback is related to its benefits.[62]

Should subordinate ratings be anonymous? Managers want to know who said what, but subordinates prefer to remain anonymous to avoid retribution. To address these concerns, collect and combine the ratings in such a manner that a manager's overall rating is not distorted by an extremely divergent opinion.[63] Like peer assessments, they provide only one perspective on performance, although evidence indicates that ratings provided by peers and subordinates are comparable, for they reflect the same underlying dimensions.[64]

Self-Appraisal   There are several arguments to recommend wider use of self-appraisals. The opportunity to participate in the performance-appraisal process, particularly if appraisal is combined with goal setting, improves the ratee's motivation and reduces her or his defensiveness during the appraisal interview.[65] On the other hand, self-appraisals tend to be more lenient, less variable, and more biased, and they tend to show less agreement with the judgments of others.[66] Thus, a study of 3,850 managers of Walgreens drugstores who were in the same store and had the same boss for two straight years found a correlation of only 0.40 between self- and boss-ratings.[67] Moreover, because U.S. employees tend to give themselves higher marks than their supervisors do (conflicting findings have been found with mainland Chinese and Taiwanese employees),[68] self-appraisals are probably more appropriate for counseling and development than for employment decisions.

Customers Served   In some situations, the consumers of an individual's or organization's services can provide a unique perspective on job performance. Examples

Customers are often able to rate important aspects of the performance of employees in frontline customer-contact positions.
Ariel Skelley/Blend Images/Getty Images

abound: subscribers to a cable-television service, bank customers, clients of a brokerage house, and citizens of a local police- or fire-protection district. Although the customers' objectives cannot be expected to correspond completely with the organization's objectives, the information that customers provide can serve as useful input for employment decisions, such as those regarding promotion, transfer, and need for training. It can also be used to assess the impact of training or as a basis for self-development. At GE, for example, the customers of senior managers are interviewed formally and regularly as part of the managers' appraisal process. Their evaluations are important, but at the same time they also build commitment, because customers are giving time and information to help GE.[69]

Are Supervisors' Ratings Affected by Other Sources of Information about Performance?

Thus far we have assumed that each source of performance information, be it the supervisor, peer, subordinate, self, or client, makes his or her judgment individually and independently from other individuals. In practice, however, assessing performance is not strictly an individual task. Thus, Salesforce.com lets people post Twitter-length questions about their performance in exchange for anonymous feedback. Two-thirds of the questions come from managers.[70] In other words, information from outside sources may influence supervisors' ratings, and they may change their ratings, particularly when a ratee's peers provide information perceived as useful.[71] Information is perceived to be most useful when it agrees with the rater's direct observation of the employee's performance.[72] In sum, although direct observation is the main influence on ratings, the presence of indirect information also is likely to affect them.[73]

Supervisors may distort their ratings to accomplish goals that they value (e.g., motivating subordinates), or to avoid negative repercussions from assigning ratings that subordinates or superiors will find objectionable.[74] Now let's consider a more formal procedure for incorporating multiple sources of performance information.

Multirater or 360-Degree Feedback

Many organizations now use input from managers, subordinates, peers, and customers to provide a perspective on performance from all angles (360 degrees). There are at least four reasons such an approach is potentially valuable[75]:

1. It includes observations from different perspectives and perhaps includes different aspects of performance that capture the complexities of an individual's performance in multiple roles.
2. Feedback from multiple sources may reinforce feedback from the boss, thereby making it harder to discount the viewpoint of that single person.
3. It may improve the reliability of performance information because it originates from multiple sources and not just one.
4. It has the potential to decrease biases, since multiple perspectives and individuals are involved.

What does the research literature on **360-degree feedback** tell us? Evidence indicates that ratings from these different sources generally do not agree closely with each other. Thus, one study found that the correlations among ratings made by self, peer, supervisor, and subordinate raters ranged from a high of 0.79 (supervisor–peer) to a low of 0.14 (subordinate–self).[76] However, evidence also indicates that ratings from the different sources are comparable, for they reflect the same underlying dimensions of performance.[77]

What about the effectiveness of feedback from such systems? Does it improve subsequent job performance? A comprehensive review found that the effects of multisource feedback have been mixed at best.[78] Perhaps the biggest problem is that conflicting feedback information often generated from 360-degree rating systems can actually make the feedback less useful and even problematic. This finding has led many practitioners to become quite negative about these systems, even though they had been quite positive when the systems were first introduced.[79]

To overcome these potential problems, decision makers need to be aware of the personal biases of raters and attempt to control their effects. To do this, consider taking the following steps[80]:

- Make sure that 360-degree feedback has a single, clear purpose—development.
- Train all raters to understand the overall process as well as how to complete forms and avoid common rating errors. UPS, for example, explains the 360-degree feedback process and discusses how data will be used. Recognize, however, that no amount of training is going to be of any help if the organizational climate is politically charged and trust is low.[81] Figure 10-8 identifies six leader behaviors to build trust, as well as employee responses to those behaviors.
- Seek a variety of types of information about performance, and make raters accountable to upper-level review. Allowing employees to nominate raters who will provide information about their performance (Goldman Sachs allows a maximum of six) increases acceptance of the results.[82]

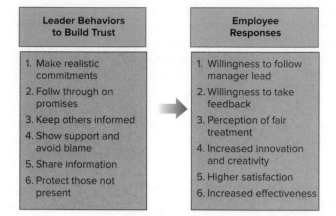

Figure 10–8

Leader behaviors to build trust and employee responses to them.

Source: Society for Human Resource Management. (2012). *Building a High-Performance Culture: A Fresh Look at Performance Management.* Alexandria, VA: SHRM.

- Help employees interpret and react to the ratings, perhaps with the aid of a personal coach.[83] Longitudinal research demonstrates convincingly that a key ingredient in producing positive changes in the ratee's behavior is organizational support that facilitates both the feedback and development process.[84]
- Link 360-degree feedback to other HR systems (e.g., training, rewards), and take the time to evaluate their effectiveness.[85] Today, many organizations administer 360-degree feedback via the Internet in order to minimize paperwork and to reduce the time involved in collecting, organizing, and summarizing the data. Such "talent-management" systems allow organizations to manage data about employees in a systematic and coordinated way.[86]

Finally, the written report should contain the following elements: a summary that integrates the main themes from the scores (assuming quantitative results are part of the process) and a detailed summary of ratings from each source.[87] Careful attention to these action steps is an integral component of performance management. Another important consideration is the timing and frequency of performance appraisal.

WHEN AND HOW OFTEN SHOULD APPRAISAL BE DONE?

Traditionally, formal appraisals were done once, or at best twice, a year. Research, however, has indicated that once or twice a year is far too infrequent.[88] Unless he or she keeps a diary, considerable difficulties face a rater who is asked to remember what several employees did over the previous 6 or 12 months. This is why firms such as Adobe, GE, Cisco, Accenture, and Deloitte have shifted to more frequent "check-ins."[89]

Research indicates that if a rater is asked to assess an employee's performance over a 6- to 12-month period, biased ratings may result, especially if information has been stored in the rater's memory according to irrelevant, oversimplistic, or otherwise faulty categories.[90] Unfortunately, faulty categorization seems to be the rule more often than the exception.[91]

There should be no surprises in appraisals, and one way to ensure this is to do them frequently. We noted earlier that social-networking–style systems now let employees post Twitter-length questions, such as "How can I run meetings better?" in exchange for anonymous feedback. Such "micro-feedback" enables them to get job-related developmental information as often as they want. The latest generation of performance-management software goes even further. For example, Salesforce Work.com, offers real-time 360 feedback, uses drag-and-drop performance reviews, lets employees track team goals, and ties those goals to metrics. It also incorporates social-networking tools and rewards employees with prizes, both virtual and real. The biggest change, however, is that the annual performance review is rapidly becoming a year-round activity.[92]

EVALUATING THE PERFORMANCE OF TEAMS

Our discussion so far has focused on the assessment and improvement of *individual* performance. However, numerous organizations (80 percent of U.S. corporations) are structured around teams.[93] Team-based organizations do not necessarily outperform organizations that are not structured around teams,[94] but there seems to be an increased interest in organizing how work is done around teams.[95] Therefore, given the popularity of teams, it makes sense for performance-management systems to target not only individual performance but also an individual's contribution to the performance of his or her team(s)—as well as the performance of teams as a whole.

The assessment of team performance does not imply that individual contributions should be ignored. On the contrary, if individual performance is not assessed and recognized, social loafing may occur.[96] Even worse, when other team members see there is a "free rider," they are likely to withdraw their effort in support of team performance.[97] Assessing team performance, therefore, should be seen as complementary to the assessment and recognition of (1) individual performance (as we have discussed so far) and (2) individuals' behaviors and skills that contribute to team performance (e.g., self-management, communication, decision making, collaboration).[98]

Not all teams are created equal, however. Different types of teams require different emphases on performance measurement at the individual and team levels. Depending on the complexity of the task (from routine to nonroutine) and membership configuration (from static to dynamic), we can identify three types of teams[99]:

- *Work or service teams.* Intact teams engaged in routine tasks (e.g., manufacturing or service tasks).
- *Project teams.* Teams assembled for a specific purpose and expected to disband once their task is completed. Their tasks are outside the core production or service of the organization and therefore less routine than those of work or service teams.
- *Virtual teams.* Teams that include membership not constrained by time or space and membership is not limited by organizational boundaries (i.e., they are typically geographically dispersed and stay in touch via e-collaboration technology). Their work is extremely nonroutine.

Table 10–2 shows a summary of recommended methods for rating the performance of each of the three types of teams.

Table 10–2

PERFORMANCE-RATING METHODS FOR DIFFERENT TYPES OF TEAMS

Team type	Who is being rated?	Who provides rating?	What is rated?			How is the rating used?		
			Outcome	Behavior	Competency	Development	Evaluation	Self-regulation
Work or service team	Team member	Manager	✓	✓	✓	✓	✓	
		Other team members		✓	✓	✓		
		Customers		✓		✓		
		Self	✓	✓	✓	✓		✓
	Entire team	Manager	✓	✓	✓	✓	✓	
		Other teams		✓				
		Customers		✓				
		Self	✓	✓	✓	✓		✓
Project team	Team member	Manager	✓		✓	✓	✓	
		Project leaders		✓	✓	✓		
		Other team members		✓	✓	✓		
		Customers		✓				
		Self	✓	✓	✓	✓		✓
	Entire team	Customers	✓	✓			✓	
		Self	✓	✓	✓	✓		✓
Virtual team	Team member	Manager		✓	✓	✓	✓	
		Team leaders		✓	✓	✓		
		Coworkers		✓	✓	✓		
		Other team members		✓	✓	✓		
		Customers		✓	✓	✓		
		Self	✓	✓	✓	✓		✓
	Entire team	Customers	✓				✓	

Source: Adapted from Scott, S. G., and Einstein, W. O. (2001, May). Strategic performance appraisal in team-based organizations: One size does not fit all. *Academy of Management Executive*, 15, p. 111.

INTERNATIONAL APPLICATION
The Impact of National Culture on Performance Management

It is one thing to institute a performance-management system with a home-country manager on an international assignment. It is quite another to do so with a local manager or local employees whose customs and culture differ from one's own. Western expatriate managers are often surprised to learn that their management practices have unintended consequences when applied in non-Western cultures. For example, we know that concepts such as individual rewards for individual performance and making explicit distinctions in performance among employees are not universally accepted. Indeed, where the prevailing view is that it takes contributions from everyone to achieve continuous improvement (i.e., the concept of kaizen in Japanese enterprises), the practice of singling out one employee's contribution may actually cause that employee to "lose face" among his or her fellow work-group members. In other cultures, where nepotism is common and extended family members work together, the primary objective is to preserve working relationships. That objective may cause host-country managers to overlook results that more objective observers might judge to be inadequate.[a]

As a general conclusion, managers will need to modify the performance-management process that is familiar to them when working with cultures other than their own. Doing so shows respect and recognizes the importance of groups as well as individuals in the organization.

[a]Gelfand, M. (2018). *Rule makers, rule breakers: How tight and loose cultures wire our world.* New York: Scribner. Peretz, H., and Fried, Y. (2012). National cultures, performance appraisal practices, and organizational absenteeism and turnover: A study across 21 countries. *Journal of Applied Psychology* 97(2), pp. 448–59. Cascio, W. F. (2011). The puzzle of performance management in the multinational enterprise. *Industrial and Organizational Psychology* 4, pp. 190-93.

For example, regarding project teams, end-of-project outcome measures may not benefit the team's development because the team is likely to disband once the project is over. Instead, measurements taken during the project can be implemented so that corrective action can be taken if necessary before the project is over. This is what HP uses with its product-development teams.[100]

Regardless of whether performance is measured at the individual level or at the individual and team levels, raters are likely to make intentional or unintentional mistakes in assigning performance scores.[101] The good news, however, is that raters can be trained to minimize such biases. We address this topic next.

APPRAISAL ERRORS AND RATER-TRAINING STRATEGIES

The use of ratings assumes that the human observer is reasonably objective and accurate. As we have seen, raters' memories are quite fallible, and raters subscribe to their own sets of likes, dislikes, and expectations about people, expectations that may or may not be valid.[102] These biases produce rating errors, or deviations between the true rating an employee deserves and the actual rating assigned.[103] We discussed some of the most common types of rating errors previously: leniency, severity, and central tendency. Three other types are halo, contrast, and recency errors.

1. **Halo error** is not as common as is commonly believed.[104] Raters who commit this error assign their ratings on the basis of global (good or bad) impressions of ratees. An employee or a team is rated either high or low on many aspects of job performance because the rater knows (or thinks she or he knows) that the employee or team is high or low on some specific aspect. In practice, halo is probably due to situational factors or to the interaction of a rater and a situation (e.g., a supervisor who has limited opportunity to observe her subordinates because they are in the field, dealing with customers).[105] Thus, halo is probably a better indicator of how raters process cognitive information than it is as a measure of rating validity or accuracy.[106]

2. **Contrast error** results when a rater compares several employees to one another rather than to an objective standard of performance.[107] If, say, the first two workers are unsatisfactory, whereas the third is average, the third worker may well be rated outstanding because, in contrast to the first two, her or his average level of job performance is magnified. Likewise, average performance could be downgraded unfairly if the first few workers are outstanding. In both cases, the average worker receives a biased rating.

3. **Recency error** results when a rater assigns his or her ratings on the basis of the employee's most recent performance. It is most likely to occur when rating is done only after a long period. Here is how one manager described the dilemma of the recency error: "Many of us have trouble rating for the entire year. If one of my people has a stellar three months prior to the review . . . [I] don't want to do anything that impedes that person's momentum and progress."[108] Of course, if the subordinate's performance peaks 3 months prior to review *every year*, that suggests a different problem!

Evidence indicates that training raters clearly improves the overall effectiveness of performance management.[109] Conversely, implementing a performance-management system without training all parties in how to use it as designed is a waste of time and money. Training managers, but then not holding them accountable for implementing what they have been trained on, is just as bad. What can be done? Begin by identifying some key topics to address with respect to performance-management training. These include the following[110]:

For both managers and employees:

- Building trust.
- Learning strategies for communication.
- Ongoing expectations and feedback.
- Developing through experience.

For managers:

- Communicating the big picture.
- Diagnosing and addressing performance issues.
- Deep-diving on feedback and coaching skills.

For employees:

- Ensuring clear expectations.
- Seeking feedback.
- Reacting well to feedback.

Of the many types of rater-training programs available today, meta-analytic evidence has demonstrated reliably that **frame-of-reference (FOR) training**[111] is most effective at improving the accuracy of performance appraisals.[112] The addition of training in performance dimensions, rater errors, and observation, in combination with FOR training improves rating accuracy even further.[113] Such FOR training proceeds as follows[114]:

1. Participants are told that they will evaluate the performance of three ratees on three separate performance dimensions.
2. They are given rating scales and instructed to read them as the trainer reads the dimension definitions and scale anchors aloud.
3. The trainer then discusses ratee behaviors that illustrate different performance levels for each scale. The goal is to create a common performance theory (frame of reference) among raters such that they will agree on the appropriate performance dimension and effectiveness level for different behaviors.
4. Participants are shown a video of a practice vignette and are asked to evaluate the manager using the scales provided.
5. Ratings are then written on a blackboard and discussed by the group of participants. The trainer seeks to identify which behaviors participants used to decide on their assigned ratings, and to clarify any discrepancies among the ratings.
6. The trainer provides feedback to participants, explaining why the ratee should receive a certain rating (target score) on a given dimension.

FOR training provides trainees with a *theory of performance* that allows them to understand the various performance dimensions, how to match these performance dimensions to rate behaviors, how to judge the effectiveness of various ratee behaviors, and how to integrate their judgments into an overall rating of performance.[115] Rater training is clearly worth the effort, and research indicates that the kind of approach advocated here is especially effective in improving the meaningfulness and usefulness of the performance-management process.[116]

SECRETS OF EFFECTIVE PERFORMANCE-FEEDBACK INTERVIEWS

The use of performance feedback (GE calls it "insights") is widespread. Managers at financial services and planning company TIAA use "one-page conversation guides" to structure conversations with employees. Its "Get Feedback" tool facilitates peer-to-peer exchanges.[117] As is well known, however, the existence of a policy is no guarantee that it will be implemented, or implemented effectively. Consider just two examples. First, we know that feedback is most effective when it is given immediately following the behavior in question.[118] How effective can feedback be if it is given only once a year during a performance-review interview?

Second, we have known for decades that when managers use a problem-solving approach, subordinates express a stronger motivation to improve performance than when other approaches are used.[119] Yet evidence indicates that many organizations still use a "tell-and-sell" approach in which a manager completes a review independently, shows it to the subordinate, justifies the rating, discusses what must be done to improve performance, and then asks for the subordinate's reaction and sign-off.[120] This is a compliance approach, not a developmental one. Are the negative reactions of subordinates really that surprising?

IMPACT OF PERFORMANCE MANAGEMENT ON PRODUCTIVITY, QUALITY OF WORK LIFE, AND THE BOTTOM LINE

Performance management is fundamentally a feedback process, and research indicates that feedback may result in increases in performance varying from 10 to 30 percent, although it is not uniformly effective.[a] Feedback is a fairly inexpensive way to improve productivity, but, to work effectively, feedback programs require sustained commitment. The challenge for managers, then, is to establish clear goals, and then to provide feedback or "progress reports" regularly to all their employees.[b]

From an employee's perspective, lack of regular feedback about performance detracts from his or her quality of work life. Most people want to improve their performance on the job, to receive constructive suggestions regarding areas they need to work on, and to be commended for things that they do well. The payoff for managers who do performance management well, compared to those who do not, is striking. They have 50 percent less staff turnover, 10–30 percent higher customer-satisfaction ratings, 40 percent higher ratings of employee commitment, and double the net profits. In sum, the myth that employees know how they are doing without adequate feedback from management can be an expensive fantasy.[c]

[a]DeNisi, A. S., and Sonesh, S. (2011). The appraisal and management of performance at work. In S. Zedeck (Ed.), *APA Handbook of Industrial and Organizational Psychology*, Vol. 2. Washington, DC: American Psychological Association, pp. 255–79. The Ken Blanchard Companies. (2009). *The High Cost of Doing Nothing: Quantifying the Effect of Leadership on the Bottom Line*. Escondido, CA: Author.

[b]Colquitt, A. L. (2020, Apr. 21). Has feedback lost its way? the case for progress instead. Retrieved from *https://www.alancolquitt.com/single-post/2020/04/21/Has-Feedback-Lost-its-Way-The-Case-for-Progress-Instead* on Apr. 22, 2020.

[c]Schumpeter. (2016, Feb. 20). Reports of the death of performance reviews are exaggerated. *The Economist*, p. 59. Hymowitz, C. (2007, Mar. 19). Managers lose talent when they neglect to coach their staffs. *The Wall Street Journal*, p. B1.

If organizations really are serious about fostering improved job performance as a result of performance-feedback interviews, the kinds of activities shown in Table 10–3 are essential before, during, and after the interview. Let's briefly examine each of these important activities.

Supervisory Activities

Communicate Frequently   Research on the appraisal interview at GE indicated clearly that once-a-year performance appraisals are of questionable value and that coaching should be a day-to-day activity–particularly with poor performers or new employees.[121] To appreciate this, consider the difference between formal and informal feedback, as shown in Figure 10–9. Feedback has maximum impact when it is given as close as possible to the action. If a subordinate behaves effectively (ineffectively), tell him or her immediately. Don't wait to discuss incidents in 6 to 9 months.

Research strongly supports this view. Thus, one study found that communication of performance feedback in an interview is most effective when the subordinate already has relatively accurate perceptions of her or his performance before the session.[122]

Get Training in Performance Feedback and Appraisal Interviewing   As we noted earlier, this includes topics unique to managers and unique to employees, as well as topics appropriate for both groups. Use a problem-solving, rather than a "tell-and-sell," approach, as noted earlier.

Table 10–3

SUPERVISORY ACTIVITIES BEFORE, DURING, AND AFTER PERFORMANCE-FEEDBACK INTERVIEWS

Before

Communicate frequently with subordinates about their performance.

Get training in performance-appraisal interviewing.

Plan to use a problem-solving approach rather than "tell-and-sell."

Encourage subordinates to prepare for performance-feedback interviews.

During

Encourage subordinates to participate.

Judge performance, not personality and mannerisms.

Be specific.

Be an active listener.

Set mutually agreeable goals for future improvements.

Avoid destructive criticism.

After

Communicate frequently with subordinates about their performance.

Periodically assess progress toward goals.

Make organizational rewards contingent on performance.

Figure 10–9

Comparing formal to informal feedback.

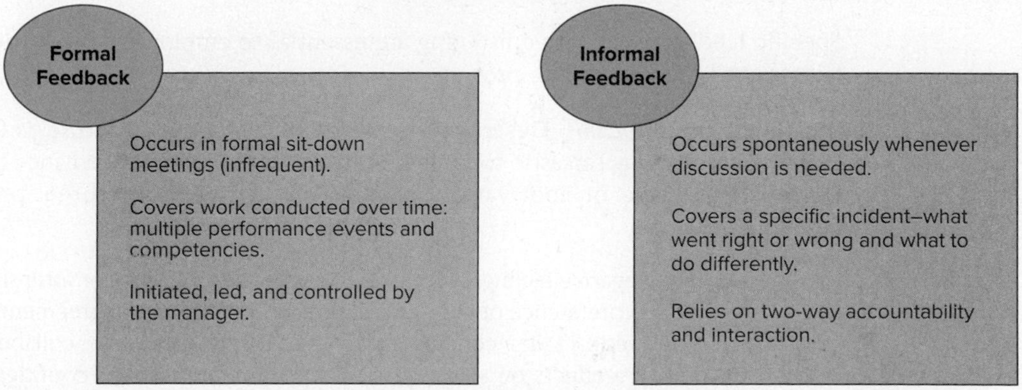

Formal Feedback

Occurs in formal sit-down meetings (infrequent).

Covers work conducted over time: multiple performance events and competencies.

Initiated, led, and controlled by the manager.

Informal Feedback

Occurs spontaneously whenever discussion is needed.

Covers a specific incident—what went right or wrong and what to do differently.

Relies on two-way accountability and interaction.

Source: Society for Human Resource Management. (2012). *Building a High-Performance Culture: A Fresh Look at Performance Management.* Alexandria, VA: SHRM.

Encourage Subordinates to Prepare   Research conducted across a variety of organizations has yielded consistent results. Subordinates who spend more time prior to performance-feedback interviews analyzing their job responsibilities and duties, problems they encounter on the job, and the quality of their performance are more likely to be satisfied with the performance-management process, more likely to be motivated to improve their performance, and more likely actually to improve.[123]

Encourage Participation   A perception of ownership–a feeling by the subordinate that his or her ideas are genuinely welcomed by the manager–is related strongly to subordinates' satisfaction with the feedback interview, the fairness of the performance management system, and their motivation to improve.[124] Participation provides an opportunity for employee voice. It encourages the belief that the feedback process was fair and constructive, that some current job problems were cleared up, and that future goals were set.[125]

Judge Performance, Not Personality   In addition to the potential legal liability of dwelling on personality rather than on job performance, supervisors are far less likely to change a subordinate's personality than they are his or her job performance. Maintain the problem-solving, job-related focus established earlier because evidence indicates that supervisory support enhances employees' motivation to improve.[126] Emphasizing the employee's personality, as opposed to the work to be done, is likely to lead to lower levels of future performance.[127]

Be Specific, and Be an Active Listener   By being candid and specific, the supervisor offers clear feedback to the employee about his or her past actions. She or he also demonstrates knowledge of the employee's level of performance and job duties. By being an active listener, the supervisor demonstrates genuine interest in the employee's ideas. **Active listening** requires that you do five things well:

1. Take the time to listen–hold all phone calls and do not allow interruptions.
2. Communicate verbally and nonverbally (e.g., by maintaining eye contact) that you genuinely want to help.
3. As the employee begins to tell his or her side of the story, do not interrupt and do not argue.
4. Watch for verbal as well as nonverbal cues regarding the employee's agreement or disagreement with your message.
5. Summarize what was said and what was agreed to.

Specific feedback and active listening are essential to employees' perceptions of the fairness and accuracy of the process.[128]

Avoid Destructive Criticism   **Destructive criticism** is general in nature; is frequently delivered in a biting, sarcastic tone; and often attributes poor performance to internal causes (e.g., lack of motivation or ability). It leads to three predictable consequences:

1. It produces negative feelings among recipients and can initiate or intensify conflict.
2. It reduces the preference of individuals for handling future disagreements with the giver of the feedback in a conciliatory manner (e.g., compromise, collaboration).
3. It has negative effects on self-set goals and on feelings of self-confidence.[129]

Needless to say, this is one type of communication to avoid.

Set Mutually Agreeable Goals   How does goal setting work to improve performance? Studies demonstrate that goals direct attention to the specific performance in question, that they mobilize effort to accomplish higher levels of performance, and that they foster persistence for higher levels of performance.[130] The practical implications of this work are clear: Set specific, challenging goals, because this clarifies for the subordinate precisely what is expected and leads to high levels of performance. We cannot change the past, but interviews that include goal setting and specific feed back can affect future job performance.

Continue to Communicate, and Assess Progress toward Goals Regularly   Periodic tracking of progress toward goals has three advantages:

1. It helps keep behavior on target.
2. It provides a better understanding of the reasons behind a given level of performance.
3. It enhances the subordinate's commitment to perform effectively.

All of this helps to improve supervisor/subordinate work relationships. Improving those work relationships, in turn, has positive effects on performance.[131]

Tie Organizational Rewards to Performance   Research results are clear-cut on this point. If subordinates see a link between the feedback they receive and employment decisions regarding issues such as merit pay and promotion, they are more likely to prepare for performance-feedback interviews, to participate actively in them, and to be

---

IMPLICATIONS FOR MANAGEMENT PRACTICE*

The chief talent officer for Deloitte Australia remarked that when it comes to performance management, employees really just want three things: "something to believe in, someone to believe in, and someone who believes in me." Likewise, through its Project Oxygen, designed to identify and build better bosses, Google found that effective leadership is synonymous with effective performance management. By analyzing performance reviews, feedback surveys, and nominations for managerial awards, Google identified eight habits of highly effective managers and three pitfalls that hamper success. What employees valued most were even-keeled bosses who made time for one-on-one meetings, helped them solve problems by asking questions rather than by dictating answers, and took an interest in their lives and careers. Effective managers also expressed a clear vision and strategy for the team. Surprisingly, the manager's ability to perform technical work ranked last among the top eight behaviors. Conversely, the three pitfalls were managers who had trouble transitioning to the team (empowering it, and not micromanaging), lack of a consistent approach to performance management and career development, and those who spent too little time managing and communicating. In short, Google discovered that bosses have a great impact on employees' performance and job attitudes. Better bosses translate into bottom-line results.

*Sources: Bashinsky, A. (2014, Apr.). *Shaping the Workforce of the Future*. Kingscliff, Australia: HR Forum for Professional Services. Bryant, A. (2011, Mar. 12). Google's quest to build a better boss. *The New York Times*. Retrieved from *http://www.nytimes.com/2011/03/13/business/13hire.html?pagewanted=all&r=0* on Mar. 14, 2011.

satisfied with the overall performance-management system.[132] In 2019, for example, star performers received raises of 4.6 percent, 70 percent higher than the 2.7 percent increase granted to those rated average. That kind of differentiation makes pay for performance meaningful.[133]

Human Resource Management in Action: Conclusion

PERFORMANCE REVIEWS ARE DEAD; LONG LIVE PERFORMANCE REVIEWS!

Only about 20 percent of companies are considering giving up ratings, and fewer than that have actually done it. In reality, even when companies get rid of performance reviews, ratings still exist. Employees just can't see them. Facebook is an exception, with 87 percent of surveyed employees wanting to keep performance ratings. One focus-group participant noted that ratings serve as a punctuation mark, because they are clear. Performance management at Facebook focuses on three themes: fairness, transparency, and development.

Facebook begins by having peers write reviews, which they share with managers and with one another. Then managers make decision about performance by sitting together and discussing their reports face-to-face, defending and championing, debating and deliberating, and incorporating peer feedback. Then managers write the performance reviews and a team of analysts examines them for bias (after the names of managers have been removed). The company then uses a formula to translate mangers' ratings directly into compensation. Managers have no discretion in compensation decisions, and that turns out to be a huge time saver.

German online fashion retailer Zalando launched an app to collect real-time performance and developmental feedback from a variety of sources. A performance dashboard allows employees to see, in one place, all of the feedback they have received for both development and evaluation. The dashboard shows how their feedback compares to average scores on their teams and of people who hold similar jobs.

Critics of performance reviews have suggested that ratings produce fight-or-flight responses. In fact, many people have stronger reactions to not being rated. In the interests of improving the overall process, therefore, here are three practical suggestions:

1. Train all frontline managers and give them the tools they need–such as real-time performance-management software–to initiate frequent and productive conversations with workers. Remember, the goal is to raise performance, not blood pressure.
2. Link employees' goals to business priorities and maintain a strong element of flexibility.
3. Get executive buy-in. To do that, consider reporting return-on-investment data for financial executives, customer satisfaction for sales leaders, and employee engagement for HR executives. Record baseline metrics under your old review system, and track changes as managers roll out real-time feedback.

Performance reviews will probably never be perfect, but making the kinds of changes suggested here can lead to better outcomes for everyone involved in the process.

SUMMARY

Performance management requires the willingness and commitment to focus on improving performance at the level of the individual or team *every day*. Like a compass, an ongoing performance-management system provides instantaneous, real-time information that describes the difference between the current and the desired course. To practice sound performance management, managers must do the same thing–provide timely feedback about performance while constantly focusing everyone's attention on the ultimate objective (e.g., world-class customer service).

At a general level, the broad process of performance management requires that you do three things well: define performance (through goals, measures, and assessments), facilitate performance (by identifying obstacles to good performance and providing resources to accomplish objectives), and encourage performance (by providing fair and timely rewards that people care about in a sufficient amount).

Performance appraisal (the systematic description of the job-relevant strengths and weaknesses of an individual or a team) is a necessary, but not sufficient, part of the performance-management process. It serves two major purposes in organizations: (1) to improve the job performance of employees and (2) to provide information to employees and managers for use in making decisions. In practice, many performance-appraisal systems fail because they do not satisfy one or more of the following requirements: relevance, sensitivity, reliability, acceptability, and practicality. The failure is frequently accompanied by legal challenge to the system based on its adverse impact against one or more protected groups.

Performance appraisal is done once or twice a year in most organizations, but research indicates that this is far too infrequently. It should happen upon the completion of projects or upon the achievement of important milestones. Managers should provide informal feedback even more frequently–for example, through "check-ins" or "touch-base" sessions. Choose a rating method based on the purpose for which it is intended. Comparisons among employees are best for generating rankings for pay purposes, whereas MBO, work planning and review, and narrative essays are least appropriate for this purpose. For employee development, critical incidents or behaviorally anchored rating scales are most appropriate. Finally, rating methods that focus on describing rather than evaluating behavior (e.g., BARS, behavioral checklists) are the most interpretable across raters.

Performance management and ratings may be done at the level of the individual or the team. Because different types of teams exist, such as work or service teams, project teams, and virtual teams, different rating methods are most appropriate for each team type (see Table 10-2). Recognize, however, that rater judgments are subject to various types of biases: leniency; severity; central tendency; and halo, contrast, and recency effects. To improve the reliability and validity of ratings, use frame-of-reference training to help raters observe behavior more accurately. To improve the value of performance-feedback interviews, communicate frequently with subordinates; encourage them to prepare and to participate in the process; judge performance, not personality; be specific; avoid destructive criticism; set goals; assess progress toward goals regularly; and make rewards contingent on performance.

KEY TERMS

performance management	paired comparisons
performance appraisal	forced distribution
performance facilitation	leniency
performance encouragement	severity
relevance	central tendency
performance standards	Likert method of summed ratings
sensitivity	critical incidents
reliability	graphic rating scales
acceptability	behaviorally anchored rating scales (BARS)
practicality	management by objectives (MBO)
applicant group	work planning and review
behavior-oriented rating methods	360-degree feedback
relative rating systems	halo error
absolute rating systems	contrast error
results-oriented rating methods	recency error
narrative essay	frame-of-reference (FOR) training
simple ranking	active listening
alternation ranking	destructive criticism

DISCUSSION QUESTIONS

10-1. What would an effective performance-management system look like?

10-2. What is the difference between performance management and performance appraisal?

10-3. You have been asked to design a rater-training program. What types of elements will be specific to managers, specific to employees, and common to both?

10-4. Working in small groups, develop a performance-management system for a cashier in a neighborhood grocery with little technology but lots of personal touch.

10-5. The chief counsel for a large corporation comes to you for advice. She wants to know what makes a firm's review system legally vulnerable. What would you tell her?

10-6. How is performance appraisal for teams different from performance appraisal for individuals?

10-7. How can we overcome employee defensiveness in performance-feedback interviews?

10-8. Should discussions of employee job performance be separated from salary considerations?

10-9. Google's Project Oxygen found that technical skill is the least important characteristic of a good boss. What kinds of other skills are more important?

10-10. In performance reviews, why is it more important to focus on the future than to dwell on the past?

APPLYING YOUR KNOWLEDGE

Avoiding a "Me" versus "We" Dilemma: Using Performance   *Case 10–1*
Management to Turn Teams into a Source of Competitive Advantage

The gold medal performance of the U.S. ice hockey team in the 1980 Winter Olympics has been described as the "Miracle on Ice." The "miracle" was the product of an effective performance management system implemented by the U.S. team's head coach, Herb Brooks. This article discusses common ways in which teams can get out of control and cause harm in the absence of a properly designed performance management system. It then provides six best-practice recommendations for the proper design of a performance management system that considers team performance explicitly, thereby avoiding a "me" versus "we" dilemma.

The link to the article is: *http://www.hermanaguinis.com/BHTeams.pdf.*

How would you apply the best-practice recommendations to answer the following questions?

Questions

1. Your boss is not happy with the performance of the cross-functional teams that are working on an enterprisewide risk-analysis project. She asks you to suggest some possible reasons why the teams are not performing well. What would you tell her?

3. Your boss likes the suggestions you made in your answer to question 1 above. Based on that information, she asks for recommendations about how to improve the performance of these teams. What would you say?

4. When it comes to rewarding members of these teams, for example, using bonuses, your boss asks whether she should consider peer ratings as an input to her decisions. What would you recommend?

REFERENCES

1. Colquitt, A., Ramesh, A., and Killen, T. (2017, Apr.). Redesigning Performance Management: Assumptions, Choices, and Roadblocks. Workshop presented at the annual conference of the Society for Industrial and Organizational Psychology, Orlando, FL. *See also* Meyrowitz, M., Mueller-Hanson, R., O'Leary, R., and Pulakos, E. D. (2012). *Building a High-Performance Culture: A Fresh Look at Performance Management.* Alexandria, VA: SHRM Foundation. *See also* Cascio, W. F. (1996, Sept.). Managing for maximum performance. *HRMonthly* (Australia), pp. 10-13.

2. Light, J. (2010, Nov. 8). Human-resources executives say reviews are off the mark. *The Wall Street Journal,* p. B8.

3. Bernthal, P. R., Rogers, R. W., and Smith, A. B. (2003, Apr.). *Managing Performance: Building Accountability for Organizational Success.* Pittsburgh, PA: Development Dimensions International. *See also* Colquitt et al. (2017), op. cit.

4. Aguinis, H. (2019a). *Performance Management for Dummies.* Hoboken, NJ: Wiley. *See also* Colquitt et al. (2017), op. cit.

5. Locke, E. A., and Latham, G. P. (Eds). (2012). *New Developments in Goal Setting and Task Performance.* New York: Routledge. *See also* Latham, G. P. (2009). *Becoming the Evidence-Based Manager: Making the Science of Management Work for You.* Boston: Davies-Black. *See also* Locke, E. A., and Latham, G. P. (2002). Building a practically useful theory of goal setting and task motivation. *American Psychologist* 57, pp. 705-17.

6. Latham, G. P., and Locke, E. A. (2017). Goal-setting theory. In S. G. Rogelberg (Ed.), *The Sage Encyclopedia of Industrial and Organizational Psychology* (2nd ed., Vol. 2). Thousand Oaks, CA: Sage, pp. 556-59. *See also* Tubbs, M. E. (1986). Goal setting: A meta-analytic examination of the empirical evidence. *Journal of Applied Psychology* 71, pp. 474-83.

7. Knight, D., Durham, C. C., and Locke, E. A. (2001). The relationship of team goals, incentives, and efficacy to strategic risk, tactical implementation, and performance. *Academy of Management Journal* 44, pp. 326-38.

8. Colquitt et al. (2017), op. cit.

9. Pulakos, E. D., and O'Leary, R. S. (2011). Why is performance management broken? *Industrial and Organizational Psychology* 4, pp. 146-64. *See also* Stokes, W., quoted in Grossman, R. J. (2010, Apr.). Tough love at Netflix. *HRMagazine*, p. 40.

10. Wood, R. E., Mento, A. J., and Locke, E. A. (1987). Task complexity as a moderator of goal effects: A meta-analysis. *Journal of Applied Psychology* 72, pp. 416-25.

11. Kaiser, R. B., Hogan, R., and Craig, S. B. (2008). Leadership and the fate of organizations. *American Psychologist* 63, pp. 96-110.

12. Kerr, S., in Sherman, S. (1995, Nov. 13). Stretch goals: The dark side of asking for miracles. *Fortune*, p. 31.

13. Delaney, K. J. (2006, Oct. 23). Google adjusts hiring process as needs grow. *The Wall Street Journal*, pp. B1, B8. *See also* Morris, B. (2008, Mar. 3). What makes Apple golden. *Fortune*. Retrieved from *money.cnn.com/2008/02/29/news/companies/amac_apple.fortune/index.htm* on Sept. 2, 2011.

14. Hancock, B., Hioe, E., and Schaninger, B. (2018, Apr.). The fairness factor in performance management. *McKinsey Quarterly*. Retrieved from *https://www.mckinsey.com/business-functions/organization/our-insights/the-fairness-factor-in-performance-management* on May 1, 2018. Greenberg, J. (2011). Organizational justice: The dynamics of fairness in the workplace. In S. Zedeck (Ed.), *APA Handbook of Industrial and Organizational Psychology* (Vol. 3). Washington, DC: American Psychological Association, pp. 271-327. *See also* Kanovsky, M. (2000). Understanding procedural justice and its impact on business organizations. *Journal of Management* 26, pp. 489-511.

15. Tulgan, B. (2004, June 28). The under-management epidemic. Retrieved from *www.rainmakerthinking.com/backwttw/2004/june30.htm* on Sept. 13, 2004. *See also* Pfeffer, J. (2009, Aug. 3). Low grades for performance reviews. *BusinessWeek*, p. 68.

16. Goler, L., Gale, J., and Grant, A. (2016, Nov.). Let's not kill performance evaluations yet. *Harvard Business Review*. Retrieved from *https://hbr.org/2016/11/lets-not-kill-performance-evaluations-yet* on Dec. 2, 2016. *See also* Schoenberger, C. R. (2015, Oct. 26). The risks of reviews. *The Wall Street Journal*, p. R5. *See also* Feintzeig, R. (2015, Apr. 22). The trouble with grading employees. *The Wall Street Journal*, pp. B1, B7. *See also* McIlvaine, A. R. (2012, July 16). There's got to be a better way. *HRExective Online*. Retrieved from *http://www.hreonline.com/HRE/view/story.jhtml?id=533349219* on July 8, 2013.

17. Cascio, W. F., and Aguinis, H. (2019). *Applied Psychology in Talent Management* (8th ed.). Thousand Oaks, CA: Sage. *See also* Murphy, K. R. (2008). Explaining the weak relationship between job performance and ratings of job performance. *Industrial and Organizational Psychology* 1, pp. 148-60.

18. Roche, K. (2017, Dec.). To review or not to review: Legal considerations in eliminating the performance review. *HR Professionals Magazine* 7(12), pp. 40, 41. *See also* Schumpeter. (2016, Feb. 20). Reports of the death of performance reviews are exaggerated. *The Economist*, p. 59. *See also* Silverman, R. E. (2016, July 26). GE does away with employee ratings. *The Wall Street Journal*. Retrieved from *www.wsj.com/articles/ge-does-away-with-employee-ratings-1469541602* on July 27, 2016.

19. Aguinis, H. (2019b). *Performance Management* (4th ed.). Chicago, IL: Chicago Business Press. *See also* Cascio, W. F. (1982). Scientific, legal, and operational imperatives of workable performance appraisal systems. *Public Personnel Management* 11, pp. 367-75.

20. DeNisi, A., and Murphy, K. R. (2017). Performance appraisal and performance management: 100 years of progress? *Journal of Applied Psychology* 102, pp. 421-33. *See also*

Zedeck, S., and Cascio, W. F. (1982). Performance appraisal decisions as a function of rater training and purpose of the appraisal. *Journal of Applied Psychology* 67, pp. 752-58.

21. Ones, D. S., Viswesvaran, C., and Schmidt, F. L. (2008). No new terrain: Reliability and construct validity of job performance ratings. *Industrial and Organizational Psychology* 1, pp. 174-79. *See also* Viswesvaran, C., Ones, D. S., and Schmidt, F. L. (1996). Comparative analysis of the reliability of job performance ratings. *Journal of Applied Psychology* 81, pp. 557-74.

22. DeNisi, A. S., and Sonesh, S. (2011). The appraisal and management of performance at work. In S. Zedeck (Ed.), *APA Handbook of Industrial and Organizational Psychology* (Vol. 2). Washington, DC: American Psychological Association, pp. 255-79.

23. Lawler, E. E. III, Benson, G., and McDermott, M. (2012). *How Can Performance Appraisals Be More Effective?* Los Angeles, CA: USC Center for Effective Organizations.

24. Colquitt et al. (2017), op. cit. *See also* Mayer, R. C., and Davis, J. H. (1999). The effect of the performance appraisal system on trust for management: A field quasi-experiment. *Journal of Applied Psychology* 84, pp. 123-36. *See also* Cawley, B. D., Keeping, L. M., and Levy, P. E. (1998). Participation in the performance appraisal process and employee reactions: A meta-analytic review of field investigations. *Journal of Applied Psychology* 83, pp. 615-33. *See also* Taylor, M. S., Masterson, S. S., Renard, M. K., and Tracy, K. B. (1998). Managers' reactions to procedurally just performance management systems. *Academy of Management Journal* 41, pp. 568-79.

25. LeBoeuf, M. (1987). *The Greatest Management Principle in the World.* New York: Berkley. *See also* McShane, S. L., and Von Glinow, M. A. (2021). *Organizational Behavior* (9th ed.). New York: McGraw-Hill-Irwin.

26. Silverman (2016), op. cit.

27. DeNisi, A., and Smith, C. E. (2014). Performance appraisal, performance management, and firm-level performance: A review, a proposed model, and new directions for future research. *Academy of Management Annals* 8(1), pp. 127-79. *See also* Gerhart, B., & Newman, J. M. (2020). *Compensation* (13th ed.). New York: McGraw-Hill. *See also* Aguinis (2019), op. cit.

28. Buzachero, V., quoted in Wells, S. J. (2009, Jun.). Prescription for a turnaround. *HRMagazine* 54(6), p. 94.

29. Miller, S. (2012, May 25). Integrating performance management and rewards at Microsoft. Retrieved from *http://www.shrm.org/hrdisciplines/compensation/articles/pages/rewardsatmicrosoft.aspx* on July 14, 2013. *See also* SHRM Foundation. (2016, Oct. 14). *Ethics: The Fabric of Business.* Available at *https://www.youtube.com/watch?v=ONeS5tnUy6E.*

30. Cascio, W. F. (2012). Global performance management systems. In I. Bjorkman, G. Stahl, and S. Morris (Eds.), *Handbook of Research in International Human Resource Management* (2nd ed.). London: Edward Elgar, pp. 183-204. *See also* Engle, A. D., Sr., Dowling, P. J., and Festing, M. (2008). State of origin: Research in global performance management, a proposed research domain and emerging implications. *European Journal of International Management* 2, pp. 153-69.

31. DeNisi and Murphy (2017), op. cit. *See also* Cascio & Aguinis (2019), op. cit.

32. DeNisi and Sonesh (2011), op. cit. *See also* Bommer, W. H., Johnson, J. L., Rich, G. A., Podsakoff, P. M., and Mackenzie, S. B. (1995). On the interchangeability of objective and subjective measures of employee performance: A meta-analysis. *Personnel Psychology* 48, pp. 587-605. *See also* Heneman, R. L. (1986). The relationship between supervisory ratings and results-oriented measures of performance: A meta-analysis. *Personnel Psychology* 39, pp. 811-26.

33. O'Boyle, E., and Kroska, S. (2017). Star performers. In D. G. Collings, K. Mellahi, and W. F. Cascio (Eds.), *The Oxford Handbook of Talent Management.* Oxford, UK: Oxford University Press, pp. 43-65. *See also* Joo, H., Aguinis, H., and Bradley, K. J. (2017). Not all non-normal distributions are created equal: Improved theoretical and measurement precision. *Journal of Applied Psychology* **102**, pp. 1022-53. *See also* O'Boyle, E. H., Jr., and Aguinis, H. (2012). The best and the rest: Revisiting the norm of normality of individual performance. *Personnel Psychology* 65, pp. 79-119.

34. Cheng, K. H. C., Hui, H., and Cascio, W. F. (2017, Apr.). Leniency bias in performance ratings: The Big-Five correlates. *Frontiers in Psychology* **8**, doi: 10.3389/fpsyg.2017.00521. *See also* Bernardin, H. J., Cooke, D. K., and Villanova, P. (2000). Conscientiousness and agreeableness as predictors of rating leniency. *Journal of Applied Psychology* 85, pp. 232-34.

35. Moon, S. H., Scullen, S. E., and Latham, G. P. (2016). Precarious curve ahead: The effects of forced distribution rating systems on job performance. *Human Resource Management Review* 26, pp. 166-79.

36. Schleicher, D. J., Bull, R. A., and Green, S. G. (2009). Rater reactions to forced-distribution rating systems. *Journal of Management* 35, pp. 899-927. *See also* Roch, S. G., Sturnburgh, A. M., and Caputo, P. M. (2007). Absolute vs. relative rating formats: Implications for fairness and organizational justice. *International Journal of Selection and Assessment* 15, pp. 302-16.

37. DeNisi and Sonesh (2011), op. cit. *See also* Stockford, L., and Bissell, H. W. (1949). Factors involved in establishing a merit rating scale. *Personnel* 26, pp. 94-116.

38. DeNisi and Murphy (2017), op. cit. *See also* Hennessy, J., Mabey, B., and Warr, P. (1998). Assessment centre observation procedures: An experimental comparison of traditional, checklist and coding methods. *International Journal of Selection and Assessment* 6, pp. 222-31.

39. Hirsch, A. S. (2016, Mar. 22). Managing the challenge of constant feedback with emerging adult employees. Retrieved from *www.shrm.org/resourcesandtools/hr-topics/behavioral-competencies/global-and-cultural-effectiveness/pages/viewpoint-managing-challenge-constant-feedback-emerging-adult-employees.aspx* on Mar. 24, 2016. *See also* Wright, G. (2015, Sept. 14). Employee feedback apps on the rise. Retrieved from *www.shrm.org/resourcesandtools/hr-topics/technology/pages/employee-feedback-apps.aspx* on Sept. 15, 2015.

40. Aguinis (2019b), op. cit. *See also* Murphy (2008), op. cit. *See also* Landy, F. J., and Rastegary, H. (1988). Criteria for selection. In M. Smith and I. Robertson (Eds.), *Advances in Personnel Selection and Assessment*. New York: Wiley, pp. 68-115.

41. Cascio and Aguinis (2019), op. cit.

42. Bernardin, H. J., and Smith, P. C. (1981). A clarification of some issues regarding the development and use of behaviorally anchored rating scales. *Journal of Applied Psychology* 66, pp. 458-63.

43. Cascio and Aguinis (2019), op. cit.

44. Aguinis, H. (2019a). *Performance Management for Dummies*. Hoboken, NJ: Wiley.

45. Cappelli, P., and Tavis, A. (2016, Oct.). The performance management revolution. *Harvard Business Review*, pp. 58-67.

46. Albrecht, K. (1978). *Successful Management by Objectives: An Action Manual*. Englewood Cliffs, NJ: Prentice-Hall. *See also* Odiorne, G. S. (1965). *Management by Objectives: A System of Managerial Leadership*. Belmont, CA: Fearon.

47. Pulakos and O'Leary (2011), op. cit. *See also* Barton, R. F. (1981). An MCDM approach for resolving goal conflict in MBO. *Academy of Management Review* 6, pp. 231-41.

48. Pulakos and O'Leary (2011), op. cit. *See also* Kondrasuk, J. N. (1981). Studies in MBO effectiveness. *Academy of Management Review* 6, pp. 419-30.

49. Meyer, H. H., Kay, E., and French, J. R. P. (1965). Split roles in performance appraisal. *Harvard Business Review* 43, pp. 123-29.

50. Miller (2017), op. cit. See also Margolis, J., Mackinnon, P., and Norris, M. (2015, Sept. 11). Gap Inc.: Refashioning performance management. Harvard Business School case 9-416-019. Boston, MA: Harvard Business Publishing.

51. Bernardin, H. J., and Beatty, R. W. (1984). *Performance Appraisal: An Organizational Perspective*. Boston: Allyn & Bacon.

52. Hirsch (2016), op. cit. *See also* Wright (2015), op. cit.

53. Hartel, C. E. J. (1993). Rating format research revisited: Format effectiveness and acceptability depend on rater characteristics. *Journal of Applied Psychology* 78, pp. 212-17.

54. Miller (2017), op. cit. *See also* Fox (2009), op. cit.

55. Cascio and Aguinis (2019), op. cit. *See also* Greguras, G. J. (2005). Managerial experience and the measurement equivalence of performance ratings. *Journal of Business and Psychology* 19, pp. 383-97.

56. Ewenstein, B., Hancock, B., and Komm, A. (2016, May). Ahead of the curve: The future of performance management. *McKinsey Quarterly*. Retrieved from *www.mckinsey.com/business-functions/organization/our-insights/ahead-of-the-curve-the-future-of-performance-management* on June 16, 2016.

57. Becker, T. E., and Klimoski, R. J. (1989). A field study of the relationship between the organizational feedback environment and performance. *Personnel Psychology* 42, pp. 353–58.

58. McEvoy, G. M., and Buller, P. F. (1987). User acceptance of peer appraisals in an industrial setting. *Personnel Psychology* 40, pp. 785–87.

59. Dierdorff, E. C., and Surface, E. A. (2007). Placing peer ratings in context: Systematic influences beyond ratee performance. *Personnel Psychology* 60, pp. 93–126.

60. Jhun, S., Bae, Z., and Rhee, S. (2012). Performance change of managers in two different uses of upward feedback: A longitudinal study in Korea. *International Journal of Human Resource Management* **23**, pp. 4246–64. *See also* Reilly, R. R., Smither, J. W., and Vasilopoulos, N. L. (1996). A longitudinal study of upward feedback. *Personnel Psychology* 49, pp. 599–612. *See also* Smither, J. W., London, M., Vasilopoulos, N. L., Reilly, R. R., Millsap, R., and Salvemini, N. (1995). An examination of the effects of an upward feedback program over time. *Personnel Psychology* 48, pp. 1–34.

61. Greguras, G. J., Robie, C., Schleicher, D. J., and Goff, M. (2003). A field study of the effects of rating purpose on the quality of multisource ratings. *Personnel Psychology* 56, pp. 1–21.

62. Walker, A. G., and Smither, J. W. (1999). A five-year study of upward feedback: What managers do with their results matters. *Personnel Psychology* 52, pp. 393–423.

63. Antonioni, D. (1994). The effects of feedback accountability on upward appraisal ratings. *Personnel Psychology* 47, pp. 249–56.

64. Maurer, T. J., Raju, N. S., and Collins, W. C. (1998). Peer and subordinate performance appraisal measurement equivalence. *Journal of Applied Psychology* 83, pp. 693–702.

65. Bortz, D. (2014, Mar.). Ace your annual review. *Money*, p. 35. *See also* Campbell, D. J., and Lee, C. (1988). Self-appraisal in performance evaluation: Development versus evaluation. *Academy of Management Review* 13, pp. 302–14.

66. van Hooft, E. A. J., van der Flier, H., and Minne, M. R. (2006). Construct validity of multi-source performance ratings: An examination of the relationship of self-, supervisor-, and peer-ratings with cognitive and personality measures. *International Journal of Selection and Assessment* 14, pp. 67–81. *See also* Atkins, P. W. B., and Wood, R. E. (2002). Self- versus others' ratings as predictors of assessment center ratings: Validation evidence for 360-degree feedback programs. *Personnel Psychology* 55, pp. 871–904. *See also* Cheung, G. W. (1999). Multifaceted conceptions of self-other ratings disagreement. *Personnel Psychology* 52, pp. 1–36. *See also* Harris, M., and Schaubroeck, J. (1988). A meta analysis of self-supervisory, self-peer, and peer-supervisory ratings. *Personnel Psychology* 41, pp. 43–62.

67. King, J. F. (2008). How managers think: Why the mediated model makes sense. *Industrial and Organizational Psychology* 1, pp. 180–82.

68. Barron, L. G., and Sackett, P. R. (2008). Asian variability in performance-rating modesty and leniency bias. *Human Performance* 21, pp. 277–90. *See also* Yu, J., and Murphy, K. R. (1993). Modesty bias in self-ratings of performance: A test of the cultural relativity hypothesis. *Personnel Psychology* 46, pp. 357–63. *See also* Farh, J. L., Dobbins, G. H., and Cheng, B. S. (1991). Cultural relativity in action: A comparison of self-ratings made by Chinese and U.S. workers. *Personnel Psychology* 44, pp. 129–47.

69. Ulrich, D. (1989, Summer). Tie the corporate knot: Gaining complete customer commitment. *Sloan Management Review* 10(4), pp. 19–27, 63.

70. McGregor, J. (2009, Mar. 30). Job review in 140 keystrokes. *BusinessWeek*, p. 58. *See also* Silverman (2016), op. cit.

71. Makiney, J. D., and Levy, P. E. (1998). The influence of self-ratings versus peer ratings on supervisors' performance judgments. *Organizational Behavior & Human Decision Processes* 74, pp. 212–22.

72. Uggerslev, K. L., and Sulsky, L. M. (2002). Presentation modality and indirect performance information: Effects on ratings, reactions, and memory. *Journal of Applied Psychology* 87, pp. 940–50.

73. Schmidt, J. A. (2018). Do trends matter? The effects of dynamic performance trends and personality traits on performance appraisals. *Academy of Management Discoveries* 4, pp. 449–71. *See also* Martell, R. F., and Leavitt, K. N. (2002). Reducing the performance-cue bias in work behavior ratings: Can groups help? *Journal of Applied Psychology* 87, pp. 1032–41.

74. Schumpeter. (2016, Feb. 20). Reports of the death of performance reviews are exaggerated. *The Economist*, p. 59. *See also* Murphy, K. R. (2008a). Perspectives on the relationship between job performance and ratings of job performance. *Industrial and Organizational Psychology* 1, pp. 197–205. *See also* Harris, M. M., Ispas, D., and Schmidt, G. F. (2008). Inaccurate performance ratings are a reflection of larger organizational issues. *Industrial and Organizational Psychology* 1, pp. 190–93.

75. Campion, M. C., Campion, E. D., and Campion, M. A. (2015). Improvements in performance management through the use of 360 feedback. *Industrial and Organizational Psychology* 8, pp. 85–93. *See also* Waldman, D., and Atwater, L. E. (1998). *The Power of 360-Degree Feedback: How to Leverage Performance Evaluations for Top Productivity.* Houston: Gulf. *See also* Borman, W. C. (1997). 360-degree ratings: An analysis of assumptions and a research agenda for assessing their validity. *Human Resource Management Review* 7, pp. 299–315.

76. Conway, J. M., and Huffcutt, A. I. (1997). Psychometric properties of multisource performance ratings: A meta-analysis of subordinate, supervisor, peer, and self-ratings. *Human Performance* 10, pp. 331–60.

77. Ones et al. (2008), op. cit. *See also* Facteua, J. D., and Craig, S. B. (2001). Are performance appraisal ratings from different rating sources comparable? *Journal of Applied Psychology* 86, pp. 215–27.

78. Smither, J. W., London, M., and Reilly, R. R. (2005). Does performance improve following multisource feedback? A theoretical model, meta-analysis, and review of empirical findings. *Personnel Psychology* 58, pp. 33–66.

79. DeNisi and Sonesh (2011), op. cit. *See also* DeNisi, A. S., and Kluger, A. N. (2000). Feedback effectiveness: Can 360-degree appraisals be improved? *Academy of Management Executive* 14(1), pp. 129–39.

80. Toegel, G., and Conger, J. A. (2003). 360-degree assessment: Time for reinvention. *Academy of Management Learning & Education* 2, pp. 297–311.

81. Ghorpade, J. (2000). Managing the five paradoxes of 360-degree feedback. *Academy of Management Executive* 14(1), pp. 140–50. *See also* Waldman, D. A., Atwater, L. E., and Antonioni, D. (1998). Has a 360-degree feedback gone amok? *Academy of Management Executive* 12(2), pp. 86–94.

82. Gellman, L., and Baer, J. (2016, May 26). Goldman Sachs to stop rating employees with numbers. *The Wall Street Journal.* Retrieved from *www.wsj.com/articles/goldman-sachs-dumps-employee-ranking-system-1464272443* on May 27, 2016. *See also* Becton, J. B., and Schraeder, M. (2004). Participant input into rater selection: Potential effects on the quality and acceptance of ratings in the context of 360-degree feedback. *Public Personnel Management* 33, pp. 23–32.

83. Hancock et al., 2018, op. cit. Luthans, F., and Peterson, S. J. (2003). 360-degree feedback with systematic coaching: Empirical analysis suggests a winning combination. *Human Resource Management* 42, pp. 243–56.

84. Bailey, C., and Austin, M. (2006). 360-degree feedback and developmental outcomes: The role of feedback characteristics, self-efficacy and importance of feedback dimensions to focal managers' current role. *International Journal of Selection and Assessment* 14, pp. 51–66.

85. Morgan, A., Cannan, K., and Cullinane, J. (2005). 360-degree feedback: A critical enquiry. *Personnel Review* 34, pp. 663–80. *See also* Kozlowski, S. W. J., Chao, G. T., and Morrison, R. F. (1998). Games raters play. In J. W. Smither (Ed.), *Performance Appraisal: State of the Art in Practice.* San Francisco: Jossey-Bass, pp. 163–205. *See also* Mount, M. K., Judge, T. A.,

Scullen, S. E., Sytsma, M. R., and Hezlett, S. A. (1998). Trait, rater, and level effects in 360-degree performance ratings. *Personnel Psychology* 51, pp. 557-76.

86. Davis, S., and Nosal, D. (2010, Aug. 6). Companies reinvent their workforce, talent management systems. Retrieved from *www.shrm.org/hrdisciplines/orgempdev/articles/Pages/ReinventTheWorkforce.aspx* on July 21, 2011.

87. Bailey and Austin (2006), op. cit.

88. Cunningham, L., and McGregor, J. (2015, Aug. 17). More U.S. companies moving away from traditional performance reviews. *The Washington Post*. Retrieved from *www.washingtonpost.com/business/economy/more-us-companies-moving-away-from-traditional-performance-reviews/2015/08/17/d4e716d0-4508-11e5-846d-02792f854297_story.html?utm_term=.df9ec12205e7* on Aug. 16, 2015. *See also* Wilkie, D. (2015, Dec. 7). If the annual performance review is on its way out, what can replace it? Retrieved from *www.shrm.org/resourcesandtools/hr-topics/employee-relations/pages/performance-reviews-dead.aspx* on Dec. 9, 2015. *See also* Meyrowitz et al. (2012), op. cit.

89. Miller (2017), op. cit. *See also* Cunningham and McGregor (2015), op. cit. *See also* Knowledge@Wharton. (2016, Sept. 19). The end of annual performance reviews: Are the alternatives any better? Retrieved from *http://knowledge.wharton.upenn.edu/article/the-end-of-annual-performance-reviews/* on Sept. 20, 2016.

90. DNisi and Murphy (2017), op. cit. *See also* DeNisi and Sonesh (2011), op. cit. *See also* Fisher, C. D. (2008). What if we took within-person performance variability seriously? *Industrial and Organizational Psychology* 1, pp. 185-89. *See also* Mount, M. K., and Thompson, D. E. (1987). Cognitive categorization and quality of performance ratings. *Journal of Applied Psychology* 72, pp. 240-46.

91. Hogan, E. A. (1987). Effects of prior expectations on performance ratings: A longitudinal study. *Academy of Management Journal* 30, pp. 354-68.

92. App Info. (2017, Mar. 23). Salesforce Work.com. Retrieved from *www.getapp.com/hr-employee-management-software/a/salesforce-work-dot-com/* on May 11, 2017. *See also* Lev-Ram, M. (2012, Oct. 29). Performance reviews remade. *Fortune*, p. 60.

93. Hollenbeck, J. R., Beersma, B., and Schouten, M. E. (2012). Beyond team types and taxonomies: A dimensional scaling conceptualization for team description. *Academy of Management Review* 37, pp. 82-106. *See also* White-collar workers shoulder together—Like it or not. (2008, Apr. 28). *BusinessWeek*, p. 58.

94. Hackman, J. R. (1998). Why teams don't work. In R. S. Tindale and L. Heath (Eds.), *Theory and Research on Small Groups*. New York: Plenum Press, pp. 245-67.

95. Mathieu, J. E., Hollenbeck, J. R., van Knippenberg, D., and Ilgen, D. R. (2017). A century of work teams in the *Journal of Applied Psychology*. *Journal of Applied Psychology* 102, pp. 452-67. *See also* Salas, E., Tannenbaum, S., Cohen, D., and Latham, G. P. (Eds.). (2013). Developing and enhancing teamwork in organizations. San Francisco: Jossey-Bass. *See also* Useem, J. (2006, June 12). What's that spell? Teamwork! *Fortune*, pp. 65, 66. *See also* Naquin, C. E., and Tynan, R. O. (2003). The team halo effect: Why teams are not blamed for their failures. *Journal of Applied Psychology* 88, pp. 332-40.

96. Scott, S. G., and Einstein, W. O. (2001). Strategic performance appraisal in team-based organizations: One size does not fit all. *Academy of Management Executive* 15, pp. 107-16.

97. DeNisi and Smith (2014), op. cit. *See also* Fox, A. (2010, Dec.). Taking up slack. *HRMagazine*, pp. 26-31. *See also* Heneman, R. L., and von Hippel, C. (1995). Balancing individual and group rewards: Rewarding individual contributions to the team. *Compensation and Benefits Review* 27, pp. 745-59.

98. Cannon-Bowers, J. A., and Bowers, C. (2011). Team development and functioning. In S. Zedeck (Ed.), *APA Handbook of Industrial and Organizational Psychology*, 1. Washington, DC: American Psychological Association, p. 597-650.

99. Roepe, L. R. (2020). Scattered. *HRMagazine*, 65(1), pp. 37-42. *See also* Dulebohn, J. H., and Hoch, J. E. (2017). Virtual teams in organizations. *Human Resource Management Review* 27, pp. 569-74. *See also* Scott and Einstein (2001), op. cit.

100. Ibid. *See also* Hoffman, L. (2017, Apr. 22). Goldman makes feedback shift. *The Wall Street Journal*, pp. B1, B2.

101. DeNisi and Smith (2014), op. cit. *See also* DeNisi and Sonesh (2011), op. cit. *See also* Naquin and Tynan (2003), op. cit.

102. DeNisi and Murphy (2017), op. cit. *See also* Murphy (2008a), op. cit. *See also* Varma, A., DeNisi, A. S., and Peters, L. M. (1996). Interpersonal affect and performance appraisal: A field study. *Personnel Psychology* 49, pp. 341-60.

103. Ones et al. (2008), op. cit. *See also* Guion, R. M. (1998). *Assessment, Measurement, and Prediction for Personnel Decisions.* Mahwah, NJ: Lawrence Erlbaum.

104. Murphy, K. R., Jako, R. A., and Anhalt, R. L. (1993). Nature and consequences of halo error: A critical analysis. *Journal of Applied Psychology* 78, pp. 218-25.

105. DeNisi and Smith (2014), op. cit. *See also* Murphy, K. R., and Anhalt, R. L. (1992). Is halo error a property of the rater, ratees, or the specific behavior observed? *Journal of Applied Psychology* 77, pp. 494-500.

106. Cascio and Aguinis, 2019, op. cit. *See also* Balzer, W. K., and Sulsky, L. M. (1992). Halo and performance appraisal research: A critical examination. *Journal of Applied Psychology* 77, pp. 975-85.

107. Sumer, H. C., and Knight, P. A. (1996). Assimilation and contrast effects in performance ratings: Effects of rating the previous performance on rating subsequent performance. *Journal of Applied Psychology* 81, pp. 436-42. *See also* Maurer, T. J., Palmer, J. K., and Ashe, D. K. (1993). Diaries, checklists, evaluations, and contrast effects in the measurement of behavior. *Journal of Applied Psychology* 78, pp. 226-31.

108. Source: Longenecker, C. O., and Gioia, D. A. (1994, Winter). Delving into the dark side: The politics of executive appraisal. *Organizational Dynamics*, p. 47-58.

109. Rosales Sánchez, C., Díaz-Cabrera, D., and Hernández-Fernaud, E. (2019). Does effectiveness in performance appraisal improve with rater training? *PLoS ONE* 14(9), e0222694. https://doi.org/10.1371/journal.pone.0222694.

110. Ibid. *See also* Meyrowitz, M., Mueller-Hanson, R., O'Leary, R., and Pulakos, E. D. (2012). *Building a High-Performance Culture: A Fresh Look at Performance Management.* Alexandria, VA: SHRM Foundation.

111. Bernardin, H. J., and Buckley, M. R. (1981). A consideration of strategies in rater training. *Academy of Management Review* 6, pp. 205-12.

112. DeNisi and Murphy (2017), op. cit. *See also* Dierdorff, E. C., Surface, E. A., and Brown, K. G. (2010). Frame-of-reference training effectiveness: Effects of goal orientation and self-efficacy on affective, cognitive, skill-based, and transfer outcomes. *Journal of Applied Psychology* 95, pp. 1181-91. *See also* Woehr, D. J., and Huffcutt, A. I. (1994). Rater training for performance appraisal: A quantitative review. *Journal of Occupational and Organizational Psychology* 67, pp. 189-205.

113. Rosales Sanchez et al. (2019), op. cit.

114. Pulakos, E. D. (1984). A comparison of rater training programs: Error training and accuracy training. *Journal of Applied Psychology* 69, pp. 581-88. *See also* Pulakos, E. D. (1986). The development of training programs to increase accuracy with different rating tasks. *Organizational Behavior and Human Decision Processes* 38, pp. 76-91.

115. DeNisi and Murphy (2017), op. cit. *See also* Fox (2009), op. cit. *See also* King (2008), op. cit. *See also* Sulsky, L. M., and Day, D. V. (1992). Frame-of-reference training and cognitive categorization: An empirical investigation of rater memory issues. *Journal of Applied Psychology* 77, pp. 501-10.

116. DeNisi and Smith (2014), op. cit. *See also* Meyrowitz et al. (2012), op. cit. *See also* Sanchez, J. I., and DeLaTorre, P. (1996). A second look at the relationship between rating and behavioral accuracy in performance appraisal. *Journal of Applied Psychology* 81, pp. 3-10. *See also* Day, D. V., and Sulsky, L. M. (1995). Effects of frame-of-reference training and information configuration on memory organization and rating accuracy. *Journal of Applied Psychology* 80, pp. 159-67.

117. Colquitt et al. (2017), op. cit. *See also* Silverman (2016), op. cit. *See also* London, M. (2003). *Job Feedback: Giving, Seeking, and Using Feedback for Performance Improvement* (2nd ed.). Mahwah, NJ: Lawrence Erlbaum.

118. Murphy, K. R., and Cleveland, J. N. (1995). *Understanding Performance Appraisal: Social, Organizational, and Goal-Based Perspectives.* Thousand Oaks, CA: Sage.

119. Wexley, K. N., Singh, V. P., and Yukl, G. A. (1973). Subordinate participation in three types of appraisal interviews. *Journal of Applied Psychology* 58, pp. 54–57.

120. Feintzeig, R. (2015, Apr. 22). The trouble with grading employees. *The Wall Street Journal,* pp. B1, B7. *See also* Schoenberger, C. R. (2015, Oct. 26). The risks of reviews. *The Wall Street Journal,* p. R5. *See also* Schellhardt, T. D. (1996, Nov. 19). Annual agony: It's time to evaluate your work and all involved are groaning. *The Wall Street Journal,* pp. A1, A5.

121. Colquitt (2020), op. cit. *See also* Pulakos and O'Leary (2011), op. cit. *See also* Sulkowicz (2007), op. cit. *See also* McGregor (2006), op. cit. *See also* Meyer, H. H. (1991). A solution to the performance appraisal feedback enigma. *Academy of Management Executive* 5(1), pp. 68–76. *See also* Cederblom, D. (1982). The performance appraisal interview: A review, implications, and suggestions. *Academy of Management Review* 7, pp. 219–27.

122. Meyrowitz et al. (2012), op. cit. *See also* Ilgen, D. R., Mitchell, T. R., and Frederickson, J. W. (1981). Poor performers: Supervisors' and subordinates' responses. *Organizational Behavior and Human Performance* 27, pp. 386–410.

123. Cawley et al. (1998), op. cit.

124. Ibid.

125. Dulebohn, J. H., and Ferris, G. R. (1999). The role of influence tactics in perceptions of performance evaluations' fairness. *Academy of Management Journal* 42, pp. 288–303. *See also* Nathan, B. R., Mohrman, A. M., Jr., and Milliman, J. (1991). Interpersonal relations as a context for the effects of appraisal interviews on performance and satisfaction: A longitudinal study. *Academy of Management Journal* 34(2), pp. 352–69.

126. Dorfman, P. W., Stephan, W. G., and Loveland, J. (1986). Performance appraisal behaviors: Supervisor perceptions and subordinate reactions. *Personnel Psychology* 39, pp. 579–97.

127. DeNisi, A. S., and Kluger, A. N. (2000). Feedback effectiveness: Can 360-degree appraisals be improved? *Academy of Management Executive* 14, pp. 129–39.

128. Itzchakov, G., Kluger, A. N., and Castro, D. R. (2017). I am aware of my inconsistencies but can tolerate them: The effect of high-quality listening on speakers' attitude ambivalence. *Personality and Social Psychology Bulletin* 43, pp. 105–20. *See also* Latham (2009), op. cit. *See also* Landy, F. J., Barnes-Farrell, J., and Cleveland, J. N. (1980). Perceived fairness and accuracy of performance evaluation: A follow-up. *Journal of Applied Psychology* 65, pp. 355–56.

129. Sulkowicz (2007), op. cit. *See also* Baron, R. A. (1988). Negative effects of destructive criticism: Impact on conflict, self-efficacy, and task performance. *Journal of Applied Psychology* 73, pp. 199–207.

130. Latham (2009), op. cit. *See also* Locke and Latham (2002), op. cit. *See also* Locke and Latham (1990), op. cit.

131. Lev-Ram (2012), op. cit. *See also* O'Leary and Pulakos (2011), op. cit. *See also* Judge, T. A., and Ferris, G. R. (1993). Social context of performance evaluation decisions. *Academy of Management Journal* 36, pp. 80–105.

132. Latham (2009), op. cit. *See also* Lawler (2003), op. cit. *See also* Burke, R. S., Wertzel, W., and Weir, T. (1978). Characteristics of effective employee performance review and development interviews: Replication and extension. *Personnel Psychology* 31, pp. 903–19.

133. Willis Towers Watson. (2019, Aug. 8). U.S. employers plan to hold the line on pay raises in 2020, Willis Towers Watson survey finds. Retrieved from *https://www.willistowerswatson.com/en-US/News/2019/08/us-employers-plan-to-hold-the-line-on-pay-raises-in-2020* on Apr. 22, 2020.

4

COMPENSATION

Compensation is a critical component of the employment relationship. It includes direct cash payments, indirect payments in the form of employee benefits, and incentives to motivate employees to strive for higher levels of productivity. Compensation is affected by forces as diverse as labor market factors, collective bargaining, government legislation, and top management's philosophy regarding pay and benefits. This is a dynamic area, and Chapters 11 and 12 present the latest developments in compensation theory and examples of company practices. Chapter 11 is a nontechnical introduction to the subject of pay and incentive systems, whereas Chapter 12 focuses on employee benefits. You will find that the material in each chapter has direct implications for sound management practice.

11 | PAY AND INCENTIVE SYSTEMS

Questions This Chapter Will Help Managers Answer

LO 11-1 How can we tie compensation strategy to general business strategy?

LO 11-2 What economic and legal factors should we consider in establishing pay levels for different jobs?

LO 11-3 What is the best way to develop pay systems that are understandable, workable, and acceptable to employees at all levels?

LO 11-4 How can we tie incentives to individual, team, or organizationwide performance?

LO 11-5 In implementing a pay-for-performance system, what key traps must we avoid to make the system work as planned?

THE TRUST GAP*

Over the years, few topics have generated as much controversy as executive compensation. CEOs say, "We're a team; we're all in this together." But employees look at the difference between their pay and the CEO's. They see top management's perks—oak dining rooms and heated garages—versus cafeterias for lower-level workers and parking spaces a half mile from the plant. And they wonder, Is this togetherness? As the disparity in pay widens, the wonder grows. CEO pay has risen 940 percent since 1978, while the typical worker's pay has risen only 12 percent since that time. Hourly workers and supervisors indeed agree that "we're all in this together," but what we're in turns out to be a frame of mind that mistrusts senior management's intentions, doubts its competence, and resents its self-congratulatory pay. What's at stake is nothing less than the public trust essential to a thriving free-market economy.

Study after study, involving hundreds of companies and thousands of workers, have found evidence of a **trust gap**—and it is growing. Indeed, the attitudes of middle managers and professionals toward the workplace are becoming more like those of hourly workers, historically the most disaffected group.

Whereas roughly half of CEO pay is now tied to changes in the value of company stock, 70 percent of the nation's college graduates have seen their after-inflation hourly wages decline since 2000, according to the Economic Policy Institute. A big reason for the gap is that bonuses and equity are routinely awarded to top managers but not to other employees.

What about shareholder pressure to limit CEO pay? The 2010 Dodd-Frank Wall Street Reform and Consumer Protection Act grants shareholders a "say on pay" vote on executive compensation. The votes are nonbinding, but companies sometimes act when there is clear disapproval from shareholders.

To be sure, much of the trust gap can be traced to inconsistencies between what management says and what it does—between saying "People are our most important asset" and in the next breath ordering layoffs, or between promoting quality while continuing to evaluate workers by how many pieces they push out the door.

There are other causes as well: competition for jobs from low-cost countries, automation, the rising cost of health-care benefits, and, sometimes, faulty incentive systems that reward financial engineering and greed rather than prudent risk management and value creation.

The result is a world in which top management thinks it's sending crucial messages but employees never hear a word. Thus, a recent survey of 7,600 business leaders and 71,000 employers from U.S. and Canadian organizations found that although 73 percent of employers say they pay their workers fairly, only 36 percent of employees agree. Although 78 percent of employers believe that employees are valued at work, only 45 percent of workers agree.

Sources: Kelly, J. (2020, Mar. 30). CEOs are cutting their own salaries in response to the coronavirus. *Forbes.* Retrieved from *https://www.forbes.com/sites/jackkelly/2020/03/30/ceos-are-cutting-their-own-salaries-in-response-to-the-coronavirus/#7db5bb263e91* on Apr. 27, 2020. Mishel, L., & Wolfe, J. (2019, Aug. 14). CEO compensation has grown 940% since 1978. *Economic Policy Institute.* Retrieved from *https://www.epi.org/publication/ceo-compensation-2018/* on Apr. 27, 2020. Lublin, J. S. (2017, May 3). How Millennial bosses can gain trust. *The Wall Street Journal,* p. B5. Schuman, M. J. (2017, Sept. 25). Why wages aren't growing. *Bloomberg Businessweek,* pp. 12–14. Francis, T., and Lublin, J. S. (2016, June 3). Divide persists between pay, performance. *The Wall Street Journal,* pp. B1, B5. Miller, S. (2016, Apr. 5). Bridge the "comp chasm" with trust, transparency. Retrieved from *www.shrm.org/resourcesandtools/hr-topics/compensation/pages/bridge-comp-chasm.aspx* on Apr. 14, 2016.

Confidence in top management's competence is collapsing. The days when top management could say "Trust us; this is for your own good" are over. Employees have seen that if the company embarks on a new strategic tack and it doesn't work, employees are the ones who lose their jobs–not management.

Whereas competence may be hard to judge, pay is known, and to the penny. The rate of increase in CEOs' pay split from workers' in 1979 and has rocketed upward ever since. What is rare are policies like those of Whole Foods Market, which prevent any executive from earning more than 14 times what the average worker makes. Said one observer, "The gap is widening beyond what the guy at the bottom can even understand. There's very little common ground left in terms of the experience of the average worker and the CEO."

Although most workers are willing to accept substantial differentials in pay between corporate highs and lows and acknowledge that the highs should receive their just rewards, more and more of the lows–and the middles–are asking, "Just how just is just?"

Challenges

1. To many people, a deep-seated sense of unfairness lies at the heart of the trust gap. How do perceptions of unfairness develop?
2. What are some of the predictable consequences of a trust gap?
3. Can you suggest alternative strategies for reducing the trust gap?

The chapter-opening vignette illustrates important changes in the current thinking about pay: Employees will always evaluate levels of pay in terms of fairness, and unless pay systems are acceptable to those affected by them, they will breed mistrust and lack of commitment. Pay policies and practices are critical because they affect every employee, from the janitor to the CEO. This chapter begins by exploring four major questions: (1) What economic and legal factors determine pay levels within a firm? (2) How do firms link their compensation and business strategies? (3) How do firms develop pay structures that reflect different levels of pay for different jobs? (4) What key policy issues in pay planning and administration must managers address? These challenges are shown graphically in Figure 11-1.

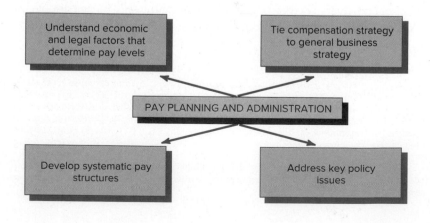

Figure 11–1

Four key challenges in planning and administering a pay system.

We will then consider what is known about incentives at the individual, team, and organizationwide levels. As a worker or manager, it is important that you become knowledgeable about these important issues. This chapter will help you develop that knowledge base.

CHANGING PHILOSOPHIES REGARDING PAY SYSTEMS

Today there is a continuing effort to tie more of workers' pay to performance.[1] Managers are asking, "What have you done for me lately?" Current performance is what counts, and every year performance standards are raised. In this atmosphere, we are seeing three major changes in company philosophies concerning pay and benefits:

1. Increased willingness to reduce the size of the workforce, to outsource jobs, and to restrict pay to control the costs of pay and benefits.
2. Less concern with pay position relative to that of competitors and more concern with what the company can afford.
3. Implementation of programs to encourage and reward performance–thereby making pay more variable. In fact, a recent study revealed that this is one of the most critical compensation issues facing large companies today.[2]

We will consider each of these changes, as well as other material in this and the following chapter, from the perspective of the line manager, not from that of the technical compensation specialist.

Cost-Containment Actions

Given that wage and salary payments may account for more than 50 percent of total operating costs, employers have an obvious interest in controlling them.[3] To do so, they are attempting to contain staff sizes, payrolls, and benefits costs. Some of the cutbacks are only temporary, such as pay cuts and furloughs.[4] Other changes are meant to be permanent: firing executives or offering them early retirement; asking employees to work longer hours, to take fewer days off, and to shorten their vacations; reducing the coverage of medical plans or asking employees to pay part of the cost; and trimming expense accounts, with restrictions on phone calls and entertainment. If such a strategy is to work, however, CEOs will first need to demonstrate to employees at all levels, by means of tangible actions, that they are serious about closing the trust gap (see the chapter-opening vignette).

Paying What the Company Can Afford

A start-up organization typically can't afford to pay what established competitors do. Thus, that an employer's ability to pay depends on its ability to compete in product or service markets.[5] Key factors in those markets are the degree of competition among producers (e.g., fast-food outlets) and the level of demand for the products or services. Both affect the ability of a firm to change the prices of its products or services. If an employer cannot increase prices without losing revenues due to decreased sales, that employer's ability to raise the level of pay is limited. If the employer does pay more, it has two options: pass the increased costs on to consumers or don't raise prices and accept smaller profit margins to cover labor costs.[6]

In order for cost-containment measures to work, CEOs need to demonstrate in tangible ways their commitment to closing the trust gap.
Shutterstock

Programs That Encourage and Reward Performance

Firms are continuing to relocate to areas where organized labor is weak and pay rates are low. They are developing pay plans that channel more dollars into incentive awards and fewer into fixed salaries. Entrepreneurs in high-risk start-up organizations, salespeople, piecework factory workers, and rock stars have long lived with erratic incomes.[7] People in other jobs are used to fairly fixed paychecks that grow a bit every year. It is a bedrock of the U.S. compensation system, but it is gradually being nudged aside by programs that put more pay at risk.[8] These programs are being linked to profit and productivity gains–usually a moving, ever-rising target.

At lower levels, such variable-pay systems almost guarantee cost control. In many new plans, any productivity gains are shared 25 percent by the employees and 75 percent by the company. If business takes off, more pay goes to workers. If it doesn't, the company is not locked into high fixed costs of labor. In the United States and globally, almost 80 percent of large- and medium-sized companies now offer some kind of variable pay–such as profit-sharing and bonus awards–up from 47 percent in 1990.[9] Later in this chapter, we will discuss pay-for-performance more fully and how it can be put into effect.

The International Application below focuses on the *outcomes* of bonus decisions. However, the *process* is also important. To a large extent, the relative emphasis managers place on performance versus relationships varies with cultural factors. Thus, when making bonus decisions, Chinese managers tend to place less emphasis on employees' work performance than do American managers. However, when making decisions about employee recognition, Chinese managers tend to place more emphasis on employees' relationships with coworkers and managers than do their American counterparts. Finally, Chinese managers tend to give larger bonuses to employees with greater personal needs, whereas American managers tend not to take personal needs into consideration when making bonus decisions.[10]

INTERNATIONAL APPLICATION
Tying Pay to Performance in the United States, Europe, and Japan[a]

In an effort to hold down labor costs, thousands of U.S. companies are changing the way they increase workers' pay. Instead of the traditional annual increase, millions of workers in industries as diverse as supermarkets and aircraft manufacturing are receiving cash bonuses. For most workers, the plans mean less money. The bonuses take many names: "profit-sharing" at Abbott Laboratories and Caterpillar, "gain sharing" at Mack Trucks and Panhandle Energy, and "lump-sum payments" at Boeing. All have two elements in common: (1) They can vary with the company's fortunes and (2) they are not permanent. Because the bonuses are not folded into base pay (as merit increases are), there is no compounding effect over time. They are simply provided on top of a constant base level of pay. This means that both wages and benefits rise more slowly than they would have if the base level of pay were rising each year. The result: a flattening of wages.

Flexible pay—tied mostly to profitability and promising better job security, but not guaranteeing it—is at the heart of the evolving bonus system. Employees are being asked to share the risks of the new global marketplace.

How large must the rewards be? Although hard data on this question are scarce, most experts agree that employees don't begin to notice incentive payouts unless they are at least 10 percent of base pay, with 15 to 20 percent more likely to evoke the desired response.[b] In the United States and most European Union countries, bonus payments have been averaging about 12 percent of a worker's base pay annually.[c] Conversely, the Japanese currently pay many workers a bonus that represents about 25 percent of base pay. For workers in all nations, a significant amount of their pay is at risk.

Have such plans generated greater productivity in the U.S. manufacturing sector in recent years? Maybe, but an equally plausible explanation is that the gains were due to automation; to company efforts to give workers more of a say in how they do their jobs; and to workers' fear that if they did not improve their productivity, their plants would become uncompetitive and be closed. In short, the jury is still out on the productivity impact of bonus systems, but evidence does indicate that bonus satisfaction is a separate and distinct component of overall pay satisfaction.[d]

[a]Podsada, J. (2016, Sept. 6). More companies are doing away with automatic annual pay raises, but will workers buy in? *Omaha World-Herald.* Retrieved from *https://www.omaha.com/money/more-companies-are-doing-away-with-automatic-annual-pay-raises/article_a81d4c77-83f3-5d12-aa5e-b409db03368a.html* on Apr. 27, 2020. Kelleher, J. B. (2013, Sept. 1). Analysis: Caterpillar plan illustrates risk of variable pay plans. Retrieved from *http://www.reuters.com/article/2013/09/01/us-usa-workers-pay-analysis-idUSBRE98005N20130901* on May 27, 2014.

[b]Gerhart, B., and Newman, J. M.. (2020). *Compensation* (13th ed.). New York: McGraw-Hill.

[c]Greenfield, R. (2016, June 21). Say goodbye to the annual pay raise. *Bloomberg.* Retrieved from *www.bloomberg.com/news/articles/2016-06-21/say-goodbye-to-the-annual-pay-raise* on May 29, 2017.

[d]Sturman, M. C., and Short, J. C. (2000). Lump-sum bonus satisfaction: Testing the construct validity of a new pay satisfaction dimension. *Personnel Psychology* 53, pp. 673–700.

COMPONENTS AND OBJECTIVES OF ORGANIZATIONAL REWARD SYSTEMS

At a broad level, an **organizational reward system** includes anything an employee values and desires that an employer is able and willing to offer in exchange for employee contributions. More specifically, such **compensation** includes both financial and nonfinancial rewards. **Financial rewards** include direct payments (e.g., salary) plus indirect payments in the form of employee benefits (see Chapter 12). **Nonfinancial rewards** include everything in a work environment that enhances a worker's sense of self-respect and esteem by others (e.g., work environments that are physically, socially, and mentally healthy; opportunities for training and personal development; effective supervision; recognition; and a positive employer brand). These ideas are shown graphically in Figure 11–2.

Although money is obviously a powerful tool used to capture the minds and hearts of workers and to maximize their productivity, don't underestimate the impact of nonfinancial rewards. In an improved economy, one way companies are trying to keep their employees satisfied is by promoting well-being, remote work, flexible hours, and other amenities. As an example, consider goodmortgage.com, a 56-employee business in Charlotte, North Carolina. Employees gather in the morning to follow exercise videos on a large flat-screen TV in the full gym and to eat breakfast cooked for them by management. After one employee won a $500 gas card in one of the company's ongoing sales contests, she remarked, "I have a lot of friends in the mortgage industry and a lot of people have tried to recruit me, but no one treats their employees like we're treated here."[11]

Companies are doing these things because they don't have much choice. Giving their workers more ease and freedom is simply enlightened self-interest. As one executive noted, "In yesteryear you worked 9 to 5 and that was work–life balance. Today, people look for more flexibility." With tight labor markets and a generational shift in the workforce, fully two-thirds of companies have enhanced their total rewards systems. Why? To attract and retain the best talent.[12]

Rewards bridge the gap between organizational objectives and individual expectations and aspirations. To be effective, organizational reward systems should provide four things: (1) a sufficient level of rewards to fulfill basic needs, (2) equity with the external labor market, (3) equity within the organization, and (4) treatment of each member of the organization in terms of his or her individual needs.[13] More broadly, pay systems are designed to attract, retain, and motivate employees. This is the ARM concept. Indeed, much of the design of compensation systems involves working out trade-offs among more or less seriously conflicting objectives.[14]

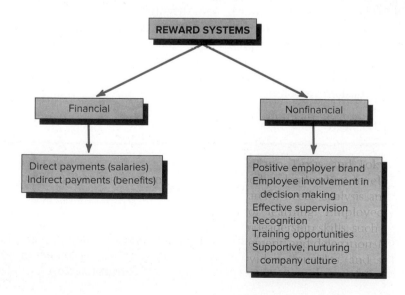

Figure 11–2

Organizational reward systems include financial as well as nonfinancial components.

Perhaps the most important objective of any pay system is fairness or equity. Equity can be assessed on at least three dimensions:

1. **Internal equity.** Are pay rates fair in terms of the relative worth of individual jobs to an organization?
2. **External equity.** Are the wages paid by an organization fair in terms of competitive market rates outside the organization?
3. **Individual equity.** Is each individual's pay fair relative to that of other individuals doing the same or similar jobs?

Researchers have proposed several bases for determining equitable payment for work.[15] They have three points in common:

1. Each assumes that employees perceive a fair return for what they contribute to their jobs.
2. All include the concept of social comparison, whereby employees determine what their equitable return should be after comparing their inputs (e.g., skills, education, effort) and outcomes (e.g., pay, promotion, job status) with those of their peers or coworkers (comparison persons).
3. The theories assume that employees who perceive themselves to be in an inequitable situation will seek to reduce that inequity. They may do so by mentally distorting their inputs or outcomes, by directly altering their inputs or outcomes, or by leaving the organization.

Reviews of both laboratory and field tests of equity theory are quite consistent: Individuals tend to follow the equity norm and to use it as a basis for distributing rewards. They report inequitable conditions as distressing, although there may be individual differences in sensitivity to equity.[16]

A final objective is **balance**—the relative size of pay differentials among different segments of the workforce. If pay systems are to accomplish the objectives set for them, ultimately they must be perceived as adequate and equitable. For example, there should be a balance in pay relationships between supervisors and the highest-paid subordinates reporting to them. This differential typically varies from 5 to 30 percent.[17] Pay ratios of 275 to 1 (or greater) between CEOs and typical workers are generally regarded as out of balance.[18]

STRATEGIC INTEGRATION OF COMPENSATION PLANS AND BUSINESS PLANS

Unfortunately, the rationale behind many compensation programs is "Two-thirds of our competitors do it" or "That's corporate policy." Compensation plans need to be tied to an organization's strategic mission and should take their direction from that mission. They must support the general business strategy—for example, differentiation (setting yourself apart from the competition) or cost leadership.[19] Further, evidence now shows that inferior performance by a firm is associated with a lack of fit between its pay policy and its business strategy.[20] From a managerial perspective, therefore, the most fundamental question is "What do you want your pay system to accomplish?"

As an example, consider Nucor Steel, a company that states in its corporate mission that it succeeds by "working together" to generate high productivity, high-quality, and low-cost products. The company focuses on all of its customers,

ETHICAL DILEMMA
Does Being Ethical Pay?*

Social responsibility has become big business for many corporations. Companies spend billions of dollars doing good works–everything from boosting diversity in their ranks to developing eco-friendly technology–and then trumpeting those efforts to the public. Do those efforts pay off?

In a series of experiments, consumers were shown the same products–coffee and T-shirts. One group was told that the items were made using high ethical standards, another was told that the items were made using low ethical standards, and a third group (the control group) received no information. In the case of coffee, consumers were willing to pay $9.71 for a pound produced using high ethical standards, $5.89 for a pound produced using unethical standards, and $8.31 when given no information about the ethical standards used in coffee production. Results for T-shirts were similar. The researchers concluded that consumers are willing to pay a small premium for goods produced ethically, but they will punish a product made unethically even more harshly, by buying it only at a steep discount.

The implication of this research is that companies should segment their overall markets and make special efforts to reach out to consumers with high ethical standards. Those are the customers who can deliver the biggest potential profits on ethically produced goods.

In an effort to attract, retain, and motivate top talent, do you believe that companies should also trumpet their ethical standards? Is there a payoff? How might organizations encourage ethical behavior in the workplace?

*Source: The Manifest. (2018, Dec. 12). How can companies encourage ethics in the workplace? Retrieved from *https://medium.com/@the_manifest/how-can-companies-encourage-ethics-in-the-workplace-5c36318e98a4* on Apr. 27, 2020. Trudel, R., and Cotte, J. (2008, May 12). Does being ethical pay? *The Wall Street Journal*, p. R4.

including its employees. It pays below the market in base pay, but bonuses based on plant production and company profits make it a market leader for total cash compensation. In a good year, its hourly workers can make $75,000 or more, compared to an average annual wage in U.S. manufacturing of about $47,000. The company has never had a layoff, even when sales dropped by more than 50 percent during the Great Recession. That's working together![21]

This approach to managing compensation and business strategies dictates that actual levels of compensation should not be strictly a matter of what is being paid in the marketplace. Instead, compensation levels derive from an assessment of what must be paid to attract and retain the right people, what the organization can afford, and what will be required to meet the organization's strategic goals. The idea is to align the interests of managers and employees.

When compensation is viewed from a strategic perspective, therefore, firms do the following:

1. They recognize compensation as a pivotal control and incentive mechanism that can be used flexibly by management to attain business objectives.
2. They make the pay system an integral part of strategy formulation.
3. They integrate pay considerations into strategic decision-making processes, such as those that involve planning and control.
4. They view the firm's performance as the ultimate criterion of the success of strategic pay decisions and its compensation programs.[22]

DETERMINANTS OF PAY STRUCTURE AND LEVEL

Marginal revenue theory in labor economics holds that unless an employee can produce a value equal to the value received in wages, it will not be worthwhile to hire that worker.[23] In practice, a number of factors interact to determine wage levels. Some of the most influential of these are labor market conditions, legislation, collective bargaining, management attitudes, and an organization's ability to pay. Let us examine each of these.

Labor Market Conditions

As noted in Chapter 6, whether a labor market is "tight" or "loose" has a major impact on wage structures and levels. Thus, if the demand for certain skills is high while the supply is low (a tight market), there tends to be an increase in the price paid for these skills. Conversely, if the supply of labor is plentiful, relative to the demand for it, wages tend to decrease. As an example, consider Jordan Machine Company.

JORDAN MACHINE COMPANY

HR BUZZ

Small Business Contends with Tight Labor Markets

Jordan Machine Company of Birmingham, Alabama, has never worked so hard to find so few employees. "We've turned over barrels and drums and searched just about everywhere we can think," says Jerry Edwards, chief executive officer. The company needs skilled machinists to help manufacture molds for everything from fishing lures to submarine hatch covers.[a]

Despite his efforts–including offers of high pay, full health benefits, and a company-sponsored savings program–Edwards estimated that his company lost more than half a million dollars last year, simply because it couldn't find enough workers to meet the demand for new orders.

Jordan Machine Company is not alone. Companies, high-tech and low-tech alike, simply cannot find workers when labor markets are tight. In tight labor markets, labor shortages are the number 1 headache for many employers. In some cases, tight labor markets have curbed growth and expansion possibilities, and in others they have forced operators to shut down early for lack of staff.[b] Such tight labor markets have predictable effects on wages. Consider auto-repair technicians, long stereotyped as low-paid grease monkeys. With increasing computerization and complex diagnostics in autos, many older mechanics are choosing to change careers rather than go back for more training. The scarcity is forcing some dealers to poach other shops, and it has driven up auto-repair costs as well as the wages of repair technicians. Their average wages were $42,090 in 2019, and demand for them is projected to remain stable through 2028. For qualified jobseekers, opportunities are good.[c]

---

[a]Jordan Machine Company. Retrieved from *http://www.jordanmachine.com/about/*on Apr. 27, 2020. Jaffe, G. (1997, Jan. 15). South's growth rate hits speed bump. *The Wall Street Journal*, p. A2.

[b]Simon, R. (2019, May 12). Tight U. S. job market squeezes smallest businesses the most. *The Wall Street Journal*. Retrieved from *https://www.wsj.com/articles/tight-u-s-job-market-squeezes-smallest-businesses-the-most-11557658804* on May 12, 2019.

[c]Bureau of Labor Statistics. Automotive service technicians and mechanics. *Occupational Outlook Handbook*. Retrieved from *www.bls.gov/ooh/installation-maintenance-and-repair/automotive-service-technicians-and-mechanics.htm* on Apr. 27, 2020.

Another labor market phenomenon that causes substantial differences in pay rates, even among people who work in the same field and are of similar age and education, is the payment of wage premiums by some employers to attract the best talent available and to enhance productivity in order to offset any increase in labor costs. This is known as the *efficiency wage hypothesis* in labor economics, and it has received some support among economic researchers.[24] The forces discussed thus far affect pay levels to a considerable extent. So also does government legislation.

Legislation

As in other areas, legislation related to pay plays a vital role in determining internal organization practices. Although we cannot analyze all the relevant laws here, Table 11-1

Table 11–1

FOUR MAJOR FEDERAL WAGE-HOUR LAWS

	Scope of coverage	Major provisions	Administrative agency
Fair Labor Standards Act (FLSA) of 1938 (as amended)	Employers involved in interstate commerce or in the production of goods for interstate commerce. Exemption from overtime provisions for managers, supervisors, executives, outside salespersons, and professional workers	*Minimum wage:* $7.25 per hour for covered employees; *overtime pay:* time and one-half for working more than 40 hours within a period of 7 consecutive days, no extra pay required for weekends, vacations, holidays, or severance; *child labor:* under age 14 usually cannot be employed; ages 14–15 may work in safe occupations outside school hours, but not more than 3 hours on a school day; when school is not in session, can work up to 40 hours per week; ages 16–17, no hourly restrictions, but cannot work in hazardous jobs	Wage and Hour Division of the Employment Standards Administration, U.S. Department of Labor
Equal Pay Act (1963)	Men and women doing "substantially similar" work in terms of skill, effort, responsibility, and working conditions	Wage differentials based exclusively on gender are prohibited.	Equal Employment Opportunity Commission
Sarbanes–Oxley Act (SOX, 2002)	Executives (CEOs and CFOs)	These individuals cannot retain bonuses or profits from selling company stock if they mislead the public about the financial health of the company.	Public Company Accounting Oversight Board, Securities and Exchange Commission
Dodd-Frank Wall Street Reform and Consumer Protection Act (2010)	All public companies	Requires reporting of the ratio of CEO pay to worker pay; gives shareholders a non-binding vote to approve or disapprove executive pay ("Say on Pay")	Securities and Exchange Commission

presents a summary of the coverage, major provisions, and federal agencies charged with administering four major federal laws that affect compensation.

Of the four laws shown in Table 11-1, the Fair Labor Standards Act (FLSA) affects almost every organization in the United States. It is the source of the terms *exempt employees* (exempt from the overtime provisions of the law) and *nonexempt employees.* It established the first national minimum wage (25 cents an hour) in 1938; subsequent changes in the minimum wage and in national policy on equal pay for equal work for both sexes (the Equal Pay Act of 1963) were passed as amendments to this law. About 1.3 million employees are covered by federal overtime rules adopted in 2019, and those rules apply to salaried and hourly workers alike.[25] At the same time, many of today's employees no longer fit into the law's outdated categories (see Figure 11-3).

There are many loopholes in FLSA minimum-wage coverage.[26] Certain workers, including casual baby-sitters and most farm workers, are excluded, as are employees of small businesses and firms not engaged in interstate commerce. State minimum-wage laws are intended to cover these workers. At the same time, if a state's minimum is higher than the federal minimum, the state minimum applies. For example, although the federal minimum wage is $7.25, as of 2020, 29 states and the District of Columbia had higher minimums. For example, the state of Washington's was $13.50, California's was $12, Connecticut's was $12, and Maryland's was $11.[27] More than 120 cities and counties pay their workers or contractors a *living wage,* which is tailored to living costs in an area and may be more than double the federal or state minimums. Although opponents argue that such laws will force some

---

Figure 11–3

Who must be paid overtime?

THE RULES REFLECT OLD ASSUMPTIONS . . .

When Congress passed a law in 1938 mandating overtime pay, it also created a series of exemptions listing various types of workers who weren't entitled to it

EXECUTIVE:
The boss, of course, is not entitled to overtime. An executive is defined as a manager who supervises at least two employees, with authority to hire, fire, and promote.

PROFESSIONALS AND CREATIVES:
Overtime is also denied to those whose job requires advanced training, a professional degree, or artistic imagination.

ADMINISTRATIVE:
Nor are many white-collar worker bees able to collect overtime. This exemption covers people who primarily do office work and exercise "independent judgment."

OUTSIDE SALESPEOPLE:
Think Willy Loman. No overtime for salespeople who are regularly away from the employer's place of business.

. . . THAT DON'T ALWAYS APPLY IN TODAY'S WORKPLACE

A big reason that wage and hour litigation is exploding is that so many employees no longer fit into the law's outdated categories

STARBUCKS STORE MANAGER:
The company claims they are executives, but store managers may spend more time serving than supervising. The company settled a case in California, where state law says you have to spend more than 50% of your time actually managing, but is fighting a case in Florida under more flexible federal rules.

MERCK SALES REPRESENTATIVE:
Drug company reps don't actually sell anything. They merely attempt to influence doctors' prescribing, so the sales exemption may be invalid. And the administrative exemption requires exercise of discretion, but the pitches to physicians are tightly scripted. Cases have been filed against every major drug manufacturer, and the legal status of these workers is unclear.

ERNST & YOUNG ACCOUNTANT:
If someone with an accounting degree is actually exercising his judgment as a CPA, the professional exemption applies. But a worker who simply gathers audit data and enters it in a spreadsheet can't—licensed or not—be classified as a professional. Litigation pending against Ernst & Young makes overtime claims on behalf of E&Y staff, including some with professional degrees.

Source: Orey, M. Wage wars. *Business Week,* October 1, 2007, p. 58. Bloomberg L.P.

businesses to close, at least some academic research suggests that living wage laws do more good than harm. They have imposed little—if any—cost to the cities that have passed them, they have led to few job losses, and they have lifted many families out of poverty.[28]

Collective Bargaining

Another major influence on wages in unionized as well as nonunionized firms is collective bargaining. Nonunionized firms are affected by collective bargaining agreements made elsewhere because they must compete with unionized firms for the services and loyalties of workers. Collective bargaining affects two key factors: (1) the level of wages and (2) the behavior of workers in relevant labor markets. In an open, competitive market, workers tend to gravitate toward higher-paying jobs. To the extent that nonunionized firms fail to match the wages of unionized firms, they may have difficulty attracting and keeping workers. Furthermore, benefits negotiated under union agreements have had the effect of increasing the package of benefits in firms that have attempted to avoid unionization. In addition to wages and benefits, collective bargaining is also used to negotiate procedures for administering pay, procedures for resolving grievances regarding compensation decisions, and methods used to determine the relative worth of jobs.[29]

Managerial Attitudes and an Organization's Ability to Pay

Managerial attitudes and an organization's ability to pay have a major impact on wage structures and levels. Earlier we noted that an organization's ability to pay depends, to a large extent, on the competitive dynamics it faces in its product or service markets. Therefore, regardless of its espoused competitive position on wages, an organization's ability to pay ultimately will be a key factor that limits actual wages.

This is not to downplay the role of management philosophy and attitudes on pay. On the contrary, management's desire to maintain or improve morale, attract high-caliber employees, reduce turnover, and improve employees' standards of living also affects wages, as does the relative importance of a given position to a firm.[30] For example, a safety engineer is more important to a chemical company than to a bank. Wage structures tend to vary across firms to the extent that managers view any given position as more or less critical to their firms. Ultimately, top management renders judgments regarding the overall competitive pay position of the firm (above-market, at-market, or below-market rates), factors to be considered in determining job worth, and the relative weight to be given seniority and performance in pay decisions. Those judgments are key determinants of the structure and level of wages.[31]

AN OVERVIEW OF PAY-SYSTEM MECHANICS

The procedures described in this section for developing pay systems should help those involved to apply their judgments in a systematic manner. The hallmarks of success in compensation management, as in other areas, are understandability, workability, and acceptability. The broad objective is to assign a monetary value to each job in the organization (a base rate) and an orderly procedure for increasing the base rate (e.g., based on merit, inflation, experience, or some combination of these). To develop such a system, we need four basic tools:

1. Updated job descriptions.
2. A job evaluation method (i.e., one that will rank jobs in terms of their overall worth to the organization).
3. Pay surveys.
4. A pay structure.

Figure 11-4 presents an overview of this process.

Job descriptions are key tools in the design of pay systems, and they serve two purposes:

1. They identify important characteristics of each job, so that the relative worth of jobs can be determined.
2. From them we can identify, define, and weight **compensable factors** (common job characteristics that an organization is willing to pay for, such as skill, effort, responsibility, and working conditions).

Once this has been done, the next step is to rate the worth of all jobs using a job evaluation system.

A number of **job evaluation** methods are available. Their purpose is to provide a work-related and business-related rationale to support decisions about pay. All of the methods also have the same final objective: to rank jobs in terms of their relative

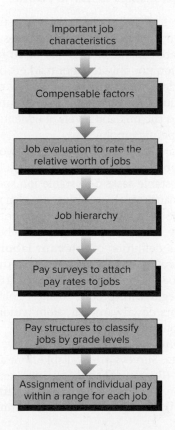

Figure 11–4

Traditional job-based compensation model.

worth to the organization so that an equitable rate of pay can be determined for each job. However, different job evaluation methods yield different rank-orders of jobs, and, therefore, different pay structures.[32] In short, method matters.

As an illustration, consider the point method of job evaluation, the approach most commonly used in the United States and Europe.[33] The first step is to analyze and define each job in terms of the compensable factors an organization has agreed to adopt. Members of a job evaluation committee then assign points to the appropriate level (or degree) of each compensable factor, such as responsibility. To compute the total points for each job, they sum the points assigned. When they rank-order the point totals from highest to lowest, the result is a **hierarchy of job worth**.

Although job evaluation provides a business-related order and logic that supports pay differences among jobs, not all firms use it. One reason is that several policy issues must be resolved first, including[34]

- Does management perceive meaningful differences among jobs?
- Is it possible to identify criteria to make distinctions among jobs?
- Will job evaluation result in meaningful distinctions in the eyes of employees?
- Are jobs stable, and will they remain stable in the future?
- Is job evaluation consistent with the organization's goals and strategies? For example, if the goal is to ensure maximum flexibility among job assignments, a knowledge- or skill-based pay system may be most appropriate. We will address that topic more fully in a later section.

Linking Internal Pay Relationships to Market Data

In the point method of job evaluation, the next task is to translate the point totals into a pay structure. Two key components of this process are identifying and surveying pay rates in relevant labor markets. This can often be a complex task because employers must pay attention not only to labor markets but also to product markets (e.g., level of demand and degree of competition).[35] Pay practices must be designed not only to attract and retain employees but also to ensure that labor costs (base pay levels, incentive awards, and the mix and levels of benefits) do not become excessive in relation to those of competing employers.

The definition of relevant labor markets requires two key decisions: which jobs to survey and which markets are relevant for each job. Jobs selected for a survey are generally characterized by stable tasks and stable job specifications (e.g., computer programmers, purchasing managers). Jobs with these characteristics are known as *key jobs*, or **benchmark jobs**. Jobs that do not meet these criteria, but that are characterized by high turnover or are difficult to fill, should also be included.

As we noted earlier, the definition of **relevant labor markets** should consider geographical boundaries (local, regional, national, or international) as well as product-market competitors (e.g., banks compared to banks, auto dealers to auto dealers). Such an approach might begin with product-market competitors as the initial market, followed by adjustments downward (e.g., from national to regional markets) on the basis of geographical considerations.

Once target populations and relevant markets have been identified, the next task is to obtain survey data. Surveys are available from a variety of sources, including the federal government (Bureau of Labor Statistics), employers' associations, trade and professional associations, users of a given job evaluation system (e.g., the Hay Group's point-factor system), and compensation consulting firms.[36]

Managers should be aware of two potential problems with pay-survey data.[37] The most serious is the assurance of an accurate job match. If only a "thumbnail sketch" (i.e., a very brief description) is used to characterize a job, there is always the possibility of legitimate misunderstanding among survey respondents. To deal with this, some surveys ask respondents if their salary data for a job are direct matches or somewhat higher or lower than those described (and therefore worthy of more or less pay).

A second problem has resulted from the explosion of *at-risk* forms of pay, some of which are based on individual performance and some on the profitability of an organization. As we noted earlier, base pay is becoming a smaller part of the total compensation package for a broad range of employees. This makes it difficult to determine the actual pay of job incumbents and can make survey results difficult to interpret. For example, how do we compare salary figures that include only base pay or direct cash payouts with at-risk pay that may take the form of a lump-sum bonus, additional time off with pay, or an employee stock-ownership plan? Despite these potential problems, all indications are that pay surveys will continue to be used widely.

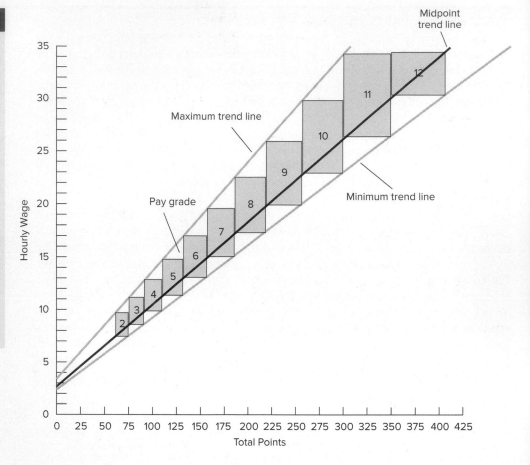

The end result is often a chart, as in Figure 11-5, that relates current wage rates to the total points assigned to each job. For each point total, a trend line is fitted to indicate the average relationship between points assigned to the benchmark jobs and the hourly wages paid for those jobs. Once a midpoint trend line is fitted, two others are also drawn: (1) a trend line that represents the minimum rate of pay for each point total and (2) a trend line that represents the maximum rate of pay for each point total.[38]

Developing a Pay Structure

The final step in attaching dollar values to jobs using the point method is to establish pay grades, or ranges, characterized by a point spread from minimum to maximum for each grade. Starting wages are given by the trend line that represents the minimum rate of pay for each pay grade, whereas the highest wages that can be earned within a grade are given by the trend line that represents the maximum rate of pay. The pay structure is described numerically in Table 11-2.

For example, consider the job of administrative clerk. Let's assume that the job evaluation committee arrived at a total allocation of 142 points across all compensable factors. The job therefore falls into pay grade 6. Starting pay is $13.12 per hour, with a maximum pay rate of $17.06 per hour. Actual rates of pay may be adjusted above or below market rates based on the local cost of labor or cost of living. Depending on where a job is located in the United States, salaries may vary by up to 23 percent.[39]

Table 11–2

ILLUSTRATIVE PAY STRUCTURE SHOWING PAY GRADES, THE SPREAD OF POINTS WITHIN GRADES, THE MIDPOINT OF EACH PAY GRADE, AND THE MINIMUM AND MAXIMUM RATES OF PAY PER GRADE

Grade	Point spread	Midpoint	Minimum rate of pay	Maximum rate of pay
2	62–75	68	$ 7.50	$ 9.75
3	76–91	83	8.63	11.21
4	92–110	101	9.92	12.90
5	111–132	121	11.41	14.83
6	133–157	145	13.12	17.06
7	158–186	172	15.09	19.62
8	187–219	203	17.35	22.56
9	220–257	238	19.95	25.94
10	258–300	279	22.95	29.83
11	301–350	325	26.39	34.31
12	351–407	379	30.35	34.45

The actual development of a pay structure is a complex process, but there are certain rules of thumb to follow:

- Jobs of the same general value should be clustered into the same pay grade.
- Jobs that clearly differ in value should be in different pay grades.
- There should be a smooth progression of point groupings.
- The new system should fit realistically into the existing allocation of pay within a company.
- The pay grades should conform reasonably well to pay patterns in the relevant labor markets.[40]

BROAD BANDING*   HR BUZZ

In order to introduce greater flexibility into their salary structures, organizations such as Merck, the U.S. Navy, Medtronic, and 3M have collapsed salary grades into only a few broad bands, each with a sizable range. This technique, known as **broad banding**, consolidates as many as four or five traditional grades into a single band with one minimum and one maximum.

Broad bands support redesigned, downsized, or boundary-less organizations that have eliminated layers of managerial jobs. Organizations with global operations, such as 3M and Medtronic, use bands to move managers among worldwide

*Sources: Gerhart, B., and Newman, J. M. (2020). *Compensation* (13th ed.). New York: McGraw-Hill. Martocchio, J. J. (2020). *Strategic Compensation* (10th ed.). Upper Saddle River, NJ: Pearson/Prentice Hall.

(continued)

assignments. Broad bands also facilitate mergers and acquisitions because there are relatively few pay levels to argue over. Yet broad banding is no cure-all. It changes *how* compensation dollars are allocated, but not *how much* is allocated. Fewer levels mean fewer promotions. Emphasis shifts to lateral moves with no pay adjustments, as employees move across functions within a band in order to gain depth of experience. Whereas pay grades and pay ranges (minimum to maximum) ensure consistency across managers, those using broad bands have greater flexibility and only a total salary budget limiting them. Not surprisingly, organizations use grades and ranges almost 10 times more often than they use broad bands.

Once such a pay structure is in place, the determination of each individual's pay (based on experience, seniority, and performance) becomes a more systematic, orderly procedure. A compensation-planning worksheet, such as that shown in Figure 11-6, can be very useful to managers confronted with these weighty decisions.

Alternatives to Pay Systems Based on Job Evaluation

There are at least two alternatives to pay systems based on job evaluation: market-based pay and skill- or knowledge-based pay, also referred to as competency-based pay.

Figure 11–6

Sample annual compensation-planning worksheet.

ORG. UNIT _____
MGR. OR SUPV. _____

ANNUAL COMPENSATION-PLANNING WORKSHEET

EMPLOYEE NAME	JOB TITLE	LAST SALARY ADJUSTMENT				CURRENT SALARY	RANGE MINIMUM	RANGE MIDPOINT	RANGE MAXIMUM	PERFORMANCE RATING	FORECAST SALARY ADJUSTMENT (If Any)				
		Amt.	%	Date	Type*						Amt.	%	Date	New Salary	Inter-val

*Code for "Type"
1—Promotion
2—Merit

PREPARED BY _____

Market-Based Pay

The **market-based pay system** uses a direct market-pricing approach for all of a firm's jobs. This type of pay structure is feasible if all jobs are benchmark jobs and direct matches can be found in the market (e.g., senior-executive positions). Pay surveys can then be used to determine the market prices of the jobs in question. If competitors' pay decisions determine a company's pay structure, though, then the level of pay or the mix of pay forms is no longer a source of potential competitive advantage. It is neither unique nor difficult to imitate. In contrast, a firm may choose to differentiate its pay strategy from those of its competitors to execute its own strategy more effectively.[41]

Competency-Based Pay

Under a **competency-based pay system**, workers are paid not on the basis of the job they currently are doing, but rather on the basis of their skills or on their depth of knowledge, both of which are termed "competencies." Skill-based plans are usually applied to so-called blue-collar work and competencies to so-called white-collar work. The distinctions are not hard and fast. They can focus on depth (specialists in corporate law, finance, or welding and hydraulic maintenance), on breadth (generalists with knowledge in all phases of operations, including marketing, manufacturing, finance, and HR), or on self-management (gaining skills that might previously have been reserved for higher levels in the organization, such as planning, training, or budgeting).[42] In a world of slimmed-down big companies and agile small ones, the last thing any manager wants to hear from an employee is "It's not my job."

In such learning environments, the more workers learn, the more they earn. Companies view skill- and competency-based pay plans as a way to develop the critical behaviors and abilities employees need to achieve specific business results. By linking compensation directly to individual contributions that make a difference to the organization, a company can maintain the highest caliber of workers, regardless of their particular specialties or roles. Such plans also provide a mechanism for cross-training employees to ensure that people in different functional areas have the behavioral or technical skills to take on additional responsibilities as needed.[43]

On the other hand, both skill- and competency-based plans become increasingly expensive as the majority of employees become certified at the highest pay levels. As a result, the employer may have an average wage higher than competitors who use conventional job evaluation. Unless the increased flexibility permits leaner staffing, the employer may also experience higher labor costs. This is what caused Motorola and TRW to abandon their plans after just a few years.[44]

Research at nine manufacturing plants concluded that the number of managers in plants using skill-based pay was as much as 50 percent lower than in traditional plants. Of course, this is also likely to dampen managers' enthusiasm for using skill-based pay![45] Is there any impact on productivity, quality, or labor costs? A 37-month study in a component-assembly plant found a 58 percent improvement in productivity, a 16 percent reduction in the cost of labor per part, and an 82 percent reduction in scrap, compared to a similar facility that did not use skill-based pay.[46] Another study linked the ease of communication and understanding of skill-based plans to employees' general perceptions of being treated fairly by the employer.[47] Finally, a study analyzed the relationship between competencies and performance among managers. Managers' competencies were related to their performance ratings, but there was no relationship to unit-level performance.[48] The lesson from these studies is that each organization must weigh the advantages and disadvantages of such plans, relative to its own context and strategy.

In summary, if compensation systems are to be used strategically, it is important that management (1) understand clearly what types of behavior it wants the compensation system to reinforce, (2) recognize that compensation systems are integral components of planning and control, and (3) view the firm's performance as the ultimate criterion of the success of strategic pay decisions and operational compensation programs.

Now let us consider some key policy issues.

POLICY ISSUES IN PAY PLANNING AND ADMINISTRATION

Pay Secrecy

Do workers know what the person in the next office makes? The answer: not really. Pay secrecy is a difficult policy to maintain, particularly as so much pay-related information is now available on the Web. Anyone with access to the Internet can find out fairly easily what a position is worth in the job market. What about discussing salaries within a particular firm–say, your own employer? As a general matter, salary discussions among employees are protected by the National Labor Relations Act, under which employees have the right to discuss their wages, their hours, and other terms and conditions of their employment.[49]

Managers need to realize that pay disclosure is happening whether they like it or not. Millennials are four times more likely than baby boomers to discuss pay with their coworkers.[50] Anonymous messaging apps, like Memo and Blind, encourage employees to share information free of employer control, and company-rating sites such as Glassdoor and Vault open corporate life to the world.[51]

Pay openness versus secrecy is not an either/or phenomenon. Rather, it is a matter of degree. For example, organizations may choose to disclose one or more of the following: (1) the work- and business-related rationale on which the system is based, (2) pay ranges, (3) pay-increase schedules, and (4) the availability of pay-related data from the compensation department.[52] Posting salary ranges, experts contend, is a public show of trust in employees. It demonstrates that the employer values them and will help them to advance.[53] It is also an important step toward **pay equity**–that is, paying men and women the same when they perform the same or similar job duties, while accounting for other factors, such as experience, job performance, pay grade, location, and tenure with the employer. Here are some additional steps to take:

- Keep job descriptions current to ensure that the work done and the skills required are reflected accurately.
- To ensure consistency, create transparent pay systems and objective metrics around recruitment, performance, advancement, and compensation.
- To build trust, communicate regularly and honestly with employees about the metrics and their progress.[54]

In general, open-pay systems tend to work best under the following circumstances: Individual or team performance can be measured objectively, performance measures can be developed for all the important aspects of a job, and effort and performance are related closely over a relatively short time span.

The Effect of Inflation

All organizations must make some allowance for inflation in their salary programs. Given an inflation rate of 4 percent, for example, the firm that fails to increase its salary ranges at all over a 2-year period will be 8 percent behind its competitors. Needless to say, it becomes difficult to recruit new employees under these circumstances, and it becomes difficult to motivate present employees to remain and, if they do remain, to produce.

How do firms cope? Average increases for salaried employees were 3 percent in 2019, for example, whereas consumer prices rose an average of 2.3 percent. The result: a slight increase in real wages for the average employee.[55] Companies such as Sprint, WD-40, BetterWorks, DuPont, and Merck are tying pay more to performance in an attempt to make the costs of labor more variable and less fixed. More and more companies, large and small, feel the same way.

Pay Compression

Pay compression is related to the general problem of inflation. It occurs when the difference in pay between newly hired or less qualified employees and more experienced ones is small or even negative.[56] Failure to address pay compression may cause long-serving employees to rethink their commitment to a company they think does not value or reward loyalty. Their frustration also can translate to lower productivity, reluctance to work overtime, and unwillingness to cooperate with higher-paid new recruits.[57]

One solution to the problem of pay compression is to adjust salary ranges and structures to keep them current with market conditions. Thus, Ford regularly benchmarks its pay for various categories of white-collar workers against 23 other companies.[58] Another approach is to grant sign-on bonuses to new hires in order to offer a competitive total compensation package, especially to those with scarce skills. Because bonuses do not increase base salaries, the structure of differences in pay between new hires and experienced employees does not change. A third approach is to offer more employer stock to long-term employees.[59] Thus, although the difference between the direct pay of this group and that of their shorter-service coworkers may be slim, senior employees have a distinct advantage when the entire compensation package is considered.

A common cause of pay compression is "hot skills" that lead a company to pay more to attract the right talent, such as in information technology, engineering/science, and finance. It's important to train managers to discuss this and other pay issues with current employees, for example, by addressing the factors that go into setting pay and bonuses, where an employee's salary falls within his or her pay range, and how they can help employees acquire skills to advance.[60] What really matters is that employees feel that the pay process is fair and transparent.[61]

Pay Raises

Coping with inflation is the biggest hurdle to overcome in a pay-for-performance plan. On the other hand, the only measure of a raise is how much it exceeds the increase in the cost of living. In 2019, for example, real wages in Singapore rose an average of 3.3 percent over the inflation rate.[62]

Figure 11–7					

Sample merit guide chart.

EMPLOYEE PERFORMANCE	PERCENT INCREASE				
Distinguished	12%	10%	9%	8%	7%
Commendable	9%	8%	7%	6%	Ceiling
Competent	7%	6%	5%	Ceiling	
Adequate	4%	0	Ceiling		
Provisional	0	Ceiling			
Salary (as % of midpoint) is:	80% → 88% → 96% → 104% → 112% → 120%				

The simplest, most effective method for dealing with inflation in a merit-pay system is to increase salary ranges. By raising salary ranges (e.g., based on a survey of average increases in starting salaries for the coming year) without giving general increases, a firm can maintain competitive hiring rates while maintaining the merit concept surrounding salary increases.

The size of the merit increase for a given level of performance should decrease as the employee moves further up the salary range. Merit guide charts provide a means for doing this. Guide charts identify (1) an employee's current performance rating and (2) his or her location in a pay grade. The intersection of these two dimensions identifies a percentage of pay increase based on the performance level and location of the employee in the pay grade. Figure 11-7 shows an example of such a chart. The rationale for the merit guide-chart approach is that a person at the top of the range is already making more than the going rate for that job. Hence, she or he should have to demonstrate more than satisfactory performance in order to continue moving further above the going rate. Performance incentives, one-time awards that must be re-earned each year, allow employees to supplement their income. Let's turn now to this topic.

PERFORMANCE INCENTIVES

"Using strong incentives opens up the possibility of obtaining substantial performance gains, but it also increases the possibility of something going terribly wrong."[63] To illustrate something going terribly wrong, consider the Wells Fargo scandal in the HR Buzz box.

Today, incentives comprise 12 percent of payroll, up from only 4 percent in 1990.[64] Evidence indicates that they work.[65] Thus, a quantitative review of

HOW HIGH-PRESSURE SALES TACTICS AND PERVERSE INCENTIVES LEAD TO UNETHICAL BEHAVIOR

Branch employees of banking giant Wells Fargo & Company opened more than 3.5 million accounts without customers' knowledge from 2009 to 2016. According to former Wells Fargo employees, this occurred as bankers tried to meet unrealistic and unattainable sales goals (open eight accounts per customer), fueled by an incentive structure that rewarded employees for selling more products. Executives made branch managers' bonuses dependent on the degree to which that sales goal was being achieved. The managers, in turn, began checking their people's progress toward those goals twice a day or, in some cases, even hourly, thereby creating a toxic, high-pressure culture at work. When some employees lost their jobs for falling short of the goals, and others observed their peers being terminated, the ethical fabric of the organization began to fray.[a]

Over a 5-year period related to the misconduct, the bank fired more than 5,300 retail bank employees. However, in testimony before Congress, the CEO characterized the problem as an ethical lapse limited to the 5,300 employees, most of them low-level bankers and tellers, who had been fired for their actions since 2011. Subsequent investigation revealed an organizational culture, orchestrated from higher levels in the organization, that condoned, or in some cases even encouraged, the unethical practices.[b]

Ultimately, the scandal cost the CEO his job. He and other former executives forfeited $182.8 million in pay, and the bank paid more than $4 billion in settlements and fines to federal, state, and local regulators and to customers in all 50 states and the District of Columbia.[c]

To prevent such scandals, experts recommend the following steps: (1) Limit the amount of pay at risk (e.g., to 15 percent of base pay); (2) think carefully about the metrics used to track incentives (service quality versus reducing costs) and their unintended ripple effects; and (3) monitor not only *what* employees or managers achieve, but also *how* they achieve those results. Financial rewards can be powerful motivators of behavior, but they should be used only in situations where management has created a culture and goal-setting process that leads to reasonable goals and there is comprehensive measurement of all of the behaviors that people can use to accomplish them.[d]

[a]Ensign, R. L., and Ackerman, A. (2019, Mar. 13). Regulator, lawmakers rebuke Wells Fargo. *The Wall Street Journal*, pp. B1, B12. Berliner, U. (2017, Aug. 31). Wells Fargo admits to nearly twice as many possible fake accounts–3.5 million. Retrieved from *https://www.npr.org/sections/thetwo-way/2017/08/31/547550804/ wells-fargo-admits-to-nearly-twice-as-many-possible-fake-accounts-3-5-million* on Sept. 6, 2017. Bistrong, R., and Hodak, M. (2017, Jan. 26). Wells Fargo: How reasonable pay plans morphed into perverse incentives. Retrieved from *www.fcpablog.com/blog/2017/1/26/wells-fargo-how-reasonable-pay-plans-morphed-into-perverse-i.html* on May 31, 2017.

[b]Cowley, S. (2016, Sept. 29). Wells Fargo's reaction to scandal fails to satisfy angry lawmakers. *The New York Times*. Retrieved from *www.nytimes.com/2016/09/30/business/dealbook/wells-fargo-ceo-john-stumpf-house-hearing.html?r=0*. Andriotis, A. M., and Glazer, E. (2016, Oct. 11). Wells pushed overdraft services. *The Wall Street Journal*, pp. C1, C2. Glazer, E. (2016a, Sept. 17). Wells Fargo tripped by its sales culture. *The Wall Street Journal*, pp. A1, A8.

[c]Eisen, B. (2020, Feb. 23). Wells Fargo settles U.S. probes. *The Wall Street Journal*, pp. A1, A10. Glazer, E. (2018, Dec. 30). Wells settles with 50 states. *The Wall Street Journal*, pp. A1, A2. Glazer, E. (2017, April 11). Wells slams former bosses' high-pressure sales tactics. *The Wall Street Journal*, pp. A1, A9. Avalos, G. (2016, Sept. 27). Wells Fargo execs lose pay in scandal linked to bogus bank accounts. *The Mercury News*. Retrieved from *www.mercurynews.com/2016/09/27/wells-fargo-execs-lose-pay-in-scandal-linked-to-bogus-bank-accounts/* on Sept. 29, 2016.

[d]Sammer, J. (2017, Jan. 3). When bonus incentives go bad–And how to prevent it. Retrieved from *www.shrm.org/resourcesandtools/hr-topics/compensation/pages/bonus-incentives-gone-bad.aspx* on Jan. 6, 2017. Lawler, E. E. III. The Wells Fargo debacle: How proper reward practices can remedy a toxic culture. *Forbes*. Retrieved from *www.forbes.com/sites/edwardlawler/2016/11/01/the-wells-fargo-debacle-how-proper-reward-practices-can-remedy-a-toxic-culture/#4b065ed1ac63* on Nov. 6, 2016.

39 studies containing 47 relationships revealed that financial incentives were not related to performance quality but were related fairly strongly (correlation of 0.34) to performance quantity.[66] It is important, though, to be attentive to possible unintended consequences, for as we have seen, financial incentives *may lead to unethical behavior, fuel employee turnover, and foster envy and discontent.*[67]

When it comes to performance incentives, the possibilities are endless. Because each has different consequences, each needs special treatment. One way to classify them is according to the level of performance targeted–individual, team, or total organization. Within these broad categories, hundreds of different approaches for relating pay to performance exist. Before we consider incentives at each of these levels though, let's first examine some fundamental requirements of all incentive systems.

REQUIREMENTS OF EFFECTIVE INCENTIVE SYSTEMS

At the outset, it is important to distinguish merit systems from incentive systems. Both are designed to motivate employees to improve their job performance. Most commonly, merit systems are applied to exempt employees in the form of permanent increases to their base pay. The goal is to tie pay increases to each employee's level of job performance. **Incentives** (e.g., sales commissions, bonuses, profit-sharing) are one-time supplements to base pay. They are also awarded on the basis of performance (individual, team, organization, or some combination of those) and are applied to broader segments of the labor force, including nonexempt and unionized employees.

Properly designed incentive programs work because they are based on two well-accepted psychological principles: (1) Increased motivation improves performance and (2) recognition is a major factor in motivation.[68] Unfortunately, however, many incentive programs are improperly designed, and they do not work. They violate one or more of the following rules (shown graphically in Figure 11-8):

1. *Be simple.* The rules of the system should be brief, clear, and understandable.
2. *Be specific.* It is not sufficient to say "Produce more" or "Stop accidents." Employees need to know precisely what they are expected to do.

Figure 11-8

Requirements of effective incentive systems.

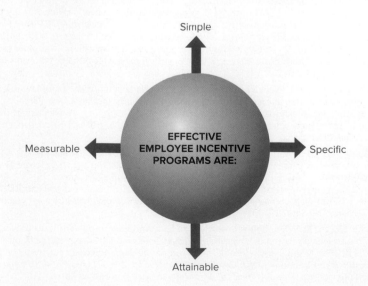

3. *Be attainable.* Every employee should have a reasonable chance to gain something.
4. *Be measurable.* Measurable objectives are the foundation on which incentive plans are built. Program dollars will be wasted (and program evaluation hampered) if managers cannot tie specific accomplishments to money spent on incentives.

MERIT-PAY SYSTEMS

Surveys show that about 90 percent of U.S. employers use **merit-pay systems**.[69] Unfortunately, many of the plans don't work. Here are some reasons why[70]:

1. *The incentive value of the reward offered is too low.* Give someone a $5,000 raise and she keeps $250 a month after taxes. The stakes, after taxes, are nominal.
2. *The link between performance and rewards is weak.* PayScale's survey of 71,000 employees revealed that most have no idea whether or not they are paid fairly.[71] Another by SAP and Oxford Economics of employees and executives in 27 countries revealed that base pay and bonus pay were extremely important to top performers and that the difference between a 6 percent raise and a 2 percent raise, as is common in many organizations, is not sufficient to keep them from leaving.[72]
3. *Supervisors often resist honest feedback.* Few supervisors are trained in the art of giving feedback accurately, comfortably, and with a minimum likelihood of creating other problems (see Chapter 8). As a result, many are afraid to make distinctions among workers—and they do not.[73] When the best performers receive rewards that are no higher than those of the worst performers, motivation plummets.
4. *Union contracts influence pay-for-performance decisions within and between organizations.* Failure to match union wages over a 3- or 4-year period (especially during periods of high inflation) invites dissension and turnover among nonunion employees.
5. *The "annuity" problem.* As past merit payments are incorporated into an individual's base salary, the payments form an annuity (a sum of money received at regular intervals) and allow formerly productive individuals to slack off for several years and still earn high pay—an effect called the **annuity problem**.

These reasons are shown graphically in Figure 11-9.

Barriers Can Be Overcome

Lincoln Electric, a Cleveland-based manufacturer of welding machines and motors, boasts a productivity rate more than double that of other manufacturers in its industry. It follows two cardinal rules:

1. Pay employees for productivity, and only for productivity.
2. Promote employees for productivity, and only for productivity.[74]

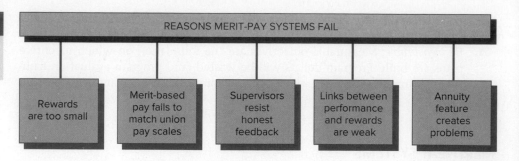

Figure 11–9

Why merit-pay systems fail.

Although this formula works for Lincoln, it may not work elsewhere because it may not fit the industry, organization, or cultural context. Despite the problems of merit pay, 69 percent of organizations continue to award merit pay but are also supplementing it with performance bonuses.[75] Meaningful differences in merit pay produce a **sorting effect**; that is, those who do not want to have their pay tied to their performance don't accept jobs at such companies, or else they leave when pay-for-performance is implemented. This leaves a residual workforce that is more productive and more responsive to merit rewards.[76]

GUIDELINES FOR EFFECTIVE MERIT-PAY SYSTEMS

Those affected by the merit-pay system must support it if it is to work as designed. This is in addition to the requirements for incentive programs shown in Figure 11-8. From the very inception of a merit-pay system, it is important that employees feel a sense of ownership of the system. Involve them in the design process, if possible. Here are five other steps to follow:

1. *Establish high standards of performance.* Low expectations tend to be self-fulfilling prophecies. In the military, sports, and education, great leaders have demanded excellence. Excellence rarely results from expectations of mediocrity.
2. *Develop and implement sound performance-management systems.* As we noted in Chapter 9, such systems include clear definitions of what good performance looks like, the elimination of roadblocks that might impede performance, regular coaching and feedback, and timely rewards that encourage good performance.
3. *Train supervisors in the mechanics of performance appraisal and in the art of giving feedback to subordinates.* Train them to manage ineffective performance constructively.
4. *Tie rewards closely to performance.* For example, review performance at least quarterly as a basis for merit increases (or no increases). One review found that 40 of 42 studies looking at merit pay reported increases in performance when pay was tied closely to performance.[77]
5. *Use a wide range of increases.* Make pay increases meaningful.

Merit-pay systems can work, but they need to follow these guidelines if they are to work effectively. Figure 11-10 depicts them graphically.

Figure 11–10
Guidelines for effective merit-pay systems.

MERIT-PAY SYSTEMS THAT WORK

Establish high standards of performance	Develop accurate performance appraisal systems	Teach supervisors how to do appraisals and how to give feedback	Link rewards closely to performance	Use a wide range of increases

INCENTIVES FOR EXECUTIVES

"It took me a long while to learn that people do what you pay them to do, not what you ask them to do," says Hicks Waldron, former chairman and CEO of Avon Products Inc.[78]

Companies with a history of outperforming their rivals, regardless of industry or economic climate, have two common characteristics: (1) a long-term strategic view of their executives and (2) stability in their executive groups.[79] It makes sense, therefore, to develop integrated plans for total executive compensation, so that rewards are based on achieving the company's long-term strategic goals. This may require a rebalancing of the elements of executive reward systems: base salary, annual (short-term) incentives, long-term incentives, employee benefits, and perquisites.[80]

Among CEOs of publicly traded companies, base pay comprises just over 9 percent, while long-term incentives (performance awards, restricted stock, stock options) comprise about 80 percent. Why place such emphasis on long-term incentives?[81]

1. Annual, or short-term, incentive plans encourage the efficient use of existing assets. They are usually based on indicators of corporate performance, such as net income, expenses, or customer loyalty measures. In light of the salary freezes and pay cuts that many companies implemented during the Great Recession, firms such as Home Depot, Cisco, and Xerox started awarding twice-a-year bonuses. Despite their clear focus on achieving short-term objectives, advocates argue that they boost morale, improve retention, and allow boards to raise goals quickly if economic conditions improve.[82]

2. Long-term plans encourage the development of new processes, plants, and products that open new markets and restore old ones. Hence, long-term performance encompasses qualitative progress as well as quantitative accomplishments. Long-term incentive plans are designed to reward strategic gains rather than short-term contributions to profits. Two examples of long-term incentives are **performance awards** (stock grants awarded for meeting goals) and performance-accelerated shares (stock that vests sooner if the executive meets goals ahead of schedule).[83] Two others are **restricted stock** (common stock that vests after a specified period) and **restricted stock units** (shares awarded over time to defer taxes).[84] In 2019, performance awards comprised 58 percent of long-term incentives, restricted stock comprised 23 percent, and stock options comprised 19 percent.[85] Executive action based on a long-term strategic perspective is the kind of view we should be encouraging among executives, for it relates consistently to company success.

In the face of widespread criticism of executive pay practices, some firms are rethinking the way they reward top executives.[86] Take stock options, for example. They are less attractive now because their fair value must be expensed on financial statements (thereby reducing earnings). Moreover, even enthusiasts can't prove that options motivate executives to perform better. Critics contend that stock options reward executives not just for their own performance, but for a booming stock market. To a large extent, they are right; as much as 70 percent of the change in a company's stock price depends only on changes in the overall market.[87] In response, some firms are trying to link executive pay more closely to company performance through stock awards or performance targets. See the HR Buzz box on Starbucks, for example.

HR BUZZ

TYING CEO PAY TO PERFORMANCE AT STARBUCKS*

Starbucks Corp. CEO Kevin Johnson's 2019 pay increased by almost $6 million, for a total compensation of $19.2 million. He received more options and stock in 2019 than in 2018, but his pay increased mainly because of a cash bonus of $4.3 million, linked to performance targets. Such structures appeal to companies and shareholders because payouts are tied to how well a company does.

Equity, or stock-based, pay now comprises 63 percent of CEO total compensation, according to a recent *Wall Street Journal* analysis of S&P 500 companies. While many CEOs rode a decade-long bull market to record paydays, the drop in the 2020 market that was fueled by the coronavirus caused hundreds of millions in losses. That is the flip side of stock-based compensation, and it has prompted companies to recalibrate how executive compensation is set. Starbucks' CEO sidestepped the stock market swoon by receiving a large cash bonus tied to other measures of firm performance, such as growth in revenues or net income, and not just to the change in the company's stock price.

Sources: Pacheco, I. (2020, March 24. Leap in CEO pay turns into a dive. *The Wall Street Journal*, p. B3. Sparks, D. (2016, Dec. 8). Starbucks Corporation's ambitious new five-year plan in five key points. *Motley Fool*. Retrieved from *www.fool.com/investing/2016/12/08/starbucks-corporations-new-ambitious-5-year-plan-i.aspx* on May 31, 2017. Francis, T., and Lublin, J. S. (2016, June 3). Divide persists between pay, performance. *The Wall Street Journal*, pp. B1, B5.

INCENTIVES FOR LOWER-LEVEL EMPLOYEES

As noted earlier in this chapter, a common practice is to supplement employees' pay with additions related to improvements in job performance. One example is a **lump-sum bonus**, in which employees receive an end-of-year bonus (based on employee or company performance) that does not build into base pay. Its purpose is to create shock waves in an entitlement culture. By giving lump-sum bonuses for several years, a company is essentially freezing base pay and repositioning itself relative to competitors.[88] Another is the **spot bonus**. Thus, if an employee's performance has been exceptional—such as filling in for a sick colleague or working nights and weekends to complete a project—the employer may reward the worker with a one-time bonus of $50, $100, or $500 shortly after the noteworthy actions. About 40 percent of companies now offer such programs.[89]

Individual incentive plans have a *baseline*, or normal, performance standard; productivity above this standard is rewarded. The baseline should be high enough that employees are not given extra rewards for what is really just a normal day's work. On the other hand, the baseline should not be so high that it is impossible to earn additional pay.

It is more difficult to specify performance standards in some jobs than in others. At the top-management level, for instance, what constitutes a normal day's output? As one moves down the organizational hierarchy, however, jobs can be defined more clearly, and shorter-run goals and targets can be established.

Setting Performance Standards

All incentive systems depend on **performance standards**. The standards provide a relatively objective definition of the job, they give employees targets to shoot for, and they make it easier for supervisors to assign work equitably. Make no mistake about it, though, effective performance is often hard to define. For example, when a Corning group set up a trial program to reward workers for improving their efficiency, a team in one business unit struggled to figure out "What's a meaningful thing to measure? What's reasonable?" The measures finally settled on included safety, quality, shipping efficiency, and forecast accuracy.[90] Once performance standards are set, employees have an opportunity to earn more than their base salaries, sometimes as much as 20 to 25 percent more. In short, they have an incentive to work both harder and smarter.

In setting performance standards for production work, the ideal job (ideal only in terms of the ability to measure performance, not in terms of improving work motivation or job satisfaction) should (1) be highly repetitive, (2) have a short job cycle, and (3) produce a clear, measurable output. The standards themselves will vary, of course, according to the *type* of product or service (e.g., a hospital, a factory, a telecommunications company); the *method of service delivery*; the degree to which service can be *quantified*; and *organizational needs*, including legal and social pressures. In fact, the many different forms of incentive plans for lower-level employees really differ along only two dimensions:

1. How premium rates are determined.
2. How the extra payments are made.

Incentives oriented toward individuals might become less popular as work increasingly becomes interdependent in nature, but they remain popular in industries like manufacturing. Lincoln Electric (see the HR Buzz box below) is a prime example.

Union Attitudes

A unionized employer may establish an incentive system, but it will be subject to negotiation through collective bargaining. Unions may also wish to participate in the day-to-day management of the incentive system, and management ought to consider that demand seriously. Employees often fear that management will manipulate the system to the disadvantage of employees. Joint participation helps reassure employees that the plan is fair.

Union attitudes toward incentives vary with the type of incentive offered. Unions tend to oppose individual piece-rate systems because they pit worker against worker and can create unfavorable intergroup conflict. However, unions tend to support organization-wide systems, such as profit-sharing, because of the extra earnings they provide to their members.[91] We will have more to say about profit-sharing shortly.

HR BUZZ

Individual Incentives

LINCOLN ELECTRIC*

Founded in 1895, Lincoln Electric Company of Cleveland, Ohio, has charted a unique path in worker-management relations, featuring high wages, guaranteed employment, few supervisors, a lucrative bonus incentive system, and piecework compensation. The company is the world's largest maker of arc-welding equipment. With $3 billion in revenue in 2019, Lincoln has 59 manufacturing locations in 18 countries and a network of distributors and sales offices in 160 countries. Among the innovative management practices that set Lincoln apart are these:

- Guaranteed employment for all full-time workers with more than 2 years' service, and no mandatory retirement. No worker has been laid off since 1948, and turnover is less than 4 percent for those with more than 180 days on the job.
- High wages, including a substantial annual bonus (up to 100 percent of base pay) based on the company's profits. Wages at Lincoln are roughly equivalent to wages for similar work elsewhere in the Cleveland area, but the bonuses the company pays make its compensation substantially higher. In 2017, for example, the average worker earned $73,955, including a bonus of $25,131. Lincoln has never had a strike and has not missed a bonus payment since the system was instituted in 1934. Individual bonuses are set by a formula that judges workers on five dimensions: quality, output, dependability, ideas, and cooperation. The ratings determine how much of the total corporate bonus pool each worker will get, on top of his or her hourly wage.
- Piecework. More than half of Lincoln's workers are paid according to what they produce, rather than an hourly or weekly wage. If a worker is sick, he or she does not get paid.
- Promotion almost exclusively from within, according to merit, not seniority.
- Few supervisors, with a supervisor-to-worker ratio of 1:100, far lower than in much of the industry. Each employee is supposed to be a self-managing entrepreneur, and each is accountable for the quality of his or her own work.
- No break periods, and mandatory overtime. Workers must work overtime, if ordered to, during peak production periods and must agree to change jobs to meet production schedules or to maintain the company's guaranteed employment program.

Although the company insists on individual initiative—and pays according to individual effort—it works diligently to foster the notion of teamwork. If a worker is overly competitive with fellow employees, he or she is rated poorly in terms of cooperation and team play on his or her semiannual rating reports. Thus, that worker's bonus will be smaller. Says one company official, "This is not an easy style to manage; it takes a lot of time and a willingness to work with people."

Sources: Lincoln Electric Company, corporate profile. Retrieved from *https://ir.lincolnelectric.com/investor-relations* on Apr. 29, 2020. Koller, F. (2018, April 30). 2017 at Lincoln Electric, no layoffs for 69 years and 84 years of amazing profit-sharing bonuses. Retrieved from *http://www.frankkoller.com/2018/04/2017-at-lincoln-electric-no-layoffs-for-69-years-and-84-years-of-amazing-profit-sharing-bonuses/* on Apr. 29, 2020. Koller, F. (2010). *Spark: How Old-Fashioned Values Drive a Twenty-First-Century Corporation.* New York: Perseus. Wiley, C. (1993, Aug.). Incentive plan pushes production. *Personnel Journal,* pp. 86–91.

TEAM INCENTIVES

To provide broader motivation than is furnished by incentive plans geared to individual employees, several other approaches have been tried. Their aim is twofold: increase productivity and improve morale by giving employees a feeling of participation in and identification with the company. Team, or workgroup, incentives are one such plan.

Team incentives provide an opportunity for each team member to receive a bonus based on the output of the team as a whole. Teams may be as small as 4 to 7 employees or as large as 35 to 40 employees, but the effect of team-based rewards on performance decreases as teams become large.[92] Team incentives are most appropriate when jobs are highly interrelated and individual efforts are difficult to quantify. In fact, highly interrelated jobs are the wave of the future and, in many cases, the wave of the present. Roughly 25 percent of firms currently use team incentives, but it is highly likely that more of them will do so in the future.[93] The accompanying HR Buzz box shows how one company does it.

NUCOR CORPORATION

HR BUZZ

*Team Incentives That Fit the Organization's Culture**

Nucor, the largest steel producer in the United States with 200 facilities in 41 states and Canada, lives and dies by the spirit of teamwork. That is evident in its organizational design, management philosophy, and incentive plans. Every one of its 26,000 employees participates in one of four incentive plans. The purest team-based compensation plan, however, is the one aimed at groups of 12 to 20 production employees, including maintenance workers and supervisors.

Perhaps the most striking feature of the plan is its simplicity: quality tons out the door and pay weekly. Nucor's plan is a true incentive because workers can gain from good performance (bonuses average 170 to 180 percent of weekly base salaries) or lose money for poor performance. That happens when the tonnage of subpar products is subtracted from total output—in increasing multiples the farther bad products travel from the source. If a team catches inferior goods in its work area, the tonnage is simply subtracted. If it reaches the next internal customer or the shipping department, the amount of bad product subtracted is doubled. If it reaches a customer, the bad tonnage is tripled and then subtracted from total output.

With bonuses included, the typical Nucor steel mill worker makes $84,000 a year and participates in a profit-sharing plan on top of that. On any given day, nearly every production worker can tell you within a tenth of a percent what his or her weekly bonus will be. Says the company's manager of HR and organizational development, "It's truly remarkable how much information the employees know. It's a beautiful thing to see." Since Nucor adopted its incentive plan in 1966, the company has been profitable every quarter and not a single employee has been laid off. Case 11-1 at the end of this chapter describes Nucor in more detail.

Sources: Nucor–Who we are. (n.d.). Retrieved from *https://nucor.com/who-we-are* on Apr. 29, 2020. Brewer, R. G. (2017, Aug. 20). 7 fascinating things you probably didn't know about Nucor Corp. *Motley Fool.* Retrieved from *https://www.fool.com/investing/2017/08/20/7-fascinating-things-you-probably-didnt-know-about.aspx* on Apr. 29, 2020. Hampton, J. (2013, Dec. 1). Fireworks: Nucor steel plant in Hertford Co. growing. *Virginia Pilot.* Retrieved from *http://hamptonroads.com/2013/11/fireworks-nucor-steel-plant-hertford-co-growing* on May 31, 2014. Bolch, M. (2007, Feb.). Rewarding the team. *HR,* pp. 91–93.

Team incentives have the following advantages:

1. They make it possible to reward workers who provide essential services to line workers (so-called indirect labor), yet who are paid only their regular base pay. These employees do things like transport supplies and materials, maintain equipment, or inspect work output.
2. They encourage cooperation, not competition, among workers.

On the other hand, team incentives also have disadvantages:

1. Competition between teams.
2. Inability of workers to see their individual contributions to the output of the team. If they do not see the link between their individual effort and increased rewards, they will not be motivated to produce more.
3. Top performers who grow disenchanted with having to carry "free riders" (those who don't carry their share of the load).

Large-scale research with work groups has revealed the critical relationship between employees' understanding of the work-group incentive plan and their perceptions of the fairness of that plan. Managers should ensure that all members of work groups understand how pay-plan goals are established, what the goals and performance standards themselves are, how the plan goals are evaluated, and how the payouts are determined.[94] To overcome the first two disadvantages of team incentives, many firms have introduced organizationwide incentives.

ORGANIZATIONWIDE INCENTIVES

In this final section, we consider three broad classes of organizationwide incentives: profit-sharing, gain-sharing, and employee stock-ownership plans. As we shall see, each is different in its objectives and implementation.

Profit-Sharing

Profit-sharing plans pay out if a firm meets its profitability target (e.g., return on assets or net income). Profit-sharing can be either deferred (i.e., to fund retirement), paid in cash, or both, and payouts may be either formula-based (e.g., a fixed percentage of net income) or discretionary. Firms use it for one or more of the following reasons: (1) to provide a group incentive for increased productivity, (2) to provide retirement income for their employees, (3) to institute a flexible reward structure that reflects a company's actual economic position, (4) to enhance employees' security and identification with the company, (5) to attract and retain workers more easily, and/or (6) to educate individuals about the factors that underlie business success and the capitalistic system.[95]

On the downside, most employees don't feel that their jobs have a direct impact on profits, or at least they can't see that link. Why? Because profits depend on numerous factors in addition to operating efficiency—such as the strength of consumer demand, global competition, and accounting practices.

In most plans, employees receive a bonus that is normally based on a percentage (e.g., 10 to 30 percent) of the company's profits beyond a minimum level. Does profit-sharing improve productivity? One review of 27 econometric studies found that profit-sharing was positively related to productivity in better than 9 of every 10 instances. Productivity was generally 3 to 5 percent higher in firms with profit-sharing plans than in those without plans.[96]

Despite profit-sharing's modest positive relationship with productivity, it is not clear that one of these *causes* increases in the other. In addition, the potential to make labor costs variable in relation to profitability will be realized only if profit-sharing plans survive years when no payouts are made.[97] At Ford Motor Company, for example, there were no bonuses in 2010, but in 2011 each of its workers received profit-sharing checks that exceeded $8,200. In 2019, the company paid each of its 53,000 U.S. workers $6,600 in profit-sharing.[98] Although profit-sharing can stimulate innovation and creativity, the actual success of such plans depends on the stability and security of the overall work environment, the company's overall HR management policy, and the state of labor-management relations.[99] This is even more true of gain-sharing plans.

Gain-Sharing

Gain-sharing is a results-based program that generally links pay to performance at the facility level.[100] In contrast to profit-sharing, where many employees cannot see the link between what they do and company profits, **gain-sharing** focuses on achieving savings in areas over which employees do have control—for example, reduced scrap or lower labor or utility costs. As the name suggests, employees share in the gains achieved. Gain-sharing is a reward system that has existed in a variety of forms for decades. Sometimes known as the Scanlon plan, the Rucker plan, or Improshare (improved productivity through sharing), gain-sharing comprises three elements[101]:

1. A philosophy of cooperation.
2. An involvement system.
3. A financial bonus.

The philosophy of cooperation refers to an organizational climate characterized by high levels of trust, two-way communication, participation, and harmonious industrial relations. *The involvement system* refers to the structure and process for improving organizational productivity. Typically, it is a broadly based suggestion system implemented by an employee-staffed committee structure that usually reaches all areas of the organization. Sometimes this structure involves work teams, but usually it is simply an employee-based suggestion system. The employees involved develop and implement ideas related to productivity. The third component, the financial bonus, is determined by a calculation that measures the difference between expected and actual costs during a bonus period.

The three components mutually reinforce one another. High levels of cooperation lead to information sharing, which in turn leads to employee involvement, which leads to new behaviors, such as offering suggestions to improve organizational productivity. This increase in productivity then results in a financial bonus (based on the amount of the productivity increase), which rewards and reinforces the philosophy of cooperation.

Gain-sharing differs from profit-sharing in three important ways[102]:

1. Gain-sharing is based on a measure of productivity. Profit-sharing is based on a global profitability measure.

2. Gain-sharing, productivity measurement, and bonus payments are frequent events, often distributed monthly, in contrast to the quarterly or annual rewards of profit-sharing plans.

3. Gain-sharing plans are current-distribution plans, in contrast to most profit-sharing plans, which have deferred payments. Hence, gain-sharing plans are true incentive plans rather than employee benefits. As such, they are more directly related to individual behavior and therefore can motivate worker productivity.

When gain-sharing plans work, they work well, with improvements in sales, customer satisfaction, and profits in the 4 to 5 percent range and labor-cost savings of approximately 29 percent.[103] Nevertheless, in the 50 years since the inception of gain-sharing, it has been abandoned by firms about as often as it has been retained. Here are some reasons why:

1. Generally, it does not work well in piecework operations.
2. The returns from gain-sharing programs appear to dwindle with increasing plan size.
3. Some firms are uncomfortable with bringing unions into business planning.
4. Some managers may feel they are giving up their prerogatives.[104]

Some features of gain-sharing plans clearly favor success, though. These include employee (and union) participation in the design of the plan, positive managerial attitudes, the number of years a company has had such a plan, favorable and realistic employee attitudes, and involvement by a high-level executive.[105] To develop an organizationwide incentive plan that has a chance to survive, let alone succeed, careful, in-depth planning must precede implementation. It is true of all incentive plans, though, that *none will work well except in a climate of trustworthy labor-management relations and sound human resource management practices.*

Employee Stock–Ownership Plans

Employee stock-ownership plans (ESOPs) have become popular in both large and small companies in the United States (e.g., PepsiCo, Lincoln Electric, DuPont, Procter & Gamble) as well as in Western Europe, some countries in Central Europe, and China.[106] The typical ESOP company is a privately held, small-to-midsize firm, with a few hundred employees. In the United States, there were an estimated 6,624 ESOPs in 2019, with 14.2 million participants.[107] The goal is to increase employee involvement in decision making, and hopefully this will build the business. Recent evidence indicates that ESOPs do just that. During the Great Recession (2007–2009), for example, revenue at ESOP firms grew an average of 15.1 percent, compared to a decline of 3.4 percent for all private-industry revenue. ESOP firms also showed employment growth, faster wage growth, and higher average wages, compared to declines in those metrics at other firms.[108] They also resort to layoffs much less frequently. Not surprisingly, workers in employee-owned companies tend to out-earn their peers, stay longer, and accumulate larger retirement savings.[109]

Generally, ESOPs are established for any of the following reasons:

■ As a means of tax-favored, company-financed transfer of ownership from a departing owner to a firm's employees. This is often done in small firms with closely held stock.[110]

- As a way of borrowing money relatively inexpensively. A firm borrows money from a bank, using its stock as collateral, and places the stock in an employee stock-ownership trust. As the loan is repaid, the trust distributes the stock at no cost to employees. Companies can deduct the principal as well as interest on the amount borrowed, and lenders pay taxes on only 50 percent of their income from ESOP loans.

- To fulfill a philosophical belief in employee ownership. In 2016, for example, Greek-yogurt maker Chobani, based in New Berlin, New York, gave all of its 2,000 full-time workers equity awards worth up to 10 percent of the company's future value, if and when it becomes public or is sold. In 2017, private-equity firm KKR & Co. awarded shares worth $100 million to about 6,000 employees of Gardner Denver Holdings, a firm it controls. Says the firm's chairman, "Treating employees like owners and business partners—that's how you can create value and make this more than just a feel-good story."[111]

Do ESOPs improve employee motivation and satisfaction? Longitudinal research spanning 45 case studies found that stock ownership alone does not make employees work harder or enjoy their day-to-day work more.[112] At the same time, however, ESOP satisfaction tends to be highest in companies where (1) the company makes relatively large annual contributions to the plan; (2) management is committed to employee ownership and is willing to share power and decision-making authority

IMPACT OF PAY AND INCENTIVES ON PRODUCTIVITY, QUALITY OF WORK LIFE, AND THE BOTTOM LINE

High salary levels alone do not ensure a productive, motivated workforce. It is not *how much* a company pays its workers but, more importantly, *how the pay system is designed, communicated, and managed.*[a] Excessively high labor costs can bankrupt a company.[b] This is especially likely if, to cover its labor costs, the company cannot price its products competitively. If that happens, productivity and profits both suffer directly, and the quality of work life suffers indirectly. Conversely, when the interests of employees and their organizations are aligned, then employees are likely to engage in behavior that goes above and beyond the call of duty (such as helping others accomplish their goals), that is not recognized by the formal reward system, and that contributes to organizational effectiveness.[c] This improves both quality of work life and productivity. What's the bottom line? When sensible policies on pay and incentives are established using the principles discussed in this chapter, everybody wins: the company, the employees, and employees' families.

[a]Gerhart, B., & Newman, J. M. (2020). *Compensation* (13th ed.). New York: McGraw-Hill. Jackson, N. M. (2010, June 17). ESOP plans let founders cash out and employees cash in. *Money*. Retrieved from money.cnn.com/2010/06/03/smallbusiness/esop_plans/index.htm on Aug. 5, 2011.

[b]Francis, T., and Lublin, J. S. (2016, June 3). Divide persists between pay, performance. *The Wall Street Journal*, pp. B1, B5. Martocchio, J. J. (2011). Strategic reward and compensation plans. In S. Zedeck (Ed.), *APA Handbook of Industrial and Organizational Psychology* (Vol. 1). Washington, DC: American Psychological Association, pp. 343–72.

[c]Kelleher, R. (2014). *Employee Engagement for Dummies*. New York: Wiley. Stajkovic, A. D., and Luthans, F. (2001). Differential effects of incentive motivators on work performance. *Academy of Management Journal* 44(3), pp. 580–90.

with employees; and (3) there are extensive company communications about the ESOP, the company's current performance, and its future plans.[113]

How does employee stock ownership affect economic performance? In a longitudinal study, researchers matched 234 pairs of ESOP and non-ESOP companies on size, industry, and region and then examined sales and employment data from 3 years prior to the adoption of the ESOP and 3 years after its adoption. ESOPs appear to increase sales, employment, and sales per employee by about 2.3 to 2.4 percent per year over what would have been expected absent an ESOP. ESOP companies are somewhat more likely to still be in business several years later and considerably more likely to offer retirement plans.[114] All ESOPs are not created equally, though, for there appears to be a declining pattern of economic returns by firm size.[115]

These results do not prove that employee stock ownership causes success; it may be that successful firms are more likely to make employees part owners. They do suggest, however, that if implemented properly, ESOPs can improve employee attitudes and economic productivity. At the same time, they are not risk-free to employees. ESOPs are not insured, and if a company goes bankrupt, its stock may be worthless.

IMPLICATIONS FOR MANAGEMENT PRACTICE

In thinking about pay and incentives, expect to see these trends:[a]

1. The movement to performance-based pay plans at all levels. Workers will put more of their pay at risk in return for potentially higher rewards tied to individual, team, business-unit, and organizational performance. Recognize, however, that average and low performers might well leave. This is the "sorting" effect of variable pay.

2. Use of a wide range of pay increases, in an effort to make distinctions in performance as meaningful as possible.

3. Increased need to reward people fairly to attract and retain top talent. That trend is being driven by

   - The movement toward greater internal and external transparency of pay levels, such as on social-media sites.

- Increasing transparency in executive pay, including published ratios of CEO pay to average worker pay.
- Pay-equity case law and legislation. Gender pay gap and broad pay-equity analysis is becoming standard practice for organizations.
- Pressure to increase levels of minimum and living wages.

[a]Miller, S. (2020, Jan. 2). Money talks: 5 compensation trends to watch in 2020. Retrieved from *https://www.shrm.org/resourcesandtools/hr-topics/compensation/pages/compensation-trends-to-watch-in-2020.aspx* on Jan. 3, 2020. De Lea, B. (2019, Nov. 4). Bank of America accelerates timeline for $20 minimum wage. Retrieved from *https://finance.yahoo.com/news/bank-america-accelerates-timeline-20-210912033.html* on Nov. 4, 2019. Sammer, J. (2019, Jan. 4). Keeping compensation fresh in 2019. Retrieved from *https://www.shrm.org/resourcesandtools/hr-topics/compensation/pages/keeping-compensation-fresh-in-a-tight-labor-market.aspx* on Jan. 4, 2019.

THE TRUST GAP

What steps can companies take to sew corporate top and bottom back together? Here are seven suggestions:

1. **Start with the obvious.** Forge a closer link between CEO compensation and company performance. In response to the coronavirus pandemic and the economic collapse in the hotel industry that followed, Marriott CEO Arne Sorenson relinquished his entire salary for 2020, while his executive team took a 50 percent pay cut.

2. **Consider instituting profit-sharing, gain-sharing, or some other program** that lets employees profit from their efforts. At Aflac, an insurer based in Columbus, Georgia, all of the company's 4,500 employees, from those in the call center to top executives, receive a percentage of their annual salaries in the form of profit-sharing bonuses. Southwest Airlines has done this since its inception.

3. **Rethink perquisites.** Now that proxy-disclosure rules require that all perks of the top five officers that exceed $10,000 be revealed, they just don't have the same appeal to executives. Yet they still have the same downside with the rank and file.

4. **Make sure the board's pay consultants don't work for management.** Adopt a written policy that outlaws such an obvious conflict of interest.

5. **Make sure your door is really open.** If that means meeting with employees at unorthodox times, such as when their shifts end, then do it. Not a single one of the CEOs interviewed by *Fortune* could recall employees ever abusing an open-door policy. The lesson is clear for managers at all levels: Employees don't walk through your door unless they have to.

6. **If you don't survey employee attitudes now, start.** What you find can help identify problems before they become crises. Share findings, and be sure employees know how subsequent decisions may be related to them. As one executive commented, "Employees by and large are reasonable people. They understand you can't do everything they want. As long as they know their views are being considered and they get some feedback from you to that effect, you will be meeting their expectations."

7. **Explain things–personally.** Although one study found that 97 percent of CEOs believe that communicating with employees has a positive impact on job satisfaction and 79 percent think it benefits the bottom line, only 22 percent do it weekly or more often.

There is no doubt that these seven steps can help close the trust gap that exists in so many U.S. organizations today. On the other hand, virtually all experts cite one important qualification: It is suicidal to start down this road unless you are absolutely sincere.

SUMMARY

Outside the entertainment industry and professional sports, pay systems are characterized by cost containment, pay and benefit levels commensurate with what a company can afford, and programs that encourage and reward performance.

Generally speaking, pay systems are designed to attract, retain, and motivate employees; achieve internal, external, and individual equity; and maintain a balance in relationships between direct and indirect forms of compensation and between the pay rates of supervisory and nonsupervisory employees. Pay systems need to be tied to the strategic mission of an organization, and they should take their direction from that strategic mission. However, actual wage levels depend on labor market conditions, legislation, collective bargaining, management attitudes, and an organization's ability to pay. The broad objective in developing pay systems is to assign a monetary value to each job or skill set in the organization (a base rate) and to establish an orderly procedure for increasing the base rate. To develop a job-based system, we need four basic tools: job analyses and job descriptions, a job-evaluation plan, pay surveys, and a pay structure. In addition, it's important to address the following pay-policy issues: pay secrecy versus openness, the effect of inflation on pay systems, pay compression, and pay raises.

In terms of incentive plans, the most effective ones are simple, specific, attainable, and measurable. Consider merit pay, for example. Merit pay works best when these guidelines are followed: (1) Establish high standards of performance, (2) develop sound performance management systems, (3) train supervisors in the mechanics of performance appraisal and in the art of giving constructive feedback, (4) tie rewards closely to performance, and (5) provide a wide range of possible pay increases.

Long-term incentives, in the form of stock awards, restricted stock, or performance shares, are becoming a larger proportion of executive pay packages. Finally, there is a wide variety of individual, group, and organizationwide incentive plans (e.g., profit-sharing, gain-sharing, employee stock-ownership plans) with different impacts on employee motivation and economic outcomes. Blending fixed versus variable pay in a manner that is understandable and acceptable to employees will present a management challenge for years to come.

KEY TERMS

trust gap	benchmark jobs
organizational reward system	relevant labor markets
compensation	broad banding
financial rewards	market-based pay system
nonfinancial rewards	competency-based pay system
internal equity	pay openness
external equity	pay equity
individual equity	pay compression
balance	incentives
compensable factors	merit-pay systems
job evaluation	annuity problem
hierarchy of job worth	sorting effect

performance awards

restricted stock

restricted stock units

lump-sum bonus

spot bonus

performance standards

profit-sharing

gain-sharing

employee stock-ownership plans
  (ESOPs)

DISCUSSION QUESTIONS

11-1. What steps can a company take to align its compensation system with its general business strategy?

11-2. What can companies do to ensure internal, external, and individual equity for all employees?

11-3. Discuss the advantages and disadvantages of competency- or skill-based pay systems.

11-4. What cautions would you advise in interpreting data from pay surveys?

11-5. In your opinion, why are more firms tying executive incentives to long-term (3 years or more) company performance?

11-6. Distinguish profit-sharing from gain-sharing.

11-7. If you were thinking of offering an employee stock-ownership plan, what key factors would you consider?

11-8. In your view, what might cause an incentive plan to fail?

11-9. In setting pay policy, a firm can lead, match, or lag the market rate of pay for various jobs. When might it choose each of these strategies?

11-10. How do tight versus loose labor market conditions affect wage rates?

APPLYING YOUR KNOWLEDGE

Nucor: The Art of Motivation*   *Case 11–1*

Steel and steel-products company Nucor's egalitarian culture places a premium on teamwork and idea-sharing between frontline workers and management. Result: A highly profitable partnership.

Pay-for-Performance

On average, two-thirds of a Nucor steelworker's pay is based on the amount of "prime" steel produced each day, with profit-sharing on top of that, and for managers, how well the company does overall. At Nucor, pay is well above the industry average, as are productivity levels, but the risks are real. When demand drops, so does pay, both for workers and for managers.

Listen to the Frontline

Execs say almost all of *the best ideas come from the factory floor*—and the newest workers often come up with them. In the wake of its recent acquisitions, Nucor is sending new workers to existing plants to hunt for improvement opportunities and is having older workers see what they can learn from newly acquired plants.

---

*Sources: Nucor: Who we are. Retrieved from *https://nucor.com/who-we-are/* on Apr. 30, 2020. Nucor. (2006, May 1). The art of motivation: What you can learn from a company that treats workers like owners. Inside the surprising performance culture of steelmaker Nucor. *BusinessWeek*, p. 59.

Push-Down Authority
To minimize layers of management, Nucor has pushed work that used to be done by supervisors, such as ordering parts, down to line workers and has pushed the duties of plant managers down to supervisors. According to the CEO, *executive vice-presidents are like "mini CEOs, and I'm their board."*

Protect Your Culture
As Nucor grows, protecting its egalitarian philosophy and team spirit is more of a challenge. A decentralized structure helps, but management makes *cultural compatibility a big focus of its acquisition research.* In visits to potential acquisitions, careful attention is paid to how plant workers and managers interact.

Try Unproven Technologies
Forays into new technologies haven't always paid off for Nucor, but it realizes *the importance of taking risks.* One project to make wire from steel failed miserably, and a $200 million attempt to build up a supply of raw materials in the Caribbean had to be scrapped. But successes such as thin-slab casting of sheet metal have made Nucor an industry leader.

Questions
1. What does Nucor's approach to managing its people require of managers?
2. Suggest several ways that a company might encourage its more experienced workers to listen to ideas from newer employees.
3. What might an organization do to preserve its culture among newly hired employees and those who arrive through acquisition?
4. Guaranteed pay at Nucor is considerably lower than that of the industry. Yet Nucor workers earn much more in total compensation than comparable workers in their industry. Why?

REFERENCES

1. Harrison, C. (2019, Jan. 8). 77% of organizations offering variable pay plans. *Salary.com*. Retrieved from *https://www.salary.com/blog/compensation-trends-organizations-embracing-variable-pay/* on Apr. 27, 2020. *See also* Miller, S. (2016a, Feb. 8). Employers seek better approaches to pay for performance. Retrieved from *www.shrm.org/resourcesandtools/hr-topics/compensation/pages/better-pay-for-performance.aspx* on Feb. 10, 2016.
2. Miller, S. (2016b, Aug. 11). Bonus binge: Variable pay outpaces salary. Retrieved from *www.shrm.org/resourcesandtools/hr-topics/compensation/pages/variable-pay-outpaces-raises.aspx* on Aug. 12, 2016. *See also* Cohen, P. (2015, May 25). One-time bonuses and perks muscle out pay raises for workers. *The New York Times.* Retrieved from *www.nytimes.com/2015/05/26/business/one-time-bonuses-and-perks-muscle-out-pay-raises-for-workers.html?r=0* on June 1, 2015.
3. Gerhart, B., and Newman, J. M. (2020). *Compensation* (13th ed.). New York: McGraw-Hill.
4. de Leon, R., and Geller, J. (2020, Mar. 13). Here's what every major company is doing about the coronavirus pandemic. *CNBC.* Retrieved from *https://www.cnbc.com/2020/03/13/workforce-wire-coronavirus-heres-what-every-major-company-is-doing-about-the-pandemic.html* on Apr. 27, 2020.
5. Gerhart and Newman (2020), op. cit. *See also* Osterman, P. (Ed.) (2019). *Creating Good Jobs.* Cambridge, MA: MIT Press.
6. Ibid. *See also* Nassauer, S. (2017, Jan. 29). Wal-Mart reworks pay. *The Wall Street Journal*, p. B2.
7. Stroh, L. K., Brett, J. M., Baumann, J. P., and Reilly, A. H. (1996). Agency theory and variable pay compensation strategies. *Academy of Management Journal* **39**, pp. 751–67.

8. Harrison (2019), op. cit. *See also* Wilkie, D. (2016, June 9). Companies rethink the annual pay raise. Retrieved from *www.shrm.org/resourcesandtools/hr-topics/employee-relations/pages/companies-rethink-the-annual-pay-raise.aspx* on June 10, 2016.

9. Harrison (2019), op. cit. *See also* Miller, S. (2010, Mar. 1). Companies worldwide rewarding performance with variable pay. Retrieved from *www.shrm.org/hrdisciplines/compensation/Articles/Pages/VariableWorld.aspx* on July 31, 2011.

10. Zhou, J., and Martocchio, J. J. (2001). Chinese and American managers' compensation-award decisions: A comparative policy-capturing study. *Personnel Psychology* **54**, pp. 115-45.

11. Kucera, D. (2010, Jul. 25). Companies ramp up perks to keep workers as economy improves. Retrieved from *www.wopular.com/companies-ramp-perks-keep-workers-economyimproves* on July 26, 2010. *See also* Minaja, E. (2018, Oct. 29). U.S. companies increase focus on pay packages. *The Wall Street Journal.* Retrieved from *https://blogs.wsj.com/cfo/2018/10/29/u-s-companies-increase-focus-on-pay-packages/* on Oct. 30, 2018.

12. Sammer, J. (2019a, Jan. 3). Keeping compensation fresh in 2019. *Dynamic HR.* Retrieved from *https://www.dynamichr.com/keeping-compensation-fresh-in-2019/* on Jan. 4, 2019. *See also* Minaya (2018), op. cit.

13. Gerhart and Newman (2020), op. cit.

14. Sammer, J. (2019b, Mar. 7). What to do when new workers out-earn current staff. *SHRM Online.* Retrieved from *https://www.shrm.org/resourcesandtools/hr-topics/compensation/pages/when-new-hires-out-earn-current-workers-pay-attention.aspx* on Mar. 7, 2019. *See also* Garvey, C. (2005, Jan.). Philosophizing compensation. *HRMagazine.* Retrieved from *www.shrm.org* on July 14, 2008.

15. Trevor, C. O., and Wazeter, D. L. (2006). A contingent view of reactions to objective pay conditions: Interdependence among pay structure characteristics and pay relative to internal and external referents. *Journal of Applied Psychology* **91**, pp. 1260-75. *See also* Gerhart, B., and Rynes, S. (2003). *Compensation: Theory, Evidence, and Strategic Implications.* Thousand Oaks, CA: Sage.

16. Greenberg, J. (2011). Organizational justice: The dynamics of fairness in the workplace. In *APA Handbook of Industrial and Organizational Psychology* (Vol. 3), pp. 271-327. Washington, D.C.: American Psychological Association. *See also* Huseman, R. C., Hatfield, J. D., and Miles, E. W. (1987). A new perspective on equity theory: The equity sensitivity construct. *Academy of Management Review* **12**, pp. 222-34.

17. Gerhart and Newman (2020), op. cit.

18. Mishel, L., and Wolfe, J. (2019, Aug. 14). CEO compensation has grown 940% since 1978. *Economic Policy Institute.* Retrieved from *https://www.epi.org/publication/ceo-compensation-2018/* on Apr. 27, 2020.

19. Thompson, A. A., Petcraf, M. A., Gamble, J. E., and Strickland, A. J. III. (2020). *Crafting and Executing Strategy* (22nd ed.). New York: McGraw-Hill.

20. Shaw, J. D. (2015). Pay dispersion, sorting, and organizational performance. *Academy of Management Discoveries* **1**(2), pp. 165-79. *See also* Grossman, W., and Hoskisson, R. E. (1998). CEO pay at the crossroads of Wall Street and Main: Toward the strategic design of executive compensation. *Academy of Management Executive* **12**(1), pp. 43-57. *See also* Montemayor, E. (1996). Congruence between pay policy and competitive strategy in high-performing firms. *Journal of Management* **22**, pp. 889-908.

21. Gerhart and Newman (2020), op. cit.

22. Gerhart and Newman (2020), op. cit. *See also* Gerhart and Rynes (2003), op. cit.

23. Gerhart and Newman (2020), op. cit.

24. Lazear, E. P., and Gibbs, M. (2015). *Personnel Economics in Practice* (3rd ed.). New York: Wiley. *See also* Klaas, B. S., and Ullman, J. C. (1995). Sticky wages revisited: Organizational responses to a declining market-clearing wage. *Academy of Management Review* **20**, pp. 281-310. *See also* Cappelli, P., and Chauvin, K. (1991). An interplant test of the efficiency wage hypothesis. *Quarterly Journal of Economics* **106**, pp. 769-94.

25. U.S. Department of Labor. (2019, Sept. 24). Overtime pay. Retrieved from *https://www.dol.gov/general/topic/wages/overtimepay* on Apr. 27, 2020.

26. Weber, L. (2015, May 21). Overtime pay for answering late-night emails? *The Wall Street Journal*, pp. B1, B6. *See also* Orey (2007), op. cit.

27. TheBalanceCareers. (2020). 2020 federal and state minimum wage rates. Retrieved from *https://www.thebalancecareers.com/2018-19-federal-state-minimum-wage-rates-2061043* on Feb. 1, 2020.

28. Living wage calculator. Retrieved from *https://livingwage.mit.edu/* on Apr. 27, 2020. *See also* The Harvard living wage fact sheet. Retrieved from *www.hcs.harvard.edu/~pslm/livingwage/factsheet.html* on Apr. 27, 2020. *See also* Quinton, S. (2013, Mar. 25). The Trader Joe's lesson: How to pay a living wage and still make money in retail. *The Atlantic*. Retrieved from *www.theatlantic.com/business/archive/2013/03/the-trader-joes-lesson-how-to-pay-a-living-wage-and-still-make-money-in-retail/274322/* on Apr. 6, 2013.

29. Budd, J. W. (2021). *Labor Relations: Striking a Balance* (6th ed.). New York: McGraw-Hill. *See also* Fossum, J. A. (2015). *Labor Relations: Development, Structure, Process* (12th ed.). New York: McGraw-Hill.

30. Gerhart and Newman (2020), op. cit. *See also* Hellerman, M. (2019, Oct. 26). How to use compensation survey data to set executive pay. *SHRM Online*. Retrieved from *https://www.shrm.org/resourcesandtools/hr-topics/compensation/pages/how-to-use-compensation-survey-data-to-set-executive-pay.aspx* on Oct. 26, 2019. *See also* Pfeffer, J., and Davis-Blake, A. (1987). Understanding organizational wage structures: A resource dependence approach. *Academy of Management Journal* **30**, pp. 437-55.

31. Boyle, M. (2018, Jan. 11). Wal-Mart raises hourly wage to $11 in wake of tax overhaul. Retrieved from *https://www.bloomberg.com/news/articles/2018-01-11/wal-mart-raises-u-s-hourly-wage-to-11-in-wake-of-tax-overhaul* on Jan. 11, 2018. *See also* Klaas, B. (1999). Containing compensation costs: Why firms differ in their willingness to reduce pay. *Journal of Management* **25**, pp. 829-50.

32. Van Sliedregt, T., Voskiujl, O. F., and Thierry, H. (2001). Job evaluation systems and pay-grade structures: Do they match? *International Journal of Human Resource Management* **12**(8), pp. 1313-24. *See also* Collins, J. M., and Muchinsky, P. M. (1993). An assessment of the construct validity of three job evaluation methods: A field experiment. *Academy of Management Journal* **36**(4), pp. 895-904. *See also* Madigan, R. M., and Hoover, D. J. (1986). Effects of alternative job evaluation methods on decisions involving pay equity. *Academy of Management Journal* 29(1), pp. 84-100.

33. Gerhart and Newman (2020), op. cit.

34. Ibid. *See also* Martocchio, J. J. (2020). *Strategic Compensation* (10th ed.). Upper Saddle River, NJ: Pearson Education.

35. Trevor, C., and Graham, M. E. (2000). Deriving the market wage: Three decision areas in the compensation survey process. *WorldatWork Journal* **9**(4), pp. 69-77. *See also* Klaas, B., and McClendon, J. A. (1996). To lead, lag, or match: Estimating the financial impact of pay level policies. *Personnel Psychology* **49**, pp. 121-40. *See also* Rynes, S. L., and Milkovich, G. T. (1986). Wage surveys: Dispelling some myths about the "market wage." *Personnel Psychology* **39**, pp. 71-90.

36. See, for example, *http://www.aon.com/human-capital-consulting/default.jsp*, *www.haygrouppaynet.com*, or *www.mercer.com*.

37. Hellerman (2019), op. cit. *See also* Greene, R. J. (2014, 1st Qtr.). Compensation surveys: The Rosetta stones of market pricing. *WorldatWork Journal*, pp. 23-31.

38. Gerhart and Newman (2020), op. cit. *See also* Martocchio (2020), op. cit.

39. Mercer. (2019, Apr. 10). U.S. geographic salary differential tool. Retrieved from *https://www.imercer.com/ecommerce/articleinsights/US-Geographic-Salary-Differential-Tool* on Apr. 28, 2020. *See also* Kolakowski, M. (2016, Oct. 19). Geographic and location pay differentials. *The Balance*. Retrieved from *www.thebalance.com/geographic-and-location-pay-differentials-1286877* on May 30, 2017.

40. Sibson, R. E. (1991). *Compensation* (5th ed.). New York: American Management Association.

41. Hellerman (2019), op. cit. *See also* Gerhart and Newman (2020), op. cit.

42. Ledford, G. E., Jr., and Heneman, H. G. III. (2011, June). *Skill-Based Pay*. Society for Industrial & Organizational Psychology, Inc. "SIOP Science" Series. Alexandria, VA: Society for Human Resource Management.

43. Zingheim, P., and Schuster, J. R. (2009). Competencies replacing jobs as the compensation/HR foundation. *WorldatWork Journal*, 18(3), pp. 6-20. *See also* Dierdorff, E. C., and Surface, E. A. (2008). If you pay for skills, will they learn? Skill change and maintenance under a skill-based pay system. *Journal of Management* **34**, pp. 721-43.

44. Southall, D., and Newman, J. (2000). *Skill-Based Pay Development*. Buffalo, NY: HR Foundations Inc.

45. Ledford, G. (2008, 1st Qtr.). Factors affecting the long-term success of skill-based pay. *WorldatWork Journal*, pp. **6**-18. *See also* Canavan, J. (2008, 1st Qtr.). Overcoming the challenge of aligning skill-based pay levels to the external market. *WorldatWork Journal*, pp. 18-24. *See also* Batt, R. (2004). Who benefits from teams? Comparing workers, supervisors, and managers. *Industrial Relations* **43**, pp. 183-212.

46. Murray, B., and Gerhart, B. (1998). An empirical analysis of a skill-based pay program and plant performance outcomes. *Academy of Management Journal* **41**, pp. 68-78.

47. Lee, C., Law, K. S., and Bobko, P. (1999). The importance of justice perceptions on pay effectiveness: A two-year study of a skill-based pay plan. *Journal of Management* **25**(6), pp. 851-73.

48. Levenson, A. R., Van der Stede, W. A., and Cohen, S. G. (2006). Measuring the relationship between managerial competencies and performance. *Journal of Management* **32**, pp. 360-80.

49. Bolden-Barrett, V. (2019, Feb. 13). Pay secrecy is illegal. Pay transparency is on the rise. *Zenefits*. Retrieved from *www.zenefits.com/workest/pay-secrecy-illegal-pay-transparency-on-rise/* on Apr. 28, 2020. *See also* Dreisbach, T. (2014, Apr. 13). "Pay secrecy" policies at work: Often illegal, and misunderstood. National Public Radio. Retrieved from *www.npr.org/2014/04/13/301989789/pay-secrecy-policies-at-work-often-illegal-and-misunderstood* on May 28, 2014.

50. Gee, K. (2017, Oct. 26). Pay is less secret in Millennial workforce. *The Wall Street Journal*, pp. B1, B6.

51. Colvin, G. (2015, Dec. 10). The benefit of baring it all. *Fortune*, p. 34.

52. Gerhart & Newman, 2020, op. cit.

53. Deal, J. (2016, Mar. 14). Why companies should make their pay transparent. *The Wall Street Journal*. Retrieved from *https://blogs.wsj.com/experts/2016/03/14/why-companies-should-make-their-pay-transparent/* on March 16, 2016. *See also* Silverman, R. E. (2013, Jan. 30). Psst ... this is what your co-worker is paid. *The Wall Street Journal*, p. B6.

54. Nagele-Piazza, L. (2020, Spring). The importance of pay equity. *HRMagazine* **65**(1), pp. 16-18. *See also* Lytle, T. (2019, Summer). A question of fairness. *HRMagazine* 64(7), pp. 41-44. *See also* Goodman, J. (2018, Apr. 2). Why pay equality is still out of reach. *Bloomberg Businessweek*, pp. 21-24.

55. Current U.S. inflation rates: 2009-2020. Retrieved from *www.usinflationcalculator.com/inflation/current-inflation-rates/* on Apr. 28, 2020. *See also* Society for Human Resource Management. Salary-increase projections 2020. Retrieved from *https://www.shrm.org/resourcesandtools/tools-and-samples/exreq/pages/details.aspx?erid=145* on Apr. 28, 2020.

56. Sammer, J. (2019c, March 7). What to do when new workers out-earn current staff. *SHRM Online*. Retrieved from *https://www.shrm.org/resourcesandtools/hr-topics/compensation/pages/when-new-hires-out-earn-current-workers-pay-attention.aspx* on Mar. 7, 2019. *See also* Miller, S. (2018, June 1). Address pay compression or risk employee flight. Retrieved from *https://www.shrm.org/resourcesandtools/hr-topics/compensation/pages/address-pay-compression-or-risk-employee-flight.aspx* on June 2, 2018.

57. Ibid.

58. Miller (2018), op. cit. See also Sammer, J. (2018, Feb. 16). What to do when workers hit the top of their pay range. Retrieved from *https://www.shrm.org/hr-today/news/hr-magazine/0318/pages/what-to-do-when-workers-hit-the-top-of-their-pay-range.aspx* on

Feb. 16, 2018. *See also* Priddle, A. (2012, Jan. 20). Ford sharing wealth of recent gains. *Chicago Tribune*. Retrieved from *http://articles.chicagotribune.com/2012-01-20/business/ct-biz-0120-ford-bonus-20120120_1* on May 14, 2012.

59. Sammer (2019c), op. cit.

60. Sammer (2019c), op. cit. *See also* Miller (2018), op. cit.

61. Wilkie, D. (2018, Sept. 10). Some companies boost starting salaries, but getting a raise is hard. Retrieved from www.shrm.org/resourcesandtools/hr-topics/compensation/pages/getting-a-raise-is-hard.aspx on April 28, 2020.

62. ECA International. (2019, Nov. 11). Real salary increases in Singapore set to be lower in 2020. Retrieved from *https://www.eca-international.com/news/november-2019/real-salary-increases-in-singapore-set-to-be-lower* on Apr. 28, 2020.

63. Gerhart and Rynes (2003), op. cit., p. 176.

64. Halzack, S. (2012, Nov. 7). Companies turn to bonuses instead of raises. *Boston Globe*. Retrieved from *http://www.bostonglobe.com/business/2012/11/07/companies-turn-bonuses-instead-raises/43VtTRNPV5B2Te8fzNaaYK/story.html* on Jan. 14, 2013. *See also* Mantell (2011), op. cit.

65. Garbers, Y., and Konradt, U. (2014). The effect of financial incentives on performance: A quantitative review of individual and team-based financial incentives. *Journal of Occupational and Organizational Psychology* 87, pp. 102–37. *See also* Sturman, M. C., Trevor, C. O., Boudreau, J. W., and Gerhart, B. (2003). Is it worth it to win the talent war? Evaluating the utility of performance-based pay. *Personnel Psychology* 56, pp. 997–1035. *See also* Stajkovic, A. D., and Luthans, F. (2001). Differential effects of incentive motivators on work performance. *Academy of Management Journal* **44**, pp. 580–90.

66. Jenkins, G. D., Jr., Mitra, A., Gupta, N., and Shaw, J. D. (1998). Are financial incentives related to performance? A meta-analytic review of empirical research. *Journal of Applied Psychology* 83, pp. 777–87.

67. Boue, G., and Corredino, D. M. (2019, June 5). Does incentive pay work? *HRMagazine* 64(2), pp. 28, 29. *See also* Knowledge@Wharton. (2011, Mar. 30). The problem with financial incentives–And what to do about it. Retrieved from *knowledge.wharton.upenn.edu/article.cfm?articleid=2741* on Mar. 31, 2011. *See also* Cascio, W. F., and Cappelli, P. (2009, Jan.). Lessons from the financial services crisis. *HRMagazine*, pp. 47–50.

68. Latham, G. P. (2009). *Becoming the Evidence-Based Manager: Making the Science of Management Work for You*. Boston: Davies-Black. *See also* Bolger, B. (2004, Spring). Ten steps to designing an effective incentive program. *Employment Relations Today*, pp. 25–33. *See also* Heneman, R. L. (2002). *Strategic Reward Management: Design, Implementation, and Evaluation*. Greenwich, CT: Information Age Publishing.

69. Gerhart and Newman (2020), op. cit. *See also* Gerhart, B., Rynes, S. L., and Fulmer, I. S. (2009). Pay and performance: Individuals, groups, and executives. *Academy of Management Annals* **3**, pp. **251**–315. *See also* Bennett, A. (1991, Sept. 10). Paying workers to meet goals spreads, but gauging performance proves tough. *The Wall Street Journal*, pp. B1, B2.

70. Wallace, C. (2008, Feb. 13). How to make great teachers. *Time*. Retrieved from *www.time.com/time/magazine/article/0,9171,1713473-1,00.html* on Mar. 18, 2008. *See also* Waldman, S., and Roberts, B. (1988, Nov. 14). Grading "merit pay." *Newsweek*, pp. 45, 46.

71. Smith, D. (2015, Dec.). Most people have no idea whether they're paid fairly. *Harvard Business Review*. Retrieved from *https://hbr.org/2015/10/most-people-have-no-idea-whether-theyre-paid-fairly* on Apr. 29, 2020.

72. Willyerd, K. (2014, Dec.). What high performers want at work. *Harvard Business Review*. Retrieved from *https://hbsp.harvard.edu/download?url=%2Fcatalog%2Fsample%2FH01PCG-PDF-ENG%2Fcontent&metadata=eyJlcnJvck1lc3NhZ2UiOiJZb3UgbXVzdCBiZSByZWdpc3RlcmVkIGFzIGEgUHJlbWl1bSBFZHVjYXRvciBvbiBOaGlzIHdlYiBzaXRlIHRvIHNlbGVjdGVkIEVkdWNhdG9yIEDb3BpXMgYW5kIEZyZWUgVHJpYWxzLiBOb3QgcmVnaXN0ZXJlZD8gQXBwbHkgbm93LiBBY2Nlc3MgZXhwaXJlZD8gUmVhdXRob3JpememUgbm93LiJ9* on Apr. 29, 2020.

73. Sammer, J. (2019d, Apr. 25). How to prepare managers to talk about pay. *SHRM Online.* Retrieved from *https://www.shrm.org/resourcesandtools/hr-topics/compensation/pages/ how-to-prepare-managers-to-talk-about-pay.aspx* on Apr. 25, 2019.

74. Koller, F. (2016, Dec. 9). 2016 ends at Lincoln Electric, no layoffs for now, 68 years and 83 years of amazing profit-sharing bonuses. Retrieved from *http://www. frankkoller.com/2016/12/2016-ends-at-lincoln-electric-no-layoffs-for-now-68-years-and- 83-years-of-amazing-profit-sharing-bonuses/* on Dec. 10, 2016. *See also* Koller, F. (2010). *Spark: How Old-Fashioned Values Drive a Twenty-First-Century Corporation.* New York: Perseus.

75. Renzulli, K. A. (2019, Feb. 12). Companies are worried about retention, but 69% don't plan to offer more than a 3% raise this year. *CNBC.* Retrieved from *https://www.cnbc. com/2019/02/12/companies-need-workers-but-69percent-wont-meaningfully-raise-worker- salaries-payscale-study-finds.html* on Feb. 12, 2019.

76. Gerhart and Newman (2020), op. cit. *See also* Shaw (2015), op. cit.

77. Lawler, E. E. III. (2003). Reward practices and performance management system effectiveness. *Organizational Dynamics* **32**(4), pp. 396–404. *See also* Heneman, R. L. (2002). A survey of merit pay-plan effectiveness: End of the line for merit pay or hope for improvement? In R. L. Heneman (Ed.), *Strategic Reward Management.* Greenwich, CT: Information Age Publishing, pp. 167–92.

78. Bennett, A. (1991, Apr. 17). The hot seat: Talking to the people responsible for setting pay. *The Wall Street Journal*, p. R3.

79. Collins, J. (2009). *How the Mighty Fall: And Why Some Companies Never Give In.* New York: Harper Collins.

80. Ellig, B. (2014). *The Complete Guide to Executive Compensation* (3rd ed.). New York: McGraw-Hill. See also Grossman, R. J. (2009, April). Executive pay: Perception and reality. *HRMagazine*, pp. 26–32.

81. Gerhart and Newman (2020), op. cit. *See also* FW Cook. *2019 top 250 report.* Downloaded from *https://www.fwcook.com/content/documents/Publications/11-20-19_ FWC_2019_Top_250_Final.pdf* on Apr. 1, 2020.

82. Sammer, J. (2017, Jan. 9). Is the annual pay raise obsolete? Retrieved from *www.shrm. org/resourcesandtools/hr-topics/compensation/pages/annual-pay-raise-obsolete.aspx* on Jan. 9, 2017. *See also* Wilkie (2016), op. cit. *See also* Cohen (2015), op. cit.

83. FW Cook (2019), op. cit.

84. Ibid. *See also* Francis, T. (2014, May 28). "Bargain" bosses are getting harder to find. *The Wall Street Journal*, p. B4. *S*

85. FW Cook (2019), op. cit.

86. Morgenson, G. (2014, Apr. 12). Pay for performance? It depends on the measuring stick. *The New York Times.* Retrieved from *www.nytimes.com/2014/04/13/business/pay-for- performance-it-depends-on-the-measuring-stick.html?r=0* on May 4, 2014. *See also* Lytle, T. (2013, Sept.). Linking executive pay to performance. *HRMagazine*, p. 59.

87. Ontario Securities Commission. (n.d.). Factors that can affect stock prices. Retrieved from *https://www.getsmarteraboutmoney.ca/invest/investment-products/stocks/factors- that-can-affect-stock-prices/* on Apr. 29, 2020. *See also* Bennett, A. (1992, Mar. 11). Taking stock: Big firms rely more on options but fail to end pay criticism. *The Wall Street Journal*, pp. A1, A8.

88. Gerhart and Newman (2020), op. cit.

89. Lesonsky, R. (2020, Feb. 4). Five different types of employee bonus programs for your small business. *Small Business Trends.* Retrieved from *https://smallbiztrends. com/2019/05/employee-bonus-small-business.html* on Apr. 29, 2020.

90. Bates, S. (2003b, Jan.). Goalsharing at Corning. *HRMagazine* 48(1), p. 33. *See also* Bennett (1992), op. cit.

91. Budd, J. W. (2021). *Labor Relations* (6th ed.). New York, NY: McGraw-Hill. *See also* Kurtulus, F. A., Kruse, D., and Blasi, J. (2011). Worker attitudes toward employee ownership, profit sharing, and variable pay. *Advances in the Economic Analysis of Participatory and Labor-Managed Firms* **12**, pp. 143–68.

92. Garbers and Konradt (2014), op. cit.

93. Lesonsky (2020), op. cit. *See also* Hoffman, J. (2017). Team-based rewards. In S. G. Rogelberg (Ed.), *The Sage Encyclopedia of Industrial and Organizational Psychology* (2nd ed., Vol. 4). Thousand Oaks, CA: Sage, pp. 1581-83. *See also* Gerhart et al. (2009), op. cit.

94. Fotsch, B., and Case, J. (2018, May 15). The key to an effective incentive plan. *Forbes.* Retrieved from *www.forbes.com/sites/fotschcase/2018/05/15/the-key-to-an-effective-incentive-plan/#2fb107dc31a7* on Apr. 29, 2020. *See also* Hoffman (2017), op. cit. *See also* Dulebohn, J. H., and Martocchio, J. J. (1998). Employee perceptions of the fairness of work-group incentive plans. *Journal of Management* **24**, pp. 469-88.

95. Svyantek, D. J. (2017). Gainsharing and profit sharing. In S. G. Rogelberg (Ed.), *The Sage Encyclopedia of Industrial and Organizational Psychology* (2nd ed., Vol. 2). Thousand Oaks, CA: Sage, pp. 521-24. *See also* Gerhart et al. (2009), op. cit. *See also* Florkowski, G. W. (1987). The organizational impact of profit sharing. *Academy of Management Review* **12**, pp. 622-36.

96. Kruse, D. L. (1993). *Profit Sharing: Does It Make a Difference?* Kalamazoo, MI: Upjohn Institute for Employment Research. *See also* Banerjee, N. (1994, Apr. 12). Rebounding earnings stir old debate on productivity's tie to profit sharing. *The Wall Street Journal*, pp. A2, A12.

97. Svyantek (2017), op. cit. *See also* Gerhart et al. (2009), op. cit.

98. Noble, B. (2020, Feb. 4). Ford to pay UAW members $6,600 in profit-sharing. *Detroit News.* Retrieved from *https://www.detroitnews.com/story/business/autos/ford/2020/02/04/ford-uaw-profit-sharing-2019/4626817002/* on Apr. 30, 2020.

99. Svyantek (2017), op. cit. *See also* Colvin, G. (1998, Aug. 17). What money makes you do. *Fortune*, pp. 213, 214.

100. Merritt, C., and Donohoe, A. (2019, Feb. 12). Difference between gainsharing & profit sharing. *The Nest.* Retrieved from *https://budgeting.thenest.com/difference-between-gainsharing-profit-sharing-23893.html* on Apr. 30, 2020. *See also* Gerhart et al. (2009), op. cit.

101. Imberman, W. (2008, July). Gainsharing: Tying pay to performance. Retrieved from *www.peoriamagazines.com/ibi/2008/jul/gainsharing* on May 31, 2017. *See also* Collins, D., Hatcher, L., and Ross, T. L. (1993). The decision to implement gainsharing: Role of work climate, expected outcomes, and union status. *Personnel Psychology* **46**, pp. 77-104. *See also* Graham-Moore, B., and Ross, T. L. (1990). Understanding gainsharing. In B. Graham-Moore and T. L. Ross (Eds.), *Gainsharing.* Washington, DC: Bureau of National Affairs, pp. 3-18.

102. Merritt and Donohoe (2019), op. cit. *See also* Hammer, T. H. (1988). New developments in profit sharing, gainsharing, and employee ownership. In J. P. Campbell and R. J. Campbell (Eds.), *Productivity in Organizations.* San Francisco: Jossey-Bass, pp. 328-66.

103. Svyantek (2017), op. cit. *See also* Gerhart and Newman (2020), op. cit. *See also* Shives, G. K., and Scott, K. D. (2003, 1st Quarter). Gainsharing and EVA: The U.S. postal experience. *WorldatWork Journal*, pp. 1-30.

104. Gerhart, B., Rynes, S. L., and Fulmer, I. S. (2009). Pay and performance: Individuals, groups, and executives. *Academy of Management Annals 3*, pp. 251-315.

105. Kim, D. (1999). Determinants of the survival of gainsharing programs. *Industrial and Labor Relations Review* 53(1), pp. 21-42. *See also* White, J. K. (1979). The Scanlon plan: Causes and consequences of success. *Academy of Management Journal* 22, pp. 292-312.

106. National Center for Employee Ownership. (2019, Sept.). Employee ownership by the numbers. Retrieved from *https://www.nceo.org/articles/employee-ownership-by-the-numbers#1* on Apr. 30, 2020. *See also* U.S. Securities and Exchange Commission. Employee stock ownership plans (ESOPs). Retrieved from *www.sec.gov/answers/esops.htm* on Apr. 30, 2020.

107. National Center for Employee Ownership (2019), op. cit. *See also* Melin, A. and Mittleman, M. (2017, June 19). Letting workers have a share. *Bloomberg Businessweek*, pp. 37, 38.

108. Jackson, N. M. (2010, June 17). ESOP plans let founders cash out and employees cash in. *Money.* Retrieved from *money.cnn.com/2010/06/03/smallbusiness/esop_plans/index.htm* on Aug. 5, 2011.

109. Melin and Mittleman (2017), op. cit. *See also* Loten, A. (2013, Apr. 18). Founders cash out, but do workers gain? *The Wall Street Journal*, p. B4.

110. Klein, K. E. (2010, Mar. 26). ESOPs on the rise among small businesses. *Business Week*. Retrieved from *www.businessweek.com/smallbiz/content/mar2010/sb20100325_591132.htm* on Aug. 5, 2011. *See also* Sammer (2007), op. cit.

111. P. Stavros, quoted in Melin and Mittleman (2017), op. cit., p. 37. *See also* Miller, S. (2016d, Apr. 29). Chobani gives employees equity with big potential value. Retrieved from *www.shrm.org/resourcesandtools/hr-topics/compensation/pages/chobani-gives-employees-equity-with-big-potential-value.aspx* on Apr. 30, 2016.

112. Klein, K. J., and Hall, R. J. (1988). Correlates of employee satisfaction with stock ownership: Who likes an ESOP most? *Journal of Applied Psychology* **73**, pp. 630–38. *See also* Klein, K. J. (1987). Employee stock ownership and employee attitudes: A test of three models. *Journal of Applied Psychology* **72**, pp. 319–32. *See also* Rosen, C., Klein, K. J., and Young, K. M. (1986). When employees share the profits. *Psychology Today* **20**, pp. 30–36.

113. Gerhart et al. (2009), op. cit. *See also* An ESOP to the workers. (2007, Apr. 14). *The Economist*, pp. 26–28. *See also* Sammer (2007), op. cit. *See also* Labich, K. (1996, Oct. 14). When workers really count. *Fortune*, pp. 212–14.

114. Kruse, D., and Blasi, J. (2002). Largest study yet shows ESOPs improve performance and employee benefits. Retrieved from *www.nceo.org/main/article.php/id/25/* on Sept. 30, 2004.

115. Gerhart et al. (2009), op. cit. *See also* Elmer, V. (2011, Feb. 1). How to deal with an invisible promotion. *Fortune*. Retrieved from *management.fortune.cnn.com/2011/02/01/how-to-deal-with-an-invisible-promotion* on Aug. 5, 2011. *See also* Tullar, W. L. (1998). Compensation consequences of reengineering. *Journal of Applied Psychology* **83**, pp. 975–80.

12 | INDIRECT COMPENSATION: EMPLOYEE BENEFIT PLANS

Questions This Chapter Will Help Managers Answer

LO 12-1   What strategic considerations should guide the design of benefits programs?

LO 12-2   What options are available to help a business control the rapid escalation of health-care costs?

LO 12-3   What are some of the key trends in benefits offered and strategies to pay for them?

LO 12-4   What cost-effective benefits options are available to a small business?

LO 12-5   In view of the considerable sums of money that are spent each year on employee benefits, what is the best way to communicate this information to employees?

THE NEW WORLD OF EMPLOYEE BENEFITS*

Major trends are changing the structure and function of employee benefits. Here are just a few: a multigenerational workforce, the global pandemic that pushed work and home lives under the same roof, the need to integrate financial wellness with physical and emotional health, the digitization of benefits, and the need to present an array of benefits options that address employees' needs during all stages of life. As the competition to attract and retain talent continues, it's more important than ever that employers understand the concerns that employees share, as well as their distinct needs. Why? Because according to Glassdoor, nearly two-thirds of job applicants focus on benefits almost as much as salary.

It wasn't always this way. In the past, major corporations offered their employees a wide array of company-paid insurance and retirement benefits. Corporations decided what was best for their employees. Now, in no small measure due to rising expenses and greater diversity than ever in their workforces, most employers are not only changing the range of benefit choices they offer, but also changing the basic structure of their benefits. Take telemedicine and virtual care, for example. As consumers and employers become more comfortable with healthcare delivered via digital technology, and as the coronavirus pandemic forced many to engage in "virtual visits" to medical providers, telemedicine took off and a new era of primary-care benefits arrived.

Economics and demographics are driving these changes. For example, the employee portion of most workers' health-care insurance has risen at a rate three times greater than their average salary increases over the past 10 years. Employers warn that this rate is not sustainable. Increasing life expectancy has made pensions more costly as well. Trends like these are causing employers to rethink their entire approach to employee benefits dramatically.

To illustrate the challenge, consider financial wellness—a major concern of each generation. Yet the major issues that drive financial wellness vary with employee life stages. A "one-size-fits-all" approach to these issues doesn't work. High levels of student debt are a primary concern for Millennials and Gen Z. Gen-Xers share concerns about managing debt as well as paying for their children's education. Fear of not saving enough for retirement is a major issue across age groups but it is most pressing for older workers for whom retirement is imminent. So rather than attempt to fashion a single approach that suits all of these interests, many employers determine a sum they'll spend on each employee, and then establish a menu of voluntary benefits that make it easy for employees to select options that best suit their individual needs. Those might include legal insurance, tuition reimbursement, onsite child care,

Sources: Wilkie, D. (2020, May 1). Into the future: How a pandemic might reshape the world of work. *SHRM Online.* Retrieved from *https://www.shrm.org/ResourcesAndTools/hr-topics/people-managers/Pages/ coronavirus-future-of-work-.aspx* on May 4, 2020. Ladika, S. (2020, Feb. 7). Virtual primary care "visits"? That future is already here. *Managed Care.* Retrieved from *https://www.managedcaremag.com/archives/2019/12/ virtual-primary-care-visits-future-already-here* on May 4, 2020. Reed, E,. H. (2020, Feb.). 2020 financial benefits trends. *HR Professionals Magazine* 10(2), pp. 34, 35. Miller, S. (2020, Jan. 2). Perk up: 6 benefits trends to watch in 2020. *SHRM Online.* Retrieved from *https://www.shrm.org/resourcesandtools/hr-topics/benefits/ pages/perk-up-six-key-benefit-trends-to-watch-in-2020.aspx* on Jan. 3, 2020. Baker, A. (2019, Nov.) Driving the future of benefits. *HR Professionals Magazine* 9(11), pp. 24, 25. Healy, D. (2019, Sept.). Meeting the benefits needs of five generations. *WorldatWork.* Retrieved from *https://www.worldatwork.org/workspan/articles/ meeting-the-benefits-needs-of-five-generations* on Oct. 8, 2019. Miller, S. (2019a, Jan. 3). 6 big benefits trends for 2019. *SHRM Online.* Retrieved from h*ttps://www.shrm.org/resourcesandtools/hr-topics/benefits/pages/ big-benefit-trends-2019.aspx* on Jan. 6, 2019.

student debt assistance, caregiver leave, or pet insurance. The result is a personalized benefits package. If necessary, employers can trim benefits merely by raising the prices of the various options on the benefits menu.

These changes reflect more than demographic diversity, however. A fundamental change in philosophy is taking place as employees assume more responsibility and self-management of their benefits options. Indeed, the new approach might well be described as one of "sharing costs, sharing risks." The conclusion to this case will showcase some major areas that are emerging or changing.

Challenges

1. Do you think companies should provide a broader menu of benefits (e.g., child care, veterinary care, financial counseling) or improve the menu of core benefits (e.g., health care, insurance, pensions)? Why?
2. How might your preference for various benefits change as you grow older or as your family situation changes?
3. What role do benefits play, in your opinion, in attracting and retaining workers? Might that role be different for different generations or for employees at different stages of their careers?

In 2019, U.S. organizations spent an average of 29.9 percent of total compensation on employee benefits. Of this sum, they spent 7.7 percent on legally required benefits (Social Security, Medicare, workers' compensation, and unemployment insurance) and the remainder on voluntary benefits.[1] Here are some reasons benefits have grown:

- Millennials, especially working parents, prize the freedom to work remotely, and businesses are finding that flexible compensation in the form of one-time bonuses, paid time off, and increased contributions to employee health insurance meet the needs of many employees.[2]
- The interest by unions in bargaining over benefits has grown, particularly because employers are pushing for more cost-sharing by employees.[3]
- The tax treatment of benefits makes them preferable to wages. Many benefits remain nontaxable to the employee and are deductible by the employer. With other benefits, taxes are deferred. Hence, employees' disposable income increases because they are receiving benefits and services that they would otherwise have to purchase with after-tax dollars.
- Granting benefits (in a nonunionized firm) or bargaining over them (in a unionized firm) confers an aura of social responsibility on employers; they are "taking care" of their employees.[4]

STRATEGIC CONSIDERATIONS IN THE DESIGN OF BENEFITS PROGRAMS

As is the case with compensation systems in general, managers need to think carefully about what they wish to accomplish by means of their benefits programs. After all, for every dollar that an employee earns in direct compensation, he or she earns almost 30 cents more in benefits. Over all employed individuals, that's almost $22,000 per employee each year.[5] It is no exaggeration to say that for most firms, benefits represent substantial annual expenditures. To leverage their impact, managers should be prepared to answer questions such as the following:

- Are the type and level of our benefits coverage consistent with our long-term strategic business plans?
- Given the characteristics of our workforce, are we meeting the needs of our employees?
- What legal requirements must we satisfy in the benefits we offer?
- Are our benefits competitive in cost, structure, and value to employees and their dependents?
- Is our benefits package consistent with the key objectives of our total compensation strategy—namely, adequacy, equity, cost control, and balance?

In the following sections, we discuss each of these points.

Long-Term Strategic Business Plans

Long-term strategic plans outline the basic directions in which an organization wishes to move in the next 3 to 5 years. One strategic issue that should influence the design of benefits is an organization's stage of development. For example, a start-up venture probably will offer low base pay and benefits but high incentives; a mature firm with well-established products and substantial market share will probably offer much more generous pay and benefits combined with moderate incentives.

Other strategic considerations include the projected rate of employment growth or downsizing, geographic redeployment, acquisitions, and expected changes in profitability. Each of these conditions suggests a change in the optimum mix of benefits in order to be most consistent with an organization's business plans.

EDUCATING EMPLOYEES ABOUT THEIR BENEFITS

HR BUZZ

Nearly 40 percent of North American organizations have budgets specifically devoted to benefits communication. Yet only 19 percent of employers say their workers have a high level of understanding about their benefits packages. Indeed, a recent survey from the nonprofit International Foundation of Employee Benefit Plans revealed the following:

- Plan participants do not open or read communication materials (80 percent).
- Participants don't understand the materials (49 percent).
- Participants don't perceive value in their benefits (31 percent).

Innovative Strategies for Communication[a]

---

[a] *Sources:* Grensing-Pophal, L. (2020, March 4). Benefits communications require balancing act. *SHRM Online.* Retrieved from *https://www.shrm.org/resourcesandtools/hr-topics/benefits/pages/benefits-communications-require-balancing-act.aspx* on Mar. 4, 2020. Miller, S. (2016c, Mar. 9). When employees don't read benefit materials. Retrieved from *shrm.org/resourcesandtools/hr-topics/benefits/pages/unread-benefits-materials.aspx* on Mar. 10, 2016. Benz, J. (2016, Jan.). Communication: Spreading the word about benefits. *HR,* p. 44.

(continued)

Despite the failure of traditional communications, fewer than half of the organizations surveyed tried nontraditional benefits-communication platforms, like video (29 percent), social media (23 percent), or texts (10 percent). To make matters worse, employees spend, on average, only 17 minutes electing their benefits during open enrollment.

In response, some organizations are building engaging channels that support frequent communication, such as branded, user-friendly, mobile-optimized websites outside corporate firewalls. Small employers, like Cannon Construction, a utilities contractor in Lakewood, Washington, have taken a different tack. Cannon engaged its benefits broker to do onsite presentations, did a GoToMeeting recording of the presentation, and then posted it on the company's YouTube channel as an unlisted link, which isn't searchable by the public. Cannon gave the URL to employees and encouraged them to view the video.

The video allowed employees to review the information presented at their leisure, with their spouses, as they decided which plans to elect. The video also allowed employees to scroll through to specific topics they wanted more information about. It had more than 300 views among the company's 130 employees during the benefits open-enrollment period.

Diversity in the Workforce Means Diversity in Benefits Preferences

Young employees who are just starting out are likely to be more concerned with direct pay (e.g., for a house purchase) than with a generous pension program. Older workers may desire the reverse. Unionized workers may prefer a uniform benefits package, whereas single parents, older workers, or workers with disabilities may place heavy emphasis on flexible work schedules. Employers that hire large numbers of temporary or part-time workers may offer entirely different benefits to these groups. Evidence indicates that the perceived value of benefits rises when employers introduce choice through a flexible benefits package. Benefits, along with direct compensation, job security, opportunities to use one's skills and abilities, and relationship with one's immediate supervisor, are the top five drivers of overall job satisfaction.[6]

Legal Requirements

The government plays a central role in the design of any benefits package. Whereas controlling the cost of benefits is a major concern of employers, the social and economic welfare of citizens is the major concern of government.[7] As examples of such concern, consider the four income-maintenance laws shown in Table 12–1.

Income-maintenance laws were enacted to provide employees and their families with income security in case of death, disability, unemployment, or retirement. For example, during the pandemic, the Families First Coronavirus Response Act required certain employers to provide paid sick leave or expanded family and medical leave.[8] In terms of tax policy, two principles have had the greatest impact on benefits.[9] One is the **doctrine of constructive receipt**, which holds that an individual must pay taxes on benefits that have monetary value when the individual receives them. The other principle is the **anti-discrimination rule**, which holds that employers can obtain tax advantages only for those benefits that do not discriminate in favor of highly compensated employees.

Table 12–1

FOUR MAJOR INCOME-MAINTENANCE LAWS

Law	Scope of coverage	Funding	Benefits	Administrative agency
Social Security Act (1935)	Full coverage for retirees, dependent survivors, and disabled persons insured by 40 quarters of payroll taxes on their past earnings or earnings of heads of households. Federal government employees hired prior to January 1, 1984, and railroad workers are excluded.	For 2020, payroll tax of 6.2 percent each for employees and employers on the first $137,700 in earnings. Self-employed persons pay the full 12.4 percent of this wage base. Employees and employers also each pay 1.45 percent for Medicare (2.9 percent if self-employed) on all wages and self-employment income. High earners ($250,000 for married taxpayers filing jointly, $200,000 for singles) pay 0.9 percent additional Medicare tax. Authorized under the Patient Protection and Affordable Care Act, these thresholds are not inflation adjusted and thus apply to more employees each year.	*Full retirement* payments after age 67 (for those born in 1960 or later), or at reduced rates after 62, to worker and spouse. Size of payment depends on past earnings. *Survivor benefits* for the family of a deceased worker or retiree. At full retirement age, a widow or widower receives the full pension granted to the deceased. A widow or widower of any age with dependent children under 16, and each unmarried child under 18, receives a 75 percent benefit check. *Disability benefits* to totally disabled workers, after a 5-month waiting period, as well as to their spouses and children. *Health insurance* for persons over 65 (Medicare). All benefits are adjusted upward whenever the consumer price index (CPI) increases more than 3 percent in a calendar year and trust funds are at a specified level. Otherwise, the adjustment is based on the lower of the CPI increase or the increase in average national wages (1983 amendments).	Social Security Administration

(continued)

Table 12–1 (cont.)

FOUR MAJOR INCOME-MAINTENANCE LAWS

Law	Scope of coverage	Funding	Benefits	Administrative agency
Federal Unemployment Tax Act (1935)	All employees except some state and local government workers, domestic and farm workers, railroad workers, and some nonprofit employees.	Payroll tax of 6.0 percent of first $7,000 of earnings paid by employer. If employers pay their state unemployment insurance in full and on time, they are eligible to receive a federal tax credit of up to 5.4 percent. States may raise both the percentage and base earnings taxed through legislation. Employer contributions may be reduced if state experience ratings for them are low.	Benefits are based on a percentage of average weekly earnings and are available for up to 26 weeks. Those eligible for benefits have been employed for some specified minimum period and have lost their jobs through no fault of their own. Most states exclude strikers. During periods of high unemployment, federal benefits may begin after an unemployed worker has used 26 weeks of state benefits. The duration of the extended benefits is determined by a state's jobless rate.	U.S. Department of Labor, Employment and Training Administration, and the several state employment security commissions
Workers' compensation (state laws)	Generally, employees of nonagricultural, private-sector firms are entitled to benefits for work-related accidents and illnesses leading to temporary or permanent disabilities.	One of the following options, depending on state law: self-insurance, insurance through a private carrier, or payroll-based payments to a state insurance system. Premiums depend on the riskiness of the occupation and the experience rating of the insured.	Benefits average about two-thirds of an employee's weekly wage and continue for the term of the disability. Supplemental payments are made for medical care and rehabilitative services. In case of a fatal accident, survivor benefits are payable.	Various state commissions

Table 12–1 (cont.)

FOUR MAJOR INCOME-MAINTENANCE LAWS

Law	Scope of coverage	Funding	Benefits	Administrative agency
Employee Retirement Income Security Act (ERISA) (1974)	Private-sector employees over age 21 enrolled in noncontributory (100 percent employer-paid) retirement plans who have 1 year's service.	Employer contributions.	Under the Pension Protection Act of 2006, employer contributions made after 2006 to a defined-contribution plan must become **vested** at 100 percent after 3 years or under a second- to sixth-year gradual-vesting schedule (20 percent per year beginning with the second year of service–i.e., 100 percent after 6 years). Different rules apply with respect to employer contributions made before 2007. Employee contributions are always 100 percent **vested**. Once an employee is vested, receipt of the pension is not contingent on future service. Authorizes tax-free transfer of vested benefits to another employer or to an individual retirement account ("portability") if a vested employee changes jobs and if the present employer agrees. Employers must fund plans on an actuarially sound basis. Pension trustees ("fiduciaries") must make prudent investments. Employers may insure vested benefits through the federal Pension Benefit Guaranty Corporation.	Department of Labor, Internal Revenue Service, Pension Benefit Guaranty Corporation

These two tax-policy principles define the conditions for the preferential tax treatment of benefits. Together they hold that if benefits discriminate in favor of highly paid or key employees, both the employer and the employee receiving those benefits may have to pay taxes on the benefits when the employee receives them.

Competitiveness of the Benefits Offered

The issue of benefits-program competitiveness is much more complicated than that of salary competitiveness.[10] In the case of salary, both employees and management focus on the same item: direct pay (fixed plus variable). However, in determining the competitiveness of benefits, senior management tends to focus mainly on cost, whereas employees are more interested in value. The two may conflict. Thus, employees' perceptions of the value of their benefits as competitive may lead to excessive costs, in the view of top management. On the other hand, achieving cost competitiveness provides no assurance that employees will perceive the benefits program as valuable to them.

Total Compensation Strategy

The broad objective of the design of compensation programs (i.e., direct as well as indirect compensation) is to integrate salary and benefits into a package that will encourage the achievement of an organization's goals. For example, although a generous pension plan may help retain employees, it probably does little to motivate them to perform on a day-to-day basis. This is because the length of time between performance and reward is too great. On the other hand, a generous severance package offered to targeted segments of the employee population may facilitate an organization's objective of downsizing to a specified staffing level. In all cases, considerations of adequacy, equity, cost control, and balance should guide decision making in the context of a total compensation strategy.

HR BUZZ

SMALL BUSINESS GETS STRATEGIC WITH VOLUNTARY BENEFITS*

Voluntary benefits programs allow smaller companies to offer a wider array of benefits than they otherwise would be able to. "We must continuously find ways to remain competitive and attract and retain top talent while evaluating costs associated with those benefits," says Cathy E. Hulsey, vice president of human resources for EPL Inc., a Birmingham, Alabama–based, 90-employee provider of services to credit unions. EPL currently offers dental, vision, life, accidental death and dismemberment, and optional life insurance and is considering offering supplemental health, long-term-care, and cancer insurance during its next open-enrollment period. "The costs of our voluntary benefits are minimal in comparison to the benefits derived from employee engagement, morale, productivity and retention," Hulsey says. Because certain voluntary benefits, such as supplemental medical coverage, can be paid for with pretax dollars, the resulting reduction in payroll taxes could offset any administrative or other costs associated with offering these programs.

Moreover, insurance-based products frequently are offered at group rates that are much lower than what most employees would pay for an individual policy.

Figuring out which voluntary benefits to offer is an important decision. "We consider many things, such as current and future workforce demographics, culture, utilization rates, competitive data, and employee survey information," says Jeff Tomschin, vice president, human resources, for Phillips Service Industries Inc., a diversified holding company with 500 full-time employees based in Livonia, Michigan. The company's goal for the program is to supplement the overall benefits strategy by allowing individual employees to choose additional benefits that may be important to them. In addition to long-term-care coverage, the company supplements its medical insurance with accident and critical-illness insurance that can help employees cover the deductible within a high-deductible health plan. "Our survey data indicate that employees are willing to pay 100 percent of the costs of certain benefits," says Alyssa Williams, a voluntary benefits consultant with consulting firm Mercer in Atlanta. "They just want the employer to serve as the access point."

With these considerations in mind, let us now examine some key components of the benefits package.

COMPONENTS OF THE BENEFITS PACKAGE

There are many ways to classify benefits, but we will follow the classification scheme used by the U.S. Chamber of Commerce. According to this system, benefits fall into three categories: security and health, payments for time not worked, and employee services. Within each of these categories is a bewildering array of options. The following discussions consider only the most popular options and cover only those that have not been mentioned previously.

Security and Health Benefits

Security and health benefits include

- Life insurance
- Workers' compensation
- Disability insurance
- Health insurance
- Other medical coverage
- Maternity and paternity leaves
- Sick leave
- Pension plans
- Social Security
- Unemployment insurance
- Supplemental unemployment insurance
- Severance pay

Note that three benefits in this list are legally required of every employer in the United States: workers' compensation, Social Security (including Medicare), and unemployment insurance. At a broad level, insurance is the basic building block of almost all benefits packages, because it protects employees against income loss caused by death, accident, or ill health. Most organizations provide group coverage for their employees. The plans may be **contributory** (in which employees share in the cost of the premiums) or **noncontributory** (in which the employer pays the full cost of the premiums).

It used to be that when a worker switched jobs, he or she lost health insurance coverage. No longer. Under the Consolidated Omnibus Budget Reconciliation Act (COBRA) of 1986, companies with at least 20 employees must make medical coverage available at group insurance rates (100 percent premium plus a 2 percent administration fee) for as long as 18 months after the employee leaves–whether the worker left voluntarily, retired, or was dismissed. The law also provides that, following a worker's death or divorce, the employee's family has the right to buy group-rate health insurance for as long as 3 years. After that, participants can opt into the Health Insurance Marketplace created by the Affordable Care Act (discussed in a later section).[11]

With respect to health information, the Health Insurance Portability and Accountability Act (HIPAA) includes strict provisions to safeguard employee privacy. Thus, an individual or group health plan that provides or pays the cost of medical care may not use or disclose **protected health information** (medical information that contains any of a number of patient identifiers, such as name or Social Security number), except with the consent or authorization of the individual in question.[12] With this in mind, let us consider the major forms of security and health benefits commonly provided to employees.

Group Life Insurance

This type of insurance is usually **yearly renewable term insurance**–that is, each employee is insured 1 year at a time. The actual amounts of coverage vary, but typical group term life insurance coverage is one to two times the employee's annual salary. This amount provides a reasonable financial cushion to the surviving spouse during the difficult transition to a different way of life. Thus, a manager making $75,000 per year may have a group term life policy with a face value of $150,000. Keep in mind, however, that the more expenses and dependents you have, the more life insurance you will need.[13] Eighty-two percent of companies offer this benefit.[14] To discourage turnover, almost all of them cancel it if an employee terminates.

Life insurance has been heavily affected by **flexible-benefits** programs. Typically, such programs provide a core of basic life coverage (e.g., $25,000) and then permit employees to choose greater coverage (e.g., in increments of $10,000 to $25,000) as part of their optional package. Employees purchase the additional insurance through payroll deductions.

Workers' Compensation

Workers' compensation is a benefit required by law in all 50 states. It provides payments to workers who are injured on the job or who contract a work-related illness. The payments cover three areas: payments to replace lost wages, medical treatment and rehabilitation costs, and retraining to perform a different type of work (if necessary). As shown in Table 12-1, these payments vary by state, and the differences in costs may be substantial. Workers' compensation costs employers $95 billion per year and the average cost of a claim is $40,000.[15]

A state's industrial structure also plays a big part in setting insurance rates. Thus, serious injuries are more common and costly among Oregon loggers and Michigan

WORKERS' COMPENSATION

As we have seen, workers' compensation is a major cost of doing business. Some of the driving forces behind these costs are higher medical costs, the increasing involvement of attorneys, and fraud.[a] What are states and companies doing to control costs?

California set up a fund, financed by employers, that pays for special teams to go after fraud. Job-injury claims declined to 8.4 per 100 workers, from nearly 10 two years earlier. Connecticut no longer awards disability benefits for mental or psychological disorders unless they are the result of an injury. It has eliminated cost-of-living adjustments on disability benefits and has cut some benefits by a third. Two years later, insurance premiums in the state fell 24 percent.

Finally, workers' compensation insurers are forming alliances with managed-care providers in order to take advantage of case-management methods and volume discounting. At Coca-Cola Bottling Company in New York, the company did exactly that and also addressed long-standing safety issues in its plants. Six years later, its average claim dropped by 60 percent.[b]

Is there an underlying theme in these approaches? Yes, and it's simple: Aggressive management of workplace safety issues pays dividends for workers and for their employers.

Controlling the Costs

---

[a]The Horton Group. (2018, June 18). Controlling workers' compensation claims and costs. Retrieved from *https://www.thehortongroup.com/resources/controlling-workers-compensation-claims-and-costs* on May 5, 2020. Lynch, T. (2014, Apr. 18). Where's Aristotle when ABC needs him? Retrieved from *www.workerscompinsider. com/compensability/* on June 9, 2014. Treaster, J. B. (2003, June 23). Cost of insurance for work injuries soars across U.S. *The New York Times.* Retrieved from *http://nyti.ms/v6m0ef* on July 21, 2008.

[b]Fleming, C. M. (2013, May 30). Controlling workers' compensation claim costs: 3 things every self-insured should know. Retrieved from *http://www.milliman.com/insight/2013/Controlling-workers-compensation-claim-costs-3-things-every-self-insured-should-know/* on June 9, 2014. Martin, T. M. (2013, Apr. 12). When your M. D. is an algorithm. *The Wall Street Journal,* pp. B1, B6.

---

machinists than among assembly-line workers in a Texas semiconductor plant. Small businesses pay, on average, $560 per year for coverage. That number is deceptively simple, however, because actual rates depend on the state(s) where employees work, the employer's annual payroll, industry, the type of work performed, and the employer's history of claims.[16]

At present, all 50 states have workers' compensation laws. Although specific terms and levels of coverage vary by state, all state laws share the following features[17]:

- All job-related injuries and illnesses are covered.
- Coverage is provided regardless of who caused the injury or illness (i.e., regardless of who was "at fault").
- Payments are usually made through an insurance program financed by employer-paid premiums.
- A worker's loss is usually not covered fully by the insurance program. Most cash payments are at least two-thirds of the worker's weekly wage, but, together with disability benefits from Social Security, the payments may not exceed 80 percent of the worker's weekly wage.
- Workers' compensation programs protect employees, dependents, and survivors against income loss resulting from total disability, partial disability, or death; medical expenses; and rehabilitation expenses.

Disability Insurance

An illness or accident will keep one in four 20-something employees out of work for at least a year before retirement.[18] Disability coverage provides a supplemental, one-time payment when death is accidental, and it provides a range of benefits when employees become disabled—that is, when they can't perform the main functions of their occupations.[19] **Long-term disability (LTD) plans** (offered by 71 percent of employers in 2019) and **short-term disability plans** (offered by 61 percent of employers in 2019) provide income replacement for employees whose illness or injury causes a longer absence from work. Short-term disability usually starts after a 1- to 2-week absence, and LTD usually goes into effect after 6 weeks to 3 months.[20]

Whereas paid sick leave usually covers an employee's entire salary, short- and long-term disability benefits may cover only a portion of that salary. For example, LTD recipients typically receive no more than 60 percent of their base pay, until they begin receiving pension benefits. The HR Buzz box below, "Controlling Disability Costs," shows what progressive firms are doing to control these costs.

Although disability benefits traditionally were divided into salary continuation, short-term disability, and long-term disability, combined **disability-management** programs now merge all three. Doing so allows for a single claim-application process and uniform case management. An employee whose short-term illness turns into a lengthy disability doesn't have to reapply for benefits or start over with a new case manager; the process is uniform and seamless, regardless of the length of the disability.

Another developing trend is toward outsourcing disability management as part of a broader effort to manage employee absences. Doing so may create common reporting systems for all absences, including those related to workers' compensation.[21]

HR BUZZ

Controlling Disability Costs*

CANADIAN IMPERIAL BANK OF COMMERCE

To control disability-leave costs, Canadian Imperial Bank of Commerce (CIBC) turned to disability-management programs that emphasize a partnership among the physician, the employee, the manager, and the HR representative, known as a *facilitator*. The physician's role is to specify what the employee can and cannot do. Ongoing discussions between the employee and manager, assisted by the facilitator, determine what tasks an employee is actually capable of doing—the opposite of traditional disability management, which focuses on what the employee cannot do. This approach balances flexibility in meeting individual needs with consistency and fairness.

Does disability management work? At CIBC, the average duration for short-term disability dropped by 32 percent in the first 9 months of the program. In addition, the firm's long-term disability (LTD) insurance carrier reported that employees on LTD were back to work 38 percent faster than the average for LTD claimants in general.

---

*Sources: Beckman, K. (2017, May 1). Integrated disability makes a comeback. Retrieved from *https://www.businessinsurance.com/article/00010101/NEWS08/912313171/Integrated-disability-makes-a-come-back-#* on May 5, 2020. Lawrence, L. (2000, Dec.). Disability management partnerships save time, money. *HR News*, pp. 11, 17. Tobenkin, D. (2010, May). Keeping disability payments in check. *HR*, pp. 81-85. Quick, E. (2011, Mar. 25). Integrated disability management in a challenging economy. Retrieved from *www.shrm.org/hrdisciplines/benefits/Articles/Pages/DisabilityManagement.aspx* on Aug. 11, 2011.

Health Insurance

Health insurance is an essential benefit for most working Americans. Self-insurance is out of the question because the costs incurred by one serious, prolonged illness could easily wipe out a lifetime of savings and assets and place a family in debt for years to come. The U.S. health insurance system is based primarily on group coverage provided by employers.

Yet there is widespread anxiety about the reliability of the system.[22] Indeed, if current trends continue, health care spending will be a quarter of the economy in 2035. Consider those trends. Over the past decade, health insurance premiums for family coverage increased by 48 percent, whereas workers' contributions to those premiums increased 71 percent. At the same time, their earnings increased 25 percent, and inflation rose 19 percent. Those increased contributions depressed wage increases workers otherwise would have received. Figure 12-1 shows these trends graphically. Figure 12-2 shows the growth in annual premiums for family coverage from 1999 to 2019 for small and large employers.

Because employers pay most of the nation's health-care premiums (about 82 percent),[23] over time such increases may make them less competitive in global markets. In fact, Australia, Britain, Canada, Germany, the Netherlands, and New Zealand (all of which provide universal health-care coverage for their citizens) spend half as much of their gross domestic product on health care as the United States does. In an effort to reform the U.S. health-care system, Congress passed the Patient Protection and Affordable Care Act (ACA) in March 2010. As of January 1, 2019, the Tax Cuts and Jobs Act repealed the requirement that individuals are required to have ACA-compliant health coverage or else pay a penalty. The following sections describe the ACA's major provisions as of 2020.[24]

Figure 12-1

Cumulative Increases in Family Coverage Premiums, General Annual Deductibles, Inflation, and Workers' Earnings, 2009-2019

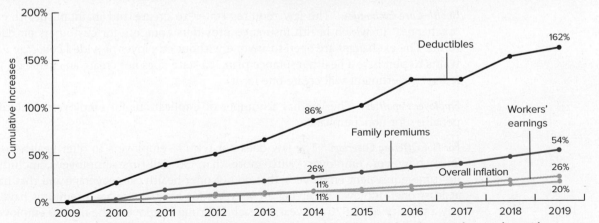

Note: Average general annual deductibles are for single coverage and are among all covered workers. Workers in plans without a general annual deductible for in-network services are assigned a value of 0.

Source: KFF Employer Health Benefits Survey, 2018-2019; Kaiser/HRET Survey of Employer-Sponsored Health Benefits, 2009-2017. Bureau of Labor Statistics, Consumer Price Index, U.S. City Average of Annual Inflation (April to April), 2009-2019; Bureau of Labor Statistics, Seasonally Adjusted Data from the Current Employment Statistics Survey, 2009-2019 (April to April).

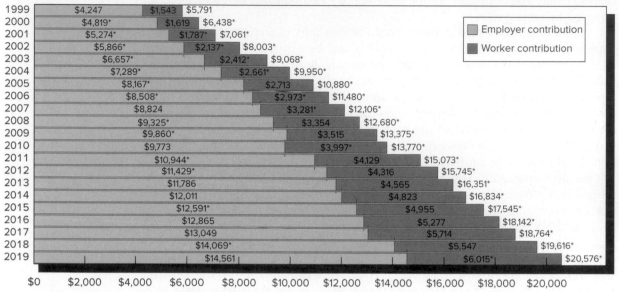

Figure 12-2

Average Annual Worker and Employer Contributions to Premiums and Total Premiums for Family Coverage, 1999-2019

*Estimate is statistically different from estimate for the previous year shown (p < .05).

Source: KFF Employer Health Benefits Survey, 2018-2019; Kaiser/HRET Survey of Employer-Sponsored Health Benefits, 1999-2017.

Mandated Benefits   All existing health insurance plans must

- Prohibit lifetime limits of insurance coverage.
- Prohibit exclusions of coverage for preexisting conditions.
- Prohibit annual limits of insurance coverage.
- Include a requirement to provide coverage for nondependent children up to age 26.

Health-Care Exchanges   The law requires states to create and maintain health-care "exchanges" in which health insurance providers compete for customers on equal terms. The exchanges are open to anyone without employer-provided coverage who wants to purchase a health insurance plan. If a state does not create an exchange, the federal government will create one for it.

Employer Penalties   The law has a number of implications for employers, including penalties for noncompliance.

For Not Offering Coverage   The law does not require employers to offer health insurance; however, employers with more than 50 full-time employees, including full-time-equivalent employees, that do not offer health-care coverage and that have at least one employee receiving a tax credit for health-coverage premiums have to pay a penalty of $2,570 per year for each full-time employee. The first 30 employees are excluded from that headcount.[25]

For Unaffordable Coverage   If an employee opts out of an employer plan because coverage is "unaffordable"—that is, if the premium exceeds 9.78 percent of family income—the employer must pay a $3,860 penalty for each full-time employee who receives a government subsidy and purchases coverage through an exchange.[26]

No Penalty for Waiting Periods   Employers will not be required to pay a penalty for employees during a waiting period that is required before an employee can enroll in an employer-provided health insurance plan. A waiting period cannot exceed 90 days.

Automatic Enrollment Procedure   The law requires employers with more than 200 employees to enroll employees automatically into health insurance plans offered by the employer, allowing for an employee opt-out. The law is silent as to the effective date of this requirement.

Restrictions on Cafeteria Plans   The law caps flexible spending account (FSA) contributions at $2,750 in 2020 and excludes over-the-counter medications without a doctor's prescription as reimbursable expenses.

Incentives for Wellness   The law allows employers to adopt wellness initiatives that offer an employee incentive of up to 30 percent of the cost of employee-only coverage. Further, with the approval of various federal agencies, wellness incentives could reach 50 percent of the cost of employee-only coverage. The law provides for grants for up to 5 years for small employers that establish wellness programs.

Tax on High-Value ("Cadillac") Plans   As of 2020, this tax is delayed until 2022. It is a tax on high-cost health coverage (40 percent tax on the value of coverage over specified thresholds).

Required W-2 Reporting   Employers are required to report the value of employees' health benefits on W-2 forms that show the amount of taxes withheld from their paychecks for the year. Those health benefits are not taxable.

Changes in Healthcare Costs over Time

Between March 2009 and March 2020, the consumer price index (CPI) for all items increased about 21 percent, whereas the CPI for medical costs increased by 39 percent. What's driving these increases in the cost of health care? In addition to an aging population, experts cite an increase in obesity (about 36 percent of the American adult population), surging drug costs, administrative costs that add millions to the country's health-care spending, mergers among local hospitals, and the cost of new technology.[27]

What about the effects of the Affordable Care Act? Its impact on companies varies greatly, depending on factors such as a firm's number of employees and whether it already provides health insurance. The law has not meant big changes for every company. In fact, some small businesses can now offer employees a benefit they would not be able to afford without the law. That said, organizations everywhere are still searching for strategies to contain the rise in health-care costs.[28]

Cost-Containment Strategies

Strategies to contain the high costs of health care are taking center stage in the boardroom as well as in the health-care industry itself. Here are some measures that firms have taken to gain tighter management control over the cost of health care:

1. *Band together with other companies to form a "purchasing coalition" to negotiate better rates with insurers.* Such coalitions have become key cost-control devices for small businesses, but Rochester, New York, took it further. Six big companies, including Xerox and Kodak, set up a health and fitness program for all of the metropolitan area's 1.04 million people. They also had their own efficiency

experts help three hospitals streamline their operations free of charge, and they contributed $685,000 toward establishing a regional electronic health records system. Four years later, Rochester's health costs dropped from 5 percent below the national average to 15 percent below it.[29]

2. *Analyze data on cost drivers, participation rates, and employee satisfaction to gain insight into benefits usage and costs.* Here are some key questions to address. *Cost drivers*: What employee health conditions or behaviors are the most expensive? Health-plan providers and employers can then implement voluntary programs for affected groups, such as smoking-cessation programs. *Participation rates*: How many employees use wellness programs? Communicate the value of underused programs and consider implementing different ones. *Satisfaction*: How do employees rate their health plans or wellness benefits? That analysis could lead to changes in plan design or to new health-plan vendors.[30]

3. *Encourage the use of generic drugs.* Fully 95 percent of companies offer prescription drug program coverage.[31] Given the dramatic increases in drug costs, it is not surprising that generics now account for 89 percent of all prescriptions dispensed at pharmacies.[32]

4. *Contract directly with health care providers.* Organizations are designing plans to steer employees to health care providers that offer high-quality, competitively priced care, whether those are doctors, hospitals, or national centers of excellence that specialize in areas such as cancer treatment, eye, or joint surgery. Others are narrowing the number of in-network doctors and hospitals, or offering tiered networks that reduce out-of-pocket costs for employees.[33]

5. *Use a managed-care approach.* **Managed care** relies on a *gatekeeper* system of cost controls. The **gatekeeper** is a primary-care physician who monitors the medical history and care of each employee and his or her family. The doctor orders testing, makes referrals to specialists, and recommends hospitalization, surgery, or outpatient care, as appropriate. Managed care takes a variety of forms. Table 12–2 presents a summary of alternative types of managed-care plans: health maintenance organizations (HMOs), preferred provider organizations (PPOs), and point-of-service (POS) plans. Evidence indicates that when given a choice, employees are moving away from the more stringent HMO and POS plans toward preferred provider organizations, even though PPOs are more expensive. In 2019, for example, 44 percent of covered workers were enrolled in PPOs, 19 percent in HMOs, and 7 percent in POS plans. Another 30 percent were enrolled in high-deductible health plans with a savings option.[34]

6. *Adopt a* **consumer-driven health plan (CDHP)**. A CDHP is a health insurance plan that allows employers, employees, or both to set aside pretax money to help pay for qualified medical expenses not covered by their health plan. To establish a CDHP, the employer must offer a high-deductible insurance plan where higher coverages don't kick in until the participant pays a larger deductible, as compared with traditional health plan offerings that may have a lower deductible. If an employer offers a qualifying plan, it may offer participants the option to save part of their income in a tax-advantaged savings account. Three different types are available[35]:

   ▪ **HSA**—A health savings account (HSA) is an employee-owned account designed to work specifically with a qualified high-deductible plan to allow tax-free payments of current and future qualified medical expenses. Employees, the employer, or both may contribute a maximum amount set by the IRS annually ($3,550 and $7,100, respectively, for individual and family coverage in 2020).

Table 12–2			
THE ABCs OF MANAGED CARE*			
Plan	**How it works**	**What you pay**	**Benefits**
Health maintenance organization (HMO)	A specified group of doctors and hospitals provides the care. A gatekeeper must approve all services before they are performed.	Average deductible for family coverage is $2,905. Copays average $30 per visit depending on the service performed.	Virtually all services are covered, including preventive care. Out-of-pocket costs tend to be lower than for any other managed-care plan.
Preferred provider organization (PPO)	In-network care comes from a specified group of physicians and hospitals. Patients can pay extra to get care from outside the network. There generally is no gatekeeper.	The typical yearly family deductible is $2,883. The plan pays 80 to 100 percent for what is done within the network but only 50 to 70 percent for services rendered outside it.	Preventive services may be covered. There are lower deductibles and copayments for in-network care than for out-of-network care.
Point-of-service (POS) plan	POSs combine the features of HMOs and PPOs. Patients can get care in or out of the network, but there is an in-network gatekeeper who must approve all services.	In addition to an average deductible of $4,347, there is a flat (average $30) fee for in-network care, and patients pay 20 to 60 percent of the bills for care they get outside the network.	Preventive services are generally covered. And there are low out-of-pocket costs for the care patients get in the network.

*Sources of 2019 deductible amounts: Kaiser Family Foundation (2019), op. cit.

- **FSA**—In a flexible spending account (FSA), employees can save pretax income (up to $2,750 in 2020) to pay for qualifying health-care expenditures, such as prescriptions or copays. At the end of each plan year, employers may allow a 2.5-month grace period or permit up to $500 to be rolled over to the next year. The employee loses any remaining unused balances that haven't been spent on qualified medical expenses by the end of the plan year or grace period.
- **HRA**—A health reimbursement arrangement (HRA) is an employer-owned account that works with employer-provided health-care plans and is solely funded by the employer with tax-free contributions. Employees benefit from tax-free reimbursements of qualified expenses up to a limit that the employer determines.

High-deductible plans are attractive for many people, especially young, healthy workers who are less likely to generate big health-care bills, making the higher deductible less of a concern and lowering their monthly premiums.[36]

Toward the Future

A variety of trends are helping to shape the future in health-care coverage. Here are a few of them[37]:

- Expect to see more experimentation with health-care designs as electronic medical records are introduced, more research is conducted on medical effectiveness, and results are built into treatment and payment structures.
- Fewer companies will provide health-care coverage for retirees; that means the government and individuals will pay in the decades ahead, although large employers may facilitate value purchasing.
- Expect to see refinements in payments for wellness and preventive care, chronic disease, and prescription drugs. The good news is that 73 percent of American workers would enroll in employer wellness programs to improve personal health if offered an incentive. At Johnson & Johnson, employees who enroll in such programs get a $500 discount on their insurance premiums. About 90 percent of them participate.[38]
- As for consumer-driven health care, it will continue to grow—unless the plans fail to show proven savings, or if workers find themselves stuck only with the higher bills and none of the new information and control that are supposed to be part of the package.
- Finally, as individuals, we are increasingly expected to check prices and shop around before undergoing surgery or popping a pill. Some may not like this, but failure to do so could cost them thousands of dollars. Beyond that, it could mean a lot to their health!

Other Medical Coverage

Medical coverage in areas such as employee assistance programs and mental health is offered by about 79 percent and 83 percent of large companies, respectively.[39] As for dental care, dental HMOs, PPOs, and indemnity (traditional fee-for-service) plans are growing fast. As with medical HMOs, a dental plan is usually paid a set annual fee per employee (usually about 10 to 15 percent of the amounts paid for medical benefits). Dental coverage is a standard inclusion for 97 percent of U.S. employers. Fully 91 percent offer their employees some form of vision care insurance as well.[40]

Maternity and Paternity Leaves

The share of moms who are working either full- or part-time in the United States has increased over the past half-century from 51 percent to 72 percent, and almost half of two-parent families now include two full-time working parents. At the same time, fathers—virtually all of whom are working—are taking on more child care responsibilities, as fatherhood has grown to encompass far more than just earning money to provide for one's family.

Despite these transformations, the United States is the only country among 92 nations that does not require any paid leave for new parents. The only federal law that guarantees parental leave in the United States—the Family and Medical Leave Act—is unpaid, and it only applies to employers with more than 50 employees. As we noted in Chapter 4, the law protects a mom's or dad's job for up to 12 weeks after childbirth or adoption. In addition, if both parents work for the same company, it only needs to offer a total of 12 weeks to split between the two of them.[41]

As of 2020, only New York, California, New Jersey, New Hampshire, and Washington, DC, require paid parental leave. Yet a number of companies now offer it voluntarily.

Citigroup, Facebook, Juniper Networks, TD Ameritrade, and Alphabet (the parent company of Google) offer 4 months of paid parental leave. American Express, Estee Lauder, and Twittter offer 5 months, DocuSign offers 6 months, and Prudential offers 6.5 months. Why? Because years of research have shown that such policies have health and career benefits for both parents.

Sick-Leave Programs

Sick leave programs provide short-term insurance to workers against loss of wages due to short-term illness. In 2020, emergency legislation, the Families First Coronavirus Response Act, required employers with fewer than 500 employees to provide up to 80 hours of paid sick leave to employees who are sick, need to quarantine or self-isolate, care for a sick or quarantined family member, or care for a child whose school has been closed. Employers received a tax credit to fully offset this benefit. As of 2019, 95 percent of U.S. firms offered stand-alone paid sick-leave benefits.[42] To control potential abuse of these benefits, 62 percent of firms offer paid-time-off (PTO) plans that combine sick leave, vacation, and personal days into one plan.[43] The number of PTO days that employees receive varies across employers. For example, at Pinnacol Assurance, employees receive 20 days of PTO at the start of employment, 25 after 5 years, and 30 after 9 years. Employees manage their own sick and vacation time and are free to take a day off without having to offer an explanation. If an employee uses up all of this time before the end of the year and needs a day off, that time is unpaid.

What about unused sick time? "Buy-back" programs allow employees to convert unused time to vacation or to accrue time and be paid for a portion of it. Employers rate PTO plans as the most effective of all absence-control programs.[44]

Pensions

A **pension** is a promise by an employer to pay workers who are eligible a set amount of money after they retire. In its financial statements, the employer is required to show that promise as a liability.[45]

In 1974, Congress passed the Employee Retirement Income Security Act (ERISA; see Table 12-1). It does not require employers to establish pension plans or to provide a minimum level of benefits. Instead, it regulates the operation of a pension plan once it has been established. ERISA was enacted to protect the interests of participants and their beneficiaries by requiring the disclosure to them of financial and other information concerning the plan. It also established standards of conduct for plan fiduciaries (individuals who act on behalf of others in circumstances that assume a relationship of trust and confidence), and it provides appropriate remedies for abuses and access to the federal courts.[46]

Money set aside by employers to cover pension obligations has become the nation's largest source of capital, with total assets (private employers plus local, state, and federal government pensions) of $25.3 trillion.[47] This is an enormous force in the nation's (and the world's) capital markets.

To ensure that covered private-sector workers will receive their accrued benefits even if their companies fail, ERISA created the Pension Benefit Guaranty Corporation (PBGC). This agency acts as an insurance company, collecting annual premiums from companies with defined-benefit plans (in 2020, $83 per participant for single-employer plans and $30 per participant for multi-employer plans) that spell out specific payments upon retirement.[48] A company can still walk away from its obligation to pay pension benefits to employees entitled to receive them, but it must then hand over up to 30 percent of its net worth to the PBGC for distribution to the affected employees.

The PBGC insures nearly 25,000 single-employer pension plans that cover 24 million workers and retirees. In 2019, the PBGC paid more than $6 billion in benefits to 932,000 retirees and their surviving beneficiaries because their pension plans could not.[49] If a company terminates its pension plan, the PBGC guarantees the payment of *vested* benefits–that is, when receipt of the benefits does not depend on future service, up to a maximum amount set by law. In 2020, that maximum amount for a worker at full retirement age was $69,750.[50]

Despite these protections, the consequences of pension plan termination can still be devastating to some pensioners. Executives whose accrued benefits are bigger than the PBGC's guaranteed limits can see their monthly checks shrivel. Employees who haven't worked at a company long enough to be vested (at least 3 years for "cliff vesting" of 100 percent of benefits, up to 6 years for "graduated vesting"[51])–aren't entitled to any benefits. So they wind up having to get by with less to support them than they had planned. Nevertheless, as a matter of social policy, it is important that, as retirees, most workers end up getting nearly all that is promised to them–and they do.

How Pension Plans Work   Contributions to pension funds are typically managed by trustees or outside financial institutions, frequently insurance companies. As an incentive for employers to begin and maintain such plans, the government defers taxes on the pension contributions and their earnings. Retirees pay taxes on the money as they receive it.

Traditionally, most big corporate plans have been **defined-benefit plans**, under which an employer promises to pay a retiree a stated pension, often expressed as a percentage of preretirement pay. In 2019, 21 percent of companies offered them, including such big companies as ExxonMobil, Coca-Cola, United Parcel Service, and 3M.[52] The most common formula is 1.5 percent of average salary over the last 5 years prior to retirement ("final average pay") times the number of years employed. In determining final average pay, the company may use base pay alone or base pay plus bonuses and other compensation. An example of a monthly pension for a worker earning a final average pay of $75,000 a year, as a function of years of service, is shown in Figure 12-3. When combined with Social Security benefits, that percentage is often about 50 percent of final average pay.[53] The company then pays into the fund each year whatever is needed to cover expected benefit payments.

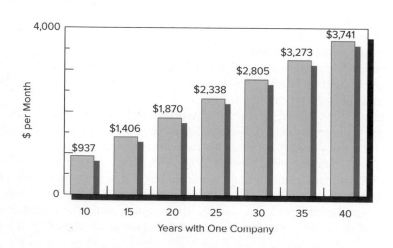

Figure 12–3

Monthly pension for a worker whose final average pay is $75,000 per year.

A second type of pension plan, popular either as a support to an existing defined-benefit plan or as a stand-alone retirement-savings vehicle, is called a **defined-contribution plan**. Fully 93 percent of U.S. employers offered some form of such a plan in 2019.[54] Examples include stock bonuses, savings plans, profit-sharing, and various kinds of employee stock-ownership plans. Brief descriptions of five types of such plans are shown in Table 12-3.

Defined-contribution plans fix a rate for employer contributions to the fund. Future benefits depend on how fast the fund grows. Such plans therefore favor young employees who are just beginning their careers because they contribute for many years. Defined-benefit plans favor older, long-service workers—and they are on their way out as more employers freeze or terminate them. In recent years, for example, companies such as DuPont, General Electric, IBM, and L.L.Bean froze their defined-benefit plans and shifted employees into defined-contribution plans.[55]

Defined-contribution plans have great appeal for employers because a company will never owe more than what was contributed. However, because the amount of benefits received depends on the investment performance of the monies contributed, employees cannot be sure of the size of their retirement checks.

A third type of pension plan is known as a **cash-balance plan**, offered by 5 percent of large employers.[56] Under it, everyone gets the same, steady annual credit toward an eventual pension, adding to his or her pension account "cash balance." Employers contribute a percentage of an employee's pay, typically 4 percent. The balance earns an interest credit, usually around 5 percent. It is portable when the employee leaves, but cash-balance plans do not vest any sooner than traditional

Table 12–3

FIVE TYPES OF DEFINED-CONTRIBUTION PENSION PLANS

- **Profit-sharing plan.** The company puts a designated amount of its profits into each employee's account and then invests the money. ESOPs are a form of profit-sharing.

- **ESOP.** An employee stock-ownership plan pays off in company stock. Each employee gets shares of company stock that are deposited into a retirement account. Dividends from the stock are added to the account.

- **401(k) plan.** A program in which an employee can deduct up to $19,500 of his or her income (in 2020, $26,000 for workers over 50) from taxable income and place the money into a personal retirement account. Many employers add matching funds, and the combined contributions grow tax-free until they are withdrawn.

- **Money-purchase plan.** The employer contributes a set percentage of each employee's salary, up to 25 percent of net income, or $57,000 (whichever is less), to each employee's account. Employees must be vested to be eligible to receive funds. Withdrawals after age 59½ are taxed at ordinary income tax rates.

- **Simplified employee pension (SEP).** Under SEP, a small-business employer can contribute up to the lesser of 100 percent of an employee's salary or $57,000. The employee is vested immediately for the amount paid into the account. The employee cannot withdraw any funds before age 59½ without penalty.

Sources: IRS. (2019, Nov. 6). 401(k) contribution limit increases to $19,500 for 2020; catch-up limit rises to $6,500. Retrieved from *https://www.irs.gov/newsroom/401k-contribution-limit-increases-to-19500-for-2020-catch-up-limit-rises-to-6500* on May 6, 2020.

pension plans. One big advantage, however, is that cash-balance plans provide insulation from stock market swings that can whipsaw 401(k) accounts.[57]

For the young, 4 percent of pay each year is more than what they were accruing under a defined-benefit plan. But for those nearing retirement, the amount is far less. So an older employee who is switched into a cash-balance system can find his or her eventual pension reduced by 20 to 50 percent, and in rare cases even more.[58]

HR BUZZ

Retirement Benefits and Small Business*

THE SUPER 401(K)

Devon Energy of Oklahoma City, Oklahoma, like 38 percent of other employers, is automatically enrolling workers in its 401(k) plan at a 3 percent contribution level. What is different, though, is that rather than rely on employees to take the initiative to save, Devon plans to save for them—by making annual contributions to these accounts in line with what it would have spent to provide a traditional pension benefit.

Depending on an employee's tenure, the company will put 8 to 16 percent of annual compensation into the 401(k), regardless of whether the employee kicks in a dime. For those who put money into the plan, the company will also match it dollar for dollar up to 6 percent of salary. Add it all up, and Devon workers who divert 6 percent of their pay into the super 401(k) could receive as much as 22 percent per year from the company.

Devon is not alone. Communications company Broadcom offers a maximum match of 5 percent of pay. The company also contributes another 5 percent, whether or not the employee contributes. On top of that, employees vest immediately. HR executives at both firms are betting that the super 401(k) will be attractive to younger workers, who prefer such plans, in part because they can take the money with them if they change jobs.

---

*Sources: Hymowitz, C., and Collins, M. (2014, Mar. 16). In 401(k) plans, a little more makes a big difference. *Bloomberg Businessweek*, pp. 47–49. Society for Human Resource Management. (2019, Jun.). *2019 Employee Benefits.* Alexandria, VA: Author. Tergesen, A. (2007, Dec. 10). Redrawing the route to retirement. *BusinessWeek*, pp. 78–82.

At a broader level, empirical research shows that employees differ in their preferences for various features of defined-benefit, defined-contribution, and cash-balance plans. Allowing employees to choose plans that are consistent with their personal characteristics and needs should lead to greater satisfaction with the plans and serve as an effective tool in attracting and retaining employees.[59]

The Pension Protection Act (PPA) of 2006   This law made extensive changes to the Employee Retirement Income Security Act (ERISA) of 1974.[60] For example, it:

- Establishes higher limits on the annual amount of compensation that can be taken into account for retirement-plan benefits.
- Establishes higher limits on the annual amount of permissible benefit and employer contributions.
- Allows individuals age 50 and older to make "catch-up" salary-deferral contributions.

In addition, the PPA permits automatic-enrollment of employees. It also permits employers to adopt cash-balance pension plans and to convert existing defined-benefit plans into cash-balance plans. Finally, the PPA also provides "safe-harbor" protection for employers if they:

- Automatically enroll workers in the company plan at a default savings-contribution rate.
- Establish default investments–for example, those that automatically invest a worker's 401(k) contributions in an age-appropriate "life-cycle" diversified fund (larger equity exposure for younger participants, greater fixed income for older ones).
- Automatically escalate workers' contributions to their 401(k) accounts on a periodic basis.

Under the PPA, 401(k) participants can still exercise individual control over their investments if they want to, but the law encourages sponsors to set up 401(k)s in a manner that helps workers to help themselves simply by doing nothing. By 2019, 42 percent of employers adopted automatic enrollment.[61]

Social Security

Table 12–1 outlined provisions for this program. Social Security is an income-maintenance program, not a pension program. It is the nation's best defense against poverty for the elderly, and it has worked well. Social Security lifts about 35 percent of older Americans out of poverty by providing regular, guaranteed income.[62] Table 12–4 shows average Social Security benefits for 2020.[63]

Current Social Security recipients are benefiting from the massive surplus accumulated in the first decade of the 21st century, as baby boomers hit their peak earning potential. This will allow full payment of scheduled benefits on a timely basis until 2035. After that, benefits would need to be reduced by about 25 percent to match revenue.[64] Remember, Social Security is a pay-as-you-go system. Payroll taxes earned by current workers are distributed to pay benefits for those who are already retired. Right now there are 2.8 workers for every retiree in our society, but by 2040 there will be only 2.2 workers per retiree.[65] In addition, people are living substantially longer. In 2020, the life expectancy for 65-year-old men and women is 84 and 86.5 years, respectively. To meet such long-term funding needs, the system will have to be reformed soon–by raising revenues, adjusting benefits for high versus low earners, or some combination of the two.[66]

Table 12–4

AVERAGE 2020 SOCIAL SECURITY BENEFITS—MONTHLY

Retired worker	$1,503
Retired couple	2,531
Disabled worker	1,258
Disabled worker with a spouse and child	2,176
Widow or widower	1,422
Widow or widower with two children	2,934

INTERNATIONAL APPLICATION
Social Security in Other Countries

An ever-increasing number of countries are publicizing their social security programs on the World Wide Web. For a listing of them, see *www.ssa.gov/policy/docs/progdesc/ssptw/*. Here is a brief sample of countries that have adopted pension programs that combine social security with private retirement accounts.

In Britain, workers can opt out of part of the state pension system by applying up to 44 percent of their social security tax to their own private individual investment accounts. Japan, Finland, Sweden, France, and Switzerland have similar programs. In these countries, the social-security component of the pension system remains on a pay-as-you-go basis in which current tax receipts are used to pay for both current benefits and other government programs.

In contrast, Chile's retirement system is 100 percent privatized, with a mandatory 10 percent of employees' pay going into individual accounts. Australia is moving to a privatization plan that calls for 9 percent of workers' pay to go into private retirement accounts, up from 6 percent previously. The employer chooses a menu of investment options, which employees can use to allocate their retirement savings.

Singapore uses a payroll tax to fund retirement through a mandatory savings scheme that works as a private pension system. Employees must contribute about 20 percent of their salaries to their individually owned accounts, with employers contributing another 13 percent. At full retirement age (62), a worker gets a lump-sum payment equal to the total worker and employer contributions, plus at least 2.5 percent in compound interest. At age 55, however, workers must put about $42,000 in a retirement account to ensure income after age 62. Employees can withdraw money from their retirement funds to purchase housing (or to pay for a child's education or for medical expenses); as a result, 80 percent of Singapore's citizens own their own residences. If an employee is dissatisfied with the return earned by the public fund, he or she can transfer the account to investments in the Singapore stock market or other approved vehicles. The asset balance in a Singaporean's retirement fund passes to his or her beneficiaries upon death. Among the countries that have systems similar to Singapore's are India, Kenya, Malaysia, Zambia, and Indonesia.[a]

---

[a]Social Security Administration. (n.d.). Social security programs throughout the world. Retrieved from *www.ssa.gov/policy/docs/progdesc/ssptw/* on May 6, 2020. Lev, M. A. (2005, Mar. 2). Singapore's plan for retirees offers lessons for U.S. *Chicago Tribune*, p. 3.

Keep in mind, however, that Social Security was never intended to cover 100 percent of retirement expenses. For a worker earning $60,000 a year, for example, experts estimate that he or she will need about 75 percent of that in retirement. Social Security will replace about 40 percent of preretirement income; pensions and personal savings will have to make up the rest. How does this compare to the actual distribution of retirees' income?

Figure 12-4 shows the distribution of retirees' income, on average. Note that 54 percent comes from Social Security plus pensions; the rest comes primarily from personal savings and current earnings in retirement. By contrast, the percentage of final salary that Social Security replaces depends on the actual final salary of the retiree. For a worker whose final salary is $100,000, Social Security replaces about 33 percent of that in retirement.[67]

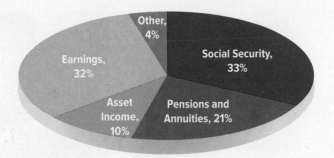

Figure 12–4

Where retirees get their income.
Source: U.S. Department of Health and Human Services. (2013). *A profile of older Americans: 2012.* Retrieved from *www.aoa. gov/AgingStatistics/Profile/ 2012/docs/2012profile. pdf* on June 11, 2014.

Unemployment Insurance

Although 97 percent of the workforce is covered by federal and state unemployment insurance laws, each worker must meet eligibility requirements in order to receive benefits. That is, an unemployed worker must (1) be able and available to work and be actively seeking work; (2) not have refused suitable employment; (3) not be unemployed because of a labor dispute (except in Rhode Island and New York); (4) not have left a job voluntarily; (5) not have been terminated for gross misconduct; and (6) have been employed previously in a covered industry or occupation, earning a designated minimum amount for a minimum amount of time. Many claims are disallowed for failure to satisfy one or more of these requirements.

The unemployment insurance system is a financial partnership between the federal and state governments. It is intended to be countercyclical—that is, to accumulate and hold significant funds during good economic times, pay out benefits during bad ones, and stimulate stagnant economies.[68]

Every unemployed worker's benefits are charged against one or more companies. The more money paid out on behalf of a firm, the higher the unemployment insurance rate for that firm (see Table 12-1). The tax rate may fall to 0 percent in some states for employers who have had no recent claims by former employees, and it may rise to 10 percent for organizations with large numbers of layoffs.

Benefits ordinarily last 26 weeks in most states. During the coronavirus pandemic, Congress expanded the eligibility for benefits, added 13 weeks of coverage, and an additional $600 per week for four months. The average weekly payment rose to $978 from the $378 that was paid, on average in late 2019.[69] Benefits are subject to federal income taxes. In general, they are based on a percentage of a worker's earnings over a recent 52-week period, up to a state maximum amount. In 2019, weekly benefits replaced about 45 percent of laid-off workers' wages.[70]

Severance Pay

Severance pay is not legally required and, because of unemployment compensation, many firms do not offer it. However, severance pay has been used extensively by some firms that are downsizing in order to provide a smooth outflow of employees.[71] This is a good example of the strategic use of compensation. For example, General Motors offered workers at bankrupt parts maker Delphi severance payments up to $140,000.[72] In Germany, as part of a restructuring effort, Volkswagen offered severance packages of as much as €249,480, or about $385,000 each, to 85,000 workers.[73] In general, however, as a 19-country study revealed, severance policies appear to be well established in both emerging markets and developed economies, with 80 percent and 73 percent, respectively, having formal, written policies in place.[74]

Unemployment insurance benefits provide a "safety net" for individuals who qualify. Other agencies help them prepare for new jobs by providing services such as résumé and interview preparation.
FangXiaNuo/Getty Images

Length of service, organization level, size of the organization, and cause of the termination are key factors that affect the amount of severance pay. For example, the typical employee gets 1 to 2 weeks of severance pay per year of service, whereas senior executives may get up to a month's pay for each year of service or whatever was negotiated in an employment contract.[75] Chief executive officers with employment contracts may receive 2 to 3 years' salary in the event of a takeover.[76]

To avoid legal problems, offer the same severance agreement to similarly situated employees and don't require them to waive their right to file a charge with a government agency or to participate in a government investigation. Don't try to prevent employees from filing a legal claim after the waiver is executed, and don't require employees who file a whistle-blower claim to forgo their right to receive a monetary reward.[77]

Payments for Time Not Worked

Included in this category are such benefits as the following:

Vacations	Paid parental leave
Holidays	Grievances and negotiations
Reporting time	Sabbatical leaves

Less than a quarter of global workers disconnect from work during a vacation, and of those, Millennials are least likely to go off the grid.[78] Even worse, nearly 60 percent of American workers leave vacation time unused. In contrast, the French take the most vacation, typically using all 30 days available to them.[79] Numerous studies show that job stress is far and away the major source of stress for American adults. Increased levels of job stress, the perception of having little control but lots of demands, are associated with increased rates of heart attack, hypertension, and other disorders.[80] The one thing a person can do to avoid the negative effects of chronic stress and burnout is to take time to recharge.

Here are four science-based reasons to use your vacation days: (1) reduce stress, (2) cut your risk for a heart attack, (3) improve productivity, and (4) sleep better. Research shows that the mental health benefits are also significant. The more active you are with your leisure time–and the more control you have over your free time–the more likely you are to be satisfied with your life overall. Beyond that, workers who take regular time to relax are less likely to experience burnout, making them more creative and productive than their overworked, under-rested counterparts.[81] Bottom line: Vacations can improve our health, motivation, relationships, job performance, and perspective and give us the break we need to return to our lives and jobs refreshed and better able to handle whatever arises in our daily work.[82]

To provide even more encouragement, some companies actually help pay for your vacation. Every February, e-commerce firm Bonanza physically moves its office to a tropical location for the month and gives employees five bonus days off to enjoy the vacation. Software solutions company BambooHR offers employees what they call "paid-paid vacation"–$2,000 each year to travel as they please.[83]

AMERICAN EXPRESS, CHOBANI, IKEA,

Paid Parental Leaves*

Increasing work demands intensify the strain on families already stretched thin by the rise of two-worker households. As employers claim more time from both spouses, juggling the needs of children, aging parents, and other family members verges on the impossible. Yet smart employers know that accommodating family needs can be an advantage in the contest for talent. They know that employees who stagger into work after a sleepless night caring for a sick child or a hospitalized parent aren't exactly at their best. Here's what three progressive companies are doing.

American Express offers paid parental leave for 20 weeks for all U.S.-based salaried employees–mothers and fathers. Greek-yogurt company Chobani offers 6 weeks of fully paid parental leave for both mothers and fathers. All full-time hourly and salaried workers are eligible. IKEA also treats hourly and salaried workers the same. Work for IKEA for at least a year and receive full base pay for the first 6 weeks of leave and half of that for 6 more weeks. Stay with IKEA for 3 years or more and receive 8 weeks of full pay and 8 weeks of half pay. The firm offers 6 to 8 weeks of short-term disability regardless of employee tenure. This boomlet in flexible workplace policies is a welcome sign that employers are starting to understand the costs of an always-on workforce.

*Sources: Zillman, C. (2016, Dec. 6). Ikea is giving all U.S. employees paid parental leave no matter how many hours they work. *Fortune.* Retrieved from *http://fortune.com/2016/12/06/ikea-maternity-leave-parental/* on Dec. 9, 2016. Cahill, J. (2016, Sept. 16). Is work-life balance becoming less of an oxymoron? *Crain's Chicago Business.* Retrieved from *www.chicagobusiness.com/article/20160916/BLOGS10/160909830/is-work-life-balance-becoming-less-of-an-oxymoron* on Sept. 18, 2016. Sahadi, J. (2016, Dec. 12). American Express will give all parents 20 weeks of paid leave. *CNNMoney.* Retrieved from *http://money.cnn.com/2016/12/12/pf/paid-parental-leave-american-express/index.html* on Dec. 14, 2016. Margolin, E. (2016, Oct. 6). Chobani offers moms, dads 6 weeks of parental leave at full pay. *NBC News.* Retrieved from *http://www.nbcnews.com/business/business-news/chobani-offers-moms-dads-6-weeks-parental-leave-full-pay-n660701* on Oct. 8, 2016.

Employee Services

A broad group of benefits falls into the employee-services category. Employees qualify for them purely by virtue of their membership in the organization, not because of performance or merit. Some examples include the following:

Tuition aid[84]	Thrift and short-term savings plans
Credit unions	Stock-purchase plans
Auto insurance	Fitness and wellness programs
Food service	Moving and transfer allowances
Company car	Transportation and parking[85]
Career clothing	Merchandise purchasing
Financial planning[86]	Professional-association memberships
Legal services	Christmas bonuses
Counseling	Service and seniority awards
Child adoption	Umbrella liability coverage
Child care	Social activities
Elder care	Referral awards
Gift matching	Purchase of used equipment
Student-loan aid[87]	Family leaves
Domestic-partner benefits	Flexible work arrangements

National survey data now indicate that people are more attached and committed to organizations that offer work–life benefits, regardless of the extent to which they benefit personally from them.[88] Such benefits include onsite child care, subsidized child care on site and off site, child adoption, elder care, flexible work schedules (flex-time and flex-place), and the ability to convert sick days into personal days that

---

ETHICAL DILEMMA
What to Do with Bad News?*

Consider this situation. You are the chief HR officer (CHRO) of a company whose stock is publicly traded. A supervisor tells you about an impending penalty from a federal regulatory agency, a penalty large enough to make headlines and to slam the company's stock price. The supervisor wants you to convince the CEO to begin making 401(k) matches with cash instead of company stock and to advise employees to move their company stock in the 401(k) plan into one of the other fund selections.

As CHRO, you are a member of the company's executive committee but not a member of the committee that oversees the 401(k) plan. Administration of the plan is outsourced to a company that provides general financial education to all employees on saving for retirement in the 401(k) plan but that offers no third-party advice on how the funds should be invested. What should you do? Would doing something about it constitute insider trading?

Source: What to do with bad news. (2002, July). HR, pp. 58-63.

employees can use to care for a sick child or family member (see the HR Buzz box on paid parental leaves).

Following the U.S. Supreme Court's decision to allow same-sex couples to marry in 2015, 86 percent of employers now provide benefits to same-sex spouses. However, less than half provide benefits to unmarried same-sex domestic partners.[89] The main reason is to provide consistent coverage for opposite-sex and same-sex couples.[90]

BENEFITS ADMINISTRATION

Benefits and Equal Employment Opportunity

Equal employment opportunity requirements also affect the administration of benefits. Consider as examples health-care coverage and pensions. The Age Discrimination in Employment Act has eliminated mandatory retirement at any age. It also requires employers to continue the same group health insurance coverage offered to younger employees to employees over the age of 70. This is another example of government **cost shifting** to the private sector.

With regard to pensions, the IRS considers a plan *discriminatory* unless the employer's contribution for the benefit of lower-paid employees covered by the plan is comparable to contributions for the benefit of higher-paid employees. To illustrate, consider the 401(k) salary-reduction plan described briefly in Table 12-3. The plan permits significant savings out of pretax compensation, produces higher take-home pay, and results in lower Social Security taxes. The catch: *The plan has to be available to everyone in any company that implements it.* Maximum employee contributions each year ($19,500 in 2020 for workers under 50, $26,000 for those 50 or over) are based on *average* company participation. Poor participation by lower-paid employees curbs the ability of the higher-paid to make full use of the 401(k).[91]

Costing Benefits

Despite the high cost of benefits, many employees take them for granted. A major reason for this is that employers have failed to do in-depth cost analyses of their benefit programs and thus have not communicated their value to employees. There are four approaches to express the costs of benefit programs. Although each has value individually, a combination of all four often enhances their impact on employees. The four methods are[92]:

- *Annual cost of benefits for all employees:* valuable for developing budgets and for describing the total cost of the benefits program.
- *Cost per employee per year:* the total annual cost of each benefits program divided by the number of employees participating in it.
- *Percentage of payroll:* the total annual cost divided by total annual payroll (this figure is valuable in comparing benefits costs across organizations).
- *Cost per hour:* the total annual cost of benefits divided by the total number of hours worked by all employees during the year.

Table 12-5 presents a company example of actual benefits costs for a fictitious firm named Sun Inc. The table includes all four methods of costing benefits. Can you find an example of each?

Table 12–5

EMPLOYEE BENEFITS: THE FORGOTTEN EXTRAS

Listed below are the benefits for the average full-time employee of Sun Inc. (annual salary $80,000°).

Benefit	Who pays	Sun's annual cost	Percentage of base earnings	What the employee receives
Health, dental, and life insurance	Sun and employee	$6,408	8.01	Comprehensive health and dental plus life insurance equivalent to the employee's salary
Holidays	Sun	4,000	5.00	13 paid holidays
Annual leave (vacation)	Sun	3,080	3.85	10 days of vacation per year (additional days starting with sixth year of service)
Sick days	Sun	3,688	4.61	12 days annually
Company retirement	Sun	7,104	8.88	Vested after 5 years of service
Social Security	Sun and employee	6,120	7.65	Retirement and disability benefits as provided by law
Workers' compensation and unemployment insurance	Sun	800	1.00	Compensation if injured on duty and if eligible; income while seeking employment
Total		$31,200, or $15.00 per hour	39.00	

°The dollar amount and percentages will differ slightly depending on the employee's salary. If an employee's annual salary is less than $80,000, the percentage of base pay will be greater. If the employee's salary is greater than $80,000, the percentage will be less but the dollar amount will be greater. Benefit costs to Sun Inc. on behalf of 5,480 employees are almost $171 million per year.

Cafeteria, or Flexible, Benefits

The theory underlying the **cafeteria-benefits** approach is simple: Instead of all workers at a company getting the same benefits, each worker can choose among alternative options cafeteria-style. Thus, an elderly bachelor might pass up maternity coverage for additional pension contributions. A mother whose children are covered under her husband's health insurance may choose legal and auto insurance instead.

The typical plan works like this. Workers are offered a package of benefits that includes basic and optional items. Basics might include modest medical coverage, life insurance equal to a year's salary, vacation time based on length of service, and some retirement pay. Then employees can use flexible credits to choose among such additional benefits as full medical coverage, dental and eye care, more vacation time, additional disability income, and higher company payments to the retirement fund. Two studies examined employees' satisfaction with their benefits and understanding of them both before and after the introduction of a flexible-benefits plan. Both found substantial improvements in satisfaction and understanding after the plan was implemented.[93]

There are advantages for employers as well. Under conventional plans, employers risked alienating employees if they cut benefits, regardless of increases in the costs of coverage. Flexible plans allow them to pass some of the increases on to workers

IMPACT OF BENEFITS ON PRODUCTIVITY, QUALITY OF WORK LIFE, AND THE BOTTOM LINE

Generally speaking, employee benefits do not enhance productivity. Rather, they are powerful tools for attracting and retaining talent and for improving the quality of life of employees and their dependents. Today's employees want choices. In fact, 76 percent of Millennials say customized benefits increase loyalty to their employers, and the good news is that they don't always expect their employers to pay for these benefits.[a] As long as employees perceive that their total compensation is equitable and that their benefit options are priced fairly, benefits programs can achieve the strategic objectives set for them. The challenge for executives will be to maintain control over the costs of benefits while providing genuine value to employees in the benefits offered. If they can do this, everybody wins.

[a] MetLife. (2020). 2020 employee benefit trends study. Retrieved from *https://www.metlife.com /employee-benefit-trends/ebts2020-holistic-well-being-drives-workforce-success/* on May 7, 2020. Baker, A. (2017, May). Simple, modern, and personal approach to benefits communication and enrollment. *HR Professionals Magazine*, pp. 26, 27.

more easily. Instead of providing employees a set package of benefits, the employer says, "Based on your $80,000 annual salary, I promise you $24,000 to spend any way you want." If health-care costs soar, the employee–not the employer–decides whether to pay more or to take less coverage.

There's help for employees even under these circumstances if they work for firms that sponsor **flexible-spending accounts** (offered by 68 percent of firms). Employees can save for expenses such as additional health insurance or day care with pretax dollars, up to a specified amount ($2,750 in 2020). As a result, it's a win-win situation for both employer and employee.[94]

To realize these potential advantages, major communications efforts are needed to help employees understand their benefits fully. In fact, careful attention to communication can enhance recruitment efforts, help cut turnover, and make employees more aware of their total package of benefits.

SAFEGUARDING BENEFIT PLANS FROM CYBERATTACKS*　　　　　　HR BUZZ

Employees' health and retirement data–and account funds–are tempting targets for hackers. The cyber-risks to benefits plans are real, and the plans are particularly susceptible because they store large amounts of sensitive employee information and share it with multiple third parties. For example, when hackers breached more than 90 deferred-compensation retirement accounts of Chicago municipal employees they were able to access secured personal information and withdrew loans from

Sources: Merritt, J. (2020, March 14). Cybersecurity and employee benefit plans. Retrieved from *https:// www.lbmc.com/blog/cybersecurity-and-employee-benefit-plans/* on May 7, 2020. Schulberg, N. S., and Dubin, M. S. (2017, May). Cyberattacks on benefit plans: The risks and liabilities of data breaches. *Benefits Magazine*, pp. 22-27.

(continued)

58 accounts, totaling about $2.6 million. The city returned funds taken from participant accounts and offered credit-monitoring services to account holders.

Cyberthreats will continue to be a significant risk facing benefit plans, but they can be managed. Experts advise organizations to take steps such as the following:

- Develop and implement a framework for addressing cybersecurity issues.
- Address third-party vendor vulnerabilities that could add risk—for example, the electronic transfer of sensitive data to third parties.
- Back up sensitive data and store it off-network.
- Augment password access to data systems with multifactor authentication (a security system that requires more than one method of authentication from separate types of evidence, such as a code sent to one's smartphone).
- Increase investment in security software and systems, and get boards of directors more involved in security matters.
- Consider purchasing cyber-liability insurance.

Inevitably, benefit plans will continue to be targeted by cybercriminals who are encouraged by lax cybersecurity measures and motivated by black-market prices for participant data. Given the potential for significant harm to the plan and its participants from a data breach, plan sponsors and administrators should take proactive steps in order to mitigate these risks.

Communicating the Benefits

Try to make a list of good reasons a company should *not* make a deliberate effort to market its benefits package effectively. It will be a short list. Generally speaking, there are four broad objectives in communicating benefits:

1. To make employees *aware* of them. This can be done by reminding them of their coverages periodically and of how to apply for benefits when needed.
2. To help employees *understand* the benefits information they receive in order to take full advantage of the plans.
3. To make employees confident that they can *trust* the information they receive.
4. To show employees how their benefits will meet their needs and help them reach their personal goals. After all, it's their "hidden paycheck."[95]

A growing number of companies are personalizing their benefits packages.[96] After all, employees are used to getting personalized recommendations from Amazon and Netflix, and the same sort of approach is an emerging trend in benefits communication. Aircraft manufacturer Boeing personalizes benefits through its "Pay & Benefits Profile," accessed through the company's intranet portal. The profile includes salary and bonuses as well as special services that Boeing offers its employees, such as travel and child-care referral services, wellness programs from the Mayo Clinic, and elder-care services. Employees can see every component of their overall rewards rolled into a total-compensation statement, and they can see what those benefits cost the company. In addition, employees have access to interactive tools they can use for financial planning.[97]

During open-enrollment periods, employees spend, on average, only 17 minutes electing their benefits.[98] Those who don't fully understand the choices they make may be leaving money on the table. Employees need decision-support tools, like smartphone apps and electronic interfaces, together with tailored advice from trusted sources, to help them navigate benefits options and make choices that are right for them. As one observer noted, "Trying to give them all of that information during open enrollment is like cramming for a final."[99] Give employees a choice of communication channels, such as one-on-one meetings, benefits fairs, and online platforms that let employees track and manage their benefits. Provide ongoing information and education on how to make the best use of benefits.[100]

One channel that has proven particularly useful is video. Thanks to YouTube and smartphones, video is commonly found on the Internet, social media, and increasingly in employee-benefits communication. Videos are most effective when used to explain complex topics or when conveying emotional content, such as employee testimonials. Do they work? A 2017 study found that 78 percent of 173,000 employees who received a video e-mail "postcard" related to benefits viewed the video at least once. Of those, 94 percent took some action, such as logging on to online enrollment software and accessing benefits information.[101]

THE NEW WORLD OF EMPLOYEE BENEFITS

Evidence indicates a strong link between employee satisfaction with benefits programs and overall employee satisfaction and retention. Among those who are highly satisfied, 85 percent expect to be working for their employers 18 months hence, versus only 50 percent of those who are not satisfied with their benefits. Here are five areas that affect employee satisfaction profoundly: benefits technology, health insurance, programs to integrate financial wellness with physical and emotional health, help for caregivers, and student-loan repayment aid.

- **Benefits technology.** As Millennials become influencers and employers seek out technology solutions, the growth of decision-support technology using online platforms for benefits enrollment and management will continue. Thus, a tool from BenefitExpress helps employees choose a health plan based on factors such as how they expect to use the plan, family size, projected spending on prescription drugs, expected number of provider visits, and their financial capacity to pay out-of-pocket costs. Using artificial intelligence, the tool ranks the employers' available health plans based on information the employee provides. Navigators, concierge services, and virtual resources will help reduce the complexity of the decision-making process.[102]
- **Health insurance.** Expect to see more direct contracting with health-care providers and, in some cases, direct contributions that provide employees with subsidies to purchase health coverage on an exchange. The objective of direct contracting is to improve access to evidence-based care at higher quality and lower cost. Direct contributions to employees may appeal to those burdened by rising group-insurance costs, those who were previously uninsured, or those who previously had to pay for individual insurance with no subsidy from an employer.[103]

- **Integrating financial wellness with physical and emotional health.** One of the most important themes in employee benefits is prevention: limiting health-care claims by keeping employees and their families healthier. Financial struggles cause stress, anxiety, and unease in every aspect of life. Many companies are providing financial-planning tools and personal financial coaches to address these issues.[104] Others, like Starbucks, provide access to behavioral health services to include on-site and telehealth counseling. Travelers Insurance Companies thoroughly studied its own programs in this area and found that the funds it spent on health promotion helped it save $7.8 million in employee-benefits costs. That's a savings of $3.40 for every dollar spent. The biggest payoffs came from education programs, including efforts to discourage smoking and drinking and to encourage healthier diets.[105]

- **Help for caregivers.** More than one-sixth of working adults in the United States are also caregivers. Whether it is caring for children or aging parents, or spouses caring for each other during the coronavirus pandemic or during chronic illnesses, more organizations are offering care-assistance resources, care subsidies, and flexible work options. They are also expanding leave benefits for new parents. Microsoft even requires its U.S. suppliers with more than 50 employees to offer 12 weeks of paid parental leave to bring the benefits of workers indirectly employed by the company closer in line with those enjoyed by its own corporate workforce.[106]

- **Student-loan repayment aid.** To attract and keep debt-challenged workers, employers are creating benefit packages that not only help pay student debt off sooner, but also help them manage their expenses and forecast their financial needs. Insurance firm, Unum, for example, allows employees to exchange accrued but unused paid time off for payments against their student loans. Since Fidelity Investments began its program in 2016, almost 9,000 employees have saved $22.5 million in principal and interest. Currently 8 percent of organizations offer contributions to help employees repay their student loans, but expect to see that benefit grow rapidly.[107]

The upshot of all of these changes is that workers who are fortunate enough to be offered benefits that fit their life stages can expect to be more involved in decision making about those benefits and to be more satisfied with them.

SUMMARY

Managers need to think carefully about what they wish to accomplish by means of their benefits programs. At an average cost of almost 30 percent of base pay for every employee on the payroll, benefits represent substantial annual expenditures. Factors such as the following are important strategic considerations in the design of benefits programs: the long-term plans of a business, its stage of development, its projected rate of growth or downsizing, the characteristics of its workforce, legal requirements, the competitiveness of its overall benefits package, and its total compensation strategy.

IMPLICATIONS FOR MANAGEMENT PRACTICE

As you think about the design and implementation of employee benefit plans, consider three practical issues:[a]

1. What are you trying to accomplish with your benefits package? Review its ability to meet diverse employee needs and to achieve business goals. Survey employees to learn what benefits matter most to them and to ask what is missing.
2. Assess the value of enhancing demographically targeted programs, voluntary benefits, and wellness programs as a means of differentiating your benefits package.
3. Develop an effective strategy for communicating benefits regularly to all employees.

[a] Reed, E. H. (2020). 2020 financial benefits trends. *HR Professionals Magazine* 10(2), pp. 34, 35. *See also* Meckle, D. (2019). Cut through the benefits communication clutter. *HR Professionals Magazine* 9(8), p. 28. *See also* Schramm, J. (2016, July 1). Survey: employee benefits trends show shifting priorities. Retrieved from *www.shrm.org/hr-today/news/hr-magazine/0716/pages/employee-benefits-trends-show-shifting-priorities.aspx* on July 2, 2016.

There are three major components of the benefits package: security and health, payments for time not worked, and employee services. Despite the high cost of benefits, many employees take them for granted. A major reason for this is that employers have not done in-depth cost analyses or communicated the value of their benefits programs. This is a multimillion-dollar oversight. Certainly, the counseling that must accompany the wide array of offerings on the benefits menu, coupled with the use of personalized financial information, can do much to alleviate this problem.

KEY TERMS

vesting
doctrine of constructive receipt
anti-discrimination rule
contributory plans
noncontributory plans
protected health information
yearly renewable term insurance
flexible benefits
workers' compensation
long-term disability (LTD) plans
short-term disability plans
disability management
managed care
gatekeeper
health maintenance organization (HMO)

preferred provider organization (PPO)
point-of-service plan (POS)
consumer-driven health plan (CDHP)
pension
defined-benefit plans
defined-contribution plan
cash-balance plan
profit-sharing plan
employee stock-ownership program (ESOP)
401(k) plan
money-purchase plan
simplified employee pension (SEP)
cost shifting
cafeteria benefits
flexible-spending accounts

DISCUSSION QUESTIONS

12-1. What should a company do over the short and long term to maximize the use and value of its benefits choices to employees?

12-2. The new world of employee benefits is best described as "sharing costs, sharing risks." Discuss the impact of that philosophy on the broad areas of health care and pensions.

12-3. In terms of the "attract-retain-motivate" philosophy, how do benefits affect employee behavior?

12-4. What can large firms do to control health-care costs? What about small firms?

12-5. Your company has just developed a new, company-sponsored savings plan for employees. Develop a strategy to publicize the program and to encourage employees to participate in it.

12-6. A major problem with benefits is that many employees don't know much about them–until they need to use them. What can organizations do to deal with that problem?

12-7. How do voluntary benefits programs allow smaller companies to offer a wider array of benefits than they otherwise would be able to?

12-8. If you could change just one feature of the Patient Protection and Affordable Care Act to make it more effective, what would you suggest?

12-9. What changes might you suggest to Social Security to ensure that it can meet the needs of younger generations?

12-10. What might be some advantages and some disadvantages of cafeteria-style benefits?

APPLYING YOUR KNOWLEDGE

Case 12–1

Encouraging employees to save more for retirement

As you have seen in this chapter, many employers are offering company-sponsored savings programs known as 401(k) plans. While experts advise that workers need to save about 15 percent of their annual salaries each year to to be able to retire comfortably, many, if not most, do not save that much. In an attempt to change those behaviors, some employers are raising their contributions, both to attract and retain employees, and also to ensure that older workers retire on time to make room for younger ones. Read more about this issue here:

https://www.wsj.com/articles/u-s-companies-have-a-new-401-k-fix-spend-more-1500283804

Discussion Questions

1. Will generous 401(k) contributions attract and retain top talent?

2. During the coronavirus pandemic, and also during the Great Recession (2007-2009), many employers suspended or reduced their contributions to 401(k) plans. Should a firm's contributions be tied to its financial results each year?

3. Will automatic enrollment of all new hires and current employees in 401(k) plans, coupled with increasing contributions each year (unless an employee opts out), actually boost savings?

4. Should employees be able to take loans from their 401(k) plans during their working years?

REFERENCES

1. U.S. Department of Labor, Bureau of Labor Statistics. (2020, Mar. 19). Employer costs for employee compensation–December 2019. Retrieved from *https://www.bls.gov/news.release/pdf/ecec.pdf* on May 4, 2020.

2. Miller, S. (2020, Jan. 2). Perk up: 6 benefits trends to watch in 2020. *SHRM Online.* Retrieved from *https://www.shrm.org/resourcesandtools/hr-topics/benefits/pages/perk-up-six-key-benefit-trends-to-watch-in-2020.aspx* on Jan. 3, 2020. *See also* Miller, S. (2016a, Aug. 17). Parents rank flextime benefits ahead of salary. Retrieved from *www.shrm.org/resourcesandtools/hr-topics/benefits/pages/parents-rank-flextime-above-salary.aspx* on Aug. 18, 2016. *See also* Miller, S. (2016b, June 28). Labor demand gives push to paid time off benefits. Retrieved from *www.shrm.org/resourcesandtools/hr-topics/benefits/pages/pto-banks-parental-leave.aspx* on June 29, 2016.

3. Pryzbylski, D. J., and Payne, T. C. (2020, May 4). Do you have to bargain with your union over your coronavirus response measures? *National Law Review.* Retrieved from *https://www.natlawreview.com/article/do-you-have-to-bargain-your-union-over-your-coronavirus-response-measures* on May 4, 2020. *See also* Smith, A. (2007, Oct. 5). GM-UAW deal shows benefits' central role in labor negotiations. Retrieved from *www.shrm.org/LegalIssues/FederalResources/FederalLegalNews/Pages/XMS 023245.aspx* on Oct. 12, 2007.

4. Healy, D.(2019, Sept.) Meeting the benefits needs of five generations. *WorldatWork.* Retrieved from *https://www.worldatwork.org/workspan/articles/meeting-the-benefits-needs-of-five-generations* on Oct. 8, 2019. *See also* Shellenbarger, S. (2009, Mar. 18). Perking up: Some companies offer surprising new benefits. *The Wall Street Journal,* pp. B1, B2.

5. Bureau of Labor Statistics. (2020, Mar. 19). Employer costs for employee compensation–December 2019. Retrieved from *https://www.bls.gov/news.release/pdf/ecec.pdf* on May 4, 2020.

6. Society for Human Resource Management. (2017). Employee job satisfaction and engagement: The doors of opportunity are open. Retrieved from *https://www.shrm.org/hr-today/trends-and-forecasting/research-and-surveys/Documents/2017-Employee-Job-Satisfaction-and-Engagement-Executive-Summary.pdf* on May 4, 2020.

7. Gerhart, B., and Newman, J. M. (2020). *Compensation* (13th ed.). New York: McGraw-Hill.

8. U.S. Department of Labor. (2020). Families First Coronavirus Response Act: Employee Paid Leave rights. Retrieved from *www.dol.gov/agencies/whd/pandemic/ffcra-employee-paid-leave* on Apr. 30, 2020.

9. Ibid. *See also www.investopedia.com.*

10. Gerhart and Newman (2020), op. cit.

11. Gerhart and Newman (2020), op. cit.

12. U.S. Department of Health & Human Services. Privacy, security, and electronic health records. Retrieved from *www.hhs.gov/sites/default/files/ocr/privacy/hipaa/understanding/consumers/privacy-security-electronic-records.pdf* on June 5, 2017.

13. For a calculator to determine how much life insurance you need, go to *www.bankrate.com/calculators/insurance/life-insurance-calculator.aspx. See also www.smartmoney.com/personal-finance/insurance/how-much-life-insurance-do-you-need-12949.*

14. Society for Human Resource Management. (2019). 2019 employee benefits. Retrieved from *https://www.shrm.org/hr-today/trends-and-forecasting/research-and-surveys/pages/benefits19.aspx* on July 1, 2019.

15. National Safety Council. (2020). Injury facts: Workers' compensation costs. Retrieved from *https://injuryfacts.nsc.org/work/costs/workers-compensation-costs/* on May 5, 2020. *See also* Gerhart and Newman (2020), op. cit.

16. What does workers' compensation cost? Retrieved from *https://www.insureon.com/small-business-insurance/workers-compensation/cost* on May 5, 2020.

17. Society for Human Resource Management. (2020). Workers' compensation training for supervisors. Retrieved from *https://www.shrm.org/resourcesandtools/tools-and-samples/presentations/pages/workerscompensationtraining.aspx* on May 5, 2020.

18. Farm Bureau Financial Services. (2020, April 24). How does disability insurance work and do you need it? Retrieved from *https://www.fbfs.com/learning-center/everything-you-needed-to-know-about-disability-insurance* on May 5, 2020.

19. Young, L. (2009, Feb. 9). Weaving that safety net. *BusinessWeek*, p. 62. *See also* Clark, M. M., and Bates, S. (2003, Dec.). A torn safety net? *HRMagazine*. Retrieved from *www.shrm.org/Publications/hrmagazine/EditorialContent/Pages/1103clark.aspx* on July 21, 2008.

20. Society for Human Resource Management. (2019). 2019 employee benefits, op. cit. *See also* Miller, S. (2016, Oct. 12). Get disability benefits on employees' radar. Retrieved from *www.shrm.org/resourcesandtools/hr-topics/benefits/pages/get-disability-benefits-on-employees-radar.aspx* on June 5, 2017.

21. JRP Employee Benefit Solutions. (2013, Sept. 1). 5 best practices of disability management. Retrieved from *jrpinsurance.com/disability-benefits-management-2/* on June 5, 2017. *See also* Sammer, J. (2006, Oct.). Outsourcing disability management. Retrieved from *www.shrm.org/hrdisciplines/Pages/CMS_018708.aspx* on Aug. 8, 2011.

22. Walker, J. (2018, Aug. 1). Why we spend so much on health care. *The Wall Street Journal*, p. A6. *See also* Walker, J. (2017, May 30). Surging drug costs inflict pain. *The Wall Street Journal*, pp. B1, B2.

23. Kaiser Family Foundation. (2019). *Employer Health Benefits 2019*. Menlo Park, CA: Author.

24. Integrity Data. (2020, April 13). Affordable Care Act in 2020: What do employers need to know? Retrieved from *https://www.integrity-data.com/blog/affordable-care-act-2020-employers-need-know/* on May 5, 2020. *See also* Society for Human Resource Management. (2020). How to comply with the Affordable Care Act in 2020. Retrieved from *https://www.shrm.org/resourcesandtools/tools-and-samples/how-to-guides/pages/how-to-comply-with-the-affordable-care-act-in-2020.aspx* on May 5, 2020. *See also* Patient Protection and Affordable Care Act of 2010. (2014, Apr. 25). Retrieved from *www.shrm.org/legalissues/federalresources/federalstatutesregulationsandguidanc/pages/patientprotecionandaffordablecareact.aspx* on June 10, 2014.

25. Cigna. (2020). Employer mandate fact Sheet. Retrieved from *https://www.cigna.com/assets/docs/about-cigna/informed-on-reform/employer-mandate-fact-sheet.pdf* on May 5, 2020.

26. Ibid.

27. Miller (2020), op. cit. *See also* Walker (2018), op. cit. *See also* Walker (2017), op. cit.

28. Miller (2020), op. cit. *See also* Walker, J. (2017b, May 3). Drug-price revolt prods a pioneer to cash out. *The Wall Street Journal*, pp. A1, A8. *See also* Murphy, T. (2014, Mar. 20). Health care law has uneven impact on companies. Retrieved from *http://news.yahoo.com/health-care-law-uneven-impact-companies-153843871.html* on Mar. 22, 2014.

29. Arnst, C. (2009, Nov. 23). 10 ways to cut health-care costs now. *BusinessWeek*, pp. 34–39.

30. Bates, S. (2015, Sep. 4). "Big data" is shaping employers' benefits strategies. Retrieved from *www.shrm.org/hr-today/news/hr-magazine/pages/0915-benefits-analytics.aspx* on Sept. 8, 2015. *See also* Deam, J. (2015, Sep. 2). 5% of employees cost Texas companies most in health care. *Houston Chronicle*. Retrieved from *http://www.houstonchronicle.com/business/medical/article/Five-Percent-of-Employees-Cost-Texas-Companies-6480449.php* on Sept. 8, 2015.

31. SHRM (2019), op. cit.

32. Association for Accessible Medicines. (2020). The generic drug supply chain. Retrieved from *https://accessiblemeds.org/resources/blog/generic-drug-supply-chain* on May 5, 2020.

33. Miller (2020), op. cit. *See also* Miller (2019a), op. cit.

34. Kaiser Family Foundation (2019), op. cit.

35. Paychex. (2019, July 2). Understanding consumer-driven health plans (CDHPs). Retrieved from *https://www.paychex.com/articles/employee-benefits/consumer-driven-health-plan-might-be-right-for-you* on May 5, 2020.

36. Ibid. *See also* Utilize the best retirement plan you've never heard of. (2014, May). *Money*, p. 60.

37. Miller (2020), op. cit. *See also* Miller (2019a), op. cit. *See also* Quick, B. (2013, Dec. 9). A three-point plan to fix health care in the U.S. *Fortune*, p. 66. *See also* Lee, A. C. (2013, Sept. 16). 5 things to know about electronic health records. *Money*, p. 53.

38. Bartz, A. (2018, Feb. 25). This healthcare company is determined to have the healthiest employees in the world. Retrieved from *https://www.jnj.com/innovation/how-johnson-johnson-is-improving-workplace-wellness-for-healthiest-employees* on May 6, 2020. *See also* Luhby, T. (2014, Oct. 17). Employers measure workers' waistlines. *CNNMoney*. Retrieved from h*ttp://money.cnn.com/2014/10/17/news/economy/lose-weight-employee-wellness-program/index.html* on Oct. 19, 2014.

39. SHRM (2019), op. cit.

40. Ibid.

41. Livingston, G., and Thomas, D. (2019, Dec. 16). Among 41 countries, only U.S. lacks paid parental leave. Pew Research Center. Retrieved from *https://www.pewresearch.org/fact-tank/2019/12/16/u-s-lacks-mandated-paid-parental-leave/* on May 6, 2020. *See also* Green, A. (2018, May 8). Everything you need to know about maternity. *The Cut*. Retrieved from *https://www.thecut.com/article/maternity-leave-usa.html* on May 6, 2020.

42. Desilver, D. (2020, March 12). As coronavirus spreads, which U.S. workers have paid sick leave–and which don't? Pew Research Center. Retrieved from *https://www.pewresearch.org/fact-tank/2020/03/12/as-coronavirus-spreads-which-u-s-workers-have-paid-sick-leave-and-which-dont/* on May 6, 2020. *See also* SHRM (2019), op. cit. *See also* Silverman, R. E. (2016, Sep. 28). Varying sick-leave laws vex some firms. *The Wall Street Journal*, p. B8.

43. SHRM (2019), op. cit. *See also* Miller (2016b), op. cit.

44. Frase, M. (2010, Mar.). Taking time off to the bank. *HRMagazine*, pp. 41-46.

45. Kozlowski, R. (2014, Feb. 3). Corporate pension plans mark sad milestone. *Pensions & Investments*. Retrieved from *http://www.pionline.com/article/20140203/PRINT/302039977/corporate-pension-plans-mark-sad-milestone* on Feb. 4, 2014. *See also* Monga, V. (2013, Feb. 26). Price to offload pension liabilities dropping. *The Wall Street Journal*, pp. B1, B8.

46. U.S. Department of Labor. Employee Retirement Income Security Act. Retrieved from *https://www.dol.gov/general/topic/retirement/erisa* on May 6, 2020.

47. Retirement assets total $25.3 trillion in fourth quarter 2016. (2017, Mar. 22). Retrieved from *www.ici.org/research/stats/retirement/ret_16_q4* on June 8, 2017.

48. Pension Benefit Guaranty Corporation. (2020). Premium rates. Retrieved from *www.pbgc.gov/prac/prem/premium-rates* on May 6, 2020.

49. Pension Benefit Guaranty Corporation. *Annual Report 2019*. Retrieved from *https://www.pbgc.gov/sites/default/files/pbgc-fy-2019-annual-report.pdf* on May 6, 2020.

50. Pension Benefit Guaranty Corporation. (2020). Maximum monthly guarantee tables. Retrieved from *www.pbgc.gov/wr/benefits/guaranteed-benefits/maximum-guarantee* on May 6, 2020.

51. Internal Revenue Service. (2020, Jan. 9). Retirement topics–vesting. Retrieved from *https://www.irs.gov/retirement-plans/plan-participant-employee/retirement-topics-vesting* on May 6, 2020.

52. Olya, G. (2019, June 6). 14 companies that still offer pensions. *Yahoo Finance*. Retrieved from *https://finance.yahoo.com/news/14-companies-still-offer-pensions-100000381.html* on May 6, 2020. See also SHRM (2019), op. cit.

53. Butrica, B., Iams, H. M., Smith, K. E., and Toder, E. J. (2009). The disappearing defined benefit pension and its impact on the retirement incomes of baby boomers. *Social Security Bulletin* **69**(3). Retrieved from *sa.gov/policy/docs/ssb/v69n3/v69n3p1.html* on May 6, 2020.

54. SHRM (2019), op. cit.

55. Waggoner, J. (2019, Oct. 16). What to do if your pension plan is frozen. *AARP*. Retrieved from *https://www.aarp.org/retirement/planning-for-retirement/info-2019/pension-plan-freeze.html* on May 6, 2020. *See also* Monga, V. (2016, Mar. 3). More companies

freezing corporate pension plans. *The Wall Street Journal*. Retrieved from *blogs.wsj.com/cfo/2016/03/03/more-companies-freezing-corporate-pension-plans/* on Mar. 4, 2016.

56. SHRM (2019), op. cit. *See also* Sammer, J. (2009, May). Rescuing pension plans. *HRMagazine*, pp. 38–43.

57. Konish, L. (2020, Mar. 6). Investors move to safer 401(k) assets amid coronavirus market swings. *CNBC*. Retrieved from *https://www.cnbc.com/2020/03/05/investors-move-to-safer-401k-assets-amid-coronavirus-market-swings.html* on May 6, 2020.

58. Fitch, A. (2006, Dec.). Is my new pension plan worth less? *Money*, p. 50. *See also* Schultz, E. E., and Francis, T. (2006, Aug. 8). IBM ruling paves way for changes to pensions. *The Wall Street Journal*, p. A3.

59. Metropolitan Life Insurance Company. (2020). *2020 Employee Benefit Trends Study*. New York: Author. *See also* Dulebohn, J. H., Murray, B., and Sun, M. (2000). Selection among employer-sponsored pension plans: The role of individual differences. *Personnel Psychology* **53**, pp. 405–32.

60. U.S. Department of Labor. (n.d.). Pension Protection Act. Retrieved from *https://www.dol.gov/agencies/ebsa/laws-and-regulations/laws/pension-protection-act* on May 6, 2020.

61. SHRM (2019), op. cit. *See also* Young, L. (2009, Jan. 12). Supersizing the 401(k). *BusinessWeek*, pp. 38, 39. *See also* Laise, E. (2009, Oct. 18). Employers begin driving your 401(k). *The Wall Street Journal*, pp. B1, B2.

62. Stone, C. (2016, Oct. 28). Social Security isn't just for seniors. *US News & World Report*. Retrieved from *https://www.usnews.com/opinion/economic-intelligence/articles/2016-10-28/social-security-lifts-people-of-all-ages-out-of-poverty* on May 6, 2020. *See also* Shelton, A. (2013, July 1). Social Security: Still lifting many older Americans out of poverty. Retrieved from *http://blog.aarp.org/2013/07/01/social-security-still-lifting-many-older-americans-out-of-poverty/* on June 11, 2014.

63. Social Security Administration. 2020 Social Security changes. Retrieved from *https://www.ssa.gov/news/press/factsheets/colafacts2020.pdf* on May 6, 2020.

64. Social Security Administration. (2020). 2020 annual report of the Social Security and Federal Disability Boards of Trustees. Retrieved from *https://www.ssa.gov/oact/tr/2020/tr2020.pdf* on May 6, 2020.

65. Social Security Administration. (2020). Fact Sheet: Social Security. Retrieved from *https://www.ssa.gov/legislation/2020Fact%20Sheet.pdf* on May 6, 2020.

66. Lew, J., Aaron, H., Apfel, K., and Reischauer, R. (2019, Oct. 17). How to reform Social Security for future generations of Americans. *The Hill*. Retrieved from *https://thehill.com/opinion/finance/466274-how-to-reform-social-security-for-future-generations-of-americans* on May 6, 2020.

67. Frankel, M. (2020, Feb. 8). How much will I get from Social Security if I make $100,000? *Motley Fool*. Retrieved from *https://www.fool.com/retirement/2020/02/08/how-much-will-i-get-from-social-security-if-i-make.aspx* on May 6, 2020.

68. Murray, S. (2010, July 6). Long recession ignites debate on jobless benefits. *The Wall Street Journal*. Retrieved from *online.wsj.com/article/SB10001424052748704334604575338691913994892.html?KEYWORDS=Long+recession+ignites+debate+on+jobless+benefits* on July 10, 2010. *See also* Wells, S. J. (2009, July). Unemployment insurance: How much more will it cost? *HRMagazine*, pp. 35–38.

69. Morath, E. (2020, April 29). Half of workers get more pay laid off. *The Wall Street Journal*, pp. A1, A2. *See also* Chaney, S. (2020, March 27). Jobless benefits, eligibility grow. *The Wall Street Journal*, p. A2.

70. Morath (2020), op. cit.

71. Rietsema, D. (2020, March 16). What is severance pay? *HR Payroll Systems*. Retrieved from *https://www.hrpayrollsystems.net/severance-pay/* on May 7, 2020. *See also* Heathfield, H. (2017, Mar. 13). Reasons why an employer might want to provide severance pay. *The Balance*. Retrieved from *www.thebalance.com/severance-pay-1918252* on June 8, 2017.

72. Maurer, H. (2006, June 26). Shelling out in Detroit. *BusinessWeek*, p. 32.

73. VW seeks return to longer work week in Germany. (2006, June 13). *The Wall Street Journal*, p. A11.

74. Kuhnert, E. (2020, March 15). Employment termination around the world. Retrieved from *https://papayaglobal.com/blog/termination-processes-around-the-world/* on May 7, 2020. *See also* Manpower Group. (2014). Severance practices around the world. Retrieved from *https://www.manpowergroup.com/wcm/connect/1537631a-4d15-42ad-8fd1-d005992e043f/RM_Severance_Whitepaper.pdf?MOD=AJPERES&CVID=kPDMnpA* on May 14, 2018.

75. Heathfield (2017), op. cit. *See also* Olson, L. (2012, May 8). Three severance pay questions every employee should ask. *US News & World Report*. Retrieved from *http://money.usnews.com/money/blogs/outside-voices-careers/2012/05/08/3-severance-pay-questions-every-employee-should-ask* on June 11, 2014.

76. Broughman, B. (2017, Feb.). CEO side payments in mergers and acquisitions. *BYU Law Review, pp.* **67**-115. See also Grossman, R. J. (2009, Apr.). Executive pay: Perception and reality. *HRMagazine*, pp. 26-32.

77. Zeidner, R. (2017, June-July). Severance under scrutiny. *HRMagazine*, pp. 90-98.

78. Holmes, T. E. (2019, July 30). Less than quarter of global workers disconnect from work during vacation. Retrieved from *www.valuepenguin.com/news/less-than-quarter-global-workers-disconnect-from-work-during-vacation* on Aug. 24, 2019.

79. Simons, J. (2016, Oct. 11). Bosses are to blame for unused vacation time. *The Wall Street Journal*. Retrieved from *https://www.wsj.com/articles/bosses-are-to-blame-for-unused-vacation-time-1476241201* on Oct. 13, 2016. *See also* Alsever, J. (2015, Dec. 15). Take it easy. That's an order! *Fortune*, p. 46. *See also* Shellenbarger, S. (2014, Aug. 13). A message from your team: Enjoy your vacation, already! *The Wall Street Journal*, pp. D1, D2.

80. The American Institute of Stress. (n.d.). Workplace stress. Retrieved from *www.stress.org/workplace-stress* on May 7, 2020.

81. Borenstein, J. (2019, July 27). The importance of taking vacation time to de-stress and recharge. Brain & Behavior Research Foundation. Retrieved from *www.bbrfoundation.org/blog/importance-taking-vacation-time-de-stress-and-recharge* on May 7, 2020.

82. Ibid.

83. Jay, R. (2020, Feb. 28). 14 flexible companies that help pay for your vacation. Retrieved from *www.flexjobs.com/blog/post/flexible-companies-that-help-pay-for-your-vacation/* on May 7, 2020.

84. Fujita, A. (2019, April 20). Disney, Starbucks, Walmart: Big companies are increasingly offering education benefits for employees. *Yahoo Finance*. Retrieved from *https://finance.yahoo.com/news/disney-starbucks-walmart-big-companies-are-increasingly-5-offering-education-benefits-for-employees-141316405.html* on Apr. 21, 2019.

85. Sammer, J. (2017, Mar. 6). 2017 transit and parking benefits: Design programs to increase workers' engagement. *SHRM Online*. Retrieved from *www.shrm.org/resourcesandtools/hr-topics/benefits/pages/transit-benefits-design.aspx* on July 17, 2017.

86. Miller, S. (2019b, April 10). Benefit mix can help financially stressed Generation X. *SHRM Online*. Retrieved from *www.shrm.org/resourcesandtools/hr-topics/benefits/pages/generation-x-financially-stressed-benefits-help.aspx* on Apr. 10, 2019. *See also* Miller, S. (2017, June 2). Employers sharply increased financial well-being benefits in 2017. *SHRM Online*. Retrieved from *www.shrm.org/resourcesandtools/hr-topics/benefits/pages/navigate-financial-wellness-options.aspx* on July 6, 2017.

87. Miller, S. (2019b, June 5). Younger workers put student loan aid near top of desired benefits. *SHRM Online*. Retrieved from *www.shrm.org/resourcesandtools/hr-topics/benefits/pages/younger-workers-seek-student-loan-aid-and-career-development.aspx* on June 5, 2019. *See also* Paquette, D. (2019, Jan. 15). More companies want to pay off your student loan debt. *Mercury News*. Retrieved from *www.mercurynews.com/2019/01/15/more-companies-want-to-pay-off-your-student-loan-debt/* on Jan. 20, 2019.

88. Galinsky, E., and Matos, K. (2011). The future of work-life fit. *Organizational Dynamics* **40**(4), pp. 267-80. *See also* Galinsky, E., Bond, J. T., and Sakai, K. (2008, June). *2008*

National Study of Employers. New York: Families and Work Institute. *See also* Demby, E. R. (2004, Jan.). Do your family-friendly programs make cents? *HRMagazine* 49(1), pp. 74–79. *See also* Grover, S. L., and Crooker, K. J. (1995). Who appreciates family responsive human resource policies: The impact of family-friendly policies on the organizational attachment of parents and non-parents. *Personnel Psychology* **48**, pp. 271–88.

89. Eisenberg, A. (2017, Aug. 16). Employers dropping domestic partner benefits. *Employee Benefit News.* Retrieved from *www.benefitnews.com/news/employers-dropping-domestic-partner-benefits* on May 7, 2020. *See also* Liptak, A. (2015, June 26). Supreme Court ruling makes same-sex marriage a right nationwide. *The New York Times.* Retrieved from *www.nytimes.com/2015/06/27/us/supreme-court-same-sex-marriage.html?_r=0* on June 6, 2017.

90. Miller, S. (2017, Aug. 18). Employers are dropping domestic partner health care benefits. *SHRM Online.* Retrieved from *www.shrm.org/resourcesandtools/hr-topics/benefits/pages/employers-dropping-domestic-partner-benefits.aspx* on Aug. 20, 2017.

91. Rae, D. (2020, Jan. 16). How much can you contribute to your 401(k) for 2020? *Forbes.* Retrieved from *https://www.forbes.com/sites/davidrae/2020/01/16/401k-for-2020/#427138307903* on May 1, 2020.

92. McCaffery, R. M. (1992). *Employee Benefit Programs: A Total Compensation Perspective* (2nd ed.). Boston: PWS-Kent.

93. Sturman, M. C., Hannon, J. M., and Milkovich, G. T. (1996). Computerized decision aids for flexible-benefits decisions: The effects of an expert system and decision-support system on employee intentions and satisfaction with benefits. *Personnel Psychology* **49**, pp. 883–908. *See also* Barber, A. E., Dunham, R. B., and Formisano, R. A. (1992). The impact of flexible benefits on employee satisfaction: A field study. *Personnel Psychology* **45**, pp. 55–75.

94. Miller (2020), op. cit. *See also* Society for Human Resource Management (2019), op. cit.

95. Robb, D. (2011, May). Benefits choices: Educating the consumer. *HRMagazine*, pp. 29–34. *See also* Heuring, L. (2003). Laying out enrollment options. *HRMagazine*, pp. 65–70.

96. Grensing-Pophal (2020), op. cit. See also Miller (2020), op. cit.

97. Baker (2017), op. cit. *See also* Robb, D. (2007, Aug.). A total view of employee rewards. *HRMagazine*, pp. 93–95.

98. Grensing-Pophal (2020), op. cit.

99. M. Zielke, quoted in Grensing-Pophal (2020), op. cit.

100. Ibid. *See also* Miller (2020), op. cit. *See also* Baker (2019), op. cit.

101. Sammer, J. (2017, May 31). Ready for prime time? Using video in benefits communication. Retrieved from *www.shrm.org/resourcesandtools/hr-topics/benefits/pages/using-video-benefits-communication.aspx* on June 1, 2017.

102. Reed, E,. H. (2020, Feb.). 2020 financial benefits trends. *HR Professionals Magazine* 10(2), pp. 34, 35. *See also* Miller, S. (2020, Jan. 2). Perk up: 6 benefits trends to watch in 2020. *SHRM Online.* Retrieved from *https://www.shrm.org/resourcesandtools/hr-topics/benefits/pages/perk-up-six-key-benefit-trends-to-watch-in-2020.aspx* on Jan. 3, 2020.

103. Ibid. *See also* Miller, S. (2019, Jan. 3). 6 big benefits trends for 2019. *SHRM Online.* Retrieved from *https://www.shrm.org/resourcesandtools/hr-topics/benefits/pages/big-benefit-trends-2019.aspx* on Jan. 6, 2019.

104. Miller, S. (2019c, April 10.). Benefit mix can help financially stressed Generation X. *SHRM Online.* Retrieved from *www.shrm.org/resourcesandtools/hr-topics/benefits/pages/generation-x-financially-stressed-benefits-help.aspx* on Apr. 10, 2019.

105. Reed, E,. H. (2020, Feb.). 2020 financial benefits trends. *HR Professionals Magazine,*10(2), pp. 34, 35. *See also* Baker, A. (2019, Nov.). Driving the future of benefits. *HR Professionals Magazine* 9(11), pp. 24, 25. *See also* Sammer, J. (2019, Sept. 10). Does AI have a place in open enrollment? *SHRM Online.* Retrieved from *https://www.shrm.org/resourcesandtools/hr-topics/benefits/pages/does-ai-have-a-place-in-open-enrollment.aspx* on Sept. 10, 2019.

106. Valinsky, J. (2018, Aug. 30). Microsoft requires contractors to offer paid parental leave. *CNNMoney.* Retrieved from *https://money.cnn.com/2018/08/30/technology/business/microsoft-contractor-paid-leave/index.html* on Aug. 30, 2018.

107. Miller (2020), op. cit. *See also* Miller, S. (2019d, Feb. 7). New benefit lets employees trade PTO for student loan relief. *SHRM Online.* Retrieved from *https://www.shrm.org/resourcesandtools/hr-topics/benefits/pages/employees-trade-pto-for-student-loan-relief.aspx* on Feb. 8, 2019. *See also* Fidelity Investments. (2018, May 8). Fidelity's student debt employer contribution program continues to be selected by leading businesses to attract and retain top talent. Retrieved from *https://www.fidelity.com/about-fidelity/employer-services/fidelitys-student-debt-employer-contribution-program* on May 4, 2020.

5

LABOR–MANAGEMENT ACCOMMODATION

Harmonious working relations between labor and management are critical to organizations. Traditionally, both parties have assumed a win–lose, adversarial posture toward each other. This must change if U.S. firms are to remain competitive in the international marketplace. Part 5 is entitled "Labor-Management Accommodation" to emphasize a general theme: To achieve long-term success, labor and management must learn to accommodate each other's needs, rather than repudiate them. By doing so, management and labor can achieve two goals at once: increase productivity and improve the quality of work life. In the current climate of wants and needs, there is no other alternative.

The focus of Chapter 13 is on union representation and collective bargaining. Chapter 14 focuses on procedural justice, ethics, and concerns for privacy in employee relations. These are vital issues in this field. As managers, you must develop and implement sound practices with respect to them. Chapters 13 and 14 will help you do that.

13

UNION REPRESENTATION AND COLLECTIVE BARGAINING

Questions This Chapter Will Help Managers Answer

LO 13-1 How have changes in product and service markets affected the way labor and management relate to each other?

LO 13-2 How should management respond to a union-organizing campaign?

LO 13-3 How might labor and management work together more productively?

LO 13-4 What kinds of dispute-resolution mechanisms should be established in order to guarantee due process for all employees?

RESTRUCTURING THROUGH UNION–MANAGEMENT COLLABORATION*

The forces of globalization and technology that began pounding labor's manufacturing strongholds in the 1970s have intensified in recent years as the economy recovered from the global financial crisis and a prolonged recession. In the United States, a strengthening economy and tight labor markets have given workers more confidence to demand employer concessions through strikes. For their part, employers face an endless struggle to keep costs down, including wages and benefits.

With more employees and retirees losing company-paid health coverage and ballooning costs of health-care coverage for current employees, coupled with worker anxiety about job security, it is clear that the old, adversarial "us-versus-them" approach to labor–management relations has long passed its "sell-by" date. Concerns about all of those issues have led to unprecedented levels of union–management cooperation in recent years.

The 2020–2023 agreements between automakers Ford, General Motors, and Fiat Chrysler and the United Auto Workers, for example, provided immediate and longer-term economic benefits to almost 150,000 workers as well as to the companies. Overall, the Big 3 automakers retained much of the flexibility they gained in recent contract negotiations but were unable to reduce health-care costs. Employees continued to contribute just 3 percent of health-care premiums, far lower than the average for other private-sector workers.

The union secured $18.2 billion in new investments in plants and the creation or retention of 25,400 U.S. jobs through 2023. It also agreed to the closures of a handful of plants. Workers at GM received one-time bonuses of $11,000 for ratifying the contract, whereas employees at Ford and Fiat Chrysler each got $9,000. The disparity in bonus checks was determined by the different financial conditions at each of the three companies.

Closing the gap in wages between newer workers and veteran employees raised overall labor costs for all three automakers, but the companies made big profits in North America because of surging sales of trucks and sport utility vehicles. The automakers need to share some of those profits with factory workers to ensure labor peace and maintain their momentum in the marketplace.

Autoworkers do receive profit sharing, and in 2019, profits were good. Workers at General Motors received an average of $8,000 each, those at Ford $6,600, and those at Fiat Chrysler $7,280. For the workers and their families, it's all about job security, steady wages, and health coverage. At a broader level, new investments in plants mean a lot to economically depressed communities in states such as Ohio, Michigan, and Pennsylvania.

*Sources: Wayland, M. (2019, Dec. 11). UAW approves labor deal with Fiat Chrysler, closing unprecedented talks with Big 3 Detroit automakers marked by a strike, corruption, and litigation. *CNBC*. Retrieved from *www.cnbc.com/2019/12/11/uaw-members-approves-deal-with-fiat-chrysler-ending-2019-negotiations.html* on May 11, 2020. Lawrence, E. D. (2020, Feb. 6). Fiat Chrysler workers to get profit sharing of $7,280. *The Detroit Free Press*. Retrieved from *www.freep.com/story/money/cars/chrysler/2020/02/06/fiat-chrysler-2019-profit-sharing-checks-earnings/4675843002/* on May 11, 2020. Maher, K., and Morath, E. (2018, Sept. 24). Tight labor market fuels strike threat. *The Wall Street Journal*, p. A3. Shingler, D. (2019, Jan. 28). Goodyear facing bumpy road as market conditions take toll on tire industry. *Rubber& Plastics News*. Retrieved from *www.rubbernews.com/article/20190128/NEWS/190129947/goodyear-facing-bumpy-road-as-market-conditions-take-toll-on-tire-industry* on May, 11, 2020. Goodyear offering contract buyouts at Gadsden tire plant. *Rubber& Plastics News*. Retrieved from *www.rubbernews.com/tire/goodyear-offering-contract-buyouts-gadsden-tire-plant* on May 11, 2020. USW locals ratify Goodyear contract. (2017, Aug. 24). *Tire Business*. Retrieved from *https://www.tirebusiness.com/article/20170824/NEWS/170829978/usw-locals-ratify-goodyear-contract* on May 11, 2020.

Now consider two related industries, steel and rubber (tire makers). Both had been sliding toward extinction until union leaders stepped forward to work with management in the development of innovative agreements that keep these industries profitable and competitive through higher worker productivity.

Thus, when the leaders of the United Steelworkers (USW) union sat down with Goodyear Tire & Rubber Company to negotiate a new labor agreement, they knew they were headed for trouble. The nation's largest tire maker faced high raw materials costs, a tough market for price increases, and lower demand for its tires in the United States, and some other countries. The union's options? Allow Goodyear to replace some of its U.S. plants with ones in Asia or fight the company with a strike that could force it into bankruptcy.

Instead, the USW came up with a third choice. Its goal: to make Goodyear globally competitive in a way that would preserve as many of the union's 19,000 jobs as possible. In the conclusion to this case, we will see what happened, but one thing is clear: Both sides would have to agree to major changes in the way the business is run if there was to be any hope of keeping this old-line manufacturing industry competitive—and keeping it in the United States.

Challenges

1. What are some key obstacles in the way of true cooperation by labor and management?
2. Is labor–management cooperation just a short-term solution to economic problems, or can it become institutionalized into the very culture of an organization?
3. Will widespread labor–management cooperation lead to a loss of union power?

WHY DO EMPLOYEES JOIN UNIONS?

Visualize this scenario: It's 7:30 on a cool December evening in Las Vegas, and 105 off-duty hotel maids, cooks, and bellhops are waiting for their monthly union meeting to start. It has been a long day working in the big casino hotels, but still the room buzzes with energy. One by one, a dozen or so members recount their success in recruiting 2,700 fellow employees at the MGM Grand, the world's largest hotel, to support the union. After a 3-year campaign of street demonstrations, mass arrests, and attacks on the company's HR practices that helped oust a stridently anti-labor CEO, MGM Grand recognized the union a year later without an election.

This is the essence of a **labor union:** a group of workers who join together to influence the nature of their employment. Perhaps they are seeking improved wages and benefits, protection against arbitrary treatment and discharge, or a greater voice in workplace decision making. For employers, in contrast, labor relations are about managing relationships with employees and unions in ways that promote organizational goals such as profitability (in the private sector) or cost-effective service delivery (in the public sector). Nonunion employers typically pursue these goals by trying to remain union free—either through aggressive anti-union tactics or through progressive HR management tactics that seek to make unions unnecessary.[1]

To be sure, the attitudes of workers toward unions are not based simply on expected economic gains; much deeper values are at stake.[2] As one union leader noted, "Our union has never seen itself as just a collective-bargaining agent, but as an agent for social change."[3] Indeed,

> if one talks to any worker long enough, and candidly enough, one discovers that his loyalty to the union is not simply economic. One may even be able to show him that, on a strictly cost-benefit analysis, measuring income lost from strikes, and jobs lost as a result of contract terms, the cumulative economic benefits are delusions. It won't matter. In the end, he will tell you, the union is the only institution that ensures and protects his "dignity" as a worker, that prevents him from losing his personal identity, and from being transformed into an infinitesimal unit in one huge and abstract "factor of production."[4]

Managers who fail to treat workers with respect, or companies that view workers only as costs to be cut rather than as assets to be developed, *invite* collective action by employees to remedy these conditions.[5] A 2019 Gallup poll found that 64 percent of Americans approve of labor unions, the third year in a row that favorability ratings exceeded 60 percent.[6] However, unions are not without sin, either, and workers will vote against them to the extent that the unions are seen as unsympathetic to a company's need to remain viable, or if they feel unions abuse their power by calling strikes or have fat-cat leaders who selfishly promote their own interests at the expense of the members' interests.[7]

UNION MEMBERSHIP IN THE UNITED STATES

Union membership shrank from a high of 35 percent of the workforce in 1945 to 22 percent in 1980 to 10.3 percent in 2019. Unions still represent 14.57 million workers, but that's just about 1 in every 10 employees. Excluding public-sector membership, unions represented just 6.2 percent of private-sector employees in 2019.[8] Figure 13-1 shows the percentage of non-farm employees represented by unions between 1930 and 2019.

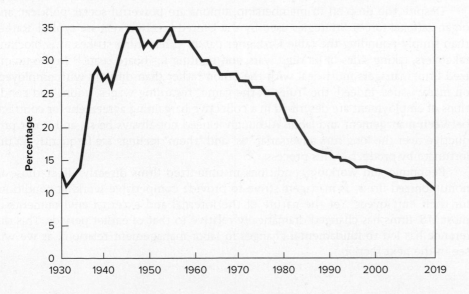

Figure 13–1

Percentage of nonfarm employees represented by unions between 1930 and 2019.

Sources: Bureau of the Census, *Historical Statistics of the United States, Colonial Times to 1970;* Bureau of Labor Statistics, *Handbook of Labor Statistics,* Bulletin 2070, Dec. 1980; Bureau of Labor Statistics, *Employment and Earnings,* Jan., various years, 1983–2013. Bureau of Labor Statistics. (2020, Jan. 22). Union members–2019. Originally prepared by the AFL-CIO.

Several economic and demographic forces favor a resurgence of unions. Prior to the coronavirus pandemic, employees were bombarded with messages of a booming economy, corporate profits, and record stock market prices. Yet they saw little of this bounty in their own paychecks. Indeed, the growing gulf between the haves and the have-nots provides fertile ground for organizing.[9] And it is not just blue-collar workers who are organizing. In fact, many of the fastest-growing unions in the United States represent white-collar professionals, including graduate students at public and private universities, physicians, nuclear engineers, psychologists, and tech-company employees.[10]

Finally, minority-group members and women, who are expected to continue entering the workforce at a high rate, tend to favor unions. Evidence indicates that women's participation is likely to be enhanced to the extent that there is greater representation of women in local union offices. As of 2019, 10.7 percent of men were union members, and 9.7 percent of women.[11]

Despite these factors, a large-scale resurgence of unions seems unlikely. Organized labor complains that U.S. labor laws favor employers,[12] but what complicates organizing efforts is that workers in many fast-growing occupations have traditionally been nonunion—in fields as diverse as insurance, information technology, and electronics. Their goals and desires are different from those of labor's traditional blue-collar stalwarts, who seem to want little more than high wages and steady work. As one expert noted, "people want something that looks more like a voice in the workplace—and less like collective bargaining and conflict with management." And because so many young workers are highly mobile (average job tenure for workers ages 25 to 34 was just 3.2 years in 2018[13]), they may not be willing to support a 6-month unionization drive that could culminate in a strike to win a first contract. Finally, many young workers are taking jobs in the rapidly growing service sector—banking, computer programming, and financial services—92 percent of which remains unorganized.[14]

The very nature of high-tech industry also hampers organizing efforts. Many software designers and biotechnology engineers work for small, start-up companies that unions find difficult and expensive to organize. Many are focused on earning stock options and other rewards for performance instead of the wage increases and steady work that unions typically seek.

Despite the drop-off in membership, unions are powerful social, political, and organizational forces. Strategies used by the United Steelworkers are typical. Rather than simply pounding the table for higher pay or threatening strikes, it is blocking takeovers, taking sides in bidding wars, and fighting for board seats.[15] In the unionized firm, managers must deal with the union rather than directly with employees on many issues. Indeed, the "rules of the game" regarding wages, hours, and conditions of employment are described in a collective-bargaining agreement (or contract) between management and labor. Although it need not always be so, and is not productive over the long run, adversarial "us" and "them" feelings are frequently an unfortunate by-product of this process.

Economic and working conditions in unionized firms directly affect those in nonunionized firms, as managers strive to provide competitive working conditions for their employees. Yet the nature of the internal and external environments of most U.S. firms has changed dramatically relative to that of earlier periods. This difference has led to fundamental changes in labor-management relations, as we will see in the next section.

THE CHANGING NATURE OF INDUSTRIAL RELATIONS IN THE UNITED STATES

Fundamentally, labor–management relations are about power—who has it and how they use it. As the chapter-opening vignette illustrated, both parties are finding that they achieve the best results when they share power rather than revert to a win–lose orientation.[16] In recent years, unions have lost power as a result of six interrelated factors: global competition, nonunion domestic competition, deregulation, the growth of service industries, corporate downsizing (which has depleted the membership of many unions), and the willingness of firms to move operations overseas. In today's world, firms face more competitive pressures than ever before. That competition arises from abroad (e.g., Toyota, Nissan, Hyundai, Sanyo, Pohang, and steelmakers from developing countries); from domestic, nonunion operators (e.g., Nucor in steel); and from nonregulated new entities (e.g., in the financial services industry).

The deregulation of many product markets created two key challenges to existing union relationships. First, it made market entry much easier—for example, in over-the-road trucking, airlines, and telecommunications. Second, under regulation, management had little incentive to cut labor costs because high labor costs could be passed on to consumers; conversely, labor-cost savings could not be used to gain a competitive advantage in the product market. Under deregulation, however, even major airlines (which are almost entirely organized) found that low costs translated into low fares and a competitive advantage. As a result, all carriers need to match the lowest costs of their competitors by matching their labor contracts.[17]

These competitive pressures have forced business to develop the ability to shift rapidly, to cut costs, to innovate, to enter new markets, and to devise a flexible labor-force strategy. As managers seek to make the most cost-effective use of their human resources, and as companies move forward into a more integrated, globalized world economy, they need to understand the legal and employment implications of different systems that underlie the infrastructure and operations of unions in nations where they do business.[18]

Traditionally, the power of unions to set industrywide wage levels through so-called **pattern bargaining** across employers was based on the market power of strong domestic producers or industries sheltered by regulation. As employers lost their market power in the 1970s and 1980s, union wage dominance shrank and fragmented. One union segment had to compete with another and with nonunion labor, both in the United States and abroad. Management's objective was (and is) to get labor costs per unit of output to a point below that of the competition. Out of this approach have come wage-level differences and the breakdown of pattern bargaining. As a result, even under union bargaining pressures, wages are now far more responsive to economic conditions at the industry and firm levels, and even at the product-line level, than they traditionally have been.[19]

The labor relations system that evolved during the 1940s and lasted until the early 1980s was institutionalized around the market power of the firm and around those unions that had come to represent large proportions, if not nearly all, of an industry's domestic workforce. The driving force for change in the new millennium has been business conditions in the firm. Those conditions have changed for good—and so must the U.S. industrial relations system. To put that system into better perspective, let us consider some of its fundamental features.

FUNDAMENTAL FEATURES OF THE U.S. INDUSTRIAL RELATIONS SYSTEM

Six distinctive features of the U.S. system, compared with those in other countries, are as follows:[20]

1. *Exclusive representation.* Only one union in a given job territory (**exclusive representation**), selected by majority vote. However, multiple unions may represent different groups of employees who work for the same employer (e.g., pilots, flight attendants, and mechanics at an airline). This situation is in contrast to that existing in continental Europe, where affiliations by religious and ideological attachment exist in the same job territory.

2. *Collective agreements that embody a sharp distinction between negotiation of and interpretation of an agreement.* Most agreements are of fixed duration, often 3 or 4 years (sometimes shorter in uncertain economic times),[21] and they result from legitimate, overt conflict that is confined to a negotiations period. They incorporate no-strike (by employees) and no-lockout (by employer) provisions during the term of the agreement, as well as interpretation of the agreement by private arbitrators or umpires. In contrast, the British system features open-ended, unenforceable agreements.

INTERNATIONAL APPLICATION
Comparing Industrial Relations Systems around the World

Direct comparisons among industrial relations (IR) systems are almost impossible, for the following three reasons:[a]

1. *The same concept may be interpreted differently in different industrial relations contexts.* For example, consider the concept of collective bargaining. In the United States, it is understood to mean negotiations between a labor union local and management. In Sweden and Germany, however, the term refers to negotiation between an organization of employers and a trade union at the industry level.[b]

2. *The objectives of the bargaining process may differ in different countries.* For example, European unions view collective bargaining as a form of class struggle, but in the United States, collective bargaining is viewed mainly in economic terms.

3. *No IR system can be understood without an appreciation of its historical origins.* Such historical differences may be due to managerial strategies for labor relations in large companies, ideological divisions within the trade-union movement, the influence of religious organizations on the development of trade unions, the methods of union regulation by governments, or the mode of technology and industrial organization at critical stages of union development.[c]

[a]Tarique, I., Briscoe, D., and Schuler, R. (2016). *International Human Resource Management* (5th ed.). New York: Routledge. Pucik, V., Evans, P., Bjorkman, I., and Morris, S. (2016). *The Global Challenge: International Human Resource Management* (3rd ed.). Chicago: Chicago Business Press.

[b]Budd, J. W. (2021). *Labor Relations* (6th ed.). New York: McGraw-Hill. Katz, H. C., Kochan, T. A., and Colvin, A. J. S. (2008). *An Introduction to Collective Bargaining and Industrial Relations* (4th ed.). Burr Ridge, IL: McGraw-Hill/Irwin.

[c]Fossum, J. A. (2015). *Labor Relations: Development, Structure, Process* (12th ed.). Burr Ridge, IL: McGraw-Hill/Irwin. Poole, M. (1986). *Industrial Relations: Origins and Patterns of National Diversity.* London: Routledge & Kegan Paul.

3. *Decentralized collective bargaining*, largely due to the size of the United States, the diversity of its economic activity, and the historic role of product markets in shaping the contours of collective bargaining. By contrast, in Sweden, the government establishes wage rates, and in Australia, some wages are set by arbitration councils and others by bargaining at the enterprise level.[22]

4. *Relatively high union dues and large union staffs* to negotiate and administer private, decentralized agreements, including grievance arbitration to organize against massive employer opposition and to lobby before legislative and administrative tribunals. Typical union dues are 2.5 hours of pay a month plus 1.15 percent of any bonuses paid.[23]

5. *Opposition by both large and small employers to union organization*, in contrast to countries such as France and Germany. Such opposition has been modified in terms of the constraints placed on management only slightly by more than 85 years of legislation.

6. *The role of government* in the U.S. industrial relations system, as compared with other systems, such as those of Mexico and Australia. The U.S. government has been relatively passive in dispute resolution and highly legalistic, both in administrative procedures and in the courts.[24] In the United States, the traditional view is that the role of government is not to establish labor standards, only to promote competition.[25]

Let's now examine the U.S. system in greater detail.

THE UNIONIZATION PROCESS

The Legal Basis

The Wagner Act, or *National Labor Relations Act*, of 1935 affirmed the right of all employees to engage in union activities, to organize, and to bargain collectively without interference or coercion from management. It also created the National Labor Relations Board (NLRB) to supervise representation elections and to investigate charges of unfair labor practices by management. The *Taft-Hartley Act* of 1947 reaffirmed those rights and specified unfair labor practices for both management and unions. The unfair labor practices are shown in Table 13-1. The act was later amended (by the *Landrum Griffin Act* of 1959) to add the **secondary boycott** as an unfair labor practice. A secondary boycott occurs when a union appeals to firms or other unions to stop doing business with an employer who sells or handles a struck product.

ETHICAL DILEMMA
Are Unfair Labor Practices Unethical?

Are the unfair labor practices shown in Table 13-1 also unethical? Are there circumstances under which activities might  be legal (e.g., cutting off health-care benefits for striking workers, as GM did in 2019) but at the same time also unethical?

Table 13–1		

UNFAIR LABOR PRACTICES FOR MANAGEMENT AND UNIONS UNDER THE TAFT-HARTLEY ACT OF 1947

Management
1. Interference with, coercion of, or restraint of employees in their right to organize.
2. Domination of, interference with, or illegal assistance of a labor organization.
3. Discrimination in employment because of union activities.
4. Discrimination because the employee has filed charges or given testimony under the act.
5. Refusal to bargain in good faith.
6. "Hot cargo" agreements: refusals to handle another employer's products because of that employer's relationship with the union.

Union
1. Restraint or coercion of employees who do not want to participate in union activities.
2. Any attempt to influence an employer to discriminate against an employee.
3. Refusal to bargain in good faith.
4. Excessive, discriminatory membership fees.
5. Make-work or featherbedding provisions in labor contracts that require employers to pay for services that are not performed.
6. Use of pickets to force an organization to bargain with a union, when the organization already has a lawfully recognized union.
7. "Hot cargo" agreements: that is, refusals to handle, use, sell, transport, or otherwise deal in another employer's products.

A so-called **free-speech clause** in the act specifies that management has the right to express its opinion about unions or unionism to employees, provided that it does not threaten or promise favors to employees to obtain anti-union actions. Finally, the act permits states to enact **right-to-work laws** under which employees represented by a union cannot be compelled to join the union or to pay dues as a condition of continued employment. As of 2020, 27 states have passed such laws.[26]

The Taft-Hartley Act covers most private-sector employers and nonmanagerial employees, except railroad and airline employees (they are covered under the *Railway Labor Act* of 1926). Federal-government employees are covered by the *Civil Service Reform Act* of 1978. That act affirmed their right to organize and to bargain collectively over working conditions, established unfair labor practices for both management and unions, established the Federal Labor Relations Authority to administer the act, authorized the Federal Services Impasse Panel to take whatever action is necessary to resolve impasses in collective bargaining, and prohibited strikes in the public sector.

The Organizing Drive

There are three ways to kick off an organizing campaign: (1) Employees themselves may begin it; (2) employees may request that a union begin one for them; or (3) in some instances, national and international unions may contact employees in

WHEN IS REFUSAL TO HIRE A UNION SYMPATHIZER UNLAWFUL?

Note unfair labor practice no. 3 for management in Table 13-1. It is unlawful for management to discriminate in employment because of union activities. The Supreme Court decided in *NLRB v. Town & Country Electric Inc.* that paid union organizers, despite their employment relationship with the union, are nonetheless "employees" and therefore are protected against discrimination in hiring based on their union affiliation. Once hired, however, they are subject to the same work rules and performance standards as are other employees. Subsequently, in *Masiongale Electrical-Mechanical Inc. v. NLRB*, the 7th Circuit Court of Appeals provided the following four-part test in order to establish a discriminatory refusal to hire:

1. The employer was hiring, or had concrete plans to hire, at the time of the alleged unlawful conduct.
2. The applicants had experience or training relevant to the announced or generally known requirements of the positions.
3. The employer did not adhere uniformly to such requirements, or the requirements themselves were a pretext for discrimination.
4. Anti-union bias contributed to the decision not to hire the applicants.

At the same time, the sympathizers must also have a genuine interest in working for the employer.[a] Once this is established, the burden shifts to the employer to show that it would not have hired the applicants even in the absence of their union activity or affiliation.[b]

---

[a]Zimolong, W. (2018, Jan. 8). Cutting the salt out: Tips for avoiding union salting charges. Retrieved from *www.supplementalconditions.com/2018/01/cutting-the-salt-out-tips-for-avoiding-union-salting-charges/* on May 12, 2020. Society for Human Resource Management.(2017, Jan. 10). Union organizing: What does the term "salting" as a union organizing tactic mean? Retrieved from *www.shrm.org/resourcesandtools/tools-and-samples/hr-qa/pages/whatdoestheterm"salting"asaunionorganizingtacticmean.aspx* on June 12, 2017.

[b]Clark, M. M. (2003, Oct.). When the union knocks . . . on the recruiter's door: Legal rules on the hiring of union "salts." *Legal Report*, pp. 7–8.

---

organizations that have been targeted for organizing. In all three cases, employees are asked to sign **authorization cards** that designate the union as the employees' exclusive representative in bargaining with management.

Well-defined rules govern organizing activities:

1. Employee organizers may solicit fellow employees to sign authorization cards on company premises, but not during working time. They may not use an employer's e-mail system, however, for union-organizing activity. The only exception is when there are not other reasonable means to communicate on nonworking time.[27]
2. Outside organizers may not solicit on premises if a company has an existing policy of prohibiting all forms of solicitation and if that policy has been enforced consistently. As of 2019, this includes public spaces within an employer's business, such as restaurants and cafeterias.[28]
3. Management representatives may express their views about unions through speeches or videos to employees on company premises. They are legally prohibited, however, from interfering with an employee's freedom of choice concerning union membership.[29]

The organizing drive usually continues until the union obtains signed authorization cards from 30 percent of the employees. At that point, it can petition the NLRB for a representation election. If the union secures authorization cards from more than 50 percent of the employees, however, it may ask management directly for the right to exclusive representation. This is known as a **card check** (referring to the index-card-sized slips of paper that workers sign). Its goal is to circumvent management's power to influence an election. The proposed Employee Free Choice Act, not yet passed by Congress, would make card-check recognition of the union automatic, thus bypassing a secret-ballot election. Needless to say, this is a controversial provision of the proposed law.[30]

The Bargaining Unit

When the petition for election is received, the NLRB conducts a hearing to determine the appropriate (collective) **bargaining unit**–that is, the group of employees eligible to vote in the representation election. Sometimes labor and management agree jointly on the appropriate bargaining unit. When they do not, the NLRB must determine the unit. The NLRB is guided in its decision, especially if there is no previous history of bargaining between the parties, by a concept called **community of interest.** That is, the NLRB will define a unit that reflects the shared interests of the employees involved. Such elements include similar wages, hours, and working conditions; the physical proximity of employees to one another; common supervision; the amount of interchange of employees within the proposed unit; and the degree of integration of the employer's production process or operation.[31] Under the Taft-Hartley Act, however, professional employees cannot be forced into a bargaining unit with nonprofessionals without their majority consent.

The *size* of the bargaining unit is critical for both the union and the employer because it is strongly related to the outcome of the representation election. The larger the bargaining unit, the more difficult it is for the union to win. In fact, if a bargaining unit contains several hundred employees, the unit is almost invulnerable.[32]

The Election Campaign

Emotions on both sides run high during a representation election campaign. However, management typically is unaware that a union campaign is under way until most or all of the cards have been signed. At that point, management has some tactical advantages over the union. It can use company time and premises to stress the positive aspects of the current situation, and it can emphasize the costs of unionization and the loss of individual freedom that may result from collective representation. Supervisors may hold information meetings to emphasize these anti-union themes. However, certain practices by management are prohibited by law (see Table 13–1, unfair labor practices). These include:

1. Physical interference, threats, or violent behavior toward union organizers.
2. Interference with employees involved with the organizing drive.
3. Discipline or discharge of employees for pro-union activities.
4. Promises to provide or withhold future benefits depending on the outcome of the representation election.

These illegal activities are *TIPS*–that is, management may not *T*hreaten, *I*nterrogate, *P*romise, or *S*py.[33] To illustrate, expressions of distaste for union organizing efforts by the president of Griffin Electric, one of the largest nonunion electrical contractors in the northeastern United States, were interpreted by the 4th U.S. Circuit Court of Appeals as threats. The president's remarks that the company would "never be union" and that employees who signed union cards would be "stabbing him in the back" were interpreted as threats because of his direct involvement with employee discipline and promotional opportunities.[34]

Companies can share facts with employees (such as what the company and the union can do legally), opinions (e.g., that the decision to be represented by a union is each employee's choice but managers prefer to work directly with employees to resolve concerns), and examples (e.g., examples of positive actions your worksite has experienced as a result of managers and employees working directly with each other).[35]

Unions are also prohibited from unfair labor practices (see Table 13-1), such as coercing or threatening employees if they fail to join the union. In addition, the union can picket the employer *only* if (1) the employer is not currently unionized, (2) the petition for election has been filed with the NLRB in the past 30 days, and (3) a representation election has not been held during the previous year. Unions tend to emphasize three themes during organizing campaigns:

- The union's ability to help employees satisfy their economic and personal needs.
- The union's ability to ensure that workers are treated fairly.
- The union's ability to improve working conditions.[36]

The campaign tactics of management and the union are monitored by the NLRB. If the NLRB finds that either party engaged in unfair labor practices during the campaign, the election results may be invalidated and a new election conducted. However, a federal appeals court has ruled that the NLRB cannot force a company to bargain with a union that is not recognized by a majority of the workers, even if the company has made "outrageous" attempts to thwart unionization.[37] For example, firing union activists—as companies do in fully one-quarter of such campaigns, according to studies of NLRB cases—is difficult to prove, takes years to work through the courts, and takes place long after an organizing drive has lost steam.[38]

The Representation Election and Certification

If management and the union jointly agree on the size and composition of the bargaining unit, a representation election occurs shortly thereafter. However, if management does not agree, a long delay may ensue. Because such delays often erode rank-and-file union support, they work to management's advantage. Not surprisingly, therefore, few employers agree with unions on the size and composition of the bargaining unit. In 2019 the NLRB modified election rules by lengthening the timeline between the filing of an election petition and the holding of the election. The new rules protect employers from what they call "ambush" or "quickie" elections.[39]

When a date for the representation election is finally established, the NLRB conducts a **secret-ballot election.** If the union receives a majority of the ballots *cast* (not a majority of votes from members of the bargaining unit), the union becomes certified as the **exclusive bargaining representative** of all employees in the unit. Once a representation election is held, regardless of the outcome, no further elections can be held in that bargaining unit for 1 year. The entire process is shown graphically in Figure 13-2.

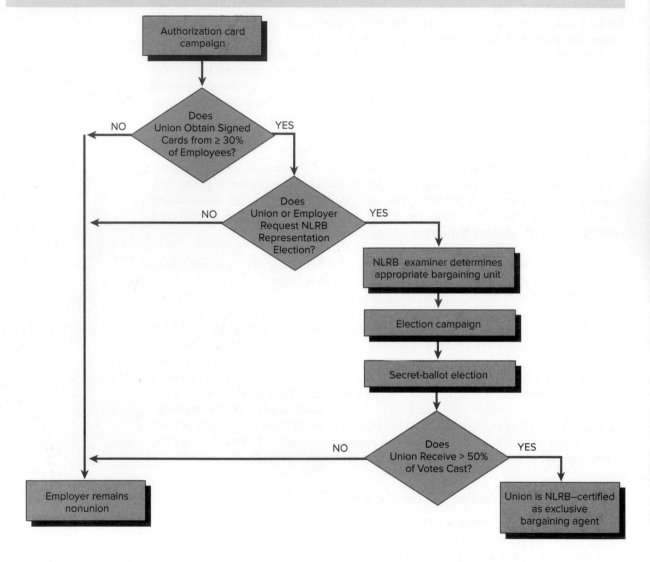

Figure 13–2

Steps involved and decisions to be made in a union-organizing campaign.

The records of elections won and lost by unions and management have changed little since the 1950s. In the 1950s, unions won more than 70 percent of representation elections. In 2018, they won 70.6 percent of them. At the same time, however, they are organizing fewer workers.[40]

The Decertification of a Union

If a representation election results in union certification, the first thing many employers want to know is when and how they can *decertify* the union. Under federal law, a union has 12 months as an exclusive representative to reach a contract for the newly organized workers. After that, it risks facing decertification campaigns or challenges from rival unions. Under NLRB rules, an incumbent union can be decertified if a majority of employees within the bargaining unit vote to rescind the union's status as their collective-bargaining agent in another representation election conducted by the NLRB. In 2019, unions lost 63 percent of decertification elections, but such elections may not be held while a contract is in effect.[41]

Because **decertification** is most likely to occur the first year or so after certification, unions will often insist on multiyear contracts. Once both parties agree to the terms and duration of the labor contract, the employer is obligated to recognize the union and to follow the provisions of the contract for the specified contract period.

To call for a decertification election, employees must collect signatures from at least 30 percent of workers in a unit. A majority of votes decides the outcome. Employees might cite evidence such as the following:[42]

- Statements about other employees' views of union representation.
- Statements expressing dissatisfaction with the union's performance.
- A majority of employees did not support the union during a strike.
- The union has become less active as a representative of employees.
- There was substantial turnover among employees subsequent to certification.
- The union has admitted a lack of majority support.

Following a decertification election, a full year must elapse before another representation election can take place.

Once a union is legally certified as the exclusive bargaining agent for workers, the next task is to negotiate a contract that is mutually acceptable to management and labor. We will examine this process in more detail next.

COLLECTIVE BARGAINING: CORNERSTONE OF AMERICAN LABOR RELATIONS

Alternative Bargaining Strategies

Negotiation is a two-party transaction whereby both parties intend to resolve a conflict.[43] What constitutes a good settlement of a negotiation? To be sure, the best outcome occurs when both parties win. Sometimes negotiations fall short of this ideal. A really bad bargain is one in which both parties lose, yet this is a risk that is inherent in the process. Despite its limitations, abuses, and hazards, negotiation has become an indispensable process in free societies in general and in the U.S. labor movement in particular. The fact is that negotiation is the most effective device thus far invented for realizing common interests while compromising on conflicting interests.[44] Any practice that threatens the process of collective bargaining will be resisted vigorously by organized labor.

In general, there are two postures that the parties involved in bargaining might assume: win-lose and win-win. In win-lose, or **distributive bargaining,** the goals of the parties initially are irreconcilable—or at least they appear that way. Central to the conflict is the belief that there is a limited, controlled amount of key resources available—a "fixed-pie" situation. Both parties may want to be the winner; both may want more than half of what is available.[45]

Evidence indicates that when one party adopts a distributive, contentious posture, the other party tends to reciprocate with contentious communications.

To break the spiral of conflict, use mixed communications—that is, use both contentious and cooperative problem-solving communications in one speaking turn. For example, a negotiator might threaten, "If you persist in these demands, we'd prefer to see you in court, where we expect the judge to find in our favor." The other party might respond with the following mixed communication: "We are prepared to let a judge decide, but we think that we will both be better off if we reach an agreement based on interests. Tell me again what your software needs are."[46]

In contrast, in win–win, or **integrative bargaining,** the goals of the parties are not mutually exclusive. If one side pursues its goals, this does not prohibit the other side from achieving its own goals. One party's gain is not necessarily at the other party's expense. The fundamental structure of an integrative bargaining situation is that it is possible for both sides to achieve their objectives.[47] Although the conflict initially may appear to be win–lose to the parties, discussion and mutual exploration usually will suggest win–win alternatives.

In practice, distributive and integrative bargaining styles contrast sharply with each other. To do well in a distributive bargaining situation, negotiators typically find it valuable to, among other things, overstate demands, withhold information, and project a stern, tough image. Effective integrative bargaining, on the other hand, involves first identifying, then solving, problems. Effective tactics include the open exchange and sharing of information and the airing of multiple voices. The problem is that it is difficult to be effective at both distributive and integrative bargaining in the same negotiations. One side might move into distributive mode, just at the moment when the other side is ready for integrative problem solving. Confronted with hard, distributive tactics, the other side might become discouraged about the possibility of integrative bargaining, making it difficult for such bargaining ever to occur.[48]

The Art of Negotiation

To be sure, there is no shortage of advice on negotiation tactics. Consider six lessons from skilled negotiators:[49]

- Respect the customs and cultures of your counterparts.
- The single biggest tool in any negotiation is the willingness to get up and walk away from the table without a deal.
- Many people listen, but few actually hear. You can't learn anything if you are doing all of the talking.
- There is no substitute for thorough preparation.
- Look for areas of mutual interest and opportunities to collaborate.
- The very best negotiators debrief themselves after every negotiation They keep notes on their own performance as well as that of their opponents. You never know when that information may be gold.

As you should be able to appreciate by now, negotiations are full of strategy and at least a little bit of drama and gamesmanship. Thus far, we have assumed that negotiation takes place face-to-face. Suppose, however, that virtual teams negotiate online. One study found that relative to face-to-face negotiations, those conducted online yielded lower levels of interpersonal trust *both* before and after negotiations. Online negotiators also were less satisfied with their outcomes and less confident in the quality of their performance, despite the absence of differences in the quality of economic outcomes relative to face-to face negotiations. These results suggest that

Table 13–2		

MAJOR SUBJECTS OF COLLECTIVE-BARGAINING IN THE UNITED STATES

Compensation: wages, benefits, vacations, holidays, shift premiums, profit sharing.

Employment policies and procedures: layoff, promotion, and transfer policies; overtime and vacation rules.

Employee rights and responsibilities: seniority rights, job standards, workplace rules.

Employer rights and responsibilities: management rights, just-cause discipline and discharge, subcontracting, safety standards.

Union rights and responsibilities: recognition as bargaining agent, union security, dues checkoff, shop stewards, no-strike clauses

Dispute resolution and ongoing decision making: grievance procedures, committees, consultation, renegotiation procedures.

Sources: Adapted from Budd, J. W. (2021). *Labor Relations: Striking a Balance* (6th ed.). New York: McGraw-Hill, p. 11.

the greatest problems for online negotiations are associated with creating positive relationships and feelings, rather than with the creation of low-quality agreements.[50]

There is one important qualifier in any discussion of negotiation strategies: national culture. Evidence indicates that managers from the United States, Japan, and Germany use different strategies to negotiate conflict. Americans value individualism, egalitarianism, and multitasking. They try to integrate their interests with those of the other party. Germans value explicit contracting, which leads them to rely on independent, objective standards as a basis for resolving conflict. Finally, the Japanese value collectivism and hierarchy and tend to resolve conflict by emphasizing status differences between the parties.[51] What is the bottom line in all this? If you want to become a win–win negotiator, be aware of the behaviors to imitate and those to avoid, and make an effort to understand the cultural norms that influence the behavior of the other party.[52]

Successful collective bargaining results in an agreement that is mutually acceptable both to labor and to management. Table 13–2 shows some of the major subjects that comprise a typical agreement.

Unfortunately, contract negotiations sometimes fail because the parties are not able to reach a timely and mutually acceptable settlement of the issues—economic, noneconomic, or a combination of both. When this happens, the union may strike, management may shut down operations (a lockout), or both parties may appeal for third-party involvement. Let's examine these processes in some detail.

BARGAINING IMPASSES: STRIKES, LOCKOUTS, AND THIRD-PARTY INVOLVEMENT

Strikes

In every labor negotiation, there exists the possibility of a strike. The right of employees to strike in support of their bargaining demands is protected by the Landrum-Griffin Act. However, there is no unqualified right to strike. A work stoppage by employees must be the result of a lawful labor dispute and not in violation of an existing agreement between management and the union. Strikers engaged in activities protected by law may not be discharged, but they may be replaced during the strike. Strikers engaged in activities that are not protected by law need not be rehired after the strike.[53]

Types of Strikes

As you might suspect, there are several types of strikes. Let's consider the major types.

Unfair Labor Practice Strikes   Unfair labor practices of the employer cause or prolong **unfair labor practice strikes.** Employees engaged in this type of strike are afforded the highest degree of protection under the act, and under most circumstances they are entitled to reinstatement once the strike ends. Management must exercise great caution in handling unfair labor practice strikes because the NLRB will become involved and company liability can be substantial.

Economic Strikes   Actions by the union of withdrawing its labor in support of bargaining demands, including those for recognition or organization, are **economic strikes.** Economic strikers have limited rights to reinstatement.

Unprotected Strikes   These include all remaining types of work stoppages, both lawful and unlawful, such as sit-down strikes, strikes in violation of federal laws (e.g., the prohibition of strikes by employees of the federal government), slowdowns, wildcat strikes that occur while a contract is in force, and partial walkouts. Participants in **unprotected strikes** may be discharged by their employers.

Sympathy Strikes   Strikes in support of other workers on strike (e.g., when more than one union is functioning in an organization) are **sympathy strikes.** Although the NLRB and the courts have recognized the right of the sympathy striker to stand in the shoes of the primary striker, the facts of any particular situation ultimately will determine the legal status of a sympathy strike.[54]

Intermittent Strikes   **Intermittent strikes** occur when workers walk out for a relatively short time (e.g., an 8-hour shift), then return to work, with the intention of striking again later. Associates who joined Organization United for Respect at Walmart (OUR Walmart), for example, were not agitating for legal recognition or collective bargaining rights. Rather, they used intermittent strikes to seek higher wages, more hours, and better access to health care. Walmart argued that intermittent

Union members have a legal right to strike in support of their bargaining demands after their collective-bargaining contract expires.
Andrew Resek/McGraw-Hill

Table 13–3
RULES OF CONDUCT DURING A STRIKE

- People working in or having any business with the organization have a right to pass freely in and out.
- Pickets must not block a door, passageway, driveway, crosswalk, or other entrance or exit.
- Profanity on streets and sidewalks may be a violation of state law or local ordinances.
- Company officials, with the assistance of local law-enforcement agents, should make every effort to permit individuals and vehicles to move into and out of the facility in a normal manner.
- Union officials and pickets have a right to talk to people going in or out. Intimidation, threats, and coercion are not permitted, either by verbal remarks or by physical action.
- The use of sound trucks may be regulated by state law or local ordinance with respect to noise level, location, and permit requirements.
- If acts of violence or trespassing occur on the premises, officials should file complaints or seek injunctions. If you are the object of violence, sign a warrant for the arrest of the person or persons causing the violence.
- Fighting, assault, battery, violence, threats, and intimidation are not permissible under the law. The carrying of knives, firearms, clubs, and other dangerous weapons may be prohibited by state law or local ordinance.

strikes are hard to distinguish from absenteeism, and in firing some workers, it merely enforced its policies about being away from work. The NLRB ruled in 2019 that such "hit and run" guerrilla tactics are not genuine strikes and, thus, are not protected by the National Labor Relations Act. In short, the intermittent strikers at Walmart were lawfully disciplined.[55]

During a strike, certain rules of conduct apply to both parties; these are summarized in Table 13-3. In addition, certain special rules apply to management. *Management must not*

- Offer extra rewards to non-strikers.
- Threaten non-strikers or strikers.
- Promise benefits to strikers in an attempt to end the strike or to undermine the union.
- Threaten employees with discharge for taking part in a lawful strike.
- Discharge non-strikers who refuse to take over a striker's job.

When the Strike Is Over

The period of time immediately after a strike is critical because an organization's problems are not over when the strike is settled. There is the problem of conflict between strikers and their replacements (if replacements were hired) and the reaccommodation of strikers to the workplace. After an economic strike is settled, the method of reinstatement is best protected by a written memorandum of agreement with the union that outlines the intended procedure. A key point of consideration in any strike aftermath is misconduct by some strikers. To refuse reinstatement for such strikers following an economic strike, management must be able to present evidence (e.g., videos, photos) to prove the misconduct.

The most important human aspect at the end of the strike is the restoration of harmonious working relations as soon as possible, so that full operations can be resumed. A letter, a video, or a speech to employees welcoming them back to work can help this process along, as can meetings with supervisors, indicating that no resentment or ill-will is to be shown toward returning strikers. In practice, this may be difficult to do. However, keep these points in mind:

- Nothing is gained by allowing vindictiveness of any type in any echelon of management.
- The burden of maintaining healthy labor–management relations now lies with the organization.
- There is always another negotiation ahead, and rancor has no place at any bargaining table.[56]

HR BUZZ

WHY THERE ARE FEWER STRIKES IN THE UNITED STATES*

The number of strikes involving 1,000 workers or more has been declining for more than 50 years (see Figure 13-3). Today they occur only in about 5 percent of all labor–management negotiations. To a large extent, this is due to major economic, legislative, and social changes that are prompting both companies and union leaders to reassess their tactics. Here are two of them:

1. Companies have proven their willingness to hire replacement workers and wait out strikers. With only 6.2 percent of private-sector Americans belonging to a union, strikes don't carry the same resonance with the public as they did in the past. Members of the public who are most likely to support a strike support unions in general, and they believe that the contract offered to the strikers was unfair. At the same time, many companies have little desire to provoke a fight, especially during times of economic weakness and pressure on profits. Although that may appear to give unions an advantage at the bargaining table, unions also recognize the reality that companies may need concessions to prosper. In short, tough demands are being made on both sides.

2. Technology and global markets make it easier than ever for big companies to reduce their labor costs–either through outsourcing or by relocating plants to cheaper, foreign sites, such as Mexico. One reason for the drop in membership at the United Auto Workers (UAW), from a peak of 1.5 million in the mid-1970s to 391,000 in 2020, is that much of the work traditionally done in automakers' own factories has been outsourced to suppliers' plants, which tend to be non-union. Any labor disruption would affect not only the union members but also thousands more hourly workers in the factories that supply the manufacturers. This is exactly what happened when the UAW struck GM in 2019, closing 30 U.S. factories for 40 days. The ripple effect through the broader U.S. economy caused temporary layoffs for thousands of non-UAW workers.

Sources: Bartash, J. (2020, Jan. 23). Share of union workers in the U. S. falls to a record low in 2019. *MarketWatch*. Retrieved from *www.marketwatch.com/story/share-of-union-workers-in-the-us-falls-to-a-record-low-in-2019-2020-01-22* on Jan. 24, 2020. United Auto Workers. (2020, May 12). *Wikipedia*. Retrieved from *https://en.wikipedia.org/wiki/United Auto Workers* on May 12, 2020. Naughton, N. (2019, Oct. 25). As GM workers approve new labor deal, UAW ends 40-day strike. *The Wall Street Journal*. Retrieved from *www.wsj.com/articles/as-gm-workers-approve-new-labor-deal-uaw-ends-40-day-strike-11572036798* on Oct. 25, 2019. Kelloway, E. K., Francis, L., Catano, V. M., and Dupre, K. E. (2008). Third-party support for strike action. *Journal of Applied Psychology* 93, pp. 806–17.

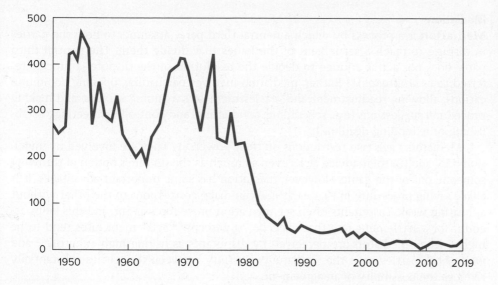

Figure 13–3

Number of work stoppages involving 1,000 employees or more.
Source: Bureau of Labor Statistics. Work stoppages involving 1,000 or more workers, 1947-2019. Retrieved from *www.bls.gov/web/ wkstp/annual listing. htm* on May 12, 2020.

Lockouts

A **lockout** may occur when a collective-bargaining agreement has expired. If the parties cannot agree on a contract, an employer may legally *lock out* its employees in order to put economic pressure on a union to settle a contract on terms favorable to the employer. Lockouts are legitimate employer tactics to decrease union power in situations where the lockout is done to avoid economic loss.[57] This is what the National Football League's owners did when the collective-bargaining agreement with the players expired in 2011.[58] The lockout lasted 159 days, with both sides making concessions in order to reach a 10-year collective-bargaining agreement. The lockout put heavy pressure on both sides, but especially on the players because their playing lives average just 3.6 years. Missing a year of competition and salary has huge consequences on lifetime earnings.[59]

It is legal for a company to replace the locked-out workers with temporary replacements in order to continue operations during the lockout. However, the use of permanent replacements (without first consulting the union) is not permissible, according to the National Labor Relations Board, because such an action would completely destroy the bargaining unit and represent an unlawful withdrawal of recognition of a duly designated union.[60]

Third-Party Involvement

A **bargaining impasse** occurs when the parties are unable to move further toward settlement. Because there is no clear formula to determine if or when an impasse in negotiations has been reached, litigation often ensues, and a judge must decide the issue.[61] In an effort to resolve the impasse, a neutral third party may become involved. In most private-sector negotiations, the parties have to agree voluntarily before any third-party involvement can be imposed on them. Because employees in the public sector are prohibited by law from striking, the use of third parties is more prevalent there.[62]

Three general types of third-party involvement are common: mediation, factfinding, and interest arbitration. Each becomes progressively more constraining on the freedom of the parties.

Mediation

Mediation is a process by which a neutral third party attempts to help the parties in dispute to reach a settlement of the issues that divide them. The neutral third party does not act as a judge to decide the resolution of the dispute (a process referred to as *arbitration*).[63] Rather, mediation involves persuading, opening communications, allowing readjustment and reassessment of bargaining stances, and making procedural suggestions (e.g., scheduling, conducting, and controlling meetings; establishing or extending deadlines).

Mediators have two restrictions on their power: (1) They are involved by invitation only and (2) their advice lacks even so much as the umpire's option of throwing someone out of the game. However, mediation has some important advantages. It is a face-saving procedure in that each side can make concessions to the other without appearing weak. Disputants often see mediation procedures as fair, and this helps account for a settlement rate that exceeds 70 percent.[64] Settlement rates tend to be higher when mediators are perceived by disputants as having high expertise[65] and when both parties trust the mediator.[66] Hostility between the parties substantially reduces the possibility of an agreement.

Fact-Finding

Fact-finding is a dispute-resolution mechanism that is commonly used in the public sector to help resolve an impasse in negotiation. Essentially, it is nonbinding arbitration. In a fact-finding procedure, each party submits whatever information it believes is relevant to a resolution of the dispute. A neutral fact-finder then examines the evidence and prepares a report on the facts. The assumption is that a neutral

---

LEGALITIES

DOES THE ADA OVERRIDE SENIORITY RIGHTS?*

Does the requirement in the Americans with Disabilities Act for "reasonable accommodation" supersede collectively bargained seniority rights? A federal appeals court ruled on this issue in a case that involved an employee of Consolidated Rail Corporation who was diagnosed with epilepsy. Medical restrictions prevented him from returning to his night-time shift. So he sought to invoke a provision in the collective-bargaining agreement that permitted an employee with a disability, upon written agreement of the employer and the union, to "bump" a more senior employee or to occupy a more senior position and be immune from bumping by more senior employees. When the union refused to sign the agreement, the employee brought suit under the ADA.

The court rejected the employee's argument, finding that "collective-bargaining seniority rights have a preexisting special status in the law and that Congress to date has shown no intent to alter this status by the duties created by the ADA." In fact, the majority of courts have held that the employer need not violate a seniority clause in a collective-bargaining agreement in order to give a light-duty job to a worker with a disability, as opposed to the most senior worker.

---

*Sources: U.S. Department of Labor. (n.d.). Americans with Disabilities Act. Retrieved from *www.dol.gov/general/topic/disability/ada* on May 13, 2020. Labor and employment. Seniority can trump disability. (2008, March 26). Retrieved from *https://corporate.findlaw.com/litigation-disputes/labor-and-employment-seniority-can-trump-disability.html* on May 13, 2020. McGlothlen, C. A. and Savine, G. N. (1997). *Eckles v. Consolidated Rail Corp.: Reconciling the ADA with Collective Bargaining Agreements: Is This the Correct Approach?* 46 DePaul L. Rev. 1043. Available at *https://via.library.depaul.edu/law-review/vol46/iss4/8.*

report will bring sufficient pressure on the parties to induce them to accept the recommendations of the fact-finder or to use the fact-finder's report as a basis for a negotiated settlement.[67]

Actually, the term *fact-finding* is a misnomer because fact-finders often proceed, with statutory authority, to render a public recommendation of a reasonable settlement. In this respect, fact-finding is similar to mediation. However, neither fact-finding nor mediation necessarily results in a contract between management and labor. Consequently, the parties often resort to arbitration of a dispute, either as a matter of law (*compulsory arbitration*) or by mutual agreement between union and management (*interest arbitration*).

Interest Arbitration

Like fact-finding, **interest arbitration** is used primarily in the public sector. However, arbitration differs considerably from mediation and fact-finding. As one author noted, "While mediation assists the parties to reach their own settlement, arbitration hears the positions of both and decides on binding settlement terms. While fact-finding would recommend a settlement, arbitration dictates it."[68]

Interest arbitration is controversial because imposition of a settlement eliminates the need for the parties to negotiate on their own. If they reach an impasse, settlement by an outsider is certain.[69] Although the use of interest arbitration in the public sector has reduced the probability of strikes more than fact-finding, there is little evidence of excessive use of interest arbitration. Even in systems that have been followed for as long as 30 years, the rate of cases going to interest arbitration rarely has exceeded 25 percent. The overall effect of interest arbitration on wage levels appears to be modest—5 to 10 percent higher than wages in jurisdictions where arbitration is not available.[70]

ADMINISTRATION OF THE COLLECTIVE-BARGAINING AGREEMENT

To many union and management officials, the real test of effective labor relations comes after the agreement is signed—that is, in its day-to-day administration. At that point, the major concern of the union is to obtain in practice the employee rights that management has granted on paper. The major concern of management is to establish its right to manage the business and to keep operations running.[71] A key consideration for both is the form of union security that governs conditions of employment.

Union-Security Clauses

Section 14b of the Taft-Hartley Act enables states to enact **right-to-work laws** that prohibit compulsory union membership (after a probationary period) as a condition of continued employment. Understandably, unions oppose these laws because they create a "free-rider" problem. That is, employees who do not pay dues still receive the same wages, benefits, and protections as those who do. Table 13-4 illustrates the forms that such **union-security clauses** can take and indicates that most of them are illegal in the 27 states that have passed right-to-work laws. In the remaining non-right-to-work states, unions are allowed to negotiate union- or agency-shop provisions into their contracts with employers. In 2018, however, the Supreme Court ruled that mandatory public-sector union dues are unconstitutional, thereby making every state a right-to-work state for the public sector.[72]

Table 13–4

FORMS OF UNION SECURITY AND THEIR LEGAL STATUS IN RIGHT-TO-WORK STATES

	Legal	Illegal
Closed shop. An individual must join the union that represents employees in order to be considered for employment.		X
Union shop. As a condition of continued employment, an individual must join the union that represents employees after a probationary period (typically a minimum of 30 days).		X
Preferential shop. Union members are given preference in hiring.		X
Agency shop. Employees need not join the union that represents them, but, in lieu of dues, they must pay a service charge for representation.		X
Maintenance of membership. An employee must remain a member of the union once he or she joins.		X
Checkoff. An employee may request that union dues be deducted from his or her pay and be sent directly to the union.	X	

Grievance Procedures in the Unionized Firm

Occasionally during the life of a contract, disputes arise about the interpretation, application, or enforcement of the collective-bargaining agreement. Under these circumstances, an aggrieved party may file a grievance. A **grievance** is an alleged violation of the rights of workers on the job.[73] A formal process known as a **grievance procedure** is then invoked to help the parties resolve the dispute. Grievance procedures are the keystone of labor-management relations because of their ability to resolve disputed issues while work continues without litigation, strikes, or other disruptions.[74]

In addition to providing a formal mechanism for resolving disputes, the grievance procedure defines and narrows the nature of the complaint. Thus, each grievance must be expressed in writing. The written grievance identifies the grievant, when the incident leading to the grievance occurred (it could, of course, be ongoing), and where the incident happened. The written statement also indicates why the complaint is considered a grievance and what the grievant thinks should be done about the matter.[75] A typical grievance procedure in a unionized firm works as shown in Figure 13-4. As the figure indicates, unresolved grievances proceed progressively to higher and higher levels of management and union representation and culminate in voluntary, binding arbitration. Specific time limits for management's decision and the union's approval are normally imposed at each step–for example, 3 days for each party at step 1, 5 days for each party at steps 2 and 3, and 10 days for each party at step 4.

Typical grievance rates in unionized employers are about 10 per 100 employees per year. The vast majority of those are resolved without resorting to arbitration.

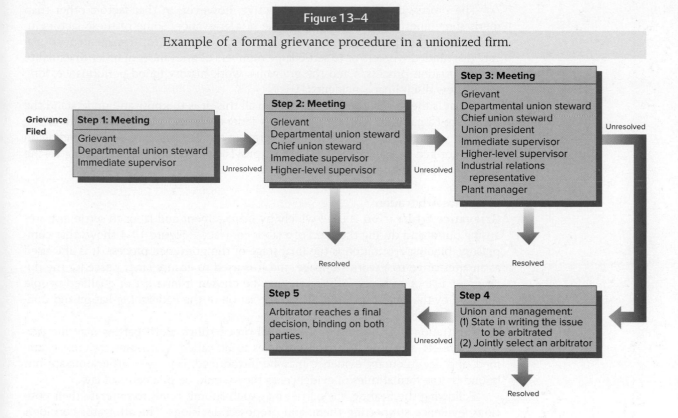

Figure 13–4

Example of a formal grievance procedure in a unionized firm.

In fact, for every 100 grievances, only about 2 percent require arbitration to resolve them—and that takes time. How much time? Data indicate an average length of time between the appointment of an arbitrator and the issuance of an award of 184 days.[76] Grievance administration can be expensive as well. Thus, the American Postal Workers Union allocates fully 20 percent of its members' dues to the costs of processing grievances.[77]

Resolving Grievances

Unions and management each win about half the time. However, unions tend to win more grievances related to such issues as the denial of sick benefits, termination, transfer, suspension, and disciplinary memoranda. Ordinarily, the burden of proof in a grievance proceeding is on the union. Because fewer issues of interpretation are involved in the areas that unions usually win, this pattern of grievance resolution is not surprising.[78]

In summary, there are two key advantages to the grievance procedure. First, it ensures that the complaints and problems of workers can be heard, rather than simply allowed to fester. Second, grievance procedures provide formal mechanisms to ensure due process for all parties. Research indicates that employees who have access to such a system are more willing to continue working for their organizations after filing a grievance than are employees who do not have access to such a system.[79] On the other hand, the job performance of grievance filers is likely to be lower after they learn the outcome of their grievances.[80]

The process is not completely objective, however, in that factors other than merit sometimes determine the outcome of a grievance. Some of these factors include the cost of granting a grievance, the perceived need for management to placate disgruntled workers or to settle large numbers of grievances in order to expedite the negotiation process,[81] and the grievant's work history (good performance, long tenure, few disciplinary incidents).[82]

What is the role of the line manager in all this? It is to know and understand the collective-bargaining contract, as well as federal and state labor laws. Above all, whether you agree or disagree with the terms of the contract, it is legally binding on both labor and management. Respect its provisions, and manage according to the spirit as well as the letter of the contract.

Grievance Arbitration

Grievance arbitration is used widely by management and labor to settle disputes arising out of and during the term of a labor contract.[83] Figure 13-4 shows that compulsory, binding arbitration is the final stage of the grievance process. It is also used as an alternative to a work stoppage, and it is used to ensure labor peace for the duration of a labor contract. Arbitrators may be chosen from a list of qualified people supplied by the American Arbitration Association or the Federal Mediation and Conciliation Service.

Arbitration hearings are quasi-judicial proceedings. Both parties may file pre-hearing briefs, along with lists of witnesses to be called. Witnesses are cross-examined, and documentary evidence may be introduced. However, arbitrators are not bound by the formal rules of evidence, as they would be in a court of law.

Following the hearing, the parties may each submit briefs to reiterate their positions, evidence supporting them, and proposed decisions. The arbitrator considers the evidence, the contract clause in dispute, and the powers granted the arbitrator under the labor agreement. The arbitrator then issues a decision. In the rare instances where a losing party refuses to honor the arbitrator's decision, the decision can be enforced by taking that party to federal court.[84]

Generally, an arbitration award cannot be appealed in court simply because one party believes the arbitrator made a mistake in interpreting an agreement. Courts have held that arbitrator awards are extensions of labor contracts, and court deference is the rule.[85]

We noted earlier that only 10.3 percent of U.S. workers belong to unions. To put this issue into perspective, let us examine rates of union membership in other countries.

UNION MEMBERSHIP IN COUNTRIES OTHER THAN THE UNITED STATES

Figure 13-5 shows current union membership as a percentage of total employees in 15 countries. Union membership is highest in Iceland (90.4 percent) as well as in the Scandinavian economies (e.g., Sweden, at 66.1 percent). In 1985, average trade union membership in Organization for Economic Cooperation and Development (OECD) countries was 30 percent; today, that has fallen to just 16 percent.[86] The OECD includes 37 member states with market economies.[87] In Figure 13-5, union membership is lowest in France, but it is important to note that many nonunionized French workers are covered by collective bargaining agreements. Under them, unions often

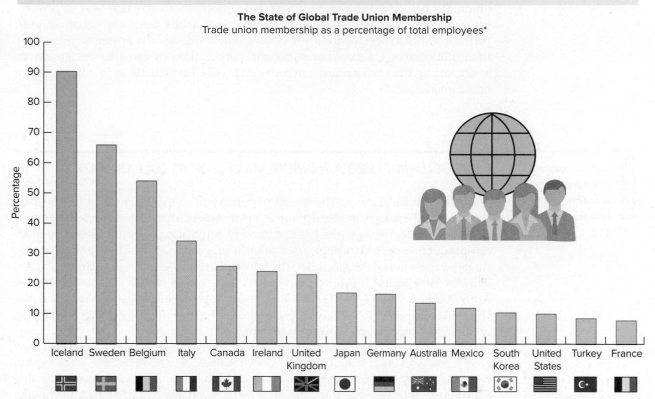

Figure 13-5

The State of Global Trade Union Membership

The State of Global Trade Union Membership
Trade union membership as a percentage of total employees*

*Selected OECD countries (2018 or latest year)

Source: Source: McCarthy, N. (2019, May 6). The state of global trade union membership (infographic). *Forbes.* Retrieved from *www.forbes.com/sites/niallmccarthy/2019/05/06/the-state-of-global-trade-union-membership-infographic/#527d258a2b6e* on May 13, 2020.

negotiate terms of employment for entire companies or even industries.[88] Unions remain powerful forces, largely because of wage premiums in unionized firms and the *spillover effect* on nonunion employers. Our next section explores these issues in more detail.

UNION WAGE PREMIUMS AND THE SPILLOVER EFFECT

In the United States, workers represented by unions are estimated to earn wages that are 14.7 percent higher than comparable nonunion workers.[89] For example, unionized registered nurses make roughly 20 percent more than their nonunion peers.[90] This is not true in all industries, and there are important differences. For example, in durable goods manufacturing and retail trade, the union wage premium is below 10 percent. Conversely, the largest union wage premiums are in the construction, trucking, warehousing, education, and health-care sectors. In short, wage differentials reflect a variety of influences in addition to coverage by a collective-bargaining agreement, such as occupation, firm size, geographical region, and industry.[91]

The impact of unions in general would be understated if we did not account for what is called the **spillover effect;** that is, employers seek to avoid unionization by offering workers the wages, benefits, and working conditions that rival unionized firms do. The nonunion employer continues to stay that way, and workers receive the spillover of rewards already obtained by their unionized counterparts. Another aspect of spillover occurs when U.S. unions attempt to increase their influence on U.S.-based multinational corporations by assisting foreign unions in organizing the corporations' offshore employees, particularly in low-wage, developing economies.[92]

Human Resource Management in Action: Conclusion

RESTRUCTURING THROUGH UNION–MANAGEMENT COLLABORATION

Make no mistake about it: The recent popularity of cooperation stems largely from the sweeping changes in the economic environment that have occurred. Another reason is new technology–the Internet, factory automation, robotics, and more modern production systems. Cooperation offers a pragmatic approach to problems that threaten the survival of companies, the jobs and income security of their employees, and the institutional future of their unions. Progressive unions such as the United Auto Workers (UAW), the Service Employees International Union (SEIU), and the United Steelworkers (USW) are at the forefront of a revolutionary change in the way unions view cooperation with management.

That was exactly the case with the USW–Goodyear agreement in 2017 that covered 7,200 workers at five plants. The USW ratified a 5-year contract–not the typical 3-year agreement–that runs through 2022. In addition to wage increases and closing gaps between labor-grade tiers, the agreement maintains cost-of-living adjustments and extends plant protection to ensure that none of the five plants closes during the contract's duration. By 2019, however, things turned much worse for the company. To strengthen its U.S. competitiveness, Goodyear cut the production of tires for less profitable segments of the tire market. It exercised a provision in its 2017 agreement with the USW, offering buyouts to workers at its Gadsden, Alabama, plant while investing up to $180 million to expand capacity at its Fayettteville, North Carolina, plant for larger-rim-diameter passenger tires.

In this new era of collaboration, here are five tips from former SEIU president Andy Stern on how labor and management can work together more effectively:

1. *Relationships are not a matter of chance; they are a matter of choice.* We don't see our employers as enemies. We need to build successful employers–to understand markets, competition, and where we can be helpful in increasing creativity, innovation, and entrepreneurial activity. To do that, everyone needs to be involved, to have a voice, and to share in the employers' success.
2. *Approach partnerships by making "finding a solution" a higher priority than placing blame.*
3. *Learn to disagree without being disagreeable.*
4. *Offer incentives that encourage others to take prudent risks.*
5. *Keep an open mind, rather than an open mouth, be willing to change, and stay focused on shared goals.*

IMPACT OF COOPERATIVE LABOR RELATIONS ON PRODUCTIVITY, QUALITY OF WORK LIFE, AND THE BOTTOM LINE*

As the company that practically invented the modern automobile assembly line, Ford understands quite clearly the importance of collaboration between labor and management. From the day CEO Allan Mulally arrived at a troubled Ford Motor Company in 2006 until he retired in 2014, he had a plan to make the company successful, and he never wavered from it. He stressed that everything was up for review and that nothing was off the table. He sold off brands that diluted Ford's resources (Volvo and Jaguar), closed down struggling brands (Mercury), and closed plants that were no longer needed in the face of reduced demand. At the same time, he encouraged executives to emulate leaner competitors, like Toyota, and to adopt team-oriented procedures, and he forced executives to put aside their internal rivalries.

As the company appeared headed for bankruptcy in 2009, Mulally and his union counterparts at the United Auto Workers had long, frequent, and open discussions, with the intent to bring about "constructive collaboration." The CEO and the board of directors were determined that Ford would emerge from the Great Recession as a solvent company, with its legacy intact, and that it would be well prepared for the future. Mulally presented a clear and incontrovertible business case to the UAW for what absolutely had to happen to make things work. According to UAW officials, "Utter transparency of data convinced labor that if the company [i.e., management] was going to save the place, we'd save it together." Moved by his gesture of transparency, the union agreed to tough terms. Labor and management were able to coalesce around the goal of working together to create profit for labor, management, and, for the first time in recent automotive history, shareholders.

As employees warmed to this approach, improvements in the safety, styling, and fuel efficiency of each new Ford model followed. So also did improvements in market share in North America, China, and more globally. The result? Nineteen consecutive quarters of profitable operations, profit-sharing with employees ($6,600 to each of 53,000 union workers in the United States in 2020), continual investments to upgrade and modernize assembly plants, vastly improved quality, and security for workers and their families. CEO Mulally's optimism, his emphasis on collaboration with the United Auto Workers, and his mantra, "Profitable growth for all," were critical to making that happen.

Sources: Noble, B. (2020, Feb. 4). Ford to pay UAW members $6,600 in profit sharing. *The Detroit News.* Retrieved from *www.detroitnews.com/story/business/autos/ford/2020/02/04/ford-uaw-profit-sharing-2019/4626817002/* on May 13, 2020. Vlasic, B. (2014, May 1). A complete U-turn: The head of Ford retires, having rejuvenated the carmaker. *The New York Times.* Retrieved from *www.nytimes.com/2014/05/02/business/ford-motor-chief-to-retire.html?r=0* on June 18, 2014. Vlasic, B. (2013, Mar. 15). Ford chiefs benefit from auto comeback. *The New York Times.* Retrieved from *www.nytimes.com/2013/03/16/business/another-lucrative-year-for-car-executives.html* on June 18, 2014. Kirkland, R. (2013, Nov.) Leading in the 21st century: An interview with Ford's Alan Mulally. Retrieved from *www.mckinsey.com/insights/strategy/leading_in_the_21st_century_an_interview_with_fords_alan_mulally* on June 18, 2014. Smith, A. (2012, Dec. 7). Ford VP: Good labor relations saved company. Retrieved from. *www.shrm.org/ResourcesAndTools/hr-topics/labor-relations/Pages/Ford-UAW.aspx* on June 15, 2014.

As we have seen, the business world has changed dramatically, largely due to changes in technology and global competition. If U.S. labor leaders let today's opportunities for labor-management cooperation slip by, they may not get another chance to be part of the solution to the continuing challenge to improve productivity, quality of work life, and profits.

IMPLICATIONS FOR MANAGEMENT PRACTICE

In a globalized, technology-based world, a distributive (win-lose) orientation toward labor is simply inefficient. Whether you are managing people in Boston, Budapest, or Beijing, view your employees as a source of potential competitive advantage. Treat them with dignity and respect, and they will respond in kind. As a cover of *Fast Company* magazine noted, "The best leaders know where all great companies start. (It's the people, stupid!)"[a]

More flexibility and less confrontation, with workers' views being heard and respected, will help companies succeed in the global marketplace. Then workers can seek higher wages without putting their jobs at risk.[b] Toward that end, nonunion employers should consider using employee-involvement teams to improve their companies. To avoid being defined as a labor organization under the NLRA, case law suggests two lessons for employers. One, make sure that such teams do not discuss issues that typically are the domain of collective bargaining: wages, hours, and conditions of work. Two, make sure that management does not dominate the committees or have a majority of members.[c]

[a]*Source:* Peoplepalooza. (2001, Jan.). *Fast Company* 42, pp. 80, 81.

[b]Agovino, T. (2020, March 14). Unions struggle to hold on. *SHRM Online*. Retrieved from *www.shrm.org/hr-today/news/all-things-work/pages/unions-struggle-to-gain-a-toehold.aspx* on Mar. 14, 2020.

[c]Mahoney, T., and Drutchas, A. (2016, June 9). Could your employee participation program be illegal? *SHRM Online*. Retrieved from *www.shrm.org/resourcesandtools/hr-topics/labor-relations/pages/could-your-employee-participation-program-be-illegal.aspx* on May 13, 2020.

SUMMARY

At a general level, the goal of unions is to improve economic and other conditions of employment. Although unions have been successful over the years in achieving these goals, more recently they have suffered membership losses. At the same time, many of the fastest-growing unions in the United States represent white-collar professionals, including physicians, nuclear engineers, psychologists, and tech-company employees.

Six features characterize the U.S. industrial relations system: exclusive representation, collective agreements that embody a sharp distinction between negotiation and interpretation of an agreement, decentralized collective bargaining, relatively high union dues and large union staffs, opposition by both large and small employers to union organization, and a government role that is relatively passive in dispute resolution and highly legalistic in administrative proceedings and in the courts.

The National Labor Relations Board, created by the Wagner Act of 1935, supervises organizing campaigns and representation elections. If the union wins, it becomes the sole bargaining agent for employees. For the U.S. labor movement, collective bargaining is a cornerstone and anything that threatens its continued viability will be resisted vigorously by organized labor.

Unfortunately, bargaining sometimes reaches an impasse, at which point the parties may resort to a strike (workers) or a lockout (management). Alternatively, the parties may request third-party intervention in the form of mediation, fact-finding, or interest arbitration. In the public sector, such intervention is usually required.

Occasionally during the life of a contract, disputes arise about the interpretation of the collective-bargaining agreement. Under these circumstances, an aggrieved party may file a grievance. A grievance is an alleged violation of the rights of workers on the job. A formal process known as a grievance procedure is then invoked to help the parties resolve the dispute. Compulsory, binding arbitration is the final stage of the grievance process. It is also used as an alternative to a work stoppage, and it is used to ensure labor peace for the duration of a labor contract.

Unionized workers still enjoy a wage premium over their nonunion counterparts, but factors other than union status may account for the difference. A spillover effect occurs when nonunion employers raise compensation in an effort to maintain their nonunion status, or when U.S. unions attempt to increase their influence on U.S.-based multinational corporations by assisting foreign unions in organizing offshore employees. Finally, as the chapter-opening vignette illustrated, labor and management are cooperating more often in an effort to enhance the productivity and overall competitiveness of their enterprises. In the current climate of global competition and the migration of technology and capital across borders, this is more productive than the old adversarial win-lose approach.

KEY TERMS

labor union	economic strikes
pattern bargaining	unprotected strikes
exclusive representation	sympathy strike
secondary boycott	intermittent strikes
free-speech clause	lockout
right-to-work laws	bargaining impasse
authorization cards	mediation
card check	fact-finding
bargaining unit	interest arbitration
community of interest	right-to-work laws
secret-ballot election	union-security clause
exclusive bargaining representative	grievance
decertification	grievance procedures
distributive bargaining	grievance arbitration
integrative bargaining	spillover effect
unfair labor practice strike	

DISCUSSION QUESTIONS

13-1. Are the roles of labor and management inherently adversarial?

13-2. Discuss the rights and obligations of unions and management during a union-organizing drive.

13-3. Why is it so difficult to be effective at both distributive and integrative bargaining in the course of the same negotiations?

13-4. What are the key features of the U.S. industrial relations system?

13-5. Compare and contrast mediation, interest arbitration, and grievance arbitration.

13-6. Why is it in the best interests of management and labor to work together? Or is it?

13-7. Your company has just learned that it is the target of a union-organizing campaign. How will you advise managers about what they can and cannot say to employees?

13-8. Prepare three arguments to support each of the following positions: (a) unions are no longer relevant today and (b) unions are still relevant today.

13-9. It's sometimes been said, "The best union organizer is the boss." Do you agree? Why or why not?

13-10. Why is it so difficult to compare industrial relations systems in different countries?

APPLYING YOUR KNOWLEDGE

Exercise 13–1   ***Contract Negotiations at Moulton Machine Shop***

Collective bargaining is the cornerstone of American labor relations. Face-to-face negotiations involving give-and-take on the part of both management and labor representatives are an inherent part of our present system. It is through these negotiations that both sides attempt to understand the positions of the other and attempt to persuade the other side of the fairness of their own demands.

The purpose of this exercise is for you to experience the collective-bargaining process and to gain an awareness of the nature and complexity of labor negotiations.

Background Information

Moulton Machine Shop is a 60 year-old shop located near Lake Erie in Pennsylvania. The company manufactures a wide variety of made-to-order products, but its primary business is the repair of mechanical airplane parts and components, a business that it conducts on an international basis. The firm has developed a reputation for quality and timely work on difficult machining projects. The mostly blue-collar workforce at Moulton consists of about 200 workers who were organized 40 years ago by the International Machinists Union (IMU). The labor relations climate at Moulton has been fairly good over the past 20 years (after a rather stormy beginning), with no strikes in the last 9 years. In the past 2 years, however, the number of grievances has increased substantially.

Recent economic conditions have been difficult for Moulton. Over the past 5 years, increased competition from lower-priced, foreign-based machine shops has pruned Moulton's profit margins. Overall, sales are down about 10 percent compared with projections made earlier in the year. Moulton's management believes that competition will intensify in the near future, creating even more problems for the firm. The union is aware of the financial situation at Moulton and is sympathetic, but it has been very clear in its overtures to management that it intends to fight for an improved contract for its members because they have fallen behind equivalent workers in recent years.

CURRENT CONTRACT PROVISIONS	
Clause	**Current contract**
Wages	Average hourly wage is $24.73.
Benefits	Company-paid life insurance and a $200-deductible medical insurance plan.
Overtime	Time and a half.
Layoffs	A 2-week notice is required to lay off any union member who has been at Moulton more than 2 months.
Vacations	2 weeks for all employees except those with more than 20 years' service, who receive 3 weeks.
Holidays	9 paid per year.
Sick leave	4 paid days per year; if verified by doctor, the leave can be up to 10 days.
Length of contract	2 years.

Additional Information

1. Hourly wage rates for union members doing similar work elsewhere in the local vicinity average $26.80.
2. A $200-deductible dental insurance plan would cost about $75 per employee.
3. Overtime averaged 185 hours per employee last year.
4. Among competitors, the most frequent vacation, holiday, and sick-leave schedules are as follows: (1) 2 weeks' vacation for starters, 3 weeks after 10 years of service, and 4 weeks after 25 years; (b) 10 paid holidays per year; and (c) 6 paid sick-leave days per year (although there is a wide variation here, with a few firms having no paid sick leave at all).
5. Contract length at similar firms varies from 1 to 3 years.

Procedure

Divide the class into groups of three. Each group consists of a union negotiator, a management negotiator, and an observer. The instructor will provide a role statement for each negotiator. These role statements should not be shared with the other negotiator or with the observer. Each group's task is to negotiate a contract between Moulton Machine Shop and the IMU. Your instructor will tell you how much time you have available for this task. It is important that you settle this contract in the limited time available, so that you can avert a costly strike.

As the negotiations proceed, observers should record significant events. Use the following sample observation form (Contract Negotiations Observation Form). When the negotiations end, observers will be asked to report the final agreed-upon contract provisions to the rest of the class and to describe the process by which the negotiations took place in each group.

CONTRACT NEGOTIATIONS OBSERVATION FORM

Clause	Final settlement
Wages	_____
Benefits	_____
Overtime	_____
Layoffs	_____
Vacations	_____
Holidays	_____
Sick leave	_____
Length of contract	_____
Other provisions	_____

Questions

1. How do the negotiations begin? Which side talks the most in the beginning? Does each side have a clear understanding of the purpose of the negotiations?
2. What behaviors of the negotiators seem either to bring the parties closer together or to drive them further apart?
3. How does the climate of the negotiations change over time? Which side talks the most as the negotiations wear on? Do the parties agree more or less as time passes?
4. How do the negotiations end? Are the parties friendly with each other? Do they both seem committed to the final solution? Are future union-management relations likely to get better or worse as a result of this agreement?

REFERENCES

1. Budd, J. W. (2021). *Labor Relations* (6th ed.). New York: McGraw-Hill.
2. Agovino, T. (2020, March 14). Unions struggle to hold on. *SHRM Online*. Retrieved from *www.shrm.org/hr-today/news/all-things-work/pages/unions-struggle-to-gain-a-toehold.aspx* on Mar. 14, 2020. See also Eidelson, J. (2015, Mar. 1). VW and UAW are odd bedfellows at a southern U. S. plant. *Bloomberg Businessweek*, pp. 21, 22.
3. Bunn, E., quoted in Whitford, D. (2007, Sept. 17). UAW's latest gamble. *BusinessWeek*, p. 27.
4. Kristol, I. (1978, Oct. 23). Understanding trade unionism. *Wall Street Journal*, p. 28.
5. Agovino (2020), op. cit. See also Cunningham, J. (2012, June). State of the unions. *NACD Directorship*, pp. 23-26. See also Fiorito, J. (2001). Human resource management practices and worker desires for union representation. *Journal of Labor Research* 22(2), pp. 35-54.
6. Agovino (2020), op. cit.
7. Scheiber, N., and Boudette, N. E. (2019, Dec. 26). Behind a U.A.W. crisis: Lavish meals and luxury villas. *The New York Times*. Retrieved from *www.nytimes.com/2019/12/26/business/uaw-gary-jones-investigation.html* on May 11, 2020.
8. Bureau of Labor Statistics. (2020, Jan. 22). Union members–2019. Retrieved from *www.bls.gov/news.release/pdf/union2.pdf* on May 11, 2020.
9. Agovino (2020), op. cit.
10. Isidore, C. (2014, Jan. 27). Union membership at businesses grows. *CNNMoney*. Retrieved from *http://money.cnn.com/2014/01/27/news/economy/union-membership/* on June 15, 2014. See also Maher, K. (2005, Sept. 27). The new union worker. *The Wall Street Journal*, pp. B1, B11.

11. Bureau of Labor Statistics (2020), op. cit. *See also* Schmitt, J., and Warner, K. (2009, Nov.). *The Changing Face of Labor, 1983–2008.* Washington, DC: Center for Economic and Policy Research. *See also* Mellor, S. (1995). Gender composition and gender representation in local unions: Relationships between women's participation in local office and women's participation in local activities. *Journal of Applied Psychology* 80, pp. 706-20.

12. Maher, K. (2007, Jan. 22). Are unions relevant? *The Wall Street Journal*, p. R5. *See also* Greenhouse, S. (2000, Oct. 24). Labor law hinders unions, leaders say. *The Denver Post*, p. 20A.

13. Bureau of Labor Statistics. (2018, Sept. 20). Employee tenure summary. Retrieved from *www.bls.gov/news.release/tenure.nr0.htm* on May 11, 2020.

14. Bureau of Labor Statistics (2020), op. cit. *See also* Fields, G., Aeppel, T., Maher, K., and Adamy, J. (2005, July 27). Reinventing the union. *The Wall Street Journal*, pp. B1, B2.

15. Lajoux, A. R. (2012, June). Unions as shareholders. *NACD Directorship*, pp. 26–30. *See also* Soltis, C. (2012, May 24). Unions' new playbook. *NACD Directorship*, pp. 30–34. *See also* Wysocki, B., Jr., Maher, K., and Glader, P. (2007, May 9). A labor union's power: Blocking takeover bids. *The Wall Street Journal*, pp. A1, A12.

16. Smith, A. (2012, Dec. 7). Ford VP: Good labor relations saved company. Retrieved from *www.shrm.org/hrdisciplines/laborrelations/articles/Pages/Ford-UAW.aspx* on June 15, 2014. *See also* Volkswagen's lasting lesson for labor. (2014, Feb. 20). *Bloomberg Businessweek*, p. 8.

17. Reed, D. (2016, Dec. 16). Low-fare international airlines threaten to end the party for American, Delta, and United. *Forbes.* Retrieved from *www.forbes.com/sites/daniel-reed/2016/12/16/is-the-party-over-already-low-fare-international-competitors-threaten-to-end-u-s-airlines-boom/#ea6a9017118a* on June 12, 2017.

18. Budd (2021), op. cit. *See also* Fossum, J. A. (2015). *Labor Relations: Development, Structure, Process* (12th ed.). Burr Ridge, IL: McGraw-Hill/Irwin.

19. Wayland, M. (2019, Dec. 11). UAW approves labor deal with Fiat Chrysler, closing unprecedented talks with Big 3 Detroit automakers marked by a strike, corruption, and litigation. *CNBC.* Retrieved from *www.cnbc.com/2019/12/11/uaw-members-approves-deal-with-fiat-chrysler-ending-2019-negotiations.html* on May 11, 2020. *See also* Lawrence, E. D. (2020, Feb. 6). Fiat Chrysler workers to get profit sharing of $7,280. *The Detroit Free Press.* Retrieved from *www.freep.com/story/money/cars/chrysler/2020/02/06/fiat-chrysler-2019-profit-sharing-checks-earnings/4675843002/* on May 11, 2020.

20. Budd (2021), op. cit. *See also* Katz, H. C., Kochan, T. A., and Colvin, A. J. S. (2008). *An Introduction to Collective Bargaining and Industrial Relations* (4th ed.). Burr Ridge, IL: McGraw-Hill/Irwin. *See also* Dunlop, J. T. (1988, May). Have the 1980s changed U.S. industrial relations? *Monthly Labor Review*, pp. 29-34.

21. Buckley, B., and Rubin, D. K. (2011, June 27). Hard times draw the line for bargaining. *ENR 2Q Cost Report*, pp. 16-19. Retrieved from *enr.construction.com/engineering/pdf/quarterly_cost_reports/2011-2Q_Cost_Report.pdf* on Aug. 17, 2011.

22. Lansbury, R. D., and Wailes, N. (2016). Employment relations in Australia. In G. J. Bamber, R. D. Lansbury, N. Wailes, and Wright, C. F. (Eds.), *International and Comparative Employment Relations: Globalization and Change.* London: Sage, pp. 117–37.

23. Boudette, N. E. (2014, Feb. 10). UAW holds breath on VW vote. *The Wall Street Journal*, pp. B1, B6.

24. Budd (2021), op. cit.

25. Epstein, R. A. (1995). *Simple Rules for a Complex World.* Cambridge, MA: Harvard University Press.

26. Nagele-Piazza, L. (2018, Aug. 9). Missouri voters strike down right-to-work law. *SHRM Online.* Retrieved from *www.shrm.org/resourcesandtools/legal-and-compliance/state-and-local-updates/pages/missouri-voters-strike-down-right-to-work-law.aspx* on Aug. 9, 2018.

27. Kanu, H. (2019, Dec. 17). Companies can ban use of work email in union organizing (1). *Daily Labor Report.* Retrieved from *https://news.bloomberglaw.com/daily-labor-report/companies-get-ok-to-ban-work-email-for-use-in-union-organizing* on Jan. 8, 2020.

28. Day, F. L., Jr., and Wildmann, M. K. (2019, Sept.). NLRB rules employers may bar union solicitation in their facilities. *HR Professionals Magazine* **9**(9), pp. 12, 13. *See also NLRB v. Babcock & Wilcox* (1956). 105 U.S. 351.

29. Nagele-Piazza, L. (2019, Aug. 13). Employer's statements against unionizing were not coercive. *SHRM Online*. Retrieved from *www.shrm.org/resourcesandtools/legal-and-compliance/employment-law/pages/employer-statements-against-unionizing-were-not-coercive. aspx* on Aug. 14, 2019.

30. The Employee Free Choice Act. (2019, Dec. 8). *Wikipedia*. Retrieved from *https:// en.wikipedia.org/wiki/Employee_Free_Choice_Act* on May 12, 2020. *See also* H.R. 5000 (114th): Employee Free Choice Act of 2016. (2016, Apr. 20). Retrieved from *www.gov-track.us/congress/bills/114/hr5000* on June 12, 2017.

31. Budd (2021), op. cit. *See also* Fossum (2015), op. cit.

32. Day, F. L., Jr. (2017, Oct.). Are you prepared for a union campaign? *HR Professionals Magazine* **7**(10), pp. 10, 11. *See also* Gurrieri, V. (2016, Mar. 10). 8th Circuit backs NLRB test for bargaining unit size. Retrieved from *www.law360.com/articles/770025* on June 12, 2017. *See also* Farber, H. S. (2001). Union success in representation elections: Why does unit size matter? *Industrial and Labor Relations Review* 54, pp. 329–48.

33. For more on the tactics both sides use, see Budd (2021), op. cit. *See also* Fossum (2015), op. cit. *See also* Berfield, S. (2015, Nov. 24). Surveillance in aisle 4: How Walmart keeps an eye on its massive workforce. *Bloomberg Businessweek*, pp. 52–57.

34. *Wayne J. Griffin Electric v. NLRB and IBEW* (2002, June 7). 4th Cir., Nos. 01-2258 and 01-2423. *See also* Loose lips: Anti-union remarks amount to unlawful threats. (2002, Aug.). *HR News*, p. 8.

35. Nagele-Piazza (2019), op. cit. *See also* Purdie, C., and Rhollans, J. (2016, Apr. 26). Union communication guidance: TIPS and FOE. Retrieved from *www.shrm.org/resourcesand-tools/hr-topics/labor-relations/pages/tips-foe.aspx* on June 13, 2017.

36. Fossum (2015), op. cit. *See also* Paleta, D. (2014, Mar. 16). UAW's southern push faces another defeat. *The Wall Street Journal*, p. B3. *See also* Maher, K. (2012, Nov. 1). Unions slip in strongholds. *The Wall Street Journal*, p. A3.

37. Wermiel, S. (1983, Nov. 16). NLRB can't force companies to bargain with minority unions, U.S. court rules. *The Wall Street Journal*, p. 12.

38. Zellner, W. (2002, Oct. 28). How Wal-Mart keeps unions at bay. *BusinessWeek*, pp. 94–96.

39. Calfee First Alert. (2019, Dec. 17). NLRB revises election rules to avoid "ambush" elections. Retrieved from *www.calfee.com/newsletters-156* on May 12, 2020.

40. Combs, R.(2019, April 24). Analysis: Five metrics that explain the state of the unions. *Bloomberg Law*. Retrieved from *https://news.bloomberglaw.com/bloomberg-law-analysis/ analysis-five-metrics-that-explain-the-state-of-the-unions* on May 12, 2020.

41. National Labor Relations Board. (2020). Decertification petitions. Retrieved from *https:// nlrb.gov/reports/nlrb-case-activity-reports/representation-cases/intake/decertification-petitions-rd* on May 12, 2020. *See also* Union decertification and deauthorization: What is the process to decertify a union? (2012, June 1). Retrieved from *www.shrm.org/ TemplatesTools/hrqa/Pages/decertifyaunion.aspx* on June 18, 2014.

42. Ibid. *See also* McGolrick, S. (2001, May). NLRB revises standards for employers to withdraw union recognition. *HR News*, pp. 7, 22.

43. Shell, G. R. (2018). *Bargaining for advantage* (3rd ed.). New York: Penguin Books. *See also* Fisher, R., Ury, W., and Patton, B. (2011). *Getting to Yes* (3rd ed.). New York: Penguin.

44. Ibid.

45. Lewicki, R. J., Saunders, D. M., and Barry, B. (2021). *Essentials of Negotiation* (7th ed.). New York: McGraw-Hill. *See also* Tinsley, C. H., O'Connor, K. M., and Sullivan, B. A. (2002). Tough guys finish last: The perils of a distributive reputation. *Organizational Behavior & Human Decision Processes* 88, pp. 621–42.

46. Brett, J. M., Shapiro, D. L., and Lytle, A. L. (1998). Breaking the bonds of reciprocity in negotiations. *Academy of Management Journal* 41, p. 410–24.

47. Ibid. *See also* Lewicki et al. (2021), op. cit. *See also* Walton, R. E., and McKersie, R. B. (1965). *A Behavioral Theory of Labor Negotiations.* New York: McGraw-Hill.

48. Katz, H. C., Kochan, T. A., and Colvin, A. J. S. (2017). *An Introduction to Collective Bargaining and Labor Relations* (5th ed.). Ithaca, NY: Cornell University ILR Press.

49. Salacuse, J. (2020, March 10). Lessons for business negotiators: Negotiation techniques from international diplomacy. Program on Negotiation, Harvard Law School. Retrieved from *www.pon.harvard.edu/daily/dealmaking-daily/the-art-of-deal-diplomacy/* on May 12, 2020. *See also* Russell, J. E. A. (2010, Dec. 6). Improve your negotiating skills. *The Washington Post.* Retrieved from *www.washingtonpost.com/wp-dyn/content/article/2010/12/03/AR2010120306007.html* on June 18, 2014.

50. Naquin, C. E., and Paulson, G. D. (2003). Online bargaining and interpersonal trust. *Journal of Applied Psychology* 88, pp. 113–20.

51. Rudd, J. E., and Lawson, D. R. (2007). *Communicating in Global Business Negotiations.* Thousand Oaks, CA: Sage. *See also* Tinsley, C. H. (2001). How negotiators get to yes: Predicting the constellation of strategies used across cultures to negotiate conflict. *Journal of Applied Psychology* 86, pp. 583–93.

52. Salacuse (2020), op. cit. *See also* Gelfand, M. J., Fulmer, C. A., and Severance, L. (2011). The psychology of negotiation and mediation. In S. Zedeck (Ed.), *APA Handbook of Industrial and Organizational Psychology* (Vol. 3). Washington, DC: American Psychological Association, pp. 495–554. *See also* Gelfand, M. J., Higgins, M., Nishii, L. H., Raver, J. L., Dominguez, A., Murakami, F., Yamaguchi, S., and Toyama, M. (2002). Culture and egocentric perceptions of fairness in conflict and negotiation. *Journal of Applied Psychology* 87, pp. 833–45. *See also* Adair, W. L., Okumura, T., and Brett, J. M. (2001). Negotiation behaviors when cultures collide: The United States and Japan. *Journal of Applied Psychology* 86, pp. 371–85. *See also* Brett, J. M., and Okumura, T. (1998). Inter- and intra-cultural negotiation: U.S. and Japanese negotiators. *Academy of Management Journal* 41, pp. 495–510.

53. Budd (2021), op. cit. *See also* Fossum (2015), op. cit. *See also* Katz et al. (2017), op. cit. *See also* Smith, A. (2016, June 10). NLRB limits right to permanently replace strikers. Retrieved from *www.shrm.org/resourcesandtools/hr-topics/labor-relations/pages/nlrb-limits-right-to-permanently-replace-strikers.aspx* on June 12, 2016.

54. USLegal. (n.d.). Sympathy strike law and legal definition. Retrieved from *https://definitions.uslegal.com/s/sympathy-strike/* on May 12, 2020. *See also* National Labor Relations Board. (2012, Aug. 2). Important information about strikes. Retrieved from *www.nlrb.gov/news-outreach/news-story/important-information-about-strikes* on May 12, 2020.

55. Morris, K., and Bolesta, J. (2019, Aug. 1). The NLRB confirms that intermittent strikes in furtherance of the same goal are unprotected. Retrieved from *www.laboremploymentlaw-blog.com/2019/08/articles/national-labor-relations-board/intermittent-strikes-unprotected/* on May 12, 2020. *See also* Banjo, S., and Trotman, M. (2014, Feb. 3). Wal-Mart fights back on strikes. *The Wall Street Journal,* pp. B1, B4.

56. Grossman, R. J. (1998, Sept.). Trying to heal the wounds. *HRMagazine,* pp. 85–92.

57. Budd (2021), op. cit.

58. Peralta, E. (2011, July 25). Football is back: Players, owners strike deal to end NFL lockout. Retrieved from *www.npr.org/blogs/thetwo-way/2011/07/25/138671825/reports-nfl-owners-players-agree-to-new-deal-ending-lockout* on July 26, 2011.

59. Iyer, V., and Brown, C. (2011, July 25). NFL lockout ends as owners, player reps agree to 10-year CBA. *Sporting News.* Retrieved from *aol.sportingnews.com/nfl/feed/2010-09/nfl-labor-talks/story/nfl-lockout-ends-owners-nflpa-10-year-deal-2011-season-cba-labor-agreement* on July 26, 2011.

60. Budd (2021), op. cit. *See also* Brown, E. (2002, Oct. 28). Fallout. *Fortune,* p. 32.

61. Fossum (2015), op. cit. *See also* Oviatt, C. R., Jr. (1995, Oct.). Case shows difficulty of declaring negotiating impasse. *HR News,* pp. 13, 16.

62. Budd (2021), op. cit. *See also* Fossum (2015), op. cit.

63. Carbonneau, T. E. (2017). *Arbitration Law in a Nutshell* (4th ed.). St. Paul, MN: West. *See also* Ross, W. H., and Conlon, D. E. (2000). Hybrid forms of third-party dispute resolution: Theoretical implications of combining mediation and arbitration. *Academy of Management Review* 25, pp. 416–27.

64. 10 mediation FAQs. (2017, May 17). OsborneClarke. Retrieved from *www.osborneclarke.com/insights/10-mediation-faqs/* on May 13, 2020. *See also* Holtzman, P. (2015, Sept.). Why litigate when you can mediate? *HRMagazine*, p. 86.

65. Arnold, J. A., and O'Connor, K. M. (1999). Ombudspersons or peers? The effect of third-party expertise and recommendations on negotiation. *Journal of Applied Psychology* 84, pp. 776–85.

66. Goldberg, S. B. (2005). The secrets of successful mediators. *Negotiation Journal* 21, pp. 365–76.

67. Budd (2021), op. cit. *See also* Katz et al. (2017), op. cit.

68. Fossum, J. A. (2015). *Labor Relations: Development, Structure, Process* (12th ed.). Burr Ridge, IL: McGraw-Hill/Irwin.

69. Budd (2021), op. cit. *See also* Katz et al. (2017), op. cit.

70. Ibid.

71. Fossum (2015), op. cit.

72. Bravin, J. (2018, June 28). Ruling on public unions strikes at labor finances. *The Wall Street Journal*, pp. A1, A4b. *See also* National Conference of State Legislatures. (2020). Right-to-work resources. Retrieved from *www.ncsl.org/research/labor-and-employment/right-to-work-laws-and-bills.aspx* on May 13, 2020.

73. Budd (2021), op. cit.

74. De Dreu, C. K. (2011). Conflict at work: Basic principles and applied issues. In S. Zedeck (Ed.), *APA Handbook of Industrial and Organizational Psychology* (Vol. 3). Washington, DC: American Psychological Association, pp. 461–93. *See also* Colvin, A. J. S. (2001). The relationship between employment arbitration and workplace dispute-resolution procedures. *Ohio State Journal on Dispute Resolution* 16, pp. 643–68. *See also* Labig, C. E., and Greer, C. R. (1988). Grievance initiation: A literature survey and directions for future research. *Journal of Labor Research* 9, pp. 1–27.

75. Fossum (2015), op. cit.

76. Fossum (2015), op. cit. *See also* Katz et al. (2017), op. cit.

77. Leonard, D. (2011, June 5). The end of mail. *BusinessWeek*, pp. 59–65. *See also* Brooks, R. (2001, June 28). Mail disorder: Blizzard of grievances joins a sack of woes at U.S. Postal Service. *The Wall Street Journal*, pp. A1, A4.

78. Mesch, D. J., and Dalton, D. R. (1992). Unexpected consequences of improving workplace justice: A six-year time series assessment. *Academy of Management Journal* 35, pp. 1099–114. *See also* Dalton, D. R., and Todor, W. D. (1985). Gender and workplace justice: A field assessment. *Personnel Psychology* 38, pp. 133–51.

79. Aryee, S., and Chay, Y. W. (2001). Workplace justice, citizenship behavior, and turnover intentions in a union context: Examining the mediating role of perceived union support and union instrumentality. *Journal of Applied Psychology* 86, pp. 154–60.

80. Olson-Buchanan, J. B. (1996). Voicing discontent: What happens to the grievance filer after the grievance? *Journal of Applied Psychology* 81, pp. 52–63.

81. Meyer, D., and Cooke, W. (1988). Economic and political factors in the resolution of formal grievances. *Industrial Relations* 27, pp. 318–35.

82. Klaas, B. S. (1989). Managerial decision-making about employee grievances: The impact of the grievant's work history. *Personnel Psychology* 42, pp. 53–68. *See also* Dalton, D. R., Todor, W. D., and Owen, C. L. (1987). Sex effects in workplace justice outcomes: A field assessment. *Journal of Applied Psychology* 72, pp. 156–59. *See also* Dalton and Todor (1985), op. cit.

83. Budd (2021), op. cit. *See also* Katz et al. (2017), op. cit.

84. Carbonneau (2017), op. cit. *See also* Loughran, C. S. (2006). *How to Prepare and Present a Labor Arbitration Case: Strategy and Tactics for Advocates* (2nd ed.). Washington, DC: Bureau of National Affairs.

85. Budd (2021), op. cit. *See also* Petersen, D. J., and Boller, H. R. (2004, Jan.). Applying the public-policy exception to labor arbitration awards. *Dispute Resolution Journal*. Retrieved from *findarticles.com/p/articles/mi_qa3923/is_200311/ai_n9463726* on July 31, 2008.

86. McCarthy, N. (2019, May 6). The state of global trade union membership (infographic). *Forbes*. Retrieved from *www.forbes.com/sites/niallmccarthy/2019/05/06/the-state-of-global-trade-union-membership-infographic/#527d258a2b6e* on May 13, 2020.
87. OECD. (2020). Who we are. Retrieved from *www.oecd.org/about/* on May 13, 2020.
88. *The Globalist*. (2017, Sept. 3). The state of organized labor in France. Retrieved from *www.theglobalist.com/the-state-of-organized-labor-in-france/* on May 13, 2020.
89. Douglas, C. C. (2016, July 27). The union wage premium, difficult to calculate, likely overblown. Retrieved from *www.mackinac.org/22643* on June 14, 2017.
90. Gaines, K. (2019, Oct. 7). Nurses unionizing: Benefits of working in a union hospital. Retrieved from *https://nurse.org/articles/benefits-of-nursing-union-hospital/* on May 13, 2020.
91. Douglas (2016), op. cit. *See also* Hirsch, B. T. (2004). Reconsidering union wage effects: Surveying new evidence on an old topic. *Journal of Labor Research* 25, pp. 233–66.
92. Marzan, C. F. R. (2014). Organizing with international framework agreements: An exploratory study. *UC Irvine Law Review* 4, pp. 725–80. *See also* Dolan, M., and Boudette, A. N. (2011, Mar. 23). UAW to send activists abroad. *The Wall Street Journal*, p. B2. *See also* Fong, M., and Maher, K. (2007, June 22). U.S. labor leader aided China's Wal-Mart coup. *The Wall Street Journal*, pp. A1, A4.

14 | PROCEDURAL JUSTICE AND ETHICS IN EMPLOYEE RELATIONS

Questions This Chapter Will Help Managers Answer

LO 14-1   How can I ensure procedural justice in the resolution of conflicts between employees and managers?

LO 14-2   How can I administer discipline without simultaneously engendering resentment toward me or my company?

LO 14-3   How do I fire people legally and humanely?

LO 14-4   What should I include in a policy on fair information practices?

LO 14-5   What is ethical decision making in employee relations? What steps or considerations are involved?

ALTERNATIVE DISPUTE RESOLUTION: GOOD FOR THE COMPANY, GOOD FOR EMPLOYEES?*

At the McGraw-Hill Companies, word came down from the chief executive officer: It was time to supplement the open-door policy with a formal, in-house **alternative dispute resolution (ADR) program.** He told attorneys in the legal department to develop something that settled disputes quickly, something good for morale.

After 6 months of work with consultants and meetings with employees and managers, as well as executives from JPMorgan Chase Bank, Cigna, JCPenney, and the KBR construction company—all of whom have ADR programs—McGraw-Hill unveiled its Fast and Impartial Resolution (FAIR) ADR program. The three-step program is voluntary and starts with bringing in a supervisor or an HR representative to resolve a dispute. If that doesn't work, it moves to mediation with a third party. If mediation is fruitless, the third step is binding arbitration with a written decision. The company pays the costs of mediation and arbitration.

The FAIR program is typical of the programs many organizations are developing. Others incorporate multilevel, internal appeals procedures or waivers of jury trials. Such programs save employers time and money. According to JAMS/Endispute, based in Irvine, California, it takes up to 6 weeks from the time that company is contacted to the time mediation actually begins. The parties spend an average of 12.5 hours in the process, and problems are resolved in up to 90 percent of cases. Says David Gage, a professional mediator, "Mediation is really a teaching experience for people in the workplace. We sit down and we actually listen. We give everybody a chance to talk. We try to identify problems, and then we brainstorm for alternative solutions." The Equal Employment Opportunity Commission has been promoting voluntary mediation of employment discrimination claims for years, and with good reason. Charges that go to mediation are disposed of in an average of 86 days—about half the time required for charges that are not mediated. In addition, the cost of settling an EEOC charge has increased by almost 79 percent since the early 1990s.

Houston-based Brown & Root has had about 1,100 ADR cases, with 17 going to arbitration. Roughly 75 percent of the cases are resolved within 2 months, as opposed to several years in the courts. In Irvine, California, American Savings Bank's four-step program is enjoying similar success, reducing legal costs by more than 60 percent. The American Arbitration Association (AAA) (*www.ADR.org*), whose ADR programs cover more than 7 million U.S. employees, has found that 80 percent of disputes are resolved at the first step, just by people sitting down and talking to each other. Of those that aren't, about 1,100 move to the next step, mediation, where a mediator helps both sides to agree. Only about 300 result in binding arbitration, but even in those cases, each side has veto power over the choice of an arbitrator. To control the costs of such cases, AAA offers the parties several options: limiting the number of arbitrators presiding on a case, offering expedited procedures, and

Sources: Janoce, J. (2020, Feb. 6). You don't have to pay the hidden costs of employment litigation. Retrieved from *www.shrm.org/resourcesandtools/hr-topics/employee-relations/humanity-into-hr/pages/you-don%E2%80%99t-have-to-pay-the-hidden-costs-of-employment-litigation.aspx* on May 18, 2020. Shonk, K. (2019, Nov. 26). What is alternative dispute resolution? Retrieved from *www.pon.harvard.edu/daily/dispute-resolution/what-is-alternative-dispute-resolution/* on May 18, 2020. Bravin, J. (2018, May 22). High court rules for bosses on arbitration. *The Wall Street Journal*, p. A3. Holtzman, P. (2015, Sept.). Why litigate when you can mediate? *HRMagazine*, pp. 86, 87. Posthuma, R. A. (2010). *Workplace Dispute Resolution*. Alexandria, VA: Society for Human Resource Management. Slate, W. K. II. (2007, May 21). The positive side of arbitration. *BusinessWeek*, p. 22. Orey, M. (2007, Apr. 30). The vanishing trial. *BusinessWeek*, pp. 38, 39.

even allowing for the entire process to be conducted over the Internet (to reduce travel costs).

On the other hand, compulsory arbitration agreements–in which employees sign agreements to arbitrate rather than litigate future disputes over alleged violations of employment law–are the subject of intense debate. Although arbitration offers significant benefits with respect to speed, cost, and the specialized expertise of arbitrators, some fear that it may unfairly favor employers. In the conclusion to this case, we will examine what a fair ADR program looks like.

Challenges

1. What do you see as some key advantages and disadvantages of ADR programs?
2. Should an employee's agreement to binding arbitration be a condition of employment or a condition of continuing employment?
3. Working in small groups, identify characteristics that would make an ADR program fair for both employees and employers.

The chapter-opening vignette illustrates another facet of labor-management accommodation: the use of workplace due process to resolve disputes. It is another attempt to enhance the productivity and quality of life of employees. Indeed, the broad theme of this chapter is "justice on the job." We will consider alternative methods for resolving disputes, such as nonunion grievance and arbitration procedures. We will also examine discipline and termination in the employment context. Finally, we will examine the growing concern for employee privacy and ethical issues in three areas: fair information practice in the Internet age, the assessment of job applicants and employees, and whistle-blowing. Let us begin by defining some important terms.

SOME DEFINITIONS

In this chapter, we are concerned with three broad issues in the context of employee relations: (1) procedural justice, (2) due process, and (3) ethical decisions about behavior. Let's begin by defining these terms.

Employee relations includes all the practices that implement the philosophy and policy of an organization with respect to employment.[1]

Justice refers to the maintenance or administration of what is just, especially by the impartial adjustment of conflicting claims or the assignment of merited rewards or punishments.[2] It is one of the fundamental bases of cooperative action in organizations.[3]

Procedural justice focuses on the fairness of the procedures used to make decisions. Procedures are fair to the extent that they are consistent across persons and over time, free from bias, based on accurate information, correctable, and based on prevailing moral and ethical standards.[4]

Distributive justice focuses on the fairness of the outcomes of decisions–for example, in the allocation of bonuses or merit pay, or in making reasonable accommodations for employees with disabilities.[5]

Due process in legal proceedings provides individuals with rights such as the following: prior notice of prohibited conduct; timely procedures adhered to at each step of the procedure; notice of the charges or issues prior to a hearing; impartial judges or hearing officers; representation by counsel; opportunity to confront and to cross-examine adverse witnesses and evidence, as well as to present proof in one's own defense; notice of decision; and protection from retaliation for using a complaint procedure in a legitimate manner. These are **constitutional due-process rights.** They protect individual rights with respect to state, municipal, and federal government processes. However, they normally do not apply to work situations. Hence, employee rights to due process are based on a collective-bargaining agreement, legislative protections, or procedures provided unilaterally by an employer.[6]

Ethical decisions about behavior concern conformity to moral standards or to the standards of conduct of a given profession or group. Ethical decisions about behavior take account not only of a person's own interests but also, equally, of the interests of those affected by the decision.[7]

WHY ADDRESS PROCEDURAL JUSTICE?

In the wake of decisions that affect employees, such as those involving pay, promotions, or assignments, employees often ask, "Was that fair?" Judgments about the fairness or equity of procedures used to make decisions—that is, procedural justice—are rooted in the perceptions of employees. Strong research evidence indicates that such perceptions lead to important consequences, such as employee behavior and attitudes, as well as business outcomes, such as customer-satisfaction ratings.[8] In short, the judgments of employees about procedural justice matter. Perceptions of fairness are especially important in the context of HR management—for example, in the hiring process, in performance management, and in compensation.

Procedurally fair treatment has been demonstrated to result in reduced stress[9] and increased performance, job satisfaction, commitment to an organization, trust, and **organizational citizenship behaviors (OCBs).** OCBs are discretionary behaviors performed outside of one's formal role that help other employees perform their jobs or that show support for and conscientiousness toward the organization.[10] They account for 15 to 30 percent of business outcomes, and as many as 40 percent of the outcomes in customer-service settings.[11] OCBs include behaviors such as the following:

- Altruism (e.g., helping out when a coworker is not feeling well).
- Conscientiousness (e.g., staying late to finish a project).
- Civic virtue (e.g., volunteering for a community program to represent the firm).
- Sportsmanship (e.g., sharing the failure of a team project that would have been successful if the team had followed your advice).
- Courtesy (e.g., being understanding and empathetic, even when provoked).[12]

Procedural justice affects citizenship behaviors by influencing employees' perceptions of **organizational support,** the extent to which the organization values employees' general contributions and cares for their well-being. In turn, this prompts employees to reciprocate with organizational citizenship behaviors.[13] These effects have been demonstrated to occur at the level of the work group as well as at the level of the individual.[14] In general, perceptions of procedural justice are most relevant and important to employees during times of significant organizational change. When employees experience change, their perceptions of fairness become especially potent factors that determine their attitudes and their behavior.[15] Because the only constant in organizations is change, considerations of procedural justice will always be relevant.

COMPONENTS OF PROCEDURAL JUSTICE

Although there is disagreement in the professional literature about the number of components of the broad topic of organizational justice,[16] we will address three of the most important ones. The first of these is **employee voice,** illustrated by organizational policies and rules that offer individuals and groups the capacity to be heard, a way to communicate their interests upward. Voice systems serve four important functions:

1. They ensure fair treatment to employees.
2. They provide a context in which unfair treatment can be appealed.
3. They help to improve the effectiveness of an organization.
4. They sustain employee loyalty and commitment.[17]

Here are some examples of voice systems that are commonly used:

- Grievance or internal complaint procedures, by which an employee can seek a formal, impartial review of an action that affects him or her.[18]
- Ombudspersons, who may investigate claims of unfair treatment or act as intermediaries between an employee and senior management and recommend possible courses of action to the parties.[19]
- **Open-door policies** by which employees can approach senior managers with problems that they may not be willing to take to their immediate supervisors. A related mechanism, particularly appropriate when the immediate supervisor is the problem, is a **skip-level policy,** whereby an employee may proceed directly to the next higher level of management above his or her supervisor.
- Participative management systems that encourage employee involvement in all aspects of organizational strategy and decision making.
- Committees or meetings that poll employee input on key problems and decisions.
- Senior-management visits, where employees can meet with senior company officials and openly ask questions about company strategy, policies, and practices or raise concerns about unfair treatment.
- Question/answer newsletters, in which employee questions and concerns are submitted to a newsletter editor and investigated by that office, and then answered and openly reported to the organizational community.[20]
- Toll-free telephone numbers that employees can use anonymously to report waste, fraud, or abuse.
- Electronic communication between remote workers, as well as online bulletin boards.[21]

Interactional justice is the second component. It is the quality of interpersonal treatment that employees receive in their everyday work. Treating others with dignity and respect is the positive side of interactional justice. Derogatory judgments, deception, invasion of privacy, inconsiderate or abusive actions, public criticism, and coercion represent the negative side of interactional justice.[22] Violating any of these elements of interactional justice leads to decreased perceptions of fair treatment. Evidence indicates that employee perceptions of interactional justice that stem from the quality of their relationships with their supervisors are positively related to their performance, citizenship behaviors directed toward their supervisors, and job satisfaction.[23]

Informational justice is the third component of procedural justice. It is expressed in terms of providing explanations or accounts for decisions made. Consider layoffs, for example. Evidence indicates that layoff survivors who were provided explanations for the layoffs, or who received advance notice of them, had more positive reactions to layoffs and higher commitment to the organization.[24] Survivors had the most negative reactions to layoffs when they identified with the victims and when they perceived the layoffs to be unfair.[25]

Think about your own experiences in times of change. Was the fairness of procedures important to you? Did your perceptions affect your attitudes toward your employer and your behavior at work? Did you wish you had more say in decisions that might affect you? This is the role of procedural justice. The next few sections describe how it is applied in practice. Let's begin by examining nonunion grievance procedures.

GRIEVANCE PROCEDURES IN NONUNION COMPANIES: WORKPLACE DUE PROCESS

Conflicts in which employees feel unfairly treated, harassed, overlooked in promotions, or deserving of a raise may arise in any workplace, union or nonunion. Methods for resolving such conflicts are needed. Grievance procedures serve that purpose because they introduce workplace justice systems that provide at least some elements of due process to individual employees. Today they are found in almost all workplaces of 100 or more employees, and they serve the following purposes:[26]

1. Increase organizational commitment and performance by treating employees fairly and by identifying problem areas.
2. Avoid costly lawsuits.
3. Prevent unionization.

Nonunion grievance procedures can take several forms.[27] The simplest is an open-door policy, in which employees are invited to bring their concerns to a manager, who will attempt to resolve it. A second form is a **peer-review panel,** which uses fellow employees as decision makers, and a third is **nonunion arbitration,** which relies on third-party, neutral arbitrators to settle disputes. Other dispute-resolution mechanisms include internal or external **mediation** and **ombudspersons.** An ombudsperson counsels employees on how to resolve issues themselves, conducts formal or informal investigations of disputes, or simply serves as a support system for employees to defuse negative emotions, animosity, and hostility.[28]

Figure 14–1 illustrates how such a procedure works in one company. This procedure emphasizes the supervisor as a key figure in the resolution of grievances. If this is inappropriate, then the employee should feel free to contact the director of human

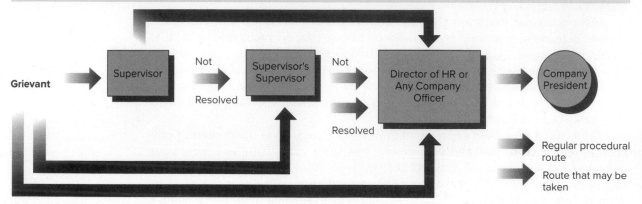

Figure 14–1

Example of a nonunion grievance procedure. This diagram indicates the possible routes a grievant may take to resolve a complaint. The regular procedural route is designed to resolve the grievance at the lowest possible level–the supervisor. However, if the grievant feels uncomfortable approaching the supervisor, the grievance may be presented directly to the supervisor's supervisor, to the director of HR, or to any officer of the company, with a final appeal to the company president.

Source: Adapted from Posthuma, R. A. (2010). *Workplace Dispute Resolution.* Alexandria, VA: Society for Human Resource Management, p. 32.

resources or any officer of the company. Employees are always encouraged to follow their chain of command. If the employee is not satisfied with the response of the appropriate officer of the corporation, the employee may bring the matter to the president's attention by filing a written copy of the request and the response or action taken.[29]

Note that this process lacks several elements of due process. Specifically, employees generally lack representation or assistance in presenting their grievances (as is the case with formal union grievance procedures), and management is the ultimate decision maker. For genuine due process to operate, a procedure must include an objective investigator and decision maker who has the power to make a binding decision on both employee and employer.[30] To address potential shortcomings of the process, one or more elements are often added to the basic nonunion grievance procedure: ombudspersons, peer-review panels, and arbitration.

As we noted earlier, an ombudsperson is a neutral facilitator between employees and managers; he or she assists them in resolving workplace disputes. That is, the ombudsperson is much more of a mediator than an arbitrator or a fact-finder.[31]

Peer-review panels sometimes constitute the appeal process in a nonunion grievance procedure. In this system, grievances can be appealed to a review panel in which employees (not managers) comprise a majority of the panel members (hence the name *peer*-review panel). Peer-review panels are established to counter perceptions of unfairness in dispute-resolution systems where managers make the final decisions.[32] For example, FedEx Corporation's "guaranteed fair-treatment process" lets employees appeal problems to a peer-review board that is chosen by the worker involved and that includes several members of management. The board rules for employees about half the time. Bosses cannot appeal decisions, but employees can appeal to a panel of top executives up to and including the chairman of the board.[33]

INTERNATIONAL APPLICATION
Perceptions of Procedural Justice across Cultures

Research indicates that perceptions of procedural justice are similar across cultures and that employee-voice systems, in particular, are associated with judgments of fairness. These findings are consistent across cultures as diverse as Argentina, the Dominican Republic, Mexico, Great Britain, the Netherlands, and the United States.[a] What about distributing rewards in the workplace (distributive justice)? Here, research indicates that different norms seem to be preferred in different nations. Whereas Americans prefer the equity norm (rewards distributed based on individual contributions), the Dutch favor equal distributions and people from India favor distributions that are sensitive to fulfilling the needs of others.[b]

Individualism and collectivism also seem to influence judgments of procedural justice. Specifically, people in individualistic cultures such as the United States prefer to have higher levels of control over the processes used to make decisions than do people in more collectivistic cultures, such as Ecuador. This may be due to the more confrontational orientation of people in individualistic cultures, in contrast to the orientation toward harmony in collectivistic cultures.[c]

Reviews of the literature in this area indicate that there is a growing body of research on culture and justice in intercultural contexts. Shared perceptions of justice are critical for the effectiveness of intercultural alliances, especially when cultural distance between the parties is high. Yet intercultural settings are precisely where there may be conflict due to differences in perceptions of justice.[d]

[a] Shao, R., Rupp, D. E., Skarlicki, D. P., and Jones, K. S. (2013). Employee justice across cultures: A meta-analytic review. *Journal of Management* 39, pp. 263–301. Cropanzano, R., Aguinis, H., Schminke, M., and Denham, D. L. (1999). Disputant reactions to managerial conflict resolution tactics: A comparison among Argentina, the Dominican Republic, Mexico, and the United States. *Group and Organization Management* 24, pp. 124–54.

[b] Greenberg, J. (2011). Organizational justice: The dynamics of fairness in the workplace. In S. Zedeck (Ed.), *APA Handbook of Industrial and Organizational Psychology* (Vol. 3). Washington, DC: American Psychological Association, pp. 271–327.

[c] Erez, M. (2011). Cross-cultural and global issues in organizational psychology. In S. Zedeck (Ed.), *APA Handbook of Industrial and Organizational Psychology* (Vol. 3). Washington, DC: American Psychological Association, pp. 807–54.

[d] Erez (2011), op. cit. Greenberg (2011), op. cit. Gelfand, M. J., Erez, M., and Aycan, Z. (2007). Cross-cultural organizational behavior. *Annual Review of Psychology* 58, pp. 479–514. Luo, Y. (2005). How important are shared perceptions of procedural justice in cooperative alliances? *Academy of Management Journal* 48, pp. 695–709.

In some but by no means all instances, arbitration is the final step of a nonunion workplace dispute-resolution system. Nonunion arbitration of grievances might provide less due process to employees than unionized grievance arbitration if there are limitations on discovery (how much information the grievant can collect from the company), if the use of outside advocates such as attorneys is restricted, or if arbitrators favor management to increase their chances of being selected for future cases.[34]

Workplace due process is a growing trend. To work effectively, however, such a procedure should meet four basic requirements:[35]

1. *All employees must know about the procedure and understand exactly how it operates.* Describe the system in the employee handbook and publicize it widely. GlaxoSmithKline goes even further. Periodically, it features its internal complaint procedure on closed-circuit television for all company employees to see.

2. *Employees must believe that there will be no reprisals taken against them for using it.*
3. *Management must respond quickly and thoroughly to all grievances.* Use trained investigators to gather facts in a timely manner. The investigator should then discuss possible actions with the manager who has the power to make a final decision, and the manager should subsequently share the decision with the complainant.
4. *Provide employees with an appeal process.*

The trend toward workplace due process represents an effort by companies to broaden employees' rights in disciplinary matters and to build an open, trusting atmosphere. Three possible reasons might explain the growth in workplace due process: (1) It is part of an effort to increase employee commitment and performance, (2) it may avoid costly lawsuits, and (3) it is part of a strategy to avoid unionization. Research supports all three explanations.[36]

Discipline

Make no mistake about it: Most employees want to conduct themselves in a manner acceptable to the company and to their fellow employees. Occasionally, problems of absenteeism, poor work performance, or rule violations arise. When informal conversations or coaching sessions fail to resolve these problems, formal disciplinary action is called for.

In a unionized firm, the *management rights* clause of the collective bargaining agreement typically retains for management the authority to impose reasonable rules for workplace conduct and to discipline employees who violate those rules–that is, for **just cause.** The concept of just cause requires an employer not only to produce persuasive evidence of an employee's liability or negligence but also to provide the employee a fair hearing and to impose a penalty appropriate to the proven offense.[37] Unions rarely object to employee discipline, provided that (1) it is applied consistently, (2) the rules are publicized clearly, and (3) the rules are considered reasonable.

Discipline is indispensable to management control. Ideally, it should serve as a corrective mechanism to create and maintain a productive, responsive workforce.[38] Unfortunately, some managers go to great lengths to avoid using discipline. To some extent, this is understandable because discipline is one of the hardest management actions to take. Managers may avoid imposing discipline because of (1) ignorance of organizational rules, (2) fear of formal grievances, or (3) fear of losing the friendship of employees.[39] Yet failure to administer discipline can result in implied acceptance or approval of the offense. Thereafter, problems may become more frequent or severe, and discipline becomes that much more difficult to administer.[40]

In fact, evidence indicates that discipline (i.e., punishment) may be beneficial.[41] Consider that

- Discipline may alert a poor performer to that poor performance and result in a change in behavior.
- Discipline may send a signal to other employees regarding expected levels of performance and standards of behavior.
- If the discipline is perceived as legitimate by other employees, it may increase motivation, morale, and performance.

Department managers in a retail store chain who used informal warnings, formal warnings, and dismissals more frequently than their peers had higher departmental performance ratings (in terms of annual cost and sales data and ratings by higher-level managers). This relationship held even when length of service was taken into account. More frequent use of sanctions was associated with improved performance. Why is this so?

The answer may lie in **social learning theory.**[42] According to that theory, individuals in groups look to others to learn appropriate behaviors and attitudes. They learn them by modeling the behavior of others, adopting standard operating procedures, and following group norms. Individuals whose attitudes or behaviors violate these norms may cause problems. Tolerance of such behavior by the supervisor may threaten the group by causing feelings of uncertainty and unfairness. On the other hand, management actions that are seen as maintaining legitimate group standards may instill feelings of fairness and result in improved performance. Failure to invoke sanctions may lead to a loss of management control and unproductive employee behavior.[43] Finally, do not underestimate the *symbolic* value of disciplinary actions, especially because punitive behavior tends to make a lasting impression on employees.[44]

Progressive Discipline

Many firms, both unionized and nonunionized, follow a procedure of **progressive discipline** that proceeds from an oral warning to a written warning to a suspension to dismissal. If progressive discipline is to be effective, however, employers need to follow four rules. Specifically, the employee needs to (1) know what the problem is, (2) know what he or she must do to fix the problem, (3) have a reasonable period of time to fix the problem, and (4) understand the consequences of inaction.[45]

At the same time, there are downsides to progressive discipline.[46] It can be frustrating for managers and employees to tolerate poor behavior and performance while they "wait out" the progressive-discipline process. It is time-consuming and requires proper documentation. Yet progressive discipline remains the policy of choice for most employers. By giving employees a second or third chance to change their inappropriate behavior to conform to the company's standards of conduct, such a policy is employee friendly and less susceptible to challenge in litigation than alternative approaches without progressive steps.[47] Severe issues, however, such as violence, theft, vandalism, and gross insubordination might warrant immediate discharge without the need for progressive discipline.[48]

At a broader level, is it possible to administer discipline without simultaneously engendering resentment by the disciplined employee? The answer is yes, if managers follow the **red-hot-stove rule.**[49] Discipline should be

- *Immediate.* Just like touching a hot stove, where feedback is immediate, there should be no misunderstanding about why discipline was imposed. People are disciplined not because of who they are (personality) but because of what they did (behavior).
- *With warning.* Small children know that if they touch a hot stove, they will be burned. Likewise, employees must know very clearly what the consequences of undesirable work behavior will be. They must be given adequate warning.

- *Consistent.* Every time a person touches a red-hot stove, he or she gets burned. Likewise, if discipline is to be perceived as fair, it must be administered consistently, given similar circumstances surrounding the undesirable behavior. In practice, evidence indicates that managers tend to be less concerned with consistency than with satisfying immediate needs within their work units.[50] That's risky because recent case law suggests that inconsistency in following a policy of progressive discipline may lead to liability for wrongful termination.[51]
- *Impersonal.* A hot stove is blind to who touches it. So also, managers cannot play favorites by disciplining subordinates they do not like while allowing the same behavior to go unpunished for those they do like.

A comprehensive review of arbitration cases and case law suggests two other guidelines for a legally defensible progressive discipline system: (1) *allow an employee the opportunity to respond* and (2) *allow employees a reasonable period of time to improve their performance.*[52]

Documenting Performance-Related Incidents

Documentation is a fact of organizational life for most managers. Prepare it with the expectation that a third party (internal or external) will review it. Include enough information so that others know what happened, what steps you took to put the employee on notice, and offer him or her an opportunity to improve. More specifically,[53]

- Describe company expectations clearly, based on a job description or company policy.
- Describe the behavior or performance that must change. Describe the conduct, not the individual, and include details such as dates and locations.
- Include the employee's explanation for why expectations aren't being met.
- Prepare a detailed action plan that the employee should use to improve performance. Focus on a few key areas.
- Set a deadline for correcting the behavior or performance, and follow up at the specified deadline.
- Describe the consequences if the behavior or poor performance continues.

Can you see the parallel with the four rules of progressive discipline described earlier? Conclude the warning by obtaining the employee's signature that he or she has read and understands the warning.

The Disciplinary Interview

Generally, disciplinary interviews are held for one of two reasons: (1) over issues of *workplace conduct*, such as attendance or punctuality or (2) over issues of *job performance*, such as low productivity. They tend to be very legalistic. In *NLRB v. J. Weingarten Inc.*, for example, the Supreme Court ruled that a *union* employee has the right to demand that a union representative be present at an investigatory interview that the employee reasonably believes may result in disciplinary action.[54] The representative may assist the employee but not obstruct reasonable questioning by the employer. While nonunion employees do not enjoy the same right, employers may voluntarily extend *Weingarten* rights to them.[55]

Having satisfied their legal burden, how should supervisors actually conduct the disciplinary interview? They must do *nine* things well:

1. Come to the interview with as many facts as possible. Check the employee's employment file for previous offenses as well as for evidence of exemplary behavior and performance.
2. Conduct the interview in a quiet, private place. "Praise in public, discipline in private" is a good rule to remember. Whether the employee's attitude is truculent or contrite, recognize that he or she will be apprehensive. In contrast to other interviews, where your first objective is to dispel any fears and help the person relax, a "light touch" is inappropriate here.
3. Avoid aggressive accusations. State the facts in a simple, straightforward way. Be sure that any fact you use is accurate, and never rely on hearsay, rumor, or unconfirmed guesswork.
4. Be sure that the employee understands the rule in question and the reason it exists.
5. Allow the employee to make a full defense, even if you think he or she has none. If any point the employee makes has merit, tell him or her so and take it into consideration in your final decision.
6. Stay cool and calm; treat the employee as an adult. Never use foul language or touch him or her. Such behaviors may be misinterpreted or grossly distorted at a later date.
7. If you made a mistake, be big enough to admit it.
8. Consider extenuating circumstances, and allow for honest mistakes on the part of the employee.
9. Even when corrective discipline is required, try to express confidence in the employee's worth as a person and ability to perform acceptably in the future. Rather than dwelling on the past, which you cannot change, focus on the future, which you can.

Employment at Will

For U.S. workers who are not covered by a collective-bargaining agreement or an individual employment contract, dismissal is an ever-present possibility.[56] The doctrine of **employment at will** or "at-will employment" refers to an employment relationship between an employer and an employee under which either party can terminate the relationship without notice, at any time, and for any reason not prohibited by law.[57] In certain situations, however, successful victims of unjust dismissal can collect sizable punitive and compensatory damages from their former employers.

In recent years, several important exceptions to the at-will doctrine have emerged. These exceptions provide important protections for workers. The first—and most important—is legislative. Federal laws limit an employer's right to terminate at-will employees for such reasons as age, race, sex, religion, national origin, union activity, reporting of unsafe working conditions, and disability.[58] However, employment at will is primarily a matter of state law.[59]

State courts have carved out three judicial exceptions. The first is a **public policy exception.** That is, an employee may not be fired because he or she refuses to commit an illegal act, such as perjury or price fixing. Second, when an employer has promised not to terminate an employee except for unsatisfactory job

HR BUZZ

The "Facebook Firing" Case

SOCIAL-MEDIA POLICIES AND AT-WILL EMPLOYMENT*

American Medical Response (AMR), a Connecticut ambulance-service company, terminated an employee after she posted negative comments about her employer and her supervisor on her Facebook page. The comments were derogatory and included profanity. AMR's policy on this issue stated "Employees are prohibited from making disparaging, discriminatory, or defamatory comments when discussing the Company or the employee's superiors, co-workers, or competitors." Following an investigation, the National Labor Relations Board issued a complaint against AMR, claiming that the discharge violated the National Labor Relations Act and its protection of the right to discuss the terms and conditions of one's employment. The case settled the day before a scheduled hearing, but subsequently it has become known as the "Facebook firing" case.

According to labor-law experts, under current law, an employer can face a charge of unfair labor practices from the NLRB *even* if the employer is nonunion *and even* if no disciplinary action is taken. Employers certainly have a legitimate interest in protecting against disclosure of trade secrets and trademarked, copyrighted, and other private information. At the same time, however, they are not permitted to restrict employees' use of social media (Facebook, YouTube, Twitter, Reddit, Instagram, blogs, etc.) and the Internet to unionize; bargain collectively; and, in general, to discuss the terms and conditions of their employment. Any social-media policy should therefore remind employees that they are prohibited from disclosing the employer's confidential information or its customers' private information. Employees have the right to express their opinions as long as they don't present themselves as company representatives. At the same time, however, once they post information on social media, they cannot claim privacy rights, even if it was communicated only to "friends."

Sources: Nagele-Piazza, L. (2017, Oct. 24). Can employees be fired for off-duty conduct? *SHRM Online.* Retrieved from *www.shrm.org/resourcesandtools/legal-and-compliance/state-and-local-updates/pages/can-employees-be-fired-for-off-duty-conduct.aspx* on Oct. 24, 2017. Hoyt, Z. W. (2017, July). Can employers discipline employees who post negative comments about the company on Glassdoor? *HR Professionals Magazine* 7(7), pp. 12, 13. Hill, K. (2011, Aug. 25). When you can and can't fire employees for social media misbehavior. *Forbes.* Retrieved from *www.forbes.com/sites/kashmirhill/2011/08/25/when-you-can-and-cant-fire-employees-for-social-media-misbehavior/* on June 24, 2014.

---

performance or other good cause, the courts will insist that the employer carry out that promise. This includes **implied promises** (such as oral promises and implied covenants of good faith and fair dealing) as well as explicit ones.[60] In addition, courts in 34 states have found that informal assurances of job security can sometimes amount to an enforceable contract.[61]

The third exception allows employees to seek damages for outrageous acts related to termination, including character defamation. This includes so-called **retaliatory discharge** cases, where a worker is fired for actions ranging from filing a workers' compensation claim to reporting safety violations to government agencies. The Supreme Court has ruled that where state law permits (as it does in 34 states), union as well as nonunion employees have the right to sue over their dismissals, even if they are covered by a collective-bargaining contract that provides a grievance procedure and remedies.[62]

It might thus appear that the at-will doctrine has been severely restricted. Think again. For example, age discrimination is still permissible for workers under age 40, and many other areas remain untouched by employment law. In what is known as **lifestyle discrimination,** workers have been fired for refusing to quit smoking, for living with someone without being married, for drinking a competitor's product, for motorcycling, and for engaging in other legal activities outside of work.[63] Although there are no federal laws that prohibit lifestyle discrimination in employment, nearly 30 states have some level of protection based on lawful off-duty activities. At a broader level, employers need to consider whether it is appropriate to use criteria that are not related to the job when making employment decisions.[64] Before implementing such a policy, carefully consider questions such as the following:[65]

- Is the employee conduct lawful or illegal?
- Is there an applicable law that protects the employees' off-duty conduct?
- What risk/cost does the policy seek to avoid or lower?
- Will the employer apply the policy consistently, or do situations exist in which it would not be able, or want to, do so?
- What effect will the policy and its application have on employee morale?
- Is it worth it?

Employment Contracts

Earlier we noted that employees with contracts (bargained collectively or individually) are not at-will employees. In fact, where a collective-bargaining contract does exist, employers cannot enter into separate employment agreements with employees covered by that contract.[66] However, more and more executives, professionals, and even middle managers are demanding contracts. Although getting a contract can be a wise career move, when is the proper time to ask for one–and how?

You should consider asking for a contract in any business where the competition for talent is intense, where ideas are at a premium, or when the conditions of your employment differ in unusual ways from a company's standard practices. A contract assures you of a job and a minimum salary for some period of time, usually 2 to 3 years, during which you agree not to quit. Other typical provisions include the job title, compensation (salary, procedures for salary increases, bonuses), benefits, stock options, length of vacation, circumstances under which you can be fired, and severance pay. However, with all these perks come a handful of restrictive covenants, or clauses, that basically limit your ability to work elsewhere. For example,[67]

- A *nonsolicitation* clause prohibits you from recruiting key clients or employees away from your former employer for a year or two.
- *Payback* clauses require that you not take another job until you have repaid the company any expenses incurred in your relocation and recruitment.
- Less common is a clause that mandates that the company must have an opportunity to *match* any employment offer that you get. If the employer matches a competing offer, you must remain.
- A *nondisclosure* clause prohibits you from divulging trade secrets or other proprietary information to outsiders during your employment at a company or after you leave.
- A *noncompete* clause bars you from working for a competitor for 6 months up to 2 years.[68] As a practical matter, however, a New York State court found

that a noncompete clause that restricted an employee from working for a competitor for 12 months was "too long" in the Internet business.[69] The clause is valid whether you are fired, your job is eliminated, or you leave voluntarily.

Noncompete agreements are most common in such highly competitive industries as computers, pharmaceuticals, toys, biotechnology, and electronics. Because information is what gives businesses their competitive edge, more of them are using noncompete agreements to make sure that inside information about products or services does not leak out to competitors. Yet such agreements may also stifle innovation, and they clearly restrict employment opportunities.[70] Thus, the 11th Circuit Court of Appeals ruled that a noncompete agreement is valid if it is reasonable and balanced with respect to three issues: duration, geographic territory, and scope of activity.[71]

Whether or not a contract has been signed, however, executives are still required to maintain all trade secrets with which their employers have entrusted them. This obligation, often called a **fiduciary duty of loyalty,** cannot keep the executive out of the job market, but it does provide the former employer with legal recourse if an executive joins a competitor and tells all. Indeed, this is precisely what Campbell's Soup claimed when it succeeded in muzzling a former key executive.

Companies say they need noncompete agreements now that growing numbers of acquisitions, bankruptcies, mergers, and layoffs regularly set loose employees with access to trade secrets and other sensitive information. It is important to recognize, however, that employment agreements are governed by state law.[72] California, North Dakota, and Oklahoma, for example, do not allow noncompete agreements.[73] To avoid having to deal with multiple interpretations of the same agreement in different states, firms generally include a **choice-of-law provision,** which designates that the laws of a particular state will be used to interpret the contract. Where feasible, companies are choosing states that tend to uphold such restrictions. Finally, a contract should state that it reflects the entire agreement of the parties and can be amended only in writing, signed by both parties. Doing so prevents employee claims that the employer made oral promises or agreements that expanded his or her rights.[74]

Now back to the negotiation process for employment contracts. In dealing with a prospective employer, do not raise the issue of a contract until you have been offered a job and have thoroughly discussed the terms of your employment. How do you broach the subject? Calmly. Say, for example, "I'd appreciate a letter confirming these arrangements." If the employer asks why, you might point out that both of you are used to putting business agreements on paper and that it's to your mutual benefit to keep all these details straight.[75] Here are some tips on how to negotiate an employment contract:

1. Keep the tone upbeat. Don't use the words *I* and *you*; talk about *we*—as though you're already aboard. People are six times more likely to make a deal with someone they like.[76]
2. Decide beforehand on three or four "make-or-break" issues (e.g., salary, job assignment, location). These are your "need-to-haves." Also make a list of secondary issues, so-called "nice-to-haves" (e.g., company car, sign-on bonus).
3. Negotiate the entire package at one time. Don't keep going back to nit-pick.
4. Be flexible (except on your "make-or-break" issues); let the company win on some things.

CAMPBELL'S SOUP

A high-profile dispute played out in front of a national audience when a key executive of Campbell's Soup, who had signed a noncompete agreement, "jumped ship" to go to work for the company's main rival, H. J. Heinz Company. After weeks of acrimonious litigation, the parties finally reached a settlement. It included an agreement that the departing Campbell's executive would not be allowed to begin working for Heinz for several months, would keep a log of all contacts he had with Heinz employees once he did start working there, and would forfeit pension and other benefits from Campbell's. For its part, Heinz agreed to permit certain of its facilities to be inspected regularly to assure Campbell's that none of its trade secrets were being used.

Protecting Trade Secrets

This case is unusual only for its high profile. Although it grabbed headlines, the fact is that every day, in courtrooms all over the country, companies, their employees, and their competitors are suing each other, seeking to enforce, limit, or get out from under noncompete agreements.[a] Some argue that these clauses are having an unintended dampening effect on U.S. entrepreneurship by preventing people from leaving the corporate world to launch their own businesses, or to hire workers when they do. One thing is quite clear, however. Companies are now playing hardball when it comes to the disclosure of trade secrets. For all parties, the stakes are high.

[a]Dougherty, C. (2017, May 16). Losing the right to a new job. *The New York Times International Edition*, pp. 10, 11. Nusco, A. (2015, July 1). Employment brawls in Silicon Valley (and beyond). *Fortune*, p. 54. Simon, R., and Loten, A. (2013, Aug. 15). When a new job leads to a lawsuit. *The Wall Street Journal*, pp. B1, B4.

Once you receive the proposed contract, have an attorney review it before you sign. Remember: Employment contracts are legally enforceable documents.

Termination

No one looks forward to firing employees, but in the case of layoffs, certain advance notification requirements may apply. The Worker Adjustment and Retraining Notification (WARN) Act requires employers of more than 100 workers to grant 60 days' written notice before closing a plant or before laying off more than one-third of a workforce in excess of 150 people. Employees entitled to notice include managers and supervisors, as well as hourly and salaried workers. WARN also provides for fewer than 60 days' notice if the layoffs result from the closure of a faltering company, unforeseeable business circumstances, or a natural disaster. Employers who violate WARN provisions are liable to each employee for an amount equal to back pay and benefits for the period of the violation, up to 60 days.[77]

The remainder of this section focuses on how to terminate employees for cause, typically for disciplinary reasons or for poor performance. Termination is one of the most difficult tasks a manager has to perform. For those fired, the perception of inequity, or procedural injustice, is often what drives them to court.

Courts expect employers to provide a full course of progressive discipline (including written and final written warnings) for employees whose job performance does not meet standards.[78] When it comes to inappropriate workplace conduct, however, such as theft, physical violence, or gross misconduct, the courts are much more lenient. As a manager, even if you choose not to terminate for inappropriate workplace conduct on the first offense, you may issue a final written warning, such as the following:[79]

> If you *ever again* engage in behavior that could be construed as hostile or intimidating, or if you violate any other company standards of performance and conduct, then you will be dismissed immediately.

Termination for cause is not an infrequent occurrence; some 2 million workers in the United States are fired every year, and that doesn't include large-scale layoffs.[80] Unfortunately, few firms provide any training to supervisors on how to conduct terminations.[81]

Although termination may be traumatic for the employee, it is often no less so for the boss. Faced with saying the words "Your services are no longer required," even the strongest person can get the shakes, sleepless nights, and sweaty palms. So how should termination be handled? Certainly not the way it was at one company that sent an e-mail to its employees around lunchtime, with instructions to call a toll-free number. When they did, they heard a voice recording saying that the company, a small technology firm, was closing its doors and all employees needed to leave right away. Is this procedural justice? Certainly not. In fact, assuming an organization is not going out of business, insensitive firings can tarnish its reputation among business partners, vendors, and customers, as well as make it difficult to recruit and retain talent.[82]

As an alternative, more humane procedure, companies should familiarize all supervisors with company policies and provide a termination checklist to use when conducting dismissals. Figure 14–2 shows one such checklist.

Before deciding to dismiss an employee, managers should conduct a detailed review of all relevant facts, including the employee's side of the story. To ensure consistent treatment, the supervisor should also examine how similar cases have been handled in the past. Once the decision to terminate has been made, the termination interview should minimize the trauma for the affected employee. Prior to conducting such an interview, the supervisor should be prepared to answer some basic questions: Who? When? Where? How?[83]

- *Who?* Typically, the employee's direct supervisor and a human resources representative will attend a termination meeting. This helps avoid a situation where it is one person's word against another's as to what occurred during the meeting.
- *When?* There is no "right" day of the week or time of day for every discharge. Unless there is a legal or security issue and the employee must be escorted off the property immediately, offer the employee the option of cleaning out his or her desk right after the meeting or coming in at a pre-arranged time during nonbusiness hours.

Figure 14–2

Termination Checklist

Type of Termination

Voluntary:

_____Received employee resignation letter. (If verbal resignation, provided employee with a written confirmation of resignation, retained copy).

_____Scheduled exit interview.   _____Completed exit interview.

Involuntary:

_____Provided employee with termination letter (for-cause terminations).

_____Provided employee with severance agreement if layoff and severance eligible.

    _____Received signed severance agreement.

_____Provided employee with WARN/OWBPA notices (if applicable).

Benefits

_____Provided employee with termination/continuation of employment insurance benefits information (COBRA, life insurance, supplemental insurance, etc.)

_____Checked FSA/HSA participation and informed employee of remaining funds and reimbursement deadlines, if applicable.

_____Checked DCAP participation and informed employee of remaining funds and reimbursement deadlines, if applicable.

_____Checked PTO balance and informed employee of any remaining PTO and how it will be processed at termination of employment.

_____Informed employee about retirement plan options.

Compensation

_____Provided notice of policy regarding any outstanding balances for money owed to company: educational loans/ pay advances.

_____Notified Payroll department to process final paycheck.

_____Informed Payroll of any unused but earned PTO amounts due to employee.

_____Notified Payroll to process severance pay and whether lump sum or salary continuation (if applicable).

Contracts/Legal

_____Provided letter reminding employee of any legal obligations that continue post-employment (such as noncompete/confidentiality agreements/employment contracts).

Immigration

_____Notified company immigration attorney of termination if employee is on temporary work visa.

Records

_____Pulled personnel file to be stored with terminated employee files.

_____Pulled Form I-9 to be stored with terminated employees' I-9s.

_____Obtained written authorization from employee to respond to employment verification requests.

(continued)

Information Technology

____ Disabled e-mail account.

____ Removed employee's name from e-mail group distribution lists; internal/office phone list; website and building directories.

____ Disabled computer access.

____ Disabled phone extension.

____ Disabled voicemail.

Facilities/Office Manager

____ Disabled security codes, if necessary.

____ Changed office mailbox.

____ Cleaned work area and removed personal belongings.

Collected the following items:

____ Keys (____ office, ____ building, ____ desk, ____ file cabinets, ____ other)

____ ID card

____ Building access card

____ Business cards

____ Nameplate

____ Name badge

____ Company cell phone

____ Laptop

____ Uniforms

____ Tools

____ Other _____

- *Where?* In private. The firing manager should arrange a neutral location and select seats that minimize the risk that an angry or violent employee will be able to block the exit.
- *How?* Advising the IT department of a pending termination can ensure that access is disabled and company data are protected from retaliatory actions. During the termination meeting, remind the employee of noncompete and confidentiality agreements, as well as his or her obligation to return company property at the time of separation. Remove the employee's name as a signatory to bank accounts or post-office boxes, and obtain adequate personal security if the situation becomes hostile.

Following these activities, the firing manager should follow five rules for the termination interview:[84]

1. *Present the situation in a clear, concise, and final manner.* Don't confuse the message to be delivered, and don't drag it out: "Tom, as you know, theft of company property is a serious offense, and the facts show clearly that you have

done that on multiple occasions." Remember: Spend only a few minutes, be honest about the reason for firing, don't make excuses, don't bargain, and don't compromise. Get to the point quickly and succinctly.

2. *Avoid debates or a rehash of the past.* Every employee has some redeeming features, so emphasize something positive about the employee, along with any deficiencies that may have contributed to the termination decision. Arguments about past performance may only compound bad feelings that already exist.

3. *Never talk down to the individual.* Be considerate and supportive, and allow the employee to maintain his or her dignity. Your objective should be to remove as much of the emotion and trauma as possible. Emphasize that it's a situation that isn't working and that the decision is made. It's a business decision–don't make excuses or apologies.

4. *Be empathetic but not compromising:* "I'm sorry that this has to happen, but the decision has been made."

5. *What's the next step?* "I'm going to give you this letter outlining remaining pay and benefit arrangements, along with a check for the full amount due to you. If you have questions about any of these issues, there is a phone number listed in the letter, where you can receive further information from HR."

Be prepared for a variety of reactions from disbelief to silent acceptance to rage. The key is to remain calm and focus on helping the employee confront the reality of the situation. Maintain your distance and composure. It does no good to argue or cry along with the employee.

How do you handle the firing of people who just don't fit in–their work is passable but they just aren't suitable for the job, for reasons ranging from personal chemistry to mismatched skills? First, be sure that as a manager, your determination of a "bad fit" isn't just a proxy for "like-me" bias. "Bad fit" or a cultural mismatch can be a legitimate factor in a termination if you can describe and document acceptable behaviors and standards of performance for the job.[85] At Banco Popular North America, for example, managers are instructed to tell employees who are not fitting in exactly where they are not meeting expectations and to offer training to fix the problem before considering dismissal. Those are important steps because many jobs at the bank have changed in recent years as a result of acquisitions and changes in marketing strategy.

If an employee must be fired, be honest, give as much notice as possible, and perhaps offer outplacement counseling or provide severance pay. "That way they walk out with their dignity and respect," says Banco Popular North America's head of HR. Remember, employees who are not fitting in well are often unhappy themselves. They may agree that they would be better off elsewhere.[86] Having examined a very public issue, termination, let us now turn our attention to a related topic, employee privacy.

EMPLOYEE PRIVACY AND ETHICAL ISSUES

In an 1890 *Harvard Law Review* article, former U.S. Supreme Court Justice Louis Brandeis defined **privacy** as the "right to be left alone."[87] It is the interest employees have in controlling the use of their personal information and in being able to engage in behavior free from regulation or surveillance.[88] Attention centers on three main issues: the kind of information collected and retained about individuals, how that

Organizations have the right to monitor the use of their computers by employees.
Monkey Business Images/ Shutterstock

information is used, and the extent to which it can be disclosed to others. For managers, these issues often lead to **ethical dilemmas**–that is, situations that have the potential to result in a breach of acceptable behavior.

But what is acceptable behavior? The difficulty lies in maintaining a proper balance between the common good and personal freedom, between the legitimate business needs of an organization and a worker's feelings of dignity and worth.[89] Although we cannot prescribe the *content* of ethical behavior across all conceivable situations, we can prescribe *processes* that may lead to an acceptable (and temporary) consensus among interested parties regarding an ethical course of action. In the remainder of this chapter, we will examine several areas that pose potential ethical dilemmas for employers and privacy concerns for employees or job applicants. Let us begin by considering fair information-practice policies.

Fair Information Practices in the Digital Age

In a recent poll by the Pew Research Center, majorities of Americans think their personal data is less secure now, that data collection poses more risks than benefits, and believe it is not possible to go through daily life without being tracked.[90] Consider three different perspectives on this issue. Together, they illustrate the complexity of the personal privacy issue. First, tracking the spread of the the coronavirus pandemic in an age of smartphones means that governments now have surveillance capabilities unimaginable during prior outbreaks. Data flowing from the world's 5.2 billion smartphones can help identify who, where, and how people get infected.[91] Second, automated eavesdropping by digital assistants like Alexa, Echo, Google Home, and Apple HomePod allows firms to target ads to your demographic characteristics and interests. By one estimate, there will be about 7.4 billion voice-controlled devices in operation by 2023. That's about one for every person on earth.[92] New 5G networks can connect billions of cameras, sensors, and other "smart" devices–and that could be trouble for personal privacy.[93]

Third, for many people, being found on social media is important to building a career, establishing a presence as an expert in one's field, and keeping in touch. Yet chances are you are also revealing more than you know on social-media sites. Fully 73 percent of social-media profiles can be found through a public search engine, and 77 percent of social-network users do not restrict access to their photo albums. The risk? Losing out on jobs, among others. Fully 70 percent of employers use social-networking sites to research job candidates, and 57 percent of those have found information that caused them not to hire a candidate.[94]

As of 2018, any business that handles the personal data of European residents must comply with the European Union's General Data Protection Regulation (GDPR), even if it has no physical presence in the EU. Here are some key provisions:[95]

- Almost any information that can be linked to individuals is covered, for example, addresses, photos, financial records, travel plans, and web-search history.
- Companies must designate a point person for data protection; certify that processes minimize the impact on privacy rights; collect only data needed immediately; disclose their data-collection policies clearly; and report any loss, destruction, or theft of data to regulators within 72 hours.
- Penalties for noncompliance can be as high as $24.5 million or 4 percent of a company's annual global revenue, whichever is higher.
- Individuals can demand to know what personal information an organization holds about them, and they have a "right to erasure," asking a business to delete their data for almost any reason.

Facebook agreed to a 20-year privacy settlement with the U.S. government that requires the company to ask users for permission before changing the way their personal information is released. Facebook also gave its more than 2.6 billion monthly users (as of 2020) new tools to manage who can see information about them. It moved a number of privacy controls–which previously required navigating to a separate settings page–to users' home pages and profile pages, next to where they view and post content. The result? Facebook is now competing on privacy.[96]

Monitoring Employees

On a company's intranet in the workplace, it is important to emphasize that, as a general matter, no absolute privacy exists, even for bosses.[97] They may view employees on video monitors; tap their phones, e-mail, and network communications; and rummage through their computer files with or without employee knowledge or consent, 24 hours a day. However, in a major statement on privacy rights in the digital age, the U.S. Supreme Court ruled that police need warrants to search the cellphones of people they arrest.[98]

What about instant messaging (IM), the immensely popular computer programs that let users exchange short text messages with online buddies in real time? Companies can pull up message logs stored locally on employees' computers, search logs stored remotely on a corporate or web-hosted server, and even establish policies to block IMs containing certain words from being sent at all.[99]

At least two-thirds of U.S. companies monitor employees for e-mail infractions, and half have fired employees for those infractions. The most common kinds of misuse tend to be violations of company policies, inappropriate language, excessive personal use, or breaches of confidentiality.[100]

Why do employers monitor their employees? They are mostly worried about two things: their legal liability for employee abuse of company information systems and employees' productivity.[101] Companies monitor e-mail and Internet activity to minimize their exposure to defamation, trade-secret, and breach-of-contract lawsuits. They also worry about copyright-infringement suits based on material employees download, including pictures, music files, and software. Their biggest concern, however, has to do with sexually explicit, racist, or other potentially offensive material that could lead to charges of a hostile work environment, as defined by harassment and discrimination laws.[102]

Some monitoring is done for the purpose of workplace wellness (wearable devices among employees who opt in) and talent analytics, but even people in those businesses say rules governing privacy are needed.[103] What about the use of biometric data–facial and voice recognition, fingerprint readers, hand and iris scans?

Roughly 6 percent of companies in the United States, Europe, and Canada track employees using biometric data–typically for timekeeping and attendance or to grant access to sensitive data. Expect more companies to embrace biometric data as it becomes more commonplace in everyday life, such as using it to unlock a smartphone or to summon a digital assistant. At the same time, only 10 percent of survey respondents believe biometrics are secure enough to be used as the sole form of authentication. Beyond that, biometric data that are stored in the cloud, transferred to third parties, and potentially subject to data breaches could expose workers to risks like identity theft.[104]

To inform employees and to minimize legal risks, transparency is paramount. Experts recommend that companies do four things well.[105]

- Have a written policy that specifies the type of devices or procedures being used and what they are being used for.
- Explain the company's plans for safeguarding biometric data.
- Describe how third-party vendors that process or store biometric data will keep it secure and require employee consent to disclose it to other parties.
- State how long biometric data will be kept and when it will be destroyed, particularly after an employee is no longer working for the company.

Developing a Fair Information-Practice Policy

Safeguards to protect personal privacy in the workplace are more important than ever. Here are some general recommendations:

1. Set up guidelines and policies to protect information in the organization: for alternative types of data, methods of obtaining the data, retention and dissemination of information, employee or third-party access to information, and release of information about former employees.
2. If you store, develop, or process data on a vendor's server running on the Internet, or "in the cloud," perform due diligence to minimize the risks of compromised data and to ensure that the service provider can meet regulatory requirements.[106]
3. Inform employees of what information is stored on them, the purpose for which it was collected, how it will be used, and how long it will be kept.
4. Collect only job-related information that is relevant for specific decisions and allow employees the right to inspect and update information stored on them.

ETHICAL DILEMMA
When a Soon-to-Be-Laid-Off Employee Asks for Advice*

As a manager, you are privy to a lot of confidential information, including knowledge that will ultimately affect the lives and pocketbooks of your employees, not just their day-to-day workflow. Unfortunately, this information may include impending layoffs, which you cannot discuss with individual employees until after the company makes an official announcement.

One of your employees would like to make summer travel plans and enroll her children in private school in the Fall. She asks for your advice because these are substantial financial commitments. You know that this employee is on the list of employees to be cut within the next weeks, but you cannot tell her this without disclosing confidential information and breaking your company's trust. However, if you don't tell her, the changes she wishes to make could lead to financial and family tension.

The problem deepens if yours is a public company implementing layoffs because of a pending merger or acquisition that has yet to be announced. If the employee you tell acts on the information or passes it on to others who do, you might incur legal problems because of violated securities regulations. What would you do?

*Sources: Green, A. (2017, Nov. 28). I found out my co-worker is getting laid off. May I tip him off? *Inc.com.* Retrieved from *www.inc.com/alison-green/i-found-out-my-coworker-is-getting laid-off-can-i-tip-him-off.html* on May 19, 2020. Quast, L. (2014, June 2). Managers: 7 tips for laying off employees due to downsizing. *Forbes.* Retrieved from *www.forbes.com/sites/lisaquast/2014/06/02/managers-7-tips-for-laying-off-employees-due-to-downsizing/#30fab5f87da2* on July 20, 2017.

5. Establish a policy that states specifically that employees and prospective employees cannot waive their rights to privacy.
6. Establish a policy that any manager or non-manager who violates these privacy principles will be subject to discipline or termination.
7. Allow employees to authorize disclosure of personal information and to maintain personal information within the organization.[107] Research has shown that an individual's perceived control over the uses of information after its disclosure is the single most important variable affecting perceptions of invasion of privacy.[108]

What about companies that allow employees to bring their own devices (BYOD)—including electronic devices such as smartphones and laptops? Legal experts advise organizations to have a policy that makes clear that the employer reserves the right to review information contained on the personal devices the employee brings to the workplace. If an employee's device contains private information that the employee wishes to keep confidential, the employer should make it clear that the employee should not bring the device to work. If the employee leaves the organization, the employer should reserve the right to wipe employer-related information off the employee's device—after advising the employee to back up personal information in case it is lost.[109]

Particularly in light of the corporate scandals that have rocked the business world over the past decade or so, people tend to give executives low marks for honesty and ethical behavior.[110] Companies that have taken the kinds of measures just described—such as IBM, 3M, AT&T, Cummins Engine, Aflac, and USAA—report that they have not been overly costly, produced burdensome traffic in access demands, or reduced the general quality of their HR decisions. Furthermore, they receive strong employee approval for their policies when they ask about them on company-attitude surveys. By matching words with deeds, companies such as these are weaving their concerns for employee privacy into the very fabric of their corporate cultures.

Assessment of Job Applicants and Employees

Decisions to hire, promote, train, or transfer are major events in individuals' careers. Frequently, such decisions are made with the aid of tests, interviews, situational exercises, performance appraisals, and other assessment techniques. Developers and users of these instruments must be concerned with questions of fairness, propriety, and individual rights, as well as with other ethical issues.

Developers, if they are members of professional associations such as the American Psychological Association, the Society for Human Resource Management, or the Academy of Management, are bound by the codes of ethical conduct put forth by those bodies.[111] Managers who use assessment instruments are subject to other ethical principles, beyond the general concerns for accuracy and equality of opportunity, including the following:[112]

- Guarding against invasion of privacy (e.g., with respect to biodata items, four areas seem to generate the greatest concern: self-incriminating items, those that require applicants to recall traumatic events, intimacy, and religion).[113]
- Guaranteeing confidentiality (treating information provided with the expectation that it will not be disclosed to others).
- Obtaining informed consent from employees and applicants before assessing them.
- Respecting employees' rights to know (e.g., regarding test content and the meaning, interpretation, and intended use of scores).
- Imposing time limitations on data (i.e., removing information that has not been used for HR decisions, especially if it has been updated).
- Using the most valid procedures available, thereby minimizing erroneous acceptances and erroneous rejections.
- Treating applicants and employees with respect and consideration (i.e., by standardizing procedures for all candidates).

What can applicants do when confronted by a question they believe is irrelevant or an invasion of privacy? Some may choose not to respond. However, research indicates that employers tend to view such nonresponse as an attempt to conceal facts that would reflect poorly on an applicant. Hence, applicants (especially those who have nothing to hide) are ill advised not to respond.[114] Clearly, it is the employer's responsibility to (1) know the kinds of questions that are being asked of candidates and (2) review the appropriateness and job relatedness of all such questions.

Whistle-Blowing

Like a referee on a playing field who can blow the whistle to stop action, **whistle-blowing** refers to disclosure by former or current organization members of illegal, immoral, or illegitimate practices under the control of their employers to persons or organizations that may be able to do something about it.[115] Research indicates that individuals can be conditioned to behave unethically (if they are rewarded for it), especially under increased competition,[116] but that the threat of punishment has a counterbalancing influence.[117] More importantly, when a formal or informal organizational policy is present that favors ethical behavior, ethical behavior tends to increase.[118]

After the wave of accounting scandals in the early 2000s, Congress passed whistle-blower protections in the 2002 Sarbanes-Oxley (SOX) corporate reform law.[119] The act

- Makes it unlawful to discharge, demote, suspend, threaten, harass, or in any manner discriminate against a whistle-blower.
- Establishes criminal penalties of up to 10 years in jail for executives who retaliate against whistle-blowers.
- Requires board audit committees to establish procedures for hearing whistle-blower complaints.
- Allows the secretary of labor to order a company to rehire a terminated whistle-blower with no court hearings whatsoever.
- Gives a whistle-blower a right to a jury trial, bypassing months or years of cumbersome administrative hearings.

Subsequently, Congress passed the 2010 Dodd-Frank Wall Street Reform and Consumer Protection Act, which contains powerful new incentives for whistle-blowers as well as enhanced anti-retaliation protections. The act creates a substantial financial incentive for whistle-blowers who voluntarily report "original information"

IMPACT OF PROCEDURAL JUSTICE AND ETHICS ON PRODUCTIVITY, QUALITY OF WORK LIFE, AND THE BOTTOM LINE

As we have seen throughout this chapter, employees and former employees are very sensitive to the general issue of "justice on the job." On a broad range of issues, they expect to be treated justly, fairly, and with due process. Doing so certainly contributes to improved productivity and quality of work life because grievances are both time consuming and costly. On the other hand, organizations that disregard employee rights can expect two things: (1) to be hit with lawsuits and (2) to find courts and juries to be sympathetic to tales of employer wrongdoing. Whistle-blower cases illustrate this trend clearly. The monetary consequences can be substantial as well. BNY Mellon paid a fine of $714 million to resolve accusations it cheated government pension funds and other investors on currency trades for more than a decade.[a] Conversely, a study of 10 years' worth of records from NAVEX Global covering financial reporting, sexual harassment, and workplace safety revealed that companies that provide employees with channels through which they can disclose unethical activity earn a higher return on assets than firms with underdeveloped whistleblowing platforms.[b] As in so many other areas of employee relations, careful attention to procedural justice and ethical decision making yields direct as well as indirect benefits. The old adage "An ounce of prevention is worth a pound of cure" says it all.

[a]Baer, J., Zuckerman, G., and Viswanatha, A. (2016, Aug. 10). Tipsters are poised for big payouts. *The Wall Street Journal*, pp. C1, C2.

[b]Towey, R. (2018, Nov. 24). Whistleblowers ultimately help their companies perform better, a new study shows. *CNBC*. Retrieved from *www.cnbc.com/2018/11/23/whistleblowers-ultimately-help-their-companies-perform-better-study.html* on Nov. 25, 2018.

directly to the Securities and Exchange Commission (SEC) or to the Commodity Futures Trading Commission (CFTC) that leads to successful enforcement and the recovery of more than $1 million in monetary sanctions. Those who qualify may be awarded 10 to 30 percent of the collected monetary sanctions, with the specific amount determined by the SEC or CFTC.

The SEC will "consider higher percentage awards for whistle-blowers who first report violations through their company's internal compliance programs." Most do.[120] As of 2018, the SEC obtained $1.7 billion in penalties for cases involving whistleblowers, and it paid out $326 million to 59 whistleblowers.[121] Finally, the Dodd-Frank Act amends SOX to lengthen the statute of limitations for a SOX retaliation claim from 90 days to 180 days and to clarify that employees are entitled to have SOX retaliation claims tried before a jury.[122]

In a dramatic expansion of whistle-blower protections in SOX, the U.S. Supreme Court ruled in 2014 that those protections apply to employees of contractors and subcontractors of a publicly traded company as well as to employees of the public firm itself.[123] More broadly, 47 federal laws protect the rights of corporate workers to report wrongdoing, as well as every state.[124]

What can a company do to make it more likely that employees will use internal channels to lodge complaints? Consider taking the following steps:[125]

- Create a culture of integrity through top-down transparency and accountability and continually communicate a commitment to ethics .
- Train managers to be receptive and supportive of employee concerns about perceived improprieties that could amount to fraud.
- Institute help lines for anonymous reports and multiple other channels for submitting complaints.
- Educate employees through training, and disseminate policies widely on the available methods for submitting complaints internally.
- Develop and disseminate comprehensive codes of conduct and ethics.
- Reward whistle-blowers for providing the company with information that enables it to identify and address incidents of fraud.
- Include the concept of "fostering a culture of ethics and accountability" among the criteria used to evaluate managers' performance.

Despite retaliation, financial loss, and high emotional and physical stress,[126] whistle-blowers continue to come forward, and they are likely to continue to do so. In a recent study of 5,101 workers by the Ethics & Compliance Initiative, 69 percent said they reported the misconduct they saw but 44 percent said they suffered retaliation for speaking up.[127] Are they social misfits? On the contrary, research indicates that most of them are well-adjusted individuals who have strong personal values, which they live by.[128]

In the case of federal contractors, disclosure of fraud, waste, and abuse can lead to substantial financial gains by whistle-blowers. Thus, under the federal False Claims Act of 1863, as amended, private citizens may sue a contractor for fraud on the government's behalf and share up to 30 percent of whatever financial recovery the government makes as a result of the charges.[129] There are no "caps" on awards; the value of the information the whistleblower provides serves as the basis for the amount of the award. The better the information, the larger the sanction. The larger the sanction, the larger the award.[130]

Whistle-blowing is likely to be effective to the extent that (1) the whistle-blower is credible and relatively powerful, (2) the reported information is clearly illegal and unambiguous, (3) the evidence is convincing, and (4) the organization itself encourages whistle-blowing and discourages retaliation against whistle-blowers.[131] If you have a tale to tell, begin by asking yourself four important questions:[132]

1. *Is this the only way?* Don't blow the whistle unless you have tried to correct the problem by reporting up the normal chain of command and gotten no results. Make sure your allegations are not minor complaints.

2. *Do I have the goods?* Gather documentary evidence that proves your case, and keep it in a safe place. Keep detailed notes, perhaps even a daily diary. Make sure you are seeing fraud, not merely incompetence or sloppiness.

3. *Why am I doing this?* Examine your motives. Don't act out of frustration or because you feel under-appreciated or mistreated. Do not embellish your case, and do not violate any confidentiality agreements you have.

4. *Am I ready?* Think through the impact on your family. Be prepared for unemployment and the possibility of being blacklisted in your profession. Last but not least, consult a lawyer.

IMPLICATIONS FOR MANAGEMENT PRACTICE

Managers who fail to address employee concerns for ethics and procedural justice do so at their peril. Companies often see whistle-blowers as motivated by revenge or greed. Studies consistently show, however, that most are driven to right a wrong. That's why more than 90 percent of them sound the alarm internally first, rather than running to the authorities or the newspapers.[a] Ethics programs are control systems whose objectives are to standardize employee behavior within the domains of ethics and legal compliance. Evidence now indicates that management, and especially top-management, commitment to an ethics program affects both its scope and its control orientation. Programs of broad scope include multiple elements, dedicated staff, and extensive employee involvement. Control may be *compliance oriented*, emphasizing adherence to rules, monitoring employee behavior, and disciplining misconduct, or it may be *values oriented*, emphasizing commitment to shared values and encouraging ethical aspirations. Some programs strive for both, so that organizational values are not perceived as empty rhetoric.[b] Multiple **meta-analyses** (quantitative cumulations of research findings) of studies of organizational justice have confirmed the beneficial effects on employee attitudes and performance of procedural-justice safeguards.[c] Provide explicit procedures for resolving conflicts and be sure that all employees know how to use them. Treat all people with dignity and respect, and they will respond with high levels of performance and commitment.

[a]The age of the whistleblower. (2015, Dec. 5). *The Economist*, pp. 61-63.

[b]Kennedy, J. A., and Schweitzer, M. E. (2018). Building trust by tearing others down: When accusing others of unethical behavior engenders trust. *Organizational Behavior and Human Decision Processes* 149, pp. 111-28. Weaver, G. R., Trevino, L. K., and Cochran, P. L. (1999). Corporate ethics programs as control systems: Influences of executive commitment and environmental factors. *Academy of Management Journal* 42, pp. 41-57.

[c]Greenberg, J. (2011). Organizational justice: The dynamics of fairness in the workplace. In S. Zedeck (Ed.), *APA Handbook of Industrial and Organizational Psychology* (Vol. 3). Washington, DC: American Psychological Association, pp. 271-327.

Conclusion

Ethical behavior is not governed by hard-and-fast rules. Rather, it adapts and changes in response to social norms. This is nowhere more obvious than in human resource management. What was considered ethical in the 1950s and 1960s (deep-probing selection interviews; management prescriptions of standards of dress, ideology, and lifestyle; refusal to let employees examine their own employment files) would be considered improper today. Indeed, as we have seen, growing concern for employee rights has placed organizational decision-making policies in the public domain. The beneficial effect of this, of course, is that it is sensitizing both employers and employees to new concerns.

To be sure, ethical choices are rarely easy. The challenge in managing human resources lies not in the mechanical application of moral prescriptions, but rather in the process of creating and maintaining genuine relationships from which to address ethical dilemmas that cannot be covered by prescription.[133]

Human Resource Management in Action: Conclusion

ALTERNATIVE DISPUTE RESOLUTION: GOOD FOR THE COMPANY, GOOD FOR EMPLOYEES?

In a 2018 decision (*Epic Systems Corp. v. Lewis*), the U.S. Supreme Court upheld class-action waivers in arbitration agreements. The ruling gave businesses the power to stop employees from banding together to file claims for work-related issues. Instead, each employee must file an individual arbitration claim when a suspected violation arises. While job applicants can be required to sign an agreement to arbitrate employment disputes as the exclusive remedy for claims against the company, current employees may require different treatment. The employer may encourage–but not require–current employees to sign such an agreement with some "additional consideration." Such consideration often takes the form of a one-time payment or bonus or some form of time off. Now that there is no question about enforceability of such agreements, opponents might point to flaws in the procedural fairness of the process as a basis for a petition to a court to nullify an agreement.

This raises another issue–what does a fair ADR program look like? According to attorneys and HR professionals, a fair ADR program is neutral and confidential, it provides due process to the employee, and it does not limit the remedies available to the employee. Moreover, it imposes fees (if any) that are no higher than what it would cost an employee to file a claim in court. In addition to these features, sound ADR programs incorporate the following principles:

- **Don't argue needlessly.** Employers with well-managed programs often use internal appeals procedures with multiple levels. The employee first discusses his or her problem with the immediate supervisor. If not resolved, the employee appeals to a higher level of management or a committee composed of management, employees, or a combination of the two.
- **Top management emphasizes that the program is not voluntary.** Everyone is expected to work to make it a success.
- **Involve all stakeholders in the design of the program.** Seek their input and support.
- **Identify metrics to measure the program's progress.** Compare your system with those of other companies.

- **Train employees and managers to address and resolve conflicts early and at the lowest possible level.**
- **Listen to any dissatisfied user of the program and make appropriate adjustments.**
- **Market the program internally to ensure trust and use and externally to publicize your company's strength.** It is an employee benefit that distinguishes your company as an open-minded, fair employer and a good place to work.

Like other HR initiatives, ADR programs have both negative and positive features. On the one hand, they may increase the number of employee claims, and unfavorable arbitration decisions are almost impossible to overturn. On the other hand, employees can pursue the same claims in arbitration that they could in court, and claims can be resolved much more quickly. Arbitrators can award damages in the same fashion that a judge or jury can. On balance, programs that incorporate features that are designed to ensure procedural justice are good for employers *and* good for employees. They will likely encourage both sides to make greater use of ADR in the future.

SUMMARY

The broad theme of this chapter is "justice on the job." This includes procedural justice, due process, and ethical decision making. Each of these processes should guide the formulation of policy in matters involving dispute resolution (e.g., through grievance procedures), arbitration, discipline, employment contracts, and termination for disciplinary or economic reasons. Indeed, such concerns for procedural justice and due process form the basis for many challenges to the employment-at-will doctrine.

Two of the most important employment issues of our time are employee privacy and ethical decision making. Three areas that involve employee privacy are receiving considerable emphasis: fair information practices in the digital age, the assessment of job applicants and employees, and whistle-blowing. Although it is not possible to prescribe the content of ethical behavior in each of these areas, processes that incorporate procedural justice can lead to an acceptable (and temporary) consensus among interested parties regarding an ethical course of action.

KEY TERMS

alternative dispute resolution
  (ADR) program
employee relations
justice
procedural justice
distributive justice

due process
constitutional due-process rights
ethical decisions about behavior
organizational citizenship behaviors (OCBs)
organizational support
employee voice

open-door policy	employment at will
skip-level policy	public policy exception
interactional justice	implied promises
informational justice	retaliatory discharge
peer-review panel	lifestyle discrimination
nonunion arbitration	noncompete agreements
mediation	fiduciary duty of loyalty
ombudspersons	choice-of-law provision
just cause	privacy
social learning theory	ethical dilemma
progressive discipline	whistle-blowing
red-hot-stove rule	meta-analysis

DISCUSSION QUESTIONS

14-1. Discuss the similarities and differences in these concepts: procedural justice, workplace due process, and ethical decisions about behavior.

14-2. What advice would you give to an executive who is about to negotiate an employment contract?

14-3. Is it ethical to record a conversation with your boss without his or her knowledge? If yes, under what circumstances?

14-4. How can a firm avoid lawsuits for employment at will?

14-5. What are some guidelines to follow in determining a reasonable compromise between a company's need to run its business and employee rights to privacy?

14-6. In the course of your job, you learn that someone is "cooking the books." Discuss the steps you would take to resolve the issue.

14-7. Discuss the similarities and differences among employee voice, interactional justice, and informational justice. Can you give an example of each one?

14-8. What might explain the finding that across cultures, employee-voice systems are associated with judgments of fairness?

14-9. How does the imposition of employee discipline for poor performance (or conversely, the failure to discipline) serve as a signal to other employees?

14-10. Develop a policy to inform employees of your organization's BYOD approach to electronic devices.

APPLYING YOUR KNOWLEDGE

Case 14–1

GM Recalls: How General Motors Silenced a Whistle-Blower

General Motors (GM) manager Courtland Kelley had been the head of a nationwide GM inspection program and then the quality manager for the Chevy Cavalier and its successor, the Chevy Cobalt. He found flaws and reported them, over and over, and repeatedly found his colleagues' and supervisors' responses wanting. He thought they were more concerned with maintaining their bureaucracies and avoiding expensive recalls than with stopping the sale of dangerous cars. Eventually, he sued GM and sought protection under Michigan's whistle-blower law. This is a story about the personal consequences for Kelley and the legal and economic consequences for GM.

To read the story, please follow this link:

http://www.consumerauto.org/wp-content/uploads/2014/10/GM-Recalls-How-General-Motors-Silenced-a-Whistle-Blower.pdf

Based on what you read, how would you answer each of the following questions?

Questions

1. What kinds of circumstances might drive employees to blow the whistle?
2. Why might some employees observe wrongdoing and come forward, whereas others do not?
3. As a manager, what procedures or processes might you suggest to encourage more employees to blow the whistle when necessary?
4. If you were Mary Barra, the CEO of General Motors who inherited the problems that led to 20 million recalls, what steps could you take to change the organization's culture?

REFERENCES

1. Fossum, J. A. (2015). *Labor Relations: Development, Structure, Process.* (12th ed.). Burr Ridge, IL: McGraw-Hill/Irwin.
2. *The Merriam-Webster Dictionary.* (2020). Retrieved from *www.merriam-webster.com/dictionary/justice* on May 18, 2020.
3. Cropanzano, R., Kirk, J., and Discorfano, S. (2017). Organizational justice. In S. G. Rogelberg (Ed.), *The Sage Encyclopedia of Industrial and Organizational Psychology* (2nd ed., Vol. 3). Thousand Oaks, CA: Sage, pp. 1118–22. *See also* Greenberg, J. (2011). Organizational justice: The dynamics of fairness in the workplace. In S. Zedeck (Ed.), *APA Handbook of Industrial and Organizational Psychology* (Vol. 3). Washington, DC: American Psychological Association, pp. 271–327.
4. Ibid. *See also* Colquitt, J. A., Conlon, D. E., Wesson, M. J., Porter, C. O. L. H., and Ng, K. Y. (2001). Justice at the millennium: A meta-analytic review of 25 years of organizational justice research. *Journal of Applied Psychology* 86, pp. 425–45.
5. Cropanzano et al. (2017), op. cit. *See also* Colella, A. (2001). Coworker distributive fairness judgments of the workplace accommodation of employees with disabilities. *Academy of Management Review* 26, pp. 100–16.
6. Wesman, E. C., and Eischen, D. E. (1990). Due process. In J. A. Fossum (Ed.), *Employee and Labor Relations.* Washington, DC: Bureau of National Affairs, pp. 4–82 to 4–133.
7. MacKinnon, B., and Fiala, A. (2018). *Ethics: Theory and Contemporary Issues* (9th ed.). Stamford, CT: Cengage Learning. *See also* Lefkowitz, J. (2006). The constancy of ethics amidst the changing world of work. *Human Resource Management Review* 16, pp. 245–68.
8. Greenberg (2011), op. cit. *See also* Simons, T., and Roberson, Q. (2003). Why managers should care about fairness: The effects of aggregate justice perceptions on organizational outcomes. *Journal of Applied Psychology* 88, pp. 432–43. *See also* Kanovsky, M. (2000). Understanding procedural justice and its impact on business organizations. *Journal of Management* 26, pp. 489–511.
9. Greenberg, J. (2010). Organizational injustice as an occupational health risk. *Academy of Management Annals,* 4, pp. 205–43. *See also* Elovainio, M., Kivimaki, M., and Helkama, K. (2001). Organizational justice evaluations, job control, and occupational strain. *Journal of Applied Psychology* 86, pp. 418–24.
10. Organ, D. W., Podsakoff, P. M., and Podsakoff, N. P. (2011). Expanding the criterion domain to include organizational citizenship behavior: Implications for employee selection. In S. Zedeck (Ed.), *APA Handbook of Industrial and Organizational Psychology* (Vol. 2). Washington, DC: American Psychological Association, pp. 281–323.

11. Ehrhart, M. (2004). Leadership and procedural justice climate as antecedents of unit-level organizational citizenship behavior. *Personnel Psychology* 57, pp. 61–94.

12. Borman, W. C., Brantley, L. B., and Hanson, M. A. (2014). Progress toward understanding the structure and determinants of job performance: A focus on task and citizenship performance. *International Journal of Selection & Assessment* 22, pp. 422–31. *See also* Organ, D. W., and Ryan, K. (1995). A meta-analytic review of attitudinal and dispositional predictors of organizational citizenship behavior. *Personnel Psychology* 48, pp. 775–802. *See also* Allen, T. D., and Rush, M. C. (1998). The effects of organizational citizenship behavior on performance judgments: A field study and a laboratory experiment. *Journal of Applied Psychology* 83, pp. 247–60.

13. Organ et al. (2011), op. cit. *See also* Moorman, R. H., Blakely, G. L., and Niehoff, B. P. (1998). Does perceived organizational support mediate the relationship between procedural justice and organizational citizenship behavior? *Academy of Management Journal* 41, pp. 351–57.

14. Organ et al. (2011), op. cit. *See also* Liao, H., and Rupp, D. E. (2005). The impact of justice climate and justice orientation on work outcomes: A cross-level multifoci framework. *Journal of Applied Psychology* 90, pp. 242–56. *See also* Naumann, S. E., and Bennett, N. (2000). A case for procedural justice climate: Development and test of a multilevel model. *Academy of Management Journal* 43, pp. 881–89.

15. Kanovsky (2000), op. cit.

16. Colquitt, J. A. (2001). On the dimensionality of organizational justice: A construct validation of a measure. *Journal of Applied Psychology* 86, pp. 386–400.

17. Sheppard, B. H., Lewicki, R. J., and Minton, J. W. (1992). *Organizational Justice: The Search for Fairness in the Workplace*. New York: Lexington.

18. Budd, J. W. (2021). *Labor Relations: Striking a Balance* (6th ed.). New York: McGraw-Hill. *See also* Soper, S. (2018, July 2). Inside Amazon's people's court. *Bloomberg BusinessWeek*, pp. 22, 23. *See also* De Dreu, C. K. (2011). Conflict at work: Basic principles and applied issues. In S. Zedeck (Ed.), *APA Handbook of Industrial and Organizational Psychology* (Vol. 3). Washington, DC: American Psychological Association, pp. 461–93.

19. Roche, W., and Teague, P. (2012, Mar.). Do conflict management systems matter? *Human Resource Management* 51(2), pp. 231–58. *See also* Hirschman, C. (2003). Someone to listen. *HRMagazine*, pp. 46–51. *See also* Arnold, J. A., and O'Connor, K. M. (1999). Ombudspersons or peers? The effect of third-party expertise and recommendations on negotiation. *Journal of Applied Psychology* 84, pp. 776–85.

20. Sheppard et al. (1992), op. cit.

21. Budd (2021), op. cit.

22. Greenberg (2011), op. cit. *See also* Leung, K., Tong, K. K., and Ho, S. S. Y. (2004). Effects of interactional justice on egocentric bias in resource allocation decisions. *Journal of Applied Psychology* 89, pp. 405–15. *See also* Bies, R. J. (2001). Interactional (in)justice: The sacred and the profane. In J. Greenberg and R. Cropanzano (Eds.), *Advances in Organizational Justice*. Lexington, MA: Lexington Press.

23. Choi, J. (2008). Event justice perceptions and employees' reactions: Perceptions of social entity justice as a moderator. *Journal of Applied Psychology* 93, pp. 513–28. *See also* Masterson, S. S., Lewis, K., Goldman, B. M., and Taylor, M. S. (2000). Integrating justice and social exchange: The differing effects of fair procedures and treatment on work relationships. *Academy of Management Journal* 4, pp. 738–48.

24. Brockner, J. (2010). *A Contemporary Look at Organizational Justice: Multiplying Insult Times Injury*. New York: Routledge. *See also* Gopinath, C., and Becker, T. E. (2000). Communication, procedural justice, and employee attitudes: Relationships under conditions of divestiture. *Journal of Management* 26, pp. 63–83.

25. Dewitt, R. L. (2012). Good downsizing. In C. L. Cooper, A. Pandey, and J. C. Quick (Eds.), *Downsizing: Is Less Still More?* Cambridge, UK: Cambridge University Press, pp. 326–55. *See also* Mishra, A. K., and Spreitzer, G. M. (1998). Explaining how survivors respond to downsizing: The roles of trust, empowerment, justice, and work redesign. *Academy of*

Management Journal 23, pp. 567–88. *See also* Brockner, J., and Wiesenfeld, B. M. (1996). An integrative framework for explaining reactions to decisions: Interactive effects of outcomes and procedures. *Psychological Bulletin* 120, pp. 189–208.

26. Budd (2021), op. cit. *See also* Colvin, A. J. S. (2014). Grievance procedures in non-union firms. In W. K. Roche, P. Teague, and A. J. S. Colvin (Eds.). *The Oxford Handbook of Conflict Management in Organizations*. Oxford, UK: Oxford University Press, pp. 168–89. *See also* Olson-Buchanan, J. B., and Boswell, W. R. (2008). Organizational dispute-resolution systems. In C. K. W. De Dreu and M. J. Gelfand (Eds.), *The Psychology of Conflict and Conflict Management in Organizations*. New York: Lawrence Erlbaum, pp. 321–52.

27. Society for Human Resource Management. (2018, June 22). Grievance procedures: Non-union. Retrieved from *www.shrm.org/resourcesandtools/tools-and-samples/policies/pages/grievance-procedures.aspx* on May 18, 2020.

28. Katz et al. (2017), op. cit. *See also* De Dreu (2011), op. cit.

29. Posthuma, R. A. (2010). *Workplace Dispute Resolution*. Alexandria, VA: Society for Human Resource Management.

30. Katz et al. (2017), op. cit. *See also* Fossum (2015), op. cit.

31. Budd (2021), op. cit. *See also* Katz et al. (2017), op. cit.

32. Budd (2021), op. cit.

33. FedEx attributes success to people-first philosophy. Retrieved from *www.fedex.com/ma/about/overview/philosophy.html* on May 18, 2020. *See also Lorenz v. FedEx Corp.* (2012). Available at *www.vawd.uscourts.gov/opinions/turk/lorenzvfedex710cv487.pdf.*

34. Budd (2021), op. cit.

35. Wilkie (2017), op. cit. *See also* Smith, A. (2011, Apr. 13). ADR is underused tool for resolving disputes. *HR News*. Retrieved from *www.shrm.org/LegalIssues/FederalResources/Pages/ADRIsUnderusedTool.aspx* on Aug. 22, 2011. *See also* Hendriks, E. S. (2000, June). Do more than open doors. *HRMagazine*, pp. 171–81.

36. Budd (2021), op. cit.

37. Katz et al. (2017), op. cit. *See also* Budd (2021), op. cit.

38. Fossum (2015), op. cit. *See also* Welch, J., and Welch, S. (2006, Nov. 13). Send the jerks packing. *BusinessWeek*, p. 136. *See also* Cottringer, W. (2003, Apr.). The abc's of employee discipline. *Supervision* 64(4), pp. 5, 7. *See also* Falcone, P. (1997, Feb.). Fundamentals of progressive discipline. *HRMagazine*, pp. 90–94.

39. Hymowitz, C. (1998, July 28). Managers struggle to find a way to let someone go. *The Wall Street Journal*, p. B1.

40. Andrews, L. W. (2004, Dec.). Hard-core offenders. *HRMagazine*, pp. 43–48.

41. Fossum (2015), op. cit. *See also* Cottringer (2003), op. cit. *See also* O'Reilly, C. A. III, and Weitz, B. A. (1980). Managing marginal employees: The use of warnings and dismissals. *Administrative Science Quarterly* 25, pp. 467–84.

42. Robbins, S. P., and Judge, T. A. (2019). *Organizational Behavior* (18th ed.). Upper Saddle River, NJ: Pearson. *See also* Bandura, A. (1986). *Social Foundations of Thought and Action: A Social Cognitive Theory*. Englewood Cliffs, NJ: Prentice-Hall.

43. Klotz, A., and Bolino, M. (2016). Saying goodbye: The nature, causes, and consequences of employee resignation styles. *Journal of Applied Psychology* 101, pp. 1386–404. *See also* Trevino, L. K. (1992). The social effects of punishments in organizations: A justice perspective. *Academy of Management Review* 17, pp. 647–76.

44. Salvo, T. (2004, July). Practical tips for successful progressive discipline. Retrieved from *www.shrm.org/Research/Articles/Articles/Pages/CMS_009030.aspx*, on Aug. 23, 2011. *See also* O'Reilly, C. A. III, and Puffer, S. M. (1989). The impact of rewards and punishments in a social context: A laboratory and field experiment. *Journal of Occupational Psychology* 62, pp. 41–53.

45. Falcone, P. (2017). The traditional progressive discipline paradigm. Retrieved from *www.shrm.org/resourcesandtools/hr-topics/employee-relations/pages/the-traditional-progressive-discipline-paradigm.aspx* on May 18, 2020. *See also* Salvo (2004), op. cit.

46. Fielkow, B. (2018, June 12). Why it's time to kill progressive discipline. *Chief Executive.* Retrieved from *https://chiefexecutive.net/why-its-time-to-kill-progressive-discipline/* on May 18, 2020.

47. Hastings, R. R. (2010, Jan. 9). Is progressive discipline a thing of the past? *HR News.* Retrieved from *www.shrm.org/hrdisciplines/employeerelations/articles/Pages/IsProgressive-DisciplineaThing.aspx* on Aug. 23, 2011.

48. Budd (2021), op. cit. *See also* Kasson, E. G. (2016, June 1). How to fire someone without getting sued. Retrieved from *www.shrm.org/hr-today/news/hr-magazine/0616/pages/how-to-fire-someone-without-getting-sued.aspx* on June 2, 2016.

49. McGregor, D. (1967). *The Professional Manager.* New York: McGraw-Hill.

50. Klaas, B. S., and Wheeler, H. N. (1990). Managerial decision making about employee discipline: A policy-capturing approach. *Personnel Psychology* 43, pp. 117–34.

51. Deschenaux, J. (2017, May 4). Failure to follow progressive discipline policy may lead to liability for wrongful termination. Retrieved from *www.shrm.org/resourcesandtools/legal-and-compliance/state-and-local-updates/pages/progressive-discipline-policy.aspx* on June 16, 2017.

52. Katz et al. (2017), op. cit. See also Falcone (2017), op. cit.

53. Meinert, D. (2016, July 1). How to create bulletproof documentation. Retrieved from *www.shrm.org/resourcesandtools/hr-topics/employee-relations/pages/performance-documentation.aspx* on July 2, 2016.

54. Thornton, G. R. (2013, Mar. 21). Complying with U.S. labor relations laws in non-union settings. Retrieved from *www.shrm.org/templatestools/toolkits/pages/lawsinnonunionsettings.aspx* on June 24, 2014. *See also NLRB v. J. Weingarten* (1975). 420 U.S. 251, 95 S. Ct. 959.

55. Budd (2021), op. cit.

56. Budd (2021), op. cit. *See also* Feffer, M. 2017, Nov. 7). "Employment at will" isn't a blank check to terminate employees you don't like. *SHRM Online.* Retrieved from *www.shrm.org/resourcesandtools/hr-topics/employee-relations/pages/employment-at-will-isnt-a-blank-check-to-terminate-employees-you-dont-like.aspx* on Nov. 7, 2017.

57. Bales, R. A. (2008). Explaining the spread of at-will employment as an inter-jurisdictional race-to-the-bottom of employment standards. *Tennessee Law Review* 75, pp. 453–71. *See also* Involuntary termination of employment in the United States. (2008, Dec. 8). *SHRM Online.* Retrieved from *www.shrm.org/Research/Articles/Articles/Pages/InvoluntaryTerminationofEmploymentintheUnitedStates.aspx* on Aug. 23, 2011.

58. Budd (2021), op. cit. *See also* Mitchell, B. (1999, Jan. 25). "At-will" employment isn't safe harbor for companies. *The Denver Post*, p. 5L.

59. At-will employment states 2020. (2020, April 6). W*orld Population Review.* Retrieved from *https://worldpopulationreview.com/states/at-will-employment-states/* on May 19, 2020. *See also* Koys, D. J., Briggs, S., and Grenig, J. (1987). State court disparity on employment-at-will. *Personnel Psychology* 40, pp. 565–77.

60. Feffer (2017), op. cit. *See also* Falcone, P. (2002, May). Fire my assistant now! *HRMagazine*, pp. 105–11. *See also* Click, J. (1999, July). Handbook created contract employer can't unilaterally alter. *HR News*, p. 8. *See also* Heshizer, B. (1984). The implied contract exception to at-will employment. *Labor Law Journal* 35, pp. 131–41.

61. Siegel (1998), op. cit.

62. Heylman, S. R. (2014, Apr. 28). Texas: No retaliatory discharge for filing comp claim. Retrieved from *www.shrm.org/legalissues/stateandlocalresources/pages/texas-no-retaliatory-discharge-for-filing-comp-claim.aspx* on June 24, 2014. *See also* Wermiel, S. (1988, June 7). Justices expand union workers' right to sue. *The Wall Street Journal*, p. 4.

63. Nagele-Piazza, L. (2017, Oct. 24). Can employees be fired for off-duty conduct? *SHRM Online.* Retrieved from *www.shrm.org/resourcesandtools/legal-and-compliance/state-and-local-updates/pages/can-employees-be-fired-for-off-duty-conduct.aspx* on Oct. 24, 2017. *See also* Rives, A. L. (2006). You're not the boss of me: A call for federal lifestyle discrimination legislation. *George Washington Law Review* 74, pp. 553–68.

64. Cook, W., and Kuhn, K.M. (2020). Off-duty deviance in the eye of the beholder: Implications of moral foundations theory in the age of social media. *Journal of Business Ethics.* https://doi.org/10.1007/s10551-020-04501-9.

65. Nagele-Piazza (2017), op. cit. *See also* David, C. (2015, Dec. 2). Understanding the legal ramifications of lifestyle discrimination. *Smart Business.* Retrieved from *www.sbnonline. com/article/understanding-the-legal-ramifications-of-lifestyle-discrimination/* on June 16, 2017.

66. LegalMatch.com (2019, Dec. 26). What is an employment agreement? Retrieved from *www.legalmatch.com/law-library/article/advantages-and-disadvantages-of-employment-agreements.html* on May 19, 2020. *See also* Obdyke, L. K. (2002, Aug). Written employment contracts–When? Why? How? Retrieved from *www.shrm.org/Publications/LegalReport/ Pages/CMS_000959.aspx* on Oct. 19, 2004.

67. Brodsky, S. (2019, Feb. 8). Restrictive covenants in employment and related contracts: Key considerations you should know. American Bar Association. Retrieved from *www. americanbar.org/groups/litigation/committees/commercial-business/practice/2019/restrictive-covenants-employment-related-contracts/* on May 19, 2020.

68. Dougherty, C. (2017, May 16). Losing the right to a new job. *The New York Times International Edition*, pp. 10, 11. *See also* Lublin, J. S. (2013, Aug. 12). Companies loosen the handcuffs on non-competes. *The Wall Street Journal*, pp. B1, B4.

69. Wirtz, D. M. (2002, Nov.). Tip the scales on non-compete agreements. *HRMagazine*, pp. 107–15.

70. Torry, H. (2019, May 18). Resistance to noncompete agreements is a win for workers. *the Wall Street Journal.* Retrieved from *www.wsj.com/articles/resistance-to-noncompete-agreements-is-a-win-for-workers-11558195200* on May 18, 2019. *See also* Dougherty (2017), op. cit. *See also* Viswanatha, A. (2016, Feb. 3). Noncompete pacts hobble rookies. *The Wall Street Journal*, pp. B1, B5.

71. Dougherty, J. A. (2013, Jan. 11). The three fatal flaws that kill non-competes. Retrieved from *www.shrm.org/LegalIssues/LegalReport/Pages/flaws-noncompetes.aspx* on June 24, 2014.

72. Foley, M. A. (2020, Jan. 30). States limit non-compete employment agreement use. *The National Law Review.* Retrieved from *www.natlawreview.com/article/competing-views-non-compete-agreements-changes-may-be-coming-across-nation-to* on May 19, 2020. *See also* Torry (2019), op. cit.

73. Torry (2019), op. cit.

74. Nagele-Piazza, L. (2018a, April 4). Employers should carefully craft noncompetes. *SHRM Online.* Retrieved from *www.shrm.org/resourcesandtools/legal-and-compliance/state-and-local-updates/pages/employers-should-carefully-craft-noncompetes.aspx* on Apr. 4, 2018. *See also* American Bar Association. (2017). The basics of employment contracts. Retrieved from *www.americanbar.org/newsletter/publications/law_trends_news_practice_area_e_newsletter_home/0705_litigation_employmentcontracts.html* on June 16, 2017.

75. Rubin Thomlinson LLP. (2015, June 19). Top 5 considerations when negotiating a new employment contract. Retrieved from *www.rubinthomlinson.com/blog/top-5-considerations-when-negotiating-a-new-employment-contract/* on June 16, 2017. *See also* Written employment contracts: Pros and cons. Retrieved from *https://www.nolo.com/legal-encyclopedia/ written-employment-contracts-pros-cons-30193.html* on May 19, 2020.

76. Tyler, K. (2015, Oct.). It's negotiable. *HRMagazine* 60(8), p. 26.

77. U.S. Department of Labor, Employment and Training Administration Fact Sheet. The Worker Adjustment and Retraining Notification Act (WARN) of 1988. Retrieved from *www.doleta.gov/programs/factsht/warn.htm* on May 19, 2020.

78. Smith. S. (2017, July 7). Take care when drafting executive employment agreements. *SHRM Online.* Retrieved from *www.shrm.org/resourcesandtools/legal-and-compliance/state-and-local-updates/pages/take-care-when-drafting-executive-employment-agreements-.aspx* on July 8, 2017.

79. Falcone (2017), op. cit.

80. Geyelin, M. (1989, Sept. 7). Fired managers winning more lawsuits. *The Wall Street Journal*, p. B13.

81. Knight, R. (2019, Feb. 6). How to decide whether to fire someone. *Harvard Business Review*. Retrieved from *www.shrm.org/resourcesandtools/hr-topics/employee-relations/pages/how-to-decide-whether-to-fire-someone.aspx* on Feb. 6, 2019. *See also* Wilkie, D. (2013, Sept. 12). Right and wrong ways to terminate. Retrieved from *www.shrm.org/hrdisciplines/employeerelations/articles/Pages/Right-Wrong-Ways-to-Terminate.aspx* on June 25, 2014.

82. Falcone, P. (2018, July 25). How to have the termination discussion. *SHRM Online*. Retrieved from *www.shrm.org/resourcesandtools/hr-topics/talent-acquisition/pages/the-termination-discussion.aspx* on July 25, 2018. *See also* Lewis, K. R. (2011, Sept. 12). The new rules of firing–And being fired. *Fortune*. Retrieved from *http://fortune.com/2011/09/12/the-new-rules-of-firing-and-being-fired/* on June 25, 2014. *See also* Needleman, S. (2008, July 8). Bad firings can hurt firm's reputation. *The Wall Street Journal*, p. D4.

83. Nagele-Piazza, L. (2018b, March 15). 12 tips for handling employee terminations and disciplinary actions. *SHRM Online*. Retrieved from *www.shrm.org/resourcesandtools/legal-and-compliance/employment-law/pages/12-tips-for-handling-employee-terminations.aspx* on Mar. 15, 2018. *See also* Kasson, E. G. (2016, June 1). How to fire someone without getting sued. *SHRM Online*. Retrieved from *www.shrm.org/hr-today/news/hr-magazine/0616/pages/how-to-fire-someone-without-getting-sued.aspx* on June 2, 2016. *See also* What technology issues should an employer consider when terminating an employee? (2012, July 13). Retrieved from *www.shrm.org/templatestools/hrqa/pages/technologyissuessterminatinganemployee.aspx* on June 25, 2014.

84. Knight (2019), op. cit. *See also* Wilkie (2013), op. cit. *See also* Coleman, F. T. (2006, July). Cardinal rules of termination. Retrieved from *www.shrm.org/Publications/LegalReport/Pages/CMS_000943.aspx* on August 5, 2008. *See also* Coleman, F. T. (2001). *Ending the Employment Relationship without Ending Up in Court*. Alexandria, VA: Society for Human Resource Management.

85. Kasson (2016), op. cit.

86. Ibid. *See also* Dvorak, P. (2006, May 1). Firing good workers who are a bad fit. *The Wall Street Journal*, p. B5.

87. Zeidner, R. (2008, Aug.). Out of the breach. *HRMagazine*. Retrieved from *www.shrm.org/Publications/hrmagazine/EditorialContent/Pages/0808zeidner.aspx* on Aug. 5, 2008.

88. Piller, C. (1993, July). Privacy in peril. *Macworld*, pp. 124–30.

89. Frye, L. (2017, May 15). Reviewing employee e-mails: When you should, when you shouldn't. *SHRM Online*. Retrieved from *www.shrm.org/resourcesandtools/hr-topics/employee-relations/pages/reviewing-employee-e-mails-when-you-should-when-you-shouldnt.aspx* on May 16, 2017. *See also* Searcey , D. (2009, Nov. 19). Some courts raise bar on reading employee email. *The Wall Street Journal*, p. A17.

90. Timberg, C. (2013, Mar. 14). Web browsers consider limiting how much they track users. *The Washington Post*. Retrieved from *www.washingtonpost.com/business/technology/web-browsers-consider-limiting-how-much-they-track-users/2013/03/14/94818d22-8bed-11e2-9f54-f3fdd70acad2_story.html* on June 25, 2014.

91. Lin, L., and Martin, T. W. (2020, Apr. 15). How coronavirus is eroding privacy. *The Wall Street Journal*. Retrieved from *www.wsj.com/articles/coronavirus-paves-way-for-new-age-of-digital-surveillance-11586963028* on Apr. 15, 2020.

92. Carr, A., Day, M., Frier, S., and Gurman, M. (2019, Dec. 16). Yes, they're listening. *Bloomberg Businessweek*, pp. 38–43.

93. FitzGerald, D. (2019, Nov. 12). 5G race could leave personal privacy in the dust. *The Wall Street Journal*, p. R6.

94. CareerBuilder. (2018, Aug. 9). More than Half of Employers Have Found Content on Social Media That Caused Them NOT to Hire a Candidate, According to Recent CareerBuilder Survey. Retrieved from *http://press.careerbuilder.com/2018-08-09-More-Than-Half-of-Employers-Have-Found-Content-on-Social-Media-That-Caused-Them-NOT-to-Hire-a-Candidate-According-to-Recent-CareerBuilder-Survey* on Feb. 1, 2019.

95. Data protection: Europe gets a grip on data. (2018, Mar. 26). *Bloomberg Businessweek*, pp. 42, 43.

96. Zuckerberg, M. (2019, Mar. 6). A privacy-focused vision for social networking. *Facebook*. Retrieved from *www.facebook.com/notes/mark-zuckerberg/a-privacy-focused-vision-for-social-networking/10156700570096634/* on May 19, 2020.

97. Frye (2017), op. cit. *See also* E-mail may be hazardous to your career. (2007, May 14). *Fortune*, pp. 24–25.

98. Liptak, A. (2014, June 25). Major ruling shields privacy of cellphones. *The New York Times*. Retrieved from *www.nytimes.com/2014/06/26/us/supreme-court-cellphones-search-privacy.html?hp&action5click&pgtype5Homepage&version5LedeSum&module5first-column-region&region5top-news&WT.nav5top-news&_r50* on June 25, 2014.

99. FindLaw. (2019, June 25). Privacy at work: what are your rights? Retrieved from *https://employment.findlaw.com/workplace-privacy/privacy-at-work-what-are-your-rights.html* on May 19, 2020.

100. Frye (2017), op. cit.

101. Frye (2017), op. cit. *See also* Searcey (2009), op. cit. *See also* Richmond, R. (2004, Jan. 12). It's 10 A.M. Do you know where your workers are? *The Wall Street Journal*, pp. R1, R4.

102. See, for example, Snowden, M. (2017, May 3). Public employee's offensive social media comments unprotected. *SHRM Online*. Retrieved from *www.shrm.org/resourcesandtools/legal-and-compliance/employment-law/pages/public-employee-offensive-social-media-posts-unprotected.aspx* on May 4, 2017.

103. Ram, A., and Boyd, E. (2018, Apr. 15). People love fitness trackers, but should employers give them out? *Financial Times*. Retrieved from *www.ft.com/content/f09c79ec-26d3-11e8-9274-2b13fccdc744* on Apr. 17, 2018. *See also* Brin, D. W. (2016, Jun.). Wearable worries. *HRMagazine* 60(5), pp. 138-40.

104. Chen, T. P. (2019, Mar. 27). Workers push back as companies gather fingerprints and retina scans. *The Wall Street Journal*. Retrieved from *https://www.wsj.com/articles/workers-push-back-as-companies-gather-fingerprints-and-retina-scans-11553698332* on Mar. 27, 2019. *See also* Maurer, R. (2018, Apr. 6). More employers are using biometric authentication. *SHRM Online*. Retrieved from *www.shrm.org/resourcesandtools/hr-topics/technology/pages/employers-using-biometric-authentication.aspx* on Apr. 6, 2018.

105. Zielinski, D. (2018, Aug. 23). Use of biometric data grows, though not without legal risks. *SHRM Online*. Retrieved from *www.shrm.org/resourcesandtools/hr-topics/technology/pages/biometric-technologies-grow-.aspx* on Aug. 24, 2018.

106. Wright, A. D. (2011, Aug. 15). Cloud computing and security: How safe is HR data in the cloud? *SHRM Online*. Retrieved from *www.shrm.org/hrdisciplines/technology/Articles/Pages/CloudSecurity.aspx* on Aug. 23, 2011.

107. Data protection: Europe gets a grip on data (2018). op. cit. *See also* Eddy, E. R., Stone, D. L., and Stone-Romero, E. F. (1999). The effects of information management policies on reactions to human resource information systems: An integration of privacy and procedural justice perspectives. *Personnel Psychology* 52, pp. 335-58.

108. Vandermey (2014), op. cit. *See also* Fusilier, M. R., and Hoyer, W. D. (1980). Variables affecting perceptions of invasion of privacy in a personnel selection situation. *Journal of Applied Psychology* 65, pp. 623-26.

109. Segal, J. A. (2013, June 16). Privacy rights: A workplace oxymoron? Paper presented at the annual conference of the Society for Human Resource Management, Chicago, Illinois.

110. Many Wall Street executives say wrongdoing is necessary: Survey. (2012, July 10). Retrieved from *www.reuters.com/article/2012/07/10/us-wallstreet-survey-idUSBRE86906G20120710* on May 9, 2013. *See also* Lewis, A. (2012, July 15). A few more bad apples. *The Wall Street Journal Sunday*, p. 5K. *See also* Wulfhorst, E. (2009, Feb. 27). Wall Street rates poorly for ethics, honesty. Retrieved from *www.reuters.com/article/2009/02/27/us-usa-ethics-idUSTRE51Q02T20090227* on Aug. 24, 2011. *See also* Alsop, R. (2004, Feb. 19). Corporate scandals hit home. *The Wall Street Journal*. Retrieved from *www.reputationinstitute.com/press/WSJ_19Feb2004.pdf* on Oct. 20, 2004.

111. See, for example, Academy of Management. AOM code of ethics. Retrieved from *https://aom.org/About-AOM/AOM-Code-of-Ethics.aspx* on May 20, 2020. *See also* American Psychological Association. Ethical principles of psychologists and code of conduct. Retrieved from *http://web.csulb.edu/~psy301/apaethicsco.html* on May 20, 2020. *See also* Society for Industrial and Organization Psychology Inc. (2018). *Principles for the Validation and Use of Personnel Selection Procedures* (5th ed.). Bowling Green, OH: Author. *See also* Society for Human Resource Management. (2014, Nov. 21). SHRM code of ethical and professional standards in human resource management. Retrieved from *www.shrm.org/about/pages/code-of-ethics.aspx* on May 20, 2020.

112. Lefkowitz, J., and Lowman, R. (2017). Ethics of employee selection. In J. L. Farr and N. T. Tippins (Eds.), *Handbook of Employee Selection* (2nd ed.). New York: Routledge, pp. 575–98. *See also* American Educational Research Association, American Psychological Association, and National Council on Measurement in Education. (2014). *Standards for Educational and Psychological Testing*. Washington, DC: American Educational Research Association.

113. Mael, F. A., Connerley, M., and Morath, R. A. (1996). None of your business: Parameters of biodata invasiveness. *Personnel Psychology* 49, pp. 614–50.

114. Stone, D. L., and Stone, E. F. (1987). Effects of missing application-blank information on personnel selection decisions: Do privacy-protection strategies bias the outcome? *Journal of Applied Psychology* 72, pp. 452–56.

115. Miceli, M. P., Near, J. P., and Dworkin, T. M. (2008). *Whistle-Blowing in Organizations*. New York: Routledge. *See also* Miceli, M. P., and Near, J. P. (1992). *Blowing the Whistle*. New York: Lexington.

116. Tugend, A. (2013, Sept. 20). Opting to blow the whistle, or choosing to walk away. *The New York Times*. Retrieved from *www.nytimes.com/2013/09/21/your-money/deciding-when-to-blow-the-whistle-and-when-to-walk-away.html?pagewanted5all&r50* on June 23, 2014. *See also* Craig, G. (2008, May 11). Fraud trial raises issues over purse strings at Kodak. Retrieved from *www.democratandchronicle.com* on May 12, 2008. *See also* A whistleblower rocks an industry. (2002, June 24). *BusinessWeek*, pp. 126–30.

117. Lunsford, J. L. (2006, June 13). Piloting Boeing's new course. *The Wall Street Journal*, pp. B1, B3. *See also* Jansen, E., and Von Glinow, M. A. (1985). Ethical ambivalence and organizational reward systems. *Academy of Management Review* 10, pp. 815–22.

118. Bates, S. (2011, Jan. 12). View of senior management critical to whistle-blowers, research finds. *SHRM Online*. Retrieved from *www.shrm.org/hrdisciplines/ethics/articles/Pages/CultureAndWhistleblowers.aspx* on Aug. 25, 2011. *See also* White, E. (2006, June 12). What would you do? Ethics courses get context. *The Wall Street Journal*, p. B3. *See also* Hegarty, W. H., and Sims, H. P., Jr. (1979). Organizational philosophy, policies, and objectives related to unethical decision behavior: A laboratory experiment. *Journal of Applied Psychology* 64, pp. 331–38.

119. Salvatore, P., and Leonard, L. S. (2006, Dec.). *The Sarbanes-Oxley Act of 2002: New federal protection for whistleblowers*. Retrieved from *www.shrm.org/Publications/LegalReport/Pages/CMS_001022.aspx* on Aug. 6, 2008.

120. DiPietro, B. (2017, Nov. 8). Whistleblowing gaining acceptance in company culture. *The Wall Street Journal*. Retrieved from *https://blogs.wsj.com/riskandcompliance/2017/11/08/the-morning-risk-report-whistleblowing-gaining-acceptance-in-company-culture/* on Nov. 8, 2017. *See also* The age of the whistleblower. (2015, Dec. 5). *The Economist*, pp. 61–63.

121. Zuckerman, G., and Michaels, D. (2018, Dec. 8). Whistleblower Inc. *The Wall Street Journal*, pp. B1, B2.

122. Lawrence-Hardy, A. J., and Peiffer, L. A. (2011, July 25). SEC's whistle-blower rules effective soon: What employers need to know now. *SHRM Legal Report*. Retrieved from *www.shrm.org/LegalIssues/EmploymentLawAreas/Pages/SECWhistleBlowerRules.aspx* on Aug. 25, 2011. *See also* Petrulakis, K. J., and Parsons, A. S. (2011, Mar. 30). April 2011: New traps–Whistle-blower protections in the Dodd-Frank Act. *SHRM Legal Report*. Retrieved from *www.shrm.org/Publications/LegalReport/Pages/NewTrapsWhistleBlowerProtections.aspx* on Aug. 25, 2011.

123. Deschenaux, J. (2014, Mar. 5). High court extends employee whistle-blower protections. Retrieved from *www.shrm.org/legalissues/federalresources/pages/high-court-extends-employee-whistle-blower-protections.aspx* on June 23, 2014.

124. FindLaw.com. (2020). State whistleblower laws. Retrieved from *https://statelaws.findlaw.com/employment-laws/whistleblower-laws.html* on May 20, 2020.

125. Smith, A. (2014, Apr. 25). SEC approves final whistle-blowing rule. Retrieved from *www.shrm.org/legalissues/federalresources/pages/secwhistleblowingrule.aspx* on June 23, 2014.

126. DiPietro (2017), op. cit. *See also* The age of the whistleblower (2015), op. cit. *See also* Tugend (2013), op. cit. *See also* Kesselheim, A. S., Studdert, D. M., and Mello, M. (2010). Whistle-blowers' experiences in fraud litigation against pharmaceutical companies. *New England Journal of Medicine* 362, pp. 1832-39.

127. DiPietro, B. (2018, Mar. 19). Whistleblower retaliation rising. *The Wall Street Journal.* Retrieved from *https://blogs.wsj.com/riskandcompliance/2018/03/19/the-morning-risk-report-whistleblower-retaliation-on-the-rise/* on Mar. 20, 2018.

128. Murphy, M. (2014, July 28). Meet the SEC's 6,500 whistleblowers. *The Wall Street Journal.* Retrieved from *www.wsj.com/articles/meet-the-secs-6-500-whistleblowers-1406591157* on July 30, 2014. *See also* A whistleblower rocks an industry (2002), op. cit. *See also* Miceli, M. P., and Near, J. P. (1988). Individual and situational correlates of whistle-blowing. *Personnel Psychology* 41, pp. 267-81.

129. Baer et al. (2016), op. cit. *See also* Rubenfeld, S. (2016, Aug. 16). SEC pursues companies for restricting whistleblowers. *The Wall Street Journal.* Retrieved from *blogs.wsj.com/riskandcompliance/2016/08/16/sec-pursues-companies-for-restricting-whistleblowers/* on Aug. 18, 2016. *See also* Berkowitz, P. M. (2005, Jul.-Aug.). Sarbanes-Oxley whistleblower claims: The meaning of "fraud against shareholders." *SHRM Legal Report*, pp. 1-8.

130. Kohn, Kohn, & Colapinto LLC. (2020). False Claims Act whistleblower protections and rewards. Retrieved from *www.kkc.com/false-claims-act-faqs/* on May 20, 2020.

131. Meinert (2011), op. cit. *See also* Bates (2011), op. cit. *See also* Near, J. P., and Miceli, M. P. (1995). Effective whistle-blowing. *Academy of Management Review* 20, pp. 679-708.

132. Tugend (2013), op. cit. *See also* Moore, B. (2011, Mar. 21). See wrongdoing on the job? Here's what you need to know. *The New York Post.* Retrieved from *www.nypost.com/p/news/business/jobs/telling_tales_mFyTtQpfqrHMVmJk0T9kcN* on Aug. 25, 2011.

133. Cascio, W. F., and Aguinis, H. (2019). *Applied Psychology in Talent Management* (8th ed.). Thousand Oaks, CA: Sage.

SUPPORT AND INTERNATIONAL IMPLICATIONS

This capstone section deals with two broad themes: organizational support for employees and the international implications of human resource management activities. Chapter 15 examines key issues involved in employee safety and health, both mental and physical. Chapter 16 considers key issues in international human resource management. Given the rapid growth of multinational corporations, it is perhaps in this area more than any other that employees and their families need special social and financial support from their firms.

15 SAFETY, HEALTH, AND EMPLOYEE ASSISTANCE PROGRAMS

16 INTERNATIONAL DIMENSIONS OF HUMAN RESOURCE MANAGEMENT

15 SAFETY, HEALTH, AND EMPLOYEE ASSISTANCE PROGRAMS

Questions This Chapter Will Help Managers Answer

LO 15-1 What is the cost-benefit trade-off of adopting measures to enhance workplace safety and health?

LO 15-2 Which approaches to job safety and health really work?

LO 15-3 How has the coronavirus pandemic changed the way organizations address health and safety?

LO 15-4 What are some key issues to consider in establishing and monitoring an employee assistance program?

LO 15-5 Does it make sound business sense to institute a worksite wellness program? If so, how should it be implemented and what should it include?

SUBSTANCE ABUSE ON THE JOB PRODUCES TOUGH POLICY CHOICES FOR MANAGERS[a]

Experts estimate that 5 to 10 percent of employees in any company have a substance-abuse problem (alcohol or drugs) serious enough to merit treatment. The situation may be even worse. Over a 2-year period, unbeknown to employees and job applicants, ChevronTexaco Corp. carried out anonymous drug testing. About 30 percent of all applicants and 20 percent of all employees tested positive for illegal drug use.

What is an appropriate policy for managers to adopt in these circumstances? Zero-tolerance policies in the workplace drive the problem underground, which does not make it go away but does reduce significantly the number of employees willing to come forward for treatment. Not only is firing workers who test positive in random drug tests without offering any treatment or rehabilitation the most expensive approach—especially when the cost of replacing a worker is compared with the cost of treatment—but this approach also passes the worker on to the next employer in no better shape than before.

Another approach is simply to demote people who have been in treatment. As one professional in the field says, "[Companies] won't have a written policy, but they'll guide that person into a position of no strategic importance. If asked, the companies won't acknowledge it. They don't want the bad publicity of being a mean guy."

Buoying these hard-liners are some very public drug- and alcohol-related accidents, of which the Exxon *Valdez* oil spill into Prince William Sound, Alaska, is probably the best known.[b] When the tanker ran aground, it spilled 11 million gallons of oil, damaged 1,300 miles of shoreline, disrupted the lives and livelihoods of people in the region, and killed hundreds of thousands of birds and marine animals. It occurred after the ship's captain, an alcoholic, left the bridge at a crucial moment. According to witnesses, he had downed five double vodkas on the night of the disaster. In a later incident, the harbor pilot of a container ship that slammed into the San Francisco-Oakland Bay Bridge, causing a huge oil spill, had a drunken-driving conviction, had a history of alcohol abuse, and took numerous prescription drugs that might have impaired him. Pilots have been arrested and convicted of operating commercial airliners while intoxicated. What should firms do? Dismissal and demotion are two obvious policy choices; rehabilitation is a third.

Among companies that endorse rehabilitation, however, there is considerable debate about whether employees should be returned to their jobs if they are successfully rehabilitated. Standard industry practice is to return people to their jobs after treatment, a policy that is consistent with the provisions of the Americans with Disabilities Act, which protects past substance abusers from discrimination. ExxonMobil, however, bucked the industry trend following the wreck of the Exxon *Valdez*. The ship's captain had previously been treated for alcoholism and returned

---

[a]Horton, R., Cromwell, L., Garrett, T., and Mallory, L. (2020, Apr.). Alcohol and substance abuse disorder under the ADAAA. *HR Professionals Magazine* 10(4), pp. 32, 33. Alcohol.org. (2019, Dec. 18). Alcohol rehab programs for airline industry pilots. Retrieved from *www.alcohol.org/professions/airline-industry/* on May 26, 2020. Liptak, A. (2008, June 26). Damages cut against Exxon in Valdez case. *The New York Times*. Retrieved from*www.nytimes.com/2008/06/26/washington/26punitive.html* on Aug 11, 2008. Oil-spill pilot's record indicated problems. (2008, Apr. 10). *The New York Times*, p. A17.

[b]The spill occurred in 1989. Over the next 19 years, a flood of litigation followed. It was finally resolved in 2008. See Gold, R., and Gleason, S. (2011, July 3). Exxon seeks to overturn $1.5 billion verdict. *The Wall Street Journal*, p. B3.

to work. After the accident, ExxonMobil took bold steps to prevent future accidents. It decided that individuals treated for alcoholism imposed too much of a risk to hold jobs that were both safety sensitive and performed without much supervision—like the job of a ship captain. For this small group of jobs only, ExxonMobil instituted a blanket exclusion of individuals with a history of substance abuse, although they will be given other jobs. The new policy embroiled the company in litigation with the EEOC that lasted many years and finally ended up in the 5th Circuit Court of Appeals. We will consider the Court's ruling and its implications in the conclusion to this case.

Those who favor returning people to work after rehabilitation argue that it is not only more humane, but also more effective. Refusing to return people to work—even in safety-sensitive positions—would be "shortsighted. It will make sure that no one who's an alcoholic ever gets help," according to the medical director of United Airlines (which regularly returns pilots to their jobs after treatment). Those who take a more hard-line attitude toward drug and alcohol abuse point out that many companies are reexamining their policies, in light of the high-profile incidents described earlier.

Challenges

1. What are some arguments for and against each of the following policies: dismissal, demotion, return to the same job following rehabilitation, return to a different job following rehabilitation?
2. Should follow-up be required after rehabilitation? If so, how long should it last and what form should it take?

As the chapter-opening vignette shows, managers face tough policy issues in the area of workplace health and safety. As we will see, a combination of external factors (e.g., the spiraling cost of health care) and internal factors (e.g., new technology) is making these issues impossible to ignore. This chapter begins by examining how social and legal policies on the federal and state levels have evolved on this issue, beginning with workers' compensation laws and culminating with the passage of the Occupational Safety and Health Act. The chapter then considers enforcement of the act, with special emphasis on the rights and obligations of management. It also examines prevailing approaches to job safety and health in other countries. Finally, it considers the new issues that businesses face in light of the coronavirus pandemic, employee assistance programs, and corporate "wellness" programs. Underlying all these efforts is a conviction on the part of many firms that it is morally right to improve job safety and health—and that doing so will enhance the productivity and quality of work life of employees at all levels.

THE EXTENT AND COST OF SAFETY AND HEALTH PROBLEMS

Consider these startling facts about U.S. workplaces:[1]

- About 14 workers die on the job each day; in general, this number has been declining over the past 10 years.
- More than 3 million workers (roughly 3 of every 100) either get sick or are injured because of their jobs each year. A study by Microsoft found that 68 percent

of office workers develop work-related ergonomic injuries, such as **repetitive-strain injuries (RSIs).** RSIs are classified as illnesses because of their long-term nature.[2] They affect 1.8 million workers per year and cost upward of $20 billion in medical expenses and lost productivity.[3]

- Overexertion and falls are the most common workplace injuries, followed by being hit by an object. They cost U.S. employers more than $1 billion per week.[4]
- Low-back injuries account for 20 percent of all workers' compensation claims and cost an average of $24,000, more than twice the average workplace claim.[5]
- For every 100 full-time workers, employers lose almost a full day away from work due to accidents and illnesses.[6]

Commercial fishing and logging are the most dangerous occupations.[7] Even though the workplace has gotten safer for employees over the years, accidents can still happen and cost businesses thousands of dollars every year in medical and other expenses. According to the National Safety Council, the average cost per death is $1.15 million, while the average cost per injury requiring medical consultation is $39,000. To offset the cost of work injuries, each worker must produce, on average, $1,100 in goods and services.

Regardless of your perspective, social or economic, these are disturbing figures. In response, public policy has focused on two types of actions: *monetary compensation* for job-related injuries and *preventive measures* to enhance job safety and health. State-run workers' compensation programs and the federal Occupational Safety and Health Administration (OSHA) are responsible for implementing public policy in these areas. Because we discussed workers' compensation in some detail in Chapter 12, we focus here on job safety and health, beginning with the Occupational Safety and Health Act of 1970.

THE OCCUPATIONAL SAFETY AND HEALTH ACT

Purpose and Coverage

The purpose of the Occupational Safety and Health Act is an ambitious one: to prevent work-related injuries, illnesses, and deaths.[8] Its coverage is equally ambitious because the law extends to any business (regardless of size) that *affects* interstate commerce. Because almost any business affects interstate commerce, most employees in the nation come under the law's jurisdiction—more than 8 million work sites and 130 million workers.[9] Federal, state, and local government workers are excluded, although the act does require federal agencies to comply with standards consistent with those for private-sector employers. The Occupational Safety and Health Administration (OSHA) also conducts inspections in response to complaints from government workers or their managers.

Administration

The 1970 act established three government agencies to administer and enforce the law:

- The *Occupational Safety and Health Administration (OSHA)* to establish and enforce the necessary safety and health standards. However, OSHA is prohibited by law from evaluating compliance officers and their supervisors on the basis of enforcement activities, such as the number of citations issued or penalties assessed.[10]

Today OSHA emphasizes three overarching goals: (1) strong, fair, and effective enforcement; (2) outreach, education, and compliance assistance; and (3) partnerships and cooperative programs.

- The *Occupational Safety and Health Review Commission* (a three-member board appointed by the president) to rule on the appropriateness of OSHA's enforcement actions when they are contested by employers, employees, or unions.
- The *National Institute for Occupational Safety and Health (NIOSH)* to conduct research on the causes and prevention of occupational injury and illness, to recommend new standards (based on this research) to the secretary of labor, and to develop educational programs.

Safety and Health Standards

Under the law, each employer has a "general duty" to provide a place of employment "free from recognized hazards." Employers also have the "special duty" to comply with all standards of safety and health established under the act.

OSHA has issued a large number of detailed standards covering numerous environmental hazards. These include power tools; machine guards; compressed gas; materials handling and storage; and toxic substances, such as asbestos, cotton dust, silica, lead, and carbon monoxide.

As an example, consider OSHA's blood-borne pathogen standard. Workers exposed to blood and bodily fluids (e.g., health-care providers, first-aid providers) are covered by the rule, but it does not apply to workers who give first aid as "good Samaritans." It requires facilities to develop exposure-control plans, to implement engineering controls and worker training to reduce the incidence of needle sticks, to provide personal protective equipment and hepatitis B vaccinations, and to communicate hazards to workers.[11]

To date, NIOSH has identified more than 15,000 toxic substances based on its research, but the transition from research findings to workplace standards is often a long, contentious process. For example, consider the group of injuries and illnesses that affect the musculoskeletal system—so-called ergonomic injuries (for which there is no single diagnosis). When OSHA proposed ergonomics rules, the process dragged on for years. As a result, OSHA developed guidelines (rather than rules) for employers in specific industries to follow.[12]

Record-Keeping Requirements

Significant record-keeping is required of employers under the act. Specifically,

- Log of work-related injuries and illnesses (OSHA Form 300) (see Figure 15–1).
- Injury and illness incident report (OSHA Form 301).
- Summary of work-related injuries and illnesses (OSHA Form 300A).

As of 2019, covered employers must submit injury and illness data electronically to OSHA that they already record on forms and keep on site.[13] Employees are guaranteed access, on request, to Form 300 at their workplaces, and the records must be retained for 5 years following the calendar year they cover. The purpose of these reports is to identify where safety and health problems have been occurring (if at all). Such information helps call management's attention to the problems, as well as that of an OSHA inspector, should one visit the workplace. Annual summaries help OSHA determine workplaces that should receive priority for inspection.

Figure 15–1

OSHA Form 300, log and summary of occupational injuries and illnesses.

OSHA's Form 300 (Rev. 01/2004)

Log of Work-Related Injuries and Illnesses

Attention: This form contains information relating to employee health and must be used in a manner that protects the confidentiality of employees to the extent possible while the information is being used for occupational safety and health purposes.

Year 20___

U.S. Department of Labor
Occupational Safety and Health Administration

Form approved OMB no. 1218-0176

You must record information about every work-related death and about every work-related injury or illness that involves loss of consciousness, restricted work activity or job transfer, days away from work, or medical treatment beyond first aid. You must also record significant work-related injuries and illnesses that are diagnosed by a physician or licensed health care professional. You must also record work-related injuries and illnesses that meet any of the specific recording criteria listed in 29 CFR Part 1904.8 through 1904.12. Feel free to use two lines for a single case if you need to. You must complete an Injury and Illness Incident Report (OSHA Form 301) or equivalent form for each injury or illness recorded on this form. If you're not sure whether a case is recordable, call your local OSHA office for help.

Establishment name _____

City _____   State _____

Identify the person			**Describe the case**			**Classify the case**							**Enter the number of days the injured or ill worker was:**		**Check the "Injury" column or choose one type of illness:**

Source: U.S. Department of Labor/OSHA.

OSHA Enforcement

In administering the act, OSHA inspectors have the right to enter a workplace (but not the home office of a teleworking employee) and to conduct a compliance inspection.[14] However, in its *Marshall v. Barlow's Inc.* decision, the Supreme Court ruled that employers could require a search warrant before allowing the inspector onto company premises.[15] In practice, only about 3 percent of employers go that far, perhaps because the resulting inspection is likely then to be an especially close one.[16] Employers are prohibited from retaliating against employees who file complaints, and an employee representative is entitled to accompany the OSHA representative during the inspection.

Because it is impossible for the 2,100 agency inspectors (most of whom are either safety engineers or industrial hygienists) to visit the nation's more than 8 million workplaces, a system of priorities has been established. OSHA assigns top priority to reports of imminent dangers—accidents about to happen. Second are fatalities or accidents serious enough to send three or more workers to the hospital. Third are employee complaints. Referrals from other government agencies are fourth, and special-emphasis programs are fifth. These involve hazardous work, such as trenching, or equipment, such as mechanical power presses.[17]

At the work site, inspectors concentrate more on dangerous hazards than on technical infractions. For example, OSHA fined industrial laundry giant Cintas Corp.

$2.8 million for the death of an employee who fell from a conveyor belt into a large dryer. According to police, he was trapped for more than 20 minutes in temperatures reaching 300 degrees. The company said he wasn't following safety rules and appealed the fine. OSHA's investigators found that employees were not trained in how to shut off equipment properly, and the investigators produced videotape taken over several weeks prior to the accident at the same plant, showing workers engaging in activities similar to what led to their coworker's death.[18]

Considerable emphasis has been given to OSHA's role of *enforcement* but not much to its role of *consultation.* For example, OSHA offers an extensive website at *www.osha.gov* that includes a special section devoted to small businesses, as well as interactive e-Tools to help employers and employees address specific hazards and prevent injuries.[19]

Employers who want help in recognizing and correcting safety and health hazards can get it from a free, on-site consultation service funded by OSHA. State governments or private-sector contractors provide this service using well-trained safety and/or health professionals (e.g., industrial hygienists). Primarily targeting small- and medium-sized businesses, this program is penalty free and completely separate from the OSHA inspection effort. An employer's only obligation is a commitment to correct serious job-safety and health hazards. Each year, OSHA's On-site Consultation Program conducts more than 26,000 visits to small-business work sites.[20]

Penalties

Fines are mandatory where serious violations are found. For each **willful violation** (one in which an employer either knew that what was being done constituted a violation of federal regulations or was aware that a hazardous condition existed and made no reasonable effort to eliminate it), an employer can be assessed a civil penalty of up to $134,937 for each violation. An employer that fails to correct a violation (within the allowed time limit) for which a citation has been issued can be fined up to $13,494 for each day the violation continues. Those amounts are indexed for inflation each year.[21]

Executives can also receive criminal penalties. Calling their conduct everything from assault and battery to reckless homicide, prosecutors have sought hard time for employers who ignore warnings to improve safety on the job. For example, former Massey Energy CEO Don Blankenship served a 1-year federal prison sentence after being convicted of conspiracy to violate federal mine safety laws. The charges stemmed from a disaster at a Massey Energy mine in West Virginia that left 29 coal miners dead.[22] Here are three other examples:

- Owners of a plumbing company pled guilty to criminal charges of willfully violating OSHA trenching safety standards after two employees were killed in a trench collapse.
- An employee fell to his death while laying steel decking at a construction site. The company had a history of OSHA violations and had been warned about its failure to install protection against falls. The company owner pled guilty to a willful violation and was sentenced to 4 months in prison.
- An employee was killed when he fell while retrieving equipment from a tower. The owners attempted to avoid disclosing that the employee was not wearing proper safety equipment. The owners pled guilty and were sentenced to 3 months in prison.[23]

Appeals

Employers can appeal citations, proposed penalties, and corrections they have been ordered to make through multiple levels of the agency, culminating with an independent federal agency, the Occupational Safety and Health Review Commission. The Commission presumes the employer to be free of violations and puts the burden of proof on OSHA.[24] Further appeals can be pursued through the federal court system.

The Role of the States

Although OSHA is a federally run program, the act allows states to develop and administer their own programs if they are approved by the secretary of labor. There are many criteria for approval, but the most important is that the state program must be judged "at least as effective" as the federal program. Currently, plans in 22 states cover private-sector as well as state and local government workers. Six others cover only state and local government workers. In 2019, federal OSHA inspected 32,020 workplaces. State-run OSHA programs conducted an additional 40,993 inspections.[25]

Workers' Rights to Health and Safety

Both unionized and nonunionized workers have walked off the job when subjected to unsafe working conditions.[26] In unionized firms, walkouts have occurred during the term of valid collective-bargaining agreements that contained no-strike and grievance and/or arbitration clauses.[27] Are such walkouts legal? Yes, the Supreme Court has ruled, as long as objective evidence is presented to support the claim that abnormally dangerous working conditions exist. This includes the coronavirus pandemic. Under those circumstances,[28]

- A walkout is legal regardless of the existence of a no-strike or arbitration clause.
- It is an unfair labor practice for an employer to interfere with a walkout under such circumstances. This is true whether a firm is unionized or nonunionized.
- Expert testimony (e.g., by an industrial hygienist) is critical in establishing the presence of abnormally dangerous working conditions.
- If a good-faith belief is not supported by objective evidence, employees who walk off the job are subject to disciplinary action.

OSHA's Impact

From its inception, OSHA's effectiveness in improving workplace safety and health has been questioned by the very firms it regulates. Employers complain of excessively detailed and costly regulations that, they believe, ignore workplace realities. However, even critics acknowledge that the agency has made the workplace safer. Since its inception in 1971, OSHA has helped cut annual workplace fatalities by two-thirds and occupational injury and illness rates by more than 74 percent. At the same time, U.S. employment has more than doubled.[29] Despite such encouraging results, some employers try to improve their competitiveness at the expense of safety. See the HR Buzz box for an example.

Management's willingness to correct hazards and to improve such vital environmental conditions as ventilation, noise levels, and machine safety is much greater now than it was before OSHA. Moreover, because of OSHA and the National Institute for Occupational Safety and Health, we now know far more about such dangerous substances as vinyl chloride, PCBs, silica, asbestos, cotton dust, and a host of other carcinogens. As a result, management has taken at least the initial actions needed to protect workers from them.

HR BUZZ

The Language of Training

PRODUCTIVITY VERSUS SAFETY IN A SMALL BUSINESS

Preoccupied with staying in business, many small businesses skimp on safety information and worker training. That can be especially risky because such companies rely more heavily than do big companies on workers who are young or who speak little English.[a] As an example, consider the case of Everardo Rangel-Jasso.

Rangel-Jasso was crushed to death at Denton Plastics Inc. in Portland, Oregon. The 17-year-old was backing up a forklift, with a box high on its fork, when he cut the rear wheels sharply and the vehicle tipped over. A posted sign, in English, warned forklift drivers to wear seat belts–but the Mexican youth didn't speak English. According to an OSHA investigator, a seat belt might have saved his life.

Employees told OSHA that Hispanic workers learned their jobs through "hand signals and body gestures." Rangel-Jasso hadn't received any forklift training and lacked a driver's license and a juvenile's work permit. Federal and state officials levied more than $150,000 in fines against the company, and two senior managers faced criminal indictments. This is not an isolated incident. To address it and others like it, OSHA requires employers to provide training in a language and vocabulary that employees can understand.[b]

[a]New challenges for health and safety in the workplace. (2010). *Workplace Visions* 3, pp. 5, 6.
[b]Optimum Safety Management. (n.d.). OSHA training requirements–language guidelines. Retrieved from *www.optimumsafetymanagement.com/blog/osha-training-requirements-language-guidelines/* on May 26, 2020.

Finally, any analysis of OSHA's impact must consider the fundamental issue of the *causes* of workplace accidents. OSHA standards govern potentially unsafe *work conditions* that employees may be exposed to. There are no standards that govern potentially unsafe *employee behaviors*. And whereas employers may be penalized for failure to comply with safety and health standards, employees are subject to no such threat. Empirical studies that control for other influences that cause worker safety to improve over time, such as changes in the industrial mix of workers, improvements in safety technology, and expanded use of employer incentives to improve safety, generally have found that OSHA's impact on safety has been modest.[30] Additional reductions in on-the-job accidents will require *behavioral* rather than *technical* modifications.

ASSESSING THE COSTS AND BENEFITS OF OCCUPATIONAL SAFETY AND HEALTH PROGRAMS

Let's face it: Accidents are expensive. According to the National Safety Council, the costs of workplace injuries each year exceeds $161 billion.[31] Aside from workers' compensation (*direct*) costs, consider the **indirect costs of an accident:**

1. Cost of wages paid for time lost.
2. Cost of damage to material or equipment.
3. Cost of overtime work by others required by the accident.

4. Cost of wages paid to supervisors while their time is required for activities resulting from the accident.
5. Costs of decreased output of the injured worker after she or he returns to work.
6. Costs associated with the time it takes for a new worker to learn the job.
7. Uninsured medical costs borne by the company.
8. Cost of time spent by higher management and clerical workers to investigate or to process workers' compensation forms.[32]

On the other hand, safety pays. Employers that have safety programs can reduce expenses related to injuries and illnesses by 40 percent and every $1 spent on safety saves an average of $3 in expenses. That return on investment (ROI) is revealed in increased productivity, improved customer service, savings from fewer injuries, and lower workers' compensation costs.[33] Here's an example.

DUPONT CORPORATION

HR BUZZ

Safety Pays

At DuPont Corp., safety experts provide feedback while engineers observe workers and then redesign valves and install key locks to deter accident-causing behavior. When injuries do happen, the company reports them quickly to workers to provide a sense of immediacy, trying to show the behavior that caused the accident without naming the offender. It also fosters peer pressure to work safely by giving units common goals—that way, workers are working together instead of independently. DuPont offers carrots, too. Its directors regularly give safety awards, and workers win modest prizes if their divisions are accident-free for 6 to 9 months. The company's incentive for doing this is not altogether altruistic—it estimates its annual cost savings to be $150 million. Says the president of DuPont safety resources, "When a business culture focuses on safety, it makes a public proclamation of its commitment to caring about the welfare of its people. A workplace noted for safe practices builds both trust and faith across the board." A large body of empirical research strongly supports this conclusion.[a]

[a]Hofmann, D.A., Burke, M. J., and Zohar, D. (2017, Jan. 26). 100 years of occupational safety research: From basic protections and work analysis to a multilevel view of workplace safety and risk. *Journal of Applied Psychology* 102, pp. 375-88. Forsman, J. (2003). New challenges for health and safety in the workplace. *Workplace Visions* 3, p. 6.

ORGANIZATIONAL SAFETY AND HEALTH PROGRAMS

As noted earlier, accidents result from two broad causes: *unsafe work conditions* (physical and environmental) and *unsafe work behaviors.* Unsafe physical conditions include defective equipment, inadequate machine guards, and lack of protective equipment. Examples of unsafe environmental conditions are noise, radiation, dust, fumes, and stress. In one study of work injuries, just over a third resulted from unsafe work conditions, whereas nearly two-thirds resulted from unsafe work behaviors.[34] However, accidents often result from an *interaction* of unsafe conditions and unsafe acts. Thus, if a particular operation forces a worker to lift a heavy part and twist around to set it on a bench, the operation itself forces the worker to perform an unsafe act.

Telling the worker not to lift and twist at the same time will not solve the problem. The *unsafe condition itself* must be corrected, either by redesigning the flow of material or by providing the worker with a mechanical device for lifting.

To eliminate, or at least reduce, the number and severity of workplace accidents, a combination of management and engineering controls is essential. These are shown in Figure 15-2. **Engineering controls** attempt to eliminate unsafe work conditions and to neutralize unsafe worker behaviors. They involve some modification of the work environment: for example, installing a metal cover over the blades of a lawn mower to make it almost impossible for a member of a grounds crew to catch his or her foot in the blades. **Management controls** attempt to increase safe behaviors. The following sections examine each of the elements shown in Figure 15-2.

Loss Control, a Safety Committee, and Safety Rules

Management's first duty is to formulate a safety policy. Its second duty is to implement and sustain this policy through a **loss-control program.** Such a program has four components: a safety budget, safety records, management's personal concern, and management's good example.[35]

To reduce the frequency of accidents, management must be willing to spend money and budget for safety. Unfortunately, it sometimes takes a tragic accident before this occurs. After the 2010 explosion of the Deepwater Horizon drilling rig in the Gulf of Mexico that left 11 workers dead and resulted in the worst oil spill in U.S. history, BP took serious steps to change its business culture to emphasize safety.[36]

Study after study has shown the crucial role that management plays in effective safety programs.[37] Such concern is manifest in a number of ways: establishing a safety committee, rewarding supervisors on the basis of their subordinates' safety records, and comparing safety results against preset objectives. Evidence indicates that employees who perceive their organizations as supporting safety initiatives and those who have high-quality relationships with their leaders are more likely to feel free to raise safety-related concerns. Such safety-related communication, in turn, is related to safety commitment and, ultimately, to the frequency of accidents.[38] The HR Buzz box illustrates the kinds of recommendations that a safety committee might make.

Figure 15–2

Causes of and responses to workplace accidents.

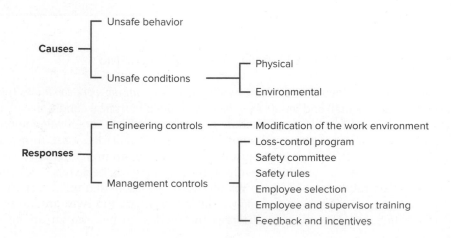

Management's good example completes a loss-control program. If hard hats or face masks are required at a workplace, then executives should wear them even if they are in business suits. If employees see executives disregarding safety rules or treating hazardous situations lightly by not conforming with regulations, they will feel that they, too, have the right to violate the rules. In short, organizations show their concern for loss control by establishing clear safety rules and by assuming the responsibility for their implementation.

AETNA LIFE & CASUALTY, GROCERY STORES, AND UNIMIN

HR BUZZ

Best Practices in Reducing Repetitive-Strain Injuries

Aetna Life & Casualty Co. (owned by CVS Health as of 2018) installed ergonomically designed chairs with lower-back supports, adjustable seats, and armrests in all offices.[a] Grocery stores rotate checkout clerks who use scanners. Mining company Unimin Corp. used to require workers at a clay plant in Tennessee to carry 40-pound buckets of silicate material down a narrow catwalk to reach a mixing tank, then bend over to tip the silicate into the tank. After analyzing the entire process, the company now uses pumps to get that material into the tank. In this case, an engineering solution eliminated a hazardous process that often resulted in workplace injuries.

These two approaches, modifying equipment and analyzing the way work is done, are the two most common preventive actions by employers. Best practices also include upper-management support, employee participation, an early reporting system, and proactive evaluation of hazards. This is a systems view of safety.[b] With ergonomic injuries accounting for as much as 40 percent of workers' compensation costs, that's smart business.[c]

---

[a]*Wikipedia.* (2020). Aetna. Retrieved from *https://en.wikipedia.org/wiki/Aetna* on May 26, 2020. Hagerty, J. (2011, Dec. 28). Keeping boomers fit for work. *The Wall Street Journal,* pp. B1, B2.

[b]Hofmann, D.A., Burke, M. J., and Zohar, D. (2017, Jan. 26). 100 years of occupational safety research: From basic protections and work analysis to a multilevel view of workplace safety and risk. *Journal of Applied Psychology* 102, pp. 375-88.

[c]Aon Risk Solutions. (2012). Repetitive motion claims strategy. Retrieved from *www.aon.com/attachments/risk-services/California-MSD-Strategy-white-paper.pdf* on June 29, 2014.

OSHA standards require that *employers furnish* and *employees use* suitable protective equipment (e.g., hard hats, goggles, face shields, earplugs, respirators) where there is a "reasonable probability" that injuries can be prevented by such equipment. Companies often find that it is in their own best interests to do so as well. Thus, a 5-year study of 36,000 Home Depot Inc. employees found that back-support devices reduced low-back injuries by about a third. The study compared the incidence of such injuries before and after the company made corsets mandatory for all store employees.[39]

Sometimes employees don't obey safety rules because they are not enforced. Yet it is also possible that they don't obey the rules because of flaws in employee-selection practices, because of inadequate training, or because there is simply no incentive for doing so.

Employee Selection

To the extent that keen vision, dexterity, hearing, balance, and other physical or psychological characteristics (such as the personality dimensions agreeableness and conscientiousness) make a critical difference between success and failure on a job, they should be used to screen applicants.[40] However, there are two other factors that also relate strongly to accident rates among workers: *age* and *length of service*.[41] According to OSHA, 40 percent of injured workers have been on the job less than a year.[42] Regardless of length of service, the younger the employee, the higher the accident rate. In fact, accident rates are substantially higher during the first month of employment than in all subsequent time periods, regardless of age. And when workers of the same age are studied, accident rates decrease as length of service increases. One large-scale study found that workers over age 55 are a third less likely than their younger colleagues to be injured at work seriously enough to lose work time. The injuries they do report, however, are two to three times more costly than those for younger workers.[43] The lesson for managers is clear: *New worker equals high risk!*

Training for Employees and Supervisors

Accidents often occur because workers lack one vital tool to protect themselves: information.[44] Consider the following data collected by the Bureau of Labor Statistics:

- Nearly one out of every five workers injured while operating power saws received no safety training on the equipment.
- Of 724 workers hurt while using scaffolds, 27 percent had received no information on safety requirements for installing the kind of scaffold on which they were injured.
- Of 554 workers hurt while servicing equipment, 61 percent were not told about lockout procedures that prevent the equipment from being turned on inadvertently while it is being serviced.

Study after study shows that safety training leads to reductions in accidents and injuries. To generate maximum benefits, safety training should focus on four general areas: using personal protective equipment, following safe practices to reduce risk, communicating health and safety information, and worker involvement in the training (see the following HR Buzz box).[45] What about non-English speakers? To address that issue, OSHA's Training Standards Policy Statement requires employers to provide instruction in a language and vocabulary that employees can understand.[46]

On the other hand, evidence indicates that training by itself is not the answer. Rather, employers need to pay more attention to the design of jobs—to reduce employees' exposure to physical hazards and heavy workloads and to increase autonomy and task variety. Supervisors also need to learn about and look for signs of substance abuse on the job because it relates strongly to the incidence of work injuries. Evidence indicates that these three factors—employee training, job design, and employer monitoring—can contribute to safer workplaces.[47] So also can "right-to-know" rules, which affect workers exposed to high levels of chemicals.

The notification rules come under OSHA's hazard-communication standard, also known as the Right-to-Know Law.[48] It requires all chemical manufacturers and importers to do four things: (1) classify all health and physical hazards according to specific criteria; (2) provide a label that includes a signal word, like "Danger" or "Warning," a pictogram, and a statement for each hazard; (3) include Safety Data Sheets that describe the ingredients and hazards of dangerous materials, safe

SAFETY TRAINING MOVES ONLINE*

Miami University, Which offers a course of study in video-game development, partnered with Cincinnati Children's Hospital to train staff members in emergency procedures, such as an evacuation. When an alarm goes off in a hospital, there is no room for error. Everyone on staff must immediately respond, evacuating patients according to predetermined plans. The staff must know which medications are needed for each patient and which exit they are required to use.

Students are building a virtual replica of the hospital. Staff members will put on goggles and immerse themselves into the virtual world, where emergency drills, including a fire or a tornado, will take place. Staff will have to answer questions, virtually pick up items they need, and choose escape routes. Following the virtual training, a real life evacuation will take place and the hospital will measure the effectiveness of the new system.

Building interactivity, gaming techniques, and lots of feedback into workplace safety training has several key advantages:

- All employees receive the same training in the same way.
- Employees working in remote locations can access it at any time.
- It provides highly efficient reporting upon completion of safety-training classes, which is essential to meet regulatory requirements.

OSHA itself has released interactive, game-based training designed to help employers and workers effectively identify common hazards in manufacturing and construction. Using the scenario "OSHA Visual Inspection Training," for example, users can view equipment from 360 degrees to look for hazards. The player can speak to the employee game character and observe the character at work to identify additional hazards. Scenarios include inspecting a character working with a saw, an industrial chemical mixer, and scaffolding and fall protection.

As these examples show, more organizations are turning to blended, flexible, or mobile versions of safety training. Of course, the biggest issue is how training affects employees' behavior on the job. Given the serious, often life-and-death nature of safety lapses in the workplace, the stakes are high to deliver the kind of training that facilitates the highest standards of safe behavior in hazardous workplaces.

Sources: Arcade Classics. (2016, May 5). Untapped potential: Using video games for safety training? Retrieved from *www.arcadeclassics.net/blog/untapped-potential-using-video-games-for-safety-training/* on May 27, 2020. Maurer, R. (2014, June 16). New OSHA video game trains for hazard detection. Retrieved from *www.shrm.org/hrdisciplines/safetysecurity/articles/pages/new-osha-video-gametrains-hazard-detection.aspx* on June 30, 2014.

handling, use and storage, and first-aid steps to take in the event of exposure; and (4) train all workers on the new elements of labels and safety data sheets so they can recognize and understand them.[49]

Lack of information and training is unfortunate, but a problem that is just as serious occurs when safety practices that are taught in training are not reinforced on the job. Regular feedback and incentives for compliance are essential.

"Right-to-know" rules inform employees about workplace hazards as well as protective measures to ensure their safety.
endomedion/123RF

Feedback and Incentives

Previous chapters have underscored the positive impact on the motivation of employees when they are given feedback and incentives to improve productivity. The same principles can also be used to improve safe behavior.[50] Thus, in one study of a wholesale bakery that was experiencing a sharp increase in work accidents, researchers developed a detailed coding sheet for observing safe and unsafe behaviors. Observers then used the sheets to record both safe and unsafe employee behaviors over a 25-week period before, during, and after a safety-training program. Pictures illustrated both safe and unsafe behaviors. Trainees saw data on the percentage of safe behaviors in their departments and established a goal of 90 percent safe behaviors. Each week, the actual percentage of safe behaviors was posted in each department. Supervisors were trained to use positive reinforcement (praise) when they observed safe behaviors. Compared to departments that received no training, workers in the trained departments averaged almost 24 percent more safe behaviors. Not only did employees react favorably to the program, but the company was able to maintain it. One year prior to the program, the number of lost-time injuries per million hours worked was 53.8. Even in highly hazardous industries, this figure rarely exceeds 35. One year after the program, it was less than 10.[51]

Newport News Shipbuilding cut its injury rate in half by using a similar behavioral approach to safety management. The company's bottom-up approach empowers employees to correct others' unsafe behavior and take it upon themselves to fix unsafe things they observe.[52] The results of these studies suggest that training, goal setting, and feedback, coupled with a positive safety climate and a culture featuring strong management support, are key elements. They provide useful alternatives to disciplinary sanctions to encourage compliance with the rules. As one safety consultant noted, "It's better to recognize a guy for success than to beat him up for failure."[53]

As we have seen, in the United States there is considerable pressure to improve plant safety. We consider the situation in some other countries in the following International Application box.

INTERNATIONAL APPLICATION
The Darker Side of Fast Fashion*

Traditionally, companies ordered clothing for each season, and a garment took as long as a year to travel from concept to store. Then in the 1990s, chains such as Inditex's Zara and Hennes & Mauritz (H&M) changed the game by proving it was possible to cut lead times while still keeping costs low. Today shoppers have become accustomed to the steady stream of colorful clothing that so-called fast-fashion apparel chains turn out—introducing new styles as often as every 2 weeks. That new business model encourages some fashion chains to push for the lowest prices from subcontracted factories in countries, such as Bangladesh, that already have some of the leanest production costs in the world.

Now consider the darker side of fast fashion. To keep their contracts in the face of demands for constant product turns, some factories put concerns about production schedules before those of worker rights or safety. This is exactly what happened in Bangladesh, where the worst garment-industry accident in history occurred in 2013, when the Rana Plaza building collapsed, killing 1,130 people and injuring 2,500, mostly women. That incident happened just months after more than 100 workers died in a fire at the Tazreen Fashions Ltd. factory near Dhaka.

The Rana Plaza Building housed roughly 5,000 workers and was owned by a local politician, who did not obtain mandatory permits from the municipal agency that oversees building safety. To make matters worse, the building sat on unstable land that had previously been a swamp. Instead, the mayor issued a permit, although he had no authority to do so. When asked why he did that, the mayor said the municipal agency took too long to issue permits at a time when Bangladesh's garment industry was booming.

In Bangladesh, clothing is king, accounting for four out of every five export dollars. The country exports more garments than any other in the world, except China. Why Bangladesh? One big reason is rock-bottom wages of $94 per month. Two, Bangladesh, as one of the world's poorest countries, can export to the European Union without paying any duties. Three, labor leaders and garment workers face major obstacles as they try to form unions, including beatings, sexual intimidation, and threats of termination.

At the same time, it can be very difficult for retailers to assume responsibility for ensuring worker safety at all the factories they work with because the average supply chain can include dozens of countries and hundreds of primary factories. Benetton, for example, hires more than 700 suppliers to sew its clothes and seek an edge over rivals. Walmart has become the largest buyer, sourcing more than $1 billion in garments annually, according to the Bangladesh Garment Manufacturers and Exporters Association. Beyond that, apparel retailers don't have long-term relationships with the same factories; they change depending on what needs to be produced. Even if outside auditors do inspect factories, they focus on factory-floor issues, not the structural soundness of the buildings themselves.

In 2014, inspectors from the Bangladesh Accord on Fire and Building Safety, backed by 150 mostly European retailers, began inspecting the country's garment factories. Several were closed after inspectors found overloaded ceilings, exposed cables, and locked fire escapes. As of 2020, 1,101 factories remain behind schedule in addressing safety hazards, with 45 percent still lacking adequate fire detection and alarm systems. Yet there are some positive steps. The government hired more than 350 factory inspectors and passed legislation to set up a workers' welfare fund and to allow stronger union representation. The garment industry itself invested more than $1 billion in safety improvements.

These kinds of efforts are paying off, yet much more remains to be done. Factory conditions in many developing countries still fail to meet basic health and safety standards. They remain under enormous pressure to churn out billions of dollars worth of goods at costs low enough to beat out the competition for business from foreign companies. This is unlikely to change until economic pressure from multinational customers forces garment factories and their owners to become as much trendsetters in labor as they are in the cutting-edge fashions they manufacture.

Sources: Paton, E. (2020, Mar. 1). After factory disaster, Bangladesh made big safety strides. Are the bad days coming back? *The New York Times.* Retrieved from *www.nytimes.com/2020/03/01/world/asia/rana-plaza-bangladesh-garment-industry.html* on May 27, 2020. Emont, J. (2018, Mar. 30). Bangladesh still grapples with safety lapses. *The Wall Street Journal*, pp. B1, B2. Al-Mahmood, S. Z., Passariello, C., and Rana, P. (2013, May 5). The global garment trail: From Bangladesh to a mall near you. *The Wall Street Journal*, pp. A1, A11; Devnath, A., and Townsend, M. (2013, Feb. 17). The hidden cost of fast fashion. *Businessweek*, pp. 15–17; Al-Mahmood, S. Z., and Wright, T. (2013, Apr. 26). Collapsed factory was built without permit. *The Wall Street Journal*, p. A9; Al-Mahmood, S. Z., and Banjo, S. (2013, Apr. 25). Deadly collapse. *The Wall Street Journal*, pp. A1, A10; Al-Mahmood, S. Z., and Banjo, S. (2014, Apr. 14). In Bangladesh, labor activists say they were beaten. *The Wall Street Journal*, p. B3.

HEALTH HAZARDS AT WORK

The Need for Safeguards

The National Institute of Occupational Safety and Health has identified more than 15,000 toxic substances, of which some 500 might require regulation as carcinogens (cancer-causing substances). The list of harmful chemical, physical, and biological hazards is a long one. It includes carbon monoxide, vinyl chloride, dusts, particulates, gases and vapors, radiation, excessive noise and vibration, and extreme temperatures. When present in high concentrations, these agents can lead to respiratory, kidney, liver, skin, neurological, and other disorders. Scary, isn't it?

There have been some well-publicized lawsuits against employers for causing occupational illnesses as a result of lack of proper safeguards or technical controls.[54] The U.S. Supreme Court has ruled that the states can prosecute company officials under criminal statutes for endangering the health of employees, even if such hazards are also regulated by OSHA.[55] Nevertheless, some of the criticism against employers is not fair. To prove negligence, it must be shown that management *knew* of the connection between exposure to the hazards and negative health consequences and that management *chose* to do nothing to reduce worker exposure. Yet few such connections were made until recent years. Even now, alternative explanations for the causes of disease or illness cannot be ruled out in many cases.[56] This has led to ethical dilemmas such as the one described in the Ethical Dilemma box.

As for OSHA, budgetary limitations force it to make choices, and in recent years it has chosen to focus on immediate dangers, rather than taking a leadership role in the coronavirus crisis[57] or preventing chronic ailments, such as black lung, asbestosis, and pneumoconiosis. Those take far more lives over the long term. They are silent killers. Since the late 1970s, OSHA has written new standards with exposure limits for some of the most deadly workplace hazards, such as lead, asbestos, and arsenic.

ETHICAL DILEMMA
What to Do When Scared Workers Don't Want to Report for Work Due to a Pandemic?

You manage a restaurant that does not offer outside seating. During the coronavirus pandemic, a number of workers refuse to come to work out of fear of contracting the virus. You assure them that in addition to taking customers' temperatures before they enter the restaurant, you are following guidelines for restaurant owners from the Centers for Disease Control and Prevention.[a] These include, among others, promoting healthy hygiene practices, such as hand washing and employees wearing cloth face coverings. You stress that you have intensified cleaning, sanitization, and disinfection. In addition, you encourage social distancing and enhance spacing at your restaurant by maintaining 6 feet between tables. You also limit the size of parties to six people and close all self-serve stations. Finally, you communicate regularly with local authorities and monitor ongoing developments.

Four of your employees tell you that they appreciate everything you are doing, but they are afraid that they will contract the virus from customers who may not show any symptoms. They refuse to come to work. How will you respond?

---

[a]Centers for Disease Control and Preventioon. (2020). Restaurants and bars during the COVID-19 pandemic. Retrieved from *www.cdc.gov/coronavirus/2019-ncov/downloads/community/restaurants-and-bars-decision-tree.pdf* on May 26, 2020.

Yet workers handle literally tens of thousands of other dangerous substances every day, and exposure limits for most of them are left up to employers.

Every year, more than 200,000 workers in the United States are incapacitated due to inhaling toxic workplace air, and more than 40,000 die from exposure to toxic substances at work. That's 10 times as many who perish from refinery explosions, mine collapses, and other accidents.

All of this costs the American economy an estimated $250 billion per year because of medical expenses and lost productivity. Although it is relatively straightforward to tally the cost in terms of hospital bills and lost wages, it is far more difficult to express the ways, large and small, that life changes for the sickened workers. Yet on one issue, all parties agree: The nature of these silent killers makes it difficult for workers to protect themselves from exposure.[58]

Recently, another health hazard has entered the workplace. Although its origins lie outside the workplace, businesses cannot ignore either its costs or its consequences. That health hazard is coronavirus.

Managing a Workforce in a Time of Crisis

The coronavirus pandemic that swept the world in 2020 forced businesses everywhere to address biological hazards in the workplace and reexamine their basic business models. Many workers deemed essential had no choice but to report to the workplace, with appropriate safeguards, while millions of others were able to work remotely from home.[59] While many organizations made management decisions on the fly, others relied on tried and true approaches used in planning for disasters or other crises.[60] As a leader in a time of crisis, consider taking steps such as the following:[61]

- *Recognize the biggest challenge: uncertainty.* Employees want answers to the "me" questions: How long will this last? What about my job? Will I continue to get paid? Will my benefits continue?
- *Develop an overall strategy* with two elements: have a plan and give people hope. In both civilian and military contexts, these elements have proven successful.[62]
- *Develop a plan.* Business continuity is key, so begin by asking, What problems/ issues are central to our business strategy? What must we continue to execute well through the crisis? What kind of culture do we need to make the business strategy work? To answer these questions, involve employees in building a supportive culture, identify deliverables for each department and employee, establish timelines and quality standards for delivery, and provide resources to help employees adjust to changes.
- *Employee communication is the linchpin of your entire plan.* HR should have access to all employee contact information, and managers should have contact information for each of their direct reports. Use multiple channels, such as e-mail, Zoom meetings, Slack messages, and phone. Do you need to make special efforts for employees with disabilities? Tell employees what actions you are taking and what they need to do. Recognize employees for particularly effective actions and coach, counsel, or discipline poor performers.
- *Offer tips about how to work remotely.*[63] Here, in brief, are six of them. (1) Establish a regular schedule—for example, core hours—and schedule and take breaks. (2) Consider regular teleconference/video calls to hear/see one another and to check in. (3) Ask employees: Does your workspace set you up for success? (4) Identify your optimum working style and your best hours. (5) Take time for self-care; commit to a fitness routine; eat healthy, nutritious meals. (6) Know when to "log off." Remember: You don't have to be available 24/7.
- *Model self-awareness and self-control.* The longer a crisis continues, the harder it becomes for leaders to stay calm and confident, but they need to do that—or at least project it. Senior management team(s) should meet daily (perhaps virtually during the crisis) to discuss key issues facing the business. To the extent possible, communicate regularly with employees—not only to inform them, but also to ease their anxieties.
- *Managers need help too.* It is the responsibility of HR to sensitize managers to the types of issues employees are facing. Advise them on how to deal with these issues. Once they do, schedule debriefing sessions to identify and follow-up on issues. If managers themselves need help, refer them to an Employee Assistance Plan (discussed in the next section).
- *Make time to keep things light.* Provide the kind of support that offers peace of mind, for example, through "virtual happy hours," "virtual talent shows," or video chats where employees can talk about anything. Humor is welcome!
- *Returning to regular work.* Recognize that things will not return to "normal" because your life and others' lives have been permanently altered. Be visible and compassionate. Increase "face time" with with employees; let them see and hear you. Explain how your organization will be even more successful going forward, and encourage employees to talk and tell their stories. Finally, involve employees in co-creating the future strategy and culture that will work best for your organization. After all: Storms don't last forever.

HR BUZZ

The investigation Process*

WHAT IF A WORKER IS INJURED WHILE WORKING FROM HOME?

A key concern for employers is the risk of a "work injury" and a potential workers' compensation claim. The primary question is whether the injury arises out of the work. Is there a direct causal connection between the employee's work duties and the injury he or she sustained? Begin by answering three questions.

First, are employees working from home for their own convenience or with the employer's approval and authorization? Second, what are the employee's specific work activities, duties, and working conditions? What does the employee need to do to perform his or her work activities and what risks or hazards exist in performing them in the home-office setting? What risks or hazards were present in the home office regardless of the work activities? Finally, did the employee have a preexisting work-related injury? If so, is his or her current physical problem a direct consequence of that work injury? Did the activities while working aggravate that preexisting work-related injury?

Carefully investigate and document the situation. Obtain a detailed statement from the employee regarding what he or she was doing when the claimed injury occurred. How did it unfold? Obtain photos of the workplace setup. If photographs would be appropriate in the usual work setting, then there should be no objection to an employer seeking them in an off-premise work-injury claim.

Source: Adapted from Thompson, J. V. (2020, May). Managing work injuries in the new "work from home" era. *HR Professionals Magazine* 10(5), pp. 38, 39.

EMPLOYEE ASSISTANCE PROGRAMS

Another (brighter) side of the employee health issue is reflected in **employee assistance program (EAPs).** Such programs represent an expansion of traditional work in occupational alcoholism-treatment programs. From a handful of programs begun in the 1940s (led by DuPont), EAPs have become a core benefit today, with almost 80 percent of companies offering them.[64]

By its very title, "employee assistance program" signals a change both in application and in technique from the traditional occupational alcoholism-treatment program. Modern EAPs are comprehensive management tools that address behavioral risks in the workplace by extending professional counseling and medical services to all "troubled" employees.[65] A **troubled employee** is an individual who is confronted by unresolved personal or work-related problems. Such problems run the gamut from alcoholism, drug abuse, and high stress to marital, family, and financial problems. Although some of these may originate outside the work context, they most certainly will have spillover effects to the work context.

Do Employee Assistance Programs Work?

As a general matter, the U.S. Department of Health and Human Services reports that "all published studies indicate that EAPs are cost-effective." The U.S. Department of Labor reports that for every dollar invested in an EAP, employers generally save from $5 to $16.[66] In a before-after study of more than 24,300 employees collected from 30 EAPs, absenteeism dropped 27 percent for workers who used the EAP, employee engagement grew 8 percent, and life satisfaction jumped 22 percent.[67]

Despite this rosy picture, these services often go unused. Employees may not know about them or understand what they provide. They also may feel there is a stigma associated with using them, despite strict confidentiality safeguards.[68] Yet by offering assistance to troubled employees, the companies promote positive employee-relations, contribute to their employees' well-being, and enhance their ability to function productively at work, at home, and in the community.[69]

From a business perspective, well-run programs seem to pay off handsomely. In well-run programs, management at various levels expresses support for the program; educates employees about the program and provides necessary training on its use; makes the program accessible to employees; and ensures that it operates in a confidential, credible, and neutral manner.[70] The following are two examples of well-run programs.

General Motors Corp., whose EAP counsels more than 6,500 employees with alcohol problems each year, reports a 65 to 75 percent success rate and estimates that it gains $3 for every $1 spent on care. In addition, blue-collar workers who resolve their alcohol- and drug-abuse problems through an EAP file only half as many grievances as they did before treatment. With respect to referrals for substance abuse and other problems, Chevron determined that its *annual* savings from referrals to the EAP were approximately $10 million. In addition, employees treated for substance abuse had no more on- or off-the-job lost-time accidents than the broader employee population.[71]

On the other hand, not all programs are equally effective. *Beware of making strong statements about a program's impact at least until repeated evaluations have demonstrated the same findings for different groups of employees.*[72] It is also important to emphasize that findings do not generalize across studies unless the EAP is implemented in the same way. For example, as we noted earlier, in some companies, counselors are available on-site. In others, it may only be possible to access an EAP counselor through video- or phone-based channels. Evidence indicates that when counselors are available on-site, as opposed to being accessible through a toll-free number, the programs are more effective.[73]

Next-Generation EAPs

Health-care technology and information provider Cerner Corp. recently expanded its EAP offerings as part of a larger campaign focusing on the importance of mental health. It rebranded its EAP as "My Life Resources," which now includes more diverse benefits, such as legal services, financial coaching, identity-theft insurance, text therapy, and online cognitive-behavioral therapy. Believing that the sources of stress are complex, Cerner wanted to present different ways to alleviate it.[74]

Like other benefits, EAPs are now app-accessible, allowing participants to interact with counselors online and through telemedicine, although some prefer to chat by phone or to interact face to face. Beacon Health started providing therapists via video conferencing, and it has proven quite popular. It gives EAP participants access to therapists and counselors beyond their immediate vicinity, which is an advantage amid the shortage of mental health professionals.

EAPs are also becoming more holistic. For example, at Sun Life Financial Group, the EAP can assemble a team that collaborates on an individual action plan. Such a team might include a vocational/rehabilitation consultant, a behavioral health specialist, a nurse clinician, and a case manager. The team can coordinate with doctors or other treatment providers to devise reasonable workplace accommodations or, if necessary, a return-to-work plan.[75]

The goal is early intervention, before a condition becomes debilitating and requires a leave from work. Yet employees can't take advantage of an EAP if they don't know about it. Hence, it is critical to establish a planned program of communications to employees to announce (and periodically to remind them) that the service is available and that it is confidential.

EAPs are relatively inexpensive. Costs vary from about 75 cents to $1.50 per employee per month, though richer plans can go up to $2. According to the chief people officer at plumbing-supply wholesaler the Granite Group, "I would never *not* have an EAP. It's low cost and if two people get something out of it, the program is worth it."[76]

More on the Role of the Supervisor

In the traditional alcoholism-treatment program, the supervisor had to look for symptoms of alcoholism and then diagnose the problem. Under an EAP, however, the supervisor is responsible only for identifying declining work performance. If normal corrective measures do not work, the supervisor confronts the employee with evidence of his or her poor performance and offers the EAP. Recognize, however, that classic warning signs, such as chronic tardiness and absenteeism, are not always evident at companies where some employees telework or where workers may be geographically separated from their supervisors. Nevertheless, here are some recommendations on how to proceed:[77]

1. Once you suspect a problem, begin documenting instances in which job performance has fallen short. Absenteeism (leaving early, arriving late for work, taking more days off than allowed by policy), accidents, errors, a slackened commitment to completing tasks, and a rise in conflicts with other employees (due to changes in mood swings) may become evident.
2. Having assembled the facts, set up a meeting that includes an HR representative. Keep the discussion focused on performance, and don't try to make a diagnosis. Outline the employee's shortcomings, insist on improvement, and then say, "do we have your approval to reach out to the EAP on your behalf?" With permission, the EAP would then reach out to the worker.
3. Often, managers are scared of potential liability and scared to be wrong. They worry, Can the person sue me? As long as the discussion focuses on declining job performance, legal experts say that a defamation claim is highly unlikely. Besides, confrontation without focusing on job performance is usually ineffective, anyway.

Now that we understand what EAPs are, their effects, and how they work, let us examine three of today's most pressing workplace problems: alcoholism, drug abuse, and violence.

Alcoholism

Management's concern over alcoholism is understandable, for alcohol misuse by employees is costly in terms of productivity, time lost from work, and treatment. According to the National Institute on Alcohol Abuse and Alcoholism (NIAAA), **harmful patterns of drinking** are defined as drinking *too much, too fast* (more than 4 drinks in 2 hours for men, and more than 3 in 2 hours for women) or *too* *much, too often* (more than 14 drinks per week for men, and more than 7 for women).[78] How prevalent is alcoholism, and how costly is it?[79]

- About 10 percent of full-time employees have a serious drinking problem. This percentage has remained constant for the past 15 years. That's about 1 in every 12 adults.[80]
- Annual deaths due to alcohol number about 105,000.
- Of all hospitalized patients, about 25 percent have alcohol-related problems.
- Alcohol results in about 500 million lost workdays annually, and it is involved in 40 percent of industrial fatalities and 47 percent of industrial accidents.
- Fully half of all auto fatalities involve alcohol.
- Alcohol abusers drain resources and reduce productivity. They use more sick days, show up late more often, and stay in jobs for shorter amounts of time. They are 3.5 times more likely to cause accidents at work and in transit, and their health costs are double their peers'.[81]

Alcoholism affects employees at every level, but it is costliest at the top. Experts estimate that it afflicts at least 10 percent of senior executives. As an example, consider an executive who makes $200,000 per year, is unproductive, and files large health claims. That cost is certainly far higher than a $10,000 outpatient treatment program.[82] Residential treatment programs of 60–90 days typically cost $12,000 to $60,000.

A study done for McDonnell Douglas Corp. (now part of Boeing) shows how expensive it is to ignore substance-abuse problems in the workplace. The company found that in the previous 5 years, each worker with an alcohol (or drug) problem was absent 113 more days than the average employee and filed $38,000 more in medical claims (in 2020 dollars). Their dependents also filed some $59,000 more in claims than the average family. Intervention works, as long as it includes ongoing case management and post-treatment monitoring.[83] Recovered alcoholics frequently credit such programs with literally saving their lives. Companies win, too—by reclaiming employees whose gratitude and restored abilities can result in years of productive service.

Drug Abuse

Drug abuse is no less insidious. About 4.2 percent of the full-time, adult American workforce tested positive for illegal drug use in 2017, according to the National Safety Council.[84] For young adults, the numbers are higher—double that for marijuana alone.[85] Drug abuse cuts across all job levels and types of organizations and, together with employee alcohol abuse, costs U.S. businesses $160 billion per year in increased health-care and insurance costs, lost productivity, and workplace accidents.[86]

Evidence clearly shows that drug abuse affects on-the-job behaviors.[87] A typical drug user in today's workforce

- Is late three times as often as fellow employees.
- Requests early dismissal or time off during work 2.2 times as often.
- Has three times as many absences of 8 days or more.
- Uses three times the normal level of sick-leave benefits.
- Is four times more likely to be involved in a workplace accident.

- Is five times as likely to file a workers' compensation claim.
- Is one-third less productive than fellow workers.

A longitudinal study of 5,465 applicants for jobs with the U.S. Postal Service found that after an average of 1.3 years of employment, employees who had tested positive for illicit drugs (typically about 5 percent) had an absenteeism rate 59.3 percent higher than employees who had tested negative. Those who had tested positive also had a 47 percent higher rate of involuntary turnover than those who had tested negative.[88] At a national level, 80 percent of drug abusers steal from their employers to support their illegal drug use, and drug abuse is the third leading cause of workplace violence.[89]

Violence at Work

What do Xerox, NASA, and the U.S. Postal Service have in common? They have employees who died violently while at work. **Workplace violence** includes assaults and other violent acts or threats that occur in or are related to the workplace. It may involve employees, customers, or vendors and entails a substantial risk of physical or emotional harm to individuals or damage to company resources or capabilities. Indeed, the most common but least reported types of workplace violence involve bullying, intimidation, or threats.[90] With respect to workplace homicides, it is important to note that most do *not* involve murderous assaults between coworkers in an organization. Rather, they occur in connection with robberies and related crimes.[91] Those most at risk are taxi drivers, police officers, retail workers, people who work with money or valuables, and people who work alone or at night.

Violence disrupts productivity, causes untold damage to those exposed to the trauma, is related to workplace abuse of drugs or alcohol and absenteeism, and costs employers billions of dollars.[92] In a stressed-out, downsized business environment, people are searching for someone to blame for their problems. With the loss of a job or other event the employee perceives as unfair, the employer may become the focus of a disgruntled individual's fear and frustration. Under these circumstances, some form of **workplace aggression**—that is, efforts by individuals to harm others with whom they work, or have worked, or their organization itself—is likely.[93]

What can organizations do? Although many American employers have a formal anti-violence policy, among those that do not, the key obstacle seems to be a widespread assumption that violence is more or less random—that there is no way to predict when a troubled worker will suddenly snap. Yet according to a former FBI agent, "People don't suddenly 'just go crazy.' Workplace violence is one of the few types of violent behavior that follows a clear pattern."[94] To be sure, fair treatment (procedural justice) on the job, adequate compensation, a climate of honesty by leaders, communicating a policy about counterproductive behavior, consistently punishing unacceptable behavior, and taking steps to reduce job stress can reduce the likelihood of workplace violence and aggression.[95] In addition, both employees and supervisors should be alert to warning signs, such as the following:[96]

- *Verbal threats.* Take seriously remarks from an employee about what he or she may do. Experts say that individuals who make such statements usually have been mentally committed to the act for a long period of time. It may take very little provocation to trigger the violence.

- *Physical actions.* Employees who demonstrate threatening physical actions at work are dangerous. The employer, working with experts trained to assess a possibly violent situation, needs to investigate and intervene. Failure to do so may be interpreted as permission to do further or more serious damage.
- *Behaviors.* Watch for changes such as irritability and a short temper. Is the employee showing a low tolerance to work stress or frustrations?[97]

Here are some additional preventive steps:[98]

- *Develop a plan to identify, defuse, and recover from a violent event.* To do that, audit your hiring and access polices and consult specialists–professionals in the area of facility security, violence assessment, EAP counseling, community support services, and local law enforcement.
- *Create, communicate, and enforce a written, zero-tolerance workplace-violence policy.* Explain the organization's position on intimidating, threatening, or violent behavior; establish a procedure for investigating all threats or acts of violence; and provide multiple channels for employees to make complaints.
- *Establish a crisis-management team* with the authority to make decisions quickly. This group should meet regularly to share information, evaluate problems, and develop plans for activities such as counseling for victims and dealing with the media.
- *Offer training and employee orientation.* Train supervisors and managers in how to recognize aggressive behavior, identify the warning signs of violence, be effective communicators, and resolve conflict. They need to know what they should do and whom they can call if they see disturbing behavior. Orient all employees on facility-security procedures and on how to recognize and report threats of violence.

IMPACT OF SAFETY, HEALTH, AND EAPs ON PRODUCTIVITY, QUALITY OF WORK LIFE, AND THE BOTTOM LINE

We know that the technology is available to make workplaces safe and healthy for the nation's men and women. We also know that legislation can never substitute for managerial commitment to safe, healthy workplaces based on demonstrated economic and social benefits. We noted earlier that the return on investment of investments in job safety and health is typically 3:1, according to the Liberty Mutual Research Institute for Safety. In light of the global coronavirus pandemic that began in 2020, business leaders everywhere need to rethink their priorities on health and wellness for their employees. According to Alex Gorsky, CEO of Johnson & Johnson, "in that scenario, every business leader in some way is going to be a health care leader going forward."[a]

On balance, commitment to job safety, health, and EAPs to promote employee well-being is a win–win situation for employees and their companies. Productivity, quality of work life, and the bottom line all stand to gain.

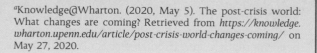

[a]Knowledge@Wharton. (2020, May 5). The post-crisis world: What changes are coming? Retrieved from *https://knowledge.wharton.upenn.edu/article/post-crisis-world-changes-coming/* on May 27, 2020.

- *Help employees adjust to change*–for example, in the event of a downsizing, a merger, or an acquisition, give employees advance notice to keep them informed about impending changes. Providing additional benefits, such as severance pay or EAP stress-management counseling, can help employees adjust to the change.
- *Be aware of potential risks and respond appropriately.* Do not ignore remarks such as "I'll kill you" or "I'd like to put out a contract on him." Experts say that in many cases an individual who becomes violent has given multiple clues of potentially violent behavior to a number of people within the organization. Be proactive; don't assume the employee doesn't mean it because when employees feel powerless, there is a greater likelihood of violence. Report the incident to management for investigation.[99]

CORPORATE HEALTH PROMOTION: THE CONCEPT OF "WELLNESS"

Consider these sobering facts about the U.S. population:

- Employees with chronic diseases such as asthma, diabetes, and congestive heart failure, all of which can be managed, account for 75 percent of the typical employer's total medical costs.[100]
- More than 42 percent of U.S. adults are obese.[101] Medical expenses for each of those employees are $1,429 higher than those for employees with healthy weights.[102] More than a million back injuries occur in U.S. workplaces each year,[103] with a median time away from the job of 6 to 7 days.[104]
- About 21 percent of the population still smoke. According to the American Lung Association, smokers die, on average, 13 to 14 years before nonsmokers. Tobacco use is responsible for one in five U.S. deaths; excess medical costs and productivity losses cost employers more than $193 billion a year; and, for individual employers, a smoker is 18 percent more expensive than a nonsmoker.[105]
- Twenty-nine percent have high blood pressure (one-third are unaware of it).
- A majority don't exercise regularly.
- Fifty percent don't wear seat belts.
- Approximately 1.5 million heart attacks and strokes occur every year in the United States, causing one in three deaths among people under age 65 and accounting for 1 in every 6 dollars spent on health care.[106]

Keep in mind that health plans do not promise good health. They simply pay for the cost of ill health and the associated rehabilitation. Because 8 of the 10 leading causes of death are largely preventable, however, employers are beginning to look to health promotion and disease management as one way to reduce health-care spending. **Disease management** is a combination of strategies developed to reduce the costs of chronic conditions that require significant changes in behavior. Its goals are to reduce episodes of acute illness, avoid repeated hospitalizations, and lower mortality risks. To do that, it is necessary to do three things well: (1) identify the condition in its early stages, (2) provide appropriate levels of care (treatment matched to the severity of the problem), and (3) deliver intensive follow-up to reinforce compliance.[107]

Is it possible that health-care costs can be tamed through on-the-job exercise programs and health-promotion efforts? Apparently, most U.S. employers think so, because more than 85 percent of organizations with more than 200 employees, and almost 60 percent of smaller ones, offer some form of employee **wellness program** or activity, such as smoking cessation, weight loss, or other lifestyle-modification programs.[108] Do such programs work? In a moment, we will consider that question, but first let's define our terms and look at the overall concept.

The process of corporate health promotion begins by promoting health awareness–that is, knowledge of the present and future consequences of behaviors and lifestyles and the risks they may present. The objective of wellness programs is not to eliminate symptoms and disease; it is to help employees build lifestyles that will enable them to achieve their full physical and mental potential. Wellness programs differ from EAPs in that wellness focuses on prevention, whereas EAPs focus on rehabilitation. **Health promotion** is a four-step process:[109]

1. Educating employees about health-risk factors–life habits or body characteristics that may increase the chances of developing a serious illness. For heart disease (the leading cause of death), some of these risk factors are high blood pressure, cigarette smoking, high cholesterol levels, diabetes, a sedentary lifestyle, and obesity. Some factors, such as smoking, physical inactivity, stress, and poor nutrition, are associated with many diseases.[110]
2. Identifying the health-risk factors that each employee faces.
3. Helping employees eliminate or reduce these risks through healthier lifestyles and habits.
4. Helping employees maintain their new, healthier lifestyles through self-monitoring and evaluation. The central theme of health promotion is "No one takes better care of you than you do."

There's actually a fifth element, and it may be the most important of all. Managers, particularly middle managers, must lead by example. The things they do and say, and the opportunities they create, are critically important to employee wellness, or as some say, well-being.[111] Only about 13 percent of employers include all five elements described here. In well-designed programs that offer incentives, 60 to 70 percent of employees can be expected to participate.[112] However, it's the 10 to 20 percent of high-risk employees who account for up to 80 percent of all claims that are the most difficult to reach.[113] The next section explains why it is important to try.

Linking Sedentary Lifestyles to Health-Care Costs

Based on data from more than 58,000 individuals, researchers at the Centers for Disease Control and Prevention collected data on minutes of physical activity per week. Then they examined each individual's average cost of health care two years later. After controlling for age, sex, body mass index, and socioeconomic status, they found that individuals who exercised more than 2.5 hours per week spent about $4,500 per year on health-care costs. Those who exercised between zero and 2.5 hours a week spent $5,076 per year, and those who didn't exercise at all spent $5,813 per year. Compared to those who are active, sedentary adults spend $1,313 more on health care every year. In the aggregate, the researchers determined that 11.1 percent of the total health-care cost of the United States is directly related to inadequate physical activity.[114] Other studies have shown that of the $3 trillion spent on health care in the United States, 70 percent is due to individuals eating the wrong kinds of foods, not moving around enough, using tobacco, or having other unhealthy lifestyle behaviors.[115] Results like these may form the basis for incentive programs to (1) improve workers' health habits and (2) reduce employees' contributions to health insurance costs or increase their benefits. Roughly a third of companies with more than 200 workers use incentives to entice workers to participate in their wellness programs.[116] The HR Buzz box shows what two companies are doing.

IBM AND THE WILLIAMS COMPANIES

HR BUZZ

Reaching "High-Risk" Employees

IBM has added an incentive dubbed the "Personal Vitality Rebate" to encourage lifestyle changes to build energy, better health, and vitality through personal well-being. The program joined four similar healthy-living rebates promoting physical activity and nutrition, preventive care, children's health, and new-hire healthy living. Each offers $150 cash incentives available to all full-time U.S. employees. Employees choosing to participate in any two programs receive up to $300 cash per year. The payoff? Over a 3-year period, IBM invested $79 million in wellness programs and saved about $191 million in lower health-care costs for participants, as compared to nonparticipants.

At energy company Williams, employees can get up to $300 off medical-plan premiums by agreeing to send biometric data to health-data analytics engine Limeade (via mobile apps or wearable devices) and reaching certain goals. Almost 60 percent of eligible employees participate. The payoff? Over 4 years, medical-claims costs increased just 1.8 percent annually, far below the industry average. It was also able to avoid raising monthly employee premiums.[a]

---

[a]IBM. (2020). IBM's culture of health. Retrieved from *www.ibm.com/ibm/responsibility/employee well being. shtml* on May 28, 2020. IBM. (2012). 2012 corporate social responsibility report. Retrieved from *www.ibm.com/ibm/responsibility/2012/the-ibmer/employee-well-being.html* on June 28, 2017; Clancy, H. (2015, Sept. 1). Gym class heroes. *Fortune*, p. 42.

Evaluation: Do Wellness Programs Work?

Wellness programs are especially difficult to evaluate, for at least six reasons:[117]

1. Health-related costs that actually decrease are hard to identify.
2. Program sponsors use different methods to measure and report costs and benefits.
3. Program effects may vary depending on *when* they are measured (immediate versus lagged effects) and *how long* they are measured.
4. Potential biases exist as a result of self-selection and exclusion of drop-outs.
5. Few studies use control groups.
6. Data on effectiveness are limited in the choice of variables, estimation of the economic value of indirect costs and benefits, estimation of the timing and duration of program effects, and estimation of the present value of future benefits.

Although a growing number of studies report favorable cost–benefit results, it is difficult to evaluate and compare them because different authors use different assumptions in their estimates of wellness-intervention costs and dollar benefits. A recent meta-analysis of 51 studies in nine industries across 12 countries found that the higher the quality of the methodology in a study, the lower the financial returns.[118]

ETHICAL DILEMMA
Should Employees Be Punished for Unhealthy Lifestyles?

A University of Michigan study of more than 223,000 employees in seven industries found that 26 percent of corporate health-care costs stem from employees' unhealthy lifestyles.[a] As a result, individuals may not be hired, might even be fired, and could wind up paying a monthly penalty based on their after-hours activities, such as smoking, skydiving, piloting a private aircraft, mountain climbing, or motorcycling.

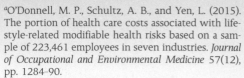

Federal civil rights laws generally don't protect against **lifestyle discrimination** because smokers and skydivers aren't named as protected classes. However, about 30 states and the District of Columbia have passed laws that protect employees and job applicants from any adverse employment actions if their use of a lawful product (such as tobacco) occurs outside of work.[b] Should employers be able to implement "lifestyle policies"?

[a]O'Donnell, M. P., Schultz, A. B., and Yen, L. (2015). The portion of health care costs associated with life-style-related modifiable health risks based on a sample of 223,461 employees in seven industries. *Journal of Occupational and Environmental Medicine* 57(12), pp. 1284–90.

[b]Nagele-Piazza, L. (2017, Oct. 24). Can employees be fired for off-duty conduct? *SHRM Online*. Retrieved from *www.shrm.org/resourcesandtools/legal-and-compliance/state-and-local-updates/pages/can-employees-be-fired-for-off-duty-conduct.aspx* on Oct. 30, 2017. Wechsler, P. (2011, July 10). And you thought cigarettes were pricey. *Bloomberg Businessweek*, pp. 24–26. Deschenaux, J. (2011, July). Is a "smoker-free" workplace right for you? *HR*, pp. 43-45.

Unfortunately, only about 25 percent of companies offering wellness programs are even collecting data to assess financial outcomes, and many small companies just don't have the resources to conduct a study.[119]

Depending on the number of options an employer wants to include, the costs of running a wellness program vary from $150 to $1,200 per employee per year.[120]

Peer-reviewed evaluations and meta-analyses show that the return on investment (ROI) is achieved through improved worker health, reduced benefit expense, and enhanced productivity.[121] A review of 72 studies concluded that health-promotion programs achieve an average ROI of $3.48 per $1 invested when considering health-care costs alone, $5.82 when considering absenteeism, and $4.30 when both are considered.[122] In a separate investigation, researchers at the Cleveland Clinic offered relentless support from management at all levels, together with cash rewards for meeting goals, such as for healthy weight and blood pressure. Over a 10-year period, while overall health-care costs rose 54 percent, those at the Cleveland Clinic rose only 14.6 percent. That saved the organization $261 million.[123]

Meta-analysis suggests that the ability to reduce risks for high-risk employees is the critical element in achieving positive cost outcomes.[124] This takes time, and studies show that a positive impact on medical costs generally requires 3 to 5 years of program participation.[125]

Clearly, wellness programs can yield significant payoffs to organizations that adopt them. It also is clear, however, that the programs do not work under all circumstances and that the problems associated with assessing relative costs and benefits may be complex. Results from large companies may not translate to small ones, and the variety of program offerings makes it difficult to generalize results.[126] Nevertheless, if companies are successful in attracting at-risk employees, and if they can create an employee experience focused on engagement, inclusion, resilience, communication, and management support, then their programs will flourish.

Wellness Programs and the Americans with Disabilities Act

Employers violate the ADA if they *require* employees to submit to wellness initiatives, such as health-risk appraisals (questionnaires about one's health history and current lifestyle) and assessments (physical and biomedical tests that screen for specific health conditions). This is because the act forbids employers from conducting mandatory medical exams once an employee is hired, unless the inquiry is "job-related and consistent with business necessity."[127]

What types of wellness programs do not violate the ADA? Companies such as American Honda, AstraZeneca, and Cal-Neva Resort, Spa & Casino encourage employees to use health-monitoring kiosks in cafeterias and employee break rooms that measure users' blood pressure, heart rate, and weight noninvasively. Using touch screens, employees answer questions about their lifestyles and health choices (e.g., level of exercise, smoking habits). Based on their answers, the computer generates a personalized health-risk appraisal that places users in government-defined health-risk categories. Use of the kiosks is completely up to the employee. In keeping with medical-information privacy law, neither employers nor the vendor can access employee-specific information in the kiosks. Employers can get aggregate data, however, to see what employee populations are using the monitoring stations and what their health concerns are. Employers can then use those data to develop health programs to address issues that employees have identified.[128] By helping employees to take an interest in their future health, employers should ultimately be able to keep at least a loose lid on claims and major expenses.

SUBSTANCE ABUSE ON THE JOB PRODUCES TOUGH POLICY CHOICES FOR MANAGERS

Human Resource Management in Action: Conclusion

In *EEOC v. Exxon USA Inc.*, the 5th Circuit Court of Appeals ruled in favor of Exxon. An employer can justify a general safety requirement–applied to all employees in a given job classification–by showing that the requirement is job-related and consistent with business necessity. There was no further review by the Supreme Court. The ruling emphasized that, ordinarily, it is not the role of the courts to question or interfere with an employer's business objectives. The practical implications of this decision for employers are clear. A review of safety-related job qualifications under a simple standard of job-relatedness will allow employers to exclude individuals with impairments based on considerations of safety, even if there is a possibility that the impairments are ADA disabilities.

Not all employers will adopt such a policy. In fact, given the amounts of time and money invested in employees, especially highly skilled knowledge workers, many firms try to rehabilitate those with substance-abuse problems. But how do firms get problem employees into rehabilitation programs? The most popular approaches are self-referral and referral by family, friends, or coworkers. Among the thousands of pilots who have gone through the airline industry's alcohol-rehabilitation program and regained their licenses, a program in effect since 1973, 85 percent were initially turned in by family, friends, or coworkers.

According to the Air Line Pilots Association, one of the hallmarks of the industry's program is a willingness of people to turn in an alcoholic pilot. That willingness, in turn, depends on knowing that the pilot can return to work. If people know that by turning in a pilot they will also be taking away his or her livelihood, they may not do it.

The key to returning to work, in the opinion of most professionals in the field of substance abuse, is follow-up because substance abuse is a recurring disease.[129] Under United's program, rehabilitated pilots are monitored for at least 2 years. During this time, the pilot is required to meet monthly with a committee comprising counselors and representatives of both union and management in a kind of group-therapy session with other recovering pilots. They may also be required to undergo periodic surprise alcohol or drug tests. United has never had an alcohol-related accident.

Companies with the best success rates in rehabilitating employees with alcohol or drug problems have the most heavily structured follow-up programs. Chevron, Shell, DuPont, American Airlines, and others have demonstrated that a 75 percent success rate is attainable, provided there are mechanisms in place to monitor and reinforce the recovery process.

IMPLICATIONS FOR MANAGEMENT PRACTICE

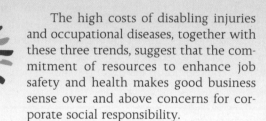

In the coming years, we can expect to see three developments in occupational safety and health:

1. Increased emphasis on prevention programs–ranging from healthy hygiene practices to multilingual safety training, to health promotion, to counterproductive behaviors that involve substance abuse or violence at work.
2. Promotion of OSHA's consultative role, particularly as small businesses recognize that this is a no-cost, no-penalty option available to them.
3. Wider use of analytics, data visualization, and data mapping to identify patterns of injuries, accidents, and unsafe conditions.[a]

The high costs of disabling injuries and occupational diseases, together with these three trends, suggest that the commitment of resources to enhance job safety and health makes good business sense over and above concerns for corporate social responsibility.

[a]Carey, S. (2016, Sept. 29). United taps criminology students to uncover patterns in accident data: Interns' finding help airline reduce employee injuries and prevent damage to its aircraft. *The Wall Street Journal.* Retrieved from *www.wsj.com/articles/united-taps-criminology-students-to-uncover-patterns-in-accident-data-1475161313?mg=prod/accounts-wsj* on Sept. 30, 2016.

SUMMARY

Public policy regarding occupational safety and health has focused on state-run workers' compensation programs for job-related injuries and federally mandated preventive measures to enhance job safety and health. OSHA enforces the provisions of the 1970 Occupational Safety and Health Act, under which employers have a "general duty" to provide a place of employment "free from recognized hazards." Employers also have the special duty to comply with all standards of safety and health established under the act. OSHA's effectiveness has been debated for decades, but it is important to note that workplace accidents can result either from *unsafe work conditions* or from *unsafe work behaviors*. OSHA can affect only unsafe work conditions. There are no standards that govern potentially unsafe employee behaviors.

A major concern of employers today is the possible health hazards associated with coronaviruses; high-technology products, such as semiconductors; and diseases related to radiation or carcinogenic substances that may have long latency periods. In response, OSHA has established or toughened workplace exposure limits for many carcinogenic substances. Management's first duty in this area is to develop a safety and health policy. Management's second duty is to establish controls that include a loss-control program, a safety committee, safety rules, careful selection of employees, extensive training, and feedback and incentives for maintaining a safe work environment.

Employee assistance programs represent a brighter side of the health issue. Such programs offer assistance to all "troubled" employees (e.g., as a result of drug or alcohol abuse or financial difficulties). Under an EAP, supervisors need be concerned only with identifying declining work performance, not with involving themselves in employee problems. Treatment is left to professionals. Finally, health promotion, or "wellness," programs differ from EAPs in that their primary focus is on prevention, not rehabilitation. Both EAPs and wellness programs hold considerable promise for improving productivity, quality of work life, and profits.

KEY TERMS

repetitive-strain injuries (RSIs)

willful violation

indirect costs of an accident

engineering controls

management controls

loss-control program

employee assistance programs (EAPs)

troubled employee

harmful patterns of drinking

workplace violence

workplace aggression

disease management

wellness programs

health promotion

lifestyle discrimination

DISCUSSION QUESTIONS

15-1. Should OSHA's enforcement activities be expanded? Why or why not?

15-2. What can firms do to encourage all employees to behave safely on the job?

15-3. Discuss the relative effectiveness of engineering versus management controls to improve job safety and health.

15-4. Explain how a disease-management program might be used to address substance-abuse problems.

15-5. If the benefits of EAPs cannot be demonstrated to exceed their costs, should EAPs be discontinued?

15-6. Outline a workplace response to a coronavirus crisis.

15-7. Should organizations be willing to invest more money in employee wellness? Why or why not?

15-8. Identify three preventive steps that an employer might take to avoid incidents of workplace violence.

15-9. Your company wants to encourage more employees to participate in work site wellness programs. Would you recommend rewards for participating or punishments for not participating?

15-10. What steps should multinational companies take to ensure that their suppliers meet at least minimum standards for workplace health and safety?

APPLYING YOUR KNOWLEDGE

Case 15–1

Skyline Machine Shop

Skyline Machine Shop is a medium-sized firm located in San Jose, California. It employs almost 1,000 workers when business is good. Skyline specializes in doing precision machining on a subcontract basis for several large aerospace companies. Skilled machinists are always in short supply and, therefore, command high salaries and generous benefits packages.

Recently, one of the plant foremen, Len Fulkner, paid a visit to Skyline's HR manager, Jamie Trenton, to discuss a problem at work.

Fulkner: You know, Jamie, I've been around the barn a time or two. I've seen all kinds of people-type problems over the years. But I guess maybe I'm over the hill–53 is no spring chicken, you know! The other day I ran into a situation like I've never seen before, and I need your help.

Trenton: What happened, Len?

Fulkner: Well, last Thursday one of my best machinists, Harry Boecker, began acting really weird. He seemed to be in a daze, couldn't seem to concentrate on the part he was milling, and began dropping tools and engineering drawings all over. At first, I thought he'd been drinking. But I smelled his breath and couldn't smell anything. When I asked him what was wrong, he mumbled something about "coke."

Trenton: What did you do?

Fulkner: I called a taxi and sent him home for the rest of the day. I didn't know what else to do, but I knew he was a danger to himself and to others, so I had to get him out of the plant. I hope I did the right thing. I'm really worried about the guy, Jamie. I'd hate to lose a good machinist like that, but I don't know the first thing about drugs or how to handle workers who have been taking them. Can you help me?

The next day, Trenton had a meeting scheduled with the president of Skyline. She had been thinking for some time about recommending an employee assistance program (EAP) to the president, and her conversation with Fulkner convinced her that now was the appropriate time. Quite a few other firms in the San Jose area had instituted EAPs–seemingly with some success. However, Trenton knew that Skyline's president was skeptical of "follow-the-leader" approaches to employee benefits.

Questions

1. Did Len Fulkner handle the situation with Harry Boecker correctly? Why or why not?
2. Prepare an outline of a cost-benefit analysis that Jamie Trenton could use in presenting her EAP proposal to Skyline's president. In particular, what categories of benefits might be quantifiable?
3. If Trenton's proposal is accepted, what key steps would you recommend to her in implementing a new EAP at Skyline Machine Shop?

REFERENCES

1. U.S. Department of Labor, Occupational Safety and Health Administration. (2020). Commonly used statistics. Retrieved from *www.osha.gov/data/commonstats* on May 26, 2020.
2. Repetitive motion accident statistics. (2018, June 21). *LegalMatch.* Retrieved from *www.legalmatch.com/law-library/article/repetitive-motion-accident-statistics.html* on May 26, 2020.
3. Bierma, P. (2020, Jan. 1). Repetitive stress injury. (RSI). *Consumer HealthDay.* Retrieved from *https://consumer.healthday.com/encyclopedia/pain-management-30/pain-health-news-520/repetitive-stress-injury-rsi-646236.html* on May 26, 2020.
4. Liberty Mutual Research Institute for Safety. (2019, April 10). 2019 Liberty Mutual Workplace Safety Index reveals workplace injuries cost U.S. companies over $1 billion per week. Retrieved from *www.libertymutualgroup.com/about-lm/news/documents/2019-workplace-safety-index.pdf* on May 26, 2020.
5. FMP Global. (2018, Sept. 17). The back-breaking cost of back pain in the U.S. Retrieved from *https://fmpglobal.com/blog/the-back-breaking-cost-of-back-pain-in-the-us/* on May 26, 2020.
6. Workplace injury statistics–2019 year-end data. *Work Injury Source.* Retrieved from *https://workinjurysource.com/workplace-injury-statistics-2019/* on May 26, 2020.
7. Johnson, D. (2016, May 13). The most dangerous jobs in America. *Time.* Retrieved from *http://time.com/4326676/dangerous-jobs-america/* on June 21, 2017.
8. U.S. Department of Labor. (2018). About OSHA. Retrieved from *www.osha.gov/Publications/all_about_OSHA.pdf* on May 26, 2020.
9. U.S. Department of Labor. (2020). OSHA–Commonly Used Statistics. Retrieved from *www.osha.gov/data/commonstats* on May 26, 2020.
10. OSH Act is changed to emphasize cooperation. (1998, Sept.). *HR News,* p. 14.
11. U.S. Department of Labor, Occupational Safety and Health Administration. (2017). Quick reference guide to the bloodborne pathogens standard. Retrieved from *www.osha.gov/SLTC/bloodbornepathogens/bloodborne_quickref.html* on June 21, 2017.
12. U.S. Department of Labor, Occupational Safety and Health Administration. (2020). Ergonomics: Standards and enforcement FAQs. Retrieved from *www.osha.gov/SLTC/ergonomics/faqs.html* on May 26, 2020. *See also* Meier, B., and Ivory, D. (2017, June 6). Industry given a louder voice on job safety. *The New York Times,* pp. A1, A16.
13. Nagele-Piazza, L. (2017, Dec. 19). OSHA is accepting electronic injury and illness records through Dec. 31. *SHRM Online.* Retrieved from *www.shrm.org/resourcesandtools/legal-and-compliance/employment-law/pages/risk-management-osha-electronic-injury-and-illness-records.aspx* on Dec. 19, 2017.
14. OSHA kept out of homes. (2000, Feb. 28). *The Denver Post,* p. 4A.
15. *Marshall v. Barlow's Inc.* (1978). 1978 OSHD, Sn. 22,735. Chicago: Commerce Clearing House.
16. Etter, I. B. (1993, Sept.). You can't hide from an OSHA inspector. *Safety & Health,* p. 3.
17. About OSHA (2018), op. cit.
18. Bandler, J., and Maher, K. (2008, Apr. 23). House panel to examine Cintas plants' safety record. *The Wall Street Journal,* pp. B1, B2. *See also* Maher, K. (2007, Dec. 5). Safety issues beset industrial laundries. *The Wall Street Journal,* p. A14.
19. About OSHA (2018), op. cit.
20. U.S. Department of Labor (2020). OSHA: On-Site Consultation. Retrieved from *www.osha.gov/consultation* on May 26, 2020.
21. U.S. Department of Labor, Occupational Safety and Health Administration. (2020, Jan. 15). OSHA penalties. Retrieved from *www.osha.gov/penalties/* on May 26, 2020.
22. Bravin, J., and Kendall, B. (2017, Oct. 10). Supreme Court rejects appeal by former Massey Energy CEO Blankenship. *The Wall Street Journal.* Retrieved from *www.wsj.com/articles/supreme-court-rejects-appeal-by-former-massey-energy-ceo-blankenship-1507646414* on Oct. 10, 2017.

23. Hilder, P. H. (2011). Criminal prosecution for safety violations is no accident. Retrieved from *www.docstoc.com/docs/86307999/CRIMINAL-PROSECUTION-FOR-SAFETY-VIOLATION-IS-NO-ACCIDENT* on Aug. 27, 2011. *See also* Fischer, H. (2010, Apr. 17). Corporations on hook for employee deaths. *East Valley Tribune.* Retrieved from *www.eastvalleytribune.com/local/article_be482066-061f-5691-b5ab-eed1154991e1.html* on Aug. 19, 2010.

24. The Occupational Safety and Health Review Commission. (2020). About the Commission. Retrieved from *www.oshrc.gov/* on May 26, 2020.

25. U.S. Department of Labor. OSHA commonly used statistics (2020), op. cit.

26. Can workers walk off the job due to fears of exposure to the COVID-19 virus? (2020, Apr. 9). *PKLaw.* Retrieved from *www.jdsupra.com/legalnews/can-workers-walk-off-the-job-due-to-59454/* on May 26, 2020. *See also NLRB v. Jasper Seating Co.* (1988). CA 7, 129 LRRM 2337. *See also Whirlpool Corporation v. Marshall* (1981, Feb. 26). *Daily Labor Report,* Washington, DC: Bureau of National Affairs, pp. D3–D10.

27. Audi, T. (2008, June 10). Worker deaths at Las Vegas site spur safety debate. *The Wall Street Journal,* pp. B1, B3. *See also Gateway Coal Co. v. United Mine Workers of America* (1974). 1974 OSHD, Sn. 17,085. Chicago: Commerce Clearing House.

28. Can workers walk off the job due to fears of exposure to the COVID-19 virus? (2020), op. cit. *See also* U.S. Department of Labor. (n.d.). Workers' right to refuse dangerous work. Retrieved from *www.osha.gov/right-to-refuse.html* on May 26, 2020.

29. U.S. Department of Labor. OSHA commonly used statistics (2020), op. cit.

30. Leeth, J., and Hale, N. (2013, Apr. 23). Evaluating OSHA's effectiveness and suggestions for reform. Retrieved from *http://mercatus.org/publication/evaluating-oshas-effectiveness-and-suggestions-reform* on June 29, 2014. *See also* Cook, W. N., and Gautschi, F. H. (1981). OSHA plant safety programs and injury reduction. *Industrial Relations* 20(3), pp. 245–57.

31. AmTrust Financial Services, Inc. (2019), op. cit.

32. NARFA. (2014, Jan. 25). Workplace injury costs. Retrieved from *www.narfa.com/the-direct-and-indirect-costs-of-workplace-injury/* on June 29, 2014. *See also* Colford, J. (2005, Sept. 12). The ROI of safety. *BusinessWeek,* pp. 68–74. *See also* Adams, S. (2003, Jan.). Costs drive safety-training needs. *HRMagazine,* pp. 63–66.

33. AmTrust Financial Services, Inc. (2019). ROI of safety: How to create a long-term profitable workplace safety program. Retrieved from https://amtrustfinancial.com/getmedia/d6d1ecf6-1ad1-4e19-84ae-f0fd1991f761/ROI-Safety-Final-Report.pdf on June 2, 2020.

34. Liberty Mutual Research Institute for Safety (2019), op. cit. *See also* Follmann, J. F., Jr. (1978). *The Economics of Industrial Health.* New York: AMACOM.

35. Elkind, P., and Whitford, D. (2011, Feb. 7). An accident waiting to happen. *Fortune,* pp. 105–32. *See also* Roughton, J. (2011). Management's role in developing an effective safety culture. Retrieved from *ezinearticles.com/?Managements-Role-in-Developing-an-Effective-Safety-Culture&id=1285414* on Aug. 27, 2011. *See also* Krause, T. R. (2010, Sept. 20). Oil CEOs must all be chief safety officers now. *Forbes.* Retrieved from *www.forbes.com/2010/09/20/chief-safety-officer-oil-companies-leadership-citizenship-ceos.html* on Sept. 22, 2010.

36. Ciccarelli, M. C. (2011, Mar.). BP's bubbling cauldron. *Human Resource Executive,* pp. 1, 18–21. *See also* Chazan, G, Faucon, B., and Casselman, B. (2010, June 30). Safety and cost drives clashed as CEO Hayward remade BP. *The Wall Street Journal,* pp. A1, A8.

37. Hofmann et al. (2017), op. cit. *See also* Zohar, D. (2014). Safety climate: Conceptualization, measurement, and improvement. In B. Schneider & K. M. Barbera (Eds.), *The Oxford Handbook of Organizational Climate and Culture.* Oxford Handbooks Online, DOI: 10.1093/oxfordhb/9780199860715.013.0017. *See also* Christian, M. S., Bradley, J. C., Wallace, J. C., and Burke, M. J. (2009). Antecedents of occupational safety performance and outcomes: A meta-analysis. *Journal of Applied Psychology* 94, pp. 1103–27. *See also* Newnam, S., Griffin, M. A., and Mason, C. (2008). Safety in work vehicles: A multilevel study linking safety values and individual predictors to work-related driving crashes. *Journal of Applied Psychology* 93, pp. 632–44. *See also* Zohar, D., and Luria, G. (2005). A multilevel model of safety climate: Cross-level relationships between organization and group-level climates.

Journal of Applied Psychology 90, pp. 616–28. *See also* Hofmann, D. A., and Morgeson, F. P. (1999). Safety-related behavior as a social exchange: The role of perceived organizational support and leader-member exchange. *Journal of Applied Psychology* 84, pp. 286–96.

38. Zohar, D., and Polachek, T. (2014). Discourse-based intervention for modifying supervisory communication as leverage for safety climate and performance improvement: A randomized field study. *Journal of Applied Psychology* 90, pp. 616–28. *See also* Kaplan, S., and Tetrick, L. E. (2011). Workplace safety and accidents: An industrial and organizational psychology perspective. In S. Zedeck (Ed.), *APA Handbook of Industrial and Organizational Psychology* (Vol. 1). Washington, DC: American Psychological Association, pp. 455–72. *See also* Zohar, D., and Luria, G. (2004). Climate as a social-cognitive construction of supervisory safety practices: Scripts as proxy of behavior patterns. *Journal of Applied Psychology* 89, pp. 322–33. *See also* Hofmann, D. A., and Stetzer, A. (1998). The role of safety climate and communication in accident interpretation: Implications of learning from negative events. *Academy of Management Journal* 41, pp. 644–57.

39. Burke, M. J., Sarpy, S. A., Tesluk, P. E., and Smith-Crowe, K. (2002). General safety performance: A test of a grounded theoretical model. *Personnel Psychology* 55, pp. 429–57. *See also* Rundle (1996), op. cit.

40. Beus, J. M., Dhanani, L. Y., and McCord, M. A. (2015). A meta-analysis of personality and workplace safety: Addressing unanswered questions. *Journal of Applied Psychology* 100, pp. 481–98.

41. Kaplan and Tetrick (2011), op. cit. *See also* Breslin, F. C., Tompa, E., Mustard, C., Zhao, R., Smith, P., and Hogg-Johnson, S. (2007). Association between the decline in workers' compensation claims and workforce composition. *American Journal of Public Health* 97, pp. 453–55. *See also* Liao, H., Arvey, R. D., and Butler, R. J. (2001). Correlates of work injury frequency and duration among firefighters. *Journal of Occupational Health Psychology* 6(3), pp. 229–42. *See also* Graham, S. (1996, Jan.). Debunk the myths about older workers. *Safety & Health*, pp. 38–41. *See also* Siskind, F. (1982). Another look at the link between work injuries and job experience. *Monthly Labor Review* 105(2), pp. 38–41. *See also* Root, N. (1981). Injuries at work are fewer among older employees. *Monthly Labor Review* 104(3), pp. 30–34.

42. AmTrust Financial Services, Inc. (2019), op. cit.

43. Hagerty (2011), op. cit. *See also* Maurer, R. (2009, July 7). The future of work: Safety and health issues of an aging workforce. *SHRM Online*. Retrieved from *www.shrm.org/hrdisciplines/safetysecurity/articles/Pages/SafetyAgingWorkforce.aspx* on July 14, 2009.

44. Burke, M. J., Sarpy, S. A., Smith-Crowe, K., Chan-Serafin, S., Salvador, R. O., and Islam, G. (2006). Relative effectiveness of worker safety and health training methods. *American Journal of Public Health* 96, pp. 315–24.

45. Hofmann et al. (2017), op. cit. *See also* Kaplan and Tetrick (2011), op. cit. *See also* Burke et al. (2002), op. cit.

46. Michaels, D. (2010, Apr. 28). OSHA training standards policy statement. Retrieved from *www.osha.gov/dep/standards-policy-statement-memo-04-28-10.html* on Oct. 5, 2010.

47. Kaplan and Tetrick (2011), op. cit. *See also* Barling, J., Kelloway, E. K., and Iverson, R. D. (2003). High-quality work, job satisfaction, and occupational injuries. *Journal of Applied Psychology* 88, pp. 276–83. *See also* Frone, M. R. (1998). Predictors of work injuries among employed adolescents. *Journal of Applied Psychology* 8, pp. 565–76.

48. OSHA hazard communication standard. (2010, July 1). 29 CFR 1910.1200.

49. U.S. Department of Labor, Occupational Safety and Health Administration. (2012, Mar. 26). Hazard communication. Retrieved from *www.osha.gov/dsg/hazcom/* on June 22, 2017.

50. Zohar (2014), op. cit. *See also* Kaplan and Tetrick (2011), op. cit. *See also* Barling, J., and Frone, M. R. (Eds.). (2004). *The Psychology of Workplace Safety.* Washington, DC: American Psychological Association. *See also* Zohar, D. (2002). Modifying supervisory practices to improve subunit safety: A leadership-based intervention model. *Journal of Applied Psychology* 87, pp. 156–63.

51. Komaki, J., Barwick, K. D., and Scott, L. R. (1978). A behavioral approach to occupational safety: Pinpointing and reinforcing safe performance in a food manufacturing plant. *Journal of Applied Psychology* 63, pp. 434–45. *See also* Zohar, D., and Luria, G. (2004). Climate as a social-cognitive construction of supervisory safety practices: Scripts as proxy of behavior patterns. *Journal of Applied Psychology* 89, pp. 322–33.

52. Yandrick, R. M. (1996, Feb.). Behavioral safety helps shipbuilder cut accident rates. *HR News*, pp. 3, 11. *See also* Neal, A., and Griffin, M. A. (2006). A study of the lagged relationships among safety climate, safety motivation, safety behavior, and accidents at the individual and group levels. *Journal of Applied Psychology* 91, pp. 946–53. *See also* Reber, R. A., and Wallin, J. A. (1984). The effects of training, goal setting, and knowledge of results on safe behavior: A component analysis. *Academy of Management Journal* 27, pp. 544–60.

53. Milbank, D. (1991, Mar. 29). Companies turn to peer pressure to cut injuries as psychologists join the battle. *The Wall Street Journal*, pp. B1, B3.

54. Waldman, P., and Mehrotra, K. (2018, Jan. 8). Life and death on the third shift. *Bloomberg Businessweek*, pp. 36–41. *See also* Urbina, I. (2013, Mar. 30). As OSHA emphasizes safety, long-term health risks fester. *The New York Times*. Retrieved from *http://www.nytimes.com/2013/03/31/us/osha-emphasizes-safety-health-risks-fester.html?pagewanted=all&_r=0* on July 2, 2014. *See also*, Parloff, R. (2005, June 13). Diagnosing for dollars. *Fortune*, pp. 95–110.

55. Wermiel, S. (1989, Oct. 3). Justices let states prosecute executives for job hazards covered by U.S. law. *The Wall Street Journal*, p. A11.

56. Bellon, T. (2020, Jan. 31). What are the obstacles to Bayer settling Roundup lawsuits? *Reuters*. Retrieved from *www.reuters.com/article/us-bayer-glyphosate-lawsuit-q-a/what-are-the-obstacles-to-bayer-settling-roundup-lawsuits-idUSKBN1ZU28H* on May 27, 2020. *See also* Worker safety. (2015, Sept. 13). *Bloomberg Businessweek*, pp. 27, 28. *See also* Parloff (2005), op. cit.

57. Scheiber, N. (2020, April 22). Protecting workers from coronavirus: OSHA leaves it to employers. *The New York Times*. Retrieved from *www.nytimes.com/2020/04/22/business/economy/coronavirus-osha-workers.html* on May 26, 2020.

58. Centers for Disease Control and Prevention. Health and economic costs of chronic diseases. Retrieved from *www.cdc.gov/chronicdisease/about/costs/index.htm* on May 26, 2020. *See also* U.S. Department of Labor, OSHA. Chemical hazards and toxic substances. Retrieved from *www.osha.gov/SLTC/hazardoustoxicsubstances/* on May 26, 2020. *See also* Urbina (2013), op. cit. *See also* Center for Occupational and Environmental Health. (2012). Annual price tag for occupational injuries and illnesses reaches $250 billion. Retrieved from *www.coeh.berkeley.edu/bridges/Spring2012/OccupationalInjuriesIllnesses.html* on Sept. 9, 2014.

59. Eisenberg, R. (2020, Apr. 10). Is working from home the future of work? *Forbes*. Retrieved from *www.forbes.com/sites/nextavenue/2020/04/10/is-working-from-home-the-future-of-work/#2a6369be46b1* on May 27, 2020. *See also* Austin, P. L. (2020, Mar. 12). 5 tips for staying productive and mentally healthy while you're working from home. *Time*. Retrieved from *https://time.com/5801725/work-from-home-remote-tips/* on May 26, 2020. *See also* Bond, S. (2020, May 21). Facebook expects half its employees to work remotely permanently. *National Public Radio*. Retrieved from *www.npr.org/sections/coronavirus-live-updates/2020/05/21/860382831/facebook-expects-half-its-employees-to-work-remotely-forever* on May 26, 2020.

60. Ladika, S. (2019). Better safe than sorry. *HRMagazine* 64(4), pp. 62–69. *See also* McKee, K., and Guthridge, L. (2006). *Leading people through disasters*. San Francisco: Berrett-Kohler.

61. Cascio, W. F. (2020, April 1). Workforce management in a time of crisis. Webinar presented to the Australian Human Resources Institute. See also Jackson, S. (2020, Apr.). Pandemics: Plan but don't panic. *HR Professionals Magazine* 10(4), pp. 40, 41.

62. See, for example, Alexander, C. (1998). *The Endurance: Shackleton's Legendary Antarctic Expedition*. New York: Alfred A. Knopf.

63. Austin (2020), op. cit. *See also* Noguchi, Y. (2020, Mar. 15). 8 tips to make working from home work for you. *National Public Radio.* Retrieved from *www.npr. org/2020/03/15/815549926/8-tips-to-make-working-from-home-work-for-you* on May 26, 2020.

64. Society for Human Resource Management. (2019). *2019 Employee Benefits.* Alexandria, VA: Author.

65. Miller, S. (2019, Aug. 14). Underused EAPs are a missed opportunity to help workers. *SHRM Online.* Retrieved from *www.shrm.org/resourcesandtools/hr-topics/benefits/pages/ under-used-eaps-are-a-missed-opportunity.aspx* on May 27, 2020.

66. Hirsch, A. S. (2016, Oct. 12). Taking a fresh look at EAP counseling. *SHRM Online.* Retrieved from *www.shrm.org/resourcesandtools/hr-topics/employee-relations/pages/taking- a-fresh-look-at-eap-counseling.aspx* on Oct. 17, 2016.

67. Attridge, M., Sharar, D., DeLapp, G., and Veder, B. (2018). EAP Works: Global results from 24,363 counseling cases with pre-post data on the Workplace Outcome Suite. *International Journal of Health and Productivity* 10(2), pp. 5–25.

68. Miller (2019), op. cit. *See also* Agovino, T. (2019). So close, yet so far. *HRMagazine* 64(4), pp. 50–55.

69. Hirsch (2016), op. cit. *See also* Stone, D. L., and Kotch, D. A. (1989). Individuals' attitudes toward organizational drug-testing policies and practices. *Journal of Applied Psychology* 74, pp. 518–21.

70. National Business Group on Health (2009), op. cit. *See also* Milne, S. H., Blum, T. C., and Roman, P. M. (1994). Factors influencing employees' propensity to use an employee assistance program. *Personnel Psychology* 47, pp. 123–45.

71. Collins, K. R. (2003, Jan.). Identifying and treating employee substance abuse problems. Retrieved from *www.shrm.org/Research/Articles/Articles/Pages/CMS_000187.aspx* on Oct. 27, 2004.

72. Cascio, W. F., Boudreau, J. W.. and Fink, A. (2019). *Investing in People: Financial Impact of Human Resource Initiatives* (3rd ed.). Alexandria, VA: SHRM Publishing. *See also* Foote, A., and Erfurt, J. (1981, Sept.–Oct.). Evaluating an employee assistance program. *EAP Digest,* pp. 14–25.

73. Grossman (2010), op. cit. *See also* Collins (2003), op. cit. *See also* Collins, K. (2001b, Apr.). HR must find new ways to battle substance abuse in the workplace. *HR News,* pp. 11, 16.

74. Agovino (2019), op. cit.

75. Miller (2019), op. cit.

76. Sponenberg, T., quoted in Agovino (2019), op. cit., p. 53.

77. Miller (2019), op. cit. *See also* Wilkie, D. (2017, Jan. 31). Drunk at work: What HR can do about employees drinking on the job. *SHRM Online.* Retrieved from *www.shrm.org/ resourcesandtools/hr-topics/employee-relations/pages/drunk-on-the-job-.aspx* on Feb. 1, 2017. *See also* Falcone, P. (2003, May). Dealing with employees in crisis. *HRMagazine,* pp. 117–21.

78. Beck, M. (2008, Jan. 8). Are you an alcoholic? *The Wall Street Journal,* pp. D1, D2.

79. Wilkie (2017), op. cit. *See also* Grossman (2010), op. cit. *See also* National Institute on Alcohol Abuse and Alcoholism. (2011). FAQs for the general public. Retrieved from *www.niaaa.nih.gov/FAQs/General-English/Pages/default.aspx* on Aug. 29, 2011. *See also* Gurchiek, K. (2007b, July 20). Few organizations deal proactively with substance abuse. *HR News.* Retrieved from *www.shrm.org/Publications/HRNews/Pages/CMS_022375.aspx* on Aug. 29, 2011.

80. Wilkie (2017), op. cit. *See also* Grossman (2010), op. cit. *See also* Frone, M. R. (2006). Prevalence and distribution of alcohol use and impairment in the workplace: A U.S. national survey. *Journal of Studies of Alcohol* 76, pp. 147–56.

81. Grossman (2010), op. cit. *See also* Lockwood, N. R. (2004b, Sept.). Employee assistance programs: Targeting substance and alcohol abuse. Retrieved from *www.shrm.org/Research/ Articles/Articles/Pages/EAP_20Series_20Part_20II_20_20EAP%27s_20Targeting_20Substance_2 0and_20Alcohol_20Abuse.aspx* on Oct. 27, 2009.

82. Addiction Center. (2020, Apr. 28). Cost of drug and alcohol rehab. Retrieved from *www.addictioncenter.com/rehab-questions/cost-of-drug-and-alcohol-treatment/* on May 27, 2020.

83. Lytle, T. (2014, June). Marijuana maelstrom. *HRMagazine,* pp. 42–48. *See also* Grossman (2010), op. cit. *See also* Collins (2003), op. cit.

84. *Safety and Health.* (2018, June 7). Positive drug tests among U.S. workers remain at 13-year high: Annual index. Retrieved from *www.safetyandhealthmagazine.com/articles/17132-positive-drug-tests-among-us-workers-remain-at-13-year-high-annual-index* on May 27, 2020.

85. Lytle, T. (2014, June). Marijuana maelstrom. *HRMagazine,* pp. 42–48.

86. DWI Resource Center. (2018). What does alcohol and drug abuse cost your business? Retrieved from *https://dwiresourcecenter.org/index.php/what-does-alcohol-drug-use-cost-your-business/* on May 27, 2020.

87. Ibid. *See also* Canadian Centre for Occupational Health and Safety. Substance abuse in the workplace. Retrieved from *www.ccohs.ca/oshanswers/psychosocial/substance.html* on June 28, 2017. *See also* Drug Free Idaho. (2010). How drug use affects the workplace: Statistics. Retrieved from *www.drugfreeidaho.org/?s=How+drug+use+affects+the+workplace&x=0&y=0* on Aug. 30, 2011. *See also* Lehman, W. E. K., and Simpson, D. D. (1992). Employee substance abuse and on-the-job behaviors. *Journal of Applied Psychology* 77, pp. 309–21.

88. Drug tests keep paying off, but continued gains are tougher. (1998, May 5). *The Wall Street Journal,* p. A1. *See also* Normand, J., Salyards, S. D., and Mahoney, J. J. (1990). An evaluation of pre-employment drug testing. *Journal of Applied Psychology* 75, pp. 629–39.

89. DWI Resource Center (2018), op. cit. *See also* Is substance abuse costing your company? Retrieved from www.summitholdings.com/wc/News/2011/3/31/Is+Substance+Abuse+Costing+Your+Company%3F on July 1, 2014.

90. Sahadi, J. (2015, Aug. 26). How common is workplace violence? *CNNMoney.* Retrieved from *http://money.cnn.com/2015/08/26/news/workplace-violence-virginia-shooting/index.html* on June 28, 2017.

91. Romano, S. J., Levi-Minzi, M. E., Rugala, E. A., and Van Hasselt, V. B. (2011, Jan.). Workplace violence prevention. *FBI Law Enforcement Bulletin.* Retrieved from *www.fbi.gov/stats-services/publications/law-enforcement-bulletin/january2011/workplace_violence prevention* on Aug. 30, 2011. *See also* Neuman, J. H., and Baron, R. A. (1998). Workplace violence and workplace aggression: Evidence concerning specific forms, potential causes, and preferred targets. *Journal of Management* 24, pp. 391–419.

92. Lebron, A. (2020, Apr. 28). The latest on workplace violence statistics. *Rave Mobile Safety.* Retrieved from *www.ravemobilesafety.com/blog/latest-workplace-violence-statistics* on May 27, 2020. *See also* Romano et al. (2011), op. cit. *See also* Fisher, A. (2005, Feb. 21). How to prevent violence at work. *Fortune,* p. 42.

93. Romano et al. (2011), op. cit. *See also* Dewan, S., and Hubbell, J. M. (2008, Aug. 15). Arkansas suspect quit job on day of killing. *The New York Times.* Retrieved from *www.nytimes.com/2008/08/15/us/15arkansas.html?scp=1&sq=Arkansas%20suspect%20quit%20job%20on%20day%20of%20killing&st=cse* on Aug. 15, 2008. *See also* Madkour, R. (2007, Apr. 22). Job review spurred shooting. *The Denver Post,* p. 2A.

94. Romano et al. (2011), op. cit. *See also* Kane, D., quoted in Fisher (2005), op. cit., p. 42.

95. Greenberg, J. (2010). Organizational injustice as an occupational health risk. *Academy of Management Annals* 4, pp. 205–43.

96. Biro, M. M. (2013, Sept. 8). Is your workplace prepared for violence? *Forbes.* Retrieved from *www.forbes.com/sites/meghanbiro/2013/09/08/is-your-workplace-prepared-for-violence/print/* on July 2, 2014. *See also* Hoey, B. (2013, Nov.). Defuse workplace violence. *HRMagazine,* pp. 67–69. *See also* Romano et al. (2011), op. cit. *See also* Thelen, J. B. (2009, Dec.). Is that a threat? *HRMagazine,* pp. 61–63.

97. Lebron (2020), op. cit. *See also* Romano et al. (2011), op. cit. *See also* Fisher (2005), op. cit.

98. Nagele-Piazza, L. (2018, Oct. 15). 4 ways to reduce the risk of violence in the workplace. *SHRM Online.* Retrieved from *www.shrm.org/resourcesandtools/legal-and-compliance/ employment-law/pages/reducing-the-risk-of-violence-in-the-workplace.aspx* on Oct. 15, 2018. *See also* Hoey (2013), op. cit. *See also* Romano et al. (2011), op. cit.

99. American National Standards Institute. (2011, Sept. 2). *Workplace Violence Prevention and Intervention.* Alexandria, VA: ASIS/SHRM. *See also* Romano et al. (2011), op. cit. *See also* Thelen (2009), op. cit. *See also* Bush (2002), op. cit.

100. Thorpe, K., and Lever, J. (2011). Prevention: The answer to curbing chronically high healthcare costs. Retrieved from *www.kaiserhealthnews.org/Columns/2011/May/ 052411thorpelever.aspx* on July 2, 2014.

101. Centers for Disease Control and Prevention. (2020, Feb. 27). Adult obesity facts. Retrieved from *www.cdc.gov/obesity/data/adult.html* on May 28, 2020.

102. Ibid.

103. Back injury statistics (2020, Jan. 30). *The Good Body.* Retrieved from *www.thegoodbody. com/back-injury-statistics/* on May 28, 2020. *See also* Hollenbeck, J. R., Ilgen, D. R., and Crampton, S. M. (1992). Lower back disability in occupational settings: A review of the literature from a human resource management view. *Personnel Psychology* 45, pp. 247–78.

104. Spine Research Institute. (2014, Aug. 15). Addressing the high corporate costs of back pain (and other MSDs). Retrieved from *https://spine.osu.edu/blog/2014/08/addressing-high-corporate-costs-back-pain-and-other-msds* on June 28, 2017. See also Grossman, R. J. (2001, Aug.). Back with a vengeance. *HRMagazine,* pp. 36–46.

105. Centers for Disease Control and Prevention. (2020, May 28). Fact sheet: Health effects of cigarette smoking. Retrieved from *www.cdc.gov/tobacco/data_statistics/fact_sheets/health_ effects/effects_cig_smoking/index.htm* on May 28, 2020. *See also* American Lung Association. (2020, May 13). Tobacco facts. Retrieved from *www.lung.org/research/sotc/by-the-numbers* on May 28, 2020.

106. U.S. Department of Health and Human Services. (2020). Cardiovascular disease: Costs and consequences. Retrieved from *https://millionhearts.hhs.gov/learn-prevent/cost-conse-quences.html* on May 28, 2020.

107. Mathews, A. W. (2016, Aug. 23). Health services get smarter about nudging employees. *The Wall Street Journal,* p. D2. *See also* Brandt, S., Hartmann, J., and Hehner, S. (2010, Oct.). How to design a successful disease-management program. *McKinsey Insights.* Retrieved from *www.mckinsey.com/insights/health_systems_and_services/how_to_design_a_successful_ disease-management_program* on July 2, 2014.

108. Katsnelson, A. (2018, July 31). Do "workplace wellness" programs work? *Knowable Magazine.* Retrieved from *www.knowablemagazine.org/article/health-disease/2018/do-work-place-wellness-programs-work* on May 28, 2020. *See also* Chenoweth, D. (2012). *Wellness Strategies.* Alexandria, VA: Society for Human Resource Management Foundation.

109. Terborg, J. (1998). Health psychology in the United States: A critique and selected review. *Applied Psychology: An International Review* 47(2), pp. 199–217. *See also* Epstein, S. S. (1989). *A Note on Health Promotion in the Workplace.* Boston: Harvard Business School.

110. Centers for Disease Control and Prevention (2020), op. cit. *See also* American Lung Association (2020), op. cit.

111. Putnam, L. (2018, May 1). From gatekeeper to multiplier. *T+D Magazine.* Retrieved from *www.td.org/magazines/td-magazine/from-gatekeeper-to-multiplier* on May 2, 2018.

112. Katsnelson (2018), op. cit. *See also* Jones, J. R. (2015, July). Wellness incentives are here to stay. *HR Professionals Magazine,* p. 22. *See also* Berry, L. L., Mirabito, A. M., and Baun, W. B. (2010, Dec.). What's the hard return on employee wellness programs? *Harvard Business Review,* pp. 104–12. *See also* Wells, S. J. (2010, Feb.). Getting paid for staying well. *HRMagazine,* pp. 59–62.

113. Miller, S. (2013, Apr. 24). More employers link premiums to wellness. Retrieved from *www.shrm.org/hrdisciplines/benefits/articles/pages/premiums-wellness-link.aspx* on July 2, 2014. *See also* Aeppel, T. (2003, June 17). Ill will: Skyrocketing health costs start to pit worker vs. worker. *The Wall Street Journal,* pp. A1, A6. *See also* Schlosser, J. (2003, Feb. 3). Uphill battle. *Fortune,* p. 64.

114. Carlson, S. A., Fulton, J. E., Pratt, M., Yang, Z., and Adams, E. K. (2015). Inadequate physical activity and health care expenditures in the United States. *Progress in Cardiovascular Diseases* 57, pp. 315–23.

115. Aldana, S. (2020, Jan. 2). This is the impact of your employee wellness on healthcare costs. *WellSteps*. Retrieved from *www.wellsteps.com/blog/2020/01/02/impact-employee-wellness-health-care-costs/* on May 28, 2020.

116. Katsnelson (2018), op. cit.

117. Cascio et al. (2019), op. cit.

118. Baxter, S., Sanderson, K., Venn, A. J., Blizzard, C. L., and Palmer, A. J. (2014). The relationship between return on investment and quality of study methodology in workplace health-promotion programs. *American Journal of Health Promotion* 28(6), pp. 347-63.

119. Jones (2015), op. cit.

120. Passport Health. (2020). How much do employee wellness programs cost? Retrieved from *www.passporthealthusa.com/employer-solutions/blog/2019-5-how-much-do-wellness-programs-cost/* on May 28, 2020.

121. Aldana (2020), op. cit.

122. Aldana, S. G. (2015). Three years of worksite wellness. *WellSteps*. Retrieved from *www.wellsteps.com/files/three_years_of_wellness.pdf* on May 28, 2020. *See also* Aldana, S. G. (2001). Financial impact of health-promotion programs: A comprehensive review of the literature. *American Journal of Health Promotion* 15(5), pp. 295-320.

123. Katsnelson (2018), op. cit.

124. Feltman, R. (2014, Jan. 7). Companies could be wasting money on wellness programs for employees who don't need them. Retrieved from *http://qz.com/164374/companies-could-be-wasting-money-on-wellness-programs-for-employees-who-dont-need-them/* on July 2, 2014. *See also* Miller (2013), op. cit. *See also* Pelletier, K. R. (2001). A review and analysis of the clinical and cost-effectiveness studies of comprehensive health-promotion and disease-management programs at the worksite: 1998-2000 update. *American Journal of Health Promotion* 16(2), pp. 107-16.

125. Ibid. *See also* Katsnelson (2018), op. cit. *See also* Edington, M. D., Karjalainen, T., Hirschland, D., and Edington, D. W. (2002). The UAW-GM health-promotion program: Successful outcomes. *AAOHN Journal* 50(1), pp. 25-31.

126. Miller, S. (2019, May 1). Wellness programs' value disputed, defended. *SHRM Online*. Retrieved from *www.shrm.org/resourcesandtools/hr-topics/benefits/pages/wellness-programs-value-disputed-defended.aspx* on May 28, 2020. *See also* Berry et al. (2010), op. cit. *See also* Chenoweth (2012), op. cit.

127. EEOC (2020), op. cit. *See also* Nemeth, P., and Myers, K. (2014, Jan. 24). Legal implications of employer-sponsored wellness programs. Retrieved from *www.shrm.org/legalissues/federalresources/pages/wellness-programs.aspx* on July 2, 2014.

128. Overman (2010), op. cit. *See also* Onley, D. (2005, Jan.). Doc in a box. *HRMagazine*, pp. 83-85.

129. Lytle (2014), op. cit. *See also* Witkiewitz, K., and Marlatt, A. (2004). Relapse prevention for alcohol and drug problems. *American Psychologist* 59, pp. 224–35.

16 INTERNATIONAL DIMENSIONS OF HUMAN RESOURCE MANAGEMENT

Questions This Chapter Will Help Managers Answer

LO 16-1 What makes cultures different?

LO 16-2 How should I approach expatriate recruitment, selection, orientation, and training?

LO 16-3 How should an expatriate compensation package be structured?

LO 16-4 What factors should I consider in assessing the performance of managers and employees from a different culture?

LO 16-5 What special issues deserve attention in the repatriation of overseas employees?

WHAT'S IT LIKE TO BE A GLOBAL MANAGER?*

My first day on the job is turning into a nightmare. I am about to meet with a promising young manager who has just botched a new assignment, and in just a few hours, I'm scheduled to make a strategy presentation to my new boss. But the phone won't stop ringing, and I'm being deluged with e-mail.

It's a good thing this isn't really happening. I'm at a makeshift office in suburban London, taking part in a workplace-simulation exercise. It's just like the one that hundreds of Motorola Inc. (now Motorola Solutions) executives around the world will go through in the coming months as part of a wide-ranging effort at the company to identify and evaluate tomorrow's top international managers.

Like many multinationals, Motorola is pressing to find talented leaders to run its increasingly complicated global business (more than 100,000 customers in 100 countries). As companies cross borders to make acquisitions and expand operations, the demand for employees with international management skills is growing exponentially. The consequences can be dire for firms that fail to build up a cadre of competent global managers. Poor decisions can lead to multibillion-dollar flubs, as products flop and marketing campaigns go awry.

Motorola's Internet-based assessment, developed with Aon Consulting Worldwide (now Aon Hewitt), can be administered remotely anyplace in the world. As Aon Hewitt executives explained to me how the simulation would work, I imagined myself enduring several hours of awkward play-acting. In practice, the experience is startlingly lifelike.

My role is Chris Jefferson, regional manager in the finance unit of a fictitious conglomerate, Globalcom. My tablet computer allows me to send and receive e-mail and texts, look up information about my employer, and consult my calendar–where several meetings have already been scheduled. An Aon Hewitt psychologist will play several roles, phoning me from an adjacent office and popping in at the end in the role of Jean Dubois, my boss.

As soon as I settle in to my windowless, brick-walled office, the phone calls, texts, and e-mails begin, and unexpected visitors arrive. Urgent tasks come so fast and furiously that I quickly forget it is all a game. Several calls and e-mails concern a promising middle manager who has let several details of a critical new assignment slip.

Another Aon Hewitt psychologist is playing the role of the manager, and he enters my office for our meeting. I try teasing out of him information about what's going wrong. We talk for several minutes before a voice in the back of my brain reminds me that it's all only make-believe.

The meeting is over and I have less than 2 hours to get my presentation ready. I hurry to prepare, scouring my computer for information about Globalcom. I find things like market research, news reports, results of an employee survey, and corporate press releases, but just like one of those bad dreams, I keep getting sidetracked by a steady stream of phone calls. An irate customer rails shrilly at me about poor service and threatens to bolt to the competition. Texts and e-mails, some of them demanding immediate attention, keep popping up on my computer screen.

Source: About Motorola Solutions. Retrieved from *www.motorolasolutions.com/en_us/about.html* on June 1, 2020. Lamson, M. (2018, June 20). New global managers: Tools and tips you'll need to be successful. *Inc.* Retrieved from *www.inc.com/melissa-lamson/10-never-fail-strategies-for-new-global-manager.html* on June 1, 2020. Woodruff, D. (2000, Nov. 21). Your career matters: Distractions make global manager a difficult role. *The Wall Street Journal.*

Challenges

1. Can you identify any differences between managing domestically and managing internationally?
2. How accurate are such workplace simulations?
3. Do simulations like Motorola's "travel well"? That is, do you think they will work in different cultures?

Increasingly, the world is becoming a "global village" as multinational investment continues to grow. All the HR management issues that we have discussed to this point are interrelated conceptually and operationally and are particularly relevant in the international context: strategic workforce planning, recruitment, selection, orientation, training and development, career management, compensation, and labor relations. In examining all these issues, as well as considering the special problems of **repatriation** (the process of reentering one's native culture after being absent from it), this chapter thus provides a capstone to the book.

THE GLOBAL CORPORATION: A FACT OF MODERN ORGANIZATIONAL LIFE

As we noted in Chapter 1, globalization is the ability of any individual or company to compete, connect, exchange, or collaborate globally. We noted that the ability to digitize so many things, to send them anywhere, and to pull them in from everywhere via our mobile phones and the Internet has unleashed a torrent of global flows of information and knowledge that is interlacing markets, media, central banks, companies, schools, communities, and individuals more tightly together than ever before.[1] To begin to appreciate the magnitude of this trend, consider a snapshot of the 2019 *Fortune* Global 500 (the largest 500 firms in the world). Their aggregate revenues were $32.7 trillion, with profits of $2.15 trillion, and they provided jobs for 69.3 million of the world's people.[2]

Labor Markets Have Become Global

Cheap labor and plentiful resources, combined with ease of travel and communication, have created global labor markets. This is fueling mobility as more companies expand abroad and people consider foreign postings as a natural part of their professional development. Beyond the positive effects that such circulation of talent brings to both developed and developing countries, it enables employment opportunities well beyond the borders of one's home country.[3] This means that competition for talent will come not only from the company down the street but also from the employer on the other side of the world. It will be a seller's market, with talented individuals having many choices. Countries as well as companies will need to brand themselves as employers of choice in order to attract this talent.[4]

At the same time, the World Wide Web is changing the ways people live and work. Consider e-commerce as an example. During the coronavirus pandemic, as millions of people around the world sheltered in place, Amazon touched nearly every part of life–from household essentials and groceries to streaming, gaming, crafts, news, and entertainment. The web is also making leaps in creativity possible, enabling mass collaboration through file-sharing, blogs, and social-networking services.[5] These trends are shaping three others.

The first is increasing workforce flux as more roles are automated or outsourced and more workers are contract-based, are mobile, or work flexible hours.[6] This may allow companies to leverage global resources more efficiently, but it also will increase the complexity of management's role. Second, expect more diversity as workers come from a greater range of backgrounds. Those with local knowledge of an emerging market, a global outlook, and an intuitive sense of the corporate culture will be particularly valued. Not surprisingly, talented young people will more frequently choose their employers based, at least in part, on opportunities to gain international experience. Finally, technical skills, although mandatory, will be less defining of the successful manager than the ability of that manager to work across cultures and to build relationships with many different constituents.

The Backlash against Globalization

Open borders have allowed new ideas and technology to flow freely around the globe, accelerating productivity growth and allowing companies to be more competitive than they have been in decades. Yet there is a growing fear on the part of many people that globalization benefits big companies instead of average citizens, as stagnating wages and growing job insecurity in developed countries create rising disenchantment. In theory, less-developed countries win from globalization because they get jobs making low-cost products for rich countries. Rich countries win because, in addition to being able to buy inexpensive imports, they also can sell more sophisticated products, like financial services, to emerging economies.[7] The problem, according to many experts, is that workers in the West are not equipped for today's pace of change, in which jobs come and go and skills can quickly become redundant.[8]

The coronavirus pandemic highlighted the downsides of extensive international integration. Large multinationals suddenly realized the risks of relying on complex global supply chains. At the same time, governments of all stripes rushed to impose travel bans, additional visa requirements, and export restrictions, thereby escalating nationalism and protectionism. The pandemic is likely to have a lasting impact, although the exact extent is, as yet, unknown. It may deal a blow to fragmented international supply chains, reduce the hypermobility of global business travelers, and encourage nationalists who favor greater protectionism and immigration controls.[9]

Localization requirements are also part of the backlash against globalization. Since 2008, governments have imposed nearly 350 regulations worldwide requiring local sourcing, hiring, or operations. Government-backed development banks require projects to buy or build domestically in exchange for inexpensive financing.[10]

In the public eye, multinational corporations are synonymous with globalization. In all of their far-flung operations, therefore, they bear responsibility to be good corporate citizens, to preserve the environment, to uphold labor standards, to provide decent working conditions and competitive wages, to treat their employees fairly, and to contribute to the communities in which they operate. Some have done so admirably. Levi Strauss & Co. has ethical manufacturing standards for its overseas operations. Home Depot Inc. has adopted an eco-friendly lumber-supply program with the Rainforest Action Network. Starbucks is working with Conservation

International to buy coffee from farmers preserving forests.[11] Actions like these make a strong case for continued globalization.

Multinational enterprises (MNEs), those that operate in more than one country, together with their foreign affiliates, account for one third of world output and GDP and two-thirds of international trade.[12] Before proceeding further, let's define some terms that we will use throughout the chapter:

- An **expatriate**, or *foreign-service employee*, is a generic term applied to anyone working outside her or his home country with a planned return to that or a third country.
- **Home country** is the expatriate's country of residence.
- **Host country** is the country in which the expatriate is working.
- A **third-country national** is an expatriate who has transferred to an additional country while working abroad. A German working for a U.S. firm in Spain is a third-country national.

Expatriates staff many, if not most, overseas operations of multinational enterprises, and the costs can be astronomical.

The Costs of Overseas Executives

One of the first lessons global corporations learn is that it is far cheaper to hire competent host-country nationals (if they are available) than to send their own executives overseas. Foreign-service employees typically cost at least twice the salary of a comparable domestic employee, and often many more times the salary of a local national employee in the assignment country. Factors like the following all work to boost costs: differences in the costs of goods and services as well as housing; assignment allowances, such as education, home leave, and tax-preparation fees; relocation expenses, such as airfares, pre-move house-hunting expenses, shipping costs in and out, lump-sum relocation allowances in and out, and language training; and extra taxes due in home and host countries. Thus, an employee with a $200,000 base salary can easily cost his or her firm more than $1.5 million for a 3-year assignment.

Although the exact number of U.S. expatriates is not known, the State Department estimates it at about 9 million, and the number is growing. Indeed, the Millennial generation views overseas assignments as a rite of passage. A 2019 study by Mercer HR Consulting revealed that the number of employees on international assignments has doubled over the last 3 years. The major reason is business growth. The duration of those assignments is changing, however. Over the next 5 years, MNEs expect to rely more on shorter-duration assignments (i.e., extended business trips, developmental/training assignments). They expect the use of long-term assignments (e.g., 3–5 years) to decrease.[13]

According to the Economist Intelligence Unit, the 10 most expensive cities in the world for expatriates in 2020 were Singapore, Osaka (Japan), Hong Kong (tied for 1st); New York; Paris and Zurich (Switzerland) (tied for 5th); Tel Aviv; Los Angeles and Tokyo (tied for 8th); and Geneva (Switzerland).[14]

Of course, costs fluctuate with international exchange rates relative to the U.S. dollar. In view of these high costs, firms are working hard to reduce these costs—for example, through the use of **efficient-purchaser indexes** for established expatriates. Such indexes assume that a person is not completely new to a location, has learned about some local brands and outlets, and therefore pays prices that are lower

Experiencing new foods is an important aspect of the expatriate experience.
Yurii Vasyliev/Shutterstock

than a newcomer would pay.[15] Firms also are working hard to reduce the failure rate among their expatriates, where failure is defined as a return home before the period of assignment is completed or as unmet business objectives. That rate is about 5 to 10 percent of expatriate assignments but may be as high as 50 percent in developing countries.[16] For companies, the costs of mistaken expatriation include the costs of initial recruitment, relocation expenses, premium compensation, repatriation costs (i.e., costs associated with resettling the expatriate), replacement costs, and the tangible costs of poor job performance. When an overseas assignment does not work out, it still costs a company, on average, twice the employee's base salary. For employees, the costs are more personal: diminished self-esteem, impaired relationships, and interrupted careers.[17]

Although the costs of expatriates are considerable, there are also compensating benefits to multinational firms. In particular, overseas postings allow managers to develop international experience outside their home countries–the kind of experience needed to compete successfully in the global economy that we now live in.

Nevertheless, it is senseless to send people abroad who do not know what they are doing overseas and cannot be effective in the foreign culture. More specifically, companies need to consider the impact of culture on international HR management. But what is culture? **Culture** refers to characteristic ways of doing things and behaving that people in a given country or region have evolved over time. It helps people to make sense of their part of the world and provides them with an identity. It is rooted in fundamental values and beliefs.

THE ROLE OF CULTURAL UNDERSTANDING IN INTERNATIONAL MANAGEMENT PRACTICE

Managers who have no appreciation for cultural differences have a **local perspective**. They believe in the inherent superiority of their own group and culture, and they tend to look down on those considered "foreign." Rather than accepting differences as legitimate, they view and measure foreign cultures in terms of their own.

By contrast, managers with a **cosmopolitan perspective** are sensitive to cultural differences, respect the distinctive practices of others, and make allowances for such factors when communicating with representatives of different cultural groups. Recognizing that culture and behavior are relative, they are more tentative and less absolute in their interactions with others.[18]

Such cultural understanding can minimize **culture shock**–"frustrations, conflict, anxiety, and feelings of alienation when entering an unfamiliar culture"–and allows managers to be more effective with both employees and customers. The first step in this process is an increase in general awareness of differences across cultures because such differences deeply affect human resource management practices.[19]

HUMAN RESOURCE MANAGEMENT PRACTICES AS A CULTURAL VARIABLE

Particularly when business does not go well, those returning from overseas assignments tend to blame the local people, calling them irresponsible, unmotivated, or downright dishonest. Such judgments are pointless, for many of the problems are a matter of fundamental cultural differences that profoundly affect how different people view the world and operate in business. This section presents a systematic framework of 10 broad classifications that will help managers assess any culture and examine its people systematically. It does not consider every aspect of culture, and by no means is it the only way to analyze culture. Rather, it is a useful beginning for cultural understanding. The framework comprises the following 10 factors:[20]

- Sense of self and space.
- Dress and appearance.
- Food and eating habits.
- Communication and language.
- Time and time consciousness.
- Relationships.
- Values and norms.
- Beliefs and attitudes.
- Work motivation and practices.
- Mental processes and learning.

Sense of Self and Space

Self-identity may be manifested by a humble bearing in some places and by macho behavior in others. Some countries (e.g., the United States) promote independence and creativity, whereas others (e.g., Japan) emphasize group cooperation and conformity. Americans have a sense of space that requires more distance between people, whereas Latins and Vietnamese prefer to get much closer. Each culture has its own unique ways of doing things.

Dress and Appearance

Dress includes outward garments as well as body decorations. Many cultures wear distinctive clothing–the Japanese kimono, the Indian turban, the Polynesian sarong, the "organization-man or -woman" look of business, and uniforms that distinguish wearers from everybody else. Cosmetics are more popular and accepted in some cultures than in others, as is cologne or after-shave lotion for men.

Food and Eating Habits

The manner in which food is selected, prepared, presented, and eaten often differs by culture. Most major cities have restaurants that specialize in the distinctive cuisine of various cultures–everything from Afghan to Zambian. Eating habits also differ, ranging from bare hands to chopsticks to full sets of cutlery. Subcultures exist as well, including the executive's dining room, the soldier's mess hall, and the worker's sandwich shop. Knowledge of food and eating habits often provides insights into customs and culture.

Communication and Language

The axiom "Words mean different things to different people" is especially true in cross-cultural communication. When an American says she is "tabling" a proposition, it is generally accepted that it will be put off. In England, "tabling" means to discuss something now. Translations from one language to another can generate even more confusion as a result of differences in style and context. As an example, consider the word *retaliation* in the context of the workplace.

In English, retaliation refers to any negative job action, such as demotion, discipline, reassignment, or termination. In many other languages, however, retaliation is translated as "revenge" or some other concept that incorporates physical violence. This is obviously not what is intended as a response to an employee who complains about a workplace issue.[21]

In many cultures, directness and openness are not appreciated. An open person may be seen as weak and untrustworthy, and directness can be interpreted as abrupt, hostile behavior. Providing specific details may be seen as insulting to one's intelligence. Insisting on a written contract may suggest that a person's word is not good.

Nonverbal cues may also mean different things. In the United States, one who does not look someone in the eye arouses suspicion and is called "shifty-eyed." In some other countries, however, looking someone in the eye is perceived as aggression. Just as communication skills are key ingredients for success in U.S. business, such skills are basic to success in international business. There is no compromise on this issue; ignorance of local customs and communications protocol is disrespectful.[22]

Time and Time Consciousness

To Americans, time is money. We live by schedules, deadlines, and agendas; we hate to be kept waiting, and we like to "get down to business" quickly. In many countries, however, people simply will not be rushed. They arrive late for appointments, and business is preceded by hours of social rapport. People in a rush are thought to be arrogant and untrustworthy.

In the United States, the most important issues are generally discussed first when making a business deal. In Ethiopia, however, the most important things are taken up last. Although being late seems to be the norm for business meetings in Latin America, the reverse is true in Switzerland, Sweden, and Germany, where prompt efficiency is the watchword.[23] The lesson for Americans doing business overseas is clear: *Be flexible about time and realistic about what can be accomplished.* Adapt to the process of doing business in any particular country.

Relationships

Cultures fix human and organizational relationships by age, gender, status, and family relationships, as well as by wealth, power, and wisdom. Relationships between and among people vary by category–in some cultures, the elderly are honored; in others, they are ignored. In some cultures, women must wear veils and act deferentially; in others, the female is considered the equal, if not the superior, of the male.

In some cultures (e.g., France, Japan, Korea, and to some extent the United States and Great Britain), where a person went to school may affect his or her status.[24] Often, lifelong relationships are established among individuals who attend the same school. Finally, the issue of nepotism is viewed very differently in different parts of the world. Whereas most U.S. firms frown upon the practice of hiring or contracting work directly with family members, in Latin America and Arab countries, it only makes sense to hire someone you can trust.[25]

Values and Norms

Values reflect what is important in a society. For example, in Arab culture, dignity, honor, and reputation are considered to be paramount virtues. America is a country in the midst of a values revolution. While Americans have become far more socially tolerant of different lifestyles, they see a decline in family values and worry about their children's future. At the same time, they believe they can achieve anything they want through sheer hard work.[26]

From its value system, a culture sets **norms of behavior**, or what some call "local customs." One such norm is that in Eastern countries, businesspeople strive for successful business outcomes after personal relationships have been established, whereas Westerners develop social relationships after business interests have been addressed. International managers ignore such norms at their peril.[27] For example, consider the impact of values and norms on management styles and HR practices in the European Union. See the nearby International Application feature.

Beliefs and Attitudes

To some degree, religion expresses the philosophy of a people about important facets in life. Whereas Western culture is largely influenced by Judeo-Christian traditions and Middle Eastern culture by Islam, Asian and Indian cultures are dominated by Buddhism, Confucianism, Taoism, and Hinduism. In cultures where a religious view of work still prevails, work is viewed as an act of service to God and people and is expressed in a moral commitment to the job or quality of effort. In Japan, the cultural loyalty to family is transferred to the work organization. It is expressed in work-group participation, communication, and consensus.[28]

T. Fujisawa, cofounder of Honda Motor Co., once remarked: "Japanese and American management is 95 percent the same, and differs in all important respects." In other words, although organizations are becoming more similar in terms of structure and technology, people's emotions, attitudes, and behavior within those organizations continue to reveal culturally based differences.[29]

INTERNATIONAL APPLICATION
Human Resource Management in the European Union

The European Union (EU) comprises 27 countries (after the United Kingdom left on January 31, 2020). The oldest members are Austria, Belgium, Denmark, Finland, France, Germany, Ireland, Italy, Greece, Luxembourg, Netherlands, Portugal, Spain, and Sweden. The newest members include Bulgaria, Croatia, Cyprus, Czech Republic, Estonia, Hungary, Latvia, Lithuania, Malta, Poland, Romania, Slovakia, and Slovenia. With its new members, the EU represents a consumer market of 445 million people. It is the largest single trading block in the world and the top trading partner for 80 countries.[a] A central EU theme is respect for differences that we live with; we do not fight about them.

The EU represents the economic and political unification of Europe—the free movement of capital, goods, and people and the harmonization of EU legislation. Does this mean that multinationals operating in Europe can deal with people in the various EU countries in a universal manner? Is there such a thing as "European HRM"? The answer is no. There is no harmonized manner in which HR services are delivered across or within the various European countries. Rather, Euro-HRM is a mosaic of practices that differ primarily on the basis of the size of a company and the different national, cultural, legal, and geographic contexts. Outsiders should know eight key things about HRM in the EU countries:[b]

1. Each country has a unique set of intricate laws that govern employment and labor relations.
2. Each country has a unique culture that impacts management styles and the corporate cultures of companies.
3. Within some EU countries there are different subcultures that influence HRM.
4. The power of the labor unions is decreasing, but labor relations issues remain very important.
5. Each country has developed a set of institutions that reflects its traditions and influences the way HR is practiced.
6. Distinct underlying social models have an impact on the way HR is practiced in each country. For example, in the Dutch social-justice model, the government plays an active, interventionist role to provide social justice in areas such as occupational health, safety, and terminations. In contrast, the Italian social model is a mixture of Christian and Marxist values. It emphasizes the individual's need for protection and solidarity and is less meritocratic and competitive than Protestant cultures.
7. There are formal consultation processes in place that allow for greater involvement of employees and trade unions in the decision-making processes of companies.
8. Importing HR practices from abroad without attempting to localize them to the specific culture, laws, and languages of the country provides little chance of successful implementation.

---

[a]EU position in world trade. (2020). Retrieved from *https://ec.europa.eu/trade/policy/eu-position-in-world-trade/#:~:text=The%20EU%20is%20the%20largest,the%20world's%20largest%20trading%20block.&text=The%20EU%20is%20the%20top%20trading%20partner%20for%2080%20countries* on June 1, 2020.

[b]Brin, D. W. (2020, Spring). Smoother sailing. *HRMagazine* 65(1), pp. 75-81. Reiche, S., Harzing, A. W., and Tenzer, H. (2019). *International Human Resource Management* (5th ed.). Thousand Oaks, CA: Sage. Tarique, I., Briscoe, D., and Schuler, R. (2016). *International Human Resource Management*. (5th ed.) New York: Routledge.

Work Motivation and Practices

Knowledge of what motivates workers in a given culture, combined with (or based on) a knowledge of what they think matters in life, is critical to the success of the international manager. Europeans pay particular attention to power and status, which results in more formal management and operating styles in comparison to the informality found in the United States. In the United States, individual initiative and achievement are rewarded, but in Japan managers are encouraged to seek consensus before acting, and employees work as teams. Reward systems, job designs, decision-making and goal-setting processes, quality-improvement programs, and other management practices that are consistent with the dominant values of a culture are most likely to motivate employees to perform well. Practices that are not consistent with the dominant values of a culture are less likely to have positive effects on employees' performance and behavior.[30]

Mental Processes and Learning

Linguists, anthropologists, and other experts who have studied mental processes and learning have found vast differences in the ways people think and learn in different cultures. Whereas some cultures favor abstract thinking and conceptualization, others prefer rote memory and learning. The Chinese, Japanese, and Korean written languages are based on ideograms, or "word pictures." On the other hand, English is based on precise expression using words. Western cultures stress linear thinking and logic–that is, A, then B, then C, then D. Among Arabic and Asian cultures, however, nonlinear thinking prevails–that is, A may be followed by C, then back to B and on to D. This has direct implications for negotiation processes. Such an approach, in which issues are treated as independent and not linked by sequence, can be confusing and frustrating to Westerners because it does not appear logical. What can we conclude from this? What seems to be universal is that each culture has a reasoning process, but each manifests the process in its own distinctive way.[31] Managers who do not understand or appreciate such differences may conclude (erroneously and to their detriment) that certain cultures are "inscrutable."

HR BUZZ

Cultural Differences among Workers Worldwide

CLASSIFYING CULTURES

Culture determines the uniqueness of a human group in the same way that personality determines the uniqueness of an individual.[a] The 10 dimensions of culture that we just discussed reflect the enormous variation and diversity in human behavior around the world. Researchers, and especially MNEs pursuing strategies of global talent management, find it extremely helpful to classify cultures along various dimensions. Doing so provides perspective on the application of current theories of work motivation, leadership, organizational behavior, and talent management practices.

---

[a]Ronen, S., and Shenkar, O. (2017). *Navigating global business: A cultural compass*. Cambridge, UK: Cambridge University Press.

One of the earliest efforts to classify cultures began in 1968, using employees in IBM subsidiaries in 72 countries. Dutch researcher Geert Hofstede identified five dimensions of cultural variation in values. They reflect basic problems that any society has to cope with but for which solutions differ: power distance, uncertainty avoidance, individualism, masculinity, and long-term versus short-term orientation.[b]

Power distance refers to the extent that members of an organization accept inequality and whether they perceive much distance between those with power (e.g., top management) and those with little power (e.g., rank-and-file workers). **Uncertainty avoidance** is the extent to which a culture programs its members to feel either comfortable or uncomfortable in unstructured situations (novel, unknown, surprising, different from usual). **Individualism vs. collectivism** reflects the extent to which people emphasize personal or group goals. **Masculinity vs. femininity** reflects the extent to which a society differentiates roles by gender (strong vs. minimal, respectively). Masculine cultures tend to emphasize ego goals—the centrality of work, careers, and money. Feminine cultures tend to emphasize social goals—quality of life, helping others, and relationships. Finally, **long-term versus short-term orientation** refers to the extent to which a culture programs its members to accept delayed gratification of their material, social, and emotional needs.

A meta-analysis of almost 600 studies based on these dimensions (except for long-term versus short-term orientation, for which there were too few studies), revealed that cultural values predict country-level differences quite well, with an average meta-correlation of 0.35.[c]

Later studies, such as the Global Leadership and Organizational Effectiveness (GLOBE) research project, categorized countries on nine cultural dimensions: assertiveness, future orientation, gender differentiation, uncertainty avoidance, power distance, institutional collectivism, in-group collectivism, performance orientation, and humane orientation.[d] Those dimensions reveal much overlap, even synthesizing, of the factors reported by Hofstede. At the same time, there have been methodological and theoretical developments in the study of culture. Among those, "country" may not be the most appropriate unit of analysis for cross-cultural research. Cross-cultural variability can be captured at the state, ethnic/racial, religious, or socioeconomic levels.[e]

---

[b]Hofstede, G. (2011). *Culture's Consequences: Comparing Values, Behaviors, Institutions, and Organizations Across Nations.* (2nd ed.). Thousand Oaks, CA: Sage.

[c]Taras, V., Kirkman, B. L., and Steel, P. (2010). Examining the impact of *Culture's Consequences:* A three-decade, multilevel, meta-analytic review of Hofstede's cultural value dimensions. *Journal of Applied Psychology Monograph* 95, pp. 405–39; Taras, V., Steel, P., and Kirkman, B. (2012). Improving national cultural indices using a meta-analysis of Hofstede's dimensions. *Journal of World Business* 47(3), pp. 329–41.

[d]Dorfman, P., Javidan, M., Hanges, P., Dastmalchian, A., and House, R. (2012). Globe: A twenty-year journey into the intriguing world of culture and leadership. *Journal of World Business* 47(4), pp. 504–18.

[e]Gelfand, M. J., Aycan, Z., Erez, M., and Leung, K. (2017). Cross-cultural industrial organizational psychology and organizational behavior: A hundred-year journey. *Journal of Applied Psychology* 102, pp. 514–29. Taras, V., Steel, P., and Kirkman, B. (2016). Does country equal culture? Beyond geography in the search for cultural boundaries. *Management International Review* 56, pp. 455–87. Ronen and Shenkar (2017), op. cit.

(*continued*)

A newer approach to classifying cultures is in terms of the strength of **social norms**—socially agreed-upon standards of behavior that form the building blocks of social order.[f] In **tight cultures**, such norms are clear, pervasive, and often entail strong punishments for people who don't follow them. In **loose cultures**, social norms are less clear and fewer in number; people follow them less often, and they are punished less for deviance. Tightness-looseness is a continuum, with extreme cases at either end and varying degrees in between. The tightest cultures are Pakistan, Malaysia, India, Singapore, South Korea, Norway, Turkey, Japan, and China. The loosest are Spain, the United States, Australia, New Zealand, Greece, Venezuela, Brazil, the Netherlands, and Israel. These countries do not share any obvious qualities in common, such as language, location, religion, or traditions. Yet they do share some common features.

Tight societies focus on social order and self-regulation. Loose societies emphasize tolerance, creativity, and openness to change. There is no direct relationship between nations' scores on tightness-looseness and their economic development, and this approach also differs from previous ways that scholars have compared cultures, such as whether they are collectivist or individualist. In short, the tightness-looseness lens is a new way of viewing cultures on the global map.[g] It raises a tantalizing question, namely, to what extent is there convergence or standardization of specific HR or talent-management practices in tight versus loose cultures? The answer is important for MNEs as they seek to develop global talent management strategies.

---

[f]Gelfand, M. J. (2018). *Rule makers, rule breakers: How tight and loose cultures wire our world.* New York: Scribner.

[g] Ibid.

Lessons Regarding Cross-Cultural Differences

There are three important lessons to be learned from this brief overview of cross-cultural differences:

1. *Do not export headquarters-country bias.* As we have seen, the HR management approach that works well in the headquarters country might be totally out of step in another country. Managers who bear responsibility for international operations need to understand the cultural differences inherent in the management systems of the countries in which their firms do business.
2. *Think in global terms.* We live in a world in which a worldwide allocation of physical and human resources is necessary for continued survival.
3. *Recognize that no country has all the answers.* Flexible work hours, statistical process control, and various innovative approaches to productivity have arisen outside the United States. Effective multinational managers must not only think in global terms but also be able to synthesize the best management approaches to deal with complex problems.

As companies become more global in their operations, cross-cultural interaction becomes more common.
FatCamera/E+/Getty Images

HUMAN RESOURCE MANAGEMENT ACTIVITIES OF GLOBAL CORPORATIONS

Before we consider recruitment, selection, training, and other international HR management issues, it is important that we address a fundamental question: Is this subject worthy of study in its own right? The answer is yes, for two reasons–scope and risk exposure.[32] In terms of *scope*, there are at least four important differences between domestic and international operations. International operations have

1. More HR activities, such as taxation, foreign work visas, coordination of dependents, international relocation, and coordination of salaries in multiple currencies.
2. More involvement in employees' personal lives, such as housing, health, education, and recreation.
3. Management of a much wider mix of employees, coupled with complex equity issues, as the workforce mix of expatriates and locals varies.
4. Broader external influences, such as multiple governments, country laws, cultures, and languages.

Heightened *risk exposure* is a second distinguishing characteristic of international HR management. This includes legal compliance issues in each country, political risk, and the HR risk of early return of international assignees. For example, the direct cost of an early return of a family of four with two school-aged children within the first year averages $400,000 (U.S. dollars).[33] On top of that, terrorism is now an ever-present risk for executives overseas, and it clearly affects how they assess international assignments.[34] The U.S. State Department has added a "k" to its travel advisories to indicate a risk of being kidnapped or held hostage.[35]

All of this has had an important effect on how people are prepared for and are moved to and from international assignment locations. In light of these considerations, it seems reasonable to ask, "Why do people accept overseas assignments?" Why *do* they go? As companies' global ambitions grow, fast-track executives at companies such as General Mills, Procter & Gamble, Gillette, GE, and ExxonMobil see foreign tours as necessary for career advancement.[36] Evidence indicates that U.S.-based multinationals actually do perform better when they have CEOs with international-assignment experience.[37]

Organizational Structure

Traditionally, businesses tended to evolve from domestic (exporters) to international (manufacturing and some technology resources allocated outside the home country) to multinational (allocating resources among national or regional areas) to global (treating the entire world as one large company) organizations.[38] Today, a new form is evolving among high-technology companies–**transnational corporations**. What makes them different is that even the executive suite is virtual. They use geodiversity to great advantage, placing their top executives and core corporate functions in different countries to gain a competitive edge through the availability of talent or capital, low costs, or proximity to their most important customers. Of course, it is all made possible by the Internet, as improved communication facilitates an integrated global network of operations.[39]

Consider Lenovo. It was a Chinese computer maker until it bought IBM's personal computer business in 2005. Initially, it planned to move its corporate headquarters to New York from Beijing, but the executive team decided that having a central base slowed the company down. Today Lenovo is incorporated in Hong Kong, where its stock is listed, but its top managers and corporate functions are scattered across the globe. Its chief executive is based in Singapore, and its chairman is in Raleigh, North Carolina. The chief financial officer is in Hong Kong, and the chief HR officer is in Seattle. Worldwide marketing is coordinated in India, and the company's top 20 leaders meet monthly in a different place.[40]

The development of transnationals has led to a fundamental rethinking about the nature of a multinational company. Does it have a home country? What does *headquarters* mean? Is it possible to fragment corporate functions globally? To be sure, organizational structure directly affects all HR functions from recruitment through retirement because, to be effective, HR management must be integrated into the overall strategy of the organization. Indeed, from the perspective of strategic management, the fundamental problem is to keep the strategy, structure, and HR dimensions of the organization in direct alignment.[41]

Strategic Workforce Planning

Strategic workforce planning is particularly critical for firms doing business overseas. They need to analyze the local *and* international external labor markets, as well as their own internal labor markets, in order to estimate the supply of people with the skills that will be required at some time in the future, relative to the demand for them. Unfortunately, the seemingly inexhaustible pools of cheap labor from China, India, and elsewhere are drying up as demand outstrips the supply of people with the needed skills. Indeed, as a panel of experts recently noted,

As executives work to attract, retain, and develop top talent in a volatile and hypercompetitive market, an unsettling realization sinks in: talent is both an organization's single biggest asset and its single biggest risk. Success depends on finding and keeping the right people. . . . This reality is intensifying as industries struggle to embrace millennials and a more transient workforce.[42]

An ongoing challenge for multinational corporations, therefore, is to make the most of the global labor pool, wherever it exists. In developed countries, national labor markets can usually supply the skilled technical and professional people needed. However, developing countries and second-tier cities are characterized by severe shortages of qualified managers and skilled workers and by great surpluses of people with little or no skill, training, or education. Firms that plan to stay in those countries focus on two things: identifying top-management potential early and providing lots of training to employees at all levels.[43] Unfortunately, most companies are far from having an accurate talent picture. Recent data indicate that only 13 percent of MNEs have comprehensive workforce plans.[44]

Recruitment

Broadly speaking, companies operating outside their home countries follow three basic models in the recruitment of executives: (1) They may select from the national group of the parent company only, (2) they may recruit only from within their own country and the country where the branch is located, or (3) they may adopt an international perspective and emphasize the unrestricted use of all nationalities.[45] Each of these strategies has both advantages and disadvantages.

Ethnocentrism: Home-Country Executives Only

A strategy of **ethnocentrism** may be appropriate during the early phases of international expansion because firms at this stage are concerned with transplanting a part of the business that has worked in their home countries. Hence, detailed knowledge of that part is crucial to success. On the other hand, a policy of ethnocentrism, of necessity, implies blocked promotional paths for local executives. Moreover, if there are many subsidiaries, home-country nationals must recognize that their foreign service may not lead to faster career progress. Finally, there are cost disadvantages to ethnocentrism as well as increased tendencies to impose the management style of the parent company.[46]

Limiting Recruitment to Home- and Host-Country Nationals

Limiting recruitment may result from acquisition of local companies. In South Korea, for example, foreigners are clearly "outsiders," so acquisition of a local firm is a common market-entry strategy.[47] Hiring nationals has some clear advantages. It eliminates language barriers, expensive training periods, and cross-cultural adjustment problems of managers and their families. It also allows firms to take advantage of (lower) local salary levels while still paying a premium to attract high-quality employees.

Yet these advantages are not without cost. Local managers may have difficulty bridging the gap between the subsidiary and the parent company because the business experience to which they have been exposed may not have prepared them to work as part of a global enterprise.[48] Finally, consideration of only home- and host-country nationals may result in the exclusion of some very able executives.

Geocentrism: Seeking the Best Person for the Job Regardless of Nationality

At first glance, it may appear that a strategy of **geocentrism** is optimal and most consistent with the underlying philosophy of a global corporation, but there are potential problems. Such a policy can be very expensive, it can take a long time to implement, and it requires a great deal of centralized control over managers and their career patterns. To implement such a policy effectively, companies must make it very clear that cross-national service is important and that it will be rewarded.

The good news is, international experience is almost universally looked at positively by employers. They know that overcoming the challenges of living and working abroad–going without your support network, building trust and problem-solving in new environments, adapting to different work practices, and experiencing a different culture–make you more interesting *and* skillful. Companies like HP, BlackRock, Booking.com, Intel, Udemy, and TripAdvisor place special emphasis on such experience.[49]

For another, very serious problem that confronts many executives offered overseas assignments, see the International Application box.

International Staffing

Staffing systems for international assignees are unique because their focus is on predicting success in a given context (a foreign country) rather than in a specific role (such as bank manager or brand manager).[50] Recent reviews indicate that the selection process for international managers is, with few exceptions, largely based on their willingness to go.[51] As a result, the selection of people for overseas assignments often is based *solely* on their technical competence and job knowledge.[52] This is a mistake; technical competence per se has nothing to do with one's ability to adapt to a new environment, to deal effectively with foreign coworkers, or to perceive–and if necessary, imitate–foreign behavioral norms.[53] Unfortunately, only 29 percent of multinationals use candidate assessment tools to select expatriates.[54] Research has demonstrated, however, that a variety of personal characteristics predict success in international assignments, as the following sections show.

General Mental Ability

General mental ability (GMA) may be defined broadly as the ability to learn. It includes any measure that combines two, three, or more specific aptitudes, or any measure that includes a variety of items that measure specific abilities (e.g., verbal, numerical, spatial relations).[55] As we noted in Chapter 7, the validity of GMA as a predictor of job performance as well as performance in training is well established in the United States, on the basis of meta-analyses of hundreds of studies.[56] Researchers have found similar results in the European Community.[57]

In terms of job complexity, results in the European Community were similar to those reported in the United States for job performance (0.64 for high-complexity jobs, 0.53 for medium-complexity, and 0.51 for low-complexity) and training (0.74 for high-complexity, 0.53 for medium-complexity, and 0.36 for low-complexity jobs). These results indicate that there is international validity generalization for GMA as a predictor of performance in training and on the job in the United States and in the European Community. Similar findings have been reported in meta-analyses of GMA in the United Kingdom, Germany, and South Korea.[58] GMA tests are therefore robust predictors for expatriate assignments, although there is still room for additional research across other cultural regions.

INTERNATIONAL APPLICATION
Job Aid for Spouses of Overseas Executives

Both parents work in more than 64 percent of married couples with children.[a] Spouses accompany 73 percent of expatriates, and 47 percent take children with them.[b] In many parts of the world, spouses of expatriates face difficult obstacles to finding jobs. Here is a scenario likely to become more and more common in the future: A company offers a promotion overseas to a promising executive. But the executive's spouse has a flourishing career in the United States. What should the company– and the couple–do?

Employers and employees are wrestling with this dilemma more often these days. Job aid for the so-called trailing spouse is a popular benefit for domestic transfers but less so for international transferees. While 43 percent of companies provide an allowance or payment to be used for job-search assistance or education, only 33 percent of companies offer job-search assistance in the host country. Interviews with 100 trailing spouses indicated that their greatest needs were for networking information to assist in their job search and for a go-to person for practical settling-in assistance.[c]

To fill their international needs, more firms are turning to short-term assignments (3 to 12 months) or "commuter assignments," in which spouses move to adjoining countries or regions. Another option is intercompany networking, in which one multinational employer (MNE) attempts to place an expatriate's spouse in a suitable job with another MNE in the same city or country. Sometimes this takes the form of a reciprocal arrangement, such as, "You find my expatriate's spouse a job and work visa, and I will do the same for you."[d]

Despite company efforts, it is often very difficult to place spouses abroad. Where there are language barriers or barriers of labor laws, tradition, or underemployment, it can be almost impossible.

Moreover, an international assignment can slow a spouse's professional progress and sometimes stir resentment. Perhaps this is why only 16 percent of spouses were employed both before the overseas assignment and also during it.[e] On the other hand, some spouses find their overseas experiences as personally and professionally rewarding as their spouses do. One American tax lawyer received permission to work in Brussels as an independent legal consultant. A German travel executive followed his wife to Britain and, 7 months later, landed a job organizing exhibitions between Britain and Germany. Because 91 percent of married female expatriates (and 50 percent of married male expatriates) are in dual-career marriages, it is not surprising that spousal income loss is a key factor determining an executive's decision to accept or reject an overseas position.[f]

[a]U.S. Bureau of Labor Statistics. (2020, Apr. 21). Employment characteristics of families–2019. Retrieved from *www.bls.gov/news.release/famee.nr0.htm* on June 2, 2020.

[b]Brookfield GRS. (2016). 2016 global mobility trend survey. Retrieved from *http://globalmobilitytrends.bgrs.com/assets2016/downloads/Full-Report-Brookfield-GRS-2016-Global-Mobility-Trends-Survey.pdf* on July 4, 2017.

[c]KPMG International. (2019). 2019 Global Assignment and Practices Survey. Retrieved from *https://assets.kpmg/content/dam/kpmg/xx/pdf/2019/10/2019-gapp-survey-report-web.pdf* on June 2, 2020. Mohn, T. (2011, Jun. 20). Plight of the expat spouse. *The New York Times*. Retrieved from *www.nytimes.com/2011/06/21/business/21expats.html?pagewanted=all&r=0* on July 15, 2014.

[d]Dowling, P. J., Festing, M., and Engle, A. D., Sr. (2017). *International Human Resource Management* (7th ed). Boston: Cengage Learning.

[e]Brookfield GRS (2016), op. cit.

[f]Wright, A. D. (2017, June 7). Why employees are less inclined to move abroad. *SHRM Online*. Retrieved from *www.shrm.org/resourcesandtools/hr-topics/global-hr/pages/why-employees-are-less-inclined-to-move-abroad.aspx* on July 5, 2017; Tyler, K. (2003, May). Cut the stress. *HR*, pp. 101-6.

Personality

When success is defined in terms of completing the expatriate assignment and supervisory ratings of performance on the assignment, evidence indicates that three personality characteristics are related to ability to complete the assignment. These are **extroversion** and **agreeableness** (which facilitate interactions and making social alliances with host nationals and other expatriates) and **emotional stability**. **Conscientiousness** is a general work ethic that supervisors look for in their subordinates, and this affects their performance ratings. Finally, **openness**, the extent to which an individual is creative, curious, and has broad interests, is positively related to cross-cultural adjustment. In short, each of these Big Five personality characteristics relates to international assignee success in a unique way and should be included as part of the staffing process.[59]

Because personality characteristics are stable, organizations should think of selection (on the basis of personality) as the precursor to cross-cultural training: First identify expatriate candidates with the requisite personality characteristics; then offer cross-cultural training to those identified.[60] This sequence is reasonable because cross-cultural training may only be effective when trainees are predisposed to success in the first place.

Other Characteristics Related to Success in International Assignments

A comprehensive study examined the validity of a broad set of predictors for selecting European managers for a cross-cultural training program in Japan.[61] The selection procedure assessed GMA, personality (in terms of the five characteristics described earlier), plus dimensions measured by an assessment center and a behavior-description interview. Two assessment-center exercises, an analysis-presentation exercise and a group-discussion exercise, were designed to measure personal characteristics related to performance in an international context. They included tenacity/resilience, communication, adaptability, and organizational and commercial awareness. In addition to these dimensions, the group-discussion exercise assessed teamwork and the behavior-description interview assessed self-discipline and cross-cultural awareness.

Results indicated that GMA was significantly correlated with a test measuring language acquisition (corrected correlation of 0.27), openness was significantly related to instructors' ratings of cross-cultural training performance (corrected correlation of 0.33), and agreeableness correlated significantly negatively with instructors' ratings of cross-cultural training performance (corrected correlation of –0.26). Although agreeableness may be universally positive for forming social relationships, individuals who are too agreeable may be seen as "pushovers" in some cultures. Hence, agreeableness may be culturally bound in terms of perceptions of professional competence.[62]

All dimensions measured in the group-discussion exercise were significantly correlated with instructor ratings (corrected correlations ranged from 0.31 to 0.40) and from 0.33 to 0.44 with the test of language acquisition.

Three dimensions, all measured by the group-discussion exercise, also predicted performance in cross-cultural training: teamwork, communication, and adaptability. This study selected people for cross-cultural training, provided the training to those selected, and then sent abroad those who passed the training. Performance in the cross-cultural training significantly predicted executives' performance in the Japanese companies (correlations of 0.38 for instructors' ratings and 0.45 for Japanese-language proficiency). An important advantage of this process is that it may reduce the costs of international assignees because only people who pass the selection process, and who therefore are predisposed for expatriate success, are sent to the training and abroad.

What about motivation to succeed in an overseas assignment? Longitudinal research with 70 expatriates during their first 4 months of assignment revealed that those with higher levels of cross-cultural motivation and empowerment demonstrated higher initial levels of work adjustment. To maintain those levels of adjustment, managers should emphasize opportunities for personal achievement and growth, such as high levels of responsibility, or "stretch" assignments that serve as stepping-stones for promotion.[63] Although motivation is often difficult to assess reliably, firms should at least try to eliminate from consideration those who are only looking to get out of their own country for a change of scenery. One way to do that is to have candidates (and their spouses) complete self-assessments, in order to gauge their fit with the personality and lifestyle requirements of the international assignment. Here is an example.[64]

AT&T

Only 5 percent of multinational enterprises use candidate self-assessments.[a] AT&T, a worldwide player in telecommunications, is one that does.[b] Here are some typical questions it uses to screen candidates for overseas transfers:[c]

Interviewing Potential Expatriates

- Would your spouse be interrupting a career to accompany you on an international assignment? If so, how do you think this will affect your spouse and your relationship with each other?
- Do you enjoy the challenge of making your own way in new situations?
- How able are you in initiating new social contacts?
- Are you prepared to have less contact with your extended family?
- How important is it for you to spend significant amounts of time with people of your own ethnic, racial, religious, and national background?
- As you look at your personal history, can you isolate any episodes that indicate a real interest in learning about other people and cultures?
- Has it been your habit to vacation in foreign countries?
- Do you enjoy sampling foreign cuisines?
- What is your tolerance for waiting for repairs?
- Upon reentry, securing a job will primarily be your responsibility. How do you feel about networking and being your own advocate?

---

[a]KPMG International. (2019). 2019 Global Assignment and Practices Survey. Retrieved from *https://assets.kpmg/content/dam/kpmg/xx/pdf/2019/10/2019-gapp-survey-report-web.pdf* on June 2, 2020.

[b]Parietti, M. (2020, Mar. 5). The world's top 10 telecommunications companies. *Investopedia.* Retrieved from *www.investopedia.com/articles/markets/030216/worlds-top-10-telecommunications-companies.asp* on June 2, 2020.

[c]Fuchsberg, G. (1992, Jan. 9). As costs of overseas assignments climb, firms select expatriates more carefully. *The Wall Street Journal,* pp. B1, B5.

Applicability of U.S. Employment Laws to Multinational Employers

The following four employment laws may apply to U.S. citizens working abroad: Title VII of the Civil Rights Act, the Age Discrimination in Employment Act (ADEA), the Americans with Disabilities Act (ADA), and the Uniformed Services Employment and Reemployment Rights Act (USERRA). They also apply to U.S. citizens of foreign corporations doing business in the United States, even if those corporations employ fewer than 20 workers. However, they do not apply to foreign employees of a U.S.-based multinational who are not U.S. citizens.

USERRA applies only to veterans and reservists working overseas for the federal government or a firm under U.S. control. Title VII, the ADEA, and the ADA are more far reaching, covering all U.S. citizens who are either employed outside the United States by a U.S. firm, or employed by a company under the control of a U.S. firm. In determining whether a non-U.S. firm is under U.S. control, the Equal Employment Opportunity Commission will review

- The degree of interrelated operations.
- The extent of common management.
- The degree of centralized control of labor relations, common ownership, and financial control.
- The place of incorporation.[65]

Each of the four laws contains an exemption if compliance with the U.S. law would cause a company to violate a law of the country in which it is located. For example, if the laws of a particular country prohibit the hiring of women for certain jobs, a U.S. company operating within that country must follow that country's law. This is consistent with the general principle that MNEs are accountable to the laws of the countries where they operate. Those laws can be quite complex and MNEs must follow them carefully.[66] The Legalities box addresses one such issue: the requirement to consult with European works councils.

Orientation

Orientation is particularly important in overseas assignments, both before departure and after arrival. Formalized orientation efforts—for example, elaborate multimedia presentations for the entire family, supplemented by presentations by representatives of the country and former expatriates who have since returned to the United States—are critical. Research indicates clearly that MNEs should provide realistic job previews that offer honest information about what it is like to live and work in a given location. The expatriate needs information about his or her role in an international assignment, the discretion he or she has in shaping that role, and the purpose of the role relative to the company's strategic objectives.[67]

A number of firms go further. Federal Express, Colgate-Palmolive, and Apache Corp., for example, send prospective expatriates and their families on familiarization trips to the foreign location in question. While there, they have to live as the natives do by taking public transportation, shopping in local stores, and visiting prospective schools and current expatriates.[68] As of 2019, 87 percent of organizations provide a formal pre-assignment visit to the host location, with the majority (57 percent) authorizing both the assignee and the spouse/partner for the trip.[69]

LEGALITIES
Consultation with European Works Councils

In Europe, works councils—comprised of elected representatives of a firm's workforce—are critical components of employment relations. Employers with more than 50 employees in all member countries, or 20 in a single country, must inform and consult with their workforces on matters such as job security, work organization, and terms and conditions of employment. Employers with more than 1,000 employees throughout the EU and with at least 150 employees in each of two countries, must establish a European-wide works council (EWC) to receive information and consultation on all decisions that cross country boundaries.[a] Firms that operate in Europe, but that come from countries where the concept of a works council does not exist, must learn to adapt to EU requirements.

In October 2018, Alcoa Spain, part of a group of companies involved in the production of aluminum, initiated a consultation process with the Spanish works councils about the possibility of laying off 700 employees through the closure of two plants in Spain. That reduction would represent more than 20 percent of its entire European workforce. At the same time, Alcoa informed its EWC about the possible reorganization and also held talks with the trade unions.

The EWC felt that it should have been the first organization to be notified so that it could have extended some real influence over the decision-making process. It took the matter to a European court in Rotterdam and sought an order against the company to terminate the negotiations with the Spanish works councils and reverse all the consequences of those negotiations. In response, Alcoa contended that it was under no obligation to consult the EWC first, before entering into negotiations with the Spanish works councils and the trade unions. It asked the court to dismiss the EWC's claims.

The court addressed two questions: (1) whether the company had a duty to consult with the EWC at all and (2) whether the EWC must be consulted prior to the local works councils. As to the first issue, the court acknowledged that the EWC has authority in relation to cross-border situations under the terms of the European Works Councils Directive. In this case, and consistent with prior case law, the Dutch court ruled that the company's decision to close two plants, although confined to a single member state (Spain), constituted a cross-border situation because it might have repercussions for companies in other member states. For example, the closure of the plants in Spain might result in a shrinkage at the company's Shared Service Centre in Hungary because there would be less support and backroom work to be done for the Spanish plants.

The court also held that Alcoa did not need to consult the EWC before beginning consultations with the Spanish works councils and trade unions. The court explained that the EWC directive imposes no such obligation because it assumes that the consultations will go on simultaneously. Moreover, the specific EWC agreement, which governs the establishment and operations of the EWC, likewise said nothing about any order of negotiations. As a result, the EWC had no express authority to support its claim, and the court dismissed the action. In brief, while MNEs often consult the EWC ahead of local works councils, it is not necessarily entitled to that preferential treatment.[b]

---

[a]European Commission. (2018, May 14). Employee involvement—European Works Councils. Retrieved from *https://ec.europa.eu/social/main.jsp?catId=707&langId=en&intPageId=211* on June 3, 2020.

[b]Pelser, A. (2019, Feb. 14). Dutch court recognizes limit on European Works Councils. *SHRM Online*. Retrieved from *www.shrm.org/resourcesandtools/legal-and-compliance/employment-law/pages/global-european-works-councils-limit.aspx* on Feb. 14, 2019.

In fact, there may be three separate phases to orientation, all of which are designed to provide potential expatriates and their families with realistic assignment previews.[70] The first is called *initial orientation*, which may last as long as 2 full days. Key components are as follows:

- *Cultural briefing:* traditions, history, government, economy, living conditions, clothing and housing requirements, health requirements, and visa applications. (Drugs get a lot of coverage, both for adults and for teenagers–whether they use drugs or not. Special emphasis is given to the different drug laws in foreign countries. Alcohol use also gets special attention when candidates are going to Muslim countries, such as Saudi Arabia.)
- *Assignment briefing:* length of assignment, vacations, salary and allowances, tax consequences, and repatriation policy.
- *Relocation requirements:* shipping, packing, or storage; home sale or rental; and information about housing at the new location.

During this time, it is important that employees and their families understand that there is no penalty attached to changing their minds about accepting the proposed assignment. It is better to bail out early than reluctantly to accept an assignment that they will regret later.

The second phase is *pre-departure orientation*, which may last another 2 or 3 days. Its purpose is to make a more lasting impression on employees and their families and to remind them of material that may have been covered months earlier. Topics covered at this stage include

- Introduction to the language.
- Further reinforcement of important values, especially open-mindedness.
- En route, emergency, and arrival information.

The final aspect of overseas orientation is *post-arrival orientation*. Upon arrival, employees and their families should be met by assigned company sponsors. This phase of orientation usually takes place on three levels, and a dedicated support staff may provide it. The purpose is to reduce the stress associated with clashing work and family demands:[71]

- *Orientation toward the environment.* Schools, housing, medical facilities, transportation, shopping, and other subjects that–depending on the country–may become understandable only through actual experience, such as dealing with local government officials.
- *Orientation toward the work unit and fellow employees.* Often a supervisor or a delegate from the work unit will describe host-office norms and politics, as well as introduce the new employee to his or her fellow workers, discuss expectations of the job, and share his or her own initial experiences as an expatriate. The ultimate objective, of course, is to relieve the feelings of strangeness or tension that the new expatriate feels.
- *Orientation to the actual job.* This may be an extended process that focuses on cultural differences in the way a job is done. Only when this process is complete can one begin to assess the accuracy and wisdom of the original selection decision.

Throughout the assignment, some companies arrange periodic, company-sponsored social functions to provide opportunities for expatriates and their families to interact with host-country nationals. Doing so facilitates cross-cultural adjustment and overall satisfaction with the assignment.[72]

Cross-Cultural Training and Development

Cross-cultural training refers to formal programs designed to prepare persons of one culture to interact effectively in another culture or to interact more effectively with persons from different cultures.[73] To survive, cope, and succeed, managers need training in three areas: the culture, the language, and practical day-to-day matters. Female expatriates (who account for 25 percent of expatriates) need training on the norms, values, and traditions that host nationals possess about women and on how to deal with challenging situations they may face as women.[74] Reviews of research on cross-cultural training have reported modest effects in terms of the impact of such training on an individual's development of skills, on his or her adjustment to the cross-cultural situation, and on his or her performance in such situations.[75] To an unknown extent, however, conclusions may well depend on moderating variables such as *training-design factors* (e.g., the duration of the cross-cultural training program, its timing–pre-departure or post-arrival–training rigor, and type of training content– country-oriented experiential versus lecture) and *trainee characteristics* such as personality, previous international experience, and previous experience with cross-cultural training.[76]

Evidence also indicates that training should take place prior to departure and after arrival in the new location. Can pre-departure training reduce the early-return rate of expatriates? Consider Shell Oil Company in the United States. Before the company provided any training to its employees being sent to Saudi Arabia, the early-return rate was 60 percent. With 3 days of training, however, that rate dropped to 5 percent. With a 6-day pre-departure program, the figure dropped to 1.5 percent.[77] Formal mentoring for expatriates by host-country nationals also shows organizational support, boosts motivation, and can help to improve both language skills (see the HR Buzz box) and the ability to interact effectively. Those, in turn, increase retention.[78]

To a very great extent, expatriate failure rates can be attributed to the culture shock that usually occurs 4 to 6 months after arrival in the foreign country. The symptoms are not pleasant: homesickness, boredom, withdrawal, a need for excessive amounts of sleep, compulsive eating or drinking, irritability, exaggerated cleanliness, marital stress, family tension and conflict (involving children), hostility toward host-country nationals, loss of ability to work effectively, and physical ailments of a psychosomatic nature.[79]

To be sure, many of the common stresses of everyday living become amplified when a couple is living overseas with no support other than from a spouse. To deal with these potential problems, spouses are taught to recognize stress symptoms in each other, and they are counseled to be supportive. One exercise, for example, is for the couples periodically to list what they believe causes stress in their mates, what the other person does to relieve it, and what they themselves do to relieve it. Then they compare lists.[80] To help avoid, or at least minimize culture shock, experts recommend that MNEs invest in awareness training (see the accompanying International Application) and that expatriates visit their home countries as often as possible, for example, twice a year.[81]

LOCAL-LANGUAGE PROFICIENCY

More and more U.S. companies are now owned by overseas parents—including Bertelsmann, Diageo PLC, and Anglo-Dutch Unilever PLC, to name a few. Yes, e-mails are written in English and English often is spoken at board meetings, even in Asian and European companies, but failing to speak the native language of a parent company could hamper a manager's advancement. Whether at companies based in the United States or overseas, executives can miss out on informal conversations or risk being misinterpreted if they don't speak the local language. Says an investment banker, "Speaking and understanding the local language gives you more insight, you can avoid misunderstandings, and it helps you achieve a deeper level of respect." As of 2019, only 40 percent of MNEs offer pre-departure language training.

At Munich-based Siemens, country managers must learn the local language of their posts: The head of Siemens's China business speaks fluent Mandarin, for example. All managers must speak either German or English, but Siemens has an internal rule about corporate meetings: If one or more individuals don't speak German, the others are obliged to speak English. In France, however, meetings may take place in French even if one or more attendees do not speak French. As one global recruiter noted, "Language is always going to give somebody an edge, as long as they have the other requirements."[a]

[a]*Sources:* KPMG International. (2019). 2019 Global Assignment and Practices Survey. Retrieved from *https://assets.kpmg/content/dam/kpmg/xx/pdf/2019/10/2019-gapp-survey-report-web.pdf* on June 2, 2020. Smith, A. D. (2019, Summer). Dealing with culture shock. *HRMagazine* 64(2), pp. 22, 23. Roberts, D., and Zhao, J. (2014, June). The war on English. *Businessweek*, pp. 17, 18. Bhaskar-Shrinivas, P., Harrison, D. A., Shaffer, M. A., and Luk, D. M. (2005). Input-based and time-based models of international adjustment: Meta-analytic evidence and theoretical extensions. *Academy of Management Journal* 48, pp. 257-81.

A key characteristic of successful global managers is adaptability. Numerous studies show that adaptability is important for expatriate success, yet nearly 80 percent of firms do not formally assess the adaptability of candidates for international assignments.[82] Empirical research has revealed eight dimensions of adaptability: handling emergencies or crisis situations; handling work stress; solving problems creatively; dealing with uncertain and unpredictable work situations; learning work tasks, technologies, and procedures; and demonstrating interpersonal adaptability, cultural adaptability, and physically oriented adaptability.[83] This implies that an effective way to train employees to adapt is to expose them to situations like those they will encounter in their assignments that require adaptation. Such a strategy has two benefits: (1) It enhances transfer of training and (2) it is consistent with the idea that adaptive performance is enhanced by gaining experience in similar situations.

Integration of Training and Business Strategy

Earlier, we noted that firms tend to evolve from domestic (exporters) to international (or multidomestic) to multinational to global, and, in some cases, to transnational. Not surprisingly, the stage of globalization of a firm influences both the type of training activities offered and its focus. In general, the more a firm moves away from the

INTERNATIONAL APPLICATION
Bridging the U.S.–India Culture Gap*

When Axcelis Technologies, a maker of tools for manufacturing semiconductors, outsourced some jobs to India, the company worried that some of its employees might resent their new Indian colleagues. So it hired one of India's premier awareness trainers to offer a course on working effectively with Indians. The day-long course starts with a quiz to assess how much students already know about India. The trainer then discusses aspects of India's religious and linguistic diversity and its differences with the United States, after which the trainer divides the class into groups to analyze different case studies of working situations. The trainer follows that with a tutorial on communication tips, including pointers on shaking hands, business protocol, and business attire in India. Sometimes the class ends with an Indian meal.

"At first I was skeptical and wondered what I'd get out of the class," says the firm's HR director. "But it was enlightening for me. Not everyone operates like we do in America." The knowledge the trainees gain may be basic, but it can help avoid business misunderstandings. For example, when Indians shake hands, they sometimes do so rather limply. That isn't a sign of weakness or dislike; instead, a soft handshake conveys respect. When an Indian avoids eye contact, that is also a sign of deference. Another tip that trainees learn is not to plunge right into business talk right away during meetings, but first to chat about current events and other subjects. The rationale? Culturally, Indians prefer a more roundabout way into business issues. Says the trainer, "When people understand these differences they're less likely to make mistakes with each other."[a]

[a]*Sources:* Barhat, V. (2015, Aug. 27). How to do business in India. *BBC.* Retrieved from *www.bbc.com/capital/story/20150826-the-challenges-of-setting-up-shop-in-india* on July 6, 2017. Cappelli, P. Singh, H. Singh, J., and Useem. M. (2010). *The India way: How India's top business leaders are revolutionizing management.* Boston: Harvard Business School Press. Tam, P. W. (2004, May 25). Culture course. *The Wall Street Journal,* pp. B1, B12.

export stage of development, the more rigorous the training should be, including its breadth of content. At the multinational and global stages, managers need to develop a global mindset and be able to socialize host-country managers into the firm's corporate culture and other firm-specific practices. This added managerial responsibility intensifies the need for rigorous training.[84]

An example of such integration is JDA Software. The company develops its future international leaders through workshops that include action-learning projects. Such projects focus on current strategic business issues facing the company. In these workshops, cross-national teams of high-potential employees work through strategic issues together. Future leaders learn, through the process of working with each other, how to work with people from a variety of cultures.[85]

International Compensation

Compensation policies can produce intense internal conflicts within a company at any stage of globalization. Indeed, few other areas in international HR management demand as much top-management attention as does compensation.

The principal problem is straightforward: *Salary levels for the same job differ among countries in which a global corporation operates.* Compounding this problem is the fact that fluctuating exchange rates require constant attention in order to maintain constant salary rates in home-country currency.

Ideally, an effective international compensation policy should meet the following objectives:

- Attract and retain employees who are qualified for overseas service.
- Facilitate transfers between foreign affiliates and between home-country and foreign locations.
- Establish and maintain a consistent relationship between the compensation of employees of all affiliates, both at home and abroad.
- Maintain compensation that is reasonable in relation to the practices of leading competitors.
- Contribute to organization strategy—that is, support organizational goals, promote the corporate culture, and motivate employees to contribute their efforts to make the organization successful.[86]

As firms expand into overseas markets, they are likely to create an international division that becomes the home of all employees involved with operations outside the headquarters country. Three types of expatriate compensation plans typically found during this stage of development are:[87]

- Localization.
- Local-plus.
- Balance sheet.

Localization refers to the practice of paying expatriates on the same scale as local nationals in the country of assignment. It implies paying a Saudi a British salary and benefits in London, and an American an Argentine package in Buenos Aires. Salary and benefits may be supplemented with one-time or temporary transition payments.

Localization works well under certain conditions—for example, when transferring an employee with very limited home-country experience, such as a recent college graduate, to a developed country. It also works well in the case of permanent, indefinite, or extremely long (e.g., 10-year) transfers to another country. Although it is designed to reduce costs, and may do so effectively in the short term, there can be long-term tax and retirement-benefit complications that make localization less desirable, particularly for expatriates who plan to return to their home countries.[88]

Local-plus compensation localizes expatriates in the host-country salary program. It then adds some allowances, such as assistance with housing, education for minor children, and international medical coverage. In Asia, two-thirds of employers are using local plus, and it is becoming popular in the United States, Europe, and the United Arab Emirates. It is commonly used when employees are coming from lower-wage to higher-wage countries as well as for permanent transfers and localized expatriates. Increasingly, local plus is used for training or developmental assignments, for roles with significant incentive compensation (e.g., financial services), and for self-initiated assignments.[89]

The **balance-sheet approach** is used by 80 percent of multinational organizations to compensate expatriates. Its primary objective is to ensure that expatriates

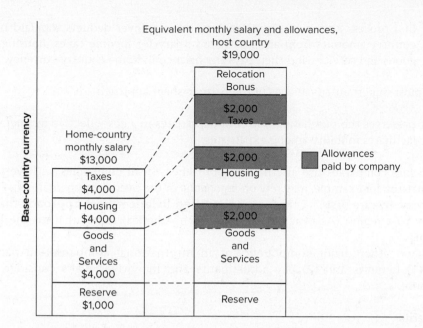

Figure 16–1

The balance-sheet approach to international compensation.

neither gain nor lose financially compared with their home-country peers. If there is no financial advantage to being in one country instead of another, then this objective will be realized. It also facilitates mobility among the expatriate staff in the most cost-effective way possible.[90]

Figure 16-1 illustrates this approach. Note the labels on the left and right columns of Figure 16-1. The left is is "home-country monthly salary." Each of the four categories identified in this column is a "norm" that represents the typical proportion of income that someone at the stated income level and family size spends (e.g., a $150,000-a-year manager with a wife and two small children). Each category behaves differently as income increases and family size changes. In most countries, as income rises, income taxes and the reserve (net disposable income that can be saved, invested, or spent at home) increase at increasing rates while housing and goods and services increase at decreasing rates.

The costs of income taxes, housing, and goods and services tend to be higher abroad than in most home countries, while the reserve remains the same. The right column, labeled "Equivalent monthly salary and allowances, host-country," demonstrates that if expatriates are responsible for the same level of expenditures abroad as at home and overall purchasing power is maintained, the employer becomes responsible for costs that exceed "normal" expatriate home-country costs. Thus, if housing is more expensive abroad than at home, the employer is responsible for the remainder. These differentials are shown in the darker-colored blocks within the right column of Figure 16-1.

The net effect of the balance sheet is to provide the expatriate with the same purchasing power as a peer at home, plus any premiums and incentives necessary to induce him or her to accept a particular foreign assignment.

Two philosophies characterize the balance-sheet approach:

1. **Protection**, which is paying expatriates the supplements in home-country currency suggested by the darker-colored blocks in the right column of Figure 16-1.

2. In a process known as **equalization**, the employer deducts standard home-country amounts from an expatriate's salary for income taxes, housing, and goods and services and then pays the balance in home-country currency.

The most important advantages of the balance-sheet approach are

- It preserves the purchasing power of expatriates in a cost-effective manner.
- It facilitates mobility among expatriates.

Some companies use alternative approaches. Small companies with very few expatriates, for example, may rely on *negotiation* of the overall compensation package on a case-by-case basis.[91] Others use a **modified balance-sheet approach** that ties salary to a region (Asia-Pacific, Europe, North America) rather than to the home country.[92]

Two other major components of an international compensation package are (1) benefits and (2) pay adjustments and incentives. Let's consider each of these.

Benefits

Benefits may vary drastically from one country to another. For example, most developed and emerging economies have some form of national health care supplied by employer- and employee-paid premiums. In Europe, employees have statutory rights that vary from country to country. These include pensions, sick pay, minimum wages, holiday pay, overtime pay, minimum work time, and dismissal procedures (including legally required severance benefits).

To deal with such variation, MNEs try to develop both qualitative and quantitative parity in benefits across countries. **Qualitative parity** is a commitment to offer employees worldwide something from each of the following categories of benefits:[93]

- *Core benefits*–basic items the company commits to making available to all employees worldwide, such as a certain level of health-care insurance.
- *Required benefits*–a cash or noncash item required by local law (e.g., mandatory profit-sharing).
- *Recommended benefits*–available wherever cost considerations permit, such as life insurance.
- *Optional benefits*–available if there is a competitive practice in a local market, such as local transportation or meal support. In the United States, for example, 70 percent of MNEs sponsor employment-based green cards (which allow permanent residency) for foreign-national employees.[94]

At Verizon Communications, **quantitative parity** is an effort to treat employees from around the globe equitably from a total-cost perspective. If an employee is assigned to a country with a rich health-care or pension system, such as France, the company does not want to add a layer of benefits on top of those coverages because that would create a situation in which some employees were clearly getting more than others. To avoid that, Verizon reviews each country from a total-rewards perspective to ensure quantitative parity.[95]

Most U.S. multinationals also offer various types of premiums and incentives. Their purpose is to provide for the difference in living costs (i.e., the costs of goods, services, and currency realignments) between the home country and the host country. Premiums may include any one or more of the following components:

- *Housing allowance.* This can be substantial, especially considering that the monthly rent for a two-bedroom apartment in 2020 in the world's top 10 most expensive cities for housing ranged from $3,685 in Hong Kong (#1) to $1,903 in Tokyo (#10).[96]
- *Education allowance.* This pays for schools, uniforms, and other educational expenses that would not have been incurred had the expatriate remained in the United States.
- *Income tax–equalization allowance* (as described earlier).
- *Hardship pay.* This is usually a percentage of base pay provided as compensation for living in an area with climactic extremes, political instability, or poor living conditions.
- *Danger pay.* This compensates for living in an area where physical danger is present, such as a war zone. For example, contractors working to rebuild Iraq typically get bonuses that equal at least 50 percent of their salaries.[97]
- *Home leave.* Commonly, one trip per year is provided for the entire family to the expatriate's home country. Hardship posts normally include more frequent travel for rest and relaxation.[98]

Finally, it is common practice for companies to pay for security guards in many overseas locations, such as in Middle Eastern countries, in the Philippines, and in Indonesia.

Pay Adjustments and Performance Management

In the United States, adjustments in individual pay levels are based, to a great extent, on how well people do their jobs, as reflected in a performance review that is part of a broader performance-management process. In most areas of the Third World, however, objective measures for rating employee or managerial performance are uncommon. Social status is based on characteristics such as age, religion, ethnic origin, and social class. Pay differentials that do not reflect these characteristics will not motivate workers.

Beyond those considerations, there are at least four broad constraints on expatriates with respect to the achievement of goals in the international context.[99] First, differences in local accounting rules or labor laws may make it difficult to compare the relative performance of host-country managers in different countries. Second, in turbulent international environments, objectives tend to be more fluid and flexible. Third, separation by time and distance may make it difficult for performance-management systems to take into account cultural factors. Fourth, business development in foreign subsidiaries is generally slower and more difficult than at home. Hence, managers need more time to achieve results. Figure 16–2 illustrates these issues graphically.

Some have argued that performance-management systems are "broken."[100] Evidence from a 20-year review of 64 articles published in the academic literature on international performance management indicates that although that may be the case domestically, the situation is even worse when the same systems are used in contexts and cultures outside the home countries where they were developed.[101]

Three key cultural differences to consider are communications (gestures, eye contact, and body language in high-context cultures versus precision with words in

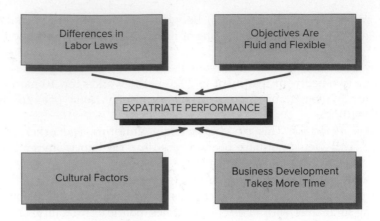

Why it is difficult to assess the performance of expatriates.

low-context cultures), goal setting, and reward systems (individual versus teamwide or organizationwide).[102] These concepts might be interpreted and implemented very differently in individualistic versus collectivistic cultures.

We know that concepts such as giving individual rewards for individual performance and making explicit distinctions in performance among employees are not universally accepted. Indeed, where the prevailing view is that it takes contributions from everyone to achieve continuous improvement (i.e., the concept of *kaizen* in Japanese enterprises), the practice of singling out one employee's contribution may actually cause that employee to "lose face" among his or her fellow work-group members. In other cultures, where nepotism is common and extended family members work together, the primary objective is to preserve working relationships. That objective may cause host-country managers to overlook results that more objective observers might judge to be inadequate. Implementation of performance feedback across cultures is fraught with even more difficulties.

In individualistic cultures, such as the United States, Great Britain, and Australia, a popular topic in first-level supervisory training programs is how to conduct performance-feedback interviews. Indeed, the ability to conduct them well and the ability to communicate "bad news" are considered key skills for a successful manager in those cultures. By contrast, in collectivist societies, such as Korea, Guatemala, and Taiwan, discussing a person's performance openly with him or her is likely to clash head-on with the society's norm of harmony, and the employee may view it as an unacceptable loss of face. Such societies have more subtle, indirect ways of communicating feedback, as by withdrawing a normal favor or by communicating concerns verbally via a mutually trusted intermediary.[103]

In addition, the target of the feedback matters. In one study, for example, individual versus group performance feedback induced more positive evaluations from individualists and collectivists, respectively.[104] Little research, however, has been done on feedback in intercultural settings, but one study found that Japanese managers provide implicit and informal feedback, although that is slowly changing.[105] In other contexts, political motives may dominate the process.[106] As these studies demonstrate, it is crucial to be sensitive to local customs with respect to the process used to communicate feedback.

The general conclusion from this brief review is that it is unwise to presume that the approach that works well in one's own culture will work similarly elsewhere. It is certainly possible to improve the process of performance management, but what is not realistic is the assumption that one size fits all.[107]

Despite such differences, research indicates that there are also important similarities in reward-allocation practices across cultures. The most universal of these seems to be the **equity norm**, according to which rewards are distributed to group members based on their contributions.[108] In general, the more expatriates perceive that the methods the parent organization uses to plan and implement decisions are fair (procedural justice), the better their adjustment to and performance in overseas assignments.[109]

When implementing performance management overseas, therefore, first determine its purpose (rewards, professional development, etc.). Second, whenever possible, set standards of performance against quantifiable objectives. Third, allow more time to achieve results abroad than is customary in the domestic market. Fourth, keep the objectives flexible and responsive to potential market and environmental conditions.[110]

Indeed, as firms evolve from multinational to global, they want their expatriates to understand that the greatest organizational growth—and their fastest career-development opportunities—are outside their home or base country. Increasingly, therefore, a large part of the compensation of these individuals will be performance-based, not just a package of costly allowances and premiums that represent fixed costs.[111]

Labor Relations in the International Arena

Labor relations structures, laws, and practices vary considerably among countries.[112] Unions may or may not exist. Management or government may dictate terms and conditions of employment. Labor agreements may or may not be contractual obligations. Management may conclude agreements with unions that have little or no membership in a plant or with nonunion groups that wield more bargaining power than the established unions do. And principles and issues that are relevant in one context may not be in others—for example, seniority in layoff decisions or even the concept of a layoff.[113]

In general, unions may constrain the choices of global companies in three ways: (1) influencing wage levels to the extent that cost structures may become noncompetitive, (2) limiting the ability of companies to vary employment levels at their own discretion, and (3) hindering or preventing global integration of such companies (i.e., by forcing them to develop parallel operations in different countries).[114] At the same time, however, unions have found global corporations particularly difficult to deal with in terms of union power and difficult to penetrate in terms of union representation.[115] Here are some of the special problems that global corporations present to unions:

1. Whereas national unions tend to follow the development of national companies, union expansion typically cannot follow the expansion of a company across national boundaries, with the exception of Canada. Legal differences, feelings of nationalism, and differences in union structure and industrial relations practices are effective barriers to such expansion.
2. The nature of foreign investment by global corporations has changed. In the past, they tended to invest in foreign sources of raw materials. As a result, the number of processing and manufacturing jobs in the home country may actually have increased. However, in recent years, there has been a shift toward the development of parallel, or nearly parallel, operations in other countries.[116] Foreign investment of this type threatens union members in the home country with loss of jobs or with a slower rate of job growth, especially if their wages are higher than those of workers in the host country.[117]

3. When a global corporation has parallel operations in other locations, the firm's ability to switch production from one location shut down by a labor dispute to another location is increased. This, of course, assumes that the same union does not represent workers at each plant or that, if different unions are involved, they do not coordinate their efforts and strike at the same time. Another assumption is that the various plants are sufficiently parallel that their products are interchangeable.

ETHICAL DILEMMA
Bribery to Win Business?*

In the United States, the Foreign Corrupt Practices Act of 1977 (amended in 1988 to increase criminal fines for organizations and civil sanctions for individuals) prohibits payments by U.S. firms and their managers to win foreign business. It has cost them billions. Worldwide, an estimated $1 trillion in bribes changes hands each year.[a] In an analysis of bribery on a global scale (427 cases), the Organization for Economic Cooperation and Development (OECD) reached five major conclusions:[b] (1) Higher-ups knew, or were at least aware, of the bribery. (2) Three-fourths of cases involved intermediaries such as agents, distributors, brokers, or subsidiary companies. (3) Bribes were mostly paid to get public procurement contracts. (4) Enforcement peaked in 2011, followed by a decline. (This was not the case in the United States.) (5) Most cases (70 percent) were resolved through a settlement involving penalties. Eighty individuals received prison sentences.

Until recently, German engineering conglomerate Siemens paid the largest fines, $800 million in the United States, almost $840 million in Germany, and another $100 million to the World Bank. Siemens does business in more than 200 countries and apparently paid "commissions" to secure orders.[c] Under the FCPA, prosecutors have extended their reach overseas, targeting alleged corruption by foreign companies with links to the U.S. financial system. Thus, two Brazilian firms paid more than $3.5 billion in fines to U.S., Brazilian, and Swiss authorities.[d] In the United Kingdom, the Bribery Act outlaws "grease payments," small bribes that are common in some countries to get mail service, phone hookups, or other services that otherwise would be delayed.[e] Such payments are legal under the FCPA, as long as they are recorded. Conflicting requirements in antibribery laws across countries have created huge headaches and potential liabilities for U.S. companies that rely on local agents to get deals done. Are grease payments ethical?

*Sources: Hersher, R. (2016, Dec. 21). Justice Department announces largest corporate bribery penalty ever. *NPR.* December 21, 2016. Retrieved from *www.npr.org/sections/thetwo-way/2016/12/21/506297795/justice-department-announces-largest-corporate-bribery-penalty-ever* on Dec. 22, 2016; Verbergt, M., and Gauthier-Villars, D. (2016, Sept. 15). Telia asked to pay $1.4 billion to settle bribery probe. Retrieved from *www.wsj.com/articles/telia-to-pay-1-4-billion-in-bribery-probe-1473921293* on Sept. 17, 2016.

[a]United Nations. (2018, Sept. 10). Global cost of corruption at least 5 percent of world gross domestic product. Retrieved from *www.un.org/press/en/2018/sc13493.doc.htm* on June 4, 2020.

[b]Rubenfeld, S. (2014, Dec. 2). 5 takeaways from the OECD report on foreign bribery. *The Wall Street Journal.* Retrieved from *https://blogs.wsj.com/briefly/2014/12/02/5-takeaways-from-the-oecd-report-on-foreign-bribery/* on June 1, 2015.

[c]Wayne, L. (2012, Sept. 3). Foreign firms most affected by a U.S. law barring bribes. *The New York Times.* Retrieved from *www.nytimes.com/2012/09/04/business/global/bribery-settlements-under-us-law-are-mostly-with-foreign-countries.html?pagewanted=all&r=0* on July 17, 2014.

[d]Viswanatha, A., and Nassauer, S. (2017, May 9). U.S. asks Wal-Mart to pay $300 million to settle bribery probe. *The Wall Street Journal.* Retrieved from *www.wsj.com/articles/u-s-asks-wal-mart-to-pay-300-million-to-settle-bribery-probe-1494366397* on May 10, 2017.

[e]Searcey, D. (2010, Dec. 28). U.K. law on bribes has firms in a sweat. *The Wall Street Journal,* pp. B1, B2.

One solution to the problems that global corporations pose for union members is **transnational collective bargaining**, in which unions in more than one country negotiate jointly with the same company. For this to work, though, coordination of efforts and the cooperation of the unions are required. That is beginning to occur. A recent investigation of the organization and policies of all 12 European industry federations found that they have developed from providing forums for the exchange of information to becoming platforms for the definition of binding guidelines and minimum standards.[118] Yet persistent problems stand in the way of such collaboration:[119]

1. National and local labor leaders would have to be willing to relinquish their autonomy to an international level. This is a major stumbling block because the local union or enterprise union is essentially an autonomous organization.
2. National laws that restrict sympathy strikes, secondary boycotts, and affiliations of labor unions with international federations all hamper transnational cooperation.
3. Language barriers; cultural, religious, and ideological differences; fear of losing domestic autonomy; legal constraints; differences in union structures and goals—not to mention employer resistance—make true transnational collective bargaining exceptionally rare.

Toward International Labor Standards

In view of the lack of success with transnational collective bargaining, unions have taken a different tack. Labor unions in the United States, for example, are attempting to influence the international labor practices of U.S.-based corporations.[120]

Four forces are driving the trend toward adoption of international labor standards: labor unions, pressure from social-advocacy groups, resentment in some developing countries against multinationals, and U.S. and European proposals for linkages between trade policy and human rights. The international labor standards advocated by these groups include

- Prohibitions on child labor.
- Prohibitions on forced labor.
- Prohibitions against discrimination.
- Protection for workers' health.
- Payment of adequate wages.
- Provision of safe working conditions.
- Freedom of association.

Industry is making progress. For example, the Responsible Business Alliance Code of Conduct (updated in 2018) is a set of industry standards on social, environmental, and ethical issues. Its 150 members include retail, auto, and toy companies with combined annual revenue greater than $5 trillion, directly employing over 6 million people. However, it leaves inspection and enforcement to each member company.[121] In the apparel industry, many retailers signed an accord on fire and building safety in Bangladesh, following the 2013 building collapse there, led by the International Labor Organization, unions, and other activist groups. The accord commits them to rigorous, independent inspections of their suppliers' factories. Although there have been some improvements, as of 2020, safety, labor, and other issues persist. For its part, the government of Bangladesh hired more than 350 new factory inspectors and passed legislation setting up a workers' welfare fund.[122] Another strategic development is regional trading blocks, of which the United States-Mexico-Canada Agreement is just one example.

The United States–Mexico–Canada Agreement

As of 2020, the United States-Canada-Mexico (USMCA) replaced the the North American Free Trade Agreement (NAFTA), which began in 1994. As North America's strategic response to the global economy, NAFTA eliminated trade barriers on goods and services within the United States, Canada, and Mexico over 15 years.[123] Since NAFTA took effect in 1994, trade among Canada, the United States, and Mexico more than tripled, to $1.1 trillion annually. Of that amount, roughly 60 percent represented trade with Canada and 40 percent trade with Mexico.[124] NAFTA changed Mexico in some fundamental ways, boosting real income per person from about $10,000 in 1994 to $19,000 in 2017. Although it helped the U.S. auto industry, its effects were uneven, and it hurt some workers, industries, and towns.[125] NAFTA and the USMCA do not differ significantly, but there are differences. Here, in brief, are four of them.[126]

Autos. The USMCA requires 75 percent of a vehicle's parts to be made in one of the three countries–up from the current 62.5 percent rule–in order to remain free from tariffs when moving among the three countries. It also requires more vehicle parts to be made by workers earning at least $16 an hour.

Labor laws. An interagency committee will monitor implementation of Mexico's labor reforms and compliance with labor obligations. It also, for the first time in any U.S. trade agreement, allows for "rapid response" panels to review whether specific facilities are violating workers' rights and to levy duties or penalties on products made at those facilities.

Data protection. The USMCA prohibits Canada and Mexico from forcing U.S. companies to store their data on in-country servers. It also ensures that U.S. companies cannot be sued in Canada and Mexico for much of the content appearing on their platforms.

Environmental protections. The agreement provides $600 million to address environmental problems in the region–like sewage spillovers from Tijuana that affect San Diego–and makes regulations easier to enforce by doing away with a requirement to prove a violation affects trade.

REPATRIATION

Consider these sobering **repatriation** statistics:[127]

- Only 12 percent of companies have a strategy for advance, proactive repatriation planning.
- Fifty percent of companies have first discussions about repatriation within 6 months of assignment completion. Only 8 percent discuss repatriation before the assignment starts.
- Sixty percent rely on informal networking or the originating department to identify positions for repatriates.
- In terms of the impact on employees' careers, 43 percent of companies say repatriates are more likely to be future leaders, and 23 percent say they will receive more rapid or frequent promotions.
- Seventy-seven percent of repatriates have less disposable income when they return home.

The results are unmet expectations, feelings of being undervalued, and concerns about one's future career. Furthermore, having become accustomed to foreign ways, upon re-entry expatriates often find home-country customs strange and, at the extreme, annoying. Such **reverse culture shock** may be more challenging than the culture shock experienced when going overseas![128] Here are three things companies can do: (1) have champions back home who look after their interests, (2) pay as much attention to "re-boarding" repatriates as they do to "on-boarding" new employees, and (3) find ways to help repatriates use what they have learned abroad.[129] Key issues fall into three areas: planning, career management, and compensation.

Planning

Both the expatriation assignment and the repatriation move should be examined as parts of an integrated whole—not as unrelated events in an individual's career.[130] To improve this process, it is necessary to define a clear strategic purpose for the move prior to the assignment. Is it executive development, coordination, and control between headquarters and foreign operations, or training of local employees?[131] Research shows that unless there is a planned purpose in repatriation, the investment of $1 million or more to send an expatriate overseas is likely to be squandered completely because turnover among repatriates may be 30 percent or more within the first year back in their home countries, and 50 percent within two years, compared with about 13 percent for all turnover.[132]

Beyond that, returning expatriates need a crash course on how to live in their homelands again. PricewaterhouseCoopers holds cocktail parties at which returning staff can meet each other, and it provides them with mentors to help them fit back in. The objective is to reduce the uncertainties and fear that often accompany the repatriation process.[133]

Career Management

Career management is the number 1 issue for expatriates. As an Australian expat living in Singapore noted, "Most expatriates are actually thinking that far ahead in terms of 'Where will this assignment take me in three years' time if I agree to go?'"[134] If companies want to retain this key talent, they need to give them a reason to stay beyond only financial rewards. They need to leverage their international experience in appropriate and challenging roles. Unfortunately, research with 111 expatriates from 23 countries who returned to their home countries within the previous year tells a different story. Compared to their expatriate job assignments, 16 percent of the repatriates were in a job that they considered a demotion, 57 percent were in a job considered a lateral move, and 27 percent were in a job considered a promotion. Receiving a promotion upon repatriation, however, signaled that the organization valued international experience and it contributed to repatriates' beliefs that the organization met their expectations regarding training and career development. These two perceptions, in turn, related positively to career satisfaction and to intentions to stay.[135]

Compensation

The loss of a monthly premium to which the expatriate has been accustomed is a severe shock financially, whatever the rationale. To overcome this problem, some firms have replaced the monthly foreign-service premium with a one-time **mobility**

premium (e.g., 3 months' pay) for each move–overseas, back home, or to another overseas assignment. A few firms also provide low-cost loans or other financial assistance so that expatriates can get back into their hometown housing markets at a level at least equivalent to what they left. Finally, there is a strong need for financial counseling for repatriates. Such counseling has the psychological advantage of demonstrating to repatriates that the company is willing to help with the financial problems that they may encounter in uprooting their families once again to bring them home.[136]

Human Resource Management in Action: Conclusion

WHAT'S IT LIKE TO BE A GLOBAL MANAGER?

Says Kelly Brookhouse, an industrial/organizational psychologist who directs Motorola's executive development program, "We put people into a simulated environment and throw business challenges at them to see how they respond. We get a fairly comprehensive picture of people's leadership profile."

"It was hard. A lot harder than I had expected," says Mandy Chooi, a Beijing-based HR executive at Motorola who recently went through the exercise. "It's surprising how realistic and demanding it is."

Companies that use such assessments often see a quick payoff. French food group Danone SA reduced its failure rate among expatriate managers to 3 percent from about 35 percent in the 3 years since it started using such assessment programs.

IMPACT OF INTERNATIONAL HRM ON PRODUCTIVITY, QUALITY OF WORK LIFE, AND THE BOTTOM LINE

The ways in which a company operates overseas can have fundamental, long-term impacts on all three of these indicators. Economic theory says that increased economic integration, free trade, and international capital mobility improve aggregate welfare in the long run, whereas short-run issues are dismissed as "adjustment costs." The economics of globalization are certainly important, but it also is critical not to overlook its broader effects on individuals, communities, cultures, and the environment. Globalization has brought many benefits to people around the world, but it also has closed U.S. factories, hollowed out entire communities, brought sweatshops to other countries, and placed great strains on the environment.[a] At the same time, many firms have practiced good corporate citizenship in every market in which they do business.[b]

To be sure, many of these effects are beyond the purview of HR management. Within organizations, however, providing professional development opportunities, challenging work, and competitive pay–in a climate of respect and inclusion, with supportive team members and leaders–can go a long way toward improving the working lives of the millions of people who toil in the global economy every day. In short, progressive HR policies can enhance productivity, quality of work life, and profits–and that benefits everyone.

[a]Short, J. R. (2016, Nov. 30). Why there's a backlash against globalization and what needs to change. *PBS Newshour.* Retrieved from *www.pbs.org/newshour/making-sense/column-theres-backlash-globalization-needs-change* on July 7, 2017; Society for Human Resource Management. (2017, Jan. 28). Global sustainability: Doing well by doing good. *YouTube.* Available at *www.youtube.com/watch?v=yYEwnUqTqJw.*

[b]Budd, J. W. (2021). *Labor relations: Striking a balance* (6th ed.). New York: McGraw-Hill.

IMPLICATIONS FOR MANAGEMENT PRACTICE

No one has discovered a single best way to manage. But before a company can build an effective management team, it must understand thoroughly its own culture, the other cultures in which it does business, and the challenges and rewards of blending the best of each.

In the immediate future, there will certainly be international opportunities for managers at all levels, particularly those with the technical skills needed by developing countries. In the longer run, global companies will have their own cadres of **globalites**, sophisticated international executives drawn from many countries, as firms such as Procter & Gamble, Schlumberger, Nestlé, and Sony do now. There is a bright future for managers with the cultural flexibility to be sensitive to the values and aspirations of foreign countries.

Finally, there is one thing of which we can be certain. Talent–social, managerial, and technical–is needed to make global business work. Competent HR management practices can find that talent, recruit it, select it, train and develop it, motivate it, reward it, and profit from it. This will be the greatest challenge of all in the years to come.

Sources: Ashman, L. (2019, July 10). Find a job abroad: Why moving abroad is great for your career. Retrieved from *https://graduateland.com/article/why-moving-abroad-can-be-great-for-your-career* on June 4, 2020. Johnson, K. (2015, Feb. 9). Career boost for CFOs: A stint abroad. *The Wall Street Journal.* Retrieved from *www.wsj.com/articles/career-booster-for-cfos-work-experience-abroad-1423527358,*on July 4, 2017. Kwoh, L. (2012, May 9). Don't unpack that suitcase. *The Wall Street Journal,* p. B10.

Back in suburban London (see the Human Resource Management in Action box that begins this chapter), I'm starting to sweat. Ms. Dubois is going to walk through the door in about 20 minutes, and I'm far from ready. There's a flipchart on an easel in the corner, but my handwriting is illegible. So I'm feverishly typing up a sheet of key points to hand her.

The phone rings. "Damn," I mutter. A persistent colleague wants me to send a team member to Holland for 3 months to help land a big new client. I put her off politely and promise to call back later. But I've lost precious time, and when Ms. Dubois strolls in, the presentation is still humming through the printer on my desk.

Sounds a lot like real life, doesn't it?

SUMMARY

Foreign investment by the world's leading corporations is a fact of modern organizational life. For executives transferred overseas, the opportunities are great, but the risks of failure are considerable. This is because there are fundamental cultural differences that affect how different people view the world and operate in business. The lesson for companies doing business overseas is clear: Guard against the exportation of home-country bias, think in global terms, and recognize that no country has all the answers.

Recruitment for overseas assignments is typically based on one of three basic models: (1) ethnocentrism, (2) limiting recruitment to home- and host-country nationals, or (3) geocentrism. Selection is based on five criteria: personality, skills, attitudes, motivation, and behavior. Orientation for expatriates and their families often takes place in three stages: initial, pre-departure, and post-arrival. Cross-cultural training may incorporate a variety of methods and techniques, but to be most effective it should be integrated with the firm's long-range global strategy and business planning. International compensation presents special problems because salary levels differ among countries. To be competitive, firms normally follow local salary patterns in each country. Expatriates, however, receive various types of premiums (foreign-service, tax-equalization, cost-of-living) in addition to their base salaries—according to the balance-sheet and local-plus approaches. To deal with the wide variation in benefits across countries, MNEs try to provide both qualitative and quantitative parity. An overseas assignment is not complete, however, until repatriation issues have been resolved. These fall into three areas: personal finances, reacclimation to the U.S. lifestyle, and readjustment to the corporate structure. Finally, because global companies operate across national boundaries but unions typically do not, the balance of power in the multinational arena clearly rests with management. To provide a more level playing field, unions are pushing hard for international labor standards.

KEY TERMS

multinational enterprise (MNE)
expatriate
home country
host country
third-country national
efficient-purchaser indexes
culture
local perspective
cosmopolitan perspective
culture shock
norms of behavior
power distance
uncertainty avoidance
Individualism vs. collectivism
masculinity
Femininity
long-term versus short-term orientation
social norms
tight cultures
loose cultures
transnational corporation
ethnocentrism

geocentrism
general mental ability (GMA)
extroversion
agreeableness
emotional stability
conscientiousness
openness
cross-cultural training
localization
local-plus compensation
balance-sheet approach
protection
equalization
modified balance-sheet approach
qualitative parity
quantitative parity
equity norm
transnational collective bargaining
repatriation
reverse culture shock
mobility premium
globalites

DISCUSSION QUESTIONS

16-1. What advice would you give to a prospective expatriate regarding questions to ask before accepting the assignment?

16-2. Discuss the special problems that women face in overseas assignments.

16-3. What effects might international labor standards have on workers, companies, and consumers?

16-4. Describe the conditions necessary for a geocentric recruitment policy to work effectively.

16-5. What key characteristics would you look for in selecting a prospective expatriate?

16-6. Describe the balance-sheet approach to international compensation.

16-7. Your boss asks for suggestions about ways to reduce the high rate of attrition among repatriates. What advice would you offer?

16-8. What are some differences between local and cosmopolitan perspectives?

16-9. Melissa chooses to accept international assignments her entire career. Over time, it is not clear where her "home" is. How might a local-plus approach to compensation help smooth her international transfers?

16-10. You have just returned from a 3-year posting in Buenos Aires. Your boss asks if there are any special concerns she should consider before doing a performance review of your replacement. What would you tell her?

APPLYING YOUR KNOWLEDGE

Expatriate Orientation Role-Play   *Exercise 16–1*

Business is increasingly international in scope. Many problems can arise when citizens of one country attempt to conduct business in another without an awareness of the local culture and customs. The obvious solution to these problems is education and training—in particular, a series of briefings for expatriates before they are sent on overseas assignments.

The purpose of this exercise is to familiarize you with the culture and customs of one foreign country and with the process of developing and implementing a cultural-briefing program for expatriates.

Procedure

Select a foreign country in which you have some interest. Then search your college's library and find other, online resources that discuss the customs and cultural dimensions of your chosen country that would be important for a businessperson to know.

On the basis of the information you have collected, develop a mock cultural briefing to be given to the rest of the class. Your cultural briefing should cover such topics as traditions, history, geography, living conditions, clothing and housing requirements, health requirements, drug and alcohol laws, and political and economic systems.

Collect visual aids for your briefing. For instance, your school or public library may have posters, videos, photos, or other visual aids available through online services that you can borrow to give students a visual overview of the country you have chosen. Another possibility is to develop a brief role-play that demonstrates a "rude" foreigner insulting his or her host through ignorance of local customs. Such a demonstration can be built right into your overall cultural briefing.

Be creative! The main idea is to teach the other students in your class about the conduct of business in another country and the importance of a cultural briefing for expatriates before they leave their home countries.

REFERENCES

1. Friedman, T. L. (2016). *Thank You for Being Late: An Optimist's Guide to Thriving in the Age of Accelerations.* New York: Farrar, Straus & Giroux.

2. Global 500. (2019). *Fortune.* Retrieved from *https://fortune.com/global500/* on June 1, 2020.

3. Dulebohn, J. H., and Hoch, J. E. (2017). Virtual teams in organizations. *Human Resource Management Review* 27, pp. 569–74.

4. Cascio, W. F. (2020). Implications of the changing nature of work for recruitment and retention. In B. J. Hoffman, M. K. Shoss, and L. A. Wegman (Eds.), *The Cambridge Handbook of the Changing Nature of Work.* Cambridge, UK: Cambridge University Press, pp. 318–39.

5. Miranda, L. (2020, May 1). Amazon has been indispensable during the pandemic—but it's clear who really wins. *NBC News.* Retrieved from *www.nbcnews.com/business/business-news/amazon-has-been-indispensable-during-pandemic-it-s-clear-who-n1197341* on June 1, 2020. *See also* Friedman (2016), op. cit.

6. Kessler, S. (2018). *Gigged: The Gig Economy, the End of the Job, and the Future of Work.* New York: Random House Business. *See also* McGovern, M. (2017). *Thriving in the Gig Economy: How to Capitalize and Compete in the New World of Work.* Wayne, NJ: Career Press/New Page Books.

7. Autor, D. H., Dorn, D., and Hanson, G. H. (2016). The China shock: Learning from labor-market adjustment to large changes in trade. *Annual Review of Economics* 8, pp. 205–40.

8. McKinsey Global Institute. (2016, Feb.) Digital globalization: The new era of global flows. Retrieved from *www.mckinsey.com/business-functions/digital-mckinsey/our-insights/digital-globalization-the-new-era-of-global-flows* on Apr. 7, 2016. *See also* Brynjolfsson, E., and McAfee, D. (2014). *The Second Machine Age: Work, Progress, and Prosperity in a Time of Brilliant Technologies.* New York: W. W. Norton.

9. Legrain, P. (2020, March 12). The coronavirus is killing globalization as we know it. *Foreign Policy.* Retrieved from *https://foreignpolicy.com/2020/03/12/coronavirus-killing-globalization-nationalism-protectionism-trump/* on June 1, 2020.

10. Mann, T., and Spegele, A. B. (2017, June 30). Why GE builds more factories overseas. *The Wall Street Journal,* pp. A1, A9.

11. Conservation International. (2017). Follow Starbucks' 15-year journey to 100% ethically sourced coffee. Retrieved from *www.conservation.org/partners/Pages/starbucks.aspx* on July 3, 2017. *See also* SHRM Foundation. (2011). *Global Sustainability: Doing Well by Doing Good* (DVD). Alexandria, VA: Society for Human Resource Management.

12. De Backer, K., Miroudot, S., and Rigo, D. (2019, Sept. 25). Multinational enterprises in the global economy: Heavily discussed, hardly measured. *VoxEU.* Retrieved from *https://voxeu.org/article/multinational-enterprises-global-economy* on June 1, 2020.

13. American Management Association. (2019, Jan. 24). Expatriate assignments are on the rise. Retrieved from *www.amanet.org/articles/expatriate-assignments-are-on-the-rise/* on June 1, 2020. *See also* KPMG International. (2019). 2019 global assignment policies and practices survey. Retrieved from *https://assets.kpmg/content/dam/kpmg/xx/pdf/2019/10/2019-gapp-survey-report-web.pdf* on June 2, 2020.

14. Economist Intelligence Unit (2020, Mar. 18). Worldwide cost of living 2020. Retrieved from *www.eiu.com/n/campaigns/worldwide-cost-of-living-2020* on June 1, 2020.

15. Mercer. (2020). Cost-of-living information services. Retrieved from *www.imercer.com/uploads/GM/pdf/cost-of-living-services-brochure.pdf* on June 1, 2020.

16. Wang, C.-H., and Varma, A. (2019). Cultural distance and expatriate failure rates: The moderating role of expatriate management practices. *The International Journal of Human Resource Management* 30(15), pp. 2211–30. *See also* AllianzCare. (2018, Sept. 13). Reasons

for expatriate failure and how HR can help. Retrieved from *www.allianzcare.com/en/employers/employer-blogs/2018/09/expat-failure.html* on June 1, 2020.

17. Chipman, R. (2016, June 16). The real costs of expatriate failure. Retrieved from *www.fidi.org/blog/real-cost-expatriate-assignment-failure* on June 1, 2020. *See also* Shaffer, M. A., and Harrison, D. A. (1998). Expatriates' psychological withdrawal from international assignments: Work, non-work, and family influences. *Personnel Psychology* 51, pp. 87–118.

18. Abramson, N. R., and Moran, R. T. (2018). *Managing Cultural Differences* (10th ed.). New York: Routledge. *See also* Middleton, J. (2014). *Cultural Intelligence, CQ: The Competitive Edge for Leaders Crossing Borders.* London, UK: Bloomsbury. *See also* Ang, S., and Van Dyne, L. (Eds.). (2008). *Handbook of Cultural Intelligence: Theory, Measurement, and Applications.* Armonk, NY: M. E. Sharpe.

19. For more on this, see Smith, A. D. (2019, Summer). Dealing with culture shock. *HRMagazine* 64(2), pp. 22, 23. *See also* Gelfand, M. J., Aycan, Z., Erez, M., and Leung, K. (2017). Cross-cultural industrial and organizational psychology and organizational behavior: A hundred-year journey. *Journal of Applied Psychology* 102, pp. 514–29. *See also* Devinney, T. M., Kirkman, B. L., Caprar, D. V., and Caligiuri, P. M. (2015). What is culture and how do we measure it? *Journal of International Business Studies* 46(9) [Special Issue].

20. Abramson and Moran (2018), op. cit.

21. Nagele-Piazza, L. (2019, Feb. 15). Should multinational employers have a global handbook? *SHRM Online.* Retrieved from www.shrm.org/resourcesandtools/legal-and-compliance/employment-law/pages/should-multinational-employers-have-a-global-handbook.aspx on Feb. 15, 2019.

22. Morrison, T., and Conaway, W. A. (2006). *Kiss, Bow, or Shake Hands* (2nd ed.). Avon, MA: Adams Media.

23. UK Department of International Trade. (2020). Doing business in Switzerland. Retrieved from *http://www.switzerland.doingbusinessguide.co.uk/the-guide/* on June 1, 2020. *See also* Bryant, S. (2019, Feb. 20). Understanding Germans: Top 12 tips on business etiquette. *Country Navigator.* Retrieved from *https://countrynavigator.com/blog/cultural-intelligence/germans/* on June 1, 2020.

24. Weisbart, M. (2010, Nov. 8). South Korea: So fast, so dynamic–Yet still hierarchical. *The Wall Street Journal*, p. R6. *See also* Needleman, S. E. (2008, July 31). Ivy Leaguers' big edge: Starting pay. *The Wall Street Journal.* Retrieved from *online.wsj.com/article/SB121746658635199271.html* on Aug. 19, 2008. *See also* Rhee, Z., and Chang, E. (2002). *Korean Business and Management.* Elizabeth, NJ: Hollym International.

25. Abramson and Moran (2018), op. cit. *See also* Muthukrishna, M. (2017, Oct. 23). In Latin America, as in the wider world, corruption is rooted in our relationships. *London School of Economics.* Retrieved from *https://blogs.lse.ac.uk/latamcaribbean/2017/10/23/in-latin-america-as-in-the-wider-world-corruption-is-rooted-in-our-relationships/* on June 1, 2020.

26. Six basic American cultural values. (2020). Retrieved from https://vintageamericanways.com/american-values/#:~:text=This%20system%20of%20values%20consists,Equality%20of%20opportunity%20and%20competition on June 1, 2020.

27. Abramson and Moran (2018), op. cit. *See also* Ralston, D. A., Holt, D. H., Terpstra, R. H., and Kai-Cheng, Y. (1997). The impact of national culture and economic ideology on managerial work values: A study of the United States, Russia, Japan, and China. *Journal of International Business Studies* 28, 177–207.

28. Abramson and Moran (2018), op. cit.

29. Taras, V., Steel, P., and Kirkman, B. L. (2011). Three decades of research on national culture in the workplace: Do the differences still make a difference? *Organizational Dynamics* 40(3), pp. 189–98.

30. Examining cross-cultural motivation in employees. (2015, Mar. 23). *UK Essays.* Retrieved from *www.ukessays.com/essays/management/examinating-cross-cultural-motivation-in-employees-management-essay.php* on July 3, 2017. *See also* Naor, M., Jones, J. S., Bernardes, E.

S., Goldstein, S. M., and Schroeder, R. (2014). The culture-effectiveness link in a manufacturing context: A resource-based perspective. *Journal of World Business* 49, pp. 321–31. *See also* Gelfand, M. J., Erez, M., and Aycan, Z. (2007). Cross-cultural organizational behavior. *Annual Review of Psychology* 58, pp. 479–514.

31. Abramson and Moran (2018), op. cit.

32. Dowling, P. J., Festing, M., and Engle, A. D., Sr. (2017). *International Human Resource Management* (7th ed.). Boston: Cengage Learning. *See also* Khilji, S. E., and Schuler, R. S. (2017). Talent management in the global context. In D. G. Collings, K. Mellahi, and W. F. Cascio (Eds.), *The Oxford Handbook of Talent Management*. Oxford, UK: Oxford University Press, pp. 399–419. *See also* Tarique et al. (2016), op. cit.

33. Chipman, R. (2016, June 16). The real cost of expatriate assignment failure. *FIDI*. Retrieved from *www.fidi.org/blog/real-cost-expatriate-assignment-failure* on July 4, 2017.

34. Reiche, S. (2014, July 7). Latest research: How does terrorism influence expats? Retrieved from *http://blog.iese.edu/expatriatus/2014/07/24/latest-research-how-does-terrorism-influence-expats/* on July 4, 2017.

35. NBC News. (2019, Apr. 13). These are the 35 countries with the U.S. State Department's new travel warning for kidnapping risk. Retrieved from *www.nbcnewyork.com/news/local/us-travel-warning-kidnapping-risk-abroad-which-countries/1777585/* on June 2, 2020.

36. Johnson, K. (2015, Feb. 9). Career boost for CFOs: A stint abroad. *The Wall Street Journal*. Retrieved from *www.wsj.com/articles/career-booster-for-cfos-work-experience-abroad-1423527358* on July 4, 2017. *See also* Baruch, Y., and Bozionelos, N. (2011). Career issues. In S. Zedeck (Ed.), *APA Handbook of Industrial and Organizational Psychology* (Vol. 2). Washington, DC: American Psychological Association, pp. 67–113. *See also* Kraimer, M. L., Shaffer, M. A., and Bolino, M. (2009). The influence of expatriate and repatriate experiences on career advancement and repatriate retention. *Human Resource Management* 48, pp. 27–47.

37. Meier, O., and Zihlmann, C. (2014). How emerging markets are changing expatriate policies. Retrieved from *www.imercer.com/uploads/GM/papers/mastering-challenges-of-global-mobility.pdf?aliId=68083484* on July 15, 2014. *See also* Carpenter et al. (2001), op. cit.

38. Tarique et al. (2016), op. cit.

39. Cashel, J. (2019, July 16). How businesses should prepare for global Internet access. *Harvard Business Review*. Retrieved from *https://hbr.org/2019/07/how-businesses-should-prepare-for-global-internet-access* on June 2, 2020. *See also* Melter, J. (2014, Feb.). Supporting the Internet as a platform for international trade. *The Brookings Institution*. Retrieved from *www.brookings.edu/wp-content/uploads/2016/07/02-internet-international-trade-meltzer.pdf* on June 2, 2020.

40. Company headquarters: Here, there, and everywhere. (2014, Feb. 22). *The Economist*. Retrieved from *www.economist.com/news/business/21596976-why-some-businesses-choose-multiple-corporate-citizenships-here-there-and-everywhere* on July 15, 2014. *See also* Dvorak, P. (2007, Nov. 19). Why multiple headquarters multiply. *The Wall Street Journal*, pp. B1, B3.

41. Thompson, A. A., Peteraf, M. A., Gamble, J. E., and Strickland, A. J. III. (2018). *Crafting and Executing Strategy: The Quest for Competitive Advantage* (21st ed.). New York: McGraw-Hill.

42. Gibson, P., Langel, E. M., and Sulkowicz, K. (2016, Mar. 15). Talent is your biggest risk. Retrieved from *www.heidrick.com/Knowledge-Center/Publication/Talent-is-your-biggest-risk* on June 2, 2020.

43. Bolden-Barrett, V. (2020, Jan. 22). Global talent shortage has nearly doubled in the past decade. *HR Dive*. Retrieved from *www.hrdive.com/news/global-talent-shortage-has-nearly-doubled-in-the-past-decade/570731/* on June 2, 2020. *See also* Medland, M. E. (2004, Jan.). Setting up overseas. *HRMagazine*, pp. 68–72. *See also* Spreitzer, G. M., McCall, M. W., Jr., and Mahoney, J. D. (1997). Early identification of international executive potential. *Journal of Applied Psychology* 82, pp. 6–29.

44. Vorhauser-Smith, S. (2014, Sept. 29). How to overcome the workforce planning disconnect. *Forbes*. Retrieved from *www.forbes.com/sites/sylviavorhausersmith/2014/09/29/yes-its-important-but-overcoming-the-workforce-planning-disconnect/#65197b804a0d* on June 2, 2020. *See also* Meier and Zihlmann (2014), op. cit.

45. Tarique et al. (2016), op. cit. *See also* Dowling et al. (2017), op. cit.

46. Ibid.

47. Weisbart (2010), op. cit.

48. Society for Human Resource Management Foundation. (2017, Feb. 6). *From Local, to Regional, to Global Player: Evolution of the HR Role at Aramex. (Dubai)*. Available at *www.youtube.com/watch?v=Yq1TCdICUuM*. *See also* Jossi, F. (2002, Oct.). Successful handoff. *HRMagazine*, pp. 48–52.

49. Giolando, E. (2016, Dec. 8). What do employers think of international experience? *Go Overseas*. Retrieved from *www.gooverseas.com/blog/what-do-employers-think-of-international-experience* on June 2, 2020. *See also* TheMuse. (n.d.). Want to work abroad? These companies will make your dreams come true. Retrieved from *www.themuse.com/advice/companies-where-you-can-work-abroad* on June 2, 2020.

50. Caligiuri, P., and Paul, K. B. (2017). Selection in multinational organizations. In J. L. Farr and N. T. Tippins (Eds.), *Handbook of Employee Selection* (2nd ed.). New York: Routledge, pp. 797–811. *See also* Caligiuri, P., and Brucker, J. J. L. E. (2015). Selection for international assignments. In D. Collings, G. Wood, and P. Caligiuri (Eds.), *Companion to International Human Resource Management*. New York: Routledge, pp. 275–88.

51. Kraimer, M., Bolino, M., and Mead, B. (2016). Themes in expatriate and repatriate research over four decades: What do we know and what do we still need to learn? *Annual Review of Organizational Psychology and Organizational Behavior* 3, pp. 83–109. *See also* Caligiuri, P., and Tarique, I. (2012). International assignee selection and cross-cultural training and development. In I. Bjorkman, G. Stahl, and S. Morris (Eds.), *Handbook of Research in International Human Resource Management* (2nd ed.). London, UK: Edward Elgar Ltd., pp. 321–42.

52. Caligiuri and Paul (2017), op. cit. *See also* Caligiuri and Brucker (2015), op. cit. *See also* Collings, D. G., and Scullion, H. (2012). Global staffing. In I. Bjorkman, G. Stahl, and S. Morris (Eds.), *Handbook of Research in International Human Resource Management* (2nd ed.). London, UK: Edward Elgar Ltd., pp. 142–61.

53. Pucik, V., Evans, P., Bjorkman, I. , and Morris, S. (2016). *The Global Challenge: International Human Resource Management* (3rd ed.). Chicago: Chicago Business Press.

54. KPMG International. (2019). 2019 Global Assignment and Practices Survey. Retrieved from *https://assets.kpmg/content/dam/kpmg/xx/pdf/2019/10/2019-gapp-survey-report-web.pdf* on June 2, 2020.

55. Schmidt, F. L. (2002). The role of general cognitive ability and job performance: Why there cannot be a debate. *Human Performance* 15, pp. 187–210.

56. Ones, D. S., Dilchert, S., Viswesvaran, C., and Salgado, J. F. (2017). Cognitive ability: Measurement and validity for employee selection. In J. L. Farr and N. T. Tippins (Eds.), *Handbook of Employee Selection* (2nd ed.). New York: Routledge, pp. 251–76. *See also* Schmidt, F. L., and Hunter, J. E. (1998). The validity and utility of selection methods in personnel psychology: Practical and theoretical implications of 85 years of research findings. *Psychological Bulletin* 124, pp. 262–74.

57. Salgado, J. F., Anderson, N., Moscoso, S., Berua, C., de Fruyt, F., and Rolland, J. P. (2003). A meta-analytic study of general mental ability validity for different occupations in the European Community. *Journal of Applied Psychology* 88, pp. 1068–81.

58. Ones et al. (2017), op. cit. *See also* Hülsheger, U. R., Maier, G. W., and Stumpp, T. (2007). Validity of general mental ability for the prediction of job performance and training success in Germany: A meta-analysis. *International Journal of Selection & Assessment* 15, pp. 3–18. *See also* Bertua, C., Anderson, N., and Salgado, J. F. (2005). The predictive validity of cognitive ability tests: A UK meta-analysis. *Journal of Occupational & Organizational Psychology* 78, pp. 387–409.

59. Caligiuri and Paul (2017), op. cit. *See also* Shaffer, M. A., Harrison, D. A., Gregersen, H., Black, J. S., and Ferzandi, L. A. (2006). You can take it with you: Individual differences and expatriate effectiveness. *Journal of Applied Psychology* 91, pp. 109–15. *See also* Caligiuri, P. M. (2000). The Big Five personality characteristics as predictors of expatriates' desire to terminate the assignment and supervisor-rated performance. *Personnel Psychology* 53, pp. 67–88. *See also* Silverman (2006), op. cit.

60. Caligiuri and Tarique (2012), op. cit.

61. Lievens, F., Harris, M. M., Van Keer, E., and Bisqueret, C. (2003). Predicting cross-cultural training performance: The validity of personality, cognitive ability, and dimensions measured by an assessment center and a behavior description interview. *Journal of Applied Psychology* 88, pp. 476–89.

62. Caligiuri (2000), op. cit.

63. Firth, B. M., Chen, G., Kirkman, B. L., and Kim, K. (2014). Newcomers abroad: Expatriate adaptation during early phases of international assignments. *Academy of Management Journal* 57, pp. 280–300.

64. Caligiuri, P., and Phillips, J. (2003). An application of self-assessment realistic job previews to expatriate assignments. *International Journal of Human Resource Management* 14, pp. 1102–16.

65. Florida Labor Lawyer. (2018, Sept. 24). U.S. citizens working abroad for a multinational employer: Your basic rights. Retrieved from *www.floridalaborlawyer.com/u-s-citizens-working-abroad-for-a-multinational-employer-your-basic-rights/* on June 3, 2020. *See also* Lau, S. (2008, Feb.). HR solutions: U.S. laws abroad. *HRMagazine*, p. 32.

66. Baker and McKenzie (2016). The global employer: A primer on international labor and employment issues. Retrieved from *www.lexology.com/library/detail.aspx?g=ca5d70cf-5055-4e81-bc17-40d66403cc6e* on June 3, 2020.

67. Kraimer et al. (2016), op. cit.

68. Pucik et al. (2016), op. cit. *See also* Pucik, V., and Saba, T. (1999). Selecting and developing the global versus the expatriate manager: A review of the state of the art. *Human Resource Planning*, pp. 40–54.

69. KPMG, 2019 global assignment policies and practices survey, op. cit.

70. Caligiuri and Tarique (2012), op. cit. *See also* Shaffer and Harrison (1998), op. cit. *See also* Black, J. S., Gregersen, H. B., and Mendenhall, M. E. (1992). *Global Assignments*. San Francisco: Jossey-Bass.

71. Gurchiek, K. (2016, Mar. 22). HR best practices can lead to a better expat experience. *SHRM Online*. Retrieved from *www.shrm.org/resourcesandtools/hr-topics/global-hr/pages/hr-best-practices-can-lead-to-better-expat-experience.aspx* on Apr. 7, 2016. *See also* Krell, E. (2005, June). Budding relationships. *HRMagazine*, pp. 114–18. *See also* Aryee, S., Fields, D., and Luk, V. (1999). A cross-cultural test of a model of the work-family interface. *Journal of Management* 25, pp. 491–511.

72. Gurchiek (2016), op. cit. *See also* Evans et al. (2011), op. cit. *See also* Shaffer, M. A., and Harrison, D. A. (2001). Forgotten partners of international assignments: Development and test of a model of spouse adjustment. *Journal of Applied Psychology* 86, pp. 238–54.

73. Reiche, B. S., Lee, Y. T., and Quintanilla, J. (2015). Cross-cultural training and support practices of international assignees. In D. G. Collings, G. T. Wood, and P. M. Caligiuri (Eds.), *The Routledge Companion to International Human Resource Management*. New York: Routledge, pp. 308–23. *See also* Bhawuk, D. P. S., and Brislin, R. W. (2000). Cross-cultural training: A review. *Applied Psychology: An International Review* 49, pp. 162–91.

74. Brookfield GRS (2016), op. cit. *See also* Napier, N. K., and Taylor, S. (2002). Experiences of women professionals abroad: Comparisons across Japan, China, and Turkey. *International Journal of Human Resource Management* 13, pp. 837–51. *See also* Caligiuri, P., and Cascio, W. F. (2000). Sending women on global assignments. *WorldatWork Journal* 9(2),

pp. 34–40. *See also* Fisher, A. (1998, Sept. 28). Overseas, U.S. businesswomen may have the edge. *Fortune*, p. 304.

75. Kraimer et al. (2016), op. cit. *See also* Caligiuri and Tarique (2012), op. cit. *See also* Littrell, L., Salas, E., Hess, K., Paley, M., and Riedel, S. (2006). Expatriate preparation: A critical analysis of 25 years of cross-cultural training research. *Human Resource Development Review* 5, pp. 355–88. *See also* Harrison, J. K. (1992). Individual and combined effects of behavior modeling and the cultural assimilator in cross-cultural management training. *Journal of Applied Psychology* 77, pp. 952-62. *See also* Black, J. S., and Mendenhall, M. (1990). Cross-cultural training effectiveness: A review and a theoretical framework for future research. *Academy of Management Review* 15, pp. 113–36.

76. Caligiuri and Tarique (2012), op. cit.

77. Tarique et al. (2016), op. cit.

78. Kraimer et al. (2016), op. cit. *See also* Gurchiek (2016), op. cit. *See also* Firth et al. (2014), op. cit. *See also* Ren, H., Shaffer, M. A., Harrison, D. A., Fu, C., and Fodchuk, K. M. (2014). Reactive adjustment or proactive embedding? Multistudy, multiwave evidence for dual pathways to expatriate retention. *Personnel Psychology* 67, pp. 203-37. *See also* Kraimer, M. L., Wayne, S. J., and Jaworski, R. A. (2001). Sources of support and expatriate performance: The mediating role of expatriate adjustment. *Personnel Psychology* 54, pp. 71-99.

79. Abramson and Moran (2017), op. cit.

80. Tyler, K. (2003, May). Cut the stress. *HR Magazine*, pp. 101-6.

81. Smith, A. D. (2019, Summer). Dealing with culture shock. *HRMagazine* 64(2), pp. 22, 23.

82. KPMG, 2019 Global Assignment and Practices Survey (2019), op. cit. *See also* Kraimer et al. (2016), op. cit. *See also* Brookfield GRS 2016 global mobility trends survey, op. cit.

83. Pulakos, E. D., Arad, S., Donovan, M. A., and Plamondon, K. E. (2000). Adaptability in the workplace: Development of a taxonomy of adaptive performance. *Journal of Applied Psychology* 85, pp. 612-24.

84. Tarique et al. (2016), op. cit. *See also* Distefano, M., and Schulman, S. (2011, 3rd Quarter). Building global cultures. *Korn/Ferry Institute Briefings on Talent and Leadership*, pp. 46–52. *See also* Dowling et al. (2017), op. cit.

85. Rathbone, C. L. H. (2014). Expatriate attraction, selection, and retention: The symbiosis between mobility and leadership development. Retrieved from *www.imercer.com/uploads/GM/papers/mastering-challenges-of-global-mobility.pdf?aliId=68083484* on July 15, 2014.

86. Bonache, J., and Stirpe, L. (2012). Compensating global employees. In G. K. Stahl, I. Bjorkman, and S. Morris (Eds.), *Handbook of Research in International Human Resource Management* (2nd ed.). Cheltenham, UK: Edward Elgar, pp. 162-82. *See also* Wright, G. (2011, June). Deliver pay worldwide. *HRMagazine*, pp. 111-14. *See also* Gerhart, B., and Newman, J. M. (2020). *Compensation* (13th ed.). New York: McGraw-Hill.

87. Herod, R. (2017, May 15). "Local-plus" expatriate policies are on the rise. *SHRM Online*. Retrieved from *www.shrm.org/resourcesandtools/hr-topics/global-hr/pages/local-plus-expatriate-policies-are-on-the-rise.aspx* on May 16, 2017. *See also* Gerhart and Newman (2020), op cit. *See also* Dowling et al. (2017), op. cit.

88. Ibid.

89. Herod (2017), op. cit. *See also* Gaster, S., Hannibal, E., and O'Neill, J. (2014). Alternative international assignment compensation approaches. Retrieved from *www.imercer.com/uploads/GM/papers/mastering-challenges-of-global-mobility.pdf?aliId=68083484* on July 15, 2014. *See also* Dowling et al. (2017), op. cit.

90. KPMG, 2019 Global assignment policies and practices survey, op. cit. *See also* Gaster, S., Hannibal, E., and O'Neill, J. (2013). Alternative international assignment compensation approaches. Retrieved from *www.imercer.com/uploads/Europe/pdfs/2013/2013_Expat_Conference/emc_booklet_final_low_res.pdf* on July 1, 2015.

91. See, for example, Meyer, E. (2015, Dec.). Getting to si, ja, oui, hai, and da. *Harvard Business Review*, pp. 74–80.

92. Gerhart and Newman (2020), op. cit.

93. Tarique et al. (2016), op. cit.

94. Maurer, R. (2018, April 12). Employers offering more perks to attract talent from abroad. *SHRM Online*. Retrieved from *www.shrm.org/resourcesandtools/hr-topics/talent-acquisition/pages/employers-offering-perks-attract-foreign-talent.aspx* on Apr. 12, 2018.

95. Spindell, A. (2013, Sept. 24). Hiring pitfalls of expanding overseas and how to avoid them. Retrieved from *http://news.thomasnet.com/IMT/2013/09/24/hiring-pitfalls-of-expanding-overseas-and-how-to-avoid-them/* on Sept. 27, 2013. *See also* Woodward, N. H. (2007, Aug.). Using "cost of living adjustments" to compensate expats. *Global HR News*. Retrieved from *www.shrm.org* on Aug. 15, 2007.

96. Hoffower, H. (2020, Jan. 14). The 25 most expensive cities around the world to rent a 2-bedroom apartment. *Business Insider*. Retrieved from *www.businessinsider.com/most-expensive-cities-worldwide-to-rent-an-apartment-2019-5* on June 3, 2020.

97. Danger-zone jobs. (2012). Retrieved from *https://civiliancontractors.wordpress.com/tag/danger-pay/* on July 16, 2014.

98. Smith (2019), op. cit. *See also* Woodward (2007), op. cit.

99. Dowling et al. (2017), op. cit.

100. Pulakos, E. D., and O'Leary, R. S. (2011). Why is performance management broken? *Industrial and Organizational Psychology: Perspectives on Science and Practice* 4(2), pp. 146–64.

101. Claus, L., and Briscoe, D. (2009). Employee performance management across borders: A review of relevant academic literature. *International Journal of Management Reviews* 11(2), pp. 175–96.

102. Cascio, W. F. (2012). Global performance management systems. In I. Bjorkman, G. Stahl, and S. Morris (Eds.), *Handbook of Research in International Human Resource Management* (2nd ed.). London: Edward Elgar Ltd., pp. 183–204. *See also* Cascio, W. F. (2011). The puzzle of performance management in multinational enterprises. *Industrial and Organizational Psychology: Perspectives on Science and Practice* 4(2), pp. 190–93.

103. Hofstede, G. (2001). *Culture's Consequences: Comparing Values, Behaviors, Institutions, and Organizations across Nations* (2nd ed.). Thousand Oaks, CA: Sage. *See also* Hofstede, G., and Hofstede, G. J. (2005). *Cultures and Organizations: Software of the Mind* (revised and expanded 2nd ed.). New York: McGraw-Hill.

104. Van de Vliert, E., Shi, K., Sanders, K., Wang, Y., and Huang, X. (2004). Chinese and Dutch interpretations of supervisory feedback. *Journal of Cross-Cultural Psychology* 35, pp. 417–35.

105. Barton, E. (2016, Aug. 23). Why you don't give praise in Japan. *BBC*. Retrieved from *www.bbc.com/capital/story/20160822-why-you-dont-give-praise-in-japan* on July 5, 2017. *See also* Matsumoto, T. (2004). Learning to "do time" in Japan: A study of U.S. interns in Japanese organizations. *International Journal of Cross-Cultural Management* 4, pp. 19–37.

106. Shore, T., and Strauss, J. (2008). The political context of employee appraisal: Effects of organizational goals on performance ratings. *International Journal of Management* 25(4), pp. 599–612.

107. Varma, A., Budhwar, P. S., and McCusker, C. (2015). Performance management in the global organization. In D. G. Collings, G. T. Wood, and P. M. Caligiuri (Eds.), *The Routledge Companion to International Human Resource Management*. New York: Routledge, pp. 172–89. *See also* Engle, A. D., Festing, M., and Dowling, P. J. (2014). Proposing processes of global performance management: An analysis of the literature. *Journal of Global Mobility* 2(1), pp. 5–25. *See also* Cascio (2011), op. cit.

108. Toh, S. M., and DeNisi, A. S. (2003). Host-country national reactions to expatriate pay policies: A model and implications. *Academy of Management Review* 28, pp. 606-21. *See also* Kim, K. I., Park, H. J., and Suzuki, N. (1990). Reward allocations in the United States, Japan, and Korea: A comparison of individualistic and collectivistic cultures. *Academy of Management Journal* 33, pp. 188-98.

109. Minton-Eversole, T. (2009). Best expatriate assignments require much thought, even more planning. *HR Trendbook*, pp. 74-75. *See also* Garonzik, R., Brockner, J., and Siegel, P. A. (2000). Identifying international assignees at risk for premature departure: The interactive effect of outcome favorability and procedural fairness. *Journal of Applied Psychology* 85, pp. 13-20.

110. Cascio (2012), op. cit.. *See also* Engle, A. D., Sr., Dowling, P. J., and Festing, M. (2008). State of origin: Research in global performance management, a proposed research domain, and emerging implications. *European Journal of International Management* 2, pp. 153-69.

110. Rosman, K. (2007, Oct. 26). Expat life gets less cushy. *The Wall Street Journal*, pp. W1, W10. *See also* White, E. (2005, Jan. 25). Executives with global experience are among the most in-demand. *The Wall Street Journal*, p. B6.

112. Budd, J. W. (2021). *Labor Relations: Striking a Balance* (6th ed.). New York: McGraw-Hill. *See also* Lamare, J. R., Farndale, E., and Gunnigle, P. (2015). Employment relations and IHRM. In D. G. Collings, G. T. Wood, and P. M. Caligiuri (Eds.), *The Routledge Companion to International Human Resource Management*. New York: Routledge, pp. 99-137.

113. Brin (2020), op. cit. *See also* Dieterling, C. (2019, March 29). 10 requirements to know when employing staff in France. *SHRM Online*. Retrieved from *www.shrm.org/resourcesandtools/legal-and-compliance/employment-law/pages/global-france-overview-mandates.aspx* on Mar. 29, 2019. *See also* Bamber, G. J., Lansbury, R. D., Wailes, N.. and Wright, C. F. (Eds.). (2016). *International and Comparative Employment Relations* (6th ed.). Thousand Oaks, CA: Sage. *See also* Roberts, D. (2016, Nov. 20). Beijing wants one union to rule them all. *Bloomberg Businessweek*, pp. 38-40.

114. Dowling et al. (2017), op. cit. *See also* Movassaghi, H. (1996). The workers of nations: Industrial relations in a global economy. *Compensation & Benefits Management* 12(2), pp. 75-77.

115. Ales, E., and Dufresne, A. (2012). Transnational collective bargaining: Another (problematic) fragment of the European multilevel industrial relations system. *European Journal of Industrial Relations* 18, pp. 95-105. *See also* Katz, H. C., Kochan, T. A., and Colvin, A. J. S. (2008). *An Introduction to Collective Bargaining and Industrial Relations* (4th ed.). New York: McGraw-Hill/Irwin.

116. Mann and Spegele (2017), op. cit. *See also* Budd (2021), op. cit. *See also* Tarique et al. (2016), op. cit. *See also* Khan, M. A. (2016). *Multinational Enterprise Management Strategies in Developing Countries*. Hershey, PA: IGI Global.

117. Agarwal, P. (2017, Aug. 12). Labor arbitrage. *Intelligent Economist*. Retrieved from *www.intelligenteconomist.com/labor-arbitrage/* on June 4, 2020. *See also* Boudette, N. E. (2013, Nov. 8). A new alliance: UAW and Germany. *The Wall Street Journal*, pp. B1, B2. *See also* Katz, H. C., Kochan, T. A., and Colvin, A. J. (2017). *An Introduction to U.S. Collective Bargaining and Labor Relations* (5th ed.). Ithaca, NY: ILR Press, Cornell University.

118. Ales, E. Wien, W., and Carli, L. G. (2018, Mar.). Transnational collective agreements: The role of trade unions and employers' associations. *European Commission*. Retrieved from *https://eu.eventscloud.com/file_uploads/185fe09c1a16e079ad008e8927fc6c8a_Ales_Final_EN3.pdf* on June 4, 2020. *See also* Mueller, T., Platzer, H. W., and Rueb, S. (2010). Transnational company policy and coordination of collective bargaining—New challenges and roles for European industry federations. *European Review of Labour and Research* 16(4), pp. 509-24.

119. Budd (2021), op. cit. *See also* Katz et al. (2017), op. cit.

120. International Labour Organization. (2020). The benefits of international labour standards. Retrieved from *www.ilo.org/global/standards/introduction-to-international-labour-standards/the-benefits-of-international-labour-standards/lang-en/index.htm* on June 4, 2020. *See also* One big union? (2008, June 9). *BusinessWeek*, p. 6. *See also* Batson, A. (2007, May 23). How U.S. labor leaders chart a global course. *The Wall Street Journal*, p. A6.

121. Code of Conduct, 6.0 (2018). *Responsible Business Alliance*. Retrieved from *www.responsiblebusiness.org/code-of-conduct/* on June 4, 2020. *See also* Burrows, P. (2006, June 19). Stalking hi-tech sweatshops. *BusinessWeek*, pp. 62, 63.

122. Paton, E. (2020, March 1). After factory disaster, Bangladesh made big safety strides. Are the bad days coming back? *The New York Times*. Retrieved from *www.nytimes.com/2020/03/01/world/asia/rana-plaza-bangladesh-garment-industry.html* on Apr. 7, 2020. *See also* Alam, J. (2017, Apr. 24). Report: Companies not complying with Bangladesh garment plan. Retrieved from *https://sg.news.yahoo.com/report-companies-not-complying-bangladesh-110043381.html* on Apr. 25, 2017.

123. Free exchange. (2017, Feb. 4). Better than a wall: Understanding NAFTA, a disappointing but underappreciated trade deal. *The Economist*, p. 63.

124. Knowledge@Wharton. (2016, Sept. 6). NAFTA's impact on the U.S. economy: What are the facts? Retrieved from *http://knowledge.wharton.upenn.edu/article/naftas-impact-u-s-economy-facts/* on Sept. 7, 2016. *See also* Sergie, M. A. (2014, Feb. 14). NAFTA's economic impact. Retrieved from *www.cfr.org/trade/naftas-economic-impact/p15790* on July 17, 2014.

125. Althaus, G., and Rogers, A. C. (2016, Nov. 11). Global car industry runs on NAFTA. *The Wall Street Journal*, pp. A1, A12. *See also* Porter, E. (2016, Mar. 29). NAFTA may have saved many autoworkers' jobs. *The New York Times*. Retrieved from *www.nytimes.com/2016/03/30/business/economy/nafta-may-have-saved-many-autoworkers-jobs.html* on Mar. 30, 2016. *See also* Black, T., and Cota, I. (2016, Apr. 24). A tale of two NAFTA towns. *Bloomberg Businessweek*, pp. 12, 13.

126. Schwartz, D., and Salins, R. (2020, Feb. 6). Labor law implications of the United States-Mexico-Canada agreement. *New York Law Journal*. Retrieved from *www.law.com/newyorklawjournal/2020/02/06/labor-law-implications-of-the-united-states-mexico-canada-agreement/?slreturn=20200504165351* on June 4, 2020. *See also* Lobosco, K., Fung, B., and Luhby, T. (2019, Dec. 17). 6 key differences between NAFTA and the USMC deal that replaces it. *CNN*. Retrieved from *www.cnn.com/2019/12/10/politics/nafta-us-mexico-canada-trade-deal-differences/index.html* on June 4, 2020.

127. KPMG International, 2019 Global assignment and practices survey (2019), op. cit. *See also* Gerhart and Newman (2020), op. cit. *See also* Brookfield GRS (2016), op. cit.

128. Schumpeter. (2015, Nov. 7). Not-so-happy returns: Big businesses fail to make the most of employees with foreign experience. *The Economist*, p. 62. *See also* Andors, A. (2010, Mar.). Happy returns. *HRMagazine*, pp. 61–63. *See also* Gregersen, H. B. (1992). Commitments to a parent company and a local work unit during repatriation. *Personnel Psychology* 45, pp. 29–54.

129. Schumpeter (2015), op. cit.

130. Kraimer et al. (2016), op. cit. *See also* Andors (2010), op. cit. *See also* Minton-Eversole (2009), op. cit. *See also* Before saying yes to going abroad. (1995, Dec. 4). *BusinessWeek*, pp. 130, 132.

131. Gerhart and Newman (2020), op. cit.

132. Kraimer, M. L., Shaffer, M. A., Harrison, D. A., and Ren, H. (2012). No place like home? An identity strain perspective on repatriate turnover. *Academy of Management Journal* 55, pp. 399–420. Estimates of repatriate turnover vary widely; see, for example, Lazarova, M. (2015). Taking stock of repatriate research. In D. G. Collings, G. T. Wood, and P. M. Caligiuri (Eds.), *The Routledge Companion to International Human Resource Management*. New York: Routledge, pp. 378–98.

133. Schumpeter (2015), op. cit.

134. Andors (2010), op. cit.

135. Kraimer et al. (2012), op. cit. *See also* Kraimer et al. (2009), op. cit.

136. Shaffer, M. A., Kraimer, M. L., Chen, Y. P., and Bolino, M. C. (2012). Choices, challenges, and career consequences of global work experiences: A review and future agenda. *Journal of Management* 38, pp. 1282–327. *See also* Lazarova, M. B., and Cerdin, J. L. (2007). Revisiting repatriation concerns: Organizational support versus career and contextual influences. *Journal of International Business Studies* 38(3), pp. 404–29.

GLOSSARY

360-degree feedback Performance assessments from above, below, and at the same level as an employee. It may also include feedback from customers.

401(k) plan A defined-contribution pension plan in which an employee can deduct a certain amount of his or her income from taxes and place the money into a personal retirement account; if the employer adds matching funds, the combined sums grow tax-free until they are withdrawn, usually at retirement.

absenteeism Any failure of an employee to report for or to remain at work as scheduled, regardless of reason.

absolute rating systems Rating formats that evaluate each employee in terms of performance standards, without reference to other employees.

acceptability The extent to which a performance measure is deemed to be satisfactory or adequate by those who use it.

action learning A process in which participants learn through experience and application.

active listening Listening in which five things are done well: taking time to listen, communicating verbally and nonverbally, not interrupting or arguing, watching for verbal and nonverbal cues, and summarizing what was said and what was agreed to.

adjustment The managerial activities intended to maintain compliance with the organization's human resource policies and business strategies.

adverse-impact discrimination Unintentional discrimination that occurs when identical standards or procedures are applied to everyone, despite the fact that such standards or procedures lead to a substantial difference in employment outcomes for the members of a particular group.

affirmative action Action intended to overcome the effects of past or present discriminatory policies or practices, or other barriers to equal employment opportunity.

age grading Subconscious expectations about what people can and cannot do at particular times of their lives.

agreeableness The degree to which an individual is cooperative, warm, and agreeable versus cold, disagreeable, and antagonistic.

alternation ranking A ranking method in which a rater initially lists all employees on a sheet of paper and then chooses the best employee, worst employee, second best, second worst, and so forth until all employees have been ranked.

alternative dispute resolution (ADR) program A formal, structured policy for dispute resolution that may involve third-party mediation and arbitration.

annuity problem The situation that exists when past merit payments, incorporated into an employee's base pay, form an annuity (a sum of money received at regular intervals), allowing formerly productive employees to slack off for several years while still earning high pay.

anti-discrimination rule A principle that holds that employers can obtain tax advantages only for those benefits that do not discriminate in favor of highly compensated employees.

applicant An individual who formally applies for a job.

applicant group Individuals who are eligible for and formally apply for a job.

applicant-tracking systems Systems that track where each applicant is in the recruitment process, generate reports that analyze the relative performance of alternative recruitment sources and strategies, and record/analyze data to meet EEO and government-contractor requirements.

assessment phase The phase of training whose purpose is to define what the employee should learn in relation to desired job behaviors.

assessment-center method A process that evaluates a candidate's potential for management on the basis of multiple assessment techniques, standardized methods of making inferences from such techniques, and pooled judgments from multiple assessors.

assistive technology In this context, computer-based technology that enables people with disabilities to perform work-related tasks.

attitudes Internal states that focus on particular aspects of or objects in the environment.

authority For managers at all levels, the organizationally granted right to influence the actions and behavior of the workers they manage.

authorization cards Cards, signed by employees, that designate the union as the employee's exclusive representative in bargaining with management.

available labor pool Individuals who possess the necessary skills or minimum qualifications that jobs require.

baby-boom generation People born between 1946 and 1964, currently 54 percent of the workforce; many believe that the business of business includes leadership in redressing social inequities.

balance In a pay system, the relative size of pay differentials among different segments of the workforce.

balance-sheet approach A method of compensating expatriates in which the primary objective is to ensure that the expatriates neither gain nor lose financially compared with their home-country peers.

bargaining impasse The situation that occurs when the parties involved in negotiations are unable to move further toward settlement.

bargaining unit A group of employees eligible to vote in a representation election.

behavior modeling Acting as a role model. The fundamental characteristic of modeling is that learning takes place by observation of the role model's behavior or by imagining his or her experience.

behavior-oriented rating method An appraisal method in which employee performance is rated either by comparing the performance of employees to that of other employees or by evaluating each employee in terms of performance standards without reference to others.

behaviorally anchored rating scales (BARS) Graphic rating scales that define the dimensions to be rated in behavioral terms and use critical incidents to describe various levels of performance.

benchmark jobs Jobs that are characterized by stable tasks and stable job specifications; also known as *key jobs*.

best of breed When choosing an HRIS, organizations select the best applications in each HR area from multiple vendors.

big data The collection and analysis of the digital history created when people shop or surf the Internet, but it also includes the tests and measures of aptitudes, behaviors, and competencies that employers compile about applicants and employees.

biometrics Unique physical and behavioral features (such as fingerprints or eye pupils) that can be sensed by devices and interpreted by computers to bond digital data to personal identities.

bona fide occupational qualification Otherwise prohibited discriminatory factors (such as gender or age) that are exempted from coverage under Title VII of the Civil Rights Act of 1964 when they are considered reasonably necessary to the operation of a particular business or enterprise.

broad banding A technique used in compensation in which as many as four or five traditional pay grades are collapsed into a single pay band with one minimum and one maximum value.

business strategy The means that firms use to compete in the marketplace (e.g., cost leadership). It provides an overall direction and focus for the organization as a whole, as well as for each functional area.

buying power A person's disposable income after taxes that allows him or her to make purchases.

cafeteria benefits A package of benefits offered to workers; both "basic" and "optional" items are included, and each worker can pick and choose among the alternative options.

card check A process in which a union secures authorization cards from more than 50 percent of employees, giving it the right to ask management directly for the right to exclusive representation.

case law The courts' interpretations of laws and determination of how those laws will be enforced, which serve as precedents to guide future legal decisions.

cash-balance plan A pension plan in which each employee receives steady annual credit toward an eventual pension, adding to his or her pension account "cash balance."

central tendency In rating employees, a tendency to give employees an average rating on each criterion.

choice-of-law provision Specifies that the laws of a particular state will be used to interpret a contract.

circumstantial evidence Statistical evidence used as a method of proving the intention to discriminate systematically against classes of individuals.

collaborative media platforms Specialized tools that support processes in various disciplines, including HR, for example, recruitment and performance management. Other tools include file-sharing sites and spaces where teams can collaborate on projects to share information in a private, secure setting.

community of interest A defined unit that reflects the shared interests of the employees involved.

compensable factors Common job characteristics that an organization is willing to pay for, such as skill, effort, responsibility, and working conditions.

compensation The human resource management function that deals with every type of reward that individuals receive in return for performing work.

competencies Characteristics of individuals that are necessary for successful performance, with behavioral indicators associated with high performance.

competency models Attempts to identify variables related to overall organizational fit and to identify personality characteristics consistent with the organization's vision.

competency-based pay system   A pay system under which workers are paid on the basis of the number of jobs they are capable of doing—that is, on the basis of the skills or depth of knowledge they possess that define various competencies.

competitive strategy   The means that firms use to compete for business in the marketplace and to gain competitive advantage.

conscientiousness   The degree to which an individual is hard-working, organized, dependable, and persevering versus lazy, disorganized, and unreliable.

constitutional due-process rights   Such rights, such as notice of charges or issues prior to a hearing, representation by counsel, and the opportunity to confront and to cross-examine adverse witnesses and evidence, protect individuals with respect to state, municipal, and federal government processes. However, they normally do not apply to work situations.

consumer-driven health plan (CDHP)   Such plans involve a high-deductible insurance plan combined with a health-care spending account from which unreimbursed health-care costs are paid.

contract compliance   Adherence of contractors and subcontractors to equal employment opportunity, affirmative action, and other requirements of federal contract work.

contrast effects   A tendency among interviewers to evaluate a current candidate's interview performance relative to the performances of immediately preceding candidates.

contrast error   A rating error occurring when an appraiser compares several employees with one another rather than with an objective standard of performance.

contributory plans   Group health-care plans in which employees share in the cost of the premiums.

cosmopolitan perspective   A perspective that comprises sensitivity to cultural differences, respect for distinctive practices of others, and making allowances for such factors in communicating with representatives of different cultural groups.

cost shifting   In health care, a situation in which one group of patients pays less than the true cost of their medical care.

critical incidents   In job analysis, vignettes consisting of brief actual reports that illustrate particularly effective or ineffective worker behaviors; a behavior-oriented rating method consisting of such anecdotal reports.

cross-cultural training   Formal programs designed to prepare persons of one culture to interact effectively in another culture or to interact more effectively with persons from different cultures.

cross-training   Providing exposure to and practice with the tasks, roles, and responsibilities of an employee's teammates in an effort to increase shared understanding and knowledge among team members.

culture   The characteristic customs, social patterns, beliefs, and values of people in a particular country or region, or in a particular racial or religious group.

culture shock   The frustrations, conflict, anxiety, and feelings of alienation experienced by those who enter an unfamiliar culture.

decertification   Revocation of a union's status as the exclusive bargaining agent for the workers.

decision-support system (DSS)   An interactive computer program designed to provide relevant information and to answer what-if questions; may be used to enhance communication about and understanding of employee benefit programs.

defined-benefit plans   Pension plans under which an employer promises to pay a retiree a stated pension, often expressed as a percentage of preretirement pay.

defined-contribution plan   A type of pension plan that fixes a rate for employer contributions to a pension fund; future benefits depend on how fast the fund grows.

demographic analysis   In the analysis of training needs, such analysis is helpful in determining the special needs of a particular group, such as older workers, women, or managers at different levels.

dependent-care assistance plan   A form of flexible spending account that provides a tax-free vehicle for employees to pay for certain dependent-care expenses.

descriptive analytics   Data-based HR analyses that help managers understand what happened in the past and why.

destructive criticism   Criticism that is general in nature; that is frequently delivered in a biting, sarcastic tone; and that often attributes poor performance to internal causes.

development   The managerial function of preserving and enhancing employees' competence in their jobs by improving their knowledge, skills, abilities, and other characteristics.

direct evidence   Intentional discrimination—for example, open expressions of hatred, disrespect, or inequality—knowingly directed against members of a particular group.

disability   A physical or mental impairment that substantially limits one or more major life activities.

disability management   A method of controlling disability-leave costs that emphasizes a partnership among physician, employee, manager, and human resources representative.

discrimination   The giving of an unfair advantage (or disadvantage) to the members of a particular group in comparison with the members of other groups.

disease management   A combination of strategies developed to reduce the cost of chronic conditions that require significant changes in behavior.

distributed practice   Practice sessions with rest intervals between the sessions.

distributive bargaining   In negotiations, the bargaining posture that assumes that the goals of the parties are irreconcilable; also known as *win-lose bargaining*.

distributive justice   Justice that focuses on the fairness of the outcomes of decisions–for example, in the allocation of bonuses or merit pay, or in making reasonable accommodations for employees with disabilities.

diversity   The ability to live and work with people who are different from us.

diversity-based recruitment with preferential hiring   An organization's recruitment policy that systematically favors women and minorities in hiring and promotion decisions; also known as a *soft-quota system*.

doctrine of constructive receipt   The principle that holds that an individual must pay taxes on benefits that have monetary value when the individual receives them.

downsizing   The planned elimination of positions or jobs in an organization.

due process   In legal proceedings, a judicial requirement that treatment of an individual may not be unfair, arbitrary, or unreasonable.

e-Verify   A free web-based tool from the Social Security Administration and the Department of Homeland Security to verify a match between employees' names, Social Security numbers, and immigration information.

economic strikes   Actions by a union of withdrawing its labor in support of bargaining demands, including those for recognition or organization.

efficient-purchaser indexes   Such indexes assume that a person is not completely new to a situation, has learned about some local brands and outlets, and therefore pays prices that are lower than a newcomer would pay.

electronic (e-) learning   Technology-based training that can be accessed via the Internet.

emotional intelligence   The ability to perceive, appraise, and express emotion. It includes four domains, each with associated competencies: self-awareness, self-management, social awareness, and relationship management.

emotional stability   The degree to which an individual is calm, self-confident, and cool; it is the opposite pole of neuroticism.

employee assistance programs (EAPs)   Programs that offer professional counseling, medical services, and rehabilitation opportunities to all troubled employees.

employee relations   All the practices that implement the philosophy and policy of an organization with respect to employment.

employee stock-ownership plans (ESOPs)   Organizationwide incentive programs in which employees receive shares of company stock, thereby becoming owners or part owners of the company; shares are deposited into employees' accounts and dividends from the stock are added to the accounts.

employee stock-ownership program (ESOP)   Organizationwide incentive programs in which employees receive shares of company stock, thereby becoming owners or part owners of the company; shares are deposited into employees' accounts and dividends from the stock are added to the accounts.

employee voice   A method of ensuring procedural justice within an organization by providing individuals and groups with an opportunity to be heard–a way to communicate their interests upward.

employment at will   An employment situation in which an employee agrees to work for an employer but there is no specification of how long the parties expect the agreement to last.

engineering controls   Modifications of the work environment that attempt to eliminate unsafe work conditions and neutralize unsafe worker behaviors.

equal employment opportunity (EEO)   Nondiscriminatory employment practices that ensure evaluation of candidates for jobs in terms of job-related criteria only, and fair and equal treatment of employees on the job.

equal employment opportunity (EEO) for women   The raising of awareness of issues among both men and women so that women can be given a fair chance to think about their interests and potential, to investigate other possibilities, to make intelligent choices, and then to be considered for openings or promotions on an equal basis with men.

equalization   An approach to international compensation in which an employer deducts standard home-country amounts from an expatriate's salary for income taxes, housing, and goods and services and then pays the balance in home-country currency.

equity norm   A reward-allocation practice, common across cultures, in which rewards are distributed to group members on the basis of their contributions.

essential functions   Parts of a job that cannot be delegated to others; typically serious consequences of error or nonperformance are associated with them.

ethical decisions about behavior   Decisions that concern a person's conformity to moral standards or to the standards of conduct of a given profession or group; decisions that take into account not only a person's own interests but also, equally, the interests of all others affected by the decisions.

ethical dilemmas   Situations that have the potential to result in a breach of acceptable behavior.

ethnic minorities   Under-represented groups of people classified according to common traits and customs.

ethnocentrism   The view of an organization that the way things are done in the parent country is the best way, no matter where the business is conducted.

evaluation phase   A twofold training process that involves establishing indicators of success in training as well as on the job and determining exactly what job-related changes have occurred as a result of the training.

exclusive bargaining representative   In a union-representation election, if a union receives a majority of the ballots cast, that union is certified as the sole representative of all employees in the bargaining unit.

exclusive representation   The concept that only one union, selected by majority vote, will exist in a given job territory, although multiple unions may represent different groups of employees who work for the same employer.

expatriate   Anyone working outside her or his home country with a planned return to that or a third country; also known as a *foreign-service employee.*

extended leave   A policy in some companies to grant longer leaves of absence, with or without pay, as a way to retain talent.

external equity   Fairness in the wages paid by an organization, in terms of competitive market rates outside the organization.

extroversion   Gregariousness, assertiveness, and sociability in an individual, as opposed to reservation, timidness, and quietness.

fact-finding   A dispute-resolution mechanism in which each party submits whatever information it believes is relevant to a resolution of a dispute, and a neutral fact-finder then makes a study of the evidence and prepares a report on the facts.

feedback   Evaluative or corrective information transmitted to employees about their attempts to improve their job performance.

femininity   Masculinity vs. femininity is the extent to which a society differentiates roles by gender and the extent to which it emphasizes work, careers, and money versus quality of life, helping others, and relationships.

fiduciary duty of loyalty   An obligation by employees to maintain all trade secrets with which their employers have entrusted them; also provides a former employer with legal recourse if an executive joins a competitor and reveals trade secrets.

financial rewards   The component of an organizational reward system that includes direct payments, such as salary, and indirect payments, such as employee benefits.

flexible benefits   Benefits provided under a plan that allows employees to choose their benefits from among the alternatives offered by the organization.

flexible scheduling   An option granted to workers to set the times they will work, within specified boundaries.

flexible-spending accounts   Accounts into which employees can deposit pretax dollars (up to a specified amount) to pay for additional benefits.

forced distribution   A rating method in which the overall distribution of ratings is forced into a normal, or bell-shaped, curve, under the assumption that a relatively small portion of employees is truly outstanding, a relatively small portion is unsatisfactory, and all other employees fall in between.

frame-of-reference (FOR) training   A form of rater training that attempts to establish a common perspective and standards among raters.

free-speech clause   The right of management to express its opinion about unions or unionism to employees, provided that it does not threaten or promise favors to employees to obtain anti-union actions.

gain-sharing   An organizationwide incentive program in which employee cooperation leads to information sharing and employee involvement, which in turn lead to new behaviors that improve organizational productivity; the increase in productivity results in a financial bonus (based on the amount of increase), which is distributed monthly or quarterly.

gamification   The application of gaming technology to engage employees and direct behavior through interactive games and competition.

gatekeeper   A primary-care physician who monitors the medical history and care of each employee and his or her family.

general mental ability (GMA)   The ability to learn. It includes any measure that combines two, three, or more specific aptitudes, or any measure that includes a variety of items that measure specific abilities (e.g., verbal, numerical, or spatial relations).

Generation X   People born between 1965 and 1980, who grew up in times of rapid change, both social and economic; also known as baby busters.

Generation Y   People born between 1981 and 1995; includes offspring of baby boomers as well as an influx of immigrants through the 1990s. These people have grown up with sophisticated technologies, having been exposed to them much earlier in life than members of Generation X.

Generation Z   Born 1996-2010, this is the first generation of true digital natives. They are attracted to careers that promise both purpose and pragmatism.

geocentrism   In the recruitment of executives for multinational companies, a strategy with an international perspective that emphasizes the unrestricted use of people of all nationalities.

globalites   Sophisticated international executives drawn from many countries.

globalization   The interdependence of business operations internationally; commerce without borders.

goal theory   The theory that an individual's conscious goals or intentions regulate her or his behavior.

graphic rating scales Those that identify, and may define, each dimension to be rated and present the rater with alternative scale points (response categories) that may or may not be defined.

grievance An alleged violation of the rights of workers on the job.

grievance arbitration The final stage of the grievance process, which consists of compulsory, binding arbitration; used as an alternative to a work stoppage and to ensure labor peace for the duration of a labor contract.

grievance procedures Procedures by which an employee can seek a formal, impartial review of a decision that affects him or her; a formal process to help the parties involved resolve a dispute.

guided team self-correction Providing guidance to team members in reviewing team events; identifying errors and exchanging feedback; developing plans for the future.

halo error A rating error occurring when an appraiser rates an employee high (or low) on many aspects of job performance because the appraiser believes the employee performs well (or poorly) on some specific aspect.

hard quotas In an organization's recruitment and selection process, a mandate to hire or promote specific numbers or proportions of women or minority-group members.

harmful patterns of drinking Drinking too much, too fast (more than 4 drinks in 2 hours for men, and more than 3 in 2 hours for women) or too much *and* too often (more than 14 drinks per week for men, and more than 7 for women).

health maintenance organization (HMO) An organized system of health care, with the emphasis on preventive medicine, that assures the delivery of services to employees who enroll voluntarily under a prepayment plan, thereby committing themselves to using the services of only those doctors and hospitals that are members of the plan.

health promotion A corporation's promotion of health awareness through four steps: educating employees about health-risk factors; identifying health-risk factors faced by employees; helping employees eliminate these risks; and helping employees maintain their new, healthier lifestyles.

hierarchy of job worth In the point method of job evaluation, such a hierarchy results when jobs are rank-ordered from highest point total to lowest point total.

home country An expatriate's country of residence.

host country The country in which an expatriate is working.

hostile-environment harassment Verbal or physical conduct that creates an intimidating, hostile, or offensive work environment or interferes with an employee's job performance.

HR dashboard A means of providing high-level, real-time, graphically formatted data to managers.

HR risk The uncertainty arising from changes in a wide range of workforce and people-management issues that affect a company's ability to meet its strategic and operating objectives.

HR strategy The decisions, processes, and choices organizations make regarding how they manage their people.

human resource management (HRM) An overall approach to management, comprising staffing, retention, development, adjustment, and managing change.

human resources information system The method used by an organization to collect, store, analyze, report, and evaluate information and data on people, jobs, and costs.

implied promises Oral promises and implied and explicit covenants of good faith and fair dealing.

in-basket test A situational test in which an individual is presented with items that might appear in the in-basket of an administrative officer, is given appropriate background information, and then is directed to deal with the material as though he or she were actually on the job.

incentives One-time supplements, tied to levels of job performance and to the base pay of employees, including nonexempt and unionized employees.

inclusion A work environment in which all individuals are treated fairly and respectfully, have equal access to opportunities and resources, and can contribute fully to the organization's success.

indirect costs of accidents Costs other than those incurred for the treatment and rehabilitation of an injured worker, such as wages paid for time lost, cost of damage to material or equipment, and any other expense created in conjunction with the accident.

individual analysis In the assessment of training needs, the level of analysis that determines how well each employee is performing the tasks that make up his or her job.

individual equity Determination of whether or not each individual's pay is fair relative to that of other individuals doing the same or similar jobs.

individualism vs. collectivism The extent to which members of a culture emphasize personal rather than group goals.

informational justice Justice expressed in terms of providing explanations or accounts for decisions made.

integrative bargaining In negotiations, the bargaining posture that assumes that the goals of the parties are not mutually exclusive, that it is possible for both sides to achieve their objectives; also known as *win-win bargaining*.

integrity tests (1) Overt (clear-purpose) tests that are designed to assess directly attitudes toward dishonest behaviors, and (2) personality-based (disguised-purpose) tests that aim to predict a broad range of counterproductive behaviors at work.

interactional justice The quality of interpersonal treatment that employees receive in their everyday work.

interest arbitration A dispute-resolution mechanism in which a neutral third party hears the positions of both parties and decides on binding settlement terms.

intermittent strikes Sporadic, but repeated actions in which workers walk out for a relatively short time (e.g., an 8-hour shift), and then return to work.

internal equity Determination of whether or not pay rates are fair in terms of the relative worth of individual jobs to an organization.

job description A written summary of task requirements for a particular job.

job design The processes and outcomes that describe how work is structured, organized, experienced, and enacted.

job evaluation Assessment of the relative worth of jobs to a firm.

job posting The advertising of available jobs internally through the use of bulletin boards (electronic or hard-copy) or in lists available to all employees.

job satisfaction A pleasurable feeling that results from the perception that a job fulfills or allows for the fulfill-ment of its holder's important job values.

job specification A written summary of worker require-ments for a particular job.

just cause As it pertains to arbitration cases, the concept that requires an employer not only to produce persuasive evidence of an employee's liability or negligence but also to provide the employee a fair hearing and to impose a penalty appropriate to the proven offense.

justice The maintenance or administration of what is just, especially by the impartial adjustment of conflicting claims or the assignment of merited rewards or punishments.

labor market A geographical area within which the forces of supply (people looking for work) interact with the forces of demand (employers looking for people) and thereby determine the price of labor.

labor union A group of workers who join together to influence the nature of their employment.

LAMP *Logic, analytics, measures*, and *process*—four critical components of a measurement system that drives strategic change and organizational effectiveness.

leaderless group discussion (LGD) A situational test in which a group of participants is given a job-related topic and is asked to carry on a discussion about it for a period of time, after which observers rate the perfor-mance of each participant.

leniency The tendency to rate every employee high or excellent on all criteria.

lifestyle discrimination Firing of workers for engaging in legal activities outside of work, such as refusing to quit smoking, living with someone without being married, using a competitor's product, and motorcycling.

Likert method of summed ratings A type of behav-ioral checklist with declarative sentences and weighted response categories; the rater checks the response cate-gory that he or she thinks best describes the employee and sums the weights of the responses that were checked for each item.

local perspective A viewpoint that includes no appre-ciation for cultural differences.

local-plus compensation Localizes expatriates in a host country's salary program, and then adds some allowances, such as housing, education, and medical coverage.

localization The practice of paying expatriates on the same scale as local nationals in the country of assignment.

lockout The shutting down of plant operations by management when contract negotiations fail.

logic diagram In the context of talent analytics, a dia-gram that links investments in an HR program to finan-cial and nonfinancial outcomes that decision makers care about.

long-term disability (LTD) plans Disability insurance plans that provide benefits when an employee is disabled for 6 months or longer, usually at no more than 60 percent of base pay.

long-term versus short-term orientation The extent to which members of a culture accept delayed gratifica-tion of their material, social, and emotional needs.

loose cultures Those in which social norms are less clear and fewer in number; people follow them less often, and they are punished less for deviance.

loss-control program A way to sustain a safety policy through four components: a safety budget, safety records, management's personal concern, and management's good example.

lump-sum bonus An end-of-year bonus given to employees that does not build into base pay.

managed care A health-care system in which a doctor's clearance for treatment is required for an employee before he or she enters a hospital.

management by objectives (MBO) A philosophy of management with a results-oriented rating method that relies on goal setting to establish objectives for the organization as a whole, for each department, for each manager, and for each employee, thus providing a mea-sure of each employee's contribution to the success of the organization.

management controls Measures instituted by manage-ment in an attempt to increase safe worker behaviors.

managing change The ongoing managerial process of enhancing the ability of an organization to anticipate and respond to developments in its external and internal environments, and to enable employees at all levels to cope with the changes.

managing diversity Establishing a heterogeneous workforce (including white men) to perform to its potential in an equitable work environment where no member or group of members enjoys an advantage or suffers a disadvantage.

market-based pay system A pay system that uses a direct market-pricing approach for all of a firm's jobs.

masculinity The extent to which members of a culture differentiate very strongly by gender, and the dominant cultural values are work-related.

massed practice Practice sessions that are crowded together.

meaningfulness Material that is rich in associations for trainees and is therefore easily understood by them.

mediation A process by which a neutral third party attempts to help the parties in a dispute reach a settlement of the issues that divide them.

merit-pay systems Pay systems, most commonly applied to exempt employees, under which employees receive permanent increases, tied to levels of job performance, in their base pay.

meta-analysis A statistical summary of research results across studies.

micro-learning apps Brief, Internet-based video and interactive lessons that take fewer than five minutes to complete and that include a quiz.

midcareer plateaus Performance by midcareer workers at an acceptable but not outstanding level, coupled with little or no effort to improve performance.

mixed-motive case A discrimination case in which an employment decision was based on a combination of job-related as well as unlawful factors.

mobility premium A one-time payment to an expatriate for each move—overseas, back home, or to another overseas assignment.

modified balance-sheet approach In terms of international compensation, linking salary to a region rather than to the home country.

money-purchase plan A defined-contribution pension plan in which the employer contributes a set percentage of each vested employee's salary to his or her retirement account; annual investment earnings and losses are added to or subtracted from the account balance.

multifactor authentication In order to log in to a website, a user must provide not only a password and user name but also something that only a user has, such as a code sent to his or her smartphone.

multinational enterprise (MNE) Any public- or private-sector organization that operates in more than one country.

narrative essay Simplest type of absolute rating system, in which a rater describes, in writing, an employee's strengths, weaknesses, and potential, together with suggestions for improvement.

negligent hiring The failure of an employer to check closely enough on a prospective employee, who then commits a crime in the course of performing his or her job duties.

neuroticism The degree to which an individual is insecure, anxious, depressed, and emotional; it is the opposite of emotional stability—calm, self-confident, and cool.

noncompete agreements Clauses in a contract that bar an individual from working for a competitor for a fixed period of time if he or she is fired, if the job is eliminated, or if the individual leaves voluntarily.

noncontributory plan One in which the employer pays the full cost of insurance premiums for employees.

nonfinancial rewards The component of an organizational reward system that includes everything in a work environment that enhances a worker's sense of self-respect and esteem by others, such as training opportunities, involvement in decision making, and recognition.

nonunion arbitration Grievance arbitration in a nonunion firm. May provide fewer due-process rights than unionized grievance arbitration—for example, if there are limitations on discovery (how much information the grievant can collect from the company).

norms of behavior Rules or guides to acceptable behavior.

obsolescence As it pertains to human resource management, the tendency for knowledge or skills to become out of date.

ombudspersons People designated to investigate claims of unfair treatment or to act as intermediaries between an employee and senior management and recommend possible courses of action to the parties.

on-boarding A process that helps a newcomer to transition from an outsider to an effective and integrated insider.

on-premise systems Software platforms housed in privately controlled data centers.

open-door policy An organizational policy that allows employees to approach senior managers with problems that they may not be willing to take to their immediate supervisors.

openness The degree to which an individual is creative, curious, and cultured versus practical with narrow interests.

operations analysis In the assessment of training needs, the level of analysis that attempts to identify the content of training—what an employee must do in order to perform competently.

organization analysis In the assessment of training needs, the level of analysis that focuses on identifying where within the organization training is needed.

organizational citizenship behaviors (OCBs) Discretionary behaviors performed outside an employee's formal role, that help other employees perform their jobs or which show support for and conscientiousness toward an organization.

organizational commitment The degree to which an employee identifies with an organization and is willing to put forth effort on its behalf.

organizational culture The way that the values and actions of managers and employees create a unique business environment.

organizational reward system A system for providing both financial and nonfinancial rewards; includes anything an employee values and desires that an employer is able and willing to offer in exchange for employee contributions.

organizational support The extent to which an organization values employees' general contributions and cares for their well-being.

orientation The process of becoming familiar with and adapting to a situation or environment.

overlearning Practicing far beyond the point where a task has been performed correctly only several times to the point that the task becomes "second nature."

paired comparisons A behavior-oriented rating method in which an employee is compared to every other employee; the rater chooses the "better" of each pair and each employee's rank is determined by counting the number of times she or he was rated superior.

passive nondiscrimination An organization's commitment to treat all races and both sexes equally in all decisions about hiring, promotion, and pay, but with no attempt to recruit actively among prospective minority applicants.

pattern bargaining Negotiating the same contract provisions for several firms in the same industry, with the intent of making wages and benefits uniform industrywide.

Paul principle The phenomenon that over time, people become uneducated, and therefore incompetent, to perform at a level at which they once performed adequately.

pay compression A narrowing of the ratios of pay between jobs or pay grades in a firm's pay structure.

pay equity Paying men and women the same when they perform the same or similar job duties, while accounting for other factors, such as experience, job performance, pay grade, location, and tenure with the employer.

pay openness Disclosure of pay-related information on a scale from very little (work- and business-related rationale on which the system is based) to very much (availability of pay-related data from the compensation department).

peer-review panel Common in nonunion settings, a panel in which employees (not managers) comprise a majority of the panel members.

pension A sum of money paid at regular intervals to an employee who has retired from a company and is eligible to receive such benefits.

people analytics A set of quantitative approaches that answer two questions: (1) What do we need to know about our organization and workforce to operate more effectively? and (2) How do we turn that knowledge into action?

performance appraisal A review of the job-relevant strengths and weaknesses of an individual or a team in an organization.

performance awards Typically, stock-denominated shares that are earned on the basis of performance against predetermined objectives over a defined period of more than one year.

performance encouragement Provision of a sufficient amount of rewards that employees really value, in a timely, fair manner.

performance facilitation An approach to management that emphasizes eliminating roadblocks to successful employee performance, providing adequate resources to get a job done right and on time, and paying careful attention to the selection of employees.

performance management A broad process that requires managers to define, facilitate, and encourage performance by providing timely feedback and constantly focusing everyone's attention on the ultimate objectives.

performance standards Criteria that specify *how well*, not *how*, work is to be done, by defining levels of acceptable or unacceptable employee behavior.

personality The set of characteristics of a person that account for the consistent way he or she responds to situations.

pivotal jobs Those jobs in which a change in the number or quality of employees makes a big difference in business outcomes.

point-of-service (POS) plan Health-care plan that offers the choice of using the plan's network of doctors and hospitals (and paying no deductible and only small copayments for office visits) or seeing a physician outside the network (and paying 30 to 40 percent of the total cost); an in-network gatekeeper must approve all services.

potential labor pool Individuals who might eventually become applicants to a specific organization once they acquire necessary skills or minimum qualifications.

power distance The extent to which members of a culture accept the unequal distribution of power.

practicality Implies that appraisal instruments are easy for managers and employees to understand and use.

practice The active use of training content. It includes active practice, overlearning, and the length of the practice session.

predictive analytics   Data-based HR analyses that use statistical modeling techniques to forecast what will happen in a future time period.

preferred provider organization (PPO)   A health care system, generally with no gatekeeper, in which medical care is provided by a specified group of physicians and hospitals; care from outside the network is available at additional cost to the individual employee.

prescriptive analytics   Data-based analyses whose objective is to develop multiple scenarios about the future.

prima facie case   A body of facts that is presumed to be true until proved otherwise.

privacy   The interest employees have in controlling the use that is made of their personal information and in being able to engage in behavior free from regulation or surveillance.

procedural justice   Justice that focuses on the fairness of the procedures used to make decisions.

productivity   A measure of the output of goods and services relative to the input of labor, capital, material, and equipment.

profit   Financial gain; the income remaining after total costs are deducted from total revenue.

profit-sharing   An organizationwide incentive program in which employees receive a bonus that is normally based on some percentage of the company's profits beyond some minimum level.

profit-sharing plan   An organizationwide incentive program in which employees receive a bonus that is normally based on some percentage of a company's profits beyond some minimum level.

progressive discipline   A discipline procedure that proceeds from an oral warning to a written warning to a suspension to dismissal.

protected health information   Medical information that contains any of a number of patient identifiers, such as name or Social Security number.

protection   In the context of international compensation, paying supplements to expatriates in home-country currency.

public-policy exception   An exception to employment at will; an employee may not be fired because he or she refuses to commit an illegal act, such as perjury or price fixing.

pure diversity-based recruitment   An organization's concerted effort to expand actively the pool of applicants so that no one is excluded because of past or present discrimination; the decision to hire or to promote is based on the best-qualified individual regardless of race or sex.

Pygmalion effect   The phenomenon of the self-fulfilling prophecy; with regard to training, the fact that the higher the expectations of the trainer, the better the performance of the trainees.

qualified job applicants   Applicants with disabilities who can perform the essential functions of a job with or without reasonable accommodation.

qualitative parity   In terms of benefits provided by multinationals, a commitment to offer employees worldwide something from each of four categories of benefits: core, required, recommended, and optional.

quality of work life (QWL)   A set of objective organizational conditions and practices designed to foster quality relationships within the organization; employees' perceptions of the degree to which the organizational environment meets the full range of human needs.

quantitative parity   In terms of benefits provided by multinationals, an effort to treat employees around the globe equitably from a total-cost perspective.

quid pro quo harassment   Sexual harassment—when sexual favors are a condition of gaining or keeping employment.

race-norming   Within-group percentile scoring of employment-related tests.

realistic job preview (RJP)   A recruiter's job overview that includes not only the positive aspects but also the unpleasant aspects of a job.

recency error   A rating error that occurs when an appraiser assigns a rating on the basis of the employee's most recent performance rather than on long-term performance.

recruitment   A market-exchange process in which employers attempt to differentiate their "products" (job opportunities) among "consumers" (job applicants) who vary in their levels of job-relevant knowledge, abilities, and skills.

red-hot-stove rule   The theory that discipline should be immediate, consistent, and impersonal and should include a warning.

relational databases   Multiple databases that store data in separate files that can be linked by common elements, such as name, Social Security number, hiring status (full- or part-time), training courses completed, job location, mailing address, or birthdate.

relative rating systems   Rating formats that compare the performance of an employee with that of other employees.

relevance   In an effective appraisal system, a requirement that there be clear links between the performance standards for a particular job and the organization's goals, and clear links between the critical job elements identified through a job analysis and the dimensions to be rated on an appraisal form.

relevant labor market   Determined by which jobs to survey and which markets are relevant for each job, considering geographical boundaries as well as product-market competitors.

reliability The consistency or stability of a measurement procedure.

repatriation The process of reentering one's native culture after being absent from it.

repetitive-strain injuries (RSIs) Injuries caused by performing the same task (or similar tasks) repeatedly, such as typing or using a computer mouse, for extended periods of time.

restricted stock Common stock that vests after a specified period.

restricted stock units Shares awarded over time to defer taxes.

restructuring The process of changing a company by selling or buying plants or lines of business, or by laying off employees.

results-oriented rating methods Rating formats that place primary emphasis on what an employee produces.

retaliatory discharge Retaliation for filing a claim or bringing a charge against an employer; in such cases, the employee may seek damages under an exception to the employment-at-will doctrine.

retention Initiatives taken by management to keep employees from leaving, such as rewarding employees for performing their jobs effectively; ensuring harmonious working relations between employees and managers; and maintaining a safe, healthy work environment.

return on investment (ROI) A measure of the gain or loss generated on an investment relative to the amount of money invested. ROI is usually expressed as a percentage and is often used to compare the efficiency of different investments.

reverse culture shock A condition experienced by an expatriate who has become accustomed to foreign ways and who, upon re-entry, finds his or her home-country customs strange and even annoying.

reverse discrimination Discrimination against whites (especially white males) and in favor of members of protected groups.

right-to-work laws Laws that prohibit compulsory union membership as a condition of continued employment.

screening Sometimes called "initial screening," it refers to the process of identifying unqualified candidates and separating them from those who meet minimum qualifications.

secondary boycott A boycott occurring when a union appeals to firms or other unions to stop doing business with an employer who sells or handles struck products.

secret-ballot election An election supervised by the National Labor Relations Board, in which each eligible member of a bargaining unit casts a secret ballot for or against union representation.

selection The process of choosing among qualified candidates or employees for hire or promotion.

selection ratio The percentage of applicants hired, which is used in evaluating the usefulness of any predictor.

self-service portals Websites or apps that enable users to perform transactions without the aid of an in-house professional, such as HR or a customer-service representative.

seniority system An established business practice that allots to employees ever-improving employment rights and benefits as their relative lengths of pertinent employment increase.

sensitivity The capability of a performance-appraisal system to distinguish effective from ineffective performers.

severity The tendency to rate every employee low on the criteria being evaluated.

sexual harassment Unwelcome sexual advances, requests for sexual favors, and other verbal or physical conduct of a sexual nature when submission to or rejection of this conduct explicitly or implicitly affects an individual's employment; unreasonably interferes with an individual's work performance; or creates an intimidating, hostile, or offensive work environment.

short-term disability plans Insurance plans that provide income replacement for employees whose illness or injury causes absence from work. Short-term disability usually starts after a 1- to 2-week absence.

shrinkage Losses due to bookkeeping errors and employee, customer, and vendor theft.

silent generation People born between 1930 and 1945, who dedicated themselves to their employers, made sacrifices to get ahead, and currently hold many positions of power.

simple ranking Requires only that the rater order all employees from highest to lowest, from "best" employee to "worst" employee.

simplified employee pension (SEP) A defined-contribution pension plan under which a small-business employer can contribute a certain percentage or amount of an employee's salary tax-free to an individual retirement account; the employee is vested immediately for the amount paid into the account but cannot withdraw any funds before age 59 1/2 without penalty.

skip-level policy An employee-voice mechanism that allows an employee with a problem to proceed directly to the next higher level of management above his or her supervisor.

SMART objectives Objectives that are Specific, Measurable, Appropriate (consistent with the vision and mission), Realistic (challenging but doable), and Timely.

social learning theory Individuals in groups look to others to learn appropriate behaviors and attitudes.

social norms Socially agreed-upon standards of behavior that form the basic building blocks of social order.

software-as-a-service (SaaS) systems Subscription-based software paid on a month-to-month basis.

sorting effect An effect of variable pay, in which people who do not want to have their pay tied to their performance don't accept jobs at companies that offer it, or else they leave when pay-for-performance is implemented.

spillover effect A situation in which employers seek to avoid unionization by offering their workers the wages, benefits, and working conditions that rival unionized firms do.

spot bonus If an employee's performance has been exceptional, the employer may reward him or her with a one-time bonus shortly after the noteworthy actions.

stackable credentials Over time, individuals can assemble, or stack, a series of traditional degree-based or nontraditional credentials, such as certificates, certifications, licenses, digital badges, or apprenticeships, that recognize achievements and provide an accurate assessment of knowledge, skills, and abilities.

staffing The managerial activities of identifying work requirements within an organization; determining the numbers of people and the skills mix necessary to do the work; and recruiting, selecting, and promoting qualified candidates.

strategic workforce planning (SWP) Identification of the numbers of employees and the skills needed to perform available jobs at some future time period, including changes in jobs required by corporate goals.

succession plan A systematic process whose objective is to supply qualified candidates to assume management or nonmanagement roles, should they become available.

succession planning The process of identifying replacement candidates for key positions, assessing their current performance and readiness for promotion, identifying career-development needs, and integrating the career goals of individuals with company goals to ensure the availability of competent executive talent.

sympathy strikes Refusals by employees of one bargaining unit to cross a picket line of a different bargaining unit.

systemic discrimination Any business practice that results in the denial of equal employment opportunity.

talent The potential and realized capacities of individuals and groups and how they are organized, including those within the organization and those who might join the organization.

team A group of individuals who are working together toward a common goal.

team-coordination training Focusing on teamwork skills that facilitate information exchange, cooperation, and coordination of job-related behaviors.

technology The application of scientific knowledge for practical purposes, especially in industry, for example, "*advances in computer technology.*"

teleworking Work carried out in a location that is remote from central offices or production facilities, where the worker has no personal contact with coworkers but is able to communicate with them using electronic means.

third-country national An expatriate who has transferred to an additional country while working abroad.

tight cultures Those in which social norms are clear and pervasive. They often entail strong punishments for people who don't follow them.

training Planned programs designed to improve performance at the individual, group, and/or organizational levels.

training-and-development phase The phase of training whose purpose is to design the environment in which to achieve the objectives defined in the assessment phase by choosing methods and techniques and by delivering them in a supportive environment based on sound principles of learning.

training paradox The seemingly contradictory fact that training employees to develop their skills and improve their performance increases their employability outside the company while simultaneously increasing their job security and desire to stay with their current employer.

transfer of training The extent to which competencies learned in training can be applied on the job.

transnational collective bargaining Unions in more than one country negotiate jointly with the same company.

transnational corporation A corporation that uses geodiversity to great advantage, placing its top executives and core corporate functions in different countries to gain a competitive edge through the availability of talent, capital, low costs, or proximity to its most important customers.

troubled employee An individual with unresolved personal or work-related problems.

trust gap A frame of mind in which employees mistrust senior management's intentions, doubt its competence, and resent its self-congratulatory pay.

turnover Any permanent departure of employees beyond organizational boundaries.

ubiquitous computing Information and communication environments in which computer sensors (such as radio frequency identification tags, wearable technology, smart watches) and other equipment (tablets, mobile devices) are unified with various objects, people, information, and computers as well as the physical environment. The result is a world where an Internet of everyone is linked to an Internet of everything.

uncertainty avoidance The extent to which members of a culture feel threatened by ambiguous situations and thus emphasize ritual behavior, rules, and stability.

unequal treatment Disparate treatment of employees based on an intention to discriminate.

unfair-labor-practice strikes Strikes that are caused or prolonged by unfair labor practices of the employer.

union-security clause In a contract, a clause designed to force all employees to join the union in order to remain working.

unprotected strikes Both lawful and unlawful work stoppages, such as sit-down strikes, slowdowns, and wildcat strikes, in which participants' jobs are not protected by law; thus, the participants may be discharged by their employer.

usability The interface between humans and technology, typically measured in terms of efficiency (time to complete a task), effectiveness (error rate), and user satisfaction.

validity Evidence regarding the appropriateness or meaningfulness of inferences about scores from a measurement procedure.

validity generalization The assumption that the results of a validity study conducted in one situation can be generalized to other similar situations.

vesting The legal right of an employee to receive the employer's share of retirement benefits contributed on his or her behalf after a certain length of employment.

virtual career fair Computer-based use of video, voice, and text to connect job seekers with recruiters. Online visitors can listen to presentations; visit booths; leave résumés and business cards; participate in live chats; and get contact information from recruiters, HR managers, and even hiring managers.

virtual organization An organizational form in which teams of specialists come together through technology to work on a project, and disband when the project is finished.

virtual workplace A new organizational form based on the idea of working anytime, anywhere–in real space or in cyberspace.

wellness programs Programs that focus on prevention to help employees build lifestyles that will enable them to achieve their full physical and mental potential.

whistle-blowing Disclosure by former or current organization members of illegal, immoral, or illegitimate practices under the control of their employers.

willful violations Violations of OSHA requirements in which an employer either knew that what was being done constituted a violation of federal regulations or was aware that a hazardous condition existed and made no reasonable effort to eliminate it.

work planning and review Emphasizes periodic review of work plans by both supervisor and subordinate in order to identify goals attained, problems encountered, and needs for training.

work-sample tests Standardized measures of behavior whose primary objective is to assess the ability to *do* rather than the ability to *know* through miniature replicas of actual job requirements; also known as *situational tests*.

workers' compensation Programs that provide payments to workers who are injured on the job, or who contract a work-related illness.

workforce forecasting The estimation of labor requirements at some future time period.

workplace aggression Efforts by individuals to harm others with whom they work or have worked, or their organization.

workplace violence Assaults and other violent acts or threats that occur in or are related to the workplace.

work-life program An employer-sponsored benefit or working condition that helps employees to balance work and nonwork demands.

yearly renewable term insurance Group life insurance in which each employee is insured 1 year at a time.

NAME INDEX

Aamodt, M. G., 242
Aaron, H., 439
Abramson, N. R., 139, 590
Achille, R. S., 104
Adams, E. K., 568
Agarwal, P., 615
Agovino, T., 72, 465
Aguinis, H., 218, 239, 284, 297, 326, 329, 338, 528
Ahearn, T., 241
Albrecht, K., 339
Aldana, S. G., 569, 570
Ales, E., 615, 617
Allen, A. G., 220
Alonso, A., 219
Althaus, G., 618
Alton, L., 146
Anderson, N., 600
Andrews, L. W., 508
Anhalt, R. L., 348
Antonioni, D., 341
Apfel, K., 439
Arad, S., 608
Armstrong, M., 215
Arnold, D. W., 243
Arnold, J. A., 482
Arnold, J. D., 117, 240
Arnst, C., 432
Arthur, M., 76
Arthur, W. J., Jr., 254, 284
Aryee, S., 485
Ashford, S. J., 297
Attridge, M., 561
Audi, T., 549
Aumann, K., 81
Austin, J. M., Jr, 254
Austin, M., 344
Auten, D., 153
Autor, D. H., 587
Avery, B., 117
Avolio, B. J., 287

Babcock, P., 13, 147, 216
Bae, Z., 341
Baer, J. C., 8, 343
Bailey, C., 344

Bakker, A. B., 65
Baldwin, T. T., 297
Bales, R. A., 511
Bandler, J., 548
Bandura, A., 294
Barber, A. E., 210
Bardoel, E. A., 76
Barkman, S. J., 139
Barrett, P. M., 14
Barron, L. G., 341
Barry, B., 475
Barton, F., 614
Bartz, A., 434
Barwick, K. D., 556
Bates, S., 397, 432, 525
Bauer, T. N., 245
Baumann, J. P., 372
Baxter, S., 569
Bayern, M., 147
Beatty, R. W., 340
Beck, M., 564
Becker, T. E., 250, 340
Beersma, B., 345
Bell, S. T., 284
Bellon, T., 558
Bennett, A., 395
Bennett, W. J, 284
Benoit, D., 12
Benson, G., 331
Bernardin, H. J., 338, 340, 349
Bernthal, P. R., 325
Berrgren, E., 8
Bersin, J., 146, 284
Berua, C., 600
Beus, J. M., 554
Bierma, P., 545
Binkley, R., 105
Biro, M. M.., 565
Bisqueret, C., 602
Bjorkman, I., 600
Blanchard, P. N., 293
Blasi, J., 404
Blizzard, C. L., 569
Blume, B. D., 297
Bobko, P., 254, 387
Bolden-Barrett, V., 113, 137, 388, 599

Bolesta, J., 479
Bolino, M. C., 509–600, 620
Bonache, J., 610
Boon, C., 8
Borenstein, J., 443
Borman, W. C., 248, 254, 503
Bortz, D., 341
Boselie, P., 8
Boudette, N. E., 465, 469
Boudreau, J. W., 37, 39, 58, 59, 63, 71, 75, 166, 178, 181, 186, 219, 284, 297, 304, 562
Boue, G., 392
Bowers, C., 345
Bowman, J., 26
Boyatzis, R., 249
Boyd, E., 522
Boyle, M., 380
Bradford, K., 213
Bradley, J. C., 256
Brandon, E., 150
Brannick, M. T., 169
Brantley, L. B., 503
Bravin, J., 110, 483, 548
Breaugh, J. A., 207, 250
Brett, J. M., 372, 476
Brin, D. W., 209
Brinkmeyer, K., 249
Briscoe, D., 139, 613
Britt, L. P., 116
Brockner, J., 505
Brodsky, S., 513
Brooks, C., 242
Broughman, B., 442
Brown, C., 481
Brown, K. G., 302
Bryant, R. H., 254
Brynjolfsson, E., 58
Buckley, B., 468
Buckley, M. R., 349
Budd, J. W., 380, 397, 464, 504, 615
Budhwar, P. S., 614
Bull, R. A., 335
Buller, P. F., 341
Bunn, E., 465
Burke, M. J., 553, 554

647

SUBJECT INDEX